PENGUIN REFE

THE PE

GERMAN–ENGLIS

Timothy Buck was born at Broadbridge Heath, West Sussex, in 1940 and educated at Collyer's School, Horsham, and Southampton University. After completing his postgraduate studies he taught for two years in the English Department of the University of Göttingen and also lectured for the British Council in Germany. A lecturer in German at Edinburgh University since 1966, he has published a number of articles on literary and linguistic subjects in various learned journals, and has also contributed several articles to the West German weeklies *Die Zeit* and *Der Spiegel* on topics connected with the contemporary German language.

THE PENGUIN
GERMAN–ENGLISH
DICTIONARY

COMPILED BY TIMOTHY BUCK

PENGUIN BOOKS

PENGUIN BOOKS

Published by the Penguin Group
27 Wrights Lane, London W8 5TZ, England
Viking Penguin Inc., 375 Hudson Street, New York, New York 10014, USA
Penguin Books Australia Ltd, Ringwood, Victoria, Australia
Penguin Books Canada Ltd, 2801 John Street, Markham, Ontario, Canada L3R 1B4
Penguin Books (NZ) Ltd, 182–190 Wairau Road, Auckland 10, New Zealand

Penguin Books Ltd, Registered Offices: Harmondsworth, Middlesex, England

First published 1990
1 3 5 7 9 10 8 6 4 2

Printed in England by Clays Ltd, St Ives plc
Typeset in Linotron Times

CONTENTS

LADY BRACKNELL
... But German sounds a thoroughly respectable language, and indeed, I believe is so.

Oscar Wilde,
The Importance of Being Earnest, I

PREFACE

This German–English dictionary, which will in due course form part of a complete two-way *Penguin German Dictionary*, has been compiled with the needs of both the beginner and the more advanced student in mind.

The aim has been to provide as full a coverage as possible of the contemporary German vocabulary: some 42,000 words are given.

Three categories of word have been treated in greater depth than is usual in dictionaries of comparable size:

(1) So-called *Fremdwörter* or 'foreign' words, e.g. *ambitioniert*, *Barsoi*, *Cäsium*, *Desinformation*, *Egozentrik*, *Embolie*, *Empirie*, *Epigone*, *Fötus*, *Klimakterium*, *Komparatistik*, *konziliant*, *Metaphorik*, *offiziös*, *Prämisse*, *telegen*, *Triptychon*, *Visagist*, *Voliere*.

(2) Proper names, e.g. *Aristoteles*, *der Ätna*, *Bozen*, *die ČSSR*, *Dick und Doof*, *Dschingis-Khan*, *Kapstadt*, *der Kilimandscharo*, *Maria Stuart*, *Neusüdwales*, *Petrarca*, *Pompeji*, *Posen*, *die „Prawda"*, *Raffael*, *der Sankt-Lorenz-Strom*, *Tripolis* (Lebanon, Libya), *Tschechow*.

(3) Austrian, Swiss and East German words, e.g. *Check*, *Diversion*, *eindrücklich*, *Hausbesorger*, *Maut*, *Mistkübel*, *Nationale*, *Normativ*, *Pastmilch*, *Plast*, *pragmatisieren*, *Präsenzdienst*, *schubladisieren*. (Also included – some for the first time in a German–English dictionary – are individual *senses* of words specific to Austrian, Swiss or East German usage, e.g. at *ausforschen* (as in 'Dort lag das Mädchen ... zwei Tage, bis seine Eltern ausgeforscht werden konnten' – Bernhard, *An der Baumgrenze*), *Industrie* (as in 'Das Tal war wieder sichtbar, auch menschlicher. Überall Höfe, hie und da kleine Industrien' – Dürrenmatt, *Das Versprechen*), *orientieren* (as in 'Wir sind die Stärkeren ... und darum beginnen sie, sich auf uns zu orientieren' – H. Kant, *Die Aula*), *Rettung* (as in 'Die beiden Burschen wurden mit der Rettung in das Krankenhaus Steyr eingeliefert' – *Kurier*, Vienna), *Tochter* (as in 'Gesucht so bald wie möglich, arbeitsfreudige, nette Tochter ... Bei gegenseitiger Zuneigung spätere Heirat erwünscht' – advertisement, *Berner Zeitung*).)

The extensive coverage of the vocabulary has been made possible by the economical style in which the entries are written, together with the space-saving grouping of compounds in so-called 'nests'. Economy has not, however, been achieved at the expense of clarity: thus the common practice of giving derivatives in truncated form has not been followed, and no short cuts have been taken in the case of nouns with 'regular' plurals (the plural is shown for *all* nouns that normally have one); also, for ease of reference major entries have been paragraphed.

The user of a dictionary tends, not unnaturally, to take its accuracy on trust. Yet it is a fact that, while impressive advances have been made in German–English lexicography since the late Trevor Jones's observations (1963) on the inadequacies of the dictionaries available after the war, standards of accuracy in both Britain and Germany have rather faltered in recent years. One thinks, for example – skating on thin ice though one manifestly is – of novel grammatical statements to the effect that *antizipieren* is an inseparable verb, that *handhaben* goes like *haben*, that *sollen* referring to what is destined to happen (e.g. *er sollte sie nie wiedersehen*) takes the subjunctive, that *fern* as in *fern der Heimat* governs the genitive and *wert* as in *Berlin ist eine Reise wert* the nominative, and so on; or of 'off-beat' renderings as in the case of *Aspirant* (E.Ger.) 'young scholar designed for teaching at a university', *darf man?* 'is it allowed to?', *Idiotikon* (= dialect dictionary) 'dictionary of idioms', *das nackte Leben* 'the naked life', *kursorische Lektüre* 'course reading', *Nabelschau* (= contemplation of one's navel) 'navel inspection', *nachdatieren* (= to antedate) 'to postdate', *parat haben* 'to have at one's fingers' ends', *Raumklang* (= stereophonic sound) 'stereoscopic sound', *sturmfreie Bude* 'trouble-free digs', 'unmolested diggings', *Überraschungsmoment* (= element of surprise) 'moment of surprise', *Vogel-Strauß-Politik* 'ostrich policy', *Volksbefragung* (= referendum) 'public opinion poll', *zügeln* 'to cheque', *aufs Töpfchen gehen* 'to go pottie'. This brief catalogue – many more examples could have been quoted – is given not in any spirit of complacency, but simply to illustrate the extent of the problem. The present dictionary, it should be added, is *meant* to uphold traditional standards; but of course, the proof of the lexicographical pudding is, as ever, in the eating ...

The writing of the dictionary – to turn to the not unproblematic question of sources – has been somewhat hampered by the absence of an authoritative comprehensive dictionary of the contemporary German language. Unhappily, neither Duden's *Das große Wörterbuch der deutschen Sprache in sechs Bänden* – a very detailed inventory marred by an astonishing multiplicity of errors that make it a veritable minefield for the user (e.g. the representation of at least fifty strong verbs such as *auswachsen*, *beleihen*, *kopfstehen*, *verschlafen* as weak, the frequent mixing up of the auxiliaries *haben* and *sein* (*hat entartet*, *hat fortgeeilt*, *hat niedergesunken*, etc.) and the inclusion of non-existent usages like 'Swiss' *abstellen* (instead of *abstehen*) as a result of incorrectly copied quotations) – nor the avowedly ideological East German *Wörterbuch der deutschen Gegenwartssprache* – which presents a much less full, if more carefully executed coverage of the German vocabulary – has proved to be such a dictionary; and it has been found necessary to draw additionally on a number of smaller but rather sounder works, including the other – highly useful – dictionaries produced by the Bibliographisches Institut in Mannheim, in order to gain a more balanced and reliable picture of today's German. (For standard Austrian German the excellent *Österreichisches Wörterbuch* has been regularly consulted.) To ensure an adequate fund of illustrative quotations – which as authentic examples of usage are valuable aids in the selection of real, workable equivalents – some 39,000 new quotations, supplementing the illustrative material given in the six-volume Duden and its East German counterpart, have been excerpted from modern works of fiction and non-fiction, the press and television programmes; a limited number are reproduced in the dictionary. It is hoped that, with the help of these measures, the *Penguin German–English Dictionary* may prove to be a practical, thoroughly up-to-date tool providing a set of translations that live up to Samuel Johnson's simple but exacting formulation: 'TO TRANSLATE ... to change into another language retaining the sense.'

*

I should like to record my gratitude to two West German institutions – Inter Nationes and the DAAD – for their most generous assistance over the years, and to various individuals who have helped in a variety of ways. My special thanks are due to my research assistant, Gudrun Buck, née Utpadel, whose help with a whole range of tasks, including the checking of the galley and page proofs, has been quite invaluable. I am also indebted to Dr Jeffrey Ashcroft (St Andrews) and Professor Paul Salmon (Oxford), who kindly read the proofs of the guides to German grammar and pronunciation and made a number of illuminating suggestions; Brenda Atkinson, née Hassan (Northampton), who contributed substantially to my collection of quotations; Thomas Diethelm (St Gallen), Dr Hans Köberl (Klagenfurt) and Harald Strobl (Graz), who patiently fielded my questions on Swiss and Austrian usage; Dr David Guild of this university's Russian Department, who vetted the transliteration table for me; Mark Handsley, who skilfully piloted the book through all the various stages of production; and finally, this dictionary's guardian Penguin, Donald MacFarlan, whose judgement, expertise and support stood it in such good stead.

TIMOTHY BUCK

Edinburgh University
June 1989

NOTES ON THE ENTRIES

1. *Vocabulary*

Words are arranged in alphabetical order, except in the case of compounds, which immediately follow, in uninterrupted sequence, the entry for the word or compounding element (e.g. **Einzel–**, **Räucher–**) forming their first component. If a compound is not listed, its constituent parts should be looked up; these may be connected by a linking element (**–e–**, **–en–**, **–er–**, **–s–**, etc.) – for examples see p. lxxi. To save space, two types of noun are normally omitted, namely feminine nouns in **–in** (unless the stem-vowel is mutated and/or the English term for the female differs from that for the male) and those in **–heit** or **–keit** translated by adding '-ness' to the translation(s) given for the adjective from which they are formed.

Proper names, including Christian names such as **Heinrich** and **Maria** that are normally translated in the case of monarchs, popes, saints and so on, are entered at the appropriate alphabetical places in the dictionary, as are abbreviations and acronyms.

2. *Orthography*

Duden Rechtschreibung and (with reference to Austrian German) the *Österreichisches Wörterbuch* have been used as guides for German orthography.

ß/ss: Where masculine and neuter nouns in **–ß** are shown with the spelling **ss** in the plural (e.g. **der Kompaß, –(ss)e**), this is also used in the genitive singular (**Kompasses**). Adjectives in **–ß** which have the spelling **ss** when inflected or compared (e.g. **naß**) are marked '(**–ss–**)'. (For general rules regarding the correct use of **ß** and **ss** see p. lxvi.)

A capital or small letter preceding the tilde (~) replaces an initial small or capital letter in the headword; thus at **bewußt**, **B~sein** signifies **Bewußtsein**, and at **Abbruch**, **a~reif** signifies **abbruchreif**. In compound nouns in which the last element is represented by the tilde it is understood that the initial capital letter of the headword is replaced by a small letter; thus at **Prima**, **Unter~** stands for **Unterprima**.

3. *Symbols*

~ stands for the headword.

| may indicate (i) the point within a compound at which one component ends and the next begins *or* (ii) a glottal stop (which prevents liaison) (see p. lxxiv).

* (see 4(iii), below.)

4. *Grammatical indications*

(i) *Nouns*

Each entry begins with the article **der**, **die** or **das** to show the gender of the noun (masculine, feminine or neuter respectively). The noun itself is followed by the *plural* form, where one is (normally) in use; this is also shown in the case of compounds. (For the *genitive singular* ending **–s** or **–es** attached to most masculines and neuters see p. xx, 'Singular' (a).) 'Weak masculine' nouns are identified as such in the relevant entries; particulars of their declension are given on p. xx under 'Singular' (b).

(ii) *Adjectives and adverbs*
Irregular comparative and superlative forms are shown in full, except when only mutation of the stem-vowel is involved, in which case the symbol ⸗ is used.

(iii) *Verbs*
The parts of strong and irregular verbs are shown at the entries concerned. They include the past subjunctive if the stem-vowel differs from that of the indicative.

Where a compound verb is asterisked (e.g. **herausfinden***) this signifies that it is either strong or irregular, and is conjugated like the simple verb (e.g. **finden**); in the case of inseparable verbs the **ge–** of the past participle is omitted (e.g. **erfinden***, past participle **erfunden**).

Verbs conjugated with **sein** are marked '(*sn*)'.

(iv) '+*gen*', '*usu*+*gen*'
The formula '+*gen*' signifies that the genitive is used if possible, but is replaced by **von** when it is not possible to show the genitive case. Prepositions marked '*usu*+*gen*' normally govern the genitive (e.g. **statt dieser Bücher** 'instead of these books'), but take the dative (e.g. **statt Büchern** 'instead of books') when the genitive plural form is not distinctive. (See also (v).)

(v) '+*dat*', '+*gen*' *used with verbs*
The formulas '+*dat*' and '+*gen*' indicate that a verb takes a dative or genitive object respectively (accompanied, in the case of transitive verbs, by an accusative object): e.g. **gehorchen** (+*dat*) 'obey', **bedürfen** (+*gen*) 'need'; (with accusative object) **abkaufen** (+*dat*) 'buy from' (as in **er kaufte ihr einen Blumenstrauß ab** 'he bought a bunch of flowers from her'), **berauben** (+*gen*) 'rob of' (as in **sie beraubten ihn seiner Würde** 'they robbed him of his dignity').

5. *Pronunciation*

Guidance on the pronunciation of German is given in the Pronunciation Guide on pp. lxxiv–lxxxiii. In addition, the following information is provided in the entries:

(i) *Stress* is shown when it falls on a syllable *other than the first*, by means of a dot beneath short vowels or a line beneath long vowels or diphthongs. (Verbs with the prefixes **durch–**, **über–**, **um–** and **unter–** that function as both separable and inseparable verbs have the stress shown in *both* cases.)

(ii) A *phonetic transcription* (in square brackets) is given, where necessary, to show the pronunciation of a word or part of a word. The IPA symbols used in these transcriptions are listed on p. lxxvi. (*Note*: For Anglicisms the usual Germanized pronunciation is shown, e.g. **die Band** [bɛnt], **live** [laͅef]; a pronunciation more closely resembling that used in English may, however, sometimes be heard in some words.)

For the pronunciation of abbreviations (**CDU**, **LPG**, etc.) the user is referred to the table 'The German Alphabet' on p. lxxxiii.

6. *Labels*

Labels – defining usage on a regional, temporal or stylistic basis, or indicating restriction to a particular field of knowledge or activity – take the form of italic abbreviations: *Aust*, *arch*, *vulg*, *comput*, etc. (see Abbreviations, pp. xiii–xiv).

The regional label *SGer* signifies 'South German', and indicates items that are current in South Germany and in many instances also in Austria and/or Switzerland.

7. *Translations*

When two or more successive lexical items share the same translation, the information is shown in the following manner:

schluchzen, der Schluchzer, – sob

To avoid ambiguity an explanatory gloss may be given in brackets, e.g. **die Anzahl** 'number (= quantity)', **wohnen** 'live (= reside) ...' Approximate equivalents are marked '*approx* =', e.g. **der Morgen** '... (measurement) *approx* = acre'; where no equivalent or approximate equivalent exists a more descriptive rendering may be necessary, e.g. South German **fensterln: ~ bei** 'pay a nocturnal visit to (one's sweetheart) by climbing through her bedroom window'.

In certain entries the translation of the word in question is accompanied by italicized explanatory matter – usually consisting of a definition – in brackets, e.g. **das Grundgesetz** 'the Basic Law (*W. German constitution*)', **der/die Volksdeutsche** 'ethnic German (*person of German origin but other nationality resident outside the 1937 frontiers of Germany and Austria*)'. In other instances only a definition is provided, in which case the German term can normally be left untranslated, e.g. **das Missingsch** '(*form of High German containing Low German elements*)'.

LIST OF ABBREVIATIONS

acc	accusative
adj	adjective, adjectival
admin	administration
adv	adverb(ial)
aer	aeronautics
agr	agriculture
angl	angling
anthrop	anthropology
approx	approximately
arch	archaic
archaeol	archaeology
archit	architecture
art	art; article
astrol	astrology
astron	astronomy
athl	athletics
attrib	attributive
Aust	Austrian
aux	auxiliary
bibl	biblical
bill	billiards
biol	biology
bookb	bookbinding
bot	botany
box	boxing
build	building
carp	carpentry
cer	ceramics
chem	chemistry
cin	cinema
civ eng	civil engineering
coll	colloquial
collect	collective
comm	commerce
comp	comparative
compd	compound
comput	computer technology
conj	conjunction
conjug	conjugation
corresp	corresponding
cost	costume
cul	culinary
cycl	cycling
cycle rac	cycle racing
danc	dancing
dat	dative
decl	declined
def	definite
dem	demonstrative
dent	dentistry
dial	dialect
dim	diminutive
dressm	dressmaking
eccles	ecclesiastical
econ	economics
educ	education
eg	for example
EGer	East German
elect	electricity
emot	emotive
emph	emphatic
eng	engineering
Eng	English
ent	entomology
equest	equestrianism
esp	especially
etw.	*etwas*
euph	euphemistic
exc	except (in the case of)
fash	fashion
fem	feminine
fig	figurative
fish	fishing
folkl	folklore
footb	association football
for	forestry
Fr hist	French history
freq	frequently
gen	genitive
geneal	genealogy
geog	geography, geographical
geol	geology
ger	gerund
Ger	German
gramm	grammar
gym	gymnastics
her	heraldry
hist	history, historical
hock	hockey
horse rac	horse racing
hort	horticulture
hunt	hunting
ie	that is
imp	imperative
impers	impersonal
incl	including
ind	indirect
indecl	indeclinable
indef	indefinite
infin	infinitive
insep	inseparable
interrog	interrogative
interj	interjection
iron	ironical
jewel	jewellery
jmd.	*jemand*
jmdm.	*jemandem*
jmdn.	*jemanden*
jmds.	*jemandes*
joc	jocular
journ	journalism
knit	knitting
leg	legal
ling	linguistics
lit	literary
liter	literature
masc	masculine

math	mathematics
mech	mechanics
med	medical
metall	metallurgy
meteor	meteorology
mil	military
min	mining
miner	mineralogy
mot	motoring
mot cycl	motor cycling
mot cycle rac	motor cycle racing
mount	mountaineering
mus	music
myth	mythology
naut	nautical
needl	needlework
neg	negative
neut	neuter
NGer	North German
nom	nominative
nucl tech	nuclear technology
num	numeral
numis	numismatics
obj	object
occ	occasionally
oil tech	oil technology
opp	opposite of, as opposed to
ornith	ornithology
pass	passive
pej	pejorative
pers	person(al)
pharm	pharmacy
philat	philately
philos	philosophy
phot	photography
phr	phrase
phys	physics
pl	plural
poet	poetic
pol	politics
pop	popularly
poss	possessive
p/part	past participle
pred	predicative
pref	prefix
prep	preposition(al)
pres	present
pres/part	present participle
print	printing
pron	pronoun
pros	prosody
Prot	Protestant
psych	psychology
p/t	past tense
rad	radio
rail	railways
RC	Roman Catholic
recip	reciprocal
refl	reflexive
reg	regional
rel	relative
relig	religion
Rom hist	Roman history
row	rowing
sep	separable
SGer	South German (see p. xii)
sing	singular
skat	skating
ski	skiing
(*sn*)	with auxiliary *sein*
sociol	sociology
sp	sport
space	space exploration/technology
stats	statistics
subj	subject; subjunctive
suff	suffix
superl	superlative
surv	surveying
swim	swimming
tail	tailoring
tech	technical
tel	telephone
text	textiles
theat	theatre
theol	theology
univ	university
usu	usually
var	various
vbl	verbal
vet	veterinary science
v/i	verb intransitive
v/t	verb transitive
vulg	vulgar
weight-lift	weight-lifting
wk masc	weak masculine
wrestl	wrestling
zool	zoology

A Concise Guide to German Grammar
Index

A CONCISE GUIDE TO GERMAN GRAMMAR

CASE AND GENDER

CASE

German has four cases: the *nominative* (indicating the subject of a sentence), the *accusative* (indicating the direct object), the *genitive* (indicating possession), and the *dative* (indicating the indirect object). The nominative is also used for the complement of **sein** 'to be', **werden** 'to become' and **bleiben** 'to remain'. The oblique cases (accusative, genitive and dative) are also used after prepositions; for example, **für** 'for' governs the accusative, **trotz** 'in spite of' (usually) the genitive, **mit** 'with' the dative.

Examples (in each the phrase **unser Lehrer** 'our teacher' is used to represent the case concerned):

(nominative) subject: **unser Lehrer fährt einen Mercedes** 'our teacher drives a Mercedes'; complement: **das ist unser Lehrer** 'that's our teacher'

(accusative) direct object: **kennst du unseren Lehrer?** 'do you know our teacher?'; following preposition: **für unseren Lehrer** 'for our teacher'

(genitive) possession: **das Haus unseres Lehrers** 'our teacher's house'; following preposition: **trotz unseres Lehrers** 'in spite of our teacher'

(dative) indirect object: **wer hat unserem Lehrer den Mercedes verkauft/gestohlen?** 'who sold the Mercedes to/stole the Mercedes from our teacher?'; following preposition: **mit unserem Lehrer** 'with our teacher'

Some verbs whose English equivalents take a direct object govern the dative (e.g. **danken** 'to thank', **folgen** 'to follow', **helfen** 'to help'); a few verbs take the genitive (e.g. **sich enthalten** 'to abstain from').

The genitive is also used in various contexts where English has 'of', e.g. **der Start des Flugzeugs** 'the take-off of the aircraft', **die Beibehaltung der Monarchie** 'the retention of the monarchy', **90% aller Aktionäre** '90% of all shareholders' (see also p. xxxix). Where the genitive case cannot be shown, it is replaced by **von**, e.g. **der Export von Kohle** 'the export of coal', **als Übersetzer von Storms Gedichten** 'as a translator of Storm's poems', **die Lösung von Problemen** 'the solving of problems' (as opposed to **die Lösung schwieriger Probleme** 'the solving of difficult problems', where the **–er** ending indicates the genitive plural).

In spoken German the genitive is commonly replaced by **von** + the dative.

The accusative and genitive cases are also used in certain expressions of time. The adverbial accusative indicates 'definite time' (e.g. **jeden Morgen** 'every morning', **dieses Jahr** 'this year'), while the adverbial genitive expresses 'indefinite time' (e.g. **eines Morgens/Tages** 'one morning/day'). In addition, the adverbial accusative serves to indicate (*a*) duration of time (the phrase often being reinforced by **lang**; e.g. **es hat den ganzen Morgen (lang) geschneit** 'it's been snowing *or* it snowed all morning'), and (*b*) distance covered (e.g. **er ist mit dem Auto den Berg hinuntergefahren** 'he drove down the mountain in the car'). The adverbial genitive also occurs in certain set phrases expressing manner, e.g. **gemessenen Schrittes** 'with measured tread', **schweren Herzens** 'with a heavy heart', **allen Ernstes** 'in all seriousness', **erster/zweiter Klasse fahren** 'to travel first/second class'.

Nouns in apposition (i.e. positioned after another noun or a pronoun and used – in G.N. Garmonsway's handy definition – to 'amplify and parallel' it) take the same case as the noun or pronoun they refer to, e.g. **sie hat ihrem Onkel, dem Zollbeamten, lange nicht geschrieben** 'she hasn't written to her uncle, the customs officer, for a long time'.

GENDER

German has three genders: *masculine*, *feminine* and *neuter*; the gender of each noun is shown in the dictionary by means of the definite article (**der** masculine, **die** feminine, **das** neuter) printed in front of the noun. In the plural no distinction of gender is made, **die** denoting all three genders. Compound nouns, e.g. **der Hurrapatriotismus** 'jingoism', always take the gender of their last component (in this instance **der Patriotismus** 'patriotism').

ARTICLES

DEFINITE ARTICLE

	SINGULAR			PLURAL
	masc.	*fem.*	*neut.*	*all genders*
nom.	**der**	**die**	**das**	**die**
acc.	**den**	**die**	**das**	**die**
gen.	**des**	**der**	**des**	**der**
dat.	**dem**	**der**	**dem**	**den**

Certain other words take the same endings as the definite article, namely **dieser**, **diese**, **dieses** 'this, that', **jeder**, **jede**, **jedes** 'each, every', **jener**, **jene**, **jenes** 'that', **mancher**, **manche**, **manches** 'many a', **solcher**, **solche**, **solches** 'such a', **welcher**, **welche**, **welches** 'which' – with the exception that where the definite article takes the form **die** they have the ending **–e** (e.g. **diese**), and in the nominative and accusative neuter they have the ending **–es** (e.g. **dieses**).

The use of the definite article in German broadly corresponds to that of English 'the'. There are, however, certain differences in usage:

(i) = no article in English: (*a*) *abstract nouns* (e.g. **die Natur** 'nature', **das Leben** 'life', **das Schicksal** 'fate', **die Liebe** 'love', **die Jugend** 'youth', **die Zeit** 'time', **die Wissenschaft** 'scholarship, science', **das Bankwesen** 'banking', **die Gesellschaft** 'society', **die Klassik** 'classicism', **der Kommunismus** 'Communism', **das Christentum** 'Christianity'); sometimes, however, the article is omitted – e.g. **(die) Politik** 'politics', **(die) politische Freiheit** 'political freedom' – its use (or non-use) often being as much a question of style and usage as of grammar; (*b*) concepts such as **der Himmel** 'heaven', **die Hölle** 'hell', **das Paradies** 'paradise', and the institutions **das Parlament** 'Parliament', **die Schule** 'school', **das Gefängnis** 'prison', **das Krankenhaus** 'hospital', **die Kirche** 'church'; (*c*) **der Mensch** 'man', **die Leute** 'people'; (*d*) the *names of the seasons*, *months* and also *meals* (e.g. **der Frühling** 'spring', **der Juni** 'June', **das Frühstück** 'breakfast'), although in certain contexts – e.g. **es war Frühling/Juni** 'it was spring/June' – the article is dropped; in the case of the *days of the week* the article is sometimes used (e.g. **(der) Montag** 'Monday'; 'on Monday etc.' is **am Montag** etc.);

(*e*) masculine and feminine *geographical names* (e.g. **die Schweiz** 'Switzerland', **die Provence** 'Provence', **die Schellingstraße** 'Schellingstrasse', **der Petersplatz** 'St. Peter's Square', **der Hydepark** 'Hyde Park', **der Kilimandscharo** 'Kilimanjaro', **der Vesuv** 'Vesuvius', **der Titicacasee** 'Lake Titicaca'), also **das Elsaß** ['ɛlzas] 'Alsace' (see also p. xxiv); (*f*) *proper names preceded by an adjective* (e.g. **die kleine Susi** 'little Susi', **das heutige Frankreich** 'present-day France'); (*g*) in certain phrases, e.g. **im/ins Ausland** 'abroad', **im Bett** 'in bed', **in der Stadt** 'in town', **mit der Bahn, dem Schiff,** etc. 'by rail, ship, etc.', **mit der Post** 'by post'.

(ii) = possessive adjective in English – referring to *parts of the body or articles of clothing* (e.g. **er steckte die Hände in die Taschen** 'he put his hands in his pockets', **er zog die Jacke aus** 'he took off his jacket', **ich schüttelte ihm die Hand** 'I shook his hand', **sie wusch sich** (dat.) **die Haare** 'she washed her hair', **das Blut schoß ihr ins Gesicht** 'blood rushed to her face'); the possessive adjective is, however, used for the subject, e.g. **seine Augen sind blau** 'his eyes are blue'.

(iii) = 'a, an' – used distributively, e.g. **fünf Mark das Pfund** 'five marks a pound'.

INDEFINITE ARTICLE

	masc.	*fem.*	*neut.*
nom.	**ein**	**eine**	**ein**
acc.	**einen**	**eine**	**ein**
gen.	**eines**	**einer**	**eines**
dat.	**einem**	**einer**	**einem**

The negative **kein** 'not a/any, no' takes the same endings in the singular as **ein**; the plural forms are (*nom.*, *acc.*) **keine,** (*gen.*) **keiner**, (*dat.*) **keinen.**

The use of the indefinite article broadly corresponds to that of English 'a, an'. There are, however, certain differences in usage:

(i) no article in German = 'a, an' – with nouns indicating *profession* or *nationality* (or other geographical identification) used as the complement of **sein, werden** or **bleiben** (e.g. **er war Architekt** 'he was an architect', **sie ist Neuseeländerin** 'she's a New Zealander', **er ist Bayer/Berliner** 'he's a Bavarian/Berliner'); the article is also as a rule omitted with other nouns referring to an individual belonging to a category of persons, although in some cases usage vacillates between using and omitting the article (e.g. **sie ist Witwe** 'she's a widow', **er wollte Junggeselle bleiben** 'he wanted to stay a bachelor', **er ist (ein) Katholik** 'he's a Catholic', **er war schon immer (ein) Optimist** 'he was always an optimist'); where the noun is preceded by an adjective the article is always used, e.g. **er war ein hervorragender Architekt** 'he was an outstanding architect', **ich bin ein unverbesserlicher Optimist** 'I'm an incurable optimist'.

(ii) **als** without article = 'as a(n)' (or, in appropriate contexts, 'as the'), e.g. **als Mensch** 'as a human being', **als Warnung** 'as a warning'; in a case like **er starb als Christ** 'he died a Christian' 'a' or 'an' alone is used.

(iii) **ein** = 'a pair of ...s', e.g. **eine Brille** 'a pair of glasses', **eine Schere** 'a pair of scissors', **eine Zange** 'a pair of tongs', **eine Hose** 'a pair of trousers'.

(iv) **ein** = 'a piece of ...' or is rendered by the English noun alone, e.g. **eine Information** '(a piece of) information', **eine Nachricht** '(a piece of) news', **ein Rat** '(a piece of) advice'.

(v) 'not a(n)' is expressed by **kein**, e.g. **kein Laut war zu hören** 'not a sound was to be heard', **ich hatte kein Auto** 'I didn't have a car'.

(vi) The indefinite article is omitted in many descriptive phrases of the type *preposition + adjective + noun* where English has 'a, an', e.g. **ein Haus mit flachem Dach** 'a house with a flat roof', **auf geheimnisvolle Weise** 'in a mysterious manner', **in hohem Alter** 'at an advanced age', **mit lauter/leiser Stimme** 'in a loud/low voice', **mit großer Mehrheit** 'by a large majority'.

NOUNS

SINGULAR

German nouns, which are written with a capital initial letter, may be divided into three main groups in the singular:

(a) *Masculines* (except weak masculines) and *neuters*. These form the genitive by adding **–s** or, in the case of native (but not 'foreign') *monosyllables*, **–es** (e.g. **der Tag** 'day'/**des Tages, das Schiff** 'ship'/**des Schiffes**: contrast **das Gen** 'gene'/**des Gens**).[1] (Exception: monosyllables ending in a vowel or vowel + **h**, e.g. **der Schuh** 'shoe'/**des Schuhs.**) Nouns ending in a *sibilant* also add **–es** (e.g. **der Komplex** 'complex'/**des Komplexes, das Walroß** 'walrus'/**des Walrosses**),[2] with the exception of those in **–as, –os, –us**, which have *no* genitive ending (e.g. **der Kubismus** 'cubism'/**des Kubismus, das Epos** 'epic'/**des Epos**) unless the dictionary indicates otherwise.[3]

In the case of *abbreviations* the ending **–s** is optional.

The optional dative ending **–e** (after monosyllables) – so common in the writings of, for example, Thomas Mann or Hermann Broch – has fallen largely into disuse; it survives chiefly in set phrases such as **auf dem Lande** 'in the country', **in hohem Maße** 'to a high degree'.

(b) *Weak masculines*. These take the ending **–en** or (when **e** is already present) **–n** in all cases of the singular except the nominative (also throughout the plural):

nom.	**der Mensch** ('man,[4] person')	**der Hase** ('hare')
acc.	**den Menschen**	**den Hasen**
gen.	**des Menschen**	**des Hasen**
dat.	**dem Menschen**	**dem Hasen**

This category includes (i) nouns (designating chiefly persons) that end in **–ant, –ent, –ist, –graph, –loge**, e.g. **der Demonstrant** 'demonstrator', **der Student** 'student', **der Realist** 'realist', **der Geograph** 'geographer', **der Theologe** 'theologian'; and (ii) nouns in **–e** denoting nationalities, e.g. **der Chinese** 'Chinese', **der Franzose** 'Frenchman', **der Schwede** 'Swede'. (Not, however, **der Deutsche** 'German', which is declined like an adjective: see p. xxxiv.)

(c) *Feminines*. These remain unchanged throughout the singular.

1. Native monosyllabic nouns sometimes, especially in less formal usage, have the ending **–s** instead.
2. Neuter nouns in **–nis** double the **s**, e.g. **das Ereignis** 'event'/**des Ereignisses.**
3. In some disyllabic nouns with unstressed prefixes (e.g. **der Vertrag** 'contract, treaty') and, especially for reasons of euphony, certain 'foreign' nouns of more than one syllable (e.g. **das Produkt** 'product') the ending **–es** may occur as an alternative to **–s**.
4. 'Man' in the sense of *homo sapiens*.

PLURAL

The nominative, accusative and genitive plural forms are identical; the dative plural adds **–n** (e.g. **die Häuser** 'the houses', dative **den Häusern**), where **n** is not already present, except in the case of nouns that add **–s** to form the plural.

Plurals are formed in various ways in German: by adding **–e** with or without umlaut, **–en** or **–n**, **–er** with or without umlaut, **–s** (chiefly added to words of foreign origin) or – in the case of nouns ending in **–el, –en, –er** – by retaining the singular form unchanged or with umlaut.

(– or ¨): nouns in **–el, –en, –er**: (*a*) *masculines*, usually with umlaut where possible – e.g. **der Engel** 'angel'/**Engel**, **der Vogel** 'bird'/**Vögel**, **der Garten** 'garden'/**Gärten**, **der Vater** 'father'/**Väter**; (*b*) *neuters*, without umlaut (except **das Kloster** 'monastery, convent'/**Klöster**) – e.g. **das Segel** 'sail'/**Segel**, **das Zeichen** 'sign'/ **Zeichen**, **das Ufer** 'shore'/**Ufer**, **das Zimmer** 'room'/**Zimmer**; (*c*) two *feminines*: **die Mutter** 'mother'/**Mütter**, **die Tochter** 'daughter'/**Töchter**.

(**–e** or **¨e**): (*a*) most *masculines*; of those which can mutate the vowel, some do while others do not – e.g. **der Arm** 'arm'/**Arme**, **der Arzt** 'doctor'/**Ärzte**, **der Baum** 'tree'/**Bäume**, **der Fisch** 'fish'/**Fische**; (*b*) a number of major *feminine* monosyllables, always with umlaut – e.g. **die Angst** 'fear, anxiety'/**Ängste**, **die Frucht** 'fruit'/ **Früchte**, **die Gans** 'goose'/**Gänse**, **die Nacht** 'night'/**Nächte**; (*c*) some *neuter* monosyllables, without umlaut (except **das Floß** 'raft'/**Flöße**) – e.g. **das Boot** 'boat'/**Boote**, **das Jahr** 'year'/**Jahre**, **das Pferd** 'horse'/**Pferde**, **das Spiel** 'game'/**Spiele**.

(**–en** or **–n**): (*a*) most *feminines*: 1. the vast majority of those ending in a consonant take **–en** – e.g. **die Schlacht** 'battle'/**Schlachten**, **die Tat** 'deed'/**Taten**, **die Uhr** 'clock, watch'/**Uhren**, **die Zeit** 'time'/**Zeiten**; likewise nouns in **–ei, –heit, –in** (with doubling of **n** in the plural), **–keit, –schaft, –ung** – e.g. **die Bäckerei** 'bakery'/ **Bäckereien**, **die Füchsin** 'vixen'/**Füchsinnen**, **die Bemerkung** 'remark'/**Bemerkungen**; 2. all feminines ending in **–e** take **–n** in the plural – e.g. **die Blume** 'flower'/**Blumen**, **die Farbe** 'colour, paint'/**Farben**, **die Minute** 'minute'/**Minuten**, **die Schwalbe** 'swallow'/**Schwalben**; (*b*) a number of *masculines* and a few *neuters* – e.g. **der Schmerz** 'pain'/**Schmerzen**, **der See** 'lake'/**Seen**, **der Staat** 'state'/**Staaten**, **der Strahl** 'ray'/**Strahlen**; **das Auge** 'eye'/**Augen**, **das Bett** 'bed'/**Betten**, **das Ende** 'end'/**Enden**; (*c*) all *weak masculines* – e.g. **der Hase** 'hare'/**Hasen**, **der Prinz** 'prince'/**Prinzen**, **der Student** 'student'/**Studenten**; (*d*) nouns in **–or** (which shift the stress in the plural) – e.g. **der Organisátor** 'organizer'/**Organisatóren**, **der Proféssor** 'professor'/**Professóren**; (*e*) nouns of foreign origin in which **–en** replaces the singular ending to form the plural – e.g. **das Drama** 'drama'/**Dramen**, **das Epos** 'epic'/**Epen**, **das Konto** '(bank) account'/**Konten**, **das Album** 'album'/**Alben**, **das Individuum** 'individual'/ **Individuen**, **der Rhythmus** 'rhythm'/**Rhythmen**, **der Organismus** 'organism'/ **Organismen**.

(**–er** or **¨er**): most *neuters* and a few *masculines*, with umlaut where possible – e.g. **das Dorf** 'village'/**Dörfer**, **das Ei** 'egg'/**Eier**, **das Kind** 'child'/**Kinder**, **das Land** 'country'/**Länder**; **der Geist** 'mind, spirit, ghost'/**Geister**, **der Gott** 'god'/**Götter**, **der Mann** 'man, husband'/**Männer**, **der Wald** 'forest'/**Wälder**.

(**–s**): (*a*) some nouns of foreign origin – e.g. **der Bikini** 'bikini'/**Bikinis**, **der Store** 'net curtain'/**Stores**, **der Streik** 'strike'/**Streiks**; **die City** 'city centre'/**Citys**, **die Hazienda** 'hacienda'/**Haziendas**, **die Sauna** 'sauna'/**Saunas**; **das Büro** 'office'/**Büros**, **das Ensemble** 'ensemble'/**Ensembles**, **das Kino** 'cinema'/**Kinos**; (*b*) the nautical terms **das Deck** 'deck'/**Decks**, **das Dock** 'dock'/**Docks**, **das Wrack** 'wreck'/**Wracks**; (*c*) a few words which form a colloquial plural in **–s** in addition to the standard form – e.g.

der Kerl 'fellow'/**Kerle**, coll. **Kerls**, **das Fräulein** 'young lady'/**Fräulein**, coll. **Fräuleins**.

(other endings used with words of foreign origin): e.g. **das Adverb** 'adverb'/**Adverbien**, **das Prinzip** 'principle'/**Prinzipien**; **der Atlas** 'atlas'/**Atlanten**; **das Paradoxon** 'paradox'/**Paradoxa**; grammatical terms such as **das Nomen** 'noun'/**Nomina**, **das Tempus** 'tense'/**Tempora**, **der Kasus** 'case'/**Kasus** (long **u**), **der Modus** 'mood'/**Modi**.

Some nouns have different plural forms corresponding to different meanings of the singular: e.g. **der Bau** 'building'/**Bauten**, 'burrow, earth'/**Baue**; **der Faden** 'thread'/**Fäden**, 'fathom'/**Faden**; **das Wort** 'word'/**Worte** '(connected) words', **Wörter** '(single) words' as in a **Wörterbuch**.

Other nouns do not have a plural form as such, the place of the 'missing' plural being taken by a compound in the plural, e.g. **der Tod** 'death' – **Todesfälle** 'deaths' (literally 'cases of death'), **der Sport** 'sport' – **Sportarten** 'sports' (literally 'types of sport'), **der Käse** 'cheese' – **Käsesorten** 'cheeses' (literally 'kinds of cheese').

Points regarding number (including agreement in number) where German usage differs from English

(i) Some German nouns in the singular correspond to an English plural, and vice versa: (*a*) German singular = English plural, e.g. **der Hafer** 'oats', **das Gemüse** 'vegetables', **das Geweih** 'antlers', **die Treppe** 'stairs', **die Kaserne** 'barracks', **das Feuerwerk** 'fireworks', **das Uhrwerk** 'works (of a clock or watch)', **der Erlös** 'proceeds', **der Lohn** 'wages', **der Schadenersatz** 'damages', **der Dank** 'thanks', **der Inhalt** 'contents', **das Mittel** 'means', **die Umgebung** 'surroundings', **die Mathematik** 'mathematics', **die Physik** 'physics', the names of the suits in cards (**Herz** 'hearts', **Karo** 'diamonds', **Pik** 'spades', **Kreuz** 'clubs'), **das Mittelalter** 'the Middle Ages', **Westindien** 'the West Indies'; (*b*) German plural = English singular, e.g. **die Haare** (also **das Haar**) 'hair' (in collective sense), **die Möbel** 'furniture', **die Lebensmittel** 'food', **die Flitterwochen** 'honeymoon', **die Zinsen** 'interest (on money lent)', **die Fortschritte** 'progress' (as in **Fortschritte machen** 'to make progress'), **die Kenntnisse** 'knowledge (of a subject etc.)'.

(ii) In the case of masculine and neuter nouns indicating a weight or measure, as well as the feminine **Mark**, the singular form is used after numerals (or expressions such as **ein paar** 'a few', **mehrere** 'several') instead of the plural, e.g. **zwei Glas Bier** 'two glasses of beer', **drei Pfund Tee** 'three pounds of tea', **vier Dutzend Eier** 'four dozen eggs', **zehn Grad (Celsius)** 'ten degrees (Celsius)', **vier Paar Schuhe** 'four pairs of shoes', **fünf Stück (Apfelsinen** etc.) 'five (oranges etc.)', **50000 Mann** '50,000 men' (if viewed as a single unit, as when constituting a fighting force: **eine Armee von 50000 Mann** 'an army of 50,000 men'), **100 Schritt** '100 paces', **20 Pfennig** '20 pfennigs', **30 Mark** '30 marks', **50 englische Pfund** '50 pounds sterling', **100 Dollar** '100 dollars'. (Feminine nouns of this type – except **Mark** – form the plural in the usual way, e.g. **drei Tassen Tee** 'three cups of tea', **100 Drachmen** '100 drachmas'.) On the other hand, where the items referred to are conceived of essentially as individual objects, the plural form is used, e.g. **zwei Fässer Bier** 'two (individual) barrels of beer' (to be compared with **zwei Faß Bier** 'two barrels of beer' as a quantity ordered etc.).

(iii) If two or more attributes refer to identical nouns, only the last noun is given – in the singular (whereas English has the plural), e.g. **das Alte (Testament** understood) **und Neue Testament** 'the Old and New Testaments', **im 17., 18. und 19. Jahrhundert** 'in the 17th, 18th and 19th centuries'. (This also applies when two compounds share the same last element, e.g. **in der Morgen- und Abendausgabe** 'in the morning and evening editions'.)

(iv) In German the singular is used in a distributive sense (where English has the plural) with reference to something concrete or abstract that applies to a number of persons, e.g. **wir nahmen den Hut ab** 'we took off our hats', **alle hoben die rechte Hand** 'all raised their right hands', **sie redete die Leute nie mit dem Namen an** 'she never addressed people by their names', **manche Leute haben ein sehr leichtes Leben** 'some people have very easy lives'.

(v) Where a noun denoting a quantity (such as **eine Anzahl** 'a number', **eine Menge** 'a quantity', **eine Herde** 'a herd') is followed by a plural noun, it may take a singular or plural verb according to whether the emphasis is more on the noun of quantity or on the following plural noun respectively, e.g. **ein Dutzend Eier kostet 5 Mark** 'a dozen eggs cost 5 marks', **eine riesige Menge Menschen war(en) versammelt** 'a huge crowd of people was gathered' (**war** stresses the collective presence of the crowd, **waren** emphasizes the people concerned).

(vi) **Die USA** 'the USA', like **die Vereinigten Staaten** 'the United States', is treated as plural, e.g. **die USA haben den Vertrag ratifiziert** 'the USA has ratified the treaty'; the corresponding personal pronoun is therefore **sie** (plural), translated by 'it, she'.

(vii) Even if the complement precedes the verb and subject, the verb agrees in number with the subject, e.g. **seine große Leidenschaft sind Schmetterlinge** 'his great passion is butterflies'.

(viii) The English plural form in phrases of the type 'in ... respects/ways' corresponds to a German singular, e.g. **in mancher Beziehung/Hinsicht** 'in some respects', **auf verschiedene Weise** 'in various ways', **auf tausenderlei Art** 'in a thousand ways'.

PROPER NAMES

Christian names and surnames, whether masculine or feminine, take **–s** in the genitive singular, e.g. **Juttas Fahrrad** 'Jutta's bicycle', **(Richard) Wagners Opern** or **die Opern (Richard) Wagners** '(Richard) Wagner's operas', **die Ermordung Kennedys** 'Kennedy's assassination'. (After **s, ß, tz, x** or **z** an apostrophe is used, e.g. **Agnes' Hut** 'Agnes's hat', **Strauß' Walzer** 'Strauss's waltzes', **Marx' Ideen** 'Marx's ideas'; however, **von** is sometimes used instead, e.g. **die Walzer von Strauß**; especially with classical names the definite article is often used to indicate genitive case, e.g. **der Tod des Sokrates** 'the death of Socrates'; **Jesus Christus** has the genitive **Jesu Christi.**) Surnames usually add **–s** in the plural; those ending in a sibilant add **–ens**, e.g. **(die) Schulzens** 'the Schulzes'.

Geographical names also take the genitive **–s** (unless feminine like **die Schweiz** 'Switzerland'), e.g. **die Bevölkerung Dänemarks** 'the population of Denmark',

die Geschichte Roms 'the history of Rome', **außerhalb Moskaus** 'outside Moscow'. (After **s, ß, tz, x** or **z** it is customary to use **von**, e.g. **das Erbe von Byzanz** 'the heritage of Byzantium', **die Theater von Paris** 'the theatres of Paris'.[1] The genitive of masculine and neuter names that are preceded by the definite article is shown at the dictionary entries concerned, e.g. **der Nil** 'the Nile' (genitive **–(s)**).) When a name is preceded by an adjective, the genitive **–s** is often dropped, e.g. **die Vorurteile des mittelalterlichen Europa(s)** 'the prejudices of medieval Europe'. Where the name of a country (or town) occurs in the plural, it is often left uninflected, although **–s** may be added, e.g. **die zwei Deutschland(s)** 'the two Germanies', **die beiden Amerika(s)** 'the two Americas'.

The names of continents (other than **die Antarktis** 'Antarctica'), countries and regions (with certain exceptions, e.g. **der Sudan** 'the Sudan', **der Balkan** 'the Balkans', **die Schweiz**, **die Tschechoslowakei** 'Czechoslovakia', **die Türkei** 'Turkey', **die Bretagne** 'Britanny', **die Toskana** 'Tuscany', (plural) **die USA** 'the USA')[2] and cities are all used without an article, and are neuter – as becomes apparent when, exceptionally, the definite article is required, namely when an adjective precedes the name or a genitive phrase follows, e.g. **das südliche Spanien** 'southern Spain', **das Frankreich Ludwigs XIV. (= des Vierzehnten)** 'the France of Louis XIV', **das Warschau von heute** 'present-day Warsaw'.

Mountains (and mountain ranges) have the definite article, and are usually masculine, e.g. **der Brocken** 'the Brocken', **der Montblanc** 'Mont Blanc', **der Fudschijama** 'Fujiyama', **der Mount Everest** 'Mount Everest', **der Ural** 'the Urals' (but **die Eifel**). Some occur as plurals, e.g. **die Alpen** 'the Alps', **die Vogesen** 'the Vosges', **die Kordilleren** 'the Cordilleras'.

Rivers in Germany are mostly feminine (e.g. **die Mosel** 'the Moselle', **die Donau** 'the Danube'), as are foreign rivers in **–a** and **–e** (e.g. **die Wolga** 'the Volga', **die Themse** 'the Thames', **die Seine**); but several major German rivers (e.g. **der Rhein, der Main, der Neckar, der Inn**) and most foreign ones (e.g. **der Amazonas** 'the Amazon', **der Jangtse(kiang)** 'the Yangtze (Kiang)', **der Limpopo, der Mississippi, der Tweed**) have masculine gender.

The planets also have the definite article, and are mostly masculine: **der Merkur** 'Mercury', **der Mars** 'Mars', **der Jupiter** 'Jupiter', **der Saturn** 'Saturn', **der Uranus** 'Uranus', **der Neptun** 'Neptune', **der Pluto** 'Pluto'; two are feminines: **die Venus** 'Venus', **die Erde** 'Earth'.

Cars are generally masculine, e.g. **der Mercedes, der Renault, der Rolls-Royce, der Volvo, der Wartburg**. *Ships* are usually feminine, e.g. **die „Nautilus", die „Graf Spee", die „Titanic"** [ti'taːnɪk]; so too are *aircraft*, e.g. **die Boeing, die DC-8, die Messerschmitt** (but **der Airbus, der Jumbo, der Starfighter**).

The titles of *works of art*, *newspapers*, *etc.* are inflected, e.g. **hast du „Iwan den Schrecklichen" gesehen?** 'have you seen "Ivan the Terrible"?' Where a title beginning with a definite article is in an oblique case the article is placed outside

1. **Von** is also usual in e.g. **der König/Präsident von ...** 'the King/President of ...' (but **der Präsident der Vereinigten Staaten**).
2. The article is optional in masculines such as **(der) Irak** 'Iraq', **(der) Iran** 'Iran'.

the quotation marks, e.g. **als Abonnent des „Spiegels"** 'as a subscriber to "Der Spiegel"', **im „Kapital" heißt es ...** 'it says in "Das Kapital" ...'; the article is dropped following an artist's name in the genitive, e.g. **die Ouvertüre zu Wagners „Fliegendem Holländer"** 'the overture to W.'s "Flying Dutchman"'.

LANGUAGES

Languages with names in **–isch** (**–sch**) have two forms: the *uninflected* form (e.g. **Englisch**, **Deutsch**), which is neuter, although the gender is not always apparent, and the – likewise neuter – *inflected* form, consisting of the corresponding adjectival noun with definite article (e.g. **das Englische/Deutsche**); other languages such as **(das) Hindi** 'Hindi', **(das) Suaheli** 'Swahili', **(das) Haussa** 'Hausa', also **(das) Esperanto** 'Esperanto' have a single name only.

The uninflected form is used to refer either to a language in a general sense (without an article) – e.g. **Deutsch sprechen** 'to speak German', **gut/fließend Deutsch sprechen** 'to speak German well/fluently', **Serbokroatisch ist nicht mein Fall** 'Serbo-Croat is not my cup of tea' – or to a particular *type* of the language concerned, e.g. **gutes Deutsch** 'good German', **das amerikanische Englisch** 'American English', **das in der Sowjetunion gesprochene Deutsch** 'the German spoken in the Soviet Union', **mein/Luthers Deutsch** 'my/Luther's German', **das Kaufmannsdeutsch** 'commercial German', **im heutigen Arabisch** 'in present-day Arabic'. The adjectival noun, on the other hand, can only refer to a language in a general sense, = 'the ... language', e.g. **das Englische ist eine indogermanische Sprache** 'English is an Indo-European language', **die Aussprache des Russischen** 'the pronunciation of Russian', also **etwas aus dem (Deutschen** etc.) **ins (Englische** etc.) **übersetzen** 'to translate something from (German etc.) into (English etc.)'.

Adverbial use of **deutsch** *etc.*: e.g. **deutsch denken/sprechen** 'to think in German/speak (in) German', **der Brief ist deutsch** (or **in Deutsch/deutsch**) **geschrieben** 'the letter is (written) in German'.

In **auf deutsch** etc. 'in German etc.' the name of the language also begins with a small letter (e.g. **sag mal was auf chinesisch** 'say something in Chinese', **wie heißt „haggis" auf deutsch?** 'what is the German for "haggis"?'); but cf. – with adjective – **in fließendem/gebrochenem Deutsch** etc. 'in fluent/broken German etc.' 'In Hindi etc.' is **auf Hindi** etc.

PRONOUNS

PERSONAL PRONOUNS

SINGULAR

	1st pers. 'I'	*2nd pers.* 'you' (familiar form)	*3rd pers.* 'he/she/it' *masc.*	*fem.*	*neut.*
nom.	**ich**	**du**	**er**	**sie**	**es**
acc.	**mich**	**dich**	**ihn**	**sie**	**es**
gen.	**meiner**	**deiner**	**seiner**	**ihrer**	**seiner**
dat.	**mir**	**dir**	**ihm**	**ihr**	**ihm**

Singular and Plural: **Sie** 'you'

nom.	**Sie**
acc.	**Sie**
gen.	**Ihrer**
dat.	**Ihnen**

PLURAL

	1st pers. 'we'	*2nd pers.* 'you' (familiar form)	*3rd pers.* 'they'
nom.	**wir**	**ihr**	**sie**
acc.	**uns**	**euch**	**sie**
gen.	**unser**	**euer**	**ihrer**
dat.	**uns**	**euch**	**ihnen**

NOTE: The genitive forms are relatively rare, occurring chiefly with verbs and adjectives that govern the genitive.

The familiar 2nd person pronouns **du** and **ihr** are used when addressing relatives, close friends, one's peers (among certain groups such as workmen), children, animals, God (**Du**) and (in poetry) personified inanimate objects; the reader of a book, advertisement, etc. is also addressed in the familiar form, e.g. **siehe ...** 'see ...', **trink Coca-Cola** 'drink Coca-Cola', and in the plural **schützt unsere Wälder!** 'protect our forests'. Otherwise **Sie** is used.

In letter-writing the 2nd person pronouns (and corresponding possessive adjectives) are capitalized: **Du (Dein)**, **Ihr (Euer)**.

The personal pronouns of the 3rd person singular agree in gender with the noun they refer to, thus 'it' may be expressed by **er** (referring to a masculine), **sie** (referring to a feminine) or **es** (referring to a neuter), e.g. **ich liebe diesen Garten – er ist so groß** 'I love this garden – it's so large'. (The use in English of 'she' to refer to countries necessarily differs from German usage: the great majority of countries being neuter in German, they are referred to by **es**.)

Although in accordance with the rules of congruence one would expect the neuter pronoun to be used in connection with the neuter nouns **Mädchen** and **Fräulein**, in practice 'natural gender' tends to assert itself, and the feminine pronoun is widely used instead, e.g. **was hat das Mädchen? – ist sie immer so?** 'what's wrong with the girl? – is she always like that?' (Likewise, the feminine possessive adjective **ihr** is widely used instead of neuter **sein**, e.g. **das Mädchen von nebenan hat ihren Paß verloren** 'the girl next door has lost her passport'.) In the case of the relative pronoun, however, congruence is always observed, e.g. **das Fräulein, das** (neuter relative pronoun) **uns bediente** 'the young lady who served us'.

After the commoner prepositions (**an, auf, aus, bei, durch, für, gegen, hinter, in, mit, nach, neben, über, unter, um, von, vor, zu, zwischen**) the personal pronouns of the 3rd person are normally used with reference to persons, e.g. **mit ihm** 'with him'. If things are referred to, an adverbial compound consisting of **da–** (before a vowel **dar–**) + preposition is generally used instead, e.g. **damit** 'with it/them', **darauf** 'on it/them'; not infrequently, however, the construction preposition + pronoun is preferred, e.g. **mehrere Jungen stehen um einen Fußball – und wissen nicht, was sie mit ihm** (= **damit**) **anfangen sollen** (newspaper report) 'several boys are standing round a football, not knowing what to do with it'.

In a clause introduced by **wie** 'such as', a 3rd person pronoun is used to refer to the antecedent, e.g. (with pronoun as subject) **der traditionelle Empfang für die Vertreter der Kirche, wie er in der Ära Ulbricht üblich war** 'the traditional reception for the representatives of the Church, such as was customary in the Ulbricht era', (as object) **Geschichten, wie man sie überall in der Welt lesen kann** 'stories such as one may read all over the world'; the pronoun **einer, eine, ein(e)s** 'one' may be used in a similar way, e.g. **ein Sonnenaufgang, wie wir noch nie einen gesehen hatten** 'a sunrise such as we had never seen before'.

Es has a number of special functions:

(i) It is used with the verb **sein** *with demonstrative force*, e.g. **es ist der Briefträger** 'it's the postman', (with plural noun determining number of verb) **es sind meine Tanten** 'it's my aunts'.

'*It's me* etc.': The personal pronoun is here followed by the verb **sein** (the number and person of which it determines) and **es**, e.g. **ich bin's** (or **bin es**) 'it's me', **er war's** (or **war es**) 'it was him' (in questions the verb comes first, e.g. **bist du's** (or **du es**)? 'is it you?'). The same word order applies when a relative clause follows, e.g. **ich war es, der/die ...** 'it was I who ...'.

(ii) It anticipates:

(*a*) a *noun subject* (which tends to be emphasized by the construction), e.g. **es geschah etwas Merkwürdiges** 'something remarkable happened', **es wurde ein Stück aufgeführt, das ...** 'a play was performed which ...', (= 'there') **es scheint keiner zu Hause zu sein** 'there doesn't seem to be anybody at home', also the formulaic **es war einmal ...** 'once upon a time there was ...'; where the anticipated subject is in the plural, the verb is also, e.g. **es kamen viele Briefe** 'many letters came', **es sind nicht alle Schlangen giftig** 'not all snakes are poisonous', **es waren zwei Fliegen im Zimmer** 'there were two flies in the room' (see p. lvi).

(*b*) a *noun clause* or *infinitive phrase*, e.g. (as subject, = English 'it') **es ist möglich, daß ...** 'it is possible that ...', **es ist mir egal, ob ...** 'it makes no difference to me whether ...', **es lohnt sich zu ...** 'it pays to ...'; (as object – sometimes optional) **(es) verheimlichen, daß ...** 'to conceal the fact that ...', **es ablehnen zu ...** 'to decline to ...', **(es) vorziehen zu ...** 'to prefer to ...', (= English 'it') **es für richtig halten zu ...** 'to think it right to ...'

(iii) In sentences such as **er ist gutmütig und wird es immer sein** 'he is good-natured and always will be', **ihre Mutter war eine Dame, sie aber war es nicht** 'her mother was a lady, but she was not' it *completes the predicate*, in place of an adjective or a noun already referred to (here **gutmütig, eine Dame**); in English this **es** has no equivalent, the complement being understood. **Es** is also without a corresponding pronoun in English in *clauses of comparison* beginning **als/wie es ...** = English 'than/as' + inversion, e.g. **wie es Sitte ist** 'as is the custom', **wie es sich gehört** 'as is proper', **als es der Fall ist** 'than is the case'.

(iv) It is used as an *indefinite object* in many *idioms* (cf. English 'it' in 'to carry it off', 'to go it alone'), e.g. **es weit bringen** 'to go a long way, go far', **es eilig haben** 'to be in a hurry', **es gut meinen** 'to mean well', **es zu bunt treiben** 'to go too far'.

REFLEXIVE PRONOUNS

The reflexive pronouns are identical with the personal pronouns in all instances except the accusative and dative (singular and plural) of the 3rd person (**er, sie, es**; pl. **sie**) and of **Sie** – in these instances the form **sich** is used; thus the conjugation of **sich waschen** 'to wash (oneself)' runs:

ich wasche mich	**wir waschen uns**
du wäschst dich	**ihr wascht euch**
er/sie/es wäscht sich	**sie, Sie waschen sich**

The reflexive pronouns refer back to the subject performing the action concerned, as do the English equivalents 'myself', 'yourself', 'oneself', etc. English, however, frequently uses the verb on its own with the reflexive sense implied, e.g. 'to wash', 'to dress', (of door etc.) 'to open', where German always has the reflexive pronoun: **sich waschen, sich anziehen, sich öffnen**. (See also **sich** 2, 3 in the dictionary.) English also omits the '-self' ending after a preposition where the pronoun refers back to the subject, e.g. 'he closed the door behind him (= himself)'; here too German requires the reflexive pronoun: **er schloß die Tür hinter sich**.

The reflexive pronouns may also be used in the reciprocal sense 'each other, one another', e.g. **wir sehen uns bald wieder** 'we'll see each other again soon'.

POSSESSIVE PRONOUNS

There are essentially two forms of possessive pronoun in German: (*a*) (the usual form) **meiner, meine, mein(e)s** 'mine', **deiner** etc. 'yours' (familiar), **seiner** etc. 'his, its', **ihrer** etc. 'hers, its', **uns(e)rer** etc. 'ours', **eu(e)rer** etc. 'yours' (familiar plural), **ihrer** etc. 'theirs', **Ihrer** etc. 'yours'; these are declined like the definite article:

	Singular			Plural
	masc.	*fem.*	*neut.*	*all genders*
nom.	**meiner**	**meine**	**mein(e)s**	**meine**
acc.	**meinen**	**meine**	**mein(e)s**	**meine**
dat.	**meinem**	**meiner**	**meinem**	**meinen**

These forms are the same as those of the possessive adjectives (**mein** 'my' etc.: see p. xxxiii) except in the masculine nominative and neuter nominative/accusative. The genitive is not shown, being replaced by **von** + dative, e.g. **von meinem/meiner/meinen** 'of mine'. Examples: **ihr Hut ist noch da, aber meiner ist verschwunden** 'her hat's still there, but mine's disappeared', **mein Auto ist größer als deins** 'my car's bigger than yours'; (*b*) (in literary usage) with the definite article and weak endings, either with or without **-ig-**: **der/die/das ...(ig)e**, e.g. **der/die/das mein(ig)e** 'mine'.

There also exists an archaic literary form, namely uninflected **mein, dein, sein, unser, euer** (not, however, **ihr** or **Ihr**), used predicatively as the complement of **sein, werden**, etc. to express possession, e.g. **Dein ist mein Herz** 'Thine is my heart' (in Schubert's *Die schöne Müllerin*).

INTERROGATIVE PRONOUNS

	was? 'what?'	**wer?** 'who?'
nom.	**was?**	**wer?**
acc.	**was?**	**wen?**
gen.	**wessen?**	**wessen?**
dat.	–	**wem?**

The neuter pronoun **was** is replaced by **wo-** (or **wor-** before vowels) when the sense 'what' + preposition is to be conveyed; this form combines with the preposition concerned to form a compound, thus 'what ... with?' is expressed by **womit?**, 'what ... on?' by **worauf?**

RELATIVE PRONOUNS

	Singular			Plural
	masc.	*fem.*	*neut.*	*all genders*
nom.	**der**	**die**	**das**	**die**
acc.	**den**	**die**	**das**	**die**
gen.	**dessen**	**deren**	**dessen**	**deren**
dat.	**dem**	**der**	**dem**	**denen**

The relative pronoun (= English 'who', 'which', 'that') agrees in gender and number with its antecedent (the noun it refers to), while its case is determined by its function within the clause. It is never omitted. The relative clause is always separated by commas from the rest of the sentence; the finite verb goes to the end of the clause. Examples: **die Illustrierte, die** (accusative) **ich kaufen wollte** 'the magazine (which) I wanted to buy', **der Klub, dem ich angehöre** 'the club I belong to (to which I belong)'. (When the antecedent is a 1st or 2nd person pronoun, German repeats the pronoun concerned after the relative pronoun, e.g. **ich, der ich immer so geduldig bin** 'I who am always so patient'.)

Pronominal adverbs such as **womit, worin, worüber** occur, if the antecedent is a thing, in more formal prose as an alternative to the construction *preposition + relative pronoun* (e.g. **die Welt, worin** – instead of **in der** – **wir leben** 'the world in which we live'); but they are now relatively uncommon – the combination of preposition and relative pronoun being generally preferred – *except* where the antecedent is a pronoun such as **das, alles, einiges, etwas, nichts** (e.g. **etwas, wofür man bezahlt werden sollte** 'something for which one should be paid') or a clause (e.g. **der Kugelstoßer hatte acht Stunden lang trainiert, wovon er ziemlich erschöpft war** 'the shot-putter had been training for eight hours, as a result of which he was pretty worn out').

Was *as a relative*: **Was** is used after **das** or neuter indefinites – e.g. **alles, was** 'everything that', **einiges, was** 'some things that', **etwas, was** 'something that', **nichts, was**

'nothing that' – as well as neuter superlative adjectives used as nouns, e.g. **das mindeste, was du tun kannst** 'the least you can do', **das Beste, was Händel je komponiert hat** 'the best thing Handel ever composed'. It is also used where a clause is the antecedent, e.g. **das Fußballspiel mußte abgebrochen werden, was wir sehr bedauerten** 'the football match had to be stopped, which we very much regretted'.

DEMONSTRATIVE PRONOUNS

The forms are the same as those of the relative pronouns (above) – except that the *genitive plural* form **deren** is replaced by **derer** when followed by a relative clause, e.g. **die Gesichter derer, die jahrelang gewartet hatten** 'the faces of those who had been waiting for years'. For the full range of possible translations see **der/die/das** 3 in the dictionary; examples: **der/die mit der Perücke** '*the one* with the wig', **die Unfallrate der Aeroflot ist nicht höher als die vergleichbarer westlicher Fluggesellschaften** 'Aeroflot's accident rate is no higher than *that* of comparable Western airlines', **ach der!** oh *him/that one*!, **Sorgen? – wir haben deren genug** 'worries? – we have enough *of them*', **mein Rat ist der: ...** 'my advice is *this*: ...'

The genitive forms **dessen** and **deren** are sometimes used in place of the possessive adjectives **sein** ('his, its') and **ihr** ('her, its, their'); they always refer back to the last-mentioned noun. This substitution need only be employed where ambiguity could arise, e.g. **am nächsten Tag besuchten sie sein Freund und dessen Sohn** (avoiding the ambiguous **sein Sohn**) 'the next day they were visited by his friend and the latter's son'.

INDEFINITE PRONOUNS

(a) **man** 'one, you, people, they, we':
This pronoun has no oblique cases, being replaced in the accusative by **einen** and in the dative by **einem**; **sich** serves as its reflexive pronoun and **sein** as its possessive adjective ('one's, your') in the oblique cases.

In some instances constructions with **man** are rendered by the English passive. Examples of usage:

man weiß nie, was geschehen kann 'one never knows what may happen'
man behauptet, er sei nach Australien ausgewandert 'they say he has (*or* he is said to have) emigrated to Australia'
das tut einem gut 'that does one good'
man hat mir gesagt, daß ... 'I've been told that ...'

(b) **jemand** 'someone' and **niemand** 'no-one, not ... anyone':

nom.	**jemand**	**niemand**
acc.	**jemand(en)**	**niemand(en)**
gen.	**jemand(e)s**	**niemand(e)s**
dat.	**jemand(em)**	**niemand(em)**

'Someone/no-one' + adjective is expressed by **jemand/niemand** + the appropriate neuter adjectival noun, e.g. 'someone interesting' = **jemand Interessantes**, 'with someone interesting' = **mit jemand Interessantem**; 'someone/no-one else' is **jemand/niemand anders** (South German **anderer**).

Einer and **keiner** are common alternatives to **jemand** and **niemand** respectively.

(c) **etwas** 'something' and **nichts** 'nothing, not ... anything':
These pronouns are indeclinable and occur in the nominative and accusative, and after prepositions.

Etwas may be followed by a noun, with the sense 'some', e.g. **etwas (frische) Milch** 'some (fresh) milk'; or it may be an adverb meaning 'somewhat'.

'Something/nothing' + adjective is expressed by **etwas/nichts** + the appropriate neuter adjectival noun, e.g. 'something/nothing good' = **etwas/nichts Gutes**; 'something/nothing else' is **etwas/nichts anderes**, 'nothing but' **nichts anderes als**.

ADJECTIVES AND ADVERBS

FORMS

In predicative use, the adjective in German is not inflected, e.g. **die Musik ist schön** 'the music is beautiful', **das Wasser ist heiß** 'the water is hot'. Used attributively, i.e. preceding a noun, it is inflected (as shown below), e.g. **die schöne Musik** 'the beautiful music', **heißes Wasser** 'hot water'.

Most adjectives may be used as adverbs – in the uninflected form, e.g. **sie hat das Lied sehr schön gesungen** 'she sang the song very beautifully'.

The adjective is declined as follows:

(a) (*Weak declension*) Following the definite article or other words declined like the definite article (**dieser**, **jeder**, **jener**, **mancher**, **solcher**, **welcher**):

SINGULAR

	masc. ('the big dog')	*fem.* ('the big cat')	*neut.* ('the big animal')
nom.	**der groß*e* Hund**	**die groß*e* Katze**	**das groß*e* Tier**
acc.	**den groß*en* Hund**	**die groß*e* Katze**	**das groß*e* Tier**
gen.	**des groß*en* Hundes**	**der groß*en* Katze**	**des groß*en* Tieres**
dat.	**dem groß*en* Hund**	**der groß*en* Katze**	**dem groß*en* Tier**

PLURAL

nom.	**die groß*en* Tiere**
acc.	**die groß*en* Tiere**
gen.	**der groß*en* Tiere**
dat.	**den groß*en* Tieren**

(b) Following the indefinite article, **kein** 'not a, no' or possessive adjective (**mein**, **dein**, etc.):

SINGULAR

	masc.	*fem.*	*neut.*
nom.	**ein groß*er* Hund**	**eine groß*e* Katze**	**ein groß*es* Tier**
acc.	**einen groß*en* Hund**	**eine groß*e* Katze**	**ein groß*es* Tier**
gen.	**eines groß*en* Hundes**	**einer groß*en* Katze**	**eines groß*en* Tieres**
dat.	**einem groß*en* Hund**	**einer groß*en* Katze**	**einem groß*en* Tier**

PLURAL

nom.	**meine groß*en* Katzen**
acc.	**meine groß*en* Katzen**
gen.	**meiner groß*en* Katzen**
dat.	**meinen groß*en* Katzen**

(c) (*Strong declension*) Without article (here the adjective – through its ending – indicates the case of the noun):

SINGULAR

	masc. ('good wine')	*fem.* ('warm milk')	*neut.* ('fresh water')
nom.	**gut*er* Wein**	**warm*e* Milch**	**frisch*es* Wasser**
acc.	**gut*en* Wein**	**warm*e* Milch**	**frisch*es* Wasser**
gen.	**gut*en* Weines**	**warm*er* Milch**	**frisch*en* Wassers**
dat.	**gut*em* Wein**	**warm*er* Milch**	**frisch*em* Wasser**

PLURAL

nom.	**gut*e* Weine**
acc.	**gut*e* Weine**
gen.	**gut*er* Weine**
dat.	**gut*en* Weinen**

When inflected, adjectives ending in **–el** always drop **e**, e.g. **edel** 'noble' but **ein edler Ritter** 'a noble knight', **miserabel** 'awful' but **sein miserables Deutsch** 'his awful German'. Adjectives in **–en** and **–er** usually retain **e**, although in elevated style it is sometimes elided. (Exceptions: adjectives of foreign origin in **–er**, e.g. **makaber** 'macabre', and those with a diphthong + **–er**, e.g. **sauer** 'sour', which regularly elide **e**, e.g. **eine makabre Geschichte** 'a macabre story', **saure Äpfel** 'sour apples'.)

Two or more adjectives before a noun have the same ending, e.g. **ein großer, runder Tisch** 'a large round table'.

The declension of adjectives following indefinite adjectives in the plural is as follows: (*a*) after **alle** 'all', **beide** 'both', **sämtliche** 'all, complete': adjectives following these words have the weak plural ending **–en** throughout, e.g. **alle grünen Vögel** 'all (the) green birds', **die Ansichten beider jungen Männer** 'the views of both young men'; (*b*) after **manche** 'some': adjectives following this word have either weak or strong plural endings, e.g. **manche reiche(n) Leute** 'some rich people'; (*c*) after **einige** 'some', **ein paar** 'a few', **mehrere** 'several', **verschiedene** 'various', **viele** 'many', **wenige** 'few': adjectives following these words have strong plural endings, e.g. **einige alte Lieder** 'some old songs', **die Werke vieler berühmter Komponisten** 'the works of many famous composers'.

Alles Schöne, **nichts Gutes**, etc.: (*a*) adjectives following **alles**, **manches**, **vieles**, **weniges** are written (with the exception of **ander**, **übrig**) with a capital letter and take the weak neuter singular endings, e.g. (*nom.*, *acc.*) **alles Schöne** 'everything beautiful', (*gen.*) **alles Schönen**, (*dat.*) **allem Schönen**; (*b*) adjectives following **allerlei**, **etwas**, **manch**, **nichts**, **viel**, **wenig** are written (with the exception of **ander**, **übrig**) with a capital letter and take the strong neuter singular endings, e.g. (*nom.*, *acc.*) **nichts Gutes** 'nothing good', (*gen.*, rare) **nichts Guten**, (*dat.*) **nichts Gutem**.

When personal pronouns are followed by attributive adjectives or adjectival nouns, these generally take a strong ending, e.g. **[Da steh' ich nun,] ich armer Tor!** (*Faust I*) 'poor fool (that I am)!', **du Glücklicher!** 'you lucky fellow!' A weak ending, however, is usual in the nominative plural, e.g. **wir (erfahrenen) Angestellten** 'we (experienced) employees' (it is also preferred in the dative singular feminine); 'we Germans' = **wir Deutschen** (but **Deutsche** also occurs).

Three categories of adjective take no ending: (*a*) certain adjectives of foreign origin: **prima** (comm.) 'first-class', (coll.) 'great' and the colour adjectives **beige**,

chamois, **creme** 'cream', **lila** 'purple', **oliv** 'olive', **orange**, **rosa** 'pink'; of these only **prima**, **lila** and **rosa** are normally used attributively (e.g. **ein rosa Kleid** 'a pink dress'), while the others are usually compounded with **–farben** or **–farbig** ('-coloured') to avoid using the uninflected forms: **beigefarben**, **olivfarben**, etc.; (*b*) **ganz** and **halb** before geographical names without the definite article, e.g. **ganz Zypern** 'the whole of Cyprus', **halb Europa** 'half Europe'; (*c*) adjectives in **–er** derived from a place-name, e.g. **ein Wiener Walzer** 'a Viennese waltz', **die Londoner Theater** 'the London theatres', **Pariser Chic** 'Parisian chic'.

POSSESSIVE ADJECTIVES

The possessive adjectives are: **mein** 'my', **dein** 'your' (familiar form), **sein/ihr/sein** 'his/her/its', **Ihr** 'your', **unser** 'our', **euer** 'your' (familiar form, plural) and **ihr** 'their'; they are declined like **kein** (p. xix). The possessive adjectives of the 3rd person singular agree in gender with the noun they refer to, thus 'its' may be expressed by **sein** (referring to a masculine or neuter) or **ihr** (referring to a feminine), e.g. **die Partei hat ihre Anhänger enttäuscht** 'the party has disappointed its supporters'.

COMPARISON OF ADJECTIVES AND ADVERBS

The *comparative* of both adjectives and adverbs is formed by adding **–(¨)er**, e.g. **laut** 'loud(ly)': **lauter** 'louder, more loudly'; **warm** 'warm(ly)': **wärmer** 'warmer, more warmly'; **interessant** 'interesting(ly)': **interessanter** 'more interesting(ly)'. Adjectives in **–el** drop the **e** in the comparative, e.g. **dunkel** 'dark': **dunkler** 'darker'; adjectives in **–en** and **–er** sometimes drop **e** when inflected (but adjectives with a diphthong + **–er** always drop the **e**, thus **sauer** 'sour': **saurer** 'sourer', **teuer** 'expensive': **teurer** 'more expensive').

The comparative form of some adjectives has a second function, namely to indicate a fairly high degree of the quality concerned, without any comparison being made; this is known as the 'absolute comparative'. Examples: **eine größere Summe** 'a largish sum', **ein jüngeres Ehepaar** 'a youngish couple', **eine längere Reise** 'a longish journey', **seit längerer Zeit** 'for some time now'; an example of adverbial use is **öfter** 'quite often'.

'—er and —er' is expressed in German by **immer** + comparative, e.g. **immer schneller** 'faster and faster', **immer lauter** 'louder and louder'.

The *superlative* of the adjective is formed by adding **–(¨)st** + ending, e.g. **(der, die, das) langsamste** 'slowest'. An **e** is inserted before the **s**, for euphony's sake, in monosyllables and words stressed on the last syllable if they end in **–d**, **–s**, **–sch**, **–ß**, **–st**, **–t**, **–tz**, **–x**, **–z**, e.g. (**der** etc.) **mildeste** 'mildest', **hübscheste** 'prettiest', **berühmteste** 'most famous' (unlike polysyllables *not* stressed on the last syllable, e.g. (**der** etc.) **malerischste** 'most picturesque', **reizendste** 'most charming', **gefürchtetste** 'most feared'); in the case of diphthongs and vowels followed by **h** the insertion of **e** is optional, e.g. (**der** etc.) **frei(e)ste** 'freest', **früh(e)ste** 'earliest'. The superlative of the adverb is formed according to the pattern **am —sten**, e.g. **am schnellsten** 'fastest'; this form is also used with the copula (**sein** 'to be') as the predicative superlative, e.g. **der Vierwaldstätter See ist im Frühling am schönsten** 'the Lake of Lucerne is (at its) loveliest in spring'.

Certain adjectives and adverbs are compared irregularly:

groß 'big, tall, great': **größer: (der, die, das) größte/am größten**
gut 'good, well': **besser: (der, die, das) beste/am besten**
hoch 'high': **höher: (der, die, das) höchste/am höchsten**
nah 'near, close': **näher: (der, die, das) nächste/am nächsten**
viel 'much': **mehr: (der, die, das) meiste/am meisten**
bald 'soon': **eher: am ehesten**
gern 'gladly': **lieber: am liebsten**

Where the stem vowel of an adjective/adverb is mutated in the comparative and superlative this is indicated at the dictionary entry concerned.

ADJECTIVES USED AS NOUNS

German adjectives – and adjectival participles – may be used as nouns. They are written with a capital letter and are declined like ordinary adjectives, e.g. **der Erwachsene** '(male) adult':

SINGULAR

nom.	**der Erwachsen*e***	**ein Erwachsen*er***
acc.	**den, einen Erwachsen*en***	
gen.	**des, eines Erwachsen*en***	
dat.	**dem, einem Erwachsen*en***	

PLURAL

nom.	**die Erwachsen*en***	**Erwachsen*e***
acc.	**die Erwachsen*en***	**Erwachsen*e***
gen.	**der Erwachsen*en***	**Erwachsen*er***
dat.	**den Erwachsen*en***	**Erwachsen*en***

Die Erwachsene '(female) adult' is declined with the corresponding feminine adjectival endings.

In the masculine, feminine or plural, adjectival nouns denote persons, e.g. **der/die Alte** 'old man/woman' (from **alt** 'old'), **der/die Fremde** 'stranger' (from **fremd** 'strange'), **der/die Deutsche** 'German' (from **deutsch** 'German'), **der/die Reisende** 'traveller' (from **reisend** 'travelling'), **der/die Geschiedene** 'divorcee' (from **geschieden** 'divorced'); although without adjectival counterpart, **der Beamte** 'official' is included in this category as it is declined like an adjective.

Neuter adjectival nouns express abstract concepts, e.g. **das Edle** 'that which is noble' (from **edel** 'noble'), **das Gute** 'the good, what is good' (from **gut** 'good'); sometimes the English equivalent is a full (abstract) noun, e.g. **sie hat einen ausgeprägten Sinn für das Schöne** 'she has a keen sense of beauty'. They are also used to refer to a particular feature or quality, where English has 'the ... thing', e.g. **das Interessante an diesem Buch** 'the interesting thing about this book'. Neuter past participles used as nouns express what has been done or has happened, e.g. **das Erreichte** 'what has been/was achieved', **das soeben Geschehene** 'what has just happened'.

Used without the article, neuter adjectival nouns are collective in sense, often being rendered by '... things' (e.g. **er hat auf diesem Gebiet Erstaunliches**

geleistet 'he has done amazing things in this field'); likewise the neuter indefinite pronouns – spelt with a small letter – e.g. **mehreres** 'several things', **verschiedenes** 'various things'. (Small letters are also used in a number of set prepositional phrases: **bei weitem** 'by far', **fürs erste/nächste** 'for the time being', **im großen und ganzen** 'on the whole', **vor kurzem** 'recently', etc.) Neuter substantival past participles without the article are often used as collectives, e.g. **Geräuchertes** 'smoked foods' (from **geräuchert** 'smoked'), **Handgearbeitetes** 'handmade articles' (from **handgearbeitet** 'handmade'), **Gefälschtes** 'forgeries' (from **gefälscht** 'forged'). All these words are in the singular and therefore take a singular verb, unlike their English translations: **Wichtiges ist vernachlässigt worden** 'important things have been neglected', **verschiedenes war noch zu besprechen** 'there were still various things to be discussed'.

EMOTIVE PARTICLES

A number of German adverbs also serve as emotive (or modal) particles. The function of these heavily-used words – which include **aber**, **auch**, **bloß**, **denn**, **doch**, **eben**, **(ein)mal**, **erst**, **etwa**, **ja**, **nur**, **schon**, **vielleicht**, **wohl**, and which also occur in a variety of combinations – is to indicate a speaker's *attitude* to what he or she is saying; while English has one or two words of this type such as *just*, *surely* it often relies on emphasis or tone of voice (or else a phrase like *I suppose*, *I dare say*) to convey the same kind of emotive nuance. A few examples follow (for fuller information and further examples see the dictionary entries):

sie ist *aber* groß geworden! 'my, how she's grown!'
warum bist du *auch* so spät gekommen! 'well, why *were* you so late?'
nimm *doch* Platz! 'do sit down', **ich bin *doch* kein Roboter!** 'I'm not a robot!'
du weißt *ja*, wie das so ist 'you know how it is'
sag *mal* 'tell me'
was hat er *nur*? 'what's wrong with him?'
Steffi ist *schon* ein ganz besonderes Mädchen 'S. really is a very special girl', **es wird *schon* werden** '(don't worry,) it'll be all right'
da habe ich *vielleicht* gelacht! 'did I laugh!'
du spinnst *wohl*! 'you must be crazy!', **er wird *wohl* kommen** 'I expect he'll come', **ob es *wohl* stimmt?** 'is it true, I wonder?'

NUMERALS

CARDINAL NUMBERS

0	**null**	21	**einundzwanzig**
1	**eins**	22	**zweiundzwanzig**
2	**zwei**	23	**dreiundzwanzig** etc.
3	**drei**		
4	**vier**	30	**dreißig**
5	**fünf**	40	**vierzig** ['fɪr-]
6	**sechs** [-ks]	50	**fünfzig**
7	**sieben**	60	**sechzig** [-ç-]
8	**acht**	70	**siebzig**
9	**neun**	80	**achtzig** [-xts-]
10	**zehn**	90	**neunzig**
11	**elf**	100	**hundert**
12	**zwölf**	101	**hunderteins** etc.
13	**dreizehn**	200	**zweihundert**
14	**vierzehn** ['fɪr-]	1,000	**tausend**
15	**fünfzehn**	10,000	**zehntausend**
16	**sechzehn** [-ç-]	100,000	**hunderttausend**
17	**siebzehn**	1,000,000	**eine Million**
18	**achtzehn** [-xts-]	2,000,000	**zwei Millionen**
19	**neunzehn**	1,000,000,000	**eine Milliarde**
20	**zwanzig**	1,000,000,000,000	**eine Billion**

Numbers are written as one word, starting with the greatest magnitude, but units – followed by **und** – precede tens, e.g. 2468 is **zweitausendvierhundertachtundsechzig.**

'One' is **eins**, unless prefixed to another number or **und** + another number, when **ein** is used, e.g. 71 = **einundsiebzig. Ein** is uninflected in **ein bis zwei**, **ein oder zwei** (e.g. **ein oder zwei Minuten lang** 'for a minute or two'); also in **ein Uhr** 'one o'clock'.

A special alternative to **zwei** exists in the shape of (the originally feminine) **zwo**, which is used – for example, on the telephone or when a judge announces a score at some sporting event – to avoid confusion between **zwei** and **drei**. **Zwei** and **drei** have genitive forms, **zweier** 'of two' and **dreier** 'of three', but in everyday German **von zwei/drei** is usual.

Uninflected and written with a small letter, **hundert** and **tausend** may be used adjectivally, e.g. **einige hundert/tausend Menschen** 'a few hundred/thousand people'; capitalized and with a plural in **–e**, they function as nouns, e.g. **Hunderte/Tausende von quakenden Fröschen** 'hundreds/thousands of croaking frogs' (thus also compounds, e.g. **Hunderttausende von Käfern** 'hundreds of thousands of beetles').

Eine Million, **eine Milliarde** 'a thousand million, a billion' and **eine Billion** 'a million million', U.S. 'a trillion' are nouns and are always inflected in the plural, e.g. **zwei Millionen Einwohner** 'two million inhabitants', **Millionen von Sternen** 'millions of stars'.

Decimals are separated from whole numbers by a comma, e.g. 17.5 = **17,5** (read **siebzehn Komma fünf**).

ORDINAL NUMBERS

1st **erst-**
2nd **zweit-** (**zwot-**: see previous section)
3rd **dritt-**
Other ordinals up to 19th are formed by adding **–t** to the cardinal number, e.g. **viert-** 'fourth'; 'seventh' is **siebent-** or **siebt-**, 'eighth' is **acht-** (with the loss of one **t**). Ordinals from 20th upwards are formed by adding **–st** to the cardinal, e.g. **zwanzigst-** 'twentieth', **tausendst-** 'thousandth'.

When written as figures – Roman numerals included – they are followed by a full stop (period), e.g. **3. [dritter] Versuch** '3rd attempt', **der 2. [Zweite] Welt-krieg** 'the 2nd World War', **Johannes XXIII. [der Dreiundzwanzigste]** 'John XXIII'.

Being adjectives, the ordinal numbers are declined according to the standard adjectival patterns. Ordinals may combine with a superlative, e.g. **zweitgrößt-** 'second largest', **dritthöchst-** 'third highest'.

FRACTIONS

Die Hälfte 'half' is feminine; all others are neuter, and are formed by adding **–tel** (a reduced form of **Teil** 'part') to the ordinal (whose final **t** is suppressed), e.g. **ein Viertel** ['fɪr-] 'a quarter, fourth', **ein Sechstel** 'a sixth', **ein Zwanzigstel** 'a twentieth', **ein Tausendstel** 'a thousandth', **zwei Drittel** 'two thirds'.

'... and a half' is expressed by **–(und)einhalb**, e.g. **sechs(und)einhalb** 'six and a half'; 'one and a half' is usually **anderthalb**, although **ein(und)einhalb** also occurs.

SUFFIXES ADDED

–ens added to the ordinal number = '-ly', e.g. **drittens** 'thirdly'.
–erlei = '... kinds of', e.g. **dreierlei** 'three kinds of'.
–fach = '-fold', e.g. **zweifach** 'twofold'.
–mal = '... times', e.g. **vierhundertmal** 'four hundred times'.

USE AS NOUNS

Cardinal numbers may be used as nouns; they have feminine gender, and add **–en** to form the plural, e.g. **zwei römische Achten** 'two Roman eights', **die Eins ist gerade abgefahren** 'the (number) one has just left'.

DATES

For the days of the month the ordinals are used, as in English, e.g. **der 17.** (pronounced **siebzehnte**) **Juli** '17th July'; as the date on a letter, this is written (e.g.) **Hamburg, den 17. Juli** (or **17.7.** = **siebzehnten siebten**) **1990**. 'On 17th July' is **am 17. Juli**. 'In 19—, 20—, etc.' is expressed either by the date alone (e.g. **1920 trat er zurück** 'in 1920 he resigned') or by the phrase **im Jahre 1920** etc. A date in the 11th century begins **tausend...**, e.g. 1066 = **tausendsechsundsechzig**; in the same way 21st century dates begin **zweitausend...**

'The twenties etc.' of a century are known as **die zwanziger** etc. **Jahre**. Here **-er** is added to the cardinal number (**zwanzig** etc.); the word so formed is invariable (**die zwanziger Jahre, in den zwanziger Jahren** 'in the twenties', etc.). 'He's in his twenties' = **er ist in den Zwanzigern**; 'she's in her early/mid-/late twenties' = **sie ist Anfang/Mitte/Ende Zwanzig**.

PREPOSITIONS

Prepositions in German govern particular cases: accusative (e.g. **für** 'for', **ohne** 'without'), genitive (e.g. **trotz** 'in spite of', **während** 'during')[1] or dative (e.g. **aus** 'out of, from', **mit** 'with'). Some prepositions govern two cases – accusative and dative – depending on circumstances: if the preposition indicates rest or motion within a place the dative is used (e.g. **Nebel lag über der Stadt** 'fog lay over the town', **das Bild hängt an der Wand** 'the picture is hanging on the wall', **sie gingen im Garten spazieren** 'they went for a walk in the garden'), while if movement to a place is involved the accusative is used (e.g. **er fuhr über die Brücke** 'he drove across the bridge', **er hängt das Bild an die Wand** 'he is hanging the picture on the wall', **sie gingen in den Garten hinaus** 'they went out into the garden').

In the case of **auf** and **über** the accusative is also the case normally used in figurative contexts, e.g. (with **auf** + accusative) **eifersüchtig/stolz auf** 'jealous/proud of', **auf diese Weise** 'in this way', **warten auf** 'to wait for', **sich verlassen auf** 'to rely on'; (with **über** + accusative) **über alles Lob erhaben** 'beyond praise', **herrschen über** 'to rule over', **reden/schreiben über** 'to talk/write about', **sich wundern über** 'to be surprised at'. (Two important exceptions are **beruhen auf** (+ dative) 'to be based on' and **bestehen auf** (+ dative) 'to insist on'.)

Some prepositions may follow the word they govern, e.g. **allen Erwartungen entgegen** 'contrary to all expectations', **der Schule gegenüber** 'opposite the school', **Ihren Anordnungen gemäß** 'in accordance with your instructions', **meiner Ansicht nach** 'in my opinion'.

In other instances a preposition is used in conjunction with another word, either preceding the noun (in the case of **bis**, e.g. **bis zu** 'as far as, up to, until') or enclosing it. Examples of the latter type are: **um ... willen** 'for the sake of', the noun concerned being placed in the genitive, and phrases consisting of preposition (+noun) + adverb, such as

an (dat.) ... **entlang** 'along' (coast etc.)
auf (acc.) ... **zu** 'towards, up to'
hinter (dat.) ... **her** (run etc.) 'after'
hinter/unter (dat.) ... **hervor** 'from behind/under'
nach ... hin 'towards'
um ... herum 'round'
von ... an 'from ... (onwards)'
von ... aus 'from'
zu ... hinaus 'out of' (door, window)

1. These and other prepositions governing the genitive case take the *dative* instead under certain circumstances (see entries concerned).

Some prepositions combine with the definite article in contracted forms:

am = **an dem**	**im** = **in dem**	**unters** (coll.) = **unter das**
ans = **an das**	**ins** = **in das**	**vom** = **von dem**
aufs = **auf das**	**überm** (coll.) = **über dem**	**vorm** (coll.) = **vor dem**
beim = **bei dem**	**übers** (coll.) = **über das**	**vors** (coll.) = **vor das**
durchs = **durch das**	**ums** = **um das**	**zum** = **zu dem**
fürs = **für das**	**unterm** (coll.) = **unter dem**	**zur** = **zu der**
hinterm (coll.) = **hinter dem**		
hinters (coll.) = **hinter das**		

*

German does not always use a preposition where English has one:

(i) Sometimes German uses a *grammatical case* where English has a preposition to indicate the relationship between words, notably (*a*) the *dative* as the equivalent of 'to' (with verbs of giving etc. to indicate the indirect object, e.g. 'why did you give it to him?' **warum hast du es ihm gegeben?**, 'she wrote to him often' **sie hat ihm oft geschrieben**; also such verbs as 'to belong to' **gehören** + dative, 'to correspond to' **entsprechen** + dative, 'to listen to' **zuhören** + dative, 'it seems to me that ...' **mir scheint, daß ...**; usages such as 'she was a good mother to him' **sie war ihm eine gute Mutter**; and with some adjectives such as 'similar to' **ähnlich** + dative, 'superior to' **überlegen** + dative, 'loyal to' **treu** + dative, 'unknown to' **unbekannt** + dative, e.g. 'their intentions are unknown to me' **ihre Absichten sind mir unbekannt**), and (*b*) the *genitive* where English has 'of' (e.g. 'the coast of Italy' **die Küste Italiens**, 'a sense of relief' **ein Gefühl der Erleichterung**), 'in' (e.g. 'a bend in the road' **eine Biegung der Straße**, 'a change in the weather' **eine Änderung des Wetters**), 'to' (e.g. 'visitors to the museum' **die Besucher des Museums**, 'to be witness to a scene' **Zeuge einer Szene sein**).

(ii) In other cases a *prefix* is the German equivalent of an English preposition; thus 'from' is expressed by the separable prefix **ab–** in 'to buy (something) from' **abkaufen** (+dative), and by the inseparable prefix **ent–** in 'to snatch (something) from' **entreißen** (+dative), while 'at' is rendered by the separable prefix **zu–** in 'to smile at' **zulächeln** (+dative). (For further examples see 'Separable and Inseparable Verbs', p. liv.)

(iii) In certain instances *apposition* occurs in German where English has 'of', e.g. 'a glass of water' **ein Glas Wasser**, 'the city of Cologne' **die Stadt Köln**, 'the University of Louvain' **die Universität Löwen**, 'the Isle of Man' **die Insel Man**, 'in the month of May' **im Monat Mai**.

If the second noun is qualified by an adjective, German has two possibilities: (*a*) apposition (with case agreement) – the usual construction, thus 'a glass of cold water' **ein Glas kaltes Wasser**, 'I'd like a cup of hot coffee' **ich möchte eine Tasse heißen Kaffee**, 'with a piece of French cake' **mit einem Stück französischem Kuchen**; (*b*) the genitive – now little used, but occasionally encountered in literary style, e.g. **ein Glas kalten Wassers**.

(iv) German often has a *compound noun* where English has two nouns linked by a preposition, most frequently 'of', e.g.:

(*of*)
'corner of the mouth' **der Mundwinkel**
'side of the street' **die Straßenseite**
'year of manufacture' **das Baujahr**
'colour of (one's) skin' **die Hautfarbe**
'work of art' **das Kunstwerk**
'voyage of discovery' **die Entdeckungsfahrt**
'head of state' **das Staatsoberhaupt**
'point of departure/view' **der Ausgangspunkt/Standpunkt**
'sense of direction' **der Ortssinn**
'knowledge of English' **die Englischkenntnisse**

(*for*)
'need for adventure' **das Abenteuerbedürfnis**
'suggestion for improvement' **der Verbesserungsvorschlag**

(*in*)
'difference in meaning' **der Bedeutungsunterschied**

(*to*)
'claim to power' **der Machtanspruch**
'damage to property' **der Sachschaden**

(v) In *time phrases* signifying 'at the beginning/in the middle/at the end of' German dispenses with a preposition, e.g. 'at the beginning of May/this month' **Anfang Mai/dieses Monats**, 'in the middle of next week' **Mitte nächster Woche**, 'at the end of 1984/the eighties' **Ende 1984/der achtziger Jahre**. Similarly, 'in' in dates is not translated, thus 'in 1996' is simply **1996** (see also p. xxxvii).

The converse is sometimes true: thus (*a*) the sense of the German preposition **bei** is often expressed in English by other means, e.g. (= English genitive) **48 Prozent aller Männer sehen bei Frauen zunächst nach dem Haar** '48 per cent of all men look at a woman's hair first', (= English conjunction) **beim Überqueren der Straße** 'when/while crossing the road', **bei ausgeschalteter Maschine** 'when the machine is/was switched off', **bei nasser Fahrbahn** 'if the road is/was wet' (see entry for further examples); (*b*) where German uses an intransitive verb with the preposition **mit** to express certain acts carried out using a part of the body (or something held in the hand, e.g. a stick or whip) English employs a transitive verb, e.g. **mit dem Kopf nicken** 'to nod one's head', **mit den Armen/Händen herumfuchteln** 'to wave one's arms/hands about', **mit den Füßen stampfen** 'to stamp one's feet', **mit der Zunge schnalzen** 'to click one's tongue', **mit den Hüften wackeln** 'to wiggle one's hips', **mit dem Schwanz wedeln** 'to wag its tail', **mit der Peitsche knallen** 'to crack one's whip'; (*c*) **in** (+accusative) and **zu** denoting a change of state have no equivalent in English in instances such as **ein britischer General hat Fort Duquesne in Pittsburgh umbenannt** 'a British general renamed Fort Duquesne Pittsburgh', **er wurde zum Bundeskanzler gewählt** 'he was elected Federal Chancellor'.

VERBS

German verbs, like English verbs, fall broadly into two groups: weak and strong verbs. *Weak* verbs form the past tense by adding **–te** to the stem, and the past participle by prefixing **ge–** to the stem and adding **–t**; there are also some irregular verbs that are conjugated weak but which also exhibit vowel change in the past tense and past participle. *Strong* verbs change the stem vowel in the past tense and, in most cases, the past participle; the latter has the prefix **ge–** and ends in **–en**.

Examples:

(weak) **leben** 'to live' (stem: **leb–**), past **lebte** 'lived', past participle **gelebt** 'lived'

(irregular weak) **nennen** 'to name', past **nannte** 'named', past participle **genannt** 'named'

(strong) **singen** 'to sing', past **sang** 'sang', past participle **gesungen** 'sung'

*

The conjugation of weak and strong verbs is as follows:

INDICATIVE

	WEAK (Examples: **leben** 'to live', **arbeiten** 'to work')		STRONG (Examples: **singen** 'to sing', **graben** 'to dig')	
Present tense				
ich	**lebe**	**arbeite**	**singe**	**grabe**
du	**lebst**	**arbeitest**	**singst**	**gräbst**
er/sie/es	**lebt**	**arbeitet**	**singt**	**gräbt**
wir	**leben**	**arbeiten**	**singen**	**graben**
ihr	**lebt**	**arbeitet**	**singt**	**grabt**
sie, Sie	**leben**	**arbeiten**	**singen**	**graben**
Past tense				
ich	**lebte**	**arbeitete**	**sang**	**grub**
du	**lebtest**	**arbeitetest**	**sangst**	**grubst**
er/sie/es	**lebte**	**arbeitete**	**sang**	**grub**
wir	**lebten**	**arbeiteten**	**sangen**	**gruben**
ihr	**lebtet**	**arbeitetet**	**sangt**	**grubt**
sie, Sie	**lebten**	**arbeiteten**	**sangen**	**gruben**

Perfect tense

= present tense of the auxiliary **haben** (p. xlvi) + past participle (usually at end of clause); in the case of verbs of motion or change of state (e.g. **kommen** 'to come', **einschlafen** 'to fall asleep'), **bleiben** 'to remain' and **sein** 'to be', the auxiliary **sein** (p. xlvi) is used instead of **haben** (cf. archaic English 'I am come', 'Christ is risen', etc.); e.g.:

ich habe etc. ... **gelebt**   **ich bin** etc. ... **gekommen**

Pluperfect tense

= past tense of the auxiliary **haben** (or **sein** where appropriate) + past participle (usually at end of clause), e.g.:

ich hatte etc. ... **gelebt**   **ich war** etc. ... **gekommen**

Future tense

= present tense of the auxiliary **werden** (p. xlvi) + infinitive (usually at end of clause), e.g.:

ich werde etc. ... **kommen**

STRONG VERBS
(grouped according to vowel change)

Only a selection of verbs is given here, to illustrate the various types; details of conjugation are given for all strong verbs in the entries concerned.
The parts shown are: (i) the infinitive, (ii) (*only shown – in brackets – where vowel change is involved*) the 2nd and 3rd persons singular of the present tense, (iii) the past tense, (iv) the past participle.

a – (ä) – ie – a
(*a*) **schlafen** 'to sleep' – **(schläfst, schläft)** – **schlief** – **geschlafen**
blasen 'to blow' – **(bläst, bläst)** – **blies** – **geblasen**
raten 'to advise' – **(rätst, rät)** – **riet** – **geraten**
(*b*) **fallen** 'to fall' – **(fällst, fällt)** – **fiel** – **gefallen**
halten 'to hold etc.' – **(hältst, hält)** – **hielt** – **gehalten**
lassen 'to let etc.' – **(läßt, läßt)** – **ließ** – **gelassen**

a – (ä) – u – a
(*a*) **fahren** 'to go, drive' – **(fährst, fährt)** – **fuhr** – **gefahren**
laden 'to load' – **(lädst, lädt)** – **lud** – **geladen**
tragen 'to carry, wear' – **(trägst, trägt)** – **trug** – **getragen**
(*b*) **wachsen** 'to grow' – **(wächst, wächst)** – **wuchs** – **gewachsen**
waschen 'to wash' – **(wäschst, wäscht)** – **wusch** – **gewaschen**

e – (ie *or* **i) – a – e**
(*a*) **sehen** 'to see' – **(siehst, sieht)** – **sah** – **gesehen**
lesen 'to read' – **(liest, liest)** – **las** – **gelesen**
geben 'to give' – **(gibst, gibt)** – **gab** – **gegeben**
treten 'to step etc.' – **(trittst, tritt)** – **trat** – **getreten**
(*b*) **messen** 'to measure' – **(mißt, mißt)** – **maß** – **gemessen**
vergessen 'to forget' – **(vergißt, vergißt)** – **vergaß** – **vergessen**
essen 'to eat' – **(ißt, ißt)** – **aß** – **gegessen**
(*c*) (with **i** or **ie** in infinitive and present):
bitten 'to ask' – **bat** – **gebeten**
liegen 'to lie' – **lag** – **gelegen**
sitzen 'to sit' – **saß** – **gesessen**

e – (i *or* **ie) – a – o**
(*a*) **helfen** 'to help' – **(hilfst, hilft)** – **half** – **geholfen**
sterben 'to die' – **(stirbst, stirbt)** – **starb** – **gestorben**
werfen 'to throw' – **(wirfst, wirft)** – **warf** – **geworfen**
(*b*) **sprechen** 'to speak' – **(sprichst, spricht)** – **sprach** – **gesprochen**
treffen 'to hit, meet' – **(triffst, trifft)** – **traf** – **getroffen**
(*c*) **stehlen** 'to steal' – **(stiehlst, stiehlt)** – **stahl** – **gestohlen**
befehlen 'to order' – **(befiehlst, befiehlt)** – **befahl** – **befohlen**
(*d*) **nehmen** 'to take' – **(nimmst, nimmt)** – **nahm** – **genommen**

i – a – o *or* **u**

(*a*) **schwimmen** 'to swim' – **schwamm** – **geschwommen**
beginnen 'to begin' – **begann** – **begonnen**

(*b*) **finden** 'to find' – **fand** – **gefunden**
klingen 'to sound' – **klang** – **geklungen**
trinken 'to drink' – **trank** – **getrunken**

ei – i – i, ei – ie – ie

(*a*) **reiten** 'to ride' – **ritt** – **geritten**
beißen 'to bite' – **biß** – **gebissen**
pfeifen 'to whistle' – **pfiff** – **gepfiffen**

(*b*) **bleiben** 'to remain' – **blieb** – **geblieben**
schweigen 'to be silent' – **schwieg** – **geschwiegen**

ie – o – o

(*a*) **schießen** 'to shoot' – **schoß** – **geschossen**
riechen 'to smell' – **roch** – **gerochen**

(*b*) **fliegen** 'to fly' – **flog** – **geflogen**
frieren 'to freeze' – **fror** – **gefroren**
ziehen 'to pull, draw' – **zog** – **gezogen**

Four major verbs

(past in **ie**; same vowel or diphthong in infinitive and past participle)

heißen 'to be called' – **hieß** – **geheißen**
laufen 'to run' – **(läufst, läuft)** – **lief** – **gelaufen**
rufen 'to call' – **rief** – **gerufen**
stoßen 'to push etc.' – **(stößt, stößt)** – **stieß** – **gestoßen**

Future perfect tense
= present tense of the auxiliary **werden** + (usually at end of clause) past participle + **haben** (or **sein** where appropriate), e.g.:

ich werde etc. ... **gelebt haben** **ich werde** etc. ... **gekommen sein**

NOTES *on verb forms*:

(i) *Weak verbs in* **–eln**,.**–ern**: The stem of these verbs is obtained by removing the final **n**; thus **rudern** 'to row' has as its stem **ruder–** (present indicative **rudere, ruderst, rudert**, pl. **rudern, rudert, rudern**; past **ruderte** etc.; past participle **gerudert**). In the 1st singular present the **e** is often omitted in verbs in **–eln** (e.g. **ich hand(e)le 'I** act'), seldom in **–ern** verbs.

(ii) *Verbs with stem ending in* **d** *or* **t**: (*a*) In weak verbs of this type the stem is followed by **e** throughout (present indicative **–e, –est, –et**, pl. **–en, –et, –en**; past **–ete** etc.; past participle **ge—et**), e.g. **arbeiten** (see tables above), **reden** 'to talk'. (*b*) In the present tense of strong verbs which do not change the stem vowel (e.g. **leiden** 'to suffer') the stem is likewise followed by **e** (thus 2nd and 3rd singular **leidest, leidet**). Those that do change the stem vowel, e.g. **halten** 'to hold, keep, etc.', add **–st, –** (zero ending) to the stem in the 2nd and 3rd singular respectively, thus **hältst, hält**; but several verbs deviate slightly from this pattern, e.g. **laden** 'to load': 2nd, 3rd singular **lädst, lädt**. In the past tense, **e** is inserted in the 2nd plural (e.g. **littet, hieltet**).

(iii) *Weak verbs with stem ending in a consonant* (*except* **l, r**) + **m, n**: As with weak verbs in the preceding category, the stem is followed throughout by **e**, e.g. (with the same endings as those shown at (ii) for weak verbs) **widmen** 'to dedicate', **atmen** 'to breathe', **leugnen** 'to deny', **öffnen** 'to open', **zeichnen** 'to draw'.

(iv) *Verbs with stem ending in* (*a*) **s, ss, ß, tz, z**: the 2nd singular present normally has the ending **–t** and thus coincides with the 3rd singular, e.g. (**wachsen** 'to grow') **wächst**, (**beißen** 'to bite') **beißt**, (**schwitzen** 'to sweat') **schwitzt**; (*b*) **sch**: the 2nd singular present retains the **s** of the normal **–st** ending, e.g. (**waschen** 'to wash') **wäschst**. The 2nd singular past of strong verbs (*a*, *b*) has **–est**, e.g. (**wachsen**) **wuchsest**, but informally the ending may be reduced to **–t**, e.g. **wuchst**.

(v) Many *strong verbs change the stem vowel* in the 2nd and 3rd singular present (**a>ä, e>i** or **ie, o>ö, au>äu**), e.g. (**graben**, see above) **gräbst, gräbt**; (**helfen** 'to help') **hilfst, hilft**; (**lesen** 'to read') **liest, liest**; (**stoßen** 'to push') **stößt, stößt**; (**laufen** 'to run') **läufst, läuft**.

SUBJUNCTIVE

	Present		*Past*	
	(weak)	(strong)	(weak)	(strong)
ich	**lebe***	**grabe***	**lebte**	**grübe**
du	**lebest***	**grabest***	**lebtest**	**grüb(e)st**
er/sie/es	**lebe**	**grabe**	**lebte**	**grübe**
wir	**leben***	**graben***	**lebten**	**grüben**
ihr*	**lebet***	**grabet***	**lebtet**	**grüb(e)t**
sie, Sie	**leben***	**graben***	**lebten**	**grüben**

*The asterisked forms of the present subjunctive do not normally occur in practice, being *replaced by the corresponding forms of the past subjunctive*.

The *past subjunctive of strong verbs* is formed with the endings shown above (**grübe** etc.). Where possible, the vowel of the past indicative is mutated (e.g. **sang** 'sang', subjunctive **sänge**); in certain instances a mutated vowel not corresponding to that of the indicative is used (e.g. **half** 'helped', subjunctive **hülfe**; **starb** 'died', subjunctive **stürbe**; **schalt** 'scolded', subjunctive **schölte**), although such forms sound stilted and are avoided except in formal style; while in a few cases both forms of past subjunctive exist side by side (e.g. **stand** 'stood', subjunctive **stünde, stände**). The past subjunctive – rarely used – of the *irregular weak verbs* **brennen, kennen, nennen** and **rennen** has the same vowel as the present tense (**brennte** etc.); **senden** and **wenden** have **sendete, wendete; bringen** and **denken** mutate the vowel of the indicative: **brächte, dächte.**

The *compound tenses* are formed as for the indicative, except that the subjunctive forms of the auxiliaries **haben, sein** and **werden** are used in place of the indicative forms.

Imperatives: e.g. (singular) **leb(e)!, grab(e)!**; (plural) **lebt!, grabt!**; (**Sie** form) **leben Sie!, graben Sie!** Where the ending **–e** is optional the form without **–e** is generally preferred except in more elevated style, e.g. **frag deinen Onkel!** 'ask your uncle!', **schlaf gut!** 'sleep well!'

Verbs such as **atmen, öffnen** (see p. xliv, Note (iii)) do not drop the ending, e.g. **atme!** 'breathe!', **öffne!** 'open!'; verbs in **–eln** likewise retain it, but often omit the penultimate **e**, e.g. **hand(e)le!** 'act!' Strong verbs that change **e** to **i** or **ie** in the 2nd and 3rd singular present also have this change of vowel in the imperative singular (**–e** is not added, except in **siehe** – see entry for **sehen**), e.g. (**helfen**) **hilf!**, (**lesen**) **lies!** (Strong verbs that mutate in the 2nd and 3rd singular, on the other hand, do not mutate in the imperative.)

Participles: e.g. (present) **lebend, grabend**; (past: *weak*) **gelebt, gearbeitet,** (*strong*) **gesungen, gegraben.**

Past participles:

(i) The prefix **ge–** is omitted from the past participle of verbs not stressed on the first syllable, i.e. verbs with an inseparable prefix (e.g. **beginnen** 'to begin', past participle **begonnen**), those ending in **–ieren** (e.g. **halbieren** 'to halve', past participle **halbiert**) and a handful of other verbs such as **offenbaren** 'to reveal', **prophezeien** 'to prophesy', **schmarotzen** 'to sponge'. It is also omitted where a separable prefix is attached to such verbs, e.g. **anerkennen** 'to acknowledge', **ausrangieren** 'to discard' (past participles **anerkannt, ausrangiert**).

(ii) The modal verbs (**dürfen, können**, etc. – see below) have two past participles: one formed with **ge–** (**gedurft, gekonnt**, etc.) and one identical with the infinitive, used when a dependent infinitive precedes the past participle. A few other verbs also have a second past participle analogous to those of the modal verbs, notably **brauchen** (with a negative, e.g. **er hat nicht zu schießen brauchen** 'he didn't need to shoot'), **hören** 'to hear' and **sehen** 'to see' (e.g. **ich habe ihn kommen sehen** 'I saw him come') and **lassen** in its causative sense (e.g. **er hat die Teller fallen lassen** 'he dropped the plates'; also in compounds, e.g. **liegenlassen: sie hat es auf der Fensterbank liegenlassen** 'she left it on the window-sill' – although the participle with **–ge–** (**liegengelassen** etc.) may, and in the passive must, be used).

PASSIVE VOICE

The passive is formed by using the appropriate tense of **werden** together with the past participle of the verb concerned (which usually goes to the end of the clause). In the perfect and pluperfect tenses the past participle of **werden** takes the form **worden**. The future passive is often replaced by the present passive.

Present tense
e.g. **ich werde** etc. ... **gefragt** 'I am etc. asked'
Past tense
e.g. **ich wurde** etc. ... **gefragt** 'I was etc. asked'
Perfect tense
e.g. **ich bin** etc. ... **gefragt worden** 'I have etc. been/was etc. asked'
Pluperfect tense
e.g. **ich war** etc. ... **gefragt worden** 'I etc. had been asked'
Future tense
e.g. **ich werde** etc. **gefragt werden** 'I shall etc. be asked'
Future perfect tense
e.g. **ich werde** etc. ... **gefragt worden sein** 'I shall etc. have been asked'

Conjugation of haben, sein *and* werden

	haben		**sein**		**werden**	
	Indic.	Subj.	Indic.	Subj.	Indic.	Subj.
Present tense						
ich	**habe**	**habe***	**bin**	**sei**	**werde**	**werde***
du	**hast**	**habest***	**bist**	**sei(e)st**	**wirst**	**werdest***
er/sie/es	**hat**	**habe**	**ist**	**sei**	**wird**	**werde**
wir	**haben**	**haben***	**sind**	**seien**	**werden**	**werden***
ihr	**habt**	**habet***	**seid**	**seiet***	**werdet**	**werdet***
sie, Sie	**haben**	**haben***	**sind**	**seien**	**werden**	**werden***

(The asterisked forms are in practice normally replaced by the past subjunctive.)

Past tense						
ich	**hatte**	**hätte**	**war**	**wäre**	**wurde**	**würde**
du	**hattest**	**hättest**	**warst**	**wär(e)st**	**wurdest**	**würdest**
er/sie/es	**hatte**	**hätte**	**war**	**wäre**	**wurde**	**würde**
wir	**hatten**	**hätten**	**waren**	**wären**	**wurden**	**würden**
ihr	**hattet**	**hättet**	**wart**	**wär(e)t**	**wurdet**	**würdet**
sie, Sie	**hatten**	**hätten**	**waren**	**wären**	**wurden**	**würden**

The *compound tenses* are formed in the usual way (**sein** and **werden** take the auxiliary **sein**): (perfect) **ich habe** etc. ... **gehabt**, **ich bin** etc. ... **gewesen**, **ich bin** etc. ... **geworden**; (pluperfect) **ich hatte** etc. ... **gehabt**, **ich war** etc. ... **gewesen**, **ich war** etc. ... **geworden**; (future) **ich werde** etc. ... **haben/sein/werden**; (future perfect) **ich werde** etc. ... **gehabt haben/gewesen sein/geworden sein**. (For the subjunctive substitute the corresponding subjunctive forms of the auxiliaries **haben** or **sein** as appropriate.)
Imperatives: (singular) **hab(e)!**, **sei!**, **werde!**; (plural) **habt!**, **seid!**, **werdet!**; (Sie form) **haben Sie!**, **seien Sie!**, **werden Sie!**
Participles: (present) **habend**, **seiend**, **werdend**; (past) **gehabt**, **gewesen**, **geworden** or (in passive constructions) **worden**.

Conjugation of modal verbs and **wissen**

German has a set of verbs called 'modal' verbs – related to the English modals 'can', 'may', etc. – which are used, chiefly in conjunction with a dependent infinitive, to express possibility, permission, necessity, obligation, inclination or volition; unlike their English cognates, they also have an infinitive form. They are **dürfen** 'to be allowed to' (present **darf** etc. also 'may'), **können** 'to be able to' (**kann** etc. also 'can'), **mögen** 'to like (to)' (**mag** etc. also 'may'), **müssen** 'to have to' (**muß** etc. also 'must'),[1] **sollen** 'to be (supposed) to', **wollen** 'to want (to)'. These verbs (the meanings and uses of which are treated more fully in the dictionary) exhibit several special features: (*a*) the 1st and 3rd singular present forms are identical (like their English counterparts: 'I can, he can'); (*b*) the vowel of the present singular differs from that of the plural and infinitive (except in the case of **sollen**); (*c*) each modal verb has two past participles, one with **ge–** and one (used with a dependent infinitive) identical with the infinitive; (*d*) a dependent infinitive is used without **zu**, e.g. **man wollte es nicht wahrhaben** 'people did not want to admit it'.

The conjugation of the modal verbs is shown together with that of the similarly-conjugated **wissen** 'to know':

	dürfen	**können**	**mögen**	**müssen**	**sollen**	**wollen**	**wissen**
Present tense (indicative)							
ich	**darf**	**kann**	**mag**	**muß**	**soll**	**will**	**weiß**
du	**darfst**	**kannst**	**magst**	**mußt**	**sollst**	**willst**	**weißt**
er/sie/es	**darf**	**kann**	**mag**	**muß**	**soll**	**will**	**weiß**
wir	**dürfen**	**können**	**mögen**	**müssen**	**sollen**	**wollen**	**wissen**
ihr	**dürft**	**könnt**	**mögt**	**müßt**	**sollt**	**wollt**	**wißt**
sie, Sie	**dürfen**	**können**	**mögen**	**müssen**	**sollen**	**wollen**	**wissen**

The *present subjunctive* is regular, having the vowel of the infinitive throughout: **(dürfen) ich dürfe, du dürfest, er/sie/es dürfe, wir dürfen, ihr dürfet, sie** and **Sie dürfen; (können) ich könne** etc.; **(mögen) ich möge** etc.; **(müssen) ich müsse** etc.; **(sollen) ich solle** etc.; **(wollen) ich wolle** etc.; **(wissen) ich wisse** etc.

Past tense (indicative)							
ich	**durfte**	**konnte**	**mochte**	**mußte**	**sollte**	**wollte**	**wußte**
du	**durftest**	**konntest**	**mochtest**	**mußtest**	**solltest**	**wolltest**	**wußtest**
er/sie/es	**durfte**	**konnte**	**mochte**	**mußte**	**sollte**	**wollte**	**wußte**
wir	**durften**	**konnten**	**mochten**	**mußten**	**sollten**	**wollten**	**wußten**
ihr	**durftet**	**konntet**	**mochtet**	**mußtet**	**solltet**	**wolltet**	**wußtet**
sie, Sie	**durften**	**konnten**	**mochten**	**mußten**	**sollten**	**wollten**	**wußten**

The *past subjunctive* is conjugated like the indicative, but (except in the case of **sollen, wollen**) with the vowel mutated: **(dürfen) ich dürfte** etc.; **(können) ich könnte** etc.; **(mögen) ich möchte** etc.; **(müssen) ich müßte** etc.; **(sollen) ich sollte** etc.; **(wollen) ich wollte** etc.; **(wissen) ich wüßte** etc.

The *compound tenses* are regular. A special feature of the *perfect* and *pluperfect* is that they are constructed with either (*a*) a past participle of the type **ge—t,**

1. Unlike 'must', **müssen** does not (except sometimes in the 2nd person: see entry) change its meaning when used with a negative, e.g. **ich muß es nicht lesen** 'I don't have to read it'; 'I mustn't read it' = **ich darf es nicht lesen**.

e.g. **ich habe ihn nie gemocht** 'I never liked him', or (*b*) (if another infinitive is dependent on the modal) a past participle identical with the infinitive, e.g. **ich habe es nicht lesen können** 'I was unable to read it', **sie hatte es bezahlen müssen** 'she had had to pay for it'. The forms of the *pluperfect subjunctive* are used to refer to an unrealized possibility:

hätte (kommen etc.) **dürfen** 'would have been allowed to (come etc.)'
hätte ... können 'could have, would have been able to'
hätte ... mögen 'would have liked to'
hätte ... müssen 'would have had to'; 'should have'
hätte ... sollen 'should have, ought to have'
hätte ... wollen 'would have wanted to'

– all with the implication 'but did not'. (Contrast the following two translations of 'he could have written it': 1. **er hätte es schreiben können** (but did not); 2. **er könnte es geschrieben haben** (and quite possibly did).)
Imperatives of **wissen: wisse!; wißt!; wissen Sie!**
Past participles: (*a*) **gedurft, gekonnt, gemocht, gemußt, gesollt, gewollt, gewußt;** (*b*) (modal verbs only: with dependent infinitive) **dürfen, können, mögen, müssen, sollen, wollen.**

USE OF TENSES

Unlike English, German does not have both simple and continuous forms; the context normally makes clear whether, for example, **sie ißt Pfannkuchen** means 'she eats pancakes' or 'she is eating pancakes'.

(i) The *present* tense may refer not only to present actions and events but very often also – as sometimes in English – to those in the future when the context makes it clear that future time is meant, e.g. **ich bin gleich wieder da** 'I'll be right back', **ich fahre morgen nach Köln** 'I'm going to Cologne tomorrow', **sie findet es nie** 'she'll never find it'; as the historic present it may also 'bring alive' past occurrences in vivid descriptive style. The present of **kommen** is used where English has the perfect in such statements as **ich komme wegen meiner Schuhe** 'I've come about my shoes'.

An important difference in usage between the two languages is that an action begun in the past and still going on is expressed in English by the perfect tense, in German by the present tense, e.g. **ich bin seit 3 Uhr/seit Jahren hier** 'I've been here since 3 o'clock/for years'; in negative statements both languages have the perfect, e.g. **ich habe ihn seit Jahren nicht (mehr) gesehen** 'I haven't seen him for years'.

(ii) Reporting the past: The *past* tense reports past actions and events, and is the tense in which most narrative prose is written, e.g. **sie lächelte** 'she smiled', **Im Herbst des Jahres 1787 unternahm Mozart in Begleitung seiner Frau eine Reise nach Prag** (Mörike) 'In the autumn of 1787 Mozart, accompanied by his wife, went on a journey to Prague'; it may also describe a past state or situation, e.g. **sie sah krank aus** 'she looked ill', **er saß in der Ecke und las** 'he sat in the corner reading'. In addition, the past tense is used in the introduction to credit titles: **es wirkten mit ...** 'those taking part were ...', **Sie sahen ...** 'you have been watching ...' In sentences such as **ich wartete seit 3 Uhr** 'I'd been waiting since 3 o'clock', the use of the past tense – where English has the pluperfect – is analogous to the use of the present described in (i) above, 2nd paragraph; in negative statements both languages have the pluperfect, e.g. **ich hatte ihn seit Jahren nicht (mehr) gesehen** 'I hadn't seen him for years'.

The *perfect* tense is used, like its English counterpart, to refer to past events that have a bearing on the present, e.g. **er hat viele Romane gelesen** 'he has read many novels', **es hat geschneit!** 'it's been snowing!', **ist er schon angekommen?** 'has he arrived yet?' But unlike the English perfect, it may refer to events further back in time than the recent past, e.g. **Darwin hat die Selektionstheorie begründet** 'Darwin founded the theory of natural selection'. It is also widely used instead of the past tense, with reference to past actions and events, e.g. **wir sind letztes Jahr nach Indien getrampt** 'last year we hitch-hiked to India', **in Piräus haben sie Schilder mit der Aufschrift „Not inside the grass" entdeckt** 'in Piraeus they discovered signs saying "N.i.t.g."', **sie hat in einem Hotel gearbeitet** 'she worked in a hotel'. Just as the present tense is often used to indicate future time, so the perfect is commonly employed in place of a future perfect (**ich werde ... gearbeitet haben** etc.), e.g. **bis du zurückkommst, habe ich das Buch zu Ende gelesen** 'by the time you return I'll have finished the book'; in subordinate clauses the perfect may be used in both English and German with the force of a future perfect, e.g. **ich möchte lieber warten, bis wir genug gespart haben** 'I'd prefer to wait until we've saved enough'.

'*Used to*', '*would*': The force of 'used to' is usually conveyed by the adverb **früher** (e.g. **Südtirol gehörte früher zu Österreich** 'South Tyrol used to be part of Austria', **er hat früher bei der Post gearbeitet** 'he used to work for the Post Office', **sie kommen nicht so oft wie früher** 'they don't come as often as they used to'), except where another adverb of time makes **früher** redundant; while 'would' indicating habitual action as in 'now and then a bird would call' may be expressed by the past tense: **ab und zu ertönte ein Vogelruf**.

The *pluperfect* tense is used like its English counterpart, e.g. **ich hatte den Wecker nicht gehört** 'I hadn't heard the alarm clock', **sie waren beim Fernsehen eingenickt** 'they had nodded off while watching TV'.

(iii) The *future* tense (formed with **werden**) is often replaced by the present tense (see (i), 1st paragraph). It may indicate a future event, e.g. **die Messe wird nächstes Jahr in Mailand stattfinden** 'the fair will be held in Milan next year'; it may predict, e.g. **die Preise werden wohl wieder steigen** 'prices will probably go up again'; it may express an intention, e.g. **ich werde es mir überlegen** 'I'll think about it'. (In this last function **werden** competes with **wollen**: **ich will es mir überlegen**. But only **wollen** is used (*a*) to express the idea of willingness to do something, e.g. **willst du mir helfen?** 'will you help me?', **die Russen wollen nicht unterschreiben** 'the Russians won't sign', (*b*) to make a suggestion, e.g. **wollen wir ins Museum gehen?** 'shall we go to the museum?')

The future tense, often supported by the adverbs **schon** or **wohl**, may also suggest a probability, e.g. **sie wird schon recht haben** 'I expect she's right', **es wird schon so sein, wie er sagt** 'it'll be as he says'; this is also true of the future perfect, e.g. **er wird (wohl) zuviel gegessen haben** 'I expect he's eaten too much', **sie werden inzwischen abgereist sein** 'they'll have left by now', **es wird ihm doch nichts passiert sein?** 'I trust nothing's happened to him?'

THE PASSIVE

By using **werden** 'to become', and not the equivalent of 'to be' (**sein**), to form the passive – **sein** normally denotes a state, not an action[1] – German avoids the kind of ambiguity that may characterize an English statement: 'the bridge was built' could denote an *action* (the construction of the bridge was carried out) or a *state* (the bridge was complete); in German the former would be **die Brücke wurde gebaut** (passive), the latter **die Brücke war gebaut**.

The *agent* in passive constructions is indicated by the preposition **von**, the *means* by **durch**, e.g. **er wurde von seiner Mutter/durch den Lärm geweckt** 'he was woken by his mother/the noise', **Guernica wurde von Hitlers Bombern/durch Hitlers Bomben zerstört** 'G. was destroyed by H.'s bombers/bombs'. Following a verbal noun, however, the agent is indicated by **durch**, e.g. **die Erfindung der Buchdruckerkunst durch Gutenberg** 'the invention of printing by G.'

Points about the passive:

(i) '*I was offered, told, etc.*': A significant difference between English and German usage lies in the fact that in English the indirect object of the verb (in the active) can become the subject of the passive (e.g. 'I was offered a place at London University'), whereas in German this is not possible – only the direct object (here 'a place', which is what is really being offered) can become the subject of the passive: **mir wurde ein Studienplatz an der Universität London angeboten**. Cf. 'I was told that that was not true' **mir wurde** (or **es wurde mir**) **gesagt, daß das nicht stimmte**, 'I was ordered to shoot' **mir wurde** (or **es wurde mir**) **befohlen zu schießen** (**befehlen** 'to order' takes the dative).

(ii) *Substitutes for the passive*: Often where the passive is used in English, German employs some other construction. Very commonly, when no agent is specified, **man** is used with an active verb, e.g. **man hat gesagt, daß ...** 'it has been said that ...', **man hörte ihn singen** 'he was heard singing'. In the case of verbs taking an indirect object in the active, the passive is frequently avoided: (*a*) **man** may be used instead, e.g. **man versprach uns bessere Arbeitsbedingungen** 'we were promised better working conditions', **man hat ihr einen anderen Arzt empfohlen** 'she was recommended another doctor', **man hat mir einen Studienplatz angeboten**; (*b*) it is sometimes replaced by a construction with **bekommen** + past participle, e.g. **sie hat das Buch zugeschickt bekommen** 'she has been sent the book', **ich habe einen Studienplatz angeboten bekommen**; (*c*) 'to be given something' and 'to be told something' are often expressed in German by the active verbs **bekommen** and **erfahren**, e.g. 'I was given a present by them' **ich habe von ihnen ein Geschenk bekommen**, 'at the airport I was told that the plane was two hours late' **am Flughafen erfuhr ich, daß das Flugzeug zwei Stunden Verspätung hatte**.

Sometimes German uses a *reflexive verb*, in 'cases where things come about of themselves' (George O. Curme), e.g. **sich widerspiegeln in** 'to be reflected in', **sich erfüllen** (of wish etc.) 'to be fulfilled', **sich bestätigen** (of suspicion etc.) 'to be confirmed'; and sometimes an *intransitive verb*, e.g. **heißen** 'to be called',

1. **Werden** is, however, replaced by **sein** as the auxiliary for passive statements (*a*) in the imperative and present subjunctive, e.g. **es sei darauf hingewiesen, daß ...** 'attention is drawn to the fact that ...', (*b*) (sometimes) in the infinitive, when used with a modal verb (**können**, **wollen**, etc.), e.g. **das will vorsichtig gemacht sein** 'that needs to be done carefully'.

gelten als 'to be regarded as', **erschrecken** 'to be frightened', **ertrinken** 'to be drowned', **umkommen** 'to be killed', **verlorengehen** (of thing) 'to get lost', **heiraten** 'to get married'.

Where English has 'can' + passive, German very frequently uses **lassen** + **sich** + infinitive, e.g. **das läßt sich machen** 'that can be done', **Marcel Prousts Werke lassen sich nicht leicht zusammenfassen** 'Marcel Proust's works cannot easily be summarized'.

NOTE: An active construction with inverted word order (see p. lix) in German frequently corresponds to a parallel passive construction in English, e.g. **schon am nächsten Tag besuchten ihn seine Freunde aus Neapel** 'the very next day he was visited by his friends from Naples', **mich fasziniert der Gedanke, daß...** 'I'm fascinated by the thought that...'

(iii) *The impersonal passive*: A widely-used construction in German is the impersonal passive, which is used with *intransitive* verbs to indicate an activity without reference to a specific agent. Where a collective activity is meant the most suitable English rendering is often 'there is/are' (frequently + gerund), e.g. **es wurde gestreikt** 'there was a strike', **freitags wurde getanzt** 'on Fridays there was dancing'. Other examples of the impersonal passive: **bei Glatteis muß gestreut werden** 'icy roads must be gritted', **wann wird geheiratet?** 'when's the wedding?', (with a personal subject – 'someone' – supplied in the English translation) **er muß immer fürchten, daß mitgehört wird** 'he always has to fear that someone is listening in', (with a prepositional object, again with a personal subject supplied in the translation) **an der neuen Schule wird bereits zwei Jahre gebaut** 'they've already been working on the new school for two years'. (The impersonal **es** is omitted – as in the last five examples – when not in initial position.)

THE SUBJUNCTIVE

The subjunctive mood is unfamiliar to English-speakers, having disappeared from English except in a few petrified usages such as '*be* that as it may', 'if I *were* you', '*suffice* it to say' or indeed 'Britannia *rule* the waves', and in constructions of the type 'they requested that he *withdraw* from the contest'. In German, by contrast, it continues – despite the encroachments of the indicative and of periphrastic constructions – to play a major role as the second mood of the verb alongside the indicative (especially in the usage of educated speakers and in literary style); and the student of German needs to be familiar with its forms and uses.

Chief uses of the subjunctive:

(i) *Indirect speech*: When the verb in the main clause is in the *past* tense, the verb in the subordinate clause normally goes into the subjunctive (**daß** is very frequently omitted); unlike its English counterpart, it retains the tense of the original statement/question:

sie sagte, er *habe* sie mißverstanden (original statement: **er hat mich mißverstanden**) 'she said he had misunderstood her'

ich fragte ihn, ob er teilnehmen *könne* (original question: **können Sie teilnehmen?**) 'I asked him if he could take part'

Where, however, the present subjunctive forms are identical with the indicative forms (e.g. **ich habe**) and therefore not distinctive, the past subjunctive is used instead, e.g. **sie sagte, ich hätte sie mißverstanden** 'she said I had misunderstood her'. In conversational German the present subjunctive is on the whole avoided, and the past subjunctive – or the indicative – used instead. When the verb of saying is in the *present* tense, it is commonly followed by the indicative, e.g. **er sagt, daß er an einem Reiseführer schreibt** 'he says he is writing a guide book'; but the subjunctive (again often without **daß**) may also be used, e.g. **Menschen, die sagen, zum Lesen fehle ihnen die Zeit** 'people who say they haven't time to read' – implicit here, as always, in the subjunctive of indirect speech is an attitude of detachment on the part of the speaker/writer: no view is expressed as to the truth or otherwise of the words reported.

As the subjunctive reports what has been said, it is naturally much used in newspaper reports where someone's opinion or account of something is being quoted; and since the subjunctive forms are clearly recognizable as indicating indirect speech, German is able to dispense with the phrases (of the type 'he said', 'they maintained', and so on) that from time to time may need to be used in an English text to indicate that indirect speech is continuing. The following extract from a newspaper report illustrates the use of the subjunctive to express indirect speech:

Vor Journalisten sagte er, er *werde* solange in Frankreich bleiben, bis sein Volk dem Weg der Demokratie *folge*. „Ich bin hier, um den Widerstand meines Volkes zu ermutigen." Er *habe* seit seiner Amtsenthebung in T. gelebt, und es *sei* ihm sogar möglich gewesen, „in den Straßen umherzugehen, ohne entdeckt zu werden".
(Speaking to journalists he said that he *would* stay in France until such time as his people *followed* the path of democracy. 'I am here to encourage the resistance of my people.' He *had* [, he went on,] been living in T. since his removal from office, and it *had* even been possible for him 'to walk about the streets without being discovered'.)

Sometimes verbs of saying are omitted altogether, since the subjunctive itself implies that a person's words are being reported (which in translation is conveyed by phrases of the 'he/she said' type), e.g. **Er hat mir schon beim ersten Telefongespräch einen Besuch in W. ausgeredet. Da sei nichts zu sehen** 'He talked me out of visiting W. in our very first phone call. He said there wasn't anything to see there'; or in a subordinate clause: **man schickte mich nach Uppsala zu einem Professor, der alle angelsächsischen Ortsnamen kenne** 'I was sent to a professor in Uppsala who, it was said, knew all the Anglo-Saxon place-names'.

The subjunctive is also widely used with verbs (or nouns) expressing an *opinion* or a *belief*, e.g. **ich habe geglaubt, du seist** (or indicative **bist**) **erst 20** 'I thought you were only 20', **er bildet sich ein, er sei Napoleon** 'he imagines he is Napoleon', **es ist ein Irrtum zu meinen, daß Umweltschutz wenig Geld koste** 'it's a mistake to think that conservation doesn't cost much money', **der Glaube, daß der Krieg unabwendbar sei** 'the belief that war is (was) inevitable', **er glaubte, daß er krank sei** 'he thought he was ill', **ich dachte, du hättest meinen Brief bekommen** 'I thought you'd received my letter', **man könnte fast denken, man wäre in Schottland** 'you might almost think you were in Scotland'.

(ii) *Conditional statements* (so-called 'unreal condition' – referring to an improbable eventuality, expressed by the past subjunctive, or one that was but is no longer possible, expressed by the pluperfect subjunctive):

(past subjunctive) **wenn ich ein Wörterbuch *hätte*, könnte ich das Wort nachschlagen** 'if I had a dictionary I could look the word up'
(pluperfect subjunctive) **wenn er *gekommen wäre*, hätten wir viel Spaß gehabt** 'if he had come we'd have had a lot of fun'

(If the verb in the 'if' clause is in the present tense ('open condition') the indicative is used, e.g. **wenn es regnet, können wir ins Theater gehen** 'if it rains we can go to the theatre'.)

In the main clause the past subjunctive is frequently – except in the case of **hätte, wäre** and the modal auxiliaries **dürfte, könnte, möchte, müßte, sollte, wollte** – replaced by the construction **würde** + infinitive, thus in **wenn er mit diesem Zug käme, bekämen wir noch den Anschluß nach Husum** ('if he came on this train we'd get our connection to H.') **bekämen wir** may be replaced by **würden wir ... bekommen.** In the subordinate clause **sollte** + infinitive sometimes replaces the subjunctive (e.g. **wenn die Vorstellung später beginnen sollte** 'if the performance were to begin later' – avoiding the stilted form **begönne**); **würde** + infinitive is also widely used, especially in the spoken language. (For the inversion of subject and verb as an alternative to **wenn** see 'Word Order', p. lxi, (iv)(*a*).)

(iii) *In 'as if' clauses*: The subjunctive is used in clauses introduced by **als ob/wenn** (or **als** with inversion), e.g. **sie sieht (so) aus, als ob sie krank wäre** (or **als wäre sie krank**) 'she looks as if she were ill', **ihm war, als müßte er davonlaufen** 'he felt as if he had to run away'.

(iv) *In final, relative and temporal clauses*: Especially in literary German, the subjunctive is sometimes used (instead of the indicative or a modal verb) in clauses introduced by: (*a*) **damit** or **daß** (expressing purpose) 'so that, so as to', e.g. **er beeilte sich, damit er nicht zu spät käme** 'he hurried so as not to be late'; (*b*) *relative pronouns* referring to a hypothetical antecedent, e.g. **sie suchte eine Karriere, die ihr Erfüllung brächte** 'she was looking for a career that would bring her fulfilment'; (*c*) **bevor** or **ehe** 'before', **bis** 'until' (when a future event is viewed hypothetically), e.g. **er beschloß zu warten, bis er die Seekarten gesehen hätte** 'he decided to wait until he had seen the charts'.

(v) *In concessive clauses* beginning with the equivalents of 'whatever', 'whoever', etc. the subjunctive is sometimes used, e.g. **wer (immer) sie auch sei** (or **sein mag**), **sie muß sich an die Spielregeln halten** 'whoever she may be, she must abide by the rules', **sei er auch noch so mutig** 'however courageous he may be'; also in set expressions: **wie dem auch sei** 'be that as it may', **koste es, was es wolle** 'cost what it may', **komme, was da wolle** 'come what may'. (With reference to the past only the indicative is possible.)

(vi) *Expressing a wish, command, etc.*: The present subjunctive is used to express:

(*a*) a *wish* in certain set phrases (3rd person singular, e.g. **es lebe ...!** 'long live ...!', **Dein Reich komme** 'Thy kingdom come', **Gott behüte!** 'heaven forbid!', **hol ihn der Teufel!** 'to hell with him!', also the South German greeting **grüß (dich) Gott!**; a historical example is the First World War slogan **Gott strafe England!** '(may) God punish England', from which 'to strafe' is derived); the present subjunctive of **mögen** is used in all persons to express 'may ...', e.g. **mögen Sie lange leben!** 'may you live long!'

(*b*) an *exhortation* or a *command*: in the 3rd person singular, the subjunctive may serve to exhort (in literary language, e.g. **Edel sei der Mensch, hilfreich und gut** (Goethe) 'Let man be noble, helpful and good'); it may be used with imperative force (e.g. **wer dagegen ist, der trete vor!** 'anyone not in favour step forward!', (with **man** as subject) **man wende sich an ...** 'apply to ...', in recipes etc. **man nehme ...** 'take ...') or to express a proposition (e.g. **ABC sei ein gleichschenkliges Dreieck** 'let ABC be an isosceles triangle'); in the 1st person plural[1] it is used in the sense of 'let's ...!', e.g. **seien wir ehrlich!** 'let's be honest!', **also fangen wir an!** 'let's start then!'.

The past and pluperfect subjunctives, accompanied by **doch** (or **bloß**, **nur**, **doch bloß/nur**), express a (heartfelt) wish that the speaker cannot expect to see realized, = 'if only ...', e.g. **wenn sie doch käme!** 'if only she would come!', **hätte ich doch mehr Zeit!** 'if only I had more time!', **wenn er das nur nicht gesagt hätte!** 'if only he hadn't said that!', **wollte Gott, sie wären schon zu Hause!** 'would to God they were already home!'

(vii) *Various uses* in which the subjunctive, always less direct than the indicative, adds a nuance of caution, tentativeness to a statement: (*a*) making a *polite utterance*, e.g. **eine Frage hätte ich noch** 'there's one more thing I'd like to ask', **ich hätte gern sechs Eier** 'I'd like six eggs', **ich hätte gern Herrn X gesprochen** 'I wonder if I might speak to Mr X?', **hätten Sie sonst noch einen Wunsch?** (in a shop) 'is there anything else I can get you?'; (*b*) referring to the *completion* of something, e.g. **das wär's!** 'that's that!', **da wären wir endlich!** 'here we are at last!'; (*c*) **ich wünschte**: the past subjunctive has the special sense 'I wish', e.g. **ich wünschte, ich hätte ihn nie getroffen** 'I wish I'd never met him'; (*d*) with **beinahe**, **fast** 'almost', e.g. **das Auto wäre beinahe umgekippt** 'the car nearly tipped over', **fast hätte ich den Fehler übersehen** 'I almost overlooked the mistake'; (*e*) in clauses introduced by **(an)statt daß** 'instead of (—ing)', **nicht daß** 'not that', **ohne daß** 'without (—ing)', **(zu ...,) als daß** '(too ...) to'; in these instances the (less tentative, more direct) indicative may also be used.

SEPARABLE AND INSEPARABLE VERBS

The German vocabulary contains a large number of verbs formed with prefixes, either separable and stressed (e.g. **auf–** in **aufgeben** 'to give up') or inseparable and unstressed (e.g. **be–** in **bekommen** 'to get').

(a) *Separable verbs*

These have no exact counterpart in English, but may be compared with phrasal verbs such as 'give up', 'take over', 'stick out'. Unlike the adverbial element in these English verbs, however, the German separable prefix *goes right to the end* in a main clause in the present and past tenses, e.g. **ich *gehe* heute abend mit meiner Freundin *aus*** 'I'm going out with my girl-friend tonight'; but where (in a subordinate clause) the verb itself is in final position, the prefix is reunited with the simple verb in the sequence prefix – verb, e.g. **wenn ich mit meiner Freun-**

1. The forms are indistinguishable from the indicative except in the case of **sein** (**seien wir**).

din ***ausgehe*** 'if/when I go out with my girl-friend', **wußtest du nicht, daß sie mit ihm** ***ausgeht*?** 'didn't you know she's going out with him?'

Separable prefixes precede, and are joined to, the verb in the infinitive (e.g. **ausgehen**) and the present participle (e.g. **ausgehend**); where the infinitive is used with **zu** the latter is inserted between the prefix and the simple verb (e.g. **auszugehen**); in the past participle the prefix precedes the **ge–** element (e.g. **ausgegangen**).

Examples:

aufgeben 'to give up' (**ich gebe ... auf, (wenn** etc.) **ich ... aufgebe, ich habe ... aufgegeben)**

einzahlen 'to pay in' (**ich zahle ... ein, (wenn** etc.) **ich ... einzahle, ich habe ... eingezahlt)**

mithalten 'to keep up' (**ich halte ... mit, (wenn** etc.) **ich ... mithalte, ich habe ... mitgehalten)**

German separable prefixes, it should be added, translate not only English adverbs but also (in certain instances) prepositions. **Ab–**, for instance, is equivalent to 'from, out of' in verbs such as **abkaufen** (+dative) 'to buy (something) from' and **ablocken** (+dative) 'to coax (something) out of'; **an–** corresponds to 'at' as in **anstarren** 'to stare at' and 'to' as in **ansprechen** 'to speak to'; **auf–** to the preposition 'on' as in **aufoktroyieren** (+dative) 'to impose (something) on'; **nach–** to the preposition 'after' as in **nacheilen** (+dative) 'to hurry after'; **vor–** to 'to' as in **vorlesen** (+dative) 'to read (something) to'; and **zu–** to 'at' or 'to' as in **zulächeln** (+dative) 'to smile at', **zuwerfen** (+dative) 'to throw (a ball etc.) to, to cast (a glance) at'.

Some separable verbs are formed by prefixing a noun, adjective or second verb to the simple verb, e.g. **teilnehmen** 'to take part' (from **Teil** 'part' and **nehmen** 'to take'), **fernsehen** 'to watch television' (from **fern** 'far' and **sehen** 'to see'), **stehenbleiben** 'to stop' (from **stehen** 'to stand' and **bleiben** 'to remain'). These are handled in exactly the same way as other separable verbs, thus **ich nehme ... teil, (wenn** etc.) **ich ... teilnehme**, past participle **teilgenommen**; **ich sehe ... fern, (wenn** etc.) **ich ... fernsehe**, past participle **ferngesehen**; and **ich bleibe ... stehen, (wenn** etc.) **ich ... stehenbleibe**, past participle **stehengeblieben**.[1]

NOTE: The beginner needs to remember that before looking up a verb in the dictionary one should first look at the end of the clause (usually marked in German by some form of punctuation) to see whether a separable prefix is there. If so, it is the entry for the *compound verb* (consisting of prefix + (simple) verb) that must be consulted; thus in the case of a sentence such as **der Mond übt auf die Erde eine Kraft aus** it is **ausüben** 'to exert etc.', and not **üben** 'to practise etc.', that should be looked up: 'the moon exerts a force on the earth'.

(b) *Inseparable verbs*

Some verbs are formed with inseparable prefixes, e.g. **erreichen** 'to reach', **vergessen** 'to forget'. As their name suggests, these prefixes cannot be detached

1. Two special cases are **radfahren** 'to cycle' and **maschineschreiben** 'to type' (intransitive), which constitute an uncomfortable halfway house between phrases of the type **Auto fahren** 'to drive' or **Ski laufen** 'to ski' (**ich fahre ... Auto, laufe ... Ski**) and separable verbs like **teilnehmen**: in the finite forms the noun retains the capital letter (**ich fahre ... Rad, schreibe ... Maschine**) but, becoming a prefix, loses it in the infinitive (**radfahren, maschineschreiben**) and past participle (**radgefahren, maschinegeschrieben**).

from the verb. The past participle of such verbs, unlike that of separable verbs, has no **ge–**; **ge–** may, however, itself be an inseparable prefix, as in **genehmigen** 'to approve'.

There is in addition a class of compound verbs – they may conveniently also be termed inseparable – some of which are derived from compound nouns (e.g. **frühstücken** 'to have breakfast', **handhaben** 'to handle' from **das Frühstück, die Handhabe**) while others are formed by other means (e.g. **schlafwandeln** 'to walk in one's sleep'). All are stressed on the first syllable and conjugated weak; their past participles are formed with the prefix **ge–** (in contrast with the inserted **–ge–** in the past participles of separable verbs like **teilnehmen** – see (a) above): **gefrühstückt, gehandhabt, geschlafwandelt.**

NOTE: The prefixes **durch–, hinter–, über–, um–, unter–, voll–, wider–, wieder–** occur as both separable and inseparable prefixes; in some instances the same verb occurs in separable and inseparable forms, e.g. **úmfahren** 'to knock down' as opposed to **umfáhren** 'to go/drive/sail round'.

IMPERSONAL VERBS AND CONSTRUCTIONS

A number of German verbs are used impersonally (i.e. in the 3rd person singular with the impersonal pronoun **es**), some of which have impersonal equivalents in English: (concrete) **es regnet** 'it rains/is raining', **es schneit** 'it snows/is snowing', (abstract) **es handelt sich um ...** 'it's about/a question of ...' Other instances (with **es** often rendered by 'there is/are ...') are: **es klopft** 'there is a knock at the door', **es klingelt** 'the doorbell is ringing', **es zieht** 'there is a draught', **es riecht nach Gas** 'there is a smell of gas', **es rauscht** 'there is a rustling', **es knallte** 'there was a bang', **es wimmelte von Insekten/Ausländern** 'the place was swarming with insects/foreigners'.

How a person feels may also be expressed by an impersonal construction: **es ist mir warm/kalt, mir ist warm/kalt** 'I'm (feeling) warm/cold', **es graut mir** (or **mir graut**) **vor** (+dative) 'I dread', **es ist mir** (or **mir ist**), **als ob ...** 'I feel as though ...', 'it seems to me that ...'

Intransitive verbs are sometimes used in the *impersonal passive* construction, e.g. **es wurde gestreikt** 'there was a strike', (with omission of **es**) **draußen wurde gehupt** 'outside, someone hooted (honked)' (see p. li).

Translation of 'there is/are ...': These are translated by **es gibt** (+accusative), when the existence of something or someone is referred to and/or when one could logically insert 'in the nature of things' in the sentence concerned: 'there are spiders throughout Africa' **es gibt Spinnen überall in Afrika**, 'there are people who ...' **es gibt Leute, die ...**, 'is there a God?' **gibt es einen Gott?**, 'there wasn't much snow this winter' **es gab in diesem Winter wenig Schnee**, 'there was nothing to eat' **es gab nichts zu essen**, 'there's always a lot to do before Christmas' **vor Weihnachten gibt es immer viel zu tun**, 'there'll be trouble' **das wird Ärger geben.**

Es ist/sind, on the other hand, are concerned not with existence but with presence – namely in a specified, limited place – and would be used when translating e.g. 'there is someone at the door' **es ist jemand an der Tür**, 'there are two spiders in the bathroom' **es sind zwei Spinnen im Badezimmer.** (**Es** is dropped if it is not the first word: **im Badezimmer sind zwei Spinnen.**) There is a certain amount of overlap between the two constructions, and it is not always possible to draw hard-and-fast distinctions.

In many contexts other translations are used, e.g. (location: **stehen**) 'there are three apple trees in the garden' **es stehen drei Apfelbäume im Garten,** (**liegen**) 'there were many books on the table' **auf dem Tisch lagen viele Bücher**; (prevalence: **herrschen**) 'there is uncertainty as to whether ...' **es herrscht Ungewißheit darüber, ob ...**, 'there was great excitement' **es herrschte große Aufregung**; (existence: **bestehen**) 'there is the possibility/danger that ...' **es besteht die Möglichkeit/Gefahr, daß ...**, 'there is no reason to suppose/no doubt that ...' **es besteht kein Grund zur Annahme/kein Zweifel, daß ...**; (collective activity: impersonal passive – see p. li) 'there was a strike' **es wurde gestreikt**, 'on Fridays there was dancing' **freitags wurde getanzt**; (phenomena: **es** + verb used impersonally – see above) 'there is a draught' **es zieht.**

THE INFINITIVE

The position of the infinitive is treated on p. lxii.

The infinitive is in most cases preceded by **zu**, but in certain constructions it is not:

(i) *Infinitive with* **zu**: e.g. **sie versucht zu schlafen** 'she's trying to sleep', **du brauchst nicht zu warten** 'you needn't wait', **er beabsichtigte, den Brief am nächsten Tag zu schreiben** 'he intended to write the letter the next day'. (For the use of the comma with infinitive phrases see p. lxviii, 'The comma', 2nd paragraph.) Where the verb concerned has a separable prefix, **-zu-** is inserted between the prefix and the simple verb, e.g. **er beabsichtigte, dieses Hobby aufzugeben** 'he intended to give up this hobby'.

The infinitive with **zu** has *passive sense* when used with the verb **sein** (cf. English 'the house is to let'), e.g. **kein Laut war zu hören** 'not a sound was to be heard', **diese Hitze ist nicht zu ertragen** 'this heat is (not to be borne =) unbearable', **diese Frage ist leicht zu beantworten** 'this question is (easily to be answered =) easy to answer', **die Personalausweise sind am Eingang vorzuzeigen** 'identity cards are to be shown at the entrance', (elliptically) **Zimmer zu vermieten** 'room to let'.

The infinitive with **zu** is used in combination with certain prepositions: **um ... zu** '(in order) to' and – if there is no change of subject – **(an)statt ... zu** 'instead of (—ing)', **ohne ... zu** 'without (—ing)', e.g. **um/(an)statt/ohne die Tür abzuschließen** '(in order) to lock the door/instead of locking the door/without locking the door'. (The last two are replaced by **(an)statt daß, ohne daß** if there is a change of subject.) **Um ... zu** is also sometimes used without any implication of purpose, like English 'to' + infinitive, to indicate someone's destiny, e.g. **sie trennten sich, um einander nie wiederzusehen** 'they parted, never to see each other again'.

(ii) *Infinitive without* **zu**: used after certain verbs, notably (*a*) the modal verbs (**dürfen, können, mögen, müssen, sollen, wollen**), e.g. **ich wollte ihn sprechen** 'I wanted to speak to him'; (*b*) the auxiliary **lassen** 'to let (do something)', (with infinitive in passive sense) 'to have (something done)', e.g. **sie ließ den Gepard entkommen** 'she let the cheetah escape', **er ließ die Nationalhymne fünfmal spielen** 'he had the national anthem played five times'; (*c*) the verbs of perception

hören 'to hear', **sehen** 'to see', **fühlen** 'to feel', **spüren** 'to feel, sense', e.g. **sie hörte ihn kommen** 'she heard him coming', **ich fühlte mein Herz schlagen** 'I felt my heart beating'; (*d*) **bleiben** (denoting a situation) and **gehen** (referring to an activity), e.g. **sitzen bleiben** 'to remain seated', **schwimmen gehen** 'to go swimming'; (*e*) (if the infinitive stands on its own, without an object etc.) **helfen** (+dative) 'to help', **lehren** 'to teach', **lernen** 'to learn', e.g. **sie half mir abtrocknen** 'she helped me dry up', **er muß erst schwimmen lernen** 'he must learn to swim first'; contrast: **man lehrte uns, alle Fremdwörter nachzuschlagen** 'we were taught to look up all the foreign words'.

The simple infinitive is also used as an *imperative* to convey brief directions, e.g. **weitermachen!** 'carry on!', **alles aussteigen!** 'all change!', **rückwärts einsteigen!** (on Austrian tramcars) 'board at the rear', **Einfahrt freihalten!** 'keep entrance clear', (with suppression of the reflexive pronoun) **nicht hinauslehnen!** 'do not lean out of the window'.

The infinitive may be used as a *noun*, in which case it has neuter gender and is written with a capital letter, e.g. **das Reisen** 'travel(ling)', **das Lesen** 'reading'; it may form part of a compound, e.g. **das Kopfschütteln** 'shaking/shake of the head', **das Menschsein** 'being human, humanity', **das Zuhörenmüssen** 'having to listen'. The infinitive – in an infinitive phrase with **zu** – may also play a nominal role as, for example, the subject of the verb in **einen Eisbären zu füttern ist gefährlich** 'feeding a polar bear is dangerous' (here **zu** may be omitted), **zu sagen, daß sie Glück hatten, ist unrealistisch** 'to say that they were lucky is unrealistic', or as the complement in **sein Ziel war, eine Goldmedaille zu gewinnen** 'his goal was to win a gold medal'.

PARTICIPLES

The present and past participles may, as in English, be used adjectivally, e.g. **ein lächelndes Gesicht** 'a smiling face', **sie ist einfach reizend** 'she is simply delightful', **ein ausgebildeter Dolmetscher** 'a trained interpreter', **ich war entsetzt** 'I was horrified'; the present participle may also be used in the verbal sense after **finden** etc., e.g. **ich fand ihn schlafend** 'I found him asleep'. Examples of adverbial use: **fragend/entsetzt schaute sie ihn an** 'she looked at him questioningly/in horror', **überraschend früh** 'surprisingly early'.

The participles may occur (chiefly in written German) in a participial phrase preceding the noun, e.g. **die im Teich schwimmenden Hechte** 'the pike swimming in the pond', **der als Verbrecher entlarvte Präsident** 'the president (who was) exposed as a criminal' (see p. lxiv, 'Adjectival and participial phrases'); the construction with **zu** + present participle has passive force (the so-called gerundive), e.g. **das zu lösende Problem** 'the problem to be solved' (literally 'the to-be-solved problem'). In literary style – the construction is rather less common than its English counterpart – the present participle sometimes occurs in a participial phrase with adverbial force (with the participle coming last), e.g. **die Route verläuft, etwa der tschechischen Grenze folgend, durch den Bayrischen Wald** 'roughly following the Czech border, the route runs through the Bavarian Forest', (with this literary-sounding construction used to telling ironic effect) **... Dettmar Cramer, der nichts sagte, dies aber perfekt artikulierend** (from a review of a TV programme: '... Dettmar Cramer, who said nothing, albeit with perfect articulation'). The similar past participle construction may have the participle at the beginning or the end, e.g. **von seiner schauspielerischen Anlage überzeugt** (or **überzeugt von seiner schauspielerischen Anlage**), **ging er zum Theater** 'convinced of his talent as an actor, he went on the stage'.

The English present participle (—ing) is rendered by other constructions in German in a number of situations:

(= relative clause) e.g. 'a teacher driving a minibus' **ein Lehrer, der einen Kleinbus fährt/fuhr**

(causal: **da ...**) e.g. 'having nothing to do, I went for a walk' **da ich nichts zu tun hatte, ging ich spazieren**, 'this being the case, ...' **da dies der Fall ist/war, ...**

(temporal: **als ..., nachdem ..., während ...**) e.g. 'hearing the doorbell, he went to open the door' **als er die Klingel hörte, ging er die Tür öffnen**, 'having written the article, I went to bed' **nachdem ich den Artikel geschrieben hatte, ging ich ins Bett**, 'and then, raising his baton, he looks up at the box' **und dann sieht er, während er den Dirigentenstab hebt, zur Loge hinauf**; sometimes two clauses linked by **und** are used, e.g. 'taking out his knife, he opened the letter' **er nahm sein Messer heraus und öffnete den Brief**, 'he left early, only later realizing that he had left his umbrella behind' **er ging früh und merkte erst später, daß er seinen Schirm vergessen hatte**, (simultaneous actions) 'there she stood waiting' **da stand sie und wartete**, 'he sat peeling potatoes' **er saß und schälte Kartoffeln**

(with verbs of perception): expressed by the infinitive, e.g. 'she heard him coming' **sie hörte ihn kommen** (see p. lvii, 'The infinitive' (ii) (*c*)); frequently, especially with more complex sentences, a clause with **wie** is used, e.g. 'he could see Donald being propped against the wall' **er sah, wie Donald gegen die Wand gelehnt wurde**, 'he heard the rain falling' **er hörte, wie der Regen fiel**

('spend time —ing', 'be busy —ing'): here the participle is rendered by **mit** + infinitive noun or, if followed by an object etc., by **damit** + infinitive phrase, e.g. 'he spends most of his time reading/collecting beer-mats' **er verbringt die meiste Zeit mit Lesen/damit, Bierdeckel zu sammeln**, 'she was busy hanging out the washing' **sie war damit beschäftigt, Wäsche aufzuhängen**

('come —ing'): translated by **kommen** + past participle of the verb of motion concerned, e.g. 'they came running along' **sie kamen angelaufen**

The German past participle is also used as an *imperative*, to express peremptory – especially military – commands, e.g. **stillgestanden!** 'attention!' (from **stillstehen** 'to stop'), **abgesessen!** 'dismount!' (from **absitzen** 'to dismount').

WORD ORDER

MAIN CLAUSES

In a main clause (except in the case of a question or an imperative) the finite verb forms the *second element* in the sentence. It may, as usually in English, follow the subject, e.g. **der Mann reitet auf dem Pferd** 'the man is riding the horse'; but it may also follow another element, in which case the subject comes after the finite verb, as happens in English in cases like 'no sooner was she ...', 'only later did they ...' – this is known as *inversion*.

Examples:

(finite verb follows adverb) **gestern *habe* ich im Garten gearbeitet** 'yesterday I worked in the garden'
(finite verb follows complement) **ein Experte *ist* er nicht, aber ...** 'he's no expert, but ...'
(finite verb follows object) **dieses Wort *kenne* ich nicht** 'I don't know this word'
(finite verb follows appositional phrase) **Däne von Geburt, *lebt* er jetzt auf Kreta** 'a Dane by birth, he now lives in Crete'
(finite verb follows past participle: i) **viele haben diesen Roman gelesen, verstanden *haben* ihn nur wenige** 'many people have read this novel, but few have understood it'
(finite verb follows past participle: ii) **sie forderten, daß die Wiedervereinigung Deutschlands aufgegeben werden solle; begründet *wurde* diese Forderung mit dem Argument, daß ...** 'they demanded that the reunification of Germany should be abandoned, basing their demand on the argument that ...'
(finite verb follows infinitive) **„Setzen wir Deutschland, sozusagen, in den Sattel! Reiten *wird* es schon können"** (Bismarck, 1867) 'Let us put Germany, so to speak, in the saddle! She'll be able to ride all right'
(finite verb follows subordinate clause) **weil es heute so warm ist, *können* wir draußen essen** 'because it's so warm today we can eat outdoors'

Inverted word-order is often used (as in the second example above) to emphasize the word or phrase placed before the verb, and may serve to underline a contrast (fifth example); not all inversion, however, is emphatic (see e.g. the first and last examples). Inverted order may also establish a link with the preceding sentence or clause (sixth example).

Exceptionally, inversion does not occur in main clauses *following a concessive clause* beginning with the equivalent of 'whatever', 'whoever', 'however', etc., e.g. **was (immer) du auch sagst, ich halte an meiner Meinung fest** 'whatever you say, I'm sticking to my opinion'.

The verb precedes the subject in the *imperative* (**Sie** form) and *direct questions* (unless the subject is an interrogative pronoun), e.g. **stehen Sie auf!** 'get up!', **warum hast du es getan?** 'why did you do it?'; likewise in the 1st person plural present subjunctive used in exhortations, e.g. **gehen wir nach Hause!** 'let's go home'.

Inverted order occurs in some *exclamations*, e.g. **hab ich's mir doch gedacht!** 'I thought as much!', **war das eine Hetze!** 'what a rush that was!', **hat die aber Glück gehabt!** 'was she lucky!', (expressing a wish) **wären wir doch in Göteborg geblieben!** 'if only we'd stayed in Gothenburg!'

While it is quite usual for an English sentence to begin with two adverbs (or adverbial phrases), in German the position of the finite verb as the second element rules out such a word order, and in an equivalent German sentence the verb stands *between* the adverbs, e.g. 'two weeks ago, under similar circumstances, she would not have hesitated to do it' ***vor zwei Wochen* hätte sie *unter ähnlichen Umständen* nicht gezögert, es zu tun**. (Compare, however, 'on the right, next to the piano, stood the two American ladies' **rechts, neben dem Klavier, standen die beiden amerikanischen Damen**: adverbs of the same type, which effectively form a unit, are not separated.)

SUBORDINATE CLAUSES

In a subordinate clause (a clause that cannot stand on its own) the finite verb *goes to the end.*

Examples:

wir wußten, daß sie nicht kommen konnten 'we knew that they couldn't come'
ich fragte, wann er angekommen sei 'I asked when he had arrived'
das Mädchen, das eine blaue Bluse anhatte 'the girl (who was) wearing a blue blouse'
Solange der Wagen gleichförmig fährt, ... (A. Einstein) 'As long as the carriage is moving uniformly, ...'

Exceptions to this rule:

(i) After the conjunction **denn** 'for' the word order is that of a main clause, e.g. **sie gingen langsam, denn es war sehr heiß in der Wüste** 'they walked slowly, for it was very hot in the desert'.

(ii) When the conjunction **daß** is omitted after **sagen**, **glauben**, etc., the word order is that of a main clause, e.g. **er sagte, er habe von dieser grammatischen Einleitung kein Wort verstanden** 'he said he hadn't understood a word of this grammatical introduction'.

(iii) The auxiliary **haben** precedes the dependent infinitive in constructions with modal verbs (or other verbs having a second past participle identical with the infinitive), e.g. **wenn ich das *hätte* aussprechen können** 'if I'd been able to pronounce that', **sie beklagte sich, daß sie die Insel nicht *habe* besuchen dürfen** 'she complained that she hadn't been allowed to visit the island'. The auxiliary **werden** sometimes precedes the dependent infinitive in constructions with modal verbs.

(iv) Inversion occurs (*a*) when in a conditional clause **wenn** 'if' + verb at the end of the clause is replaced by inversion of subject and verb, e.g. **kommt der Pianist nicht, dann kann das Konzert nicht stattfinden** 'if the pianist doesn't come the concert can't take place', **wäre ich sofort aufgestanden, hätte ich den Zug noch erreicht** 'if I'd (had I) got up immediately I would have caught the train'; (*b*) when **als** is used in the sense of 'as if', e.g. **es sieht aus, als würde es bald regnen** 'it looks as if it'll rain soon'; (*c*) (in literary style) when used with **doch** to convey causal force, e.g. **das Dorf ist sehr ruhig, liegt es doch abseits der Hauptverkehrsstraßen** 'the village is very quiet, situated as it is away from the trunk roads'.

If two (or more) clauses have compound tenses *with the same auxiliary*, the latter is 'held over' until the end of the second (last) clause, e.g. **nachdem ich gebadet und mein Haar gewaschen *hatte*, machte ich mir ein Omelett** 'after I'd had a bath and washed my hair I made myself an omelette'.

It follows from the rule regarding the position of the verb in a subordinate clause that when *one subordinate clause is enclosed within another* the verb goes to the end in both clauses, e.g. **er wußte, daß sich das junge Paar, das sehr wenig Geld *hatte*, die neue Sitzgarnitur nicht leisten *konnte*** 'he knew that the young couple, who had very little money, could not afford the new suite'.

INFINITIVES, PAST PARTICIPLES AND SEPARABLE PREFIXES

Infinitives, past participles and separable prefixes go to the end of a main clause, e.g. **Indonesien wird auf seinen Anspruch nicht verzichten** (infinitive) 'Indonesia will not give up her claim', **wir haben viel Geld verloren** (past participle) 'we've lost a lot of money', **der Schäferhund hielt die Herde zusammen** (separable prefix) 'the sheepdog kept the flock together'. (An infinitive follows a past participle, e.g. **die Räder müssen ausgewuchtet werden** 'the wheels need balancing'.) This rule, helpful though it is as a general guideline for the student of German, is not rigidly observed in that (*a*) for stylistic reasons, one or more prepositional phrases sometimes follow such words (e.g. **er wird sich bestimmt entschuldigen für seinen Fehler** 'he's sure to apologize for his mistake', **dieses Auto wird gern gekauft wegen der geringen Unterhaltungskosten** 'this car sells well because of its low maintenance costs', **wir schalten um nach München** (TV announcement) 'we're going over to Munich'), (*b*) phrases introduced by **als** 'than' or **wie** 'as, like' may also follow them (e.g. **sie hätte keinen besseren Begleiter haben können als diesen schneidigen jungen Flieger** 'she could have had no better escort than this dashing young aviator', **man muß den Kopf drehen wie ein Flamingo** 'you have to turn your head like a flamingo'). When a subordinate clause follows a main clause containing an infinitive, past participle or separable prefix as final element, the latter separates the subordinate clause from the word it refers back to (e.g. **all das war in einer Nation *entstanden*, die ...** 'all this had come into being in a nation which ...', **er sprach die Hoffnung *aus*, daß ...** 'he expressed the hope that ...').

In a subordinate clause infinitives and past participles occupy the penultimate position, immediately before the finite verb (e.g. – to return to the examples given under 'Subordinate clauses' above – **... daß sie nicht *kommen* konnten, ... wann er *angekommen* sei**); separable prefixes are compounded with the verb (e.g. **... das eine blaue Bluse *an*hatte**).

COMPLEMENTS

Noun complements normally come last, e.g. **er ist seit vielen Jahren Dirigent** 'he's been a conductor for many years', **sie ist trotz all ihrer Schwächen eine bewundernswerte Frau** 'she's an admirable woman in spite of all her weaknesses'. Predicative adjectives frequently go to the end of a clause, e.g. **Pferde sind in der Regel gehorsam** 'horses are obedient as a rule', **die Tage sind im Winter kurz** 'the days are short in winter'.

POSITION AND ORDER OF OBJECTS AND ADVERBS

(i) *Position of the pronoun object* (*including reflexive pronoun*): (*a*) In a main clause with the subject first, it comes immediately after the finite verb, e.g. **man hat es in Sambia entdeckt** 'it was discovered in Zambia', **der Werbespot rentiert sich nicht mehr** 'the commercial no longer pays'. (*b*) In a subordinate clause or when there is inversion in the main clause, it generally precedes the subject if the latter is a noun (or indefinite pronoun such as **jemand, nichts**) but always follows if it is a personal pronoun, e.g. **da mir der Zollbeamte (da er mir) den**

Paß wegnehmen wollte 'as the customs officer (he) wanted to take away my passport', **früher glaubte man, daß sich die Sonne (daß sie sich) um die Erde bewege** 'it used to be thought that the sun (it) moved round the earth', **letztes Jahr hat ihn ein Hund (hat er ihn) gebissen** 'last year a dog (it) bit him', **plötzlich öffnete sich sein Fallschirm (öffnete er sich)** 'suddenly his parachute (it) opened', **kann sich ein Popstar (kann er sich) so ein großes Haus leisten?** 'can a pop star (he) afford such a big house?'[1]

(ii) *Direct and indirect objects of the verb*:

(*a*) two nouns: dative precedes accusative, e.g. **er gab dem Jungen ein Spielzeug** 'he gave the boy a toy'.

(*b*) two pronouns: accusative precedes dative, e.g. **er gab es ihm** 'he gave it to him'.

(*c*) pronoun precedes noun, e.g. **er gab es dem Jungen** 'he gave it to the boy', **er gab ihm ein Spielzeug** 'he gave him a toy'.

(iii) *Adverbs and adverbial phrases*: The usual order is Time–Manner–Place (although this is not rigidly applied and variations may occur for the sake of emphasis), e.g. **sie sind gestern** (T) **mit dem Bus** (M) **nach Zürich** (P) **gefahren** 'they went by bus to Zurich yesterday'. Where there are two or more adverbs (or adverbial phrases) of time the more general precedes the more specific, e.g. **sie kommt jeden Abend um 8 nach Hause** 'she comes home at 8 every evening'.

Numerous adverbial phrases are used in conjunction with a verb to form a set phrase of the type **in Betracht ziehen** 'to take into account'. (Other examples are **in Frage stellen** 'to call in question', **zur Folge haben** 'to lead to'; phrases such as **zustande** (formerly **zu Stande**) **bringen** 'to bring about, achieve' also belong here.) They effectively function like separable prefixes, occupying the same position in the sentence as the latter (e.g. **hinzu kam, daß der Vulkanausbruch in ganz Europa Wetterveränderungen zur Folge hatte** 'added to which the eruption of the volcano led to changes in the weather throughout Europe').

(iv) *Adverbs and noun objects*: When both an adverb (or adverbial phrase) and a direct noun object are present, the former generally precedes the latter, e.g. **wir erwarten seit fünf Monaten eine Gehaltserhöhung** 'we've been expecting a salary increase for five months', **Amnesty International erhielt 1977 den Friedensnobelpreis** 'A.I. received the Nobel peace prize in 1977'; emphasis may, however, reverse this order, e.g. (with the time stressed) **wir erwarten eine Gehaltserhöhung seit fünf Monaten.**

(v) *Position of* **nicht** '*not*': (*a*) **Nicht** is normally placed after an object (but before an infinitive, past participle or separable prefix) when it negatives an entire sentence or clause, e.g. **wir brauchen ihre Hilfe nicht** 'we don't need her/their help', **ich habe es nicht gelesen** 'I haven't read it', **sag das nicht!** 'don't say that!', **warum liest du das Buch nicht?** 'why don't you read the book?' But it precedes an adjective or noun complement (e.g. **diese Bemerkung war nicht sehr freundlich** 'that remark was not very friendly', **das ist nicht meine Schuld** 'that's not my fault') or a prepositional phrase (e.g. **steig nicht auf den Berg!** 'don't climb the mountain!'). (*b*) If a particular word or phrase is negatived, **nicht** then precedes that word or phrase, e.g. **nicht jeder kann das** 'not everyone can do that', **ich**

1. It is not uncommon, however, for the pronoun object (including the reflexive pronoun) to follow the noun subject, e.g. **da der Zollbeamte mir den Paß wegnehmen wollte, ... daß die Sonne sich um die Erde bewege.**

habe nicht dich gemeint, sondern Jürgen 'I didn't mean you, I meant Jürgen', **ich bin nicht im geringsten beleidigt** 'I'm not in the least offended'. (*c*) Common combinations (with **nicht** placed second): **auch nicht** 'not ... either', **noch nicht** 'not yet', **gar/überhaupt nicht** 'not at all'.

ADJECTIVAL AND PARTICIPIAL PHRASES (ATTRIBUTIVE)

A common feature of written German is the adjectival or participial phrase preceding the noun, e.g. **der für die Schulen zuständige Minister** 'the minister responsible for schools' (literally 'the for schools responsible minister'), **ein nach Kapstadt bestimmtes Schiff** 'a ship bound for Cape Town' (literally 'a for Cape Town bound ship'), (with a direct object) **diese Fußball spielenden Mädchen** 'these girls playing football' (literally 'these football playing girls').

This construction can be a stumbling-block for the beginner, not only because the order of words is unfamiliar but also because the article is separated (sometimes considerably) from the noun it refers to. To translate the construction it is necessary first to identify and translate the article (or similar word) and the noun it refers to, which will always follow the adjective or participle concerned:

1	4	3	2
der	**[für die Schulen**	**zuständige]**	**Minister**
ein	**[nach Kapstadt**	**bestimmtes]**	**Schiff**
diese	**[Fußball**	**spielenden]**	**Mädchen**

The adjective or participle (3) is then translated, and finally any words (4) that come between the article etc. and the adjective or participle.

The adjectival or participial phrase may immediately follow an adjective (plus comma), whereas in English their equivalents would be separated by the noun concerned, e.g. **auf jene sorglose, für die Jugend typische Weise** 'in the carefree manner typical of the young'.

This construction may also occur where an adjective or participle functions as a noun, e.g. **der von der Polizei Gesuchte** 'the man wanted by the police', **die Hoffnungslosigkeit der politisches Asyl Suchenden** 'the hopelessness of those seeking political asylum' (**politisches Asyl** = object).

GERMAN SPELLING

HISTORICAL NOTE

German spelling was standardized as recently as the beginning of the 20th century, a strong impetus towards orthographical unity having been provided by the political union of 1871. It was in 1902 that the Prussian spelling rules – prescribed for use in that state's schools and widely propagated within and beyond Prussia's boundaries by Konrad Duden's *Orthographisches Wörterbuch*, published in 1880 – were finally given the blessing of the German state following a special conference held in Berlin (and subsequently accepted by Austria and Switzerland). At that conference changes in the spelling of certain words were decided on, as a result of which books and articles published before 1902 contain words with spellings no longer given in dictionaries. The changes consisted of the replacement of the **c** that remained in some words of foreign origin, which meant that **Citrone** 'lemon' became **Zitrone** and **Accusativ** 'accusative'

Akkusativ, and the substitution of **t** for **th** (except in words of foreign origin), whereby for example **Thal** 'valley' – preserved in the English (but no longer German) spelling *Neanderthal* – and **thun** 'to do' became **Tal** and **tun** respectively.

The authoritative *Duden Rechtschreibung* of the present day (now published in separate West and East German editions) is the direct descendant of Konrad Duden's original dictionary.

SPECIAL POINTS

(a) **fff>ff, nnn>nn**, *etc.*:

Three identical consonants in a compound word are reduced to two before a vowel (except when the word is divided at the end of a line), e.g. **die Schiffahrt** [-ff-] 'shipping, navigation' (for **Schiff-fahrt**), **die Brennessel** [-nn-] 'stinging-nettle' (for **Brenn-nessel**), **das Bettuch** [-tt-] 'sheet' (for **Bett-tuch**). Before a consonant there is no reduction, e.g. **fetttriefend** 'dripping with fat'.

(b) *Hyphenation*:

The hyphen is used especially (*a*) when part of a compound word is omitted to avoid repetition, e.g. **Buch- und Zeitungstitel** 'titles of books and newspapers' (**Buch-** standing for **Buchtitel**), **ein- und ausatmen** 'to breathe in and out' (**ein-** for **einatmen**), **bergauf und -ab** 'uphill and downhill' (**-ab** for **bergab**); (*b*) to break up compounds consisting of more than three components if such compounds are felt to be unwieldy, e.g. **das Arbeiter-Unfallversicherungsgesetz** 'workers' accident insurance law'; and to avoid a sequence of three identical vowels in a compound, e.g. **die Hawaii-Inseln** 'the Hawaiian Islands'; (*c*) in compounds of which one element is a letter, abbreviation or numeral, e.g. **die U-Bahn** 'underground (railway)', **die CDU-Führung** 'the C.D.U. leadership', **die US-Flotte** 'the U.S. fleet', **der Kfz-Fahrer** 'driver of a motor vehicle', **die 10-Pfennig-Marke** '10 pfennig stamp'; (*d*) in many compounds incorporating proper names, especially if more than one of the components is a name, e.g. **die Max-Planck-Gesellschaft** 'the Max Planck Society', **der Dortmund-Ems-Kanal** 'the Dortmund-Ems Canal', **der Sankt-Gotthard-Paß** 'the St. Gotthard Pass', **der Konrad-Adenauer-Platz, die Friedrich-Schiller-Allee** (but cf. – with a single name component – **der Adenauerplatz, die Schillerallee**), **die James-Bond-Filme** 'the James Bond films'; in the case of geographical names beginning with an adjectival element or one denoting a point of the compass, such as **Neu-, Groß-, Nord-**, etc., the compound is formed without hyphenation, e.g. **Kleinasien** 'Asia Minor', **Südafrika** 'South Africa', unless the second component is the name of a city, in which case the hyphen is used (except in derivatives), e.g. **Groß-London** 'Greater London', **West-Berlin** 'West Berlin'; geographical names of which the first element ends in an uninflected **–isch** also have a hyphen, e.g. **Britisch-Kolumbien** 'British Columbia' (more prevalent, of course, in colonial times: **Belgisch-Kongo** 'the Belgian Congo', **Deutsch-Ostafrika** 'German East Africa', etc.); (*e*) in compounds such as **die Lohn-Preis-Spirale** 'wage-price spiral', **der Hals-Nasen-Ohren-Arzt** 'ear, throat and nose specialist'; (*f*) to link two adjectives (see concluding paragraph of 'Compound adjectives', p. lxxii).

When, at the end of a line, a word is divided at the combination **ck** (as in **locker** 'loose') the latter takes the form **kk** (**lok-ker**).

(c) *The symbol* **ß**; **ß** *or* **ss**?:

ß (known as **Eszett**, which indicates its origin as (long) **s** + **z**) is a ligature peculiar to the German language. It is replaced by **SS** when capital letters are used. Except in Switzerland, where ss is regularly used in its place, it is considered incorrect to use ss instead of **ß** where it is prescribed.

The rules governing the use of **ß** and **ss** are as follows:

(i) *between vowels*: **–ss–** is used if the preceding vowel is *short*, while **–ß–** is the spelling after a *long* vowel or a diphthong:

die Gasse 'alley etc.'	**die Straße** 'street, road'
russisch 'Russian'	**rußig** 'sooty'
müssen 'to have to'	**füßeln** 'to play footsie'

gewissermaßen 'so to speak, in a way'

(ii) *in other positions* the symbol **ß** is *always used*, irrespective of the length of the preceding vowel: at the end of a word[1] or an element in a compound (e.g. **der Fuß** 'foot' with long **u**, **der Eßapfel** 'eating apple' with short **e**) or if followed by a suffix (e.g. **häßlich** 'ugly' with short **ä**); and before a consonant, usually **t** (e.g. **grüßt** 'greets' with long **ü**, **wußte** 'knew' with short **u**).

Accordingly, words ending in **–ß** following a short vowel always have **–ss–** when inflected, e.g. **der Fluß** 'river' (gen. **Flusses**, pl. **Flüsse**), **blaß** 'pale' (**blass-** as in **blasse Haut** 'pale skin').

(d) *Capital letters*:

All nouns are written with an initial capital letter, except in a number of common phrases including **außer acht lassen** 'to disregard', **sich in acht nehmen** 'to be careful', **in bezug auf** 'with regard to', **ein bißchen** 'a little', **ein paar** 'a few' (as opposed to **ein Paar** 'a pair/couple (of)'), **recht/unrecht haben** 'to be right/wrong', **schuld haben/sein (an)** 'to be to blame (for)'.

The names of languages have a capital letter, *except* in phrases of the type 'in + (name of language)', e.g. **auf deutsch** 'in German'. (See p. xxv.)

Initial capitals are also used in the following instances:

(i) *2nd person personal pronouns* ('you'): (*a*) **Sie** always; (*b*) **du, ihr** (familiar forms) in letter-writing: **Du, Ihr**.

(ii) *Adjectives* following **alles**, **etwas**, **nichts**, etc., e.g. **alles Schöne**, **nichts Gutes** (see p. xxxii); also *adjectives used as nouns*, e.g. **das Gute** (see p. xxxiv).

(iii) Certain *adjectives connected with names*, *titles*: (*a*) when forming part of a geographical, historical or institutional name, e.g. **das Tote Meer** 'the Dead Sea', **die Französische Revolution** 'the French Revolution', **der Dreißigjährige Krieg** 'the Thirty Years' War', **der Eiserne Vorhang** 'the Iron Curtain', **das Auswärtige Amt** 'the (West German) Foreign Ministry'; (*b*) if derived from a personal name when the noun so qualified is the work or property of the person concerned, e.g. **die Luthersche Bibelübersetzung** 'Luther's translation of the Bible', **das Ohmsche Gesetz** 'Ohm's Law', **eine Mahlersche Sinfonie** 'a symphony by Mahler' (but adjectives used in a more general way, to convey the idea of

1. A few surnames are spelt with final **-ss**, e.g. **(Günter) Grass**, **(Carl) Zeiss**, **(Richard) Strauss** (but the Austrian composers, father and son, are spelt **Johann Strauß**).

'(done) in the manner or spirit of' are not capitalized, e.g. **die platonische Liebe** 'Platonic love', **drakonische Gesetze** 'Draconian laws', **lutherische Kirchenlieder** 'Lutheran hymns').

Initial capitals are *not* used in the following instances:

(i) The particle **von** in personal names is written with a lower-case initial (but has a capital at the beginning of a sentence, unless it is abbreviated to **v.**).

(ii) *Adjectives of nationality*, e.g. **britisch** 'British', **südafrikanisch** 'South African'. (Adjectives in official titles do, however, have a capital letter, e.g. **die Deutsche Bank, die Österreichischen Bundesbahnen.)**

(e) *Transliteration of Russian names*:
The differences between the customary German and English transliterations of Russian characters are shown in the following table. In the examples the German transliteration is given in roman, the English in italics. (The abbreviation *EG* indicates East German practice, as recorded in the Leipzig *Duden Rechtschreibung*.)

Russian character	*Transliteration German*	*English*	*Examples*
В в	w	v	Wladimir *Vladimir*, Rostow *Rostov*
Е е *initially, after vowel, etc*:	je	ye, e	Jewtuschenko *Yevtushenko*
Ё ё	jo	yo	Pjotr *Pyotr*
—*after certain consonants*:	o	e, o	Gorbatschow *Gorbachev* (*-chov*)
Ж ж	sch, *EG* sh	zh	Schukow (*EG* Sh-) *Zhukov*
З з	s	z	Sinowjew *Zinoviev*, Kasan *Kazan*
И и *after* **ь**:	ji	yi	Iljitsch *Ilyich*
Й й	i	y, i	Tolstoi *Tolstoy* (also representing **-ий**: Dostojewski *Dostoyevsky*)
—*initially*:	j	y	Joschkar-Ola *Yoshkar-Ola*
С с *between vowels*:	ss	s	Nekrassow *Nekrasov*
Х х	ch	kh	Charkow *Kharkov*
Ц ц	z	ts	Winniza *Vinnitsa*, Solschenizyn *Solzhenitsyn*
Ч ч	tsch	ch	Tschernobyl *Chernobyl*, Schostakowitsch *Shostakovich*
Ш ш	sch	sh	Timoschenko *Timoshenko*
Щ щ	schtsch, *EG* stsch	shch	Chruschtschow (*EG* -stsch-) *Khrushchev*
Ю ю	ju	yu	Iljuschin *Ilyushin*
Я я	ja	ya	Jakutsk *Yakutsk*

A typographical note: In order to emphasize a word or phrase in German, printers use either *italics*, as in English, or *letter-spacing* **(Sperrdruck)**, e.g. **im Plural dagegen ...** 'in the *plural*, on the other hand, ...'

PUNCTUATION

German punctuation differs from English punctuation in a number of important points:

The comma: The use of the comma in German is strictly *syntactical*, whereas the English comma is often used as a stylistic device to indicate a pause in the sentence: 'he, however, was convinced that ...' (compare: **er aber war überzeugt, daß ...**), 'luckily, she was in when I rang' (**zum Glück war sie zu Hause, als ich anrief**).

The German comma *separates clauses* (e.g. **er sagte, er sei zu Fuß gekommen** 'he said he came on foot', **sie sucht einen Partner, der sie versteht** 'she is looking for a partner who understands her', **ich konnte ihn schlecht verstehen, weil das Radio so laut war** 'I had difficulty in understanding him because the radio was so loud'). It also *introduces infinitive phrases* (e.g. **sie waren nicht bereit, an den Olympischen Spielen teilzunehmen** 'they were not prepared to take part in the Olympic Games'); where, however, only an infinitive with **zu** is involved there is no comma, unless it is a perfect or passive infinitive, e.g. **sie waren nicht bereit teilzunehmen, sie fingen an zu singen** 'they began to sing'. These functions of the comma are neatly illustrated in the following sentence: **... E. Rhoodie, der behauptete, im Besitz von Informationen zu sein, aus denen hervorgehe, daß auch J.B. Vorster und andere Mitglieder der Regierung belastet seien** '... E. Rhoodie, who claimed to be in possession of information showing that J.B. Vorster and other members of the government were also implicated'.

The German comma is often placed *between main clauses*, where English would have a semi-colon. The following examples from modern narrative prose are given with the corresponding sentences in published translations:

Die Tür war nur mit Draht gesichert, sie bogen ihn auseinander und traten in die Hütte, ... 'The door was secured only by wire; they bent it apart and stepped into the cabin, ...' (S. Lenz, *Der Verzicht*, transl. S. Spencer); **Wir kletterten hinüber, Großvater blutete an der Hand, ich am Knie** 'We clambered over; grandfather's hand was bleeding, so was my knee' (G. de Bruyn, *Fedezeen*, transl. P. Anthony).

Another function not shared with the English comma is as an alternative to a dash or bracket, to indicate the beginning or end of a parenthesis, e.g. **Eines Tages, es war mitten im Winter, stand ein Hirsch in unserem Garten** 'One day – it was midwinter – there was a stag standing in our garden'.

Two clauses linked by **und** do not have a comma before the conjunction unless the second has a new grammatical subject (which may denote the same person or thing): **sie blieb zu Hause und sah fern** 'she stayed at home and watched television' as against **sie blieb zu Hause, und ihre Mutter ging einkaufen** 'she stayed at home and her mother went shopping'. (Where, however, two subordinate clauses are joined by **und** there is no comma after the first clause: **... daß**

sie zu Hause blieb und ihre Mutter einkaufen ging.) The same rules apply to **oder** 'or'.

In numerals the comma marks the *decimal point*, e.g. **17,5** (read as **siebzehn Komma fünf**). Spaces, not commas, are used to indicate thousands in numbers of more than four figures, e.g. **10 000.**

The colon: The colon is used broadly as in English. (For its use in introducing direct speech see 'Quotation marks' below.) It also appears in the score of games, where English has the dash, e.g. **sie haben 3:4 [drei zu vier] verloren** 'they lost 3–4', **es** (or **das Spiel**) **steht 1:0 [eins zu null]** 'the score is 1–0'.

A word following a colon is as a rule written with a *capital letter* if the colon introduces an utterance that is effectively a self-contained sentence, e.g. **Wir alle sind einer Meinung: Er ist ein Mensch, dem man voll vertrauen kann** 'We are all of the same opinion: he is a person who can be fully trusted'. Otherwise a small letter is used, as when factors etc. are enumerated or the consequence of some action is stated, e.g. **Das Ende war vorauszusehen: er verlor alles, was er hatte** 'The end was foreseeable: he lost everything he had'.

The full stop (*period*): (*a*) *After a numeral*, a full stop indicates that it represents an ordinal number, e.g. **am 10.** [read as **zehnten**] **Mai** 'on 10th May', **Heinrich VIII. [der Achte]** 'Henry VIII', **12. [zwölfte] Auflage** '12th edition'. (*b*) It is used *in abbreviations* when the words abbreviated are spoken in full, e.g. **d.h. [das heißt]** 'i.e.', **z.B. [zum Beispiel]** 'e.g.', **Frankfurt a.M. [am Main]**, (after the last letter) **Frl. [Fräulein]**, **usw. [und so weiter]** 'etc.' The full stop is *not* used in abbreviations in which the letters are pronounced individually, e.g. **CDU**, **DDR**, **DNS**, **EG**, **LKW** or **Lkw**, **LPG**, **SPD**, nor in acronyms like **NATO**, nor in the abbreviations of metric weights and measures, e.g. **g** for **Gramm**, **m** for **Meter**.

The exclamation mark: Unlike the English exclamation mark, the German symbol is also used in public notices: **Zutritt verboten!** 'No admittance', **Abflüge werden nicht ausgerufen!** 'Departures will not be announced', **Vorsicht, Glas!** 'Glass – with care', **Vorsicht, Kurve!** 'Bend'. It is sometimes used in addressing someone at the beginning of a letter: **Sehr geehrter Herr Schmidt!**, **Liebe Anna!** (Here a comma may be used instead, in which case the first word of the text of the letter does not have an initial capital unless capitalized anyway.) Closing formulas such as **herzliche Grüße** 'kind regards' do not have the exclamation mark.

The dash: Over and above the functions it shares with its English counterpart, the German dash has one special use, namely to indicate some kind of transition, for instance to a new topic, as in the first example (from a letter) that follows; in the second (from a narrative) the passage of time is evoked:

... Und ich kann die Arbeiten nachholen, die ich während der Schönwetterperiode vernachlässigt habe. – Da gleich meine Familie nach Hause kommt, muß ich nun schnell mit dem Mittagessenkochen beginnen '... And I can catch up on the jobs I've neglected during this spell of lovely weather. As my family will be coming home in a minute I must get on with cooking lunch'; **... Ich kann sagen, daß es der am härtesten verdiente Penny meines Lebens war. – Der Abend kam, und die Stühle wurden leer ...** '... I may say that it was the hardest-earned penny of my life. [*New paragraph*] Evening came, and the chairs emptied ...' (A. Spoerl, *Memoiren eines mittelmäßigen Schülers*).

Brackets: In German square brackets are used when brackets within brackets are required.

Quotation marks: The normal quotation marks are „“. Officially called **Anführungszeichen**, they are informally known as **Gänsefüßchen**. Quotations are introduced by a colon: **er sagte: „..........“**; if the quotation comes first, then a comma follows the quotation: **„..........“, dachte sie**. In literary texts speech or thoughts are sometimes quoted without quotation marks, e.g. **Er sollte ausspannen, sagte die alte Frau, sorgen Sie doch dafür, ihr habt doch noch keine Ferien gehabt in diesem Jahr** '"He ought to take a rest," the old lady said. "Why don't you arrange it? After all, you haven't had a holiday yet this year"' (I. Bachmann, *Das Gebell*, transl. F. Kyle); **Frau Andrew legt ihren Arm um die Tochter, das hätten wir längst tun sollen, denkt sie, einmal heraus aus dem Alltag, und alles wird gut** 'Mrs Andrew put her arm round her daughter. "We should have done this long ago," she thought. "Once we get away from the daily routine, everything will be all right again"' (M.L. Kaschnitz, *Jennifers Träume*, transl. H. Taylor). 'Quotes within quotes' have single quotation marks. (For the position of quotation marks in e.g. **als Abonnent des „Spiegels“** see p. xxv.)

WORD FORMATION

The German vocabulary is rich in derivatives and compound words. The various prefixes and suffixes are dealt with in the dictionary, and so are not considered here; some observations on compound words follow.

COMPOUND NOUNS

The combination of two (or more) elements to form a new word is an old-established practice in the Germanic languages (cf. English *teapot*, Norwegian *kattemusikk* 'caterwauling', Afrikaans *kameelperd* 'giraffe'); in German it has always been a fertile source of new vocabulary, and remains so.

The German convention of writing compounds (including long ones) as single words sometimes leads beginners to regard them – or German – as difficult; and Mark Twain complains, in his tongue-in-cheek essay on 'The Awful German Language', of these 'mountain-ranges stretching across the page', suggesting they should only be allowed to be uttered with intervals. (One wonders what he would have made of some of the coinages current in present-day computerese, for instance **das Unterbrechungsanforderungsflipflop**, alias 'interrupt request latch'.) In fact, however, English and German are not so different here – it is merely a matter of orthography: English does not always join up the elements to make a formal compound, whereas German does, e.g 'life insurance company' = **die Lebensversicherungsgesellschaft**, 'media research' = **die Medienforschung**. A more substantial difference between the two languages in the matter of compounds lies in the fact that German often has a compound where English uses something else, for example a phrase with nouns linked by 'of' ('work of art' = **das Kunstwerk**), adjective + noun ('man-made fibre' = **die Kunstfaser**, 'human geography' = **die Kulturgeographie**), or a word consisting of one element only ('desk' = **der Schreibtisch**, 'skunk' = **das Stinktier**).

German compound nouns may be composed of the following elements: (*a*) noun + noun, e.g. **der Marktplatz** 'market-place'; (*b*) adjective or participle + noun, e.g. **der Billigflug** 'cheap flight', **der Gebrauchtwagen** 'used car'; (*c*) numeral + noun, e.g. **der Dreifuß** 'tripod'; (*d*) verb-stem + noun, e.g. **das Rennpferd** 'racehorse' (cf. **rennen** 'to run'), **das Lesebuch** 'reader' (cf. **lesen** 'to read'); (*e*) preposition + noun, e.g. **der Nachsommer** 'Indian summer'; (*f*) pronoun + noun, e.g. **das Selbstvertrauen** 'self-confidence'.

Not even the largest dictionary can include all possible compound nouns, and if a word is not given in the dictionary it should be broken down into its component parts, consideration of which should suggest a possible translation. In this connection, it is helpful to have a knowledge of how compounds of type (*a*) (noun + noun: the commonest type) are put together:

(i) noun 1 + noun 2, directly joined: e.g. **der Milchmann** 'milkman', **die Hausfrau** 'housewife', **das Zahnfleisch** 'gums'.

(ii) noun 1 (with loss of final **–e**) + noun 2: e.g. **die Kirschblüte** 'cherry blossom' (cf. **die Kirsche**), **das Endstadium** 'final stage' (cf. **das Ende**).

(iii) noun 1 + linking element + noun 2:

(*a*) **–e–**: e.g. **die Mausefalle** 'mousetrap' (cf. **die Maus**), **das Tagebuch** 'diary' (cf. **der Tag**).

(*b*) **–(e)n–**: e.g. **der Schwanengesang** 'swan-song' (cf. **der Schwan**), **die Sonnenuhr** 'sundial' (cf. **die Sonne**), **die Menschenrechte** 'human rights' (cf. **der Mensch**).

(*c*) **–(e)ns–**: e.g. **der Schmerzensschrei** 'scream of pain' (cf. **der Schmerz**), **die Willensfreiheit** 'free will' (cf. **der Wille**).

(*d*) **–er–**: e.g. **der Kinderschuh** 'child's shoe' (cf. **das Kind**), **die Bildersprache** 'imagery' (cf. **das Bild**), **der Eierlikör** 'advocaat' (cf. **das Ei**).

(*e*) **–s–**, also **–es–**: e.g. **der Geburtstag** 'birthday' (cf. **die Geburt**), **der Produktionsausfall** 'loss of production' (cf. **die Produktion**), **die Schönheitskönigin** 'beauty queen' (cf. **die Schönheit**), **das Volkslied** 'folk-song' (cf. **das Volk**), **das Hilfsverb** 'auxiliary (verb)' (cf. **die Hilfe**); **der Freundeskreis** 'circle of friends' (cf. **der Freund**), **die Bundesregierung** 'the (Federal) Government' (cf. **der Bund**), **das Liebesgedicht** 'love-poem' (cf. **die Liebe**).

Sometimes the first noun appears in different forms: e.g. (**die Geburt** 'birth') **die Geburtenkontrolle** 'birth control', **der Geburtsort** 'place of birth'; (**der Mann** 'man') **das Mannloch** 'manhole', **das Mannesalter** 'manhood', **die Männerstimme** 'male voice'.

A few regional variations occur: North German **Rinder–**, **Schweine–** and **Gänse–** (followed by e.g. **–braten** 'roast beef, pork, goose') become **Rinds–**, **Schweins–** and **Gans–** on southern menus. Austrian usage replaces **e** by **s** in words such as **die Aufnahmsprüfung** 'entrance examination', **der Ausnahmsfall** 'exception(al case)', **die Einnahmsquelle** 'source of income'; and inserts linking **s** in e.g. **der Fabriksarbeiter** 'factory hand', **der Gesangsverein** 'choral society', **die Zugsverbindung** 'train connection'.

COMPOUND ADJECTIVES

German compound adjectives may be composed of the following elements:

(*a*) *noun + adjective* (*or participle*) – sometimes directly joined, sometimes connected by a linking element or with the loss of final **–e**: e.g. (with noun as object of present participle) **atemberaubend** 'breathtaking'; (corresponding to genitive construction) **siegessicher** 'sure of victory', (to dative construction) **umweltfeindlich** 'damaging to the environment'; (corresponding to prepositional constructions) **kalorienreich** 'rich in calories', **schrankfertig** 'washed and ironed' (literally 'wardrobe-ready'), **krisenfest** 'stable' (literally 'crises-proof'); (with participles: instrumental) **efeuumrankt** 'ivy-clad', **handgemalt** 'hand-painted', **fetttriefend** 'dripping with fat'; (with participles: locative) **stadtbekannt** 'known all over the town', **endbetont** 'with final stress'; (comparison, intensification) **stocksteif** 'stiff as a poker', **splitter(faser)nackt** 'stark naked'.[1]

(*b*) *adjective + adjective*: e.g. **kleinlaut** 'meek', **dunkelrot** 'dark red'; ('copulative' compounds with two elements of equal weight) **naßkalt** 'cold and wet', **bittersüß** 'bitter-sweet', **schwarzweiß** 'black and white'; (colour adjectives denoting a particular shade) **blaugrün** 'bluish-green'; (adverb + adjective or participle) **schwerkrank** 'seriously ill', **tiefgreifend** 'far-reaching', **gleichgesinnt** 'like-minded'; ('parasynthetic' compounds in **–ig**) **blauäugig** 'blue-eyed', **kurzlebig** 'short-lived', **viertürig** 'four-door'.

(*c*) *verb-stem + adjective*: e.g. **kauflustig** 'in a buying mood' (cf. **kaufen**), **experimentierfreudig** 'keen on experimenting' (cf. **experimentieren**), **schreibfaul** (literally 'writing-lazy') **sein** 'to be a poor correspondent' (cf. **schreiben**).

Hyphenated adjectival combinations represent a looser kind of association of two adjectives, the hyphen indicating that they retain their separate force, e.g. **seine nüchtern-kalte Beurteilung der Situation** 'his sober, cold assessment of the situation'. The hyphen is used in combinations such as **deutsch-englisch** (of relations etc.) 'Anglo-German', **römisch-katholisch** 'Roman Catholic' and **griechisch-orthodox** 'Greek Orthodox', **maria-theresianisch** (of furniture etc.) 'Maria Theresa', **original–** 'genuine ...' (e.g. **original-französischer Käse** 'genuine French cheese'), **gelb-grün** 'yellow and green' (as opposed to **gelbgrün** 'yellowish-green' – see (*b*) above).

COMPOUND VERBS

A number of compound verbs have been formed by joining a noun, adjective/adverb or second verb to a simple verb, often with the same economy of expression that characterizes many compound nouns and adjectives. Examples: (*a*) *noun + verb*: (separable) **standhalten** (+dative) 'to stand up to', **teilnehmen** 'to

1. Certain compounds which combine a noun with a past participle are neither instrumental nor locative in sense. A number of formations with **–betont** are used in the sense 'with ... emphasized', e.g. **taillenbetont** 'with the waist emphasized', i.e. 'emphasizing the waist', **gefühlsbetont** 'emotional, emotive'; in the similar formation **hirnverbrannt** 'hare-brained' the French *cerveau brûlé* 'hothead' is reproduced, in form if not in meaning. Cf. the group of adjectives ending in **–vergessen** (explained by the old use of the participle **vergessen** + genitive 'forgetful of'), e.g. **pflichtvergessen** 'forgetful of one's duty'.

take part'; (only in the infinitive and past participle) **probefahren** 'to test-drive', **punktschweißen** 'to spot-weld'; (inseparable) **brandmarken** 'to brand', **schlafwandeln** 'to walk in one's sleep'; (*b*) *adjective/adverb + verb*: (separable) **freisprechen** 'to acquit', **totschweigen** 'to hush up', **schwarzhören** 'to listen to the radio without a licence'; (inseparable) **vollenden** 'to complete'; (*c*) *verb + verb* (separable): **kennenlernen** 'to get to know', **sitzenlassen** 'to leave in the lurch, jilt', **spazierengehen** 'to go for a walk'.

PRONUNCIATION GUIDE

German tends to be articulated more clearly and vigorously than English. Stress falls on the first syllable – with certain exceptions, notably:

(*a*) **lebéndig** 'alive', **die Forélle** 'trout', **die Hornísse** 'hornet', **der Holúnder** 'elder', **der Wachólder** 'juniper'; (*b*) most words of foreign origin, e.g. **die Geographíe** 'geography', **der Theológe** 'theologian', **der Patiént** 'patient', **die Existénz** 'existence', **romántisch** 'romantic', **europäisíeren** 'to Europeanize', and nouns ending in **–ei**, e.g. **die Heucheléi** 'hypocrisy'; (*c*) inseparable verbs, together with nouns and adjectives derived from them, e.g. **begínnen** 'to begin', **entdécken** 'to discover', **erhéblich** 'considerable', **die Vernúnft** 'reason'; (*d*) (with the prefix **ab–**) **abschéulich** 'abominable', **das Abtéil** 'compartment', **die Abtéilung** 'department'; (with the prefix **un–**) **unéndlich** 'infinite', as well as some adjectives which may also have initial stress, e.g. **unerréichbar** 'unattainable'; (*e*) certain compounds, e.g. **das Jahrhúndert** 'century', **die Apfelsíne** 'orange', **die Zweidríttelmehrheit** 'two-thirds majority', **willkómmen** 'welcome', **beiséite** 'aside', **zusámmen** 'together'; (*f*) some place-names, e.g. **Bayréuth**, **Bremerháven**, **Hannóver** 'Hanover', **Heilbrónn**, **Paderbórn**, also names in **–in** (with final stress), e.g. **Schwerín**; (*g*) most abbreviations in which the names of the letters are pronounced (the final letter being stressed), e.g. **der BH́** 'bra', **die DDŔ** 'East Germany', **die DNŚ** 'D.N.A.'

Compound adjectives of the type **steinalt** 'as old as the hills', **stockfinster** 'pitch-dark' take level stress.

An important feature of German speech is the phenomenon known as the glottal stop (as heard, for example, in Cockney *wa'er* for *water*). It occurs before vowels in initial position or following a prefix as well as at the junction of compounds in which the second element begins with a vowel, e.g. **der | Arzt** 'doctor', **ver|achten** 'to despise', **die Hoch|ebene** 'plateau'; here a consonant must not be carried over to the vowel that follows, as happens in English: contrast **für | Eva** with *for‿Eve*, **ein | Eis** with *an‿ice*.[1]

Vowels are pure and never diphthongized as in Southern English (e.g. *say*, *boat*). They are usually short if followed by two or more consonants (e.g. **der Mann** 'man', **die Kunst** 'art'), long if followed by a single consonant or silent **h** (e.g. **der Rat** 'advice', **die Kuh** 'cow'), if doubled (e.g. **das Boot** 'boat') or if final and stressed (e.g. **das Büro** 'office'); a long stem vowel as in **loben** 'to praise' remains long in derived forms, e.g. **lobt**, **lobte**. Exceptions to these general rules (e.g. **der Papst** 'pope', **die Erde** 'earth', **Ostern** 'Easter', **düster** 'gloomy' with long vowels, and **das Kap** 'cape (geog.)', **ob** 'whether', **weg** 'away' with short vowels) are shown at the entries concerned. Before final **ß** or **ß** + suffix vowels are short (e.g. **der Paß** 'passport', **häßlich** 'ugly') unless the contrary is indicated in the dictionary; before **ß** + vowel they are always long (e.g. **mäßig** 'moderate').

1. In English it has been possible, for example, for *an ewt* to evolve into *a newt*; such developments are phonetically impossible in German.

The glottal stop is *not* sounded in certain compounds, e.g. **allein**, **einander**, **vollenden**, also such adverbs as **darauf**, **heraus**, **hinein**, **vorüber**.

The German consonant system possesses a special feature relating to the voiced consonants (**b**, **d** and **g**): these are pronounced like **p**, **t** and **k** at the end of a word or element of a compound, or when followed by a suffix, e.g. **gab** 'gave', **die End/station** 'terminus', **mög/lich** 'possible'. (The suffix **–ig** is a special case dealt with below under **g**.) There are no silent consonants, apart from silent **h** (mostly a sign of vowel length); thus, the **p** in **pn–**, **ps–** and **pt–** (e.g. **pneumatisch** 'pneumatic', **der Psychologe** 'psychologist', **Ptolemäus** 'Ptolemy') and the **k** in **kn–** (e.g. **das Knie** 'knee') are always pronounced.

PHONETIC SYMBOLS

VOWELS

[a] a *Mann*
[aː] a *Vater*, aa *Maat*, ah *Sahne*
[ɛ] ä *lächeln*, e *setzen*
[ɛː] ä *Mädchen*, äh *zählen*
[e] e *Dezember*
[eː] e *eben*, ee *Schnee*, eh *gehen*
[ə] e *Sonne*
[ɐ] er *Fenster*, r *mehr*
[ɪ] i *Zimmer*
[i] i *direkt*
[iː] i *gib*, ie *lief*, ieh *sieh*, ih *ihr*
[ĭ] i *Australien*
[ɔ] o *Motte*
[o] o *Drogist*
[oː] o *Sog*, oh *Bohne*, oo *Boot*
[ŏ] (in *oi*, *oy*) *Memoiren*, *loyal*
[ʊ] u *lustig*
[u] u *Duell*
[uː] u *Fuß*, uh *Kuh*
[ŭ] u *Suite*
[œ] ö *fördern*
[ø] ö *Zölibat*
[øː] ö *böse*, öh *Söhne*
[ʏ] ü *Lücke*
[y] ü *Büro*, y *dynamisch*
[yː] ü *Küken*, üh *Mühe*, y *typisch*

Nasal vowels: [ãː] = am, an, em, en (*Elan*, *Amüsement*), [ɛ̃ː] = aim, ain, ein, en (after *i* or *y*), im, in (*Terrain*, *Teint*, *Bassin*), [ɔ̃ː] = om, on (*Affront*), [œ̃ː] = um (*Parfum*). (They are shortened in unstressed syllables, e.g. *Enquete* [ã-].)

DIPHTHONGS

[ae̯] ai *Mai*, ei *reich* [ɔø̯] äu *Häuptling*, eu *Reue* [ao̯] au *auch*

CONSONANTS

[b] b *haben*, bb *Ebbe*
[ç] ch *Licht*, g (in *-ig*) *zwanzig*
[d] d *Ding*, dd *Widder*
[dʒ] dsch *Dschungel*, g *Gin*, j *jetten*
[f] f *fünf*, ff *Affe*, v *vier*, ph *Phobie*
[g] g *gehen*, gg *Dogge*
[h] h *Humor*
[j] j *jung*
[k] k *König*, ck *backen*, kk *Akkord*, c *Café*, ch *Charakter*, -g *trug*
[ks] chs *Lachs*, cks *Klecks*, ks *Koks*, x *Lexikon*
[kv] qu *Quelle*
[l] l *lachen*, ll *voll*
[m] m *amüsant*, mm *hämmern*
[n] n *Sohn*, nn *Henne*
[ŋ] ng *Klingel*, n *krank*
[p] p *Pilz*, -b *Dieb*
[r] r *rosa*, rh *Rhabarber*
[s] s *Haus*, ss/ß *hassen*, *Haß*
[ʃ] sch *Wunsch*, sk *Ski*, ch *Branche*, s (in *sp-*, *st-*) *Sport*, *stehen*
[t] t *Zeit*, th *Thema*, dt *Stadt*, -d *Land*
[ts] z *Zahn*, zz *Skizze*, ts *Lotse*, tz *benutzen*, ds *Landsmann*, c *Cäsar*, t *Aktion*
[tʃ] tsch *Quatsch*, ch *Couch*
[v] w *Wald*, v *Version*
[x] ch *lachen*
[z] s *so*
[ʒ] g *Regime*, j *Journalist*

OTHER SYMBOLS

[ʔ] glottal stop [ˈ] stress mark [ˌ] indicates a syllabic consonant

THE SOUNDS OF GERMAN

SPELLING	SYMBOL	EXAMPLE(S)	REMARKS
a(1) long	[aː]	*sagen*	like *a* in 'father'
(2) short	[a]	*Mann*, *akut*	like Southern English *u* in 'fun', Northern English *a* in 'man'
aa, ah	[aː]	A*a*l, *n*ah	= **a**(1)
ai	[a̯e]	*Mai*	like *y* in 'my' (but with the mouth open wider for the first component than for that of the English diphthong)
au	[a̯o]	*Haus*	like *ou* in 'house' (but with the mouth open wider for the first component than for that of the English diphthong)
ä(1) long	[ɛː]	*Mädchen*	as **ä**(2), but with the vowel lengthened; similar to *ai* in 'hair' (many North Germans use **e**(1) instead)
(2) short	[ɛ]	*hätte*	like *e* in 'set'
äh	[ɛː]	*wählen*	= **ä**(1)
äu	[ɔø]	*Fräulein*	like *oi* in 'noise'
b(1)	[b]	*Bär*, *haben*	as in English
(2)	[p]	*Kal*b, *Hub-raum*, *lie*b-*lich*; *a*b*strakt*, *O*b*jekt*, *Su*b*jekt*; *lie*b*t*, *hü*b*sch*, *Gelü*b*de*	like English *p*; *b* is unvoiced when final, at the end of an element in a compound, or before a suffix; also in the prefixes *ab-*, *ob-*, *sub-*, and before an unvoiced consonant or *d*, *g*
c(1)	[k]	*Clou*	(before *a*, *o*, *u* and *l*, *r*) = **k**
(2)	[ts]	*Cäsar*	(elsewhere) = **z**
ch(1)	[x]	*auch*	(after *a*, *o*, *u*, *au*) like *ch* in Scots 'loch'
(2)	[ç]	*lächeln*, *Bücher*, *Eiche*; *Mil*ch, *manche*, *dur*ch; Ch*emie*; *Mädchen*	(after other vowels and diphthongs; after consonants; at the beginning of words when followed by *e* or *i*; also in the suffix *-chen*) like the *h* in 'hue'
(3)	[k]	*Charakter*	(in words of Greek origin, before *a*, *o* and *l*, *r*) = **k**
chs	[ks]	*Fuchs*	(if the *s* is part of the stem) like English *x* (but *ch* and *s* are articulated separately in e.g. (*des*) *Loch-s*, (*du*) *lach-st*)
ck	[k]	*Bock*	= **k**
d(1)	[d]	d*u*, *laden*	as in English
(2)	[t]	*run*d, *Wan*d*-uhr*, *freun*d*-lich*, *Mä*d*-chen*; A*djektiv*; *Wodka*, *widmen*	like English *t*; *d* is unvoiced when final, at the end of an element in a compound, or before a suffix; also in the prefix *ad-*, and before an unvoiced consonant or *g*, *m*, *n*, *v*, *w*

SPELLING	SYMBOL	EXAMPLE(S)	REMARKS
dt	[t]	*Stadt, sandte*	like English *t*
e(1) long	[eː]	*Leben*	like *ay* in Scots 'say' or *eh* in Northern English 'eh lad'
	[e]	*Medizin*	(in words of foreign origin, in unstressed syllables) as **e**(1) but shortened
(2) short	[ɛ]	*Bett*	like *e* in 'set'; the prefixes *er-*, *ver-* and *zer-* are also pronounced with this vowel
(3) neutral	[ə]	*Liebe, beginnen*	(in unstressed syllables) like *a* in 'ago'; in the unstressed endings *-el*, *-eln*, *-em*, *-en* the *e* is generally dropped in ordinary speech after certain consonants, e.g. *Nebel, betteln, messen* (cf. the usual pronunciation of 'petal', 'dozen') *-er*: this ending is pronounced [-ɐ], a short vowel close to the *u* in 'fun', e.g. *ein guter Lehrer*; similarly *-ern* [-ɐn], e.g. *wandern*
ee, eh	[eː]	*See, sehen*	= **e**(1)
ei	[ae̯]	*mein*	like *y* in 'my'
eu	[ɔø̯]	*heute*	like *oi* in 'noise'
f	[f]	*fliegen*	as in English
g(1)	[g]	*gehen, Geologie*	as in English ('hard' *g*)
(2)	[k]	*Tag, Weg-weiser, trag-bar; sagt, Jagd*	like English *k*; *g* is unvoiced when final, at the end of an element in a compound, or before a suffix; also before an unvoiced consonant or *d* (*Note*: in North German speech *g* is generally pronounced here like **ch** instead, e.g. *lag* [laːx], *Berg* [bɛrç] – see **ch**(1) and (2))
(3) **-ig**	[-ɪç]	*König, zwanzig*	*g* is here pronounced like **ch**(2), except in the South which uses [-ɪk]; similarly before a consonant (e.g. *Königs* and, with a suffix, *Königtum, Ewigkeit*) except before *-lich* (e.g. *königlich*) and in *Königreich*, where *-ig-* is pronounced [-ɪk-]; before a vowel *-ig-* = [-ɪg-], e.g. *Könige, Zwanziger* *-igst*, *-igt*(*e*) in verbs ending in *-igen* also have [ç]: [-ɪçst, -ɪçt(ə)]
h(1)	[h]	Herz	as in English
(2) silent	–	*nehmen; Theater*	see (*a*) **ah**, **eh**, etc., in which *h* is used to show that the preceding vowel is long, (*b*) **th**
i(1) long	[iː]	*Bibel, Musik*	like *i* in 'machine', only closer
	[i]	*Zitrone*	(in words of foreign origin, in unstressed syllables) as **i**(1) but shortened
(2) short	[ɪ]	*ich, Logik*	like *i* in 'sick'

SPELLING	SYMBOL	EXAMPLE(S)	REMARKS
(3) non-syllabic	[ĭ]	*asiatisch*, *Patient*, *Milieu*, *Station*, *seriös*; (before unstressed vowel) *Linie* [-ĭə], *Spanien*, *Cäsium*	(in words of foreign origin, before a stressed or unstressed vowel – except after certain consonantal combinations difficult to unite with [ĭ], e.g. *Bibliothek*, *Adria*; here *i* = [i])
ie, ieh, ih	[iː]	*Diesel*, *Vieh*, *ihn*	= **i**(1); exceptions are *vierzehn*, *vierzig*, *Viertel* (*ie* = [ɪ]) and *vielleicht* (*ie* = [i])
j	[j]	*jung*	like *y* in 'young'
k	[k]	*kalt*	as in English, but with more aspiration before a stressed vowel
l	[l]	*Salz*	'clear' *l* (formed with the tip of the tongue against the teeth-ridge or the upper front teeth)
m	[m]	*Mann*	as in English
n	[n]	*Name*	as in English
ng(1), **n**	[ŋ]	*bringen*, *Ingwer*, *England*, *lang*, *Bank*, *Sphinx*	like *ng* in 'singer'
(2)	[ŋg]	*Linguist*, *Mangan*, *Tango*, *Ungarn*, *Kongo*	(in words of foreign origin, medially before a full vowel – i.e. any other vowel than [ə] – or *r*) like *ng* in 'finger'
o(1) long	[oː]	*Zone*	like *o* in Scots 'no'
	[o]	*moralisch*, *anthropoid*	(in words of foreign origin, in unstressed syllables) as **o**(1) but shortened
(2) short	[ɔ]	*Osten*, *geworden*	like *o* in 'got', but with lip-rounding
oh, oo	[oː]	*Sohn*, *Moos*	= **o**(1)
ö(1) long	[øː]	*schön*	lips protruded and rounded with tongue in position for **e**(1)
	[ø]	*ökonomisch*	(in words of foreign origin, in unstressed syllables) as **ö**(1) but shortened
(2) short	[œ]	*Köln*	lips protruded and rounded with tongue in position for **e**(2)
öh	[øː]	*Höhle*	= **ö**(1)
p	[p]	*Post*	as in English, but with more aspiration before a stressed vowel
ph	[f]	*Phonetik*	as in English
qu	[kv]	*bequem*	like *kv*
r(1)	[r]	*rot*, *hart*, *groß*, *stören*	entirely different from the retroflex *r* (as in 'run') of most English speakers; produced either by vibrating the uvula (the sound is similar to French *r* as in 'rue') or – chiefly in Southern German – by lightly trilling with the tip of the tongue[1]

1. The latter pronunciation is the one used in the singing of classical music.

SPELLING	SYMBOL	EXAMPLE(S)	REMARKS
(2) vocalic	[ɐ]	*Oh*r, *we*r*den*	following a long vowel *r*, in final position or before a consonant, is regularly realized as [ɐ], a (short) *a*-like sound close to the *u* in 'fun'
(3) **-er**	[-ɐ]	*gut*er, *Lehr*er	see note at **e**(3)
rh	[r]	Rh*abarber*	= **r**(1)
s(1) voiced	[z]	s*o*, s*ouverän*, *Schick*-s*al*, *lang*-s*am*; *ro*s*ig*; *Am*s*el*, *impul*s*iv*	like English *z*: initially before a vowel, and in the suffixes *-sal*, *-sam*; between vowels; and in *-ls-*, *-ms-*, *-ns-*, *-rs-*; in the South *s* is unvoiced in all these positions
(2) unvoiced	[s]	*Ei*s, *hoffnung*s*-lo*s, *bö*s*-artig*, *lö*s*-lich*; S*zene*, *Fen*s*ter*, *Pri*s*ma*; *Erb*s*e*, *Rät*s*el*; S*ujet*	like *s* in 'sit': finally, at the end of an element in a compound, or before a suffix; before a consonant (but see *sp-*, *st-* at (3)); after a consonant (except in *-ls-*, *-ms-*, *-ns-*, *-rs-*); and initially before a vowel in some words of foreign origin
(3) in **sp-**, **st-**	[ʃ]	s*prechen*, *Ge*-s*präch*, S*pirale*; s*tehen*, *er*-s*taunen*, S*tudent*	like *sh* in 'ship': initially or following a prefix – except in a few words of foreign origin in which [s] is retained, e.g. *Stewardeß* (in some both [s] and [ʃ] occur, e.g. S*pektrum*, s*teril*)
sch	[ʃ]	*Fi*sch	like *sh* in 'ship'; where *-chen* follows *s, s* and *ch* are pronounced separately, e.g. *Häus-chen*
ss, ß	[s]	*la*ss*en*, *So*ß*e*, *mu*ß	like *ss* in 'miss'
t(1)	[t]	*Zei*t	as in English, but with more aspiration before a stressed vowel
(2) in **-ti-**	[ts]	*Ter*t*ia*, *par*t*iell*, *Pa*t*ient*, *Na*t*ion*, *sta*t*ionär*, *ra*t*ionieren*	(in words of foreign origin, when *-ti-* is followed by a vowel) like *ts* in 'nuts' (*Note*: before a stressed [iː] as in *Demokratie t* is pronounced as in English)
th	[t]	Th*eater*, *Timo*th*eus*	= **t**(1)
tz	[ts]	*Ka*tz*e*	like *ts* in 'nuts'
u(1) long	[uː]	*r*u*fen*	like the second element in the diphthongized pronunciation [ʊu] of *oo* as in 'zoo'; lips strongly rounded and protruded
	[u]	*M*u*sik*, z*u*-*zusammen*	(in words of foreign origin and *zu*-compounds, in unstressed syllables) as **u**(1) but shortened
(2) short	[ʊ]	*M*u*tter*, U*rteil*	like *u* in 'put', but with more lip-rounding
(3) non-syllabic	[ŭ]	*S*u*ada*, *ak*t*uell*, *Stat*u*e*	(in words of foreign origin)
uh	[uː]	*Sch*uh	= **u**(1)
ü(1) long	[yː]	*drüben*	lips positioned for pronouncing **u**(1) (long *u*), with tongue in position for **i**(1) (long *i*); like French *u* as in 'rue'

SPELLING	SYMBOL	EXAMPLE(S)	REMARKS
	[y]	*Büro*	(in words of foreign origin, in unstressed syllables) as **ü**(1) but shortened
(2) short	[ʏ]	*hübsch*	lips rounded with tongue in position for **i**(2) (short *i*)
üh	[y:]	*kühl*	= **ü**(1)
v(1)	[f]	*von, freveln, aktiv*	like *f* in 'fire'; final *-v* in words of foreign origin is always pronounced [f]
(2)	[v]	*Vase, Klavier, nervös*	like *v* in 'very': the usual pronunciation of initial and medial *v* in words of foreign origin (where a loanword has [f] instead – e.g. V*ers*, *Larve* – this is shown in the dictionary)
w, wh	[v]	W*asser*, Wh*isky*	like *v* in 'very'
x	[ks]	X*ylophon*, *Sex*	like *x* in 'six'
y(1) long	[y:]	*Lyrik*	= **ü**(1)
	[y]	*Zypresse*	(in words of foreign origin, in unstressed syllables) as **y**(1) but shortened; in *Zylinder* it is pronounced [i]
(2) short	[ʏ]	*Rhythmus*	= **ü**(2)
z	[ts]	*zu, Herz*	like *ts* in 'nuts'

Additional pronunciations occurring in words of foreign origin

In words of foreign origin, the letters of the German alphabet (and their combinations) may have different values – normally approximating to their pronunciation(s) in the language of origin – from those listed above. Thus **ai** in words of French origin is pronounced [ɛ:] e.g. *Baisse*, [ɛ] e.g. *Baiser*, [a̯e] e.g. *Detail*, while **au** is realized as [o:] e.g. *Hausse*, [o] e.g. *Fauxpas*, [ɔ] e.g. *Chauffeur*; **oi** and **oy** are pronounced [ŏa(:)] e.g. *Memoiren*; and the French nasal vowels are similarly nasalized in German, e.g. *El*an with [ã:], *Parf*um with [œ̃:] (sometimes a denasalized pronunciation is used instead, as in *Ball*on [-'lɔŋ]). Similarly, vowels in words from English are pronounced in an approximately English fashion: **a** is reproduced either as [ɛ] e.g. *trampen* or as [e:] e.g. *Cape*, long **i** as [a̯e] e.g. *live* [la̯ef], long **o** (variously spelt) as [o:] e.g. *Toast*, *Sh*ow, **u** as [a] e.g. *Run*, **y** as [a̯e] e.g. *Nylon* or as [i] e.g. *Party*, and so on.

A number of consonants may have values not found in native German words: **c** is pronounced [s] in e.g. *City*, *Aktrice* [-sə], **ch** is [tʃ] in English words, e.g. ch*artern* (also [ʃ-]) but [ʃ] in Gallicisms, e.g. Ch*ef*; **g** and **j** are both [dʒ] e.g. G*in*, J*et* and [ʒ] e.g. *Genie*, J*ournal*; **gn** is [nj] in French and Italian words, e.g. *Champagner*; **ll** is [lj] in *Billard*, *Medai*lle [-'daljə], *Tai*lle ['taljə]; **z** is realized as [z] in *Gaze*, as [s] in *Bronze* ['brɔ̃:sə]. Certain consonants are silent in final position as in the source-language French, e.g. *Premi*er, *Eta*t, *Palai*s. Finally, the combination **dsch**, used to render English *j* in words of Oriental origin, is pronounced [dʒ] e.g. Dsch*ungel*.

PROPER NAMES: A SELECTION

The list that follows contains a selection of well-known personal and place names from the German-speaking countries and outside that are not treated in the body of the dictionary and whose pronunciation is in some way worthy of note.

Several spellings are peculiar to proper names; others may have values found only in proper names:

ae	[ɛː]	*Baer*
ay	[ae̯]	*Bayern, May*
ey	[ae̯]	*Meyer, Loreley*
oe	[øː]	*Schroeder*
	[œ]	Oe*tker*
oe, oi	[oː]	*Itzehoe, Troisdorf, Voigt* [foːkt]
oey	[øː]	*Bad* Oey*nhausen*
-ow	[-o]	*Trept*ow (but = [-ɔf] in Russian names)
ue	[uː]	*Kues*
	[ʏ]	*Mueller*
ui	[yː]	*Juist*
y	[iː]	*Schwyz*

NOTE: Where no phonetic transcription is given, the name concerned is included to show where the stress falls; this is indicated by means of a line (= long vowel or diphthong) or dot (= short vowel).

Bach [bax]
Baedeker ['bɛːdəkɐ]
Bayreuth [bae̯'rɔø̯t]
Beethoven, van ['beːthoːfn̩ (fan)]
Berchtesgaden
Berlin [bɛr'liːn]
Bethmann Hollweg
Beuys [bɔø̯s]
Bismarck ['bɪsmark]
Blücher ['blʏçɐ]
Bochum ['boːxʊm]
Bremerhaven [breːmɐ'haːfn̩]
Breughel ['brɔø̯gl̩]
Büchner ['byːçnɐ]
Buxtehude
Calvin [kal'viːn]
Cambridge ['keːmbrɪtʃ]
Cervantes [sɛr'vantɛs]
Chiemsee ['kiːmzeː]
Chur [kuːɐ]
Cuxhaven [kʊks'haːfn̩]
Dante ['dantə]
Darwin ['darviːn]
Dresden ['dreːsdn̩]
Duisburg ['dyːsbʊrk]
Erfurt ['ɛrfʊrt]
Erlangen ['ɛrlaŋən]
Freud [frɔø̯t]
Gelsenkirchen
Goes [gøːs]
Goethe ['gøːtə]
Gogh, van [gɔx (fan)]
Goya ['goːja]
Grosz [grɔs]
Gstaad [kʃtaːt]
Haydn ['hae̯dn̩]
Heilbronn
Hohenstaufen
Hohenzollern
Ibsen ['ɪpsn̩]
Johannesburg [jo'hanəsbʊrk]
Johnson ['joːnzɔn]
Kaiserslautern
Lenin ['leːniːn]
Liverpool ['lɪvɐpuːl]
London ['lɔndɔn], *commonly* ['lɔndn̩] *with unvoiced* d
Los Angeles [lɔs 'ɛndʒələs]
Luther ['lʊtɐ]
Magdeburg ['makdəbʊrk]
Manchester ['mɛntʃɛstɐ]
Melbourne ['mɛlbɐn]
Mercedes [mɛr'tseːdəs]
Montreal [mɔntre'aːl]
Musil ['muːzɪl]
Napoleon [na'poːleɔn]
Osnabrück [ɔsna'brʏk]
Ottawa ['ɔtava]
Oxford ['ɔksfɔrt]
Pachelbel ['paxɛlbl̩]
Paderborn
Potsdam ['pɔtsdam]
Recklinghausen
Reclam ['rɛklam, 'reː-]
Roosevelt ['roːzəvɛlt]
Roth [roːt]
Saarbrücken
San Francisco [sanfran'tsɪsko]
Schleswig ['ʃleːsvɪç]
Seghers ['zeːgɐs]
Soest [zoːst]
Southampton [sao̯'θɛmptn̩]
Stalin ['staːliːn, ʃt-]
Telemann ['teːləman]
Vancouver [vɛn'kuːvɐ]
Velazquez [ve'laskɛs]
Virchow ['fɪrço, 'vɪr-]
Washington ['wɔʃɪŋtn̩]
Wilhelmshaven [vɪlhɛlms'haːfn̩]
Zermatt [tsɛr'mat]

THE GERMAN ALPHABET

The names of the letters of the German alphabet are pronounced as follows:

A	[aː]	**H**	[haː]	**N**	[ɛn]	**T**	[teː]
B	[beː]	**I**	[iː]	**O**	[oː]	**U**	[uː]
C	[tseː]	**J**	[jɔt, *Aust* jeː]	**P**	[peː]	**V**	[faʊ̯]
D	[deː]			**Q**	[kuː, *Aust* kveː]	**W**	[veː]
E	[eː]	**K**	[kaː]			**X**	[ɪks]
F	[ɛf]	**L**	[ɛl]	**R**	[ɛr]	**Y**	['ʏpsilɔn]
G	[geː]	**M**	[ɛm]	**S**	[ɛs]	**Z**	[tsɛt]

Additional symbols: **Ä** [ɛː], **Ö** [øː], **Ü** [yː], (lower case) **ß** [ɛs'tsɛt].

A

^das^ **A** [aː] A (*gen*, *pl* –, *coll* [aːs]) A; **das a, A** *mus* (the note) A; (*key*) **A** A major, **a** A minor; **das ~ und O** the essential thing; **von ~ bis Z** *coll* from A to Z

à *comm* at (... each)

a. = **am**

^der^ **Aal, –e** eel; **aal|glatt** slippery as an eel

aalen: sich ~ *coll* laze; bask

a. a. O. (= **am angeführten Ort**) loc. cit.

^der^ **Aar, –e** *poet* eagle

^das^ **Aas, –e** carcass; (*pl* **Äser**) *vulg* 'louse'; 'bitch'; devil; **kein ~** *coll* not a damn soul

aasen *coll*: **~ mit** squander

ab [ap] 1 *prep* (+ (*usu*) *dat*) from (... onwards); ex (store, works); 2 *adv* off; (*eg* **Hamlet ~**) exit (H. *etc*); (*in timetable*, *eg* **Bonn ~**) departs from (B. *etc*); **ich bin ganz ~** I'm all in; **... ist ~** ... has come off; **~ und zu** now and then

---

ab– *sep pref – general senses*:

(*i*) ... off; ... away (*eg* **~beißen** bite off, **~segeln** sail away); *cf* **~schrecken** deter, **~trennen** separate, detach;

(*ii*) ... down (*eg* **~stellen** put down, **~schwellen** go down);

(*iii*) de–, dis–, un–, *etc* (*eg* **~bauen** dismantle, **~schnallen** unbuckle); *cf* **~bestellen** cancel;

(*iv*) (+*dat*) ... from (someone), ... (someone) out of ... (*eg* **jmdm. etw. ~kaufen** buy sth. from s.o., **jmdm. etw. ~listen** trick s.o. out of sth.);

(*v*) *indicates treatment applied to something* (*eg* **~tupfen** dab, **~schmieren** lubricate), *formal performance* (*eg* **~spielen** play (national anthem *etc*)), *a process of copying* (*eg* **~schreiben** copy (something written)), *or a thorough search* (*eg* **~grasen** scour)

---

ab|ändern alter; modify; *parl* amend

^die^ **Ab|änderung, –en** alteration; modification; *parl* amendment

ab|ängstigen: sich ~ worry oneself sick

ab|arbeiten work off; work (passage); **sich ~** wear oneself out

^die^ **Ab|art, –en** variety

ab|artig abnormal; perverse

Abb. (= **Abbildung**) fig.

^der^ **Abbau** dismantling; demolition; reduction; cutback; breaking down (of barriers); (gradual) elimination; decline; *min* extraction; working; *chem* decomposition

abbauen take down; dismantle; break down; (gradually) eliminate; reduce, cut back; *min* extract; work (seam); *chem* decompose; (*v/i*) *coll* grow feeble; flag

abbeißen* bite off

abbekommen* get off; get (as one's share); **etwas/nichts ~** get some/none; get/not get damaged *or* hurt

abberufen*, die Abberufung, –en recall

abbestellen cancel

^die^ **Abbestellung, –en** cancellation

abbetteln (+*dat*) cadge from

abbezahlen pay off

abbiegen* bend; *coll* ward off; parry; steer (conversation) onto another topic; (*v/i sn*) turn off; **nach links/rechts ~** turn left/right

^das^ **Abbild, –er** picture; image; reflection

abbilden portray; **... ist (auf S. 6** *etc***) abgebildet** there is a picture of ... (on p. 6 *etc*); **sich ~ in** (*dat*) be reflected in

^die^ **Abbildung, –en** *vbl noun*; *also* representation; illustration; *math* mapping

abbinden* untie; *med* (remove by) ligature; (*v/i* cement) set

Abbitte: ~ leisten bei ask for forgiveness

abbitten* (+*dat of pers*) ask (s.o.'s) forgiveness for

abblasen* blow off; release (gas); *coll* call off

abblättern (*sn*) lose its leaves; flake off; peel off

Abblend–: das ~licht, –er dipped headlights, dimmed headlights *US*; **der ~schalter, –** dip-switch, dimmer *US*

abblenden dim; screen; dip, dim *US* (one's headlights); *phot* stop down

abblitzen (*sn*) *coll* be given the brush-off (**bei** by); **~ lassen** give (s.o.) the brush-off

abblocken block (*also sp*)

abblühen (*sn*) finish flowering

abborgen (+*dat*) borrow from

abbrausen give (s.o.) a shower; (*v/i sn*) roar off; **sich ~** take a shower

abbrechen* break off; demolish; call off (strike); stop; (*v/i sn*) break off; **das Lager ~** strike camp

abbremsen brake; stop (vehicle); slow down (development); curb

abbrennen* (*see also* **abgebrannt**) burn off;

let off (rocket); *Aust coll* tan; *tech* pickle; (*v/i sn*) burn down; *coll* have one's house burn down

abbringen*: ~ **von** get (s.o.) to give up; talk out of; get off (topic); **vom rechten Weg** ~ lead astray; **davon läßt er sich nicht** ~ he won't budge

abbröckeln (*sn*) crumble away; flake off; *comm* ease off

der **Abbruch** breaking-off; demolition; (+*dat*) ~ **tun** impair; harm || **a~reif** fit for demolition

abbrühen (*see also* **abgebrüht**) scald

abbrummen *coll* serve (sentence); do (... years *etc*); (*v/i sn*) drive off noisily

abbuchen [–u:–] write off; **von einem Konto** ~ debit an account with

abbürsten brush off; brush (down)

abbüßen serve (sentence); atone for; **mit Geld** ~ pay a fine for

das **Abc** [a:be:'tse:], – ABC, ABC's *US*; **nach dem** ~ alphabetically || **der ~-schütze, –n** (*wk masc*) beginner at primary school

abchecken [–tʃ–] *coll* check out; (on list) tick off, check off *US*

abdachen: sich ~ slope

abdämmen dam (up); dike (land); curb

der **Abdampf, ¨–e** exhaust steam

abdampfen evaporate; (*v/i sn*) steam off; evaporate; *coll* shove off

abdämpfen muffle; tone down

abdanken resign; (monarch) abdicate

die **Abdankung, –en** resignation; abdication; *Swiss* funeral

abdecken (storm) take the roof off; cover (over); settle (debt); *sp* cover, mark; *comput* mask; **(den Tisch)** ~ clear the table; **sich** ~ kick off the bedcover

abdichten make airtight/watertight; seal; caulk; insulate

die **Abdichtung, –en** *vbl noun*; *also* seal

abdienen *mil* serve (period)

abdrängen push aside/away

abdrehen turn off (gas, tap, *etc*); twist off; wring (neck); turn (face) away; *cin* shoot; (*v/i, also sn*) *naut etc* turn off; **sich** ~ turn away

abdrosseln throttle (down); cut back

der **Abdruck, –e** copy; printed version; reprinting; (*pl* ¨–e) impression; cast; (finger *etc*) print

abdrucken print

abdrücken fire (**auf** *acc* at); take an impression/a cast of; *coll* give (s.o.) a hug; **sich** ~ (foot *etc*) leave an impression

ab|ebben (*sn*) die down

abend: gestern/heute/morgen ~ last/this/tomorrow evening

der **Abend, –e** evening; **guten** ~! good evening!; **eines** ~**s** one evening; **am** ~ in the evening; **zu** ~ **essen** have supper/dinner; **es ist noch nicht aller Tage** ~ don't count your chickens before they're hatched || **das ~brot** *NGer* = **das ~essen** supper; dinner; **a~füllend** full-length; **die ~kasse, –n** box-office (at evening performance); **der ~kurs, –e** evening classes; **das ~land** the West; **a~ländisch** western; **das ~mahl** the Last Supper; *Prot* holy communion; **das ~rot** = **die ~röte** sunset glow; **die ~schule** night school

abendlich evening

abends in the evening; in the evening(s)

das **Abenteuer, –** adventure; (brief) affair

abenteuerlich adventurous; risky; weird

der **Abenteurer, –** adventurer

die **Abenteurerin, –nen** adventuress

aber but; however; (*as emotive particle*) really; certainly; *or rendered by stressing the verb* (*eg* **du kommst** ~ **früh!** you *are* early!); ~, ~! come, come!; **(hundert** *etc*) **und** ~ **(hundert** *etc*) (hundreds *etc*) and (hundreds *etc*); ~ **und** ~**mals** again and again; **ich** ~ (but) *I* do/did/can/have *etc*; **oder** ~ or else; **das Aber, –** objection; snag || **der A~glaube** (*like* **Glaube**) superstition; **~gläubisch** superstitious; **~malig** renewed; **~mals** (once) again; **~witzig** crazy

ab|erkennen* (+*dat of pers*) deprive (s.o.) of; deny that (s.o.) has (quality)

die **Ab|erkennung** deprivation (of right, citizenship)

ab|essen* eat clean; pick (bone); eat (currants *etc* on cake); **abgegessen haben** have finished eating

Abessinien [–ĭən] *hist* Abyssinia; *joc* nudists' beach

Abf. (= **Abfahrt**) dep.

abfahren* take away (on vehicle); wear out (through driving); use up (ticket); knock off (piece of wall), sever (leg *etc* in accident); *cin, rad, TV* start; (*also sn*) drive along/all over (*esp* in search of sth.); (*v/i sn*) leave; drive off; *ski* run downhill; (+*dat*) slip out of (s.o.'s) hands; **ihm wurde (ein Bein** *etc*) **abgefahren** he lost (a leg *etc*); ~ **auf** (*acc*) (*sn*) *coll* go for; ~ **lassen** *coll* send packing

sich ~ (tyre) wear out

die **Abfahrt, –en** departure; (autobahn) exit; *ski* downhill run

der **Abfall, ¨–e** refuse; waste; slope; defection; drop (*gen* in); **der ~eimer, –** dustbin, garbage can *US*; **das ~produkt, –e** waste product; **die ~stoffe** *pl* waste

abfallen* (*sn*) fall/drop off; be left over; (terrain) fall away; (pressure) drop; *athl* fall back

~ **für: für ... fallen (1 000 Mark** *etc*) **ab** ... get(s) (1,000 marks *etc*); **was fällt für mich dabei ab?** what's in it for me?

~ **gegen** compare unfavourably with
~ **von** come off; fall off; desert (person), defect from (party *etc*), renounce (faith); (fear *etc*) leave

abfällig disparaging; adverse

Abfang–: der ~jäger, – *aer* interceptor

abfangen* catch; intercept; ward off; head off; absorb (impact, costs); *aer*, *mot* bring under control; *sp* intercept; catch up with; *build*, *tech* prop up; (+*dat*) steal (customers) from

abfärben: es färbt ab the colour runs; **die Wand färbt ab** the paint comes off the wall; ~ **auf** (*acc*) (views *etc*) rub off on

abfassen write; catch

abfaulen (*sn*) rot off

abfeilen file down/off

abfertigen get (sth.) ready for dispatch; (customs) clear; deal with (*esp* in a business-like manner); process; *sp* dispose of; ~ **mit** fob off with; **kurz** ~ *coll* be short with

die **Abfertigung, –en** *vbl noun*; *also* (customs) clearance; rebuff; dispatch office; *aer* check-in desk

abfeuern fire (**auf** *acc* at)

abfinden* pay off; pay compensation to; ~ **mit** put off with (promise *etc*); **sich ~ mit** resign oneself to; put up with

die **Abfindung, –en** *vbl noun*; *also* settlement; compensation

abfischen fish out

abflachen flatten; (*v/i sn*) fall off, decline; **sich** ~ flatten out

abflauen (*sn*) (wind) drop; (interest *etc*) flag; fade; *comm* (business) fall off; (prices) drop

abfliegen* fly out; (*also sn*) *aer* fly along; (*v/i sn*) fly away/off; *aer* take off (**nach** for)

abfließen* (*sn*) drain away; (traffic) flow; (bath) empty; *fin* flow out; *elect* leak out; *med* be discharged; ~ **lassen** drain off

der **Abflug, ⸚e** *aer* take-off; departure; **die ~zeit, –en** departure time

der **Abfluß, ⸚(ss)e** draining away; flow (of traffic); outflow (of capital); drain; = **das ~rohr, –e** waste-pipe

die **Abfolge, –n** sequence; succession

abfordern (+*dat*) demand from; ask to see (passport *etc*)

abformen model (in clay *etc*)

abforsten deforest

abfragen test, quiz *US* (child orally); test/quiz *US* the class (orally) on; *tel* test (line); *comput* interrogate; (+*dat*) test/quiz *US* (child orally) on

abfressen* browse on, crop; strip (vegetation); (rust *etc*) eat away

abfrieren* (*sn if v/i*) be frostbitten; **sich** *dat* **...** ~ get frostbite in; **abgefroren** frostbitten

die **Abfuhr, –en** removal; *coll* rebuff; *coll sp* trouncing

Abführ–: das ~mittel, – laxative

abführen lead away; take into custody; draw off (gas); pay (amount) (**an** *acc* to); (*v/i*) open the bowels; ~ **von** take away from; (*v/i* road) leave

abfüllen decant; ~ **in** (*acc*) pour into; **auf Flaschen** ~ bottle

der **Abfüller, –** bottler

die **Abfüllung, –en** *vbl noun*; *also* bottled wine; **„eigene ~“** ‘bottled by the grower’

abfüttern[1] feed

abfüttern[2] line

die **Abgabe, –n** tax; duty; handing in/over; delivery; sale; emission; making (of statement); casting (of vote); firing (of shot); *sp* pass(ing); **a~frei** duty-free; **a~(n)|pflichtig** dutiable; taxable

der **Abgang, ⸚e** departure; retirement; *theat* exit; *gym* dismount; *comm* loss(es); sale; *med* discharge (of); (*pl*) persons leaving/discharged

der **Abgänger, –** school-leaver

abgängig missing

das **Abgas, –e** exhaust gas; waste gas; (*pl*) exhaust fumes

abgaunern (+*dat of pers*) swindle out of

das **ABGB** = **Allgemeines Bürgerliches Gesetzbuch** Austrian Civil Code

abgeben* hand in/over; cast (vote); make (statement *etc*); give (opinion); fire (shot) (**auf** *acc* at); give off (heat, oxygen, *etc*); give up (post *etc*); sell; let, rent *US* (accommodation); make (a good lawyer *etc*); provide (framework *etc*); *sp* pass (ball); concede (points *etc*); (+*dat*/**an** *acc*) make over to; **jmdm. etwas (von ...)** ~ let s.o. have some (of ...); ~ **bei** leave with; **... (billig) abzugeben** ... for sale (cheap)

sich ~ mit concern oneself with; *coll* associate with

abgebrannt *p/part*; *coll* broke

abgebrüht *p/part*; *coll* callous, hardened

abgedroschen *coll* hackneyed

abgefeimt cunning

abgegriffen *p/part*; *also* well-thumbed; (coin) worn; (phrase) well-worn, hackneyed

abgehackt *p/part*; *also* jerky; staccato

abgehärmt *p/part*; *also* careworn

abgehen* (*also sn*) inspect; *mil* patrol; (*v/i sn*) leave; go off, be sent; come off; go off (well *etc*); sell; (shot) be fired; (road) branch off; *theat* exit; *med* be discharged/passed; *comm* be deducted; ~ **von** (*sn*) leave; (road) branch off; digress from; give up, drop; *comm* be deducted from; **(eine Eigenschaft** *etc*) **geht mir ab** I lack (a quality *etc*); **geht ab** (stage direction) exit; **ihm geht nichts ab** he doesn't want for anything

abgekämpft battle-weary; worn-out

abgekartet *p/part*; **~es Spiel** *coll* put-up job
abgeklappert *p/part*; *coll* clapped-out; hackneyed
abgeklärt *p/part*; *also* mellow
abgelebt *p/part*; *also* decrepit; outmoded
abgelegen *p/part*; *also* remote; secluded
abgelten* pay off; satisfy (claim)
abgemagert *p/part*; *also* emaciated
abgemessen *p/part*; *also* measured
abgeneigt: (+*dat*) **nicht ~** not averse to
abgenutzt *p/part*; *also* worn-out; shabby
der **Abge|ordnete** (*fem* **die ~**) (*decl as adj*) deputy (in assembly); member of parliament
abgerissen *p/part*; *also* ragged; disjointed; incoherent
abgerundet *p/part*; *also* well-rounded
abgesagt *p/part*; *also* avowed
der **Abgesandte** (*fem* **die ~**) (*decl as adj*) emissary
abgeschabt *p/part*; *also* shabby
abgeschieden *p/part*; *also* secluded; deceased
die **Abgeschiedenheit** seclusion
abgeschlagen *p/part*; *also* chipped; *sp* beaten
abgeschlossen *p/part*; *also* self-contained; enclosed; complete; (existence) secluded
abgeschmackt absurd
abgesehen *p/part*; **~ von** apart from
abgespannt *p/part*; *also* tired out
abgestanden *p/part*; *also* stale; flat
abgestorben *p/part*; *also* (plant *etc*) dead
abgestumpft *p/part*; *also* (who has *etc* become) insensitive; (conscience *etc*) dulled
abgetakelt *p/part*; *coll* worn-out; who has *etc* seen better days
abgewetzt *p/part*; *also* worn-out
abgewinnen* (+*dat*) get out of; win from; discover (aspect *etc*) of; reclaim (land) from; (+*dat*) **Vertrauen** *etc* **~** win (s.o.'s) confidence *etc*; (+*dat*) **Geschmack ~** take pleasure in
abgewirtschaftet *p/part*; *also* run-down
abgewöhnen (+*dat of pers*) get (s.o.) to give up (habit); **sich** *dat* **... ~** give up (habit); **sich** *dat* **das Rauchen/Trinken ~** give up smoking/drinking
abgezehrt *p/part*; *also* emaciated
abgießen* pour off; strain; cast (statue *etc*)
der **Abglanz** reflection
abgleiten* (*sn*) slip; (glance *etc*) stray; *fin* fall; **~ an** (*dat*) have no effect on; **~ in** (*acc*) lapse into
der **Abgott, ¨-er** idol
die **Abgötterei** idolatry
abgöttisch idolatrous; **~ lieben** worship (beloved)
abgraben* divert (by digging a trench); level; (+*dat*) **das Wasser ~** take the bread from (s.o.'s) mouth
abgrasen graze; *coll* scour (**nach** for)
abgreifen* (*see also* **abgegriffen**) feel (all over); measure off (with fingers, compasses); wear out (by constant handling)
abgrenzen divide off; delimit; define (rights *etc*); **~ gegen** differentiate from; **sich ~** stand aloof
die **Abgrenzung, -en** *vbl noun*; *also* delimitation; definition; drawing a distinction
der **Abgrund, ¨-e** abyss; precipice; gulf (between); ruin; **abgrund|häßlich** extremely ugly; **abgrund|tief** profound
abgründig inscrutable; immense
abgucken (+*dat*) *coll* copy from; learn from
der **Abguß, ¨-(ss)e** (plaster *etc*) cast
abhaben* *coll* have (taken) off; **ich möchte etwas ~** I'd like some
abhacken (*see also* **abgehackt**) chop off
abhaken unhook; take off the hook; tick off, check off *US* (items)
abhalftern take the halter off; *coll* get rid of
abhalten* keep away/out; hold (meeting *etc*); hold (child) (over pot *etc*); **~ von** keep from; stop from (doing); **(von sich) ~** hold away from oneself; **laß dich nicht ~** don't let me disturb you
abhandeln deal with; get (sth.) knocked off the price; (+*dat*) obtain from (by bargaining)
abhanden: ~ kommen get lost; **... ist mir ~ gekommen** I've lost ... || **das A~kommen** loss (of)
die **Abhandlung, -en** treatise; essay
der **Abhang, ¨-e** slope
abhängen uncouple; take down (picture); *coll* drop; shake off; (*v/i*) *tel* hang up; (**~***, *like* **hängen** *v/i*) (meat) hang; **~* von** depend on; be dependent on
abhängig dependent (**von** on)
die **Abhängigkeit** dependence (**von** on)
abhärmen: sich ~ grieve
abhärten harden; **sich ~** toughen oneself
abhaspeln unreel; *coll* reel off
abhauen* cut down/off; (*v/i sn*) (*p/t only* **haute ab**) *coll* shove off
abhäuten skin
abheben* lift; take off; withdraw (money); (*v/i*) *aer* become airborne; **(die Karten) ~** cut (the cards); **sich ~ gegen/von** stand out against/from
abheften file (away); *needlew* tack (hem)
abheilen (*sn*) heal up
abhelfen* (+*dat*) remedy; redress; do something about; meet (need)
abhetzen exhaust (animal); **sich ~** wear oneself out
die **Abhilfe** remedy; **~ schaffen** take remedial measures
abhobeln plane off; plane smooth
abhold (*following dat*) averse (to); ill-disposed (towards)
abholen call for; collect; meet (person arriv-

ing); take away
abholzen clear of trees
Abhör– monitoring ...; (telephone) tapping ...; **das ~gerät, –e** hidden microphone; monitoring device
abhorchen listen (in) to; *med* sound
abhören listen in to; monitor; listen to (recording, station); *tel* tap; *med* sound; = **abfragen** (*first 3 senses*)
abhungern: sich *dat* **...** ~ lose (... pounds) (by going on a starvation diet); starve oneself to pay for; **sich** ~ starve oneself
das **Abi** ['a–] *coll* = **Abitur**
ab|irren (*sn*) stray; **vom Weg** ~ lose one's way
das **Abitur** school-leaving examination (at the *Gymnasium*)
der **Abiturient, –en** (*wk masc*) candidate for the *Abitur*
abjagen (+*dat*) retrieve from (after a chase); steal (customer) from; **sich** ~ *coll* wear oneself out
Abk. (= **Abkürzung**) abbrev.
abkämmen comb off; comb (**nach** for)
abkanzeln *coll* haul over the coals
abkapseln: sich ~ cut oneself off
abkarten (*see also* **abgekartet**) *coll* plot
abkassieren *coll* collect (contribution *etc*); collect the contributions/fares *etc* of
abkaufen (+*dat*) buy from; *coll* 'buy' (s.o.'s story)
die **Abkehr** turning away (**von** from); abandonment (of); break (with)
abkehren[1] turn away, avert; **sich** ~ **von** turn away from; abandon; break with
abkehren[2] sweep; sweep up
abketteln cast off (stitch)
abketten unchain; *knit* cast off (stitch)
abklappern (*see also* **abgeklappert**) *coll* scour; traipse round
abklären *esp Swiss* clear up, clarify
der **Abklatsch** (poor) imitation
abklemmen clamp; disconnect
abklingen* (*sn*) fade away; abate; die down
abklopfen knock off; brush off; dust down; pat; tap; scrutinize (**auf** *acc* for); *med* sound; (*v/i*) *mus* stop the orchestra (by rapping one's baton)
abknabbern nibble off; pick (bone)
abknallen *coll* shoot down
abknapsen *coll* dock (from pocket-money *etc*); **sich** *dat* **...** ~ stint oneself of; snatch (time for sth.); +**von** squeeze out of (housekeeping *etc*)
abkneifen* nip off
abknicken snap off; bend; (*v/i sn*) bend
abknöpfen unbutton; (+*dat*) *coll* get (money *etc*) out of
abkochen boil; cook outdoors, cook out *US*
abkommandieren *esp mil* detail; ~ **nach** order to
abkommen* (*sn*) get away; go out of fashion; (marksman) aim; ~ **von** get off (course, ground, point); stray from; give up; revise (opinion); **vom Wege** ~ lose one's way
das **Abkommen, –** agreement
abkömmlich available; **ich bin** ~ I can be spared/get away
der **Abkömmling, –e** descendant; *chem* derivative
abkoppeln uncouple
abkratzen scrape; scrape off; scratch off; (*v/i sn*) *coll* kick the bucket; shove off
abkriegen *coll* get; get off; **etwas** ~ **von** get some of
abkühlen cool; (*v/i sn*) = **sich** ~ cool (down/off); **es kühlt (sich) ab** it's turning cooler
die **Abkühlung** cooling(-off); drop in temperature
die **Abkunft** origin
abkuppeln uncouple
abkürzen shorten; abbreviate; cut short; **den Weg** ~ take a short cut
die **Abkürzung, –en** abbreviation; short cut; curtailment
abküssen smother with kisses
Ablade– unloading ...
abladen* unload; vent (anger) (**bei** on); *coll* drop (passenger); ~ **auf** (*acc*) shift (blame) onto
die **Ablage, –n** place to keep/put sth.; filing department; *Swiss* branch; *zool* laying (of egg)
ablagern deposit; (*v/i, also sn*) mature; season; **sich** ~ be deposited
die **Ablagerung, –en** *vbl noun*; *also* deposit; sediment
der **Ablaß, ⸗(ss)e** *eccles* indulgence
ablassen* let off/out; release; drain; *coll* leave off; (+*dat*) let have (**für** for); ~ **von** leave alone; give up; **vom Preis** ~ knock off the price; **nicht** ~ **zu ...** not stop (+*ger*)
der **Ablativ, –e** ablative
der **Ablauf, ⸗e** expiry; course (of events); drain; waste-pipe; outflow; *sp* start
ablaufen* wear out (shoe); (*also sn*) go along; scour (**nach** for); (*v/i sn*) drain (away); unwind; (clock *etc*) stop; expire; go (off) (well *etc*); *sp* start; ~ **an** (*dat*) (*sn*) leave cold; ~ **von** (*sn*) run off; **sich** *dat* **die Beine nach ...** ~ *coll* walk one's legs off in search of; ~ **lassen** let out; let drain; pay out (rope *etc*); run (film); play (tape)
ablauschen (+*dat*) learn from (by listening to); base on (real life)
der **Ablaut** vowel-gradation
das **Ableben** decease
ablecken lick; lick off; lick clean
ablegen take off (coat *etc*); discard; file; put

down; drop (habit, title, *etc*); take (examination, oath); (*v/i*) take one's things off; *naut* set sail; **es darauf ~ zu ...** be out to ...

^der **Ableger, –** *hort* layer; cutting; *comm* subsidiary

ablehnen turn down; reject; disclaim (responsibility); (+*vbl noun*, *eg* **die Behandlung von ... ~**) refuse to (treat ... *etc*); **es ~ zu ...** refuse to ...; **~d** disapproving; (answer *etc*) negative

^die **Ablehnung** *vbl noun*; *also* refusal; rejection

ableiern *coll* intone

ableisten complete (military service *etc*); fulfil

ableiten divert; draw off; **~ aus** derive from; trace from; draw (conclusion) from; **~ von** derive from; trace from; **sich ~ aus/von** be derived from

^die **Ableitung, –en** diversion; derivation; deduction; *ling* derivative

ablenken deflect; divert; distract; take (s.o.'s) mind off things; *phys* refract; **(vom Thema) ~** change the subject

^die **Ablenkung, –en** deflection; diversion; distraction; *phys* refraction; **das ~s|manöver, –** diversion(ary tactic); red herring

ablesen* read (speech, meter, *etc*); read off; pick off

  ~ an (*dat*) read in, tell from (s.o.'s face); **... läßt sich ~ an ...** can be seen in

  ~ aus deduce from

  ~ von read in, tell from (s.o.'s face); **von den Lippen ~** lip-read (words)

ableuchten inspect with a light; (searchlight) sweep

ableugnen deny

^die **Ableugnung, –en** denial

ablichten photostat; *coll* photograph

abliefern deliver; hand over

^die **Ablieferung, –en** *vbl noun*; *also* delivery

abliegen* (*see also* **abgelegen**): **weit ~** be a long way off; **+von** be a long way from

ablisten (+*dat of pers*) trick (s.o.) out of; wangle out of

ablocken (+*dat*) coax out of

ablöschen extinguish; blot; wipe (blackboard *etc*); wipe off; *cul* add water to

Ablöse–: die ~summe, –n *sp* transfer fee

ablösen detach; peel off; take over from; relieve; take the place of; supersede; *fin* redeem; **sich ~** come off; peel off; (*recip*) take turns (**bei** at); work in shifts; alternate

^die **Ablösung, –en** *vbl noun*; *also* detachment (from); relief (of sentry); replacement; *fin* redemption

abluchsen [–ks–] (+*dat of pers*) trick (s.o.) out of; learn from (by watching carefully)

ablutschen *coll* suck off; suck clean

abmachen remove; agree (on); settle; *coll* do (time in prison *etc*); **mit sich selbst ~** work out for oneself; **abgemacht!** it's a deal!

^die **Abmachung, –en** *vbl noun*; *also* agreement; arrangement

abmagern (*see also* **abgemagert**) (*sn*) grow thin; **bis zum Skelett ~** be reduced to a skeleton

^die **Abmagerung** growing thin; emaciation; **die ~s|kur, –en** slimming diet

abmalen paint (a picture of); **sich ~ in** (*dat*) be reflected in

^der **Abmarsch** marching off; departure

abmarschieren (*sn*) march off

abmelden cancel (paper *etc*), have (telephone) disconnected; take (vehicle) off the road; (**polizeilich ~**) notify the police that (person) is moving away; *educ* give notice that (child) is leaving; *sp coll* neutralize; **... ist bei mir abgemeldet** *coll* I want nothing more to do with ...

  sich ~ announce one's departure/resignation; check out; (**sich polizeilich ~**) notify the police that one is moving away

^die **Abmeldung, –en** *vbl noun*; *also* cancellation

abmessen* (*see also* **abgemessen**) measure; measure off; assess

^die **Abmessung, –en** measurement; assessment; (*pl*) dimensions

abmontieren dismantle; take down/off

abmühen: sich ~ toil; **sich ~ mit** struggle with

abmurksen *coll* bump off; *mot* stall

abmustern *naut* pay off; (*v/i*) *naut* sign off

abnagen gnaw; pick (bone); gnaw off

abnähen *dressm* take in

^der **Abnäher, –** *dressm* dart

^die **Abnahme** decrease (*gen* in); removal; administration (of oath); (official) inspection; *comm* purchase; *mil* review; *med* amputation

abnehmen* remove; take down/off; take (fingerprints); inspect; hold (examination); lose (... pounds *etc*); *tel* lift (receiver); *med* amputate; (+*dat*) take from; buy from; relieve (s.o.) of; administer (oath) to; obtain (promise) from; charge; *coll* 'buy' (s.o.'s story); (*v/i*) lose weight; decrease; go down; abate; decline; grow weak; wane; (days) grow shorter; (**Maschen**) ~ decrease; **die Parade ~** review the troops

^der **Abnehmer, –** buyer; customer

^die **Abneigung, –en** aversion (**gegen** to)

abnọrm [ap–] abnormal

^die **Abnormitạ̈t** [ap–], **–en** abnormality; freak

abnötigen (+*dat*) wring from; command (s.o.'s respect); **sich** *dat* **ein Lächeln ~** force a smile

abnutzen, *esp SGer* **abnützen** (*see also* **abgenutzt**), **sich ~** wear out

[die] **Abnutzung** wear (and tear)
[das] **Abonnement** [–ə'mã:], **–s** subscription; = **die ~(s)|karte, –n** *theat* season-ticket
[der] **Abonnent, –en** (*wk masc*) subscriber; *theat* season-ticket holder
abonnieren = **abonniert sein auf** (*acc*) subscribe to
ab|ordnen: ~ nach/zu send as a representative to
[die] **Ab|ordnung, –en** *vbl noun*; *also* delegation
[der] **Abort**[1], **–e** *med* miscarriage; abortion
[der] **Abort**[2], **–e** *dated* lavatory
abpacken pack (in bags *etc*)
abpassen *dressm* adjust the length of; *coll* watch out for; waylay
abpatrouillieren [–trulj–] patrol
abpausen trace
abpfeifen*: (das Spiel) ~ blow the (final) whistle
[der] **Abpfiff, –e** final whistle
abpflücken pick
abplagen: sich ~ toil; **sich ~ mit** struggle with
abplatzen (*sn*) flake off; fly off
[der] **Abprall, –e** rebound; ricochet
abprallen (*sn*) rebound; ricochet; **~ an** (*dat*) bounce off; ricochet off; have no effect on
abpressen squeeze out; (+*dat*) extort from
abputzen wipe; wipe off; plaster (wall); **sich ~** wipe one's bottom
abquälen: sich *dat* **… ~** force oneself to produce; **sich ~** slave away; **sich ~ mit** slave away at; struggle with
abqualifizieren dismiss
abrackern: sich ~ *coll* slave away; **sich ~ mit** struggle with
abrahmen skim
abrasieren shave off; *coll* raze to the ground
abraten*: (+*dat*) **~ von** advise against
abräumen clear (the table); clear away
abreagieren work off; *psych* abreact; **~ an** (*dat*) take out on; **seine Wut ~** let off steam
sich ~ simmer down
abrechnen deduct; (*v/i*) settle accounts; **~ mit** settle with; get even with; **(die Kasse) ~** cash up; **… abgerechnet** leaving aside …
[die] **Abrechnung, –en** deduction; settlement (of accounts); statement (of account); settling of accounts; **Tag der ~** day of reckoning; **in ~ bringen** deduct || **die ~s|stelle, –n** clearing-house; **der ~s|verkehr** clearing
[die] **Abrede** agreement; **in ~ stellen** dispute
abregen: sich ~ *coll* calm down
abreiben* rub down/off; wipe (down); *cul* grate; **sich ~** rub oneself down
[die] **Abreibung, –en** *vbl noun*; *also* rub-down; *coll* beating; telling-off
[die] **Abreise, –n** departure
abreisen (*sn*) leave (**nach** for); **~ von** leave
Abreiß– tear-off …
abreißen* (*see also* **abgerissen**) tear off; pull down (building); *coll* do (military service), serve (time); (*v/i sn*) come off; break (off); **… reißt nicht ab** there is no end to …
abreiten* (*also sn*) ride along; patrol; (*v/i sn*) ride off
abrennen* *coll* scour (**nach** for); (*v/i sn*) run off; **sich ~** run oneself off one's feet
abrichten train (animal)
abriegeln bolt; cordon off
abringen* (+*dat*) wrest from
[der] **Abriß, –(ss)e** outline; demolition
abrollen unroll; unwind; (*v/i sn*) unroll; unwind; (vehicle) move off, *aer* taxi off; pass off; unfold (before s.o.'s eyes); **sich ~** unwind; unfold (before s.o.'s eyes)
abrücken move away; (*v/i sn*) move away; *mil* march off; *coll* clear out; **~ von** (*sn*) move away from; dissociate oneself from
Abruf: auf ~ on call
abrufen* call away; *comput* retrieve; *comm* request delivery of; *fin* withdraw
abrunden (*see also* **abgerundet**) round off; **~ auf** (*acc*) round up/down to; **nach oben/unten ~** round up/down; **sich ~** be rounded off
abrupfen pluck off
abrupt [ap–] abrupt
abrüsten disarm
[die] **Abrüstung** disarmament
abrutschen (*sn*) slip (down); *aer*, *ski* sideslip
[die] **Abruzzen** *pl* the Abruzzi
Abs. = **Absatz, Absender**
absäbeln *coll* hack off
absacken (*sn*) *coll* sink, *aer* lose height; fall off (in performance); go to pot
[die] **Absage, –n** refusal (of invitation); rejection (**an** *acc* of); *rad* sign-off
absagen (*see also* **abgesagt**) cancel, call off; (*v/i*) cry off; (+*dat*) renounce; tell (s.o.) one can't come; **eine Sendung ~** *rad* sign off
absägen saw off; *coll* fire
absahnen skim the cream off; *coll* rake in
absatteln unsaddle
[der] **Absatz, ⸚e** paragraph; heel; (stairs) landing; *comm* sales; *geol* deposit; **reißenden ~ finden** sell very fast
Absatz– *esp* sales …; marketing …; **die ~chancen** *pl* sales opportunities; **der ~direktor, –en** marketing director; **a~fähig** marketable; **die ~förderung** sales promotion; **die ~forschung** market research; **das ~gebiet, –e** market (for goods); **der ~markt, ⸚e** market, outlet; **a~weise** paragraph by paragraph
absaufen* (*sn*) *coll* drown; (ship) go to the bottom; (carburettor) flood
absaugen (*see* **saugen**) draw off (by suction); siphon off; vacuum-clean
abschaben (*see also* **abgeschabt**) scrape;

scrape off

abschaffen get rid of; abolish, do away with

die **Abschaffung** *vbl noun*; *also* abolition

abschälen strip the bark from; peel off; **sich** ~ peel off

abschalten switch off (*also v/i coll*)

abschattieren shade; nuance

abschätzen estimate; assess; size up

abschätzig disparaging

die **Abschätzung, -en** *vbl noun*; *also* valuation; assessment; estimate

der **Abschaum** scum

abschäumen *cul* skim

abscheiden* (*see also* **abgeschieden**) *physiol* secrete; *chem* precipitate; (*v/i sn*) pass away; **sich** ~ *physiol* be secreted; *chem* be precipitated

abscheren* shave off; shave; shear

der **Abscheu** loathing, abhorrence (**gegen/vor** *dat* of); **a~erregend** repulsive

abscheuern scrub; scrub off; scrape off (skin); wear out; **sich** ~ wear out

abscheulich abominable; horrible

die **Abscheulichkeit, -en** repulsiveness; abomination

abschicken send (off)

abschieben* push away; deport (alien); *coll* get rid of (by transferring elsewhere); (*v/i sn*) *coll* push off; ~ **auf** (*acc*) shift (blame) onto; (**von sich**) ~ disclaim (responsibility)

die **Abschiebung, -en** *vbl noun*; *also* deportation

der **Abschied, -e** parting, farewell; dismissal; *mil* discharge; ~ **nehmen** say goodbye (**von** to); **seinen** ~ **nehmen** resign one's post/*mil* commission; (+*dat*) **zum** ~ **winken** wave goodbye to

Abschieds- farewell ...; parting ...; **das** ~**gesuch, -e** letter of resignation

abschießen* fire; shoot (**auf** *acc* at); shoot off/*aer* down; *mil* knock out (tank); *coll* oust

abschinden (*p/part* **abgeschunden**): **sich** ~ *coll* slave away

abschirmen shield; cover (lamp); keep off/out; ~ **gegen** shield from

abschlachten, die Abschlachtung, -en slaughter

der **Abschlag, ⸚e** reduction (in price); instalment; *footb* punt; *golf* drive; tee; *hock* bully; **auf** ~ on account

abschlagen* (*see also* **abgeschlagen**) knock off; cut down/off; turn down; repel; *sp* punt (ball)

abschlägig: ~e Antwort refusal

die **Abschlags|zahlung, -en** payment on account

abschleifen* (*like* **schleifen**[1]) remove by grinding; sand (down); **sich** ~ wear down

Abschlepp- towing ...; **der ~dienst** breakdown service, wrecking service *US*; **die ~stange, -n** tow-bar; **der ~wagen, -** breakdown lorry, tow truck *US*

abschleppen tow away/off; *coll* drag off; **sich** ~ **mit** *coll* struggle with

abschließen* (*see also* **abgeschlossen**) lock (up); seal (hermetically); complete, conclude; close; take out (insurance); make (bet); *comm* balance (books); settle (account); (*v/i*) conclude, close; conclude a deal; sign a contract; ~ **mit** end in/with; finish with; *comm* close with

sich ~ cut oneself off

abschließend concluding; (*adv*) in conclusion

der **Abschluß, ⸚(ss)e** conclusion; taking out (of insurance); border; *comm* deal, transaction; contract (**über** *acc* for); balancing (of books); settlement (of account); *coll* final exam; **zum** ~ in conclusion; **zum** ~ **bringen** bring to a conclusion; **zum** ~ **kommen** be completed/concluded/settled; +**mit** bring to a conclusion; *comm* close with

Abschluß- final ...

abschmatzen *coll* kiss noisily

abschmecken taste (to judge flavour); season

abschmeicheln (+*dat*) wheedle out of

abschmelzen* melt; *tech* separate by fusion; (*v/i sn*) melt away

abschmieren lubricate, grease; *coll* copy (untidily); (*v/i sn*) *aer coll* crash

abschminken remove the make-up from; **jmdn./sich** ~ remove s.o.'s/one's make-up

abschmirgeln rub with emery

abschnallen unfasten, undo; (*v/i*) *coll* switch off (mentally); **sich** ~ undo one's seat-belt

abschneiden* cut off; cut (nails *etc*); (*v/i*) take/be a short cut; do (well *etc*) (**bei** in); **den Weg** ~ take a short cut; (+*dat*) head off; **das Abschneiden** *vbl noun*; *also* performance

abschnippeln *coll* snip off

der **Abschnitt, -e** section; period; stub, counterfoil; *EGer* district; *mil* sector; *math* segment; **der ~s|bevollmächtigte** (*decl as adj*) *EGer* district police officer

abschnüren cut off; *med* ligature

abschöpfen skim off; cream off (profits *etc*); siphon off

abschrägen slope; bevel

abschrauben unscrew

abschrecken deter; *cul* run cold water over (boiled egg); *tech* quench; **~d** deterrent; repulsive; **~des Beispiel** warning

die **Abschreckung** *vbl noun*; *also* deterrence; = **das ~s|mittel, -** deterrent

abschreiben* copy (out); wear out (with writing); *comm* allow for the depreciation of; deduct; *coll* write off; (*v/i*, +*dat*) decline (s.o.'s) invitation (by letter)

die **Abschreibung, -en** *vbl noun*; *comm* (allowance for) depreciation; deduction

abschreiten* pace out; (*also sn*) walk along;

mil inspect
die **Abschrift, –en** copy
abschuften: sich ~ *coll* slave away
abschürfen graze
die **Abschürfung, –en** *vbl noun*; *also* graze; abrasion
der **Abschuß, ⸚(ss)e** firing, launch; *aer* shooting down; *mil* knocking out; **die ~rampe, –n** launching pad
abschüssig steep
abschütteln shake off; shake down; shake out; shrug off
abschütten pour off
abschwächen weaken; lessen; tone down; soften; *phot* reduce; **sich ~** diminish
abschwatzen (+*dat of pers*) talk (s.o.) out of
abschweifen (*sn*) stray; digress
die **Abschweifung, –en** digression
abschwellen* (*sn*) go down; subside
abschwenken (*sn*) swing round; *mil* wheel; **~ von** turn off; *coll* move away from (policy *etc*); **von ... zu ... ~** *coll* switch from ... to ...
abschwindeln (+*dat of pers*) swindle (s.o.) out of
abschwirren (*sn*) whirr off; *coll* buzz off
abschwitzen sweat off
abschwören* (+*dat*) renounce; **dem Alkohol ~** take the pledge
absegnen [–eː–] *coll* give one's blessing to
absehbar foreseeable; **in ~er Zeit** in the foreseeable future
absehen* (*see also* **abgesehen**) foresee; (+*dat*) copy from; learn by watching; read (wish); **~ von** disregard; refrain from; **es abgesehen haben auf** (*acc*) be after; have it in for; **abgesehen sein auf** (*acc*) be meant for; **es ist kein Ende abzusehen** there is no end in sight
abseifen soap down
abseihen strain
abseilen lower on a rope; **sich ~** lower oneself on a rope; *mount* abseil
abseitig out-of-the-way; perverse
abseits to one side; out of the way; *sp* off-side; (+*gen*/**von**) off; away from; **~ stehen** be on the outside; *sp* be off-side; **im Abseits** *sp* off-side; **im Abseits stehen** (outsider) stand on the sidelines; *sp* be off-side
absenden* send (off)
der **Absender, –** sender
abservieren clear (the table); clear away (crockery); *coll* get rid of; *coll sp* 'thrash'
absetzbar deductible (for tax purposes); marketable; dismissible
absetzen put down; deposit (sediment *etc*); (horse) throw; push off (boat); remove; cancel; discontinue (treatment); wean; deduct; set off (colours); *comm* sell; *print* start (new line); **~ mit** trim with; **es setzt etwas ab** *coll* there'll be trouble; **ohne abzusetzen** without a break
sich ~ be deposited; collect; *mil* retreat; *coll* take off (**nach** for); *coll sp* break away; **sich ~ gegen** stand out against; **sich ~ von** dissociate oneself from
die **Absetzung, –en** *vbl noun*; *also* removal; deposition; cancellation; deduction
absichern make secure (**gegen** against); safeguard (against); guarantee (loan); **sich ~** cover oneself (**gegen** against)
die **Absicht, –en** intention; **in der ~ zu ...** with the intention of (+*ger*); **mit ~** deliberately; **ohne ~** unintentionally
absichtlich intentional
Absichts–: die ~erklärung, –en declaration of intent; **a~los** unintentional
absingen* sing (through); sight-read
absinken* (*sn*) sink (**auf** *acc* to); drop; (performance *etc*) fall off
der **Absinth** [apˈzɪnt] absinth
absitzen* wear out (by sitting); *coll* serve (sentence); while away (while sitting); (*v/i sn*) dismount (**von** from); *Swiss* sit down; (**zu weit** *etc*) **~ von** sit (too far *etc*) away from
absolut [apz–] absolute; **~ nicht** simply ... not
die **Absolution** [apz–], **–en** absolution
der **Absolutismus** [apz–] absolutism
absolutistisch [apz–] absolutist
der **Absolvent** [apz–], **–en** (*wk masc*) school-leaver; graduate
absolvieren [apz–] complete (studies *etc*); pass (examination); *eccles* absolve
absonderlich odd
absondern isolate; separate; *physiol* secrete; discharge; **sich ~ von** cut oneself off from
die **Absonderung, –en** isolation; separation; *physiol* secretion; discharge
absorbieren [apz–] absorb
die **Absorption** [apz–], **–en** absorption
abspalten (*p/part also* **abgespalten**) split off; *chem*, *phys* separate; **sich ~ von** break away from
der **Abspann, –e** credit titles
abspannen (*see also* **abgespannt**) unhitch; unyoke; *tech* stay; (*v/i*) relax
die **Abspannung** *vbl noun*; *also* exhaustion; guy-ropes
absparen: sich *dat* **... ~** save up for (**von** out of); save up (amount) (out of); **sich** *dat* **... vom Munde ~** scrimp and scrape to get
abspecken *coll* lose (... pounds)
abspeisen feed; **~ mit** fob off with
abspenstig: (+*dat*) **~ machen** entice away from
Absperr–: der ~hahn, ⸚e stopcock
absperren cordon off; shut off; *SGer* lock
die **Absperrung, –en** *vbl noun*; *also* barrier;

cordon

abspiegeln reflect; **sich ~ in** (*dat*) be reflected in

[das] **Abspiel** *sp* pass

abspielen play (through); sight-read; wear out by playing; *sp* pass; **sich ~** take place; **da spielt sich nichts ab!** nothing doing!

absplittern splinter off; (*v/i sn*) splinter off; flake off; **sich ~** break away

[die] **Absprache** [–aː–], **–n** agreement

absprechen* agree on; (+*dat of pers*) dispute (s.o.'s right *etc*); deny that (s.o.) has (talent *etc*)

abspreizen spread out (arms *etc*)

abspringen* (*sn*) jump (off); bale out; come off; rebound; *coll* back out; take one's custom elsewhere; **~ von** bounce off; *coll* back out of

abspritzen spray; hose down, spray off; *Nazi* dispose of by means of a lethal injection; (*v/i sn*) splash off; race off

[der] **Absprung, ⸚e** jump; *athl* take-off

abspulen unwind; unreel; **sich ~** unwind

abspülen wash; wash away/off; **das Geschirr ~** wash up, wash the dishes *US*

abstammen: ~ von be descended/derived from

[die] **Abstammung** origin; descent; **die ~s|lehre** theory of evolution

[der] **Abstand, ⸚e** distance; gap; interval; compensation; **~ halten** keep one's distance; **~ nehmen von** refrain from (doing); **in Abständen von** at intervals of; **mit ~** by far || **die ~s|summe, –n** compensation

abstatten: (+*dat*) **einen Besuch/seinen Dank ~** pay a visit/express one's thanks to

abstauben dust; *sp* snatch (goal); *coll* help oneself to

abstechen* cut (turf *etc*); cut the throat of (animal); stick (pig); drain; rack (wine); *tech* tap; **~ gegen/von** contrast with

[der] **Abstecher, –** detour; digression

abstecken mark out; establish; unpin; *dressm* fit (with pins)

abstehen* (*see also* **abgestanden**) spend standing; (*v/i*) (ears) stick out; (*sn*) *Swiss* touch bottom; **~ von** be (... feet *etc*) away from; (*also sn*) abandon; **sich** *dat* **die Beine ~** *coll* wear one's legs out (by standing); **~d** (ears) that stick out

Absteige–: das ~quartier, –e overnight accommodation; hotel of dubious repute

absteigen* (*sn*) get off; dismount; stay (in accommodation); *mount* make one's descent; *sp* be relegated; **~d** descending

[der] **Absteiger, –** relegated team; team facing relegation

Abstell–: der ~bahnhof, ⸚e railway yard, railroad yard *US*; **das ~gleis, –e** siding; **der ~hahn, ⸚e** stopcock; **der ~raum, ⸚e** storeroom

abstellen put down; park; switch off; put an end to; *mil* detail; *sp* release; **~ auf** (*acc*) gear to

abstempeln stamp; **~ als/zu** label; brand as

absteppen quilt; stitch

absterben* (*see also* **abgestorben**) (*sn*) go numb; (cell *etc*) die; (custom *etc*) die out

[der] **Abstich, –e** cutting; racking (of wine); *tech* tapping

[der] **Abstieg, –e** descent; decline; *sp* relegation

abstimmen *rad* tune; (*v/i*) vote (**über** *acc* on); **~ auf** (*acc*) harmonize with; gear to; *rad* tune to; **~ mit** agree (plan *etc*) with; **sich ~ mit** come to an agreement with

[die] **Abstimmung, –en** *vbl noun*; *also* ballot; harmonization; **zur ~ bringen** put to the vote

abstinent [ap–] abstemious; teetotal

[die] **Abstinenz** [ap–] abstinence; teetotalism

[der] **Abstinenzler** [ap–], **–** teetotaller

abstoppen halt; stop; *sp* time; (*v/i*) pull up

[der] **Abstoß** [–oː–], **⸚e** push-off; *footb* goal-kick

abstoßen* knock off; chip; fray; scuff; graze; damage (furniture); pay off; get rid of; repel (*also phys*); *med* reject; *comm* dispose of; *biol* shed; (*v/i*) be repulsive; **(den Ball) ~** take a goal-kick; **(das Boot) ~** push off

sich ~ push off; *biol* be shed; (*recip*) *phys* repel one another

abstoßend *pres/part*; *also* repellent

abstottern *coll* buy on hire-purchase/the installment plan *US*

abstrahieren [ap–] abstract

abstrakt [ap–] abstract

[die] **Abstraktion** [ap–], **–en** abstraction

[das] **Abstraktum** [ap–], **–(t)a** abstract concept/noun

abstrampeln: sich ~ *coll* slave away; pedal furiously

abstrapazieren: (sich) ~ *coll* wear (oneself) out

abstreichen* scrape off; knock off; skim off; wipe off; wipe; strop (razor); search (**nach** for); (searchlight) sweep (for); (*v/i sn*) fly away; **~ von** deduct from; disregard (part of what is said)

abstreifen slip off; cast (skin); knock off (ash); rid oneself of (habit *etc*); scour (**nach** for)

abstreiten* deny; (+*dat of pers*) dispute (s.o.'s right *etc*); deny that (s.o.) has (quality)

[der] **Abstrich, –e** cut (**an** *dat* in); downstroke; *med* smear; swab

abstrus [ap–] abstruse

abstufen terrace; layer (hair); grade; downgrade (in salary scale)

[die] **Abstufung, –en** *vbl noun*; *also* shade

abstumpfen (*see also* **abgestumpft**) blunt;

dull (senses *etc*); make indifferent (**gegen** to); (*v/i sn*) become blunt/dulled/ indifferent

der **Absturz, ⸚e** precipice; fall; *aer* crash

abstürzen (*sn*) fall; (rock face) fall away steeply; *aer* crash

abstützen prop up; back up; **sich ~ von** push oneself away from

absuchen [–uː–] search (**nach** for); sweep (sky) (for)

der **Absud, –e** decoction

absurd [apz–] absurd

die **Absurdität** [apz–], **–en** absurdity

der **Abszeß** [aps–], **–(ss)e** abscess

der **Abt** [apt], **⸚e** abbot

Abt. (= **Abteilung**) dept.

abtakeln (*see also* **abgetakelt**) unrig

Abtast– scanning ...

abtasten feel (all over); search (**nach** for); *tech*, *comput* scan

abtauen thaw; defrost; (*v/i sn*) thaw (out)

die **Abtei** [ap–], **–en** abbey

das **Abteil, –e** *rail* compartment

abteilen divide up (**in** *acc* into); partition off

die **Abteilung, –en** dividing up; partitioning; **die Abteilung, –en** department; section; (hospital) unit; *mil* detachment; **der Abteilungs|leiter, –** head of department

abteufen sink (shaft)

abtippen *coll* type out

die **Äbtissin** [ɛp–], **–nen** abbess

abtöten kill; mortify (the flesh)

abtragen* level; demolish; (water) erode; clear away; pay off; wear out

abträglich (*following dat*) detrimental (to)

abtrainieren [–trɛ–] work off by exercise/ training

der **Abtransport** removal (by vehicle); *mil* evacuation

abtransportieren take away (on vehicle); *mil* evacuate

abtreiben* drive/carry off course; drive (cattle) down from the mountain pasture; *med* expel; abort; *esp Aust cul* whisk; (*v/i*) have an abortion; (*sn*) drift/be driven off course

die **Abtreibung, –en** *vbl noun*; *also* abortion

abtrennbar detachable; separable

abtrennen detach; take off (button *etc*); sever; separate; partition off

die **Abtrennung** *vbl noun*; *also* separation

abtreten* wear down/out; stamp (snow *etc*) from one's shoes *etc*; detach (by treading on it/them); (+*dat*) give up (seat *etc*) to; cede to; transfer to; (*v/i sn*) resign; *mil* stand down; *theat* make one's exit; **~ an** (*acc*) cede to; transfer to; **sich** *dat* **die Füße ~** wipe one's feet; **~ lassen** allow to stand down; *mil* dismiss

der **Abtreter, –** doormat

die **Abtretung, –en** *vbl noun*; *also* transfer; cession

der **Abtritt, –e** resignation; *theat* exit; *dated coll* privy

abtrocknen dry (hands, tears); (*v/i sn*) dry out; (**das Geschirr**) **~** dry up, dry the dishes *US*; **sich ~** dry oneself

abtropfen (*sn*) drip; drain; **~ lassen** (let) drain; let drip

abtrotzen (+*dat*) wrest from

abtrumpfen: (+*dat*) **eine Karte ~** trump (s.o.'s) card

abtrünnig disloyal; apostate; (+*dat*) **~ werden** desert; defect from; **der/die Abtrünnige** (*decl as adj*) renegade; apostate

abtun* dismiss (**als** as); **lachend ~** laugh off; **mit einer Handbewegung ~** wave aside; **abgetan sein** (matter) be disposed of; **es damit abgetan sein lassen** leave it at that

abtupfen dab

ab|urteilen [–ʊr–] pass sentence on; condemn, censure

der **ABV, –(s)** *EGer* = **Abschnittsbevollmächtigte**

abverlangen (+*dat*) demand of

abvermieten *coll* sublet

abwägen* weigh up; weigh (one's words); (**gegeneinander**) **~** balance

abwählen vote out (of office); *educ* opt out of

abwälzen roll away; **~ auf** (*acc*) shift onto; push (job) onto; pass (cost) on to; **die Verantwortung von sich ~** shift the responsibility onto someone else

abwandeln vary

abwandern (*also sn*) hike through; (*v/i sn*) move away; *meteor* move; **~ in** (*acc*) (*sn*) migrate to; move into; find its way into; **~ zu** (*sn*) switch to

die **Abwanderung, –en** *vbl noun*; *also* migration; exodus

die **Abwandlung, –en** variation

abwarten wait for; bide (one's time); wait for (rain *etc*) to stop; (*v/i*) wait (and see); **das bleibt abzuwarten** it remains to be seen; **~d** (attitude) wait-and-see; **sich ~d verhalten** bide one's time

abwärts downward(s); **~gehen*** (*sep*; *sn*) (**es geht ~ mit** ... ... is *etc* going downhill)

der **Abwasch** washing-up, dirty dishes *or* dishwashing *US*; **der ~lappen, –** dishcloth; **das ~mittel, –** washing-up liquid, dishwashing liquid *US*; **das ~wasser** dishwater

die **Abwasch, –en** *Aust* sink

abwaschbar washable

abwaschen* wash (face *etc*); wash off; wipe out (disgrace); (**das Geschirr**) **~** wash up, wash the dishes *US*

das **Abwasser, ..wässer** sewage; effluent; **der ~kanal, ⸚e** sewer

abwechseln [–ks–]: (**sich**) **~** take turns (**bei**

at); alternate; **~d** alternating; alternate; (*adv*) alternately, by turns

die **Abwechslung, -en** change; alternation; variety; **zur ~** for a change || **a~s|reich** varied

Abwege: auf ~ führen/geraten lead/go astray

abwegig inept; misguided

die **Abwehr** defence; resistance; warding off; counter-espionage service; *sp* defence; save

Abwehr- defence ...; defensive ...; protective ...; **der ~dienst** counter-espionage service; **die ~kräfte** *pl* (body's) defences; **der ~spieler, -** *sp* defender; **der ~stoff, -e** antibody

abwehren ward off; avert; keep away/off; dismiss (objection *etc*); *sp* parry (blow); (*v/i*) decline; **den Ball ~** make a save

abweichen[1]* (*like* **weichen[1]**) (*sn*): **~ von** deviate from; depart from; swerve from; differ from; **vom Thema ~** get off the point; **voneinander ~** diverge; **~d** divergent; **~d von** unlike

abweichen[2] soak off; (*v/i sn*) come off (after soaking)

der **Abweichler, -** deviationist

die **Abweichung, -en** *vbl noun*; *also* divergence; deviation

abweiden graze

abweisen* turn away; reject, turn down; beat off; *leg* dismiss; **sich nicht ~ lassen** refuse to be put off; **~d** unfriendly; (gesture *etc*) of refusal

die **Abweisung** *vbl noun*; *also* rejection; refusal; *leg* dismissal

abwendbar avoidable; preventable

abwenden* turn away (eyes *etc*); avert; ward off; **sich ~** turn away; **sich ~ von** turn away from; turn one's back on

abwerben* poach (employee *etc*)

abwerfen* drop (bomb); jettison; (horse) throw; throw off; *cards* throw away; *bot*, *zool* shed; *comm* yield; *sp* knock off; get (player) out; (*v/i*) *sp* throw the ball into play; **viel ~** be very profitable

abwerten [-eː-] devalue; depreciate (ideal *etc*); **~d** derogatory

die **Abwertung, -en** devaluation; depreciation

abwesend absent; absent-minded

die **Abwesenheit** absence; absent-mindedness; **durch ~ glänzen** be conspicuous by one's absence

abwetzen wear smooth; (*v/i sn*) *coll* hare off

abwickeln unwind; conduct; carry out; handle (imports *etc*); organize; *comm* wind up (company); **sich ~** pass off; run

die **Abwicklung** *vbl noun*; *also* organization; *comm* liquidation

abwiegeln mollify; (*v/i*) play the matter down

abwimmeln *coll* get rid of; get out of

abwinken *mot rac* wave down; stop (race); (*v/i*) make a gesture of refusal; say no, decline

abwirtschaften (*see also* **abgewirtschaftet**) ruin/(*v/i*) be ruined by mismanagement; **abgewirtschaftet haben** be finished/a spent force

abwischen wipe; wipe away; **sich ~** wipe one's bottom

abwohnen *coll* make (accommodation) shabby; **die Miete ~** stay the full period for which rent has been paid

abwracken break up (ship)

der **Abwurf, ⸚e** dropping; *sp* throwing of the ball into play (by goalkeeper)

abwürgen stifle (discussion *etc*); *mot* stall

abzahlen pay for/repay by instalments

abzählen count; count out; *mil* number off, count off *US*; **bitte das Fahrgeld abgezählt bereithalten!** please have the exact fare ready

die **Abzahlung, -en** *vbl noun*; *also* repayment; instalment; **auf ~ kaufen** buy on hire-purchase/the installment plan *US*

abzapfen draw off; (+*dat*) **Blut ~** *coll* take blood from; (+*dat*) **Geld ~** *coll* get money out of

abzappeln: sich ~ *coll* wear oneself out with frantic activity

abzäumen unbridle

abzäunen fence off

abzehren (*see also* **abgezehrt**) emaciate; **sich ~** pine away (**vor** *dat* with)

das **Abzeichen, -** badge; distinguishing mark; *zool* (*usu* white) marking

abzeichnen draw; initial; **sich ~** show (in face); be visible (through garment); emerge; become apparent; loom up; **sich ~ gegen/von** stand out against

das **Abzieh|bild, -er** transfer

abziehen* take off; take out (key); sharpen; strop (razor); surface (floor); let off (firearm); strip (bed); skin; peel; *phot* print; *print* run off; pull; *fin* withdraw (capital); *mil* pull out; *coll* throw (party); (*v/i*) pull the trigger; (*sn*) move off; (smoke *etc*) escape; *meteor* move away; *coll* go away; **~ von** deduct from; subtract from; distract from; **(auf Flaschen) ~** bottle

abzielen: ~ auf (*acc*) aim at; be aimed at

abzirkeln measure meticulously; weigh (words) very carefully

der **Abzug, ⸚e** deduction; discount; departure; escape (of gas); vent, outlet; trigger; *mil* withdrawal; *phot* print; *print* copy; proof; (*pl*) deductions (from pay); **in ~ bringen** deduct

abzüglich (+*gen*) less

abzugs|fähig deductible

abzupfen pull off (petal *etc*)

abzwacken *coll* nip off; **sich** *dat* **...** ~ stint oneself of; snatch (time for sth.); +**von** squeeze out of

die **Abzweig|dose, -n** junction-box

abzweigen set aside; (*sn*) branch off; **sich** ~ fork

die **Abzweigung, -en** *vbl noun*; *also* turn-off; *rail* branch line

abzwicken nip off

abzwingen* (+*dat*) wring from; command (s.o.'s respect); **sich** *dat* **ein Lächeln** ~ force a smile

die **Accessoires** [aksɛ'sõaːʁs] *pl* (fashion) accessories

ach! oh!; **ach so** oh so; **ach so!** (oh,) I see; **ach was/wo** (*introducing remark*) oh come on; no no; **mit Ach und Krach** *coll* by the skin of one's teeth || **der Ach-Laut, -e** 'hard' *ch*

der **Achat** [-x-], **-e** agate

Achill(es) [a'xɪl(ɛs)] Achilles

Achs- [-ks-] axle ...; **der ~abstand, ⸗e** wheelbase; **die ~last, -en** axle load

die **Achse** [-ks-], **-n** axle; axis; **auf (der)** ~ *coll* on the road/move

die **Achsel** [-ks-], **-n** shoulder; **auf die leichte ~ nehmen** make light of; **über die ~ ansehen** look down on || **die ~höhle, -n** armpit; **das ~zucken** shrug of the shoulders; **a~zuckend** with a shrug of the shoulders

Achsen- axle ...; *math*, *phys* axial ...; **der ~bruch, ⸗e** broken axle; **die ~mächte** *pl* *hist* the Axis powers

-achsig [-ks-] -axled; -axial

acht[1] eight; ~ **Tage** a week

acht[2]**: zu** ~ (*see* **zu** 1 (*i*)); **acht..** eighth

acht[3]**: außer ~ lassen** disregard; **sich in ~ nehmen** be careful; +**vor** (*dat*) beware of

die **Acht**[1], **-en** eight

die **Acht**[2] *hist* outlawry; **in ~ und Bann tun** ostracize

acht- eight ...; **das A~eck, -e** octagon; **~eckig** octagonal; **acht|einhalb** eight and a half; **~fach** eightfold; **~geben*** (*sep*) take care (**a. auf** (*acc*) pay attention to; keep an eye on; mind); **~los** careless; **die A~losigkeit** carelessness; **~mal** eight times; **~malig** occurring eight times

achtbar estimable; (performance *etc*) respectable

achtel: ein ~ ... an eighth of a ...

das **Achtel, -** eighth; **die ~note, -n** quaver, eighth note *US*

achten respect; esteem; ~ **auf** (*acc*) pay attention to; keep an eye on

ächten ostracize; *hist* outlaw

achtens eighthly

der **Achter, -** *sp* figure of eight; *row* eight; **die ~bahn, -en** switchback, roller coaster *US*; **das ~deck, -s** after-deck

achtsam attentive; careful

die **Achtung** respect (**vor** *dat* for); **~!** look out!; *mil* attention!; *sp* on your marks!; **alle ~!** good for you/her *etc*! || **a~gebietend** imposing; **der ~s|erfolg, -e** succès d'estime

achtzehn eighteen

achtzehnt.., das Achtzehntel, - eighteenth

achtzig eighty; **auf ~** *coll* livid; **auf ~ bringen** *coll* make (s.o.'s) blood boil

achtziger: die ~ Jahre the eighties; **der Achtziger, -** octogenarian; (*pl*) eighties

achtzigst.., das Achtzigstel, - eightieth

ächzen groan; creak

der **Acker,** *pl* **Äcker** (ploughed) field; **der ~bau** agriculture; **a~bau|treibend** farming; **der ~boden = das ~land** arable land

ackern plough; (*v/i*) *coll* slog away

a conto on account

Acryl- acrylic ...

a. D. [aː'deː] (= **außer Dienst**) retd.

ad absurdum [at ʔapz-]: ~ **führen** demonstrate the absurdity of

der **ADAC = Allgemeiner Deutscher Automobil-Club** (*W. German motoring organization*)

ad acta [at ʔ...]: ~ **legen** regard as closed

Adam ['aːdam] Adam; **nach ~ Riese** *coll* according to the rules of arithmetic || **der ~s|apfel, ..äpfel** Adam's apple; **~s|kostüm** *joc* (**im A.** (of male) in one's birthday suit)

adaptieren adapt; *Aust* redecorate

adäquat appropriate

Addier-: die ~maschine, -n adding-machine

addieren add (up)

Addis Abeba Addis Ababa

die **Addition, -en** addition

ade! farewell!; **das Ade, -s** farewell

der **Adel** nobility; title; ~ **verpflichtet** noblesse oblige

adeln ennoble

Adels- ... of (the) nobility; **das ~prädikat, -e** nobiliary particle (**von,** *de*); **der ~stand** nobility; **der ~titel, -** title

die **Ader, -n** vein (*also bot*, *geol*, *zool*); (musical *etc*) bent; streak; *elect* core (of cable); **keine ~ haben für** have no feeling for; **zur ~ lassen** bleed || **der ~laß** blood-letting

die **Adhäsion** [at-] adhesion

das **Adjektiv** ['at-], **-e** adjective

adjektivisch ['at-] adjectival

adjustieren [at-] *tech* adjust

der **Adjutant** [at-], **-en** (*wk masc*) adjutant; aide-de-camp

der **Adler** ['aː-], **-** eagle; **der ~blick** eagle eye; **der ~horst, -e** eyrie; **die ~nase, -n** aquiline nose

adlig ['aː-] noble; **der/die Adlige** (*decl as adj*) nobleman/woman; **die A~en** *pl* the nobility

die **Administration** [at-], **-en** administration; *EGer* (bureaucratic) issuing of regulations

administrativ [at-] administrative; *EGer*

bureaucratic

der **Administrator** [at–], **–(or)en** administrator

administrieren [at–] administer; (*v/i*) *EGer* issue regulations in bureaucratic fashion

der **Admiral** [at–], **–e** admiral; *ent* red admiral; **das ~s|schiff, –e** flagship

die **Admiralität** [at–] the Admiralty

der **ADMV** = **Allgemeiner Deutscher Motorsportverband** (*E. German motoring association*)

der **ADN** = **Allgemeiner Deutscher Nachrichtendienst** (*official E. German news agency*)

Adonis [–ɪs] *myth*, **der ~** (*gen* **–**), **–se** Adonis

adoptieren adopt (child)

die **Adoption, –en** adoption

Adoptiv– adopted ...; adoptive ...

das **Adrenalin** adrenalin

Adreß–: das ~buch, ⸗er directory

der **Adressant, –en** (*wk masc*) sender

der **Adressat, –en** (*wk masc*) addressee

die **Adresse, –n** address (*also comput*); **an die falsche ~ geraten** *coll* come/go to the wrong person

Adressier–: die ~maschine, –n addressograph

addressieren address (*also comput*)

adrett smart

die **Adria** ['aː–] the Adriatic

adsorbieren [at–] adsorb

die **Adsorption** [at–] adsorption

das **Adstringens** [at–, –ɛns] (*gen* **–**), **–(en)zien** [–ĭən] astringent

der **Advent** [at–] Advent; (**erster** *etc*) **~** (first *etc*) Sunday in Advent || **die ~s|zeit** Advent

das **Adverb** [at–], **–ien** [–ĭən] adverb

adverbial [at–] adverbial

der **Advokat** [at–], **–en** (*wk masc*) advocate (of cause); *esp Aust*, *Swiss* lawyer

die **AEG** = **Allgemeine Elektricitäts-Gesellschaft**

Aero– [aero–] aero–

die **Aerodynamik** [–ɪk] aerodynamics

aerodynamisch aerodynamic

das **Aerogramm, –e** air-letter

die **Aeronautik** [–ɪk] aeronautics

aeronautisch aeronautical

das **Aerosol, –e** aerosol

die **Affäre, –n** affair; **sich aus der ~ ziehen** extricate oneself (from awkward situation)

der **Affe, –n** (*wk masc*) monkey; ape; *coll* fool; *mil* knapsack; **einen ~n gefressen haben an** (*dat*) *coll* be crazy about

der **Affekt, –e** (strong) emotion; **im ~** in the heat of the moment || **die ~handlung, –en** act committed in the heat of the moment

affektiert affected

äffen make a fool of

Affen– monkey('s) ...; *coll* tremendous ...; **a~artig** monkey/ape-like (**mit a~artiger Geschwindigkeit** *coll* like greased lightning); **die ~hitze** *coll* scorching heat; **die ~liebe** doting; **~schande** *coll* (**es ist eine A.** it's scandalous); **das ~theater, –** *coll* (complete) farce; **~zahn** *coll* (**mit A.** at breakneck speed)

affig *coll* stuck-up

die **Äffin, –nen** female monkey/ape

äffisch ape/monkey-like

der **Affront** [–'frɔ̃ː], **–s** affront (**gegen** to)

der **Afghan** ['afgaːn], **–s** afghan (= carpet)

der **Afghane, –n** (*wk masc*) Afghan; Afghan hound

afghanisch Afghan

Afghanistan Afghanistan

Afrika ['aː–] Africa

der **Afrikaner, –, afrikanisch** African

der **Afrikanist, –en** (*wk masc*) Africanist

die **Afrikanistik** [–ɪk] African studies

Afro–: der ~-Look Afro look; **afro-asiatisch** Afro-Asian

der **After, –** anus; *in compds* anal ...

die **AG, –s** = **Aktiengesellschaft**; *cf* PLC, plc

die **Ägäis** [–ɪs] the Aegean Sea

ägäisch Aegean; **das Ä~e Meer** the Aegean Sea

die **Agave, –n** agave

das **Agens** ['aːgɛns] (*gen* **–**) **–(en)zien** [–ĭən] *chem* agent

der **Agent, –en** (*wk masc*) secret agent; agent

die **Agentur, –en** agency

das **Agglomerat, –e** agglomerate; agglomeration

das **Aggregat, –e** aggregate; *tech* unit; **der ~zustand, ⸗e** *phys* state

die **Aggression, –en** aggression

aggressiv aggressive

die **Aggressivität** aggressiveness

der **Aggressor, –(or)en** aggressor

Ägide: unter der ~ (+*gen*) under the aegis of

agieren act

agil agile

die **Agilität** agility

die **Agitation** (political) agitation; *EGer* propaganda (*not pej*)

der **Agitator, –(or)en** agitator; *EGer* propagandist (*not pej*)

agitatorisch rabble-rousing; *EGer* propagandist (*not pej*)

agitieren agitate; make propaganda

der **Agnostiker, –, agnostisch** agnostic

der **Agnostizismus** agnosticism

die **Agonie, –(ie)n** death-throes

die **Agraffe, –n** clasp

Agrar– agricultural ...; agrarian ...; **die ~politik** agricultural policy

der **Agrarier** [–ĭɐ], **–** *hist* big landowner

agrarisch agrarian

der **Agronom, –en** (*wk masc*) agronomist

die **Agrotechnik** ['aːgrotɛçnɪk] *EGer* agricultural technology

Ägypten Egypt

der **Ägypter, –, ägyptisch** Egyptian

ah! ah!; oh!; **ah so!** (oh,) I see
äh! ugh!
aha! I/you see!; **das Aha-Erlebnis, -se** sudden realization
die **Ahle, -n** bradawl
Ahn-: die ~frau, -en ancestress; **der ~herr, -en** (*like* **Herr**) ancestor
ahnden punish
ähneln (+*dat*) resemble; be like
ahnen sense; have a foreboding of; suspect; **mir ahnt nichts Gutes** I fear the worst; **(ach,) du ahnst es nicht!** would you believe it!; **(nur) zu ~ sein** be (only) faintly discernible; **~ lassen** (painting *etc*) suggest, hint at; **nichts ~d** unsuspectingly
die **Ahnen** *pl* ancestors; *in compds* ... of ancestors; ancestor ...; ancestral ...; **der ~kult** ancestor-worship; **die ~tafel, -n** genealogical table
ähnlich similar (*following dat* to); **-ähnlich** -like; (+*dat*) **~ sehen** look like; **das sieht ihm ~!** that's just like him!; **oder so ~** or something like that; **und ~es** etc
die **Ähnlichkeit, -en** similarity; **~ haben mit** bear a resemblance to
die **Ahnung, -en** premonition; hunch, suspicion; idea (= inkling); **hast 'du eine ~!** that's what *you* think!; **keine ~!** search me!; **keine blasse ~ haben von** not have the foggiest idea about || **a~s|los** unsuspecting; **a~s|voll** full of foreboding
ahoi! ahoy!
der **Ahorn, -e** maple
die **Ähre, -n** ear (of grain)
das **Aids** [eːts] (*gen* -; *usu no art*) AIDS
der **Airbus** ['ɛːɐbʊs] (*gen* **-ses**), **-se** airbus
das **ais, Ais** ['aːɪs] (*gen* -), **-** *mus* (the note) A sharp; (*key*) **Ais** A sharp major, **ais** A sharp minor
Ajax ['aː-] Ajax
die **Akademie, -(ie)n** academy; college; *Aust* literary/musical gathering
der **Akademiker, -** (university) graduate
akademisch academic
die **Akazie** [-ĭə], **-n** acacia
die **Akelei, -en** columbine
die **Akklamation, -en** *esp Aust* applause; acclamation
akklamieren *esp Aust* applaud; elect by acclamation
die **Akklimatisation, -en** acclimatization
akklimatisieren: sich ~ acclimatize oneself
der **Akkord, -e** chord; **im ~ arbeiten** be on piece-work || **die ~arbeit, -en** piece-work
das **Akkordeon** [-ɔn], **-s** accordion
akkreditieren *fin* give (s.o.) credit facilities; *pol* accredit
das **Akkreditiv, -e** *fin* letter of credit; *pol* credentials
der **Akku, -s = der Akkumulator, -(or)en** accumulator
akkumulieren accumulate
akkurat meticulous; precise
die **Akkuratesse** meticulousness
der **Akkusativ, -e** accusative
die **Akne** [-nə] acne
die **Akonto|zahlung, -en** payment on account
der **Akquisiteur** [-'tøːɐ], **-e** *comm* canvasser
die **Akribie** meticulousness
akribisch meticulous
der **Akrobat, -en** (*wk masc*) acrobat
die **Akrobatik** [-ɪk] acrobatics
akrobatisch acrobatic
die **Akropolis** [-ɪs] the Acropolis
der **Akt, -e** act (*also theat etc*); ceremony; sex act; *art* nude; *in compds* nude ...
die **Akte, -n** document; file, record; **zu den ~n legen** file away; regard as closed || **der ~n|deckel, -** folder; **der ~n|koffer, -** attaché case; **die ~n|mappe, -n** file; briefcase; **die ~n|notiz, -en** memorandum; **der ~n|schrank, ⸚e** filing cabinet; **die ~n|tasche, -n** briefcase; **das ~n|zeichen, -** reference (number)
der **Akteur** [-'tøːɐ], **-e** actor; protagonist
die **Aktie** [-tsĭə], **-n** *comm* share; **die ~n|gesellschaft, -en** joint-stock company, corporation *US*; **der ~n|markt, ⸚e** stock market
die **Aktion, -en** action; campaign; operation
der **Aktionär, -e** shareholder, stockholder *US*
Aktions- ... of action; **die ~art, -en** *gramm* aspect; **der ~radius, -(i)en** range; sphere of action
aktiv active (*also gramm*); *comm* (balance of trade) favourable; *mil* regular; **der/die Aktive** (*decl as adj*) *sp* regular competitor
das **Aktiv**[1] *gramm* active (voice)
das **Aktiv**[2], **-e/-s** *EGer* action-group
Aktiv-: der ~posten, - asset; **der ~saldo, -s/-(d)en** credit balance; **der ~urlaub, -e** activity holiday
die **Aktiva** *pl* assets
aktivieren get (s.o.) moving/(sth.) going; *comm* enter on the assets side; *chem, phys* activate
aktivisch *gramm* active
der **Aktivismus** activism
der **Aktivist, -en** (*wk masc*) activist (*EGer: worker who achieves distinction through his exemplary efforts or initiative*)
die **Aktivität, -en** activity
die **Aktrice** [-sə], **-n** *dated* actress
aktualisieren make topical; *comput* update
die **Aktualität** topicality; **das ~en|kino, -s** news theatre
aktuell topical; current; in fashion
akupunktieren treat with acupuncture
die **Akupunktur** acupuncture
die **Akustik** [-ɪk] acoustics
akustisch acoustic

akut acute; pressing
der **Akut, –e** acute accent
der **Akzent, –e** accent; stress; **den ~ legen auf** (*acc*) place the accent on; **neue ~e setzen** introduce a new note; **die modischen ~e sind ...** the accent is on ... || **a~frei** without an accent; **die ~verschiebung, –en** shift of accent/emphasis
akzentuieren stress; accentuate
das **Akzept, –e** *comm* acceptance
akzeptabel acceptable
der **Akzeptant, –en** (*wk masc*) *comm* acceptor
akzeptieren accept
die **Akzise, –n** *esp EGer* excise duty
Aladin ['aladi:n] Aladdin
der **Alarm, –e** alarm; *mil* alert; **blinder ~** false alarm; **~ schlagen** sound the alarm || **die ~anlage, –n** alarm (system); **a~bereit** on the alert; **die ~bereitschaft** state of readiness (**in A.** on stand-by)
alarmieren alert; call out; alarm; **~d** alarming
der **Alaun, –e** alum
der **Albaner, –** Albanian
Albanien [–ĭən] Albania
der **Albanier** [–ĭɐ], **–** Albanian
albanisch, (*language*) **A~** Albanian
der **Albatros** [–ɔs], **–se** albatross
Alben *pl of* **Album**
albern[1] fool about
albern[2] silly
die **Albernheit, –en** silliness; (*pl*) tomfoolery
der **Albino, –s** albino
Albrecht Albert
das **Album, –(b)en** album
die **Alchimie** [–ç–] alchemy
der **Alchimist** [–ç–], **–en** (*wk masc*) alchemist
alemannisch Alemannic
die **Aleuten** *pl* the Aleutians
Alexander Alexander
die **Algarve** [–və] the Algarve
die **Alge, –n** alga
die **Algebra** ['al–] algebra
algebraisch algebraic
Algerien [–ĭən] Algeria
der **Algerier** [–ĭɐ], **–**, **algerisch** Algerian
Algier ['alʒi:ɐ] Algiers
alias ['a:lĭas] alias
das **Alibi** ['a:–], **–s** alibi
die **Alimente** *pl* maintenance (paid for illegitimate child)
der **Alk, –e** (*or* **–en** *wk masc*) auk
das **Alkali, –en** [–ĭən] alkali
alkalisch alkaline
der **Alkohol, –e** alcohol; **unter ~ setzen** make drunk || **a~frei** non-alcoholic; **a~haltig** alcoholic; **der ~spiegel, –** level of alcohol (in blood); **das ~verbot, –e** ban on alcohol
die **Alkoholika** *pl* alcoholic drinks
der **Alkoholiker, –** alcoholic; **Anonyme ~** Alcoholics Anonymous
alkoholisch alcoholic
der **Alkoholismus** alcoholism
der **Alkoven** [–v–], **–** alcove
all (*see also* **alle**[1], **alles**) all (the); every; any; **~e zwei Tage** every other day; **vor ~en Dingen** above all
das **All** universe; outer space
all– *esp* all–; universally ...; (*eg* **~deutsch**) pan– (German *etc*);
~abendlich every evening; **~bekannt** universally known; **~fällig** *Aust, Swiss* possible; any; **all|gegenwärtig** omnipresent; **~gemein** general; universal (**~gemeine Redensarten** generalities; **~gemein gesprochen** generally speaking; **im ~gemeinen** in general); **A~gemein–** general ...; **~gemein|gültig** universal, universally valid; **A~gemein|gut** (**A. sein/werden** be/become generally known); **die A~gemeinheit, –en** generality; (the) general public; **~gemein|verständlich** easily understood; popular; **das A~heil|mittel, –** panacea; **~jährlich** yearly; every year; **die A~macht** omnipotence; **~mächtig** omnipotent, all-powerful; **~mählich** gradual; (*adv*) gradually, *or expressed by* ... begin(s) to ... (*eg* **ich begreife a., was du meinst** I'm beginning to understand what you mean); **~monatlich** monthly; **~nächtlich** nightly; **~seitig** all-round; general; (*adv*) *also* (consider *etc*) from every angle; = **~seits** on all sides; **~stündlich** hourly; **der A~tag** everyday life/routine (**grauer A.** monotony of everyday life); **~täglich** daily; (**~täglich**) everyday; ordinary; **~tags** on weekdays; **A~tags–** everyday ...; ordinary ...; **~umfassend** all-embracing; **A~wetter–** all-weather ...; **all|wissend** omniscient; **~wöchentlich** weekly; **~zu–** all/only too; far too; **all|zu|sehr, all|zu|viel** too much; **all|zu|wenig** too little; **A~zweck–** all/general-purpose ...
Allah Allah
alle[1] (*see also* **all**) all; everyone
alle[2] *coll* all gone; worn out; **~ machen** finish off; **~ werden** run out
alle–: ~dem (**bei** *etc* **a.** for *etc* all that); **~mal** always; every time; *coll* certainly (**ein für a.** once and for all); **alle|samt** all (together)
die **Allee, –(ee)n** avenue
die **Allegorie, –(ie)n** allegory
die **Allegorik** [–ɪk] allegory (= use of allegory)
allegorisch allegorical
allein 1 *adj/adv* alone; on one's/its own; 2 *adv* only, solely; ... alone (*eg* **~ Schweden** Sweden alone); 3 *conj* however; **~ der Gedanke** the very thought of it; **von ~** on one's/its own; automatically

Allein– exclusive ...; sole ...; solo ...; **der ~gang, ⸚e** solo effort (**im A.** on one's own; **etw. im A. machen** go it alone); **der ~gänger, –** person who goes it alone; **die ~herrschaft** autocratic rule; **der ~herrscher, –** autocrat; **das ~sein** being alone; loneliness; **allein|selig|machend** *RC* (faith *etc*) only true; **a~stehend** single; (house) detached; **der/die ~stehende** (*decl as adj*) single person; **der ~vertrieb** exclusive selling rights (**den A. haben für** be the sole agent(s) for)

alleine *coll* = **allein**

alleinig sole; exclusive; *Aust* (person) single

alle|mal *see* **alle**

allen|falls at most; if need be; perhaps

allent|halben on all sides

aller– (+*superl*) ... of all; very ... (*eg* **~best** best of all; very best); (*in absolute sense, translated by superlative alone*) most ... (*eg* **~gnädigst** most gracious, **~herzlichst** most cordial); **das ~(wichtigste** *etc*)/**am ~(wichtigsten** *etc*) **ist, daß ...** the most (important *etc*) thing of all is that ...; **das A~(schönste** *etc*) the (loveliest *etc*) thing; **am ~(besten** *etc*) (best *etc*) of all (*cf* **an** 3); **aufs ~(beste** *etc*) in the (best *etc*) possible way (*cf* **auf** 3);

aller|aller– (+*superl*) very ... of all (*eg* **allerallerletzt** very last of all); **aller|äußerst** outermost; (caution *etc*) extreme; (case *etc*) most extreme; **das Aller|äußerste** the very utmost; the worst; **~dings** however; albeit; it is true; ... though (**a.!** certainly!); **~hand** (*indecl*) all kinds of (things); a lot (of) (**das ist (doch/ja) ~hand!** that's a bit thick/quite something!); **Aller|heiligen** All Saints' Day; **das Aller|heiligste** (*decl as adj*) the holy of holies; *RC* the Blessed Sacrament; **~lei** (*indecl*) all kinds of (things); **das A~lei** mixture, miscellany (**Leipziger A.** mixed vegetables); **aller|letzt** very last/latest; *coll* most awful; **aller|liebst** very favourite; delightful; **am aller|meisten** most of all; **aller|nächst** very next; very closest (**in ~nächster Zeit** in the very near future); **aller|neuest** very latest; **aller|nötigst** most necessary; **aller|orten** = **aller|orts** everywhere; **Aller|seelen** All Souls' Day; **~seits** on all sides; (*in greeting*) everyone; **Aller|welts–** ordinary ...; **der Aller|welts|kerl, –e** *approx* = tremendous guy (referring to someone extremely versatile); **die aller|wenigsten ...** very few ...; **der Aller|werteste** (*decl as adj*) *joc* posterior

^die^ **Allergie, –(ie)n** allergy

allergisch allergic (**gegen** to)

alles everything; all; *coll* everyone; **~ (Schöne** *etc*) everything (beautiful *etc*); **das ~** all that; **~, was** everything that; **~ in allem** altogether; all in all; **über ~** above all else; more than anything else; **vor allem** especially; above all; **was er ~ (weiß** *etc*)! the things he (knows *etc*)! || **der A~fresser, –** omnivore; **der A~kleber, –** all-purpose adhesive

alle|samt *see* **alle**

allg. = **allgemein**

all|gemein *etc*: *see* **all–**

^die^ **Allianz, –en** alliance

^der^ **Alligator, –(or)en** alligator

alliieren: sich ~ mit ally oneself with; **alliiert** allied; **der Alliierte** (*decl as adj*) ally; **die Alliierten** the Allies (in Second World War)

^das^ **Allotria** (*gen* **–(s)**) larking about; **~ treiben** lark about

^die^ **Allüren** *pl* airs and graces

^die^ **Alm, –en** alpine pasture

^der^ **Almanach, –e** (illustrated) year-book

^die^ **Almosen** *pl* alms; charity; **für ein ~** for a pittance

^die^ **Aloe** ['a:loe], **–n** [–oən] aloe

Alp–: das ~drücken nightmares; **das ~horn, ⸚er** alpenhorn; **der ~traum, ⸚e** nightmare

^die^ **Alpen** *pl* Alps; *in compds* alpine ...; **das ~veilchen, –** cyclamen

^das^ **Alphabet, –e** alphabet; **nach dem ~ ordnen** arrange in alphabetical order

alphabetisch alphabetical

alphabetisieren put in alphabetical order; teach (illiterate) to read and write

alpin alpine

^der^ **Alpinismus** alpinism

^der^ **Alpinist, –en** (*wk masc*) alpinist

^die^ **Alpinistik** [–ɪk] alpinism

^die^ **Alraune, –n** mandrake

als as (a/the) (*or not translated, eg* **~ gute Freunde auseinandergehen** to part good friends); (*following comp*) than; (*past time or in synopsis*) when; as; *if followed immediately by verb in subjunctive*, = **~ ob/wenn ...** (+*subj*) as if ...; **... ~ einzige(r)/erste(r)/letzte(r) ...** (am, was, *etc*) the only one/first/last to ...; **zu ..., ~ daß ...** too ... (for ...) to ... || **~bald** forthwith

also so; (*summarizing*) that is (to say); (*emotive particle*) then; so; well (then); *arch* thus; **~ gut!** all right then!; **~ los!** right, let's go!; off you go!; fire away!; **na ~!** you see!

alt (*comp, superl* ⸚) old; ancient; *in certain instances, expressed by* age (*eg* **so ~ wie ...** *also* the same age as ..., **doppelt so ~ wie ...** twice (s.o.'s) age, **nicht so ~ aussehen, wie man ist** not look one's age); **~ und jung** young and old; **~ kaufen** buy second-hand; **~ werden** grow old, age; **hier/heute werde ich nicht ~** *coll* I won't be staying here long/be staying up long tonight; **es bleibt**

alles beim ~en everything stays the same; **alles beim ~en lassen** leave things as they are; **älter..** older; elder; elderly; senior; **ältest..** oldest; eldest; **der Alte** (*decl as adj*) old man; *coll* boss; **die Alte** (*decl as adj*) old woman; **die A~en** *pl* old folk; the ancients; *ornith* the parent birds; **ganz der ~e sein** be the same as ever; **der/die Älteste** (*decl as adj*) eldest (son/daughter); *eccles etc* elder

der **Alt, -e** (= voice) alto; contralto; **die ~sängerin, -nen** contralto

alt- old ...; ancient ...; ex- ...; scrap ...; **~backen** stale; old-fashioned; **die A~bau|wohnung, -en** flat/apartment *US* in an old building; **~bekannt** familiar; **~berühmt** famous old; **~bewährt** well-tried; long-standing; **~ehr|würdig** venerable; time-honoured; **~eingesessen** old-established; **~gedient** veteran; **~gewohnt** familiar; **~hergebracht** traditional; **~hoch|deutsch, A~hoch|deutsch** Old High German; **~jüngferlich** old-maidish; **~klug** precocious; **das A~material** scrap; **der A~meister, -** doyen; *sp* ex-champion; **das A~metall** scrap metal; **~modisch** old-fashioned; **das A~papier** waste-paper; **der A~philologe, -n** (*wk masc*) classicist; **die A~philologie** (the) classics; **~sprachlich** (studies) classical; **die A~stadt** old (part of the) town/city; **die A~stein|zeit** the Palaeolithic; **~stein|zeitlich** Palaeolithic; **~testamentlich** Old Testament; **~väterlich** patriarchal; **die A~vordern** *pl* forbears; **die A~waren** *pl* second-hand goods; **der A~weiber|sommer** Indian summer; gossamer

der **Altan, -e** balcony

der **Altar, ⸚e** altar

Alten-: das ~heim, -e old people's home; **das ~teil, -e** part of farm retained by retiring farmer (**sich auf das A. zurückziehen** *also* retire from public life)

das **Alter** age; old age; **ein hohes ~ erreichen** live to a ripe old age; **im ~ von** at the age of; **im besten ~** in one's prime; **im gleichen ~ stehen** be the same age; **von hohem ~** of great antiquity

altern (*sn*) age; (wine) mature

alternativ (*in compds* **A~-**), **die Alternative, -n** alternative

alters: seit ~ = von ~ her since ancient times

Alters- ... of (old) age; age ...; old-age ...; **die ~erscheinung, -en** sign of old age; **die ~fürsorge** care of the aged; **der ~genosse, -n** (*wk masc*) contemporary; **die ~grenze, -n** age limit; retirement age ; **die ~gruppe, -n** age-group; **das ~heim, -e** old people's home; **die ~klasse, -n** age-group; **a~schwach** old and infirm; dilapidated; **die ~stufe, -n** age(-group); **das ~werk, -e** late work

das **Altertum** antiquity (= period); **die Altertümer** *pl* antiquities

altertümelnd archaizing

altertümlich ancient; old-fashioned

Altertums-: der ~forscher, - archaeologist; **die ~kunde = die ~wissenschaft** archaeology

der **Ältesten|rat** council of elders; (*W. Germany*) *committee advising* Bundestagspräsident *on conduct of parliamentary business etc*

die **Altistin, -nen** contralto

ältlich oldish

Alu- aluminium ..., aluminum ... *US*

das **Aluminium** aluminium, aluminum *US*; **die ~folie** tin foil

am = an dem; (*non-standard usage*) **~ (Schreiben** *etc*) **sein** be +*pres/part* (writing *etc*); *for* **~ ...sten** *see* **an** 3

a. M. = am Main

das **Amalgam, -e** amalgam

der **Amateur** [-'tøːɐ], **-e** amateur; *in compds* amateur ...

der **Amazonas** [-as] (*gen* -) the Amazon

die **Amazone, -n** *myth* Amazon; *equest* woman show-jumper

das **Ambiente** ambience

die **Ambition, -en** ambition

ambitioniert ambitious

ambitiös ambitious

ambivalent ambivalent

die **Ambivalenz** ambivalence

der **Amboß, -(ss)e** anvil

die **Ambra** ambergris

ambulant itinerant; *med* (as an) out-patient; **~er Patient** out-patient

die **Ambulanz, -en** ambulance; = **das Ambulatorium, -(i)en** *EGer* out-patients' department

die **Ameise** ['aː-], **-n** ant; **der ~n|bär, -en** (*wk masc*) ant-eater; **der ~n|haufen, -** ant-hill; **die ~n|säure** formic acid

das **Amen** ['aːmɛn], **-** amen; **sein ~ geben zu** give one's consent to; **zu allem ja und amen sagen** *coll* agree to everything

Amerika America

der **Amerikaner, -, amerikanisch** American

amerikanisieren Americanize

der **Amerikanismus, -(m)en** Americanism

der **Amerikanist, -en** (*wk masc*) specialist in/student of American language and literature

die **Amerikanistik** [-ɪk] American studies

der **Amethyst, -e** amethyst

der **Ami** ['a-], **-s** *coll* Yank

die **Amino|säuren** *pl* amino-acids

die **Amme, -n** wet-nurse; **das ~n|märchen, -** cock-and-bull story

die **Ammer, -n** bunting

das **Ammoniak** ammonia

das **Ammonium** ammonium
die **Amnesie, –(ie)n** amnesia
die **Amnestie, –(ie)n, amnestieren** amnesty
die **Amöbe, –n** amoeba
Amok ['aːmɔk]: ~ **laufen** run amok
amoralisch ['a–] amoral
amorph amorphous
die **Amorphie, –(ie)n** amorphism
die **Amortisation, –en** amortization; recovery of cost through profits
amortisieren amortize; recover (cost) through profits
amourös [–mu–] amorous
die **Ampel, –n** traffic lights/light *US*; hanging lamp/flowerpot
das **Ampere** [am'pɛːɐ] (*gen* –(s)), – ampere
der **Ampfer, –** dock
die **Amphibie** [–ĭə], **–n** *zool* amphibian; **das ~n|fahrzeug, –e, das ~n|flugzeug, –e** amphibian
amphibisch amphibious
das **Amphitheater, –** amphitheatre
amplifizieren amplify
die **Amplitude, –n** *phys* amplitude
die **Ampulle, –n** *anat* ampulla; *med* ampoule
die **Amputation, –en** amputation
amputieren amputate
die **Amsel, –n** blackbird
Amsterdam Amsterdam
das **Amt, ⸚er** office; duty; (administrative) department, office; *tel* exchange; *RC* sung mass; **seines ~es walten** discharge one's duties; **von ~s wegen** officially; by virtue of one's office || **der ~mann, ⸚er** (*senior official in middle grade of civil service*)
amtieren hold office; officiate; act; **~d** *also* incumbent
amtlich official
Amts– … of office; official …;
die ~anmaßung, –en unauthorized assumption of authority; **die ~dauer** term of office; **das ~deutsch** officialese; **das ~gericht, –e** district court; **die ~gewalt** authority; **die ~handlung, –en** official act; **die ~miene** official air; **der ~mißbrauch** abuse of authority; **die ~person, –en** official (**als A.** in an official capacity); **der ~schimmel** *coll* red tape; **der ~sitz, –e** official residence; office; **die ~stunden** *pl* office hours; **~weg** (**auf dem A.** through official channels); **das ~zeichen, –** dialling tone, dial tone *US*; **die ~zeit, –en** term of office
das **Amulett, –e** amulet
amüsant amusing
das **Amüsement** [–zə'mãː], **–s** amusement
amüsieren amuse; **sich ~** enjoy oneself; **sich ~ über** (*acc*) be amused at; **amüsiert** amused; (*adv*) in amusement
amusisch ['a–] lacking in aesthetic sense
an [an] **1** *prep* (+*acc*, *indicating motion*) on; against (wall *etc*); to (*also of letters etc*, *in dedications*); (sit down *etc*) by;

2 *prep* (+*dat*) (*see also* **am**) (*a*) (*indicating place*) at (place, crossroads, *etc*); in (the sky); on (chin, wall, coast, (= beside) the Danube, *Aust*, *Swiss* one's back, *etc*); (leaning *etc*) against; by; (hang *etc*) from;

(*b*) (*indicating time*) on (a certain day, afternoon, *etc*); in (**am Morgen/Nachmittag/Abend** in the morning/afternoon/evening); *SGer* at (Easter *etc*);

(*c*) (*indicating means*) (lead, recognize, *etc*) by; (illustrate) by means of; (*cause*) (die) of; (suffer) from;

(*d*) (*other senses*) in the way of (ideas, luggage, *etc*); (the best thing *etc*) about; (betrayal, consumption, criticism, loss, *etc*) of; (increase, boom, *etc*) in; (rich *etc*) in; (wealth) of;

3 am …sten (*eg* **schönsten**) most …(ly) (*eg* beautiful(ly)) (*in relative sense – contrast* **auf** 3);

4 *adv* on; (*in timetable*, *eg* **Bonn ~**) arrives at (B. *etc*)
es ist ~ … (*dat*) **zu …** it is up to … to …
~ – aus on–off
es ist ~ dem/nicht ~ dem it is a fact/not so
~ die … roughly …
~ … (*dat*) **entlang** along (the side of sth.)
~ sich in itself/themselves; as such; = **~ und für sich** basically; **er hat etwas (Komisches** *etc*) **~ sich** there is something (funny *etc*) about him; **das hat er so ~ sich** that's just his way; **es so ~ sich haben zu …** have this habit of (+*ger*)
von … ~ from … on(wards); **von heute ~** (as) from today
~ … (*dat*) **vorbei** past

---

an– *sep pref – general senses*:
(*i*) … on (*eg* **~löten** solder on);
(*ii*) … at …; … to … (*eg* **~lächeln** smile at, **~schreiben** write to);
(*iii*) *indicates treatment applied to something* (*eg* **~fetten** grease); *often* = … lightly, … slightly (*eg* **~braten** roast lightly, **~schmutzen** soil slightly);
(*iv*) begin to … (*eg* **~brennen** begin to burn); *cf* **~beißen** take a (first) bite of, **~lesen** read a few pages of;
(*v*) *indicates growth, accumulation* (*eg* **~sammeln** amass, **~schwellen** swell);
(*vi*) (+*dat*) *indicates imposition of something on someone* (*eg* **jmdm. etw. ~hängen** palm sth. off on s.o., pin sth. on s.o., saddle s.o. with sth.);
(*vii*) (+*dat*) *indicates recognition of a*

quality etc (*see* **anhören, anmerken, ansehen**);

(*viii*) **an(ge)... kommen** come ...ing along (*eg* **angerast/anmarschiert kommen** come tearing/marching along); *see the simple verb*, *eg* **rasen, marschieren**

---

die **Anabolika** *pl* anabolic steroids

der **Anachronismus** [–kr–], **–(m)en** anachronism

anachronistisch [–kr–] anachronistic

das **Anagramm, –e** anagram

anal (*in compds* **A~–**) anal

das **Analgetikum, –(k)a** analgesic

analog analogous; **der A~rechner, –** analog computer

die **Analogie, –(ie)n** analogy

der **Analphabet, –en** (*wk masc*) illiterate

das **Analphabetentum** illiteracy

analphabetisch illiterate

die **Analyse, –n** analysis

analysieren analyse

der **Analytiker, –** analyst

analytisch analytical

die **Anämie, –(ie)n** anaemia

anämisch anaemic

die **Ananas** ['ananas], **–(se)** pineapple

die **Anarchie** [–ç–], **–(ie)n** anarchy

anarchisch [–ç–] anarchic

der **Anarchist** [–ç–], **–en** (*wk masc*) anarchist

anarchistisch [–ç–] anarchistic

die **Anästhesie** anaesthesia

der **Anästhesist, –en** (*wk masc*) anaesthetist

anästhe(ti)sieren anaesthetize

Anatolien [–ĭən] Anatolia

der **Anatolier** [–ĭɐ], **–, anatolisch** Anatolian

der **Anatom, –en** (*wk masc*) anatomist

die **Anatomie, –(ie)n** anatomy; anatomical institute

anatomieren dissect

anatomisch anatomical

anbacken (*p/part* **angebacken**) bake lightly; (*v/i sn*) stick to the cake tin

anbahnen prepare the ground for; **sich ~** begin to develop; be in the offing

anbändeln: ~ mit *coll* get off with

der **Anbau** building (on); *agr* cultivation; (*pl* **–ten**) extension, annexe; **a~fähig** cultivable; **die ~fläche, –n** cultivable land; **die ~küche, –n** kitchen unit; **die ~möbel** *pl* unit furniture

anbauen add (building); *agr* cultivate, grow; (*v/i*) build an extension; **~ an** (*acc*) build onto

der **Anbeginn** beginning; **von ~** from the beginning

anbehalten* keep on

anbei enclosed

anbeißen* take a bite of, bite into; (*v/i*) swallow the bait; **zum Anbeißen sein/aussehen** *coll* look a treat

anbelangen: was ... anbelangt as far as ... is *etc* concerned

anbellen bark at

anberaumen arrange, fix (date, meeting, *etc*)

anbeten worship; adore

der **Anbeter, –** admirer; worshipper

Anbetracht: in ~ (+*gen*) in view of

anbetreffen*: was ... anbetrifft as far as ... is *etc* concerned

anbetteln beg from

die **Anbetung** worship; adoration

anbiedern: sich ~ bei try to ingratiate oneself with

anbieten* offer; **sich ~** offer oneself/one's services; present itself; (solution *etc*) suggest itself

anbinden* (*see also* **angebunden**) tie up (**an** *acc/dat* to); tether (to); **~ mit** pick a quarrel with

anblasen* blow at; *tech* blow in; *mus* blow the first notes on; *coll* bawl out; **~ mit** blow (smoke) at

anblecken bare its teeth at

anblenden flash one's lights at

der **Anblick, –e** sight; contemplation (of); **beim ~** (+*gen*) at the sight of

anblicken look at

anblinzeln squint at; wink at

anblitzen look daggers at

anbohren drill a hole in; tap; open up (oilfield); *coll* pump (for information)

anbranden (*sn*) surge

anbraten* brown; **kurz ~** sauté

anbräunen brown gently

anbrechen* crack; start (bottle *etc*); break into (banknote, savings); (*v/i sn*: day, era) dawn; (night) fall

anbremsen: (den Wagen) ~ brake gently

anbrennen* light; (*v/i sn*) catch fire; (food) burn

anbringen* (*see also* **angebracht**) install; put up; fix (**an** *dat* to); bring (along); make (complaint *etc*) (**bei** to); show off (knowledge); *coll* find a job/husband/buyer for

der **Anbruch** dawning; **bei/vor ~ des Tages/der Nacht** at/before daybreak/nightfall

anbrüllen roar at; bellow at

die **Andacht, –en** devotions; rapt attention; *eccles* short service

andächtig devout; rapt; (silence) solemn; (*adv*) *also* with rapt attention

Andalusien [–ĭən] Andalusia

der **Andalusier** [–ĭɐ], **–, andalusisch** Andalusian

andauern go on; last; persist; **~d** continual; constant; (*adv*) continually; constantly; *or conveyed by* ... keep(s) on ...

die **Anden** [–dn̩] *pl* the Andes

das **Andenken, –** memory (of); souvenir; memento; **zum ~ an** (*acc*) in remembrance of

ander.. other; different; (something *etc*) else; (day *etc*) next; **~es** something/anything else; other/different things; **alles ~e/nichts ~es als** anything/nothing but; **unter ~em** among other things; **zum ~en** secondly

ander–: ein ~mal some other time; **~wärtig, ~wärts** elsewhere; **~weitig** other; (*adv*) elsewhere; to someone else; otherwise

ander(e)n–: ~falls otherwise; **~orts** elsewhere; **~tags** the next day; **~teils** on the other hand

anderer|seits on the other hand

ändern, sich ~ alter; change; **ich kann es nicht ~** I can't help it; there's nothing I can do about it; **es ändert nichts an** (*dat*) it makes no difference to; **es ist nicht zu ~ = es läßt sich nicht ~** it can't be helped

anders (someone *etc*) else; differently; another way; (look *etc*) different; *coll* otherwise; **~ (Herr X** *etc*) not so (Mr X *etc*); **irgendwie ~** some other way; **~ als** different(ly) from; unlike; **~ ausgedrückt** to put it another way; **~ werden** change; **es geht nicht ~** there's no other way; **ich kann nicht ~** I can't help it; **ich kann nicht ~ als zu ...** I have no choice but to ...; **es kam ganz ~** it turned out quite differently

anders– differently ...; (*eg* **~farbig**) of a different (colour *etc*); **~artig** different; **die A~artigkeit** different nature; **~denkend** of a different opinion; dissenting; **~ge|artet** different; **~gläubig** of a different faith; **~herum** the other way round; *coll* 'queer'; **~lautend** (report) to the contrary; **~sprachig** written in/speaking another language; **~wie** *coll* some other way; **~wo** somewhere else; **~woher** from somewhere else; **~wohin** (go *etc*) somewhere else

andert|halb one and a half

die **Änderung, –en** change; alteration; **der ~s|antrag, ⸚e** *parl* amendment; **der ~s|vorschlag, ⸚e** suggested change

andeuten hint at; indicate; outline; (line *etc*) suggest; (+*dat*) intimate to; **sich ~** become apparent

die **Andeutung, –en** *vbl noun*; *also* allusion; indication; innuendo; hint

andichten write a poem to; (+*dat*) impute to

andicken thicken (soup)

andienen (+*dat*) press on

andocken: ~ an (*dat*) (spacecraft) dock with

andonnern *coll* roar at; **angedonnert kommen** come roaring along

der **Andrang** crowd; rush

andrängen (*sn*) press forward

Andreas [–as] Andrew

andrehen turn on; screw on; tighten; (+*dat*) *coll* palm off on

andrer *etc* = **anderer** *etc*; **~seits** on the other hand

androhen (+*dat of pers*) threaten (s.o.) with

die **Androhung, –en** threat

andrücken press on/together; **~ an** (*acc*) press against; **sich ~ an** (*acc*) snuggle up to

Äneas [–as] Aeneas

an|ecken (*sn*) bump into something; *coll* get people's backs up; **~ bei** *coll* get (s.o.'s) back up

die **Äneide** the Aeneid

an|eignen: sich *dat* **... ~** acquire; learn (language); adopt; appropriate

die **An|eignung, –en** acquisition; adoption; appropriation; **widerrechtliche ~** misappropriation

an|einander to *etc** each other (**see* **an**); **~ vorbei** past each other

an|einander– *sep pref* ... together; **~fügen** fit together; **~geraten*** (*sn*) come to blows; **~grenzen** be adjacent; **~grenzend** adjacent; **~prallen** (*sn*) collide; **~reihen** line up; string together; **~rücken** (*sn*) move closer together; **~stoßen*** (*sn*) collide; meet

die **Äneis** [–ɪs] the Aeneid

die **Anekdote, –n** anecdote

anekdotenhaft anecdotal

an|ekeln disgust

die **Anemone, –n** anemone

an|empfehlen* (*also insep*) (+*dat*) recommend to

an|empfunden simulated

–aner (*pl* –), *fem* **–anerin** (*pl* **–nen**) (*forming nouns*), **–anisch** (*forming adjectives*) –an, *eg* **der Mexikaner, die Mexikanerin, mexikanisch** Mexican

an|erbieten* (*also insep*): **sich ~ zu ...** offer to ...

das **An|erbieten, –** offer

an|erkannt *p/part*; *also* recognized; accepted;

an|erkannter|maßen by common consent

an|erkennen* (*also insep*) (*see also* **anerkannt**) acknowledge; recognize; **~d** approving; appreciative; **~s|wert** commendable

die **An|erkennung, –en** acknowledgement; recognition; approval

an|erziehen* (+*dat*) instil in

anfachen fan (embers); stir (up)

anfahren* head for; approach (corner); run into; bring (in vehicle); let fly at; *tech* bring into operation; (*v/i sn*) move off; drive up; **~ an** (*acc*) (*sn*) run into

die **Anfahrt, –en** journey, drive (to a place); (road) drive; approach

der **Anfall, ⸚e** attack; fit; yield (**an** *dat* of); amount (of work *etc*) accumulating; **einen ~ bekommen** have an attack/*coll* a fit

anfallen* set upon; (emotion) come over; (*v/i sn*) arise; accrue; accumulate; (gas *etc*) be produced (as by-product)

anfällig delicate; ~ **für** susceptible to

die **Anfälligkeit** delicacy; susceptibility

der **Anfang, ⸚e** beginning; (*pl*) beginnings; rudiments; ~ (**Januar** *etc*) at the beginning of; ~ (**Fünfzig/der Fünfziger** *etc*) **sein** be in one's early (fifties *etc*); **den ~ machen** start; **seinen ~ nehmen** (thing) begin

in prepositional phrases:

am ~ at first; (+*gen*) at the start of

für den ~ for a start

in den Anfängen stecken be in its infancy

von ~ an from the very start

zu ~ at first; to begin with

anfangen* begin, start; start up; set about; (*v/i*) begin, start

~ **mit** do with; (*v/i*) start with; begin; **mit ... nichts ~ können/nichts anzufangen wissen** not know what to do with; not know what to make of; **mit ... ist nichts anzufangen** ... is *etc* useless; **angefangen mit** starting with; **angefangen mit ... bis zu ...** from ... to ...

~ **von** *coll* start talking about; **immer wieder von ... ~** keep on about; **von vorne ~** start at the beginning; = **wieder von vorne ~** start all over again; **angefangen von** = **angefangen mit** (*see* ~ **mit** *above*)

der **Anfänger, –** beginner

anfänglich initial; (*adv*) at first, initially

anfangs 1 *adv* at first; 2 *prep* (+*gen*) *coll* at the beginning of

Anfangs– initial ...; starting ...; elementary ...; **der ~buchstabe, –n** (*like* **Buchstabe**) initial; **die ~gründe** *pl* rudiments

anfassen touch; take (s.o.) by the hand; treat; tackle; **mit ~** lend a hand; **sich ~** feel (rough *etc*)

anfauchen snap at; (cat) spit at

anfaulen (*sn*) begin to rot

anfechtbar disputable; open to question

anfechten* dispute; contest; challenge; (emotion) disquiet

die **Anfechtung, –en** *vbl noun*; *also* temptation

anfeinden show hostility towards

die **Anfeindung, –en** hostility

anfeixen *coll* smirk at

anfertigen make; produce; write; draw up; make up (medicine); ~ **lassen** have (sth.) made (up)/done

die **Anfertigung, –en** *vbl noun*; *also* production; preparation

anfeuchten moisten; sprinkle (linen)

anfeuern light (stove); spur on

anflehen implore (**um** for)

die **Anflehung, –en** entreaty

anfliegen* (aircraft) approach; operate to; (emotion) come over; (*v/i sn*) (aircraft) approach; (+*dat*) come easily to

der **Anflug, ⸚e** approach (of aircraft); touch (of); hint (of)

anfordern request; send for

die **Anforderung, –en** *vbl noun*; *also* request (*gen* for); (*pl*) demands; **große ~en stellen an** (*acc*) make great demands on

die **Anfrage, –n** enquiry; *parl* question (**kleine ~:** *dealt with in written reply*, **große ~:** *dealt with in session of Bundestag*); **auf ~** on request

anfragen inquire (**bei** of)

anfressen* nibble at; corrode; eat away

anfreunden: sich ~ become friends; **sich ~ mit** make friends with; get used to

anfügen add; (+*dat*) add to; enclose with

anfühlen feel; **sich ~** feel (rough *etc*)

die **Anfuhr** transport(ing)

anführen lead; command; cite; adduce; *coll* take in; **zu seiner Entschuldigung ~** make (sth.) one's excuse

der **Anführer, –** leader; ringleader

Anführungs–: die ~striche *pl* = **die ~zeichen** *pl* quotation marks

anfüllen fill (up)

die **Angabe, –n** indication; giving; *Aust* down-payment; *sp* service; *coll* showing off; (*pl*) information; data; details; instructions; (**genaue** *etc*) **~n machen über** (*acc*) give (accurate *etc*) information about; **nach ~n** (+*gen*) according to

angängig permissible; feasible

angeben* state; give; indicate; set (pace *etc*); *leg* name; (*v/i*) *cards* deal first; *sp* serve; *coll* show off; ~ **mit** estimate at; (*v/i*) *coll* show off with; boast about

der **Angeber, –** informer; *coll* show-off

angeberisch *coll* boastful

das **Angebinde, –** (small) gift

angeblich alleged; (*adv*) allegedly; reputedly; *or conveyed by* ... is *etc* said to ...

angeboren innate; *med* congenital

das **Angebot, –e** offer; first bid; range (**an** *dat* of); output (of films *etc*); *comm* supply (of); tender; **ein ~ machen für** make an offer for; *comm* tender for; ~ **und Nachfrage** supply and demand

angebracht *p/part*; *also* appropriate

angebunden *p/part*; **kurz ~** brusque, curt

angedeihen: (+*dat*) ~ **lassen** grant; bestow on; give (education *etc*)

angegangen *p/part*; *also* (gone) bad

angegossen: wie ~ passen/sitzen fit like a glove

angegraut greying

angegriffen *p/part*; *also* worn-out; *med* affected

angeheiratet (related) by marriage; **~e Verwandtschaft** in-laws

angeheitert 'merry'

angehen* (*see also* **angegangen**) approach (with a request); attack; tackle (task *etc*); (matter) concern; *sp* tackle, *equest* go at (fence), *mount* make an assault on, *mot* take (corner); (*v/i sn*) (fire) begin to burn; (light) go on; (plant) take root; **das geht noch/nicht an** that is tolerable/won't do; **sobald** *etc* **es angeht** as soon *etc* as possible; **was ... angeht** as far as ... is *etc* concerned; **was geht mich das an?** what has that got to do with me?

~ **gegen** (*sn*) fight (prejudice, verdict, *etc*)

~ **um** ask for

angehend budding; (star) in the making; (father *etc*) prospective; **ein ~er (Vierziger** *etc*) **sein** be rising (forty *etc*)

angehören (+*dat*) belong to; be a member of; **der Vergangenheit** ~ be a thing of the past

der **Angehörige** (*fem* **die** ~) (*decl as adj*) member; relative; (*pl*) family

der **Angeklagte** (*fem* **die** ~) (*decl as adj*) accused; defendant

angeknackst *p/part*; *coll* shaky

angekränkelt sickly

die **Angel, -n** hinge; fishing-rod; **aus den ~n heben** take (door) off its hinges; turn upside down

Angel- fishing ...; **das ~gerät, -e** fishing tackle; **der ~haken, -** fish-hook; **der ~punkt, -e** central point; keystone; **die ~rute, -n** fishing-rod; **der ~sachse, -n** (*wk masc*), **a~sächsisch** Anglo-Saxon; **der ~sport** angling

angelegen *p/part*; **sich** *dat* **... ~ sein lassen** make (sth.) one's concern; **es sich** *dat* **~ sein lassen zu ...** make a point of (+*ger*)

die **Angelegenheit, -en** matter; business; **auswärtige ~en** foreign affairs

angelegentlich insistent; eager

angelernt *p/part*; *also* semi-skilled

angeln catch; (*v/i*) fish (**auf** *acc*/**nach** for); **sich** *dat* **...** ~ *coll* hook (husband)

die **Angeln** *pl* the Angles

angemessen *p/part*; *also* appropriate, fitting; (price) reasonable; (*following dat*) appropriate (to); in keeping (with)

angenehm pleasant; **~e Reise!** have a good trip!; **~e Ruhe!** sleep well!; **(sehr) ~!** pleased to meet you!; (+*dat*) **~ sein** be welcome

angenommen *p/part*; **~, (daß) ...** assuming ..., supposing ...

angeregt *p/part*; *also* lively

angesäuselt *coll* tipsy

angeschlagen *p/part*; *also* groggy; *coll* shaky

angeschmutzt slightly soiled; *comm* shop-soiled

angeschrieben *p/part*; **gut/schlecht ~ bei** *coll* in (s.o.'s) good/bad books

angesehen respected; (firm) reputable

das **Angesicht** countenance; **im** ~ (+ *gen*) in the face of; **von ~ zu ~** face to face

angesichts (+*gen*) in view of; in the face of

angespannt *p/part*; *also* tense; (attention) close; *comm* tight; (*adv*: work) strenuously

angestammt inherited

angestaubt slightly dusty

der **Angestellte** (*fem* **die** ~) (*decl as adj*) (salaried) employee; clerk; **leitende(r) ~(r)** executive || **~n|verhältnis (im A. stehen** be employed as a salaried employee)

angestrengt *p/part*; *also* (attention) close; (*adv*) intently; strenuously

angetan *p/part*; **~ mit** clad in; **~ von** taken with; **danach/dazu ~ zu ...** such as to ...; calculated to ...; suitable for (+*ger*)

angetrunken *p/part*; *also* tipsy

angewandt *p/part*; *also* applied

angewiesen *p/part*; **~ auf** (*acc*) dependent on; **auf sich selbst ~ sein** be on one's own

angewöhnen (+*dat of pers*) get (s.o.) used to; **sich** *dat* **... ~** get into the habit of; (*eg* **sich Pünktlichkeit ~**) make a habit of (being punctual *etc*); **jmdm./sich** *dat* **~ zu ...** get s.o. into/get into the habit of (+*ger*); **sich** *dat* **das Trinken ~** take to drink

die **Angewohnheit, -en** habit

angewurzelt: wie ~ rooted to the spot

angezeigt *p/part*; *also* advisable

die **Angina, -(n)en** angina; tonsillitis

angleichen* (+*dat*) bring into line with; adjust to; **sich ~** (+*dat*) adapt to; fall into line with

die **Angleichung, -en** *vbl noun*; *also* adaptation (**an** *acc* to); adjustment (to)

der **Angler, -** angler

angliedern (+*dat*) incorporate in; attach to

die **Angliederung, -en** *vbl noun*; *also* incorporation (**an** *acc* into)

der **Anglikaner, -, anglikanisch** Anglican

anglisieren anglicize

der **Anglist, -en** (*wk masc*) English scholar; student of English

die **Anglistik** [-ɪk] English studies

der **Anglizismus, -(m)en** Anglicism

anglophil anglophile

anglophob anglophobe

die **Anglophobie** anglophobia

anglotzen *coll* gape at

Angola Angola

der **Angolaner, -, angolanisch** Angolan

Angora- angora ...

angreifen* (*see also* **angegriffen**) attack (*also sp*); draw on (reserves, savings, *etc*); affect; take it out of

der **Angreifer, -** attacker (*also sp*)

angrenzen: ~ an (*acc*) border on; **~d** bordering; neighbouring

der **Angriff, -e** attack (**auf** *acc*/**gegen** on) (*also* *sp*); *aer* raid; **in ~ nehmen** tackle

Angriffs– … of attack; attacking …; offensive …; **die ~fläche, –n** weak point; chink in s.o.'s armour; **die ~lust** aggressiveness; **a~lustig** aggressive; **der ~punkt, –e** point of attack; chink in s.o.'s armour; **die ~spitze, –n** *mil* spearhead (**die A. bilden** spearhead the attack); **das ~ziel, –e** *mil* objective

angrinsen grin at

angrunzen grunt at

angst: mir ist/wird ~ (und bange) I am/get scared (**vor** *dat* of); (+*dat*) **~ (und bange) machen** scare

die **Angst, ⸚e** fear (**vor** *dat* of); anxiety; **~ bekommen/haben** get/be frightened (**vor** *dat* of); **es mit der ~ zu tun bekommen** get scared; (+*dat*) **~ machen** scare; **keine ~, …** don't worry, …; **in ~ versetzen** frighten; **in tausend Ängsten schweben** be in a terrible state || **a~erfüllt** frightened; **das ~gefühl, –e** sense of anxiety; **der ~hase, –n** (*wk masc*) *coll* = **der ~meier, –** *coll* scaredy-cat; **der ~schweiß** cold sweat; **a~voll** frightened

ängstigen frighten; **sich ~** be frightened (**vor** *dat* of); worry (**um** about)

ängstlich anxious; timid; **~ darauf bedacht sein, daß …** be anxious that …; **~ bemüht sein zu …** be anxious to …

angucken *coll* look at

angurten: sich ~ fasten one's seat-belt

Anh. = **Anhang**

anhaben* *coll* have on; **… kann (mir** *etc***) nichts ~** … cannot harm; … cannot touch

anhaften (+*dat*) stick to; (smell) cling to; attach to; be inherent in

anhaken: ~ an (*acc*) hook onto

der **Anhalt** clue; grounds (for suspicion)

anhalten* stop; hold (breath, note); urge (to); (+*dat*) hold up against; (*v/i*) stop; persist, (weather) hold; **mit angehaltenem Atem** with bated breath; **~ um** ask for (a girl's) hand in marriage; **zur Ordnung/Pünktlichkeit ~** get (s.o.) to be orderly/punctual; **~d** persistent; (applause) prolonged

der **Anhalter, –** hitch-hiker; **per ~ fahren** *coll* hitch-hike

der **Anhalts|punkt, –e** clue; grounds; guide

anhand (+*gen*) with the aid of

der **Anhang, ⸚e** appendix; family; followers

Anhänge–: das ~schloß, ⸚(ss)er padlock

anhängen hang up (**an** *acc* on); attach (to); join on (to); append (*dat*/**an** *acc* to); *coll* do (… terms *etc*) in addition; (+*dat*) *coll* pin on, saddle with; palm off on; (*v/i*: **~***, *like* **hängen** *v/i*) (+*dat*) be an adherent of; (reputation *etc*) stay with; **die Krankheit hängt mir noch an** I still feel the effects of the illness

sich ~ hang on; **sich ~ an** (*acc*) hang on to; tag on to

der **Anhänger, –** supporter; trailer; pendant; tie-on label, tag

die **Anhängerschaft** following; adherents

anhängig (lawsuit) pending; **~ machen** institute (proceedings)

anhänglich devoted

die **Anhänglichkeit** devotion

das **Anhängsel, –** appendage; pendant

der **Anhauch** touch (of)

anhauchen breathe on; *coll* bawl out; **rosig angehaucht** tinged with pink; **(romantisch** *etc***) angehaucht** (romantically *etc*) inclined

anhauen* start chopping; (*p/t only* **haute an**) *coll* accost; **~ um** *coll* touch for

anhäufen accumulate, amass; **sich ~** accumulate

die **Anhäufung, –en** accumulation

anheben* raise; (*v/i*) (*p/t also* **hub an**) *poet* begin

anheften attach (**an** *acc*/*dat* to); clip on(to); pin up (notice) (on); tack on(to); (+*dat*) **einen Orden ~** pin a medal on

anheim– *sep pref*

anheimeln make (s.o.) feel at home; give (s.o.) a cosy feeling; **~d** homely, cosy

anheimfallen* (*sn*) (+*dat*) pass to; fall a victim to; fall into (oblivion)

anheimgeben* (+*dat*) entrust to; **sich ~** (+*dat*) entrust oneself to; give oneself up to

anheimstellen (+*dat*) leave to (s.o.'s) discretion; **sich dem Schicksal ~** abandon oneself to one's fate

anheischig: sich ~ machen zu … undertake to …

anheizen light (stove); stimulate; exacerbate

anherrschen bark at

anheuern sign on; *coll* hire

anheulen howl at

Anhieb *coll*: **auf ~** at the first attempt; right away

anhimmeln *coll* idolize; gaze adoringly at

die **Anhöhe, –n** (small) hill

anhören hear (witness *etc*); (*also* + **sich** *dat*) listen to; (+*dat*) hear in (s.o.'s) voice; be able to tell from (s.o.'s) voice; **mit ~** overhear; **man hört ihm den Deutschen an** you can tell he's German (by his accent); **sich (gut** *etc***) ~** sound (good *etc*)

die **Anhörung, –en** *parl* hearing

anhupen honk at

das **Anhydrid, –e** anhydride

das **Anilin** aniline

animalisch animal

Animier–: die ~kneipe, –n *coll* = **das ~lokal, –e** bar (with hostesses); **das ~mädchen, –** hostess (in bar *etc*)

animieren encourage (to); *cin* animate; **animiert** in high spirits

die **Animosität** animosity

der **Anis, –e** aniseed; *bot* anise

Ank. (= **Ankunft**) arr.

ankämpfen: ~ gegen battle with; fight; fight back (tears)

der **Ankauf, ⸚e** purchase

ankaufen purchase; **sich ~ in** (*dat*) buy a place in

der **Ankäufer, –** buyer

der **Anker, –** anchor; *elect* armature; **vor ~ gehen** cast anchor; *coll* settle down; **vor ~ liegen** ride at anchor || **die ~kette, –n** cable; **der ~platz, ⸚e** anchorage; **die ~winde, –n** capstan

ankern anchor; lie at anchor

anketten chain (up) (**an** *acc/dat* to)

die **Anklage, –n** accusation, *leg* charge; indictment (**gegen** of: abuses *etc*); *leg* prosecution (= prosecuting party); **~ erheben gegen** bring charges against; **unter ~ stellen** charge (**wegen** with); **unter ~ stehen** be charged (**wegen** with); be on trial (for) || **die ~bank** dock (**auf der A. sitzen** be in the dock); **die ~schrift, –en** indictment; **der ~vertreter, –** counsel for the prosecution

anklagen accuse (*gen*/**wegen** of), *leg* charge (with); be an indictment of

der **Ankläger, –** accuser; *leg* prosecutor

anklägerisch accusing

anklammern peg, pin *US* (**an** *acc* on); clip (to); **sich ~ an** (*acc*) cling to

der **Anklang, ⸚e** echo (**an** *acc* of); **~ finden** go down well (**bei** with)

ankleben stick on/up; hang (wallpaper); **~ an** (*dat*) (*sn*) stick to

ankleckern *coll*: **angekleckert kommen** come bothering one; come in dribs and drabs

Ankleide–: die ~kabine, –n cubicle; **der ~raum, ⸚e** changing/dressing-room

ankleiden, sich ~ dress

anklingen* be discernible; **~ an** (*acc*) be reminiscent of; **in seinen Worten klingt ... an** there is a hint of ... in his words

anklopfen: (an die/der Tür) ~ knock at the door; **~ bei** knock at (s.o.'s) door; **bei ... um/wegen ... ~** *coll* ask (s.o.) if one may have

anknabbern nibble at; eat into (savings)

anknacksen (*see also* **angeknackst**) *coll* crack; crack a bone in; dent (pride)

anknipsen *coll* switch on

anknöpfen button on; **~ an** (*acc*) button onto

anknüpfen tie on; establish (relations), start up; **~ an** (*acc*) tie to; (*v/i*) take up (remarks); continue (tradition); **~ mit** establish contact with

Anknüpfung: in ~ an (*acc*) with reference to || **der ~s|punkt, –e** point of contact; starting-point (for conversation)

anknurren growl at

ankommen* (*sn*) (feeling) come over; (*v/i*) arrive; approach; **(gut) ~** go down well; **hart ~** be hard for

~ auf (*acc*) depend on; **es kommt auf ... an** ... matter(s); **es kommt mir auf ... an** what matters to me is ... ; **es kommt darauf an** it all depends; **darauf kommt es (nicht) an** that's (not) the point; **es auf ... ~ lassen** risk

~ bei go down well with; get a job with; **bei ... nicht ~ mit** not get anywhere with

~ gegen stand up to; get the better of; **nicht ~ gegen** be no match for

~ mit: immer wieder ~ mit keep on asking (questions)

der **Ankömmling, –e** newcomer

ankönnen* *coll*: **nicht ~ gegen** be no match for

ankoppeln couple on

ankotzen *vulg* puke over; make sick

ankratzen scratch (slightly); harm (reputation *etc*); **sich** *dat* **einen/eine ~** *coll* get a boy/girl-friend; **sich ~ bei** *coll* suck up to

ankreiden (+*dat*) hold against

ankreuzen put a cross against

ankündigen announce; herald; **sich ~** (spring *etc*) be in the air; **sich ~ durch** (illness *etc*) be preceded by

die **Ankündigung, –en** announcement

die **Ankunft** arrival; **die ~s|tafel, –n** arrivals board; **die ~s|zeit, –en** time of arrival

ankuppeln couple on

ankurbeln boost; step up; *mot* crank up (engine)

Anl. (= **Anlage**) encl.

anlächeln smile at

anlachen beam at; (sun) smile on; **sich** *dat* **... ~** *coll* get off with; **der Kuchen lacht mich an** the cake looks very tempting

die **Anlage, –n** installation; construction; laying out; arrangement; lay-out; structure (of play *etc*); composition (of painting); enclosure (in letter); predisposition; aptitude, talent (**zu** for); *fin* investment; (*pl*) grounds; park; installations; facilities; plant; **in der/als ~** enclosed || **das ~kapital** invested capital

anlangen (*sn exc* **was ... anlangt**) arrive; **~ bei** reach; **was ... anlangt** as regards

der **Anlaß, ⸚(ss)e** reason, cause (**zu** for); occasion; **aus ~** (+*gen*) on the occasion of; **beim geringsten ~** on the slightest pretext; **~ geben zu** give rise to

anlassen* start (engine); keep on; leave on/burning; *tech* anneal; **sich gut ~** start well; make a good start

der **Anlasser, –** starter

anläßlich (+*gen*) on the occasion of

anlasten (+*dat of pers*) accuse (s.o.) of; blame (s.o.) for; put (blame) on

der **Anlauf, ⸚e** attempt; start; *sp* run-up; *ski* approach run; *mil* assault; ~ **nehmen** take a run-up; +**zu** prepare for; **einen neuen ~ nehmen** start afresh || **die ~zeit, -en** time for preparations; *mot* warming-up time

anlaufen* (ship) call at; (*also sn*) *sp* run (at a certain speed *etc*); (*v/i sn*) start (up); (metal) tarnish; (glass) cloud over; (costs) mount up; *sp* run up; (**rot** *etc*) ~ turn (red *etc*); ~ **lassen** start up (engine); **angelaufen kommen** come running up

der **Anlaut, -e** *ling* initial sound; **im** ~ in initial position

anläuten *sp* ring the bell for

Anlege-: die ~brücke, -n = der ~steg, -e landing-stage; **die ~stelle, -n** landing-place; mooring

anlegen put on; chain up; give (child) the breast; (horse *etc*) put back (ears); apply (criterion); start; lay in (stock); design; lay out (garden); draw up (list *etc*); *fin* invest; (+*dat*) put on; (*v/i*) take aim; (ship) put in; **(mit) Hand** ~ lend a hand; **(die) letzte Hand** ~ put the finishing touches; **groß angelegt** on a grand scale; **angelegt in** (*dat*) present in embryo in

~ **an** (*acc*) place against; apply (criterion) to

~ **auf** (*acc*) take aim at; **es darauf ~ zu ...** make a point of (+*ger*); be set on (+*ger*); **es darauf angelegt haben zu ...** be out to ...; **angelegt sein auf** be aimed at

~ **für** spend on

sich ~ mit pick a fight with; take on

anlehnen leave ajar/slightly open; ~ **an** (*acc*) lean against; **sich ~ an** (*acc*) lean against; follow (model); **angelehnt** ajar; slightly open

die **Anlehnung** dependence (**an** *acc* on); borrowing (from author *etc*); ~ **suchen an** (*acc*) look to (s.o.) for support; **in ~ an** (*acc*) following || **das ~s|bedürfnis** need of affection; **a~s|bedürftig** needing affection

die **Anleihe, -n** loan; **eine ~ machen bei** borrow from

anleimen glue on

anleinen put on the lead

anleiten instruct; ~ **zu** teach (s.o. sth.)

die **Anleitung, -en** instruction; guidance; instructions

Anlern-: der ~beruf, -e job requiring 1–2 years' training (but not apprenticeship); **die ~zeit** period of training for an *Anlernberuf*

anlernen (*see also* **angelernt**) train; **sich** *dat* **...** ~ acquire (knowledge) by learning

der **Anlernling, -e** trainee

anlesen* read a few pages of; **sich** *dat* **...** ~ acquire (knowledge) from books

anliefern deliver

die **Anlieferung** delivery

anliegen* (*see also* **angelegen**) (+*dat*) be of concern to; **eng** ~ be a tight fit; **~d** adjacent; enclosed; **eng ~d** tight-fitting

das **Anliegen, -** request; wish; concern; **ein ~ haben an** (*acc*) have a favour to ask of

der **Anlieger, -** resident (of road)

anlocken lure; attract

anlöten solder on

anlügen* lie to

Anm. = Anmerkung

anmachen switch on; light (fire); put up; mix; dress (salad); *coll* chat up (with sexual intent)

anmahnen send (s.o.) a reminder about

anmalen paint; **sich** ~ *coll* paint one's face

der **Anmarsch** *mil* advance; **im** ~ advancing; *coll* on the way

anmaßen: sich *dat* **...** ~ arrogate to oneself; assume; **sich** *dat* ~ **zu ...** take it upon oneself to (do sth.); claim to (be sth.); **sich** *dat* **ein Urteil ~ über** (*acc*) presume to express an opinion on; **~d** arrogant, presumptuous

die **Anmaßung, -en** arrogance, presumption; arrogation (of); assumption (of)

Anmelde- registration ...; **das ~formular, -e** application/entry/registration form; **die ~pflicht** compulsory registration

anmelden announce; enrol (**zu** for); enter (for); register; apply for (patent); express (doubts), make known (wishes), assert (claim), lodge (protest); *tel* book, place *US* (call); **haben Sie etwas anzumelden?** have you anything to declare?; **angemeldet sein** have an appointment (**bei** with)

sich ~ report (on arrival); register (**polizeilich** with the police); enrol (**zu** for); enter (for); make an appointment (**bei** with); **ein Kind hat sich angemeldet** a baby is on the way

die **Anmeldung, -en** *vbl noun*; *also* registration; application (for patent); enrolment; *tel* booking, placing *US* (of call); announcement (of visitor); reception (desk); **nur nach vorheriger** ~ only by appointment || **das ~s|formular, -e** application/entry/registration form

anmerken mark (in red *etc*); remark; (+*dat*) notice about; notice (s.o.'s embarrassment *etc*); **man merkt ihm an, daß er ...** one can tell that he ...; **sich** *dat* **...** ~ **lassen** show (emotion *etc*); **sich** *dat* **nichts ~ lassen** not let on

die **Anmerkung, -en** (foot)note; **Ausgabe mit ~en** annotated edition

anmessen* (*see also* **angemessen**) (+*dat of*

pers) measure for (suit *etc*); **sich** *dat* **... ~ lassen** be measured for

die **Anmut** grace; charm (of landscape *etc*)

anmuten seem (odd *etc*) (to)

anmutig graceful; charming

Anna Anne

annageln nail on/up; **~ an** (*acc/dat*) nail to

annähen sew on

annähern (+*dat*) bring closer to/more into line with; **sich ~** approach; (+*dat*) come closer to; **sich** *dat pl* **(einander) ~** come closer to one another; **~d** approximate; **nicht ~d** nowhere near

die **Annäherung, -en** approach; approximation (**an** *acc* to); coming closer; *pol* rapprochement; **der ~s|versuch, -e** overtures, advances; **a~s|weise** approximately; **der ~s|wert, -e** approximate value

die **Annahme, -n** acceptance, (refuse *etc*) to accept; adoption; assumption; taking (on); passing; counter/office for handing in lottery coupons/laundry *etc*; **~ an Kindes Statt** adoption; **der ~ sein, daß ...** assume that ...; **in der ~, daß ...** on the assumption that ...; **„~ von ..."** '... repaired'; 'we buy ...' || **die ~stelle, -n** counter/office for handing in lottery coupons/laundry *etc*

die **Annalen** *pl* annals

annehmbar acceptable; decent (= quite good)

annehmen* (*see also* **angenommen**) accept; assume, take on; adopt (custom *etc*); fall into (habit); pass (resolution *etc*); assume, presume; (substance) take; *sp* receive (ball); **(an Kindes Statt) ~** adopt; **Gestalt ~** take shape; **Vernunft ~** see reason; **man sollte ~, daß ...** you'd think that ...

sich ~ (+*gen*) look after; take on; take up

die **Annehmlichkeit, -en** convenience; (*pl*) amenities

annektieren annex

die **Annexion, -en** annexation

annieten rivet on

Anno: ~ (1749 *etc*) *arch* in the year; **~ dazumal** in the olden days; **aus/von ~ Tobak** from the olden days

die **Annonce** [-'nɔ̃:sə], **-n** advertisement

annoncieren [-nɔ̃s-] (*also v/i*) advertise

annullieren cancel (contract *etc*); *leg* annul; quash

die **Anode, -n** anode

an|öden *coll* bore; pester

anomal ['a-] anomalous; abnormal

die **Anomalie, -(ie)n** anomaly; abnormality

anonym anonymous

die **Anonymität** anonymity

der **Anorak** ['anorak], **-s** anorak

an|ordnen arrange; order (release *etc*)

die **An|ordnung, -en** arrangement; order

anorganisch ['anˀ-] inorganic

anormal ['a-] abnormal

anpacken take hold of; tackle; treat; **mit ~** lend a hand

anpassen (+*dat*) make (sth.) fit; adapt to; tailor to; bring into line with; **sich ~** adapt (*dat* to)

die **Anpassung** adaptation (**an** *acc* to); adjustment (to); **a~s|fähig** adaptable; flexible; **die ~s|fähigkeit = das ~s|vermögen** adaptability; flexibility

anpeilen take a bearing on; *coll* set one's sights on

anpfeifen* (*also* **das Spiel ~**) *sp* blow the whistle (for play to start); *coll* bawl out

der **Anpfiff, -e** *sp* whistle (at kick-off); *coll* dressing-down

anpflanzen plant; cultivate

die **Anpflanzung, -en** planting; cultivation

anpflaumen *coll* pull (s.o.'s) leg

anpinseln paint

anpirschen: sich ~ an (*acc*) stalk; creep up on

anpöbeln *coll* hurl abuse at

der **Anprall** impact

anprallen (*sn*): **~ an** (*acc*)/**gegen** strike; collide with; (rain) beat against

anprangern denounce

anpreisen* extol

die **Anprobe, -n** fitting

anprobieren try on

anpumpen *coll* touch (for a loan)

der **Anrainer, -** *SGer* resident (of road); neighbour

anranzen *coll* bawl out

der **Anranzer, -** *coll* telling-off

anrasen: angerast kommen come tearing along

anraten* recommend (*dat* to); (+*dat*) **dringend ~ zu ...** urge to ...; **auf Anraten** (+*gen*) on the recommendation of

anräuchern smoke lightly

anrechnen charge (price); make s.o. an allowance on (car *etc*); (+*dat*) charge for; count (towards sth.); **~ als** count as; **jmdm./sich** *dat* **... als/zum Verdienst ~** give s.o./take the credit for; **~ auf** (*acc*) count towards; (+*dat*) **~ für** allow (amount) on; (+*dat*) **hoch ~** think highly of ... for; **zuviel ~** overcharge; **zuwenig ~** undercharge

Anrechnung: in ~ bringen = anrechnen

das **Anrecht, -e** right (**auf** *acc* to); claim (to); *theat etc* subscription

die **Anrede, -n** form of address

anreden speak to (**auf ...** (*acc*) **hin** about); address (**mit** as/by); **~ gegen** make oneself heard above

anregen (*see also* **angeregt**) suggest; stimulate; *phys* excite; **~ zu** stimulate to; encourage to do; give (s.o.) the idea for;

prompt (thoughts); **~d** stimulating; **~des Mittel** stimulant

[die] **Anregung, -en** suggestion; idea (**zu** for); stimulation; *phys* excitation; **das ~s|mittel, -** stimulant

anreichern enrich; increase

[die] **Anreicherung, -en** enrichment

anreihen (*in 1st sense also p/t* **rieh an,** *p/part* **angeriehen**) tack on; **~ an** (*acc*) add to; **sich ~** join the queue/line *US*; **ein Unglück** *etc* **reiht sich an das andere an** one misfortune *etc* follows another

[die] **Anreise, -n** journey (to a place); arrival

anreisen (*sn*) travel (to a place); arrive; **angereist kommen** arrive

anreißen* make a slight tear in; start up; strike (match); broach (topic); *tech* scribe; *coll* break into (savings *etc*); start

[der] **Anreiz, -e** incentive

anreizen stimulate; whet; spur on (**zu** to); encourage (to)

anrempeln barge into

anrennen* (*sn*): **~ an** (*acc*) run into; **~ gegen** run into; fight (prejudice *etc*); *mil* storm; **angerannt kommen** come running along

[die] **Anrichte, -n = der ~tisch, -e** sideboard

anrichten prepare (food) for serving; cause, do; **~ mit** garnish with; **es ist angerichtet** dinner *etc* is served

anrollen roll up (barrels *etc*); (*v/i sn*) roll up; begin to roll; *aer* taxi up

anrüchig disreputable; shady

anrucken start with a jolt

anrücken move up; (*v/i sn*) approach; *coll* turn up; **~ an** (*acc*) move (object) up to

[der] **Anruf, -e** *tel* call; *mil* challenge; **~ genügt** just give us a call || **der ~be|antworter, -** telephone-answering machine

anrufen* call to; hail; call on, invoke; appeal to (*also leg*); *mil* (sentry) challenge; *tel* ring (up), call (up); **~ bei** *tel* ring, call

[der] **Anrufer, -** caller

anrühren touch (*usu with neg*); mix; touch on (topic); move, affect

ans = an das

ansäen sow

[die] **Ansage, -n** announcement; *cards* call

ansagen announce; *cards* call; (+*dat*) dictate to; (+*dat*) **den Kampf ~** declare war on; **sich ~ bei** let (s.o.) know that one is coming

[der] **Ansager, -** announcer; compère

ansammeln accumulate; amass; **sich ~** gather; accumulate; build up

[die] **Ansammlung, -en** accumulation; collection; crowd

ansässig, der/die Ansässige (*decl as adj*) resident; **sich ~ machen** take up residence

[der] **Ansatz, ⸚e** beginning(s), first signs (**zu** of); attempt (at); approach; base (of neck *etc*); layer; formation; *comm* estimate; *math* formulation; *mus* intonation; embouchure; *tech* extension; attachment; **in ~ bringen** estimate || **der ~punkt, -e** point of departure; **das ~stück, -e** attachment; extension

ansaufen* *coll*: **sich** *dat* **einen ~** get plastered

ansaugen (*see* **saugen**) suck in; attract, draw; **sich ~** attach itself (by suction)

anschaffen (*also* + **sich** *dat*) get (oneself), acquire

[die] **Anschaffung, -en** acquisition; purchase

anschalten switch on

anschauen *esp SGer* look at; **sich** *dat* **... ~** have a look at

anschaulich graphic; vivid; (visually) clear; **~ machen** illustrate

[die] **Anschauung, -en** view; contemplation; **aus eigener ~** from experience; **der ~ sein, daß ...** take the view that ... || **das ~s|material** visual aids; **der ~s|unterricht** instruction using visual aids; object-lesson; **die ~s|weise, -n** approach

[der] **Anschein** appearance; impression; **sich** *dat* **den ~ geben, als (ob) ...** pretend that ...; **es hat den ~, als (ob) ...** it looks as if ...; **allem ~ nach** to all appearances

anscheinend apparently

anscheißen* *vulg* give (s.o.) hell; play a dirty trick on; **angeschissen kommen** show up (though unwelcome)

anschicken: sich ~ zu ... prepare to ...

anschieben* push-start

anschielen cast a sidelong glance at

anschießen* wound (by shooting)

[der] **Anschiß, -(ss)e** *vulg* bawling-out

[der] **Anschlag, ⸚e** notice (on board *etc*); touch (of pianist *etc*); beating (of waves); striking (of key by typist); space (in typing); attack (**auf** *acc* on), attempt (on s.o.'s life); *comm* estimate; *tech* stop; *swim* touch; **in ~ bringen** take into account; **das Gewehr in ~ bringen** take aim

anschlagen* (*see also* **angeschlagen**) strike; chip; nail on; put up (notice); aim (gun) (**auf** *acc* at); broach (topic, *Aust* cask); adopt (tone); estimate; (*v/i*) strike the keys (in typing); (bell) ring; (clock) strike; (dog) bark; (medicine) take effect; *swim* touch; **~ an** (*acc*) (*sn*) (waves) beat against; **~ bei** *coll* make (s.o.) put on weight; **mit dem Kopf** *etc* **~** (*sn*) bump one's head *etc* (**an** *acc* against); **hoch ~** rate highly

anschleichen* creep up on; **sich ~** creep up (**an** *acc* on); **angeschlichen kommen** come creeping up

anschleppen drag along; bring along; *mot* tow (to get it started)

anschließen* padlock (**an** *dat* to); chain (to); connect (**an** *acc* to; *also tech*, *elect* (to system, supply, *etc*)); add (observation *etc*);

(+*dat*) affiliate to; attach to; add to; **eng ~** be a tight fit; **~ an** (*acc*) adjoin; follow
sich ~ (+*dat*) join; subscribe to (view); **sich ~ an** (*acc*) adjoin; follow; make friends with; **sich leicht/schwer ~** make/not make friends easily; **an ... schloß sich ... an** ... was followed by ...; **darf ich mich ~?** may I join you?

anschließend adjacent; following, ensuing; (*adv*) afterwards; **~ an** (*acc*) after, following

der **Anschluß, ⸚(ss)e** connection (**an** *acc* to: mains, water supply, *etc*); contact (**an** *acc* with); affiliation (to); *tel* line; *comput* link; *rail* connection; *pol* incorporation (**an** *acc* in); **(der ~)** the Anschluss (*Germany's annexation of Austria, 1938*); **~ bekommen** get a connection; catch up (**an** *acc* with); *tel* get through (to); **~ finden** get to know people; **+an** (*acc*) catch up with; **~ haben an** (*acc*) connect with; **wann habe ich ~ nach ...?** when is there a connection to ...?; **keinen ~ haben** not know anyone; **~ suchen** try to get to know people; **den ~ verpassen** miss one's connection; *coll* miss the boat; **kein ~ unter dieser Nummer** *tel* number unobtainable; **im ~ an** (*acc*) following; further to (letter)

Anschluß– connecting ...; **die ~dose, –n** wall-socket; **das ~kabel, –** lead; **das ~tor, –e** goal bringing a team within one goal of the opposition; **der ~zug, ⸚e** connecting train

anschmachten gaze at languishingly

anschmieden forge on

anschmiegen: sich ~ an (*acc*) snuggle up to; fit snugly

anschmiegsam affectionate

anschmieren daub (wall *etc*); *coll* take for a ride; **sich ~** make oneself dirty; daub oneself; **sich ~ bei** *coll* suck up to

Anschnall–: der ~gurt, –e seat-belt

anschnallen strap on; put on (skates, skis); strap in; **sich ~** fasten one's seat-belt

anschnauzen *coll* bawl out

der **Anschnauzer, –** *coll* dressing-down

anschneiden* cut into; broach (topic); *archaeol* discover (while excavating); *phot* show a section of; *sp* cut (corner); put spin on

der **Anschnitt, –e** first slice; cut end

die **Anschovis** [–ɪs], **–** anchovy

anschrauben screw on

anschreiben* (*see also* **angeschrieben**) write up; write to (officially); start using (pen); *Swiss* label; **~ gegen** attack (by writing); **Punkte ~** score; **~ lassen** buy on credit

anschreien* yell at

die **Anschrift, –en** address

anschuldigen accuse (*gen*/**wegen** of)

die **Anschuldigung, –en** accusation

anschüren stoke up; foment

anschwärmen idolize

anschwärzen blacken; *coll* run down

anschweigen* say nothing to

anschweißen weld on

anschwellen swell; increase; (*v/i*: **~***, *like* **schwellen** *v/i*) (*sn*) swell; **~ zu** blow up into; (*v/i* sn*) swell into

die **Anschwellung, –en** swelling

anschwemmen (sea *etc*) wash up

die **Anschwemmung, –en** *vbl noun*; *also* alluvial deposit

anschwindeln *coll* tell (s.o.) a fib

ansegeln make for (port *etc*)

ansehen* (*see also* **angesehen**) look at; view (matter); **sich** *dat* **... ~** have a look at; watch (programme); see (film, sights, *etc*); look into (matter); (+*dat*) be able to tell (**an** *dat* from); **~ als/für** regard as; take for; **mit ~** watch (passively); witness; **ich kann es nicht mit ~** I can't bear to see/watch it; **man sieht ihm (den Bayern/die schlechte Laune** *etc*) **an** you can tell he's (a Bavarian/in a bad mood *etc*); **man sieht ihm sein Alter nicht an** he doesn't look his age; **sieh mal (einer) an!** fancy that!; **sieh dir das an!** I *ask* you!
sich (schön *etc*) **~** look (lovely *etc*); **sich ~ als** regard oneself as

das **Ansehen** reputation; standing; **ein anderes ~ bekommen** assume a different complexion; **in hohem ~ stehen** be held in high regard (**bei** by); **ohne ~ der Person** without respect of persons; **vom/von ~** by sight

ansehnlich considerable; handsome

anseilen rope up; rope (together); **sich ~** rope up

ansengen singe

ansetzen put into position; apply (knife *etc*); raise to one's lips; put (pen) to paper; add; join on; sew on; become coated with; arrange (meeting *etc*); estimate; *bot* bear (fruit); *cul* prepare (punch *etc*); *math* set up; (*v/i*) begin; *cul* stick to the pan; *bot* set; **Blätter ~** come into leaf; **(Fett) ~** put on weight; **(Knospen) ~** bud; **Rost ~** rust; **angesetzt kommen** come bounding along
~ an (*acc*) put up against; apply (tool *etc*) to; **~ an** (*acc/dat*) add to; join onto; sew onto
~ auf (*acc*) arrange (meeting *etc*) for; put on (s.o.'s) trail; put onto (project *etc*); estimate at; **auf die Fährte ~** put (dog) on the trail
~ für arrange (meeting *etc*) for; allow (time) for
~ zu begin (sprint finish *etc*); (*followed by vbl noun, eg* **zum Sprechen ~**) begin to (speak *etc*); **zur Landung ~**

come in to land; **zum Sprung ~** get ready to jump
sich ~ form; *cul* stick to the pan

die **Ansicht, -en** view; opinion, view; **nach ~** (+*gen*) according to; **meiner ~ nach** in my opinion; **der ~ sein, daß ...** take the view that ... ; **zur ~** on approval; for inspection

ansichtig: (+*gen*) **~ werden** catch sight of

Ansichts-: die ~(post)karte, -n picture postcard; **~sache (das ist A.** that's a matter of opinion)

ansiedeln, sich ~ settle; **... ist (hier** *etc*) **anzusiedeln** ... belongs (here *etc*)

der **Ansiedler, -** settler

die **Ansiedlung, -en** settlement

das **Ansinnen, -** (unreasonable) request

ansonst *Aust, Swiss* otherwise

ansonsten otherwise

anspannen (*see also* **angespannt**) harness; yoke; tauten, tighten; tense (muscles); strain; concentrate (attention *etc*); summon up (energy); **sich ~** tauten

die **Anspannung** *vbl noun*; *also* exertion; strain

anspeien* spit on

das **Anspiel, -e** start of play

anspielen *sp* pass the ball to; *mus* play a few notes on/bars of; (*v/i*) *cards* lead; *sp* start playing, *footb* kick off; **~ auf** (*acc*) allude to

die **Anspielung, -en** *vbl noun*; *also* allusion (**auf** *acc* to)

anspinnen* start up; **sich ~** develop, start up

anspitzen sharpen; *coll* keep on his/her toes

der **Ansporn** spur, stimulus (**zu** to)

anspornen spur (horse); spur on

die **Ansprache** [-a:-], **-n** address, speech; *SGer* someone to talk to

ansprechbar free; responsive (**auf** *acc* to)

ansprechen* speak to; address; speak about; (thing) appeal to; (*v/i*) go down well; (medicine) work; (instrument) play (well *etc*); **~ als** describe as, call; **sich angesprochen fühlen** believe one is meant by sth.
~ auf (*acc*) ask about; (*v/i*) respond to
~ bei go down well with; (medicine) work with
~ mit address by
~ um approach for

ansprechend appealing

anspringen* leap up at; pounce on; (emotion) overcome; (*v/i sn*) *mot* start; *coll* take up the offer; **~ auf** (*acc*) (*sn*) *coll* take up (offer); **angesprungen kommen** come bounding along

anspritzen spray; splash

der **Anspruch, ⸚e** claim (**auf** *acc* to); **~ erheben auf** (*acc*) lay claim to; **Ansprüche stellen an** (*acc*) make demands on; **den Ansprüchen gerecht werden** meet the requirements; **in ~ nehmen** claim; enlist; draw on; (thing) take (up) (time); **völlig in ~ nehmen** take up all of (s.o.'s) time; **in ~ genommen** busy (**von** with) || **a~s|los** unassuming; unpretentious; simple; lowbrow; **a~s|voll** demanding, exacting; discerning; sophisticated; high-quality

ansprühen spray

anspucken spit at

anspülen (sea *etc*) wash up

anstacheln spur on

die **Anstalt, -en** establishment, institution; home; institute; *rad, TV* station; **~en machen zu ...** prepare to ...; **keine ~en machen zu ...** show no sign of (+*ger*); **~en treffen** make arrangements (**zu** for); **+zu ...** take steps to ...; prepare to ...

der **Anstand, ⸚e** (good) manners; decorum; *hunt* (raised) hide, (raised) blind *US*; *SGer* trouble (with s.o.); **den ~ wahren** observe the proprieties

anständig decent; seemly; *coll* (sum) tidy; (hiding) proper; (achievement *etc*) respectable

die **Anständigkeit** decency; seemliness

Anstands-: der ~besuch, -e formal call; **die ~dame, -n** chaperon; **a~halber** out of politeness; **a~los** readily, without hesitation; **die ~regeln** *pl* etiquette; **der ~wauwau, -s** *joc* chaperon

anstänkern *coll* lay into (verbally)

anstarren stare at

anstatt (*usu* + *gen*) instead of; **~ zu ...** instead of (+*ger*)

anstauen dam up; **sich ~** accumulate; become bottled up; **angestaut** pent-up

anstaunen stare in amazement at; marvel at

anstechen* prick; broach (cask); *archaeol* open up; **angestochen** (fruit) eaten into by an insect; **wie angestochen** *coll* like a scalded cat

Ansteck-: die ~nadel, -n pin, brooch; badge

anstecken put on; pin on; light; set fire to; infect; (*v/i*) be infectious; be contagious; **sich ~** become infected; **sich bei ... mit ... ~** catch from

ansteckend infectious; contagious

die **Ansteckung** infection; contagion; **der ~s|herd, -e** source of infection

anstehen* queue up, line up *US* (**nach** for); be outstanding/pending; *geol* outcrop; *leg* be fixed (**auf** *acc* for); (+*dat*) become, befit; **~ auf** (*acc*) (*sn*) *Aust* be dependent on; **es steht ihm schlecht an** it ill becomes him; **nicht ~ zu ...** have no hesitation in (+*ger*); **~ lassen** defer; defer payment of; **~d** outstanding; pending; **~des Gestein** outcrop

ansteigen* (*sn*) rise, (road) climb; (temperature *etc*) rise (**auf** *acc* to)

anstelle (+*gen*) instead of

anstellen place (**an** *acc* against); switch on; employ; carry out; draw (comparison); manage (to do); *coll* get up to; **alles mögliche** ~ try everything; **sich** ~ queue up, line up *US*; *coll* act (stupidly *etc*); **stell dich nicht so an!** don't make such a fuss!

die **Anstellerei** (making a) fuss; (perpetual) queueing

anstellig able

die **Anstellung, –en** *vbl noun*; *also* employment; job

anstemmen: sich ~ **gegen** push against; set one's face against

ansteuern head for

der **Anstich, –e** broaching (of barrel); **frischer** ~ beer from a fresh barrel

der **Anstieg, –e** incline; rise, increase (*gen* in); ascent; **im** ~ on the increase

anstieren stare at

anstiften instigate; cause; ~ **zu** incite (s.o.) to commit

der **Anstifter, –** instigator; *leg* abettor

die **Anstiftung** incitement; instigation; *leg* abetment

anstimmen strike up; break into (laughter *etc*)

anstinken* *vulg* make sick; **nicht** ~ **können gegen** be unable to do a thing about

der **Anstoß** [–o:–], **⸚e** impetus; *sp* kick-off; ~ **erregen** give offence; ~ **nehmen an** (*dat*) take offence at

anstoßen* knock; give (s.o., sth.) a push; prompt (to do sth.); (*v/i*) *sp* kick off; (*sn*) bump into something; give offence; **(mit dem Ellbogen)** ~ nudge; **mit dem Kopf** ~ (*sn*) bump one's head; **(mit der Zunge)** ~ lisp; **(mit den Gläsern)** ~ clink glasses; **angestoßen** (fruit) bruised
 ~ **an** (*acc*) adjoin; (*sn*) bump into
 ~ **auf** (*acc*) drink to
 ~ **bei** (*sn*) give offence to

anstoßend adjoining

anstößig offensive

anstrahlen shed its rays on; illuminate; floodlight, *theat* spotlight; beam at

anstreben strive after; ~ **gegen** strive against; **es wurde angestrebt zu ...** the aim was to ... || ~**s|wert** worth striving after

anstreichen* paint; mark; underline (mistake); strike (match); **rot** ~ (in text *etc*) mark in red

der **Anstreicher, –** house-painter

anstreifen touch lightly, brush; slip on; ~ **an** (*acc*)/**gegen** brush against

anstrengen (*see also* **angestrengt**) exert; rack (brains); tire; be a strain on; (*v/i*) be tiring; **einen Prozeß** ~ **gegen** bring an action against; **sich** ~ try hard; make an effort; go to a lot of trouble; ~**d** strenuous; a strain

die **Anstrengung, –en** *vbl noun*; *also* effort, exertion; strain (**für** on)

der **Anstrich, –e** coat (of paint); painting; (artistic *etc*) touch; air

anstücke(l)n *coll* lengthen (by adding a piece); ~ **an** (*acc*) add to

der **Ansturm, ⸚e** onrush; onslaught (**auf** *acc* on); rush (for)

anstürmen (*sn*): ~ **gegen** charge; storm; (waves) dash against; battle against (prejudice *etc*); **angestürmt kommen** come storming along

anstürzen: angestürzt kommen come dashing along

ansuchen [–u:–] *esp Aust*: ~ **um** request; apply for

das **Ansuchen** [–u:–], **–** request; **auf** ~ (+*gen*) at the request of

der **Antagonismus, –(m)en** antagonism

der **Antagonist, –en** (*wk masc*) antagonist

antagonistisch antagonistic

antanzen (*sn*) *coll* turn up; **angetanzt kommen** turn up

die **Antarktis** [ant'ʔarktɪs] the Antarctic

antarktisch [antʔ–] Antarctic

antasten touch; touch on (topic); encroach on; cast a slur on

der **Anteil, –e** share (**an** *dat* in, of); proportion (of); *fin* interest (in); ~ **haben an** (*dat*) participate in; ~ **nehmen an** (*dat*) take an interest in; take part in; sympathize with s.o. in (his/her loss *etc*); share in (s.o.'s joy *etc*) || **a**~**mäßig** proportional, proportionate; pro rata; **die** ~**nahme** sympathy (**an** *dat* with); interest; participation (**an** *dat* in)

anteilig proportional, proportionate; pro rata

antelefonieren *coll* phone

die **Antenne, –n** aerial, antenna; *zool* antenna; **eine/keine** ~ **haben für** *coll* have a/no feeling for

die **Anthologie, –(i)e)n** anthology

der **Anthrazit** anthracite

anthropoid [–o'i:t], **der Anthropoid, –en** (*wk masc*) anthropoid

der **Anthropologe, –n** (*wk masc*) anthropologist

die **Anthropologie** anthropology

anthropologisch anthropological

anti– anti–

der **Anti|alkoholiker, –** teetotaller

anti|autoritär anti-authoritarian

die **Antibaby|pille** [–'be:bi–], **–n** contraceptive pill

das **Antibiotikum, –(k)a, antibiotisch** antibiotic

antichambrieren [–ʃãb–] bow and scrape

das **Antidepressivum, –(v)a** anti-depressant

der **Antifaschist, –en** (*wk masc*), **antifaschistisch** anti-Fascist

der **Antiheld, –en** (*wk masc*) anti-hero

antik classical, of antiquity, (Greece, Rome)

ancient; antique

[die] **Antike** (classical) antiquity; **die ~n** *pl* classical works of art

antikisierend written in the classical style

[das] **Antiklopf|mittel, –** antiknock

[der] **Antikörper, –** antibody

Antillen *pl*: **die (Großen/Kleinen) ~** the (Greater/Lesser) Antilles

[die] **Antilope, –n** antelope

[die] **Antimaterie** [–ĭə] anti-matter

[das] **Antimon** antimony

[der] **Antipassat, –e** antitrade

[die] **Antipathie, –(ie)n** antipathy (**gegen** for, to)

[der] **Antipode, –n** (*wk masc*) person living on the opposite side of the world; person of opposite views

antippen tap (on shoulder *etc*), touch lightly; touch on; **~ bei** *coll* sound out

[die] **Antiqua** *print* roman

[der] **Antiquar, –e** second-hand bookseller

[das] **Antiquariat, –e** second-hand bookshop

antiquarisch second-hand

antiquiert antiquated

[die] **Antiquitäten** *pl* antiques; *in compds* antique …

[der] **Antisemit, –en** (*wk masc*) anti-Semite

antisemitisch anti-Semitic

[der] **Antisemitismus** anti-Semitism

[das] **Antiseptikum, –(k)a, antiseptisch** antiseptic

[die] **Antithese, –n** antithesis

antithetisch antithetical

[die] **Antizipation, –en** anticipation

antizipieren anticipate

[die] **Antizyklone, –n** anticyclone

[das] **Antlitz, –e** *poet* countenance

[der] **Antrag, ⸗e** application (**auf** *acc* for); proposal (of marriage); offer; application form; *parl* motion; *leg* petition (**auf** *acc* for); **einen ~ stellen auf** (*acc*) make application for || **der ~steller, –** applicant; *parl* mover

antragen* (+*dat*) offer

[das] **Antrags|formular, –e** application form

antreffen* find (in a certain place/state); encounter

antreiben* drive (*also mech*); (curiosity *etc*) drive on; wash ashore; *hort* force; (*v/i sn*) be washed ashore; **zur Arbeit ~** keep hard at work; **zur Eile ~** hurry up

[der] **Antreiber, –** slave-driver (= hard taskmaster)

antreten* tread down (earth); kick-start; set out on; start; take up (office); come into (inheritance); furnish (proof); (*v/i sn*) line up, *mil* fall in; *sp* compete; (team) turn out; put in a burst of speed; **an(ge)treten!** fall in!

~ **an** (*acc*) (*sn*) *ling* be added to

~ **gegen** (*sn*) *sp* compete against; play

~ **zu** (*sn*) line up for; take our *etc* places for (dance); report for (duty)

[der] **Antrieb, –e** impulse; impetus; drive; *mech* drive; propulsion; (+*dat*) **neuen ~ geben** give a fillip to; **aus eigenem ~** of one's own accord

Antriebs– driving …; **die ~welle, –n** driving shaft

antrinken* (*see also* **angetrunken**) drink a little from/of; **sich** *dat* **einen ~** *coll* = **sich** *dat* **einen Rausch/Schwips ~** get tipsy; **sich** *dat* **Mut ~** give oneself Dutch courage

[der] **Antritt** start (of journey *etc*); taking up (of office); *sp* burst of speed; *in compds* **~s–** inaugural …; **der ~s|besuch, –e** formal call (made on taking up office)

antun* (*see also* **angetan**) (+*dat*) do to; (+*dat*) **Böses ~** do (s.o.) harm; **sich** *dat* **etwas ~** do away with oneself; **… hat es mir angetan** I am very taken with …

Antwerpen Antwerp

[die] **Antwort, –en** answer (*also* = solution), reply (**auf** *acc* to); **als ~ auf** (*acc*) in reply to; **zur ~ bekommen** be told (in reply); **zur ~ geben** answer || **der ~schein, –e** reply coupon; **das ~schreiben, –** (written) reply

antworten answer, reply; (+*dat*) answer (person); **~ auf** (*acc*) reply to; answer (letter, question, *etc*); respond to (stimulus); **was hat sie darauf geantwortet?** what was her reply?

an|ulken *coll* rag

anvertrauen (+*dat of pers*) entrust (s.o.) with; entrust to (s.o.'s) care; put (one's life *etc*) in (s.o.'s) hands; confide (secret) to; **sich ~** (+*dat*) confide in; put oneself in (s.o.'s) hands

anverwandeln: sich *dat* **… ~** adopt (idea *etc*)

anverwandt related (*dat* to); **der/die Anverwandte** (*decl as adj*) relative

anvisieren take aim at; take a bearing on, *astron* sight (star); aim at, set one's sights on

anwachsen* [–ks–] (*sn*) (plant) take; (amount *etc*) grow (**auf** *acc* to); **~ an** (*acc*) grow onto; **die Haut wächst an** the skingraft takes; **wie angewachsen vor dem Bildschirm hocken** *coll* be glued to one's TV set; **das Anwachsen** growth

anwählen *tel* dial

[der] **Anwalt, ⸗e** lawyer; counsel; advocate (of cause)

[die] **Anwaltschaft** lawyers (*collect*); **die ~ übernehmen** take on (s.o.'s) case

anwandeln (mood) come over

[die] **Anwandlung, –en** (sudden) mood; impulse; fit (of anger, generosity, *etc*)

anwärmen warm slightly

[der] **Anwärter, –** aspirant (**auf** *acc* to); candidate (for); contender (for)

[die] **Anwartschaft** claim (**auf** *acc* to)

anwehen blow on; drift; (feeling) come over

anweisen* (*see also* **angewiesen**) instruct (to); *fin* remit (**an** *acc* to); (+*dat*) allocate to; ~

bei instruct in; (+*dat*) **einen Platz** ~ show to his/her seat

die **Anweisung, -en** instruction(s); allocation; *fin* remittance; money-order; *comput* statement

anwendbar applicable (**auf** *acc* to)

die **Anwendbarkeit** applicability

anwenden* (*see also* **angewandt**) use, employ; apply (**auf** *acc* to); take (pains) (**auf** *acc* over)

der **Anwender, –** *comput* user

die **Anwendung, -en** application (**auf** *acc* to); use; (*pl*) *med* therapy (as part of cure at spa); ~ **finden** be applied; **zur** ~ **bringen** employ || **die** ~**s\|möglichkeit, -en** (possible) use

anwerben* recruit

die **Anwerbung** recruitment

anwerfen* start (engine)

das **Anwesen, –** property

anwesend present; **der/die Anwesende** (*decl as adj*) person present

die **Anwesenheit** presence; **in** ~ (+*gen*) in the presence of || **die** ~**s\|liste, -n** attendance sheet

anwettern *coll* bawl at

anwidern disgust

anwinkeln bend

anwinseln whimper at

der **Anwohner, –** resident (of street)

die **Anzahl** number (= quantity)

anzahlen pay (as a deposit); make a down payment on

anzählen *box* start giving (s.o.) the count

die **Anzahlung, -en** *vbl noun*; *also* down payment

anzapfen tap; *coll* get money out of; pump (for information); ~ **um** *coll* 'touch' for

das **Anzeichen, –** sign; symptom (*also med*); **wenn nicht alle** ~ **trügen** unless I am very much mistaken

die **Anzeige, -n** advertisement; (printed) announcement; reporting (to authorities); indicator; (instrument) reading; *comput* indicator, display; **kleine** ~ small ad; ~ **erstatten gegen** = **zur** ~ **bringen** report to the police || **die** ~**pflicht** obligation to notify the authorities/police; **a**~**pflichtig** notifiable; **die** ~**tafel, -n** *sp* scoreboard; *comput* indicator chart

anzeigen (*see also* **angezeigt**) report (**bei** to); announce (marriage *etc*); indicate; show; (instrument) read

der **Anzeigen\|teil, -e** advertisement section

der **Anzeiger, –** indicator; (*in newspaper titles*) Gazette

anzetteln instigate; hatch

anziehen* attract (*also phys*); absorb (moisture); dress; put on (clothes); draw in (reins); draw up (knees); tighten; apply (brakes); (*v/i*) (horses) begin to pull; (train) pull away; (car *etc*) accelerate; *fin* rise; *chess* make the first move; **wieder** ~ change back into; **ich habe nichts anzuziehen!** I haven't a thing to wear!; **gut angezogen** well-dressed; **sich angezogen fühlen von** feel attracted to; **angezogen kommen** come marching along

sich ~ dress; (*recip*: opposites) attract one another; **sich warm** ~ put on warm clothes

anziehend attractive

die **Anziehung** attraction; pull; **die** ~**s\|kraft** attraction; magnetism (of person); *phys* attractive force (**eine große A. ausüben auf** (*acc*) have a great attraction for)

anzielen aim at

anzischen hiss at; **angezischt kommen** *coll* come whizzing up

der **Anzug, ⸚e** suit; *mot* acceleration; *Swiss parl* motion; **im** ~ approaching; in the offing; (cold *etc*) coming on; **gut im** ~ **sein** have good acceleration

anzüglich suggestive; pointed; ~ **werden** get personal

die **Anzüglichkeit, -en** suggestiveness; personal/suggestive remark

anzünden light; set fire to

der **Anzünder, –** lighter

anzweifeln call in question

anzwinkern wink at

a. O. = **an der Oder**

die **AOK** = **Allgemeine Ortskrankenkasse** (*compulsory health insurance scheme*)

die **Aorta, -(t)en** aorta

apart striking; distinctive; stylish

das **Apartment** [a'partmənt], **-s** (luxury) flat/apartment *US*; **das** ~**haus, ⸚er** block of flats, apartment house *US*

die **Apathie** apathy

apathisch apathetic

die **Apenninen** *pl* the Apennines

der **Aperitif, -s** aperitif

der **Apfel,** *pl* **Äpfel** apple; **in den sauren** ~ **beißen** bite the bullet || **der** ~**baum, ⸚e** apple-tree; **der** ~**most** apple-juice; **das** ~**mus** apple-purée; **der** ~**saft, ⸚e** apple-juice; **der** ~**schimmel, –** dapple-grey horse; **die** ~**sine, -n** orange; **der** ~**strudel, –** apple strudel (*pastry with apple filling*); **der** ~**wein, -e** cider, hard cider *US*

äpfeln (horse) drop manure

der **Aphorismus, -(m)en** aphorism

das **Aphrodisiakum, -(k)a** aphrodisiac

apodiktisch dogmatic; *philos* apodictic

die **Apokalypse, -n** apocalypse

apokalyptisch apocalyptic

die **Apokryphen** *pl* the Apocrypha

apolitisch ['a-] non-political

Apoll(o) Apollo

[der] **Apologet, –en** (*wk masc*) apologist

[die] **Apologie, –(ie)n** apologia

[die] **Apoplexie, –(ie)n** apoplexy

[der] **Apostel, –** apostle; **die ~geschichte** the Acts of the Apostles

apostolisch apostolic

[der] **Apostroph, –e** apostrophe (')

apostrophieren refer to; **~ als** describe as

[die] **Apotheke, –n** (dispensing) chemist's, drugstore *US*; *coll* expensive shop

[der] **Apotheker, –** pharmacist

[die] **Apotheose, –n** apotheosis

[die] **Appalachen** [–x–] *pl* the Appalachians

[der] **Apparat, –e** apparatus; (administrative) machinery; *tel* telephone; (*with number*) extension; *phot* camera; *rad*, *TV* set; = **Hand~**; **am ~** on the telephone; (*replying*) speaking; **bleiben Sie am ~** hold the line; **wer ist am ~?** who is speaking/calling?

[die] **Apparatur, –en** apparatus; equipment

[das] **Appartement** [–(ə)'mãː], **–s** (hotel) suite; = **die ~wohnung, –en** luxury flat/apartment *US*

[der] **Appell, –e** appeal; *mil* roll-call; **zum ~ antreten** fall in for roll-call

appellieren: ~ an (*acc*) appeal to

[der] **Appetit** appetite (**auf** *acc* for); **~ haben auf** (*acc*) feel like; **guten ~!** enjoy your meal || **a~anregend** appetizing; **die ~losigkeit** lack of appetite

appetitlich appetizing; pleasant-looking

applaudieren, ~ (*+dat*) applaud

[der] **Applaus** applause

[die] **Applikation, –en** application; *needlew* appliqué

[die] **Applikatur, –en** *mus* fingering

applizieren apply; *needlew* appliqué

apport! fetch!

apportieren retrieve

[die] **Apposition, –en** apposition

appretieren, die Appretur, –en *text* finish

[die] **Approbation, –en** licence to practise

approbiert (doctor *etc*) licensed to practise

approximativ approximate

[das] **Après-Ski** [aprɛ'ʃiː], **–s** après-ski; après-ski clothes

[die] **Aprikose, –n** apricot

[der] **April** (*gen* –(s)), **–e** April; **im ~** in April; **in den ~ schicken** make an April fool of; **~, ~!** April fool!

apriorisch a priori

apropos [–'poː] by the way

[die] **Apsis,** *pl* **Apsiden** apse

[der] **Aquädukt, –e** (*also* **das**) aqueduct

[der] **Aquamarin, –e** aquamarine

[das] **Aquaplaning** aquaplaning

[das] **Aquarell, –e** water-colour; **~ malen** paint in water-colours

[der] **Aquarellist, –en** (*wk masc*) water-colourist

[das] **Aquarium, –(i)en** aquarium

[der] **Äquator** equator; **die ~taufe, –n** 'crossing-the-line' ceremony

äquatorial equatorial

[der] **Aquavit** aquavit

Aquin: Thomas von ~ Thomas Aquinas

[das] **Äquinoktium** [–ts–], **–(i)en** equinox

Aquitanien [–ĭən] Aquitaine

äquivalent, das Äquivalent, –e equivalent

[die] **Äquivalenz, –en** equivalence

äquivok equivocal

[das] **Ar, –e**/(*following num*) **–** are (*100 square metres*)

[die] **Ära, –(r)en** era

[der] **Araber** ['ara–], **–** Arab (*also* = horse)

[die] **Arabeske, –n** arabesque

Arabien [–ĭən] Arabia

arabisch Arab; Arabian; Arabic; **A~** (*language*) Arabic; **die A~e Liga** the Arab League; **das A~e Meer** the Arabian Sea

[der] **Arabist, –en** (*wk masc*) Arabist

[die] **Arabistik** [–ɪk] Arabic studies

[die] **Arbeit, –en** work; labour; job; piece of work; workmanship; *educ* (academic) paper; (school) test; (*pl*) work (on sth.); **an/bei der ~** at work; **an die ~ gehen** set to work; **in ~** being made; employed (**bei** by); **in ~ geben** have (sth.) made; **in ~ haben** be working on; **in ~ nehmen** start work on; employ || **der ~geber, –** employer; **der ~nehmer, –** employee; **a~sparend** labour-saving

arbeiten work (**an** *dat* on); operate, (organ) function; ferment; warp; (dough) rise; (*v/t*) make; work (material); **~ gehen** go out to work; (*+dat*) **in die Hände ~** play into (s.o.'s) hands

sich ~ durch work one's way through; **sich krank/müde ~** make oneself ill/wear oneself out with work; **sich nach oben ~** work one's way up

[der] **Arbeiter, –** worker; *in compds* worker(s') ..., working-class ...; labour ...; **die ~klasse** working class

[die] **Arbeiterschaft** workers (*collect*); work force

Arbeits– ... of work/labour; work ...; labour ...; working ...;

das ~amt, ⸚er job centre; **der ~dienst, –e** *mil* fatigue; *Nazi* (compulsory) labour service; **der ~eifer** enthusiasm for one's work; **die ~erlaubnis, –se** work permit; **der ~gang, ⸚e** operation; **die ~gemeinschaft, –en** team; study-group; association; **a~intensiv** labour-intensive; **der ~kampf, ⸚e** industrial dispute; **die ~kraft, ⸚e** working capacity; worker; (*pl*) labour, manpower; **a~los** unemployed; **die ~losen|unterstützung** unemployment benefit; **die ~losigkeit** unemployment; **das ~pferd, –e** work-horse; **der ~platz, ⸚e** job; place of work; **a~scheu** work-shy; **die**

~studie, -n time and motion study; der ~tag, -e working day; a~teilig based on the division of labour; die ~teilung division of labour; das ~tier, -e working animal; (person) work-horse; workaholic; der ~titel, - provisional title; das ~verhältnis, -se contractual relationship between employer and employee; (*pl*) working conditions (in einem A. stehen be employed); die ~weise, -n working method; *tech* mode of operation; a~willig willing to work; die ~zeit, -en working hours/time; das ~zimmer, - study

arbeitsam hard-working

archaisch [-ç-] archaic

archaisierend [-çai-] (diction) archaic

der **Archaismus** [-ç-], -(m)en archaism

Archangelsk [-'çaŋ|sk] Archangel

der **Archäologe** [-ç-], -n (*wk masc*) archaeologist

die **Archäologie** [-ç-] archaeology

archäologisch [-ç-] archaeological

die **Arche** [-çə], -n ark; **die ~ Noah** Noah's Ark

der **Archetyp** [-ç-], -en archetype

archetypisch [-ç-] archetypal

Archimedes [-ç-,-ɛs] Archimedes

Archimedisch [-ç-]: **das ~e Prinzip** Archimedes' principle

der **Archipel** [-ç-], -e archipelago

der **Architekt** [-ç-], -en (*wk masc*) architect

architektonisch [-ç-] architectural

die **Architektur** [-ç-] architecture

das **Archiv** [-ç-], -e archives; record office

der **Archivar** [-ç-], -e archivist

der **ARD** = **Arbeitsgemeinschaft der öffentlich-rechtlichen Rundfunkanstalten der Bundesrepublik Deutschland** (*regionally-based first channel of W. German television*)

die **Ardennen** *pl* the Ardennes; **die ~schlacht** the Battle of the Bulge

die **Are**, -n *Swiss* = **Ar**

das **Areal**, -e area

areligiös ['a-] non-religious

die **Arena**, -(n)en arena; (circus) ring

arg (*comp*, *superl* ¨) bad; serious; nasty; (*adv*) badly; *coll* ever so; **im ~en liegen** be in a bad state || **die A~list**, **~listig** cunning; **~los** unsuspecting; innocent; **der A~wohn** suspicion; **~wöhnen** (*insep*) suspect; **~wöhnisch** mistrustful (**gegen** of)

Argentinien [-ĭən] Argentina

der **Argentinier** [-ĭɐ], -, **argentinisch** Argentine

der **Ärger** annoyance; indignation; trouble; (+*dat*) **~ bereiten/machen** cause (s.o.) a lot of trouble; **so ein ~!** how annoying!

ärgerlich annoying; annoyed (**auf** *acc* with, **über** *acc* about, with)

ärgern annoy, irritate; tease (animal); **sich ~** be annoyed (**über** *acc* about, with); **sich zu Tode ~** be hopping mad; **„Mensch, ärgere dich nicht!"** ludo

das **Ärgernis**, -se offence (caused); nuisance; (*pl*) annoyances; **zum ~** (+*gen*) to the annoyance of

das **Argument**, -e argument (put forward)

die **Argumentation**, -en line of argument

argumentieren argue

Argus|augen: mit ~ Argus-eyed

die **Arie** [-ĭə], -n aria

der **Arier** [-ĭɐ], -, **arisch** Aryan

Ariost Ariosto

arisieren *Nazi* Aryanize

der **Aristokrat**, -en (*wk masc*) aristocrat

die **Aristokratie**, -(ie)n aristocracy

aristokratisch aristocratic

Aristophanes [-ɛs] Aristophanes

Aristoteles [-ɛs] Aristotle

aristotelisch Aristotelian

die **Arithmetik** [-ɪk] arithmetic

arithmetisch arithmetical

die **Arkade**, -n arch; (*pl*) arcade

Arkadien [-ĭən] Arcadia

arkadisch Arcadian

die **Arktis** [-ɪs] the Arctic

arktisch Arctic

arm (*comp*, *superl* ¨) poor (**an** *dat* in); **-arm** with a low ... content; **~ dran** badly off; **ärmer sein/werden um** have lost/lose; **der/die Arme** (*decl as adj*) poor man/woman; **die A~en** *pl* the poor

der **Arm**, -e arm; branch (of river); **auf den ~ nehmen** *coll* pull (s.o.'s) leg; **~ in ~** arm in arm; (+*dat*) **in den ~ fallen** restrain; (+*dat*) **in die ~e laufen** *coll* run into; (+*dat*) **in die ~e treiben** drive into the arms of; (+*dat*) **unter die ~e greifen** help out

Arm-: **a~amputiert** with an amputated arm; **das ~band, ¨er** bracelet; **die ~band|uhr, -en** wrist-watch; **die ~binde, -n** arm-band; *med* sling; **der ~bruch, ¨e** broken arm; **die ~brust, ¨e** crossbow; **arm|dick** as thick as one's arm; **die ~lehne, -n** arm-rest; **der ~leuchter, -** candelabra; *coll* 'bugger'; **der ~reif, -e = der ~reifen, -** bangle; **die ~sünder|miene, -n** *coll* hangdog look

das **Armaturen|brett**, -er *aer* instrument-panel; *mot* dashboard

die **Armee**, -(ee)n army

der **Ärmel**, - sleeve; **aus dem ~ schütteln** *coll* produce on the spur of the moment || **der ~kanal** the English Channel; **ä~los** sleeveless

Armen-: **das ~haus, ¨er** *hist* poorhouse; **das ~recht** legal aid; **das ~viertel, -** poor quarter

Armenien [-ĭən] Armenia

der **Armenier** [-ĭɐ], -, **armenisch** Armenian

armieren *tech* reinforce; *elect* sheathe

-armig -armed

ärmlich poor, wretched

arm|selig wretched

die **Armut** poverty; ~ **an** (*dat*) lack of || ~**s|zeugnis (ein A. sein für** show up; **sich** *dat* **ein A. ausstellen** give oneself away)
Arnheim Arnhem
das **Aroma, -(m)en/-s** aroma; flavour; flavouring
aromatisch aromatic
das **Arrangement** [arãʒə'mã:], **-s** arrangement (*also mus*)
der **Arrangeur** [arã'ʒø:ɐ], **-e** *mus* arranger
arrangieren [arãʒ-] arrange (*also mus*); **sich** ~ **mit** come to an arrangement/to terms with
der **Arrest, -e** detention; **mit** ~ **belegen** impound
arretieren *tech* lock
arriviert successful
arrogant arrogant
die **Arroganz** arrogance
der **Arsch, ⸗e** *vulg* arse; **leck mich am** ~**!** to hell with you!; **im** ~ fucked up; (+*dat*) **in den** ~ **kriechen** suck up to || **die** ~**backe, -n** *vulg* buttock; **der** ~**lecker, -** *vulg* bumsucker, brown-nose *US*; **das** ~**loch, ⸗er** *vulg* arsehole; 'bastard'
das **Arsen** arsenic
das **Arsenal, -e** arsenal
die **Art** [a:-], **-en** nature; manner, way (**zu ...** of +*ger*); kind, sort, type; *biol* species; ~ **und Weise** manner; **,,Die Entstehung der Arten"** 'The Origin of Species'; **... aller** ~ all kinds of ...; **... daß es (nur so) eine** ~ **hat** *coll* ... with a vengeance; **das ist doch keine** ~**!** that's no way to behave!; **auf diese** ~ this/that way; **auf meine** ~ my way; **auf (natürliche** *etc***)** ~ in a (natural *etc*) way; **aus der** ~ **schlagen** turn out different from the rest of the family; **einzig in seiner** ~ unique; **nach** ~ **von** in the manner of; **nach (französischer** *etc***)** ~ à la (française *etc*) || **a~fremd** *biol* foreign; *Nazi* alien to the race; **a~verwandt** kindred; akin (*dat* to)
Art. = **Artikel**
arten ['a:-] (*see also* **geartet**) (*sn*): ~ **nach** take after
die **Arterie** [-ĭə], **-n** artery; **die** ~**n|verkalkung** hardening of the arteries
die **Arteriosklerose** arteriosclerosis
artesisch: ~**er Brunnen** artesian well
die **Arthritis** [-ɪs] arthritis
arthritisch arthritic
artig ['a:-] well-behaved, good; *arch* courteous; *arch* charming

---

-artig (*eg* **schlangen~** snake) -like; (*eg* **anders~**) of a (different *etc*) kind

---

die **Artigkeit** good behaviour; *arch* courtesy
der **Artikel, -** article (*also comm, gramm*)
die **Artikulation, -en** articulation
artikulieren articulate; express; **sich** ~ express oneself; be expressed
die **Artillerie** artillery
der **Artillerist, -en** (*wk masc*) artilleryman
die **Artischocke, -n** artichoke
der **Artist, -en** (*wk masc*) (circus, variety) artiste
die **Artistik** [-ɪk] (formal) artistry; artistry of circus/variety performers
artistisch (feat) of circus *etc* artistry, (skill) as a performer; very skilful; showing formal artistry
Artus [-ʊs]: **(König)** ~ King Arthur; *in compds* Arthurian ...
die **Arznei, -en** medicine; **das** ~**buch, ⸗er** pharmacopoeia; **die** ~**kunde** pharmaceutics; **das** ~**mittel, -** medicine; **die** ~**pflanze, -n** medicinal plant; **das** ~**schränkchen, -** medicine-chest
der **Arzt** [a:-], **⸗e** doctor; **praktischer** ~ general practitioner || **die** ~**helferin, -nen** doctor's assistant
die **Ärzteschaft** medical profession
die **Ärztin** ['ɛ:-], **-nen** (woman) doctor
ärztlich ['ɛ:-] medical
das **as, As**[1] [as] (*gen* -), **-** *mus* (the note) A flat; (*key*) **As** A flat major, **as** A flat minor
das **As**[2] [as] (*gen* **-ses**), **-se** ace (in cards, tennis; *also* = person (**in** *dat* at))
der **Asbest** asbestos
Asch- ash ...; = **Aschen-; asch|blond** ash-blond(e); **asch|fahl** ashen; **asch|grau** ash-grey
die **Aschanti|nuß, ⸗(ss)e** *Aust* peanut
die **Asche** ash; ashes; cinders; *in compds* ~**n-** ... of ash(es); ash ...; cinder ...; **die** ~**n|bahn, -en** cinder-track; *mot cycle rac* speedway; **der** ~**n|becher, -** ash-tray; **das** ~**n|brödel** Cinderella; drudge; **das** ~**n|puttel** Cinderella; drudge
der **Ascher|mittwoch, -e** Ash Wednesday
Äschylus ['ɛʃ-] Aeschylus
äsen (deer) browse
aseptisch aseptic
Äser *pl of* **Aas**
der **Asiat, -en** (*wk masc*), **asiatisch** Asian
Asien [-ĭən] Asia
die **Askese** asceticism
der **Asket, -en** (*wk masc*), **asketisch** ascetic
Äskulap Aesculapius
Äsop Aesop
Äsopisch: die ~**en Fabeln** Aesop's Fables
asozial ['a-] antisocial
der **Aspekt, -e** aspect; **unter (diesem** *etc***)** ~ from (this *etc*) point of view
der **Asphalt, asphaltieren** asphalt
der **Aspik** aspic
der **Aspirant, -en** (*wk masc*) candidate; *EGer* postgraduate (studying for a doctorate and required to give a limited amount of tuition)
aspirieren *ling* aspirate; ~ **auf** (*acc*) *Aust* apply for

das **Aspirin** aspirin

aß (äße) *p/t (subj) of* **essen**

die **Assel, -n** isopod

das **Asservat, -e** *leg* exhibit

der **Assessor, -(or)en** (*assistant teacher or lawyer with civil servant status but still on probation*)

die **Assimilation, -en** assimilation

assimilieren assimilate; **sich ~** assimilate (*dat* to)

der **Assistent, -en** (*wk masc*) assistant

die **Assistenz** assistance; **der ~arzt, ⸚e** assistant physician; **der ~professor, -en** assistant professor

assistieren, ~ (+*dat*) assist

die **Assoziation, -en** association

assoziativ associative

assoziieren evoke; **~ mit** associate with; **assoziiert** associated

Assuan [-ŭ-] Aswan

Assyrien [-ĭən] Assyria

der **Assyrier** [-ĭɐ], **-, assyrisch** Assyrian

der **Ast, ⸚e** branch; knot (in wood); *coll* hump; back; **sich** *dat* **einen ~ lachen** *coll* split one's sides with laughter; **auf dem absteigenden ~** on the downgrade || **das ~loch, ⸚er** knot-hole; **ast|rein** free of knots; *coll* above board; **das ~werk** branches

der **AStA** ['asta] = **Allgemeiner Studenten-Ausschuß**

die **Aster, -n** aster

der **Ästhet, -en** (*wk masc*) aesthete

die **Ästhetik** [-ɪk] aesthetics; aesthetic sense

ästhetisch aesthetic

der **Ästhetizismus** aestheticism

das **Asthma** asthma

der **Asthmatiker, -, asthmatisch** asthmatic

der **Astrologe, -n** (*wk masc*) astrologer

die **Astrologie** astrology

astrologisch astrological

der **Astronaut, -en** (*wk masc*) astronaut

die **Astronautik** [-ɪk] astronautics

astronautisch astronautical

der **Astronom, -en** (*wk masc*) astronomist

die **Astronomie** astronomy

astronomisch astronomical

die **Astrophysik** astrophysics

das **Asyl, -e** asylum; home; **das ~recht** right of asylum

der **Asylant, -en** (*wk masc*) asylum-seeker

asymmetrisch asymmetrical

A. T. (= **Altes Testament**) O.T.

der **Atavismus** atavism

atavistisch atavistic

das **Atelier** [atə'lĭeː], **-s** studio

der **Atem** breath; breathing; **außer ~** out of breath; **~ holen** draw breath; **in ~ halten** keep in suspense/on the go; **mit angehaltenem ~** with bated breath || **a~beraubend** breathtaking; **a~los** breathless; **die ~not** shortage of breath; **die ~pause, -n** breather; breathing-space; **das ~schutz|gerät, -e** breathing apparatus; **die ~wege** *pl* respiratory tract (**... der A.** respiratory (disease *etc*)); **der ~zug, ⸚e** breath (**in einem/im selben A.** in one and the same breath)

der **Atheismus** [a-] atheism

der **Atheist** [a-], **-en** (*wk masc*) atheist

atheistisch [a-] atheistic

Athen Athens

der **Athener, -, athenisch** Athenian

der **Äther** ether

ätherisch ethereal (*also chem*)

Äthiopien [-ĭən] Ethiopia

der **Äthiopier** [-ĭɐ], **-, äthiopisch** Ethiopian

der **Athlet, -en** (*wk masc*) athlete

die **Athletik** [-ɪk] athletics

athletisch athletic

das **Äthyl** ethyl

Atlanten *pl of* **Atlas**[2]

der **Atlantik** [-ɪk] (*gen* **-s**) the Atlantic (Ocean)

atlantisch Atlantic; **der A~e Ozean** the Atlantic Ocean

der **Atlas**[1] ['atlas] (*gen* **-(ses)**), **-se** satin

der **Atlas**[2] ['atlas] (*gen* **-(ses)**), *pl* **Atlanten** atlas

der **Atlas**[3] ['atlas] (*gen* **-**) = **das ~gebirge** the Atlas Mountains

atmen ['aː-] (*also v/i*) breathe

die **Atmosphäre** atmosphere; **der ~n|druck** atmospheric pressure; **der ~n|überdruck** pressure above normal air pressure measured in atmospheres

atmosphärisch atmospheric; **~e Störungen** atmospherics

die **Atmung** breathing; respiration; *in compds* **~s-** *also* respiratory ...

der **Ätna** ['ɛt-] (*gen* **-(s)**) Mount Etna

das **Atoll, -e** atoll

das **Atom, -e** atom; *in compds* atomic ...; nuclear ...; **a~betrieben** nuclear-powered; **die ~bombe, -n** atom(ic) bomb; **der ~bunker, -** fall-out shelter; **die ~energie** nuclear energy; **der ~forscher, -** nuclear scientist; **das ~gewicht, -e** atomic weight; **die ~kraft** nuclear power; **das ~kraft|werk, -e** nuclear power station; **die ~macht, ⸚e** nuclear power (= state); **der ~müll** radioactive waste; **der ~pilz, -e** mushroom cloud (after nuclear explosion); **die ~rakete, -n** nuclear-powered rocket; *mil* nuclear missile; **der ~reaktor, -en** nuclear reactor; **der ~sperr|vertrag** non-proliferation treaty; **das ~-U-Boot, -e** nuclear submarine; **der ~versuchs|stopp** nuclear test ban; **die ~waffe, -n** nuclear weapon; **a~waffen|frei** nuclear-free

atomar = **atomisch** *Swiss* atomic; nuclear

die **Atrophie, -(ie)n** atrophy

ätsch! ['ɛː-] so there!; serves you *etc* right!

der **Attaché** [-ʃ-], **-s** attaché

die **Attacke, –n** attack (*also med*); *mil* charge; **eine ~ reiten gegen** attack (in words); *mil* charge

attackieren attack; *mil* charge

das **Attentat** ['atŋ–], **–e** attempted assassination (**auf** *acc* of); **ein ~ verüben auf** (*acc*) make an attempt on the life of

der **Attentäter** ['atŋ–], – (would-be) assassin

das **Attest, –e** certificate

attestieren testify to; **~ als** *EGer* confer the status of ... on

die **Attitüde, –n** pose; attitude

die **Attraktion, –en** attraction; draw

attraktiv attractive

die **Attraktivität** attractiveness

die **Attrappe, –n** dummy; mock-up; **das ist alles nur ~** it's all a sham

das **Attribut, –e** attribute (*also gramm*)

atü [a'ty:] = **Atmosphärenüberdruck**

atypisch ['a–] atypical

Ätz– etching ...; *chem* caustic ...; **das ~mittel, –** caustic; corrosive

ätzen etch; corrode; *med* cauterize; **~d** caustic; corrosive; acrid

die **Ätzung, –en** etching; corrosion; *med* cauterization

au! oh! (*enthusiastic*); = **aua!** ow!

die **Aubergine** [obɛr'ʒi:nə], **–n** aubergine

auch also, too, as well; so ... (*eg* **ich ~** so am/have/did *etc* I); (*followed by noun/pron*) even; (*after interrogative*) –ever (*eg* **wann ... ~ (immer)** whenever); (*reinforcing statement, seeking reassurance, etc*) really, (*conveying exasperation*) *rendered by emphasis* (*eg* **warum hast du es ~ geschrieben?** (well,) why *did* you write it?); *often left untranslated* (*eg* **er sah krank aus, und er war es ~** he looked ill, and he was, **das stimmt ~!** that's right!); *with inversion of subject and verb*, = even if (*eg* **hätte ich es ~ nicht gedacht ...** even if I hadn't thought so ...); *also used elliptically after interrogatives* (*eg* **wozu ~?** why should you *etc*?)

- **~ nicht** not ... either, neither; not even; **ich ~ nicht** neither am/have/would *etc* I
- **~ noch** also, in addition; **mag ... ~ noch so (sehr) ...** no matter how (much) ...; **~ 'das noch!** that's just what I needed!
- **~ nur** even
- **oder ~** or else
- **so (sehr) ... ~** however (much) ...; **'so (gut** *etc*) **... '~ (wieder) nicht** not all *that* (good/well *etc*)
- **~ wenn ...** even if/when ...; **wenn ... ~** even if; **wenn ... ~ noch so (sehr) ...** no matter how (much) ...; **wenn ~!** what of it?

die **Audienz, –en** audience (**bei** with)

audiovisuell audiovisual

auditiv auditory, auditive

das **Auditorium, –(i)en** lecture-hall; audience; **~ maximum** main lecture-hall

Auer–: der ~hahn, ⸚e (cock) wood grouse; **das ~huhn, ⸚er** wood grouse; **der ~ochse, –n** (*wk masc*) aurochs

auf 1 *prep* (+*acc*) (*a*) (*indicating motion etc*) on, onto; to (one's room *or esp public building*, *eg* post office, station, *or function etc*, *eg* party, wedding); into (street, the country, *etc*); (take aim *etc*) at; (view, prospect) of; at (... yards *etc*); (*indicating increase*, *limitation*, *reference*, *etc*) to;

(*b*) (*indicating time*) (go somewhere *etc*) for (... days *etc*); (month *etc*) after (month);

(*c*) (*in calculations*, *expressing ratios*, *etc*) to (... decimal places, the minute, the square kilometre, *etc*);

(*d*) (*indicating manner*) in (a certain way; *also with name of language*, *eg* **~ deutsch** in German); *ling* ending in;

(*e*) (*other senses*) in reply/response to; at (s.o.'s risk, suggestion, *etc*), on (s.o.'s initiative *etc*); (check *etc*) for;

2 *prep* (+*dat*) on (top of); in, on *US* (street); in (one's room, field, *etc*, the country, the world, the Balkans, *sp* lane, *or with name of island*, *eg* **~ Mallorca** in Majorca); at (*esp public buildings*, *eg* post office, station, *or function etc*, *eg* party, wedding);

3 ~ das/aufs ...ste (*eg* **angenehmste**) most ...ly (*eg* pleasantly) (*in absolute sense – contrast* **an** 3);

4 *adv* up (= not in bed); open

- **~!** up you get!; come on!; (**Fenster** *etc*) **~!** open (the window *etc*)!; **~ geht's!** let's go!; **~ (zum Bahnhof** *etc*)**!** let's go to (the station *etc*)!
- **~ ...** (*acc*) **aus** after; bent on
- **~ daß ...** *arch* in order that ...
- **~ ...** (*dat*) **entlang** along (the top of sth.)
- **~ ...** (*acc*) **hin** in response to; at (s.o.'s request *etc*), on (s.o.'s advice *etc*); on the basis/strength of; towards; (check *etc*) for
- **~ ...** (*acc*) **hinaus** out to (sea); for (years *etc*)
- **~ sich: es hat etwas/nichts ~ sich** there is something/nothing in it; **was es mit ... ~ sich hat** what ... really mean(s); what ... is *etc* (all) about
- **~ und ab** up and down, to and fro
- **~ und davon** *coll* gone, off; **~ und davon gehen** *coll* = **sich ~ und davon machen** *coll* make off
- **~ ...** (*acc*) **zu** up to; towards; **~ – zu** open – closed

Auf: das ~ und Ab the ups and downs

---

auf– *sep pref – general senses:*
(*i*) ... up (*eg* **~blasen** blow up, inflate, **~brauchen** use up, **~sprudeln** bubble up, **~lodern** flare up);
(*ii*) ... on (*eg* **~kleben** stick on); (+*dat*) *indicates imposition of something on someone* (*eg* **jmdm. etw. ~halsen** saddle s.o. with sth., **jmdm. etw. ~schwatzen** talk s.o. into buying sth.);
(*iii*) ... open, un– (*eg* **~brechen** break open, **~decken** uncover);
(*iv*) *indicates sudden event or utterance* (*eg* **~beben** quake (momentarily), **~schreien** cry out);
(*v*) *indicates renewal* (eg **~färben** redye, **~polieren** polish up)

---

auf|arbeiten catch up on; use up; refurbish; survey; *nucl tech* reprocess
auf|arten *Nazi* improve (race)
auf|atmen [–a:t–] draw a deep breath; breathe a sigh of relief
aufbacken (*p/part* **aufgebacken**) warm up (roll *etc*)
aufbahren put on the bier
der **Aufbau** (re)construction (*in E. Germany* **der ~** *refers to the building after 1945 of the new socialist republic*); erection; building up (of economy *etc*); structure; (*pl* **–ten**) *tech* (car) body; (*pl*) *naut* superstructure; *cin* set; **die ~jahre** *pl* (child's) years of growth; years of reconstruction
aufbauen construct; erect, put up; set up (cameras); assemble; build up (army *etc*, person as star); *chem* synthesize; **~ auf** (*dat*) base on; (*v/i*) be based on; **wieder ~** rebuild; reconstruct
sich ~ draw oneself up to one's full height; (clouds *etc*) build up; **sich ~ auf** (*dat*) be based on; **sich ~ aus** *chem* be composed of
aufbauend constructive; that builds up (health *etc*)
aufbäumen: sich ~ rear up; **sich ~ gegen** rebel against
aufbauschen fill (sail); blow up (incident) (**zu** into); **sich ~** balloon; **sich ~ zu** be blown up into
Aufbauten *pl of* **Aufbau**
aufbegehren rebel (**gegen** against); **das Aufbegehren** rebellion; protest
aufbehalten* keep on; keep open
aufbeißen* bite open; crack (nut) with one's teeth
aufbekommen* *coll* get open; manage to undo; get (hat *etc*) on; finish up (food); be set (homework)
aufbereiten process; purify (water); dress (ore); establish (text); *comput* edit
die **Aufbereitung** *vbl noun*; *also* purification
aufbessern improve; increase
die **Aufbesserung, –en** improvement; increase
aufbewahren keep; preserve; **das Gepäck ~ lassen** leave one's luggage, check one's baggage *US*
die **Aufbewahrung, –en** *vbl noun*; *also* preservation; storage; left-luggage office, checkroom *US*; **der ~s|ort, –e** place where sth. is kept
aufbieten* mobilize; summon up; bring to bear/into play; call the banns of; put up (for auction); **aufgeboten werden** have their *etc* banns called
Aufbietung: mit/unter ~ aller Kräfte summoning up all one's strength
aufbinden* untie; put up (hair), tie up; (+*dat*) *coll* tell (s.o. tall story); **~ auf** (*acc*) tie onto
aufblähen distend; fill (sail); puff out (cheeks), puff up (feathers); inflate; **sich ~** balloon; distend; give oneself airs
aufblasen* (*see also* **aufgeblasen**) blow up, inflate; distend; puff out; **sich ~** puff itself up; give oneself airs
aufbleiben* (*sn*) stay up; stay/be left open
aufblenden *cin* fade in; (*v/i*) *phot* open the diaphragm; *cin* fade in; **(die Scheinwerfer) ~** turn the headlights on main beam, turn up the high beam *US*
aufblicken look up; **~ zu** look up at; look up to
aufblinken flash
aufblitzen flash; **~ in** (*dat*) (*sn*) flash through (s.o.'s) mind
aufblühen (*sn*) blossom; flourish; come to life
aufbocken jack up
aufbrauchen use up; exhaust
aufbrausen (*sn*) bubble up; (sea) surge; (person) flare up; **(Beifall** *etc*) **braust auf** there is a roar of (applause *etc*); **~d** quick-tempered; **~des Temperament** quick temper
aufbrechen* break open; force; break into; break up (land *etc*); (*v/i sn*) set out (**nach** for, **zu** on); open, (abscess *etc*) burst; (surface) break up; (controversy *etc*) arise
aufbrennen*: einem Tier ein Zeichen ~ brand an animal
aufbringen* (*see also* **aufgebracht**) muster, summon up; find (cash); start (fashion, rumour, *etc*); infuriate; *naut* seize; *coll* get open; **~ gegen** set against; **gegen sich ~** get (s.o.'s) back up
der **Aufbruch** departure; (national *etc*) awakening; *geol* fissure
aufbrühen make (coffee, tea)
aufbrüllen let out a roar; (gun) roar
aufbrummen (+*dat*) *coll* give (as punish-

ment); (*v/i sn*) run aground; ~ **auf** (*acc*) (*sn*) *coll* run into the back of

aufbügeln press (clothes); ~ **auf** (*acc*) iron onto

aufbürden (+*dat*) load onto; burden (s.o.) with; put (blame) on

aufbürsten give (sth.) a brush

aufdecken lay (tablecloth); uncover; turn down (bedclothes); reveal; expose; **die Karten** ~ show one's hand; **sich** ~ kick off the bedclothes

die **Aufdeckung, -en** *vbl noun*; *also* exposure; disclosure

aufdonnern (*see also* **aufgedonnert**): **sich** ~ *coll* doll oneself up

aufdrängen (+*dat*) force on; **sich** ~ (+*dat*) force oneself on; (idea *etc*) force itself upon, be borne in on

aufdrehen (*see also* **aufgedreht**) turn on (tap, *SGer* light); turn up (radio *etc*); unscrew; put (hair) in curlers; twirl up (moustache); (*v/i*) *coll* step on the gas; (person) liven up

aufdringlich obtrusive; (colour *etc*) loud; (smell) overpowering

der **Aufdruck, -e** words printed; letterhead; *philat* overprint

aufdrucken: ~ **auf** (*acc*) print on

aufdrücken push open; open by pressing the button; squeeze (spot *etc*); (+*dat*) impress (seal *etc*) on; press (hat *etc*) on; ~ **auf** (*acc*) stick (plaster) on; impress (seal *etc*) on; (+*dat*) **einen Kuß** ~ place a kiss on (s.o.'s) lips; (+*dat*) **einen** ~ *coll* give (s.o.) a kiss; **die Feder/mit der Feder** ~ press on one's pen

auf|einander (*also sep pref* **auf|einander-**) on *etc**each other (**see* **auf**)

auf|einanderbeißen* clench (teeth)

auf|einanderdrücken press together

die **Auf|einanderfolge** sequence; **in rascher** ~ in rapid succession

auf|einanderfolgen (*sn*) follow one another; ~**d** successive

auf|einanderprallen (*sn*) collide; (opinions *etc*) clash

auf|einandersitzen* sit on top of one another; *coll* live/(in train *etc*) sit on top of one another

auf|einanderstoßen* (*sn*) collide, run into one another; (opinions *etc*) clash

auf|einandertreffen* (*sn*) *mil*, *sp* meet

der **Auf|enthalt** [-nt-], **-e** stay; stop, wait (at station *etc*); being (somewhere, *eg* **der** ~ **in der Kälte** being out in the cold); (place of) residence; **ohne** ~ non-stop || **die** ~**s|erlaubnis, -se** residence permit; **der** ~**s|ort, -e** (place of) residence; whereabouts; **der** ~**s|raum, ⸗e** common/day/recreation room

auf|erlegen (+*dat*) impose on

auf|erstehen* (*usu infin and p/part* **auferstanden**) (*sn*) rise again; **wieder** ~ (movement) revive; **Christus ist auferstanden** Christ is risen

die **Auf|erstehung** resurrection

auf|erwecken (*usu infin and p/part* **auferweckt**) raise from the dead; bring back

auf|essen* eat up; *coll* clear (plate)

auffädeln string (pearls *etc*)

Auffahr-: der ~**unfall, ⸗e** (nose-to-tail) collision

auffahren* bring up; cut up (road); *coll* serve up; (*v/i sn*) drive up; jump up (with a start); fly into a temper; *naut* run aground; *bibl* ascend; ~ **auf** (*acc*) (*sn*) run into; *naut* run on; **aus dem Schlaf** ~ awake with a start; **(zu) dicht** ~ drive (too) close to the car in front; ~**d** irascible

die **Auffahrt, -en** approach road; drive(way); (motorway) slip road, on-ramp *US*; drive to the summit; driving up

auffallen* (*sn*) attract attention; be conspicuous/noticeable, show; (+*dat*) strike, *or conveyed by* notice (*eg* **ist dir nichts aufgefallen?** didn't you notice anything?); ~ **auf** (*acc*) fall on; **angenehm/unangenehm** ~ make a good/bad impression; **allgemein** ~ be noticed by everybody; ~**d** striking; conspicuous; *phys* incident

auffällig conspicuous; showy; ostentatious; (colour) loud

Auffang-: das ~**lager, -** reception camp (for refugees)

auffangen* catch; collect (rainwater *etc*); pick up (message *etc*); accommodate (refugees) (in a camp); cushion (impact), absorb (losses *etc*); ward off (blow); *mil* check; *aer* pull out of a dive

auffärben redye

auffassen take in; understand; interpret; **falsch** ~ misinterpret; misconstrue; ~ **als** view as; take as

die **Auffassung, -en** view; conception; interpretation; **der** ~ **sein, daß ...** take the view that ...; **nach meiner** ~ in my view || **die** ~**s|gabe** (mental) grasp; ~**s|sache (das ist A.** that's a matter of opinion); **das** ~**s|vermögen** (mental) grasp

auffindbar discoverable; to be found

auffinden* find, discover

auffischen *coll* fish out/up; pick up

aufflackern (*sn*) flicker up; flare up, (hope) flicker

aufflammen (*sn*) light up; (rioting *etc*) flare up

auffliegen* (*sn*) fly up; (door) fly open; *coll* fail, collapse, (ring *etc*) be busted; ~ **lassen** *coll* bust (ring *etc*), cause to fail

auffordern call on (to); ask (to); ~ **zu** ask to come for (walk), ask to play (game); (*fol-*

lowed by vbl noun, eg **zur Erfüllung von …** ~) call on to (fulfil *etc* …), (*eg* **zur Teilnahme an …** ~) ask to (participate in … *etc*); **(zum Tanz)** ~ ask to dance

die **Aufforderung, -en** *vbl noun; also* request; invitation; summons

aufforsten (re)afforest

die **Aufforstung, -en** (re)afforestation

auffressen* (animal, *coll* person) eat up; *coll* eat (*eg* **ich könnte dich** ~ I could eat you), devour (with eyes); (thing) swallow up

auffrischen freshen up; touch up; refurbish; replenish; refresh (memory *etc*); brush up (knowledge); (*v/i, also sn*) (wind) freshen; **sich** ~ refresh oneself

der **Auffrischungs|kurs, -e** refresher course

aufführen perform, put on; cite; list; erect; **sich** ~ behave (badly *etc*)

die **Aufführung, -en** *vbl noun; also* performance; erection; **zur** ~ **bringen** stage

auffüllen fill up; replenish; top up; (+*dat*) put on (s.o.'s) plate; ~ **mit** add (stock *etc*) to; **Benzin** ~ fill up with petrol/gasoline *US*

auffuttern *coll* eat up

die **Aufgabe, -n** job; task; role; function; giving up; surrender; handing in; posting, mailing *US*; registering (of luggage), checking (of baggage) *US*; insertion (of advertisement); *sp* retirement (from race *etc*); *math* problem; (*pl*) homework; **es sich** *dat* **zur** ~ **machen zu …** make it one's business to …

aufgabeln *coll* pick up; dig up

der **Aufgaben|bereich, -e** area of responsibility

der **Aufgang, ⸚e** (flight of) stairs; rising (of sun *etc*); *gym* mount

aufgeben* give up; hand in; put (advertisement) in the paper; post, mail *US*; register (luggage), check (baggage) *US*; place (order); (+*dat*) set (s.o. homework)

aufgeblasen *p/part; also* conceited

das **Aufgebot, -e** notice of intended marriage, *eccles* banns; contingent; array (**an** *dat* of); **mit/unter** ~ **aller Kräfte** summoning up all one's strength

aufgebracht *p/part; also* incensed (**über** *acc* at)

aufgedonnert *p/part; coll* dolled up

aufgedreht *p/part; also* in high spirits

aufgedunsen bloated

aufgehen* (*sn*) (sun, dough, *etc*) rise; go up (in flames/smoke); open; burst; come undone; (plant) come up; *math* come out; work out; (+*dat*) dawn on; ~ **in** (*dat*) merge in; be wrapped up in (work *etc*); *math* go into

aufgeilen *vulg* get (s.o.) worked up (sexually)

aufgeklärt *p/part; also* enlightened; ~ **sein** be enlightened; know the facts of life

die **Aufgeklärtheit** enlightenment; enlightened attitude

aufgeknöpft *p/part; coll* expansive

aufgekratzt *p/part; coll* chirpy

das **Aufgeld, -er** extra charge; *fin* agio

aufgelegt *p/part; coll* barefaced; arrant; **(gut** *etc*) ~ in a (good *etc*) mood; ~ **zu** in the mood for

aufgelockert *p/part; also* relaxed

aufgelöst *p/part; also* distraught; all in

aufgeräumt *p/part; also* in a cheerful mood

aufgeregt *p/part; also* excited; worked up

die **Aufgeregtheit** excitement

aufgeschlossen *p/part; also* open-minded; ~ **für** receptive to

aufgeschmissen *coll* in a fix

aufgeschossen *p/part;* **lang** ~ lanky

aufgeschwemmt *p/part; also* bloated

aufgetakelt *p/part; coll* dolled up

aufgeweckt *p/part; also* (child) bright

aufgießen* make (coffee, tea); pour on

aufgliedern divide up (**in** *acc* into); break down (into); **in Gruppen** ~ group

die **Aufgliederung, -en** division; breakdown (of costs *etc*)

aufgraben* dig up

aufgreifen* pick up; take up; resume

aufgrund (+*gen*) as a result of; on the basis of

der **Aufguß, ⸚(ss)e** infusion; brew; rehash

aufhaben* have on; have open; have (homework) to do; *coll* have got open/undone; *coll* have finished (eating); (*v/i* shop *etc*) be open

aufhacken break up; peck a hole in

aufhaken unhook

aufhalsen (+*dat of pers*) saddle (s.o.) with

aufhalten* hold out (hand), hold open; keep open; stop, halt; stave off; hold up
 sich ~ be (in a certain place); stay; **sich** ~ **mit** spend one's time on; **sich** ~ **über** (*acc*) *coll* find fault with; **lassen Sie sich nicht** ~ don't let me keep you

aufhängen hang up/out; hang; (+*dat of pers*) saddle (s.o.) with; palm off on; tell (s.o. lie *etc*); **(den Hörer)** ~ hang up; ~ **an** (*dat*) hang from; suspend from; use as a way of introducing (subject); **sich** ~ hang oneself (**an** *dat* from)

der **Aufhänger, -** loop; peg (to hang story *etc* on)

die **Aufhängung** *vbl noun; tech* suspension

aufhäufeln heap up; earth up

aufhäufen, sich ~ pile up; accumulate

die **Aufhäufung, -en** *vbl noun; also* accumulation

aufheben* pick up; raise, lift (up); keep (*dat*/**für** for); abolish; cancel (order *etc*); rescind, *leg* quash; lift (ban *etc*), raise (siege); close (meeting); neutralize; offset (gain, loss); **sich** ~ cancel (each other) out; **gut aufgehoben** in good hands (**bei** with)

Aufheben(s): viel ~ **machen von** make a lot of

fuss about

[die] **Aufhebung** *vbl noun*; *also* abolition; cancellation; closure (of meeting); neutralization

aufheitern cheer up; **sich ~** brighten up

[die] **Aufheiterung, -en** *vbl noun*; *also* bright spell

aufheizen, sich ~ *phys*, *tech* heat up

aufhelfen* (+*dat*) help up; help back on his/her feet; boost

aufhellen lighten (the colour of); elucidate; **jmds. Gemüt ~** cheer up; **sich ~** brighten (up); be clarified, (meaning) become clear

[die] **Aufhellung** *vbl noun*; *also* elucidation

aufhetzen stir up; incite (**zu** to)

[die] **Aufhetzung** incitement

aufheulen let out a howl; (wind) howl, (siren) wail (suddenly), (engine) whine (suddenly)

aufholen make up; catch up (on); (*v/i*) catch up; *fin* (shares) pick up; **(die Verspätung) ~** make up time

aufhorchen prick up one's ears; **~ lassen** make (s.o.) sit up and take notice

aufhören stop; come to an end; **~ mit** stop (work *etc*); **~ zu ...** stop (+*ger*); **nicht ~ zu ...** keep on (+*ger*); **hör auf (damit)!** stop it!; **da hört (sich) doch alles auf!** that's the limit!

aufjauchzen = aufjubeln shout for joy

[der] **Aufkauf, ¨-e** buying up

aufkaufen buy up

[der] **Aufkäufer, -** buyer

aufkeimen (*sn*) sprout; spring up in s.o.'s mind, (love) burgeon

aufklappen open; put up; turn up (collar *etc*); (*v/i sn*) come open

aufklaren (sky) clear

aufklären (*see also* **aufgeklärt**) clear up; explain the facts of life to; *EGer* educate politically; *mil* reconnoitre; **~ über** (*acc*) explain to; educate (public) about; **sich ~** (sky) clear; (face) brighten up; be cleared up

[der] **Aufklärer, -** *mil* scout, *aer* reconnaissance aircraft; *EGer* propagandist (*not pej*); *hist* representative of the Enlightenment

aufklärerisch promoting enlightenment; rationalistic

[die] **Aufklärung** elucidation; clarification; education (of public), *EGer* political education; *mil* reconnaissance; *hist* (**die ~**) the Enlightenment; **sexuelle ~** sex education

Aufklärungs- information(al) ...; sex education ...; *mil* reconnaissance ...; **der ~film, -e** sex education film; **das ~flugzeug, -e** reconnaissance aircraft; **das ~lokal, -e** *EGer* political education centre; **das ~zeit|alter** the Age of Enlightenment

aufkleben stick on; glue on

[der] **Aufkleber, -** sticker

aufklinken open (door)

aufknacken crack (nut); *coll* break into (car), crack (safe)

aufknöpfen (*see also* **aufgeknöpft**) unbutton; **~ auf** (*acc*) button onto; **knöpf dir die Ohren auf!** wash your ears!

aufknoten untie

aufknüpfen untie; *coll* string up

aufkochen bring to the boil; reboil; (*v/i*, *also sn in 1st sense*) come to the boil; *SGer* prepare a grand spread; **~ lassen** bring to the boil

aufkommen* (*sn*) arise; (custom *etc*) come in; (wind) get up, (storm) brew; *naut* come up; *sp* catch up; **~ lassen** permit to arise; give rise to; **niemanden neben sich ~ lassen** brook no competition; **keine Mißverständnisse ~ lassen** avoid any misunderstandings

~ für pay for; meet (cost); be responsible for

~ gegen stand up to; **nicht ~ können gegen** be no match for; be powerless against

~ in (*dat*) arise in (s.o.'s) mind

[das] **Aufkommen** advent (of); *fin* revenue (from taxes); *EGer econ* target

aufkorken uncork

aufkratzen (*see also* **aufgekratzt**) scratch open; scratch (ground); (+*dat*) make (s.o.'s throat) raw

aufkreischen give a shriek

aufkrempeln roll up (sleeves *etc*)

aufkreuzen (*also sn*) *naut* tack; (*sn*) *coll* show up

aufkriegen *coll* = **aufbekommen**

aufkündigen terminate

[die] **Aufkündigung** termination

Aufl. = Auflage

auflachen give a laugh; **laut ~** laugh out loud

aufladen* load (**auf** *acc* onto); *tech* supercharge; *elect* charge; (+*dat of pers*) load (s.o.) with; burden (s.o.) with; **sich ~** charge up; **emotional aufgeladen** emotionally charged

[die] **Auflage, -n** circulation; print run; edition *or* impression (of book); condition (imposed); coating; overlay; rest, support; *econ* production (= rate); *EGer econ* target; **die ~n|höhe** circulation; (of book) print run; **a~(n)|schwach** low-circulation; **a~(n)|stark** high-circulation

auflassen* release (balloon *etc*); *SGer* close down (factory *etc*); *leg* convey; *coll* keep on; *coll* leave open; *coll* allow to get/stay up

auflauern (+*dat*) lie in wait for

[der] **Auflauf, ¨-e** crowd, *leg* unlawful assembly; *cul* (lightly-baked) savoury dish; soufflé || **die ~form, -en** soufflé dish

auflaufen* (*sn exc* **sich die Füße ~**) accumulate, mount up; (water) rise; ~ **auf** (*acc*) run into (from behind); *naut* run on; ~ **zu** *sp* join (leaders); **sich** *dat* **die Füße** ~ *coll* (walker) get sore feet; ~ **lassen** *sp* body-check

aufleben (*sn*) (plant, conversation) revive; (person) come alive; **(wieder)** ~ **lassen** revive

auflecken lick up, (animal) lap up

auflegen (*see also* **aufgelegt**) put on; lay (place at table); put (cards, elbows) on the table; publish; put out (list) for inspection; *econ* commence production of; *fin* float (loan); (+*dat*) put (saddle *etc*) on; **(den Hörer)** ~ hang up; **neu** ~ reprint; reissue

auflehnen: sich ~ **gegen** rebel against

die **Auflehnung, -en** revolt

aufleimen glue on

auflesen* pick up

aufleuchten (*also sn*) light up

aufliegen*: ~ **auf** (*dat*) rest on; **sich** ~ get bedsores; **sich** *dat* **den Rücken** ~ get bedsores on one's back

auflisten list (*also comput*)

auflockern (*see also* **aufgelockert**) loosen up; break up; make (atmosphere) more relaxed; relieve the monotony of; **sich** ~ break up; loosen up; (atmosphere) become more relaxed

auflodern (*sn*) flare up

auflösbar soluble; dissoluble

auflösen (*see also* **aufgelöst**) dissolve (in liquid); (re)solve; decipher; break up; break off (engagement); dissolve (*also parl*); wind up (company *etc*), disband; close (account); cancel (contract); undo (knot *etc*); *math* solve (equation); get rid of (brackets); *comput* solve; *mus* cancel; resolve (dissonance); *phys*, *phot* resolve; ~ **in** (*acc*) *phot* resolve into; *phys* resolve into; reduce to (atoms); **in Tränen aufgelöst** in tears

sich ~ dissolve; break up, disintegrate; disband, (club *etc*) wind itself up, *parl* dissolve itself; be resolved; (knot) come undone; **sich** ~ **in** (*acc*) break up into; turn to (slush *etc*); **sich in Luft/Rauch** ~ vanish into thin air; **sich in Tränen** ~ dissolve into tears

die **Auflösung, -en** *vbl noun*; *also* resolution; dissolution; cancellation; break-up, disintegration, (of organism) decomposition; distraught state; solution (to puzzle); *comput*, *phys*, *phot* resolution; *mus* cancellation; resolution; **das ~s|zeichen, -** *mus* natural

auflöten solder on

aufmachen open; undo; get up (book *etc*); (*v/i*) answer the door; (+*dat*) open the door to; **wieder** ~ reopen; **groß** ~ give a big spread to; **sich** ~ get oneself up; set off (**zu** on); (wind) rise

die **Aufmachung, -en** get-up; layout (of newspaper); presentation; packaging; **in großer** ~ **herausbringen** give a big spread to

aufmalen: ~ **auf** (*acc*) paint on

der **Aufmarsch, ⸚e** parade

aufmarschieren (*sn*) march up (and form up); parade

aufmerken pay attention (**auf** *acc* to)

aufmerksam attentive; observant; ~ **machen auf** (*acc*) draw (s.o.'s) attention to; ~ **werden auf** (*acc*) become aware of

die **Aufmerksamkeit, -en** attention; attentiveness; small gift

aufmöbeln *coll* buck up; revamp; brush up (image *etc*)

aufmontieren mount; fit on

aufmotzen *coll* jazz up

aufmucken *coll*: ~ **gegen** kick against

aufmuntern cheer up; buck up; encourage (to)

die **Aufmunterung** *vbl noun*; *also* encouragement

aufmüpfig *coll* rebellious

aufnageln nail on

aufnähen sew on

die **Aufnahme, -n** reception (*also* = area of hospital); admission (**in** *acc* to); taking (of minutes *etc*), taking down (from dictation); intake (of food *etc*) (**in** *acc* into); inclusion (in), *ling* borrowing; raising (of loan *etc*); establishment (of relations); commencement; *geog* mapping (of terrain); *rad etc* recording; *phot* shot; taking (of photograph); *cin* take; shooting (of scene); ~ **finden** be received/admitted/*ling* borrowed; **eine** ~ **machen** take a photograph; make a recording; **Achtung, ~!** *cin* action! || **a~fähig** receptive (**für** to); **die ~gebühr, -en** entry fee; **die ~prüfung, -en** entrance examination

Aufnahms- *Aust* = **Aufnahme-**

aufnehmen* pick up; take in (food *etc*); absorb; (ship *etc*) hold; receive; put up (guest); take up (suggestion *etc*); raise (loan); establish (contact *etc*); commence; take (minutes *etc*), take down (particulars); *Aust* take on, employ; *geog* map; *rad etc* record; *phot* photograph; *cin* shoot; **wieder** ~ resume; take up again; ~ **in** (*acc*) admit to; include in; **in sich** ~ absorb, take in; **es** ~ **mit** take on; **es ~/nicht ~ können mit** be a/no match for

aufnorden *Nazi* Nordicize

aufnötigen (+*dat*) force on

auf|oktroyieren [–trŏaj–] (+*dat*) impose on

auf|opfern sacrifice; **sich** ~ **für** sacrifice oneself for; **~d** self-sacrificing; selfless

die **Auf|opferung** sacrifice; self-sacrifice; **mit** ~

with devotion

aufpacken undo (parcel *etc*); (+*dat*) load onto; burden with

aufpäppeln *coll* feed up

aufpassen pay attention; ~ **auf** (*acc*) pay attention to; look after; keep an eye on; **paß auf!** pay attention!; look out!; ... you wait and see; (*making suggestion etc*) listen ..., look ...; **aufgepaßt!** pay attention!; **~, daß ...** take care that ...

der **Aufpasser, –** look-out; spy, snooper

aufpeitschen whip up; stir up; **sich** ~ pep oneself up

aufpflanzen set up; *mil* fix (bayonet); **sich ~ vor** (*dat*) *coll* plant oneself in front of

aufpflügen plough up

aufpfropfen graft (**auf** *acc* onto); (+*dat*) graft (alien customs *etc*) onto

aufplatzen (*sn*) burst open; split (open)

aufplustern [–u:–] ruffle up (feathers); **sich** ~ ruffle up its feathers; *coll* put on airs

aufpolieren polish up

aufprägen stamp (**auf** *acc* on); (+*dat*) **seinen Stempel** ~ leave one's mark on; **sich** ~ (+*dat*) leave its mark on

der **Aufprall** impact (**auf** *acc* on)

aufprallen (*sn*): ~ **auf** (*acc*) hit

der **Aufpreis, –e** extra charge

aufprobieren try on (hat *etc*)

aufpulvern [–lf–] *coll* pep up; buck up; **sich** ~ pep oneself up

aufpumpen pump up (the tyres of)

Aufputsch–: das ~mittel, – stimulant; pep pill; *sp* dope

aufputschen stir up; pep up, (with drugs) hype up; **sich** ~ pep/hype oneself up

der **Aufputz** (extravagant) attire

aufputzen dress up; adorn; embellish (story); **sich** ~ dress up

aufquellen* (*sn*) swell up; rise; well up

aufraffen snatch up; **sich** ~ struggle to one's feet; pick oneself up; collect oneself; **sich ~ aus** shake oneself out of; **sich ~ zu** (finally) resolve on; rouse oneself to (action); **sich ~ zu ...** (finally) resolve to ...; bring oneself to ...

aufragen tower up

aufrappeln: sich ~ *coll* struggle to one's feet; rouse oneself (to action); **sich wieder** ~ get on one's feet again

aufräumen (*see also* **aufgeräumt**) tidy up; clear away; ~ **mit** do away with; ~ **unter** (*dat*) take a heavy toll of; **gründlich** ~ make a clean sweep

die **Aufräumungs|arbeiten** *pl* clearance work

aufrechnen (+*dat*) charge to; hold against; ~ **gegen** offset against

aufrecht upright; erect; ~ **sitzen** sit upright || **~erhalten*** (*sep*) maintain; uphold; keep going; sustain; keep (peace); stand by (decision *etc*); **die A~erhaltung** maintenance; upholding

aufreden (+*dat of pers*) talk (s.o.) into buying/taking

aufregen excite; upset; **sich** ~ get worked up/upset (**über** *acc* about); **~d** exciting

die **Aufregung, –en** excitement; agitation; **in ~ geraten** get excited; **in großer** ~ in a state of great excitement

aufreiben* chafe; wear down (person); *mil* wipe out; **sich** ~ wear oneself out; **~d** wearing

aufreihen line up; string; **sich** ~ line up

aufreißen* tear open; fling open; open (eyes, mouth) wide; tear up (road surface); tear (**an** *dat* on); pull up (from chair *etc*); outline (topic); *tech* make a sketch of; *sp* open up (defence); *coll* pick up (girl); get; (*v/i sn*) burst; split; (clouds) break up; (wound) burst open; **das Maul** ~ *coll* talk big

aufreizen excite; stir up; ~ **zu** incite to; **~d** that excites the senses; provocative; maddening

aufrichten straighten up (back); prick up (ears); put up, erect; sit up; help to his/her feet; give (s.o.) courage; establish; **sich** ~ straighten up; sit up; raise itself up; **sich ~ an** (*dat*) take heart from; **sich (wieder)** ~ get to one's feet; **sich hoch** ~ draw oneself up

aufrichtig sincere; honest; heartfelt

die **Aufrichtigkeit** sincerity; honesty

aufriegeln unbolt

der **Aufriß, –(ss)e** outline (of subject); *archit* elevation

aufritzen slit open; scratch (skin)

aufrollen roll up (sleeves *etc*), furl (flag); unroll (carpet *etc*), unfurl (flag); roll open; go into (topic); **wieder** ~ reopen (case); **sich** ~ roll up; unroll

aufrücken (*sn*) move up; be promoted

der **Aufruf, –e** appeal, call; calling out (of name), *leg* calling (of witness); *fin* calling in; *comput* call; **(öffentlicher)** ~ proclamation; **nach** ~ when called

aufrufen* call (out); call (the name of), *educ* ask (s.o.) a question/to translate *etc* (in class); appeal to (conscience *etc*); *leg* call (witness); *fin* call in; *comput* call; call up; ~ **zu** appeal to (public *etc*) for, (*followed by vbl noun, eg* **zum Widerstand** ~) call on (to resist *etc*); (*v/i*) call for

der **Aufruhr** rebellion; tumult, turmoil; **in** ~ in a tumult; **in ~ geraten** rebel; be thrown into a turmoil

aufrühren stir up; rake up

der **Aufrührer, –** rebel

aufrührerisch rebellious; seditious

aufrunden round up (**auf** *acc* to)

aufrüsten (*also v/i*) arm; rearm

die **Aufrüstung** arming; rearmament
aufrütteln rouse from his/her sleep; stir (conscience); rouse (the masses); ~ **aus** shake out of
aufs = **auf das**; (*with superl*: *see* **auf** 3)
aufsagen recite; (+*dat*) **die Freundschaft** ~ break with
aufsammeln gather up; *coll* pick up (drunk *etc*)
aufsässig rebellious
aufsatteln saddle up; *tech* attach (single-axle trailer)
der **Aufsatz, ⸚e** essay, (in journal) article; attachment; top (part)
aufsaugen (*see* **saugen**) soak up; absorb
aufschauen *esp SGer* look up; ~ **zu** look up at; look up to
aufschäumen (*usu sn*) froth up; foam (with rage)
aufscheinen* (*sn*) *Aust* (name *etc*) appear
aufscheuchen scare away; startle; **aus dem Bett** ~ rout out of bed
aufscheuern chafe
aufschichten pile up, stack
aufschieben* slide open; push back; put off (**auf** *acc* until)
aufschießen* (*see also* **aufgeschossen**) (*sn*) shoot up; leap up
aufschinden (*p/part* **aufgeschunden**) graze
der **Aufschlag, ⸚e** impact; extra charge, surcharge; lapel; cuff, (trousers) turn-up, cuff *US*; *sp* service; ~ **haben** *sp* serve
aufschlagen* open; turn to (page); cut open (head *etc*); break (ice *etc*), crack (nut); pitch (tent), put up; turn back (bedclothes), turn up (collar *etc*), lift (veil); take up (quarters, residence); *knit* cast on; (*v/i*) (price, commodity) go up; put up the price(s); *sp* serve; (*sn*) hit the ground/water; fly open; (flames) leap up; **dumpf** ~ thud
~ **auf** (*acc*) put on (price); ~ **auf** (*acc/dat*) (*sn*) (falling person/object) hit
~ **mit** (*sn*): **mit dem Kopf** ~ hit one's head (**auf** *acc/dat* on); **mit dem Bauch (auf das/dem Wasser)** ~ belly-flop
aufschließen* (*see also* **aufgeschlossen**) unlock; open up (oilfield *etc*); *chem* break down, decompose; *min* crush (ore); (+*dat*) unlock (door) for; expound to; (*v/i*) (straggler *etc*) close up; (+*dat*) unlock the door for; ~ **zu** catch up with; (+*dat*) **sein Herz** ~ unburden oneself to
sich ~ (+*dat*) unburden oneself to; (new world) open up to
aufschlitzen slit open; slash
aufschluchzen give a (sudden) sob
der **Aufschluß, ⸚(ss)e** information; enlightenment; *geol* section; *chem* decomposition; (*pl*) information; ~ **geben über** (*acc*) give information about; throw light on; **sich** *dat* ~ **verschaffen über** (*acc*) inform oneself about || **a~reich** informative; revealing
aufschlüsseln classify (**nach** according to); break down (**in** *acc* into); decode
die **Aufschlüsselung, -en** classification; breakdown
aufschmieren *coll* spread on
aufschnallen unbuckle; buckle on; **sich** *dat* ... ~ strap on one's back
aufschnappen snap up; pick up (word *etc*); (*v/i sn*) snap open
aufschnaufen *SGer coll* breathe a sigh of relief
aufschneiden* cut open; cut the pages of; slice; carve (meat); *med* lance; (*v/i*) *coll* brag (**mit** about)
der **Aufschneider, -** *coll* braggart
aufschnellen (*sn*) leap up
der **Aufschnitt** (sliced) cold meats, cold cuts *US*
aufschnüren undo; unlace
aufschrammen graze
aufschrauben unscrew; unscrew the lid/cap of; ~ **auf** (*acc*) screw onto
aufschrecken startle (**aus** out of); (*v/i*; *also* **schrick(s)t auf,** *p/t* **schrak** (*subj* **schräke**) **auf**) (*sn*) start (**aus** from, **von** at)
der **Aufschrei, -e** cry; scream; ~ **der Empörung** outcry
aufschreiben* write down; (*also* + **sich** *dat*) note down; *coll* (policeman) book (**wegen** for); (+*dat*) *coll* prescribe for
aufschreien* cry out; scream
die **Aufschrift, -en** inscription; writing; **mit einer** ~ **versehen** label
der **Aufschub, ⸚e** delay; deferment; extension (of time-limit); *leg* stay of execution; **ohne** ~ without delay
aufschürfen graze
aufschürzen tuck up
aufschütteln shake up
aufschütten pour on; put on the fire; heap up; build (embankment *etc*); raise the level of *or* widen (road); *geog* deposit
aufschwatzen (+*dat of pers*) talk (s.o.) into buying/taking
aufschwellen swell; (*v/i*: ~*, *like* **schwellen** *v/i*) (*sn*) swell (up)
aufschwemmen (*see also* **aufgeschwemmt**) make bloated
aufschwingen* (*sn exc* **sich** ~) swing open; **sich** ~ soar; **sich** ~ **zu** work one's way up to; set oneself up as; bring oneself to make/write *etc*; *coll* treat oneself to; **sich (dazu)** ~ **zu ...** bring oneself to ...
der **Aufschwung, ⸚e** *esp comm* boom, upturn upswing; *gym* upward circle; **einen** ~ **nehmen** boom
aufsehen* look up; ~ **zu** look up at; look up to

das **Aufsehen** stir; ~ **erregen** cause a stir; **großes** ~ **erregen** cause a sensation || **a~erregend** sensational

der **Aufseher, –** supervisor; attendant; (prison) warder, guard *US*

aufseilen: (sich) ~ haul (oneself) up by a rope

aufsetzen put on, *build* add; put (foot) on the ground; place (pick-up) on the record; sit (child *etc*) up; draft; beach, *aer* put down; (+*dat*) put on (s.o.'s) head; (*v/i*) (pick-up) come down; *ski* land; *aer* touch down; ~ **auf** (*acc*) add (floor) to; **sich** ~ sit up

aufseufzen: (tief) ~ heave a (deep) sigh

die **Aufsicht, –en** supervision; supervisor; *math etc* top view; **die** ~ **führen** be in charge (**über** *acc* of); invigilate, proctor *US*; **unter ärztlicher** ~ under medical supervision || **der/die** ~**führende** (*decl as adj*) supervisor; invigilator, proctor *US*

der **Aufsichter, –** *EGer* assistant stationmaster

Aufsichts– supervisory ...; **der** ~**be|amte** (*decl as adj*) attendant; *rail* assistant stationmaster; **der/die** ~**führende** (*decl as adj*; = **Aufsichtführende**); **der** ~**rat, ⸚e** (member of the) supervisory board

aufsitzen* sit up; *naut* be aground; (*sn*) mount; get on; (+*dat*) (*sn*) be taken in by; ~ **auf** (*dat*) *tech* rest on; ~ **lassen** *coll* let down

aufspalten (*p/part also* **aufgespalten**) split; split up (**in** *acc* into); *chem* break down (into); **sich** ~ split open; split (up) (**in** *acc* into)

die **Aufspaltung, –en** splitting; split-up; *chem* breakdown

aufspannen put up (umbrella *etc*); spread (net *etc*); ~ **auf** (*acc/dat*) put on; stretch (canvas) on

aufsparen save up

aufspeichern store; **sich** ~ **in** (*dat*) build up inside; **aufgespeichert** (anger) pent-up

aufsperren open (wide); *SGer* unlock

aufspielen strike up; play; **sich** ~ give oneself airs; **sich** ~ **als** pose as

aufspießen stick one's fork in; impale, *ent* pin (insect); gore; *coll* lambast

aufsplittern (*sn if v/i*) splinter; split up (**in** *acc* into); **sich** ~ **in** (*acc*) split (up) into

aufsprayen [–ʃpreːən, –sp–] spray on

aufsprengen force open; blast open

aufsprießen* (*sn*) shoot up

aufspringen* (*sn*) jump up; burst open; burst; become chapped; bounce, *ski* land; (breeze) spring up; ~ **auf** (*acc*) jump onto; **aufgesprungen** chapped

aufspritzen spray on; squirt on; (*v/i sn*) splash up; spurt up

aufsprudeln (*sn*) bubble up

der **Aufsprung, ⸚e** *gym*, *ski*, *etc* landing; (on trampoline) upward leap

aufspulen wind onto a reel/spool

aufspülen (sea) wash up

aufspüren track down; nose out; ferret out

aufstacheln incite (**zu** to); spur on (to)

aufstampfen stamp the ground; stamp one's feet

der **Aufstand, ⸚e** revolt

aufständisch rebellious; **der/die Aufständische** (*decl as adj*) rebel

aufstapeln pile up

aufstauen dam up; **sich** ~ collect; **sich** ~ **in** (*dat*) build up inside; **aufgestaut** (anger) pent-up

aufstechen* prick open; *med* lance

aufstecken put up (hair), pin up; put on; *coll* (*also v/i*) give up; (+*dat*) put on

aufstehen* be open; (*sn*) get up; stand up; rise (**gegen** against); (prophet) arise; (**auf dem Boden**) ~ touch the floor/ground

aufsteigen* (*sn*) go up; rise; *aer*, *mount* climb; *sp* be promoted; ~ **lassen** fly (kite), release (balloon); give (s.o.) a lift (on motorcycle *etc*)

~ **auf** (*acc*) get onto; mount

~ **in** (*acc*) *sp* be promoted to (higher division); ~ **in** (*dat*) arise in (s.o.'s) mind; cross (s.o.'s) mind; (tears) well up in (s.o.'s) eyes

~ **vor** (*dat*) rise up before; **... steigt vor mir auf** I see ... in my mind's eye

~ **zu** rise to be; rise to (power); *mount* climb to

aufsteigend rising; *astron*, *geneal*, *mus*, *phys* ascending

der **Aufsteiger, –** *sp* promoted team; team about to be promoted; **sozialer** ~ social climber

aufstellen put up; stand up; stand, put (in position), set (trap), *mil* post (sentry); put on (to boil); (animal) prick up (ears); get (choir, team, *etc*) together, raise (army); draw up (list *etc*); put forward (theory), lay down; make (assertion, demand); *sp* set up (record); **als Kandidaten** ~ nominate; **sich** ~ **lassen** stand, run *US* (for office)

sich ~ take up one's position; line up; (hair) stand on end; **sich** ~ **längs** (*gen*) line (road *etc*)

die **Aufstellung, –en** *vbl noun*; *also* nomination; list; table; *sp* line-up

aufstemmen prise open; **sich** (**mit dem Ellbogen** *etc* **auf etw.** *acc*) ~ prop one's elbow *etc* on sth.

aufstempeln stamp on

aufsteppen stitch on

aufstieben* (*sn*) fly up

der **Aufstieg, –e** ascent (**auf** *acc* of); rise (to power *etc*), advancement, *sp* promotion (to higher division); way up; **wirtschaftlicher** ~ boom || **die** ~**s|möglichkeiten** *pl*

promotion prospects
aufstöbern unearth; hunt down; *hunt* start
aufstocken add a storey to; increase (**um** by); (*v/i*) add a storey; *comm* increase its capital
aufstöhnen give a (sudden) groan
aufstören startle (game); disturb; ~ **aus** rouse from
aufstoßen* push open; graze (knee *etc*); *comput* joggle; (*v/i*) belch, (baby) burp; (+*dat*) (*also sn*) (food) repeat on; (*sn*) (fact *etc*) strike; ~ **auf** (*acc*) (*sn*) hit, strike; **mit dem Kopf** ~ **auf** (*acc*) bang one's head on; (+*dat*) **sauer** ~ *coll* be painful for
aufstreben (building *etc*) tower; **~d** towering; up-and-coming
aufstreichen* spread on
aufstreuen scatter; sprinkle (**auf** *acc* on)
der **Aufstrich, –e** upstroke; (food) spread; *mus* up-bow
aufstufen upgrade
aufstülpen turn up; clap on (hat *etc*); ~ **auf** (*acc*) place over; **die Lippen** ~ pout; **aufgestülpt** (nose) retroussé
aufstützen prop up; ~ **auf** (*acc*) rest (head *etc*) on; **sich** ~ prop oneself up
aufsuchen [–uː–] visit, call on; go and see (doctor); visit (place), go to (room); look up (passage, place on map, name in directory, *etc*); gather up
aufsummieren *comput* sum up
auftakeln (*see also* **aufgetakelt**) *naut* rig; **sich** ~ *coll* doll oneself up
der **Auftakt, –e** start (**zu** of); prelude (to); *mus* upbeat; *pros* anacrusis
auftanken fill up (with petrol/gasoline *US*); *aer* refuel
auftauchen (*sn*) appear; turn up; crop up; (diver *etc*) surface; **wieder** ~ reappear; turn up again; crop up again
auftauen thaw; defrost; *mot* thaw out (radiator); (*v/i sn*) thaw; thaw out
aufteilen share out (**unter** *acc* among); divide up (**in** *acc* into); partition
die **Aufteilung, –en** *vbl noun*; *also* division
auftischen serve up
der **Auftrag, ⸚e** orders; instructions; assignment; task; mission; commission; application (of paint *etc*); *comm* order (**über** *acc* for); *leg* brief; **im** ~ (+*gen*) on behalf of; **in** ~ **geben** commission, *comm* order (**bei** from) || **der ~geber, –** client; **das ~s|buch, ⸚er** order-book; **a~s|gemäß** as instructed; *comm* as per order; **das ~s|werk, –e** commissioned work
auftragen* apply (paint *etc*) (**auf** *acc* to), put on (make-up); serve up; wear out (clothes); (+*dat of pers*) ask to convey (greetings); instruct (to); (*v/i*) make s.o. look fat; **dick** ~ *coll* lay it on thick
auftreffen* (*sn*): ~ **auf** (*acc*) hit
auftreiben* distend; make (dough) rise; drive out of bed; (wind) raise (dust), whip up (waves); *agr* drive to market/the mountain pasture; *coll* get hold of; (*v/i sn*) distend; (dough) rise
auftrennen unpick
auftreten* kick open; (*v/i sn*) appear (in public, *theat etc*); tread (softly *etc*); have a ... manner; occur, (difficulty *etc*) arise; ~ **als** (*sn*) act as; *leg*, *theat* appear as; ~ **gegen** (*sn*) oppose, speak out against; ~ **mit** (*sn*) state; **zum erstenmal** ~ make one's début
das **Auftreten** manner; occurrence; appearance (at *etc*); **erstes** ~ début
der **Auftrieb, –e** impetus; *agr* driving to mountain pasture; sale of cattle (at market); number (of cattle) offered for sale; *phys* buoyancy; *aer* lift; **neuen** ~ **bekommen** be given a boost; (+*dat*) ~ **geben** give (s.o., sth.) a boost, buoy up; **keinen** ~ **haben** lack drive
der **Auftritt, –e** appearance, *theat* entrance; scene (= show of anger *etc*); *theat* scene
auftrumpfen demonstrate one's superiority; be full of oneself; ~ **mit** parade
auftun* open; (+*dat*) *coll* put on (s.o.'s) plate; **sich** ~ open; open up
auftürmen pile up; **sich** ~ pile up; tower up
aufwachen (*sn*) wake up; ~ **aus** awake from; **aus der Narkose** ~ come round
aufwachsen* [–ks–] (*sn*) grow up
aufwallen (*sn*) boil up; (mist) surge up; (blood) boil; ~ **in** (*dat*) well up within; ~ **lassen** bring to the boil
die **Aufwallung, –en** upsurge (of emotion)
der **Aufwand** expenditure (**an** *dat* of); outlay (on); extravagance; ~ **an** (*dat*) *also* amount of ... expended/used; ~ **an Zeit** time spent; **das erfordert einen großen** ~ **an** (**Konzentration** *etc*) that requires a great deal of (concentration *etc*); **großen** ~ **treiben** be very extravagant || **die ~s|entschädigung, –en** expense allowance
aufwärmen warm up; rake up; **sich** ~ warm oneself; *sp* warm up
die **Aufwarte|frau, –en** charwoman, cleaning woman
aufwarten (+*dat*) wait on; *arch* call on; (+*dat*) ~ **mit** serve (s.o. sth.); ~ **mit** come up with
aufwärts upward(s); up; **von ...** ~ from ... up || **die A~entwicklung, –en** upward trend; **~gehen*** (*sep*; *sn*) *coll* (**es geht** ~ **mit ...** things are looking up for ..., ... is *etc* getting better)
Aufwartung: (+*dat*) **seine** ~ **machen** pay one's respects to
der **Aufwasch** washing-up, dirty dishes *or* dishwashing *US*; **in einem** ~ in one go

aufwaschen* wash up, wash the dishes *US*
aufwecken (*see also* **aufgeweckt**) wake up
aufweichen soak; make sodden; undermine (system); (*v/i sn*) go soft; become soggy
der **Aufweis, –e** pointing out
aufweisen* show; exhibit (symptom *etc*); have (weakness *etc*); **aufzuweisen haben** have, possess; (place *etc*) boast
aufwenden* spend (money, time) (**für** on); expend (energy) on; put in (effort); use, employ; **alles ~, (um) zu ...** do one's utmost to ...
aufwendig costly; extravagant
die **Aufwendung, –en** use, employment; expenditure (of); (*pl*) expenditure (**für** on)
aufwerfen* throw up; throw open; throw on the fire; put (card) on the table; toss (head); pout (lips); build (embankment *etc*); bring up, raise (question); **sich ~ zu** set oneself up as
aufwerten [–e:–] revalue (upwards); place a higher value on; enhance (standing)
die **Aufwertung, –en** *vbl noun*; *also* (upward) revaluation
aufwickeln unwrap; wind up (string *etc*); put (hair) in curlers; **~ auf** (*acc*) wind onto
aufwiegeln stir up; incite (**zu** to)
die **Aufwiegelung, –en** incitement
aufwiegen* (*like* **wiegen**[1]) compensate for; **nicht mit Gold aufzuwiegen** worth his/her/its weight in gold
der **Aufwiegler, –** agitator
aufwieglerisch inflammatory
der **Aufwind, –e** up-current; **~ erhalten** receive a boost
aufwinden* hoist (with a winch)
aufwirbeln (*sn if v/i*) whirl up; **Staub ~** *coll* cause a stir
Aufwisch–: der ~lappen, – floorcloth
aufwischen wipe (floor); wipe up
aufwühlen churn up; turn up; stir (emotionally)
aufzahlen *SGer* pay extra
aufzählen enumerate
die **Aufzählung, –en** enumeration
aufzäumen bridle; **das Pferd beim Schwanz ~** *coll* put the cart before the horse
aufzehren eat up; use up; **sich (innerlich) ~** eat one's heart out
aufzeichnen draw; record (*also rad etc*)
die **Aufzeichnung, –en** *vbl noun*; *also* record; *comput*, *rad*, *etc* recording; (*pl*) notes
aufzeigen show; point out; (pupil) put up one's hand
aufziehen* raise; hoist; undo; pull open (drawer), draw (curtain); uncork; unpick; mount (photograph); fit (tyre); wind up; bring up (child), rear; organize; start up; *med* fill (syringe); draw up; *coll* tease (**mit** about); (*v/i sn*) march up; (clouds *etc*) come up
die **Aufzucht** rearing
der **Aufzug, ¨–e** procession, *mil* parade; approach (of clouds); get-up; lift, elevator *US*, (for loads) hoist; *theat* act; *gym* pull-up
aufzwingen* (+*dat*) force on; impose (will *etc*) on; **sich ~** (+*dat*) force itself on
aufzwirbeln twirl up (moustache)
der **Aug|apfel, ..äpfel** eyeball; apple of (s.o.'s) eye
das **Auge, –n** eye; speck of fat (in soup), eye (on potato, butterfly's wing), pip (on dice *etc*); **blaues ~** black eye (*see also* + **mit** *below*); **(große) ~n machen** *coll* stare in amazement; (+*dat*) **schöne ~n machen** *coll* make eyes at; **ein ~ zudrücken** *coll* turn a blind eye; **kein ~ zutun** *coll* not sleep a wink
in prepositional phrases:
aus dem ~ (*in fig usage*)/**den ~n verlieren** lose sight of (*also* = lose touch with); **nicht aus den ~n lassen** not let out of one's sight; **aus den ~n, aus dem Sinn** out of sight, out of mind
in: im ~ behalten keep an eye on; bear in mind; **im ~ haben** have in mind; **~ in ~** face to face; (+*dat*) **in die ~n sehen** look (s.o.) in the face; **ins ~ fallen/springen** catch the eye; **ins ~ fassen** contemplate; envisage; **ins ~ gehen** *coll* go wrong; (+*dat*) **ins ~ sehen** face up to; look (death) in the face; (+*dat*) **ins ~/in die ~n stechen** catch (s.o.'s) eye, take (s.o.'s) fancy
mit anderen ~n sehen see in a different light; **mit einem blauen ~ davonkommen** *coll* get off lightly
unter vier ~n privately; **Gespräch unter vier ~n** tête-à-tête; (+*dat*) **nicht mehr unter die ~n treten können** be unable to face
vor aller ~n in front of everybody; (+*dat*) **vor ~n führen** show; demonstrate to; **vor ~n haben** have in front of one; see (in one's mind's eye); be aware of; **sich** *dat* **... vor ~n halten** bear in mind
äugeln: ~ mit make eyes at; **~ nach** glance furtively at
äugen look (cautiously)
Augen– ... of the eye(s); eye ...; optic ...; ophthalmic ...;
der ~arzt, ¨–e oculist; **der ~blick, –e** moment (**einen A.!** just a moment!; **im A.** at the moment; **jeden A.** any moment; **alle ~blicke** all the time); **a~blicklich** momentary; immediate; present; (*adv*) immediately; at the moment; **~blicks–** short-lived ..., momentary ...; **das ~blinzeln** blinking of the eyes; wink; **die ~braue, –n** eyebrow; **der ~brauen|stift, –e** eyebrow pencil;

a~fällig conspicuous; evident; **die ~heil|kunde** ophthalmology; **~höhe (in A.** at eye-level); **die ~höhle, -n** eye-socket; **die ~klappe, -n** eye-patch; (*pl*) blinkers; **das ~leiden, -** eye trouble; **das ~licht** eyesight; **das ~lid, -er** eyelid; **das ~maß** eye (for judging distance *etc*); judgement; **der ~mensch, -en** (*wk masc*) person with a strong visual sense; **~merk (sein A. richten auf** (*acc*) direct one's attention to); **der ~optiker, -** optician; **das ~paar, -e** pair of eyes; **die ~ränder** *pl* rings round the eyes; **der ~schein** seeing for oneself; appearances (**in A. nehmen** scrutinize; **dem A. nach** to all appearances); **a~scheinlich** evident; **der ~schirm, -e** eye-shade; **der ~schmaus** *coll* sight for sore eyes; **der ~spiegel, -** ophthalmoscope; **die ~weide** delight to the eye; **die ~wimper, -n** eyelash; **die ~wischerei, -en** eyewash; **der ~zeuge, -n** (*wk masc*) eye-witness; **der ~zeugen|bericht, -e** eyewitness account; **das ~zwinkern** wink; **a~zwinkernd** with a wink

der **Augias|stall** [-as-] the Augean stables; **den ~ ausmisten** clean up

-äugig -eyed

der **August** (*gen* -(s)), **-e** August; **im ~** in August

August ['ao-]: **dummer ~** clown

augusteisch, *Rom hist* **A~** Augustan

der **Augustiner, -** Augustinian

Augustiner- Augustinian ...

die **Auktion, -en** auction

der **Auktionator, -(or)en** auctioneer

die **Aula, -(l)en** assembly hall

das **Au-pair-Mädchen** [o'pɛːɐ-], **-** au pair (girl)

die **Aureole, -n** *art*, *astron* aureole

aus 1 *prep* (+*dat*) out of; from; made of; from, out of (fear *etc*), for (reason); 2 *adv* out (*also sp*); (switched) off; over, finished

auf ... ~ after; bent on

~ ... heraus out of; from; as a result of; over (difficulty *etc*); past (age); **~ sich heraus** on one's own initiative

~ mit: es ist ~ mit ... ... is *etc* finished/at an end; it's all up with ...

von ... ~ from; **von 'sich ~** of one's own accord; **von 'mir ~** as far as I'm concerned; **von 'mir ~!** it's O.K. with me!

weder ~ noch ein wissen be at one's wits' end

das **Aus** *coll* 'curtains'; **im/ins ~** *sp* out (of play)

---

aus- *sep pref – general senses*:

(*i*) ... out (*eg* **~treiben** drive out, expel, **~fließen** flow out);

(*ii*) un- (*eg* **~haken** unhook, **~packen** unpack);

(*iii*) *indicates completion* ... to the end, ... completely, finish ...ing, *etc* (*eg* **~lesen** read to the end, finish reading, **~heilen** cure completely, **~kosten** enjoy to the full, savour, **~pendeln** stop swinging);

(*iv*) *indicates derision or audience's rejection* (*eg* **~lachen** laugh at, **~buhen** boo)

---

aus|arbeiten work out; draw up; **sich ~** take exercise

aus|arten [-aː-] (*sn*) behave badly; (child) get out of hand; **~ in** (*acc*)/**zu** degenerate into

die **Aus|artung, -en** *vbl noun*; *also* degeneration

aus|atmen breathe out

ausbacken (*p/part* **ausgebacken**) bake thoroughly; deep-fry

ausbaden *coll*: **~ müssen** have to suffer the consequences of

ausbaggern dredge; excavate

ausbalancieren [-lãs-], **sich ~** balance

ausbaldowern (*p/part* **ausbaldowert**) *coll* scout out

der **Ausball, ⸗e** dead ball

der **Ausbau** extension; expansion; development; consolidation; conversion (of building *etc*: **zu** into); removal (of engine *etc*); **a~fähig** capable of extension/expansion/development; (job) with good prospects

ausbauen extend; expand; develop; consolidate; convert (building *etc*: **zu** into); remove (engine *etc*)

ausbedingen (*p/t* **bedang aus,** *p/part* **ausbedungen**): **sich** *dat* **... ~** stipulate; reserve (right)

ausbeißen*: **sich** *dat* **... ~** break (tooth) (**an** *dat* on); **sich** *dat* **die Zähne ~ an** (*dat*) wrestle unsuccessfully with

ausbessern, die Ausbesserung, -en repair

ausbeulen (*see also* **ausgebeult**) make baggy; make a dent in; knock out the dent(s) in, *tech* beat out

die **Ausbeute** results (of research); *min* yield

ausbeuten exploit (*also min*)

der **Ausbeuter, -** exploiter

die **Ausbeutung** exploitation

ausbezahlen pay off; buy out; (+*dat*) pay (s.o. salary *etc*)

ausbiegen* bend outwards; straighten; (*v/i sn*) swerve; (+*dat*) swerve to avoid; avoid

ausbilden (*see also* **ausgebildet, Auszubildende**) train (*also mil*, *mus* voice; **an** *dat* in the use of); develop; (plant) form; *tech* design; **sich ~** form; develop; = **sich ~ lassen** train (**als/zu** as); **sich ~ in** (*dat*) study

der **Ausbilder, -** instructor

die **Ausbildung, -en** training; development; formation; **sich in der ~ befinden** be undergoing training

ausbitten*: **sich** *dat* **... ~** request; insist on; **das möchte ich mir ausgebeten haben!** I should think so too!

ausblasen* blow out; blow (egg); *tech* shut down (blast-furnace)

ausbleiben* (*sn*) stay out; stay away; fail to materialize; not occur; *med* stop; **nicht ~ können** be inevitable; **das Ausbleiben** staying out; non-appearance; absence; non-occurrence; failure to materialize; *med* failure

ausbleichen fade; bleach (bones *etc*); (*v/i*: *p/t* **blich aus,** *p/part* **ausgeblichen/ausgebleicht**) (*sn*) fade; bleach

ausblenden *rad etc* fade out; *comput* mask

der **Ausblick, –e** view (**auf** *acc* of); outlook (for the future)

ausblicken: ~ nach look out for

ausblühen finish flowering; (*sn*) *chem* effloresce

ausbluten stop bleeding; (*sn*) lose all one's/its blood; be drained of its vitality; **~ lassen** drain the blood from (animal); allow (wound) to bleed

ausbohren drill (hole, tooth); gouge out

ausbomben bomb out; **ausgebombt werden** be bombed out

ausbooten take ashore (by boat); *coll* kick out

ausborgen *coll* (+*dat*) lend to; **sich** *dat* **... ~** borrow (**bei/von** from)

ausboxen outbox

ausbraten* fry the fat out of; roast/fry thoroughly

ausbrechen* break off; knock out (tooth, wall); let (window) into the wall; bring up (contents of stomach); (*v/i sn*) break out; erupt; *mot* skid; **mir brach der Schweiß aus** I broke out in a sweat; **~ aus** (*sn*) break out of (*also mil*); **~ in** (*acc*) (*sn*) break into (applause *etc*); explode with (rage); burst into (tears); **in Gelächter ~** burst out laughing

der **Ausbrecher, –** escaped prisoner

ausbreiten spread (out); open out; stretch out, extend (arms); display; unfold, set forth; **sich ~** spread; extend; *coll* spread oneself; **sich ~ über** (*acc*) hold forth on

die **Ausbreitung** *vbl noun*; *also* spread

ausbrennen* (*see also* **ausgebrannt**) (sun) scorch; *med* cauterize; (*v/i sn*) burn (itself) out; be gutted; *coll* be burnt out; **wie ausgebrannt** parched

ausbringen* propose (toast) (**auf** *acc* to)

der **Ausbruch, ⸚e** break-out (*also mil*), escape; outbreak; eruption; outburst; **zum ~ kommen** break out; erupt; (storm) break

ausbrüten hatch; incubate; *coll* hatch (up) (plan); *coll* be sickening for

ausbuchen [–u:–] (*see also* **ausgebucht**) *fin* write off

die **Ausbuchtung, –en** bulge; indentation (of coastline)

ausbuddeln *coll* dig up; dig out (old letters *etc*)

ausbügeln iron, press; iron out (crease, misunderstanding, *etc*)

ausbuhen boo

Ausbund: ein ~ an (*dat*)/**von** the embodiment of, ... personified

ausbürgern deprive of citizenship

ausbürsten brush out; give (sth.) a brush

die **Ausdauer** perseverance; endurance; stamina

ausdauernd persistent, persevering; *bot* perennial; *sp* with stamina

ausdehnbar capable of expansion; *tech* expansible

ausdehnen (*see also* **ausgedehnt**) stretch; extend (**auf** *acc* to); expand; **sich ~** stretch; expand; spread; (party *etc*) go on; (land) stretch out; **sich ~ auf** (*acc*) spread to; extend to

die **Ausdehnung, –en** expansion; extension; spread; extent; expanse; *math* dimension

ausdenken* think through; (*usu* + **sich** *dat*) devise, think up; make up; imagine; **es ist nicht auszudenken** it doesn't bear thinking about

ausdeuten interpret

ausdeutschen (+*dat*) *Aust coll* spell out for

die **Ausdeutung, –en** interpretation

ausdienen (*see also* **ausgedient**): **ausgedient haben** *coll* have had his/her/its day; have had it; (**das Telefon** *etc*) **hat nicht ausgedient** (the telephone *etc*) still has its uses

ausdiskutieren thrash out

ausdorren (*sn*) dry up; become parched

ausdörren dry up; parch; (*v/i sn*) dry up; become parched

ausdrehen switch off; *tech* bore

der **Ausdruck, ⸚e** expression (*also math*); term; ability to express oneself; (*pl*, *with adj*) *also* language; (*pl* **–e**) *comput* expression; print-out; *print* completion of printing; **das ist gar kein ~!** that's not the word for it!; **Ausdrücke gebrauchen** use bad language; (+*dat*) **~ geben/verleihen** express (feeling *etc*); **zum ~ bringen** voice; express; **zum ~ kommen** be expressed

ausdrucken *comput* print out; *print* finish printing; print in full

ausdrücken express, (*with adv*) put; be expressive of; squeeze (lemon, spot, *etc*); squeeze out; stub out (cigarette); **anders ausgedrückt** to put it another way; **ausgedrückt in** (*dat*) expressed in; in terms of

sich ~ express oneself; put it (*eg* **wenn ich mich so ~ darf** if I may put it that way); **sich ~ in** (*dat*) be expressed in; **in** (**seinen Worten** *etc*) **drückt sich ... aus** (his words *etc*) show ...

ausdrücklich express, explicit; (*adv*) *also* specifically

Ausdrucks– ... of expression; **die ~form, –en**

form of expression; **die ~kraft** expressiveness; **a~leer = a~los** expressionless; (look) vacant; **das ~mittel, –** means of expression; **a~voll** expressive; (*adv*) *also* with expression; **die ~weise, –n** way of expressing oneself; diction

ausdünnen thin out

ausdunsten, ausdünsten give off; *bot, physiol* transpire; (*v/i*) give off vapour/an odour; *bot, physiol* transpire

aus|einander apart; (write) as two words; from one another; **~ sein** *coll* have broken up; (engagement) be off

aus|einander– *sep pref* (*i*) ... apart; (*ii*) ... to pieces; (*iii*) ... in all directions

aus|einanderbrechen* (*sn*) break up

aus|einanderbreiten unfold, open out

aus|einanderbringen* separate; cause (people) to fall out

aus|einander|entwickeln: sich ~ grow apart

aus|einanderfallen* (*sn*) fall apart

aus|einanderfalten unfold

aus|einandergehen* (*sn*) part; diverge; break up; come apart; *coll* get fat; **~d** divergent; **das Auseinandergehen** parting; break-up; divergence

aus|einanderhalten* keep apart; keep separate; distinguish (between), tell apart

aus|einanderjagen scatter

aus|einanderklaffen gape; diverge greatly

aus|einanderklamüsern (*p/part* **auseinanderklamüsert**) *coll* disentangle; (+*dat of pers*) put (s.o.) wise to

aus|einanderkommen* (*sn*) *coll* drift apart; lose touch

aus|einanderlaufen* (*sn*) scatter; diverge; (ice cream *etc*) melt; spread; (colour) run

aus|einanderleben: sich ~ drift apart

aus|einandernehmen* take apart; *sp coll* demolish

aus|einanderreißen* tear apart

aus|einanderrollen unroll; roll in different directions; **sich ~** unroll

aus|einanderrücken move apart; (*v/i sn*) move apart; *mil* disengage

aus|einandersetzen (+*dat*) explain to; **sich ~ mit** have it out with; grapple with; deal with; *leg* come to an agreement with; **sich ~ müssen mit** *also* be up against (opponent *etc*)

die **Aus|einandersetzung, –en** discussion, debate; argument, row; difference; clash; **~ mit** grappling with; dealing with

aus|einanderstieben* (*sn*) scatter

aus|einanderstreben seek to go their *etc* separate ways; (opinions *etc*) diverge; (*sn*) go off in different directions

aus|einandertreiben* drive apart; disperse; (*v/i sn*) drift apart

aus|einanderwickeln unroll

aus|einanderziehen* pull apart; stretch; (*v/i sn*: people living together) split up; **sich ~** string out

aus|erkoren chosen

aus|erlesen choice; select; (taste) exquisite

aus|ersehen* choose (**zu** for (task), as); destine (for, to be)

aus|erwählen choose

aus|essen* eat up; clean up (plate); eat (grapefruit, melon); (*v/i*) *coll* finish eating

ausfächern fan out

ausfahrbar extendible; *aer* retractable

ausfahren* (*see also* **ausgefahren**) take for a drive/ride; deliver; cut up (road), *rail etc* wear out (rails); extend, *aer* lower (undercarriage), *naut* raise (periscope); take (bend) on the outside; *mot rac* run (vehicle) flat out; hold (motor race); (*v/i sn*) go for a drive; (spirit) leave the body; *rail* pull out of the station; *naut* put to sea

der **Ausfahrer, –** *SGer* delivery-man

die **Ausfahrt, –en** departure; outing (in car *etc*), drive; exit (from garage, motorway), mouth (of harbour)

der **Ausfall, ⸚e** loss; dropping out; failure, breakdown (of machine); absence; cancellation; (abusive) attack, *pl* invective; result; *ling* dropping; *mil* sortie; *fenc, gym* lunge, *weight-lift* split; (*pl*) days lost; *mil* losses; **die ~straße, –n** main road leading out of the city/town

ausfallen* (*see also* **ausgefallen**) (*sn*) (hair *etc*) fall out, *chem* be precipitated, *ling* be dropped; drop out; be absent; be cancelled, (wages *etc*) not be paid; not be available (for sth.); break down, fail, *comput* go down; turn out (well *etc*), prove to be (favourable *etc*); *fenc* lunge; **ihm fallen die Haare/Zähne aus** he's losing his hair/teeth; **die Schule fällt heute aus** there's no school today; **~ lassen** cancel; **~d** abusive (**gegen** towards)

ausfällen *chem* precipitate; *Swiss leg* impose

ausfällig abusive (**gegen** towards)

ausfasern (*sn*) fray

ausfechten* fight out

ausfegen sweep out

ausfeilen file; polish (style *etc*)

ausfertigen issue; draw up; sign (in official capacity)

die **Ausfertigung, –en** *vbl noun*; *also* copy; **in zweifacher/dreifacher/vierfacher ~** in duplicate/triplicate/quadruplicate

ausfindig: ~ machen trace; find (after a search)

ausfischen fish out (pond *etc*)

ausflaggen *sp* mark out with flags

ausflicken *coll* patch up

ausfliegen* fly out; (*v/i sn*) fly out (of an area); (bird) fly off; leave the nest; **der**

Vogel ist ausgeflogen *coll* the bird has flown; **ausgeflogen sein** *coll* be out

ausfließen* (*sn*) flow out; (container) leak

ausflippen (*see also* **ausgeflippt**) (*sn*) *coll* freak out; drop out

die **Ausflucht, ⸚e** excuse; **Ausflüchte machen** make excuses

der **Ausflug, ⸚e** excursion; outing, trip; *zool* flight (from nest *etc*); **einen ~ machen** go on an excursion

der **Ausflügler, –** excursionist, tripper

Ausflugs–: der ~dampfer, – pleasure-steamer; **das ~lokal, –e** restaurant/café catering for excursionists; **das ~ziel, –e** popular excursion resort

der **Ausfluß, ⸚(ss)e** outlet; outflow, *med* discharge; product (of imagination *etc*)

ausfolgen *Aust* hand over (*dat* to)

ausformen shape, form; frame (idea *etc*), fashion (work of art); **~ zu** shape into; **sich ~** take shape

ausforschen question (**über** *acc* about); find out; *Aust* trace

ausfragen question, quiz

ausfransen (*sn*) fray

ausfressen* (animal) eat up; eat up all the food in; (water) eat away; *coll* suffer for; **er hat etwas ausgefressen** *coll* he's been up to something

ausfugen point (wall *etc*)

die **Ausfuhr, –en** export (of); (country's *etc*) exports; (*pl*) exports; *in compds* export ...; **die ~bewilligung, –en** export licence; **das ~land, ⸚er** exporting country; **das ~verbot, –e** export ban; **der ~zoll, ⸚e** export duty

ausführbar feasible, practicable; *comm* exportable

ausführen take out (to dinner *etc*); take (invalid, dog) for a walk, *joc* show off (new dress *etc*); carry out (order, plan, *etc*), execute (movement, painting in oils, *etc*), *sp* take; explain (at length), expound; *comm* export; **weiter ~** develop, elaborate on; **in (Palisanderholz** *etc*) **ausgeführt** in (rosewood *etc*); **~de Gewalt** executive; **der/die Ausführende** (*decl as adj*) performer

ausführlich detailed; full; (*adv*) in detail; **sehr ~** in great detail; **~ beantworten/erklären** give a detailed answer to/explanation of; **~er** in greater detail; **Ausführlich(er)es** (*decl as adj*) (further) details

die **Ausführlichkeit** fullness (of report *etc*); **in aller ~** in great detail

die **Ausführung, –en** *vbl noun*; *also* execution; explanation, exposition; model (of car *etc*); version; finish; workmanship; (*pl*) remarks; **zur ~ bringen/kommen** carry/be carried into effect

ausfüllen fill in; fill (gap, space, position), close (loophole); fill in/out (form); occupy (one's time); occupy, take up; occupy (s.o.'s) mind; (job *etc*) give satisfaction to

ausfüttern[1] feed up

ausfüttern[2] line

Ausg. (= **Ausgabe**) ed.

die **Ausgabe, –n** distribution; issuing, *fin* issue (of shares); issue (of periodical), edition; expense, *pl* expenditure; version; *comput* output, read-out; = **die ~stelle, –n** issuing office; counter; hatch

der **Ausgang, ⸚e** exit, (at air terminal) gate; going out, (of convalescent) outing; outcome; end(ing); starting-point (of talk *etc*); (*pl*) outgoing items; **mit tödlichem ~** fatal; **~ haben** have one's day/evening off; **einen (guten** *etc*) **~ nehmen** turn out (well *etc*); **seinen ~ nehmen von** start in

ausgangs (+*gen*) at the end of

Ausgangs– initial ...; starting ...; *elect* output ...; **der ~punkt, –e** starting-point; point of departure; **die ~sperre, –n** (= **~verbot**); **die ~sprache** source language; **das ~verbot, –e** curfew; *mil* confinement to barracks

ausgeben* spend (**für** on); hand out (food *etc*), issue (tickets *etc*, *fin* shares, *mil* order); give (password); *comput* output; *coll* stand (round); **~ als/für** pass off as; **sich ~** tire oneself out; **sich ~ als/für** pass oneself off as

ausgebeult *p/part*; *also* baggy; dented

ausgebildet *p/part*; *also* trained; qualified

ausgebrannt *p/part*; *also* (person) burnt out

ausgebucht [–u:–] booked up

ausgebufft *coll* crafty

die **Ausgeburt** [–u:–], **–en** figment (of imagination); product (of sick mind *etc*)

ausgedehnt *p/part*; *also* extensive; (walk) long

ausgedient *p/part*; *mil arch* (general *etc*) retired; *coll* worn-out

ausgefahren *p/part*; *also* well-worn

ausgefallen *p/part*; *also* unusual; odd

ausgeflippt *p/part*; **~er Typ** *coll* drop-out; 'freak'

ausgefuchst [–ks–] *coll* crafty

ausgeglichen *p/part*; *also* balanced; (climate) equable; *sp* even

die **Ausgeglichenheit** balance; evenness; equability

Ausgeh–: der ~anzug, ⸚e = **die ~uniform, –en** walking-out dress; **das ~verbot, –e** curfew; orders to stay indoors; *mil* confinement to barracks

ausgehen* (*sn*) go out; (supplies *etc*) run out; (hair *etc*) fall out; (colour) run; (cigar *etc*) go out; end, turn out (well *etc*); **frei ~** get off scot-free; **leer ~** come away empty-handed; **ihm ging das Benzin aus** he ran out of petrol/gasoline *US*; **ihm ging die Geduld**

aus he ran out of patience; **es geht sich aus** *Aust* it's enough; ~ **lassen** let (s.o., sth.) go out; issue (decree *etc*), send out

~ **auf** (*acc*) aim at; be out to ... (*eg* **auf Gewinn** make a profit, **auf Stimmenfang** catch votes); go in search of; *ling* end in; **darauf ~ zu ...** set out to ...

~ **bei: aus- und eingehen bei** be in and out of (s.o.'s) house

~ **von** (roads) radiate from; start at/in/with; (idea *etc*) come from; emanate from, *or conveyed by* radiate (*with prep obj becoming subj, eg* **von der Krankenschwester ging menschliche Wärme aus** the nurse radiated human warmth), there is ... about (*eg* **ein geheimnisvolles Fluidum geht von ihr aus** there is an aura of mystery about her); (person) start from, take as a point of departure; **in (seiner Untersuchung** *etc*) **von ... ~** base (one's investigation *etc*) on; **davon ~, daß ...** go on the assumption that ...

ausgehend outgoing; (period) late; **im ~en Mittelalter** towards the end of the Middle Ages

ausgehungert *p/part*; *also* starved

ausgeklügelt *p/part*; *also* ingenious

ausgekocht *p/part*; *coll* cunning

ausgelassen *p/part*; *also* boisterous; exuberant; (dancing *etc*) wild; ~ **sein** be in high spirits

[die] **Ausgelassenheit** boisterousness; exuberance; wildness

ausgeleiert *p/part*; *also* worn-out

ausgelernt *p/part*; *also* fully-trained

[das] **Ausgeliefert|sein:** ~ **an** (*acc*) being at the mercy of

ausgemacht *p/part*; *also* certain; *coll* out-and-out, downright; **es ist eine ~e Sache, daß ...** it's a certainty that ...

ausgemergelt *p/part*; *also* emaciated

ausgenommen *p/part*; *also* except; unless

ausgepicht *coll* cunning

ausgeprägt *p/part*; *also* (face) distinctive; marked, pronounced

ausgepumpt *p/part*; *coll* all in

ausgerechnet *p/part*; *also* precisely; ... of all days/places/people/things *etc*; *eg* ~ **du** you of all people

ausgereift *p/part*; *also* mature

ausgeruht *p/part*; *also* rested

ausgeschlossen *p/part*; *also* impossible; out of the question; **es ist nicht ~, daß ...** one can't rule out the possibility that ...

ausgeschnitten *p/part*; *also* low-cut; **tief ~** with a plunging neckline

ausgesprochen *p/part*; distinct, pronounced; positive; (*adv*) decidedly, distinctly

ausgestalten organize, arrange; decorate; ~ **zu** develop into

[die] **Ausgestaltung** organization, arrangement; development; form

ausgestellt *p/part*; *also* flared

ausgestorben *p/part*; *also* extinct; **wie ~** deserted

[der] **Ausgestoßene** (*fem* **die ~**) (*decl as adj*) outcast

ausgesucht [–u:–] *p/part*; *also* choice, select; studied; exceptional; (*adv*) exceptionally; **das Angebot an ... ist schon sehr ~** there isn't much choice in the way of ... any more

ausgetreten *p/part*; *also* well-trodden; worn-down

ausgewachsen [–ks–] *p/part*; *also* full-grown; fully-fledged; full-blown; *coll* absolute, utter

ausgewählt *p/part*; *also* select, choice; (works) selected

ausgewechselt [–ks–] *p/part*; **wie ~** a different man/woman

ausgewogen *p/part*; *also* (well-)balanced

[die] **Ausgewogenheit** balance

ausgezehrt *p/part*; *also* emaciated

ausgezeichnet *p/part*; *also* excellent; ~ **(kochen** *etc*) **können** be an excellent (cook *etc*)

ausgiebig extensive; (meal) substantial; ~ (**frühstücken/schlafen** *etc*) have a good (breakfast/sleep *etc*)

ausgießen* pour out; empty; put out (by pouring on water); *tech* fill (with tar *etc*); ~ **über** (*acc*) (sun) shed (light) on; pour (scorn) on

[der] **Ausgleich, -e** compensation; counterbalance; settlement (*also fin, leg*); reconcilement (of interests *etc*); *sp* equalizer, equalization *US*; **als/zum ~** in compensation, to make up for (loss *etc*); as a counterbalance; (+*gen*) *comm* in settlement of

ausgleichen* (*see also* **ausgeglichen**) balance; equalize; even out; compensate for; counterbalance; offset; settle (difference; *also comm*); (*v/i*) *sp* equalize

sich ~ *comm* balance; (*recip*) cancel out; **sich dadurch ~, daß ...** be offset by the fact that ...

ausgleichend compensatory; (justice) poetic

Ausgleichs–: der ~fonds, – equalization fund; **das ~getriebe, –** differential gear; **die ~gymnastik** keep-fit exercises; **das ~rennen, –** handicap; **der ~sport** exercise (*eg* jogging, swimming; **als A. ...** for exercise ...); **das ~tor, -e** equalizer

ausgleiten* (*sn*) slip; (+*dat*) slip from (s.o.'s) hands

ausgliedern exclude; ~ **aus** detach from; take out of

ausglühen (sun *etc*) parch; *tech* anneal; *med* sterilize; (*v/i sn*) stop glowing; burn out

ausgraben* dig up; dig out; disinter; unearth (secret *etc*); rake up; *archaeol* excavate

die **Ausgrabung, -en** *vbl noun*; *also* disinterment; *archaeol* excavation

ausgräten bone

ausgreifen* (horse) step out; **(weit) ~d** (stride) long; (gesture) sweeping; (plan) ambitious

der **Ausguck, -e** look-out; **~ halten** keep a look-out

der **Ausguß, ¨-(ss)e** sink; drain

aushaben* *coll* have taken off; have finished; (*v/i*) finish (at school *etc*)

aushacken hoe up; peck out

aushaken unhook; **sich ~** come unhooked/undone; **es hakt bei mir aus** *coll* I give up; something in me snaps

aushalten* endure, bear, be able to stand; meet (s.o.'s gaze); sustain; stand up to (journey *etc*); *mus* hold, sustain; *coll* keep (lover, mistress); (*v/i*) hold out; **~ bei** stick with; **den Vergleich ~ mit** bear comparison with; **ich halte es vor (Kälte** *etc*) **nicht mehr aus** I can't stand the (cold *etc*) any more; **er hält es (nirgends** *etc*) **lange aus** he never stays (anywhere *etc*) for long; **es ist nicht auszuhalten** it's unbearable; **hier läßt es sich ~** it's really quite tolerable here; **sich ~ lassen von** *coll* be kept by

aushämmern beat out

aushandeln negotiate; work out (compromise)

aushändigen hand over (*dat* to)

der **Aushang, ¨-e** notice

Aushänge-: das ~schild, -er sign; figurehead, front (for); advertisement (for)

aushängen put up (notice); take off its hinges; (*v/i*: **~***, *like* **hängen** *v/i*) be (announced) on the notice-board/bulletin board *US*; **sich ~** lose its creases; come off its hinges; **sich ~ bei** *coll* take one's arm away from (s.o. else's)

ausharren hold out; wait (patiently); **auf seinem Posten ~** stay at one's post; **~ bei** stick with

aushauchen exhale; emit (odour); breathe (sigh, words); **sein Leben ~** breathe one's last

aushauen* cut (hole in ice, steps), hew (out) (path); hew (statue); thin out; clear (forest); prune

ausheben* dig up; dig (trench); take off its hinges; rob (nest); raid (hideout); pick up (gang); *Aust* empty (letter-box); *wrestl* pick up; *mil arch* levy; *coll* put out (shoulder *etc*); *coll* pump out (stomach)

aushecken *coll* cook up; hatch

ausheilen cure (completely); heal; (*v/i sn*) be cured (completely); heal (completely)

aushelfen*, ~ (+*dat*) help out

die **Aushilfe, -n** temporary assistance; temporary assistant

Aushilfs- temporary ...; **die ~kraft, ¨-e** temporary assistant; **a~weise** as a stopgap (**a. arbeiten** help out)

aushöhlen hollow out; erode; undermine (s.o.'s position *etc*)

die **Aushöhlung, -en** *vbl noun*; *also* erosion; cavity

ausholen swing one's arm back (before throwing *etc*); **mit der Hand ~** raise one's hand (before throwing *etc*); **zum Schlag/Gegenschlag ~** prepare to strike/strike back; **weit ~** go back a long way (in relating sth.); **(weit) ~d** (stride) long; (gesture) sweeping

aushorchen pump (for information) (**über** *acc* about)

aushülsen shell

aushungern (*see also* **ausgehungert**) starve; *mil* starve out

aushusten [-u:-] cough up; = **sich ~** finish coughing

aus|ixen (with typewriter) cross out (using x's), x out *US*

ausjäten pull up (weeds); weed

auskämmen comb out (*also* one's/s.o.'s hair); comb (forest *etc*); weed out

auskämpfen fight out; **er hat ausgekämpft** his suffering is at an end

auskehren sweep out

auskeilen (horse) kick; *geol* pinch

auskennen*: sich ~ know one's way around; know what's what; **sich ~ in** (*dat*) know one's way around (place); be well up in; **sich ~ mit** know; understand (women, horses, *etc*)

auskerben notch

auskernen stone

ausklammern exclude (**aus** from); *math* place outside the brackets

die **Ausklammerung, -en** *vbl noun*; *also* exclusion

der **Ausklang, ¨-e** conclusion, end; *mus* closing phrase

ausklappbar folding

ausklappen fold down

auskleiden undress; *tech* line; **sich ~** undress

ausklingen* stop ringing; (*sn*) die away; close; **~ in** (*acc*/*dat*)/**mit** close with

ausklinken release (bomb *etc*)

ausklopfen knock out (ash, pipe); beat (carpet); beat the dust out of

der **Ausklopfer, -** carpet-beater

ausklügeln (*see also* **ausgeklügelt**) think out

auskneifen* (*sn*) *coll* run away (*dat* from)

ausknipsen *coll* switch off

ausknobeln *coll* throw dice to decide; think up

ausknocken [-nɔkŋ] *box* knock out; *coll* 'lick'

auskochen (*see also* **ausgekocht**) boil; *med* sterilize; *coll* cook up

auskommen* (*sn*) manage, make do; *SGer* escape (**aus** from); ~ **mit** manage on; get on with; **gut miteinander** ~ get on well together; **mit ... ist nicht auszukommen** ... is *etc* impossible to get on with

das **Auskommen** livelihood; **sein** ~ **haben** make a living; **mit ... ist kein** ~ ... is *etc* impossible to get on with

auskosten enjoy to the full; savour; ~ **müssen** have to suffer

auskotzen *vulg*, **sich** ~ spew up

auskramen *coll* dig out; dig up

auskratzen scratch out; scrape out, *med* scrape; (*v/i sn*) *coll* run away (**vor** *dat* from)

auskriechen* (*sn*) hatch

auskristallisieren (*sn*) crystallize

auskugeln dislocate

auskühlen cool; cause to lose heat; (*v/i sn*) cool down; ~ **lassen** allow to cool

auskundschaften find out; ferret out; *mil* reconnoitre

die **Auskunft, ⸚e** information; information desk; *tel* directory enquiries/assistance *US*; (*pl*) information

die **Auskunftei, -en** information agency (giving information on creditworthiness)

Auskunfts– information ...; **die ~person, -en** informant (in survey); **die ~stelle, -n** information bureau

auskuppeln disengage the clutch

auskurieren cure completely; **sich** ~ be completely cured

auslachen laugh at; **sich** ~ have a good laugh

Auslade– unloading ...

ausladen* unload; *coll* ask (invited person) not to come; (*v/i*) project; **~d** *also* projecting; **(weit) ~d** sweeping; **breit ~d** broad

die **Ausladung, -en** *vbl noun*; *also* projection, overhang

die **Auslage, -n** show-case; display (in shop-window); *sp* starting position, *fenc* on guard position; (*pl*) expenses

auslagern remove (art treasures *etc*) to a safe place; *comm* take out of store

das **Ausland** foreign countries; **das (neutrale** *etc*) ~ (neutral *etc*) countries; **... des ~s** foreign (opinion, reaction, *etc*); **aus dem** ~ from abroad; **im/ins** ~ abroad

der **Ausländer, –** foreigner; *admin* alien

ausländisch foreign

Auslands– foreign ...; (stay *etc*) abroad; **der/die ~deutsche** (*decl as adj*) German living abroad; **das ~gespräch, -e** international call; **die ~reise, -n** trip abroad

Auslangen *Aust*: **das/sein** ~ **finden** make a living

der **Auslaß, ⸚(ss)e** *tech* outlet

auslassen* (*see also* **ausgelassen**) leave out; miss out; miss (opportunity); melt down (fat *etc*); *dressm* let out; *esp Aust* let go (of); leave in peace; *coll* leave off; ~ **an** (*dat*) vent on; **sich** ~ **über** (*acc*) speak about; **sich lang und breit** ~ **über** (*acc*) expatiate on

die **Auslassung, -en** omission; (*pl*) remarks; **die ~s|punkte** *pl* suspension points; **das ~s|zeichen, –** apostrophe

auslasten use to capacity; **ausgelastet** working to capacity; **voll ausgelastet** fully occupied

der **Auslauf, ⸚e** room to run about; chicken-run; exercise; outlet; *athl* run-out, *ski* outrun, *fenc* run-back, *row* clear water

auslaufen* (*sn exc* **sich** ~) run out, (ink *etc*) leak; empty; (colour *etc*) run; (path *etc*) end; come to a standstill, *athl* ease up (after finish); be discontinued; (contract *etc*) run out; turn out, end (well *etc*); *naut* put to sea; ~ **in** (*acc*) end in (point *etc*); lead into, (valley *etc*) open out into; **sich** ~ get some exercise (by going for a run or walk)

der **Ausläufer, –** *geog* spur; *bot* runner; *meteor* trough; ridge; *Aust*, *Swiss* errand-boy; (*pl*) outskirts; *geog* foothills

auslaugen exhaust, wear out; *chem* lixiviate; leach out

der **Auslaut, -e** *ling* final sound; **im** ~ in final position

auslauten *ling*: ~ **auf** (*acc*) end in

ausleben: sich ~ live one's life to the full (*esp* sensually)

auslecken lick clean; lick up

ausleeren empty; drain (glass)

auslegen display; lay out; lay (cable *etc*); put down (poison), put out (bait), set (snares); interpret (**als** as); pay (amount for s.o. by way of a loan); *agr* sow; *tech* design; ~ **mit** line with; pave with; inlay with; cover the floor of (room) with; **mit Teppichen** ~ carpet; **falsch** ~ misinterpret

der **Ausleger, –** interpreter; exegete; *tech* jib; cantilever; *row* outrigger; **das ~boot, -e** outrigger

die **Auslegung, -en** *vbl noun*; *also* interpretation; exegesis; **falsche** ~ misinterpretation

ausleiden: er hat ausgelitten his sufferings are at an end

ausleiern (*see also* **ausgeleiert**) *coll* wear out (elastic *etc*)

die **Ausleihe, -n** lending out; issue desk, checkout desk *US*

ausleihen* lend (*dat*/**an** *acc* to); (*also* + **sich** *dat*) borrow (**bei/von** from)

auslernen (*see also* **ausgelernt**) complete one's apprenticeship; **man lernt nie aus** you live and learn

die **Auslese** selection; élite; wine from specially selected grapes; *liter* anthology; **natürliche** ~ natural selection; **eine** ~ **treffen** make a selection || **das ~verfahren, -** selection procedure

auslesen* pick out (rotten apples *etc*); sort; select; finish reading; *comput* read out; (*v/i*) finish reading

ausleuchten illuminate

ausliefern hand over (*dat*/**an** *acc* to), *leg* extradite; *comm* supply (to retailer); **seinem Schicksal ~** abandon to his fate; (+*dat*) **(hilflos) ausgeliefert** (utterly) at the mercy of; **sich ~** (+*dat*) give oneself up to

die **Auslieferung, -en** *vbl noun*; *leg* extradition; *comm* supply; **der ~s|vertrag, ⸚e** extradition treaty

ausliegen* be on display; be available for inspection

auslöffeln eat up (with a spoon); empty (with a spoon); **~ müssen, was man sich eingebrockt hat** *coll* have to face the music

auslohnen pay off

auslöschen extinguish; wipe off (from blackboard); obliterate; wipe out (memory)

Auslöse- release ...

auslosen draw lots for; decide by lot

auslösen set off, trigger, *mech*, *phot* release; give rise to, cause; redeem (pawned object); ransom (**gegen** for)

der **Auslöser, -** trigger (for action *etc*); *phot* shutter release

die **Auslosung, -en** *vbl noun*; *also* draw

die **Auslösung, -en** *vbl noun*; *also* redemption; travel allowance; *mech* release

ausloten probe; fathom; *naut*, *tech* plumb

auslüften air; **sich ~** *coll* get a breath of fresh air

ausmachen (*see also* **ausgemacht**) put out (fire *etc*), switch off; settle; agree on; make out, spot; perceive; amount to; constitute, make up; **mit sich selbst ~** work out for oneself; **etwas ~** matter (*dat* to); **wenig/viel ~** matter little/a great deal (*dat* to); make little difference/a great deal of difference (to); **nichts ~** not matter (*dat* to); not make any difference (to); **es macht mir nichts aus zu ...** I don't mind (+*ger*); **macht es dir was aus?** do you mind?

ausmahlen (*p/part* **ausgemahlen**) grind (into flour)

ausmalen colour (woodcut *etc*); colour in; paint (in fresco *etc*), *esp SGer* paint (room); describe (graphically), paint (*eg* **etw. in düsteren Farben ~** paint a gloomy picture of sth.); **sich** *dat* **... ~** picture

ausmanövrieren outmanoeuvre

der **Ausmarsch, ⸚e** marching out, departure

ausmarschieren (*sn*) march out

das **Ausmaß, -e** extent; scale; (*pl*) dimensions; proportions; **in diesem/großem/geringem ~** on this/a large/a small scale

ausmauern line with brick

ausmeißeln chisel; remove with a chisel

ausmergeln (*see also* **ausgemergelt**) exhaust, drain of all strength; exhaust (soil)

ausmerzen destroy (vermin); cull; weed out; stamp out; eliminate (errors); obliterate (from memory)

ausmessen* measure

ausmieten *Swiss* let, rent *US* (occasionally)

ausmisten muck out; *coll* clear out

ausmontieren take out (engine *etc*)

ausmünden (*also sn*): **~ in** (*acc/dat*) open into, (river) empty into; end in

ausmustern withdraw (old model *etc*); *mil* exempt from military service

die **Ausnahme, -n** exception; **~ von der Regel** exception to the rule; **eine ~ bilden/machen** be/make an exception; **mit ~** (+*gen*) with the exception of, except for; **ohne ~** without exception

Ausnahme- special ...; **der ~fall, ⸚e** exception(al case); **der ~zustand, ⸚e** exceptional state of affairs; *pol* state of emergency

Ausnahms-: der ~fall, ⸚e *Aust* exception(al case); **a~los** without exception; **a~weise** by way of exception; for once

ausnehmen* (*see also* **ausgenommen**) remove (from nest, hive); take out (liver *etc*); rob (nest); raid (hideout), *mil* take out; gut (fish, game), draw (fowl); *Aust* make out; *coll* clean out; fleece; *coll* quiz; **~ von** except from; exclude from; **ausgenommen sein** be exempt; be excluded

sich ~ except oneself; look (good *etc*)

ausnehmend exceptional

ausnüchtern: sich ~ sober up

ausnutzen, *esp SGer* **ausnützen** use; take advantage of; cash in on; exploit; **gut/voll ~** make good/full use of

die **Ausnutzung,** *esp SGer* **Ausnützung** *vbl noun*; *also* use; exploitation

auspacken unpack; unwrap; *coll* reveal; (*v/i*) *coll* speak one's mind; spill the beans; **pack aus!** out with it!

auspeitschen flog

auspendeln *box* dodge; (*v/i*, *also sn*) stop swinging

auspfeifen* catcall

auspflanzen plant out

die **Auspizien** [-ĭən] *pl* auspices; **unter den ~** (+*gen*) under the auspices of

ausplappern blab out

ausplaudern blab out; (+*dat*) let on about (sth.) to

ausplauschen *Aust* blab out

ausplündern plunder, pillage; rob

die **Ausplünderung, -en** *vbl noun*; *also* pillage

auspolstern pad; pad the shoulders of; upholster

ausposaunen (*p/part* **ausposaunt**) *coll* shout

from the rooftops

auspowern *coll* impoverish (by ruthless exploitation)

ausprägen (*see also* **ausgeprägt**) mint; mint money from; shape; **sich ~** develop; become marked; **sich ~ in** (*dat*) be stamped on

die **Ausprägung, -en** *vbl noun*; *also* form

auspressen squeeze; squeeze out; bleed white

ausprobieren try out

der **Auspuff, -e** exhaust; **die ~gase** *pl* exhaust (fumes); **das ~rohr, -e** exhaust-pipe; **der ~topf, ⸚e** silencer, muffler *US*

auspumpen (*see also* **ausgepumpt**) pump out

auspunkten *box* outpoint

auspusten [–uː–] *coll* blow out

ausputzen *footb* act as sweeper

der **Ausputzer, –** *footb* sweeper

ausquartieren move out (temporarily); *mil* billet out

ausquatschen *coll* blab out

ausquetschen squeeze; squeeze out; *coll* quiz; grill

ausradeln, ausrädeln prick out (pattern); *cul* cut out with a pastry-wheel

ausradieren erase; wipe out

ausrangieren [–rãʒ–] discard, throw out

ausrasieren shave; shave off

ausrasten[1] (*sn*) *tech* disengage

ausrasten[2] *SGer*: **(sich) ~** rest

ausrauben rob; ransack

ausräubern rob; 'clean out'

ausräuchern smoke out; fumigate

ausraufen: sich *dat* **die Haare ~** tear one's hair

ausräumen clear out; eliminate (obstacle *etc*); clear up; *coll* (thief) clean out

ausrechnen (*see also* **ausgerechnet**) calculate, work out, figure out; **sich** *dat* **gute Chancen ~** reckon one stands a good chance; **sich** *dat* **eine Chance ~ können** stand a chance

ausrecken stretch (arm *etc*); **sich** *dat* **den Hals ~** crane one's neck **(nach** to see); **sich ~** stretch

die **Ausrede, -n** excuse

ausreden (+*dat of pers*) talk (s.o.) out of; persuade (s.o.) to give up; (*v/i*) finish speaking

ausregnen: es hat (sich) ausgeregnet it has stopped raining

ausreiben* scour; remove by rubbing; *Aust* scrub

ausreichen be sufficient; **~ mit** *coll* manage on; have enough of; **~d** sufficient

ausreifen (*see also* **ausgereift**) (*sn*) ripen; mature

die **Ausreise, -n** leaving (a country); (+*dat*) **die ~ verweigern** refuse (s.o.) permission to leave the country || **die ~erlaubnis, -se** exit permit; **das ~visum, -(s)a** exit visa

ausreisen (*sn*) leave the country; **~ aus** leave; **~ nach** go to

ausreißen* pull up; pull out (hair *etc*), tear out; (*v/i sn*) come off; tear; *sp* break away (*dat* from); *coll* run away (*dat* from); **~ aus** (*sn*) *coll* run away from (institution).

der **Ausreißer, –** *sp* runner/cyclist who breaks away from the field; *coll* runaway

ausreiten* ride (horse) full out; ride round (bend) on the outside; hold (race); (*v/i sn*) ride out; go for a ride

ausrenken dislocate

die **Ausrenkung, -en** dislocation

ausrichten line up; align; convey (message) (*dat* to); stage (championships *etc*), arrange (wedding *etc*); *SGer coll* run down; **etwas/nichts ~** achieve something/nothing; get somewhere/nowhere **(bei** with); **(links** *etc*) **ausgerichtet** with (leftist *etc*) leanings; (+*dat*) **einen Gruß ~ lassen** send one's regards to; **jmdm. ~, daß ...** tell s.o. that ...

~ auf (*acc*) align with; gear to

~ gegen: etwas ~ können gegen be able to do something about; **nichts ~ können gegen** be powerless against

~ nach align with; base on; gear to

sich ~ *mil* dress; **sich ~ auf** (*acc*) be geared to; **sich ~ nach** follow; *mil* dress by

der **Ausrichter, –** organizer

die **Ausrichtung** *vbl noun*; *also* alignment; arrangement; orientation

ausrinnen* (*sn*) *SGer* run out; become empty

der **Ausritt, -e** ride (on horseback); riding out

ausroden clear (forest); root up

ausrollen unroll; roll (dough); (*v/i*, *also sn*) roll/*aer* taxi to a standstill

ausrotten wipe out; exterminate; eradicate

die **Ausrottung** *vbl noun*; *also* extermination; eradication

ausrücken *print* set in the margin; *tech* disengage; (*v/i sn*) march out; turn out; *coll* run away (*dat* from)

der **Ausruf, -e** cry; proclamation

Ausrufe-: das ~zeichen, – exclamation mark

ausrufen* exclaim, cry; call out (s.o.'s name); call (flight, strike), proclaim (republic *etc*); cry (one's wares); put up for auction; **als/zum (König** *etc*) **~** proclaim (s.o. king *etc*); **~ lassen** put out a call for, (in hotel) page

der **Ausrufer, –** town-crier

die **Ausrufung** *vbl noun*; *also* proclamation; **das ~s|zeichen, –** exclamation mark

ausruhen: (sich) ~ rest; **ausgeruht** rested

ausrupfen pluck out; pull out

ausrüsten equip; fit out; *text* finish; **sich ~** equip oneself

die **Ausrüstung, -en** *vbl noun*; *also* equipment;

text finish || **der ~s|gegenstand, ¨-e** piece of equipment

ausrutschen (*sn*) slip; *coll* put one's foot in it

der **Ausrutscher, –** *coll* slip (on ice *etc*); gaffe; *sp* surprise defeat

die **Aussaat** sowing; seed (*collect*)

aussäen sow

die **Aussage, –n** statement; message (of work of art); *leg* statement, (of witness) testimony; *gramm* predicate; **eine ~ machen** *leg* make a statement, (witness) testify; **nach ~** (+*gen*) according to || **die ~kraft** effectiveness in communicating its message; significance (of statistics *etc*); **a~kräftig** effective in communicating its message; significant; **die ~weise, –n** *gramm* mood

aussagen state; (work of art *etc*) express; say; (*v/i*) *leg* make a statement; testify; **~d** *gramm* predicative

der **Aussatz** leprosy

aussätzig leprous; **der/die Aussätzige** (*decl as adj*) leper

aussaugen (*see* **saugen**) suck out; suck the juice from/poison out of; drain (country) of its resources, bleed (people) white

ausschaben scrape out; *med* scrape

ausschachten dig up; excavate; sink (shaft)

die **Ausschachtung, –en** *vbl noun*; *also* excavation

ausschalten switch off; eliminate (*also sp*); cut out (rival); **sich ~** switch itself off

die **Ausschaltung** *vbl noun*; *also* elimination

der **Ausschank, ¨-e** bar; sale of alcohol

ausscharren scratch up; scrape (hollow)

Ausschau: ~ halten nach keep a look-out for; be on the look-out for

ausschauen (*SGer only exc* + **nach**) look (good *etc*); **~ nach** keep a look-out for, be on the look-out for; **wie schaut's aus?** how are things?

ausschaufeln shovel out; dig up (buried person); shovel (path *etc*)

der **Ausscheid, –e** *EGer* qualifying round

ausscheiden* eliminate; *physiol* excrete; *chem* precipitate; (*v/i sn*) be ruled out; *sp* be eliminated; **~ aus** (*sn*) retire from (office); leave; *sp* be eliminated from; **~d** outgoing

die **Ausscheidung, –en** elimination; *physiol* excretion; *chem* precipitation; *sp* elimination; qualifying round; (*pl*) *physiol* excreta; **der ~s|kampf, ¨-e** qualifying round; **der ~s|lauf, ¨-e** heat; **das ~s|organ, –e** excretory organ; **das ~s|produkt, –e** waste product; **das ~s|rennen, –** heat; **das ~s|spiel, –e** qualifying match

ausschelten* scold

ausschenken pour out; sell (alcoholic beverages)

ausscheren (*sn*) pull out, *aer* peel off, *naut* haul out of the line; step out of line; pull out (of cartel *etc*)

ausschießen* shoot out (eye); shoot for (prize); *print* impose; (*v/i sn*) fade; (plant) shoot up

ausschiffen disembark; unship (cargo); **sich ~** disembark

ausschildern signpost

ausschimpfen scold

ausschlachten gut; cannibalize (for spare parts); exploit

die **Ausschlachtung** *vbl noun*; *also* cannibalization; exploitation

ausschlafen* sleep off; (*v/i*) = **sich ~** have a good (night's) sleep; **ausgeschlafen haben/sein** have had enough sleep

der **Ausschlag, ¨-e** *med* rash; *phys* deflection (of needle *etc*); **(einen) ~ bekommen** come out in a rash; **den ~ geben** clinch the matter; tip the scales || **a~gebend** decisive (**a. sein für** decide; be of crucial importance for)

ausschlagen* knock out; beat out; line; turn down (offer *etc*); (*v/i*) hit out; (horse) kick; (*also sn*) burst into leaf; swing, (needle *etc*) deflect, (divining-rod) dip; (*sn*) turn out (well *etc*); **zum Guten/Bösen ~** turn out well/badly; **ausgeschlagen haben** have stopped striking/beating

ausschließen* (*see also* **ausgeschlossen**) lock out; exclude (**von** from); expel; rule out; preclude; *print* justify; **zeitweilig ~** suspend; **... sind vom Umtausch ausgeschlossen** ... cannot be exchanged; **~, daß ...** rule out the possibility that ...

sich ~ lock oneself out; exclude oneself; (*recip*) be mutually exclusive

ausschließlich 1 *adj* exclusive; sole; (*adv*) exclusively; nothing but; 2 *prep* (*usu* + *gen*) exclusive of

die **Ausschließung** *vbl noun*; *also* exclusion; expulsion; preclusion

ausschlüpfen (*sn*) hatch out

ausschlürfen drink up noisily; suck (egg); empty (glass) noisily

der **Ausschluß, ¨-(ss)e** exclusion; expulsion; *print* spaces; **unter ~ der Öffentlichkeit stattfinden** be heard in camera

ausschmelzen* melt down (fat)

ausschmücken decorate; embellish

die **Ausschmückung, –en** decoration; embellishment

ausschnaufen: (sich) ~ *SGer coll* take a breather

ausschneiden* (*see also* **ausgeschnitten**) cut out; prune (tree *etc*); cut out the bad part from; *dressm* cut out the neck of (dress); cut out

der **Ausschnitt, –e** part cut out (of door, shutter, *etc*); neck (of dress); (newspaper) cutting, clipping; extract, excerpt (**aus** from), (of picture) detail, *cin* clip; facet; *math* sector; **tiefer ~** plunging neckline; **mit tiefem ~** low-necked; **spitzer ~** V neck || **a~weise** in extracts

ausschnüffeln *coll* nose out

ausschöpfen scoop out, (from boat) bail out; bail out (boat); exhaust (possibilities *etc*)

ausschrauben unscrew

ausschreiben* write out; make out (bill, cheque, *etc*); write out in full; copy from; announce (competition); advertise; call (meeting, election); impose (tax); *comm* invite tenders for

die **Ausschreibung, -en** *vbl noun*; *also* advertising (of post); announcement; *comm* invitation to tender

ausschreiten* pace out; (*v/i sn*) step out

die **Ausschreitungen** *pl* rioting, riots; excesses

der **Ausschuß, ¨(ss)e** committee; board; point of exit (of bullet); *comm* = **die ~ware, -n** rejects

ausschütteln shake out; shake

ausschütten pour out; spill; empty; *fin* distribute; **~ über** (*acc*) heap on; (+*dat*) **sein Herz ~** pour out one's heart to; **sich vor Lachen ~** split one's sides with laughter

die **Ausschüttung, -en** *vbl noun*; *also* fall-out; *fin* distribution; amount paid out

ausschwärmen (*sn*) swarm out; *mil* fan out

ausschwatzen *coll* let out (secret)

ausschweifen (*sn*) indulge in excess; lead a dissolute life; **~d** dissolute; unbridled; **~d leben** lead a dissolute life

die **Ausschweifung, -en** excess; (*pl*) debauchery

ausschweigen*: sich ~ remain silent

ausschwemmen wash out; wash (for gold *etc*); *geol* erode

ausschwenken rinse out; swivel outwards; (*v/i sn*) swing out; swing round

ausschwitzen sweat out; exude; *cul* extract the moisture from (by heating); (*v/i sn*) exude

aussehen* look (good *etc*); **wie sieht ... aus?** what does ... look like?; **wie siehst du denn aus?** what *do* you look like!; **so siehst du gerade aus!** that's what *you* think!, not likely!

mit ... sieht es schlimm aus ... is *etc* in a bad way; things look bad for ...; **wie sieht es mit ... aus?** what is the situation regarding ...?

~ nach look like; look out for; **es sieht danach aus, als ob ...** it looks as if ...; **er/sie/es sieht auch danach aus** he/she/it looks it; **nach etwas/nichts ~** *coll* look good/not look anything special

~ zu: gut ~ zu (garment) go well with

das **Aussehen** appearance; looks

aussehend: (*eg* **jung ~** young) -looking

außen (on the) outside; **nach ~** outwards; = **nach ~ hin** outwardly; **von ~** from the outside

Außen- outside ...; outer ...; external ...; exterior ...; outdoor ...; foreign ...;

die ~bezirke *pl* outskirts; **der ~bord|motor, -en** outboard motor; **der ~dienst** work in the field (of sales representative *etc*); **der ~handel** foreign trade; **das ~handels|defizit, -e** trade gap; **der ~minister, -** foreign minister; (*of U.K.*) Foreign Secretary; (*of U.S.A.*) Secretary of State; **das ~ministerium, -(i)en** foreign ministry; (*of U.K.*) Foreign Office; (*of U.S.A.*) State Department; **die ~politik** foreign affairs/policy; **a~politisch** relating to foreign affairs/policy; **die ~seite, -n** outside; exterior; **der ~seiter, -** outsider (*also sp*); **die ~stände** *pl* outstanding debts; **der/die ~stehende** (*decl as adj*) outsider; person not involved; **die ~stelle, -n** branch; **der ~stürmer, -** *sp* winger; **die ~welt** outer world; world outside; **der ~zoll, ¨e** external tariff

aussenden* send out; transmit; *phys* emit

außer 1 *prep* (+*dat*) except; apart from; out of (danger, sight, *etc*); beyond (doubt); 2 *conj* except; (*with subsequent* **auch/noch** *left untranslated*) in addition to; **~ daß ...** except that ...; unless ...; **~ wenn ...** unless ...; except when ...; **~ sich sein** be beside oneself (**vor** *dat* with); **~ sich geraten** go wild

außer- extra-; non-; outside ...; **~dem** besides; in addition; **~dienstlich** private; **~ehelich** extramarital; illegitimate; (*adv*) out of wedlock; **~fahrplan|mäßig** non-scheduled; **~gerichtlich** out of court; **~gewöhnlich** exceptional, unusual; **~halb** 1 *adv* outside the city/town; 2 *prep* (+*gen*) outside; **~irdisch** extraterrestrial; **außer|ordentlich** extraordinary; exceptional; (professor) associate; (*adv*) *also* extremely; **~orts** *Aust*, *Swiss* out of town; **~plan|mäßig** unscheduled; additional; **~schulisch** extracurricular; **~stande (a. zu ...** unable to ...); **~tourlich** [-tuːɐ-] *Aust* (bus *etc*) extra

äußer.. (*see also* **äußerst**) external; outer; outward; **das Äußere** (*decl as adj*) exterior; appearance(s); **Minister des Ä~en** Foreign Minister

äußerlich external; outward; superficial; (*adv*) *also* outwardly (calm *etc*); **rein ~ betrachtet** on the face of it

die **Äußerlichkeit, -en** formality; (*pl*) externals

äußerln *Aust coll*: **~ führen** take (dog) for a walk

äußern express; **sich ~** express an opinion (**über** *acc*/**zu** about); **sich ~ in** (*dat*) manifest itself in

äußerst 1 *adj* **äußerst..** extreme; farthest; outermost; highest; lowest; latest (possible); utmost; 2 *adv* extremely; **im ~en Fall** = **~enfalls; das Äußerste** (*decl as adj*) the most/worst; (risk *etc*) everything; **sein Ä~es tun** do one's utmost; **ein Ä~es an** (*dat*) the ultimate in; **bis zum Ä~en** (hold out) to the last; (go, push) to the limit; **aufs ~e** extremely || **~en|falls** if absolutely necessary; at the outside

[die] **Äußerung, -en** expression (of); remark

aussetzen abandon (infant *etc*); maroon; release (animal); put ashore; lower (boat); offer (reward *etc*); *bill* place (ball); *eccles* expose; *leg* suspend (proceedings, judgement); (+*dat*) expose to; subject to; bequeathe (inheritance) to; (*v/i*) (music *etc*) stop, (engine) fail; take time off, **(einen Tag** *etc* **~)** take (a day *etc*) off; take a break; *games* miss a turn; **ohne auszusetzen** without a break

~ **an** (*dat*): **etwas auszusetzen haben an** find fault with; **daran ist nichts/viel auszusetzen** there's nothing/a lot wrong with it; **was gibt es auszusetzen an ...?** what's wrong with ...?

~ **für** settle (annuity *etc*) on

~ **mit** discontinue; stop

sich ~ (+*dat*) expose oneself to; lay oneself open to; run (risk of ...)

[die] **Aussetzung, -en** *vbl noun*; *also* release; *leg* suspension

[die] **Aussicht, -en** view (**auf** *acc* of); prospect (of); **~ haben auf** (*acc*) stand a chance of; be in the running for; **in ~ haben** have in prospect; **in ~ nehmen** envisage; **+für** have in mind for; **in ~ stellen** promise; hold out the prospect of || **a~s|los** hopeless; **der ~s|punkt, -e** vantage point; **a~s|reich** hopeful, promising; with good prospects; **der ~s|turm, ⸗e** look-out tower; **der ~s|wagen, -** observation car

aussieben sift out, *phys* filter out; select; weed out

aussiedeln resettle (compulsorily)

[der] **Aussiedler, -** person being resettled (*esp ethnic German from Eastern Europe*)

[die] **Aussiedlung, -en** (compulsory) resettlement

aussöhnen reconcile (**mit** with); **sich ~** become reconciled; **sich ~ mit** make it up with; become reconciled to

[die] **Aussöhnung, -en** reconciliation

aussondern pick out; weed out

aussortieren pick out; discard, throw out

ausspähen spy out; spy on; find out by spying; **~ nach** keep a look-out for

ausspannen spread out (net *etc*); unharness (horse *etc*), unyoke (oxen); take out (of typewriter); (+*dat of pers*) *coll* persuade (s.o.) to let one have/to lend one; pinch (s.o.'s girl-friend *etc*); (*v/i*) take a rest; **(8 Tage** *etc*) **~** take (a week *etc*) off

[die] **Ausspannung** *vbl noun*; *also* relaxation; **~ nötig haben** need a rest

aussparen leave blank; leave (space); omit; not touch on

[die] **Aussparung, -en** *vbl noun*; *also* omission; blank space; *archit* recess

ausspeien* vomit; spew out; (*v/i*) spit

ausspeisen *Aust* provide meals for (refugees *etc*)

aussperren lock out (*also* workers); **sich ~** lock oneself out

[die] **Aussperrung, -en** *vbl noun*; *also* lock-out

ausspielen bring into play; exploit (one's superiority *etc*); *cards* lead with (card); *games*, *sp* play for; outplay; *theat* play to the full; (*v/i*) *cards* lead; **~ gegen** play off against; **(seine Rolle) ausgespielt haben** be played out

[die] **Ausspielung, -en** *vbl noun*; *also* draw (of lottery)

ausspinnen* elaborate

ausspionieren spy on; spy out

ausspotten *SGer* mock

[die] **Aussprache** [-a:-], **-n** pronunciation; accent; (frank) discussion; **das ~wörterbuch, ⸗er** pronouncing dictionary

aussprechbar pronounceable, (easy, hard) to pronounce; expressible

aussprechen* (*see also* **ausgesprochen**) pronounce; enunciate; express; *leg* pronounce; grant (divorce); (*v/i*) finish (speaking)

sich ~ unburden oneself (**bei** to); (*recip*) have a heart-to-heart talk; **sich ~ für/gegen** express one's support for/opposition to; **sich ~ in** (*dat*) be expressed in; **sich ~ mit** have a heart-to-heart talk with; **sich (anerkennend** *etc*) **~ über** (*acc*) speak (approvingly *etc*) of; **sich leicht/schwer ~** be easy/hard to pronounce

aussprengen sprinkle; blast out; circulate (rumour)

ausspritzen squirt out, *zool* (insect) eject, *physiol* ejaculate; flush out; extinguish (with a hose); *med* syringe

[der] **Ausspruch, ⸗e** saying; utterance

ausspucken spit out; *coll* spew up; cough up (money); churn out; (*v/i*) spit

ausspülen rinse (out); (water) wash away

ausstaffieren fit out; rig out; **~ mit** equip with; **sich ~** fit oneself out; rig oneself out

[die] **Ausstaffierung, -en** *vbl noun*; *also* outfit

[der] **Ausstand, ⸗e** strike; *SGer* leaving one's job/school; **im ~** on strike; **in den ~ treten** go on strike

ausständig *SGer* outstanding

ausstanzen punch out; stamp out

ausstatten equip; furnish; produce (book *etc*); ~ **mit** equip with; fit out with; vest with; endow with

die **Ausstattung, -en** *vbl noun*; *also* furnishings; fittings; equipment; get-up (of book); *theat* scenery and costumes || **das ~s|stück, -e** spectacular

Ausstech-: die ~form, -en pastry-cutter

ausstechen* cut out; gouge out; cut (peat); dig (ditch); outdo; cut out (rival); ~ **bei** replace in (s.o.'s) affections

ausstehen* endure; (*v/i*) be on display; (payment) be outstanding; (*sn*) *SGer* (employee) leave; **ich kann ... nicht** ~ I can't stand ...; **die Antwort/Entscheidung/Lösung steht noch aus** the reply hasn't come/the decision hasn't been taken/the solution hasn't been found yet; **viel auszustehen haben** have a lot to put up with (**bei/mit** from); **ausgestanden sein** be over; **~d** outstanding; pending; **~de Forderungen** arrears

aussteigen* (*sn*) get out; get off; *aer* bail out; *sp* give up; drop out; *coll* pull out; ~ **aus** get off; get out of; *sp* drop out of; *coll* pull out of; ~ **lassen** (player with the ball) beat; **alles ~!** all change!

der **Aussteiger, -** drop-out

ausstellen (*see also* **ausgestellt**) issue; make out (**auf** *acc* in (s.o.'s name), to); exhibit; put on display; post (sentry); *coll* switch off; (+*dat of pers*) issue (s.o.) with; write (testimonial) for; **einen Wechsel ~ auf** (*acc*) draw a bill on; **sich** *dat* **... ~ lassen** obtain (receipt *etc*)

der **Aussteller, -** exhibitor; issuer

die **Ausstellung, -en** *vbl noun*; *also* issue (of); exhibition; show; display; *in compds* **~s-** exhibition ...; (date, place) of issue; **das ~s|stück, -e** exhibit

Aussterbe|etat [-eta:] *coll*: **auf dem ~ sein/stehen** be on the way out

aussterben* (*see also* **ausgestorben**) (*sn*) die out; become extinct; **das Aussterben** extinction

die **Aussteuer** trousseau

aussteuern provide with a trousseau; stop paying insurance benefits to; *mot* bring under control (by steering); *elect* control the level of

der **Ausstieg, -e** exit; getting out; climbing out

ausstopfen stuff; stuff up

der **Ausstoß** [-o:-] *econ* output; *naut* discharge (of torpedo) || **das ~rohr, -e** torpedo-tube

ausstoßen* expel (air *etc*), emit (gas *etc*), *naut* fire (torpedo); utter (cry *etc*), heave (sigh); knock out (tooth *etc*); expel (**aus** from); *econ* turn out; *ling* drop

ausstrahlen radiate; illuminate; *rad* broadcast; (*v/i*) radiate; (pain *etc*) spread; ~ **auf** (*acc*) influence; have an effect on

die **Ausstrahlung, -en** radiation; illumination; aura, charisma; impact, influence; *rad* transmission; **die ~s|kraft** charisma

ausstrecken stretch out; (snail) put out (horns); **die Hand ~** hold out one's hand; **+nach** reach out for; try to lay hands on; **mit ausgestreckten Armen** with outstretched arms; **sich ~** stretch oneself out

ausstreichen* smooth out; spread; fill in; grease (baking-tin); score out; (*v/i*) *geol* outcrop

ausstreuen scatter; spread (rumour); ~ **mit** sprinkle with

der **Ausstrich, -e** *med* smear; *geol* outcrop

ausströmen radiate; give off; (*v/i sn*) pour out; escape; ~ **von** (of quality) *conveyed – with prep obj becoming subj – by* radiate (*eg* **von ihm strömt Ruhe aus** he radiates calm)

die **Ausströmung** *in vbl senses*; *also* outflow; escape

ausstülpen turn inside out; *med* evert

aussuchen [-u:-] (*see also* **ausgesucht**) pick out

austapezieren paper (room)

austarieren balance

der **Austausch** exchange; replacement; **im ~ gegen** in exchange for || **der ~motor, -en** replacement engine; **der ~stoff, -e** substitute; **a~weise** on an exchange basis

austauschbar exchangeable; interchangeable

austauschen exchange, swap (**gegen** for); replace

austeilen distribute; share out; *cards* deal out

die **Auster, -n** oyster; **die ~n|bank, ⸚e** oyster-bed; **der ~n|fischer, -** oyster-catcher

austilgen wipe out; eradicate; obliterate

austoben work off (**an** *dat* on); **sich ~** let off steam; have one's fling; (storm) spend itself

austollen: sich ~ romp about to one's heart's content

der **Austrag** settlement; *sp* holding; **zum ~ bringen** settle; **zum ~ kommen** be settled; *sp* be held

austragen* deliver; carry (child) to full term; argue out; fight out; fight (duel); delete (from list *etc*); *sp* hold; play; **sich ~** sign out

der **Austragungs|ort, -e** *sp* venue

Austr<u>a</u>lien [-ĭən] Australia

der **Austr<u>a</u>lier** [-ĭɐ], **-**, **austr<u>a</u>lisch** Australian

austräumen finish dreaming; **der Traum von ... ist ausgeträumt** the dream of ... is over

austreiben* drive out; exorcize; drive (cattle) to pasture; put forth; *Aust* roll (dough); (+*dat of pers*) cure (s.o.) of (mood *etc*); (*v/i*) sprout

die **Austreibung, -en** *vbl noun*; *also* expulsion; exorcism

austrennen take out (lining)

austreten* (*see also* **ausgetreten**) tread (path); wear down; stretch (shoes) (by wear); tread out; (*v/i sn*) flow out; escape; *med* protrude; *coll* = ~ **gehen** *coll* go to the toilet; ~ **aus** (*sn*) leave

austricksen outmanoeuvre (by means of a trick); *sp* trick (opponent)

austrinken* drink up; empty; **trink aus!** drink up!

der **Austritt, -e** outflow (of water *etc*), escape (of gas *etc*), *med* protrusion; leaving; resignation

austrocknen dry out; drain; wipe dry; (*v/i sn*) dry out; dry up; become parched

austüfteln *coll* think up; puzzle out

austupfen swab

aus|üben practise; carry on; carry out; exercise (right *etc*); ~ **auf** (*acc*) have (influence, effect) on; have (attraction) for; put (pressure) on; ~**d** practising; performing; *pol* executive

die **Aus|übung** practice; performance (of); exercise (of)

aus|ufern (*sn*) overflow its banks; get out of hand

der **Ausverkauf** clearance sale; sell-out; **heute ist** ~ there's a sale on today

ausverkaufen sell out (article); **ausverkauft** sold out

auswachsen* [-ks-] (*see also* **ausgewachsen**) outgrow; (*v/i sn*) sprout; **fast ausgewachsen vor Langeweile sein** *coll* be bored to tears; **... ist zum Auswachsen** *coll* ... is enough to drive you mad
sich ~ spread; **sich** ~ **zu** turn into

auswägen* *chem*, *phys* weigh out

die **Auswahl** selection, choice (**an** *dat* of); pick; *sp* select team; **eine** ~ **treffen** make a selection; **... stehen zur** ~ there are ... to choose from || **die** ~**mannschaft, -en** select team

auswählen (*see also* **ausgewählt**) choose, select (**aus** from)

auswalken *Aust* = **auswallen** *Swiss* roll (dough)

auswalzen roll (dough); *tech* roll out; **(lang und) breit** ~ *coll* go on about

der **Auswanderer, -** emigrant

auswandern (*sn*) emigrate

die **Auswanderung, -en** emigration

auswärtig from outside; non-resident; in another place/other places; *pol* foreign; **das A~e Amt** the (W. German) Foreign Ministry

auswärts out of town; away from home; (eat, sleep) out; *sp* away; in an away match; *in compds* A~- *sp* away ...

auswaschen* wash out; wash; *geol* erode, wash away; *chem* edulcorate

Auswechsel- [-ks-]: **die** ~**bank, ¨-e** substitutes' bench; **der** ~**spieler, -** substitute

auswechselbar exchangeable; interchangeable; replaceable

auswechseln [-ks-] (*see also* **ausgewechselt**) exchange (**gegen** for); replace (by, with); (*v/i*) *sp* make a substitution

die **Auswechslung** exchange; replacement

der **Ausweg, -e** way out; escape (from situation *etc*); **als letzter** ~ as a last resort || **a~los** hopeless; **die** ~**losigkeit** hopelessness

Ausweich- alternative ...; **das** ~**manöver, -** manoeuvre to avoid sth.; evasive action; **die** ~**möglichkeit, -en** alternative; **die** ~**stelle, -n** passing-place, turnout *US*

ausweichen* (*like* **weichen**[1]) (*sn*) get out of the way; swerve (to the left/right); be evasive; avoid the question; (+*dat*) get out of the way of; avoid; dodge, sidestep; shirk; ~ **auf** (*acc*) switch to; ~ **in** (*acc*) *mus* modulate into; ~**d** evasive, non-committal

ausweiden eviscerate

ausweinen: sich *dat* **die Augen** ~ cry one's eyes out; **sich** ~ have a good cry

der **Ausweis, -e** identification: *esp* identity card, passport, (membership) card, (reader's) ticket; *fin* (bank) return; **die** ~**papiere** *pl* (identification) papers

ausweisen* expel; demonstrate; (statistics *etc*) show, reveal; *EGer* (plan) provide for; ~ **als** identify as; show (s.o.) to be; **sich** ~ prove one's identity; establish one's credentials; **sich** ~ **als** show oneself (to be)

die **Ausweisung, -en** expulsion

ausweiten stretch (by wear); extend (**auf** *acc* to); expand (**zu** into); **sich** ~ stretch; widen; expand; **sich** ~ **zu** expand into; escalate into

die **Ausweitung, -en** *vbl noun*; *also* expansion; extension

auswendig by heart; from memory; **in- und** ~ (know) inside out

auswerfen* (sea, volcano, *etc*) throw up; cough up; eject (*also comput*); knock out (eye *etc*); dig (ditch); dig out (earth); allocate (**für** to); *naut*, *angl* cast; *tech* turn out

der **Auswerfer, -** ejector

auswerten [-e:-] evaluate; utilize

die **Auswertung, -en** evaluation; utilization

auswickeln unwrap

auswiegen* (*like* **wiegen**[1]) (*see also* **ausgewogen**) weigh; weigh out

auswirken knead; **sich** ~ make itself felt; have a ... effect; work out (to s.o.'s advantage); **sich** ~ **auf** (*acc*) affect, have an effect on

die **Auswirkung, -en** effect; consequence; repercussion

auswischen wipe out; wipe clean; wipe off; **sich** *dat* **die Augen** ~ wipe one's eyes; **sich**

dat **den Schlaf aus den Augen ~** rub the sleep from one's eyes; (+*dat*) **eins ~** *coll* play a trick on; get one's own back on
auswringen* wring out
der **Auswuchs** [-ks], **⸚e** excrescence; growth; (unhealthy) figment; (*pl*) excesses; abuses
auswuchten balance (wheels)
der **Auswurf, ⸚e** throwing up (of lava); dregs (of society); *med* expectoration
auszacken serrate
auszahlen pay out; pay off; buy out; **sich ~** pay (off)
auszählen count; *box etc* count out
die **Auszahlung, –en** payment; remittance
die **Auszählung, –en** counting; count
auszehren (*see also* **ausgezehrt**) exhaust
die **Auszehrung** exhaustion; *arch med* consumption
auszeichnen (*see also* **ausgezeichnet**) mark, *comm* price, *print* mark up (manuscript), display (heading *etc*); honour, *mil* decorate; distinguish; **~ mit** award to; **sich ~** distinguish oneself; **sich ~ durch** distinguish oneself by; (thing) be distinguished by
die **Auszeichnung, –en** *vbl noun*; *also* honour, distinction, *mil* decoration; award; *print* display
Auszieh–: die ~feder, –n drawing-pen; **die ~leiter, –n** extension ladder; **die ~platte, –n** draw-leaf; **der ~tisch, –e** draw-table; **die ~tusche, –n** drawing-ink
ausziehbar extensible; pull-out
ausziehen* undress; take off; pull out; extend (ladder), pull out the draw-leaf of (table); draw (metal); extract (substance, *also math*); (chemical) remove; excerpt (passage); make extracts from; ink in; *coll* fleece; (*v/i sn*) move out; set out; (aroma) escape; **sich ~** undress
auszischen hiss (at)
der **Auszubildende** (*fem* **die ~**) (*decl as adj*) trainee
der **Auszug, ⸚e** moving out; departure; exodus; walk-out; extract, excerpt; (bank) statement; extension (of apparatus); *chem* extract; *mus* arrangement; **a~s|weise** in extracts (**a. wiedergeben** reproduce extracts from)
auszupfen pluck out; pluck
autark self-sufficient
die **Autarkie** self-sufficiency
authentisch authentic
die **Authentizität** authenticity
das **Auto, –s** car; **~ fahren** drive; go by car; **mit dem ~** in the/by car
Auto– car ...; motor ...; road (atlas *etc*);
die ~bahn, –en motorway, expressway *US*; **das ~bahn|kreuz, –e** motorway *etc* interchange; **der ~bus** (*gen* **–ses**), **–se** bus; coach; **der ~car, –s** *Swiss* coach, bus *US*; **die ~fähre, –n** car ferry; **das ~fahren** motoring; **der ~fahrer, –** motorist; **die ~fahrt, –en** drive (in car); **die ~falle, –n** speed trap; **der ~friedhof, ⸚e** car dump; **der ~händler, –** car dealer; **das ~kino, –s** drive-in (cinema); **der ~knacker, –** *coll* thief who breaks into cars; **die ~kolonne, –n** line of cars; **der ~lenker, –** *Swiss* motorist; **die ~marke, –n** make of car; **der ~reise|zug** *cf* Motorail; **das ~rennen, –** motor-race; = **der ~renn|sport** motor-racing; **der ~salon, –s** motor show; **die ~schlange, –n** queue of cars; tailback; **der ~schlosser, –** garage mechanic; **der ~skooter, –** dodgem car; **~stop(p)** (**per A. fahren** hitch-hike); **das ~telefon, –e** car telephone; **der ~unfall, ⸚e** car accident; **der ~verleih** car hire (firm); **die ~werk|statt, ⸚en** garage; **das ~zubehör** car accessories
die **Autobiographie, –(ie)n** autobiography
autobiographisch autobiographical
der **Autodidakt, –en** (*wk masc*) autodidact, self-educated person
autodidaktisch autodidactic; self-taught
autogen autogenous; (training) autogenic; *tech* oxyacetylene
das **Autogramm, –e** autograph; **der ~jäger, –** autograph hunter
der **Autokrat, –en** (*wk masc*) autocrat
die **Autokratie** autocracy
autokratisch autocratic
der **Automat, –en** (*wk masc*) automatic machine, *esp* slot/vending machine; automaton; **das ~en|restaurant, –s** self-service restaurant, automat *US*
die **Automatik** [–ɪk], **–en** automatic mechanism/ *mot* transmission; automatic operation
die **Automation** automation
automatisch automatic
automatisieren automate
das **Automobil, –e** automobile
der **Automobilist, –en** (*wk masc*) *Swiss* motorist
autonom autonomous
die **Autonomie** autonomy
die **Autopsie, –(ie)n** autopsy
der **Autor, –(or)en** author
die **Autorin, –nen** authoress
die **Autorisation, –en** authorization
autorisieren authorize
autoritär authoritarian
der **Autoritarismus** authoritarianism
die **Autorität, –en** authority
autoritativ authoritative
die **Autorschaft** authorship
autsch! ouch!
auweh! ouch!; oh dear!
auwei(a)! dear me!
Avancen [–'vã:s–]: (+*dat*) **~ machen** make advances to

avancieren [–vãs–] (*sn*) be promoted
Avant– [–vã–]: **die ~garde, –n** avant-garde; **der ~gardist, –en** (*wk masc*) avant-gardist; **a~gardistisch** avant-garde
der **AvD** [a:faọ'de:] (= **Automobilclub von Deutschland**) (*W. German motoring organization*)
die **Aversion, –en** aversion (**gegen to**)
das **Avis** [–'vi:] (*gen* – [–(s)]), – [–s] (*or* [–'vi:s] (*gen* **–es**), **–e**) (*also* **der**) *comm* advice; **laut ~** as per advice
avisieren *comm* advise of the arrival of
die **AWG, –(s)** *EGer* (= **Arbeiterwohnungsbaugenossenschaft**) workers' house-building co-operative
axial axial
das **Axiom, –e** axiom
axiomatisch axiomatic
die **Axt, ⸚e** axe
die **Azalee** [–'le:ə], **–n** = **die Azalie** [–ĭə], **–n** azalea
das **Azetat, –e** acetate
das **Azetylen** acetylene
die **Azoren** *pl* the Azores
der **Azteke, –n** (*wk masc*), **aztekisch** Aztec
der **Azubi** (*fem* **die ~**), **–s** *coll* = **Auszubildende**
der **Azur, a~blau** azure

B

das **B** [beː] (*gen, pl* –, *coll* [beːs]) B; **das b, B** *mus* (the note) B flat; (*key*) **B** B flat major, **b** B flat minor

B *as in* **B1 = Bundesstraße**

b. (= **bei**) near; c/o

das **Baby** ['beːbi], **–s** baby; **b~sitten** [–s–] (*only infin*) baby-sit; **der ~sitter** [–sɪtɐ], **–, die ~sitterin, –nen** baby-sitter; **der ~speck** puppy-fat

Babylon ['baːbylɔn] Babylon

babylonisch Babylonian

der **Bach, ¨e** stream; **die ~stelze, –n** wagtail

Back– baking ...;

das ~blech, –e baking-sheet; **das ~bord** port (side); **b~bord(s)** to port; **der ~fisch, –e** fried fish; *dated coll* teenage girl; **die ~form, –en** baking-tin; cake-tin; **das ~hähnchen, – = das ~hendl, –(n)** *Aust* = **das ~huhn, ¨er** fried chicken; **das ~obst** dried fruit; **der ~ofen, ..öfen** oven; **die ~pflaume, –n** prune; **das ~pulver** baking-powder; **der ~stein, –e** brick; **die ~waren** *pl* bread, cakes and pastries

die **Backe, –n** cheek (*also coll* = buttock); *tech* cheek, jaw (of vice); (brake) shoe; *ski* toe-piece (of ski binding); **au ~!** crikey!

backen¹ (*p/part* **gebacken**) bake; *esp SGer* fry; **frisch gebacken** (*see* **frisch**)

backen² *esp NGer* cake; **~ an** (*dat*) stick to

Backen– cheek ...; **der ~bart, ¨e** side-whiskers; **das ~hörnchen, –** chipmunk; **der ~knochen, –** cheekbone; **die ~tasche, –n** cheek pouch; **der ~zahn, ¨e** molar

der **Bäcker, –** baker; **der ~laden, ..läden** baker's (shop)

die **Bäckerei, –en** bakery; baking

der **Background** ['bɛkgraʊnt], **–s** background

–backig –cheeked

das **Bad, ¨er** bath (*also phot*); bathroom; (public) baths; spa; swim, bathe; **ein ~ nehmen** take a bath

Bade– bathing ...; swimming ...; bath ...; spa ...; **die ~anstalt, –en** public baths; **der ~anzug, ¨e** bathing-suit; **der ~gast, ¨e** visitor to a spa/bathing-resort; bather; **die ~hose, –n** (pair of) bathing-trunks; **die ~kappe, –n** bathing-cap; **der ~mantel, ..mäntel** bathrobe; **die ~matte, –n** bath-mat; **der ~meister, –** swimming-pool attendant; **der ~ort, –e** spa; bathing-resort; **das ~trikot, –s** bathing-suit; **das ~tuch, ¨er** bath-towel; **die ~wanne, –n** bath(tub); **das ~zeug** bathing things; **das ~zimmer, –** bathroom

baden bath; bathe; (*v/i*) (take a) bath; **~ gehen** go for a swim; *coll* come a cropper

badisch (of) Baden

baff *coll* flabbergasted

BAföG ['baːføːk] *coll*: **~ kriegen** get a grant

die **Bagage** [–ʒə] *coll* rabble

die **Bagatelle, –n** trifle

bagatellisieren play down

Bagdad ['bakdat] Baghdad

der **Bagger, –** dredger; excavator

baggern dredge; excavate

bah! ugh!; yah!

bäh! ugh!; yah!; (*imitating sheep*) baa!

die **Bahn, –en** path; way; course; width (of material); *astron* orbit, (of star) course; *phys* trajectory; *mot* lane; *rail etc* railway, railroad *US*, **(Straßen~)** tram, streetcar *US*; *sp* track, (bowling) alley, (ice) rink, (toboggan) run; lane; *tech* face (of tool); (+*dat*) **~ brechen** pave the way for; pioneer; **sich** *dat* **~ brechen** (idea *etc*) gain acceptance; **aus der ~ bringen/werfen** throw off course; **mit der ~** by rail

Bahn– *astron* orbital ...; *rail* railway ..., railroad ... *US*; *sp* track ...; **b~brechend** pioneering; **der ~brecher, –** pioneer; **der ~damm, ¨e** (railway) embankment; **die ~fahrt, –en** train journey; **der ~hof, ¨e** station (**mit großem B. empfangen** *coll* give (s.o.) the red carpet treatment); **der ~hofs|vorsteher, –** stationmaster; **der ~körper, –** track; **b~lagernd** to be called for at the station; **der ~steig, –e** platform; **die ~steig|karte, –n** platform ticket; **der ~übergang, ¨e** level crossing, grade crossing *US*; **der ~wärter, –** (railway) gate-keeper and linesman/lineman *US*

bahnen: (+*dat*) **einen Weg ~** clear the way for; **sich** *dat* **einen Weg ~** clear a way for oneself; work one's way; (+*dat*) **den Weg ~** pave the way for

Bahr–: das ~tuch, ¨er pall

die **Bahre, –n** bier; stretcher

die **Bai, –en** (*esp in geographical names*) bay

das **Baiser** [bɛ'zeː], **–s** meringue

die **Baisse** ['bɛːsə], **–n** fall (in share prices)

der **Baissier** [bɛ'sǐeː], **–s** (stock exchange) bear

das **Bajonett, –e** bayonet

der **Bajuware, –n** (*wk masc*), **bajuwarisch** *hist or joc* Bavarian

die **Bake, –n** beacon; roadside sign (giving warning of autobahn exit, level crossing/grade crossing *US*)

die **Bakterie** [–ĭə], **–n** germ; (*pl*) bacteria, germs

bakteriell bacterial

Bakterien– bacterial ...; **der ~krieg** germ warfare

der **Bakteriologe, –n** (*wk masc*) bacteriologist

die **Bakteriologie** bacteriology

bakteriologisch bacteriological

die **Balance** [–'lã:sə] balance; **der ~akt, –e** balancing-act

Balancier– [–lãs–]: **die ~stange, –n** (balancing) pole

balancieren [–lãs–] balance; (*v/i*) balance (on one foot *etc*); ~ **über** (*acc*) (*sn*) walk across (while trying to keep one's balance); pick one's way across

bald (*comp* **eher,** *superl* **am ehesten**) soon; *coll* almost; **~ ..., ~ ...** now ..., now ...; **so ~ nicht** not ... in a hurry; **bis ~!** see you soon! || **~möglichst** earliest possible; (*adv*) as soon as possible

der **Baldachin** [–x–], **–e** canopy

Bälde: in ~ shortly

baldig early; speedy; **~st** as soon as possible

der **Baldrian** valerian

die **Balearen** *pl* the Balearic Islands

das **Balg, ¨–er** (*also* **der**) *coll* brat; kid

der **Balg, ¨–e** (animal's) skin; (stuffed) body (of doll); (*pl*) *mus*, *phot* bellows

balgen: sich ~, die Balgerei, –en scrap (**um** over)

der **Balkan** (*gen* **–s**) the Balkans; *in compds* Balkan ...

der **Balken, –** beam; **die ~überschrift, –en** banner headline

der **Balkon** [–'kɔŋ], **–s** balcony; *theat* dress-circle, balcony *US; coll* (large) bust; **die ~tür, –en** French door (opening onto balcony)

der **Ball¹, ¨–e** ball (= formal dance)

der **Ball², ¨–e** ball; **~ spielen** play ball; **am ~ bleiben** *coll* keep at it

Ball–: der ~besitz *sp* possession; **die ~führung** ball-control; **der ~junge, –n** (*wk masc*) ball-boy; **die ~königin, –nen** belle of the ball; **der ~saal, ..säle** ballroom; **das ~spiel, –e** ball-game; **der ~wechsel, –** *sp* rally

die **Ballade, –n** ballad

balladesk ballad-like

der **Ballast** [*also* 'bal–] ballast; burden; **die ~stoffe** *pl* roughage

ballen (*see also* **geballt**) form into a ball; clench (one's fist); **sich ~** form into a ball, agglomerate; gather; become clenched

der **Ballen, –** bale; *anat* ball (of foot *etc*), *zool* pad; *med* bunion

die **Ballerina, –(n)en** ballerina

ballern *coll* hurl; slam; (*v/i*) bang away (with gun); bang; **~ gegen** bang on

das **Ballett, –e** ballet; **der Ballettänzer, –, die Ballettänzerin, –nen** ballet-dancer; **der ~meister, –** maître de ballet; **die ~truppe, –n** ballet (company)

die **Balletteuse** [–'tø:zə], **–n** ballerina

die **Ballistik** [–ɪk] ballistics

ballistisch ballistic

der **Ballon** [–'lɔŋ], **–s** balloon; demijohn, *chem* balloon; *coll* 'nut'; **der ~fahrer, –** balloonist; **der ~korb, ¨–e** gondola (of balloon)

die **Ballung, –en** *vbl noun*; *also* concentration; **das ~s|gebiet, –e = der ~s|raum, ¨–e** densely-populated region; conurbation

der **Balsam** [–a:m], **–e** balsam; balm

balsamieren embalm

balsamisch balmy

der **Balte, –n** (*wk masc*) Balt

das **Baltikum** (*gen* **–s**) the Baltic States; (*pre-1918*) the Baltic Provinces

baltisch Baltic

die **Balustrade, –n** balustrade

die **Balz** *ornith* courtship; mating-season

balzen *ornith* display

der **Bambus** [–ʊs] (*gen* **–(ses)**), **–se** bamboo; **der ~bär, –en** (*wk masc*) giant panda; **der ~vorhang** the Bamboo Curtain

Bammel *coll*: **~ haben vor** (*dat*) be scared of

bammeln *coll* dangle (**an** *dat* from)

banal banal

banalisieren trivialize; render banal

die **Banalität, –en** banality

die **Banane, –n** banana; **die ~n|republik, –en** banana republic; **die ~n|schale, –n** banana-skin

der **Banause, –n** (*wk masc*) Philistine

das **Banausentum** philistinism

banausisch Philistine

band *p/t of* **binden**

das **Band¹, ¨–er** ribbon; tape; band (*also rad*); hoop; metal strip; *anat* ligament; *tech* conveyor belt; assembly line; **am laufenden ~** *coll* continually, (**Unfälle** *etc* **am laufenden ~**) one (accident *etc*) after another; **auf ~** on tape; **auf ~ aufnehmen** tape; **auf ~ legen** put into production

das **Band², –e** bond, tie; (*pl*) *poet* bonds, fetters; **zarte ~e knüpfen** start a romance

der **Band, ¨–e** volume; **das spricht Bände** that speaks volumes

die **Band** [bɛnt], **–s** (dance) band

Band– tape ...; band ...; ribbon ...; **die ~aufnahme, –n** tape-recording; **die ~breite, –n** range; *fin* range of fluctuation; *rad* bandwidth; **das ~gerät, –e** tape-recorder; **das ~maß, –e** tape-measure; **die ~nudeln** *pl* noodles; **die ~säge, –n** band-saw; **die ~scheibe, –n** intervertebral disc; *coll* = **der**

~scheiben|vorfall, ⸚e slipped disc; **der ~wurm, ⸚er** tapeworm; **der ~wurm|satz, ⸚e** *coll* long and involved sentence
die **Bandage** [–ʒə], **–n** bandage; **mit harten ~n kämpfen** fight tooth and nail
bandagieren [–ʒ–] bandage
die **Bande**[1], **–n** gang; band; *coll* bunch
die **Bande**[2], **–n** *sp* cushion; (of arena) fence; (of rink) boards
bände *p/t subj of* **binden**
der **Banden|führer, –** gang-leader
die **Banderole, –n** revenue stamp (on tobacco products)
–bändig –volume
bändigen tame; restrain; subdue, master
der **Bandit, –en** (*wk masc*) bandit; **das ~en|(un)wesen** banditry
bange anxious; (+*dat*) **~ machen** scare; **mir ist/wird ~** I'm/I get scared; **mir ist ~ vor** (*dat*) I'm scared of
Bange *NGer coll*: **(keine) ~ haben** (not) be scared; **nur keine ~!** don't worry! || **der ~macher, –** *coll* scaremonger
bangen: ~ um be anxious about; **mir bangt vor** (*dat*) I'm afraid of
die **Bangigkeit** anxiety
das **Banjo** ['banjo, 'bɛndʒo], **–s** banjo
die **Bank**[1], **⸚e** bench, *eccles* pew; (sand)bank; bed (of oysters, *also geol*); bank (of cloud); **auf die lange ~ schieben** *coll* put off; **(alle) durch die ~** *coll* every man jack
die **Bank**[2], **–en** bank; **der/die ~angestellte** (*decl as adj*) bank-clerk; **der ~direktor, –en** bank manager; **das ~fach, ⸚er** safe deposit box; banking; **der ~halter, –** *games* banker; **die ~note, –n** banknote, bill *US*; **b~rott** bankrupt; *coll* broke (**b. gehen** go bankrupt; **b. machen** bankrupt); **der ~rott, –e** bankruptcy (**B. machen** go bankrupt; fail); **der ~rotteur** [–'tøːɐ], **–e** bankrupt; **die ~verbindung, –en** (s.o.'s) bankers; **das ~wesen** banking
Bänkel–: das ~lied, –er street-ballad; **der ~sänger, –** ballad-singer
das **Bankett**[1], **–e** banquet
das **Bankett**[2], **–e = die Bankette, –n** shoulder (beside road)
der **Bankier** [baŋ'ki̯eː], **–s** banker
der **Bann** spell; *hist* ban, *eccles* excommunication; **in seinem ~ halten** hold spellbound; **im ~ stehen von** be held spellbound by; be under the spell of; **in seinen ~ schlagen/ziehen** captivate || **~kreis** (**in jmds. B.** under s.o.'s influence; **unter jmds. B. geraten** come under s.o.'s influence); **die ~meile** area in which public meetings are prohibited
bannen (*see also* **gebannt**) exorcize; avert (danger *etc*); captivate; *hist* banish, *eccles* excommunicate; **~ auf** (*acc*) capture on (canvas *etc*)
das **Banner, –** banner, standard
der **Baptist, –en** (*wk masc*) Baptist
bar cash; sheer; *arch* bare; (+*gen*) devoid of; (*adv*) in cash; **~es Geld** cash; **gegen/in ~** for/in cash
die **Bar, –s** bar; night-club
Bar– cash ...; bar ...; **(bar–)** bare–; **b~busig** bare-bosomed; **die ~dame, –n** barmaid; **b~fuß = b~füßig** barefoot; **das ~geld** cash; **b~geld|los** by cheque or credit transfer; **b~häuptig** bare-headed; **der ~hocker, –** bar-stool; **der ~mixer, –** bartender; **der ~scheck, –s** uncrossed cheque; **die ~zahlung, –en** cash payment

---

–bar (*added to verbs*) –able, –ible, *eg* **auffind~** discoverable (**auffinden** = discover); **leicht/schwer ...bar** easy/hard to ..., *eg* **schwer faß~** hard to grasp (**fassen** = grasp)

---

der **Bär, –en** (*wk masc*) bear; **der Große/Kleine ~** *astron* the Great/Little Bear; (+*dat*) **einen ~en aufbinden** *coll* take for a ride || **b~beißig** surly
die **Baracke, –n** hut; shack
der **Barbar, –en** (*wk masc*) barbarian
die **Barbarei, –en** barbarism; barbarity
barbarisch barbarous; barbaric; *coll* frightful
der **Barchent** [–çn̩t], **–e** fustian
der **Barde, –n** (*wk masc*) bard
Bären– bear ...; bear's ...; **~haut** *coll* (**auf der B. liegen** loaf about); **die ~mütze, –n** bearskin; **bären|stark** strong as an ox
das **Barett, –e** (flat) cap; biretta; mortar-board
barg (bärge) *p/t* (*subj*) *of* **bergen**
die **Bärin, –nen** she-bear
der **Bariton** [–ɔn], **–e** [–oːnə] baritone
die **Barkasse, –n** launch
die **Barke, –n** small boat
barmherzig merciful
die **Barmherzigkeit** mercy
barock baroque
das **Barock** (*also* **der**) baroque; baroque period
das **Barometer, –** barometer
barometrisch barometric
der **Baron, –e** baron
die **Baronesse, –n** baron's daughter
die **Baronin, –nen** baroness
der **Barras** [–as] *coll* army (life); **beim ~** in the army
das **Barrel** ['bɛ–], **–(s)** barrel (= measure)
der **Barren, –** ingot; bar; *gym* parallel bars; **das ~gold** gold bullion
die **Barriere** [–'ri̯eːrə, –ɛː–], **–n** barrier
die **Barrikade, –n** barricade; **auf die ~n gehen/steigen für** take up the cudgels for
barsch gruff
der **Barsch, –e** perch (= fish)
die **Barschaft** ready money

der **Barsoi, –s** borzoi
barst (bärste) *p/t* (*subj*) *of* **bersten**
der **Bart** [–a:–], ⸚**e** beard, (of cat *etc*) whiskers; bit (of key); *astron* tail; (+*dat*) **um den ~ gehen** *coll* butter up
Bart– beard ...; *ornith* bearded ...; **b~los** beardless; **die ~stoppeln** *pl* stubble (on chin)
Bartholomäus Bartholomew
bärtig [–ɛ:–] bearded; **–bärtig** -bearded
der **Basalt, –e** basalt
der **Basar, –e** bazaar
die **Base, –n** *chem* base
Basedowsch [–doʃ]: **die ~e Krankheit** Graves' disease
Basel Basle
Basen *pl of* **Base, Basis**
basieren: ~ auf (*dat*) be based on
die **Basilika, –(k)en** basilica
das **Basilikum** basil
die **Basis,** *pl* **Basen** base (*also archit, bot, math, mil, etc*); basis, footing; rank and file; grass roots (level); work-force
basisch *chem, geol* basic
der **Baske, –n** (*wk masc*) Basque; **die ~n|mütze, –n** beret
baskisch, (*language*) **B~** Basque
baß *arch joc*: **~ erstaunt** mighty surprised
der **Baß,** ⸚**(ss)e** bass; bass voice; = **die ~geige, –n** double-bass; **der ~schlüssel, –** bass clef
das **Bassin** [–'sɛŋ], **–s** basin (of fountain); pool
der **Bassist, –en** (*wk masc*) bass; bass player
der **Bast** bast; raffia; *zool* velvet
basta: (und damit) ~! and that's that!
der **Bastard, –e** *hist* bastard; *biol* hybrid
die **Bastei, –en** bastion
die **Bastel|arbeit, –en** handicraft (as a hobby); (piece of) handiwork
basteln build; make; (*v/i*) make things (as a hobby); **~ an** (*dat*) work on
die **Bastion, –en** bastion
der **Bastler, –** handyman
bat *p/t of* **bitten**
das **Bataillon** [batal'jo:n], **–e** battalion
bäte *p/t subj of* **bitten**
der **Batik** [–ɪk], **–en** (*also* **die**) batik
der **Batist** batiste; cambric
die **Batterie, –(ie)n** *elect, mil* battery
der **Batzen, –** lump; *hist* batz (*former coin*); **ein ~ Geld** *coll* a tidy sum
der **Bau** construction; structure; build; building-site; (*pl* **–ten**) building; (*pl*) *cin* sets; (*pl* **–e**) burrow; earth; *min* working; **–bau** *also min* -mining; *agr* -growing; **(3 Tage** *etc*) **~** *coll* (3 days *etc*) in the guardhouse; **im ~** under construction
Bau– building ...; construction(al) ...;
die ~arbeiten *pl* construction work; road works; **die ~art, –en** (method of) construction; design; **das ~fach** building trade; **b~fällig** dilapidated; **das ~gerüst, –e** scaffolding; **der ~herr, –en** (*like* **Herr**) person for whom/body for which a building is (being) built; **der ~ingenieur, –e** civil engineer; **das ~jahr, –e** year of manufacture/construction; **der ~kasten, ..kästen** construction set; box of bricks; **das ~kasten|system** unit construction; **der ~klotz,** ⸚**e** building brick; **die ~kunst** architecture; **der ~meister, –** (master) builder; **der ~plan,** ⸚**e** building project; architect's plan; **der ~platz,** ⸚**e** building-site; **b~sparen** (*usu infin*) save with a *Bausparkasse*; **die ~spar|kasse, –n** building society, building and loan association *US*; **der ~stein, –e** building stone; brick; component, *comput* module; (important) contribution; **die ~stelle, –n** building-site; road works; **der ~stil, –e** architectural style; **der ~unternehmer, –** building contractor; **die ~weise, –n** (method of) construction; architectural style; **das ~werk, –e** edifice; **das ~wesen** building trade
der **Bauch,** ⸚**e** belly; stomach; *in compds also* abdominal ...; **die ~binde, –n** band (around cigar *etc*); *med* abdominal belt; **das ~fell, –e** peritoneum; **der ~klatscher, –** *coll* belly-flop; **der ~laden, ..läden** vendor's tray; **die ~landung, –en** belly-landing; **b~pinseln** *coll* **(sich gebauchpinselt fühlen** feel flattered); **b~reden** (*usu infin*) ventriloquize; **das ~reden** ventriloquism; **der ~redner, –** ventriloquist; **die ~schmerzen** *pl* stomach-ache; **der ~speck** belly of pork; 'spare tyre'; **die ~speichel|drüse, –n** pancreas; **die ~tänzerin, –nen** belly-dancer; **das ~weh** *coll* tummy-ache
bauchig bulbous; **–bauchig** -bellied
bäuchlings on one's stomach
bauen build, construct; make; *coll* take (exam); cause (accident); (*v/i*) build; **~ an** (*dat*) be building; be working on; **~ auf** (*acc*) bank on
das **Bauer, –** (bird-)cage
der **Bauer, –n** (*wk masc*) farmer; peasant; *chess* pawn; *cards* jack
das **Bäuerchen, –** *coll* (baby's) burp
die **Bäuerin, –nen** farmer's wife; peasant woman
bäuerlich rural; rustic
Bauern– farm ...; farmer's ...; peasant('s) ...; country ...; rural ...; **der ~fänger, –** trickster; **die ~fängerei, –en** trickery; **das ~frühstück, –e** (*scrambled egg with fried potatoes and diced ham – not a breakfast dish*); **das ~gut,** ⸚**er** farm; **das ~haus,** ⸚**er** farmhouse; **der ~hof,** ⸚**e** farm; **die ~schläue** native cunning
die **Bauernschaft** farmers; peasantry
das **Bauerntum** farmers; peasantry; rustic origins
baulich structural

^die^ **Baulichkeiten** *pl* buildings

^der^ **Baum, ⸚e** tree; *naut* boom; *tech* beam (of loom); **die ~grenze, -n** tree-line; **der ~läufer, -** tree-creeper; **der ~ring, -e** tree-ring; **die ~schule, -n** nursery; **der ~stamm, ⸚e** tree-trunk; **der ~stumpf, ⸚e** tree-stump; **~woll-** cotton ...; **die ~wolle, b~wollen** cotton

baumeln dangle (**an** *dat* from); *coll* 'swing'; **~ mit = ~ lassen** dangle (one's legs)

bäumen: sich ~ rear; **sich ~ gegen** rebel against

bäurisch boorish

^der^ **Bausch, ⸚e** wad; **in ~ und Bogen** (condemn *etc*) wholesale

bauschen swell (sail *etc*); (*v/i*) bunch; **sich ~** swell out; bunch

bauschig (skirt *etc*) full

Bauten *pl of* **Bau**

^der^ **Bauxit, -e** bauxite

bauz! boomps-a-daisy!

^der^ **Bayer** [-ae-], **-n** (*wk masc*) Bavarian

bay(e)risch [-ae-] Bavarian

Bayern [-ae-] Bavaria

^der^ **Bazi, -(s)** *SGer coll* rogue

^der^ **Bazillen|träger, -** germ-carrier

^der^ **Bazillus, -(ll)en** bacillus; germ

Bd(e). (= **Band (Bände)**) vol(s).

^der^ **BDM** *Nazi* = **Bund Deutscher Mädel**

be- *insep pref* (*unstressed*)

be|absichtigen intend

be|achten observe; heed, pay attention to; **~s|wert** noteworthy

be|achtlich considerable; quite important

^die^ **Be|achtung** *vbl noun*; *also* observance; notice, attention; (+*dat*) **(keine) ~ schenken** pay (no) attention to

be|ackern plough; *coll* work through; *coll* work on (person)

^der^ **Be|amte** (*decl as adj*) official; (*status of certain government employees*) civil servant; (police) officer

^das^ **Be|amtentum** officialdom; civil servants

be|amtet employed as a civil servant

be|ängstigen alarm; **~d** alarming

be|anspruchen claim; take up; make demands on; take up (s.o.'s) time; *mech* stress; **zeitlich stark beansprucht sein** have many calls on one's time

^die^ **Be|anspruchung, -en** *vbl noun*; *also* demands (*gen* on); strain; *mech* stress

be|anstanden, *Aust* **be|anständen** object to; make a complaint about; query

^die^ **Be|anstandung, -en** complaint; objection

be|antragen apply for; propose, *parl* move, *leg* ask for

be|antworten answer; respond to

Be|antwortung: in ~ (+*gen*) in reply to

be|arbeiten work (land), *tech* dress, work; work on; deal with, handle; process; revise (manuscript), adapt (for stage *etc*), *mus* arrange; *coll* work on (person); 'work over'; pound away at; **~ mit** treat with; **maschinell ~** machine

^die^ **Be|arbeitung, -en** *in vbl senses*; *also* treatment; revision, adaptation, *mus* arrangement; **in ~** in preparation || **die ~s|gebühr, -en** administrative charge

be|argwöhnen be suspicious of

^der^ **Beat** [biːt] beat (music)

^die^ **Be|atmung** artificial respiration

be|aufsichtigen supervise

^die^ **Be|aufsichtigung** supervision

be|auftragen commission; instruct (to); **~ mit** entrust with

^der^ **Be|auftragte** (*fem* **die ~**) (*decl as adj*) (authorized) representative

be|äugen eye

bebauen build on; cultivate

^das^ **Bébé, -s** *Swiss* baby

beben tremble, shake (**vor** *dat* with); **das Beben** trembling; tremor

bebildern illustrate

bebrillt bespectacled

^der^ **Becher, -** beaker; mug; carton; (ice-cream) tub, cup *US*; cup (of happiness *etc*); *bot* cupule

bechern *coll* booze

becircen *coll* bewitch

^das^ **Becken, -** basin (*also geol*); (swimming-) pool; *anat* pelvis; (*pl*) *mus* cymbals; *in compds anat* pelvic ...

^die^ **Beckmesserei, -en** carping

bedachen roof

bedacht *p/part of* **bedenken, bedachen;** *also* cautious; **~ auf** (*acc*) concerned about; **darauf ~ zu ...** intent on (+*ger*)

Bedacht: mit ~ with deliberation; **ohne ~** without thinking

bedächtig deliberate; cautious

bedanken: sich ~ express one's thanks; **sich ~ bei** thank; **sich ~ für** express one's thanks for; **dafür bedanke ich mich bestens!** *no, thank* you!

^der^ **Bedarf** need (**an** *dat* for); requirement(s); supply (of); *comm* demand (for); **~ haben an** (*dat*) need; **bei/nach ~** if/as required || **der ~s|artikel, -** requisite; **~s|fall (im B.** if necessary); **die ~s|halte|stelle, -n** request stop

bedauerlich regrettable; **bedauerlicher|weise** unfortunately

bedauern regret; feel sorry for; **bedaure!** sorry!; **das Bedauern** regret; sympathy || **~s|wert** pitiable; regrettable; **~s|würdig** pitiable

bedecken cover; **sich ~** cover oneself; cloud over; **mit Küssen ~** smother in kisses; **bedeckt** *also* overcast

^die^ **Bedeckung, -en** cover(ing); *mil etc* escort

Bedenk–: die ~zeit time to think sth. over

bedenken* (*see also* **bedacht**) think about; bear in mind; remember (in will); **~ mit** present with; bestow on; **sich ~** reflect; **zu ~ geben, daß ...** point out that ...

das **Bedenken, –** objection; (*pl*) misgivings; scruples; **nach reiflichem ~** after careful reflection; **ohne ~** unhesitatingly || **b~los** without thinking/hesitating

bedenklich dubious; ominous; serious; (expression) doubtful; **~ stimmen** cause (s.o.) to have doubts

bedeppert *coll* dumbfounded

bedeuten mean; (+*dat*) *also* give (s.o.) to understand; **das hat nichts zu ~** it's of no consequence; **~d** important; major; considerable

bedeutsam significant

die **Bedeutsamkeit** significance

die **Bedeutung, –en** meaning; significance; importance; **ohne ~** of no importance; **von ~** important || **b~s|los** insignificant; meaningless; **b~s|voll** significant; meaningful; **der ~s|wandel** semantic change

bedienen serve; operate; *sp* pass to; *cards* play (from same suit); *fin* pay interest on; (*v/i*) *cards* follow suit; **sich ~** help oneself; (+*gen*) make use of; **bedient sein** *coll* have had enough

die **Bedienerin, –nen** *Aust* cleaner, cleaning woman

der **Bedienstete** (*fem* **die**) (*decl as adj*) public employee; servant

die **Bedienung** service; operation (of machinery); waiter *or* waitress; *Aust* cleaner; *mil* gun crew; **der ~s|aufschlag, ¨–e = das ~s|geld, –er** service charge; **die ~s|vorschrift, –en** operating instructions; **die ~s|mannschaft, –en** gun crew

bedingen cause, give rise to; determine; entail; **sich gegenseitig ~** be interdependent

bedingt *p/part*; *also* conditional; qualified, limited; (reflex) conditioned; (*adv*) *also* partially; in a limited sense; **~ durch** (*also* **–bedingt**) governed by; dependent on, determined by; conditioned by; due to

die **Bedingung, –en** condition; (*pl*) (weather *etc*) conditions; *comm* terms; **mit/unter der ~, daß ...** on condition that ... || **b~s|los** unconditional; unquestioning; **der ~s|satz, ¨–e** conditional clause

bedrängen press hard; pester; (sorrow *etc*) oppress; **in bedrängter Lage** in a tight corner

die **Bedrängnis** distress

bedrohen threaten

bedrohlich threatening; ominous; dangerous

die **Bedrohung, –en** threat (*gen* to)

bedrucken print (fabric *etc*); **~ mit** print on

bedrücken oppress; depress; **~d** depressing; oppressive; **bedrückt** dejected

der **Beduine, –n** (*wk masc*), **beduinisch** Bedouin

bedürfen* (+*gen*) need; require

das **Bedürfnis, –se** need; desire (**nach** for); **das ~ haben zu ...** feel the need to ... || **die (öffentliche) ~anstalt, –en** public convenience, comfort station *US*; **b~los** undemanding

bedürftig needy, poor; (*following gen*; *also* **–bedürftig**) in need of

die **Bedürftigkeit** need, want

beduselt *coll* tipsy; dazed

das **Beefsteak** ['bi:fste:k], **–s** steak; **deutsches ~** beefburger

be|ehren honour; **sich ~ zu ...** have the honour to ...

be|eiden declare on oath

be|eilen: sich ~ hurry

be|eindrucken impress; **~d** impressive

be|einflußbar easily influenced

be|einflussen influence

die **Be|einflussung** *vbl noun*; *also* influence

be|einträchtigen impair; detract from

be|elenden *Swiss* distress

be|enden finish; end

be|engen restrict, cramp; be too tight for; **beengt wohnen** live in cramped conditions

be|erben inherit the estate of

be|erdigen bury

die **Be|erdigung, –en** burial; funeral; **das ~s|institut, –e** undertakers, funeral parlor *US*

die **Beere, –n** berry

das **Beet, –e** (flower *etc*) bed

befähigen enable (to); **~ zu** equip for; **befähigt** able; **befähigt zu** fit for, qualified for

die **Befähigung, –en** ability; qualifications (**zu** for)

befahl (befähle) *p/t* (*subj*) *of* **befehlen**

befahrbar passable; *naut* navigable

befahren* drive on/through; use; *naut* navigate; *min* go down

der **Befall** infestation (of plant)

befallen* overcome (*usu pass*); (disease *etc*) attack

befangen self-conscious; biased; **~ in** (*dat*) prepossessed with; blinded by (prejudices); **in einem Irrtum ~ sein** labour under a misapprehension

befassen: sich ~ mit concern oneself with; attend to; deal with; spend time with

der **Befehl, –e** order; command; *comput* instruction; **auf ~** (+*gen*) by order of; **zu ~!** yes, sir!

befehlen (befiehl(s)t, *p/t* **befahl** (*subj* **befähle, beföhle**), *p/part* **befohlen**) order; (*v/i*) give orders; **~ über** (*acc*) *mil* command; **jmdm. ~ zu ...** order s.o. to ...

befehlerisch imperious

befehligen command (forces)
Befehls– … of command/an order/orders; command …; **die ~form** imperative mood; **b~gemäß** according to instructions; **der ~haber, –** commander; **b~haberisch** imperious; **die ~verweigerung, –en** refusal to obey orders; **b~widrig** contrary to instructions
befestigen fasten; fix; strengthen; *mil* fortify
die **Befestigung, –en** *vbl noun*; *mil* fortification
befeuchten moisten
befiehl *imp sing*, **befiehl(s)t** (*2nd*,) *3rd sing pres of* **befehlen**
befinden*: ~ für deem; **~ über** (*acc*) decide; **sich ~** be (in a certain place/situation); feel (well *etc*); **das Befinden** (state of) health
befindlich to be found; situated; *or not translated* (*eg* **die im Bau ~en Häuser** the houses under construction, **die im Keller ~e Pumpe** the pump in the cellar)
befingern *coll* finger
beflaggen deck out with flags; *naut* dress
beflecken stain; sully
befleißigen: sich ~ (+*gen*) cultivate; apply oneself to; **sich ~ zu …** take great pains to …
befliegen* fly (route); *bot* (bee) visit
beflissen eager; **~ um** solicitous for
beflissentlich studiously
beflügeln wing (s.o.'s steps *etc*); lend (s.o.) wings; **beflügelt** winged
beföhle *p/t subj*, **befohlen** *p/part of* **befehlen**
befolgen follow; comply with
beförderlich *Swiss* expeditious
befördern carry (passengers), transport; forward; send; promote; **an die frische Luft/ins Freie ~** *coll* chuck out
die **Beförderung, –en** transport(ation); promotion; **das ~s|mittel, –** conveyance
befrackt in tails
befragen ask; consult
befranst fringed
befreien free; liberate; **~ von** free from; rid of; exempt from; **sich ~ aus** escape from; **sich ~ von** free oneself from; rid oneself of
befreiend that relieve(s) the tension
der **Befreier, –** liberator; rescuer
die **Befreiung** freeing; liberation; exemption
befremden take aback; disconcert; **~d** odd; disconcerting; **das Befremden** surprise (mingled with displeasure)
befremdlich odd; disconcerting
befreunden: sich ~ mit make friends with; get used to; **befreundet** friendly; friends (with); *math* amicable
befrieden pacify
befriedigen satisfy; give (s.o.) satisfaction; (*v/i*) be satisfactory; give satisfaction; **sich ~** masturbate; **~d** satisfactory
die **Befriedigung** satisfaction
befristen set a time-limit on
befruchten fertilize; inseminate; fructify
die **Befruchtung** fertilization; insemination; fructification
die **Befugnis, –se** authority (to act); (*pl*) powers, authority
befugt authorized
befühlen *coll* finger; feel
befummeln *coll* touch, feel; 'grope'
der **Befund, –e** findings; result (of test)
befürchten, die Befürchtung, –en fear
befürworten advocate; support
der **Befürworter, –** advocate; supporter
die **Befürwortung** advocacy; support
begabt gifted, talented
die **Begabung, –en** gift, talent
begaffen *coll* gape at
begann (begänne) *p/t* (*subj*) *of* **beginnen**
begasen gas (foxes, badgers, *etc*)
begatten mate with; **sich ~** mate
begaunern *coll* swindle (**um** out of)
begeben*: sich ~ proceed, go (to a place); occur; (+*gen*) forgo; **sich ~ an** (*acc*) set about; **sich ~ in** (*acc*) place oneself under (s.o.'s protection); expose oneself to (danger); have (treatment)
die **Begebenheit, –en** occurrence
begegnen (*sn*) (word *etc*) occur; (+*dat*) meet; encounter; treat (politely *etc*); face (danger), counter (attack), combat (epidemic *etc*); happen to; **sich** *dat pl* **~** meet
die **Begegnung, –en** meeting; encounter
begehen* commit; make (mistake); celebrate; walk along; inspect (on foot)
begehren desire; covet; **begehrt** *also* sought-after || **~s|wert** desirable
begehrlich covetous
begeistern fill with enthusiasm; thrill; inspire; **sich ~** get enthusiastic (**für** about); **sich ~ an** (*dat*) be inspired by; **~d** inspiring; **begeistert** *also* enthusiastic (**von** about)
die **Begeisterung** enthusiasm; **in ~ geraten** be filled with enthusiasm
die **Begierde, –n** longing; desire
begierig eager (**auf** *acc*/**nach** for)
begießen* pour water on; water; *cul* baste; *coll* celebrate (with a drink)
der **Beginn** beginning; **zu ~** at the start (*gen* of)
beginnen (*p/t* **begann** (*subj* **begänne, begönne**), *p/part* **begonnen**) begin; set about; do; **~ mit** do with; (*v/i*) begin, (make a) start on; (word *etc*) begin with; **~d** incipient; (13th *etc* century) early; **das Beginnen** undertaking
beglaubigen certify; *pol* accredit
die **Beglaubigung, –en** certification; *pol* accreditation; **das ~s|schreiben, –** credentials
begleichen* pay, settle (bill)
Begleit– accompanying …; *mil* escort …; **der ~brief, –e** covering letter; **die**

~**erscheinung, –en** concomitant; accompanying phenomenon; **die ~musik** accompaniment; incidental music; **die ~person, –en** escort; **das ~schreiben, –** covering letter; **der ~umstand, ¨–e** attendant circumstance

begleiten accompany (*also mus*); escort; see (to the door *etc*); (wishes) go with

der **Begleiter, –** companion; escort; *mus* accompanist

die **Begleitung, –en** *vbl noun*; *also* company; escort; entourage; *mus* accompaniment; **in ~** (+*gen*) accompanied by

beglücken make happy; **~ mit** favour with; **beglückt** happy (**über** *acc* about)

beglückwünschen congratulate (**zu** on)

begnadet highly gifted

begnadigen, die Begnadigung, –en pardon; reprieve

begnügen: sich ~ mit content oneself with

die **Begonie** [–ĭə], **–n** begonia

begönne *p/t subj*, **begonnen** *p/part of* **beginnen**

begraben* bury

das **Begräbnis, –se** burial; = **die ~feier, –n** funeral

begradigen straighten

begreifen* (*see also* **begriffen**) understand, grasp; realize

begreiflich understandable; (+*dat*) **~ machen** make clear to || **begreiflicher|weise** understandably

begrenzen limit (**auf** *acc* to); form the boundary of

die **Begrenztheit** limitation, limited nature

die **Begrenzung, –en** limitation; boundary

der **Begriff, –e** conception, idea; concept; term; **ein ~ sein** be a household word; (+*dat*) **ein ~ sein** mean/convey something to; **sich** *dat* **einen ~ machen von** imagine; **für meine ~e** to my mind; **im ~ zu ...** about to ... ; **das geht über meine ~e** it's beyond me; **schwer von ~** *coll* slow on the uptake

begriffen *p/part*; **~ in** (*dat*) in process of; engaged in

begrifflich abstract; conceptual

Begriffs–: die ~bestimmung, –en definition; **b~stutzig**, *Aust* **b~stützig** slow-witted; **das ~vermögen** comprehension

begründen give (one's) reasons for; substantiate; found, establish; **~ mit** give as the reason for; **begründet** *also* well-founded; justified; **begründet sein in** (*dat*) be the result of

der **Begründer, –** founder

die **Begründung, –en** reason (given); grounds; foundation (of); **mit der ~, daß ...** on the grounds that ...; **zur ~** (+*gen*) in support of

begrüßen greet; welcome; *Swiss* consult; **~s|wert** welcome

die **Begrüßung, –en** *vbl noun*; *also* welcome

begucken *coll* look at

begünstigen favour; *leg* aid and abet (after crime)

begut|achten give an expert opinion on; *coll* size up; have a look at

begütert well-to-do

begütigen soothe

behaart hairy; **–behaart** -haired

behäbig portly (and easy-going); leisurely; *Swiss* well-to-do

behaftet: ~ mit afflicted with; **... ist mit einem Makel ~** a stigma attaches to ...

behagen (+*dat*) please, be to (s.o.'s) taste

das **Behagen** contentment; **mit ~** with relish

behaglich cosy; comfortable

behalten* keep; retain; keep on; remember; **bei sich ~** keep on one; keep (food) down; put up; **für 'sich ~** keep for/to oneself; **er hat von (dem Unfall** *etc*) **... behalten** (the accident *etc*) left him with ...

der **Behälter, –** container; tank

behandeln deal with; treat (*also med*: **wegen** for); handle; **sich ~ lassen** have treatment

behändigen *Swiss* take (unlawfully)

die **Behandlung, –en** treatment (*also med*); **in ~** undergoing treatment

der **Behang, ¨–e** hangings; decoration (on Christmas tree); crop (of fruit-tree)

behangen: ~ mit laden with

behängen: ~ mit hang with

beharren: ~ auf (*dat*)/**bei** persist in; stick to; **das Beharren** persistence; adherence

beharrlich persistent, persevering; steadfast; (*adv*) *also* doggedly

die **Beharrlichkeit** persistence; steadfastness

das **Beharrungs|vermögen** *phys* inertia

behauchen breathe on; *ling* aspirate

behauen* (*p/t* **behaute**) hew (stone *etc*)

behaupten assert; say; maintain; *mil* hold; **sich ~** hold one's own; *fin* remain steady

die **Behauptung, –en** statement, assertion; *math*, *philos* proposition

die **Behausung, –en** dwelling

beheben* repair; rectify; remedy; get rid of; dispel; *Aust* collect, *fin* withdraw

beheimatet: ~ in (*dat*) resident in; *bot*, *zool* indigenous to; **~ sein in** *also* come from

beheizen heat

der **Behelf, –e** makeshift

behelfen*: sich ~ make do (**mit** with)

Behelfs– temporary ...; **b~mäßig** temporary; makeshift

behelligen bother; pester

behend(e) nimble

die **Behendigkeit** nimbleness

beherbergen put up; accommodate; house

beherrschen rule; dominate; control; have a command of; be master of; **sich ~** control oneself; **~d** dominant

beherrscht *p/part*; *also* self-possessed; composed

die **Beherrschtheit** self-control

die **Beherrschung** *vbl noun*; *also* domination; control; mastery; command (of language); self-control

beherzigen take to heart

beherzt courageous

behexen bewitch

behilflich helpful; (+*dat*) ~ **sein** help (**bei** with)

behindern hinder; obstruct (*also sp*); **behindert** *also* handicapped

die **Behinderung, –en** hindrance; obstruction (*also sp*); disability

die **Behörde, –n** (public) authority

behördlich official

behost *coll* in trousers

Behuf *arch*: **zu diesem ~** to this end

behuft hoofed

behüten watch over; guard (secret); ~ **vor** (*dat*) protect from; **(Gott) behüte!** heaven forbid!; **behütet** (childhood) sheltered

der **Behüter, –** protector

behutsam cautious, careful; gentle

bei (+*dat*) (*a*) (*indicating place etc*) by, next to; near (*in addresses, eg* **Offenbach ~ Frankfurt**); (*with names of battles*) of; at (bank *etc*), at ...'s (*eg* ~ **Woolworth** at Woolworth's, **~m Bäcker** at the baker's); at (s.o.'s) house/place; with; c/o; among; in (*also = 'in the works of'*, *eg* ~ **Homer** in H.); on (= *'on (s.o.'s) person'*); (assume *etc*) on the part of; ~ **sich** on one; with one; to oneself; **nicht ganz ~ sich** not quite all there; ~ **uns** at our house; in our family/firm *etc*; in our (part of the) country;

(*b*) (*indicating means*: take, call, *etc*) by;

(*c*) (*indicating instance*) with, in the case of;

(*d*) (*indicating time, circumstances*) at (daybreak, s.o.'s birth, these words, O°, *etc*); on (occasion, closer acquaintance, *etc*); in (accident, bad weather, *etc*); by (night, moonlight, *etc*); over (a beer *etc*); with (*eg* ~ **offenem Fenster** with the window open); (*with vbl noun*) during; when ..., as ..., while ..., on (+*ger*) (*eg* ~ **der Besetzung dieses Postens** when filling this post, **~m Anflug auf München** *aer* while approaching Munich, **~m Skilaufen** while skiing, **~m Eintritt in ...** on entering ...);

(*simultaneity*) as ..., while ... (*eg* **die Emigrantenzahl fiel – ~ wachsendem Wohlstand der Bundesrepublik – auf 200 000 zurück** as West Germany's prosperity increased (so) the number of emigrants went down to 200,000, **im neuen Telefonnetz sind ~ unveränderter Gesprächigkeit der Einwohner die Gebühreneinnahmen um 20 Prozent gesunken** in the new telephone system receipts have fallen by 20 per cent while the loquaciousness of the inhabitants has remained unchanged);

(*condition*) in case/the event of, if ..., where ... (*eg* ~ **Achsenbruch** if an axle breaks, ~ **Regen/nasser Fahrbahn** if it rains/the road is wet, ~ **steigendem Ölverbrauch** where oil consumption increases, ~ **richtiger Anwendung dieses Verfahrens** if this process is properly applied);

(*e*) (*indicating state, activity*) in (good health *etc*); **~m (Lesen** *etc*) **sein** be +*pres/part* (*eg* reading);

(*f*) in view of; with; (*concessive*) for, with (all ...); in spite of; ~ **alledem** for all that;

(*g*) (*in oaths, imprecations*) by

---

bei– *sep pref*; *frequently indicates the addition of something to something else*

Bei– *signifies something additional, supplementary*

beibehalten* keep; retain; maintain; keep to

die **Beibehaltung** *vbl noun*; *also* retention; maintenance

das **Beiblatt, ⸗er** supplement

das **Beiboot, –e** dinghy

beibringen* produce (evidence *etc*); (+*dat*) teach; inflict on; (+*dat*) **das Lesen/Schreiben ~** teach to read/write; (+*dat*) **schonend ~** break (news) gently to

Beicht–: b~hören (*sep*) *Aust* hear confession; **das ~kind, –er** penitent; **der ~stuhl, ⸗e** confessional; **der ~vater, ..väter** (father) confessor

die **Beichte, –n** confession; (+*dat*) **die ~ abnehmen** confess

beichten confess

beid– *esp sp* (*eg* **~armig**) with both (arms *etc*); **~händig** ambidextrous; two-handed; (*adv*) with both hands

beide both; (*with def art etc*) two; either, (*in pronominal use*: *with neg*) either of them; *sp* (*eg* **30 ~**) all; **alle ~** both of them; **~s** both (things); either

beider–: ~lei (*indecl*) of both kinds (**b. Geschlechts** of both sexes); **~seitig** bilateral; mutual; **~seits** on both sides (*gen* of)

beidrehen *naut* heave to

bei|einander together; next to each other

der **Beifahrer, –** passenger (beside driver); pillion passenger; co-driver (*also sp*)

der **Beifall** applause; ~ **finden** meet with approval; ~ **klatschen** applaud

beifällig approving

Beifalls– ... of applause/approval; **der ~s|ruf, –e** cheer; **der ~sturm, ⸚e** storm of applause

der **Beifilm, –e** supporting film

beifügen enclose (*dat* with); add (to)

die **Beifügung, –en** *vbl noun*; *gramm* attribute; **unter ~** (+*gen*) enclosing

der **Beifuß** [–u:–] mugwort

die **Beigabe, –n** addition; *archaeol* object placed in a grave

beige [be:ʃ] (*indecl*) beige

beigeben* (+*dat*) add to; assign to; **klein ~** climb down

beige|ordnet *p/part*; *gramm* co-ordinate; **der/die Beigeordnete** (*decl as adj*) assistant (in municipal administration)

der **Beigeschmack** (slight) flavour; taste

beigesellen (+*dat*) put together with; **sich ~** (+*dat*) join

das **Beiheft, –e** supplement; special issue

beiheften (+*dat*) attach to

die **Beihilfe, –n** financial assistance; grant; subsidy; *leg* aiding and abetting

der **Beiklang, ⸚e** undertone

beikommen* (*sn*) (+*dat*) get the better of; master (difficulty *etc*); deal with

das **Beil, –e** hatchet; chopper; *hist* axe

die **Beilage, –n** supplement; *Aust* enclosure; *cul* vegetables (served with main dish)

beiläufig incidental; casual; *Aust* approximate; (*adv*) *also* in passing

beilegen enclose; settle; (+*dat*) enclose with; bestow on; ascribe to; attach (importance) to

beileibe: ~ nicht by no means; on no account

das **Beileid** sympathy; condolences; *in compds* **~s–** ... of condolence

beiliegen* (+*dat*) be enclosed with; **~d** enclosed

beim = bei dem

beimengen (+*dat*) mix with, add to

beimessen* (+*dat*) attach (importance) to

beimischen (+*dat*) mix with, add to; **sich ~** (+*dat*) mingle with

die **Beimischung, –en** *vbl noun*; *also* addition

das **Bein, –e** leg; **–bein** *also* ... bone; (+*dat*) **~e machen** *coll* make (s.o.) get a move on; (+*dat*) **ein ~ stellen** *coll* trip up; **auf den ~en** on one's feet; up and about; **auf die ~e stellen** *coll* launch; **sich auf die ~e machen** *coll* make tracks; **mit dem linken ~ zuerst aufstehen** *coll* get out of bed on the wrong side

Bein– leg ...; bone ...; **b~amputiert** with an amputated leg; **der ~bruch, ⸚e** broken leg (**das ist kein B.** *coll* it's no great disaster; **Hals- und B.!** good luck!); **die ~kleider** *pl arch* trousers; **die ~prothese, –n** artificial leg; **die ~schiene, –n** *med* splint; *sp* shinpad

beinahe almost, nearly

der **Beiname, –n** (*like* **Name**) nickname; epithet

be|inhalten contain; embrace

–beinig –legged

bei|ordnen (*see also* **beigeordnet**) *gramm* co-ordinate; (+*dat*) assign to

beipflichten (+*dat*) agree with

das **Beiprogramm, –e** *cin* supporting programme

der **Beirat, ⸚e** advisory board; adviser

be|irren: sich nicht ~ lassen not be put off/deterred

beisammen (*also sep pref* **beisammen–**) together; **~haben*** (*sep*) have got (money *etc*) together (**seine fünf Sinne nicht ganz b.** not be all there); **das B~sein** get-together

beischießen* contribute (sum)

der **Beischlaf** (sexual) intercourse

beischließen* *Aust* enclose (*dat* with)

Beisein: im ~ (+*gen*) in the presence of

beiseite aside (*also theat*); to one side; **~ lassen** disregard; **~ legen** put aside; **~ nehmen** take aside; **~ schaffen** get rid of; stash away; **~ schieben** push aside; brush aside; **~ setzen** set aside; **~ treten** step aside

das **Beisel, –n** *Aust* tavern

beisetzen bury, inter

die **Beisetzung, –en** burial, interment; funeral

der **Beisitzer, –** member (of board *etc*); *leg* associate judge

das **Beispiel, –e** example (**für** of); **sich** *dat* **ein ~ nehmen an** (*dat*) take as an example; **mit gutem ~ vorangehen** set a good example; **ohne ~** unparalleled; **zum ~** for example || **b~los** unparalleled

beispielhaft exemplary

beispiels|weise for example

beispringen* (*sn*) (+*dat*) hasten to (s.o.'s) aid

Beiß–: der ~ring, –e teething-ring; **der ~zahn, ⸚e** incisor; **die ~zange, –n** pincers

beißen (*p/t* **biß**, *p/part* **gebissen**) (*also v/i*) bite; (smoke *etc*) sting; **~ auf** (*dat*) sting (tongue); **sich** *dat* **auf die Zunge ~** bite one's tongue; **~ in** (*acc*) bite into; make (eyes) smart

sich ~ bite one another; (colours) clash

beißend biting; pungent

der **Beistand, ⸚e** assistance; *leg* legal adviser; (+*dat*) **~ leisten** aid

beistehen* (+*dat*) assist

Beistell–: der ~tisch, –e side-table

beistellen *Aust* make available; (+*dat*) place at (s.o.'s) disposal

beisteuern contribute (**zu** to)

beistimmen (+*dat*) agree with

der **Beistrich, –e** *esp Aust* comma

der **Beitrag, ⸚e** contribution (**zu** to); subscription; (insurance) premium

beitragen* (*also v/i*) contribute (**zu** to); **das Seine ~ zu** do one's bit towards; **dazu ~ zu ...** help to ...

^der **Beiträger, –** contributor
beitreiben* recover (debt)
beitreten* (*sn*) (+*dat*) join; accede to
^der **Beitritt, -e:** ~ **zu** joining (club *etc*); accession to
^der **Beiwagen, –** sidecar
^das **Beiwerk** accessories, trimmings
beiwilligen (+*dat*) *Swiss* agree to
beiwohnen (+*dat*) be present at, attend
^das **Beiwort, ¨-er** epithet; *gramm* adjective
^die **Beize**[1] *hunt* hawking
^die **Beize**[2], **-n** *tech* mordant; pickle; stain; *agr* disinfectant; *cul* marinade
beizeiten in good time
beizen[1] *hunt* go hawking
beizen[2] (smoke) sting; *tech* mordant; bate; pickle; stain; *agr* disinfect; *cul* marinate
beiziehen* *SGer* call in; consult
bejahen answer in the affirmative; approve of; have a positive attitude to; ~**d** positive; affirmative (*also gramm*)
bejahrt advanced in years
^die **Bejahung, -en** affirmative answer; positive attitude (*gen* to); approval
bejammern lament; ~**s|wert** lamentable
bejubeln cheer; acclaim
bekämpfen fight; combat
^die **Bekämpfung** fight (*gen* against); control
bekannt *p/part*; *also* well-known (**wegen** for); familiar; **... ist mir** ~ I am familiar with ...; I know ...; ~ **mit** familiar with; acquainted with; ~ **machen mit** (*cf* **bekanntmachen**) introduce to; familiarize with; **sich** ~ **machen** introduce oneself; +**mit** familiarize oneself with; ~ **werden mit** (*cf* **bekanntwerden**) make (s.o.'s) acquaintance; become acquainted with; **der/die Bekannte** (*decl as adj*) acquaintance; friend; boy/girl-friend || **die B~gabe** announcement (of); ~**geben*** (*sep*) announce; ~**machen** (*sep*) (*cf* **bekannt machen** *at* **bekannt**) announce; **die B~machung, -en** announcement; ~**werden*** (*sep*) (*cf* **bekannt werden** *at* **bekannt**) (*sn*) become known; (secret) get out
^der **Bekannten|kreis, -e** circle of acquaintances
bekannter|maßen = **bekanntlich** as is well-known
^die **Bekanntschaft, -en** acquaintance; friend; (circle of) acquaintances; **jmds.** ~ **machen** make the acquaintance of
^die **Bekassine, -n** snipe
bekehren convert; **sich** ~ **zu** become a convert to; **der/die Bekehrte** (*decl as adj*) convert
^die **Bekehrung, -en** conversion
bekennen* confess; profess (faith); **sich** ~ **zu** declare one's support for; stand by; profess (Islam *etc*); admit (guilt *etc*); openly acknowledge (proclivity *etc*)

^der **Bekenner|mut** courage of one's convictions
^das **Bekenntnis, -se** confession; profession (of faith); declaration of one's belief (**zu** in); *eccles* denomination; **die** ~**schule, -n** denominational school
beklagen mourn; lament; **sich** ~ complain (**bei** to) || ~**s|wert** deplorable; pitiable
^der **Beklagte** (*fem* **die** ~) (*decl as adj*) defendant
beklatschen applaud; *coll* gossip about
bekleben: ~ **mit** stick onto
bekleckern *coll* stain; ~ **mit** spill (soup *etc*) over; **sich** ~ make one's clothes dirty (by spilling sth.)
beklecksen spot; blot
bekleiden hold (office); clothe; cover (wall *etc*); ~ **mit** cover with; invest with
^die **Bekleidung, -en** clothing; tenure (of office)
bekleistern *coll* cover with paste; ~ **mit** plaster with
beklemmen oppress; ~**d** oppressive
^die **Beklemmung, -en** feeling of oppression
beklommen anxious
^die **Beklommenheit** anxiety
beklopfen tap; *med* percuss
bekloppt *coll* crazy
beknien *coll* keep on at
bekochen *coll* cook for
bekommen* (*a*) get (*also with complement*, *eg* s.o. out of bed, sth. through the door); receive; obtain; catch (cold, disease); have (baby, item on menu *etc*, trouble); have, get (rain *etc*); develop (cracks *etc*); acquire, take on; *bot* sprout; **Angst** ~ get frightened; **Durst/Hunger** ~ get thirsty/hungry; **was** ~ **Sie?** how much is it/are they/do I owe you?; what can I get you?; **ich bekomme** (**5 Mark** *etc*) that'll be ...; you owe me ...; ~ **Sie schon?** are you being served?;

(+*p/part*) get/have + *p/part* (*eg* **etw. verlängert** ~ get/have sth. extended); (+*p/part of verb normally governing dative of person*) be + *p/part* (*eg* **etw. angeboten/geschenkt** ~ be offered/given sth.);

(+*infin*): **zu essen/trinken** ~ get (sth.) to eat/drink; **zu hören** ~ (get to) hear; **zu sehen** ~ (get to) see; **es zu tun** ~ **mit** get into trouble with (*see also* **Angst**); **jmdn. dazu** ~ **zu ...** get s.o. to ...;

(*b*) (+*dat*) (*sn*) (food *etc*) agree with; do (s.o.) good; **wohl bekomm's!** your health!; bon appétit!; *iron* good luck to you!
bekömmlich wholesome; easy to digest; **schwer** ~ hard to digest
beköstigen provide with meals
bekrabbeln: sich ~ *coll* pick oneself up again
bekräftigen confirm; support; reinforce
^die **Bekräftigung, -en** confirmation; **zur** ~ (+*gen*) in support of
bekränzen garland; crown (with laurels)

bekreuzigen: sich ~ cross oneself
bekriegen make war on; fight; **sich** ~ war
bekritteln find fault with
bekritzeln *coll* scrawl on
bekrönen crown
bekümmern worry; **sich** ~ **um** concern oneself with; **bekümmert** worried
bekunden show, manifest; *leg* testify
die **Bekundung, -en** manifestation; *leg* testimony
belächeln smile at (in a superior manner)
belachen laugh at
beladen* load; ~ **mit** load with; burden with; **schwer beladen** heavily laden
der **Belag, ⸚e** covering; (road) surface; film, *med* fur, *dent* plaque; *cul* filling; meat/egg/cheese *etc* on a slice of bread; *mot* lining
belagern besiege
die **Belagerung, -en** *vbl noun*; *also* siege; **der ~s|zustand, ⸚e** state of siege
Belang: von/ohne ~ of importance/no importance (**für** to) || **b~los** insignificant; **die ~losigkeit, -en** insignificance; triviality
die **Belange** *pl* interests; concerns
belangen: (gerichtlich) ~ prosecute, take to court
belassen* leave (in a place/state); retain (in post); **es dabei** ~ leave it at that
belasten load; (put a) strain (on); be a burden on; weigh on; (pollutant) harm; *leg* incriminate; ~ **mit** burden with; encumber with; *fin* debit with; **zu stark** ~ overload; **belastet** *also* busy
sich ~ incriminate oneself; **sich** ~ **mit** burden oneself with
belästigen bother; molest; pester
die **Belästigung, -en** *vbl noun*; *also* molestation; annoyance
die **Belastung, -en** *vbl noun*; *also* burden; strain (*gen* on); liability; encumbrance; *fin* debit; *elect*, *tech* load (*gen* on); *leg* incrimination; **das ~s|material** incriminating evidence; **die ~s|probe, -n** test; *mech* load test; **der ~s|zeuge, -n** (*wk masc*) witness for the prosecution
belauben: sich ~ come into leaf
die **Belaubung** *vbl noun*; *also* foliage
belauern watch secretly; spy on
belaufen*: sich ~ **auf** (*acc*) amount to
belauschen eavesdrop on
beleben liven up; reinvigorate; stimulate; **neu** ~ revive; **sich** ~ come alive/to life; liven up; (face) light up; **belebt** animate; busy
das **Belebungs|mittel, -** stimulant
belecken lick; **nicht von der Kultur beleckt** *coll* untouched by civilization
der **Beleg, -e** evidence; voucher (*also comput*), receipt; example (of usage)
belegen cover; line (brakes); substantiate; testify to, attest; provide evidence of; reserve; *univ* enrol for; *sp* take (first *etc* place); **dokumentarisch** ~ document; ~ **mit** *also* impose on; give (s.o. name); *cul* put on; fill with; *mil* billet (soldiers) in/on; **mit Bomben** ~ bomb; **mit Teppichen** ~ carpet; **belegt** *also* coated; husky; occupied, taken; *ling* attested; **das Wort ist bei ... belegt** the word occurs in ...; **belegtes Brot** open sandwich; **belegtes Brötchen** half a roll with cheese/ham/wurst *etc*
die **Belegschaft, -en** employees (*collect*)
belehren instruct; inform (**über** *acc* of); **eines Besseren** ~ set right; **sich eines anderen** ~ **lassen** learn otherwise; **er läßt sich nicht** ~ he won't be told; **~d** instructive; didactic
beleibt corpulent
die **Beleibtheit** corpulence
beleidigen offend; insult
die **Beleidigung, -en** *vbl noun*; *also* insult; offence (*gen* against: good taste *etc*); **die ~s|klage, -n** action for slander/libel
beleihen* lend money on
belemmert *coll* sheepish; (weather *etc*) wretched
belesen well-read
die **Belesenheit** wide reading
beleuchten light (up), illuminate; examine
die **Beleuchtung** *vbl noun*; *also* illumination; examination; light; lighting, *mot* lights
beleum(un)det: gut/schlecht ~ of good/ill repute
Belgien [-ĭən] Belgium
der **Belgier** [-ĭɐ], -, **belgisch** Belgian
Belgrad Belgrade
belichten *phot* expose
die **Belichtung, -en** *phot* exposure; **der ~s|messer, -** exposure meter
belieben (*see also* **beliebt**) deign, be pleased (to); **wann/wie** *etc* **es jmdm. beliebt** when/as *etc* s.o. pleases
das **Belieben: in jmds.** ~ **stellen** leave to s.o.'s discretion; **in jmds.** ~ **stehen** be left to s.o.'s discretion; **nach** ~ as desired
beliebig any (... you like); arbitrary; (*adv*) at will; (*eg* ~ **oft**) as (often *etc*) as you *etc* like; **jede(r) ~e** anybody
beliebt *p/part*; *also* popular (**bei** with)
die **Beliebtheit** popularity
beliefern supply
bellen bark (out); (*v/i*) bark; *coll* cough loudly
die **Belletristik** [-ɪk] belles-lettres; fiction
belletristisch literary
belobigen commend
belohnen reward
die **Belohnung, -en** *vbl noun*; *also* reward
belügen* lie to
belustigen amuse; **sich** ~ amuse oneself; **sich** ~ **über** (*acc*) make fun of
die **Belustigung, -en** amusement; entertainment
bemächtigen: sich ~ (+*gen*) seize, take pos-

session of; (emotion) take hold of
bemäkeln *coll* find fault with
bemalen paint; decorate
bemängeln find fault with
bemannen man; **bemannt** manned; **bemannt mit** with a crew of
bemänteln disguise
bemeistern master
bemerkbar noticeable; **sich ~ machen** draw attention to oneself; make itself felt; tell
bemerken notice; remark; **~s|wert** noteworthy; remarkable
die **Bemerkung, -en** remark; note
bemessen* measure out; **~ nach** measure by; fix in accordance with; **zu knapp ~** not allow enough ...; **knapp bemessen** limited; brief; scant
bemitleiden pity; **sich selbst ~** feel sorry for oneself || **~s|wert** pitiable
bemittelt well-to-do
bemogeln *coll* cheat
bemoost moss-covered; **~es Haupt** *coll* veteran student; old-timer
bemühen trouble; call on the services of; quote (example *etc*); **bemüht um** concerned to achieve/make; attentive to; **bemüht zu ...** at pains to ...
sich ~ endeavour (to); go (to a place); **sich ~ für** exert oneself on (s.o.'s) behalf; **sich ~ um** attend to; be attentive to; try to obtain; strive to achieve/gain
das **Bemühen** endeavour(s)
die **Bemühung, -en** effort (**um** to achieve); (*pl*) (doctor's, lawyer's) services
bemüßigt: sich ~ fühlen zu ... feel obliged to ...
bemuttern mother
benachbart neighbouring; next door
benachrichtigen inform; notify
die **Benachrichtigung, -en** notification
benachteiligen put at a disadvantage; discriminate against; **benachteiligt** *also* at a disadvantage; handicapped
die **Benachteiligung** discrimination (*gen* against)
benagen gnaw at
benebeln befuddle
Benedikt Benedict
der **Benediktiner, -** Benedictine
Benediktiner- Benedictine ...
Benefiz- benefit (match *etc*)
benehmen* (*see also* **benommen**) (+*dat of pers*) deprive of; (+*dat*) **den Atem ~** take (s.o.'s) breath away; **sich ~** behave
das **Benehmen** behaviour
beneiden envy; **~ um** envy (s.o. sth.) || **~s|wert** enviable
die **Benelux|staaten** *pl* the Benelux countries
benennen* name (**nach** after); nominate
benetzen moisten
der **Bengale, -n** (*wk masc*) Bengali
Bengalen Bengal
bengalisch Bengali; **~es Feuer** Bengal light
der **Bengel, -** rascal; **süßer ~** dear little boy
der **Benimm** *coll* manners
der **Benjamin** [-i:n], **-e** youngest member
benommen *p/part*; *also* dazed
die **Benommenheit** dazed state
benoten mark
benötigen need
benutzen, *esp SGer* **benützen** use
der **Benutzer,** *esp SGer* **Benützer, -** user; borrower
die **Benutzung,** *esp SGer* **Benützung** use, utilization; **unter ~** (+*gen*) using
das **Benzin** petrol, gasoline *US*; *chem* benzine; **die ~uhr, -en** fuel gauge
das **Benzol, -e** benzene; benzole
be|obachten watch; observe; keep under observation (*also med*); **~ an** (*dat*) notice about
der **Be|obachter, -** observer
die **Be|obachtung, -en** observation; observance; **die ~s|gabe** powers of observation; **der ~s|satellit, -en** (*wk masc*) observation satellite
be|ordern order (to do sth., to a place); **zu sich ~** send for
bepacken load
bepflanzen: ~ mit plant with
bepflastern pave; *coll* put a plaster on; *coll mil* 'plaster'
bepinseln *coll* daub; fill (with writing); **~ mit** *cul* brush with; *med* paint on
bepudern powder
bequem comfortable; easy; convenient; indolent; **es sich** *dat* **~ machen** make oneself comfortable; take the easy way out
bequemen: sich ~ consent (to); **sich ~ zu** consent to give/make
die **Bequemlichkeit, -en** comfort; convenience; indolence
berappen *coll* fork out
beraten* advise (**bei** on); = **~ über** (*acc*) discuss; **sich ~ lassen** take advice (**von** from); **gut/schlecht beraten sein zu ...** be well/ill advised to ...
sich ~ mit confer with
beratend advisory; consultative
der **Berater, -** adviser; consultant
beratschlagen = **~ über** (*acc*) confer on
die **Beratung, -en** discussion; advice; guidance; *leg, med* consultation; = **die ~s|stelle, -n** advice bureau; *med* clinic
berauben rob; (+*gen*) rob of; bereave of (speech *etc*), deprive of
berauschen intoxicate; **sich ~ an** (*dat*) become intoxicated with; get carried away by
der **Berber, -** Berber
Berber- Berber ...
die **Berberitze, -n** berberis

berechenbar calculable; predictable
berechnen calculate; (+*dat of pers*) charge (s.o., +**mit** s.o. sth.) for; (+*dat*) **zuviel** ~ overcharge; ~**d** calculating
die **Berechnung, -en** calculation; **aus** ~ from motives of self-interest
berechtigen: ~ **zu** entitle (one) to; justify
berechtigt *p/part*; *also* justified; **-berechtigt** entitled to ... || **berechtigter|weise** justifiably
die **Berechtigung, -en** entitlement, right; justification
bereden discuss, talk over; gossip about; ~ **zu ...** talk into (+*ger*); **sich** ~ **mit** confer with
die **Beredsamkeit** eloquence
beredt eloquent
die **Beredtheit** eloquence
der **Bereich, -e** area (*also comput*), region; range (*also mil*, *rad*); sector, sphere; domain, field; realm; **nicht in jmds.** ~ **fallen** not be (within) s.o.'s province
bereichern enrich; enlarge; **sich** ~ enrich oneself (**an** *dat* from)
die **Bereicherung** enrichment; enlargement
bereifen[1] put a tyre/tyres on
bereifen[2] cover with hoar-frost
die **Bereifung, -en** *vbl noun*; *also* (set of) tyres
bereinigen clear up; settle
bereisen tour; *comm* (representative) work
bereit ready; prepared; **-bereit** (*eg* **marsch~**) ready to (march *etc*); (*eg* **kompromiß~**) prepared to (compromise *etc*); **sich** ~ **erklären/finden zu ...** offer *or* agree/be prepared to ...; **sich** ~ **halten** hold oneself in readiness; stand by || ~**halten*** (*sep*) have/keep ready; ~**legen** (*sep*) put out; ~**machen** (*sep*) get ready; ~**stehen*** (*sep*) be ready; ~**stehend** (car *etc*) waiting; ~**stellen** (*sep*) make available; provide; *mil* assemble; **die B~stellung** provision; *mil* assembly; ~**willig** willing; **die B~willigkeit** willingness
bereiten prepare; (+*dat*) cause (s.o. difficulties *etc*), give (s.o. pleasure *etc*); put (end) to
bereits already; as early as
die **Bereitschaft, -en** readiness; (police) squad; **in** ~ on stand-by; **in** ~ **halten** have ready || **der** ~**s|dienst** emergency service; stand-by duty (**B. haben** be on call/stand-by)
berennen* assault (fortress); *sp* storm
bereuen regret; repent of
der **Berg, -e** mountain; hill; **hinterm** ~ **halten mit** *coll* keep quiet about; **nicht hinterm** ~ **halten mit** *coll* make no bones about; **über den** ~ *coll* out of the wood(s *US*); over the worst; **über alle** ~**e** *coll* miles away; **die Haare standen ihm zu** ~**e** *coll* his hair stood on end

Berg- mountain ...; *min* mining ...;
b~ab downhill (**es geht b. mit ...** *coll* ... is *etc* going downhill); **b~an** uphill; **der ~arbeiter, -** miner; **b~auf** uphill; **der ~bau** mining; **der ~fink, -en** (*wk masc*) brambling; **der ~fried, -e** keep; **der ~gipfel, -** peak; **die ~kette, -n** mountain range; **der ~kristall** rock-crystal; **das ~land** mountainous/hilly country; **der ~mann, ..leute** miner; **b~männisch** miner's; **die ~predigt** the Sermon on the Mount; **b~reich** mountainous; **der ~rutsch, -e** landslide; **die ~schlucht, -en** ravine; **der ~schuh, -e** climbing boot; **das ~steigen** mountaineering; **der ~steiger, -** mountaineer; **der ~sturz, ¨-e** landslide; **die ~-und-Tal-Bahn, -en** switchback, roller coaster; **die ~wacht** mountain rescue service; **die ~wand, ¨-e** rock face; **das ~werk, -e** mine; **das ~wesen** mining
bergen (**birg(s)t**, *p/t* **barg** (*subj* **bärge**), *p/part* **geborgen**) (*see also* **geborgen**) rescue; recover; *naut* salvage; *agr* get in; = **in sich** ~ hold; involve; contain within itself; ~ **vor** (*dat*) protect from; **das Gesicht in seinen Händen** ~ bury one's face in one's hands
sich ~ **vor** (*dat*) take shelter from
bergig mountainous; hilly
die **Bergung, -en** *vbl noun*; *also* rescue; recovery; *naut* salvage
der **Bericht, -e** report; account; ~ **erstatten** report (**über** *acc* on) || **der ~erstatter, -** reporter; **die ~erstattung** reporting
berichten report; ~ **über** (*acc*) report on; *journ* report, cover
berichtigen correct
die **Berichtigung, -en** correction
beriechen* sniff at; **sich** ~ *coll* size each other up
berieseln spray (with water); ~ **mit** subject to a constant stream of
Bering-: das ~meer the Bering Sea; **die ~straße** the Bering Straits
beringen ring, band *US* (bird); **beringt** *also* (finger) ringed
beritten mounted
die **Berlinale, -n** Berlin Film Festival
Berliner (*indecl*) (of) Berlin; ~ **Pfannkuchen** doughnut; ~ **Weiße** (*kind of light fizzy beer, often served* **mit Schuß,** *ie with a dash of raspberry juice*)
der **Berliner, -** Berliner; *cul* doughnut
berlinern speak with a Berlin accent; speak Berlin dialect
berlinisch *esp ling* Berlin
die **Bermuda|inseln** *pl* = **die Bermudas** [-as] *pl* Bermuda
Bern Berne
Berner (*indecl*): **die** ~ **Alpen** the Bernese Alps; **das** ~ **Oberland** the Bernese Ober-

land; **die ~ Konvention** the Berne Convention

Bernhard Bernard

der **Bernhardiner, – = der ~hund, –e** St Bernard

der **Bernstein** amber

der **Berserker, –** wild man; *myth* berserk(er)

bersten (*2nd/3rd sing pres* **birst**, *p/t* **barst** (*subj* **bärste**), *p/part* **geborsten**) (*sn*) burst; crack; *naut* break up; **~ von** be bursting with; **~ vor** (+*dat*) (person) be bursting with; **vor Lachen ~** burst one's sides with laughing; **(bis) zum Bersten voll** full to bursting

berüchtigt notorious (**wegen** for)

berücken captivate; **~d** captivating; ravishing

berücksichtigen take into consideration; allow for; consider (applicant *etc*)

die **Berücksichtigung** *vbl noun*; *also* consideration; **unter ~** (+*gen*) taking into account

der **Beruf, –e** occupation; profession; trade; **die freien ~e** the professions; **im ~ stehen** be working; **von ~** by profession/trade

berufen* appoint (**zu** to); **(zu sich) ~** summon; **~ gegen** *Aust leg* appeal against; **ich will es nicht ~, aber …** I don't want to tempt providence, but …; **berufen** *also* competent; **berufen sein zu** have a vocation/be destined for

sich ~ auf (*acc*) quote (in support); refer to; plead

beruflich professional; vocational

Berufs– professional …; vocational …; occupational …;

der ~berater, – careers adviser; **das ~geheimnis, –se** professional secret/secrecy; **die ~genossenschaft, –en** trade association; **die ~krankheit, –en** occupational disease; **das ~leben** professional life (**im B. stehen** be working); **b~mäßig** professional; **das ~risiko, –(k)en** occupational hazard; **die ~schule, –n** vocational school (attended part-time); **der ~sportler, –** professional; **b~tätig** working; **das ~verbot, –e** debarment from a profession

die **Berufung, –en** appointment; vocation; reference (**auf** *acc* to); *leg* appeal (**bei** to); **~ einlegen** lodge an appeal; **unter ~ auf** (*acc*) citing (as authority) || **das ~s|gericht, –e** court of appeal

beruhen: ~ auf (*dat*) be based on; be due to; **auf Gegenseitigkeit ~** be mutual; **auf sich ~ lassen** let (matter) rest

beruhigen calm (down); reassure; salve; **sich ~** calm down; die down; **beruhigt** reassured; (*adv*) with an easy mind

die **Beruhigung** calming (down); reassurance; **das ~s|mittel, –** sedative; **die ~s|pille, –n** sedative (pill)

berühmt famous (**wegen** for); **~-berüchtigt** notorious

die **Berühmtheit, –en** fame; celebrity

berühren touch; visit (place briefly), (route) pass through, *naut* call at; touch on; move, affect; make a … impression on, *or* (**~** + *adv*) *conveyed by verb* (*eg* **schmerzlich ~** pain, **angenehm berührt** pleased)

sich ~ touch; (lips) meet; **sich ~ mit** come close to

die **Berührung, –en** *vbl noun*; *also* touch; contact; **in ~ kommen mit** come into contact with || **der ~s|punkt, –e** point of contact

berußt covered in soot

bes. (= **besonders**) esp.

besabbern *coll* dribble over

besäen sow; **besät mit** strewn with; studded with

besagen say; mean; **besagt** (afore)said

besaiten *mus* string

besamen inseminate

die **Besamung** insemination

der **Besan, –e** mizzen

besänftigen calm, pacify; **sich ~** calm down

der **Besatz, ⸗e** trimming

die **Besatzung, –en** *aer*, *naut* crew; *mil* garrison; occupation forces; *in compds* **~s–** … of occupation; occupying …; occupied …

besaufen*: sich ~ *coll* get plastered

das **Besäufnis, –se** (*also* **die**) *coll* booze-up

besäuseln: sich ~ *coll* get tipsy; **besäuselt** tipsy

beschädigen damage

die **Beschädigung, –en** *vbl noun*; *also* damage (*gen* to)

beschaffen[1] obtain

beschaffen[2]**: ich bin nun einmal so ~** that's the way I am; **so ~, daß …** such that …; so constituted that …; **es ist schlecht ~ mit …** … is *etc* in bad shape; **wie ist es mit … ~?** how is *etc* …?

die **Beschaffenheit** condition; texture; nature; constitution

beschäftigen employ; give (s.o.) something to do; occupy (s.o.'s) mind; **beschäftigt** *also* busy; **damit beschäftigt zu …** busy (+ -ing)

sich ~ occupy oneself; **sich ~ mit** occupy oneself with; consider (question); concern oneself with; devote oneself to; deal with

der **Beschäftigte** (*fem* **die ~**) (*decl as adj*) employee

die **Beschäftigung, –en** employment; occupation, pursuit; something to do; **~ mit** consideration of; study of || **b~s|los** unemployed; **der ~s|stand** level of employment; **die ~s|therapie** occupational therapy

beschämen (put to) shame; **~d** humiliating; shameful; **beschämt** ashamed, abashed

die **Beschämung** shame; humiliation

beschatten shade; cast a shadow over; shadow, tail, *sp* mark closely

die **Beschau** inspection

beschauen examine, inspect

beschaulich tranquil; contemplative

der **Bescheid, -e** notification; (official) decision; information; (+*dat*) ~ **geben/sagen** let (s.o.) know; ~ **wissen** know (all) about it/one's way around; +**in** (*dat*) know one's way around; be well up in; +**über** (*acc*) be informed about

bescheiden¹* notify; summon (to a place); **abschlägig** ~ refuse; (+*dat*) **beschieden sein** fall to (s.o.'s) lot; **ihm war kein Erfolg beschieden** success was denied him; **es war ihm nicht beschieden zu ...** he was not destined to ...

sich ~ **mit** content oneself with

bescheiden² modest; *coll* (*for* **beschissen**) rotten

die **Bescheidenheit** modesty

bescheinen* shine on

bescheinigen certify; acknowledge (receipt)

die **Bescheinigung, -en** *vbl noun*; *also* certificate; receipt

bescheißen* (*see also* **beschissen**) *vulg* swindle

beschenken give a present to; ~ **mit** present with

bescheren give (s.o.) a Christmas present; (+*dat*) give (s.o. present) for Christmas; bless with; bring (s.o. surprise); (*v/i*) give out the Christmas presents

die **Bescherung, -en** *vbl noun*; *also* distribution of Christmas presents; **eine schöne** ~ *coll* a pretty kettle of fish

bescheuert *coll* 'cracked'

-beschichtet *tech* -coated

beschicken exhibit at; send representatives/ *sp* competitors to; *tech* charge

beschießen* fire on; bombard (*also phys*); shell

die **Beschießung, -en** *vbl noun*; *also* bombardment

beschildern signpost; label

beschimpfen abuse, call (s.o.) names

die **Beschimpfung, -en** *vbl noun*; *also* insult; (*pl*) abuse

beschirmen shield (**vor** *dat* from)

der **Beschiß** *vulg* swindle

beschissen *p/part*; *also vulg* 'lousy'

beschlafen* *coll* sleep with (woman); sleep on (problem *etc*)

der **Beschlag, ⸚e** metal fitting; clasp; horseshoes; film, (on food) mould; **in** ~ **nehmen** = **mit** ~ **belegen** monopolize || **die** ~**nahme** confiscation; **b**~**nahmen** confiscate; *coll* monopolize (person)

beschlagen¹* put a metal fitting on; stud; shoe (horse); (damp) mist; (*v/i sn*) go mouldy; = **sich** ~ mist over; **-beschlagen** -mounted

beschlagen² *p/part*; **(gut)** ~ **in** (*dat*) well-versed in

die **Beschlagenheit** thorough knowledge (**in** *dat* of)

beschleichen* creep up on; stalk; creep over

beschleunigen accelerate (*also phys*), speed up; quicken; expedite; (*v/i*) *mot* accelerate; **sich** ~ increase; quicken

der **Beschleuniger,** - *phys* accelerator

die **Beschleunigung** *vbl noun*; *also* acceleration (*also mot*, *phys*); speed-up

beschließen* decide (to); decide on, *parl* pass; end; ~ **über** (*acc*) vote on; **es ist beschlossene Sache** it's settled

der **Beschluß, ⸚(ss)e** decision; resolution; **einen** ~ **fassen** pass a resolution || **b**~**fähig** (**b. sein** have a quorum); **die** ~**fassung, -en** passing of a resolution; **b**~**unfähig** (**b. sein** be without a quorum)

beschmieren smear; scrawl on; ~ **mit** smear with; spread on; scrawl on

beschmutzen dirty; besmirch

beschneiden* cut; clip; trim; prune; cut (salary *etc*); curb; *med*, *relig* circumcise

die **Beschneidung, -en** *vbl noun*; *also* cut (*gen* in); curtailment; *med*, *relig* circumcision

beschneit snow-covered

beschnüffeln = **beschnuppern** sniff at; size up; **sich** ~ sniff each other; *coll* size each other up

beschönigen gloss over; ~**der Ausdruck** euphemism

beschränken (*see also* **beschränkt**) limit, restrict (**auf** *acc* to); **sich** ~ **auf** (*acc*) restrict oneself to; be restricted to

beschrankt (crossing) with gates

beschränkt limited; simple-minded; narrow-minded; (*adv*, *eg* ~ **Zeit haben**) a limited amount of

die **Beschränkung, -en** limitation, restriction

beschreiben* describe (*also math*); write on; **nicht zu** ~ indescribable; ~**d** descriptive

die **Beschreibung, -en** description (*also math*)

beschreiten* walk along; **neue Wege** ~ strike out in a new direction

beschriften inscribe (*also comput*); caption; label

die **Beschriftung, -en** *vbl noun*; *also* inscription; caption; label

beschuldigen accuse (*gen* of)

die **Beschuldigung, -en** accusation

beschummeln *coll* cheat (**um** out of)

der **Beschuß** bombardment (*also phys*); fire (of guns); **unter** ~ **geraten** come under fire; **unter** ~ **nehmen** fire on

beschütten: ~ **mit** pour on; put on

beschützen protect (**vor** *dat* from)

der **Beschützer,** - protector

beschwatzen *coll*: ~ **zu** talk into

die **Beschwerde, -n** (formal) complaint; *leg* appeal (against court order *etc*); (*pl*) *med* difficulty, (*esp in compds*) complaint, trouble; ~ **führen** lodge a complaint || **der ~führer, -** complainant

beschweren weight; weigh heavily on; ~ **mit** burden with; **sich** ~ complain (**bei** to); **sich ~ mit** burden oneself with

beschwerlich arduous

die **Beschwerlichkeit, -en** arduousness; (*pl*) discomforts

die **Beschwerung, -en** *vbl noun*; *also* weight; ballast

beschwichtigen placate; soothe

die **Beschwichtigungs|politik** policy of appeasement

beschwindeln *coll* tell (s.o.) a fib; swindle (**um** out of)

beschwingen exhilarate; **beschwingt** elated; lively

beschwipst *coll* tipsy

beschwören* swear to (statement); invoke, raise (spirit); charm (snake); conjure up; invoke; implore (to)

die **Beschwörung, -en** *vbl noun*; *also* entreaty; invocation; incantation

beseelen endow with a soul; bring to life; inspire; **beseelt** *also* having a soul; inspired; **beseelt von** filled with

besehen* (*also* +**sich** *dat*) look at, examine

beseitigen remove; eliminate; remedy (abuse)

die **Beseitigung** removal; elimination

beseligen fill with joy; **beseligt** overjoyed; joyous

der **Besen, -** broom; *coll* 'old bag'; **der ~ginster** *bot* broom; **der ~stiel, -e** broomstick

besessen *p/part*; *also* obsessed (**von** with); possessed; (gambler) compulsive; **wie ein Besessener/eine Besessene** like one obsessed

die **Besessenheit** obsession

besetzen occupy (*also mil etc*); fill (post, *theat* part); appoint members to; ~ **mit** appoint to; stock with (fish *etc*); set with; trim with; **besetzt** *also* full; taken; engaged, occupied; *tel* engaged, busy *esp US*; *coll* (person) busy; **gut besetzt** *theat* well cast; **besetzt mit** *also* with ... occupants

das **Besetzt|zeichen, -** *tel* 'engaged' tone, 'busy' signal *US*

die **Besetzung, -en** *vbl noun*; *mil etc* occupation; *theat* cast; *sp* team; **zweite** ~ *theat* understudy

besichtigen view; tour; *mil* inspect

die **Besichtigung, -en** viewing; tour; *mil* inspection

besiedeln settle; (**dicht** *etc*) **besiedelt** populated

besiegeln seal

besiegen defeat (*also sp*); overcome

besingen* cut (disc); sing of, celebrate (in song or verse)

besinnen* (*see also* **besonnen**): **sich** ~ reflect; collect one's thoughts; think better of it; come to one's senses; remember; **sich ~ auf** (*acc*) remember; **sich anders** ~ change one's mind; **sich eines Besseren** ~ think better of it; **nach kurzem Besinnen** after a moment's reflection

besinnlich contemplative; spent in thought

die **Besinnung** reflection; consciousness; ~ **auf** (*acc*) calling to mind; **die ~ verlieren** lose consciousness/one's head; **ohne** ~ unconscious; **zur ~ bringen** bring round/to his *etc* senses; **zur ~ kommen** come to one's senses; collect one's thoughts; **nicht zur ~ kommen** not have time to think; **wieder zur ~ kommen** regain consciousness || **b~s|los** unconscious; (rage) blind (**b. vor** (*dat*) beside oneself with)

der **Besitz** possession; property; ~ **ergreifen von** take possession/hold of; **im** ~ (+*gen*) in possession/receipt of; **in (privatem/kanadischem** *etc*) ~ (privately/Canadian *etc*) -owned; **in ~ nehmen** take possession of || **b~anzeigend** *gramm* possessive; **die ~ergreifung = die ~nahme** taking possession

besitzen* (*see also* **besessen**) possess, own; have; **~d** (classes) propertied

der **Besitzer, -** owner; proprietor

das **Besitztum, ¨er** possessions; property

die **Besitzung, -en** property, estate; (*pl*) (overseas *etc*) possessions

besoffen *p/part*; *coll* 'plastered'

besohlen sole

besolden pay (soldier, government employee)

die **Besoldung** *vbl noun*; *also* salary; *mil* pay

besonder.. special; particular; exceptional; separate; **im ~en** in particular

die **Besonderheit, -en** special/unusual feature

besonders especially, particularly; separately; **nicht** ~ not very much; *coll* 'not so hot'

besonnen *p/part*; *also* level-headed; prudent

die **Besonnenheit** level-headedness; prudence

besorgen (*see also* **besorgt**) get; attend to; look after; **es jmdm.** ~ *coll* get even with s.o.; let s.o. have it

die **Besorgnis, -se** concern, anxiety; **b~erregend** alarming

besorgt *p/part*; *also* worried (**über** *acc*/**wegen** about); ~ **um** concerned about

die **Besorgtheit** concern, anxiety

die **Besorgung, -en** *vbl noun*; *also* errand; **~en machen** go shopping

bespannen string; ~ **mit** cover with; harness (horse *etc*) to

bespickt: ~ **mit** bristling with (medals)
bespiegeln portray; **sich** ~ look at oneself in the mirror; preen oneself
bespielen *theat* play (city *etc*); ~ **mit** *mus* record on
bespitzeln spy on
bespötteln ridicule
besprechen* discuss; review; make a recording (of speech) on; cure by incantation; **sich** ~ **mit** confer with
die **Besprechung, -en** *vbl noun*; *also* discussion; conference; review
besprengen sprinkle
besprenkeln speckle; sprinkle
bespritzen spray; spatter
besprühen spray
bespucken spit at
bespülen (sea *etc*) wash
besser (*comp of* **gut**) better; better-class; glorified; (*adv*) better; (*expressing view*) preferably, (*with pass*) better; *or conveyed by* ... had better ... (*eg* **du kommst** ~ **am Freitag** you'd better come on Friday), (... **hätte** ~ +*p/part*) ... would have done better to ...; **(oder)** ~ or rather; ~ **werden** get better, improve; **es** ~ **wissen** know better; **Besseres zu tun haben** have better things to do || ~**gehen*** (*sn*) (**es geht ihm besser** he's getting better; he's better off); ~**gestellt** better-off; **der B~wisser, -,** ~**wisserisch** know-all
bessern improve; reform (person); **sich** ~ improve; reform, mend one's ways
die **Besserung, -en** improvement; reform (of character); **gute** ~! get well soon! || **die** ~**s|anstalt, -en** reformatory
best.. (*superl of* **gut**) best; excellent; **am** ~**en** best; *or conveyed by* it is best to ...; ... had best ...; **aufs** ~**e** extremely well; **zum** ~**en geben** recite; sing; tell; **zum** ~**en haben** make fun of; **es steht mit ... nicht zum** ~**en** ... is *etc* not too good/not doing too well; **mein B~er** my dear fellow; **sein B~es geben/tun** give of/do one's best; **zum B~en** (+*gen*) for the benefit of || ~**gehaßt** *coll* most hated; **die B~leistung, -en** *sp* best performance; (personal) best; ~**möglich** best possible; **der B~seller** ['bɛstsɛlɐ], **-, der B~seller|autor, -en** best-seller; **der B~wert, -e** optimum; **die B~zeit, -en** *sp* fastest time; (personal) best; **B~zustand** (**im B.** in perfect condition)
bestallen install, appoint
der **Bestand, ¨-e** stock (**an** *dat* of), (of library *etc*) holdings; continued existence; **(keinen)** ~ **haben** (not) last; **von** ~ lasting || **der** ~**teil, -e** component; element; ingredient (**wesentlicher B.** integral part)
bestanden *p/part*; *Swiss* advanced in years; ~ **mit** covered with (trees)
beständig constant; (weather) settled; lasting; *chem* stable; ~ **gegen** resistant to; **-beständig** -resistant
die **Beständigkeit** constancy; settled state; resistance (**gegen** to); *chem* stability
Bestands-: die ~**aufnahme, -n** stock-taking; taking stock (**eine B. machen** take stock); **das** ~**jubiläum, -(ä)en** *Aust* anniversary (of foundation of firm *etc*)
bestärken confirm (suspicion *etc*); ~ **in** (*dat*) confirm in (prejudice *etc*); encourage in (belief); **jmdn. in seinem Entschluß** ~ strengthen s.o.'s resolve
bestätigen confirm; bear out; *leg* uphold; *comm* acknowledge (receipt of); **sich** ~ prove true/justified; ~**d** confirmatory; (*adv*) in confirmation
die **Bestätigung, -en** confirmation; *comm* acknowledgement (of receipt)
bestatten bury
die **Bestattung, -en** burial; **das** ~**s|institut, -e** undertakers, funeral home *US*
bestauben make dusty
bestäuben *agr*, *cul* dust; *bot* pollinate
die **Bestäubung, -en** *vbl noun*; *bot* pollination
bestaunen stare at in amazement; marvel at
bestechen* bribe; captivate; (*v/i*) impress; **sich** ~ **lassen** take a bribe/bribes; ~**d** captivating; tempting; *sp* (form) splendid
bestechlich open to bribery
die **Bestechung, -en** bribery; **das** ~**s|geld, -er** bribe
das **Besteck, -e** (set of) knife, fork and spoon; cutlery; *med* set of surgical instruments
bestecken: ~ **mit** decorate with
bestehen* (*see also* **bestanden**) pass (examination); come through; (*v/i*) exist, be in existence; survive; hold one's own; **es besteht ...** there is ...
~ **auf** (*dat*) insist on; **darauf** ~ **zu ...** insist on (+*ger*)
~ **aus** consist of; be made of
~ **in** (*dat*) consist in; lie in
~ **vor** (*dat*) face; stand up to (criticism)
das **Bestehen** existence; insistence (**auf** *dat* on); passing (of examination); pass; (*eg* **hundert)jähriges** ~ (hundredth *etc*) anniversary
bestehen-: ~**bleiben*** (*sep*; *sn*) remain; endure; (objection *etc*) stand; ~**lassen*** (*sep*) maintain
bestehend existing
bestehlen* rob (**um** of)
besteigen* climb; mount (*also zool*); get on; ascend (throne)
Bestell- order ...; **der** ~**schein, -e** order-form
bestellen order (**bei** from); reserve; appoint (**zu** as); *agr* cultivate (land); (+*dat*) send (s.o. greetings); (**ins Hotel** *etc*) ~ ask (s.o.)

to meet one (at the hotel *etc*); **zu sich ~** send for; ask (s.o.) to come; **nichts zu ~ haben** have no say; **+gegen** be no match for; **er läßt dir ~, daß ...** he told me to tell you that ...; **kann ich etwas ~?** can I give him *etc* a message?; **bestellt sein** be on order; be reserved; have an appointment (**bei** with); **wie es um ... bestellt ist** what state ... is *etc* in; **es ist (schlecht** *etc*) **bestellt mit/um ......** is *etc* in a (bad *etc*) state

die **Bestellung, -en** *vbl noun*; *also* reservation; appointment; cultivation (of land); order (**auf** *acc*/**über** *acc* for); message; **auf ~** to order

besten|falls at best

bestens extremely well; **er läßt ~ grüßen** he sends his best regards

besternt starry

besteuern tax

bestialisch bestial; *coll* 'beastly'

die **Bestialität, -en** bestiality

besticken embroider

die **Bestie** [-ĭə], **-n** beast

bestimmen fix; determine; lay down; define; *bot* classify; (*v/i*) give the orders; **näher ~** *gramm* qualify; **nichts zu ~ haben** have no say; **sich ~ lassen von** be governed by

~ **für** earmark/intend for

bestimmt nach bound for

~ **über** (*acc*) decide on; decide how ... is to be spent

~ **zu** designate as; intend for/to be; destine for; (*foll. by vbl noun*) induce to

bestimmend decisive; characteristic (**für** of)

bestimmt *p/part*; *also* definite (*also gramm*); certain; particular; firm; (*adv*) certainly, definitely; for certain; I'm sure, *or conveyed by* ... is *etc* sure to ...; firmly

die **Bestimmtheit** firmness; **mit ~** definitely; for certain; **mit aller ~** most emphatically

die **Bestimmung, -en** *vbl noun*; *also* determination (of); regulation, (of will *etc*) provision; (intended) purpose; fate, destiny; *gramm* adjunct; *in compds* **~s-** ... of destination; **der ~s|ort, -e** destination

bestirnt starry

Best.-Nr. (= **Bestellnummer**) order no.

bestrafen punish

die **Bestrafung, -en** punishment

bestrahlen shine on; illuminate; *med* irradiate; give radiation treatment to

die **Bestrahlung, -en** *vbl noun*; *also* illumination; *med* irradiation; radiotherapy

bestreben: sich ~/bestrebt sein zu ... endeavour to ..., strive to ...; **das Bestreben** endeavour

die **Bestrebungen** *pl* efforts

bestreichen* sweep (sky *etc*, *also mil*); **~ mit** spread on; give (sth.) a coat of; *med* paint with; **mit Fett ~** grease

bestreiken take strike action against, strike *US*; **bestreikt** strikebound; **bestreikt werden** be hit by strike action

bestreiten* dispute, contest; challenge (right); deny; defray (costs), pay for; be responsible for (programme *etc*); **die Unterhaltung allein ~** do all the talking

bestreuen: ~ mit strew with; sprinkle with (*also cul*)

bestricken captivate; *coll* knit things for; **~d** captivating

bestücken: ~ mit equip with; *naut* arm with

bestuhlen provide with seating

die **Bestuhlung, -en** *vbl noun*; *also* seating

bestürmen *mil* storm; *sp* attack; **~ mit** pester with

bestürzen fill with dismay; **~d** disconcerting; **bestürzt** filled with dismay; (*adv*) in dismay

die **Bestürzung** dismay; **zu jmds. ~** to s.o.'s dismay

der **Besuch, -e** visit (*gen*/**bei**/**in** *dat* to: museum *etc*/person/place *respectively*); visiting; attendance (*gen* at), attending; visitor(s); **-besuch** (*eg* **der Kino~** cinema) -going; **einen ~ machen bei** call on; **~ haben** have visitors/a visitor; **auf/zu ~** on a visit (**bei** to)

besuchen visit; go to; attend; **gut/schlecht besucht** well/poorly attended

der **Besucher, -** visitor

Besuchs- visiting ...; **die ~zeit, -en** visiting hours

besudeln soil, make dirty; sully

Bet-: der ~stuhl, ⸚e prie-dieu

betagt advanced in years

betasten feel; *med* palpate

betätigen operate; **sich ~** be active (in sth.); busy oneself; **sich ~ als** act as; work as; **sich (literarisch** *etc*) **~** engage in (literary *etc*) activities

die **Betätigung, -en** operation (of); activity; **das ~s|feld, -er** sphere of activity

betäuben stun; deaden; (noise) deafen; dull (grief *etc*); *med* anaesthetize; **seinen Kummer mit Alkohol ~** drown one's sorrows; **sich ~ durch/mit** seek consolation in; **~d** deafening; (fragrance) intoxicating; (blow) stunning; *med* anaesthetic

die **Betäubung, -en** *vbl noun*; *also* daze; *med* anaesthesia; anaesthetization; **das ~s|mittel, -** anaesthetic

die **Bete: rote ~** beetroot, beet *US*

beteiligen: ~ an (*dat*) give (s.o.) a share in; **beteiligt sein an** (*dat*) be involved in; be a party to; *comm* have a share in; **der/die Beteiligte** (*decl as adj*) participant; person involved

sich ~ an (*dat*) participate in; share in; contribute to; *comm* become (financially) interested in

die **Beteiligung, –en** *vbl noun*; *also* participation (**an** *dat* in); share (in); attendance (at); *comm* interest (in)

beten say (prayer); (*v/i*) pray

beteuern declare; protest (innocence); **~, daß ...** swear that ...

die **Beteuerung, –en** declaration; protestation (of innocence)

betexten caption; write the words for

Bethlehem ['beːtlehɛm] Bethlehem

betiteln give (sth.) a title; **~ mit** address as; *coll* call (s.o. sth.)

der **Beton** [be'tɔŋ], **–s** concrete; **die ~misch|-maschine, –n** concrete-mixer; **die ~wüste, –n** concrete jungle

betonen stress; emphasize; accentuate; **betont** *also* studied; (*adv*: *eg* **betont elegant/höflich**) with studied (elegance/politeness *etc*); **–betont** (*eg* **taillenbetont**) emphasizing (the waist *etc*); *ling* (*eg* **endbetont**) with (final *etc*) stress

betonieren, betoniert concrete

die **Betonung, –en** *vbl noun*; *also* emphasis; stress; accentuation

betören captivate; **~d** captivating

Betr. (*in letter heading*, = **Betreff**), **betr.** (= **betreffend, betreffs**) re

Betracht: außer ~ bleiben/lassen not be taken into/leave out of account; **in ~ kommen** be a possible candidate/a possibility; **nicht in ~ kommen** be out of the question; **in ~ ziehen** take into account

betrachten look at; consider, view; **~ als** regard as

der **Betrachter, –** onlooker; *art* spectator

beträchtlich considerable

die **Betrachtung, –en** *vbl noun*; *also* contemplation; reflection (**über** *acc* on); **~en anstellen über** (*acc*) reflect on; **bei näherer ~** on closer inspection || **die ~s|weise, –n** approach

der **Betrag, ⸚e** amount

betragen* amount to; **sich ~** behave; **das Betragen** behaviour

betrauen: ~ mit entrust with

betrauern mourn

beträufeln: ~ mit sprinkle with (lemon juice *etc*)

betreffen* (*see also* **betroffen**) concern, affect; befall; dismay; **betroffen werden von** be hit by; be afflicted with; **was ... betrifft** as far as ... is *etc* concerned, as regards; **~d** relevant; in question; (*following acc*) concerning ...; **der/die Betreffende** (*decl as adj*) person concerned

betreffs (+*gen*) with regard to

betreiben* carry on; run; pursue; go in for; press on with; *mech* operate; (**mit Dampf** *etc*) **betrieben** (steam *etc*) –driven; **auf Betreiben** (+*gen*) at the instigation of

betreßt braided

betreten[1]* enter, step/walk on; **unbefugt ~** trespass on; **unbefugtes Betreten** trespass; **„Betreten verboten!"** 'keep out/off'

betreten[2] *p/part*; *also* embarrassed; (*adv*) *also* in embarrassment

die **Betretenheit** embarrassment

betreuen look after; be in charge of

der **Betreuer, –** person who looks after s.o.; *sp* attendant

die **Betreuung** *vbl noun*; *also* care; person who looks after s.o.

der **Betrieb, –e** concern; business; works; work(ing); operation; bustle, (hectic) activity; (heavy) traffic; rush; **in den Geschäften** *etc* **ist viel ~** the shops *etc* are very busy; **außer ~** not in use; out of order; **in ~ nehmen** put into operation/service; *rail* open; **in ~ setzen** start (sth.) working

betrieblich (relating to the) company

Betriebs– company ...; works ...; operating ...; **die ~art, –en** *comput* mode; **b~fähig** operational; in working order; **die ~gewerkschafts|leitung, –en** *EGer* works trade union council; **das ~kapital** working capital; **das ~klima** atmosphere (at work); **die ~kosten** *pl* operating costs; **der ~leiter, –** works manager; **die ~leitung, –en** management; **die ~nudel, –n** *coll* live wire; **der ~rat, ⸚e** (member of the) works council; **b~sicher** trouble-free; **der ~stoff, –e** fuel; **die ~störung, –en** breakdown; **der ~unfall, ⸚e** industrial accident; *joc* unplanned pregnancy; **der ~wirt, –e** graduate in business administration; **die ~wirtschaft** business administration

betriebsam bustling, busy

die **Betriebsamkeit** bustle

betrinken* (*see also* **betrunken**): **sich ~** get drunk

betroffen *p/part*; *also* dismayed (**über** *acc* at); taken aback (by); (*adv*) in dismay

die **Betroffenheit** dismay

betrüben (*see also* **betrübt**) grieve

betrüblich distressing

betrübt *p/part*; *also* sorrowful, sad

die **Betrübtheit** sorrow, sadness

der **Betrug** deception; swindle; *leg* fraud

betrügen* deceive; cheat (**um** out of); cheat on; *leg* defraud; **sich ~** deceive oneself

der **Betrüger, –** deceiver; cheat; impostor

die **Betrügerei, –en** cheating; trickery; *leg* fraud

betrügerisch deceitful; *leg* fraudulent

betrunken *p/part*; *also* drunk(en); **der/die Betrunkene** (*decl as adj*) drunk

die **Betrunkenheit** drunkenness

das **Bett, –en** bed (*also mech*), *rail* berth; duvet, quilt; **das ~ hüten** stay in bed; **im ~** in bed; **ins/zu ~ gehen** go to bed; **zu ~ bringen** put to bed || **der ~bezug, ⸚e** duvet cover; **die**

~couch, -en studio couch; die ~decke, -n bedspread; blanket; das ~gestell, -e bedstead; b~lägerig bedridden; das ~nässen bed-wetting; der ~nässer, - bed-wetter; ~schwere *coll* (die nötige B. haben be ready for bed); das Bettuch, ⸚er (bed)-sheet; der ~vorleger, - bedside rug; die ~wäsche bed-linen; das ~zeug bedding

Bettel– mendicant ...; **bettel|arm** destitute; **der ~brief, -e** begging letter; **~stab (an den B. bringen/kommen** reduce/be reduced to beggary)

betteln beg (**um** for)

betten: ~ auf (*acc*) lay on; **sich ~** make a bed for oneself; **er ist nicht auf Rosen gebettet** *coll* his life is not a bed of roses; **weich gebettet sein** have an easy life

der **Bettler, -** beggar

betucht *coll* well-heeled

betulich fussy, fussing

betupfen dab; dot

die **Beuge, -n** bend (of arm, leg); *gym* bend from the waist

das **Beugel, -** *Aust* croissant

beugen bend; break (s.o.'s pride); *gramm* inflect; *phys* diffract; **sich ~** bend; lean (out of window *etc*); (+*dat*) bow to

die **Beugung, -en** *vbl noun*; *gramm* inflection; *phys* diffraction

die **Beule, -n** dent; bump; bulge; **die ~n|pest** bubonic plague

be|unruhigen worry; make (s.o.) feel uneasy; **sich ~** worry; **~d** disturbing

die **Be|unruhigung** *vbl noun*; *also* uneasiness

be|urkunden certify, authenticate; register

be|urlauben grant (s.o.) leave; suspend (official); **beurlaubt** *also* on leave; **sich ~ lassen** take leave of absence

die **Be|urlaubung, -en** *vbl noun*; *also* leave; suspension

be|urteilen judge (**nach** by); assess; take a ... view of; **falsch ~** misjudge

die **Be|urteilung, -en** judgement; assessment; confidential report (*gen* on); review

die **Beute, -n** prey; booty, loot; haul; *hunt* bag; **eine ~ werden von** fall a prey to

der **Beutel, -** bag; pouch (*also zool*); (*in idioms*) pocket, purse; **die ~ratte, -n** opossum; **das ~tier, -e** marsupial

beuteln: (sich) ~ bag

bevölkern inhabit; fill; populate, settle; **sich ~** become inhabited; fill (**mit** with)

die **Bevölkerung, -en** population; (general) public; **die ~s|explosion, -en** population explosion; **der ~s|schutz (ziviler B.** civil defence); **die ~s|zahl, -en** population

bevollmächtigen authorize (to); **der/die Bevollmächtigte** (*decl as adj*) authorized representative; *pol* plenipotentiary; *leg* attorney

die **Bevollmächtigung, -en** authorization

bevor before; **~ ... nicht** until

bevormunden (*insep*) treat like a child (by taking decisions for him/her); keep (people) in tutelage

bevorrechtet privileged

bevorstehen* (*sep*) be imminent/approaching; (+*dat*) be in store for; **~d** imminent; forthcoming; approaching

bevorzugen (*insep*) prefer; favour; **bevorzugt** preferred; (position) privileged; (treatment) preferential; (*adv*) chiefly; **bevorzugt behandeln** give priority to

die **Bevorzugung** *vbl noun*; *also* priority (given to); preferential treatment (of)

bewachen guard; *sp* mark, cover *US*; **scharf ~** keep a close watch on; **bewacht** (carpark) supervised

bewachsen [-ks]: **~ mit** covered with

die **Bewachung** *vbl noun*; *also* guard

bewaffnen arm; **sich ~** arm oneself

die **Bewaffnung** *vbl noun*; *also* arms; armament

bewahren maintain; keep (secret, clear head, *etc*); retain; **sich** *dat* **... ~** retain; maintain; **~ vor** (*dat*) protect from; save from; spare; **(Gott) bewahre!** heaven forbid!

bewähren: sich ~ prove oneself/itself *or* one's/its worth; prove a success; **bewährt** proven, well-tried; reliable

bewahrheiten: sich ~ prove to be/come true

die **Bewährung** proving oneself; **zur ~ aussetzen** suspend (sentence) || **die ~s|frist, -en** probation; **der ~s|helfer, -** probation officer; **die ~s|probe, -n** test

bewaldet wooded

die **Bewaldung** afforestation; woods

bewältigen overcome (difficulty); come to terms with; cope with; accomplish; get through; manage; cover (distance)

bewandert: ~ in (*dat*) well up in, well-versed in

Bewandtnis: damit hat es folgende ~ the matter is as follows; **mit ... hat es seine eigene ~** there are special circumstances connected with; **was hat es mit ... für eine ~?** what is *etc* ... all about?

bewässern irrigate; water

die **Bewässerung** irrigation; watering

Beweg–: der ~grund, ⸚e motive

bewegen (*see also* **bewegt**) move; stir; occupy (s.o.'s) mind; exercise (horse); (*p/t* **bewog** (*subj* **bewöge**), *p/part* **bewogen**) induce (to); **sich ~** move; stir; take exercise; **sich ~ zwischen** range between; **~d** moving; (power) motive

beweglich movable; mobile; moving; flexible; agile; manoeuvrable

die **Beweglichkeit** movability; mobility; flexibility; agility; manoeuvrability

bewegt *p/part*; *also* full of emotion; eventful;

turbulent; lively (*also fin*); **stark ~** (sea) rough

[die] **Bewegtheit** emotion; turbulence; liveliness (*also fin*)

[die] **Bewegung, –en** movement; motion; exercise; emotion; **in ~** in motion; on the move; **in ~ setzen** set in motion; **sich in ~ setzen** start to move || **die ~s|energie** kinetic energy; **die ~s|freiheit** room to move; freedom of action; **b~s|los** motionless; **der ~s|mangel** lack of exercise

beweihräuchern adulate

[die] **Beweihräucherung** adulation

beweinen mourn; bewail

[der] **Beweis, –e** proof (**für** of); (piece of) evidence; sign; (*pl*) evidence; **unter ~ stellen** prove || **die ~aufnahme, –n** taking of evidence; **die ~führung** argument(ation); *leg* presentation of evidence; **der ~grund, ⸚e** argument; **die ~kraft** conclusiveness; cogency; **b~kräftig** conclusive; cogent; **die ~last** onus of proof; **das ~material** evidence; **das ~mittel, –** (piece of) evidence; **das ~stück, –e** exhibit; piece of evidence

beweisen* prove; show; **sich ~** prove oneself/itself

bewenden: es ~ lassen bei content oneself with; **es dabei ~ lassen** leave it at that

[der] **Bewerb, –e** *Aust sp* event

bewerben*: sich ~ um apply for; *dated* ask for (s.o.'s) hand in marriage

[der] **Bewerber, –** applicant; *dated* suitor

[die] **Bewerbung, –en** application; *dated* suit; **das ~s|schreiben, –** letter of application

bewerfen* plaster; rough-cast; **~ mit** pelt with

bewerkstelligen manage; effect

bewerten assess, rate; value (**mit** at)

[die] **Bewertung, –en** assessment; valuation

bewilligen authorize, approve

bewillkommnen welcome

bewirken bring about; effect; **~, daß ...** cause (s.o., sth.) to ...

bewirten entertain with food and drink

bewirtschaften run; farm (land); ration; control (foreign exchange)

[die] **Bewirtung** entertaining (of guests); hospitality

bewitzeln make fun of

bewog (bewöge) *p/t (subj)*, **bewogen** *p/part of* **bewegen** ('induce')

bewohnen live in, occupy; inhabit

[der] **Bewohner, –** inhabitant; occupant; **–bewohner** *also* –dweller

bewölken: sich ~ cloud over; (brow) cloud; **bewölkt** overcast; (brow) clouded

[die] **Bewölkung** *vbl noun*; *also* cloud(s)

[der] **Bewuchs** [–ks] vegetation

bewundern admire; **~s|wert** admirable

[die] **Bewunderung** admiration

[der] **Bewurf** plaster; rough-cast

bewußt conscious; deliberate; avowed; in question; agreed; **sich** *dat* **...** (*gen*) **~ sein/werden** be/become conscious of; **... ist/wird mir ~** I am/become aware of ...; (+*dat*) **~ werden lassen** bring home to || **~los** unconscious; **die B~losigkeit** unconsciousness (**bis zur B.** *coll* ad nauseam); **~machen** (*sep*) (+*dat*) make (s.o.) aware of; **das B~sein** consciousness; awareness; **–bewußtsein** *also* sense of ... (**bei B.** conscious; **im B.** (+*gen*) conscious of; **ohne B.** unconscious; (+*dat*) **zu(m) B. bringen** bring home to; **wieder zu(m) B. kommen** regain consciousness; (+*dat*) **zu(m) B. kommen** come home to)

[die] **Bewußtheit** consciousness

Bez. = Bezeichnung, Bezirk

bezahlen pay; pay for; **sich ~ lassen** take payment; **teuer ~ müssen** pay dearly for; **sich** *dat* **... teuer ~ lassen** charge a lot for; exact a high price for; **sich bezahlt machen** pay

[die] **Bezahlung** payment; pay

bezähmen restrain; quell; **sich ~** restrain oneself

bezaubern captivate, enchant; **~d** captivating

[die] **Bezauberung** enchantment

bezechen: sich ~ get drunk; **bezecht** drunk(en)

bezeichnen mark; indicate; denote; **~ als** refer to as; call (s.o., sth. sth.); describe as; **~d** indicative (**für** of); characteristic (of) || **bezeichnender|weise** characteristically

[die] **Bezeichnung, –en** *vbl noun*; *also* marking; indication; description; name; designation

bezeigen show; (+*dat*) express to; show (s.o. respect)

bezeugen attest; testify to

bezichtigen (+*gen*) accuse of

[die] **Bezichtigung, –en** accusation

beziehen* cover; put clean sheets/a clean slip on; string (instrument, racket); move into, *mil* take up; take (newspaper); draw (salary *etc*); adopt (standpoint); *Swiss* collect (taxes); **Prügel ~** *coll* get a thrashing

~ auf (*acc*) relate to; apply to; **auf sich ~** take personally; **bezogen auf** referring to

~ aus obtain from

sich ~ cloud over; **sich ~ auf** (*acc*) refer to

[der] **Bezieher, –** subscriber (to newspaper); person who draws (a salary *etc*)

[die] **Beziehung, –en** connection; relationship (**zu** with); (*pl*) relations; pull, influence; **~en haben** know the right people; **keine ~ haben zu** bear no relation to; (person) not relate to; **seine ~en spielen lassen** pull strings; **in dieser/jeder/keiner ~** in this/every/

no respect; **in anderer/mancher ~** in other/some respects; **in (politischer** *etc*) **~** from a (political *etc*) point of view, ...ly (politically *etc*); **in ~ bringen/setzen zu** connect with; relate to; **in ~ stehen zu** be connected with/related to; **in keiner ~ stehen zu** be unconnected with; bear no relation to || **b~s|los** unconnected; **b~s|reich** rich in associations; **b~s|voll** allusive; **b~s|weise** and ... respectively; or (as the case may be); or rather

beziffern number; **~ auf** (*acc*) assess at; **sich ~ auf** (*acc*) amount to

der **Bezirk, –e** (administrative) region (*in W. Germany* = **Regierungs~**); sphere; *EGer coll* regional government offices; **der ~s|tag, –e** regional assembly

bezirzen *coll* ensnare (man)

bezogen *p/part*; **–bezogen** –related; **der/die Bezogene** (*decl as adj*) drawee

bezug: in ~ auf (*acc*) regarding

der **Bezug, ⸚e** pillow-case, (of cushion *etc*) cover; strings (of instrument *etc*); drawing (of salary *etc*); purchase; subscribing (*gen* to); moving into; relationship (**zu** with); reference (to); (*pl*) earnings; **~ haben auf** (*acc*) relate to; **~ nehmen auf** (*acc*) refer to; **mit/unter ~ auf** (*acc*) with reference to || **die ~nahme, –n** reference (**mit/unter B. auf** (*acc*) with reference to); **der ~schein, –e** (ration) coupon

der **Bezüger, –** *Swiss* subscriber (to newspaper); collector (of taxes)

bezüglich 1 *adj gramm* relative; 2 *prep* (+*gen*) regarding; **~ auf** (*acc*) relating to

Bezugs– *also* reference ...; **b~fertig** ready for occupation; **die ~person, –en** significant other; **der ~preis, –e** purchase price; subscription rate; **der ~punkt, –e** point of reference; **die ~quelle, –n** source of supply; **das ~recht, –e** *fin* option; **der ~schein, –e** (ration) coupon; **das ~system, –e** frame of reference; **das ~wort, ⸚er** antecedent

bezuschussen subsidize

bezwecken aim at

bezweifeln call in question, doubt

bezwingen* conquer; master, overcome; *sp* beat; **sich ~** restrain oneself; **~d** winning; compelling

der **Bezwinger, –** conqueror

das **BGB = Bürgerliches Gesetzbuch**

der **BGH = Bundesgerichtshof**

die **BGL, –(s)** *EGer* (= **Betriebsgewerkschaftsleitung**) works trade union council

der **BGS = Bundesgrenzschutz**

der **BH, –(s)** *coll* (= **Büstenhalter**) bra

Bhf. (= **Bahnhof**) station

die **BHG, –(s)** *EGer* (= **Bäuerliche Handelsgenossenschaft**) farmers' trading co-operative

bibbern *coll* tremble

die **Bibel, –n** Bible; *in compds also* biblical ...; **b~fest** well-versed in the Bible

der **Biber, –** beaver

der **Bibliograph, –en** (*wk masc*) bibliographer

die **Bibliographie, –(ie)n** bibliography

bibliographisch bibliographical

die **Bibliothek, –en** library

der **Bibliothekar, –e** librarian

biblisch biblical; (age) ripe old

bieder upright; worthy; **der B~mann, ⸚er** honest citizen; petit bourgeois; **das B~meier** (*style of furniture and interior decoration in Germany after 1815*)

biegen (*p/t* **bog** (*subj* **böge**), *p/part* **gebogen**) bend; *Aust gramm* inflect; (*v/i sn*) turn (into street *etc*); (road *etc*) wind; **~ um** (*sn*) turn (corner); **auf Biegen oder Brechen** *coll* by hook or by crook; **es geht auf Biegen oder Brechen** *coll* it's all or nothing

sich ~ bend; **sich vor Lachen ~** *coll* double up with laughter

biegsam supple; pliable; ductile

die **Biegsamkeit** suppleness; pliability; ductility

die **Biegung, –en** *vbl noun*; *also* bend; curve; *Aust gramm* inflection

die **Biene, –n** bee; *dated coll* 'chick'; **das ~n|haus, ⸚er** apiary; **die ~n|königin, –nen** queen bee; **der ~n|korb, ⸚e** (straw) beehive; **der ~n|stich, –e** bee-sting; *cul: kind of cake with almond topping*; **der ~n|stock, ⸚e** beehive; **das ~n|wachs** beeswax; **die ~n|zucht** bee-keeping; **der ~n|züchter, –** bee-keeper

die **Biennale, –n** biennial festival

das **Bier, –e** beer; **der ~deckel, –** beer-mat; **die ~leiche, –n** *coll* person who is dead drunk; **die ~ruhe** *coll* tremendous calm

die **Biese, –n** tuck; piping (on uniform)

das **Biest, –er** *coll* wretched creature; confounded thing; (= person) beast

bieten (*p/t* **bot** (*subj* **böte**), *p/part* **geboten**) offer; bid (**auf** *acc* for); give; provide; present; (*v/i*) bid (**auf** *acc* for); **sich ~** present itself (*dat* to); **sich** *dat* **... nicht ~ lassen** not stand for

der **Bieter, –** bidder

die **Bigamie** bigamy

bigamisch bigamous

der **Bigamist, –en** (*wk masc*) bigamist

bigott over-devout; sanctimonious

die **Bigotterie** excessive religious zeal; sanctimoniousness

der **Bikini, –s** bikini

die **Bilanz, –en** outcome; *comm* balance; balance-sheet; **~ machen** *coll* review one's financial situation; **(die) ~ ziehen** take stock

bilanzieren take stock of; *comm* (*also v/i*)

balance

das **Bild, -er** picture; image (*also liter*); scene (*also theat*), sight; appearance (of street *etc*); **-bild** *also* (*eg* **das Deutschland~**) view of (Germany *etc*); **ein ~ von einem Mädchen** a gorgeous girl; **ein ~ machen** take a picture; **sich** *dat* **ein ~ machen von** form an impression of; **im ~e sein** be in the picture; **ins ~ setzen** put in the picture || **die ~fläche, -n** screen; (*in idioms*) *coll* scene; **der ~hauer, -** sculptor; **die ~hauerei** sculpture; **b~hauerisch** sculptural; **die ~hauer|kunst** sculpture; **bild|hübsch** pretty as a picture; **die ~kassette, -n** video cassette; **die ~platte, -n** video disc; **der ~reporter, -** photojournalist; **die ~schärfe** *phot etc* definition; **der ~schirm, -e** *comput*, *TV* screen; **das ~schirm|gerät, -e** visual display unit, V.D.U.; **der ~schirm|text** (*usu no art*) videotex; **bild|schön** lovely; **der ~stock, ⸗e** *SGer* roadside shrine; **die ~tafel, -n** plate; **das ~telefon, -e** videophone; **der ~text, -e = die ~unterschrift, -en** caption; **die ~wand, ⸗e** (projection) screen; **der ~werfer, -** projector; **die ~zuschrift, -en** reply with photograph

bilden (*see also* **gebildet**) form; shape, mould; (*v/i*) broaden the mind; **sich** *dat* **... ~** form (opinion); **sich ~** form; educate oneself; **die ~den Künste** the fine arts

Bilder- picture ...; image ...; illustrated ...; **das ~buch, ⸗er** picture-book; **~buch-** text-book ...; **der ~rahmen, -** picture-frame; **b~reich** richly illustrated; rich in imagery; **die ~schrift, -en** picture writing; **die ~sprache** imagery; **der ~stürmer, -** iconoclast

bildhaft pictorial; graphic

bildlich pictorial; figurative

das **Bildnis, -se** portrait; effigy

die **Bildung, -en** formation; *approx* = education; form, *ling* formation; **~ haben** be educated

Bildungs- educational ...; **der ~s|gang, ⸗e** education; **der ~s|grad, -e** level of education; **das ~s|gut** (body of) knowledge; cultural heritage; **die ~s|lücke, -n** gap in one's education; **der ~s|roman, -e** (*novel depicting the spiritual education of the central character*); **der ~s|stand** level of education; **der ~s|weg, -e** (type of) education (**der zweite B.** '*alternative route*' *to the* Abitur *through evening classes etc*)

das **Billard** ['bɪljart] billiards; **die ~kugel, -n** billiard-ball; **der ~stock, ⸗e** billiard cue

der **Billeteur** [*Aust* bije'tøːɐ, *Swiss* bɪljɛ-], **-e** *Aust* usher; *Swiss* conductor

das **Billett** [-lj-], **-s/-e** *Swiss* ticket

die **Billiarde, -n** thousand billions, quadrillion *US*

billig cheap; (price) low; (excuse *etc*) poor; proper; (*adv*: sell *etc*) cheap; *in compds* **B~-** cheap ...; **die B~flagge, -n** flag of convenience; **der B~preis, -e** low price

billigen approve; approve of

die **Billigung** approval

die **Billion, -en** million million, trillion *US*

bim bam! ding-dong!; **heiliger Bimbam!** hell's bells!

die **Bimmel, -n** *coll* little bell

bimmeln *coll* ring; tinkle

Bims-: **der ~stein, -e** pumice-stone

bimsen *coll* cram; drill hard

bin *1st sing pres of* **sein[1]**

binär binary; **die B~stelle, -n** binary digit

Bind-: **der ~faden, ..fäden** string (**es regnet Bindfäden** *coll* it's raining cats and dogs)

die **Binde, -n** bandage; sling; arm-band; sanitary towel/napkin *US*; **einen hinter die ~ gießen** *coll* wet one's whistle

Binde-: **das ~gewebe, -** connective tissue; **das ~glied, -er** link; **die ~haut** conjunctiva; **das ~mittel, -** binder; medium; **der ~strich, -e** hyphen; **das ~wort, ⸗er** conjunction

binden (*p/t* **band** (*subj* **bände**), *p/part* **gebunden**) (*see also* **gebunden**) tie; bind; make (garland *etc*); hoop; be binding on; tie down/up; *cul* thicken; *mus* play legato; (*v/i*) bind; **an Händen und Füßen gebunden** bound hand and foot

sich ~ commit oneself: tie oneself down

bindend binding (**für** on)

die **Bindung, -en** *vbl noun*; *also* bond, tie; attachment; commitment (**an** *acc* to); *ski* binding; *text* weave; *chem* linkage

binnen (+*dat/gen*) within

Binnen- inland ...; home ..., domestic ...; internal ...; inner ...; **das ~land, ⸗er** interior; **b~ländisch** inland; **der ~markt, ⸗e** domestic market (**der europäische B.** the Single European Market); **das ~meer, -e** inland sea; **der ~staat, -en** landlocked country

die **Binse, -n** rush; **in die ~n gehen** *coll* go west || **die ~n|wahrheit, -en = die ~n|weisheit, -en** truism

Bio- bio-; *agr*, *hort* organic ...

die **Biochemie** [-ç-] biochemistry

der **Biochemiker** [-ç-], **-** biochemist

biochemisch [-ç-] biochemical

der **Biograph, -en** (*wk masc*) biographer

die **Biographie, -(ie)n** biography

biographisch biographical

der **Biologe, -n** (*wk masc*) biologist

die **Biologie** biology

biologisch biological

die **Biophysik** biophysics

birg *imp sing*, **birg(s)t** (*2nd*,) *3rd sing pres of* **bergen**

die **Birke, –n** birch; **der ~n|zeisig, –e** redpoll

Birma Burma

der **Birmane, –n** (*wk masc*) Burmese

birmanisch, (*language*) **B~** Burmese

der **Birn|baum, ⸚e** pear-tree

die **Birne, –n** pear; (electric) bulb; *coll* 'nut'

birst *imp sing, 2nd/3rd sing pres of* **bersten**

bis [–ɪ–] 1 *prep* (+*acc*) until; by (= no later than); as far as; (count) (up) to; (*between numerals*) or; to; between ... and ...; (*between adjectives, indicating range*) to; 2 *conj* until; by the time; *Aust coll* when; **~ bald/gleich/morgen/nachher/Montag** *etc*! see you soon/in a minute/tomorrow/later/on Monday *etc*!

- **~ an** (*acc*) until; as far as; (up) to; down to
- **~ auf** (*acc*) right onto/to; to within; down to (the last ...); to (this day); except for; **~ auf weiteres** until further notice; for the time being
- **~ hin zu** right up to; down to; even to the point of
- **~ in** (*acc*) right into; (right) down to
- **~ nach** until after; as far as
- **~ über** (*acc*) to above
- **~ unter** (*acc*) up to; to below
- **von ... ~ ...** from ... to ...
- **~ vor** (*acc*) up to (place); **~ vor** (*dat*) until ... ago
- **~ wann ...?** when ... by?; how long ...?
- **~ zu** as far as; up to; to (brim *etc*); until, (= no later than) by; to the point of

bis–: ~her so far; until now (**wie b.** as hitherto); **~herig** previous; (employed) hitherto; (*following* **mein, sein,** *etc*) the ... I have/he has *etc* had until now; **~lang** so far; until now; **~weilen** at times

der **Bisam** [–am], **–e/–s** musquash (fur); **die ~ratte, –n** musquash

der **Bischof** [–ɔf], **⸚e** bishop

bischöflich [–øː–] episcopal

Bischofs– bishop's ...; episcopal ...; **die ~mütze, –n** mitre; **der ~sitz, –e** see; cathedral city; **der ~stab, ⸚e** crozier

bisexuell bisexual

bisher, bisherig *see* **bis–**

Biskaya: der Golf von ~ the Bay of Biscay

die **Biskotte, –n** *Aust* sponge finger

das **Biskuit** [–'kviːt], **–s/–e** (*also* **der**) sponge; **der ~kuchen, –** sponge cake; **die ~rolle, –n** Swiss roll; **der ~teig** sponge mixture

bis|lang *see* **bis–**

der **Bison** ['biːzɔn], **–s** bison

biß *p/t of* **beißen**

der **Biß, –(ss)e** bite

bißchen: ein ~ a little/bit (of); **das ~, was ...** what little ...; **kein ~** not a bit; no ... at all

biss(e)l *SGer coll* = **bißchen**

der **Bissen, –** mouthful; morsel; bite (to eat)

bissig (animal) vicious; snappish; **~ sein** bite; **„~er Hund!"** 'beware of the dog'

bist *2nd sing pres of* **sein**[1]

das **Bistum** ['bɪs–], **⸚er** *RC* diocese, bishopric

bis|weilen *see* **bis–**

Bitt–: der ~brief, –e petition; **der ~gang, ⸚e** approach (to s.o. for sth.); *eccles* (supplicatory) procession; **das ~gesuch, –e = das ~schreiben, –** petition; **der ~steller, –** petitioner

bitte please; **~ (schön/sehr)!** please do, by all means, go ahead; don't mention it, you're welcome *US*; *also said when offering something* (*usu not translated*); (*accepting apology*) that's all right; **~!** come in!; **~ schön/sehr?** can I help you?; what would you like?; **was, ~ schön/sehr, ...?** what, I ask you, ...?; **ja, ~?** yes?; **(na,) ~!** what did I tell you!; **(wie) ~?** pardon?; **'wie ~?** I *beg* your pardon?

die **Bitte, –n** request (**um** for); **ich habe eine ~ an dich** I want to ask you a favour; **auf jmds. ~ hin** at s.o.'s request

bitten (*p/t* **bat** (*subj* **bäte**), *p/part* **gebeten**) ask (to); ask (to one's room *etc*); (*with pers obj understood*) **~, etw. zu tun** (*eg* **er bat, sein Alter zu berücksichtigen**) request that ... should be (+ *p/part*); **darf ich ~?** would you come this way, please?; dinner is served; may I have this dance?; **wenn ich ~ darf** would you come this way, please?; may I have your attention, please?; (*accepting*) if I may; (not so loud *etc*) if you don't mind; **ich muß doch sehr ~!** I really must protest!; do you mind!; **sich lange ~ lassen** make a show of being reluctant; **ich lasse ~!** show him *etc* in; **Herr X läßt ~** Mr X will see you now

- **~ für** intercede on behalf of (**bei** with)
- **~ um** ask for, (+*vbl noun*) ask to (do sth.); (*v/i*) ask for, request; **darum möchte ich doch sehr gebeten haben!** *so* I should *think*!
- **~ zu** invite to; **zu sich ~** ask (s.o.) to come and see one

bittend pleading

bitter bitter; (chocolate) plain; dire; grievous; **der Bittere** (*decl as adj*) bitters ‖ **bitter|böse** furious; **bitter|ernst** deadly/extremely serious; **bitter|kalt** bitterly cold; **bitter|süß** bitter-sweet

die **Bitterkeit** bitterness

bitterlich slightly bitter; (*adv*) bitterly

die **Bitternis, –se** bitterness; (*pl*) bitter experiences

das **Bitumen, –** bitumen

bituminös bituminous

das **Biwak** [–ak], **–e/–s, biwakieren** bivouac

bizarr bizarre

der **Bizeps** (*gen* **–(es)**), **–e** biceps

blaffen bark

[das] **Blag, –en** *coll* = **die Blage, –n** *coll* brat

blähen swell; dilate; (*v/i*) cause flatulence; **sich ~** swell; dilate; give oneself airs

[die] **Blähung, –en** (*usu pl*) flatulence

blaken *NGer* (lamp) smoke

blamabel shameful

[die] **Blamage** [-ʒə], **–n** disgrace

blamieren disgrace; **sich ~** make a fool of oneself; disgrace oneself

blank shining, shiny; bare; sheer; (polish *etc*) till it shines; *coll* broke; (*adv*) *Aust* without a coat on; **der B~vers, –e** line of blank verse; (*pl*) blank verse

blanko blank; **der B~scheck, –s** blank cheque; **die B~voll|macht** full power of attorney; carte blanche

Blas–: das ~instrument, –e wind instrument; **die ~kapelle, –n** brass band; **die ~musik** music played by wind instruments/a brass band; **das ~rohr, –e** blow-pipe

[die] **Blase, –n** bubble; *med* blister; *anat* bladder; *coll* gang; **sich** *dat* **~n laufen** get blisters on one's feet || **der ~balg, ⸚e** bellows

blasen (*2nd/3rd sing pres* **bläst,** *p/t* **blies,** *p/part* **geblasen)** blow; blow on; *mus* play; (*v/i*) blow; *mus* play (**auf** *dat* on); **in die Hände ~** blow on one's fingers; **~ zu** *mil* sound; **dem** *etc* **werd' ich was ~!** he *etc* can get lost!

[der] **Bläser, –** player of wind instrument; (*pl*) wind (section)

blasiert blasé

[die] **Blasiertheit** blasé attitude

[die] **Blasphemie, –(ie)n** blasphemy

blasphemisch blasphemous

blaß (–ss–) pale; (recollection) faint; (performance *etc*) colourless; sheer

Bläß–: das ~huhn, ⸚er coot

[die] **Blässe** paleness, pallor; colourlessness

bläßlich palish

bläst *2nd/3rd sing pres of* **blasen**

[das] **Blatt, ⸚er** leaf; sheet (of paper); newspaper; print; blade (of oar, saw, *etc*); *cards* card; hand; *mus* reed; **vom ~ singen/spielen** sight-read; **kein ~ vor den Mund nehmen** not mince matters; **das ~ hat sich gewendet** the tables are turned; **das steht auf einem anderen ~** that is quite a different matter || **das ~gold** gold-leaf; **das ~grün** chlorophyll; **die ~laus, ⸚e** aphid, greenfly

Blatter–: die ~narbe, –n pock-mark

Blätter– … of leaves; **der ~pilz, –e** agaric; **der ~teig** puff-pastry; **der ~wald** *joc* the press

blätt(e)rig flaky; **–blätt(e)rig** –leaved

[die] **Blattern** *pl* smallpox

blättern: ~ auf (*acc*) put down on one by one; **~ in** (*dat*) leaf through

blau blue; *coll* 'tight'; **~es Auge** black eye; **~en Montag machen** *coll* take Monday off; **~e Zone** limited-parking zone; **das B~e vom Himmel (herunter)lügen** *coll* lie in one's teeth; **ins B~e hinein** *coll* at random; aimlessly; **Fahrt ins B~e** mystery tour

blau– blue …; (*with second colour-word attached*) bluey–, bluish–; **~äugig** blue-eyed; **die B~beere, –n** bilberry, blueberry *US*; **~blütig** blue-blooded; **das B~licht, –er** blue light (on police-car *etc*); **~machen** (*sep*) *coll* take time off (unofficially); **die B~meise, –n** bluetit; **die B~pause, –n** blueprint; **die B~säure** prussic acid; **der B~schimmel|käse, –** blue cheese; **der B~strumpf, ⸚e** bluestocking; **der B~wal, –e** blue whale

[die] **Bläue** blue(ness)

bläulich bluish

[der] **Blazer** ['bleːzɐ], **–** blazer

[das] **Blech, –e** *tech* sheet metal; tin; *cul* baking-sheet; *mus* brass; *coll* nonsense; *coll mil* 'gongs', 'fruit salad' *US*; **–blech** (*eg* **Eisen~**) sheet (iron *etc*)

Blech– tin …; metal …; *mus* brass …; **die ~dose, –n** tin, can; **der ~schaden, ..schäden** bodywork damage; **das ~walz|werk, –e** sheet-mill

blechen *coll* fork out

blechern metal, tin; tinny

blecken bare (one's teeth)

[das] **Blei, –e** lead; *build, naut* plumb; **b~frei** lead-free, unleaded; **b~haltig** containing lead; **blei|schwer** as heavy as lead; leaden; **der ~soldat, –en** (*wk masc*) tin soldier; **der ~stift, –e** pencil; **der ~stift|absatz, ⸚e** stiletto heel; **der ~stift|spitzer, –** pencil-sharpener

[die] **Bleibe** place to stay

bleiben (*p/t* **blieb,** *p/part* **geblieben)** (*sn*) stay, remain; keep (calm *etc*); be (*eg* **es blieb nicht ohne Konsequenzen** it was not without consequences), go (unnoticed *etc*), be left (unanswered *etc*); remain, be left, (+*dat*: **… bleibt mir)** *expressed by* I have … left/am left with …; (at sea, on crusade, *etc*) perish; **sitzen/stehen ~** remain seated/standing; **wo bleibt …?** where's … got to?; what's become of …?; **wo bist du (so lange) geblieben?** where've you been (all this time)?

~ bei stay with; stick to; stick at (one's work); **es bleibt bei …** … remain(s) unchanged; … continue(s); (arrangement) stands; *sp* the score remains unchanged at …; **es blieb bei …** *also* nothing came of …; they *etc* didn't get beyond the … stage; **es bleibt dabei** that's settled; the situation remains the same; **dabei ~, daß …** insist that …; **und dabei bleibt's!** and that's final!; **dabei blieb es** things stayed that way; that was as far as it went; **dabei blieb es nicht** that was not all; **bei der Sache ~** stick to the point

für/unter *dat* **sich** *etc* **~** keep to themselves *etc*; **das bleibt unter uns** that's strictly between ourselves

bleiben–: ~lassen* (*p/part usu* **~lassen;** *sep*) *coll* leave alone; stop

bleibend lasting; permanent

Bleibens: hier ist meines ~ nicht länger I cannot remain here any longer

bleich pale; **das B~gesicht, –er** paleface; **das B~mittel, –** bleach

bleichen (*sn if v/i*) bleach

bleiern leaden

Blend–: das ~werk deception

die **Blende, –n** shade, *mot* visor; *tail* facing; *phot* stop; aperture; *cin* fade; *archit* blind door/window *etc*; *geol* blende; **~ 11** *etc* f/11 *etc*

blenden blind; dazzle; **~d** dazzling; superb, marvellous

die **Blenden|zahl, –en** *phot* f-number

Bleß–: das ~huhn, ⸚er coot

die **Blesse, –n** blaze; animal with a blaze

bleu [blø:] (*indecl*) pale blue

der **Blick, –e** glance; look; eye (for sth.); view (**auf** *acc* of); **auf den ersten ~** at first glance/sight; **mit 'einem ~** at a glance || **der ~fang, ⸚e** eye-catcher; **das ~feld, –er** field of vision; (narrow, wide) horizon; **der ~punkt, –e** point which attracts one's gaze; standpoint (**im B. der Öffentlichkeit** in the limelight); **die ~richtung, –en** line of vision; outlook; **der ~winkel, –** standpoint, angle

blicken look (**auf** *acc* at); **sich ~ lassen** show one's face; **das läßt tief ~** *coll* that's very revealing

blieb *p/t of* **bleiben**

blies *p/t of* **blasen**

blind blind (*also archit*); clouded, (metal) tarnished; (*adv*) blindly; (trust *etc*) implicitly; **~er Passagier** stowaway; **~ für/gegen** blind to; **~ machen** blind (**für/gegen** to)

Blind– blind … (*also aer*, *archit*); *comput* dummy …; **der ~darm** caecum; *pop* appendix; **die ~darm|entzündung, –en** appendicitis; **b~fliegen*** (*sep*; *sn*) fly blind; **der ~flug, ⸚e** blind flying/flight; **der ~gänger, –** *mil* dud; *coll* dud, dead loss; **die ~schleiche, –n** slow-worm; **b~schreiben*** (*sep*) touch-type; **das ~schreiben** touch-typing

Blinde|kuh blind-man's-buff

Blinden– … for the blind; **der ~hund, –e** guide-dog, seeing-eye dog *US*; **die ~schrift** Braille

die **Blindheit** blindness

blindlings blindly; wildly; headlong

Blink–: das ~feuer, – *aer*, *naut* flashing beacon; **das ~licht, –er** flashing light; *mot* indicator, blinker *US*

blinken flash (signal); (*v/i*) gleam; glint; (star) twinkle; flash, *mot* signal

der **Blinker, –** indicator, blinker *US*

blinzeln blink; screw up one's eyes; wink

der **Blitz, –e** lightning; flash of lightning; *phot coll* flash; **wie ein ~ aus heiterem Himmel** like a bolt from the blue; **einschlagen wie ein ~** be a bombshell; **wie vom ~ getroffen** thunderstruck || **der ~ableiter, –** lightning-conductor, lightning rod *US*; **b~artig** lightning; split-second; (*adv*) like lightning; in a flash; **blitz|blank** spick and span; **das ~gerät, –e** flashgun; **das ~gespräch, –e** special priority call; **der ~kaffee** *Swiss* instant coffee; **der ~krieg, –e** blitzkrieg; **das ~licht, –er** *phot* flashlight; **die ~licht|birne, –n** flash-bulb; **blitz|sauber** *coll* spick and span; *SGer* (girl) splendid; **der ~schlag, ⸚e** (stroke of) lightning (**vom B. getroffen** struck by lightning); **blitz|schnell** lightning; (*adv*) with lightning speed; like a flash; **der ~strahl, –en** flash of lightning; **das ~telegramm, –e** special priority telegram; **der ~würfel, –** flash cube

blitze|blank spick and span

blitzen *phot coll* photograph with a flash; (*v/i*) flash; sparkle; **es blitzt** there is a flash of lightning; **bei dir blitzt es** *joc* your slip is showing; **Wut blitzte aus seinen Augen** his eyes flashed with anger

Blitzes|schnelle: mit ~ with lightning speed

der **Block, ⸚e/–s** (writing) pad; *philat* souvenir sheet; (*pl usu* **–s**) block (of houses); (*pl* **–s**) *rail*, *sp* block; (*pl* **⸚e**) block (of marble *etc*); *geol* boulder; *metall* ingot; *med* block; *pol* bloc; *hist* stocks; **die ~flöte, –n** recorder; **b~frei** non-aligned; **das ~haus, ⸚er = die ~hütte, –n** log-cabin; **die ~schokolade** cooking chocolate; **die ~schrift** block letters; **der ~wart, –e** *Nazi* block warden

die **Blockade, –n** blockade

blocken *rail*, *sp* block; (*v/i*) *hunt* perch

blockieren block; *mil* blockade; (*v/i*) jam; (wheel *etc*) lock

Blöd–: der ~mann, ⸚er *coll* stupid fool; **der ~sinn** *coll* nonsense (**B. machen** fool about); **b~sinnig** *coll* idiotic

blöd(e) feeble-minded; *coll* stupid; annoying; **es wird mir zu ~** *coll* I've just about had enough of it; **es ist zu ~, daß …** *coll* it's too bad that …

blödeln *coll* fool about; talk nonsense

die **Blödheit, –en** imbecility; *coll* stupidity; stupid remark

der **Blödian, –e** *coll* blockhead

blöken bleat

blond fair(-haired); blonde; *coll* (ale) pale
blondieren bleach (hair)
die **Blondine, –n** blonde
bloß [-o:-] bare; mere; sheer; (*adv*) only, just; merely; (*as emotive particle*: *with imper*) for goodness' sake, (*with interrog*) on earth; **mit ~em Auge** with the naked eye; **~ nicht!** heaven forbid!; for goodness' sake don't!; **wenn … ~ …!** if only …! || **~legen** (*sep*) uncover; expose; **~stellen** (*sep*) show up; expose (**sich b.** show oneself up); **die B~stellung, –en** showing up; exposure; **~strampeln** (*sep*): **sich b.** kick off the bedclothes
die **Blöße, –n** nakedness; (forest) clearing; *fenc* opening; **sich** *dat* **eine ~ geben** show a weakness
das **Blouson** [blu'zɔ̃:] (*gen* **–(s)**), **–s** (*also* **der**) blouson
blubbern *coll* mumble; (*v/i*) bubble; gurgle
der **Blues** [blu:s] (*gen* **–**), **–** blues
der **Bluff, –s, bluffen** bluff
blühen (be in) bloom; (be in) blossom; be full of flowers; thrive, flourish; (+*dat*) *coll* happen to; **~d** *also* blooming; blossoming; radiant; flourishing; (imagination) vivid; (nonsense) absolute
die **Blume, –n** flower; bouquet (of wine); head (on beer); **durch die ~ sagen** hint at || **der ~n|händler, –** florist; **der ~n|kasten, ..kästen** window-box; **der ~n|kohl** cauliflower; **das ~n|muster, –** floral pattern; **b~n|reich** flowery; **der ~n|stock, ⸚e** (flowering) pot-plant; **der ~n|strauß, ⸚e** bouquet; **der ~n|topf, ⸚e** flowerpot; **die ~n|zwiebel, –n** bulb
blumig flowery
die **Bluse, –n** blouse
das **Blut** blood; **heißes ~ haben** be hot-tempered; **kaltes ~ bewahren** keep a cool head; **ruhig ~!** keep calm!; **~ lecken** develop a liking for sth. || **die ~ader, –n** vein; **b~arm** anaemic; **(blut|arm)** *coll* as poor as a church mouse; **die ~armut** anaemia; **das ~bad, ⸚er** blood-bath; **die ~bank, –en** blood bank; **b~befleckt** blood-stained; **der ~druck** blood-pressure; **der ~egel, –** leech; **der ~farb|stoff** haemoglobin; **die ~gier** lust for blood; **b~gierig** bloodthirsty; **die ~gruppe, –n** blood group; **der ~hund, –e** bloodhound; bloodthirsty person; **blut|jung** very young; **die ~konserve, –n** stored blood (for transfusions); **das ~körperchen, –** blood corpuscle; **b~leer** bloodless; **das ~plasma** blood plasma; **die ~probe, –n** blood sample; blood test; **die ~rache** blood-vengeance; vendetta; **b~rünstig** bloodthirsty; **die ~schande** incest; **die ~senkung, –en** blood sedimentation; **der ~spender, –** blood-donor; **b~stillend** styptic; **die ~transfusion, –en** blood transfusion; **b~unterlaufen** bloodshot; **das ~vergießen** bloodshed; **der ~verlust** loss of blood; **die ~wurst** black pudding, blood sausage *US*
die **Blüte, –n** blossom; flower, bloom; flowering, blooming; blossoming; prime; flowering (of arts *etc*), heyday; *coll* forged banknote; **~n treiben** be in bloom/blossom; **seltsame ~n treiben** produce strange results; **in (voller) ~ stehen** be in (full) bloom/blossom; flourish || **die ~zeit, –en** flowering; blossom-time; heyday; golden age
bluten bleed; **schwer ~ müssen** *coll* have to pay through the nose
Blüten–: das ~blatt, ⸚er petal; **der ~kelch, –e** calyx; **der ~staub** pollen; **blüten|weiß** sparkling white
die **Bluter|krankheit** haemophilia
blutig bloody; (tears) bitter; (beginner *etc*) absolute; *cul* rare
–blütig –blooded; –blossomed
Bluts– … of blood; blood …; **b~verwandt** related by blood
die **Blutung, –en** bleeding; haemorrhage
BMW = Bayerische Motorenwerke
die **Bö, –en** gust; squall
die **Boa, –s** boa (constrictor)
der **Bob** [bɔp], **–s** bob-sleigh
Boccaccio [bɔ'katʃo] Boccaccio
der **Bock, ⸚e** buck; he-goat; ram; (coachman's) box; *tech* trestle; stand; horse; *gym* buck; **einen ~ haben auf** (*acc*) *coll* fancy; **einen ~ schießen** *coll* slip up || **b~beinig** pigheaded; **das ~bier** bock (*strong dark beer*); **das ~springen** leap-frog; *gym* vaulting the buck; **die ~wurst, ⸚e** (*type of frankfurter*)
bocken buck; *coll* be obstinate; *coll mot* play up; refuse to start
bockig pigheaded
Bocks– goat's …; **~horn** *coll* **(ins B. jagen** browbeat)
der **Boden,** *pl* **Böden** ground; land; floor; soil (= territory); bottom; attic; (+*dat*) **den ~ entziehen** knock the bottom out of; **am ~ zerstört** *coll* shattered; **(an) ~ gewinnen/verlieren** gain/lose ground; **sich auf den ~ der Tatsachen stellen** be realistic; **aus dem ~ stampfen** conjure up (from nowhere); **zu ~ fallen** fall to the ground; **zu ~ schlagen** floor || **die Boden-Boden-Rakete, –n** surface-to-surface missile; **die ~fläche** area (of land); floor-space; **b~lang** full-length; **b~los** bottomless; *coll* incredible; **die Boden-Luft-Rakete, –n** surface-to-air missile; **das ~personal** ground staff; **die ~reform** land reform; **der ~satz** sediment; dregs; **die ~schätze** *pl* mineral resources; **der ~see** Lake Constance; **b~ständig** with one's roots in one's own locality; indi-

genous; local; **die ~station, -en** tracking station

bog (böge) *p/t* (*subj*) *of* **biegen**

der **Bogen, -**/*esp SGer* **Bögen** curve; loop (over handwritten 'u'), *mus* slur; sheet (of paper); *archery*, *mus* bow; *math* arc; *ski* turn; (*pl* **Bögen**) arch; **den ~ überspannen** overdo it; **den ~ raushaben** *coll* have got the hang of it; **große ~ spucken** *coll* talk big; **einen großen ~ machen um** steer clear of || **das ~fenster, -** arched window; **b~förmig** arched; **der ~gang, ⸚e** arcade; **die ~lampe, -n** arc-light; **das ~schießen** archery; **der ~schütze, -n** (*wk masc*) archer

die **Boheme** [bo'ɛ:m] bohemian circles

der **Bohemien** [boe'mĩɛ̃:], **-s** bohemian

die **Bohle, -n** plank

der **Böhme, -n** (*wk masc*) Bohemian

Böhmen Bohemia

böhmisch Bohemian; **das sind für mich ~e Dörfer** *coll* it's all Greek to me

die **Bohne, -n** bean; **dicke/grüne/weiße ~** broad/French/haricot bean; **nicht die ~** *coll* not a scrap/fig || **der ~n|kaffee** (real) coffee; **das ~n|kraut** savory; **die ~n|stange, -n** beanpole

Bohner-: das ~wachs, -e floor-polish

bohnern polish (floor)

Bohr- drilling ...; boring ...; **die ~insel, -n** oil-rig; **das ~loch, ⸚er** borehole; **die ~maschine, -n** drill; **der ~turm, ⸚e** derrick

bohren drill; bore; drive (tunnel); (*v/i*) drill; bore; *coll* persist; **~ auf** (*acc*)/**nach** drill for; **~ in** (*acc*) plunge (knife) into; dig (nails) into; **~ in** (*dat*) pick (one's nose); drill (tooth); (fear *etc*) gnaw at

sich ~ bore (its way); pierce; penetrate

bohrend nagging; piercing; persistent

der **Bohrer, -** drill; driller

die **Bohrung, -en** *vbl noun*; *also* drill-hole; bore

böig squally; (flight) bumpy

der **Boiler** [-ɐ], **-** water-heater (on wall); boiler

die **Boje, -n** buoy

der **Bolide, -n** (*wk masc*) racing-car

der **Bolivianer, -, bolivianisch** Bolivian

Bolivien [-ĭən] Bolivia

Böller-: der ~schuß, ⸚(ss)e gun-salute

böllern fire a gun (in celebration, salute)

das **Bollwerk, -e** quay; bulwark

der **Bolschewik** [-ʃe-], **-en** (*wk masc*) (*pl also* **-i**) Bolshevik

der **Bolschewismus** [-ʃe-] Bolshevism

der **Bolschewist** [-ʃe-], **-en** (*wk masc*), **bolschewistisch** Bolshevist

der **Bolzen, -** bolt; pin

das **Bombardement** [-də'mã:], **-s** bombing; bombardment

bombardieren bomb; bombard

der **Bombast** bombast

bombastisch bombastic

Bombay ['bɔmbe] Bombay

die **Bombe, -n** bomb; *sp coll* scorcher; **wie eine ~ einschlagen** come as a bombshell

bomben *sp coll* slam (into back of net)

Bomben- bomb ...; bombing ...; *coll* tremendous ...; **der ~erfolg, -e** smash hit; **b~fest** bomb-proof; **(bombenfest)** *coll* dead certain; **das ~flugzeug, -e** bomber; **der ~räum|trupp, -s** bomb disposal squad; **b~sicher** bomb-proof; **(bombensicher)** *coll* dead certain; **der ~trichter, -** bomb-crater

der **Bomber, -** *coll* bomber

bombig *coll* great, tremendous

der **Bon** [bɔŋ], **-s** coupon, voucher; sales slip

das **Bonbon** [bɔŋ'bɔŋ], **-s** (*also* **der**) sweet, candy *US*

die **Bonbonniere** [bɔŋbɔ'nĭɛ:rə], **-n** box of chocolates

bongen *coll* ring up (on cash-register)

das **Bonmot** [bɔ̃'mo:], **-s** witticism

der **Bonze, -n** (*wk masc*) bonze; (party *etc*) boss

der **Boom** [bu:m], **-s** boom (**an** *dat* in)

das **Boot, -e** boat

Boots- boat ...; **der ~mann, ..leute** chief petty officer; boatswain

das **Bor** boron; **die ~säure** bor(ac)ic acid

das **Bord, -e** shelf

Bord *naut*: **an ~** aboard; (+*gen*) aboard; **über ~** overboard; **von ~ gehen** leave the ship/aircraft

Bord- *aer* air(craft) ...; flight ...; *naut* ship's ...; **der ~funker, -** radio operator; **die ~kante, -n** kerb, curb *US*; **die ~karte, -n** boarding-card; **die ~küche, -n** galley; **der ~stein, -e** kerb, curb *US*; **die ~wand, ⸚e** ship's side

das **Bordell, -e** brothel

die **Bordüre, -n** border

borgen (*also* + **sich** *dat*) borrow; (+*dat*) lend

die **Borke, -n** bark

der **Born, -e** *poet* spring; well; fount(ain)

borniert narrow-minded

der **Borretsch** borage

die **Börse, -n** purse; *comm* stock exchange; (the) market; **der ~n|bericht, -e** market report; **der ~n|makler, -** stockbroker; **die ~n|notierung, -en** quotation

die **Borste, -n** bristle

borstig bristly; surly

die **Borte, -n** braid

bös = böse; ~artig malicious; vicious; *med* malignant; **die B~artigkeit** maliciousness; viciousness; *med* malignance; **~willig** malevolent; **die B~willigkeit** malevolence

die **Böschung, -en** slope; embankment

böse bad; evil; malicious; angry (**auf** *acc* with); *coll* naughty; (+*dat*) **~ sein** be angry with; **das Böse** (*decl as adj*) evil; harm; **im ~n auseinandergehen** part on bad terms || **der B~wicht, -e(r)** scoundrel

boshaft malicious
die **Boshaftigkeit** spite, maliciousness
die **Bosheit, –en** malice, spite; malicious act/remark
der **Bosporus** the Bosp(h)orus
der **Boß, –(ss)e** *coll* boss
bot *p/t of* **bieten**
die **Botanik** [–ɪk] botany
der **Botaniker, –** botanist
botanisch botanical
der **Bote, –n** (*wk masc*) messenger; errand-boy; **der ~n|gang, ⸚e** errand
böte *p/t subj of* **bieten**
die **Botschaft, –en** message; *pol* embassy
der **Botschafter, –** ambassador; **~ebene (auf B.** at ambassadorial level)
der **Bottich, –e** tub; vat
die **Bouillon** [bʊl'jɔŋ], **–s** bouillon
die **Boulette** [bu–], **–n** meat-ball
der **Boulevard** [bulə'vaːɐ], **–s** boulevard; *EGer* pedestrian precinct; **das ~blatt, ⸚er** (sensationalistic) tabloid; **die ~presse** gutter press; **das ~theater** *approx* = commercial theatre
der **Bourbone** [bʊr–], **–n** (*wk masc*), **bourbonisch** Bourbon
der **Bourgeois** [bʊr'ʒo̯a] (*gen* –), **–** bourgeois
die **Bourgeoisie** [bʊrʒo̯a–] bourgeoisie
die **Boutique** [bu'tiːk], **–n** boutique
der **Bovist, –e** puff-ball
die **Bowle** ['boːlə], **–n** cold punch; punch-bowl
die **Box, –en** loose-box, box stall *US*; parking space (in garage), *mot rac* pit; stand; loudspeaker; *phot* box-camera
Box– boxing ...; **der ~kampf, ⸚e** boxing-match; **der ~sport** boxing
boxen punch; *box* fight; (*v/i*) *box* box; **sich ~** *coll* fight one's way; (*recip*) *coll* have a punch-up
der **Boxer, –** boxer (*also* = dog); **der ~aufstand** the Boxer Rebellion
boxerisch boxing
der **Boy, –s** page-boy, bell-boy *US*
der **Boykott, –e/–s, boykottieren** boycott
Bozen Bolzano
BR = Bayerischer Rundfunk
brabbeln *coll* mumble
brach¹ **(bräche)** *p/t* (*subj*) *of* **brechen**
brach² [–aː–] fallow; **~liegen*** (*sep*) lie fallow; **~liegend** lying fallow; unutilized; **der B~vogel, ..vögel** curlew
die **Brache** [–aː–], **–n** fallow; fallowing
die **Brachial|gewalt** [–x–] brute force
brachte (brächte) *p/t* (*subj*) *of* **bringen**
Brack–: das ~wasser brackish water
der **Bracke, –n** (*wk masc*) hound
brackig brackish
der **Brahmane, –n** (*wk masc*) Brahman
bramarbasieren swagger
die **Branche** ['brãːʃə], **–n** (line of) business; industry; **das ~n|verzeichnis, –se** yellow pages
der **Brand, ⸚e** fire; firing (of bricks *etc*); *med* gangrene; *bot* blight; *coll* tremendous thirst; **in ~ stecken** set fire to; **in ~ stehen** be on fire
Brand– *esp* fire ...;
der ~brief, –e *coll* urgent letter/reminder; **brand|eilig** *coll* extremely urgent; **das ~eisen, –** branding-iron; **die ~ente, –n** shelduck; **der ~fleck, –e** burn; **die ~gans, ⸚e** shelduck; **der ~geruch** burnt smell; **der ~herd, –e** source of a fire; storm-centre; **der ~leger, –** *Aust* arsonist; **die ~legung, –en** *Aust* arson; **das ~mal, –e** brand; stigma; **b~marken** (*insep*) denounce; brand, stigmatize; **brand|neu** *coll* brand-new; **das ~opfer, –** fire victim; burnt offering; **die ~rede, –n** virulent speech; **brand|rot** fiery red; **die ~salbe, –n** ointment for burns; **b~schatzen** (*insep*) pillage; **die ~sohle, –n** insole; **der ~stifter, –** arsonist; **die ~stiftung, –en** arson; **die ~wunde, –n** burn; scald; **das ~zeichen, –** brand
branden surge; **~ an** (*acc*)/**gegen** break against; **~d** (applause) thunderous
brandig smelling/tasting of burning; (smell) burnt; *med* gangrenous; *bot* blighted
die **Brandung, –en** surf; surge
Brannt–: der ~wein, –e spirits
brannte *p/t of* **brennen**
die **Brasil, –(s)** Brazil cigar
der **Brasilianer, –, brasilianisch** Brazilian
Brasilien [–ĭən] Brazil
Brat– roast(ing) ...; fried ...; frying ...; **der ~apfel, ..äpfel** baked apple; **b~fertig** oven-ready; **das ~hendl, –(n)** *SGer* = **das ~huhn, ⸚er** roast chicken; **die ~kartoffeln** *pl* fried potatoes; **die ~pfanne, –n** frying-pan; **der ~rost, –e** grill; **die ~wurst, ⸚e** fried sausage
braten (brät(st), *p/t* **briet,** *p/part* **gebraten)** roast; fry; bake (apples); (*v/i*) *coll* roast (in sun)
der **Braten, –** joint; roast; **–braten** (*eg* **der Gänse~**) roast (goose *etc*); **den ~ riechen** *coll* smell a rat
die **Bratsche** [–aː–], **–n** viola
Brau– brewing ...; **das ~haus, ⸚er** brewery
der **Brauch, ⸚e** custom
brauchbar useful; serviceable; viable; quite good
brauchen (*p/part* **gebraucht,** (*after dependent infin*) **brauchen**) need; take (... hours *etc*); use (up); **... hätte nicht zu ...** (*infin*) **~ ...** need not have +*p/part*, there was no need for ... to + *infin*
das **Brauchtum** customs; tradition
die **Braue, –n** eyebrow

brauen brew; *coll* make (coffee *etc*)

die **Brauerei, -en** brewery; brewing

braun brown; *coll* Nazi; **~gebrannt** suntanned; **die B~kohle** lignite

die **Bräune** sun-tan; brown (colour)

bräunen tan; *cul* brown; (*v/i, also sn*) get a tan; *cul* brown

bräunlich brownish

Braunschweig Brunswick

die **Brause, -n** shower; rose (of watering can); fizzy drink; **der ~kopf, ⸚e** *coll* hot-head; **die ~limonade, -n** fizzy drink

brausen give (s.o.) a shower; spray down; (*v/i*) take a shower; roar; thunder; (*sn*) roar; race; **es braust mir in den Ohren** my ears are buzzing; **sich ~** take a shower; **~d** roaring; thunderous

die **Braut, ⸚e** bride; fiancée; *in compds* bridal ...; wedding ...; **die ~jungfer, -n** bridesmaid; **die ~leute** *pl* = **das ~paar, -e** bride and groom; engaged couple; **~schau (auf B. gehen** go looking for a wife)

der **Bräutigam** [-am], **-e** bridegroom; fiancé

bräutlich bridal

brav good, well-behaved; worthy; (rendering) competent (but uninspired); *arch* brave

bravo: ~! well done!; bravo! || **der B~ruf, -e** cheer

die **Bravour** [-'vuːɐ] bravery; *mus* bravura; **das ~stück, -e** tour de force; *mus* bravura

bravourös [-vu-] brilliant; brisk

die **BRD (= Bundesrepublik Deutschland)** West Germany

Brech-: die ~bohne, -n (young) French bean; **das ~eisen, -** crowbar; jemmy, jimmy *US*; **das ~mittel, -** emetic; *coll* sickening person; **der ~reiz** nausea; **die ~stange, -n** crowbar

brechen (brich(s)t, *p/t* **brach** [-aː-] (*subj* **bräche** [-ɛː-]), *p/part* **gebrochen)** break; vomit; take precedence over; *phys* refract; (*v/i*) *coll* vomit; (*sn*) break; **die Ehe ~** commit adultery; (+*dat*) **das Herz ~** break (s.o.'s) heart

~ aus (*sn*) break out of; burst out of; gush out of

~ durch (*sn*) break through

~ mit break with; break oneself of

sich ~ *phys* be refracted; **sich ~ an** (*dat*) break against

brechend: ~ voll full to bursting

die **Brechung, -en** *phys* refraction

der **Brei, -e** pulp; pap; mush; porridge; (semolina *etc*) pudding; **wie die Katze um den heißen ~ gehen** beat about the bush; **zu ~ schlagen** *coll* beat to a pulp

breiig pulpy, mushy

breit wide; broad; diffuse; (public) general; **~beinig** with legs apart; **~gefächert** wide; **~machen** (*sep*): **sich b.** *coll* spread oneself; throw one's weight around; (thing) spread; **~schlagen*** (*sep*) *coll* talk round; **~schultrig** broad-shouldered; **die B~seite, -n** broadside; **~spurig** broad-gauge; *coll* self-important; **~treten*** (*sep*) *coll* go on at great length about; **~walzen** (*sep*) *coll* discuss at great length; **die B~wand** wide screen; **der B~wand|film, -e** wide-screen film

die **Breite, -n** width; breadth; diffuseness; *geog* latitude; **(50° *etc*) nördlicher/südlicher ~** latitude (50° *etc*) north/south; **in die ~ gehen** *coll* put on weight; **der ~ nach** breadthwise

breiten spread

Breiten-: der ~grad, -e degree of latitude; (49th *etc*) parallel; **der ~kreis, -e** parallel; **die ~wirkung** impact on a wide audience

Brems- brake ...; braking ...; **die ~backe, -n** brake-shoe; **der ~belag, ⸚e** brake-lining; **der ~klotz, ⸚e** brake-block; **die ~leistung, -en** brake horsepower; **die ~rakete, -n** retro-rocket; **die ~spur, -en** skid-mark; **die ~trommel, -n** brake-drum; **der ~weg, -e** braking distance

die **Bremse**[1], **-n** brake

die **Bremse**[2], **-n** gad-fly

bremsen brake (vehicle); restrain; curb; (*v/i*) brake; cut down (**mit** on)

der **Bremser, -** brakesman, brakeman *US*

Brenn- burning ...; **die Brennessel, -n** stinging-nettle; **das ~gemisch, -e** combustible mixture; **das ~holz** firewood; **das ~material, -ien** fuel; **der ~ofen, ..öfen** kiln; **der ~punkt, -e** focal point (**im B. des Interesses stehen** be the focus of interest); **die ~schere, -n** curling-tongs; **der ~stoff, -e** fuel; **die ~weite, -n** focal length

brennbar combustible

brennen (*p/t* **brannte** (*subj rare* **brennte**), *p/part* **gebrannt)** burn; brand; fire; distil; roast (coffee); curl (with curling-tongs); (*v/i*) burn; be on fire; (light) be on; smart; sting; (sun) beat down; **~ auf** (*acc*)/**nach** be dying for; **~ vor** (*dat*) be burning with; **es brennt!** fire, fire!; it's urgent; (in game) you're getting hot; **wo brennt's denn?** *coll* what's the hurry?; **~ lassen** let burn; leave (light) on; **~d** burning; lighted; fervent; (thirst) raging; searing; urgent; (*adv*) tremendously; (need) badly; **~d gerne tun** *coll* love doing

der **Brenner, -** distiller; *tech* burner

die **Brennerei, -en** distillery; distilling

brenzlich *Aust*, **brenzlig** (smell) burnt; *coll* tricky, dodgy

die **Bresche, -n** breach; **eine ~ schlagen für** stand up for; **in die ~ springen** step into the breach

Breslau [–ɛ–] Wroclaw, *hist* Breslau
die **Bretagne** [brəˈtanjə] Brittany
der **Bretone, –n** (*wk masc*), **bretonisch** Breton
das **Brett, –er** board; plank; shelf; (*pl*) skis; *theat* boards; *box* floor; **Schwarzes ~** notice-board, bulletin board *US*; **ein ~ vor dem Kopf haben** *coll* be slow on the uptake; have a mental block; **über die ~er gehen** be performed || **das ~spiel, –e** board-game
Bretter– wooden ...; **der ~zaun, ⸚e** wooden fence; hoarding
das **Brevier, –e** *RC* breviary; *liter* collection of extracts from the works of a single author
die **Brezel, –n** pretzel
brich *imp sing*, **brich(s)t** (*2nd,*) *3rd sing pres of* **brechen**
das **Bridge** [brɪtʃ] *cards* bridge
der **Brief, –e** letter; *bibl* epistle; **der ~beschwerer, –** paper-weight; **der ~block, –s** writing-pad; **der ~bogen, –** sheet of writing-paper; **die ~bombe, –n** letter-bomb; **der ~freund, –e** pen-friend; **die ~karte, –n** correspondence card; **der ~kasten, ..kästen** letter-box, mailbox *US*; **der ~kopf, ⸚e** letter-head; **die ~marke, –n** postage stamp; **~marken–** stamp ...; **die ~marken|kunde** philately; **der ~öffner, –** letter-opener; **das ~papier** notepaper; **die ~tasche, –n** wallet; **die ~taube, –n** carrier-pigeon; **der ~träger, –** postman, mailman *US*; **der ~umschlag, ⸚e** envelope; **der ~wechsel** correspondence (**in B. stehen mit** correspond with)
das **Briefchen, –** note; sachet; book (of matches); packet (of needles)
brieflich by letter
briet *p/t of* **braten**
die **Brigade, –n** brigade (*EGer also*: *team of workers*); **der ~general, –e/⸚e** brigadier, brigadier general *US*; (air force) air commodore, brigadier general *US*
der **Brigadier** [–ˈdi̯eː], **–s** = **Brigadegeneral;** *EGer* (*also* [–ˈdiːɐ]) brigade-leader
die **Brigg** [–k], **–s** brig
das **Brikett, –s** briquette
brillant [–lj–] brilliant; splendid
der **Brillant** [–lj–], **–en** (*wk masc*) cut diamond
die **Brillanz** [–lj–] brilliance
die **Brille, –n** (pair of) spectacles; goggles; *coll* toilet seat; **die ~n|schlange, –n** spectacled cobra; *coll* woman who wears glasses
brillieren [–lj–] shine (through achievement); give a brilliant performance
das **Brimborium** *coll* fuss
bringen (*p/t* **brachte** (*subj* **brächte**), *p/part* **gebracht**) bring; take; make (sacrifice); publish; carry (report *etc*); present; give; give rise to; *agr* bear; yield; *comm* yield; fetch; *rad*, *TV* broadcast; *the construction ~ + prep + vbl noun is sometimes employed in formal style as a substitute for a verb* (*eg* **in Abzug ~ = abziehen** deduct, **zur Ausführung ~ = ausführen** carry out)
an sich ~ take possession of
~ auf (*acc*) put (idea) into (s.o.'s) head; bring (conversation) round to; reduce to (formula); **es ~ auf** manage; make
dahin: jmdn. dahin ~, daß er ... get s.o. to ...; **du wirst** *etc* **es noch dahin ~, daß ...** you *etc* 'll make (us *etc*) + *infin*
hinter sich ~ get (sth.) over and done with; cover (distance)
mit sich ~ entail; carry with it
über: es über sich ~ zu ... bring oneself to ...
~ um deprive of; do out of; **ums Leben ~** kill
von der Stelle ~ get (s.o., sth.) to move
~ zu: es zu etwas ~ get somewhere in life; **es zum ... ~** rise to be; **wieder zu sich ~** bring round; **jmdn. zum ...** (*infin noun*) **~/dazu ~ zu ...** get s.o. to ...; make s.o. ...
brisant explosive
die **Brisanz** explosiveness
die **Brise, –n** breeze
Britannien [–ĭən] *hist* Britain
der **Brite, –n** (*wk masc*) Briton; **die ~n** the British
britisch British
bröck(e)lig crumbly
bröckeln (*also v/i*) crumble; **~ von** (*sn*) flake off
brocken: ~ in (*acc*) crumble and put in (soup *etc*)
der **Brocken, –** piece; lump; *coll* hulk; (*pl*) snatches (of); **harter ~** tough nut to crack; **ein paar ~ (Deutsch** *etc*) a few scraps of
brodeln bubble; swirl; **es brodelt** discontent is rife
der **Broiler** [–ɐ], **–** *EGer* fried chicken
der **Brokat, –e** brocade
das **Brom** bromine
die **Brombeere** [–ɔ–], **–n** blackberry
Bromberg [–ɔ–] Bydgoszcz
bronchial [–ç–] bronchial; **der B~katarrh** bronchitis
die **Bronchien** [–çĭən] *pl* bronchial tubes
die **Bronchitis** [–ˈçiːtɪs] bronchitis
die **Bronze** [ˈbrɔ̃ːsə], **–n** bronze; **die ~zeit** the Bronze Age; **b~zeitlich** Bronze Age
bronzen [ˈbrɔ̃ːsn̩] bronze; bronzed
die **Brosamen** *pl* crumbs
die **Brosche** [ˈbrɔʃə], **–n** brooch
broschiert [brɔʃ–] in paper covers
die **Broschüre** [brɔʃ–], **–n** pamphlet; booklet
der **Brösel, –** crumb
das **Brot, –e** bread; loaf; slice of bread; **= der ~erwerb** living; **der ~korb, ⸚e** bread-basket ((+*dat*) **den B. höher hängen** *coll*

put on short rations); **b~los** out of work (**das ist eine b~lose Kunst** there's no money in that); **die ~zeit, -en** *SGer* (mid-morning) snack

das **Brötchen, -** roll

brr! brr!; ugh!; whoa!

BRT = Bruttoregistertonne

der **Bruch**[1], **⸚e** breaking; break; crack; breach; crease; fold; broken china/chocolate *etc*; *math* fraction; *geol* fault; *med* fracture; hernia; **-bruch** *also* ... quarry; *med* fractured ...; **~ machen** crash-land; **in die Brüche/zu ~ gehen** break, get broken; come to nothing; break up; **zu ~ fahren** smash up

der **Bruch**[2] [-ʊ-, -u:-], **⸚e** (*also* **das**) marsh

Bruch-: die ~bude, -n *coll* 'dump'; **die ~landung, -en** crash-landing; **die ~rechnung** (use of) fractions; **die ~stelle, -n** break; crack; **das ~stück, -e** fragment; **b~stückhaft** fragmentary; **der ~teil, -e** fraction (**im B. einer Sekunde** in a split second); **die ~zahl, -en** *math* fraction

brüchig brittle; crumbling; cracked

die **Brücke, -n** bridge (*also dent, naut*); rug; *gym* back-bend; *wrestl* bridge; **alle ~n hinter sich abbrechen** burn one's boats; (+*dat*) **goldene ~n bauen** make things easy for; **~n schlagen** (music *etc*) be a link || **der ~n|kopf, ⸚e** bridgehead; **die ~n|waage, -n** weighbridge

der **Bruder,** *pl* **Brüder** brother; *eccles* friar; *coll* 'character'; **-bruder** *coll* (*eg* **der Skat~** skat) enthusiast; fellow (skat-player *etc*); **unter Brüdern** *coll* between friends

Bruder- brotherly ...; fraternal ...; **der ~mord, -e, der ~mörder, -** fratricide; **das ~volk, ⸚er** *esp EGer* sister nation

brüderlich brotherly; **~ teilen** share and share alike

die **Bruderschaft, -en** brotherhood, fraternity

die **Brüderschaft** close friendship (marked by the use of 'du'); **~ trinken** (*celebrate the mutual decision to adopt the 'du' form of address by means of a drink*)

Brügge Bruges

Brüh-: brüh|heiß boiling hot; **die ~kartoffeln** *pl* potatoes boiled in meat stock; **brüh|warm** *coll* (news) red-hot; **die ~wurst, ⸚e** (*kind of frankfurter, heated in boiling water*)

die **Brühe, -n** broth; stock; *coll* dirty water; (= drink) dishwater; **in der ~** *coll* in the soup

brühen pour boiling water over; brew (tea, coffee)

brüllen roar; bellow; **... ist zum Brüllen** *coll* ... is a scream

Brumm-: der ~bär, -en (*wk masc*) *coll* = **der ~bart, ⸚e** *coll* grouser; **der ~baß, ⸚(ss)e** *mus* double bass; *coll* deep bass voice; **der ~kreisel, -** humming-top; **der ~schädel, -** *coll* hangover; sore head

brummeln mumble

brummen growl; mumble; *coll* do (... months *etc*); (pupil) be kept in for; (*v/i*) buzz; growl; boom; drone; (top) hum; *coll* do time; (pupil) be kept in

der **Brummer, -** *coll* buzzing insect, *esp* bluebottle; noisy big plane/truck *etc*

brummig *coll* surly

brünett, die Brünette, -n (*or decl as adj*) brunette

die **Brunft, ⸚e** rut (of deer)

brunften rut

Brünn Brno

der **Brunnen, -** well; (mineral) spring; fountain; fount (of knowledge *etc*)

die **Brunst, ⸚e** rut; heat

brunsten rut; be on heat

brünstig rutting; on heat

brüsk brusque

brüskieren snub

Brüssel Brussels

die **Brust, ⸚e** breast; chest; **schwach auf der ~ sein** *coll* have a weak chest; be short of cash; **sich in die ~ werfen** give oneself airs

Brust- breast ...; chest ...; pectoral ...; thoracic ...; mammary ...; **das ~bild, -er** half-length portrait; **die ~fell|entzündung, -en** pleurisy; **der ~kasten, ..kästen** *coll* chest; **der ~korb, ⸚e** thorax; **b~schwimmen** (*only infin*) swim the breast-stroke; **das ~schwimmen** breast-stroke; **das ~stück, -e** *cul* breast; brisket; **die ~tasche, -n** breast-pocket; **der ~ton** *mus* chest-note (**im B. der Überzeugung** with great conviction); **der ~umfang** chest measurement; **die ~warze, -n** nipple

brüsten: sich ~ boast (**mit** about)

-brüstig -breasted; -chested

die **Brüstung, -en** parapet; balustrade; (under window) breast

die **Brut, -en** brooding, incubation; brood; spawn; *coll* rabble; **der ~apparat, -e** *agr* incubator; **die ~henne, -n** brooding hen; **die ~hitze** *coll* stifling heat; **der ~kasten, ..kästen** *med* incubator; **der ~reaktor, -en** breeder reactor; **der ~schrank, ⸚e** incubator; **die ~stätte, -n** breeding-ground

brutal brutal

brutalisieren brutalize

die **Brutalität, -en** brutality

brüten plot; *tech* breed; (*v/i*) brood; **~ über** (*dat*) brood over; **~d** stifling

der **Brüter, -** breeder reactor; **schneller ~** fast breeder

brutto *comm* gross; **die B~register|tonne, -n** register ton; **das B~sozial|produkt, -e** gross national product

brutzeln *coll* fry; (*v/i*) sizzle

der **Bub, –en** (*wk masc*) *SGer* boy

der **Bube, –n** (*wk masc*) *cards* jack; *arch* rogue; **der ~n|streich, –e** prank; *arch* = **das ~n|stück, –e** knavish trick

der **Bubi|kopf, ¨–e** bobbed hair

das **Buch** [–u:–], **¨–er** book; *cin* screenplay; **ein ~ mit sieben Siegeln** a closed book; **~ führen** keep the accounts; **+über** (*acc*) keep a record of; **... wie er/sie/es im ~e steht** your typical ...; **zu ~e schlagen** prove an asset; **zu ~e stehen mit** be valued at || **der ~binder, –** book-binder; **der ~drucker, –** printer; **die ~druckerei, –en** printing; press; **die ~drucker|kunst** (art of) printing; **die ~ecker, –n** beech-nut; **der ~fink, –en** (*wk masc*) chaffinch; **~form (in B.** in book form); **die ~führung** book-keeping; **die ~gemeinschaft, –en** book-club; **der ~halter, –** book-keeper; **die ~haltung, –en** book-keeping; accounts department; **der ~handel** book-trade; **der ~händler, –** bookseller; **die ~handlung, –en** bookshop, bookstore *US*; **der ~macher, –** bookmaker; **der ~stabe** (*acc, dat* **–n**, *gen* **–ns**), **–n** letter; character; **das ~staben|rätsel, –** anagram; **b~stabieren** spell; decipher (writing); **–b~stabig** –letter; **b~stäblich** literal; **der ~weizen** buckwheat; **das ~zeichen, –** book-mark

die **Buche** [–u:–], **–n** beech

buchen [–u:–] book; record; *comm* enter (in the books); **~ als** count (a success *etc*)

Buchen– beech ...

Bücher– ... of books; book ...; **der ~abschluß, ¨–(ss)e** balancing of accounts; **das ~bord, –e** = **das ~brett, –er** bookshelf; **der ~freund, –e** = **der ~liebhaber, –** bibliophile; **die ~revision, –en** audit; **der ~revisor, –en** auditor; **der ~schrank, ¨–e** bookcase; **die ~stütze, –n** book-end; **das ~verzeichnis, –se** bibliography; **die ~wand, ¨–e** (set of) bookshelves; wall lined with bookshelves; **der ~wurm, ¨–er** bookworm

die **Bücherei** [–y:–], **–en** library

der **Buchs|baum** [–ks–], **¨–e** box

die **Buchse** [–ks–], **–n** *elect* socket; *mech* bush

die **Büchse** [–ks–], **–n** tin; can; box; rifle; *in compds* **~n–** *also* canned ...; **der ~n|macher, –** gunsmith; **der ~n|öffner, –** can-opener

die **Bucht, –en** bay; **die Deutsche ~** the German Bight

buchtig indented

die **Buchung, –en** *vbl noun*; *also* booking, reservation; *comm* entry

der **Buckel, –** (hunchback's) hump; *coll* back; **einen ~ machen** hunch one's/arch its back; **einen krummen ~ machen** *coll* bow and scrape; **viel auf dem ~ haben** *coll* have a lot on one's plate

buck(e)lig hunchbacked; hilly; (road) bumpy; **der/die Buck(e)lige** (*decl as adj*) hunchback

buckeln hump; (*v/i*) arch its back; *coll* kowtow

bücken: sich ~ bend down

der **Bückling**[1], **–e** bloater

der **Bückling**[2], **–e** *coll*, **einen ~ machen** bow

Budapest Budapest

buddeln *coll* dig

Buddha ['buda] Buddha

der **Buddhist, –en** (*wk masc*), **buddhistisch** Buddhist

die **Bude, –n** stall; hut; *coll* room; digs; 'pad'; 'dump'; 'joint'; **Leben in die ~ bringen** liven the place up || **der ~n|zauber, –** *coll* rave-up (in s.o.'s lodgings)

das **Budget** [by'dʒe:], **–s** budget

das **Büfett** [–'fe:], **–s** (*or* [–'fɛt], **–e**) sideboard; bar; counter; *Swiss* station restaurant; **kaltes ~** cold buffet

der **Büffel, –** buffalo

büffeln *coll* (*also v/i*) cram (for examination)

der **Bug, –e** *naut* bow(s); *aer* nose; (*pl also* **¨–e**) *zool* shoulder; **das ~spriet, –e** (*also* **der**) bowsprit

der **Bügel, –** hanger; stirrup; frame (of saw *etc*); ear-piece (of spectacles); *tech* bow collector; **der ~automat, –en** (*wk masc*) rotary iron; **das ~brett, –er** ironing-board; **das ~eisen, –** iron; **die ~falte, –n** crease; **b~frei** non-iron; **die ~maschine, –n** rotary iron

bügeln iron; press; *sp coll* 'thrash'

bugsieren [buks–] *naut* tow; *coll* steer

buh! boo!

Buh–: der ~mann, ¨–er *coll* scapegoat; **der ~ruf, –e** boo

buhen boo

der **Buhle, –n** (*wk masc*) *poet*, **die Buhle, –n** *poet* paramour

buhlen: ~ um court (favour)

die **Buhne, –n** groyne

die **Bühne, –n** stage; theatre; *tech* platform; **hinter der ~** behind the scenes; **über die ~ gehen** *coll* pass off; **zur ~ gehen** go on the stage || **der ~n|arbeiter, –** stage-hand; **das ~n|bild, –er** set; **der ~n|bildner, –** stage designer; **das ~n|stück, –e** stage play; **b~n|wirksam** theatrically effective (**b. sein** be good theatre)

Bukarest Bucharest

das **Bukett, –s/–e** bouquet (*also* of wine)

bukolisch bucolic

die **Bulette, –n** *esp Berlin* meat-ball

der **Bulgare, –n** (*wk masc*) Bulgarian

Bulgarien [–ĭən] Bulgaria

bulgarisch, (*language*) **B~** Bulgarian

Bull–: das ~auge, –n porthole; **die ~dogge, –n** bulldog; **der ~dozer** [–zɐ], – bulldozer

der **Bulle, –n** (*wk masc*) bull; *coll* cop; hulk (of a man); *coll mil* big shot

die **Bulle, –n** (papal) bull

Bullen–: der ~beißer, – bulldog; *coll* bad-tempered character; **die ~hitze** *coll* sweltering heat

bullern *coll* (fire) roar; bubble (noisily); rage; **~ gegen** pound on

das **Bulletin** [byl'tɛ̃:], **–s** bulletin

bullig *coll* brawny; sweltering

bum! [–ʊ–] boom!

der **Bumerang, –e/–s** boomerang

der **Bummel, –** stroll; pub-crawl; **einen ~ machen** go for a stroll/pub-crawl || **das ~leben** idle life; **der ~streik, –s** go-slow, slowdown *US*; **der ~zug, ⸚e** *coll* slow train

der **Bummelant, –en** (*wk masc*) *coll* dawdler; idler

bumm(e)lig *coll* slow; lackadaisical

bummeln dawdle; loaf about; (*sn*) stroll; **~ gehen** go on a pub-crawl

der **Bummler, –** stroller; dawdler

bums! thud!

der **Bums, –e** *coll* bump; 'hop'; = **das ~lokal, –e** *coll* low dive

bumsen *footb* slam (into net); *coll* 'screw'; (*v/i*) bump; 'screw'; **~ an** (*acc*)/**gegen** pound on; (*sn*) bang against; **~ auf** (*acc*) (*sn*) thud onto; **es bumst** there is a bang/crash

das **Bund, –e** bundle; bunch

der **Bund, ⸚e** bond; association; alliance; confederation; *tail, dressm* waistband; *mus* fret; *bibl* covenant; **(der ~)** the Federal Government; *coll* (*with prep*) the *Bundeswehr*; **der Alte/Neue ~** the Old/New Testament; **im ~e mit** in league with

das **Bündel, –** bundle; bunch; *math, phys* pencil

bündeln tie into bundles/a bundle

Bundes– federal ...; Federal ... (*can often in practice be translated by* West German, Austrian *or* Swiss *according to context*);

der ~anwalt, ⸚e Federal Prosecutor; **die ~bahn(en** *in Austria, Switzerland*) Federal Railway(s); **der ~bruder, ..brüder** fellow-member of a *Verbindung*; **der ~bürger, –** West German (citizen); **b~deutsch** West German; **~ebene (auf B.** at Federal level); **b~eigen** Federal; **die ~feier** Swiss national holiday (*Aug.1st*); **das ~gebiet** (territory of) the Federal Republic/*Aust* the Republic; **der ~genosse, –n** (*wk masc*) ally; **der ~gerichts|hof** the (West German) Supreme Court; **der ~grenz|schutz** the (West German) Federal Border Police (*supraregional paramilitary force with responsibilities in the areas of border policing and internal security*); **das ~haus** (*W. German, Swiss parliament buildings*); **das ~heer** the Austrian Armed Forces; **die ~hymne** the Austrian national anthem; **der ~kanzler, –** (Federal) Chancellor; **das ~kanzler|amt** the Federal Chancellery; **das ~kriminal|amt** the Federal Criminal Investigation Bureau; **die ~lade** the Ark of the Covenant; **das ~land, ⸚er** (*Austria*) province; (*W. Germany*) Land; **die ~post** the Federal (= W. German) Post Office; **der ~präsident, –en** (*wk masc*) (*Austria, W. Germany*) (Federal) President; (*Switzerland*) President of the Bundesrat; **der ~rat, ⸚e** the Bundesrat (*in Austria, W. Germany: upper house of parliament, representing the provinces and Länder respectively; in Switzerland: the government*); *Aust, Swiss* member of the Bundesrat; **die ~regierung** the (West German, Austrian) Federal Government; **die ~republik, –en** federal republic (*usu* = **die ~republik Deutschland** the Federal Republic of Germany (*official title of* West Germany)); **b~republikanisch** West German; **der ~staat, –en** federal state; state (*eg* of U.S.A.); **die ~straße, –n** Federal highway (*cf* A-class road in U.K.); **der ~tag** the Bundestag (*lower house of the W. German parliament*); **der ~tags|präsident** (*wk masc*) President (= Speaker) of the Bundestag; **die ~tags|wahl, –en** Federal election; **der ~trainer** West German team manager; **das ~verfassungs|gericht** the Federal Constitutional Court; **die ~versammlung** the Federal Assembly (*in Austria: joint session of the Nationalrat and Bundesrat; in Switzerland: parliament; in W.Germany: body convened to elect the President*); **die ~wehr** the (West German) Armed Forces; **b~weit** nationwide

bündig succinct; conclusive; *build* flush

das **Bündnis, –se** alliance

der **Bungalow** ['bʊŋgalo], **–s** bungalow

der **Bunker, –** bunker; air-raid shelter

bunt coloured; colourful; multi-coloured; (colour) bright, gay; (cow) spotted; varied, (crowd) motley; confused; **~er Abend** social (with entertainments); **~e Platte** selection of cold meats; **in ~er Reihe** with men and women sitting alternately; **es zu ~ treiben** go too far; **jetzt wird's mir zu ~!** that's too much!

Bunt– coloured ...; **b~bemalt** painted in bright colours; **b~farbig** brightly-coloured; **b~gefiedert** with bright plumage; **b~gefleckt** spotted; **b~gemischt** varied; **b~gestreift** with coloured stripes; **das ~metall, –e** non-ferrous metal; **b~scheckig** spotted; **b~schillernd** iridescent; **der ~specht, –e** great spotted woodpecker; **der ~stift, –e** crayon; **die ~wäsche** *pl* coloureds

die **Buntheit** colourfulness; variety

die **Bürde, –n** burden

der **Bure, –n** (*wk masc*) Boer; **der ~n|krieg** the Boer War

die **Burg, –en** castle; *zool* (beaver's) lodge; **der ~friede(n)** (*acc, dat* **..en**, *gen* **..ens**), **..en** *pol* truce; **der ~graben, ..gräben** moat; **das ~verlies, –e** dungeon

der **Bürge, –n** (*wk masc*) guarantor; **~ sein für** vouch for; be a guarantee of

bürgen: ~ für vouch for; be a guarantee of; *fin* stand surety for

der **Bürger, –** citizen; member of the middle classes; bourgeois; **der ~** (*generalizing*) the public

Bürger– *also* civic ...; **die ~initiative, –n** (citizens') action-group; **der ~krieg, –e** civil war; **die ~kunde** civics; **der ~meister, –** mayor; **das ~recht, –e** citizenship; (*esp pl*) civic rights; **der ~rechtler, –** civil rights campaigner; **der ~schreck** bête noire (of society); **der ~sinn** public spirit; **der ~steig, –e** pavement, sidewalk *US*

bürgerlich civic; civil; middle-class; bourgeois (*EGer* = *esp* western, capitalist); (cooking) plain; **B~es Gesetzbuch** German Civil Code; **der/die Bürgerliche** (*decl as adj*) commoner

die **Bürgerschaft** citizens; (Bremen, Hamburg) City Parliament

das **Bürgertum** middle classes, bourgeoisie

die **Bürgschaft, –en** *leg* surety; **~ leisten für** vouch for; *leg* stand surety for

Burgund Burgundy

der **Burgunder, –** Burgundian; = **der ~wein, –e** burgundy

burgundisch Burgundian

burisch Boer

burlesk farcical

die **Burleske, –n** farce

Burma *esp EGer, Swiss* Burma

der **Burmese, –n** (*wk masc*) *esp EGer, Swiss* Burmese

burmesisch, (*language*) **B~** *esp EGer, Swiss* Burmese

das **Büro, –s** office; **–büro** *also* ... agency; **der/die ~angestellte** (*decl as adj*) office-worker; **der ~bedarf** office equipment; **die ~klammer, –n** paper-clip; **die ~stunden** *pl* office hours

der **Bürokrat, –en** (*wk masc*) bureaucrat

die **Bürokratie, –(ie)n** bureaucracy

bürokratisch bureaucratic

bürokratisieren bureaucratize

der **Bürokratismus** red tape

der **Bursche, –n** (*wk masc*) young man; lad; fellow, guy; *univ* full member of a *Verbindung*; *mil arch* orderly; **übler ~** bad lot

die **Burschenschaft, –en** students' association

burschikos casual; (female) hearty

die **Bürste, –n** brush; *coll* crew-cut

bürsten brush

der **Bürsten|schnitt, –e** crew-cut

der **Bürzel, –** *ornith* rump; *cul* parson's nose

der **Bus** [–ʊ–] (*gen* **–ses**), **–se** bus; coach; **die ~halte|stelle, –n** bus/coach-stop

der **Busch, ⸚e** bush; bunch of flowers; **der ~** *geog* the bush; **auf den ~ klopfen bei** *coll* sound out || **die ~bohne, –n** dwarf bean; **der ~mann, ⸚er** Bushman; **das ~werk** bushes; scrub

das **Büschel, –** bunch; cluster; tuft; wisp

buschig bushy

der **Busen, –** bosom; **b~frei** topless; **der ~freund, –e** bosom-friend

busig *coll* bosomy; **–busig** –bosomed

Buß– [–uː–] penitential ...; **b~fertig** penitent; **das ~geld, –er** fine; **die ~übung, –en** act of penance; **(der) ~- und Bettag** Day of Prayer and Repentance

der **Bussard, –e** buzzard

die **Buße, –n** *eccles* penance; *leg* damages; *esp Swiss* fine

büßen: ~ (für) atone for, *eccles* do penance for; pay (the penalty) for; **~ mit** *Swiss* fine (s.o. sth.); **schwer ~ müssen für** pay heavily for

der **Büßer, –** penitent; **das ~hemd, –en** hair shirt

das **Busserl, –(n), busserln** *SGer coll* kiss

die **Bussole, –n** (mariner's) compass

die **Büste, –n** bust; *tail* tailor's dummy; **der ~n|halter, –** bra

die **Busuki, –s** bouzouki

das **Butan** butane

der **Butt, –e** flounder

die **Bütte, –n** tub; vat; **die ~n|rede, –n** carnival oration

die **Butter** butter; **alles in ~!** everything's fine! || **die ~blume, –n** buttercup; dandelion; **das ~brot, –e** slice of bread and butter ((+*dat*) **aufs B. schmieren** *coll* rub sth. in; **für ein B.** *coll* for a mere pittance; for a song); **das ~brot|papier** greaseproof paper; **die ~dose, –n** butter-dish; **das ~faß, ⸚(ss)er** butter-churn; **die ~milch** buttermilk; **die ~seite, –n** buttered side (of slice); bright side (**auf die B. fallen** *coll* fall on one's feet); **butter|weich** very soft

buttern butter; (*v/i*) make butter; **~ in** (*acc*) *coll* put (money) into

der **Butze|mann, ⸚er** bogeyman

b.w. (= **bitte wenden**) P.T.O.

byzantinisch Byzantine

Byzanz Byzantium

bzgl. (= **bezüglich**) with reference to

bzw. (= **beziehungsweise**) or (... respectively)

C

[das] **C** [tseː] (*gen, pl* –, *coll* [tseːs]) C; **das c, C** *mus* (the note) C; (*key*) **C** C major, **c** C minor; **C** *phys* (= **Celsius**) C
ca. (= **circa**) approx.
[das] **Café**, **–s** café
[der] **Camion** ['kamiõ], **–s** *Swiss* van; (small) lorry, truck *US*
campen ['kɛm–] (go) camp(ing)
[der] **Camper** ['kɛm–], – camper
[das] **Camping** ['kɛm–] camping; **der ~platz, ⸗e** camp-site; **der ~wagen, –** motor caravan, camper
[der] **Cañon** ['kanjɔn, kan'joːn], **–s** canyon
[das] **Cape** [keːp], **–s** cape
[der] **Car, –s** *Swiss* = **Autocar**
Cäsar ['tsɛː–], (*title*) **der ~, –(ar)en** (*wk masc*) Caesar
[das] **Cäsium** caesium
catchen ['kɛtʃn̩] do catch-as-catch-can wrestling
[der] **Catcher** ['kɛtʃɐ], – catch-as-catch-can wrestler
Catull Catullus
[die] **CDU** = **Christlich-Demokratische Union**
[der] **Cellist** [tʃ–], **–en** (*wk masc*) cellist
[das] **Cello** [tʃ–], **–s/Celli** cello
[das] **Cellophan** [ts–] (*trade-mark*) cellophane
Celsius ['tsɛlzĭʊs] Celsius, centigrade
[der] **Cembalist** [tʃ–], **–en** (*wk masc*) harpsichordist
[das] **Cembalo** [tʃ–], **–s/–(l)i** harpsichord
[der] **Cercle** ['sɛrkl̩], **–s** *Aust* front stalls
[das] **ces, Ces** [tsɛs] (*gen* –), – *mus* (the note) C flat; (*key*) **Ces** C flat major, **ces** C flat minor
[die] **Cevennen** [se–] *pl* the Cévennes
cg = **Zentigramm**
[das] **Chamäleon** [k–, –ɔn], **–s** chameleon
chamois [ʃa'mŏa] (*indecl*) chamois
[der] **Champagner** [ʃam'panjɐ], – champagne
[der] **Champignon** ['ʃampɪnjɔŋ], **–s** mushroom
[das] **Championat** [ʃampĭ–], **–e** championship
[die] **Chance** ['ʃãːsə], **–n** chance, opportunity; (*pl*) prospects; **keine ~n haben** not stand a chance; **die ~n stehen 10 zu 1** the odds are 10 to 1 || **die ~n|gleichheit** equality of opportunity
changierend [ʃãʒ–] *text* shot
[das] **Chanson** [ʃã'sõː], **–s** (political *or* satirical) song
[das] **Chaos** ['kaːɔs] (*gen* –) chaos
[der] **Chaot** [ka–], **–en** (*wk masc*) anarchical element
chaotisch [ka–] chaotic
[der] **Charakter** [k–], **–(er)e** character (*also theat*); **c~fest** of firm character; **c~los** unprincipled; characterless; **der ~zug, ⸗e** characteristic
charakterisieren [k–] characterize
[die] **Charakteristik** [k–, –ɪk], **–en** characterization; *math* characteristic
[das] **Charakteristikum** [k–], **–(k)a** characteristic
charakteristisch [k–] characteristic (**für** of)
charakterlich [k–] of character; (qualities) personal; ~ (**einwandfrei** *etc*) of (impeccable *etc*) character
[die] **Charge** ['ʃarʒə], **–n** *mil etc* rank; *theat* minor character part; *tech* charge (of furnace)
[das] **Charisma** ['çaːrɪsma, ça'rɪsma], **–(m)en** charisma
charismatisch [ça–] charismatic
Charkow ['çarkɔf] Kharkov
charmant [ʃ–] charming
[der] **Charme** [ʃarm] charm
[der] **Charmeur** [ʃar'møːɐ], **–e** charmer
[die] **Charta** [k–], **–s** charter
Charter– ['(t)ʃartɐ–] charter …
chartern ['(t)ʃartɐn] charter; hire
[das] **Chassis** [ʃa'siː] (*gen* – [–(s)]), – [–s] chassis
Chatschaturjan [x–] Khachaturian
[der] **Chauffeur** [ʃɔ'føːɐ], **–e** chauffeur; driver (of taxi); *Swiss* driver
chauffieren [ʃɔf–] drive
[die] **Chaussee** [ʃɔ–], **–(ee)n** highway
[der] **Chauvi** ['ʃoːvi], **–s** *coll* male chauvinist pig
[der] **Chauvinismus** [ʃo–] chauvinism
[der] **Chauvinist** [ʃo–], **–en** (*wk masc*), **chauvinistisch** chauvinist; male chauvinist
[der] **Check** [ʃ–], **–s** *Swiss* cheque, check *US*
Check– [tʃ–]: **die ~liste, –n** check-list
checken [tʃ–] check
[der] **Chef** [ʃɛf], **–s** head; chief; boss; leader (of gang); *in compds* chief …; **der ~redakteur, –e** editor(-in-chief)
[die] **Chemie** [ç–] chemistry; *in compds* chemical …; **die ~faser, –n** man-made fibre
[die] **Chemikalien** [ç–, –ĭən] *pl* chemicals
[der] **Chemiker** ['çeː–], – chemist (*not* = pharmacist)
chemisch [ç–] chemical; **~e Reinigung** dry cleaning
chemisieren [ç–] *EGer* make intensive use of chemistry in

der **Chemo|techniker** [ç–], – technician (in chemical laboratory)

–chen (*pl* –) *diminutive suffix* (*making noun neuter and usually causing stem-vowel to be mutated where possible*) little ..., *eg* **das Lämm~** little lamb (**Lamm** = lamb); *nouns in* **–e** *or* **–en** *lose these endings before* **–chen,** *eg* **das Schürz~** little apron (**Schürze** = apron), **das Fäd~** little thread (**Faden** = thread)

---

der **Cherub** ['çe:rʊp], **–im** [–rubi:m]/**–inen** [çerub–] cherub
cherubinisch [ç–] cherubic
chevaleresk [ʃəvalə–] chivalrous
chic [ʃɪk] = **schick**
der **Chicorée** ['ʃɪ–] (*also* **die**) chicory
der **Chiffon** ['ʃɪfɔ̃], **–s** chiffon
die **Chiffre** ['ʃɪfrə, –fʁ], **–n** character (of cipher); box-number; symbol (**für** of); **die ~schrift, –en** cipher
chiffrieren [ʃ–] encipher; **chiffriert** in cipher
Chile ['tʃi:le] Chile
der **Chilene** [tʃ–], **–n** (*wk masc*), **chilenisch** Chilean
China [ç–] China; **der ~kohl** Chinese cabbage
der **Chinese** [ç–], **–n** (*wk masc*) Chinese
chinesisch [ç–] Chinese; **die C~e Mauer** the Great Wall of China; **das C~e Meer** the China Sea; **C~** Chinese (*language*); **–chinesisch** (*eg* **das Partei~** party) jargon
chinesisch– Sino–; (dictionary) Chinese–
das **Chinin** [ç–] quinine
der **Chip** [tʃɪp], **–s** chip (in gambling or = microchip); (potato) crisp/chip *US*
der **Chirurg** [ç–], **–en** (*wk masc*) surgeon
die **Chirurgie** [ç–], **–(ie)n** surgery; surgical unit
chirurgisch [ç–] surgical
das **Chlor** [kl–] chlorine; **die ~säure** chloric acid; **der ~wasser|stoff** hydrogen chloride
chloren [kl–] chlorinate
das **Chlorid** [kl–], **–e** chloride
chlorieren [kl–] chlorinate
chlorig [kl–] chlorous
das **Chloroform** [kl–], **chloroformieren** chloroform
das **Chlorophyll** [kl–] chlorophyll
der **Choke** [tʃo:k], **–s** = **der Choker** ['tʃo:kʁ], – choke
die **Cholera** ['ko:–] cholera
der **Choleriker** [k–], – irascible person
cholerisch [k–] choleric
das **Cholesterin** [ç–] cholesterol; **der ~spiegel,** – cholesterol level
der **Chor** [k–], **¨–e** *mus* choir; section (of orchestra); unison strings; (= piece of music) chorus; *theat* chorus; (*pl also* **–e**) *archit* choir; organ gallery; **im ~** in chorus
Chor– choir ...; choral ...; **das ~gestühl** choir-stalls; **der ~knabe, –n** (*wk masc*) choirboy; **der ~sänger,** – member of a choir
der **Choral** [k–], **¨–e** chorale; Gregorian chant
der **Choreograph** [k–], **–en** (*wk masc*) choreographer
die **Choreographie** [k–] choreography
choreographieren [k–] choreograph
choreographisch [k–] choreographic
chorisch [k–] choral
die **Chose** ['ʃo:zə], **–n** *coll* business
Christ [kr–] (*in hymns*) Christ
der **Christ** [kr–], **–en** (*wk masc*) Christian; *in compds* Christmas ...; **der ~baum, ¨–e** *esp SGer* Christmas tree; **der ~demokrat, –en** (*wk masc*), **c~demokratisch** Christian Democrat; **das ~kind** the infant Jesus; *esp SGer*, *approx* = Santa Claus; **c~sozial** (of the) C.S.U.; **der ~stollen,** – Yule loaf
Christen– Christian ...; **die ~verfolgung, –en** persecution of the Christians
die **Christenheit** Christendom
das **Christentum** Christianity
christianisieren [kr–] Christianize
christlich [kr–] Christian; (*adv*) as/like a Christian
Christophorus [kr–] St Christopher
Christus [kr–] (*gen* **Christi**) Christ
das **Chrom** [kr–] chrome; chromium
die **Chromatik** [kr–, –ɪk] *phys* chromatics; *mus* chromaticism
chromatisch [kr–] chromatic
das **Chromosom** [kr–], **–en** chromosome
die **Chronik** ['kro:nɪk], **–en** chronicle
chronisch [kr–] chronic
der **Chronist** [kr–], **–en** (*wk masc*) chronicler
die **Chronologie** [kr–] chronology
chronologisch [kr–] chronological
das **Chronometer** [kr–], – chronometer
die **Chrysantheme** [kr–], **–n** chrysanthemum
die **Chuzpe** ['xʊtspə] *coll* 'cheek', chutzpah
Cicero ['tsi:tsero] Cicero
circa [ts–] approximately
der **Circulus vitiosus** ['tsɪrkulʊs vi'tsĭo:zʊs], **–(l)i –(s)i** vicious circle
das **cis, Cis** [tsɪs] (*gen* –), – *mus* (the note) C sharp; (*key*) **Cis** C sharp major, **cis** C sharp minor
die **City** ['sɪti], **–s** city-centre
der **Clan** [klɛn], **–s** clan
clever ['klɛvʁ] clever, smart; skilful
die **Cleverness (–neß)** [–nɛs] cleverness; skill
der **Clip, –s** clip; = **der Clips** (*gen* **–es**), **–e** clip-on earring
die **Clique** ['klɪkə], **–n** clique; group, set (of friends); **das ~n|wesen** = **die ~n|wirtschaft** cliquism
der **Clou** [klu:], **–s** highlight; climax
der **Clown** [klaʊn], **–s** clown

die **Clownerie** [klaʊnə–] clowning (about)
cm (= **Zentimeter**) cm.
das **Cockpit, –s** cockpit
der **Cocktail** [–teːl], **–s** cocktail; cocktail party; *EGer* reception
der **Code** [koːt], **–s** code (*also comput*)
codieren *comput* (en)code
der **Coiffeur** [kŏa'føːɐ], **–e, die Coiffeuse** [–'føːzə], **–n** *Swiss* hairdresser
die **Cola, –s** *coll* Coke
die **Collage** [–ʒə], **–n** collage
das **Comeback** [kam'bɛk], **–s** comeback; **ein ~ feiern** make a comeback
Comer: der ~ See Lake Como
die **Comics** ['kɔmɪks] *pl* comic strips
der **Computer** [kɔm'pjuːtɐ], **–** computer; **c~gesteuert** computer-operated; **der ~satz** computer typesetting
computerisieren [kɔmpjutə–] computerize
der **Conférencier** [kɔ̃ferã'sĭeː], **–s** compère; master of ceremonies
der **Container** [kɔn'teːnɐ], **–** container; skip
die **Contenance** [kɔ̃tə'nãːs(ə)] composure
Contergan (*trade-mark*) Thalidomide
die **Contradictio in adjecto** [kɔntra'dɪktsĭo ɪn at'jɛkto] contradiction in terms
der **Contratenor, ⸚e** counter-tenor
der **Corner** ['kɔrnɐ], **–** *Aust sp* corner
die **Couch** [kaʊtʃ], **–(e)s/–en** couch; **die ~garnitur, –en** three-piece suite; **der ~tisch, –e** coffee-table
die **Couleur** [ku'løːɐ], **–s** *univ* colours (of a *Verbindung*); *cards* trump; **... jeder** *etc* **~** ... of every *etc* type/hue
der **Countdown** ['kaʊnt'daʊn], **–s** (*also* **das**) countdown
das **Coupé** [ku'peː], **–s** *mot* coupé; *Aust, Swiss rail* compartment
der **Coupon** [ku'pɔ̃ː], **–s** coupon; length of material
die **Courage** [ku'raːʒə] courage; **Angst vor der eigenen ~ bekommen** get cold feet
couragiert [kuraʒ–] courageous
die **Courtage** [kʊr'taːʒə], **–n** brokerage
der **Cousin** [ku'zɛ̃ː], **–s, die Cousine** [ku–], **–n** cousin
der **Crack** [krɛk], **–s** ace; top racehorse
creme [kreːm, krɛːm] *indecl* cream
die **Creme** [kreːm, krɛːm], **–s** (skin) cream; *cul* whip; cream (filling); **die ~ der Gesellschaft** the cream of society
die **Crew** [kruː], **–s** crew; cadets of the same year
der **Croupier** [kru'pĭeː], **–s** croupier
die **Crux** trouble; difficulty
die **ČSSR** [tʃeːˀɛsˀɛs'ˀɛr] Czechoslovakia
die **CSU** = **Christlich-Soziale Union**
cum grano salis with a pinch of salt
der **Cup** [kap], **–s** *sp* cup
das **Curry** ['kœri], **–s** curry (= dish); (*also* **der**) = **das ~pulver, –** curry(-powder); **die ~wurst, ⸚e** (*fried sausage with ketchup and curry*)
der **Cut(away)** ['kœt(əve)], **–s** morning coat
cutten ['katn̩] *cin etc* cut, edit
der **Cutter** ['katɐ], **–** *cin etc* editor
der **CVJM** (= **Christlicher Verein Junger Männer**) Y.M.C.A.

D

[das] **D** [deː] (*gen, pl* –, *coll* [deːs]) D; **das d, D** *mus* (the note) D; (*key*) **D** D major, **d** D minor

da 1 *adv* there; here; then; (*linking two events*) when; (be right *etc*) about that, there; (*circumstances*) then, (*consequence*) so; *or expressed by* that (*eg* **was sagen Sie ~?** what's that you're saying?); **... ist** *etc* **~** *also* ... has *etc* come; **der/die/das ~** that one; **~ und ~** at such and such a place; **~ und dort** here and there; now and then; **und ~ (überlegst du noch lange?** *etc*) and yet (you still hesitate? *etc*); **wieder ~** back (again); **~, wo ...** where ...;

2 *conj* as, since; *or – where the subject is also the subject of the main clause – often expressed by a pres/part construction* (*eg* **~ er blind war, hat er sie nicht gesehen** being blind he didn't see her, **~ ich wußte, daß ...** knowing that ...); **~ ... doch** when (= considering that);

3 *rel adv* (*in literary style*) (moment *etc*) when; (place, case) where

d. Ä. (= **der Ältere**) the Elder

da– (dar–) + *prep* (*see p. xxvii and the individual entries concerned*)

1 ... it/them; ... that/those (*eg* **dafür** for *etc** it/them/that/those; **darüber** over *etc** it/them/that/those)

For the full range of possible translations of the prepositional element see the preposition concerned* (*eg* **für, über) *or – where appropriate – the relevant verb or adjective entry* (*eg for* **stolz dar*auf*** proud *of* it *see* **stolz** proud (**auf** *acc* of), *for* **es hängt da*von* ab** it depends *on* it *see* **abhängen von** depend on, *for* **ich rechne da*mit*** I'm expecting it *see* **rechnen mit** expect);

da ... für/über *etc*: *in North German colloquial usage these forms may be divided, eg* **da weiß ich nichts von** I know nothing about that;

2 *arch* ... which (*eg* **darin** in which); *see note at* 1 *regarding possible translations of the prepositional element*;

3 (+**daß ..., ob** *etc* **...** *or* **zu** + *infinitive*): *the particle* **da–** *is also used to anticipate a following noun clause with* **daß, ob,** *etc or a construction with* **zu** + *infinitive*; *the constructions are translated as follows*:

(*a*) (*with* **daß**-*clause*): *the appropriate preposition* + the fact that *or* + *gerund* (...ing) (*eg* **ich machte ihn *darauf* aufmerksam, daß es regnete** I drew his attention *to the fact that* it was raining, **ihre Enttäuschung *darüber*, daß sie übergangen wurde** her disappointment *at* be*ing* passed over);

(*b*) (*with* **ob, was, wie,** *etc*): **da–** *element untranslated* (*eg* **wir haben noch nicht *darüber* entschieden, ob ...** we haven't yet decided *on* whether ..., **wir sind uns *darin* einig, wie ...** we are in agreement *on* how ...);

(*c*) (*with* **zu** +*infinitive*): *the appropriate preposition* + *gerund* (...ing), *with* **da–** *element untranslated* (*eg* **er träumte *davon*, Oberitalien zu erobern** he dreamt *of* conquer*ing* Northern Italy, **ich warnte ihn *davor*, es zu tun** I warned him *against* do*ing* it), *or* (**dazu zu ...**) to + *infinitive* (*eg* **sie brachte ihn *dazu*, seinen Job aufzugeben** she got him *to* give up his job)

dabehalten* (*sep*) keep

dabei (*emph* **dabei**) with it/them; (arising) from it; (happy) about it; there (= present); here (= in this connection); in/when doing so; at the same time; in the process; in the course of it; at it; moreover; yet; **nahe ~** nearby; **~ sein zu ...** be about to ...; be in the act/process of (+*ger*); **es ist nichts ~** there's no harm in it; there's nothing to it; **was ist schon ~?** what of it? (*see also* **bleiben**) || **~bleiben*** (*sep*; *sn*) stay; stick at it/with it; **~haben*** (*sep*) have on/with one; **~sein*** (*sep*; *sn*) be there; be involved (**ich bin ~! I'm** game!); **~stehen*** (*sep*) stand by

dableiben* (*sep*; *sn*) stay

da capo encore (*cf* **Dakapo**)

[das] **Dach, ⸚er** roof; **eins aufs ~ bekommen** *coll* get a crack on the nut; get it in the neck; (+*dat*) **eins aufs ~ geben** *coll* give (s.o.) a crack on the nut; = (+*dat*) **aufs ~ steigen** *coll* haul over the coals; **unter ~ und Fach** safely under cover; completed; signed and sealed; **unter ~ und Fach bringen** get (sth.) safely under cover; complete; wrap up (deal *etc*) || **der ~boden, ..böden** loft; **der ~decker, –** tiler; slater; thatcher; **das ~fenster, –** skylight; **die ~gesellschaft, –en** holding company; **die ~kammer, –n** garret; **die**

~organisation, -en umbrella organization; die ~pfanne, -n pantile; die ~rinne, -n gutter; ~schaden coll (einen D. haben not be quite right in the head); das ~stroh thatch; die ~stube, -n garret; der ~stuhl, ⸚e roof truss; die ~terrassen|wohnung, -en penthouse; der ~verband, ⸚e umbrella organization; der ~ziegel, - tile

der Dachs [-ks], -e badger; junger ~ coll (inexperienced) young fellow

dachte (dächte) p/t (subj) of denken

der Dackel, - dachshund

dadurch (emph dadurch; see da-) through it/them/that/those; by this means, this/that way; by it; thereby; arch through/by (means of) which; ~, daß ... because ...; by (+ger)

dafür (emph dafür; see da-) for it/them/that/those; in favour (of it/them); instead; in return; on the other hand; but then; arch for which; for ~ followed by a noun clause (daß ..., ob ..., etc) see da- 3; dafür, daß ... considering ... || ~halten* (sep) be of the opinion (nach meinem D. in my estimation); ~können* (sep) coll (ich kann nichts ~ I can't help it; it's not my fault); ~stehen* (sep) Aust coll (es steht dafür zu ... it's worthwhile (+ ger))

dagegen (emph dagegen; see da-) against it/them/that/those; in exchange; by comparison; on the other hand; arch against which; for ~ followed by a daß-clause see da- 3(a); etwas ~ haben object (to it), mind; ich habe nichts ~ I don't mind; etwas ~ tun do something about it || ~halten* (sep) compare with it/them; object (that ...)

dagewesen p/part of dasein

dahaben* (sep) have (at one's disposal); have here/there

daheim SGer at home; ~ sein in (dat) come from

das Daheim SGer home

daher (emph daher) from there; (daher) that is where ... from; hence; therefore; that is why; arch (daher) whence; von ~ from there; daher kommt es, daß ... that is why ...; es kommt daher, daß/weil ... it's because ...

daher- sep pref: (i) ... away (eg ~filmen film away); (ii) ... along (esp in construction daherge... (eg dahergelaufen) kommen come ...ing (eg running) along (see the simple verb, eg laufen)); ~gelaufen who has turned up from nowhere; ~kommen* (sep; sn) come along; ~reden (sep) say (without thinking); talk (nonsense); (v/i) talk away (without thinking)

dahin (emph dahin) there (= to that place); to that; in that direction; to that effect; ~, daß ... to the effect that ...; (agree) that ...; bis dahin until/by then; that far; ~ sein have gone; coll have had it

dahin- sep pref: (i) ... along (eg ~rasen tear along); (ii) ... away (eg ~siechen waste away); ~dämmern be in a semi-conscious state; (sn) fade away; dahingegen on the other hand; ~gehen* (sn) walk along/past; pass away; (time) pass; dahingehend to that effect (d., daß ... to the effect that ...; (agree) that ...); ~gestellt (es bleibt/sei d., ob ... it is an open question whether ...; it remains to be seen whether ...; es d. sein lassen, ob ... leave it open whether ...); ~leben live from day to day; ~raffen (epidemic etc) carry off; ~schwinden* (sn) dwindle away; fade away; (years etc) slip by; ~siechen (sn) waste away; ~stehen* (es steht dahin, ob ... it is an open question whether ...); ~vegetieren vegetate

dahinten (emph dahinten) back/over there

dahinter (emph dahinter; see da-) behind (it/them/that/those); beyond; arch behind which; da ist etwas ~ there's something in it || ~knien (sep): sich d. coll put one's back into it; ~kommen* (sep; sn) coll find out (about sth.); ~stecken (sep) coll be behind it; ~stehen* (sep) be behind it, back it; underlie it

dahinterher coll: ~ sein make a real effort

die Dahlie [-ĭə], -n dahlia

das Dakapo, -s encore (cf da capo)

die Daktylo, -s Swiss typist

der Daktylus, -(yl)en dactyl

dalassen* (sep) leave (there)

daliegen* (sep) lie (there)

dalli: ~ (~)! make it snappy!

Dalmatien [-tsĭən] Dalmatia

der Dalmatiner, - Dalmatian (also = dog)

dalmatinisch Dalmatian

Dam- [-a-]: der ~hirsch, -e fallow deer; das ~wild fallow deer (collect)

damalig of/at that time; then

damals then, at that time

Damaskus Damascus

der Damast, -e damask

das Dämchen, - precocious young lady; tart

die Dame, -n lady; draughts, checkers US; cards, chess queen; draughts/US checkers king; meine ~n und Herren! ladies and gentlemen! || das ~brett, -er draughtboard, checkerboard US; das ~spiel, -e (game of) draughts, checkers US

Damen- lady's ...; ladies' ...; die ~binde, -n sanitary towel/napkin US; der ~friseur, -e ladies' hairdresser; ~sitz (im D. sidesaddle); die ~wahl ladies' choice; die ~wäsche lingerie; die ~welt the ladies

damenhaft ladylike

damisch SGer coll daft; giddy; (adv) awfully

damit 1 *adv* (*emph* **damit;** *see* **da–**) with it/them/that/those; (mean) by it/that; thereby; thus; *arch* with which; **(damit)** with that, thereupon; whereby; 2 *conj* in order that/to; *for* ~ *followed by a noun clause etc* (**ob … etc**) *see* **da–** 3; **~, daß …** by (+*ger*) (*and see also* **da–** 3(*a*)); **~ sieht es schlecht aus** things look bad; **~ hat sich's** *coll* that's the end of that; **her ~!** give me that/those!

der **Dämlack, –s/–e** *coll* fathead

dämlich *coll* silly, stupid

der **Damm, ⸚e** embankment; dike; causeway; *esp Berlin* roadway; *med* perineum; *naut* jetty; **wieder auf den ~ bringen** *coll* put back on his/her feet; **nicht auf dem ~** *coll* out of sorts; **wieder auf dem ~** *coll* back on one's feet

Dämm–: der ~stoff, –e insulating material

dämmen dam; check

Dämmer–: das ~licht half-light; twilight; **der ~schlaf** light sleep; **der ~schoppen, –** 'sundowner' (= drink); **die ~stunde, –n** twilight; **der ~zustand, ⸚e** semi-conscious state; state between waking and sleeping

dämm(e)rig dim; dusky; (day) gloomy; **es wird ~** dusk is falling; dawn is breaking

dämmern: es dämmert day is breaking; it is getting dark; (+*dat*/**bei**) *coll* dawn on; **der Morgen dämmert** day is breaking; **der Abend dämmert** it is getting dark; **vor sich hin ~** be in a semi-conscious state

die **Dämmerung, –en** twilight; dawn; dusk

das **Damokles|schwert** [–ɛs–] sword of Damocles

der **Dämon** ['dɛːmɔn], **–(on)en** demon; demonic force

die **Dämonie** demonic force/nature

dämonisch demonic

der **Dampf, ⸚e** steam; vapour; **~ haben vor** (*dat*) be scared of; (+*dat*) **~ machen** *coll* tell (s.o.) to get a move on; **~ dahinter machen/setzen** *coll* get things moving || **der ~koch|topf, ⸚e** pressure-cooker; **die ~maschine, –n** steam-engine; **das ~schiff, –e** steamship; **die ~schiffahrt** steam navigation; **die ~walze, –n** steam-roller

dampfen (*sn if indicating motion*) steam

dämpfen (*see also* **gedämpft**) muffle; tone down; soften; cushion (blow); restrain (person), damp(en) (enthusiasm); press with a damp cloth/steam-iron; *cul* steam

der **Dampfer, –** steamship; **auf dem falschen ~ sein/sitzen** *coll* have got the wrong idea

der **Dämpfer, –** *mus* damper; mute; *cul* steamer; (+*dat*) **einen ~ aufsetzen** *coll* take down a peg or two; put a damper on

danach (*emph* **danach;** *see* **da–**) after/according to/in accordance with *etc* it/them/that/those; afterwards; accordingly; *arch* after *etc* which; *for* ~ *followed by a noun clause* (**ob … etc**) *see* **da–** 3; **er sieht ~ aus** *coll* he looks it; **… aber es ist auch ~** *coll* … and it looks it/smells *etc* like it; **mir ist (nicht) ~** *coll* I (don't) feel like it

der **Däne, –n** (*wk masc*) Dane

daneben (*emph* **daneben**) next to him/her/it/them/that/those; in comparison; in addition

daneben– *sep pref indicating error or failure*; **~benehmen*: sich d.** *coll* misbehave; **~gehen*** (*sn*) miss (the target); *coll* go wrong; misfire; **~hauen*** (*p/t* **haute daneben**) miss (with hammer *etc*); *mus* play the wrong note; *coll* slip up; **~schießen*** miss; *coll* be wide of the mark

Dänemark Denmark

danieder|liegen* (*sep*) be laid up; *comm* be depressed

dänisch, (*language*) **D~** Danish

dank (+*dat*/*gen*) thanks to

der **Dank** thanks; gratitude; (+*dat*) **~ sagen** thank; **Gott sei ~** thank heavens!; **vielen/schönen ~** many thanks! || **das ~schreiben, –** letter of thanks

dankbar grateful; appreciative; rewarding; *coll* hard-wearing

die **Dankbarkeit** gratitude; appreciation

danke: ~! thank you; no, thank you; **~ schön/sehr!** thank you very much; **~ nein!** = **nein ~!** no, thank you || **das D~schön** thank-you

danken (+*dat*) thank for; repay for; owe to; (*v/i*) thank s.o.; return s.o.'s greeting; decline; (+*dat*) thank (**für** for); **~ lassen** send one's thanks; **nichts zu ~!** don't mention it!; **na, ich danke!** no, *thank* you!; **~d** with thanks; **Betrag ~d erhalten** received with thanks || **~s|wert** rewarding; commendable

Dankes–: die ~worte *pl* words of thanks

dann then; **~ und ~** at such and such a time; **~ und wann** now and then; **~, wenn …** when …; if …; **bis ~!** see you then!

dannen *arch*: **von ~** away

Dante [–tə] Dante

Danzig Gdansk, *hist* Danzig

dar– *sep pref*; **~** +*prep*: *see the individual entries concerned and* **da–**

daran (*emph* **daran;** *see* **da–**) on/to/at *etc* it/them/that/those; about it *etc* (*eg* **das Schöne ~** the nice thing about it); in it/that (*eg* **es muß etwas ~ sein** there must be something in it); *arch* on *etc* which; *for* ~ *followed by a noun clause etc* (**daß …, ob …,** *etc*) *see* **da–** 3; **nahe ~ sein zu …** be on the point of (+*ger*) || **~gehen*** (*sep*; *sn*) set to work; **~machen** (*sep*): **sich d.** *coll* get down to it; **~setzen** (*sep*) risk (**alles d. zu …** do one's utmost to …; **sich d.** set to work)

darauf (*emph* **darauf;** *see* **da–**) on/at it/

them/that/those; (react *etc*) to it *etc*, (wait *etc*) for it *etc*, (proud) of it *etc*; (a week *etc*) later; (shortly *etc*) afterwards; *arch* on *etc* which; **(darauf)** thereupon; *for ~ followed by a noun clause etc* (**daß ..., ob ...**, *etc*) *see* **da–** 3; **darauf steht ...** the penalty (for that) is ...; ~ **aus** after it/them; ~ **aus zu ...** out to ...; ~ **zu** towards/up to it/them || ~**folgend** following; ensuing; **daraufhin** (*emph* **daraufhin**) as a result; thereupon; about it/them/that/those; (examine) for it/them/that/those

daraus (*emph* **daraus;** *see* **da–**) from/out of it/them/that/those; *arch* from/out of which; *for ~ followed by a* **daß**-*clause see* **da–** 3(*a*); ~ **folgt, daß ...** it follows that ...

darben live in want

darbieten* perform; present; (+*dat*) offer; **sich ~** present itself (*dat* to); (sight) meet s.o.'s eyes

die **Darbietung, –en** performance; presentation; item; act

darbringen* (+*dat*) make (sacrifice) to; offer; give (s.o. ovation)

die **Dardanellen** *pl* the Dardanelles

darein (*emph* **darein;** *see* **da–**) in(to)/to it/them/that/those/*arch* which; *for ~ followed by a* **daß**-*clause see* **da–** 3(*a*) || ~**finden*** (*sep*): **sich d.** resign oneself to it; ~**setzen** (*sep*) (**seinen Ehrgeiz d. zu ...** make it a point of honour to ...)

Daressalam Dar-es-Salaam

darf *1st/3rd*, **darfst** *2nd sing pres of* **dürfen**

darin (*emph* **darin;** *see* **da–**) in it/them/that/those; there, on that point; (good *etc*) at that; *arch* in which; *for ~ followed by a noun clause* (**daß ... etc**) *see* **da–** 3

Darius Darius

darlegen explain; expound

die **Darlegung, –en** explanation; exposition

das **Darlehen, –** loan

der **Darm, ⸚e** gut, intestine; skin (of sausage); *in compds* ... of the bowels; intestinal ...; **die ~entzündung, –en** enteritis; **die ~saite, –n** catgut

darob (*emph* **darob**) *arch* on account of this

die **Darre, –n** (drying-)kiln; oast; kiln-drying

darreichen (+*dat*) proffer; give

darren kiln-dry

darstellen represent; depict; describe; constitute, be; *theat* play; *chem* prepare; **falsch ~** misrepresent; **graphisch ~** plot (curve); **etwas ~** be somebody; look impressive

sich ~ appear (*dat* to); **sich ~ als** appear to be; represent oneself as

darstellend (arts) performing; *math* descriptive; ~**er Künstler** performer

der **Darsteller, –** actor

darstellerisch acting; as an actor/actress

die **Darstellung, –en** representation; depiction; portrayal (*also theat*); account; *chem* preparation; **falsche ~** misrepresentation

dartun* demonstrate; expound

darüber (*emph* **darüber;** *see* **da–**) over/above/across it/them/that/those; about it *etc*; in the meantime; in the process; more; *arch* over *etc* which; *for ~ followed by a noun clause etc* (**daß ..., ob ...**, *etc*) *see* **da–** 3; ~ **hinaus** beyond/past it/them/that/those; in addition; ~ **hinaus sein** be beyond it; be beyond that stage; **es geht nichts ~** there's nothing like it; **es geht mir nichts ~** there's nothing I like more || ~**stehen*** (*sep*) be above such things

darum (*emph* **darum;** *see* **da–**) around it/them/that/those; about it *etc*; (fight *etc*) for it *etc*; *arch* around *etc* which; **(darum)** that is why; therefore; *for ~ followed by a noun clause etc* (**daß ..., ob ...**, *etc*) *see* **da–** 3; **darum!** (*in reply*) because! || ~**kommen*** (*sep; sn*) (**d. zu ...** miss the chance of (+*ger*))

darunter (*emph* **darunter;** *see* **da–**) under it/them/that/those; underneath; (understand) by it/that; among them; including; (for) less; *arch* under which; *for ~ followed by a* **daß**-*clause see* **da–** 3(*a*)

das [–a–] (*see* **der**[1]/**die**/**das**) *nom/acc neut sing*: 1 *art* the; 2 *dem adj* (*stressed*) that; 3 *dem pron* (*stressed*) that; this; the one; (*with pl of* **sein**) they; these; those; 4 *rel pron* which, that

~ **mit ...** the business about ...; what he/she *etc* said about ...; **und ~** and that; and then; and ... too; ~ **und ~** such and such; **~, was** what; *for phrases with* **dem** *see* **dem**

dasein* (*sep; sn*) be there/present; be; exist; **noch nie dagewesen** unprecedented

das **Dasein** existence; life; **die ~s|berechtigung** raison d'être; **der ~s|kampf, ⸚e** struggle for existence

dasitzen* (*sep*) sit there; ~ **ohne** *coll* be without any

dasjenige *see* **derjenige/diejenige/dasjenige**

daß that; the fact that; (it is customary *etc*) for ... to +*infin*; so that; **~ ...!** I do hope ...!; would that ...!; mind ...!; fancy ...!; to think that ...!

dasselbe *see* **derselbe/dieselbe/dasselbe**

dastehen* (*sep*) stand there; be (alone *etc*); **einzig ~** be unique; **einzig ~d** unique; **gut/schlecht ~** be doing well/badly; **wie stehe ich jetzt da?** just look at me now!; what a fool I look now!

die **Datei** [da–], **–en** data file

Daten *pl of* **Datum;** *in compds* data ...; **die ~bank, –en** data bank; **der ~schutz** data protection; **die ~station, –en** data terminal; **d~ver|arbeitend** data-processing; **die**

~ver|arbeitung data processing; **die ~ver|arbeitungs|anlage, –n** data processor

datieren date (letter, work of art, *etc*); **~ aus/von** date from

der **Dativ, –e** dative

dato: bis ~ to date

die **Datscha, –s/Datschen,** *esp EGer* **die Datsche, –n** dacha

die **Dattel, –n** date; **die ~palme, –n** date-palm

das **Datum, –(t)en** date; datum; (*pl*) particulars; data; **welches ~ haben wir heute?** what's the date today?; **ohne ~** undated

die **Dauer** duration; period; length; **auf ~** permanently; **auf die ~** in the long run; (*with neg*) for any length of time; **für die ~** (+*gen*) for (a period of); **von ~ sein** last; **von kurzer ~** short-lived

Dauer– permanent ...; continuous ...; *mech, sp* endurance ...; **der ~auftrag, ⸚e** banker's order; **die ~karte, –n** season ticket; **der ~lauf, ⸚e** jog(ging); **der ~lutscher, –** *coll* lollipop; **der ~marsch, ⸚e** forced march; **der ~parker, –** long-stay parker; **die ~wirkung, –en** lasting effect; **die ~welle, –n** permanent wave; **die ~wurst, ⸚e** hard smoked sausage (*eg* salami, saveloy); **der ~zustand, ⸚e** permanent state of affairs

dauerhaft lasting; durable

die **Dauerhaftigkeit** durability

dauern[1] last; go on; take (... hours *etc*); be (*eg* **es wird lange ~, bis ...** it will be a long time before ...); **das dauert (seine Zeit)** it takes time; **das dauert aber!** it's taking a long time!

dauern[2] *arch*: **... dauert mich** I feel sorry for ...; I regret ...

dauernd continual, constant; permanent; (*adv*) continually, always; *or conveyed by* ... keep(s) on ...

das **Däumelinchen** Tom Thumb

der **Daumen, –** thumb; **~/Däumchen drehen** *coll* twiddle one's thumbs; (+*dat*) **den ~ drücken/halten** keep one's fingers crossed for; **über den ~ peilen** *coll* estimate roughly || **die ~schraube, –n** thumbscrew ((+*dat*) **(die) ~schrauben anlegen** *coll* put the screws on)

der **Däumling, –e** thumb (of glove); **der ~** Tom Thumb

die **Daune, –n** downy feather; (*pl*) down; **das ~n|bett, –en** eiderdown; **das ~n|kleid, –er** *ornith* down

David ['da:fɪt] David; **der ~(s)|stern, –e** Star of David

davon (*emph* **davon; *see* da–**) from it/them/that/those; from there; of it *etc*; about it *etc*; (*with pass*) by it *etc*; (eat *etc*) some (of it/them), (*with neg*) any; *arch* of *etc* which; *for ~ followed by a noun clause etc* (**daß ..., ob ...,** *etc*) *see* **da–** 3

davon– *sep pref* ... away, ... off; **~gehen*** (*sn*) leave; **~kommen*** (*sn*) escape; get off (**mit einem blauen Auge d.** *coll* get off lightly; *for* **das kommt davon** *see* **kommen**); **~laufen*** (*sn*) run away (**vor** *dat* from); (prices *etc*) get out of control; (+*dat*) run away from; (prices *etc*) outstrip; *coll* walk out on (**... ist zum D.** *coll* ... is enough to drive you up the wall); **~machen: sich d.** make off; **~stehlen*: sich d.** sneak away; **~tragen*** carry off; win, sustain (injury), suffer (damage), contract (illness) (**den Sieg d.** win the day)

davor (*emph* **davor; *see* da–**) in front of/before it/them/that/those; (protect *etc*) from it *etc*, (warn *etc*) of it *etc*; *arch* in front of *etc* which; *for ~ followed by a noun clause etc* (**daß ...** *etc*) *see* **da–** 3

dazu (*emph* **dazu; *see* da–**) for/to it/them/that/those; for this purpose; (advise, determined, *etc*) to do it/that, (capable) of doing it/that; about/on it *etc*; with it *etc*; as well as; ... into the bargain; *arch* for *etc* which; *for ~ followed by a noun clause etc* (**daß ..., ob ...,** *etc*) *see* **da–** 3; **noch ~** ... into the bargain

dazu– *sep pref denoting addition, joining*; **~gehören** belong to it/them; be part of it; go with it; (person) belong; **~gehörig** that goes with/pertaining to it/them; **~kommen*** (*sn*) come (along); be added (**dazu kommt noch ...** add to this ...); **~lernen** learn (something new); **~rechnen** add on; also consider; **~tun*** *coll* add (**ohne jmds. D.** without s.o.'s help)

dazwischen (*emph* **dazwischen; *see* da–**) between them/those, in between; among them/those; between times; **~fahren*** (*sep; sn*) intervene; cut in; **~funken** (*sep*) *coll* put one's oar in; **~kommen*** (*sep; sn*) intervene; prevent s.o. (from doing sth.) (**wenn nichts ~kommt** if all goes well); **~liegend** intervening; **~reden** (*sep*) interrupt; interfere; (+*dat*) interrupt; **~treten*** (*sep; sn*) intervene; come between them; **das D~treten** intervention

DB = Deutsche Bundesbahn

die **DBD** *EGer* = **Demokratische Bauernpartei Deutschlands**

die **DDR** (= **Deutsche Demokratische Republik**) East Germany; **der ~-Bürger, –** East German (citizen)

das **DDT** D.D.T.

das **Debakel, –** débâcle

die **Debatte, –n** debate; **zur ~ stehen/stellen** be under/bring up for discussion; **das steht nicht zur ~** that's not the issue

Debattier–: der ~klub, –s talking-shop

debattieren, ~ über (*acc*) debate

[das] **Debet** [–ɛt], **–s** debit
[das] **Debüt** [de'byː], **–s** début
[der] **Debütant, –en** (*wk masc*) performer/sportsman *etc* making his début
[die] **Debütantin, –nen** performer/sportswoman *etc* making her début; débutante
debütieren make one's début
[der] **Dechant** [–ç–], **–en** (*wk masc*) *RC* dean
dechiffrieren [–ʃ–] decipher
[das] **Deck, –s** deck; **alle Mann an ~!** all hands on deck!; **auf ~** on deck
Deck– covering ...; top ...; *naut* deck ...; **die ~adresse, –n** accommodation address, cover address *US*; **das ~bett, –en** duvet, comforter *US*; **die ~farbe, –n** body-colour; **der ~mantel** cover (**unter dem D.** (+*gen*) under the guise of); **der ~name, –n** (*like* **Name**) assumed name; pseudonym; **das ~wort, ⸚er** code-word
[die] **Decke, –n** ceiling; (table)cloth; bedspread; blanket; (road) surface; (book) cover; (tyre) outer cover; **an die ~ gehen** *coll* hit the roof; **sich nach der ~ strecken** *coll* cut one's coat according to one's cloth; **unter einer ~ stecken mit** *coll* be hand in glove with
[der] **Deckel, –** lid; cover; (+*dat*) **eins auf den ~ geben** *coll* haul over the coals; **eins auf den ~ kriegen** *coll* get it in the neck
decken (*see also* **gedeckt**) cover (*also fin, zool*); lay (table); shield; cover up for; meet (demand); *sp* cover, mark, guard *US*; *chess, box* guard; **~ über** (*acc*) spread over; **das Dach ~** roof a building
sich ~ protect oneself; cover oneself (**gegen** against); (*recip*) coincide; tally; *math* be congruent; **sich ~ mit** coincide with; tally with
Decken– ceiling ...; **die ~heizung** overhead heating
[die] **Deckung** *vbl noun*; *esp mil* cover; *math* congruence; *fin* cover; security; *sp, chess* defence; *box, fenc* guard; *zool* service; **in ~ gehen** take cover || **d~s|gleich** identical; *math* congruent
[das] **Dederon** [–ərɔn] *EGer approx* = nylon
[die] **Deduktion, –en** *philos* deduction
deduzieren *philos* deduce
De-facto– [de–] de facto ...
[der] **Defätismus** defeatism
[der] **Defätist, –en** (*wk masc*), **defätistisch** defeatist
defekt defective, faulty
[der] **Defekt, –e** defect, fault; (physical) defect, (mental *etc*) deficiency
defensiv (*in compds* **D~–**) defensive
[die] **Defensive** defensive; **in der ~** on the defensive
[das] **Defilee, –s/–(ee)n** march-past
defilieren (*also sn*) march past
definieren define
[die] **Definition, –en** definition
definitiv definitive; definite
[das] **Defizit** [–ɪt], **–e** deficit; deficiency (**an** *dat* of)
defizitär in deficit; leading to a deficit
[die] **Deflation, –en** deflation; *in compds* **~s–** deflationary ...
deflationär deflationary
deflorieren deflower
[die] **Deformation, –en** deformation
deformieren deform; distort
[die] **Deformierung, –en** deformation; distortion
deftig *coll* earthy; robust; hefty; (meal) hearty
[der] **Degen**[1], **–** sword; *fenc* épée
[der] **Degen**[2], **–** *poet* warrior
[die] **Degeneration, –en** degeneration
degenerieren (*sn*) degenerate; **degeneriert** degenerate
degoutieren [–gu–] disgust
degradieren degrade; demote; *mil* reduce to the ranks; **~ zu** reduce to
dehnbar elastic; flexible; ductile
[die] **Dehnbarkeit** elasticity; flexibility; ductility
dehnen stretch; *ling* lengthen; **sich ~** stretch; drag on; extend
dehydrieren dehydrogenate
[der] **Deibel** *coll* = **Teufel**
[der] **Deich, –e** dike
[die] **Deichsel** [–ks–], **–n** pole (of cart *etc*); shafts
deichseln [–ks–] *coll* engineer
dein (*in correspondence*: **D~**; *see p. xxxiii*) your (*familiar sing*); **~er/~e/~(e)s** (*see p. xxviii*; *also* **der/die/das ~e**) yours (*familiar sing*); (*at end of letter*) **D~(e) ...** yours, ...; **das D~e** what is yours; **das D~e tun** do your bit; **die D~en** your family
deiner (*gen of* **du**: *see p. xxvi*) of you; **~seits** for/on your part
deines|gleichen people like you(rself)
deinet–: **~wegen** because of you; = **(um) ~willen** for your sake
deinige: der/die/das ~ = **der/die/das deine** (*at* **dein**)
De-jure– [de'juːrə–] de jure ...
[das] **Deka** [–ɛ–] (*gen* **–(s)**), **–(s)** *Aust* ten grammes
[die] **Dekade, –n** (period of) ten days; decade
dekadent decadent
[die] **Dekadenz** decadence
[der] **Dekan, –e** *eccles, univ* dean
[das] **Dekanat, –e** *eccles, univ* office of a dean; *univ* dean's office, *eccles* deanery
[die] **Deklamation, –en** declamation; (*pl*) (empty) rhetoric
deklamatorisch declamatory
deklamieren declaim
[die] **Deklaration, –en** declaration
deklarieren declare
deklassieren lower the social standing of; *sp* outclass
[die] **Deklination, –en** *gramm* declension; *astron,*

phys declination

deklinieren *gramm* decline

das **Dekolleté** [–lt–], **–s** low neckline

dekolletiert [–lt–] low-necked; décolletée

die **Dekontamination, –en** decontamination

dekontaminieren decontaminate

der **Dekor, –s** (*also* **das**) decoration; *cin*, *theat* décor

der **Dekorateur** [–'tøːɐ], **–e** window-dresser; interior designer

die **Dekoration, –en** decoration (of sth.); décor; window display; decoration (*also mil*); *cin*, *theat* set; **der ~s|stoff, –e** furnishing fabric

dekorativ decorative

dekorieren decorate; dress (window)

das **Dekret, –e, dekretieren** decree

dekuvrieren expose; reveal; **sich ~** reveal one's true character

die **Delegation, –en** delegation

delegieren delegate (**an** *acc* to); **der/die Delegierte** (*decl as adj*) delegate

delektieren: ~ mit regale with; **sich ~ an** (*dat*) delight in; regale oneself with

Delhi ['deːli] Delhi

delikat delicate; delicious

die **Delikatesse, –n** delicacy; (= quality) delicacy, sensitivity; **das ~n|geschäft, –e** delicatessen

das **Delikt, –e** offence

der **Delinquent, –en** (*wk masc*) offender

delirieren be delirious

das **Delirium, –(i)en** delirium

die **Delle, –n** *coll* dent

delogieren [–ʒ–] *Aust* evict

die **Delogierung, –en** *Aust* eviction

der **Delphin, –e** dolphin; **das ~schwimmen** butterfly

delphisch Delphian, Delphic

das **Delta, –s/Delten** delta; **d~förmig** delta-shaped; deltoid

dem (*see* **der**[1]**/die/das**) 1 *art dat sing masc/neut* (to/for) the; 2 *rel pron dat sing masc/neut* (to/for) whom/which; 3 *dem pron dat sing masc/neut* (*stressed*) (to/for) that one/the one/him; 4 *dem adj dat sing masc/neut* (*stressed*) (to/for) that; **wie ~ auch sei** be that as it may; **wenn ~ so ist** if that is so

der **Demagoge, –n** (*wk masc*) demagogue

die **Demagogie, –(ie)n** demagogy

demagogisch demagogic

die **Demarkations|linie, –n** demarcation line

demaskieren unmask; **sich ~** unmask; unmask oneself

dem|entgegen against this

das **Dementi, –s** (official) denial

dementieren issue a denial of

dem|entsprechend corresponding; (*adv*) correspondingly; accordingly

demgegen|über on the other hand; in comparison

demgemäß accordingly

die **Demission, –en** *pol* resignation

demissionieren *pol* resign

demnach consequently, so; accordingly; according to that

demnächst [–ç–] shortly

demobilisieren demobilize

die **Demobilisierung, –en = die Demobilmachung, –en** demobilization

die **Demographie** demography

demographisch demographic

der **Demokrat, –en** (*wk masc*) democrat

die **Demokratie, –(ie)n** democracy

demokratisch democratic

demokratisieren democratize

demolieren wreck; *Aust* demolish

die **Demolierung, –en** *vbl noun*; *Aust* demolition

der **Demonstrant, –en** (*wk masc*) demonstrator

die **Demonstration, –en** demonstration

demonstrativ pointed; demonstrating one's (dis)approval; *gramm* demonstrative; (*adv*) pointedly; in protest; **~es Beispiel** illustration

demonstrieren (*also v/i*) demonstrate

die **Demontage** [–ʒə], **–n** dismantling

demontieren dismantle

demoralisieren demoralize; deprave

die **Demoskopie** public opinion research

demoskopisch relating to public opinion research; obtained in an opinion poll; **~e Untersuchung** opinion poll

Demosthenes [–tenɛs] Demosthenes

die **Demut** humility

demütig humble

demütigen humiliate; **sich ~** humble oneself; **~d** humiliating

die **Demütigung, –en** humiliation

demzufolge consequently

den (*see* **der**[1]**/die/das**) 1 *art acc sing masc* the; 2 *art dat pl* (to/for) the; 3 *rel pron acc sing masc* whom; which; 4 *dem pron acc sing masc* (*stressed*) that one; the one; him; 5 *dem adj acc sing masc* (*stressed*) that; 6 *dem adj dat pl* (*stressed*) those

denaturieren denature

denen (*see* **der**[1]**/die/das**) 1 *rel pron dat pl* (to/for) whom/which; 2 *dem pron dat pl* (to/for) them/those/the ones

Den Haag The Hague

Denk– … of thought; thought …; mental …; **die ~art, –en** way of thinking; mentality; **die ~aufgabe, –n** brain-teaser; **d~faul** mentally lazy; **der ~fehler, –** error in reasoning; **das ~mal, ¨–er** memorial; monument; **der ~mal(s)|schutz** protection of ancient monuments; **das ~modell, –e** blueprint; **die ~pause, –n** break (in negotiations *etc*); **die ~schrift, –en** memorandum;

der ~sport solving of puzzles; **das ~vermögen** intellectual capacity; **die ~weise, -n** way of thinking; mentality; **d~würdig** memorable; **der ~zettel, -** *coll* lesson ((+*dat*) **einen D. geben** teach (s.o.) a lesson)

denkbar conceivable; (*adv*) extremely; (*followed by superl*) ... possible; ... imaginable

denken (*p/t* **dachte** (*subj* **dächte**), *p/part* **gedacht**) (*see also* **gedacht**) think; be planning (to); **sich** *dat* **...** ~ imagine; envisage; **sich** *dat* **nichts dabei** ~ think nothing of it; mean no harm; **zu ~ geben** make one think; (+*dat*) make (s.o.) think; **ich denke, ...** (*eg* **wir warten noch 10 Minuten**) I think (we should wait another 10 minutes); (*eg* **Sie sollten in X sein**) I thought (you were supposed to be in X); **ich dächte, ...** I would have thought ...; **man sollte ~, ...** one would have thought ...; **denk mal!** imagine!; **wo denkst du hin!** good heavens no!; **denkste!** that's what *you* think!; **das läßt sich ~** I can imagine; **habe ich's mir doch gedacht!** I thought as much!; **gedacht für** intended for

~ **an** (*acc*) think of; remember; have in mind; **an ... ist nicht zu ~** ... is *etc* out of the question; **ich denke nicht dran!** I wouldn't think of it!; ~ **lassen an** be suggestive of

bei sich ~ think to oneself

~ **über** (*acc*) think about/of; **wie ~ Sie darüber?** what's your opinion?

das **Denken** thinking; thought

der **Denker, -** thinker

denkerisch intellectual

denkste! *see* **denken**

denn 1 *conj* for; (*esp before* **als**) than; 2 *adv*: *NGer coll* then; (*emotive particle*) then; *or left untranslated* (*eg* **wozu ~?** what for?); **es sei ~, ...** unless ...; ~ **auch** (and) in fact; and indeed; ~ **nun** now; (how *etc*) exactly

dennoch nevertheless; yet

denselben *see* **derselbe**

der **Denunziant, -en** (*wk masc*) informer

die **Denunziation, -en** denunciation

denunzieren inform against; denounce

das **Deodorant, -s/-e** deodorant

das **Departement** [-tə'mɛnt], **-e** *Swiss* ministry; department

die **Dependance** [depã'dã:s], **-n** (hotel) annexe; branch

die **Depesche, -n** *arch* dispatch; telegram

deplaciert [-s-], **deplaziert** out of place

die **Deponie, -(ie)n** dump

deponieren deposit

die **Deportation, -en** deportation; *hist* transportation

deportieren deport; *hist* transport

die **Depositen** *pl fin* deposits

das **Depot** [-'po:], **-s** depot; depository; strong-room

der **Depp, -e** (*or* **-en** (*wk masc*)) *SGer coll* blockhead

deppert *SGer coll* daft

die **Depression, -en** depression

depressiv depressed

deprimieren depress; **~d** depressing

die **Deputation, -en** deputation

deputieren depute; **der/die Deputierte** (*decl as adj*) deputy, representative; delegate

der[1]/die/das (*declension is shown in Guide to Grammar – see pages referred to in this article*) (*see* **das, dem**)

1 *def art* (*see p. xviii*) the, (*with part of the body*) my, your, his, her, *etc*; *or not translated* (*as in* **der Mensch** man, *or before names of substances, abstract nouns – eg* **die Zeit** time, **das Fliegen** flying – *etc*); (*used as distributive*) a (*eg* **2 Mark das Pfund** 2 marks a pound);

2 *dem adj* (*stressed*; *decl like* **1**, *not used in gen*) that; (*pl*) those;

3 *dem pron* (*for neut see* **das** 3) (*stressed*; *see p. xxx*) that one; the one; (= the following) this; (*masc*) he, (*fem*) she; (*pl*) they; those; the ones;

4 *rel pron* (*see p. xxix*) who, that; which, that; *or expressed by pres/part* ...ing (*eg* **Ortsnamen, die auf** *-itz* **ausgehen** place-names ending in *-itz*) *or* to + *infin* (*eg* **der einzige/letzte, der ihn sah** the only/last one to see him, **ein Auto, mit dem man zur Arbeit fahren kann** a car to drive to work in);

5 = *dem+rel prons* the person/one who; the one that; (*pl*) those who/that (*eg* **die nach Fidschi auswanderten** those who emigrated to Fiji);

ich, der ich/du, der du *etc* **...** I/you *etc* who ...; **der und der** such and such (a person)

der[2] (*see* **der[1]/die/das**) 1 *art gen sing fem/gen pl* of the; 2 *art dat sing fem* (to/for) the; 3 *rel pron dat sing fem* (to/for) whom/which; 4 *dem pron dat sing fem* (*stressed*) (to/for) that one/the one/her; 5 *dem adj dat sing fem* (*stressed*) (to/for) that

der|art to such an extent, so much; in such a manner; (*followed by adj/adv*) so; ~ **sein, daß ...** be such that ...

der|artig such, like this/that; (*adv*) = **derart**; **~es** this kind of thing; **etwas/nichts D~es** something/nothing like that; ~ **sein, daß ...** be such that ...

derb coarse, (joke) crude; (material) strong, tough; ~ **anfassen** be rough with

die **Derbheit, -en** coarseness, crudity; strength, toughness; coarse remark

der|einst one day; *arch* once

deren (*see* **der¹/die/das**) 1 *rel pron gen sing fem/gen pl* whose; of whom/which; 2 *dem pron gen sing fem/gen pl* of her/it/them/the one(s); (*followed by noun*) her; its; their
derent–: ~**wegen** because of her/it/them; because of whom/which; ~**willen (um d.** for her/its/their sake; for whose sake/the sake of which)
derer (*see* **der¹/die/das**) 1 *dem pron gen pl* (*followed by rel pron*) of those; 2 (= *standard* **deren** 1) of whom/which
dergestalt thus; in such a manner; ~ **sein, daß ...** be such that ...
dergleichen (*indecl*) 1 *adj* such, of this/that kind; 2 *pron* this/that kind of thing; **und** ~ **(mehr)** and the like; **nicht** ~ **tun** *coll* pretend not to notice; **nichts** ~ nothing of the kind
das **Derivat, –e** derivative
derjenige/diejenige/dasjenige 1 *adj* the, that; (*pl*) those; 2 *pron* (*followed by gen*) that; (*pl*) those; (*followed by rel pron*) the man/woman; the one; (*pl*) those; the ones
derlei (*indecl*) = **dergleichen**
dermaßen to such an extent; (*followed by adj/adv*) so
der **Dermatologe, –n** (*wk masc*) dermatologist
die **Dermatologie** dermatology
dermatologisch dermatological
derselbe/dieselbe/dasselbe (*2nd element is detached from def art when latter coalesces with a prep, eg* **zur selben Zeit**) the same; **ein und dasselbe** one and the same thing
derweil(en) meanwhile
der **Derwisch, –e** dervish
derzeit at present; *arch* then
derzeitig present; *arch* then
des [–ɛ–] (*see* **der¹/die/das**) *art gen sing masc/neut* of the
das **des, Des** [–ɛ–] (*gen* –), – *mus* (the note) D flat; (*key*) **Des** D flat major
das **Desaster, –** disaster
des|avouieren [–vu–] repudiate
der **Deserteur** [–'tøːɐ], **–e** deserter
desertieren (*sn*) desert
desgl. = **desgleichen**
desgleichen likewise
deshalb therefore; because of that; that is why; **(schon)** ~, **weil ...** (if only) because ...
das **Design** [di'zaen], **–s** design
der **Designer** [di'zaenɐ], **–** designer
designieren designate (**zu** as); **der designierte (Präsident** *etc*) the (president *etc*) designate
die **Des|illusion, –en** disillusionment
des|illusionieren disillusion
die **Des|infektion, –en** disinfection; **das** ~**s|mittel, –** disinfectant
des|infizieren disinfect; ~**d** disinfectant
die **Des|information, –en** disinformation
die **Des|integration, –en** disintegration
das **Des|interesse** lack of interest (**an** *dat* in), apathy
des|interessiert uninterested, apathetic
desodorieren deodorize
desolat wretched
des|organisieren disorganize
des|orientieren disorientate
die **Des|oxydation, –en** deoxidation
des|oxydieren deoxidize
despektierlich disrespectful
der **Despot, –en** (*wk masc*) despot
die **Despotie, –(ie)n** despotism
despotisch despotic
dessen (*see* **der¹/die/das**) 1 *rel pron gen sing masc/neut* whose; of whom/which; 2 *dem pron gen sing masc/neut* of him/it/that/the one; (*followed by noun*) his; its; ~**unge|achtet** nevertheless
dessent–: ~**wegen** because of him/it; because of whom/which; ~**willen (um d.** for his/its sake; for whose sake/the sake of which)
das **Dessert** [–'sɛːɐ], **–s** dessert
das **Dessin** [–'sɛ̃ː], **–s** design, pattern
das **Destillat, –e** distillate
die **Destillation, –en** distillation
Destillier–: der ~**apparat, –e** still
destillieren distil
desto all the; **je ...,** ~ **...** the ... the ...
destruktiv destructive
deswegen therefore; because of that; that is why; **(schon)** ~, **weil ...** (if only) because ...
das **Detail** [–'tae], **–s** detail; **ins** ~ **gehen** go into detail; **bis ins kleinste** ~ down to the last detail
Detail– detailed ...; *comm* retail ...
detailliert [–taj–] detailed
die **Detektei, –en** detective agency
der **Detektiv, –e** (private) detective
der **Detektor, –(or)en** detector
die **Detonation, –en** detonation
detonieren (*sn*) detonate
Deut *coll*: **keinen/nicht einen** ~ not a whit/brass farthing/fig; **nicht einen** ~ **verstehen von** not know the first thing about
deuteln quibble (**an** *dat* over); **daran gibt es nichts zu** ~ there can be no argument about that
deuten interpret; ~ **auf** (*acc*) point at; point to, indicate
deutlich clear; distinct; ~ **werden** not mince matters
die **Deutlichkeit** clarity; distinctness; **mit aller** ~ in no uncertain terms
deutsch, (*language*) **D**~ German; **die D**~**e Bucht** the German Bight; **der D**~**e Krieg** the Seven Weeks' (*or* Austro-Prussian) War; **die D**~**e Mark** the (deutsch)mark;

der D~e Orden *hist* the Teutonic Order; **die ~e Schweiz** German-speaking Switzerland; **auf ~** in German; **auf gut ~** *coll* in plain language; **~ reden mit** *coll* speak plainly to; **der/die Deutsche** (*decl as adj*) German; **das Deutsche** (*decl as adj*) German (*language*) || **D~land** Germany (**die beiden D.** the two Germanies); **das D~land|lied** 'Deutschland, Deutschland über alles'; **der D~schweizer, –, ~schweizerisch** German Swiss; **~sprachig** German-speaking/language; **~stämmig** of German descent

das **Deutschtum** Germanness; (the) Germans abroad

die **Deutung, –en** interpretation

die **Devise, –n** motto; guiding principle; (*pl*) foreign currency; *in compds* **~n–** (foreign) exchange ...

devot servile

die **Devotion** servility

die **Dextrose** dextrose

der **Dezember** (*gen* –(s)), – December; **im ~** in December

dezent discreet, unobtrusive; subdued

dezentralisieren decentralize

die **Dezenz** discretion; quiet elegance

das **Dezernat, –e** department

der **Dezernent, –en** (*wk masc*) head of a department

das **Dezibel** [–bɛl], – decibel

dezidiert firm

Dezimal– decimal ...; **der D~bruch, ⸚e** decimal (fraction); **die D~rechnung** decimals; **die D~stelle, –n** decimal (place)

die **Dezime, –n** *mus* tenth

dezimieren decimate

der **DFF = Deutscher Fernsehfunk** (*E. German broadcasting corporation*)

der **DGB** (= **Deutscher Gewerkschaftsbund**) Federation of German Trade Unions

dgl. = dergleichen

d. h. (= **das heißt**) i.e.

Di. (= **Dienstag**) Tues.

das **Dia, –s** slide; transparency

der **Diabetes** [–ɛs] diabetes

der **Diabetiker, –, diabetisch** diabetic

diabolisch diabolical

das **Diadem, –e** diadem

die **Diagnose, –n** diagnosis; **eine ~ stellen** make a diagnosis

diagnostizieren = ~ auf (*acc*) diagnose

diagonal diagonal; **der D~reifen, –** cross-ply tyre

die **Diagonale, –n** diagonal

das **Diagramm, –e** diagram; graph

der **Diakon, –e** (*also* **–en** (*wk masc*)) deacon

die **Diakonisse, –n** deaconess

der **Dialekt, –e** dialect

die **Dialektik** [–ɪk] dialectic(s)

dialektisch *ling* dialectal; *philos* dialectical

der **Dialog, –e** dialogue

die **Dialyse, –n** dialysis

der **Diamant, –en** (*wk masc*), **diamanten** diamond

der **Diameter, –** diameter

diametral diametrical; **~ entgegengesetzt** diametrically opposed

das **Diapositiv, –e** slide; transparency

die **Diarrhöe** [–'rø:], **–n** [–ən] diarrhoea

das **Diaskop, –e** slide-projector

diät: ~ leben (be on a) diet

die **Diät** diet; **~ halten** keep to a strict diet || **die ~kost** dietary food

die **Diäten** *pl parl* daily allowance

diatonisch diatonic

dich (*acc of* **du**; *see p. xxvi*; *in correspondence*: **D~**) you (*familiar sing*); (*refl*) yourself

dicht dense; thick; close-woven; (water)-tight; compact; (*adv, followed by prep*) right, just (behind *etc*); **–dicht** (*eg* **schall~** sound) –proof, (*eg* **wasser~** water) –tight; **~ an** (*acc/dat*)/**bei** close to; **~ halten** (*cf* **dichthalten**) be watertight; **~ machen** (*cf* **dichtmachen**) make watertight; seal; *naut* batten down; **~ stehen** stand close together; **nicht ganz ~ sein** *coll* not be all there

dicht– densely ...; **~gedrängt** closely-packed; **~halten*** (*sep*) (*cf* **dicht halten** *at* **dicht**) *coll* keep one's mouth shut; **~machen** (*sep*) (*cf* **dicht machen** *at* **dicht**) (*also v/i*) close; close down

Dicht–: die ~kunst (art of) poetry; creation of literary works; literature

die **Dichte** density; thickness; closeness (of weave); compactness

dichten[1] make (water)tight; seal; *naut* caulk

dichten[2] write (literary work); (*v/i*) write verse

der **Dichter, –** author, writer; poet; **die ~sprache** poetic diction

dichterisch literary; poetic

der **Dichterling, –e** poetaster

die **Dichtung**[1], **–en** gasket; packing; seal

die **Dichtung**[2], **–en** literature; literary work

Dichtungs–: der ~ring, –e washer

dick thick; fat; swollen; *coll* (mistake *etc*) big, (salary *etc*) fat; (friendship) close; **~ haben** *coll* have had enough of; **es nicht so ~ haben** *coll* be none too well off; **~ machen** be fattening; make one look fat; **durch ~ und dünn** through thick and thin || **der D~darm, ⸚e** colon; **~fellig** *coll* thick-skinned; **~flüssig** thick; viscous; **der D~häuter, –** pachyderm; *coll* thick-skinned person; **~häutig** thick-skinned; **der D~kopf, ⸚e** *coll* stubborn person (**einen D. haben** be stubborn); **~köpfig** *coll* stubborn; **~leibig** corpulent; bulky; **die D~milch** sour milk; **der D~schädel, –** *coll* stubborn person; **~tun*** (*sep*): **sich d.** *coll* brag (**mit** about); **der**

D~wanst, ⁻̈e *coll* pot-belly (= person)
Dick: ~ und Doof Laurel and Hardy
dicke *coll*: **~ haben** have had enough of; **~ genug** plenty
die **Dicke** thickness; fatness
das **Dickicht, -e** thicket; labyrinth, maze
dicklich thickish; plump
die **Didaktik** [-ɪk] didactics
didaktisch didactic
die (*see* **der**[1]**/die/das**) *nom/acc sing fem, nom/acc pl*: 1 *art* the; 2 *dem adj* (*stressed*) that; (*pl*) those; 3 *dem pron* (*stressed*) that one; the one; she/her; (*pl*) those; the ones; they/them; 4 *rel pron* who/who(m), that; which, that; 5 = *dem+rel prons* the person/one who; the one that; (*pl*) those who/that
der **Dieb, -e** thief; **haltet den ~!** stop thief! || **der ~stahl, ⁻̈e** theft
die **Dieberei, -en** thieving
Diebes- thief's ...; thieves' ...; **das ~gut** stolen goods; **d~sicher** burglar/theft-proof
diebisch thieving; thievish; impish, mischievous; **sich ~ freuen** be very gleeful
diejenige *see* **derjenige/diejenige/dasjenige**
die **Diele, -n** (entrance) hall; floorboard
dienen serve (*also mil*) (**als/zu** as); *hist* be in service; (*+dat*) serve; be of service to; (*+dat*) **~ mit** help with; **... dient** (*+dat vbl noun or* **zum/zur** *+vbl noun*) ... is used to *+infin*; the purpose of ... is to + *infin*; **womit kann ich Ihnen ~?** what can I do for you?; can I help you?; **mit ... ist mir nicht gedient** ... is *etc* of no use to me
der **Diener, -** servant; **einen ~ machen** *coll* bow
die **Dienerin, -nen** maid, servant
dienern bow (repeatedly) (**vor** *dat* to); bow and scrape
die **Dienerschaft** servants
dienlich: (*+dat***) ~ sein** be helpful to; serve
der **Dienst, -e** service (**an** *dat* to); work; **-dienst** *also* ... duty; (*+dat*) **einen guten/schlechten ~ erweisen** do (s.o.) a good turn/a disservice; **~ haben** be on duty; **außer ~** off duty; retired; **außer ~ stellen** withdraw from service; **im ~ sein** be on duty; **in ~ stellen** put into service; (*+dat*) **zu ~en stehen** be at (s.o.'s) disposal
Dienst- *also* official ...;
das ~alter length of service; **der/die ~älteste** (*decl as adj*) most senior member of staff/officer; **d~beflissen** zealous (in the performance of one's duties); **d~bereit** helpful; (pharmacy) open (for the dispensing of prescriptions); **der ~bote, -n** (*wk masc*) servant; **der ~eifer** devotion to duty; **d~eifrig** zealous (in the performance of one's duties); **d~fähig** fit for service; **d~frei** (**d~freier Tag** *etc* day *etc* off; **d. haben** be off duty); **der ~grad, -e** rank; **d~habend** on duty; **der ~herr, -en** (*like* **Herr**) employer; **das ~jahr, -e** year of service; **die ~kleidung, -en** uniform; **die ~leistung, -en** service (performed); **das ~leistungs|gewerbe, -** service industry; **das ~mädchen, -** maid; **das ~personal** personnel; domestic staff; **der ~plan, ⁻̈e** duty roster; **die ~reise, -n** official/business trip; **die ~stelle, -n** (competent) authority; department; office; (police) station; **die ~stunden** *pl* working/office hours; **d~tuend** on duty; **der ~wagen, -** company/official car; **der ~weg** official channels (**auf dem D.** through official channels); **d~widrig** contrary to regulations; **die ~zeit, -en** (period of) service; working hours
der **Dienstag, -e** Tuesday
dienstags on Tuesdays
dienstbar (*following dat*) subservient (to); **sich** *dat* **... ~ machen** subjugate; harness
dienstlich official
dies 1 *dem adj* = **dieses**; 2 *dem pron* this; (*with pl of* **sein**) these; **~bezüglich** regarding this; **~jährig** this year's; **~mal, ~malig** this time; **~seitig** on this side; of this world; **~seits** (*+gen*) on this side of; **das D~seits** this life
Diesel- diesel ...
dieselbe *see* **derselbe/dieselbe/dasselbe**
dieser/diese/dieses (*see p. xviii*) 1 *adj* this; (*pl*) these; 2 *pron* this (one); the latter; (*pl*) these; the latter
diesig hazy
der **Dietrich, -e** skeleton key; picklock
diffamieren defame; **~d** defamatory
die **Diffamierung, -en** defamation
Differential- differential ...
die **Differenz, -en** difference; *comm* deficit; (*pl*) differences (of opinion)
differenzieren *math* differentiate; (*v/i*) make distinctions; differentiate; **sich ~** become differentiated, *biol* differentiate; **differenziert** *also* varied; complex; subtle; sophisticated
differieren differ
diffizil difficult; complicated
diffus vague; *phys* diffuse
digital digital; **der D~rechner, -** digital computer; **die D~uhr, -en** digital clock/watch
das **Diktat, -e** dictation; dictate; *pol* diktat; **nach ~** from dictation
der **Diktator, -(or)en** dictator
diktatorisch dictatorial
die **Diktatur, -en** dictatorship
Diktier-: das ~gerät, -e = die ~maschine, -n dictating machine
diktieren dictate
das **Dilemma, -s/-ta** dilemma
der **Dilettant, -en** (*wk masc*) amateur; dilettante

dilettantisch amateurish
der **Dill, –e** dill
die **Dimension, –en** dimension
–dimensional –dimensional
das **Diminutiv, –e** diminutive
DIN [di:n] (= **Deutsche Industrie-Norm**) German Industrial Standard
das **Diner** [–'ne:], **–s** (formal) dinner
das **Ding, –e**/*coll* **–er** thing; **das ~ an sich** the thing-in-itself; **guter ~e** in good spirits; **ein ~ drehen** *coll* pull a job; **es geht nicht mit rechten ~en zu** there is something fishy about it; **vor allen ~en** above all; **das ist ein ~!** that's quite something!; did you ever hear of such a thing! || **d~fest (d. machen** take into custody)
das **Dingelchen, –** little thing
dingen (*p/part* **gedungen**) hire (killer, *arch* servant *etc*)
das **Dingi** [–ŋg–], **–s** dinghy
dinglich real (*also leg*)
das **Dings** *coll* = **das ~bums/~da** thingummy; **der/die ~bums/~da** *coll* what's-his/her-name; **~da** (*no art*, = place) what's-its-name
dinieren dine
der **Dinosaurier** [–ĭɐ], **–** dinosaur
dionysisch Dionysian
das **Dioxyd, –e** dioxide
die **Diözese, –n** *RC* diocese
die **Diphtherie** diphtheria
der **Diphthong, –e** diphthong
diphthongieren [–ŋg–] diphthongize
Dipl.– (*eg* **Dipl.-Ing./-Kfm.**) = **Diplom–(ingenieur, kaufmann,** *etc*)
das **Diplom, –e** diploma; *univ*: *approx* = degree, *eg* **der ~kaufmann** *approx* = B.Comm., **der ~physiker** *approx* = B.Sc. (in physics), **der ~volkswirt** *approx* = B.Sc. (Econ.)
der **Diplomat, –en** (*wk masc*) diplomat; *in compds* **~en–** diplomatic ...; **der ~en|koffer, –** executive case
die **Diplomatie** diplomacy; diplomatic corps
diplomatisch diplomatic
dir (*dat of* **du:** *see p. xxvi*; *in correspondence*: **D~**) (to/for) you/yourself (*familiar sing*)
direkt direct; *rail* through; *coll* sheer; downright; (*adv*) directly; direct, straight; *rad*, *TV* live; *coll* positively; **die D~übertragung, –en** live broadcast
die **Direktion, –en** management; offices (of management)
die **Direktive, –n** directive
der **Direktor, –(or)en** director; governor, warden *US* (of prison); *educ* principal; headmaster
das **Direktorat, –e** director's *etc* office; directorship; governorship, wardenship *US*; *educ* principalship; headship
das **Direktorium, –(i)en** board (of directors)
der **Dirigent, –en** (*wk masc*) *mus* conductor; **der ~en|stab, ⸚e** conductor's baton
dirigieren direct; manage; *econ* control (economy); *mus* conduct
der **Dirigismus** state intervention
dirigistisch (policy) of state intervention
das **Dirndl, –** dirndl; *SGer* girl; **das ~kleid, –er** dirndl
die **Dirne, –n** prostitute
das **dis, Dis** [–ɪ–] (*gen* –), – *mus* (the note) D sharp; (*key*) **Dis** D sharp major, **dis** D sharp minor
Discount– [–'kaont–] discount ...
die **Disharmonie, –(ie)n** disharmony
disharmonisch disharmonious
der **Diskant, –e** treble
die **Diskette, –n** floppy disk
die **Disko, –s** disco
der **Diskont, –e, diskontieren** discount
diskontinuierlich discontinuous
die **Diskothek, –en** discotheque; record library
diskreditieren discredit, bring into disrepute
die **Diskrepanz, –en** discrepancy
diskret discreet; quiet, unobtrusive; *math*, *phys* discrete
die **Diskretion** discretion
diskriminieren discriminate against; disparage
die **Diskriminierung, –en** discrimination (*gen* against); disparagement
der **Diskus, –se/Disken** discus
die **Diskussion, –en** discussion; **zur ~ stehen** be under discussion; **zur ~ stellen** bring up for discussion || **der ~s|leiter, –** chairman; **der ~s|teilnehmer, –** participant (in discussion); *rad*, *TV* panellist
diskutabel worth considering/discussing
diskutieren = **~ über** (*acc*) discuss
der **Dispatcher** [–'pɛtʃɐ], **–** production manager; *EGer* production controller, *rail* traffic controller
der **Dispens, –e** dispensation (*also RC*)
die **Dispensaire|betreuung** [–pã'sɛ:ɐ–] *EGer* (*system of medical care – based on health centres – for the prevention and treatment of diseases*)
dispensieren: ~ von exempt from; *RC* dispense from
disponibel available
disponieren make arrangements; plan; **~ über** (*acc*) have at one's disposal; do as one wishes with
disponiert *p/part*; **~ für/zu** prone to; **(gut** *etc*) **~** in (good *etc*) form
die **Disposition, –en** free use (**über** *acc* of); plan (of essay *etc*); disposition; *med* predisposition; (*pl*) arrangements
disproportioniert ill-proportioned
der **Disput, –e** dispute
disputieren debate; argue; **~ über** (*acc*) debate; argue over

die **Disqualifikation, –en** disqualification
disqualifizieren disqualify
der **Dissens, –e** dissent, disagreement
die **Dissertation, –en** (doctoral) thesis
der **Dissident, –en** (*wk masc*) dissident; *eccles* dissenter
die **Dissonanz, –en** dissonance
die **Distanz, –en** distance; detachment; **~ wahren** keep one's distance
distanzieren *sp* outdistance; **sich ~ von** dissociate oneself from; **distanziert** detached
die **Distel, –n** thistle; **der ~fink, –en** (*wk masc*) goldfinch
das **Distichon** [–çɔn], **–(ch)en** distich
distinguiert [–ŋ'giːɐt] distinguished-looking; (appearance) distinguished
der **Distrikt, –e** district
die **Disziplin, –en** discipline; *sp* event; **d~los** undisciplined
Disziplinar– disciplinary ...
disziplinarisch disciplinary
diszipliniert disciplined
dito ditto
die **Diva, –s/Diven** (female) star; prima donna
divergent divergent
die **Divergenz, –en** divergence
divergieren diverge; **~d** divergent
der **Diversant, –en** (*wk masc*) *EGer* saboteur
diverse various; **D~s** various things
die **Diversion, –en** *EGer* sabotage
die **Dividende, –n** dividend
dividieren divide
die **Division, –en** division
der **Diwan, –e** *liter* divan
d. J. (**= dieses Jahres**) of this year, (**= der Jüngere**) the Younger
die **DKP = Deutsche Kommunistische Partei**
DM = (*and pronounced as*) **D-Mark** ['deː–] (**= Deutsche Mark**) deutschmark(s)
d. M. (**= dieses Monats**) inst.
der **Dnjepr** ['dnjɛpɐ] (*gen* **–(s)**) the Dnieper
der **Dnjestr** ['dnjɛstɐ] (*gen* **–(s)**) the Dniester
die **DNS** (**= Desoxyribonukleinsäure**) D.N.A.
Do. (**= Donnerstag**) Thurs.
doch 1 *conj* but; however; 2 *adv* all the same; yet; (*as emotive particle*) after all; surely; ..., won't you/isn't she *etc*?, (*with neg*) ..., will you/is she *etc*?; (*urging*) do ... (*eg* **beeil dich ~!** do hurry!); *or conveyed by emphasis or* do (*eg* **sie hat also '~ keinen Paß!** so she *doesn't* have a passport!, **es imponiert ihm '~** it does impress him); *or left untranslated* (*eg* **das ist ~ unerhört!** it's disgraceful!, **du kennst ihn ~!** you know what he's like!); (*in response to negative utterance*) yes I do/he is/they can/we must *etc*; (*with inversion, indicates reason*) since ...; ...ing (as ... does/is *etc*) (*eg* **..., wußte er ~ ...** knowing as he did ..., **sie sah sehr bleich aus, war sie ~ wochenlang krank gewesen** she looked very pale, having been ill for weeks); (*expressing wish, eg* **hätten wir ~ ...!**) if only (we had ... *etc*)!
  ~ (ein)mal do ...; why don't you ...?; ..., will you?
  nicht ~! don't!; certainly not!
  ~ noch after all; still; yet
  oder ~ or at least; **... oder ~?** ... or is he/must we *etc*?
  wenn ... ~ ...! if only ...!
  ~ wohl = ~ 2 *above*, '*as emotive particle*' (*2nd and 3rd senses*)
der **Docht, –e** wick
das **Dock, –s** dock
die **Docke, –n** skein
docken (*also v/i*) *naut, space* dock
der **Docker, –** docker, longshoreman *US*
der **Doge** [–ʒə], **–n** (*wk masc*) doge
die **Dogge, –n** Great Dane; **englische ~** mastiff
das **Dogma, –(m)en** dogma
der **Dogmatiker, –** dogmatician; dogmatist
dogmatisch dogmatic
der **Dogmatismus** dogmatism
die **Dohle, –n** jackdaw
der **Doktor, –(or)en** doctor (academic title); *coll* (medical) doctor; **seinen ~ machen** take one's doctor's degree || **die ~arbeit, –en** doctoral thesis; **der ~hut** doctor's cap; *coll* **= der ~titel, – = die ~würde, –n** doctorate
der **Doktorand, –en** (*wk masc*) candidate for a doctor's degree
die **Doktrin, –en** doctrine
doktrinär doctrinaire
das **Dokument, –e** document; record (of events); *EGer* Party membership book; *leg* deed, instrument
Dokumentar–: der ~bericht, –e documentary; **der ~film, –e** documentary (film); **das ~spiel, –e** dramatized documentary
dokumentarisch documentary; (*adv*) by means of documents
der **Dokumentarist, –en** (*wk masc*) documentarist
die **Dokumentation, –en** documentation; record; demonstration (of goodwill *etc*)
dokumentieren document; demonstrate; **sich ~** be demonstrated
der **Dolch, –e** dagger; **der ~stoß, ⸚e** thrust of a dagger; stab in the back
die **Dolde, –n** umbel
doll *coll esp NGer* tremendous, fantastic; incredible; (*adv*) tremendously; **nicht so ~** not so hot
der **Dollar** (*gen* **–(s)**), **–s**/(*following num*) **–** dollar
der **Dolmetsch, –e** spokesman (for poor *etc*); *Aust* interpreter
dolmetschen (*also v/i*) interpret
der **Dolmetscher, –** interpreter
die **Dolomiten** *pl* the Dolomites
der **Dom, –e** cathedral; *poet* canopy; **der ~herr,**

-en (*like* **Herr**) canon; **der ~pfaff, -en** (*wk masc*) bullfinch

die **Domäne, -n** demesne; domain, province

domestizieren domesticate

dominant dominant (*also biol*)

die **Dominante, -n** dominant feature; *mus* dominant

die **Dominanz** dominance (*also biol*)

dominieren dominate; (*v/i*) dominate; predominate

der **Dominikaner, -** Dominican

Dominikaner- Dominican ...

Dominikanisch: die ~e Republik the Dominican Republic

das **Domino, -s** dominoes; **der ~stein, -e** domino

das **Domizil, -e** domicile

der **Dompteur** [dɔmp'tøːɐ], **-e, die Dompteuse** [-'tøːzə], **-n** trainer (of circus animals)

der **Don** [-ɔ-] (*gen* **-(s)**) the Don

die **Donau** the Danube; *in compds* Danubian ...; **die ~monarchie** the Austro-Hungarian Empire

der **Donner, -** thunder; **wie vom ~ gerührt** *coll* thunderstruck || **der ~schlag, ⸚e** thunderclap; **das ~wetter** *coll* row (**Donnerwetter (noch mal)!** my word!; = **zum Donnerwetter!** for heaven's sake!)

donnern hurl (into corner *etc*); slam (into goal *etc*); thunder out; (*v/i*) thunder, roar; (*sn*) thunder (across *etc*); **~ gegen** *coll* hammer on; fulminate against; (*sn*) crash into; **es donnert** it is thundering; **~d** thundering; thunderous

der **Donnerstag, -e** Thursday

donnerstags on Thursdays

Don Quichotte [dɔnki'ʃɔt] Don Quixote

doof *coll* daft

dopen [-ɔ-, -oː-] *sp* dope

das **Doping** [-ɔ-, -oː-], **-s** *sp* doping; **die ~kontrolle, -n** dope test

das **Doppel, -** duplicate; *sp* doubles; *in compds* double ...; twin ...; dual ...; **das ~bett, -en** double bed; **d~bödig** ambiguous; **der ~decker, -** double-decker; *aer* biplane; **d~deutig** ambiguous; **die ~ehe** bigamy; **das ~fenster, -** double-glazed window; (*pl*) double glazing; **der ~gänger, -** double; **das ~kinn, -e** double chin; **der ~kopf** (*card game*); **d~läufig** double-barrelled; **der ~laut, -e** diphthong; **der ~punkt, -e** colon; **d~reihig** in two rows; *cost* double-breasted; **d~seitig** double-page; double-sided; *med* (pneumonia) double; **der ~sinn** double meaning; ambiguity; **d~sinnig** ambiguous; **das ~spiel, -e** double-dealing; *sp* doubles (match); **der ~stecker, -** two-way adaptor; **die ~verdiener** *pl* (married) couple with two incomes; **der ~zentner, -** 100 kilograms; **das ~zimmer, -** double room; **d~züngig** two-faced

doppeln *Aust* resole; *comput* duplicate

doppelt double; twice; redoubled; (*adv*) twice (as ...); doubly; (see) double; **~e Moral** double standard; **in ~er Ausführung** in duplicate; **~ so groß** twice the size; **das Doppelte** (*decl as adj*) double; twice as much || **~kohlen|sauer** bicarbonate of ...

das **Dorf, ⸚er** village; **der ~bewohner, -** villager

dörflich village; rural

der **Dorn, -en** thorn; (*pl* **-e**) *tech* mandrel; pin; *athl* spike; (+*dat*) **ein ~ im Auge sein** be a thorn in (s.o.'s) flesh || **das ~röschen** [-sç-] Sleeping Beauty; **der ~röschen|schlaf** slumber

dornig thorny; beset with difficulties

Dörr- dried ...; **die ~pflaume, -n** prune

dorren (*sn*) dry up

dörren dry

der **Dorsch, -e** codling

dort there; **~, wo ...** where ...; **~ drüben/oben/unten** over/up/down there || **~her** (**von d.** from there); **~hin** there (= to that place); **~hinaus** out there (**bis dorthinaus** *coll* like/as hell)

dortig there

die **Dose, -n** box (with lid); can; jar; *elect* socket

Dosen *pl of* **Dose, Dosis**

dösen *coll* doze; day-dream

Dosen- canned ...; **der ~öffner, -** can-opener

dosieren measure out a dose of

die **Dosierung, -en** *vbl noun*; *also* dosage

dösig *coll* drowsy

die **Dosis, -(s)en** dose

das **Dossier** [-'si̯eː], **-s** dossier

Dostojewski [-to'jɛf-] Dostoyevsky

dotieren endow; (**gut** *etc*) **dotiert** (well *etc*) -paid; **der Preis ist mit ... dotiert** the prize is worth ...

das **Dotter, -** (*also* **der**) yolk

doubeln ['duː-] *cin, theat* stand in (for)

das **Double** ['duːbl̩], **-s** *cin, theat* stand-in

das **Doublé** [du-], **-s** rolled gold

doublieren [du-] *text* double; *tech* plate

down [daʊn] *coll*: **~ sein** feel low

der **Doyen** [dŏa'jɛ̃ː], **-s** doyen

der **Dozent, -en** (*wk masc*) lecturer

die **Dozentur, -en** lectureship

dozieren lecture on; (*v/i*) lecture; hold forth

DP *EGer* = **Deutsche Post** (*E. German postal service*)

dpa = **Deutsche Presse-Agentur**

DR *EGer* = **Deutsche Reichsbahn** (*E. German railways*)

Dr. (= **Doktor**) Dr

der **Drache, -n** (*wk masc*) dragon

der **Drachen, -** kite; hang-glider; *coll* 'battle-axe'; *in compds also* dragon('s) ...; **das ~fliegen** hang-gliding; **der ~flieger, -** hang-glider

die **Drachme, -n** drachma
das **Dragée** [-ʒ-], **-s** sugar-coated sweet/candy *US*; sugar-coated pill
der **Dragoner, -** dragoon; *coll* virago
der **Draht, ⸚e** wire; **heißer ~** hot line; **auf ~** *coll* on the ball || **die ~anschrift, -en** telegraphic address; **das ~haar** wiry hair; **~haar-, d~haarig** wire-haired; **d~los** wireless; **die ~schere, -n** wire-cutters; **die ~seil|bahn, -en** cable railway; **der ~seil|künstler, -** tightrope walker; **der ~zieher, -** wire-drawer; wire-puller
drahten wire
drahtig wiry
drakonisch Draconian
drall strapping; chubby
der **Drall** rifling (of gun-barrel); tendency; *phys* rotation
das **Dralon** [-ɔn] (*trade-mark*) dralon
das **Drama, -(m)en** drama
die **Dramatik** [-ɪk] drama (*collect, or of situation etc*)
der **Dramatiker, -** dramatist
dramatisch dramatic
dramatisieren dramatize
der **Dramaturg, -en** (*wk masc*) literary adviser (to theatre *etc*)
dran *coll* = **daran; ich bin ~** it's my turn; I'm for it; **gut ~** well off; **schlecht ~** in a bad way; **ich weiß nicht, wie ich mit ... ~ bin** I don't know where I am with; **es ist was ~** there's something in it; **an ...** (*dat*) **ist was ~** there's something wrong with (engine *etc*); **was ist ~ an ...** (*dat*)? what is it about ...?; **an ...** (*dat*) **ist nichts ~** there's nothing in (report *etc*)/wrong with (engine *etc*); there's no meat on; (person) is *etc* all skin and bone/nothing special
dran- *sep pref*; **~geben*** *coll* sacrifice; **~gehen*** (*sn*) (= **darangehen**); **~halten*: sich d.** *coll* get a move on; **~kommen*** (*sn*) *coll* have one's turn; (pupil) be asked a question/to read *etc* (**als erster/letzter d.** be first/last; **ich komme dran** it's my turn); **~kriegen** *coll* get (s.o.) to do it; **~machen** (= **daranmachen**); **~nehmen*** *coll* take (patient *etc*); ask (pupil) a question/to read *etc*; **~setzen** (= **daransetzen**)
der **Drang** urge; yearning (**nach** for); pressure
drang (dränge) *p/t* (*subj*) *of* **dringen**
drängeln *coll* (*also v/i*) jostle, shove; pester s.o. (to do sth.); **sich ~** push one's way (to front *etc*)
drängen (*see also* **gedrängt**) push; press (to); (*v/i*) push (one's way); be pressing; **~ auf** (*acc*) press for; **zum Aufbruch/zur Eile ~** urge (s.o.) to leave/hurry; **die Zeit drängt** time presses; **es drängt mich zu ...** I feel impelled to ...
sich ~ push one's way; (*recip*) crowd together; follow close on one another
das **Drängen** urging; **auf ~** (*+gen*) at the insistence of
die **Drangsal, -e** distress; hardship
drangsalieren harass; plague
drapieren drape
drastisch drastic; (crudely) graphic
drauf *coll* = **darauf; ~ haben** be doing (... m.p.h.); **~ und dran zu ...** on the point of (*+ger*) || **der D~gänger, -** daredevil; **~gängerisch** reckless; **~geben*** (*sep*) *coll* throw in ((*+dat*) **eins d.** land (s.o.) one; take to task); **~gehen*** (*sep*; *sn*) *coll* snuff it; go west; be used up/spent; **~hauen*** (*sep*; *p/t* **haute drauf**) *coll* (**einen d.** celebrate); **~legen** (*sep*) *coll* put on it/them; pay another ...; **~los-** *sep pref* ... away; **~zahlen** (*sep*) *coll* pay in addition
draus *coll* = **daraus**
draußen outside; outdoors; out (in garden *etc*); abroad; (out) at sea; *mil coll* at the front; **da/hier ~** out there/here; **nach ~** outside; **~ vor** (*dat*) outside
die **Drechsel|bank** [-ks-], **⸚e** lathe
drechseln [-ks-] (*see also* **gedrechselt**) turn (on lathe); produce (verses *etc*) laboriously
der **Drechsler, -** turner
der **Dreck** *coll* dirt; mud; muck; rubbish, trash; **jeder ~** every little thing; **einen ~** *vulg* = not at all, *as in* **das geht ... einen ~ an** that's none of ...'s business, **sich einen ~ kümmern um** not give a damn about; **im ~ sitzen** be in a mess; **in den ~ ziehen** drag in the mud || **der ~fink, -en** (*wk masc*) *coll* = **der ~spatz, -en** (*wk masc*) *coll* dirty little fellow
dreckig *coll* dirty; **es geht mir ~** I'm in a bad way
der **Dreh, -s** *coll* turn; knack; idea; **den ~ rausbaben** have got the knack
Dreh- ... of rotation; turning ...; rotating ...; revolving ...; rotary ...; *cin* shooting ...;
die ~arbeiten *pl cin* shooting; **die ~bank, ⸚e** lathe; **der ~bleistift, -e** propelling pencil, mechanical pencil *US*; **die ~brücke, -n** swing-bridge; **das ~buch, ⸚er** *cin* screenplay; **das ~gestell, -e** *rail* bogie; **das ~kreuz, -e** turnstile; **das ~moment, -e** torque; **die ~orgel, -n** barrel-organ; **der ~punkt, -e** pivot; fulcrum; **die ~scheibe, -n** potter's wheel; *rail* turntable; **der ~stuhl, ⸚e** swivel chair; **die ~tür, -en** revolving door; **~wurm** *coll* (**den D. haben** feel giddy); **die ~zahl, -en** (number of) revolutions; **der ~zahl|messer, -** rev(olution) counter
drehbar rotating; revolving; that can be turned
drehen turn; rotate; grind (barrel-organ); roll (cigarette); *cin* shoot; make (film); *coll*

engineer; (*v/i*) turn; *cin* film; ~ **an** (*dat*) turn; (+*dat*) **den Rücken** ~ turn one's back on; **wie man es auch dreht und wendet** whichever way you look at it

sich ~ turn; revolve; rotate; swivel; **sich** ~ **um** rotate about; be about; **es dreht sich darum, ob …** the question is whether …

die **Drehung, –en** *vbl noun*; *also* rotation; revolution; turn

drei (*gen* **–er**) three; **die Drei, –en** three (*also* = *third grade* – **'befriedigend'** – *in marking scale*) || **~dimensional** three-dimensional; **das D~eck, –e** triangle; **~eckig** triangular; **das D~ecks|verhältnis, –se** eternal triangle; **die D~einigkeit** the Trinity; **~fach** threefold, triple; **die D~faltigkeit** the Trinity; **der D~fuß, ⸗e** tripod; **das D~gespann, –e** team of three horses; trio; **„Die D~groschen|oper"** 'The Threepenny Opera'; **~jährlich** triennial; **der D~käse|hoch, –s** *coll* little fellow; **der D~klang, ⸗e** triad; **D~könige** *pl* = **das D~königs|fest** Epiphany; **~mal** three times; three tickets to/portions *etc* of; **~malig** (done) three (times); **das D~rad, ⸗er** tricycle; three-wheeler; **der D~spitz, –e** three-cornered hat; **der D~sprung, ⸗e** triple jump; **D~stufen–** three-stage …; **~teilen** (*sep*) divide into three; *math* trisect; **~teilig** three-piece/part; tripartite; **~viertel** three-quarters; (*in time phrases*) quarter to; **~viertel|lang** [–'fɪr–] three-quarter length; **der D~viertel|takt** [–'fɪr–] three-four time; **der D~zack, –e** trident

dreier *see* **drei**; *in compds* **D~–** … of three; tripartite …; **~lei** (*indecl*) three kinds of; three things; **der D~takt** triple time

drein– *sep pref*; **~blicken** wear a … expression; **~reden** interfere; **~schauen** (= **~blicken**)

dreißig thirty; **der D~jährige Krieg** the Thirty Years' War

dreißiger: die ~ Jahre the thirties; **der Dreißiger, –** man in his thirties; (*pl*) thirties

dreißigst.., das Dreißigstel, – thirtieth

dreist impudent; bold

die **Dreistigkeit, –en** impudence; boldness; **sich** *dat* **~en herausnehmen** take liberties

dreizehn thirteen; **jetzt schlägt's ~!** that *does* it!

dreizehnt.., das Dreizehntel, – thirteenth

Dresch– threshing …

Dresche *coll*: ~ **bekommen** get a thrashing

dreschen (**drisch(s)t**, *p/t* **drosch** (*subj* **drösche**), *p/part* **gedroschen**) thresh; *coll* thrash; slam (ball *etc*); ~ **auf** (*acc*) *coll* hammer; thump; **Phrasen** ~ *coll* churn out platitudes

der **Dreß, –(ss)e** (sports) outfit

der **Dresseur** [–'søːɐ], **–e** (animal) trainer

dressieren train (animal); *cul* truss; decorate; **dressiert** *also* performing

der **Dressman** [–mɛn], **..men** male (fashion) model

die **Dressur, –en** training (of animal); trick (performed by animal); *equest* dressage

dribbeln *sp* dribble

das **Dribbling, –s** *sp* dribble; (*pl*) dribbling

driften (*sn*) drift

drillen drill (*also mil*)

der **Drillich** *text* drill

der **Drilling, –e** triplet; triple-barrelled shotgun

drin *coll* = **darin;** ~ **sein** be a possibility; **nicht** ~ **sein** be out (of the question); **ich bin noch nicht wieder richtig** ~ I haven't really got back into it yet || **~sitzen*** (*sep*) *coll* be in a fix

dringen (*p/t* **drang** (*subj* **dränge**), *p/part* **gedrungen**):

an die Öffentlichkeit ~ (*sn*) get out

~ **auf** (*acc*) insist on

~ **aus** (*sn*) come from; (steam *etc*) escape from

~ **durch** (*sn*) penetrate; make one's way through; break through

~ **in** (*acc*) (*sn*) enter, penetrate; press

~ **(bis) zu** (*sn*) reach (s.o.'s) ears

dringend urgent; compelling; (suspicion) strong

dringlich urgent

die **Dringlichkeit** urgency

der **Drink, –s** (alcoholic) drink

drinnen inside; **da/hier** ~ in there/here

drisch *imp sing*, **drisch(s)t** (*2nd*,) *3rd sing pres of* **dreschen**

dritt: zu ~ (*see* **zu** 1 (*i*)); **dritt..** third; **die D~e Welt** the Third World; **der/die Dritte** (*decl as adj*) third party/person

dritt– third …; **~letzt** third from last; **~rangig** third-rate

drittel: ein ~ … a third of a …

das **Drittel, –** third

dritteln divide into three

drittens thirdly

DRK = Deutsches Rotes Kreuz

droben *esp SGer* up there

die **Droge, –n** drug; **d~n|abhängig** addicted to drugs; **der/die ~n|abhängige** (*decl as adj*) drug addict; **der ~n|mißbrauch** drug abuse

die **Drogerie, –(ie)n** chemist's, drugstore *US* (not dispensing prescriptions)

der **Drogist, –en** (*wk masc*) chemist, druggist *US*

der **Droh|brief, –e** threatening letter

drohen (danger, storm, *etc*) threaten; (+*dat*) threaten (person *etc*; *sometimes pass*, *eg* **eine Hungersnot drohte dem Land** the country was threatened by famine); ~ **mit** threaten (war *etc*); (*followed by vbl noun*, *eg* **mit dem Abbruch von …** ~) threaten to (break off … *etc*); (+*dat*) ~ **mit** shake (one's fist *etc*) at; threaten with (dismissal *etc*); **ihm droht Gefängnis/Strafe** he risks being imprisoned/punished; **ihm droht der Tod** he's in danger of his life; **~ zu ...** be in danger of (collapsing, overheating, *etc*); = **damit ~ zu ...** threaten to ...; **es droht zu regnen** there's a threat of rain; **~d** threatening; impending

die **Drohne, –n** drone

dröhnen roar; boom; resound; (head) buzz

die **Drohung, –en** threat

drollig funny; cute; quaint

das **Dromedar, –e** dromedary

der **Drops** (*gen* –), – fruit-drop

drosch (drösche) *p/t* (*subj*) *of* **dreschen**

die **Droschke, –n** (hackney) cab; *arch* taxi

die **Drossel, –n** thrush

drosseln cut down, reduce; *tech* throttle

drüben over there; across the border (*coll* = in the other Germany); on the other side; **da/dort ~** over there

drüber *coll* = **darüber**

der **Druck, ⸗e** pressure; (*pl* **–e**) printing; print; **~ machen hinter** (*acc*) *coll* get (sth.) moving; **im/in ~** pressed for time; **in ~ geben** send to press; **unter ~ setzen** put pressure on; **unter ~ stehen** be under pressure

Druck– pressure ...; pressurized ...; *print* printing ...; **der ~fehler, –** misprint; **d~fertig** ready for press; **der ~knopf, ⸗e** push-button; snap-fastener; **die ~legung** printing; **die ~luft** compressed air; **~luft–** compressed-air ...; pneumatic ...; **die ~luft|bremse, –n** air-brake; **der ~messer, –** pressure-gauge; **das ~mittel, –** lever, means of bringing pressure to bear; **d~reif** ready for publication; impeccably formulated; **die ~sache, –n** (item of) printed matter; **die ~schrift, –en** block letters; (unbound) publication; *print* type; **die ~sorten** *pl Aust* forms; **die ~taste, –n** push-button; **d~technisch** typographical

der **Drückeberger, –** *coll* shirker

drucken print

drücken (*see also* **gedrückt**) press; squeeze; force down (price *etc*); weigh heavily on; (*v/i*) pinch, be too tight; be oppressive; **~ auf** (*acc*) press; **aufs Gemüt ~** get one down; **„~"** 'push'

sich ~ slip (out of *etc*); **sich ~ um/von/vor** (*dat*) shirk; duck

drückend oppressive; heavy

der **Drucker, –** printer; **die ~schwärze** printer's ink

der **Drücker, –** door-handle; push-button; trigger; **am ~ sitzen** *coll* be in a key position; **auf den letzten ~** *coll* at the last minute

die **Druckerei, –en** printing-house; printer's

drum *coll* = **darum; sei's ~!** never mind; **alles, was ~ und dran ist** everything connected with it; **~ herum** *coll* around it/them; **das Drum und Dran** incidentals; ins and outs; **mit allem Drum und Dran** with all the trimmings

drunten *esp SGer* down there

drunter *coll* = **darunter; es geht ~ und drüber** everything is topsy-turvy

die **Drüse, –n** gland; *in compds* **~n–** glandular ...

Dschidda [dʒ–] Jedda

Dschingis-Khan ['dʒɪŋgɪs'kaːn] Genghis Khan

der **Dschungel** ['dʒʊŋl], – jungle

die **Dschunke** [dʒ–], **–n** *naut* junk

dt. = **deutsch**

dtv = **Deutscher Taschenbuchverlag**

Dtzd. (= **Dutzend**) doz.

du (*see p. xxvi*; *in correspondence*: **D~**) you (*familiar sing*); (*introducing comment, suggestion, etc*) **~, ...** I know what; you know; look, listen; **~, sag mal ...** tell me ...; **auf ~ und ~ stehen mit** be on familiar terms with; **per ~ sein** *approx* = be on first-name terms; **~, ~!** naughty, naughty!

dual dual; *comput* binary

der **Dübel, –** dowel; (wall) plug

dübeln fix (in wall) with a plug

dubios dubious

das **Dublee, –s** rolled gold

die **Dublette, –n** duplicate; *jewel* doublet

dublieren *text* double; *tech* plate

ducken duck; humiliate; **sich ~** duck; cringe (**vor** *dat* before, to)

der **Duckmäuser, –** *coll* yes-man

duckmäuserisch *coll* servile

Dudel–: der ~sack, ⸗e bagpipes; **der ~sack|pfeifer, –** piper

dudeln *coll* tootle; (instrument) drone away

das **Duell, –e** duel

der **Duellant, –en** (*wk masc*) duellist

duellieren: sich ~ fight a duel

das **Duett, –e** duet

der **Duft, ⸗e** scent; fragrance; aroma; **das ~organ, –e** scent organ

dufte *coll esp Berlin* 'great'

duften smell (nice *etc*); be fragrant; *iron* (garlic, manure, *etc*) smell; **~ nach** smell of; **es duftet nach** there is a smell of; **~d** fragrant

duftig gossamer; frothy

der **Dukaten, –** ducat

dulden tolerate; endure; (*v/i*) suffer; **stillschweigend ~** connive at

die **Dulder|miene, –n** martyred expression

duldsam tolerant

die **Duldsamkeit** tolerance

die **Duldung** toleration (of)

dumm (*comp, superl* ⸗) stupid; silly; *coll* disagreeable; (feeling) uneasy; **~es Zeug** nonsense; **es wird mir zu ~** *coll* I've had enough; **das ist 'zu ~!** what a nuisance!; **ich lasse mich nicht für ~ verkaufen** *coll* I won't be made a fool of; (+*dat*) **~ kommen** *coll* be cheeky to; **sich ~ stellen** *coll* pretend not to understand; **der D~e sein** *coll* come off worst || **~dreist** brash, impudent; **der D~kopf, ⸚e** blockhead

der **Dumme|jungen|streich, -e** (*1st element may be declined with adj endings*) (boyish) prank

das **Dummerchen, -** *coll* silly

der **Dummerjan, -e** *coll* idiot

dummer|weise foolishly; unfortunately

die **Dummheit, -en** stupidity; foolish action; **eine ~ begehen** do something foolish

dümmlich (rather) stupid

dumpf dull; stuffy; vague

das **Dumping** ['dam-] *comm* dumping

die **Düne, -n** dune

der **Dung** dung

das **Dünge|mittel, -** fertilizer

düngen manure; fertilize

der **Dünger, -** manure; fertilizer

dunkel dark; (voice) deep; obscure; vague; dubious; **im ~n lassen** leave in the dark; **das liegt noch im ~n** that is as yet uncertain; **im D~n** in the dark

das **Dunkel** darkness

der **Dünkel** conceit

dunkel- dark ...; **~häutig** swarthy; **die D~kammer, -n** dark room; **der D~mann, ⸚er** shady character (operating behind the scenes); *arch* obscurantist; **das D~werden** nightfall (**vor/nach (dem) D.** before/after dark); **die D~ziffer, -n** number of unknown cases

dünkelhaft conceited

die **Dunkelheit** darkness; **bei Einbruch der ~** at nightfall; **nach Einbruch der ~** after dark

dunkeln (*sn*: hair *etc*) darken; **es dunkelt** it is getting dark

dünken *arch* (*also* + *dat*) seem ... to; **sich ~** fancy oneself to be

Dünkirchen [-yː-] Dunkirk

dünn thin; (tea *etc*) weak; **sich ~ machen** (*cf* **dünnmachen**) squeeze up || **der D~darm, ⸚e** small intestine; **das D~druck|papier** India paper; **~flüssig** thin; **~machen** (*cf* **sich dünn machen** *at* **dünn**) (*sep*): **sich d.** *coll* make oneself scarce

dünne|machen (*sep*): **sich ~** *coll* make oneself scarce

der **Dunst, ⸚e** haze; vapour; **keinen (blassen) ~ haben von** *coll* not have the faintest idea about; (+*dat*) **blauen ~ vormachen** *coll* hoodwink || **die ~glocke, -n** pall of smog; **der ~kreis** aura

dunsten give off a smell; steam; **~ lassen** *Aust* keep (s.o.) waiting

dünsten steam; stew

dunstig hazy; smoky

die **Dünung** swell (of sea)

das **Duo, -s** pair (of crooks *etc*); *mus* duet (= composition, performers)

Duodez-: der ~fürst, -en (*wk masc*) princeling; **der ~staat, -en** tiny state

düpieren dupe

das **Duplikat, -e** duplicate

duplizieren duplicate

die **Duplizität, -en** simultaneous occurrence (of two similar cases *etc*)

das **Dur** *mus* major (key); **-Dur** *mus* ... major (*eg* **C-Dur** C major)

durch 1 *prep* (+*acc*) (*a*) (*indicating direction*) through; across; (tour) of;

(*b*) (*indicating agency*, *cause*, *etc*) by (means of), (*with passive*) by; through (friend, intermediary, *etc*); over (loudspeaker *etc*); as a result of; by reason of; *math* divided by;

(*c*) (*indicating time*): (*preceding noun*) *Aust* for (... weeks *etc*); (*following noun*) *coll* = **hindurch;**

2 *adv* through; **ich bin ~** I have got through; I have pulled through; **... ist ~ ...** is worn through/done/(cheese) ripe; (application) has gone through; (bus *etc*) has gone

es ist (7 *etc*) **Uhr ~** it's gone (7 *etc*) o'clock

~ ... hin across; over (period)

~ ... hindurch through; (*indicating time*) for; over; (*with noun qualified by* **ganz**) throughout

~ und ~ through and through; thoroughly; throughout; (know) inside out

unten ~: ... ist bei mir unten ~ *coll* I'm through with ...

---

durch- *sep* (*stressed*) *and insep* (*unstressed*) *pref – general senses*:

(*i*) ... through (*eg* **~fließen** flow through, (*with connotation 'from beginning to end'*) **~spielen** play through); *with reflexive pronoun* ... one's way through (*eg* **sich ~arbeiten** work one's way through); *with modal auxiliary eg* **~müssen** go/get through (*eg* **ich muß durch** I must get through);

(*ii*) *suggesting thoroughness* (*eg* **~rühren** stir well, **~atmen** breathe deeply);

(*iii*) (*transitive only*) *suggesting continuous activity* (*eg* **~tanzen** dance all (night *etc*) long, **eine ~tanzte Nacht** a night spent dancing)

---

durch|ackern *coll* plough through

durch|arbeiten work through; work out; work thoroughly; (*v/i*) work without a break; **sich ~, sich ~ durch** work one's way through

durch|atmen breathe deeply

durch|aus thoroughly (readable *etc*); quite; absolutely; **~ nicht** not at all; by no means; **~ tun wollen** be set on doing

durchbacken (*p/part* **durchgebacken**) (*cf next entry*) bake thoroughly; **gut durchgebacken** well-baked

durchbacken (*cf previous entry*): **~ mit** baked with

durchbeißen* (*cf next entry*) bite through/in two; **sich ~** *coll* struggle through

durchbeißen* (*cf previous entry*) (fierce animal) tear open (throat)

durchbekommen* *coll* get (s.o., sth.) through; saw through

durchbetteln: sich ~ beg one's way

durchbiegen* bend to its fullest extent; **sich ~** sag

durchblättern, durchblättern leaf through

durchbleuen *coll* give (s.o.) a good hiding

der **Durchblick, -e** view (between ...) (**auf** *acc* of)

durchblicken, ~ durch look through; **~ lassen** hint at

durchblitzen flash through (s.o.'s) mind

durchblutet blood-stained; **gut/schlecht ~** with good/poor circulation

die **Durchblutung** circulation of blood; **die ~s|störung, -en** circulatory disorder

durchbohren (*cf next entry*) bore through; bore (hole)

durchbohren (*cf previous entry*) pierce; run through; **~d** (glance) penetrating

durchboxen *coll* push through; **sich ~** battle one's way through

durchbraten* cook through; **gut durchgebraten** well done

durchbrechen* (*cf next entry*) break in two; make a hole in; make (window *etc* in wall); (*v/i sn*) break in two; fall through; (sun, *mil, sp*) break through; (bud) burst; (tooth) come through; (character) reveal itself; *med* perforate; **~ durch** (*sn*) fall through

durchbrechen* (*cf previous entry*; *see also* **durchbrochen**) break through, (water) breach, *aer* break (sound-barrier); break, violate

durchbrennen* keep burning; (*sn*) burn through; (fuse) blow; (light bulb) burn out; *coll* decamp; (+*dat*) (*sn*) *footb* elude; *coll* run away from; **~ mit** (*sn*) *coll* run away with; **von zu Hause ~** *coll* run away from home; **~ lassen** keep (stove) in

durchbringen* get (s.o., sth.) through; bring (patient) through; provide for; *coll* squander; **sich (ehrlich) ~** make a(n honest) living

durchbrochen *p/part*; *also* open-work

der **Durchbruch, ⸚e** breakthrough (*also mil*); opening, (in dyke *etc*) breach; *aer* breaking; *med* perforation; **~ der Zähne** cutting of teeth; **zum ~ kommen** manifest itself; gain acceptance; (+*dat*) **zum ~ verhelfen** help win acceptance for

durchdenken* think through; think out; think over carefully

durchdrängen: sich ~ push one's way through

durchdrehen (*see also* **durchgedreht**) put through the mincer/meat grinder *US*; put through the wringer; (*v/i*) (wheels) spin; *cin* shoot without a break; *coll* crack up

durchdringen* (*cf next entry*) (*sn*) penetrate; (idea) find acceptance; **~ (bis) zu** reach; **~ durch** penetrate; **~ mit** win acceptance for; **(mit seiner Stimme) nicht ~ können** be unable to make oneself heard

durchdringen* (*cf previous entry*) penetrate; pervade; **durchdrungen von** filled with; convinced of

durchdringend, durchdringend penetrating; pungent; piercing

durchdrücken press through a sieve *etc*; wash through gently; straighten (knees *etc*); *coll* push through (bill *etc*); **seinen Willen ~** *coll* get one's way

durch|eilen (*cf next entry*) (*sn*) hurry through

durch|eilen (*cf previous entry*) hurry through (place)

durch|einander in a muddle; confused; (eat, drink) indiscriminately; **das Durch|einander** muddle; chaos || **~bringen*** (*sep*) mix up; confuse; **~gehen*** (*sep*; *sn*) *coll* go haywire; **~geraten*** (*sep*; *sn*) get mixed up; **~reden** (*sep*) talk all at once; **~werfen*** (*sep*) jumble up; muddle up

durchfahren* (*cf next entry*) (*sn*) go through; drive/travel through (without stopping); **~ durch** drive through; travel through; **der Zug fährt in X durch** the train doesn't stop at X; **die Nacht ~** drive/travel all night; **bei Gelb/Rot ~** go through the lights at amber/red, run a yellow/red light *US*

durchfahren* (*cf previous entry*) travel through/across; drive through/across; cover (distance); (thought) cross (s.o.'s) mind; **ein Schreck durchfuhr mich I** was seized with fear

die **Durchfahrt, -en** journey through; passage; **auf der ~** on the way through; passing through; **„~ verboten!"** 'no thoroughfare' || **die ~s|straße, -n** through road

der **Durchfall, ⸚e** diarrhoea; *coll* failure; flop

durchfallen* (*cf next entry*) (*sn*) fall through; fail; (play *etc*) be a flop; **~ lassen** fail

durchfallen* (*cf previous entry*) fall (... feet *etc*)

durchfechten* fight out; fight (cause) to a successful conclusion; **sich ~** struggle through; *coll* beg one's way
durchfeilen file through; polish (piece of writing)
durchfeuchten soak
durchfinden*: ~ zu find; **sich ~** find one's way; **(sich) nicht mehr ~** be lost
durchflechten*: ~ mit weave through; **durchflochten mit** *also* interlarded with
durchfliegen* (*cf next entry*) (*sn*) fly through; fly non-stop; *coll* fail; **~ durch** fly through
durchfliegen* (*cf previous entry*) fly through; fly (distance); skim through
durchfließen* (*cf next entry*) (*sn*), **~ durch** flow through
durchfließen* (*cf previous entry*) flow through; *phys* pass through
der **Durchflug, ⸗e, ~ durch** flight through || **das ~s|recht, -e** overflying rights
der **Durchfluß, ⸗(ss)e** flow (**durch** through); opening
durchfluten (*cf next entry*) (*sn*), **~ durch** flood through, pour through
durchfluten (*cf previous entry*) flow through; (light) flood; **durchflutet von** flooded with
durchformen elaborate
durchforschen research (field); scan (**auf** *acc* for); scrutinize (for); **~ nach** search for
durchforsten thin (forest); prune (expenditure *etc*)
durchfressen* eat through; **~ durch** eat (hole) in; **sich ~ bei** *coll* sponge one's meals from; **sich ~ durch** eat/burn its way through; *coll* plough through
durchfrieren* (*sn*) freeze solid; (person) freeze; **durchgefroren = durchfroren** frozen stiff
durchfrösteln (shiver) run down (s.o.'s) back
durchfühlen sense; **~ durch** feel (ribs *etc*) through
die **Durchfuhr** *econ* transit
durchführbar feasible
die **Durchführbarkeit** feasibility
durchführen lead through/across; take through/across; show round; perform, carry out; hold (meeting); pursue to its logical conclusion; **~ durch** lead through/across; show round; lay (cable *etc*) through
die **Durchführung** *vbl noun*; *also* execution; performance (of)
durchfurcht furrowed (**von** with)
durchfüttern *coll* feed, support
die **Durchgabe, -n** passing on (of message by telephone *etc*); *rad*, *TV* broadcasting (of news), announcement
der **Durchgang, ⸗e** passageway; *sp etc* round; *astron*, *econ* transit; **~ durch** passage through; „**~ verboten!**" 'no thoroughfare'
durchgängig universal; (feature *etc*) constant; (*adv*) *also* throughout
Durchgangs- through ...; transit ...; **das ~stadium, -(i)en** transitional stage; **die ~straße, -n** through road; **der ~verkehr** through traffic
durchgeben* phone (message); *rad*, *TV* broadcast (report *etc*)
durchgedreht *p/part*; **~ sein** *coll* be a nervous wreck
durchgehen* (*sn*) go through; (*v/i*) go through; pass through; walk without a break; (rain) come through; (horse) bolt; (motion) be passed; *rail* go right through; (+*dat*) *coll* run away from; **~ lassen** let pass, overlook; (+*dat*) let (s.o.) get away with; overlook (s.o.'s error *etc*)
  ~ bis go on until; *rail* go right through to
  ~ durch go through; pass through; (rain) come through; (motif) run right through
  ~ für pass as
  ~ mit run away/off with; (feelings, imagination) run away with
durchgehend continuous; (train) through; (*adv*) from top to bottom; **~(s *Aust*) geöffnet** open all day
durchgeistigt highly intellectual
durchgeregnet *p/part*; *coll* wet through
durchgestalten develop fully
durchgießen* strain
durchgliedern, durchgliedern structure (by dividing into sections)
durchgreifen* reach through; take firm action; **energisch/hart ~** take vigorous/tough action; **~d** vigorous; sweeping; far-reaching
durchhaben* *coll* have finished (reading)
Durchhalte-: der ~befehl, -e order to fight on to the finish; **das ~vermögen** staying power; endurance
durchhalten* keep up, sustain; stand (strain); see (battle *etc*) through; (*v/i*) hold out
der **Durchhang, durchhängen*** (*like* **hängen** *v/i*) sag
durchhauen* hack through; (*p/t only* **haute durch**) *coll* give (s.o.) a good hiding; blow (fuse); **sich ~** hack one's way through; get through
durchhecheln heckle (flax); *coll* pull to pieces
durchheizen heat thoroughly; (*v/i*) keep the heating on continuously
durchhelfen*: (+*dat*) ~ durch help to get through; see through (difficulty); **sich ~** manage
durchhören hear (through wall *etc*); detect (note of ...)
durchhungern: sich ~ scrape a living
durch|irren wander through
durch|ixen (on typewriter) cross out (using

x's), x out *US*

durchjagen (*cf next entry*) chase through; rush (order *etc*) through; (*v/i sn*) race through; ~ **durch** chase through; (*v/i sn*) race through

durchjagen (*cf previous entry*) race through

durchkämmen comb thoroughly; = **durchkämmen** comb (**nach** for)

durchkämpfen fight out; achieve (after a struggle); **sich** ~ fight one's way through; struggle on

durchkauen chew thoroughly; *coll* go over (at great length)

durchklingen* (*cf next entry*) (*also sn*) be clearly audible (above din *etc*); **durch seine Worte klang ... durch** there was a note of ... in his voice

durchklingen* (*cf previous entry*): **Musik durchklingt den Raum** the room rings with the sound of music

durchkneten knead thoroughly; massage

durchkochen (*also v/i*) boil/cook thoroughly

durchkommen* (*sn*) get through (*also tel*); come through; pull through; get by (**mit** on); get on; succeed; become apparent; (bud, sun) come out; **(mit der Arbeit) nicht** ~ be unable to cope

durchkomponieren work (novel *etc*) out in great detail; *mus* set to music with an individual setting for each stanza; **durchkomponiert** through-composed

durchkosten (*cf next entry*) taste one after another; experience

durchkosten (*cf previous entry*) savour

durchkreuzen (*cf next entry*) cross out

durchkreuzen (*cf previous entry*) cross, travel across; thwart; **sich** ~ intersect

der **Durchlaß**, ⸚(ss)e opening; passage; permission to pass through; *civ eng* culvert

durchlassen* let through; let in; *coll* overlook

durchlässig permeable; porous; leaky; permitting easy transfer; **–durchlässig** pervious to ...

Durchlaucht: (Euer *etc*) ~ (Your *etc*) Serene Highness

der **Durchlauf**, ⸚e *comput* run; *sp* round; **der ~(-Wasser)erhitzer, –** (continuous-flow) water heater; geyser; **die ~zeit, –en** *comput* throughput time

durchlaufen* (*cf next entry*) wear out (shoes *etc*); (*v/i sn*) run through; run non-stop; seep through; filter through; *archit* be continuous; ~ **lassen** filter (coffee)

durchlaufen* (*cf previous entry*) run through; run (distance); pass through; run down (s.o.'s) spine; *astron* describe; **es durchlief mich heiß und kalt** I went hot and cold

durchlaufend *esp archit* continuous

durchleben live through; experience

durchlegen *coll* run (road *etc*) through

durchleiden* endure

durchlesen* read through

durchleuchten (*cf next entry*) shine through

durchleuchten (*cf previous entry*) X-ray; (sun *etc*) light up; investigate

durchliegen* wear out (mattress); **sich** ~ get bedsores

durchlöchern make holes in; riddle; undermine; **durchlöchert** full of holes

durchlösen book through

durchlüften air thoroughly

durchmachen undergo; go through; *coll* work over (weekend); (*v/i*) *coll* continue working (after hours); **die Nacht** ~ make a night of it; **er hat viel durchgemacht** he's been through a lot

der **Durchmarsch**, ⸚e, **durchmarschieren** (*sn*) march through

durchmessen* stride through; traverse

der **Durchmesser**, – diameter; **im** ~ in diameter

durchmischen (*cf next entry*) mix thoroughly

durchmischen (*cf previous entry*): **mit (Sand** *etc*) ~ mix (sand *etc*) with

durchmüssen* *coll* have to go/get through; have to go through with it

durchmustern, durchmustern scrutinize

die **Durchnahme** going through (subject-matter)

durchnässen drench; **durchnäßt** wet through

durchnehmen* go through (in class)

durchnumerieren number consecutively

durch|organisieren organize in great detail; **durchorganisiert** highly organized

durchpauken *coll* cram; railroad (through legislature)

durchpausen trace

durchpeitschen flog; rush through

durchproben run through (at rehearsal)

durchprobieren try on/out one after another

durchprügeln *coll* give (s.o.) a good hiding

durchpulsen pulse through; **durchpulst von** pulsating with

durchqueren cross; traverse

durchrationalisieren reorganize completely

durchrechnen work out

durchregnen (*see also* **durchgeregnet**): **es regnet durch** the rain comes through

durchreiben*, sich ~ wear through

die **Durchreiche, –n** serving-hatch

durchreichen pass through

die **Durchreise, –n** journey through; **auf der** ~ on the way through || **das ~visum, –(s)a** transit visa

durchreisen (*cf next entry*) (*sn*) travel through; travel non-stop; ~ **durch** travel through

durchreisen (*cf previous entry*) travel across

der **Durchreisende** (*fem* **die** ~) (*decl as adj*) person travelling through; through passenger

durchreißen* (*cf next entry*) tear in half; (*v/i*) *mil* fire prematurely; (*sn*) break (in two)
durchreißen* (*cf previous entry*) breast (tape)
durchreiten* (*cf next entry*) wear out (by riding); (*v/i sn*) ride through; ride without a break; ~ **durch** (*sn*) ride through; **sich** ~ make oneself sore by riding
durchreiten* (*cf previous entry*) ride across
durchrieseln (*cf next entry*) (*sn*) trickle through
durchrieseln (*cf previous entry*) run through; (shiver) run down (s.o.'s) spine
durchringen*: sich ~ **zu** bring oneself (after much heart-searching) to take/make/carry out; **sich dazu** ~ **zu ...** bring oneself to ...
durchrosten (*sn*) rust through
durchrühren stir well
durchrutschen (*sn*) *coll* slip through; (examinee) scrape through; **ein Fehler ist ihm durchgerutscht** he slipped up
durchrütteln shake up
durchs = durch das
durchsacken (*sn*) *aer* suddenly lose height
die **Durchsage, -n** (loudspeaker *etc*) announcement
durchsagen pass on; phone (message); *rad* announce
durchsägen saw in half
der **Durchsatz, ⸚e** *comput*, *tech* throughput
durchsausen (*sn*) *coll* hurtle through; (examinee) fail; ~ **durch** hurtle through
durchschalten *elect etc* connect up; (*v/i*) *mot* go through the gears
durchschaubar: (leicht) ~ easy to grasp; transparent; **schwer** ~ hard to grasp/fathom; enigmatic
durchschauen (*cf next entry*) *SGer* = **durchsehen**
durchschauen (*cf previous entry*) see through (ruse *etc*); grasp; fathom
durchschauern make (s.o.) shiver/shudder
durchscheinen* (*cf next entry*) shine through; show through; be apparent
durchscheinen* (*cf previous entry*) fill with light
durchscheinend transparent, diaphanous; extremely delicate
durchscheuern fray; **sich** *dat* **die Haut** ~ chafe one's skin
durchschießen* (*cf next entry*), ~ **durch** shoot (arrow *etc*) through
durchschießen* (*cf previous entry*) shoot through; interleave; shoot through (s.o.'s) mind; *print* lead; ~ **mit** interweave with
durchschimmern gleam through; show through; ~ **lassen** give a hint of
durchschlafen* sleep through
der **Durchschlag, ⸚e** carbon copy; *cul* colander; *tech* punch; **das ~papier** carbon paper
durchschlagen* (*cf next entry*) knock through; split in two; knock a hole in; make a carbon copy of; *cul* sieve; (*v/i*) (food) have a laxative effect; (*also sn*) come through; (inherited characteristic) come out (**in** *dat* in); (*sn*) (fuse) blow; ~ **auf** (*acc*) (*sn*) have an impact on; **bei ihm schlägt ... durch** he takes after ...; **sich** ~ get through; get by
durchschlagen* (*cf previous entry*) (bomb *etc*) penetrate
durchschlagend convincing; compelling; resounding
die **Durchschlags|kraft** penetration; force (of argument *etc*); *sp* punch
durchschlängeln: sich ~ thread one's way through
durchschleichen* (*sn*) slip through
durchschleppen drag through; see (person) through
durchschleusen pass through a lock; (at customs *etc*) pass through
der **Durchschlupf, ⸚e** hole (in wall *etc*)
durchschlüpfen (*sn*) slip through; (+*dat*) **(zwischen den Fingern)** ~ give (s.o.) the slip
durchschmecken (be able to) taste
durchschneiden* (*cf next entry*) cut in half; cut through; cut (throat)
durchschneiden* (*cf previous entry*) cut in half; cut through; intersect; (cry) pierce
der **Durchschnitt, -e** average; *tech* section (of building); **im** ~ on average; *tech* in section
durchschnittlich average; (*adv*) on average; ~ **betragen/erreichen/verdienen** *etc* average; ~ **(groß/intelligent** *etc*) of average (height/intelligence *etc*)
Durchschnitts- average ...
durchschreiben* make a carbon copy of
durchschreiten* stride across; stride through
die **Durchschrift, -en** carbon copy
der **Durchschuß, ⸚(ss)e** shot-wound (through the body); *text* weft; *print* space; lead
durchschütteln shake thoroughly
durchschwärmen swarm through; spend (night) in revelry
durchschwimmen* (*cf next entry*) (*sn*) swim/float through; swim without a break
durchschwimmen* (*cf previous entry*) swim (river *etc*)
durchschwitzen soak with perspiration
durchsegeln (*cf next entry*) (*sn*) sail through; *coll* (examinee) fail
durchsegeln (*cf previous entry*) sail (across)
durchsehen* look through; glance through; (*v/i*) see through; *coll* get the hang of it; ~ **durch** look through; see through; look right through
durchseihen strain, filter
durchsetzen (*cf next entry*) achieve; get car-

ried into effect; get accepted; **seinen Willen** ~ get one's way; **~, daß ...** get (s.o., sth.) to ...; (*with pass, eg* **... die Wahlen verschoben werden**) get ... *+p/part* (the elections delayed *etc*)

sich ~ assert oneself; hold one's own; succeed; get one's way; achieve recognition; (spelling *etc*) become established; (theory *etc*) gain acceptance; **sich ~ gegen** prevail against; overcome; **sich ~ mit** gain acceptance for

durchsetzen (*cf previous entry*): **~ mit** intersperse with; infiltrate with; **durchsetzt mit/von** interspersed with; dotted with

die **Durchsicht** going through; examination

durchsichtig transparent; see-through

die **Durchsichtigkeit** transparency

durchsickern (*sn*) seep through; (news *etc*) leak out

durchsieben (*cf next entry*) sift; screen

durchsieben (*cf previous entry*) riddle (with sth.); **durchsiebt von** riddled with

durchsitzen* wear through (seat of trousers)

durchspalten split in two

durchspielen play through; act out; **sich ~** *sp* penetrate the defence

durchsprechen* talk over

durchspülen rinse thoroughly

durchstarten (*sn*) accelerate away; *aer* overshoot

durchstechen* (*cf next entry*) stick through; (*v/i* needle) stick through

durchstechen* (*cf previous entry*) pierce; *civ eng* cut through

durchstehen*, durchstehen* go through; keep up (pace); *ski* perform successfully

durchsteigen* (*cf next entry*) (*sn*) climb through; **da steig' ich nicht durch** *coll* it's beyond me

durchsteigen* (*cf previous entry*) *mount* climb

durchstellen *tel* put through

der **Durchstich, -e** *civ eng* cutting (of); cut; canal

durchstöbern rummage through (**nach** for); search through (for); browse through

der **Durchstoß** [-o:-], **⸚e** *mil* breakthrough

durchstoßen* (*cf next entry*) thrust through; wear through; (*v/i sn*) *mil* break through

durchstoßen* (*cf previous entry*) break through (*also mil*)

durchstreichen* cross out; *cul* sieve

durchstreifen roam through

durchströmen (*cf next entry*) (*sn*) flow through; pour through

durchströmen (*cf previous entry*) flow through

durchsuchen search (**nach** for)

die **Durchsuchung, -en** search(ing); **der ~s|befehl, -e** search-warrant

durchtoben spend (night) in revelry; rage through

durchtrainieren [-trɛ-] get into peak condition; **durchtrainiert** in peak condition

durchtränken soak; permeate; **durchtränkt mit/von** soaked in; imbued with

durchtrennen, durchtrennen cut; sever

durchtreten* wear out; *mot* press (pedal) down to the floor; (*v/i sn*) pass through

durchtrieben, die Durchtriebenheit cunning

durchtrocknen (*sn if v/i*) dry out

durchwachen (*cf next entry*) stay awake (all night *etc*)

durchwachen (*cf previous entry*): **die Nacht ~** stay awake all night; **durchwacht** spent without sleep

durchwachsen* [-ks-] (*cf next entry*) (*sn*), **~ durch** grow through

durchwachsen [-ks-] (*cf previous entry*) (bacon) streaky; (**so**) ~ *coll* so-so

durchwählen dial direct

durchwandern walk through

durchwärmen, durchwärmen warm up; **sich durchwärmen** warm oneself

durchwaschen*: (kurz) ~ give (sth.) a quick wash

durchwaten (*cf next entry*) (*sn*) wade through

durchwaten (*cf previous entry*) wade through; ford

durchweben (*weak exc lit*): **~ mit** weave into; **durchwoben mit/von** interlaced with

durchweg [-vɛk], *esp Aust, Swiss* **durchwegs** [-ve:ks] without exception, all; wholly

durchwehen blow through; pervade

durchweichen (*cf next entry*) (*sn*) go soggy

durchweichen (*cf previous entry*) make soggy; **durchweicht** soggy

durchwinden*: sich ~ thread one's way through; wind its way through; **sich ~ durch** thread one's/wind its way through; find a way through (difficulties)

durchwirken: ~ mit weave into

durchwühlen (*cf next entry*) rummage through; rifle; **sich ~ durch** burrow through; *coll* plough through

durchwühlen (*cf previous entry*) rummage through; rifle; churn up

durchwurs(ch)teln: sich ~ *coll* muddle through

durchzählen count; (*v/i*) *mil* number off, count off *US*

durchzechen (*cf next entry*) drink (without a break)

durchzechen (*cf previous entry*) spend (night) drinking

durchzeichnen trace; draw in detail

durchziehen* (*cf next entry*) pull through; pull (oar *etc*) as far as it will go; draw (line); run (wall *etc*); *coll* see (project *etc*) through; (*v/i sn*) pass through; march through; *cul* steep; **sich ~ durch** run through

durchziehen* (*cf previous entry*) cross, travel through; (river, theme, *etc*) run through; (pain) shoot through; (odour *etc*) pervade; ~ **mit** weave into; cut (ditches *etc*) across; **durchzogen von** intersected by (canals, ravines, *etc*); (face) furrowed with; (rock *etc*) streaked with

durchzucken (lightning) light up; flash through (s.o.'s) mind; (pain) shoot through

der **Durchzug** draught; passing through; **auf ~ schalten** *coll* switch off (mentally)

durchzwängen, sich ~ squeeze through; **~ durch, sich ~ durch** squeeze through

dürfen (*pres* **darf, darfst, darf, dürfen, dürft, dürfen,** *subj* **dürfe** *etc*; *p/t* **durfte,** *subj* **dürfte;** *p/part* **gedurft,** (*after dependent infin*) **dürfen**) (*see p. xlvii*) be allowed to, (I *etc*) may; (*ellipt*) be allowed to do; be allowed to go (home, to ..., *etc*); **... darf nicht** ... may not; ... must not; (*making speech etc*) **ich darf ...** let me ...; may I ...; **das darf nicht sein!** that's not possible!; that isn't right!; **was darf es sein?** can I help you?; what will you have?;

durfte was allowed to; **dürfte** would be allowed to; (*probability*) should, ought to; must; *or expressed by* probably (*eg* **es dürfte wenige Menschen geben, die ...** there are probably few people who ...); **dürfte ich ...?** may I ...?, might I ...?);

habe ... ~ have been/was allowed to; **hätte ... ~** would have been allowed to; **hätte nicht ... ~** would not have been allowed to; should not have + *p/part*

dürftig poor; meagre; wretched

dürr dried up; arid; skinny, scrawny

die **Dürre, -n** dryness; aridity; drought

der **Durst** thirst (**nach** for); **~ haben** be thirsty || **d~löschend = d~stillend** thirst-quenching; **die ~strecke, -n** lean period.

dursten thirst

dürsten: ~ nach thirst for; **mich dürstet** *poet* I thirst (**nach** for)

durstig thirsty

Dusch-: das ~bad, ¨-er shower-bath; **die ~ecke, -n** shower (in corner of bathroom *etc*); **der ~raum, ¨-e** showers

die **Dusche, -n** shower; **eine kalte ~ sein für** damp (s.o.'s) spirits

duschen give (s.o.) a shower; (*v/i*) = **sich ~** have a shower

die **Düse, -n** nozzle; jet

der **Dusel** *coll* drowsy state; luck; **~ haben** be lucky

duselig *coll* drowsy

duseln *coll* doze; day-dream

Düsen- jet ...; **der ~antrieb** jet propulsion (**mit D.** jet-propelled); **das ~flugzeug, -e** jet (aircraft); **der ~jäger, -** jet fighter

der **Dussel, -** *coll* nitwit

duster [-u:-] *NGer coll* dark

düster [-y:-] gloomy; sombre

die **Düsterkeit** gloom(iness); sombreness

der **Dutt, -e** *coll* bun (= hair-style)

das **Dutzend, -e**/(*following num etc*) - (*gen pl* **-er** *if case not otherwise shown*) dozen; **zu ~en** in their dozens || **d~weise** by the dozen

der **Duvetine** [dvf'ti:n], **-s** duvetine

Duz-: der ~bruder, ..brüder = der ~freund, -e close friend (addressed as 'du'); **~fuß** *coll* (**auf dem D. stehen mit** be on familiar terms with)

duzen address as 'du'; **sich ~ mit** address (and be addressed by) as 'du'

die **Dynamik** [-ɪk] dynamics; dynamism

dynamisch dynamic; (pension) index-linked

das **Dynamit, mit ~ sprengen** dynamite

der **Dynamo, -s = die ~maschine, -n** dynamo

die **Dynastie, -(ie)n** dynasty

dynastisch dynastic

der **D-Zug, ¨-e** express train

E

das **E** [eː] (*gen, pl* –, *coll* [eːs]) E; **das e, E** *mus* (the note) E; (*key*) E E major, **e** E minor

die **Ebbe** low tide; **die ~ tritt ein** the tide starts to go out; **in meinem Geldbeutel ist ~** *coll* my funds are very low

ebd. (= **ebenda**) ibid.

eben 1 *adj* even; level; flat; smooth; 2 *adv* just (*temporal*); just, exactly; just, simply; **zu ~er Erde** at ground level; **~ erst** just now; **~ noch** just (= barely); just now; **(ja/na) ~!** exactly!, quite! || **das E~bild, –er** image (= exact likeness); **~bürtig** equal; *hist* of equal rank ((+*dat*) **e. sein** be (s.o.'s) equal (**an** *dat* in)); **~derselbe/~dieselbe/~dasselbe** that same; **~deswegen** for that very reason; **~erdig** at ground level; **~falls** likewise; too (**danke, e.!** thank you, the same to you!); **das E~holz** ebony; **das E~maß** harmonious proportions; evenness, regularity; **~mäßig** of harmonious proportions; even, regular; **~so** just as; likewise; **~so–** just as ...; **~sogern** just as soon; (like) just as much; **~sogut** just as well; **~solch** just such a; **~so|sehr** just as much; **~so|wenig** just as little; not ... either, nor (**e. wie ...** not any more/no more ... than ...)

die **Ebene, –n** plain; level; *math* plane; **auf (höchster** *etc*) **~** at the (highest *etc*) level

der **Eber, –** boar; **die ~esche, –n** mountain ash

ebnen ['eː–] level; (+*dat*) **den Weg ~** smooth the way for

das **Echo** ['ɛço], **–s** echo; response; **das ~lot, –e** echo-sounder

die **Echse** [–ks–], **–n** lizard

echt genuine; authentic; real; typical; (colour) fast; *math* (fraction) proper; (*adv*) *coll* really

das **Eck, –e** *SGer* corner; **über ~** diagonally

Eck– corner ... (*also sp*); *econ* guiding ...; **der ~ball, ⸗e** corner (kick/throw); **der ~pfeiler, –** corner-pillar; cornerstone (of policy *etc*); **der ~platz, ⸗e** corner/end seat; **der ~zahn, ⸗e** canine (tooth)

die **Ecke, –n** corner (*also sp*); **eine ganze ~** *coll* quite a long way; **an allen ~n und Enden** *coll* at every turn; **um die ~ bringen** *coll* bump off

eckig square; angular; awkward; **–eckig** –cornered; –angular

edel noble; (wine *etc*) fine

Edel– *esp* high-class (*eg* detective story, western) (*sometimes used with an ironical nuance, eg* **die ~schnulze** *denoting a sentimental book, film or song with artistic pretensions,* **der ~kommunist** *denoting a theoretical Communist who fights shy of revolutionary action*); **der ~mann, ..leute** *hist* nobleman; **das ~metall, –e** noble metal; **der ~mut** magnanimity; **e~mütig** magnanimous; **die ~nutte, –n** *coll* high-class tart; **der ~stahl** high-grade steel; **der ~stein, –e** precious stone; gem; **das ~weiß, –e** edelweiss

Eden: (der Garten) ~ (the Garden of) Eden

edieren edit

das **Edikt, –e** edict

Edinburg ['eːdɪn–] Edinburgh

die **Edition, –en** edition; editing

Eduard ['eː–] Edward

die **EDV** (= **elektronische Datenverarbeitung**) E.D.P.

der **Efeu** ivy

Eff|eff *coll*: **aus dem ~ können/verstehen** know inside out

der **Effekt, –e** effect; **die ~hascherei, –en** cheap showmanship; **e~voll** effective

die **Effekten** *pl* securities

effektiv effective; actual; (*adv*) *also coll* definitely

effizient efficient

die **Effizienz** efficiency

die **EG** (= **Europäische Gemeinschaft(en)**) the E.E.C., the E.C.

egal identical; **das ist mir (ganz) ~** *coll* it's all the same to me; I don't care/mind; **(ganz) ~, ob** *etc* **...** *coll* regardless of whether *etc* ...

egalisieren *sp* equal

egalitär egalitarian

der **Egalitarismus** egalitarianism

der **Egel, –** leech

die **Egge, –n, eggen** harrow

der **Egoismus** selfishness; egoism

der **Egoist, –en** (*wk masc*) egoist

egoistisch selfish; egoistic

die **Egozentrik** [–ɪk] egocentricity

egozentrisch egocentric

e. h. = **ehrenhalber**

eh[1] *SGer coll* anyway

eh[2]: **seit ~ und je** always; **wie ~ und je** as always

eh! hey!

ehe before; ~ ... **nicht** until

die **Ehe, –n** marriage; **eine ~ schließen** marry

ehe– (*cf also next sequence*): **ehe|dem** formerly; **~malig** former; ex–; **~mals** in former times

Ehe– marriage ...; marital ...; matrimonial ...; conjugal ...;

die ~beratung marriage guidance; **der ~brecher, –** adulterer; **die ~brecherin, –nen** adulteress; **e~brecherisch** adulterous; **der ~bruch, ¨–e** adultery; **die ~frau, –en** wife; **das ~gespons, –e** *joc* spouse; **der ~gespons, –e** *joc* (male) spouse; **das ~glück** wedded bliss; **das ~leben** married life; **die ~leute** *pl* married couple; **e~los** unmarried; **der ~mann, ¨–er** husband; **e~mündig** of marriageable age; **das ~paar, –e** married couple; **der ~ring, –e** wedding ring; **die ~scheidung, –en** divorce; **die ~schließung, –en** marriage; **der ~stand** matrimony; **der ~stifter, –** matchmaker

ehelich marital; legitimate; (*adv*: born) in wedlock

ehelichen wed

eher sooner, earlier; rather, sooner; more; if anything; somewhat; *or conveyed by* ... is *etc* more likely to ...; **~ möglich** more likely; **nicht ~, als bis ...** not until ...; **um so ~, als ...** the more so as ...

ehern (will *etc*) iron; *poet* made of ore

ehest.. earliest; **am ~en** (the) earliest; most easily/readily; *or conveyed by* ... is *etc* most likely to ...; **am ~en würde ich ...** most of all I should like to ...

ehestens at the earliest; *Aust* as soon as possible

Ehr–: der ~begriff, –e sense of honour; **e~erbietig** respectful; **die ~erbietung** deference; **die ~furcht** reverence; awe; **e~furcht|gebietend** awesome; **e~fürchtig** = **e~furchts|voll** reverent; **das ~gefühl** sense of honour; **der ~geiz** ambition; **e~geizig** ambitious; **e~los** disreputable; **die ~sucht** inordinate ambition; **e~süchtig** inordinately ambitious; **e~würdig** venerable; *RC* Reverend

ehrbar honourable; respectable

die **Ehre, –n** honour; *relig* glory; (*+dat*) **~ machen** do (s.o.) credit; be a credit to; **in ~n halten** cherish; **... in ~n** with all due respect to ...; **zu ~n** (*+gen*) in honour of; **wieder zu ~n kommen** come back into favour

ehren (*see also* **geehrt**) honour; do credit to

Ehren– ... of honour; honorary ...;

e~amtlich honorary; **der ~bürger, –** freeman (of city); **das ~bürger|recht, –e** freedom (of city); **der ~gast, ¨–e** guest of honour; **e~halber** (**Doktor e.** Doctor *honoris causa*); **der ~kodex, –(d)izes** code of honour; **die ~loge, –n** V.I.P. box; **das ~mal, –e/¨–er** monument; war memorial; **der ~mann, ¨–er** man of honour; **der ~preis, –e** prize; **~rechte** *pl* (**bürgerliche E.** *certain civic rights, including the right to vote and hold public office*; **Aberkennung der bürgerlichen E.** *deprivation of such rights*); **e~rührig** injurious to (s.o.'s) reputation; defamatory; **die ~runde, –n** lap of honour; **die ~sache** point of honour (**E.!** of course!); **die ~salve, –n** gun salute; **der ~tag, –e** (s.o.'s) special day (*eg* birthday, mother's day); **e~voll** honourable; **e~wert** reputable; honourable; **das ~wort** word of honour (**E.!** cross my heart!); **das ~zeichen, –** decoration

ehrenhaft honourable

ehrlich honest; sincere

die **Ehrlichkeit** honesty; sincerity

ehrsam respectable

die **Ehrung, –en** *vbl noun*; *also* honour

ei! oh!; **ei, ei!** well, well!

das **Ei, –er** egg; *biol* ovum; (*pl*) *coll* marks; *vulg* 'balls'; **das ~ des Kolumbus** strikingly simple solution || **der ~dotter** (*also* **das**), **–** yolk; **e~förmig** ovoid; **das ~gelb, –e** yolk; **der ~leiter, –** oviduct; Fallopian tube; **der ~sprung, ¨–e** ovulation; **das ~weiß** white of egg; *biol*, *chem* protein; **e~weiß|reich** high-protein; **die ~weiß|stoffe** *pl* proteins

---

–ei (*with verbs ending in* **–eln, –ern**), **–erei** (*pl* **–en**):

(*i*) –ing (*activity or product of an activity*), *eg* **die Schnitzerei** (wood-)carving (**schnitzen** = carve); *denoting a continual or repeated activity, the suffixes often have a pejorative flavour*, *eg* **die Schreiberei** (endless) writing (**schreiben** = write);

(*ii*) (**–erei** *only*) –ery, *eg* **die Bäckerei** bakery (**Bäcker** = baker)

---

eiapopeia hushaby baby

die **Eibe, –n** yew

Eich–: das ~amt, ¨–er Office of Weights and Measures, Bureau of Standards *US*; **das ~hörnchen, –** = **das ~kätzchen, –** squirrel; **das ~maß, –e** standard measure

die **Eiche, –n** oak

die **Eichel, –n** acorn; *anat* glans; **der ~häher, –** jay

eichen[1] (*see also* **geeicht**) calibrate; verify (weight, measure)

eichen[2] oak(en)

Eichen– oak ...

der **Eid, –e** oath; **Erklärung an ~es Statt** solemn affirmation; **unter ~ (stehen)** (be) under oath || **der ~genosse, –n** (*wk masc*) Swiss citizen; **~genossenschaft** (**die Schweizerische E.** the Swiss Confederation);

e~genössisch Swiss
die **Eidechse** [–ks–], **–n** lizard
die **Eider|daunen** *pl* eiderdown
Eides– ... of an oath; **e~stattlich** (affirmation) solemn
Eidg. (= **Eidgenössisch**) *Swiss* Swiss
eidlich sworn; (*adv*) on oath
Eier *pl of* **Ei**; *in compds* egg ...; **der ~becher, –** egg-cup; **die ~frucht, ¨–e** aubergine; **der ~kopf, ¨–e** *coll* egghead; **der ~kuchen, –** pancake; **der ~likör, –e** advocaat; **die ~schale, –n** eggshell; **der ~schaum** beaten white of egg; **die ~speise, –n** egg dish; *Aust* scrambled eggs; **der ~stock, ¨–e** ovary; **die ~uhr, –en** egg-timer
eiern *coll* wobble
der **Eifer** enthusiasm; zeal; **im ~ des Gefechts** in the heat of the moment || **die ~sucht** jealousy; **die ~süchtelei, –en** petty jealousy; **e~süchtig** jealous (**auf** *acc* of)
der **Eiferer, –** fanatic; zealot
eifern: ~ für/gegen agitate for/against; **~ nach** strive after
eifrig eager; enthusiastic; zealous; **~ bemüht zu ...** anxious to ...
eigen own; of one's own; separate; peculiar; (*following dat*) characteristic of; peculiar to; **–eigen** -owned; **sich** *dat* **... zu ~ machen** adopt || **die E~art, –en** peculiarity; idiosyncrasy; special character; **~artig** strange; **die E~brötelei** solitary ways; **der E~brötler, –** lone wolf; **~brötlerisch** solitary; **~händig** in one's own hand; personal; (*adv*) with one's own hands; in one's own hand; personally; **das E~heim, –e** home of one's own; **das E~leben** life of one's own; own way of life; **die E~liebe** love of self; **das E~lob** self-praise; **~mächtig** high-handed; unauthorized; (*adv*) high-handedly; on one's own authority; **die E~mächtigkeit, –en** high-handedness; unauthorized action; **der E~name, –n** (*like* **Name**) proper name; **der E~nutz** self-interest; **~nützig** selfish; **der E~sinn** obstinacy; **~sinnig** stubborn; **die E~staatlichkeit** sovereignty; **~ständig** independent; **das E~tor, –e** own goal; **die E~wärme** body heat; **der E~wert, –e** intrinsic value; **der E~wille** (*like* **Wille**) self-will; **~willig** self-willed; highly individual
die **Eigenheit, –en** peculiarity; idiosyncrasy
eigens specially; expressly
die **Eigenschaft, –en** quality; *chem*, *phys* property; **in meiner ~ als ...** in my capacity as ... || **das ~s|wort, ¨–er** adjective
eigentlich real; actual; proper (*placed after noun*, *eg* **das ~e Spanien** Spain proper); (*adv*) actually, in actual fact; really; (what *etc*) exactly
das **Eigentum** property; ownership (**an** *dat* of)
der **Eigentümer, –** owner
eigentümlich peculiar; (*following dat*) characteristic (of); **eigentümlicher|weise** oddly enough
die **Eigentümlichkeit, –en** peculiarity
Eigentums– ... of ownership; **die ~wohnung, –en** (owner-occupied) flat/apartment *US*
eignen (*see also* **geeignet**): **sich ~ als** be suitable as; **sich ~ für/zu** be suited to; **sich ~ zum ...** be suited to be .../suitable for ...
der **Eigner, –** owner (of ship)
die **Eignung** suitability; **die ~s|prüfung, –en** aptitude test
Eil– express ...; **der ~bote, –n** (*wk masc*) special messenger (**durch ~boten** express, by special delivery); **der ~brief, –e** special-delivery letter; **e~fertig** hasty; **das ~gut** express goods/freight *US*; **der ~zug, ¨–e** limited-stop train; **die ~zustellung, –en** special delivery
das **Eiland, –e** *poet* isle
die **Eile** haste; **~ haben** be in a hurry; be urgent; **damit hat es keine ~** there's no hurry; **in ~** in a hurry; **in aller ~** in great haste
eilen be urgent; (*sn*) hurry; **damit eilt es nicht** there's no hurry; **„eilt!"** 'urgent'
eilends hurriedly
eilig hurried; urgent; **es ~ haben** be in a hurry
der **Eimer, –** bucket; **im ~** *coll* down the drain; **es gießt wie aus/mit ~n** *coll* it's bucketing down || **e~weise** in bucketfuls
ein[1]**/eine/ein** (*see also* **einer/eine/ein(e)s**) (*see p. xix*) 1 *num* one; 2 *indef art* a, an; **ein und derselbe/dieselbe/dasselbe** one and the same; **ein für allemal** once and for all; **mit 'einem Wort** in a word; **wie 'ein Mann** as one man
ein[2]**: ~ – aus** on–off; **weder ~ noch aus wissen** be at one's wit's end
ein–[1] one–; single–; uni–; mono–

---

ein–[2] *sep pref – general senses*:
(*i*) ... in (*eg* **~lassen** let in, admit, **~steigen** get in);
(*ii*) ... up (*eg* **~wickeln** wrap up);
(*iii*) ... out (*eg* **~schenken** pour out);
(*iv*) *indicates an act or process of covering* (*eg* **~fetten** grease);
(*v*) *indicates destruction* (*eg* **~schlagen** smash, smash in) *or diminution* (*eg* **~schrumpfen** shrink);
(*vi*) (+*dat*) *indicates the imparting of something to someone* (*eg* **jmdm. etw. ~pauken** drum sth. into s.o.)

---

der **Ein|akter, –** one-act play
einander (*acc/dat*) one another, each other
ein|arbeiten train (new employee); **~ in** (*acc*) work into; incorporate in; **sich ~ in** (*acc*) familiarize oneself with
ein|armig one-armed

ein|äschern reduce to ashes; cremate
ein|atmen breathe in; drink in (atmosphere)
ein|äugig one-eyed
Ein-Ausgabe– *comput* input/output ...
die **Einbahn|straße, –n** one-way street
einbalsamieren embalm
der **Einband, ⸚e** binding
der **Einbau, –ten** installation; fitting; incorporation (**in** *acc* in); *in compds* built-in ...; **die ~küche, –n** fitted kitchen; **die ~möbel** *pl* unit furniture
einbauen build in; fit; install; *sp* bring in; **~ in** (*acc*) build into; fit in; install in; incorporate in; insert in; **eingebaut** built-in
der **Einbaum, ⸚e** dug-out
einbegreifen*: (mit) ~ include; **... (mit) einbegriffen** including ...
einbehalten* withhold; retain; detain
einbeinig one-legged
einbekennen* *Aust* confess, admit
einberufen* convene; convoke; *mil* call up, draft *US*; **der/die Einberufene** (*decl as adj*) conscript
die **Einberufung, –en** *vbl noun*; *also* convocation; *mil* call-up, draft *US*
Einbett–: die ~kabine, –n single-berth cabin; **das ~zimmer, –** single room
einbetten: ~ in (*acc/dat*) embed in; set in (context); **eingebettet sein in** be embedded in; nestle in
einbeziehen*: (mit) ~ in (*acc*) include in; bring into
die **Einbeziehung** inclusion (**in** *acc* in); **unter ~** (+*gen*) including
einbiegen*: ~ in (*acc*) (*sn*) turn into
einbilden (*see also* **eingebildet**): **sich** *dat* **... ~** imagine (danger, that one is ..., *etc*); **sich** *dat* **etwas/viel ~ auf** (*acc*) be conceited about; **darauf brauchst du dir nichts einzubilden** that's nothing to be proud of
die **Einbildung, –en** imagination; delusion; conceit; **die ~s|kraft** imagination
einbinden* bind; **~ in** (*acc*) tie up in; integrate into
einblasen* blow down; blow in (*also mus*); (+*dat*) *coll* put (idea) in (s.o.'s) head; whisper (gossip) in (s.o.'s) ear; **~ in** (*acc*) blow into
einblenden *cin etc* insert; fade in
die **Einblendung, –en** *cin etc* insertion; fade-in
einbleuen (+*dat*) *coll* drum into
der **Einblick** insight; (+*dat*) **~ gewähren in** (*acc*) permit to see; **~ nehmen in** (*acc*) inspect
einbrechen* break down; (*v/i*) break in; (*sn*) cave in; set in, (night) fall; **auf dem Eis ~** fall through the ice; **~ in** (*acc*) (*sn*) break into, burgle, burglarize *US*; invade; **bei uns ist eingebrochen worden** we've been burgled/burglarized *US*; **bei ~der Nacht** at nightfall
der **Einbrecher, –** housebreaker; burglar
einbrennen* burn (into wood *etc*); *cul* brown (to make a roux); (+*dat*) **ein Zeichen ~** brand; **sich ~** (+*dat*/**in** *acc*) become etched in
einbringen* bring in; get in; yield (interest); capture; *parl* introduce (bill); (+*dat*) bring (s.o. fame *etc*); **~ in** (*acc*) bring into; feed into; put (capital) into; **wieder ~** make up for; recapture
einbrocken: ~ in (*acc*) crumble (bread) and put it in (soup); **jmdm./sich** *dat* **etwas ~** *coll* get s.o./oneself into a fix
der **Einbruch, ⸚e** caving-in, *econ* slump (in prices *etc*); break-in, burglary; incursion; **~ der Dunkelheit** nightfall
einbuchten *coll* lock up
die **Einbuchtung, –en** dent; indentation; bay; *coll* locking up
einbürgern naturalize (*also bot, zool*); establish; **in (Island** *etc*) **eingebürgert sein** be a naturalized (Icelander *etc*); **sich ~** become established; be adopted; *bot, zool* become naturalized
die **Einbürgerung** naturalization; establishment
die **Einbuße, –n** loss (**an** *dat* of)
einbüßen lose; forfeit; **~ an** (*dat*) lose (*some of, eg* authority, value)
einchecken [–tʃ–] *aer* (*also v/i*) check in
eincremen cream; **sich ~** cream one's skin
eindämmen dam up; curb; check the spread of; *pol* contain
eindämmern (*sn*) doze off
die **Eindämmung, –en** *vbl noun*; *pol* containment
eindecken cover (up); **~ mit** cover with; *coll* ply with; **mit Arbeit (voll) eingedeckt sein** *coll* have plenty of work to do; **sich ~ mit** lay in a supply of
der **Eindecker, –** monoplane
eindeichen dike; embank
eindellen *coll* dent
eindeutig clear; unequivocal
eindeutschen Germanize
eindicken (*sn if v/i*) thicken
eindimensional one-dimensional
eindösen (*sn*) *coll* doze off
eindrängen: ~ auf (*acc*) (*sn*) crowd in on; **sich ~ in** (*acc*) force one's way into; intrude on; interfere in
eindrehen screw in; **sich** *dat* **die Haare ~** put one's hair in curlers
eindringen* (*sn*) get in; penetrate; **~ auf** (*acc*) set about; assail (with questions); **~ in** (*acc*) penetrate; get into; enter by force; penetrate (mystery); *mil* invade; **mit Bitten ~ auf** (*acc*) plead with
eindringlich insistent; forceful; (advice) urgent
der **Eindringling, –e** intruder

[der] **Eindruck, ⸗e** impression; **den ~ erwecken, als ob ...** give the impression that ...; **~ machen auf** (*acc*) impress; **~ schinden** *coll* show off || **e~s|voll** impressive

eindrücken dent; push in; crush; **~ in** (*acc*) press into; imprint in; **sich ~ in** (*acc*) become imprinted in; **eingedrückte Nase** flattened nose

eindrücklich *Swiss* impressive

ein|ebnen [–e:–] level

[die] **Ein|ehe** monogamy

ein|eiig (twins) identical

ein|einhalb one and a half

einen, sich ~ unite

ein|engen narrow; restrict; (garment) restrict (s.o.'s) movements

[die] **Ein|engung** *vbl noun*; *also* restriction

einer/eine/ein(e)s (*see also* **eins**) one; **einer** *also* someone, (*in question etc*) anyone; one, you; **ein(e)s** *also* one thing; **so ~** one like that; **der/die/das eine** one; the one; **das eine** *also* the one thing; **die einen ..., die anderen ...** some ..., others ...; **noch ein(e)s** another one; one other thing; **du bist mir eine(r)!** you are a one!

[der] **Einer, –** *row* single scull; *math* unit

einer–: ~lei (*indecl*) the same (**es ist mir e.** it's all the same to me; **e., ob** *etc* **...** no matter whether *etc* ...); **das E~lei** monotony; **~seits** on the one hand

eines|teils on the one hand

ein|exerzieren drill; (+*dat of pers*) drill in

einfach simple; plain; (ticket) single, one-way *US*; (*adv*) simply; (folded) once; simply, just; **~er Soldat** private; **~e Leute** ordinary folk; **~ so** just like that; **(Bonn** *etc*) **~** a single to (B. *etc*), (B. *etc*) one-way *US*

[die] **Einfachheit** simplicity

einfädeln thread (needle, film, tape); pass (thread) through the eye of a needle; *coll* engineer; **sich ~** filter (into traffic)

einfahren* get in (crop); knock down (by driving into it); run in, break in *US* (vehicle), break in (horse for driving); earn (by driving); *aer*, *naut* retract; (*v/i sn*) (train) pull in; *naut* put into port; *min* go down the pit; **sich ~** get used to driving

[die] **Einfahrt, –en** entry; entrance; (harbour) mouth; slip-road, access road (leading into motorway); *min* descent; **der Zug hat ~ auf Gleis ...** the train is now arriving at platform .../on track ... *US*

[der] **Einfall, ⸗e** (sudden) idea; invasion (**in** *acc* of); incursion; *phys* incidence

einfallen* (*see also* **eingefallen**) (*sn*) collapse; set in; cut in; (voices *etc*) come in; join in; (light) enter; (+*dat*) occur to, *or – with ind obj becoming subj – expressed by* think of, remember (*eg* **ihm fiel eine Ausrede ein** he thought of an excuse, **plötzlich fiel ihr ein, daß ...** she suddenly remembered that ...); **~ in** (*acc*) join in; cut in on (conversation); invade; **sich** *dat* **... ~ lassen** come up with; **was fällt dir ein?** what *do* you think you're doing?; **das fällt mir gar nicht/nicht im Traum ein!** I wouldn't dream of it!

Einfalls–: e~los unimaginative; **die ~losigkeit** lack of imagination; **e~reich** imaginative; **das ~tor, –e** gateway (**nach** to); **der ~winkel, –** angle of incidence

[die] **Einfalt** naïveté; simple-mindedness

einfältig naïve; simple(-minded)

[der] **Einfalts|pinsel, –** *coll* simpleton

[das] **Einfamilien|haus, ⸗er** house (for a single family)

einfangen* catch; capture (on film *etc*)

einfärben dye; *print* ink

einfarbig, *Aust* **einfärbig** in one colour; plain

einfassen enclose; edge, border; set, mount (**in Gold** in gold); **mit einer Mauer ~** wall in; **mit einem Zaun ~** fence in

[die] **Einfassung, –en** *vbl noun*; *also* border, edging; frame; mount, setting

einfetten grease; dub

einfeuchten damp, moisten

einfinden*: sich ~ turn up (**zu** for); present oneself (for examination *etc*)

einflechten* plait; **~ in** (*acc*) weave into; work into; **~, daß ...** mention in passing that ...

einflicken *coll* insert, put in

einfliegen* fly in; test-fly; make (profit) by flying; (*v/i sn*) fly in; **~ in** (*acc*) (*sn if v/i*) fly into

[der] **Einflieger, –** test-pilot

einfließen* (*sn*) flow in; (funds) come in; **~ lassen in** (*acc*) slip (remark) into; **~ lassen, daß ...** let it be known that ...

einflößen (+*dat of pers*) administer to; fill with (admiration, pity, *etc*), give (s.o. courage); inspire (s.o.'s confidence)

[der] **Einflug, ⸗e** flying in; flight (into)

[der] **Einfluß, ⸗(ss)e** influence (**auf** *acc* on, **bei** with); inflow, influx; **~ ausüben auf** (*acc*) have an influence on; **~ haben auf** (*acc*) have an influence on; affect; **unter dem ~** (+*gen*) under the influence of || **der ~bereich, –e** sphere of influence; **die ~nahme** (exercising of) influence; **e~reich** influential

einflüstern (+*dat*) insinuate into (s.o.'s) mind; **~ auf** (*acc*) speak in an insistent whisper to

einfordern call in (debt); call for

einförmig uniform; monotonous

[die] **Einförmigkeit** uniformity; monotony

einfressen*: sich ~ take hold; **sich ~ in** (*acc*) eat into; gnaw at (s.o.'s) heart

einfrieden enclose; fence in; wall in

einfrieren* deep-freeze; freeze (prices *etc*);

(*v/i sn*) freeze; freeze up; become icebound; *fin* be blocked
einfügen: ~ **in** (*acc*) put in; insert in; **sich** ~ **in** (*acc*) adapt to; fit in with
die **Einfügung, -en** insertion; interpolation
einfühlen: sich ~ **in** (*acc*) empathize with; project oneself into
einfühlsam sensitive; empathetic
das **Einfühlungs|vermögen** empathy
die **Einfuhr, -en** import (of); (country's *etc*) imports; (*pl*) imports; *in compds* import ...; **der** ~**hafen, ..häfen** port of importation; **das** ~**land, ⸚er** importing country; **der** ~**stopp, -s** = **das** ~**verbot, -e** ban on imports; **der** ~**zoll, ⸚e** import duty
einführen introduce; instruct in his/her duties; *comm* import; ~ **in** (*acc*) insert into; introduce into; introduce to (subject *etc*); install in (office); **wieder** ~ reintroduce
sich ~ introduce oneself; **sich gut** ~ *comm* become well-established
einführend introductory
die **Einführung, -en** introduction; instruction (in his/her duties); insertion; installation; *in compds* ~**s-** introductory ...
einfüllen pour in; ~ **in** (*acc*) put in; pour in; **in Flaschen** ~ bottle
die **Eingabe, -n** petition; administering; *comput* input; **die** ~**daten** *pl* input data
der **Eingang, ⸚e** entrance; beginning; *esp comm* arrival; *elect* input; (*pl*) incoming goods/mail *etc*; ~ **finden** find a market; +**in** (*acc*) gain entry to; (+*dat*) ~ **verschaffen** get (s.o.) admitted; introduce (practice *etc*); **sich** *dat* ~ **verschaffen** gain entry to; **nach** ~ (+*gen*) on receipt of
eingängig easily understood; catchy
eingangs 1 *adv* at the beginning; 2 *prep* (+*gen*) at the beginning of
Eingangs- opening ...; *comm* ... of receipt; **die** ~**halle, -n** entrance hall; **das** ~**tor, -e** gateway (**zu** to)
eingeben* *comput* read in, input; *arch* submit (**bei** to); (+*dat*) administer to; suggest (idea *etc*) to; *comput* input to
eingebildet *p/part*; *also* conceited (**auf** *acc* about); imaginary
eingeboren native; innate, inborn; **der/die Eingeborene** (*decl as adj*) native
die **Eingebung, -en** inspiration; impulse; prompting
eingedenk (+*gen*) mindful of
eingefallen *p/part*; *also* hollow; haggard
eingefleischt dyed-in-the-wool, (bachelor) confirmed; deep-rooted
eingehen* (*sn*) enter into; lay (wager); take (risk); (*v/i*) arrive; come in; shrink; (animal, plant, *coll esp hyperbolically* person) die; *coll* fold; **... geht mir leicht/schwer ein** I am quick/slow to grasp ...; **es geht mir glatt ein** I lap it up; **es will mir nicht** ~**, daß ...** it's beyond me how ...
~ **an** (*dat*) (animal, plant) die of
~ **auf** (*acc*) give one's attention to (person); deal with, go into; agree to; fall in with; **näher** ~ **auf** go into in greater detail; **nicht** ~ **auf** ignore
~ **in** (*acc*) enter (consciousness *etc*); pass into; **in die Geschichte** ~ go down in history
eingehend (mail *etc*) incoming; thorough; detailed; (*adv*) in detail; thoroughly
eingekeilt hemmed in; ~ **zwischen** sandwiched between
das **Eingemachte** (*decl as adj*) bottled fruit
eingemeinden incorporate in the town/city
die **Eingenommenheit** bias (**für** towards)
eingerostet *p/part*; *also* rusty
eingeschnappt *p/part*; *coll* miffed
eingeschneit *p/part*; *also* snowbound
eingesessen (family) old-established
das **Eingesottene** (*decl as adj*) *Aust* bottled fruit
eingestandener|maßen on (s.o.'s) own admission
das **Eingeständnis, -se** confession
eingestehen* confess, admit
eingesunken *p/part*; *also* hollow, sunken
eingetragen *p/part*; *also* registered
eingewachsen [-ks-] *p/part*; *also* (toenail) ingrown
die **Eingeweide** *pl* entrails; **der** ~**bruch, ⸚e** hernia
der **Eingeweihte** (*fem* **die** ~) (*decl as adj*) initiate, insider
eingewöhnen: sich ~ get acclimatized; settle down
eingewurzelt *p/part*; **tief** ~ deep-rooted
eingießen* pour (out)
eingipsen fix (in wall *etc*) with plaster; *med* put in plaster
eingleisig single-track
eingliedern: ~ **in** (*acc*) incorporate in; integrate into; **sich** ~ **in** (*acc*) fit into
die **Eingliederung, -en** incorporation; integration
eingraben* bury; dig in; ~ **in** (*acc*) bury in; sink (post *etc*) in; carve on; **sich** ~ dig in; **sich** ~ **in** (*acc*) (river) cut into; engrave itself on (memory)
eingravieren: ~ **in** (*acc*) engrave on
eingreifen* intervene, step in; ~ **in** (*acc*) intervene in; encroach on; *mech* mesh with; **das Eingreifen** intervention
eingrenzen enclose; restrict (**auf** *acc* to)
der **Eingriff, -e** intervention (**in** *acc* in); encroachment (on); *med* operation; *mech* meshing; **im** ~ **stehen** be in mesh
eingruppieren: ~ **in** (*acc*) place in (salary grade *etc*)
einhaken fasten (with hook); (*v/i*) *coll* cut in; **sich** ~ link arms (**bei** with)

–einhalb ... and a half
Einhalt: (+*dat*) ~ **gebieten** stop; put a stop to
einhalten* keep (promise *etc*); keep up (payments, speed); keep to (diet *etc*); keep on (course); *tail* take in; (*v/i*) stop; ~ **mit** stop (+*ger*)
einhämmern hammer in; (+*dat*) drum into (s.o.'s) head; ~ **auf** (*acc*) hammer away at
einhandeln obtain by barter; obtain (in exchange); ~ **gegen** obtain in exchange for; **sich** *dat* ... ~ *coll* get (disease, telling-off, *etc*)
einhändig one-handed
einhändigen (+*dat*) hand over to
einhängen hang (in position); *tel* put down; (*v/i*) *tel* hang up; **sich** ~ **bei** link arms with
einhauchen (+*dat*) breathe (life) into
einhauen* smash in; ~ **auf** (*acc*) lay into; ~ **in** (*acc*) knock into; carve in; (*v/i*) *coll* tuck into
einheben* *Aust* collect (taxes)
einheften put into a (loose-leaf) file; *tail* tack in
einhegen enclose
einheilen (*sn*) (transplant) take
einheimisch local; *ling* vernacular; *bot*, *zool* indigenous; *sp* home; **der/die Einheimische** (*decl as adj*) local
einheimsen *coll* rake in; reap; win (praise *etc*)
die **Einheirat:** ~ **in** (*acc*) marriage into
einheiraten: ~ **in** (*acc*) marry into
die **Einheit, –en** unity; unit (*also mil*)
einheitlich uniform; standard; integrated
die **Einheitlichkeit** uniformity
Einheits– standard ...; **die ~front** united front; **die ~liste, –n** single list; **der ~staat, –en** unitary state
einheizen heat; light; (*v/i*) heat the house *etc*; (+*dat*) *coll* make things hot for; give it (s.o.) hot
einhellig unanimous
die **Einhelligkeit** unanimity
einher– *sep pref* ... along
einhergehen* (*sn*) walk along; ~ **mit** go hand in hand with
einholen catch up with; catch up on; make up for; obtain (permission *etc*); *naut* haul down; haul in; *coll* buy; ~ **gehen** *coll* go shopping
das **Einhorn, ⸚er** unicorn
einhüllen wrap up (**in** *acc* in); envelop; **sich** ~ **in** (*acc*) wrap oneself up in; become shrouded in
einhüten *esp NGer* baby-sit; look after the house *etc* while s.o. is away
einig united; in agreement; **sich** *dat pl* ~ **sein/werden** be in/reach agreement; **mit sich selbst nicht** ~ **sein** be in two minds || ~**gehen*** (*sn*) (**e. mit** agree with)
einig.. some; ~**e** *pl* some; a few; ~**es** something; some things; quite a lot || ~**emal** a few times
ein|igeln: sich ~ curl up in a ball; shut oneself off; *mil* take up a position of all-round defence
einigen unite; **sich** ~ **auf** (*acc*) agree on
einiger|maßen fairly; somewhat, rather; to some extent; reasonably well; (*in reply to question about one's wellbeing*) not too bad
die **Einigkeit** unity; agreement
die **Einigung, –en** unification; agreement
ein|impfen (+*dat of pers*) inoculate with; *coll* drum into
einjagen: (+*dat*) **Angst/einen Schreck(en)** ~ give (s.o.) a fright
einjährig one-year-old; a year's (service *etc*); *bot* annual; ~**e Pflanze** annual
einkalkulieren include (in price); allow for
einkapseln encapsulate; **sich** ~ shut oneself off; *zool* encapsulate; encyst
einkassieren collect; *coll* help oneself to
der **Einkauf, ⸚e** buying; purchase; (*pl*) shopping; **Einkäufe machen** go shopping
einkaufen buy (*also sp*); ~ **gehen** go shopping; **ich war** ~ *coll* I've been shopping; **sich** ~ **in** (*acc*) buy a place/share in
der **Einkäufer, –** buyer (for firm)
Einkaufs– shopping ...; **das ~netz, –e** string bag; **der ~preis, –e** wholesale price; **der ~wagen, –** (shopper's) trolley
Einkehr: bei sich ~ **halten** search one's heart
einkehren (*sn*) put up (**in** *dat* at); (peace *etc*) come (**bei** to)
einkellern store in the cellar
einkerben cut a notch in; ~ **in** (*acc*) cut (initials *etc*) on
einkerkern incarcerate
einkesseln *mil* encircle
einklagen sue for (outstanding debt *etc*)
einklammern bracket
der **Einklang** harmony; *mus* unison; **in** ~ **bringen mit** reconcile with; harmonize with; **in** ~ **stehen mit** be in keeping with
einklappen fold away
Einklassen–, einklassig *educ* one-class
einkleben stick in
einkleiden provide with a new set of clothes; *eccles* clothe in the habit of the order; *mil* kit out; ~ **in** (*acc*) couch in
einklemmen wedge in, jam; catch (in door *etc*); put (tail) between its legs; ~ **in** (*acc*) clamp in; put (monocle) in; **eingeklemmter Bruch** strangulated hernia
einklinken latch; (*v/i*, *also sn*) click shut
einkneifen* press (lips) together; put (tail) between its legs
einknicken bend (slightly); (*v/i sn*) (knees) give way; **ich knicke in den Knien ein** my knees give way
einkochen preserve; (*v/i sn*) boil away

einkommen* (*sn*): ~ **um** apply for

das **Einkommen, –** income; **e~s|schwach** low-income; **e~s|stark** high-income; **die ~s|steuer** income tax; **die ~s|steuer|erklärung, –en** income-tax return

einköpfen head in

einkrachen (*sn*) *coll* collapse; **auf dem Eis ~** fall through the ice

einkratzen: ~ in (*acc*) scratch (name *etc*) on

einkreisen ring (on calendar *etc*); incorporate (town) in a *Landkreis*; home in on (problem *etc*); *mil*, *pol* encircle

die **Einkreisung, –en** *vbl noun*; *mil*, *pol* encirclement

einkriegen *coll* catch up with; **sich ~** contain oneself

die **Einkünfte** *pl* income

einkuppeln let in the clutch

einkuscheln: sich ~ snuggle down (**in** *acc* in)

einladen[1]* load (**in** *acc* into; onto)

einladen[2]* invite; ~ **in** (*acc*) take to (theatre *etc*); ~ **zu** invite to, ask to; treat to; **zu sich ~** invite home; **~d** inviting

die **Einladung, –en** invitation; **auf ~** (+*gen*) at the invitation of

die **Einlage, –n** insert; arch support (in shoe); *cul* solid ingredient (*eg* dumpling, vegetable) in soup; *dent* temporary filling; *fin* deposit; investment; *mus* interlude; *theat* intermezzo

einlagern store; **sich ~ in** (*acc/dat*) be deposited in

einlangen (*sn*) *Aust* arrive

der **Einlaß** admission; *tech* intake; **~ erhalten** gain admittance; (+*dat*) **~ gewähren** admit || **die ~karte, –n** ticket

einlassen* let in, admit; run (water); *SGer* wax (floor); varnish; ~ **in** (*acc*) run (water) into; let into; set (jewel) in

sich ~ auf (*acc*) get involved in; accept (condition *etc*); **sich ~ in** (*acc*) get involved in; **sich ~ mit** get involved with

einläßlich *Swiss* detailed; thorough; (*adv*) in detail

die **Einlassung, –en** *leg* statement (by defendant)

der **Einlauf, ⸚e** *med* enema; *sp* finish; order (at finish); (*pl*) incoming mail; **beim ~ in** (*acc*) on entering (straight *etc*)

einlaufen* break in (shoes); (*v/i sn*) flow in; come in, arrive; shrink; *sp* take the field; ~ **in** (*acc*) (*sn*) enter (harbour, station, *sp* straight, *etc*); (+*dat*) **die Bude/das Haus ~** *coll* pester with unwanted visits; **ein Bad ~ lassen** run a bath

sich ~ get going; (engine) be run in/broken in *US*; *sp* warm up

einläuten ring the bell(s) to signal the start of, ring in (year), *sp* ring the bell for (lap *etc*); signal the start of

einleben: sich ~ settle down; **sich ~ in** (*acc*) settle down in; project oneself into the mind of; get into the spirit of

Einlege–: die ~arbeit, –en inlaid work; **die ~sohle, –n** insole

einlegen put in; insert; set (hair); lay on (extra train *etc*); lodge (complaint *etc*); *row* ship (oars); *phot* load (film); *mot* engage (gear); *carp* inlay; *cul* pickle; marinate; preserve; *fin* deposit; ~ **in** (*acc*) put in; insert in; enclose with; **eine Pause ~** take a break; **ein gutes Wort ~ für** put in a good word for (**bei** with)

einleiten commence; usher in (era); initiate (negotiations *etc*), set up (enquiry), take (step), *leg* institute; write an introduction to; **künstlich ~** induce (birth); **~d** introductory; (*adv*) by way of introduction

die **Einleitung, –en** *vbl noun*; *also* commencement; initiation; introduction (to book); *in compds* **~s–** introductory …

einlenken adopt a more conciliatory attitude; ~ **in** (*acc*) (*sn if v/i*) turn into; **~d** conciliatory

einlesen* *comput* read in, input; **sich ~ in** (*acc*) get into (book *etc*)

einleuchten (+*dat*) be clear to; **das leuchtet ein** that stands to reason; **mir leuchtet nicht ein, warum …** I don't see why …; **~d** plausible

einliefern deliver; ~ **in** (*acc*) take to; **ins Krankenhaus ~** take to hospital

der **Einlieferungs|schein, –e** certificate of posting

einlochen *golf* hole; *coll* put behind bars

einlösen redeem; cash (cheque); make good (promise *etc*); *comm* honour; **sein Wort ~** keep one's word

einlullen lull to sleep; lull (s.o.'s) fears/suspicions; **in Sicherheit ~** lull into a false sense of security

die **Einmach** *Aust* roux

Einmach– preserving …; **das ~glas, ⸚er** preserving jar

einmachen preserve; bottle

einmahnen call in (debt)

einmal once; at one time; one day; for once; (*emotive particle, with imp*) just (*eg* **stell dir ~ vor!** just imagine!), *or left untranslated* (*eg* **sag ~** tell me); **~ (Frankfurt** *etc*) **einfach** a single to (F. *etc*), (F. *etc*) one-way *US*; **~ (Gurkensalat** *etc*) one (cucumber salad *etc*); **es war einmal …** once upon a time there was …

~ …, ~ … now …, now …; **~ …, zum anderen …** in the first place …, in the second place …

auf ~ all of a sudden; at once (= at the same time); at a time

da … (schon) ~ now that

nicht ~ not even; not once

noch ~ once more; again; **noch ~ so**

twice as
nun ~ (*expressing resignation*, *eg* **ich bin/es ist nun** ~ **so** that's the way I am/how it is)
schon ~ before; now and again; (*in questions*) ever
wenn ... (erst) ~ once (*conj*)
wieder ~ once again
Einmal– disposable ...; **das** ~**eins** multiplication tables; ABC (of)
einmalig unique; single; non-recurrent
Einmann– one-man ...
der **Einmarsch, ¨e** marching in; entry; invasion (**in** *acc* of)
einmarschieren (*sn*) march in; ~ **in** (*acc*) march into; enter
einmauern wall in; fix in a wall
einmeißeln carve (with a chisel) (**in** *acc* into)
einmengen: sich ~ interfere (**in** *acc* in); butt in (on)
einmieten: sich ~ **bei** take lodgings with
einmischen mix in; **sich** ~ interfere (**in** *acc* in); butt in (on)
die **Einmischung, –en** interference
einmontieren *tech* fit
einmotorig single-engine
einmotten put in mothballs; *mil* mothball
einmummeln *coll*: **(sich)** ~ wrap (oneself) up
einmünden (*also sn*): ~ **in** (*acc*) flow into, (road) lead into; end in
einmütig unanimous
die **Einmütigkeit** unanimity
einnähen sew in; *tail* take in; ~ **in** (*acc*) sew into; sew up in
die **Einnahme, –n** taking; *mil* capture; (*pl*) income; takings; revenue; **die** ~**quelle** (*Aust* **Einnahms|quelle**), **–n** source of income/revenuc
einnebeln befog; *mil* lay a smokescreen over
einnehmen* take (meal, medicine, *etc*); take (money), collect (taxes); take (one's seat); take up, occupy; hold (position); adopt (attitude); *mil* take, capture; **eingenommen von** taken with; **von sich eingenommen** full of oneself
~ **für** predispose in favour of; **für sich** ~ win over
~ **gegen** bias against
einnehmend engaging, winning
einnicken (*sn*) *coll* nod off
einnisten: sich ~ nest; install oneself; **sich** ~ **bei** park oneself on
die **Ein|öde, –n** wilderness, wilds
ein|ölen lubricate; rub oil into; **sich** ~ rub oil into one's skin
ein|ordnen arrange, order; file (*also comput*); classify; ~ **in** (*acc*) put in their places in; place in (category); **sich** ~ fit in; *mot* get into the correct lane; **„E~!"** 'get in lane'
die **Ein|ordnung, –en** *vbl noun*; *also* classification

einpacken pack (**in** *acc* in); wrap up (in); **sich gut** ~ wrap up well
einparken park (between vehicles)
Einpartei(en)– one-party ...
einpassen: ~ **in** (*acc*) fit into; **sich** ~ fit in
einpauken *coll* (+*dat*) drum into; **sich** *dat* **...** ~ cram
einpeitschen (+*dat*) drub into; ~ **auf** (*acc*) whip
der **Einpeitscher, –** (party) whip
einpendeln: sich ~ settle down; find its own level
der **Einpendler, –** commuter (travelling to work)
einpferchen pen; ~ **in** (*acc*) cram into
einpflanzen plant; (+*dat*) instil in; *med* implant in
einphasig *elect* single-phase
einpinseln *med* paint
einplanen budget for; allow for; include in one's plans
einpökeln salt down
einprägen (+*dat*) impress on; **sich** *dat* **...** ~ make a mental note of; memorize; ~ **in** (*acc*) imprint on; **sich** ~ (+*dat*) impress itself on; **sich leicht** ~ be easy to remember
einprägsam easily remembered; catchy
einpudern powder
einpumpen pump in
einpuppen: sich ~ pupate
einquartieren put up (**bei** with); *mil* billet (on); **sich** ~ **bei** put up at (s.o.'s) house
einrahmen frame
einrammen ram in
einrasten (*sn*) snap into position; *coll* take umbrage
einräumen put away; put the furniture in; concede; (+*dat*) grant; let (s.o.) have; devote to; ~ **in** (*acc*) put away in; put (books) in/on; put (furniture) in; ~**d** *gramm* concessive
die **Einräumung, –en** *vbl noun*; *also* concession
einrechnen include (in one's calculations); **... eingerechnet** including ...
die **Einrede, –n** *leg* plea
einreden (+*dat of pers*) talk into believing in/accepting; **sich** *dat* **...** ~ make oneself believe; ~ **auf** (*acc*) keep on at; talk (insistently *etc*) to
einregnen (*sn exc* **sich** ~) be drenched by the rain; be held up by the rain; **es regnet sich ein** the rain is settling in
das **Einreibe|mittel, –** embrocation
einreiben* rub in; rub (back); ~ **mit** rub with
einreichen submit; tender (resignation); *leg* file
einreihen: ~ **in** (*acc*) place in (category); incorporate into; ~ **unter** (*acc*) rank among; **sich** ~ **in** (*acc*) take one's place in; join
der **Einreiher, –** single-breasted suit
einreihig single-breasted

die **Einreise** entry (into a country); **die ~genehmigung, -en** entry permit

einreisen (*sn*) enter the country; **~ in** (*acc*) enter

einreißen* demolish; tear; (*v/i sn*) get torn; (abuse *etc*) spread

einreiten* break in; (*v/i sn*) ride in; **sich ~** get used to riding

einrenken set (limb); *coll* put right; **sich ~** *coll* sort itself out

einrennen* (by running at sth.) smash in; break open; (+*dat*) **die Bude/das Haus ~** *coll* pester with unwanted visits; **sich** *dat* **den Kopf ~ an** (*dat*) bang one's head against

einrichten furnish; fit out; arrange; set up; establish; start; *med* set; *math* reduce to an improper fraction; **~ für** *mus* arrange for; **sich ~** furnish one's house *etc*; manage (on moderate income); **sich ~ auf** (*acc*) prepare for

die **Einrichtung, -en** *vbl noun*; *also* establishment (of); furnishings; equipment; device; institution; *mus* arrangement; (*pl*) installations

der **Einriß, -(ss)e** tear; crack

der **Einritt, -e** entry (on horseback)

einritzen: ~ in (*acc*) scratch on

einrollen roll up; *sp* roll in; (*v/i sn*) roll in; (train) pull in; **sich** *dat* **die Haare ~** put one's hair in curlers; **sich ~** roll up; roll up in a ball

einrosten (*sn*) rust; *coll* get stiff; **eingerostet sein** (s.o.'s German *etc*) be rusty

einrücken put (announcement) in the paper; *mech* engage; *print* indent; (*v/i sn*) move up (into higher position *etc*); *mil* march in; *mil* report for duty

einrühren stir in

eins 1 *num* one; 2 *pron* (*see* **einer/eine/ein(e)s**) one; one thing; **~ sein mit** be one/in agreement with; **es ist mir alles ~** *coll* it's all the same to me; **die Eins, -en** one (*also = top grade* – **'sehr gut'** – *in marking scale*) || **das E~sein** oneness

einsacken[1] sack; *coll* rake in

einsacken[2] (*sn*) *coll* sink

einsalben rub with ointment

einsalzen salt down

einsam lonely; solitary; secluded

die **Einsamkeit** loneliness; solitude; seclusion

einsammeln collect; gather (fruit)

einsargen put in a coffin

der **Einsatz, ⸚e** use, employment (of); effort(s); commitment; (in gambling) stake; deposit (on sth.); insert, piece inserted, *dressm* insertion; *mil* action; mission; *mus* entry; **im ~ sein** be on duty; be in operation; *mil* see action; **unter ~ seines Lebens** at the risk of one's life; **zum ~ kommen** be brought into use/*mil* sent into action || **e~bereit** ready for use/*mil* action; **e~fähig** operational; *mil* fit for action; *sp* fit; **e~freudig** enthusiastic; **das ~kommando, -s** task force; **das ~stück, -e** insert; **der ~wagen, -** extra bus/car (put on in rush hour)

einsauen *vulg* make filthy

einsaugen (*see* **saugen**) suck in; breathe in; (bee) suck; absorb, soak up

einsäumen hem (garment); border

Einschalt-: die ~quote, -n viewing figures

einschalten switch on; call in; interpolate; *mot* engage (gear); *rad* tune in to; **sich ~** switch itself on; intervene (**in** *acc* in)

einschärfen (+*dat*) impress on

einscharren bury hastily

einschätzen assess, size up; *fin* assess provisionally; **hoch ~** have a high opinion of

die **Einschätzung, -en** assessment

einschenken pour (out); fill; (*v/i*, +*dat*) fill (s.o.'s) glass; pour (s.o.) a cup

einscheren (*sn*) get back into one's previous lane

einschicken send in

einschieben* push in; insert, interpolate; put on (extra train *etc*); fit (person) in; take (break)

das **Einschiebsel, -** interpolation

die **Einschienen|bahn, -en** monorail

einschießen* smash (with ball *etc*); demolish by gunfire; test-fire (gun); drive (dowel) into the wall; contribute (cash); *sp* shoot (ball) into the goal; *print* insert; (*v/i sn*) (water) rush in; **sich ~** get one's eye in; **sich ~ auf** (*acc*) (gun) zero in on; be gunning for

einschiffen embark; ship; **sich ~** embark

die **Einschiffung** embarkation; shipment (of)

einschirren harness

einschl. (= **einschließlich**) incl.

einschlafen* (*sn*) fall asleep; pass away; (leg *etc*) go to sleep; peter out, (custom) die out

einschläfern send to sleep; lull into a false sense of security; soothe (conscience); allay (suspicion); *vet* put to sleep; **~d** soporific

einschläfrig (bed) single

der **Einschlag, ⸚e** impact (of grenade, meteorite, *etc*); hole made by a grenade, meteorite, *etc*; felling; timber felled; element; touch (of); *mot* lock

einschlagen* knock in; smash; smash in; fell (timber); wrap (**in** *acc* in); take (route); enter on (career); *mot* turn (wheel); *agr* put (plants) (temporarily) in the ground; (*v/i*) (projectile, lightning) strike; shake hands (with s.o., when sealing bargain); *coll* be a success; **~ auf** (*acc*) rain blows on; **~ in** (*acc*) strike; **in jmds. Hand ~** shake hands with s.o. (when sealing bargain); **der**

Blitz/es hat eingeschlagen lightning has struck

einschlägig relevant; (shop) dealing in this article

einschleichen*: sich ~ creep in; **sich ~ in** (*acc*) creep into; worm one's way into (s.o.'s confidence)

einschleppen tow in; bring in (disease *etc*)

einschleusen smuggle in; **~ in** (*acc*) put into (circulation); infiltrate into

einschließen* lock up (**in** *acc/dat* in); include (**in** *acc/dat* in); enclose; *mil* surround; *athl* box in; **in Klammern ~** put in brackets; **sich ~** shut oneself in; **... eingeschlossen** inclusive of ...

einschließlich 1 *adv*: **bis (zu) ... ~** up to and including; 2 *prep* (+*gen*) including, inclusive of

einschlummern (*sn*) fall asleep; pass away peacefully; *coll* fade

der **Einschluß, ⸗(ss)e** locking up; *geol* inclusion; **mit/unter ~** (+*gen*) including

einschmeicheln: sich ~ bei ingratiate oneself with; **~d** ingratiating; enticing, (voice) silky

einschmeißen* *coll* smash (in)

einschmelzen* melt down

einschmieren grease; oil; rub cream into; *coll* make dirty; **~ mit** rub with

einschmuggeln: (sich) ~ smuggle (oneself) in

einschnappen (*sn*) snap shut; *coll* take umbrage

einschneiden* cut into; **~ in** (*acc*) carve (name *etc*) in; *cin* cut into; *cul* cut up and add to (soup); (*v/i*) (string *etc*) cut into; have a profound effect on; **~d** far-reaching; drastic; having a profound effect (on s.o.'s life)

einschneien (*see also* **eingeschneit**) (*sn*) get snowed up

der **Einschnitt, -e** cut, *med* incision; break; turning-point; *civ eng* cutting

einschnüren constrict; lace

einschränken limit, restrict (**auf** *acc* to); **sich ~** economize

die **Einschränkung, -en** restriction; reservation (about); economy; **ohne ~** unreservedly

einschrauben screw in

Einschreibe- *post* registered ...; **die ~gebühr, -en** enrolment fee; *post* registration fee

einschreiben* enter (name *etc*); enrol; register (*also post*); *comput* write; **~ lassen** send by registered post/mail *US*; **sich ~ (lassen)** enrol; register; **sich ~ in** (*acc*) enter one's name in

das **Einschreiben, -** registered letter/packet/parcel; **per ~** by registered post/mail *US*; „~!" 'registered'

einschreiten* (*sn*) step in; **~ gegen** take action against; **das Einschreiten** intervention

einschrumpfen (*sn*) shrivel up; (supplies *etc*) shrink

der **Einschub, ⸗e** interpolation

einschüchtern intimidate, cow

die **Einschüchterung** intimidation

einschulen send to school (for first time); **eingeschult werden** start school

der **Einschuß, ⸗(ss)e** bullet-hole; *fin* capital invested; *sp* shot into goal; *text* weft, woof

einschütten pour in; tip in; pour out (coffee *etc*)

einschweißen shrink-wrap (book, record); *tech* weld in

einschwenken swing inwards; (*v/i sn*) swing (left *etc*); **~ auf** (*acc*) (*sn*) go along with

einschwören*: ~ auf (*acc*) get (s.o.) to commit himself/herself to; **eingeschworen auf** (*acc*) committed to

einsegnen [-e:-] *Prot* confirm; *RC* bless

die **Einsegnung, -en** *Prot* confirmation; *RC* blessing

einsehen* see into; examine (document *etc*); realize, see; **ein Einsehen haben** show understanding; see reason

einseifen soap; lather; *coll* con

einseitig one-sided; unilateral; on one side

Einsende-: der ~termin, -e closing date

einsenden* send in

der **Einsender, -** sender

die **Einsendung, -en** *vbl noun*; *also* contribution; entry

einsenken: ~ in (*acc*) sink into

einsetzen put in; insert; put on (extra train *etc*); put into service; appoint; send in (troops *etc*); use, employ; risk; stake; *sp* play (player); (*v/i*) (weather *etc*) set in; start; *mus* come in

~ für summon up (energy) for

~ in (*acc*) install in

~ zu make (s.o. one's heir)

sich ~ exert oneself; **sich voll ~** do one's utmost; **sich ~ für** support; champion; use one's influence (**bei** with) on behalf of

die **Einsicht, -en** realization; insight; sense, reason; **~ nehmen in** (*acc*) inspect; **zur ~ bringen** get (s.o.) to see reason; **zur ~ kommen** see reason; **zu der ~ kommen, daß ...** come to realize that ... || **die ~nahme** inspection (**in** *acc* of)

einsichtig sensible; understanding; easily understood

einsichts-: ~los unreasonable; **~voll** sensible

einsickern (*sn*) seep in; infiltrate

die **Einsiedel<u>ei</u>, -en** hermitage

der **Einsiedler, -** hermit; recluse

einsiedlerisch hermit-like

einsilbig monosyllabic; taciturn

einsingen*: sich ~ get oneself into voice

einsinken* (*see also* **eingesunken**) (*sn*) sink

in; subside; (knees) give way

einsitzen* (*see also* **eingesessen**) serve a sentence

der **Einsitzer, –** single-seater

einsortieren sort out (**nach** according to); ~ **in** (*acc*) sort into

einspannen harness (to sth.); yoke; *coll* rope in; ~ **in** (*acc*) put in; clamp in; **den ganzen Tag eingespannt** on the go all day long

der **Einspänner, –** one-horse carriage; *Aust* black coffee with whipped cream; *coll* loner; bachelor

einspännig one-horse; (*adv*) with one horse; *joc* as a bachelor

einsparen save; economize on; axe (job)

die **Einsparung, –en** *vbl noun*; *also* saving; economy

einspeichern *comput*: ~ **in** (*acc*) input to

einspeisen: ~ **in** (*acc*) *comput* input to; *tech* supply to

einsperren lock up (*also* = jail) (**in** *acc/dat* in)

einspielen bring in, gross; record (title); *mus* bring to full resonance (by playing); **sich ~** get into practice; (system *etc*) get going; *sp* play oneself in; **sich ~ auf** *acc*/**bei** *tech* come to rest at; **sich aufeinander ~** get used to playing together; get used to each other's ways; **aufeinander eingespielt sein** make a good team

einspinnen*: sich ~ spin a cocoon; **sich ~ in** (*acc*) lose oneself in

die **Einsprache** [–a:–], **–n** *Aust*, *Swiss* = **Einspruch**

einsprachig monolingual

einsprechen*: ~ **auf** (*acc*) keep on at; talk (insistently *etc*) to

einsprengen sprinkle with water; ~ **in** (*acc*) blast (hole) in; **eingesprengt** *also* scattered

einspringen* (*sn*) snap shut; step into the breach; ~ **für** stand in for; **sich ~** do some practice jumps

Einspritz– *mech* injection ...

einspritzen sprinkle with water; *med*, *mech* inject (**in** *acc* into); (+*dat*) give (s.o.) an injection of

die **Einspritzung, –en** *vbl noun*; *med*, *mech* injection

der **Einspruch, ⸚e** objection (**gegen** to), protest (against); *leg* appeal (against); ~ **erheben gegen** protest against; *leg* lodge an appeal against

einspurig *rail* single-track; *mot* single-lane

einst once; some day; **~weilen** for the moment; in the meantime; **~weilig** temporary

einstampfen pulp; press (cabbage) down (into barrel *etc*)

der **Einstand, ⸚e** starting work in a new job (celebrated by a party); *tennis* deuce

einstanzen: ~ **in** (*acc*) stamp on

einstauben make dusty; *Aust* powder; (*v/i sn*) become dusty

einstäuben powder

einstechen*: ~ **auf** (*acc*) stab at; ~ **in** (*acc*) stick into; prick (hole) in; **mit einer Gabel ~ in** (*acc*) stick a fork in

einstecken put in; sheathe (sword); plug in; post, mail *US*; put in one's bag/pocket; *coll* pocket; *coll* swallow (insult *etc*), take (blows, criticism); *coll* be more than a match for

einstehen* (*sn*): ~ **für** answer for; vouch for; **dafür ~, daß ...** guarantee that ...

einsteigen* (*sn*) get on; get in; ~ **in** (*acc*) get on; get into; *mount* start climbing; *coll* go into; move into; **hart ~** tackle hard; **~!** all aboard!

Einstell–: der ~platz, ⸚e car port; parking space (in garage)

einstellbar adjustable

einstellen put away; take on, employ; stop, *leg* stay (proceedings); *rad* tune in to; *sp* equal; ~ **auf** (*acc*) adjust to; set at/to; gear to; *rad* tune to; **scharf ~** focus; **die Arbeit ~** down tools; **scharf eingestellt** in focus; (**liberal** *etc*) **eingestellt** (liberal *etc*) -minded; **eingestellt auf** (*acc*) prepared for; geared to; **eingestellt gegen** unfavourably disposed towards

sich ~ turn up; set in; appear; arise; **sich ~ auf** (*acc*) adapt (oneself/itself) to, adjust (oneself/itself) to; prepare (oneself) for

einstellig one-figure; (decimal) one-place

die **Einstellung, –en** *vbl noun*; *also* attitude (**zu** to); employment; adjustment; stoppage; discontinuation; *leg* stay; *mil* cessation; *cin* take

der **Einstieg, –e** entrance (of bus *etc*); ~ **in** (*acc*) entry into; way of getting into/approaching

einstig former

einstimmen *mus* tune up; (*v/i*) *mus* join in; ~ **auf** (*acc*) put in the mood for; ~ **in** (*acc*) join in (song, applause, *etc*); **sich ~ auf** (*acc*)/**für** get in the mood for

einstimmig unanimous; *mus* for one voice; (*adv*) unanimously; *mus* in unison

die **Einstimmigkeit** unanimity

einstöckig one-storey

einstöpseln plug in; put in (cork)

einstoßen* thrust in; push in

einstreichen* (*coll exc* + **mit**) pocket; **mit** (**Kleister** *etc*) ~ spread (paste *etc*) over

einstreuen: ~ **in** (*acc*) scatter in; intersperse (speech) with; ~ **mit** strew with; **mit Mehl ~** flour

einströmen (*sn*) pour in; stream in

einstudieren study (role); rehearse; **einstudiert** (pose) studied

die **Einstudierung, –en** *vbl noun*; *also* production

einstufen grade; classify; ~ **als** classify as; class as; ~ **in** (*acc*) put in

einstufig single-stage
die **Einstufung, –en** grading; classification
einstürmen (*sn*): ~ **auf** (*acc*) rush at; assail (with questions *etc*); crowd in on
der **Einsturz, ⸚e** collapse
einstürzen (*sn*) collapse, fall in; ~ **auf** (*acc*) (events) overtake
einsuggerieren (+*dat*) insinuate (idea *etc*) into (s.o.'s) mind
eintägig one-day; day-old
die **Eintags|fliege, –n** mayfly; flash in the pan; nine days' wonder; passing fad
der **Eintänzer, –** gigolo
eintauchen dip (in liquid); (*v/i sn*) dive in
der **Eintausch** exchange; **im ~ gegen** in exchange for
eintauschen: ~ gegen exchange for
einteilen organize (work, time); ~ **in** (*acc*) divide into; ~ **für/zu** assign to; **sein Geld ~** plan one's expenditure, budget
einteilig one-piece
die **Einteilung, –en** *vbl noun*; *also* division; organization; assignment
eintönig monotonous
die **Eintönigkeit** monotony
der **Eintopf = das ~gericht, –e** stew
die **Eintracht** harmony
einträchtig harmonious
der **Eintrag, ⸚e** entry (in book; *also comput*); (+*dat*) ~ **tun** impair
eintragen* enter (**in** *acc* in); register (in); bring in, yield; (+*dat*) earn (s.o. sympathy *etc*); **sich** ~ enter one's name; **sich ~ in** (*acc*) enter one's name in; sign
einträglich lucrative
die **Eintragung, –en** *vbl noun*; *also* registration; entry (in book)
eintrainieren [–trɛ–] (+*dat*) inculcate in (by training); **sich** ~ practise (systematically)
einträufeln (+*dat*) implant (hatred *etc*) in; ~ **in** (*acc*) put (drops) in (ear)/up (nose)
eintreffen* (*sn*) arrive; come true; happen (as predicted); **das Eintreffen** arrival
eintreiben* drive in; drive (cattle) home; collect (outstanding debts *etc*)
eintreten* kick in; break in (shoes); (*v/i sn*) enter, go/come in; occur, take place; set in; (silence) fall; **sich** *dat* **...** ~ get (thorn *etc*) in one's foot; **wenn der Fall eintritt, daß ...** in the event of (s.o.'s/sth.'s +*ger*)
~ **auf** (*acc*) kick repeatedly
~ **für** (*sn*) stick up for; support, champion
~ **in** (*acc*) tread into; (*v/i sn*) enter; join; enter into; *space* go into (orbit)
das **Eintreten** *vbl noun*; *also* entry (**in** *acc* into); occurrence; advocacy (**für** of)
eintrichtern (+*dat*) *coll* drum into
der **Eintritt, –e** entry; admission; onset (of); ~ **in** (*acc*) entry into; admission to; joining; (+*dat*) ~ **gewähren** admit; **bei** ~ (+*gen*) at the onset of; when ... sets in; if ... should arise; **„~ verboten!"** 'no admittance' || **das ~s|geld, –er** admission fee; **die ~s|karte, –n** ticket
eintrocknen (*sn*) dry up; shrivel up
eintrommeln *coll* (+*dat*) drum into; ~ **auf** (*acc*) assail (s.o.'s) ears
eintrüben: sich ~ cloud over
eintrudeln (*sn*) *coll* roll up
eintunken *coll* dunk
ein|üben practise; learn (by practising); train
einverleiben (*also insep*; *p/part* **einverleibt**) (+*dat*) incorporate into; **sich** *dat* **...** ~ acquire; *joc* get outside of (food)
die **Einverleibung, –en** incorporation
die **Einvernahme, –n** *Aust*, *Swiss leg* examination
einvernehmen* *Aust*, *Swiss leg* examine
das **Einvernehmen** understanding; **im ~ mit** in agreement with; **in gutem ~ stehen mit** be on good terms with
einverstanden: ~ sein mit agree to; agree with; approve of; **nicht ~ sein mit** disagree with; disapprove of; **sich ~ erklären mit** agree to; **~!** O.K.!
das **Einverständnis** agreement; approval; **im ~ mit** in agreement with
einwachsen*[1] [–ks–] (*like* **wachsen**[1]) (*see also* **eingewachsen**) (*sn*) take root; (nail) grow inwards
einwachsen[2] [–ks–] wax
der **Einwand, ⸚e** objection (**gegen** to); **e~frei** perfect; faultless; impeccable; (*adv*: prove) beyond any doubt
der **Einwanderer, –** immigrant
einwandern (*sn*) immigrate; ~ **in** (*acc*) settle in
die **Einwanderung, –en** immigration
einwärts inwards
einweben weave in; ~ **in** (*acc*) weave into; work into
einwechseln [–ks–] change (**in** *acc* into); *sp* bring on (as substitute)
Einweck–: das ~glas, ⸚er preserving jar
einwecken preserve, bottle
Einweg– non-returnable ...; one-way ...
einweichen soak
einweihen open (formally); *eccles* consecrate; *joc* christen; ~ **in** (*acc*) initiate into; let in on; **eingeweiht** *also* in the know
die **Einweihung, –en** *vbl noun*; *also* (official) opening, *eccles* consecration; initiation
einweisen* instruct in his/her duties; *mot* direct into a parking space *etc*; ~ **in** (*acc*) put in (home), send to (hospital); assign to (accommodation); instruct in (duties); *mot* direct into; **(in sein Amt)** ~ install in office; *eccles* induct
die **Einweisung, –en** *vbl noun*; *also* assignment

(to); instruction (in duties); installation (in office), *eccles* induction

einwenden*: etwas ~ gegen raise an objection to; **etwas/nichts einzuwenden haben gegen** have an/no objection to; **~, daß ...** object that ...

die **Einwendung, -en** objection (**gegen** to)

einwerfen* smash (by throwing sth.); insert (coin); post, mail *US*; interject, throw in; *sp* throw in

einwertig *chem* univalent

Einwickel-: das ~papier wrapping paper

einwickeln wrap (up); *coll* get round; **sich** *dat* **die Haare ~** put one's hair in curlers; **sich ~ lassen von** *coll* let (s.o.) get round one

einwiegen rock to sleep; **sich ~ lassen von** allow oneself to be deluded by

einwilligen consent (**in** *acc* to)

die **Einwilligung, -en** consent

einwinken direct (**in** *acc* into)

einwirken work in (design *etc*); **~ auf** (*acc*) influence; affect, have an effect on; act on; **aufeinander ~** interact

die **Einwirkung, -en** influence; effect; action (on)

der **Einwohner, -** inhabitant; **das ~melde|amt, ¨er** registration office for residents; **die ~zahl, -en** population

der **Einwurf, ¨e** slit; slot; insertion (of coin); posting, mailing *US*; interjection; *sp* throw-in

einwurzeln (*see also* **eingewurzelt**) (*sn*) = **sich ~** take root

die **Einzahl** singular

einzahlen pay in; **~ auf** (*acc*) pay into

die **Einzahlung, -en** *vbl noun*; *also* payment; deposit; *in compds* **~s-** paying-in ...

einzäunen fence in

die **Einzäunung, -en** *vbl noun*; *also* fence

einzeichnen draw in; mark (**auf** *dat* on); **seinen Namen/sich ~ in** (*acc*) enter one's name in

das **Einzel, -** *sp* singles

Einzel- single ...; individual ...; separate ...; **das ~bett, -en** single bed; **der ~fall, ¨e** individual/isolated case; **der ~gänger, -** lone wolf; **die ~haft** solitary confinement; **der ~handel** retail trade (**im E. verkaufen** sell retail); **der ~handels|preis, -e** retail price; **der ~händler, -** retailer; **das ~haus, ¨er** detached house; **der ~kampf, ¨e** single combat; *sp* individual contest; **das ~kind, -er** only child; **die ~person, -en** individual; **das ~spiel, -e** *sp* singles; **der ~teil, -e** component (part); **das ~wesen, -** individual (being); **das ~zimmer, -** single room

die **Einzelheit, -en** detail; **bis in alle ~en** down to the last detail

der **Einzeller, -** unicellular organism

einzellig unicellular

einzeln individual; separate; single, solitary; (sock *etc*) odd; (*adv*) *also* one by one; **~e** *pl* some; **~es** a few things; **im ~en** in detail; **ins ~e gehen** go into detail; **der/die ~e** (*decl as adj*) the individual || **~stehend** solitary

einzementieren cement in; consolidate

einziehbar (debt) recoverable; *aer* retractable

einziehen* pull in (stomach *etc*), duck (head), put (tail) between its legs; haul in (net), *aer* retract, *naut* take in (sail), haul down (flag), ship (oars); absorb; breathe in, inhale; collect (debts *etc*); withdraw (licence *etc*), call in (coins *etc*), confiscate (property *etc*); make (enquiries); *build* put in; *mil* call up, draft *US*; *print* indent; (*v/i sn*) enter; move in; (spring *etc*) come; *mil* march in; **~ in** (*acc*) (*sn*) enter; move into; be absorbed into; (peace *etc*) come to; *mil* march into; *sp* get into

einzig only, sole; single; unique; (*adv*) only; singularly (beautiful); **ein ~er/eine ~e/ein ~es ...** a/one single ...; one big/long ...; **~ dastehen** be unique; **~ und allein** solely; **als ~er/~e/~es** *conveyed by* ... is *etc* the only one to + *infin*; **das ~e** the only thing || **~artig** unique

einzuckern sugar (fruit)

der **Einzug, ¨e** entry (**in** *acc* into); moving in(to); move (into); advent; collection (of taxes *etc*); *print* indentation; **seinen ~ halten** make one's entry; (spring *etc*) make its appearance || **der ~s|bereich, -e** catchment area; area from which a labour force *etc* is drawn; **die ~s|feier, -n** house-warming; **das ~s|gebiet, -e** *geog* catchment area; = **~sbereich**

einzwängen squeeze in; constrain

das **eis, Eis** ['eːɪs] (*gen* -), - *mus* (the note) E sharp; (*key*) **Eis** E sharp major, **eis** E sharp minor

das **Eis** ice; ice-cream; **~ am Stiel** ice lolly, popsicle *US*; **das ~ brechen** break the ice; **auf ~ legen** put on ice; put (plan *etc*) into cold storage || **die ~bahn, -en** ice-rink; **der ~bär, -en** (*wk masc*) polar bear; **der ~becher, -** ice-cream tub; sundae; **das ~bein, -e** pickled and boiled knuckle of pork; (*pl*) *joc* cold feet; **der ~berg, -e** iceberg; **der ~beutel, -** ice-bag; **die ~blumen** *pl* frost pattern; **der ~brecher, -** icebreaker; **die ~decke, -n** sheet of ice; **die ~diele, -n** ice-cream parlour; **e~gekühlt** iced; **eis|grau** hoary; **die ~heiligen** *pl* the 'Ice Saints' (*cold spell in May*); **das ~hockey** ice-hockey; **der ~kaffee** iced coffee; **eis|kalt** freezing cold; (glance *etc*) icy; cold and calculating; **der ~kühler, -** ice-bucket; **der ~kunst|lauf** figure-skating; **der**

~kunst|läufer, – figure-skater; **der ~lauf** ice-skating; **e~laufen*** (*sep*: **ich laufe eis;** *p/part* **eisgelaufen;** *sn*) skate; **der ~läufer, –** skater; **das ~meer, –e** polar sea (**das Nördliche/Südliche E.** the Arctic/Antarctic Ocean); **der ~pickel, –** ice-axe, ice-pick; **das ~schießen** *approx* = curling; **der ~schnellauf** speed-skating; **die ~scholle, –n** ice-floe; **der ~schrank, ⸗e** refrigerator; **der ~tanz** ice-dancing; **der ~vogel, ..vögel** kingfisher; **der ~zapfen, –** icicle; **die ~zeit, –en** ice age

das **Eisen, –** iron; horseshoe; trap; **heißes ~** delicate/controversial matter; **mehrere ~ im Feuer haben** have several irons in the fire; **zum alten ~ gehören** be on the shelf; **zum alten ~ werfen** throw on the scrap-heap

Eisen– iron ...; ferric ...; ferrous ...; ferro–;

die ~bahn, –en railway, railroad *US* (**mit der E.** by rail); **der ~bahner, –** railway-man, railroader *US*; **der ~bahn|wagen, –** railway carriage, railroad car *US*; **das ~blech** sheet iron; **das ~erz** iron ore; **die ~feil|späne** *pl* iron filings; **die ~gießerei, –en** iron-foundry/smelting; **der ~guß** iron-casting; cast iron; **e~haltig,** *Aust* **e~hältig** containing iron; **die ~handlung, –en** ironmonger's, hardware store *US*; **eisen|hart** as hard as iron; (will) iron; **der ~hut** aconite; **die ~hütte, –n** ironworks; **der ~kies** iron pyrites; **die ~waren** *pl* hardware; **das ~werk, –e** ironworks; **die ~zeit** Iron Age

eisern iron; (energy) unflagging; (*adv*) resolutely; **~ bleiben/sein in** (*dat*) be adamant about; **~ schweigen** maintain a stony silence; **aber ~!** you bet!

eisig icy

eitel vain; *arch* idle, vain; (*indecl*) *poet* pure; sheer

die **Eitelkeit** vanity

der **Eiter** pus

eit(e)rig festering

eitern fester

EK = Eisernes Kreuz

die **EKD = Evangelische Kirche in Deutschland**

das **Ekel, –** *coll* beast

der **Ekel** disgust (**vor** *dat* at); nausea (at); **~ empfinden vor** (*dat*) be sickened by || **e~erregend** revolting

ekelhaft = ek(e)lig revolting; *coll* beastly

ekeln: mich/mir ekelt vor (*dat*) I am disgusted by; I loathe; **sich ~ vor** (*dat*) be disgusted by; loathe

das **EKG, –(s)** (**= Elektrokardiogramm**) E.C.G.

der **Eklat** [–'kla], **–s** sensation, stir; row

eklatant striking; blatant; sensational

die **Eklipse, –n** eclipse

die **Ekliptik** [–ɪk], **–en** ecliptic

die **Ekstase, –n** ecstasy; **in ~ geraten** go into ecstasies

ekstatisch ecstatic

das **Ekzem, –e** eczema

der **Elan** [–'lã:, –'la:n] zest

elastisch elastic; springy; supple; flexible; resilient

die **Elastizität** elasticity; springiness; suppleness; flexibility; resilience

die **Elbe** the Elbe

der **Elch, –e** elk; moose

der **Elefant, –en** (*wk masc*) elephant

elegant elegant

die **Eleganz** elegance

die **Elegie, –(ie)n** elegy

elegisch elegiac; melancholy

elektrifizieren electrify

die **Elektrifizierung, –en** electrification

die **Elektrik** [–ɪk] *esp mot* electrical system

der **Elektriker, –** electrician

elektrisch electric; electrical; (*adv*) *also* (cook *etc*) by electricity

elektrisieren electrify; *med* treat with electrotherapy; **sich ~** get an electric shock

die **Elektrizität** electricity; **das ~s|werk, –e** power station

Elektro– electro–; electric(al) ...; **das ~gerät, –e** electrical appliance; **der ~herd, –e** electric cooker/stove *US*; **der ~installateur, –e** electrician; **der ~motor, –en** electric motor; **e~motorisch** electromotive; **der ~rasierer, –** electric razor; **der ~schock, –s** electric shock; **die ~technik** electrical engineering; **der ~techniker, –** electrical engineer; electrician

die **Elektrode, –n** electrode

die **Elektrolyse, –n** electrolysis

das **Elektron** [–ɔn], **–(on)en** electron

Elektronen– electron ...; electronic ...; **das ~blitz|gerät, –e** electronic flash

die **Elektronik** [–ɪk] electronics

elektronisch electronic

das **Element, –e** element; *elect* cell; (*pl*, *in var senses*) elements; **in seinem ~** in one's element

elementar (*in compds* **E~–**) elementary; elemental

elend ['e:lɛnt] miserable, wretched; *coll* awful

das **Elend** ['e:lɛnt] misery; destitution, want; **das heulende ~** *coll* the blues || **das ~s|quartier, –e** hovel; **das ~s|viertel, –** slums

elf eleven; **der E~meter, –** penalty kick

der **Elf, –en** (*wk masc*), **die Elfe, –n** elf

die **Elf, –en** *sp* eleven, team

Elfen– ... of the elves/fairies; **das ~bein, e~beinern** ivory; **die ~bein|küste** the Ivory Coast; **der ~bein|turm, ⸗e** ivory tower

elfenhaft elfin

elft: zu ~ (*see* **zu** 1(*i*)); **elft..** eleventh

elftel: ein ~ ... an eleventh of a ...
das **Elftel, -** eleventh
eliminieren eliminate (*also math, sp*)
Elisabeth [-bɛt] Elizabeth
elitär élitist
die **Elite, -n** élite
das **Elixier, -e** elixir
der **Ell|bogen, -** elbow; **die ~freiheit** elbow-room
die **Elle, -n** ell; *anat* ulna; **der ~n|bogen, -** elbow; **ellen|lang** *coll* interminable
die **Ellipse, -n** *math* ellipse; *gramm* ellipsis
elliptisch elliptical
die **Eloge** [-ʒə], **-n** eulogy
die **Elritze, -n** minnow
das **Elsaß** ['ɛlzas] (*gen* -/-(ss)es) Alsace; **Elsaß-Lothringen** Alsace-Lorraine
der **Elsässer, -, elsässisch** Alsatian
die **Elster, -n** magpie
elterlich parental
die **Eltern** *pl* parents; **nicht von schlechten ~** *coll* not bad at all
Eltern- parents' ...; parental ...; **das ~haus, ⸚er** home; **e~los** orphaned; **der ~teil, -e** parent
das **Email** [-'maɐ], **-s = die Emaille** [-'maljə], **-n, emaillieren** [-mal(j)-] enamel
die **Emanze, -n** *coll* women's libber
die **Emanzipation** emancipation
emanzipatorisch emancipatory
emanzipieren emancipate
das **Emblem** [*also* ã-], **-e** emblem
die **Embolie, -(ie)n** embolism
der **Embryo, -s/-(o)nen** embryo
embryonal embryonic
emeritiert emeritus
der **Emigrant, -en** (*wk masc*) émigré
die **Emigration, -en** emigration; exile; émigrés (*collect*); **innere ~** (*state of 'inward exile' – as opposed to physical emigration – into which some opponents of the Nazi régime withdrew*); **in die ~ gehen** go into exile; **in der ~** in exile
emigrieren (*sn*) emigrate
eminent eminent; outstanding
die **Eminenz, -en** (*title of cardinal*) Eminence; **graue ~** éminence grise
der **Emir, -e** emir
das **Emirat, -e** emirate
die **Emission, -en** emission (*also phys*); *fin* issue; *Swiss rad* broadcast
die **Emotion, -en** emotion
emotional = emotionell emotional; emotive
empfahl (empfähle) *p/t* (*subj*) *of* **empfehlen**
empfand (empfände) *p/t* (*subj*) *of* **empfinden**
der **Empfang, ⸚e** reception (*also rad, TV*); receipt (of); (hotel) reception (desk); **in ~ nehmen** receive; take delivery of
empfangen* (*like* **fangen**) receive (*also rad, TV*); conceive (child)
der **Empfänger, -** recipient; receiver (*also rad, TV*); *comm* consignee
empfänglich receptive (**für** to); susceptible (to)
die **Empfänglichkeit** receptivity; susceptibility
die **Empfängnis** conception (of child); **e~verhütend** contraceptive (**e~verhütendes Mittel** contraceptive); **die ~verhütung** contraception; **das ~verhütungs|mittel, -** contraceptive
Empfangs- reception ...; receiving ...; **die ~bescheinigung, -en** (acknowledgement of) receipt; **der ~chef, -s** receptionist, desk clerk *US*; **die ~dame, -n** receptionist; **das ~s|gerät, -e** *rad, TV* receiver; **die ~s|halle, -n** foyer (of hotel)
empfehlen (empfiehl(s)t, *p/t* **empfahl** (*subj* **empfähle, empföhle**), *p/part* **empfohlen)** recommend; (+*dat*) recommend to; commend to; **sich ~** take one's leave; **... empfiehlt sich durch ...** ... is to be recommended for ...; **es empfiehlt sich zu ...** it is advisable to ...; **empfohlener Richtpreis** recommended price || **~s|wert** to be recommended; advisable
die **Empfehlung, -en** recommendation; compliments; **= das ~s|schreiben, -** letter of recommendation; testimonial
empfiehl *imp sing*, **empfiehl(s)t** (*2nd,*) *3rd sing pres of* **empfehlen**
empfinden* (*like* **finden**) feel; **das Empfinden** feeling; sense (**für** of)
empfindlich sensitive (**gegen** to); delicate; sensitive, touchy; that marks easily; (losses) heavy, (punishment *etc*) severe; (*adv*) *also* appreciably; **-empfindlich** sensitive to ...
die **Empfindlichkeit** sensitivity
empfindsam sensitive; sentimental
die **Empfindung, -en** feeling; sensation; **e~s|los** numb; unfeeling
empfing *p/t of* **empfangen**
empföhle *p/t subj*, **empfohlen** *p/part of* **empfehlen**
empfunden *p/part of* **empfinden**
die **Emphase, -n** emphasis
emphatisch emphatic
das **Empire** [ã'piːɐ] **= der ~stil** Empire (style)
die **Empirie** empirical method/knowledge
der **Empiriker, -** empiricist
empirisch empirical
der **Empirismus** empiricism
empor upwards
empor- *sep pref* ... up; ... upwards
empor|arbeiten: sich ~ work one's way up
emporblicken look up (**zu** at)
die **Empore, -n** gallery
empören fill with indignation; **sich ~** revolt (**gegen** against); **sich ~ über** (*acc*) be indignant at; **~d** outrageous; **empört** indignant (**über** *acc* at)

emporkommen* (*sn*) come up; get on
der **Emporkömmling, –e** upstart
emporragen (*also sn*) tower up; **~d** towering
emporschnellen (*sn*) leap up; shoot up, rocket
emporschwingen* swing up(wards); **sich ~** swing up(wards); **sich ~ zu** accomplish
emporsteigen* (*sn*) climb (up); (*v/i*) climb (up); rise; **~ zu** rise to become
emporstreben aim high; (*sn*) tower up
die **Empörung, –en** indignation; revolt
emsig busy; industrious
emulgieren emulsify
die **Emulsion, –en** emulsion
End– final ...; terminal ...; ultimate ...; end ...; (*of person, eg* **der ~zwanziger/die ~zwanzigerin**) person in his/her late (twenties *etc*); **der ~bahnhof, ⸚e** terminus; **~effekt** (**im E.** ultimately, in the final analysis); **das ~ergebnis, –se** end/final result; **e~gültig** final; definitive; (*adv*) *also* once and for all; **die ~gültigkeit** finality; **der ~kampf, ⸚e, der ~lauf, ⸚e** final; **e~los** endless, unending; infinite (**bis ins ~lose** endlessly); **die ~lösung** *Nazi* Final Solution; **das ~resultat, –e** final result/*sp* score; **das ~spiel, –e** final; *chess* end-game; **der ~spurt, –s** *athl* finish; **die ~station, –en** terminus; end of the line; **die ~stelle, –n** *comput* terminal; **die ~summe, –n** total; **der ~verbraucher, –** consumer; **die ~zeit** *theol* last days
–end *forms present participle* ...ing; *for use after* **zu** *see* **zu** 2 (*c*)
das **Ende, –n** end; finish; (of film *etc*) ending; *hunt* tine, point; *coll* piece, bit; *coll* way (= distance, *eg* **ein ganzes ~** quite a way); **„~"** 'over and out'; *arts* 'the end'; **~ (März/nächster Woche** *etc*) at the end of (March/next week *etc*); **~ (Fünfzig/der Fünfziger** *etc*) **sein** be in one's late (fifties *etc*); **äußerstes ~** extremity; tip; **das dicke ~** *coll* the catch; **letzten ~s** after all, when all is said and done; in the end; **oberes/unteres ~** upper/lower end, (of road, table, *etc*) top/bottom; (+*dat*) **ein ~ bereiten/machen** put an end to; **... hat ein ~** there is an end to ...; **ein ~ nehmen** come to an end; **... nimmt kein ~** there is no end to ...
in prepositional phrases:
am ~ in the end; at the end (*gen* of); *NGer coll* perhaps; **am ~ sein** *coll* be all in; **am richtigen/falschen ~ anfassen** go about (sth.) the right/wrong way
bis/gegen/nach/seit/vor ~ (+*gen*) by/towards/after/since/before the end of
zu ~ finished; at an end; (*with verb*) finish (+*ger*) (*eg* **zu ~ lesen** finish reading); **zu(m) ~** (+*gen*) at the end of; **zu ~ bringen/führen** finish; **zu ~ denken** think through; **zu ~ gehen** come to an end; run out
endemisch endemic
enden end; end up; **~ auf** (*acc*)/**mit** (word) end in; **nicht ~ wollend** unending
die **Endivie** [–ĭə], **–n** endive
endlich finite (*also math*); (*adv*) at last; finally; *expressing impatience, variously rendered* (*eg* **wann kommen die ~?** when *are* they going to come?; (*with imp*) **mach doch ~ deinen Mund auf!** for heaven's sake *say* something!, **hör ~ auf!** *will* you stop that!)
die **Endlichkeit** finite nature
die **Endung, –en** *gramm* ending
die **Energie, –(ie)n** energy; vigour; **e~geladen** full of energy; **e~los** lacking in energy
energisch energetic; vigorous; forceful; firm; **~ werden** put one's foot down
enervieren enervate; **~d** enervating; nerve-racking
eng narrow; confined, cramped; (garment) tight; (circumstances) straitened; (friend, link, *etc*) close; (*adv*) close (together); closely (printed, related, *etc*); (interpret) narrowly; **~ befreundet sein** be close friends ‖ **~anliegend** tight-fitting; **~herzig** petty; **~maschig** close-meshed; tight-knit; *sp* close; **der E~paß, ⸚(ss)e** defile; bottleneck; **~stirnig** narrow-minded
das **Engagement** [ãgaʒəˈmãː], **–s** (political *etc*) commitment; involvement; engagement (of artist)
engagieren [ãgaʒ–] engage; **sich ~** commit oneself (politically *etc*); become committed (militarily, financially, *etc*); **sich ~ für** work for (cause *etc*); **engagiert** *also* committed
die **Enge, –n** narrowness; cramped conditions; *arch* narrow place; **in die ~ treiben** drive into a corner ‖ **der ~laut, –e** fricative
der **Engel, –** angel; **der ~macher, –** *coll*, **die ~macherin, –nen** *coll* backstreet abortionist
engelhaft angelic
Engels–: die ~geduld patience of a saint; **~zungen** (**mit E. reden** speak honeyed words)
England [–ŋl–] England; Britain
der **Engländer** [–ŋl–], **–** Englishman; Briton; *tech* monkey-wrench; **die ~** the English/British
die **Engländerin, –nen** Englishwoman; Briton
englisch [–ŋl–] English; British; **~ (gebraten)** (steak) rare; (*language*) **E~** English; **englisch–(deutsch** *etc*) Anglo–, (dictionary) English– ‖ **das E~horn, ⸚er** cor anglais; **~sprachig** English-speaking; English-language; in English
en gros [ãˈgroː] *comm* wholesale

der **Enkel, –** grandson; (*pl*) grandchildren; **das ~kind, –er** grandchild; **der ~sohn, ¨e** grandson; **die ~tochter, ..töchter** granddaughter

die **Enkelin, –nen** granddaughter

die **Enklave, –n** enclave

enorm enormous, tremendous

die **Enquete** [ã'kɛːt], **–n** (official) inquiry; *Aust* symposium; **die ~kommission, –en** commission of inquiry

das **Ensemble** [ã'sãːbl̥], **–s** *cost, mus* ensemble; *theat* troupe, company; *archit esp EGer* group (of buildings)

---

ent– *insep pref* (*unstressed*) – *general senses:*
(*i*) de–; dis–; un– (*eg* **~mythologisieren** demythologize, **~erben** disinherit, **~schleiern** unveil); *the sense 'remove the ... from' is sometimes expressed in English simply by using a noun as a verb, eg* **~hülsen** husk (**Hülse** = husk), **~häuten** skin (**Haut** = skin);
(*ii*) ab–; ... away (*eg* **~führen** abduct, **~laufen** run away);
(*iii*) (+*dat*) ... from ...; ... out of ... (*eg* **jmdm. etw. ~reißen** snatch sth. from s.o.)

---

ent|arten (*sn*) degenerate (**zu** into); **entartet** degenerate

die **Ent|artung, –en** degeneration

ent|äußern: sich ~ (+*gen*) relinquish; renounce

entbehren do without; miss; (+*gen*) be without/devoid of

entbehrlich dispensable; superfluous

die **Entbehrung, –en** privation; (personal) sacrifice

entbieten* (+*dat*) send (s.o. greetings)

entbinden* deliver (woman); (*v/i*) give birth to a child; **~ von** release from; relieve of; **entbunden werden von** give birth to

die **Entbindung, –en** release; *med* delivery; **das ~s|heim, –e** maternity home

entblättern strip of its leaves; defoliate; **sich ~** lose its leaves; *joc* shed one's clothes

entbleien remove the lead from

entblöden: sich nicht ~ zu ... have the effrontery to ...

entblößen bare; *sp* leave exposed; (+*gen*) divest of; denude of

entbrennen* (*sn*) flare up; **~ in** (*dat*)/**von** become inflamed with

entdecken discover; discern; spot

der **Entdecker, –** discoverer; explorer

die **Entdeckung, –en** discovery; **die ~s|reise, –n** expedition; voyage of discovery

die **Ente, –n** duck; *coll* hoax; **kalte ~** (*drink made of white wine, champagne, lemon*)

ent|ehren disgrace; dishonour

ent|eignen expropriate

die **Ent|eignung, –en** expropriation

ent|eilen (*sn*) hasten away; (time) fly by

ent|eisen defrost; *aer* de-ice

Enten– duck('s) ...; **der ~braten, –** roast duck

Enter–: der ~haken, – grappling-iron

ent|erben disinherit

der **Enterich, –e** drake

entern *naut* board

entfachen kindle; provoke

entfahren* (*sn*) (+*dat*) slip out

entfallen* (*sn*) be cancelled; not apply; (+*dat*) slip from (s.o.'s) hands; escape (s.o.'s) memory; **~ auf** (*acc*) be allotted to; go to

entfalten unfold; display; develop; **sich ~** unfold; develop; realize one's potential

entfärben decolorize; **sich ~** lose its colour; turn pale

entfernen remove; **sich ~** move off; go away; **sich ~ von** leave; depart from (subject *etc*); grow away from

entfernt *p/part; also* distant, remote; (... metres *etc*) away; **weit ~** far (away); far removed (from sth.); **weit davon ~ zu ...** far from (+*ger*); **weit davon ~ sein zu ...** have no intention of (+*ger*); **nicht im ~esten** not in the least

die **Entfernung, –en** distance, *mil etc* range; removal; **auf eine ~ von** at a distance/range of; **aus einiger ~** from a distance; **in einer ~ von** at a distance of || **der ~s|messer, –** range-finder

entfesseln unleash

der **Entfesselungs|künstler, –** escapologist

entfetten remove the fat from; scour (wool); *tech* degrease

die **Entfettungs|kur, –en** slimming diet

entflammen inflame, fire; kindle; (*v/i sn*) break out; **~ für** fire with enthusiasm for; (*v/i sn*) become inflamed with passion for; **sich ~** ignite; **sich ~ an** (*dat*) be kindled by

entflechten* (*pres, p/t also weak*) disentangle; *econ* break up (cartel)

die **Entflechtung, –en** disentanglement; *econ* breaking up

entfliegen* (*sn*) fly away

entfliehen* (*sn*) flee; escape (**aus** from); (time, youth, *etc*) fly by; (+*dat*) escape from; escape (danger *etc*); flee

entfremden (+*dat*) alienate/estrange from; **seinem Zweck ~** use for a purpose other than that for which it was intended; **sich ~** (+*dat*) become estranged from

die **Entfremdung** alienation; estrangement

entfrosten defrost

entführen abduct, kidnap; run away with; hijack; (+*dat*) *joc* walk off with (s.o.'s) ...

der **Entführer, –** abductor, kidnapper; hijacker

die **Entführung, –en** abduction, kidnapping;

hijack(ing)
entgegen 1 *prep* (+*dat*; *often following noun*) against; contrary to; 2 *adv* (*following noun*) towards
entgegen– *sep pref* (+*dat*): (*i*) … towards …; … to meet …; (*ii*) … against …
entgegen|arbeiten (+*dat*) work against; counter
entgegenbringen* (+*dat*) bring to; show (s.o. respect *etc*); show (interest *etc*) in; show (understanding) for
entgegen|eilen (*sn*) (+*dat*) hurry towards/to meet; hasten to (one's doom)
entgegengehen* (*sn*) (+*dat*) go towards/to meet; be heading for (disaster *etc*); face (danger *etc*); be nearing (completion); **seinem Ende ~** draw to a close; be nearing one's end
entgegengesetzt *p/part*; *also* opposite; contrary; opposing; **das Entgegengesetzte** (*decl as adj*) the opposite
entgegenhalten* (+*dat*) hold out (hand) to; say in reply to, point out (to s.o.)
entgegenhandeln (+*dat*) act against; act contrary to
entgegenkommen* (*sn*) (+*dat*) come towards, approach; come to meet; be … towards; meet (wishes); (thing) accord with; be to (s.o.'s taste); (+*dat*) **auf halbem Weg(e) ~** meet half-way
das **Entgegenkommen** obliging attitude; concession; **~ zeigen** be obliging
entgegenkommend (traffic) oncoming; obliging; **entgegenkommender|weise** obligingly
entgegenlaufen* (*sn*) (+*dat*) run towards/to meet; run counter to
die **Entgegennahme** acceptance; receipt (of)
entgegennehmen* accept; receive
entgegenschlagen* (*sn*) (+*dat*) (flames) leap out at; (smoke) come surging at; (noise) strike (s.o.'s) ear; **(Feindseligkeit** *etc*) **schlägt mir entgegen** I am met with (hostility *etc*)
entgegensehen* (+*dat*) watch (s.o., sth.) coming; look forward to; await; face (danger *etc*); view (prospect)
entgegensetzen (*see also* **entgegengesetzt**) (+*dat*) offer (resistance) to; set against; say in reply to
entgegenstehen* (+*dat*) (obstacle) stand in the way of; conflict with
entgegenstellen (+*dat*) set against; **sich ~** (+*dat*) bar (s.o.'s) way; oppose
entgegenstemmen: sich ~ (+*dat*) set one's face against
entgegenstrecken (+*dat*) stretch out towards
entgegentreten* (*sn*) (+*dat*) confront, face; oppose; fight (abuse, prejudice, *etc*); **diese Erscheinung tritt einem häufig entgegen** one often encounters this phenomenon
entgegenwirken (+*dat*) counteract; counter
entgegnen reply; **~ auf** (*acc*) say in reply to
die **Entgegnung, –en** reply; rejoinder
entgehen* (*sn*) (+*dat*) escape; elude; escape (s.o.'s) attention; **sich** *dat* **… ~ lassen** miss; let slip; forgo
entgeistert dumbfounded
das **Entgelt** payment
entgelten* (+*dat*) pay for; repay for
entgiften detoxicate; decontaminate
entgleisen (*sn*) commit a faux-pas; *rail* be derailed
die **Entgleisung, –en** faux-pas; *rail* derailment
entgleiten* (*sn*) (+*dat*) slip from (s.o.'s) hands; grow away from; (control) slip from
entgräten fillet
enthaaren remove unwanted hair from
das **Enthaarungs|mittel, –** hair-remover
enthalten* contain; **sich ~** (+*gen*) refrain from; abstain from; **sich der Stimme ~** *parl etc* abstain; **enthalten in** (*dat*) *also* included in
enthaltsam abstemious; (sexually) continent
die **Enthaltsamkeit** abstemiousness; continence
enthärten soften (water)
enthaupten behead
enthäuten skin
entheben* (+*gen*) relieve of
entheiligen desecrate
enthemmen free from his/her inhibitions
enthüllen unveil; reveal; expose; **sich ~** be revealed
die **Enthüllung, –en** *vbl noun*; *also* revelation; exposure
enthülsen shell; husk
der **Enthusiasmus** enthusiasm
der **Enthusiast, –en** (*wk masc*) enthusiast
enthusiastisch enthusiastic
entjungfern deflower
entkalken decalcify
entkeimen sterilize; remove the sprouts from; (*v/i sn*) *poet* sprout from
entkernen stone; core; seed
entkleiden undress; (+*gen*) strip of; **sich ~** undress
die **Entkleidungs|nummer, –n** striptease act
entkommen* (*sn*) escape (**aus** from); (+*dat*) escape (from) (pursuers *etc*); escape (disaster *etc*)
entkorken uncork
entkräften weaken, debilitate; invalidate (argument *etc*)
die **Entkräftung** *vbl noun*; *also* debilitation; invalidation
entkrampfen relax; ease (situation)
entladen* unload; *elect* discharge; **sich ~** (storm) break; vent itself; *elect* discharge
entlang 1 *prep* (+*dat or* (*SGer*) *gen*; *may also follow noun in acc*) along; 2 *adv*: **an …** (*dat*) **~** along (the side of sth.); **auf …** (*dat*)

~ along (the surface/top of sth.); **hier ~** along here; this way

entlang– *sep pref* ... along ..., ... down ... (*eg* **die Autobahn ~fahren** drive along/down the autobahn); *with* **an** (*dat*) = along (the side of, *eg* **an der Maas ~fahren** drive along the Meuse); *with* **auf** (*dat*) = along (the surface/top of, *eg* **auf dem Dach ~kriechen** creep along the roof)

entlangziehen* (*sn exc* **sich ~**) go along; move along; **~ an** (*dat*) go/move along (the side of); **sich ~** (column *etc*) move along; **sich ~ an** (*dat*) move along (the side of); (ditch *etc*) run along; skirt; pull oneself along

entlarven unmask, expose

entlassen* dismiss; make redundant; discharge; release

die **Entlassung, –en** dismissal; discharge; release

entlasten relieve; ease the burden/load on; relieve the congestion in; *leg* exonerate; *fin* credit (account) (**für/um** with)

die **Entlastung** *vbl noun*; *also* relief; *leg* exoneration; **zu jmds. ~** to take some of the load off s.o.; *leg* in s.o.'s defence || **der ~s|zug, ̈–e** relief train

entlauben strip of its leaves; **sich ~** lose its leaves

entlaufen* (*sn*) run away (*dat*/**aus** from); **entlaufen** runaway; (pet) lost

entlausen delouse

entledigen: sich ~ (+*gen*) get rid of; remove (garment); discharge (duty)

entleeren empty; evacuate (bowels)

entlegen remote; out-of-the-way

entlehnen (+*dat*/**aus**) borrow (word *etc*) from

die **Entlehnung, –en** borrowing

entleihen* borrow (**aus/von** from)

entloben: sich ~ break off one's engagement

entlocken (+*dat*) elicit from; coax out of

entlohnen, *Swiss* **entlöhnen** pay

entlüften ventilate; *tech* bleed (brakes)

die **Entlüftung, –en** *vbl noun*; *also* ventilation

entmachten deprive of his/her/its power

entmannen castrate; emasculate

entmenschlichen dehumanize

entmenscht inhuman

entmilitarisieren demilitarize

entmündigen *leg* incapacitate

entmutigen discourage; **sich ~ lassen** get discouraged

die **Entnahme** taking (out); extraction; withdrawal

entnazifizieren denazify

entnehmen* (+*dat*/**aus**) take from/out of; gather/infer from

entnerven enervate

der **Entomologe, –n** (*wk masc*) entomologist

die **Entomologie** entomology

entpersönlichen depersonalize

entpolitisieren depoliticize

entpuppen: sich ~ emerge from the chrysalis; **sich ~ als** turn out to be

entrahmen skim

entraten* (+*gen*) *arch* do without

enträtseln unravel, puzzle out; decipher

entrechten deprive of his/her rights

das **Entrée** [ã–], **–s** entrance hall; entrée; *esp Aust* entrance fee

entreißen* (+*dat*) snatch from; wrest from

entrichten pay (amount)

entriegeln unbolt

entringen* (+*dat*) wrest from; **sich ~** (+*dat*) break free from; (sigh *etc*) escape

entrinnen* (*sn*) (*poet* time *etc*) fly by; (+*dat*) escape (from)

entrollen unroll; unfurl; (*v/i sn*, +*dat*) roll out of; **sich ~** unroll; unfold (before s.o.)

entrosten remove the rust from, derust

entrücken enrapture; (+*dat*) carry away from; **...** (*dat*) **entrückt** removed from

entrümpeln clear out (attic *etc*)

entrüsten fill with indignation; **sich ~** be indignant (**über** *acc* at); **entrüstet** indignant

die **Entrüstung** indignation

entsaften extract the juice from

der **Entsafter, –** juice-extractor

entsagen (+*dat*) renounce

die **Entsagung, –en** renunciation; self-denial; **e~s|voll** full of self-denial

entsalzen desalinate

entschädigen compensate; *leg* pay (s.o.) compensation

die **Entschädigung, –en** compensation

entschärfen defuse; tone down

der **Entscheid, –e** decision; ruling

entscheiden* (*see also* **entschieden**) (*also v/i*) decide; rule (that ...); **~ über** (*acc*) decide (s.o.'s future *etc*); decide on

sich ~ make up one's mind, decide; be decided; **sich ~ für** decide on/in favour of; **sich ~ gegen** decide against

entscheidend decisive; crucial; *sp* deciding

die **Entscheidung, –en** decision; ruling; **vor der ~ stehen** be about to be decided; have to decide (whether ...) || **die ~s|schlacht, –en** decisive battle; **das ~s|spiel, –e** play-off

entschieden *p/part*; *also* firm; decided, definite

die **Entschiedenheit** determination; **mit aller ~** firmly; categorically

entschlacken remove the slag from; *med* purge (bowels); purify

entschlafen* (*sn*) pass away

entschleiern unveil; reveal; **sich ~** unveil

entschließen* (*see also* **entschlossen**): **sich ~** make up one's mind; **sich ~ zu** resolve on; (*followed by vbl noun*, *eg* **sich zur Aufgabe von ... ~**) resolve to (give up ... *etc*)

[die] **Entschließung, –en** *parl etc* resolution
entschlossen *p/part*; *also* determined; **kurz ~** without a moment's hesitation
[die] **Entschlossenheit** determination
entschlüpfen (*sn*) slip away; (+*dat*) give (s.o.) the slip; (remark) slip out
[der] **Entschluß, ⸗(ss)e** decision; **die ~kraft** resolution
entschlüsseln decode (*also comput*); decipher; puzzle out
entschuldbar excusable
entschuldigen excuse (**mit** as due to); make (s.o.'s) excuses (**bei** to); **sich ~** apologize (**bei** to); make one's excuses; **sich ~ lassen** send one's apologies; **~ Sie!** excuse me!; sorry!
[die] **Entschuldigung, –en** excuse; apology; **um ~ bitten** apologize (to); **~!** excuse me!; sorry!
entschwinden* (*sn*) vanish; **~ aus** fade from (memory)
entseelt lifeless
entsenden* send (delegate *etc*)
entsetzen horrify; *mil* relieve; **sich ~** be horrified (**über** *acc* at); **entsetzt** horrified (**über** *acc* at); (*adv*) in horror
[das] **Entsetzen** horror; **mit ~** to s.o.'s horror
entsetzlich dreadful
entseuchen disinfect; decontaminate
entsichern release the safety-catch of
entsiegeln unseal
entsinnen*: sich ~ (+*gen*) recall
entsorgen dispose of refuse/(nuclear) waste from
[das] **Entsorgungs|zentrum, –(r)en** nuclear waste disposal facility
entspannen relax; slacken, unbend (bow), reduce the surface tension of (water); ease (situation); **sich ~** relax, unwind; (situation) ease
[die] **Entspannung** *vbl noun*; *also* relaxation; *pol* détente
entspinnen*: sich ~ develop
entsprechen* (+*dat*) correspond to; be in accordance/keeping with; answer (description); match; come up to (expectations); comply with; meet (demands *etc*); **sich** *dat pl* **~** correspond, tally; **~d** corresponding; appropriate; (*adv*) *also* accordingly; (+*dat*; *may also follow noun*) in accordance with; according to
[die] **Entsprechung, –en** equivalent; parallel; correspondence
entsprießen* (*sn*) *poet* spring up; (+ *dat*/**aus**) come of
entspringen* (*sn*) (river) rise; (+*dat*/**aus**) escape from; spring from
entstaatlichen denationalize
entstammen (*sn*) (+*dat*) be descended from; be derived from; originate in
entstauben remove the dust from; modernize
entstehen* (*sn*) arise (**aus** from); come into being; be produced/written/composed/painted/built *etc*; **im Entstehen** in the making
[die] **Entstehung** origin; genesis; emergence; *in compds* **~s–** ... of origin; **die ~s|geschichte, –n** history of the origins; genesis
entsteigen* (*sn*) (+*dat*) step from; emerge from; (fumes *etc*) rise from
entsteinen stone (fruit)
entstellen disfigure; distort
[die] **Entstellung, –en** disfigurement; distortion
entstempeln *mot* cancel the registration of
entstören fit a suppressor to
entströmen (*sn*) (+*dat*) issue from; pour from
entsühnen *relig* purify
enttäuschen disappoint; let down; (*v/i*) be a disappointment; **enttäuscht über** (*acc*) disappointed at
[die] **Enttäuschung, –en** disappointment
entthronen dethrone
enttrümmern clear of rubble
entvölkern depopulate
[die] **Entvölkerung** depopulation
entwachsen* [–ks–] (*sn*) (+*dat*) grow out of; grow away from
entwaffnen disarm; **~d** disarming
entwalden deforest
entwarnen sound the all-clear
[die] **Entwarnung, –en** all-clear
entwässern drain
entweder either; **das Entweder-Oder** (*gen* –), – either-or
entweichen* (*sn*) escape (**aus** from)
entweihen desecrate
entwenden steal (*dat*/**aus** from)
entwerfen* design, *art* make a sketch for; draft (speech *etc*); devise; **ein Bild ~ von** paint a picture of (conditions *etc*)
entwerten devalue (*also econ*); cancel (stamp, ticket)
[der] **Entwerter, –** cancelling-machine
[die] **Entwertung, –en** devaluation; depreciation; cancellation
entwickeln develop (*also phot*) (**zu** into); generate (gas *etc*); display; *EGer* train; *mil* deploy; **sich ~** develop (**zu** into); *mil* deploy
[die] **Entwicklung, –en** *vbl noun*; *also* development; evolution; generation; trend, (political *etc*) developments; *in compds* **~s–** *also* ... of development; **der ~s|dienst** (voluntary) service in a developing country; **der ~s|helfer, –** volunteer serving in a developing country; **die ~s|hilfe** aid to developing countries; **die ~s|jahre** *pl* adolescence; **das ~s|land, ⸗er** developing country; **der ~s|roman, –e** (= **Bildungsroman**); **die ~s|ten-**

denz, –en trend
entwinden* (+*dat*) wrest from
entwirren disentangle; unravel
entwischen (*sn*) *coll* slip (through window, abroad, *etc*); (+*dat*) give (s.o.) the slip; ~ **aus** escape from
entwöhnen wean; (+*gen*/**von**) wean from (habit *etc*); ... (*dat*) **entwöhnt** unused to
entwürdigen degrade
die **Entwürdigung, –en** degradation
der **Entwurf, ¨–e** sketch; design; outline; draft; **–entwurf** draft (resolution *etc*); draft of a ...
entwurzeln uproot
entzaubern free from a spell; break the spell of
entzerren *rad* equalize; *phot* rectify
entziehen* (+*dat*) take away from; withdraw from; deprive of (alcohol *etc*); stop (s.o.'s pension *etc*); take away (s.o.'s licence *etc*); extract/*bot* draw from; **sich** ~ (+*dat*) free oneself from (embrace *etc*); avoid, shun; evade, shirk; elude; escape (danger *etc*); defy (analysis *etc*); be beyond; (+*dat*) **das Wort** ~ instruct (speaker) to stop
die **Entziehungs|kur, –en** treatment for drug addicts/alcoholics
entziffern decipher; decode
entzücken delight; **~d** delightful; **das Entzücken** delight
der **Entzug** withdrawal; stopping; *bot* drawing; **die ~s|erscheinung, –en** withdrawal symptom
entzündbar inflammable; excitable
entzünden light, ignite; kindle (enthusiasm *etc*), inflame; **sich** ~ catch fire; (quarrel) be sparked off; *med* become inflamed; **sich** ~ **an** (*dat*) be kindled by; be excited by
die **Entzündung, –en** *vbl noun*; *also* ignition; *med* inflammation; **e~s|hemmend** anti-inflammatory
entzwei broken; in pieces; **entzwei–** *sep pref* ... in two; ... (in)to pieces (*eg* **~brechen** break in two/into pieces, **~schlagen** smash (to pieces))
entzweien divide; **sich ~ mit** fall out with
en vogue [ã'vo:k] in vogue
der **Enzian, –e** gentian; *also a schnapps derived from the root of yellow gentian*
die **Enzyklika, –(k)en** encyclical
die **Enzyklopädie, –(ie)n** encyclopaedia
enzyklopädisch encyclopaedic
das **Enzym, –e** enzyme
Epen *pl of* **Epos**
ephemer ephemeral
die **Epidemie, –(ie)n, epidemisch** epidemic
der **Epigone, –n** (*wk masc*) (inferior) imitator
das **Epigramm, –e** epigram
die **Epik** ['e:pɪk] narrative literature
der **Epiker, –** writer of narrative literature; epic poet
Epiktet Epictetus
Epikur Epicurus
epikureisch epicurean
die **Epilepsie, –(ie)n** epilepsy
der **Epileptiker, –, epileptisch** epileptic
der **Epilog, –e** epilogue
das **Epiphanias** [–as] Epiphany
episch epic; narrative
das **Episkopat, –e** (*also* **der**) episcopate
die **Episode, –n** episode
episodenhaft episodic
die **Epistel, –n** epistle
das **Epitaph, –e** epitaph; memorial plaque
das **Epitheton** [–ɔn], **–(t)a** epithet
das **Epizentrum, –(r)en** epicentre
epochal [–x–] epoch-making
die **Epoche** [–x–], **–n** epoch, era; ~ **machen** make history || **e~machend** epoch-making
das **Epos** [–ɔs], **–(p)en** epic (poem)
die **Eprouvette** [–pru–], **–n** *Aust* test-tube
er (*see p. xxvi*) (*referring to masc noun*) he; it; **ein Er** *coll* a he

---

er– [ɛɐ–] *insep pref* (*unstressed*); *may be added to existing verbs to form new verbs with the sense* acquire by ...ing, *eg* **~spielen** acquire by playing (**spielen** = play)

–er [–ɐ] *suffix*:

(*i*) (*pl* –) *denotes a person engaged in an activity*, *eg* **der Brauer** brewer (**brauen** = brew), *or a tool*, *eg* **der Öffner** opener (**öffnen** = open); (*added to place-names*) *denoting an inhabitant*, *eg* **der Berliner** Berliner, **der Stockholmer** inhabitant of/man from Stockholm;

(*ii*) (*added to place-names*, *forming indecl adj*) *eg* **Kölner** (of) Cologne, (*origin*) from Cologne, **Mailänder** (of) Milan, Milanese

---

er|achten: ~ als/für consider (to be); **meines Erachtens** in my estimation
er|arbeiten achieve (by working); acquire; work out
Erb– ... of inheritance; hereditary ...; inherited ...; **die ~anlage, –n** hereditary disposition; **der ~faktor, –en** gene; **der ~feind, –e** traditional enemy; **die ~folge** succession; **das ~gut** inheritance; *biol* genotype; **der ~lasser, –** testator; **e~los** without an heir; **das ~recht** law/right of inheritance; **der ~schleicher, –** legacy-hunter; **das ~stück, –e** heirloom; **die ~sünde** original sin; **das ~teil, –e** (share of) inheritance; *biol* inherited characteristic
erbarmen move to pity; **sich** ~ (+*gen*) take pity on

das **Erbarmen** pity (**mit** on); **zum ~ = e~s|wert** pitiful

erbärmlich wretched; pitiful; despicable; *coll* terrible

erbarmungs–: ~los merciless; **~voll** full of pity; **~würdig** pitiful

erbauen erect; edify; **sich ~ an** (*dat*) be edified/uplifted by; **nicht erbaut sein von** not be enthusiastic about

der **Erbauer, –** builder; architect (of scheme)

erbaulich edifying

die **Erbauung** edification

das **Erbe** inheritance; heritage

der **Erbe, –n** (*wk masc*) heir

erben inherit

erbeben (*sn*) tremble

erbetteln obtain by begging; **~ von** wheedle out of

erbeuten capture; carry off

erbieten*: sich ~ zu ... offer to ...

die **Erbin, –nen** heiress

erbitten* request

erbittern embitter; fill with resentment; **erbittert** *also* (opponent) implacable; (resistance *etc*) fierce

die **Erbitterung** bitterness; resentment

erblassen (*sn*) turn pale; **vor Neid ~** turn green with envy

erbleichen (*sn*) turn pale, blanch

erblich hereditary; **er ist** *etc* **~ belastet** it runs in the family

erblicken catch sight of; perceive

erblinden (*sn*) go blind

erblühen (*sn*) blossom

erbosen anger; **sich ~ über** (*acc*) get infuriated at; **erbost** furious (**über** *acc* at)

erbötig willing (to)

erbrechen* break open; vomit; **(sich) ~** vomit; **das Erbrochene** (*decl as adj*) vomit; **bis zum Erbrechen** *coll* ad nauseam

erbringen* produce

die **Erbschaft, –en** inheritance; **die ~s|steuer, –n** inheritance tax

die **Erbse, –n** pea

Erd– [e:–] ... of the earth; earth('s) ...; **der ~apfel, ..äpfel** *Aust* potato; **der ~ball** globe; **das ~beben, –** earthquake; **~beben–** *also* seismic ...; **der ~beben|messer, –** seismograph; **~beer–** strawberry ...; **die ~beere, –n** strawberry; **der ~boden** ground (**dem E. gleichmachen** raze to the ground); **das ~gas** natural gas; **der ~geist, –er** earth-spirit; **das ~geschoß, –(ss)e** ground-floor; **das ~innere** (*decl as adj*) interior of the earth; **das ~kabel, –** underground cable; **der ~kreis** world; **die ~kugel** globe; **die ~kunde** geography; **e~kundlich** geographical; **die ~nuß, ⸚(ss)e** peanut; **das ~öl** petroleum; **~öl–** oil ...; **das ~pech** bitumen; **der ~rutsch, –e** landslide (*also pol*); **der ~satellit, –en** (*wk masc*) earth satellite; **der ~stoß, ⸚e** earth tremor; **der ~teil, –e** continent

die **Erde** ['e:–] earth; ground; *elect* earth, ground *US*; **auf ~n** on earth; **über/unter der ~** above/below ground; **zu ebener ~** at ground level

erden ['e:–] *elect* earth, ground *US*

Erden– *esp poet* ... of the earth; earthly ...

erdenken* think up

erdenklich conceivable; possible

erdichten invent, make up

erdig ['e:–] earthy

erdolchen stab to death

erdreisten: sich ~ zu ... have the audacity to ...

erdröhnen (*sn*) boom out; resound

erdrosseln strangle

erdrücken crush; overwhelm

erdulden endure

die **Erdung** *vbl noun*; *elect* earth, ground *US*

–erei *see* **–ei**

er|eifern: sich ~ get worked up

er|eignen: sich ~ occur

das **Er|eignis, –se** event; occurrence; **e~los** uneventful; **e~reich** eventful

er|eilen (fate *etc*) overtake

die **Erektion, –en** *physiol* erection

der **Eremit, –en** (*wk masc*) hermit

er|erben inherit

erfahren[1]* learn, be told; experience; meet with; undergo; **~ von** hear of

erfahren[2] *p/part*; *also* experienced

die **Erfahrenheit** experience

die **Erfahrung, –en** experience; **die ~ machen, daß ...** find that ...; **gute/schlechte ~en machen mit** be satisfied/disappointed with; **aus eigener ~** from one's own experience; **in ~ bringen** find out || **e~s|gemäß** as experience shows

erfassen catch (hold of); (fear *etc*) overcome, seize (*esp pass*); take in, grasp; include, embrace; cover

erfinden* invent

der **Erfinder, –** inventor

erfinderisch inventive

die **Erfindung, –en** invention; **die ~s|gabe** inventiveness; **e~s|reich** inventive

der **Erfolg, –e** success; result; **~ haben** be successful; **mit ~** successfully; **ohne ~** without success || **e~los** unsuccessful; without success; **die ~losigkeit** lack of success; **e~reich** successful; **e~versprechend** promising

erfolgen (*sn*) take place; be carried out, (payment) be made; ensue

Erfolgs– ... of success; successful ...

erforderlich necessary

erfordern require, call for

das **Erfordernis, –se** requirement

erforschen explore; investigate, inquire into,

univ etc (do) research into; investigate, probe; search (conscience)

die **Erforschung** exploration; investigation

erfragen ask (way *etc*); **zu ~ bei** apply to

erfrechen: sich ~ zu ... have the audacity to ...

erfreuen delight; give pleasure to; **sich ~** (+*gen*) enjoy (privilege *etc*); **sich ~ an** (*dat*) take pleasure in

erfreulich agreeable; welcome; gratifying; **erfreulicher|weise** fortunately; gratifyingly

erfrieren* (*sn*) freeze to death; be frost-bitten/killed by frost

die **Erfrierung, -en** *vbl noun*; *also* (*pl*) frostbite

erfrischen refresh; **sich ~** refresh oneself; **~d** refreshing

die **Erfrischung, -en** refreshment; **das ~s|getränk, -e** refreshment; **der ~s|raum, ⸚e** refreshment-room; cafeteria

erfüllen fill; fulfil; carry out; serve (purpose); **sich ~** come true; **-erfüllt** full of ...

die **Erfüllung** fulfilment; carrying out; realization; **in ~ gehen** be realized

ergänzen complete; supplement; supply; complement; **~d** supplementary; additional

die **Ergänzung, -en** *vbl noun*; *also* completion; supplement(ation); complement (*also gramm*); addition (*gen* to); *in compds* **~s-** complementary ...; supplementary ...

ergattern *coll* (manage to) get hold of

ergaunern (*also* + **sich** *dat*) *coll* obtain by trickery

ergeben[1]* show; produce; come to; **sich ~** arise; *mil* surrender; (+*dat*) take to (drink *etc*), give oneself up to; **sich ~ aus** arise from; follow from; **sich ~ in** (*acc*) resign oneself to

ergeben[2] *p/part*; *also* devoted; resigned

die **Ergebenheit** devotion; resignation

das **Ergebnis, -se** result; conclusion (reached); **e~los** fruitless; inconclusive

ergehen* (*sn*) be issued; **es ist mir gut/schlecht ergangen** I fared well/badly; **~ lassen** issue; send out; **über sich ~ lassen** endure; submit to; **Gnade für Recht ~ lassen** be lenient

sich ~ take a stroll; **sich ~ in** (*dat*) indulge in; pour forth; **sich ~ über** (*acc*) hold forth on

das **Ergehen** (state of) health

ergiebig (source *etc*) rich; productive, fruitful; economical

ergießen*: sich ~ pour (into, over sth.)

erglühen (*sn*) glow; be aglow; **vor Scham ~** blush with shame

ergo therefore

ergötzen delight; **sich ~ an** (*dat*) take delight in; **zum Ergötzen** (+*gen*) to the delight of

ergötzlich delightful

ergrauen (*sn*) go grey

ergreifen* grasp, take hold of; seize (criminal *etc*); (fear *etc*) overcome, seize (*esp pass*); take up; take (measures); (music *etc*) move; **~d** moving

die **Ergriffenheit** emotion

ergrimmen (*sn*) become furious

ergründen get to the bottom of; fathom

der **Erguß, ⸚(ss)e** effusion; outpouring

erhaben lofty, elevated; sublime; **~ über** (*acc*) above; beyond; superior to

die **Erhabenheit** loftiness; sublimity

der **Erhalt** receipt (of); preservation

erhalten* receive, get; obtain; be given (chance, task, *etc*); keep; maintain; preserve; (+*p/part of verb normally governing dative of person*) be +*p/part* (*eg* **etw. zugewiesen ~** be allocated sth.); **sich ~** (custom) survive; **gut erhalten** in good condition; well preserved; **erhalten bleiben** be maintained/preserved

erhältlich obtainable

die **Erhaltung** maintenance; preservation; *phys* conservation

erhandeln obtain by bargaining

erhängen hang

erhärten harden; substantiate; (*v/i sn*) harden

erhaschen catch

erheben* raise; levy (tax *etc*), charge; make (claim *etc*); *esp SGer* establish; **~ zu** make into; **sich erhoben fühlen** feel uplifted

sich ~ rise; revolt; (question *etc*) arise; **sich ~ über** (*acc*) rise above; think oneself better than

erhebend edifying, uplifting

erheblich considerable

die **Erhebung, -en** *vbl noun*; *also* elevation; uprising; uplift; inquiry

erheischen demand

erheitern amuse

erhellen light up; elucidate; **~ aus** be evident from; **sich ~** brighten; (face) light up

erheucheln feign; **sich** *dat* **... ~** obtain by pretence

erhitzen heat; make hot; **sich ~** get hot; become heated; **erhitzt** hot; heated

erhoffen (*also* + **sich** *dat*) hope for

erhöhen raise; increase; heighten; *mus* sharpen, sharp *US*; **sich ~** rise, increase (**um** by)

die **Erhöhung, -en** *vbl noun*; *also* increase; rise; elevation; **das ~s|zeichen, -** *mus* sharp

erholen: sich ~ recover; relax (after work, on holiday, *etc*); *fin* recover, rally

erholsam restful

die **Erholung** recovery; relaxation, rest; holiday, vacation *US*

erhören hear (prayer *etc*); accept (suitor)

erigieren *physiol* become erect

[die] **Erika, -(k)en** heather
er|innerlich: ... ist mir ~ I remember ...
er|innern remind; **~ an** (*acc*) remind of; (*v/i*) remind one of; be reminiscent of; **sich ~ an** (*acc*) (*also* **sich ~** +*gen*) remember
[die] **Er|innerung, -en** memory; souvenir (**an** *acc* of); (*pl*) memoirs; (+*dat*) **in ~ bringen** remind of; **zur ~ an** (*acc*) in memory of || **das ~s|vermögen** memory
erjagen catch; hunt down
erkalten (*sn*) cool (down); grow cold
erkälten: sich ~ catch cold; **(leicht/stark) erkältet sein** have a (slight/bad) cold
[die] **Erkältung, -en** cold; chill
erkämpfen (*also* + **sich** *dat*) win (by fighting for it/them)
erkaufen (*also* + **sich** *dat*) buy (s.o.'s silence *etc*); **~ mit** pay for (success *etc*) with; **teuer ~** pay dearly for
erkennbar recognizable; perceptible
erkennen* recognize, know (**an** *dat* by); make out; realize; **~ auf** (*acc*) *leg* grant; impose a sentence of; impose; *sp* award; **zu ~ geben** indicate; **sich zu ~ geben** disclose one's identity; **~ lassen** show; indicate; **erkenne dich selbst!** know thyself!
erkenntlich: sich ~ zeigen show one's appreciation
[die] **Erkenntlichkeit** gratitude; token of one's gratitude
[das] **Erkenntnis, -se** *Aust leg* decision
[die] **Erkenntnis, -se** realization; recognition; knowledge; *philos* cognition; (*pl*) knowledge; findings; **zu der ~ kommen, daß ...** come to realize that ... || **die ~lehre** epistemology
Erkennungs-: die ~marke, -n identity disc; **das ~zeichen, -** sign (for identification); *aer* markings
[der] **Erker, -** bay-window
erkiesen (*p/t* **erkor** (*subj* **erköre**), *p/part* **erkoren;** *usu only p/t and p/part*) *arch* choose (**zu** as, to be)
erklären explain; declare; announce; **~ an** (*dat*) illustrate by; **~ für** declare (open *etc*); pronounce (dead); **sich ~ aus** be explained by; **sich von selbst ~** be self-explanatory; **~d** explanatory; (*adv*) by way of explanation
erklärlich explicable; understandable; **leicht ~** easily explained
erklärt declared; avowed; **erklärter|maßen** avowedly
[die] **Erklärung, -en** explanation; declaration; statement
erklecklich considerable
erklettern climb
erklimmen* climb; climb to (position)
erklingen* (*sn*) ring out; resound
erklügeln think up
erkranken (*sn*) be taken ill (**an** *dat* with); **erkrankt** ill
[die] **Erkrankung, -en** illness; falling ill
erkühnen: sich ~ zu ... have the audacity to ...
erkunden find out; *mil* reconnoitre
erkundigen: sich ~ enquire (**nach** about)
[die] **Erkundigung, -en** enquiry; **~en einholen/einziehen** make enquiries
[die] **Erkundung, -en** *mil* reconnaissance
erkünstelt affected
erküren (*p/t and p/part weak or identical with those shown for* **erkiesen**) *arch* = **erkiesen**

-erl *SGer* (*Swabian* **-le**) (*pl* **-**) *diminutive suffix* (*making noun neuter and sometimes causing stem vowel to be umlauted*) little ..., wee ..., *eg* **das Hunderl** little dog(gie), **das Häuserl** little house

---

[der] **Erlag|schein, -e** *Aust* (giro) inpayment slip
erlahmen (*sn*) (grow) weary; flag
erlangen achieve, attain
[der] **Erlaß, -(ss)e** decree, order; remission; exemption; issuing (of decree)
erlassen* issue (decree); (+*dat*) release from
erlauben allow; permit; **sich** *dat* **... ~** permit oneself; take (liberty); have (joke); venture; beg (to); **sich** *dat* **... ~ können** be able to afford; **~ Sie mal!** do you mind!
[die] **Erlaubnis, -se** permission; = **der ~schein, -e** permit
erlaucht illustrious
erläutern explain, elucidate
[die] **Erläuterung, -en** explanation, elucidation
[die] **Erle, -n** alder
erleben experience; have (surprise *etc*); go/live through; undergo; receive (performance), go through (editions); witness; (live to) see; know, see (in a certain state); **es erlebt haben, daß ...** have known (s.o., sth.) to ...
[das] **Erlebnis, -se** experience; adventure
erledigen settle; get (sth.) done; deal with; *coll* wear out; do in; finish (off); **sich von selbst ~** take care of itself; **erledigt** *coll* all in
erlegen kill (game *etc*); *Aust*, *Swiss* pay

-erlei (*indecl*) ... kinds of, *eg* **all~** all kinds of; *in pronominal use* ... (different) things, *eg* **zwei~** two (different) things

---

erleichtern lighten; make easier; ease; relieve; **~ um** *joc* relieve of
[die] **Erleichterung, -en** *vbl noun*; *also* relief
erleiden* suffer; sustain
erlernbar learnable; (easy *etc*) to learn
erlernen learn
erlesen choice; select

erleuchten illuminate, light up
die **Erleuchtung, –en** illumination; flash of inspiration
erliegen* (*sn*) (+*dat*) succumb to; be a victim of; **zum Erliegen bringen/kommen** bring/come to a standstill
erlisten (*also* + **sich** *dat*) obtain by cunning
der **Erlös, –e** proceeds
erlöschen (erlisch(s)t, *p/t* **erlosch** (*subj* **erlösche),** *p/part* **erloschen)** (*sn*) (fire) go out, (volcano) become extinct; (interest *etc*) die; lapse, expire; die out; **erloschen** (volcano) extinct
erlösen rescue (**aus** from); *relig* redeem; **~ von** free from; **~d** (feeling) of relief
der **Erlöser, –** rescuer; deliverer; *relig* redeemer
die **Erlösung** *vbl noun*; *also* deliverance, release; *relig* redemption
erlügen* fabricate; **das ist alles erlogen** it's all a pack of lies
ermächtigen authorize (to)
die **Ermächtigung, –en** authorization; **das ~s|gesetz, –e** enabling act
ermahnen admonish, urge (**zur Vorsicht** *etc* to be careful *etc*)
die **Ermahnung, –en** admonition
ermangeln (+*gen*) be lacking in
Ermangelung: in ~ (+*gen*) in the absence of
ermannen: sich ~ pluck up courage
ermäßigen reduce; **sich ~** be reduced
die **Ermäßigung, –en** reduction
ermatten tire; (*v/i sn*) grow weary
ermessen* assess; appreciate
das **Ermessen** judgement; discretion; **in jmds. ~** (*acc*) **stellen** leave to s.o.'s discretion; **nach menschlichem ~** as far as one can tell
ermitteln establish, ascertain; trace; (*v/i*) *leg* investigate; **~ gegen** investigate (person)
die **Ermittlung, –en** *vbl noun*; *also* establishment (of); (*pl*) *leg* investigation; **das ~s|verfahren, –** preliminary investigation
ermöglichen make possible
ermorden murder; assassinate
die **Ermordung, –en** murder; assassination
ermüden (*sn if v/i*) tire; **~d** tiring; **ermüdet** weary
die **Ermüdung** fatigue (*also tech*), weariness; **die ~s|erscheinung, –en** sign of fatigue
ermuntern encourage
die **Ermunterung, –en** encouragement
ermutigen encourage
die **Ermutigung, –en** encouragement
ernähren feed; support; **sich ~ von** live on; make a living from
der **Ernährer, –** breadwinner
die **Ernährung** feeding; nourishment, nutrition; food, diet; support (of family *etc*); *in compds* **~s–** nutritional ...; **die ~s|weise, –n** diet
ernennen* appoint (**zu** (as))
die **Ernennung, –en** appointment
erneuern renew; renovate; *mot* change (oil); **sich ~** be renewed
die **Erneuerung, –en** *vbl noun*; *also* renewal; renovation
erneut renewed; fresh; (*adv*) again
erniedrigen debase; humiliate; *mus* flatten, flat *US*
die **Erniedrigung, –en** *vbl noun*; *also* debasement; humiliation; **das ~s|zeichen, –** *mus* flat
ernst serious; **es ~ meinen** mean it; **+mit** be serious about; **~ nehmen** take seriously
der **Ernst** seriousness; **~ machen mit** carry out; **das ist mein (voller) ~** I'm quite serious; **es ist mir ~ mit ...** I'm serious about ...; **allen ~es** in all seriousness; **im ~** seriously || **der ~fall, ⸚e** emergency (**im E.** in case of emergency); **e~gemeint** serious, genuine; **e~zunehmend** (rival *etc*) serious
ernsthaft serious
ernstlich serious
die **Ernte, –n** harvest; **das ~dank|fest, –e** harvest festival
ernten harvest; reap; earn (praise *etc*)
ernüchtern sober up; bring down to earth
der **Er|oberer, –** conqueror
er|obern conquer
die **Er|oberung, –en** conquest
er|öffnen open; (+*dat*) reveal to; **sich ~** (+*dat*) unburden oneself to; open up to
die **Er|öffnung, –en** *vbl noun*; *also* disclosure; **die ~s|feier, –n** opening ceremony
erogen erogenous
er|örtern discuss
die **Er|örterung, –en** discussion
die **Erosion, –en** erosion
die **Erotik** [–ɪk] eroticism
erotisch erotic
erotisierend (music *etc*) erotic
der **Erpel, –** drake
erpicht: ~ auf (*acc*) keen on
erpressen blackmail; extort (money *etc*)
der **Erpresser, –** blackmailer
die **Erpressung, –en** blackmail; extortion
erproben test; (put to the) test; **erprobt** proven; reliable
erquicken refresh
erquicklich agreeable
erraten* guess
errechnen calculate
erregbar excitable
erregen excite; arouse; cause; **sich ~** get excited; **erregt** *also* heated
der **Erreger, –** *med* germ
die **Erregtheit** excitement
die **Erregung** *vbl noun*; *also* excitement
erreichbar available; attainable; within reach
erreichen reach; attain; achieve; catch (bus *etc*); catch up with; get in touch with;

etwas/nichts ~ bei get somewhere/nowhere with; **~, daß ...** get (s.o., sth.) to ...; (*with pass*, *eg* **... jmd. abgeschoben wird**) get ... +*p/part* (s.o. deported *etc*)

erretten save

errichten erect; found

^die^ **Errichtung** *vbl noun*; *also* erection

erringen* win; achieve

erröten (*sn*) blush (**vor** *dat* with)

^die^ **Errungenschaft, –en** achievement; *coll* acquisition; **mit den neuesten ~en der Technik** (ship *etc*) with the very latest equipment that technology has to offer

^der^ **Ersatz** replacement; substitute; compensation; *in compds also* spare ...; substitute ...; **die ~befriedigung, –en** substitute; **der ~dienst** alternative service (for conscientious objectors); **die ~kasse, –n** private health insurance; **der ~mann, ⸚er/..leute** replacement; *sp* substitute; **der ~spieler, –** *sp* substitute; **der ~teil, –e** spare part; **die ~teil|medizin** spare-part surgery

ersaufen* (*sn*) *coll* drown; *mot* be flooded

ersäufen drown (animal, *coll* sorrows)

erschaffen* (*like* **schaffen**¹) create

erschallen (*p/t* **erschallte/erscholl,** *p/part* **erschallt/erschollen**) (*sn*) ring out; resound

erschaudern (*sn*) shudder (**vor** *dat* with)

erschauern (*sn*) shiver; shudder (**vor** *dat* with)

erscheinen* (*sn*) appear; seem; **das Erscheinen** appearance; publication

^die^ **Erscheinung, –en** appearance; phenomenon; vision; publication (of); (*with adj*, = person) figure; **–erscheinung** *also* sign/symptom of ...; **in ~ treten** appear; manifest itself || **das ~s|bild, –er** appearance (of thing); *biol* phenotype; **die ~s|form, –en** manifestation; **der ~s|ort, –e** place of publication

erschießen* shoot (dead); **erschossen** *coll* worn out

erschlaffen (*sn*) grow weary; slacken; flag

erschlagen* kill; **erschlagen** *coll* worn out; dumbfounded

erschleichen* (*also* + **sich** *dat*) obtain by devious means; worm one's way into

erschließen* open up, develop; tap (resources); exploit; **~ aus** deduce from; **sich ~** open up; yield its meaning; **erschlossen** *ling* reconstructed

^die^ **Erschließung, –en** *vbl noun*; *also* development; exploitation; deduction

erschöpfen exhaust; **sich ~** exhaust oneself; **sich ~ in** (*dat*) be confined to; **~d** *also* exhaustive

^die^ **Erschöpfung** exhaustion; **bis zur ~** to the point of exhaustion

erschrecken frighten, startle; (*v/i*: **~***: **erschrick(s)t,** *p/t* **erschrak** (*subj* **erschräke**), *p/part* **erschrocken**) (*sn*) be frightened (**vor** *dat* by)/alarmed; be startled; **~d** alarming

^die^ **Erschrockenheit** (state of) fright

erschüttern shake; shock; cast doubt on; **~d** shattering

^die^ **Erschütterung, –en** *vbl noun*; *also* tremor; shock

erschweren make more difficult; hamper; **~d** *leg* aggravating

erschwindeln (*also* + **sich** *dat*) obtain by swindling

erschwingen* afford

erschwinglich within one's means

ersehen*: **~ aus** see from

ersehnen (*also* + **sich** *dat*) long for

ersetzen replace; reimburse (costs); (person) take the place of

ersichtlich apparent

ersinnen* think up

erspähen spot

ersparen save; (+*dat*) spare (s.o. sth.); **... bleibt mir erspart** I am spared ...

^die^ **Ersparnis, –se** saving (**an** *dat* of); (*pl*) savings

erspielen (*also* + **sich** *dat*) win (by one's playing)

ersprießlich profitable

erst [e:–] (*cf next entry*) first; at first; not ... until; only; (*followed by subject*) only ...; it is/was ... who/that ...; (*with inversion of subject and verb*) = **wenn ... ~** *below*; (*as emotive particle*) really, (*intensifying*) *conveyed by emphasis* (*eg* **sie ist schon hübsch, aber du solltest ~ ihre Schwester sehen!** she is pretty but you should see her sister!)

~, als ... (it was) only when

eben ~ only just

~ (ein)mal first

~ jetzt only now

~ noch first; still

~ 'recht all the more (so); really; **~ 'recht nicht** all the less (so); **jetzt ~ recht/recht nicht!** now I most certainly will/won't!

~, wenn ... only when ...; **wenn ... ~ (einmal)** once ...; **wenn ... ~ ...!** if only ...!

erst.. [e:–] first; **als ~es** first of all; **als ~er/~e/~es** *conveyed by* ... is *etc* the first to ...; **fürs ~e** for the time being; **zum ~en, zum zweiten, zum dritten!** going, going, gone!; **der/die/das ~e beste** the first ... that comes along/that one comes across

Erst– first ...; *esp comput* primary ...; **die ~aufführung, –en** première; **e~best** first ... that comes along/that one comes across; **e~klassig** first-class; **e~malig** first; (*adv*) = **e~mals** for the first time; **e~rangig** first-rate; **der ~schlag, ⸚e** first strike; **der ~täter, –** first offender

erstarren (*sn*) grow stiff; solidify; set; con-

geal; (smile) freeze; ossify; **vor Schreck ~** be paralysed with fear; **das Blut erstarrte ihm in den Adern** his blood ran cold
erstatten refund; **Bericht ~** report
erstaunen astonish, amaze; **erstaunt** astonished, amazed (**über** *acc* at)
das **Erstaunen** astonishment, amazement; **in ~ (ver)setzen** astonish, amaze
erstaunlich astonishing, amazing
erstechen* stab to death
erstehen* (manage to) buy; (*v/i sn*) arise
ersteigen* climb
erstellen construct; produce (plan *etc*)
erste|mal: das ~ the first time
ersten|mal: zum ~ for the first time
erstens firstly
ersterben* (*sn*) die; die away
ersticken suffocate; smother; stifle; (*v/i sn*) suffocate; **~ an** (*dat*) (*sn*) be suffocated by; choke on; **in der Arbeit ~** *coll* be snowed under with work; **zum Ersticken** stifling
die **Erstickung** suffocation
Erstlings– ['eː–] first ...
erstrahlen (*sn*) shine brightly
erstreben strive for; **~s|wert** desirable
erstrecken: sich ~ extend (over *etc* sth.); **sich ~ auf** (*acc*) apply to; cover
erstunken *coll*: **das ist ~ und erlogen** that's a pack of lies
erstürmen (take by) storm
ersuchen, das Ersuchen, – request
ertappen catch (doing sth., *eg* **jmdn. beim Abschreiben ~** catch s.o. copying)
erteilen give (lessons); (+*dat*) give (s.o. advice *etc*); issue to
ertönen (*sn*) ring out; sound
der **Ertrag, ¨–e** yield; proceeds; **e~reich** productive; profitable
ertragen* bear; **nicht zu ~** unbearable
erträglich tolerable
ertränken drown
erträumen: sich *dat* **... ~** dream of
ertrinken* (*sn*) drown
ertrotzen (*also* + **sich** *dat*) obtain by defiance
ertüchtigen toughen up; **sich ~** get fit
er|übrigen save; spare (time); **sich ~** be superfluous/unnecessary
eruieren ascertain; *Aust* trace
erwachen (*sn*) awake; (curiosity *etc*) be aroused; **ein böses Erwachen** a rude awakening
erwachsen[1]* [–ks–] (*sn*) arise; (+*dat*) accrue to; be incurred by; **~ aus** arise from; **aus ... erwächst jmdm. ... ...** brings/causes s.o. ...
erwachsen[2] [–ks–] *p/part*; *also* adult, grown-up; **der/die Erwachsene** (*decl as adj*) adult, grown-up
erwägen* consider
die **Erwägung, –en** consideration; **in ~ ziehen** give consideration to
erwählen choose (**zu** as)
erwähnen mention; **~s|wert** worth mentioning
die **Erwähnung, –en** *vbl noun*; *also* mention
erwärmen warm (up); **~ für** win over to; **sich ~** warm up; **sich ~ für** take to
erwarten expect; wait for; **ich kann es nicht ~ zu ...** I can't wait to ...; **über/wider Erwarten** beyond/contrary to expectation
die **Erwartung, –en** expectation; **e~s|gemäß** as expected; **e~s|voll** expectant
erwecken awaken; arouse; give (impression)
erwehren: sich ~ (+*gen*) ward off; **sich eines Lächelns/der Tränen nicht ~ können** be unable to refrain from smiling/keep back one's tears; **ich kann mich des Eindrucks nicht ~, daß ...** I can't help thinking that ...
erweichen (*sn if v/i*) soften; **sich ~ lassen** relent
Erweis: den ~ erbringen für prove
erweisen* prove; (+*dat*) do (s.o. favour, service); show (s.o. respect *etc*); **sich ~ als** show oneself (to be); prove (to be)
erweitern widen, enlarge; dilate (pupil of eye *etc*); expand; extend; broaden (horizon *etc*); *math* reduce (fraction); **sich ~** widen, enlarge; dilate
die **Erweiterung, –en** *vbl noun*; *also* enlargement; dilation; expansion; extension
der **Erwerb** acquisition; living; earnings; **seinem ~ nachgehen** earn one's living
erwerben* acquire; win (respect *etc*)
Erwerbs–: e~fähig capable of earning a living; **e~los** unemployed; **die ~losigkeit** unemployment; **die ~quelle, –n** source of income; **e~tätig** gainfully employed; **e~unfähig** unable to earn a living
die **Erwerbung, –en** acquisition
erwidern reply; return (*also mil*), reciprocate; **(scharf) ~** retort; **~ auf** (*acc*) say in reply to
erwiesener|maßen as has been shown
erwirken obtain (s.o.'s release *etc*)
erwirtschaften make (profit *etc*) (by careful management)
erwischen *coll* catch (thief *etc*, train *etc*; *also* s.o. doing sth., *eg* **beim Mogeln** cheating); get hold of; get; **es hat ... erwischt ...** has *etc* caught it/had it/got it bad
erwünscht desired; desirable; welcome
erwürgen strangle
das **Erz** [ɛ–, eː–], **–e** ore; bronze
Erz– [ɛ–] arch–; **(erz–)** utterly ...; ultra–; **der ~bischof, ¨–e** archbishop; **der ~feind, –e** arch-enemy; **der ~vater, ..väter** patriarch
Erzähl– narrative ...
erzählen tell; narrate; (*v/i*) tell a story/stories; **man erzählt sich, daß ...** people say

that …; ~**d** narrative
der **Erzähler, –** narrator; storyteller
die **Erzählung, –en** story; narration
erzeigen (+*dat*) show (s.o. respect *etc*); render (s.o. service); **sich dankbar** ~ show oneself grateful
erzeugen produce; generate (*also chem, phys, comput*); engender, give rise to; *Aust* manufacture (goods)
der **Erzeuger, –** producer; father; *Aust* manufacturer
das **Erzeugnis, –se** product, (*pl*) *agr* produce; creation
die **Erzeugung** production; generation; creation; *Aust* manufacture (of goods)
erziehen* educate; bring up (**zur Sparsamkeit** *etc* to be thrifty *etc*)
der **Erzieher, –** educator; teacher; tutor
erzieherisch educational; educative
die **Erziehung** education; upbringing; manners; *in compds* ~**s–** educational …; **die ~s|anstalt, –en** community home, reformatory *US*; **das ~s|wesen** educational system
erzielen achieve; obtain; fetch (price); *sp* score
erzittern (*sn*) tremble
erzürnen anger; **sich** ~ get angry; **erzürnt** angry (**über** *acc* about)
erzwingen* force (decision *etc*); obtain by force
es [ɛs] (*see p. xxvi*) (*nom/acc*) it; (*referring to* **das Mädchen** *etc*) she/her; (do, say, remain) so; *in certain instances left untranslated* (*eg* **er sieht intelligent aus, aber er ist** ~ **nicht** he looks intelligent, but he isn't, **ich weiß** ~ I know, **wie/als** ~ **der Fall ist** as/than is the case, **ich ziehe** ~ **vor zu …** I prefer to …); **ich bin** ~ **satt** I'm sick of it;
often used impersonally (*see p. lvi*; *eg* ~ **regnet** it's raining, ~ **drängt mich zu …** I feel an urge to …, (*cf* **werden** 3 (*b*)) ~ **darf geraucht werden** smoking is allowed); *when certain phenomena are referred to impersonal* ~ + *verb* = there is a + *noun* (*eg* ~ **riecht nach Gas** there's a smell of gas, ~ **klopfte** there was a knock (at the door), ~ **raschelte** there was a rustling sound); *when* ~ *is used to anticipate the subject, it is translated by* there (*eg* ~ **folgte(n) …** there followed …), *or by bringing the subject forward* (*eg* ~ **wurden Briefe geschrieben** letters were written); ~ **gibt,** (*esp with reference to presence in a specified place*) ~ **ist/sind** there is/are; ~ **fährt** *etc* **sich gut** (*see* **sich** 3)
das **es, Es**[1] [ɛs] (*gen* –), – *mus* (the note) E flat; (*key*) **Es** E flat major, **es** E flat minor
das **Es**[2] [ɛs], – *psych* id
die **Esche, –n** ash
der **Esel, –** donkey; *coll* ass
eselhaft asinine
Esels– donkey('s) …; ass's …; **die ~brücke, –n** mnemonic; crib, pony *US*; **das ~ohr, –en** donkey's ear; dog-ear
die **Eskalation, –en** escalation
eskalieren (*sn if v/i*) escalate
die **Eskapade, –n** escapade
der **Eskimo, –s** Eskimo
die **Eskorte, –n, eskortieren** escort
esoterisch esoteric
die **Espe, –n** aspen; ~**n|laub** (**zittern wie E.** tremble like a leaf)
der **Esprit** [ɛs'pri:] wit
Eß– eating …; dining …; **die ~ecke, –n** dining area; **das ~geschirr, –e** dinner-service; *mil* mess-tin; **die ~kastanie, –n** sweet chestnut; **der ~löffel, –** tablespoon; **die ~lust** appetite; **das ~stäbchen, –** chopstick; **die ~waren** *pl* foodstuffs; **das ~zimmer, –** dining-room (suite)
der **Essay** ['ɛse, ɛ'se:], **–s** (*also* **das**) essay
der **Essayist** [ɛse'ɪst], **–en** (*wk masc*) essayist
eßbar edible; eatable
essen (*2nd/3rd sing pres* **ißt,** *p/t* **aß** [a:s] (*subj* **äße**), *p/part* **gegessen**) eat; **kalt/warm** ~ have a cold/hot meal; ~ **gehen** go out for a meal
das **Essen, –** food; meal; (formal) dinner; eating
die **Essenz, –en** essence (*also cul etc*)
der **Esser, –** (poor *etc*) eater; mouth to feed
der **Essig** vinegar; **mit … ist es** ~ *coll* … is *etc* off || **die ~säure** acetic acid
das **Establishment** [ɪs'tɛblɪʃmənt], **–s** *pol etc* establishment
der **Este** ['e:–], **–n** (*wk masc*) Estonian
Estland ['e:–] Estonia
estnisch ['e:–], (*language*) **E~** Estonian
die **Estrade, –n** dais; *EGer* variety show
der **Estragon** [–ɔn] tarragon
der **Estrich, –e** cement *etc* floor; *Swiss* attic
das **Eszett** (*gen* –), – (the letter) ß
etablieren establish; set up; **sich** ~ establish oneself, *comm* set up (in business); become established; **etabliert** established
das **Etablissement** [–(ə)'mã:], **–s** establishment
die **Etage** [–ʒə], **–n** floor, storey; **das ~n|bett, –en** bunk bed; **die ~n|wohnung, –en** flat, apartment *US* (occupying the whole of one storey)
–etagig [–ʒ–] –storeyed
die **Etappe, –n** stage; *mil* communications zone
der **Etat** [–'ta:], **–s** budget
etepetete [e:təpə'te:tə] *coll* finicky
der **Eternit** (*also* **das**) (*trade-mark*) asbestos cement
die **Ethik** [–ɪk] ethics
ethisch ethical
ethnisch ['ɛt–] ethnic
der **Ethnograph** [ɛt–], **–en** (*wk masc*) ethnographer

^die^ **Ethnographie** [ɛt–] ethnography
^der^ **Ethnologe** [ɛt–], **–n** (*wk masc*) ethnologist
^die^ **Ethnologie** [ɛt–] ethnology
^das^ **Ethos** [–ɔs] ethical sense; ethic
^das^ **Etikett, –e/–s** label (*also comput*); price-tag
^die^ **Etikette, –n** etiquette; *Aust, Swiss* = **Etikett**
etikettieren label; attach a price-tag to
etlich.. ['ɛt–] some; (*pl*) several; a number of; ~**es** a number of things; quite a lot
^der^ **Etrusker, –, etruskisch** Etruscan
^die^ **Etsch** the Adige
^die^ **Etüde, –n** *mus* étude
^das^ **Etui** [e'tŭi:], **–s** (cigarette *etc*) case
etwa ['ɛt–] approximately; for example; *Swiss* now and again; (*as emotive particle*) perhaps; by any chance; *or left untranslated* (*eg* **du brauchst nicht ~ zu denken, ich hätte es nicht bemerkt** you needn't think I hadn't noticed); **in ~** broadly speaking; **nicht ~, daß ...** not that ...; **... und nicht ~ ...** ... and not, as one might suppose, ...
etwaig ['ɛtva(:)–] possible; any (that may occur)
etwas ['ɛt–] 1 *pron* something/anything (*also* + *substantival adj, eg* **~ Wunderbares** something wonderful); some (*also* + *noun, eg* **~ Geld** some money); 2 *adv* somewhat; **~ sein** be somebody; **~, was ...** something that ...; **noch ~** something/anything else; some more (meat *etc*); (stay *etc*) a little longer; **so ~** (*see* **so**); **das gewisse Etwas** that certain something
etwelch.. ['ɛt–] *Aust, Swiss* some
^die^ **Etymologie, –(ie)n** etymology
etymologisch etymological
Etzel Attila
euch (*acc/dat of* **ihr** 1: *see p. xxvi*; *in correspondence*: **E~**) (*a*) you (*familiar pl*); (*dat*) (to/for) you; (*b*) (*refl*) yourselves, (*recip*) each other, one another; (*dat*) (to/for) yourselves, (*recip*) (to/for) each other/one another
^die^ **Eucharistie** [–ç–], **–(ie)n** Eucharist
euer (*in correspondence*: **E~**) 1 *poss adj* (*see p. xxxiii*) your (*familiar pl*); 2 *pron* (*gen of* **ihr** 1: *see p. xxvi*) of you (*familiar pl*); **~er/~e/~(e)s** = **eurer** *etc* (*at* **eur..**)
^der^ **Eukalyptus, –/–(t)en** eucalyptus (tree)
Euklid Euclid
^die^ **Eule, –n** owl; *coll* 'bag'; **die ~n\|spiegelei, –en** prank
^der^ **Eunuch** [–x], **–en** (*wk masc*) eunuch
^der^ **Euphemismus, –(m)en** euphemism
euphemistisch euphemistic
^die^ **Euphorie** euphoria
euphorisch euphoric
^der^ **Euphrat** [–at] (*gen* **–(s)**) the Euphrates
eur.. = **euer..**; **eurer/eure/eures** (*see p. xxviii*; *also* **der/die/das ~e**) yours (*familiar pl*); **das E~e** what is yours; **das E~e tun** do your bit; **die E~en** your families
^der^ **Eurasier** [–ĭɐ], **–, eurasisch** Eurasian
eurer\|seits for/on your part
eures\|gleichen people like you(rselves)
euret–: **~wegen** because of you; = **(um) ~willen** for your sake
eurige: **der/die/das ~** = **der/die/das eure** (*at* **eur..**)
Euripides [–ɛs] Euripides
Euro– Euro–; **der ~cheque** [–ʃɛk], **–s** Eurocheque; **die ~vision** Eurovision
Europa Europe; *in compds* European ...; **der ~pokal** the European Cup; **der ~rat** the Council of Europe
^der^ **Europäer, –, europäisch** European
europäisieren Europeanize
^das^ **Euter, –** udder
^die^ **Euthanasie** euthanasia
ev. = **evangelisch**
e. V. (= **eingetragener Verein**) registered association
Eva [–f–, –v–] Eve
evakuieren evacuate
^die^ **Evakuierung, –en** evacuation
evangelisch Protestant; evangelical
^der^ **Evangelist, –en** (*wk masc*) evangelist
^das^ **Evangelium, –(i)en** gospel
evaporieren evaporate (liquid *etc*)
Evas\|kostüm *joc*: **im ~** (of female) in one's birthday suit
^die^ **Eventualität, –en** eventuality
eventuell possible; any (... that may occur); (*adv*) possibly; if necessary
Everest ['ɛvərɛst]: **der Mount ~** Mount Everest
^der^ **Evergreen** ['ɛvɐgri:n], **–s** (*also* **das**) *mus* evergreen
^die^ **Evolution, –en** evolution
evtl. = **eventuell**
^die^ **EWG** (= **Europäische Wirtschaftsgemeinschaft**) the E.E.C.
ewig eternal; perpetual; *coll* constant; (*adv*) for ever; *coll* constantly; for ages; (take) ages; **auf ~** for ever; **das ist ~ schade** *coll* it's a great pity
^die^ **Ewigkeit, –en** eternity; **eine ~** *coll* for ages; (take) ages; **(bis) in alle ~** for ever
Ex– ex–
exakt exact
exaltiert gushing; over-excited
^das^ **Examen, –/Examina** (final) examination; **im ~ stehen** be taking one's exams
examinieren examine (*also educ*)
^die^ **Exegese, –n** exegesis
^der^ **Exeget, –en** (*wk masc*) exegete
^die^ **Exekution, –en** execution
^die^ **Exekutive, –n** executive; *Aust* forces of law and order
^das^ **Exempel, –** example; **ein ~ statuieren an** (*dat*) make an example of

das **Exemplar, –e** copy; specimen
exemplarisch exemplary; (*adv*) as an example
exemplifizieren exemplify
Exerzier–: der ~platz, ¨–e parade-ground
exerzieren drill; *coll* go through, practise
der **Exhibitionismus** exhibitionism
der **Exhibitionist, –en** (*wk masc*) exhibitionist
exhumieren exhume
das **Exil, –e** exile; **im ~** in exile; **ins ~ gehen** go into exile
existentiell [–ts–] existential
die **Existenz, –en** existence; livelihood; *coll* (*with adj*) individual; **gescheiterte/verkrachte ~** *coll* failure || **die ~angst** angst; **e~fähig** viable; **das ~minimum** subsistence level; living wage
existieren exist (**von** on)
exkl. = **exklusive**
exklusiv exclusive
exklusive (+*gen*) exclusive of
die **Exklusivität** exclusiveness
die **Exkommunikation, –en** excommunication
exkommunizieren excommunicate
die **Exkremente** *pl* excrement
der **Exkurs, –e** excursus
die **Exkursion, –en** field trip
die **Exotik** [–ɪk] exoticism
exotisch exotic
die **Expansion, –en** expansion (*also phys*); **die ~s|politik** expansionism
expedieren dispatch
die **Expedition, –en** expedition; dispatch; dispatch department
das **Experiment, –e** experiment
experimentell experimental; (*adv*) by experiment
experimentieren experiment
der **Experte, –n** (*wk masc*) expert
die **Expertise, –n** expert's report
explizieren explain; explicate
explizite [–te] explicitly
explodieren (*sn*) explode
die **Explosion, –en** explosion; **zur ~ bringen** explode
explosiv explosive
das **Exponat, –e** exhibit
der **Exponent, –en** (*wk masc*) representative (of movement *etc*); *math* exponent
exponieren expose; **sich ~** stick one's neck out; **exponiert** (position) exposed
der **Export, –e** export (of); (country's *etc*) exports; (*pl*) exports; *in compds* export ...; **der ~handel** export trade
der **Exporteur** [–'tøːɐ], **–e** exporter
exportieren export
das **Exposé, –s** memorandum; outline
das **Expreß|gut** express parcels
der **Expressionismus** expressionism
der **Expressionist, –en** (*wk masc*), **expressionistisch** expressionist
expressis verbis [...iːs ...iːs] in so many words
exquisit exquisite
extemporieren extemporize
extern external (*also comput*); (pupil) day
extra extra; specially; separately; *coll* on purpose; **das E~blatt, ¨–er** special edition; **E~touren** *coll* (**sich** *dat* **E. leisten** go one's own way, be different); **die E~wurst** *coll* special treatment
extrahieren extract
der **Extrakt, –e** extract; synopsis
extravagant flamboyant; outlandish
die **Extravaganz, –en** flamboyance; outlandishness
extravertiert extrovert
extrem, das Extrem, –e extreme
der **Extremist, –en** (*wk masc*), **extremistisch** extremist
die **Extremitäten** *pl* extremities
extrovertiert extrovert
exzellent excellent
die **Exzellenz, –en** Excellency
die **Exzentrik** [–ɪk] eccentric behaviour; (in variety *etc* act) grotesque comedy
der **Exzentriker, –, exzentrisch** eccentric
die **Exzentrizität** eccentricity
exzeptionell exceptional
exzerpieren excerpt (book *etc*)
der **Exzeß, –(ss)e** excess; **bis zum ~** to excess
exzessiv excessive

F

das **F** [ɛf] (*gen, pl* –, *coll* [ɛfs]) F; **das f, F** *mus* (the note) F; (*key*) **F** F major, **f** F minor

f. (= **folgende** (**Seite**)) f., (= **für**) for

Fa. (= **Firma**) Messrs

die **Fabel, –n** fable; fantastic story; *liter* plot; *in compds also* mythical ...

fabelhaft fabulous

die **Fabrik, –en** factory; **die ~anlage, –n** manufacturing plant; **der ~arbeiter, –** factory worker; **f~mäßig** (**f. hergestellt** mass-produced); **der ~preis, –e** price ex works; **das ~schiff, –e** factory ship

der **Fabrikant, –en** (*wk masc*) manufacturer

das **Fabrikat, –e** product; make

die **Fabrikation, –en** manufacture

Fabriks– *Aust* = **Fabrik–**

fabrizieren *coll* concoct

fabulieren make up stories

das **Facelifting** ['fe:s–], **–s** face-lift

die **Facette** [–s–], **–n** facet

das **Fach, ¨er** subject; compartment; pigeon-hole; *theat* (type of) role; **Mann vom ~** expert; **das schlägt nicht in mein ~** that's not my department

Fach– specialist ...; professional ...; technical ...;

der ~arbeiter, – skilled worker; **der ~arzt, ¨e** (medical) specialist; **der ~ausdruck, ¨e** technical term; **der ~bereich, –e** field; *univ* school; **das ~gebiet, –e** field; **f~gemäß** = **f~gerecht** expert; **das ~geschäft, –e** specialist shop; **der ~händler, –** dealer; **der ~idiot, –en** (*wk masc*) *coll* narrow specialist; **f~kundig** expert; **der ~mann, ¨er/..leute** expert (**für** on), specialist (in); **f~männisch** expert; **die ~presse** technical/trade journals; **die ~richtung, –en** subject (of study); **die ~schule, –n** technical college; **die ~simpelei, –en** *coll* shop-talk; **f~simpeln** (*insep*) *coll* talk shop; **der ~verband, ¨e** professional/trade association; **die ~welt** (the) profession; **das ~werk, –e** half-timbering; **das ~werk|haus, ¨er** half-timbered house

–fach ... times; –fold

fächeln fan

der **Fächer, –** fan; **f~förmig** fan-shaped

fachlich professional; technical

die **Fackel, –n** torch

fackeln *coll* shilly-shally; **nicht lange ~** lose no time

fad(e) insipid; dull

der **Faden,** *pl* **Fäden** thread; *elect* filament; (*pl* –) *naut* fathom; **roter ~** theme (running through work); **den ~ verlieren** lose the thread; **keinen guten ~ lassen an** (*dat*) *coll* tear to shreds; **die Fäden ziehen** take out the stitches; **an einem (dünnen/seidenen) ~ hängen** hang by a thread || **die ~nudeln** *pl* vermicelli; **f~scheinig** threadbare; (excuse) feeble

die **Fadheit** insipidness; dullness

fadisieren: sich ~ *Aust coll* get bored

das **Fagott, –e** bassoon

fähig able; capable (**zu**/*gen* of); (**dazu**) **~ zu ...** capable of (+*ger*)

–fähig: (*i*) (*eg* **arbeits~**) able to (work *etc*); (*ii*) –able, –ible (*eg* **transport~** transportable), (*eg* **entwicklungs~**) capable of (development *etc*); *also in sense* '*eligible for ...*' (*eg* **gesellschafts~** socially acceptable)

---

die **Fähigkeit, –en** ability; capacity; **–fähigkeit** –ability; –ibility; ability to ...; capacity for ...

fahl pale

das **Fähnchen, –** small flag; *coll* cheap dress

fahnden: ~ nach hunt for, search for

die **Fahndung, –en** hunt, search

die **Fahne, –n** flag; banner; *mil* colours; *print* galley-proof; **die/seine ~ nach dem Wind(e) drehen** trim one's sails to the wind; **eine ~ haben** *coll* reek of alcohol || **der ~n|eid, –e** oath of allegiance; **die ~n|flucht** desertion; **der/die ~n|flüchtige** (*decl as adj*) deserter; **die ~n|stange, –n** flagpole; **der ~n|träger, –** standard-bearer

der **Fähnrich, –e** officer cadet

Fahr– driving ...;

der ~ausweis, –e ticket; *Swiss* driving licence, driver's license *US*; **die ~bahn, –en** road(way); traffic lane; **der ~damm, ¨e** *NGer esp Berlin* road(way); **die ~eigenschaften** *pl mot* handling; **der ~gast, ¨e** passenger; **das ~geld, –er** fare; **das ~gestell, –e** *mot* chassis; *aer* undercarriage; **die ~karte, –n** ticket; **die ~karten|ausgabe, –n** ticket-office; **der ~karten|automat, –en** (*wk masc*) ticket-machine; **f~lässig** negligent (**f~lässige Tötung** *see* **Tötung**); **die**

~**lässigkeit, –en** negligence; **der ~lehrer, –** driving instructor; **der ~plan, ⸚e** timetable; schedule; **f~plan|mäßig** scheduled; (*adv*) on/according to schedule; **der ~preis, –e** fare; **die ~prüfung, –en** driving test; **das ~rad, ⸚er** bicycle; **der ~schein, –e** ticket; **die ~schule, –n** driving school; **der ~schüler, –** learner driver, student driver *US*; **der ~stuhl, ⸚e** lift, elevator *US*; **die ~stunde, –n** driving lesson; **das ~verbot, –e** driving ban; **das ~wasser** channel (**im richtigen F.** in one's element); **das ~werk, –e** undercarriage; **das ~zeug, –e** vehicle

Fähr– ferry ...

fahrbar mobile

die **Fähre, –n** ferry

fahren (fähr(s)t, *p/t* **fuhr** (*subj* **führe**), *p/part* **gefahren)** drive; ride; *cin, TV* track; *tech* operate; (*sn*) take (route); do (... miles per hour); (*v/i sn*) go, travel; leave; (bus *etc*) go, run; (motorist) drive; (car *etc*) run (smoothly *etc*); do (well *etc*)

~ **aus** (*sn*) leap out of

~ **durch** (*sn*): (+*dat*) **durch den Kopf ~** flash through (s.o.'s) mind; (+*dat*) **durchs Haar ~** run one's fingers through (s.o.'s) hair

~ **gegen** (*sn*) drive into

~ **in** (*acc*) (*sn*) throw on (clothes); **was ist in ... gefahren?** what's got into ...?

~ **mit** (*sn*) go by (car, bus, *etc*)

~ **über** (*acc*) (*sn*): **mit der Hand** *etc* **~ über** run one's hand *etc* over

hier fährt es sich gut this is a good road for driving on

fahren–: ~lassen* (*p/part usu* **~lassen;** *sep*) let go of; give up

fahrend itinerant; travelling

der **Fahrer, –** driver; chauffeur; **die ~flucht** hit-and-run driving

fahrerisch driving

fahrig nervous; distracted

fähr(s)t (*2nd,*) *3rd sing pres of* **fahren**

die **Fahrt, –en** journey; trip; drive; speed; **freie ~** 'go' signal; the go-ahead; **gute ~!** have a good trip!; **~ ins Blaue** mystery tour; **eine ~ machen** go on a trip; **in ~** under way; *coll* in one's stride; furious; **in ~ bringen** *coll* get (s.o.) going; make wild; **in ~ kommen** get under way; *coll* get into one's stride; get wild; **während der ~** while the train *etc* is in motion || **die ~richtung, –en** direction (of travel); **der ~schreiber, –** tachograph; **die ~unterbrechung, –en** stopover

die **Fährte, –n** trail; scent; **auf der richtigen/falschen ~** on the right/wrong track

der **Fahrten|schreiber, –** tachograph

das **Faible** ['fɛːbl̩], **–s** liking; soft spot

fair [fɛːɐ] fair

die **Fairneß** ['fɛːɐnɛs] fairness

die **Fäkalien** [–ĭən] *pl* faeces

der **Fakir, –e** fakir

faktisch actual; (*adv*) in reality, in fact; *Aust coll* practically

der **Faktor, –(o̱r)en** factor (*also math, comput*)

das **Faktum, –(t)en** fact

die **Fakultä̱t, –en** *univ* faculty

fakultati̱v optional

falb dun-coloured

der **Falke, –n** (*wk masc*) falcon; *pol* hawk; **das ~n|auge, –n** eagle eye; **die ~n|jagd** falconry

der **Fall, ⸚e** fall; case (*also gramm, leg, med*); **das ist ganz mein ~** *coll* that's just my cup of tea; **klarer ~!** you bet!; **gesetzt/setzen wir den ~, (daß) ...** supposing ...; **auf jeden ~ = auf alle Fälle** in any event; at all events; **auf keinen ~** under no circumstances; **für den ~** (+*gen*) in the event of; **für den ~, daß ...** in case ...; **für alle Fälle** (just) in case; **im ~e** (+*gen*; *also in compds, eg* **im Krankheits~**) in the event of; **zu ~ bringen** bring down; defeat; **zu ~ kommen** fall || **das ~beil, –e** guillotine; **die ~brücke, –n** drawbridge; **das ~gitter, –** portcullis; **das ~obst** windfalls; **das ~reep, –e** *naut* gangway; **das ~rohr, –e** down-pipe; **der ~schirm, –e** parachute; **der ~schirm|jäger, –** paratrooper; **der ~schirm|springer, –** parachutist; **der ~strick, –e** trap (set for s.o.); **die ~studie, –n** case-study; **die –tür, –en** trap door; **f~weise** from case to case; *Aust* occasionally

die **Falle, –n** trap; *Swiss* door-handle; (+*dat*) **eine ~ stellen** set a trap for; **in die ~ gehen** fall into the trap; *coll* hit the hay; (+*dat*) walk into (s.o.'s) trap

fallen (fäll(s)t, *p/t* **fiel,** *p/part* **gefallen)** (*sn*) fall; drop; be made/taken/spoken/fired/*sp* scored; *mil* be killed; **~ lassen** (*cf* **fallenlassen**) drop (object, stitch); **sich ~ lassen auf** (*acc*)/**in** (*acc*) drop onto/into

~ **an** (*acc*) go to

~ **auf** (*acc*) (glance, choice, date, *etc*) fall on; go to

~ **durch** fail

~ **in** (*acc*) fall into (coma *etc*); lapse into (dialect); belong to (period); come under/within; **einem Pferd in die Zügel ~** grab a horse's reins

~ **unter** (*acc*) come under

fallen–: ~lassen* (*p/part usu* **~lassen;** *sep*) drop; let drop

fällen fell; take (decision), *leg* pronounce (sentence); *math* drop (perpendicular); *chem* precipitate

fällig due; *fin* mature

der **Fallout** [fɔːl'ʔao̯t], **–s** fall-out

falls if; in case

fäll(s)t (*2nd,*) *3rd sing pres of* **fallen, fällen**

falsch wrong; false; mis– (*eg* ~**e Aussprache** mispronunciation, ~ **darstellen** misrepresent); forged; counterfeit; **ein** ~**es Spiel treiben mit** play false; ~ **liegen** *coll* be mistaken; **ohne Falsch** without guile || **das F~geld** counterfeit money; **die F~meldung, –en** false alarm; **der F~münzer, –** counterfeiter; ~**spielen** (*sep*), **der F~spieler, –** *games* cheat

fälschen forge; fake; falsify

fälschlich erroneous; **fälschlicher|weise** erroneously, by mistake

die **Fälschung, –en** forgery; fake; falsification

das **Falsett, –e** falsetto

Falt– folding ...; collapsible ...; **das** ~**blatt, ¨–er** leaflet; **das** ~**boot, –e** collapsible boat

faltbar folding; collapsible

die **Falte, –n** wrinkle; fold (*also geol*); crease; pleat

fälteln fold in small folds

falten fold; wrinkle (brow)

Falten–: **f~los** smooth; uncreased; **der** ~**rock, ¨–e** pleated skirt; **der** ~**wurf** arrangement of the folds

der **Falter, –** butterfly

faltig creased; wrinkled

–fältig –fold

die **Faltung, –en** *geol* folding

der **Falz, –e** fold; joint; *tech* rabbet; *philat* hinge

falzen fold; *tech* rabbet

die **Fama** rumour

familiär family; informal; familiar

die **Familie** [–ĭə], **–n** family (*also biol*); ~**n|anschluß** (**F. haben** live as one of the family); **der** ~**n|name, –n** (*like* **Name**) surname; **das** ~**n|oberhaupt, ¨–er** head of the family; **der** ~**n|stand** marital status; **der** ~**n|zuwachs** addition to the family

famos *dated coll* first-rate

der **Famulus, –se/Famuli** medical student undergoing clinical training; *arch* professor's assistant

der **Fan** [fɛn], **–s** fan

das **Fanal, –e** signal

der **Fanatiker, –** fanatic

fanatisch fanatical

der **Fanatismus** fanaticism

fand (fände) *p/t* (*subj*) *of* **finden**

die **Fanfare, –n** fanfare

der **Fang, ¨–e** catching; catch; (*pl*) fangs; talons; **der** ~**arm, –e** tentacle; **das** ~**eisen, –** trap; **die** ~**frage, –n** catch question; **die** ~**leine, –n** painter; mooring-rope; **das** ~**netz, –e** net; **der** ~**stoß, ¨–e** coup de grâce; **der** ~**zahn, ¨–e** tusk; fang

fangen (fäng(s)t, *p/t* **fing,** *p/part* **gefangen)** (*see also* **gefangen**) catch; catch out; **sich** ~ recover oneself; (water *etc*) collect; **sich** ~ **in** (*dat*) get caught in; collect in

die **Fantasie, –(ie)n** *mus* fantasy

Farb– colour ...; paint ...; **das** ~**band, ¨–er** typewriter ribbon; **f~echt** colour-fast; **der** ~**fernseher, –** colour TV; **der** ~**film, –e** colour film; **die** ~**gebung** colouring; **der** ~**kasten, ..kästen** paint-box; **f~los** colourless; **der** ~**stift, –e** crayon; **der** ~**stoff, –e** dye; colouring; **der** ~**ton, ¨–e** shade

die **Farbe, –n** colour; paint; dye; ~ **bekennen** put one's cards on the table; **welche** ~ **hat ...?** what colour is ...?

färben (*see also* **gefärbt**) dye; colour; (*v/i*) run; **sich** ~ colour; turn (red *etc*)

Farben– colour ...; paint ...; **f~blind** colour-blind; **f~freudig** colourful; **die** ~**lehre** chromatics; **die** ~**pracht** blaze of colour; **f~prächtig** splendidly colourful; **f~reich** colourful

–farben (*eg* **haut**~ skin) –coloured

die **Färberei, –en** dyeing; dyeing works

farbig coloured, in colour; colourful; **–farbig** –coloured; **der/die Farbige** (*decl as adj*) coloured person

färbig *Aust* = **farbig** (*1st sense*); **–färbig** *Aust* = **–farbig**

farblich as regards colour

die **Färbung, –en** colouring; dyeing; slant

die **Farce** [–sə], **–n** farce

die **Farm, –en** (large) farm (overseas); (poultry *etc*) farm

der **Farmer, –** farmer (*cf* **Farm**)

der **Farn, –e** = **das** ~**kraut, ¨–er** fern; bracken

die **Färöer** *pl* the Faeroes

die **Färse, –n** heifer

der **Fasan, –e(n)** pheasant

faschieren *Aust* mince; **das Faschierte** (*decl as adj*) *Aust* mince, ground meat *US*

der **Fasching, –e/–s** carnival (in S. Germany, Austria)

der **Faschismus** Fascism

der **Faschist, –en** (*wk masc*), **faschistisch** Fascist

faseln *coll* blather

die **Faser, –n** fibre; **die** ~**platte, –n** fibreboard

faserig fibrous; stringy

fasern fray

das **Faß, ¨–(ss)er/**(*following num*) **–** barrel; vat; **das schlägt dem** ~ **den Boden aus!** *coll* that takes the biscuit!; ~ **ohne Boden** bottomless pit || **das** ~**bier** draught beer

die **Fassade, –n** façade; **der** ~**n|kletterer, –** cat-burglar

fassen (*see also* **gefaßt**) take hold of; seize; catch; grasp, take in; make (decision); express; set (jewel); (building *etc*) hold; (horror) seize (*esp pass*); *mil* draw; (*v/i*) grip; bite; ~ **an** (*dat*)/**bei** take by (arm *etc*); **in Worte** ~ put into words; ~ **nach** reach for; **Mut** ~ pluck up courage; **Vertrauen** ~ **zu** begin to trust; **Zuneigung** ~ **zu** take a liking to; **zu** ~ **bekommen** get hold of; **es ist nicht zu** ~! it's unbelievable!

sich ~ compose oneself; **sich kurz ~** be brief; **sich vor Freude kaum ~ können** be beside oneself with joy

faßlich comprehensible; (easy *etc*) to understand

die **Fasson** [–'sɔ̃ː], **–s** style, cut; shape; **aus der ~ geraten** go out of shape; *coll* lose one's figure

die **Fassung, –en** setting (of jewel), (spectacle) frame, *elect* socket; version; composure; **aus der ~ bringen** disconcert || **f~s|los** speechless; beside oneself; **das ~s|vermögen** capacity; comprehension

fast almost, nearly; **~ kein/nichts/niemals/niemand** hardly any/anything/ever/anyone

Fast–: die ~nacht carnival; Shrovetide, *esp* Shrove Tuesday; **der ~tag, –e** day of fasting

fasten fast

Fasten– Lent(en) ...; **die ~zeit** Lent

die **Faszination** fascination

faszinieren fascinate; **~d** fascinating

fatal disastrous; unfortunate

der **Fatalismus** fatalism

der **Fatalist, –en** (*wk masc*) fatalist

fatalistisch fatalistic

die **Fata Morgana, – –(n)en/– –s** mirage

der **Fatzke, –n** (*wk masc*)/**–s** *coll* (conceited) ass

fauchen spit, hiss

faul lazy; rotten; *coll* fishy; feeble; (joke) bad; **nicht ~** promptly || **der F~pelz, –e** *coll* lazybones; **das F~tier, –e** sloth; *coll* lazybones

faulen (*also sn*) rot; decay

faulenzen loaf about

der **Faulenzer, –** layabout

faulig rotting; putrid

die **Fäulnis** decay; rotting

der **Faun, –e** faun; lecher

die **Fauna, –(n)en** fauna

die **Faust, ⸚e** fist; **auf eigene ~** off one's own bat; **das paßt wie die ~ aufs Auge** *coll* it's quite out of place; it clashes horribly; it's just right || **f~dick** *coll* (lie) whopping great (**f. auftragen** lay it on thick; **es f. hinter den Ohren haben** be a sly customer); **der ~hand|schuh, –e** mitten; **das ~pfand, ⸚er** security; lever; **das ~recht** taking the law into one's own hands; **die ~regel, –n** rule of thumb; **der ~schlag, ⸚e** punch; **die ~skizze, –n** rough sketch

Fäustchen: sich *dat* **(eins) ins ~ lachen** laugh up one's sleeve

fausten punch (ball)

der **Fäustling, –e** mitten

der **Fauteuil** [fo'tøːj], **–s** *Aust, Swiss* armchair

der **Fauxpas** [fo'pa] (*gen* **–** [–(s)]), **–** [–s] faux-pas

favorisieren favour

der **Favorit, –en** (*wk masc*) favourite

die **Faxen** *pl coll* silly antics, tomfoolery; (funny) faces

die **Fayence** [fa'jãːs], **–n** faience

die **FAZ = Frankfurter Allgemeine Zeitung**

das **Fazit** [–ɪt], **–e/–s** conclusion (drawn); result; **das ~ ziehen** sum up

FC = Fußball-Club

der **FDGB** *EGer* = **Freier Deutscher Gewerkschaftsbund**

die **FDJ** *EGer* = **Freie Deutsche Jugend**

der **FDJler** [ɛfdeː'jɔtlɐ], **–** *EGer* member of the F.D.J.

die **FDP = Freie Demokratische Partei**

der **Feber, –** *Aust*, **der Februar** [–eː–] (*gen* **–(s)**), **–e** February; **im ~** in February

Fecht– fencing ...

fechten (ficht(st), *p/t* **focht** (*subj* **föchte**), *p/part* **gefochten)** fence

der **Fechter, –** fencer

die **Feder, –n** feather; pen; nib; *tech* spring; (*pl*) *coll* (*in idioms*) bed; **~n lassen (müssen)** *coll* not escape unscathed || **der ~ball, ⸚e** shuttlecock; badminton; **das ~bett, –en** duvet; **das ~brett, –er** springboard; **der ~busch, ⸚e** plume; *ornith* crest; **der ~fuchser** [–ks–], **–** pettifogger; pen-pusher; **f~führend** in overall charge (**für** of); **die ~führung** overall control; **die ~kraft** elasticity; **feder|leicht** light as a feather; **~lesens (ohne viel F.** without ceremony; **nicht viel ~lesens machen mit** make short work of); **das ~messer, –** (fine) penknife; **der ~strich, –e** stroke (of the pen); **das ~vieh** poultry; **die ~zeichnung, –en** pen-and-ink drawing

federn give; be springy; **~d** springy; **gefedert** sprung

die **Federung** springs; *mot* suspension

die **Fee, –n** [–ən] fairy

feenhaft ['feːən–] fairy-like

das **Fege|feuer** purgatory

fegen sweep; (*v/i sn*) sweep, rush

die **Fehde, –n** feud; **der ~hand|schuh** (*in phrases*) gauntlet

fehl: ~ am Platz out of place

Fehl– wrong ...; false ...; faulty ...; incorrect ...; mis–;

~anzeige (F.! nothing doing); **f~besetzen** (*sep*) miscast; **der ~betrag, ⸚e** deficit; **die ~geburt, –en** miscarriage; **f~gehen*** (*sep; sn*) go wrong; be mistaken; *sp* go wide; **f~geschlagen** *p/part*; *also* abortive; **der ~griff, –e** mistake; **die ~konstruktion, –en** badly-designed article/structure *etc*; **die ~leistung, –en** slip, mistake (**Freudsche F.** Freudian slip); **f~leiten** (*sep*) misdirect; **f~schießen*** (*sep*) shoot wide; be wide of the mark; **der ~schlag, ⸚e** failure; **f~schlagen*** (*sep; sn*) (*see also* **f~geschlagen**) misfire, fail; **der ~schluß, ⸚(ss)e** wrong conclusion; **der**

~schuß, ⸚(ss)e miss; **der ~start, –s** false start; **der ~tritt, –e** false step; lapse; (sexual) indiscretion; **das ~urteil, –e** error of judgement; *leg* miscarriage of justice; **der ~versuch, –e** unsuccessful attempt; **die ~zündung, –en** backfire (**F. haben** backfire; *coll* get the wrong end of the stick)

fehlbar fallible; *Swiss* guilty of an offence

fehlen be absent; be lacking; be missing; *arch* do wrong; **mir fehlt ...** I lack ...; **... fehlt mir** I miss ...; **mir fehlen die Worte** words fail me; **das hat mir gerade noch gefehlt!** that's all I needed!; **mir fehlt etwas/nichts** there is something/nothing the matter with me; **was fehlt Ihnen?** what's the matter with you?; **es fehlte nicht viel, und ...** (he, they, *etc*) very nearly ...; **weit gefehlt!** far from it!

~ **an** (*dat*): **es fehlt an ...** there is a lack of ...; **es fehlt mir an ...** I lack ...; **an mir soll es nicht ~** I'll do my bit; **es ~ lassen an ...** lack ...; **es an nichts ~ lassen** spare no pains/expense

das **Fehlen** absence; lack

fehlend absent; missing

der **Fehler, –** mistake, error; fault (*also sp*); defect; **f~frei = f~los** perfect; faultless; **der ~punkt, –e** *sp* fault; **die ~quelle, –n** source of error

fehlerhaft faulty, defective

die **Feier, –n** ceremony; celebration; **der ~abend, –e** knocking-off time; leisure time (after work) (**F. machen** knock off; **nach F.** after work); **das ~abend|heim, –e** *EGer* old people's home; **die ~stunde, –n** ceremony; **der ~tag, –e** (public) holiday; **f~täglich** (mood *etc*) holiday; **f~tags** (**sonn- und f.** on Sundays and public holidays)

feierlich solemn; ceremonial; **das ist schon nicht mehr ~** *coll* it's beyond a joke

die **Feierlichkeit, –en** solemnity; ceremony; (*pl*) festivities, celebrations

feiern celebrate; fête; (*v/i*) *coll* stay off work; be laid off

feige cowardly

die **Feige, –n** fig; **das ~n|blatt, ⸚er** fig-leaf

die **Feigheit** cowardice

der **Feigling, –e** coward

feil–: ~bieten* (*sep*) offer for sale; **die F~späne** *pl* filings

die **Feile, –n** file

feilen file; **~ an** (*dat*) polish (style *etc*)

feilschen haggle (**um** over)

fein fine; choice; delicate; subtle; (hearing *etc*) acute; refined; elegant; *coll* nice and; **~ heraussein** be sitting pretty

Fein– fine ...; precision ...; **die ~bäckerei, –en** patisserie; **f~fühlig** sensitive; **das ~gefühl** sensitivity; tact; **der ~gehalt** standard (of purity); **f~körnig** fine-grained; **die ~kost, das ~kost|geschäft, –e** delicatessen; **f~machen** (*sep*): **sich f.** dress up; **die ~mechanik** precision engineering; **das ~meß|gerät, –e** precision instrument; **der ~schmecker, –** gourmet; **f~sinnig** sensitive

feind (*following dat*) hostile (to)

der **Feind, –e** enemy; **sich** *dat* **... zum ~ machen** make an enemy of || **f~selig** hostile; **die ~seligkeit, –en** hostility

feindlich hostile; *mil* enemy; **–feindlich** (*eg* **deutsch~**) anti– (German *etc*)

die **Feindlichkeit** hostility; **–feindlichkeit** (*eg* **die England~** Anglo) –phobia

die **Feindschaft, –en** enmity

die **Feinheit, –en** fineness; delicacy; subtlety; acuteness; refinement; elegance; (*pl*) finer points, subtleties

das **Feins|liebchen, –** *poet* sweetheart

feist fat

feixen *coll* smirk

das **Feld, –er** field (*also comput, mil, phys*); open country, fields; box (on form), *games* square, *her* field; *sp* field, pitch; (= all competitors) field; **das ~ behaupten** stand one's ground; **das ~ räumen** beat a retreat; (+*dat*) give way to; **ins ~ führen** advance (as argument); **zu ~e ziehen gegen** campaign against || **der ~bau** agriculture; **das ~bett, –en** camp-bed; **die ~blume, –n** wild flower; **die ~frucht, ⸚e** crop; **f~grau** field-grey; **der ~herr, –en** (*like* **Herr**) military commander; **das ~huhn, ⸚er** partridge; **der ~jäger, –** military policeman; **die ~lerche, –n** skylark; **der ~messer, –** surveyor; **der ~spat** felspar; **der ~stecher, –** field-glasses; **Feld-Wald-und-Wiesen–** *coll* run-of-the-mill ..., common-or-garden ...; **der ~webel, –** sergeant; (air force) sergeant, staff sergeant *US*; **der ~weg, –e** track through fields; **der ~zug, ⸚e** campaign

die **Felge, –n** (wheel) rim; *gym* circle

das **Fell, –e** skin; coat; fur; **ein dickes ~ haben** *coll* have a thick skin; (+*dat*) **das ~ über die Ohren ziehen** *coll* take for a ride

der **Fels, –en** (*wk masc*) rock; **der ~block, ⸚e** boulder; **der ~vorsprung, ⸚e** ledge; **die ~wand, ⸚e** rock face

der **Felsen, –** rock; cliff; **felsen|fest** unshakeable; (*adv*) firmly; absolutely; **das ~gebirge** the Rocky Mountains

felsig rocky

feminin feminine; effeminate

das **Femininum** [*also* –'niː–], **–(n)a** feminine (noun)

der **Feminismus** feminism

der **Feminist, –en** (*wk masc*), **die Feministin, –nen, feministisch** feminist

der **Fenchel** fennel

das **Fenster, –** window (*also comput*); **weg vom ~**

sein *coll* be out of the race; **das Geld zum ~ hinauswerfen** spend money like water || **die ~bank, ⸚e** window-sill; window-seat; **das ~brett, –er** window-sill; **der ~laden, ..läden** shutter; **das ~leder, –** shammy-leather; **der ~platz, ⸚e** window-seat; **der ~rahmen, –** window-frame; **die ~scheibe, –n** window-pane

fensterln *SGer*: **~ bei** pay a nocturnal visit to (one's sweetheart) by climbing through her bedroom window

–fenstrig with … windows

Ferial– *Aust* = **Ferien–**

die **Ferien** [–ĭən] *pl* holidays, vacation *US*; *parl* recess; **~ haben** be on holiday/vacation *US*; **~ machen** take a holiday/vacation *US*; **~ vom Ich** 'getting away from it all'

Ferien– holiday …, vacation … *US*

das **Ferkel, –** piglet; *coll* mucky pup

ferkeln (sow) litter; *coll* tell dirty jokes; *coll* make a mess

fern (*see also* **ferner**) far (away); remote; distant; (+*dat*) far from; **der F~e Osten** the Far East; **von ~(e)** from a distance

Fern– long-distance/range …; remote-control …;

f~bleiben* (*sep*; *sn*) stay away (*dat* from); **das ~bleiben** absence; **f~gelenkt** remote-controlled; **das ~gespräch, –e** long-distance call; **f~gesteuert** remote-controlled; **das ~glas, ⸚er** pair of binoculars; **f~halten*** (*sep*), **sich f.** keep away; **die ~heizung** district heating; **der ~kurs, –e** correspondence course; **die ~leihe** inter-library loan; **die ~lenkung** remote control; **die ~lenk|waffe, –n** guided missile; **das ~licht, –er** *mot* full beam, high beam *US*; **f~liegen*** (*sep*) (+*dat*) be far from (s.o.'s) mind; **~melde–** telecommunications …; **die ~melde|truppe, –n** signals corps; **das ~melde|wesen** telecommunications; **f~mündlich** telephone; (*adv*) by telephone; **Fẹrn|ọst–, fẹrn|ọ̈stlich** Far Eastern; **das ~rohr, –e** telescope; **~ruf …** telephone number …; **~schreib–** telex …; **das ~schreiben, –** telex (message); **der ~schreiber, –** teleprinter; telex; teleprinter/telex operator; **f~schriftlich** by telex; **~seh–** television …; **der ~seh|apparat, –e** television set; **f~sehen*** (*sep*) watch television; **das ~sehen** television (**im F.** on television); **der ~seher, –** viewer; television set; **~seh|funk** (**Deutscher F.** (*East*) German Broadcasting Corporation); **das ~seh|gerät, –e** television set; **die ~sicht** clear view; **~sprech–** telephone …; **das ~sprech|amt, ⸚er** telephone exchange; **der ~sprecher, –** (public) telephone; **die ~sprech|zelle, –n** telephone box/booth *US*; **f~stehen*** (*sep*) (+*dat*) not be close to; have no connection with; **f~steuern** (*sep*) operate by remote control; **die ~steuerung** remote control; **das ~studium** study by correspondence course; **die ~universität** *approx* = Open University; **das ~weh** longing for faraway places

die **Ferne** distance; **aus der ~** at/from a distance; **in der ~** in the distance; **in weiter ~ liegen** be a long way off/a long time ago

ferner (*comp of* **fern**) further; continued; (*adv*) further(more); (*continuation*) *conveyed by* … continue to …; **unter „~ liefen" rangieren** be among the also-rans || **~hin** = **~** (*adv*)

die **Ferse, –n** heel; (+*dat*) **auf den ~n bleiben** dog (s.o.'s) footsteps || **~n|geld** *coll* (**F. geben** take to one's heels)

fertig finished; ready; ready-made; accomplished; mature; *coll* worn out; (*with verb*) finish (+*ger*, *eg* **etw. ~ lesen** finish reading sth.); **–fertig** (*eg* **reise~**) ready to (depart *etc*), (*eg* **back~**) ready for (baking *etc*); **~ sein** have finished; be ready; **+mit** have finished; have finished with (person); **~ haben** have finished; **~ werden** be ready/finished; manage; **+mit** finish; cope with, handle; get over; **~!** *athl* set!; **(und damit) ~!** and that's that!

Fertig– finished …; ready-made …; *build* prefabricated …; **f~bekommen*** (*sep*) = **f~bringen*** (*sep*) get finished; manage; be (quite) capable of (**ich bringe es nicht fertig zu …** I cannot bring myself to …); **das ~gericht, –e** ready-to-serve meal; **f~kriegen** (*sep*) *coll* (= **f~bringen**); **f~machen** (*sep*) finish; get ready; *coll* do for; wear out; haul over the coals (**sich f.** get ready; *coll* wear oneself out); **f~stellen** (*sep*) complete; **die ~stellung** completion

fertigen produce, manufacture

die **Fertigkeit, –en** skill

die **Fertigung, –en** production, manufacture

das **fes, Fes** [–ɛ–] (*gen* –), – *mus* (the note) F flat; (*key*) **Fes** F flat major, **fes** F flat minor

der **Fes** [–eː–] (*gen* –(es)), –(e) fez

fesch *coll* smart; **sei ~ und …** *Aust* be a sport and …

der **Feschak** [–ak], –s *Aust coll* dandy

die **Fessel**[1], **–n** ankle; *zool* pastern

die **Fessel**[2], **–n** fetter, bond

der **Fessel|ballon, –s** captive balloon

fesseln bind; shackle; hold (attention); fascinate; **~ an** (*acc*) confine to; tie to; **~d** gripping, riveting

fest firm, (jelly *etc*) set; solid (*also phys*); tight; stout, sturdy; (health) robust; (sleep) sound; steady (*also fin*); regular; permanent; (income *etc*) fixed; (phrase) set; firm, definite; **–fest** -proof

das **Fest, –e** celebration; party; (religious) feast,

festival (*often referring specifically to Christmas, Easter, etc*)

Fest-[1] festival ...; festive ...; ceremonial ...;

Fest-[2] *esp comm* fixed ...; **(fest-)** *sep pref* ... tight(ly); ... firmly; ... down

der ~akt, -e ceremony; **f~angestellt** permanent; **f~binden*** (*sep*) tie up (**f. an** (*dat*) tie to); **f~bleiben*** (*sep*; *sn*) stand firm; **das ~essen, -** banquet; **f~fahren*** (*sep*; *sn if v/i*): **(sich) f.** get stuck; get bogged down; **f~fressen*** (*sep*): **sich f.** seize up; **f~frieren*** (*sep*; *sn*) freeze solid; **f~gefügt** firmly-established; **f~gewurzelt** (**wie f.** rooted to the spot); **die ~halle, -n** hall; ballroom; **f~halten*** (*sep*) hold onto; hold, detain; capture (atmosphere); record (**f. an** (*dat*) cling to; stick to; **sich f.** hold tight; **sich f. an** (*dat*) hold onto); **f~klammern** (*sep*): **sich f. an** (*dat*) cling tightly to; **der ~körper, -** *phys* solid; **das ~land, ⸚er** mainland; continent; **f~legen** (*sep*) fix; lay down; *fin* invest (on a long-term basis) (**f. auf** (*acc*) tie down to; **sich f.** commit oneself (**auf** *acc* to)); **f~lesen*** (*sep*): **sich f.** become engrossed in the book *etc* one is reading; **f~liegen*** (*sep*) be stuck, *naut* be aground; be fixed/established; **f~machen** (*sep*) fasten (**an** *dat* to); tie up; fix (date); (*v/i*) *naut* moor; **das ~mahl, -e** feast; **f~nageln** (*sep*) nail (down); *coll* nail down (**auf** *acc* to); **die ~nahme, -n, f~nehmen*** (*sep*) arrest; **der ~ordner, -** steward; **der ~punkt, -e** *comput, phys* fixed point; **die ~rede, -n** speech (on special occasion); **der ~redner, -** speaker (on special occasion); **der ~saal, ..säle** hall; ballroom; **f~schnallen** (*sep*) (= **anschnallen**); **f~schrauben** (*sep*) screw tight; **f~schreiben*** (*sep*) establish (by treaty *etc*); **die ~schrift, -en** commemorative volume; festschrift; **f~setzen** (*sep*) fix; lay down; detain (**sich f.** collect; take root; *coll* establish oneself); **die ~setzung, -en** *vbl noun*; *also* detention; **f~sitzen*** (*sep*) be tight; be firmly embedded, (dirt) be ingrained; be stuck; **das ~spiel, -e** festival play; (*pl*) festival; **f~stehen*** (*sep*) be fixed; be certain (**fest steht, daß ...** it is a fact that ...); **f~stehend** fixed; established; (phrase) set; **f~stellen** (*sep*) ascertain, establish; realize; detect; state (that ...); **die ~stellung, -en** establishment (of); statement; comment, remark (**die F. machen, daß ...** realize that ...; remark that ...); **der ~tag, -e** (public) holiday; **f~treten*** (*sep*) tread down; **f~umrissen** clear-cut; **f~verzinslich** fixed-interest; **die ~vorstellung, -en** gala performance; **die ~wiese, -n** fairground; **die ~woche, -n** festival week; (*pl*) festival; **f~ziehen*** (*sep*) pull tight; tighten; **der ~zug, ⸚e** procession

feste *coll* heartily; soundly; with a will

festigen consolidate; strengthen; **sich ~** become stronger

der **Festiger, -** setting-lotion

die **Festigkeit** strength; firmness

die **Festigung** consolidation; strengthening

festlich festive; **~ begehen** celebrate

die **Festlichkeit, -en** festive nature; festivity

die **Festung, -en** fortress; **der ~s|wall, ⸚e** rampart

die **Fete** [-ɛ:-, -e:-], **-n** *coll* party

der **Fetisch, -e** fetish

der **Fetischismus** fetishism

der **Fetischist, -en** (*wk masc*) fetishist

fett fat; (food) fatty; rich; *print* bold

das **Fett, -e** fat; grease; **sein ~ (ab)bekommen/(ab)kriegen** *coll* get what was coming to one; **sein ~ weghaben** *coll* have got what was coming to one || **f~arm** low-fat; **das ~auge, -n** speck of fat; **der ~fleck, -e** grease spot; **f~gedruckt** in bold type; **f~leibig** corpulent; **die ~leibigkeit** corpulence; **~näpfchen** *coll* (**ins F. treten** put one's foot in it); **die ~säure, -n** fatty acid (**mehrfach ungesättigte F.** polyunsaturated fatty acid); **die ~sucht** obesity; **der ~wanst, ⸚e** *coll* potbelly; 'fat pig'

fetten grease

fettig greasy; fatty

der **Fetzen, -** scrap; shred; wisp (of smoke *etc*); *Aust* cloth; (*pl*) rags; scraps, snatches; **..., daß die ~ fliegen** *coll* ... like blazes

feucht moist; damp; humid; **feucht|fröhlich** *coll* merry; **feucht|heiß** muggy; **feucht|kalt** cold and damp; clammy

die **Feuchtigkeit** moistness; dampness; humidity; moisture; damp; **die ~s|creme, -s** moisturizer

feudal feudal; *coll* grand

der **Feudalismus** feudalism

feudalistisch feudalistic

das **Feuer, -** fire; (Olympic) flame; (*no art*) a light (for cigarette *etc*); **~ und Flamme sein** be wildly enthusiastic; **das ~ einstellen** cease fire; **~ fangen** catch fire; *coll* become enthusiastic; fall for s.o.; **durchs ~ gehen für** go through fire and water for; **die Hand ins ~ legen für** stake one's life on; **mit dem ~ spielen** play with fire; **~!** fire! (*also mil*) || **die ~bestattung, -en** cremation; **~eifer** (**mit F.** with great enthusiasm); **f~fest** fire-proof; **der ~fresser, -** fire-eater; **f~gefährlich** inflammable; **der ~haken, -** poker; **der ~kopf, ⸚e** hot-head; **~land** Tierra del Fuego; **die ~leiter, -n** fire-escape; fireman's ladder; **die ~linie, -n** firing line; **der ~löscher, -** fire-extinguisher; **der ~melder, -** fire-alarm; **die ~probe, -n** (acid) test; *hist* ordeal by fire;

feuer|rot fiery (red); scarlet; **das ~schiff, –e** lightship; **f~sicher** fire-proof; **der ~stein, –e** flint; **die ~taufe, –n** baptism of fire; **die ~treppe, –n** fire-escape; **die ~wache, –n** fire-station; **die ~waffe, –n** firearm; **die ~wehr, –en** fire-brigade, fire department *US*; **das ~werk, –e** firework display; **der ~werks|körper, –** firework; **die ~zange, –n** fire tongs; **das ~zeug, –e** lighter; **das ~zeug|benzin** lighter fuel

feuern fire (boiler *etc*); *coll* hurl, *footb* slam; *coll* fire, sack; (*v/i*) *mil* fire (**auf** *acc* at); **~ mit** use (as fuel)

die **Feuerung, –en** *vbl noun*; *also* heating; fuel

das **Feuilleton** [fœjəˈtɔ̃ː], **–s** cultural section (of newspaper)

der **Feuilletonist** [fœjəto–], **–en** (*wk masc*) contributor to the *Feuilleton*

feuilletonistisch [fœjəto–] in *Feuilleton* style; superficial

feurig fiery

ff [ɛfˈʔɛf] *coll* first-class (*cf* **Effeff**)

ff. (= **folgende (Seiten)**) ff.

der **Fiaker, –** *Aust* hackney cab; cab-driver

das **Fiasko, –s** fiasco

die **Fibel**[1], **–n** primer

die **Fibel**[2], **–n** *archaeol* fibula

ficht *imp sing*, *3rd sing pres*, **fichtst** *2nd sing pres of* **fechten**

die **Fichte, –n** spruce

der **Fick, –s** *vulg*, **ficken** *vulg* (*also v/i*) fuck

fidel *coll* jolly

der **Fidibus** (*gen* **–(ses)**), **–se** spill

die **Fidschi|inseln** [ˈfɪdʒi–] *pl* the Fiji Islands

das **Fieber** temperature; fever; **~ haben** have a temperature || **das ~thermometer, –** (clinical) thermometer; **der ~wahn** delirium

fieberhaft feverish

fiebern be feverish; **~ nach** crave for; **~ vor** (*dat*) be in a fever of

fiebrig feverish

die **Fiedel, –n, fiedeln** fiddle

fiel *p/t of* **fallen**

fies *coll* nasty

fifty-fifty [ˈfɪftiˈfɪfti] *coll*: **~ machen** go fifty-fifty; **die Sache steht ~** it's a toss-up

der **Fight** [faet], **–s, fighten** *sp* fight

die **Figur, –en** figure (*also math*, *mus*, *sp*); *liter* character; *chess* piece

figurieren appear (in list *etc*)

figürlich figurative; *arts* depicting figures; (*adv*) as regards her *etc* figure

die **Fiktion, –en** fiction

fiktiv fictitious

das **Filet** [–ˈleː], **–s** fillet

Filial–: der ~leiter, – branch manager

die **Filiale, –n** *comm* branch

das **Filigran, –e** filigree

der **Film, –e** film (*also cin* (**nach** of), *phot*); **der ~** *collect* films, the cinema; **beim ~ sein** be in films; **zum ~ gehen** go into films

Film– film …, screen …; **die ~kunst** cinematic art; **die ~rolle, –n** *phot* roll of film; *cin* film part; **der ~star, –s** film star; **das ~theater, –** cinema, movie theater *US*

der **Filme|macher, –** film-maker

filmen (*also v/i*) film

filmisch cinematic

der **Filou** [–ˈluː], **–s** *coll* rogue

der **Filter, –** (*tech* **das**) filter; **der ~kaffee** filter coffee, drip coffee *US*; **die ~zigarette, –n** filter-tipped cigarette

filtern filter

filtrieren *esp tech* filter

der **Filz, –e** felt; *coll* felt hat; **der ~schreiber, – = der ~stift, –e** felt pen

filzen (*coll exc v/i*) frisk; search; (*v/i*) felt

filzig felt-like

die **Filzokratie, –(ie)n** *coll* power structure based on 'jobs for the boys'

der **Fimmel, –** *coll* mania; **einen ~ haben** be crazy

Final–: das ~produkt, –e *EGer* end product

das **Finale, –(s)** *mus* finale; *sp* final(s)

Finanz– … of finance; finance …; financial …; **das ~amt, ⸗er** tax office; **der ~be|amte** (*decl as adj*) revenue officer; **der ~mann, ..leute** financier; **das ~wesen** finance, financial system

die **Finanzen** *pl* finances

der **Finanzer, –** *Aust coll* customs official

finanziell financial

finanzieren finance

das **Findel|kind, –er** foundling

finden (*p/t* **fand** (*subj* **fände**), *p/part* **gefunden**) find; think (= consider); meet with (reception *etc*), receive (recognition *etc*), *or expressed by verb in passive* (*eg* **Verwendung ~** be used); (*v/i*) find one's/its way (to a place); **~ Sie nicht auch?** don't you agree?; **wie ~ Sie …?** what do you think of …?; how do you like …?; **ich finde nichts dabei** I see nothing wrong in that

sich ~ be found; occur; (*recip*) find one another; **sich ~ in** (*acc*) resign oneself to; **es findet/~ sich …** there is/are …; **es wird sich ~** it'll sort itself out

der **Finder, –** finder; **der ~lohn, ⸗e** reward

findig resourceful

der **Findling, –e** foundling; *geol* erratic (boulder)

die **Finesse, –n** finesse; (*usu pl*) trick; (technical) refinement

fing *p/t of* **fangen**

der **Finger, –** finger; **überall seine ~ im Spiel haben** *coll* have a finger in every pie; **keinen ~ rühren/krumm machen** *coll* not lift a finger; **krumme/lange ~ machen** *coll* be light-fingered; **die ~ lassen von** *coll* leave alone; **das kann man sich an den (fünf) ~n abzählen** *coll* that's plain to see; (+*dat*) **auf die ~ sehen** *coll* keep a sharp eye on; **sich** *dat* ... **aus den ~n saugen** invent, make up || **der ~abdruck, ⸚e** fingerprint; **der ~breit, –** finger's breadth; **f~fertig** nimble-fingered; **der ~hut, ⸚e** thimble; *bot* foxglove; **der ~nagel, ..nägel** fingernail; **der ~satz, ⸚e** fingering; **die ~spitze, –n** fingertip; **das ~spitzen|gefühl** sure instinct; sensitivity; **der ~zeig, –e** hint; sign

fingern (*coll exc* + **an**) 'swing'; **~ an** (*dat*) fiddle about with

fingieren feign; **fingiert** fictitious

das **Finish** ['fɪnɪʃ] (*gen* **–s**), **–s** *sp, tech* finish

der **Fink, –en** (*wk masc*) finch

der **Finne, –n** (*wk masc*) Finn

finnisch, (*language*) **F~** Finnish

Finnland Finland

finster dark; gloomy; sinister; grim; shady; (look) black; **~ anblicken** glower at; **im F~n** in the dark

die **Finsternis, –se** darkness; *astron* eclipse

die **Finte, –n** ruse; *sp* feint

der **Firlefanz, –e** *coll* frippery; fooling about

die **Firma, –(m)en** firm; (*in address*) Messrs

firmen *RC* confirm

Firmen– company ...; **das ~register, –** register of companies

firmieren: ~ unter (*dat*) trade under the name of

der **Firmling, –e** *RC* candidate for confirmation

die **Firmung, –en** *RC* confirmation

der **Firn, –e** firn, névé

der **Firnis, –se, firnissen** varnish

der **First, –e** ridge (of roof)

das **fis, Fis** [–ɪ–] (*gen* **–**), **–** *mus* (the note) F sharp; (*key*) **Fis** F sharp major, **fis** F sharp minor

der **Fisch, –e** fish; (*pl*) *astron, astrol* Pisces; *in compds also* fishing ...; fishy (smell *etc*); **der ~adler, –** osprey; **der ~dampfer, –** trawler; **der ~fang** fishing; **die ~gräte, –n** fish-bone; **das ~gräten|muster, –** herring-bone; **der ~händler, –** fishmonger, fish dealer *US*; **der ~otter, –** otter; **der ~reiher, –** heron; **das ~stäbchen, –** fish-finger, fishstick *US*; **die ~zucht** fish-farming; **der ~zug, ⸚e** catch, haul

fischen fish for; (*v/i*) fish; **nach Komplimenten ~** fish for compliments

der **Fischer, –** fisherman; *in compds* fishing ...

die **Fischerei** fishing; *in compds* fishing ...

fischig fishy

die **Fisimatenten** *pl coll* fuss; excuses

der **Fiskus** exchequer, treasury

die **Fisole, –n** *Aust* French bean

die **Fistel|stimme, –n** falsetto

fit [–ɪ–] fit; **sich ~ halten** keep fit

die **Fitness** (*also* **–ß**) [–nɛs] fitness

der **Fittich, –e** pinion; **unter seine ~e nehmen** *coll* take under one's wing

fix fixed; *Aust* permanent; *coll* quick; smart; **~e Idee** obsession; **~ und fertig** *coll* all finished/ready; all in, worn out; done for; **~ und fertig machen** *coll* wear out; finish || **der F~stern, –e** fixed star

fixen *coll* have a fix

der **Fixer, –** *coll* junkie

Fixier– *phot* fixing ...; **das ~mittel, –** fixative

fixieren decide on, fix; set down (in writing); fix one's gaze on; *phot* fix; **fixiert sein an** (*acc*)/**auf** (*acc*) have a fixation on

die **Fixierung, –en** *vbl noun*; *psych* fixation

das **Fixum, –(x)a** basic salary

FKK (= **Freikörperkultur;** *no art*) nudism; *in compds* (*eg* **der ~-Strand**) nudist ...

flach flat; low; shallow; **~fallen*** (*sep*; *sn*) *coll* not come off; **das F~land** plains; lowland; **der F~mann, ⸚er** *coll* hip-flask; **das F~relief, –s** bas-relief

die **Fläche, –n** area; surface; expanse; **der ~n|inhalt, –e** *math* area; **das ~n|maß** square measure

flächig (face) flat

der **Flachs** [–ks] flax; **f~blond** flaxen

flachsen [–ks–] *coll* kid; **~ mit** kid (on)

flackern flicker

der **Fladen, –** cow-pat; *esp SGer* flat round cake

Flagg–: das ~schiff, –e flagship

die **Flagge, –n** flag; **die ~ streichen** capitulate; **unter falscher ~ segeln** sail under false colours

flaggen fly a flag

das **Flair** [flɛːɐ] aura

die **Flak** [–a–], **–(s)** (= **Flugzeugabwehrkanone**) anti-aircraft gun/artillery; *in compds* anti-aircraft ...

der **Flakon** [–'kɔ̃ː], **–s** (*also* **das**) (perfume *etc*) bottle

flambieren *cul* flame; **flambiert** flambé

der **Flame, –n** (*wk masc*) Fleming

flämisch Flemish

die **Flamme, –n** flame; **in ~n stehen** be ablaze

Flammen–: das ~meer, –e sea of flames; **der ~werfer, –** flame-thrower

flammend blazing; fiery; **~ rot** flaming red

Flandern Flanders

flandrisch Flemish

der **Flanell, –e** flannel

der **Flaneur** [–'nøːɐ], **–e** stroller

flanieren (*sn if direction indicated*) stroll

die **Flanke, –n** side; flank (*also mil*); *sp* wing; (= pass) centre; *gym* flank

flanken *sp* centre

flankieren flank

der **Flansch, –e, flanschen** flange

der **Flaps, –e** *coll* young lout

flapsig *coll* loutish

die **Flasche, –n** bottle; *coll* dud; *in compds* **~n–** *also* bottled ...; **der ~n|öffner, –** bottle-opener; **die ~n|post** message in a bottle; **der ~n|zug, ⸚e** block and tackle

flatterhaft fickle

flattern (*sn if indicating direction*) flutter; flap its wings; (hands) shake; *coll* (wheels *etc*) wobble

flau slack (*also comm*); queasy; *phot* flat; **mir ist ~** I feel queasy

der **Flaum** down, fluff; (on peaches *etc*) bloom; **flaum|weich** as soft as down; *coll* (person) soft

flaumig downy; *Aust cul* light

der **Flausch, -e** *text* fleece

flauschig fleecy

die **Flausen** *pl coll* nonsense, foolish ideas; excuses

die **Flaute, -n** *naut* calm; *comm* lull, slack period

fläzen: sich ~ *coll* sprawl

Flecht:- das ~werk wicker-work

die **Flechte, -n** plait; *bot*, *med* lichen

flechten (flicht(st), *p/t* **flocht** (*subj* **flöchte),** *p/part* **geflochten)** weave; plait; **aufs Rad ~** *hist* break on the wheel

der **Fleck, -e(n)** spot, mark; stain; patch; *coll* spot, place; **blauer ~** bruise; **vom ~ weg** *coll* on the spot; **nicht vom ~ kommen** *coll* make no progress || **der ~entferner, -** spot-remover; **das ~fieber = der ~typhus** typhus fever

der **Flecken, -** small town; **= Fleck** (*exc coll*)

fleckig marked; stained; (face) blotchy

die **Fleder|maus, ⸚e** bat

der **Flegel, -** lout

die **Flegelei, -en** loutish behaviour

flegelhaft loutish

flegeln: sich ~ auf (*acc*) sprawl across

flehen: ~ um plead for; **~ zu** beseech

flehentlich pleading; **~e Bitte** entreaty

das **Fleisch** flesh; meat; **sich** *acc/dat* **ins eigene ~ schneiden** cut off one's nose to spite one's face; (+*dat*) **in ~ und Blut übergehen** become second nature to || **die ~brühe, -n** stock; beef-tea; **f~farben** flesh-coloured; **f~fressend** carnivorous; **der ~fresser, -** carnivore; **der ~hauer, -** *Aust* butcher; **die ~hauerei, -en** *Aust* butcher's (shop); **das ~klößchen, -** meat ball; **f~los** skinny; (diet) vegetarian; **der ~salat, -e** diced meat salad; **die ~töpfe** *pl* fleshpots; **die ~waren** *pl* meats; **die ~werdung** incarnation; **der ~wolf, ⸚e** mincer, meat grinder *US*; **die ~wurst, ⸚e** (*kind of pork sausage*)

der **Fleischer, -** butcher

die **Fleischerei, -en** butcher's (shop)

die **Fleisches|lust** lusts of the flesh

fleischig fleshy; meaty

fleischlich carnal

der **Fleiß** diligence, industry; hard work || **die ~arbeit, -en** task requiring great application; laborious task

fleißig industrious, hard-working; painstaking; *coll* (churchgoer *etc*) keen; (*adv*: work *etc*) hard

flektieren (*also v/i*) inflect

flennen *coll* blubber

fletschen bare (teeth)

flexibel flexible

die **Flexibilität** flexibility

die **Flexion, -en** inflection

flicht *imp sing, 3rd sing pres*, **flichtst** *2nd sing pres of* **flechten**

Flick-: die ~arbeit, -en mending; **der ~schuster, -** cobbler; **das ~werk** poor piece of work (that has merely been thrown together); **das ~wort, ⸚er** expletive (used to fill out a sentence); **das ~zeug** (puncture) repair kit; sewing kit

flicken mend; darn; patch

der **Flicken, -** patch

der **Flieder, -, f~farben** lilac; **der ~tee** elder-flower tea

die **Fliege, -n** fly; bow-tie

fliegen (*p/t* **flog** (*subj* **flöge),** *p/part* **geflogen)** (*sn if v/i*) fly; *coll* be thrown out/fired; **~ auf** (*acc*) *coll* go for; **~ durch** *coll* fail

Fliegen- fly ...; **die ~klappe, -n** fly-swatter; **der ~pilz, -e** fly agaric; **der ~schnäpper, -** flycatcher

der **Flieger, -** airman; (air force) aircraftman, airman basic *US*; *cycle rac* sprinter; *coll* plane; *in compds* flying ...; air ...; air force ...; aerial ...; **der ~alarm, -e** air-raid warning; **der ~horst, -e** (military) airfield, air base *US*

die **Fliegerei** flying

fliegerisch flying

Flieh-: die ~kraft, ⸚e centrifugal force

fliehen (*p/t* **floh** (*subj* **flöhe),** *p/part* **geflohen)** shun; (*v/i sn*) flee (**vor** *dat* from); **~d** (chin, forehead) receding

die **Fliese, -n** tile

Fließ-: das ~band, ⸚er assembly-line; **das ~heck, -e/-s** fastback; **das ~wasser** *Aust* running water

fließen (*p/t* **floß** (*subj* **flösse),** *p/part* **geflossen)** (*sn*) flow; (blood) be shed; **~d** *also* (water) running; fluent; fluid; **~d (Englisch** *etc*) **sprechen** speak fluent (English *etc*)

der **Flimmer** shimmer; **der ~kasten, ..kästen** *coll* **= die ~kiste, -n** *coll* 'the box', 'the tube' *US*

flimmern shimmer; *cin*, *TV* flicker; **es flimmert mir vor den Augen** everything is dancing before my eyes

flink nimble; quick

die **Flinte, -n** shotgun; **die ~ ins Korn werfen** throw in the sponge

der **Flipper, -** pinball machine

flippern *coll* play pinball

flirren whirr; shimmer

der **Flirt** [-œ-], **-s** flirtation

flirten [-œ-] flirt

das **Flittchen, -** *coll* floozy

[der] **Flitter, –** sequins; cheap finery; **die ~wochen** *pl* honeymoon

flittern glitter; *coll* honeymoon

flitzen (*sn*) *coll* dash; streak

[der] **Flitzer, –** *coll* nippy little car; streaker

floaten [–o:–], **~ lassen** *fin* float

flocht (flöchte) *p/t* (*subj*) *of* **flechten**

[die] **Flocke, –n** flake; flock (of wool)

flockig fluffy; flaky

flog (flöge) *p/t* (*subj*) *of* **fliegen**

floh (flöhe) *p/t* (*subj*) *of* **fliehen**

[der] **Floh, ⸚e** flea; (*pl*) *coll* 'dough'; **das ~(hüpf)-spiel, –e** tiddlywinks; **der ~markt, ⸚e** flea-market

flöhen rid of fleas; *coll* fleece

[der] **Flop** [–ɔ–], **–s** flop (*also athl*)

[der] **Flor**[1] mass of flowers; bevy; **in ~ stehen** be in full bloom

[der] **Flor**[2], **–e** crêpe; gauze; pile (of carpet)

[die] **Flora, –(r)en** flora

[der] **Florentiner, –** Florentine (*also cul*); picture hat

florentinisch Florentine

Florenz Florence

[das] **Florett, –e** *fenc* foil

florieren flourish

[die] **Floskel, –n** empty phrase

floskelhaft cliché-ridden

floß (flösse) *p/t* (*subj*) *of* **fließen**

[das] **Floß** [–o:–], **⸚e** raft; *fish* float

[die] **Flosse, –n** fin (*also aer, naut*); flipper (*also swim*); *coll* 'mitt'

flößen float (logs)

[die] **Flöte, –n** flute; *cards* flush

flöten (bird) warble; *coll* whistle; *coll* speak in honeyed tones; **~gehen*** (*sep*; *sn*) *coll* go west; **F~töne** *coll* ((+*dat*) **die F. beibringen** teach (s.o.) what's what)

[der] **Flötist, –en** (*wk masc*) flautist

flott afloat; *coll* smart; brisk; lively; (life) gay; **ein bißchen ~!** make it snappy! || **~bekommen*** (*sep*) = **~machen** (*sep*) refloat; *coll* get (car) on the road; get (firm) on its feet

[die] **Flotte, –n** fleet; *in compds* **~n–** naval ...

[die] **Flottille, –n** flotilla; **der ~n|admiral, –e** commodore

[das] **Flöz, –e** (coal) seam

[der] **Fluch** [–u:–], **⸚e** curse

fluchen [–u:–] swear; **~ auf** (*acc*)/**über** (*acc*) curse

[die] **Flucht**[1], **–en** row; suite (of rooms)

[die] **Flucht**[2] flight (**vor** *dat* from); escape; **die ~ ergreifen** take flight; **auf der ~** on the run (**vor** *dat* from); while trying to escape; **in die ~ schlagen** put to flight

Flucht–: f~artig hasty; **der ~punkt, –e** vanishing point

flüchten (*sn*) flee; escape (**vor** *dat* from); **sich ~** take refuge (somewhere)

flüchtig fleeting, brief; cursory; fugitive; *chem* volatile; **der/die Flüchtige** (*decl as adj*) fugitive

[der] **Flüchtigkeits|fehler, –** careless mistake

[der] **Flüchtling, –e** refugee

[der] **Flug, ⸚e** flight; *ski* jump; **(wie) im ~e vergehen** fly by

Flug– flight ...; flying ...; air ...; **~abwehr–** anti-aircraft ...; **die ~bahn, –en** flight path; trajectory; **der ~ball, ⸚e** high ball; volley; **der ~begleiter, –, die ~begleiterin, –nen** flight attendant; **das ~blatt, ⸚er** leaflet; **das ~boot, –e** flying boat; **der ~gast, ⸚e** (airline) passenger; **die ~gesellschaft, –en** airline; **der ~hafen, ..häfen** airport; **der ~kapitän, –e** captain (of aircraft); **der ~körper, –** missile; **der ~lotse, –n** (*wk masc*) air-traffic controller; **das ~objekt, –e (unbekanntes F.** unidentified flying object); **das ~personal** air-crew; **der ~plan, ⸚e** (airline) timetable; **der ~platz, ⸚e** airfield; **die ~post** *Aust* airmail; **der ~preis, –e** air fare; **die ~reise, –n** flight; **der ~sand** drifting sand; **der ~schein, –e** (airline) ticket; pilot's licence; **der ~schreiber, –** flight-recorder; **das ~ticket, –s** (airline) ticket; **das ~wesen** aviation; **das ~zeug, –e** aircraft; **der ~zeug|entführer, –** hijacker; **die ~zeug|entführung, –en** hijack; **der ~zeug|führer, –** pilot; **die ~zeug|halle, –n** hangar; **der ~zeug|träger, –** aircraft-carrier

[der] **Flügel, –** wing (*also archit, pol, sp*); leaf (of double-door *etc*); *mech* blade, (of windmill) sail; *mus* grand piano; **f~lahm** with an injured wing; feeble; **der ~schlag, ⸚e** beat of its wings; **die ~tür, –en** double-door

flügge fully-fledged; **~ werden** be able to fly; stand on one's own feet

flugs [–ʊ–] in great haste

[das] **Fluidum, –(d)a** aura; atmosphere

fluktuieren fluctuate

[die] **Flunder, –n** flounder

flunkern *coll* tell stories

[der] **Flunsch, –e** *coll* pout

[das] **Fluor** fluorine

[die] **Fluoreszenz** fluorescence

fluoreszieren fluoresce; **~d** fluorescent

[das] **Fluorid, –e** fluoride

[der] **Flur, –e** (entrance) hall; corridor

[die] **Flur, –en** open fields; *agr* farmland (belonging to community); **die ~bereinigung** redistribution of farmland

[der] **Fluß, ⸚(ss)e** river; flow; **in ~ bringen** get (sth.) going; **in ~ kommen** get going; **im ~** in a state of flux || **f~abwärts** downstream; **f~aufwärts** upstream; **das ~diagramm, –e** flow-chart; **das ~pferd, –e** hippopotamus; **der ~spat** fluorspar

flüssig liquid (*also fin*); molten; (style) fluent, fluid; **~/nicht ~ sein** *coll* be in/out of funds || **das F~gas, -e** liquid gas; **~machen** (*sep*) convert into cash; realize

^die^ **Flüssigkeit, -en** liquid; liquidity; fluidity; **das ~s|maß** liquid measure

Flüster-: ~stimme (mit F. in a whisper); **~ton (im F.** in a whisper); **die ~tüte, -n** *joc* megaphone

flüstern whisper

^die^ **Flut, -en** (high) tide; flood (of); (*pl*) waters; **die ~ tritt ein** the tide starts to come in || **die ~katastrophe, -n** flood disaster; **das ~licht** floodlight; **die ~welle, -n** tidal wave

fluten *naut* flood; (*v/i sn*) flood, pour

flutschen *coll* go well; (*sn*) slip (from hand)

focht (föchte) *p/t* (*subj*) *of* **fechten**

^die^ **Fock, -en** foresail; **der ~mast, -e(n)** foremast; **das ~segel, -** foresail

^der^ **Föderalismus** federalism

^der^ **Föderalist, -en** (*wk masc*), **föderalistisch** federalist

^die^ **Föderation, -en** federation

föderativ federal

föderiert federated

fohlen foal

^das^ **Fohlen, -** foal; colt; filly

^der^ **Föhn, -e** foehn (*hot, dry Alpine wind*)

^die^ **Föhre, -n** Scots pine

^die^ **Folge, -n** consequence; sequence (*also comput, math*); succession; series; issue (of journal); *rad, TV* instalment; (+*dat*) **~ leisten** comply with; accept; **in der ~** in future; subsequently; **in rascher ~** in rapid succession; **zur ~ haben** result in, lead to; **es hat zur ~, daß ...** the effect of it is that ... || **die ~erscheinung, -en** consequence; **f~richtig** logical; consistent; **das ~ton|horn, ⸚er** *Aust* (police *etc*) siren; **~zeit (in der F.** subsequently)

folgen (+*dat*) (*sn exc in 2nd sense*) follow; obey; **~ auf** (*acc*) follow; come after; **daraus folgt, daß ...** it follows that ...; **~des** the following

folgen-: ~reich with important consequences; **~schwer** with far-reaching consequences; momentous

folgender|maßen as follows

folgern: ~ aus conclude from

^die^ **Folgerung, -en** conclusion, inference

folglich consequently, therefore

folgsam obedient

^der^ **Foliant, -en** (*wk masc*) tome; folio

^die^ **Folie** [-lĭə], **-n** foil

^die^ **Folklore** [fɔlk'loːrə] folklore

folkloristisch [fɔlk-] folkloric; ethnic

^die^ **Folter, -n** torture; torment; *hist* rack; **auf die ~ spannen** keep on tenterhooks || **die ~bank, ⸚e** *hist* rack; **der ~knecht, -e** *hist* torturer; **die ~qual, -en** agony of torture; torment

foltern, die Folterung, -en torture; torment

^der^ **Fön, -e** (*trade-mark*) hair-dryer

^der^ **Fond** [fɔ̃ː], **-s** background; foundation; *mot* back

^der^ **Fondant** [fɔ̃'dãː], **-s** fondant

^der^ **Fonds** [fɔ̃ː] (*gen* - [-(s)]), - [-s] fund

fönen blow-dry

^die^ **Fontäne, -n** fountain

^der^ **Football** ['futbɔːl] American football, football *US*

foppen *coll* make a fool of

forcieren [-s-] force; speed up; **forciert** forced

Förder- *min, oil tech* production ...; *min* winding ...; **das ~band, ⸚er** conveyor-belt; **die ~klasse, -n** special class; remedial class; **der ~korb, ⸚e** pit cage; **der ~turm, ⸚e** winding-tower

^der^ **Förderer, -** patron; sponsor

förderlich beneficial; (*following dat*) beneficial (to); conducive (to)

fordern demand; claim; challenge; *leg* summon; *sp etc* stretch

fördern support; promote; encourage, foster; *min, oil tech* extract, produce

^die^ **Forderung, -en** *vbl noun*; *also* demand

^die^ **Förderung, -en** support; promotion; encouragement; *min, oil tech* extraction

^die^ **Forelle, -n** trout; **~ blau** poached trout

Foren *pl of* **Forum**

forensisch forensic

^die^ **Forke, -n** *NGer* pitchfork

^die^ **Form, -en** form (*also sp*); shape; mould, *cul* baking-tin; (*pl*) (female) curves; (social) conventions; manners; **feste ~ annehmen** take shape; **die ~ wahren** observe the proprieties; **der ~ halber/wegen** for form's sake; **in/nicht in ~** on/off form; **gut in ~** in good form; **in ~** (+*gen*) in the form of; **in aller ~** formally || **f~beständig** that retains its shape; **das ~blatt, ⸚er** form; **der ~fehler, -** breach of etiquette; irregularity; **die ~gebung** form; design; **die ~gestaltung** design; **f~los** shapeless; amorphous; informal; **die ~sache, -n** formality; **f~schön** elegant; **f~vollendet** perfectly shaped; perfect in form

formal formal; technical

^die^ **Formalität, -en** formality

^das^ **Format, -e** size; format; calibre, stature; *comput* format

^die^ **Formation, -en** formation; *geol* system

^die^ **Formel, -n** formula; form of words; **auf eine einfache ~ bringen** reduce to a simple formula || **~-1-** formula one ...

formelhaft stereotyped; (phrase) set

formell formal

formen form; shape; mould; **sich ~** be formed

Formen– ... of forms; **die ~lehre** morphology

formieren form; *mil* draw up; **sich ~** form up

-förmig -shaped

förmlich formal; positive, downright; (*adv*) positively; literally

die **Förmlichkeit, -en** formality

das **Formular, -e** form (*also comput*)

formulieren formulate; word

die **Formulierung, -en** formulation; wording

forsch brisk, vigorous; dashing

forschen do research; **~ nach** search for; **~d** searching

der **Forscher, –** research worker; scientist; scholar; explorer

die **Forschung, -en** research; (*pl*) research(es); **das ~s|gebiet, -e** field of research; **die ~s|reise, -n** expedition; **der/die ~s|reisende** (*decl as adj*) explorer

der **Forst, -e(n)** forest; **die ~wirtschaft** forestry

der **Förster, –** forest warden/ranger *US*

die **Forsythie** [-tsĭə], **-n** forsythia

fort away; gone; **in einem ~** continuously; **und so ~** and so forth

---

fort– *sep pref – general senses*:
(*i*) ... away (*eg* **~eilen** hurry away);
(*ii*) *indicates continuation* (*eg* **~wirken** continue to be felt, **~entwickeln** develop further)

---

fort|an henceforward

der **Fortbestand** continued existence

fortbestehen* continue in existence/to exist

fortbewegen, sich ~ move

fortbilden give (s.o.) further education/training; **sich ~** continue one's education/training

die **Fortbildung** further education/training

fortbleiben* (*sn*) stay away; **das Fortbleiben** absence

fortbringen* move; take away; *sp* get (ball) away

die **Fortdauer** continuance

fortdauern persist; go on; **~d** continuing; persistent

fortdürfen* be allowed to leave

fort|eilen (*sn*) hurry away

fort|entwickeln develop further; **sich ~** develop (further)

fortfahren* drive away; (*v/i, also sn*) continue; (*sn*) depart; drive away; **~ mit** (*also sn*) continue, carry on with

der **Fortfall** dropping (of); discontinuance

fortfallen* (*sn*) be dropped; be omitted; (doubts *etc*) disappear

fortführen continue, carry on; take away

die **Fortführung** *vbl noun*; *also* continuation

der **Fortgang** progress; departure; **seinen ~ nehmen** progress

fortgehen* (*sn*) leave; go on

fortgeschritten *p/part*; *also* advanced

fortgesetzt *p/part*; *also* continual

fortjagen chase away; throw out; (*v/i sn*) race off

fortkommen* (*sn*) get away; get on; get lost; **machen Sie, daß Sie ~!** get out of here!

das **Fortkommen** livelihood; progress; **sein ~ finden** make a living

fortkönnen* be able to get away

fortlassen* let go; leave out

fortlaufen* (*sn*) run away (*dat* from); continue; **~d** continuing; (*adv*) continually; (numbered) consecutively

fortleben live on

fortmüssen* have to leave

fortnehmen* take away; (+*dat*) take away from

fortpflanzen propagate; **sich ~** reproduce; *phys* travel

die **Fortpflanzung** reproduction; propagation; *in compds* **~s–** *also* reproductive ...

fortreißen* sweep away; (eloquence *etc*) carry away; (+*dat*) snatch away from; **sich ~ lassen von** be carried away by

Forts. (= **Fortsetzung**) cont.

der **Fortsatz, ⸚e** *anat*, *bot*, *zool* process

fortschaffen remove

fortscheren: sich ~ *coll* clear out

fortschicken send off; send away

fortschleppen drag off; **sich ~** drag oneself along; drag on; (error) be perpetuated

fortschreiben* extrapolate; continue (and update) (project *etc*); *admin* reassess (property value)

die **Fortschreibung, -en** extrapolation; continuation (and updating); *admin* reassessment (of property value)

fortschreiten* (*see also* **fortgeschritten**) (*sn*) advance; progress; (time) march on; **~d** progressive

der **Fortschritt, -e** advance; progress; (*pl*) progress (made); **(große) ~e machen** make (great) progress

fortschrittlich progressive

fortsetzen (*see also* **fortgesetzt**), **sich ~** continue; **„wird fortgesetzt"** 'to be continued'

die **Fortsetzung, -en** continuation; instalment; sequel; **„~ folgt"** 'to be continued' || **der ~s|roman, -e** serialized novel

fortstehlen*: sich ~ steal away

forttreiben* drive away; carry away; (*v/i sn*) drift away; **es so ~** carry on like that

fortwährend constant

fortwirken continue to have an effect/to be felt

fortwollen* want to get away

fortziehen* pull away; drag along; (*v/i sn*) move away

das **Forum, -(r)en** forum

fossil fossilized, (fuel) fossil
das **Fossil, –ien** [–Iən] fossil
das **Foto, –s** photo(graph); **Foto–** *see* **Photo–**
fotogen photogenic
der **Fötus** (*gen* **–(ses)**), **–se/Föten** foetus
die **Fotze, –n** *vulg* cunt
das **Foul** [–aʊ–], **–s, foulen** *sp* foul
der **Fox** (*gen* **–(es)**), **–e** (*also* **der ~terrier, –**) fox-terrier; (*also* **der ~trott, –e/–s**) fox-trot
das **Foyer** [fŏa'jeː], **–s** foyer, lobby
die **FPÖ = Freiheitliche Partei Österreichs**
Fr. = Frau, *Swiss* **Franken;** (**=Freitag**) Fri.
die **Fracht, –en** freight, *aer*, *naut* cargo, freight; (= charge) freight; carriage; **der ~brief, –e** consignment note; **f~frei** carriage paid; **das ~gut, ⸗er** freight; **der ~raum, ⸗e** hold; **das ~schiff, –e** freighter
der **Frachten|bahnhof, ⸗e** *Aust* goods station, freight station *US*
der **Frachter, –** freighter
der **Frack, ⸗e** tails; **das ~hemd, –en** dress-shirt; **„~zwang"** 'tails'
frag–: ~los undoubtedly; **~würdig** dubious; questionable
die **Frage, –n** question; matter; (+*dat*) **eine ~ stellen** put a question to; **das ist gar keine ~/steht außer ~** there's no doubt about it; **in ~ kommen** be possible/a possibility; be considered (for sth.); **nicht in ~ kommen** be out of the question; **in ~ stellen** (call in) question; (thing) jeopardize; **ohne ~** without question || **der ~bogen, –** questionnaire; **der ~satz, ⸗e** interrogative sentence/clause; **der ~steller, –** questioner; **die ~stellung, –en** formulation of a question; question; **die ~stunde, –n** *parl* question-time; **das ~zeichen, –** question-mark
fragen (*see also* **gefragt**) ask; **~ nach** ask about/for; ask (the way, time, s.o.'s name, *etc*); **nicht ~ nach** *also* not care about; **sich ~** wonder; **es fragt sich, ob ...** the question is whether ...; **~d** questioning
die **Fragerei** questioning, (tiresome) questions
fraglich doubtful; in question
das **Fragment, –e** fragment
fragmentarisch fragmentary
die **Fraktion, –en** *pol* (parliamentary) party; group; *chem* fraction; **der ~s|führer, –** party leader; **der ~s|zwang** three-line whip
die **Fraktur, –en** *med* fracture; *print* Gothic type; **~ reden mit** *coll* speak one's mind to
frank: ~ und frei frankly, openly
der **Franke, –n** (*wk masc*) Franconian; *hist* Frank
Franken Franconia
der **Franken, –** (Swiss) franc
frankieren put a stamp/stamps on
fränkisch Franconian; *hist* Frankish
franko post-paid; carriage paid; **der F~kanadier, –, ~kanadisch** French Canadian

Frankreich France
die **Franse, –n** (loose) thread; (*pl*) fringe
fransen fray
fransig frayed
Franz Francis; **der ~brannt|wein** alcoholic liniment
der **Franziskaner, –** Franciscan
Franziskaner– Franciscan ...
franzisko-josephinisch *Aust* of the reign of Emperor Franz Joseph (*1848–1916*)
der **Franzose, –n** (*wk masc*) Frenchman; monkey-wrench; **die ~n** the French
französieren gallicize
die **Französin, –nen** Frenchwoman
französisch, (*language*) **F~** French; **sich (auf) ~ empfehlen** take French leave; **französisch–** Franco–; (dictionary) French–
frappant = frappierend striking
die **Fräse, –n** milling/moulding cutter; *agr* rotary hoe
fräsen mill; mould (wood)
der **Fraß** [–aː–] (animals') food; *coll* 'muck'
fraß (fräße) *p/t* (*subj*) *of* **fressen**
fraternisieren fraternize
der **Fratz, –e(n)** *coll* (*usu* = girl) scamp; *esp SGer* brat
die **Fratze, –n** grimace; grotesque face; *coll* face; **~n schneiden/ziehen** make faces
fratzenhaft grotesque
die **Frau, –en** woman; wife; (*before surname*) Mrs *or* Ms, (*referring to unmarried woman*) Miss *or* Ms
das **Frauchen** [–ç–], **–** wifie; (dog's) mistress
Frauen– woman's ...; women's ...; female ...; **der ~arzt, ⸗e** gynaecologist; **die ~bewegung, –en** feminist movement; **die ~geschichten** *pl* amorous adventures; womanizing; **die ~heil|kunde** gynaecology; **der ~held, –en** (*wk masc*) lady-killer; **das ~kloster, ..klöster** convent; **die ~rechtlerin, –nen** feminist; **das ~zimmer, –** *coll* female
frauenhaft womanly
das **Fräulein –**/*coll* **–s** young lady; girl (working in shop *etc*); (*before surname*) Miss; **älteres ~** spinster; **~!** miss!; waitress!
fraulich womanly
frech cheeky, insolent; brazen; (clothes *etc*) saucy; **der F~dachs, –e** *coll* cheeky devil
die **Frechheit, –en** cheek, insolence; piece of impudence; insolent remark
die **Freesie** [–Iə], **–n** freesia
die **Fregatte, –n** frigate; **der ~n|kapitän, –e** commander
frei free (*also chem*, *phys*); vacant; open; freelance; (*adv*) freely; unaided; (speak) without notes; **–frei** –free; non–; **~ lassen** (*cf* **freilassen**) leave (space); leave blank/bare; **~ machen** (*cf* **freimachen**) bare; clear; vacate; **den Oberkörper ~**

machen strip to the waist; **sich ~ machen** take one's clothes off; +**von** rid oneself of; **~ werden** become free/vacant; *chem* be liberated; **im F~en** in the open, outdoors; **ins F~e** into the open, outdoors || **das F~bad, ⸚er** open-air swimming-pool; **~bekommen*** (*sep*) free (arm *etc*); get released; get (day *etc*) off; **~beruflich** freelance; **der F~betrag, ⸚e** (tax) allowance; **der F~beuter, –** freebooter; **der F~brief, –e** charter; carte blanche; licence; **der F~denker, –** freethinker; **die F~frau, –en** baroness; **die F~gabe** release; decontrol; passing; opening; *aer* clearance; *fin* floating; **~geben*** (*sep*) release; decontrol; (censor) pass; open (to traffic); *aer* clear; *fin* float; (*v/i*, +*dat*) give (s.o.) time off; **~gebig** generous; **die F~gebigkeit** generosity; **der F~geist, –er** freethinker; **~haben*** (*sep*) have off; (*v/i*) have a holiday; **der F~hafen ..häfen** free port; **~halten*** (*sep*) keep free/clear; keep (seat); pay for, treat; **~händig** freehand; with no hands; (shoot) without support; **~heraus** frankly; **der F~herr, –en** (*like* **Herr**) baron; **~herrlich** baronial; **~kaufen** (*sep*) buy (s.o.'s) freedom; **~kommen*** (*sep*; *sn*) get free; **das F~konzert, –e** *Swiss* open-air concert; **die F~körper|kultur (FKK)** nudism; **~lassen*** (*sep*) (*cf* **frei lassen** *at* **frei**) (set) free; **die F~lassung** release; **der F~lauf** free wheel; **~laufen*** (*sep*): **sich f.** *sp* move into an open space; **~lebend** living in the wild; **~legen** (*sep*) expose; **F~licht–** open-air ...; **das F~los, –e** free lottery ticket; *sp* bye; **~machen** (*sep*) (*cf* **frei machen** *at* **frei**) stamp; *coll* take (day *etc*) off (**sich f.** *coll* take time off); **die F~marke, –n** (postage) stamp; **der F~maurer, –** Freemason; **die F~maurerei** Freemasonry; **der F~mut** candour; **~mütig** candid; **~pressen** (*sep*) obtain (s.o.'s) release by means of threats; **~schaffend** freelance; **der F~schärler, –** *hist* franc-tireur; **~schwimmen*** (*sep*): **sich f.** pass one's (15 minute) swimming test; stand on one's own two feet; **~setzen** (*sep*) release (*also phys*); make redundant; **die F~setzung** release (*also phys*); making redundant; **~sprechen*** (*sep*) acquit (**von** of); **der F~spruch, ⸚e** acquittal; **~stehen*** (*sep*) stand empty (**es steht mir frei zu ... I** am at liberty to ...); **~stellen** (*sep*) release; exempt; (+*dat*) leave (up) to; **die F~stellung** release; exemption; **der F~stil** *swim*, *wrestl* free-style; **der F~stoß, ⸚e** free kick; **der F~tag, –e** Friday; **~tags** on Fridays; **der F~tod** suicide; **der F~umschlag, ⸚e** stamped envelope; **das F~wild** fair game; **~willig** voluntary; **der/die F~willige** (*decl as adj*) volunteer; **die F~zeit** leisure time; *eccles* retreat; **F~zeit–** leisure ...; casual ...; **die F~zeit|gestaltung** organization of one's leisure time; **~zügig** free to move; liberal; permissive; **die F~zügigkeit** freedom of movement; liberality; permissiveness

^der^ **Freier, –** suitor

^die^ **Freiheit, –en** freedom; liberty; **dichterische ~** poetic licence

freiheitlich free; liberal

Freiheits– ... of/for freedom/liberty; freedom ...; **die ~strafe, –n** prison sentence

freilich though; admittedly; **(ja) ~!** *SGer* certainly!

fremd foreign; strange, unfamiliar; someone else's; other people's; other; (help *etc*) outside; **–fremd** not belonging to ...; alien to ...; **~er Mann/~e Frau** stranger; **~e Leute** strangers; **unter ~em Namen** under an assumed name; **ich bin hier ~** I'm a stranger here; **~ tun** be distant; **der/die Fremde** (*decl as adj*) stranger; visitor (to a place) || **der F~arbeiter, –** *esp Swiss* foreign worker; **~artig** strange; **~gehen*** (*sep*; *sn*) *coll* be unfaithful; **die F~herrschaft** foreign rule; **der F~körper, –** foreign body; alien element; **~ländisch** foreign; **die F~sprache, –n** foreign language; **~sprachig** in/speaking a foreign language; **~sprachlich** foreign; (instruction) foreign-language; **das F~wort, ⸚er** foreign word (**... ist ein F. für ... ...** doesn't/don't know the meaning of the word ...)

^die^ **Fremde** (*cf* **die Fremde** *at* **fremd**) foreign parts

fremdeln (child) be shy

Fremden–: das ~bett, –en hotel bed; spare bed; **der ~führer, –** guide (= person or book); **das ~heim, –e** guest-house; **die ~legion** the Foreign Legion; **der ~legionär, –e** Foreign Legionnaire; **der ~verkehr** tourism; **~verkehrs–** tourist ...; **das ~zimmer, –** room (in inn *etc*); guest-room

^die^ **Fremdheit** strangeness, unfamiliarity

^der^ **Fremdling, –e** stranger

frenetisch frenetic, frenzied

frequentieren frequent

^die^ **Frequenz, –en** numbers (attending); volume of traffic; *phys* frequency; *med* rate

^das^ **Fresko, –(k)en** fresco

Freß– feeding ...; **die ~gier** voracity; **f~gierig** voracious; **der ~napf, ⸚e** feeding-bowl; **der ~sack, ⸚e** *coll* 'pig'

^die^ **Fressalien** [–ĭən] *pl coll* 'grub'

^die^ **Fresse, –n** *vulg* 'kisser'

fressen (*2nd/3rd sing pres* **frißt**, *p/t* **fraß** [–aː–] (*subj* **fräße**), *p/part* **gefressen**) (animal, *coll* person) eat, *coll* eat greedily; eat up (capital, petrol, *etc*), take up (time); (rust *etc*) eat away; **~ an** (*dat*) (grief *etc*) gnaw at; (+*dat*) **aus der Hand ~** eat out of (s.o.'s) hand; **sich satt ~** gorge oneself; **gefressen haben** *coll* have had just about enough of; have got the hang of; **zum Fressen gern haben** *coll* be crazy about

das **Fressen** *vbl noun*; *also* (animal's) food; *coll* 'grub'; **ein gefundenes ~ sein für** be just what (s.o.) wanted

das **Frettchen, –** ferret

freud–: ~los joyless

die **Freude, –n** joy; pleasure; **~ haben an** (*dat*) enjoy; (+*dat*) **eine ~ bereiten/machen** give (s.o.) pleasure; **mit ~n** gladly

Freuden– ... of joy; **das ~haus, ⸚er** *dated* brothel; **das ~mädchen, –** *dated* street-walker; **f~reich** joyful; **~sprung (einen F. machen** jump for joy)

freudig happy; joyful; (surprise) pleasant; (*adv*) *also* gladly; warmly; **–freudig** (*eg* **verantwortungs~**) willing to take (responsibility *etc*); (*eg* **experimentier~**) fond of (experimenting *etc*)

Freudsch (*see also* **Fehlleistung**) Freudian

freuen please; **es freut mich** I'm pleased; **freut mich (sehr)!** pleased to meet you!

sich ~ be pleased (**über** *acc* about); **sich ~ an** (*dat*) take pleasure in; **sich ~ auf** (*acc*) look forward to

der **Freund, –e** friend; boy-friend; lover (of music *etc*)

der **Freundes|kreis, –e** circle of friends

die **Freundin, –nen** (girl-)friend

freundlich friendly; kind; pleasant; **–freundlich** (*eg* **regierungs~, england~**) pro– (government, British, *etc*); (*eg* **haut~**) kind to (the skin *etc*); **freundlicher|weise** kindly

die **Freundlichkeit, –en** friendliness; kindness; pleasantness; (*pl*) kind remarks

die **Freundschaft, –en** friendship; **~ schließen mit** make friends with

freundschaftlich friendly

Freundschafts– ... of friendship; **der ~dienst, –e** good turn; **die ~inseln** *pl* the Friendly Islands; **das ~spiel, –e** *sp* friendly

der **Frevel, –** iniquity

frevelhaft iniquitous, wicked

freveln: ~ an (*dat*) sin against; **~ gegen** violate

der **Frevler, –** evil-doer

Frhr. = Freiherr

fried–: ~fertig peaceable; **der F~hof, ⸚e** cemetery; **~liebend** peace-loving; **~los** restless

der **Frieden** peace; **~ schließen** make peace; **im ~** in peacetime; **in ~ lassen** leave in peace

Friedens– peace ...; ... of (the) peace; peacetime ...; **der ~richter, –** magistrate; **der ~schluß, ⸚(ss)e** conclusion of a peace treaty; **der ~stifter, –** peacemaker

friedlich peaceful

Friedrich Frederick

frieren (*p/t* **fror** (*subj* **fröre**), *p/part* **gefroren**) be/feel cold, freeze; (*sn*) freeze; **es friert** it is freezing; there is a frost; **mich friert** I'm freezing

der **Fries, –e** *archit*, *text* frieze

der **Friese, –n** (*wk masc*), **friesisch** Frisian

frigid(e) frigid

die **Frigidität** frigidity

die **Frikadelle, –n** (meat) rissole

das **Frikassee, –s, frikassieren** fricassee

frisch fresh; lively; (shirt *etc*) clean; **~ gebacken** freshly baked; *coll* newly-married/qualified; **„~ gestrichen!"** 'wet paint'; **auf ~er Tat ertappen** catch red-handed; **von ~em** afresh || **die F~halte|packung, –en** vacuum pack (**in F.** vacuum-packed); **der F~käse** curd cheese; **~weg** straight out; without further ado

die **Frische** freshness; liveliness

der **Friseur** [–'zøːɐ], **–e** hairdresser; barber

die **Friseuse** [–'zøːzə], **–n** hairdresser

Frisier–: die ~haube, –n hairdryer (at hairdresser's); **der ~salon, –s** hairdressing salon; **der ~tisch, –e** dressing-table

frisieren do (s.o.'s hair); *coll* doctor; cook; *coll mot* soup up; **sich ~** do one's hair

friß *imp sing*, **frißt** *2nd/3rd sing pres of* **fressen**

die **Frist, –en** (limited) period; term; deadline; extension; **f~gerecht** within the prescribed period; **f~los** (dismissal) instant; (*adv*) without notice

fristen: sein Leben ~ eke out an existence

Fristen–: die ~lösung = die ~regelung legal termination of pregnancy within a specified period

die **Frisur, –en** hair-style

fritieren deep-fry

Fritz: der Alte ~ *coll* Frederick the Great

–fritze (*wk masc* **(–n)**, *in compds*) *coll* ... fellow

frivol frivolous; risqué

die **Frivolität, –en** frivolity; flippant/risqué remark

Frl. = Fräulein

froh cheerful, happy; glad; (news) happy; **~ um** *SGer* grateful for || **~gelaunt** cheerful; **~locken** (*insep*; *p/part* **~lockt**) rejoice (**über** *acc* at); gloat (over); **die F~natur, –en** cheerful soul; cheerful disposition; **der F~sinn** cheerfulness

fröhlich cheerful, happy; gay

die **Fröhlichkeit** cheerfulness, happiness; gaiety

fromm (*comp*, *superl also* ⸚) devout; pious; docile

die **Frömmelei, –en** sanctimoniousness

frömmeln affect piety; **~d** sanctimonious

die **Frömmigkeit** piety

der **Frömmler, –** sanctimonious person

die **Fron** drudgery; *hist* = **der ~dienst, –e** *hist* corvée; **~leichnam** (*no art*) Corpus Christi

fronen toil; *hist* labour for one's feudal lord

frönen (+*dat*) indulge; be a slave to

die **Front, –en** front (*also meteor, mil, pol*); **~ machen gegen** make a stand against; **in ~ gehen/liegen** *sp* go into/be in the lead || **der ~soldat, –en** (*wk masc*) front-line soldier

frontal frontal; head-on; **der F~zusammenstoß, ⸚e** head-on collision

fror (fröre) *p/t* (*subj*) *of* **frieren**

der **Frosch, ⸚e** frog; firecracker; **sei kein ~!** don't be a spoilsport! || **der ~laich** frog-spawn; **der ~mann, ⸚er** frogman; **die ~perspektive, –n** worm's eye view (**aus der F. sehen** have a worm's eye view of; have a blinkered view of); **der ~schenkel, –** frog's leg; **der ~wechsel, –** about-turn

der **Frost, ⸚e** frost; *med* shivering; **der ~aufbruch, ⸚e** frost damage (to road); **die ~beule, –n** chilblain; **das ~schutz|mittel, –** anti-freeze

frösteln shiver; **mich fröstelt** I shiver

frostig frosty

das **Frottee** (*also* **der**) terry towelling; **das ~(hand)tuch, ⸚er** terry towel

Frottier–: das ~(hand)tuch, ⸚er terry towel

frottieren rub down

frotzeln *coll* tease

die **Frucht, ⸚e** fruit; *biol* foetus; **der ~becher, –** fruit sundae; **f~bringend** fruitful; **das ~fleisch** flesh (of fruit); **die ~folge, –n** rotation of crops; **f~los** fruitless; **der ~saft, ⸚e** fruit-juice; **der ~wechsel, –** rotation of crops

fruchtbar fertile; fruitful

die **Fruchtbarkeit** fertility; fruitfulness

das **Früchtchen, –** *coll* good-for-nothing

fruchten: wenig/nicht(s) ~ have little/no effect

früh (*see also* **früher**) early; (*adv*) early; early on; at an early age; **gestern/heute/morgen ~** yesterday/this/tomorrow morning; **Donnerstag** *etc* **~** on Thursday *etc* morning; **von ~ an** from an early age; **von ~ bis spät** from morning till night; **zu ~ kommen** be early || **~auf** (**von f.** from an early age); **der F~aufsteher, –** early riser; **die F~geburt, –en** premature birth/baby; **das F~jahr** spring; **der F~jahrs|putz, –e** spring-cleaning; **~morgens** early in the morning; **die F~pensionierung, –en** early retirement; **~reif** precocious; physically mature at an early age; *agr, hort* early; **die F~reife** precocity; early physical maturity; *agr, hort* early ripening; **der F~schoppen, –** morning drink; **der F~start, –s** false start; **das F~stück, –e** breakfast (**zweites F.** mid-morning snack); **~stücken** (*insep*) breakfast; **der F~stücks|speck** streaky bacon; **das F~warn|system, –e** early warning system; **die F~zeit** early days/period; **~zeitig** (*also adv*) early

Frühe: in aller ~ bright and early; **in der ~** *SGer* in the morning

früher (*comp of* **früh**) earlier; former; (*adv*) earlier; formerly, at one time, *or conveyed by* … used to …; **~ oder später** sooner or later

frühestens at the earliest

der **Frühling, –e** spring

der **Frust** *coll* frustration

die **Frustration, –en** frustration

frustrieren frustrate

der **Fuchs** [–ks], **⸚e** fox (*also* = crafty person); chestnut (horse); tortoiseshell (butterfly); *univ* first-year member of a *Verbindung*; *coll* redhead; **wo sich** *dat* **die Füchse/wo sich** *dat* **Hase und Fuchs gute Nacht sagen** in the middle of nowhere || **der F~schwanz, ⸚e** fox's tail; handsaw; *bot* love-lies-bleeding; **fuchs|teufels|wild** *coll* hopping mad

fuchsen [–ks–] *coll* rile

die **Fuchsie** [–ksĭə], **–n** fuchsia

fuchsig ginger; *coll* furious

die **Füchsin** [–ks–], **–nen** vixen

Fuchtel: unter jmds. ~ under s.o.'s thumb

fuchteln: ~ mit *coll* wave about

fuchtig *coll* furious

das **Fuder, –** cart-load; tun

der **Fudschijama** (*gen* **–s**) Fujiyama

Fug: mit ~ und Recht with good reason

die **Fuge**[1], **–n** joint; gap, crack; **aus den ~n gehen/geraten** fall apart; **in allen ~n krachen** creak at the joints

die **Fuge**[2], **–n** *mus* fugue

fugen joint

fügen formulate; (fate *etc*) ordain; **~ an** (*acc*) join to; **~ in** (*acc*) fit into; **fest gefügt** solidly built; firmly established

sich ~ submit; (+*dat*) submit to; comply with; **sich ~ in** (*acc*) bow to; **es fügte sich, daß …** it so happened that …

fügsam compliant

die **Fügung, –en** act of providence; *gramm* construction; **glückliche ~** stroke of luck

fühlbar perceptible; noticeable; **sich ~ machen** make itself felt

fühlen (*also v/i*) feel; **~ nach** feel for; **sich ~** feel (sad *etc*); **sich ~ als** feel oneself to be; **der fühlt sich aber!** he really fancies himself

der **Fühler, –** feeler; horn (of snail); **seine ~ ausstrecken** put out feelers

die **Fühlung, ~ nehmen mit** contact; **die ~nahme** (establishing) contact

fuhr (führe) *p/t* (*subj*) *of* **fahren**

Fuhr–: der ~mann, ⸚er/..leute carter; **der ~park, –s** fleet (of vehicles); **das ~unter-**

nehmen, – haulage firm; **das ~werk, –e** cart; **f~werken** (*insep*) *coll* bustle about

[die] **Fuhre, –n** (cart-)load

führen lead; take; (pipe) carry; wield; run (firm *etc*); hold, conduct; lead (life); keep (diary, list, *etc*); bear (title); *comm* stock; *admin* drive, *aer* pilot; (*v/i*) lead; go, (pipeline *etc*) run; *sp* (be in the) lead; **bei/mit sich ~** carry with one; **~ durch** show round; *TV* host; **~ über** (*acc*) cross; **~ zu** raise to (lips); (*v/i*) lead to

sich ~ conduct oneself

führend leading

[der] **Führer, –** leader; guide (*also* = book); **der ~schein, –** driving licence, driver's license *US*; **der ~stand, ⁼e** driver's cab

[die] **Führung, –en** *vbl noun*; *also* leadership, *mil* command; management; guidance; leadership, leaders; (guided) tour (**durch** of); conduct; *sp etc* lead; **in ~ gehen/liegen** go into/be in the lead; **unter der ~** (+*gen*) under the leadership/direction/*mil* command of || **die ~s|kraft, ⁼e** executive; **die ~s|spitze, –n** leadership; top management; **der ~s|stab, ⁼e** top management; *mil* command; **das ~s|tor, –e** goal that puts a team in the lead; **das (polizeiliche) ~s|zeugnis, –se** police certificate of conduct (giving particulars of any offences committed)

Füll– filling ...; **der ~feder|halter, –** fountain-pen; **das ~gewicht** net weight; **das ~horn, ⁼er** cornucopia; **das ~wort, ⁼er** expletive (used to fill out a sentence)

[die] **Fülle** fullness; profusion; host (of); plumpness

füllen (*see also* **gefüllt**) fill; *cul* stuff; **~ in** (*acc*) pour into; put into; **sich ~** fill; fill up

[das] **Füllen, –** foal

[der] **Füller, –** fountain-pen

füllig plump

[das] **Füllsel, –** filler; padding

[die] **Füllung, –en** *vbl noun*; *also* filling; stuffing (*also cul*); centre (of chocolate); panel (of door)

fulminant brilliant

[der] **Fummel, –** *coll* cheap dress

fummeln *coll* fumble; (sexually) 'grope'; *footb* dribble for too long; **~ an** (*dat*) fiddle about with

[der] **Fund, –e** find; discovery; **einen ~ machen** make a find || **das ~amt, ⁼er = das ~büro, –s** lost-property office, lost and found office *US*; **der ~gegenstand, ⁼e** object found; *archaeol* find; **die ~grube, –n** treasure-house (of art *etc*); mine (of information); **der ~ort, –e** place where an object is found; **die ~sache, –n** object found; (*pl*) lost property

[das] **Fundament, –e** foundation(s); *mech* base

fundamental fundamental

fundamentieren lay the foundations of

fundieren underpin; **(gut) fundiert** sound; **schlecht fundiert** unsound

fündig: ~ werden make a strike; strike lucky

[der] **Fundus, –** fund (*gen*/**an** *dat*/**von** of); *theat* equipment

fünf five; **~ gerade sein lassen** *coll* stretch a point; **die Fünf, –en** five (*also = fifth grade* – **'mangelhaft'** – *in marking scale*) || **das F~eck, –e** pentagon; **~eckig** pentagonal; **der F~jahres|plan, ⁼e** five-year plan; **~jährlich** quinquennial; **der F~kampf, ⁼e** pentathlon; **die F~tage|woche, –n** five-day week

[der] **Fünfer, –** *coll* five-pfennig piece

[der] **Fünfling, –e** quintuplet

fünft: zu ~ (*see* **zu** 1 (*i*)); **fünft..** fifth

fünftel: ein ~ ... a fifth of a ...

[das] **Fünftel, –** fifth

fünftens fifthly

fünfzehnt.., das Fünfzehntel, – fifteenth

fünfzig fifty

fünfziger: die ~ Jahre the fifties; **der Fünfziger, –** man in his fifties; *coll* fifty-pfennig piece

fünfzigst.., das Fünfzigstel, – fiftieth

fungieren: ~ als act as

[der] **Funk** radio; **das ~meß|gerät, –e** radar equipment; **das ~sprech|gerät, –e** radio telephone; walkie-talkie; **der ~spruch, ⁼e** radio message; **die ~streife, –n** police radio patrol; **der ~streifen|wagen, –** squad car; **das ~taxi, –s** radio cab; **die ~verbindung, –en** radio contact

[der] **Funke** (*acc*, *dat* **–n**, *gen* **–ns**), **–n** spark

funkel–: funkel|nagel|neu brand-new

funkeln sparkle; (star) twinkle; (eyes) twinkle, (with anger) flash

funken radio; (*v/i*) give off sparks, spark; *coll* work; **es hat bei ... gefunkt** *coll* ... has *etc* got the message

[der] **Funken, –** spark; **f~sprühend** emitting sparks; (wit) sparkling; **die ~strecke, –n** spark-gap

[der] **Funker, –** radio operator

[die] **Funktion, –en** function (*also comput*, *math*); **in ~ treten** begin to function; come into operation

[der] **Funktionär, –e** functionary

funktionell functional; *comput* logic(al)

funktionieren function; work

[die] **Funktions|störung, –en** *med* malfunction

[die] **Funzel, –n** *coll* feeble lamp

für (+*acc*) for (*also* = considering); in exchange for; in favour of; (closed, receptive, *etc*) to; (typical *etc*) of; (*indicating significance to s.o., sth.*) to (*eg* insult, value to; **~ norddeutsche Ohren** to North German ears); (step *etc*) by (step *etc*), (evening *etc*) after (evening *etc*); **~ sich** on one's own; ... **hat etwas/viel ~ sich** there's something/a lot to be said for ...; **was ~ ...** (*see* **was**); **das Für und Wider** the pros and cons

fürbaß *arch* on(wards)

die **Fürbitte, -n** intercession

die **Furche, -n, furchen** furrow; rut

die **Furcht** fear (**vor** *dat* of); **f~los** fearless

furchtbar terrible

fürchten fear; **~ für/um** fear for; **sich ~ vor** (*dat*) be afraid of

fürchterlich terrible

furchtsam timid

für|einander for each other

die **Furie** [-ĭə], **-n** *myth* fury

furios impassioned; terrific

das **Furnier, -e, furnieren** veneer

Furore: ~ machen cause a sensation

fürs = für das

die **Fürsorge** care; welfare services/work; *coll* social security

der **Fürsorger, -** welfare worker

fürsorglich solicitous

die **Fürsprache** [-a:-] recommendation; **~ einlegen für** speak on (s.o.'s) behalf (**bei** to)

der **Fürsprecher, -** person who speaks on s.o.'s behalf

der **Fürst, -en** (*wk masc*) prince (= ruler; *also as title conferred, eg* **~ Bismarck**)

das **Fürstentum, ¨-er** principality

die **Fürstin, -nen** princess (= wife of a prince); (female) ruler

fürstlich princely; prince's; sumptuous

die **Furt, -en** ford

der **Furunkel, -** (*also* **das**) boil

fürwahr *arch* truly

das **Fürwort, ¨-er** pronoun

der **Furz, ¨-e** *vulg*, **furzen** *vulg* fart

der **Fusel, -** *coll* rotgut

der **Füsilier, -e** *hist or Swiss* fusilier

die **Fusion, -en** amalgamation, *comm* merger; *biol, phys* fusion

fusionieren amalgamate, *comm* merge; *biol, phys* fuse

der **Fuß** [-u:-], **¨-e**/(*following num*) **-** foot; base; leg (of table *etc*); **kalte Füße bekommen/kriegen** *coll* get cold feet; **(festen) ~ fassen** gain a (firm) foothold; settle down

in prepositional phrases:

auf: (+*dat*) **auf dem ~e folgen** follow hard on (s.o.'s) heels; (event *etc*) follow on the heels of; **auf (gutem** *etc*) **~(e) stehen mit** be on (good *etc*) terms with; **auf eigenen Füßen stehen** stand on one's own two feet; **auf freiem ~** at liberty; **auf freien ~ setzen** set free; **auf großem ~(e) leben** live in great style; **immer auf die Füße fallen** always land on one's feet

bei ~! heel!

mit dem linken ~ zuerst aufstehen *coll* get out of bed on the wrong side; **mit Füßen treten** walk all over (person); trample on (rights *etc*)

zu ~ on foot; **gut zu ~ sein** be a good walker; (+*dat*) **zu Füßen** at (s.o.'s) feet

Fuß-: der ~abtreter, - door-mat; **die ~angel, -n** man-trap; trap; **der ~ball, ¨-e** football (= soccer, ball used); **der ~ball|spieler, -** footballer; **die ~bank, ¨-e** footstool; **der ~boden, ..böden** floor; **die ~boden|heizung, -en** underfloor heating; **der ~breit** (*in idioms*) inch; **die ~bremse, -n** foot-brake; **das ~ende, -n** foot (of bed); **~fall (einen F. machen vor** (*dat*) prostrate oneself before); **der ~gänger, -** pedestrian; **der ~gänger|streifen, -** *Swiss* = **der ~gänger|überweg, -e** pedestrian crossing, crosswalk *US*; **die ~gänger|zone, -n** pedestrian precinct; **der ~geher, -** *Aust* pedestrian; **f~hoch** ankle-deep; **f~krank** footsore; **die ~kranken** *pl* weaker members *etc*; **die ~leiste, -n** skirting, baseboard *US*; **die ~note, -n** footnote; **die ~pflege** chiropody; **der ~pfleger, -** chiropodist; **die ~spur, -en** footprint; **der ~stapfen, -** footprint (**in jmds. F. treten** follow in s.o.'s footsteps); **die ~taste, -n** pedal; **der ~tritt, -e** kick; **das ~volk** rank and file; **der ~weg, -e** footpath

die **Fussel, -n** (*also* **der**, *pl* **-(n)**) piece of fluff

fusselig *coll* covered with fluff; **sich** *dat* **den Mund ~ reden** talk till one is blue in the face

fusseln *coll* shed fluff

füßeln play footsie

fußen: ~ auf (*dat*) be based on

-füßig -footed

futsch *coll* gone; kaput

das **Futter**[1] feed; fodder; **gut im ~** well-fed

das **Futter**[2], **-** lining

Futter-: die ~krippe, -n manger; **der ~napf, ¨-e** (feeding-)bowl; **der ~neid** jealousy; **der ~sack, ¨-e** nosebag; **der ~stoff, -e** lining (material); **der ~trog, ¨-e** feeding-trough

das **Futteral, -e** case

futtern *coll* eat (heartily)

füttern[1] feed

füttern[2] line (garment *etc*)

das **Futur, -e** future (tense)

futuristisch futuristic

G

das **G** [ge:] (*gen*, *pl* –, *coll* [ge:s]) G; **das g, G** *mus* (the note) G; (*key*) **G** G major, **g** G minor

g = **Gramm,** *Aust* **Groschen**

gab (gäbe) *p/t* (*subj*) *of* **geben**

die **Gabe, –n** gift (*also* = talent); *med* dose

die **Gabel, –n** fork; *agr* pitchfork; *tel* cradle; **der ~bissen, –** canapé; fillet of pickled herring; **das ~frühstück, –e** buffet lunch; **der ~stapler, –** fork-lift truck

gabeln: sich ~ fork

die **Gabelung, –en** fork (in road *etc*)

gackern cackle

die **Gaffel, –n** *naut* gaff

gaffen gape

der **Gag** [gɛk], **–s** gimmick

der **Gagat, –e** jet

die **Gage** [–ʒə], **–n** (artist's) fee

gähnen yawn

die **Gala** evening/*mil* full dress; *in compds* formal …; evening …

galaktisch galactic

der **Galan, –e, galant** gallant

die **Galanterie, –(ie)n** gallantry (towards ladies)

die **Galaxie, –(ie)n** galaxy

der **Gäle, –n** (*wk masc*) Gael

die **Galeere, –n** *hist* galley

die **Galerie, –(ie)n** *archit*, *art* gallery

der **Galgen, –** gallows; *cin*, *TV* boom; **die ~frist, –en** respite; **der ~humor** gallows humour; **der ~strick, –e = der ~vogel, ..vögel** gallows bird

die **Galions|figur, –en** figure-head

gälisch Gaelic

die **Galle, –n** bile; gall; = **die ~n|blase, –n** gall-bladder; **der ~n|stein, –e** gall-stone

das **Gallert, –e = die Gallerte, –n** jelly

Gallien [–ĭən], **der Gallier** [–ĭɐ], **–** Gaul

gallig gall-like; (person, face, *etc*) sour

gallisch Gallic

der **Gallizismus, –(m)en** Gallicism

der **Galopp, –s/–e** gallop; **im ~** at a gallop; *coll* at top speed

galoppieren (*also sn*; *if indicating direction*, *only sn*) gallop; **~d** *econ* galloping

galt (gälte) *p/t* (*subj*) *of* **gelten**

galvanisieren electroplate

die **Gamasche, –n** gaiter; spat

gammeln *coll* loaf about

der **Gammler, –** beatnik

der **Gams|bart, ⸚e** tuft of chamois hair

gang: ~ und gäbe quite usual

der **Gang, ⸚e** gait, walk; errand; walk, stroll; course (of events *etc*, *cul* of meal); operation (of machine); passage; corridor; gangway, aisle; *mech* gear; *tech* thread (of screw); *anat* duct; *min* vein; *comput* cycle; *sp* bout; heat; **einen schweren ~ tun müssen** face a difficult task; **im ~(e)** under way; afoot; **in ~** in operation; **in ~ bringen/halten** get/keep going; **in ~ kommen** get going || **die ~art, –en** gait; **die ~schaltung, –en** gear-change, gearshift *US*; gears

gangbar passable; practicable

Gängel|band: am ~ führen/halten keep tied to one's apron-strings

gängeln treat like a child; keep tied to one's apron-strings

der **Ganges** ['gaŋgɛs, 'gaŋəs] (*gen* –) the Ganges

gängig current; *comm* in demand; **–gängig** *mech* -gear; -speed; *cul* -course

der **Gangster** ['gɛŋstɐ], **–** gangster

die **Gangway** ['gɛŋwe:], **–s** *naut* gangway; *aer* steps

der **Ganove, –n** (*wk masc*) *coll* crook

die **Gans, ⸚e** goose; *in compds SGer* = **Gänse–**

Gänse–: das ~blümchen, – daisy; **der ~braten, –** roast goose; **die ~füßchen** *pl coll* quotation marks; **die ~haut** goose-pimples; **das ~klein** goose giblets; **die ~leber|pastete, –n** pâté de foie gras; **~marsch (im G.** in single file)

der **Gänserich, –e** gander

ganz whole, entire; all (*eg* **das ~e Geld** all the money); quite (*eg* **eine ~e Menge** quite a lot); *coll* (*foll. by num*) all of; *coll* intact; in one piece; (*indecl*, *with geog names*) all; (*adv*) quite (*also in relative sense*, *eg* **~ nett** quite nice); completely; very, really; right (at the top *etc*); **~ und gar** completely; **~ und gar nicht** not at all; **~ wie** just as/like; **wieder ~ machen** *coll* mend; **durch/in ~ (Südafrika** *etc*) all over (South Africa *etc*); **~ (Aufmerksamkeit** *etc*) **sein** be all (attention *etc*); **ein Ganzes** (*decl as adj*) a whole; **das G~e** the whole thing; **als G~es** as a whole; **aufs G~e gehen** *coll* go all out/the whole hog; **im ~en** all told; in bulk; = **im großen (und) ~en** on the whole || **die G~aufnahme, –n** *phot* full-length portrait; **G~leder (in G.** leather-bound); **G~leinen**

(in G. cloth-bound); ~**seitig** full-page; ~**tägig** all-day; full-time; (*adv*) = ~**tags** all day; full-time; **die G~tags|schule, –n** all-day school

Gänze *esp Aust*: **zur ~** completely

die **Ganzheit** entirety; totality

ganzheitlich that treats sth. as a totality; (*adv*: view *etc*) in its entirety

die **Ganzheits|medizin** holistic medicine

gänzlich completely

gar[1] *cul* done; *SGer* used up

gar[2] even; (*with neg*) at all; ~ **zu** all too

Gar–: ~**aus** *coll* ((+*dat*) **den G. machen** do in; put an end to); **die ~küche, –n** (cheap) eating-house

Gär– fermenting ...

die **Garage** [–ʒə], **–n** garage

garagieren [–ʒ–] *Aust, Swiss* park (in garage)

der **Garant, –en** (*wk masc*) guarantor

die **Garantie, –(ie)n** guarantee; **der ~schein, –e** guarantee (certificate)

garantieren guarantee; ~ **für** vouch for, guarantee; **garantiert** guaranteed; (*adv*) *coll* definitely

die **Garbe, –n** sheaf; *mil* burst (of fire)

die **Garçonnière** [–'nĭɛːrə], **–n** *Aust* one-room flat/apartment *US*

die **Garde, –n** (body)guard (of monarch); **die ~** the Guards; **die alte ~** the old guard

die **Garderobe, –n** wardrobe (= stock of clothes); hall-stand; cloakroom, check room *US*; *theat* dressing-room; **die ~n|marke, –n** *approx* = cloakroom ticket, coat/hat check *US*

die **Garderobiere, –n** cloakroom attendant; *theat* wardrobe mistress

die **Gardine, –n** curtain; **die ~n|predigt, –en** *coll* telling-off; **die ~n|stange, –n** curtain-rod

der **Gardist, –en** (*wk masc*) guardsman

garen cook

gären (*p/t* **gärte/gor** (*subj* **gärte/göre**), *p/part* **gegärt/gegoren;** *in fig sense weak*) (*also sn*: wine *etc*) ferment; **(Wut** *etc*) **gärt in** (*dat*) ... is *etc* seething with (anger *etc*); **es gärt in** (*dat*) (population *etc*) is in a state of ferment; (s.o.'s) mind is in a turmoil

das **Garn, –e** yarn; thread; net

die **Garnele, –n** prawn; shrimp

garnieren decorate; *cul* garnish

die **Garnison, –en** garrison

die **Garnitur, –en** trimming; set; **erste/zweite ~ sein** *coll* be top-notch/second-rate

garstig nasty, horrid

der **Garten,** *pl* **Gärten** garden; **die ~arbeit** gardening; **der ~bau** horticulture; **das ~fest, –e** garden-party; **das ~lokal, –e** open-air café/restaurant; beer-garden; **die ~schere, –n** pruning-shears; **das ~zentrum, –(r)en** garden centre; **der ~zwerg, –e** garden gnome

der **Gärtner, –** gardener

die **Gärtnerei, –en** nursery; market garden, truck farm *US*; horticulture

gärtnerisch gardening; horticultural

die **Gärung** fermentation; ferment, unrest

das **Gas, –e** gas; ~ **geben** step on the gas || **der ~behälter, –** gasometer; **g~förmig** gaseous; **der ~hebel, –** accelerator; **die ~kammer, –n** gas-chamber; **die ~leitung, –en** gas main; **das ~pedal, –e** accelerator; **der ~zähler, –** gas meter

der **Gasa|streifen** the Gaza Strip

die **Gascogne** [–'kɔnjə] Gascony

die **Gasse, –n** alley, lane; passage (formed); *SGer* street; **der ~n|hauer, –** popular song; **der ~n|junge, –n** (*wk masc*) street-urchin

Gassi *coll*: ~ **gehen** go walkies

der **Gast, ⸚e** guest; visitor; customer; **zu ~ sein bei** be (s.o.'s) guest; **zu ~ bitten** invite || **der ~arbeiter, –** foreign worker; **g~frei** = **g~freundlich** hospitable; **die ~freundlichkeit** = **die ~freundschaft** hospitality; **der ~geber, –** host; **die ~geberin, –nen** hostess; **das ~haus, ⸚er** = **der ~hof, ⸚e** inn; **das ~land, ⸚er** host country; **der ~professor, –en** visiting professor; **das ~recht** right to hospitality; **das ~spiel, –e** guest performance; *sp* away match; **die ~stätte, –n** restaurant (serving food and drink); **die ~stube, –n** dining-room (in inn); **der ~wirt, –e** landlord; **die ~wirtschaft, –en** inn

Gäste– guests' ...; guest ...; **das ~buch, ⸚er** visitors' book

gastieren make a guest appearance

gastlich hospitable

die **Gastlichkeit** hospitality

die **Gastritis** [–ɪs] gastritis

der **Gastronom, –en** (*wk masc*) restaurateur

die **Gastronomie** catering trade; gastronomy

gastronomisch gastronomic

der **Gatte, –n** (*wk masc*) (*respectfully referring to s.o. else's*) husband; (*pl*) husband and wife; **die ~n|liebe** conjugal love

das **Gatter, –** gate (*also comput*); grating; *sp* fence

die **Gattin, –nen** (*respectfully referring to s.o. else's*) wife

die **Gattung, –en** kind, type; *bot, zool* genus; *arts* genre; **der ~s|begriff, –e** generic concept/term

der **Gau, –e** *hist* district; **der ~leiter, –** *Nazi* gauleiter

die **Gaudi** *SGer coll* fun

Gaukel–: das ~spiel, –e deception

die **Gaukelei, –en** deception; (*pl*) antics

gaukeln (*also sn*) *poet* flutter

der **Gaukler, –** conjuror; trickster

der **Gaul, ⸚e** old nag; **einem geschenkten ~ sieht man nicht ins Maul** don't look a gift-horse in the mouth

der **Gaumen, –** palate; **der ~laut, –e** palatal; **das ~segel, –** velum

der **Gauner, –** rogue; crook; **die ~sprache** underworld slang

die **Gaunerei, –en** swindle; swindling

die **Gavotte, –n** gavotte

die **Gaze** [–zə], **–n** gauze

die **Gazelle, –n** gazelle

---

ge– *insep pref* (*unstressed*): *usually indicates a past participle, but is sometimes part of the verb itself* (*eg* **gehören, gelingen**);

Ge– *noun pref*: (*i*) *prefixed to verb-stems* (*sometimes with the addition of final* **–e**) *to denote a continual activity or repeated action, often with a pejorative overtone*, *eg* **das Gebrüll** roaring, bellowing (**brüllen** = roar, bellow), **das Gegacker** (constant) cackling, cackle (**gackern** = cackle), **das Gesinge** (irksome) singing (**singen** = sing); *where such words are not given in the dictionary, see the translation*(*s*) *of the verb concerned and add* –ing; (*ii*) *prefixed to certain nouns* (*with ablaut or umlaut where possible*) *to form collective nouns*, *eg* **das Gebirge** mountains, mountain range (**Berg** = mountain), **das Gefieder** plumage (**Feder** = feather), **das Gehörn** antlers (**Horn** = horn), **das Gerippe** skeleton (**Rippe** = rib)

---

der **Ge|ächtete** (*fem* **die ~**) (*decl as adj*) outlaw; outcast

das **Ge|ächze** groaning

das **Ge|äder** veins; vein-like pattern

ge|ädert veined

ge|artet of a (certain) nature; **gut ~** good-natured; **... ist so ~, daß ...** it's (his *etc*) nature to ...; the nature of (the problem *etc*) is such that ...

das **Ge|äst** branches

geb. (= **geboren**) born, (= **geborene**) née; (= **gebunden**) bound

das **Gebäck** biscuits, cookies *US*; pastries

gebacken *p/part of* **backen**

das **Gebälk** timber-work

geballt *p/part*; *also* concentrated

gebannt *p/part*; **(wie) ~** spellbound

gebar (**gebäre**) *p/t* (*subj*) *of* **gebären**

Gebär–: die ~klinik, –en *Aust* maternity hospital; **die ~mutter, ..mütter** womb; **der ~mutter|hals, ¨–e** cervix

die **Gebärde, –n** gesture

gebärden: sich ~ behave

Gebärden–: das ~spiel gestures; **die ~sprache** sign-language

das **Gebaren** conduct

gebären (*p/t* **gebar** (*subj* **gebäre**), *p/part* **geboren**) (*see also* **geboren**) give birth to; (+*dat*) bear (s.o. a child); **geboren werden** be born; **ich bin (1982** *etc*) **geboren I** was born in (1982 *etc*)

das **Gebäude, –** building; structure

gebe|freudig generous

die **Gebeine** *pl* bones

das **Gebell(e)** barking

geben (**gib(s)t,** *p/t* **gab** (*subj* **gäbe**), *p/part* **gegeben**) give; perform; teach (subject); set (example); (tree *etc*) provide (shade), (cow, stove, *etc*) produce; (= amount to) make; (*v/i*) *cards* deal; *sp* serve; **es jmdm. ~** *coll* let s.o. have it; **es gibt** there is/are/will be; **was gibt's?** what's up?; **was gibt's zum (Mittagessen** *etc*)? what's for (lunch *etc*)?; **das gibt's nicht!** there's no such thing!; that's out of the question!; **..., da gibt's (gar) nichts** *coll* ... and no mistake; **gegeben werden** be on (at theatre *etc*); **sich** *dat* **... ~ lassen** ask for

auf (*acc*): **viel/wenig ~ auf** set great/little store by

von sich ~ utter; *coll* bring up (food)

sich ~ behave; (pain) pass; **sich ~ als** pass oneself off as

das **Gebet, –e** prayer; **ins ~ nehmen** *coll* take to task

gebeten *p/part of* **bitten**

die **Gebets|mühle, –n** prayer-wheel

gebeugt *p/part*; *also* stooping

das **Gebiet, –e** territory; area, region; sphere, field; **auf (wirtschaftlichem** *etc*) **~** in the (economic *etc*) field

gebieten* (*see also* **geboten**) command; (situation *etc*) demand; **~ über** (*acc*) rule over; have at one's disposal

der **Gebieter, –** master; ruler

gebieterisch imperious

Gebiets– territorial ...; regional ...

das **Gebilde, –** structure; formation; creation; figment

gebildet *p/part*; *also* educated; cultured, cultivated

das **Gebimmel** *coll* ringing

das **Gebinde, –** spray (of flowers); *text* skein

das **Gebirge, –** mountains; mountain range

gebirgig mountainous

Gebirgs– mountain ...; **der ~zug, ¨–e** mountain range

das **Gebiß, –(ss)e** (set of) teeth; dentures; bit

gebissen *p/part of* **beißen**

das **Gebläse, –** *tech* blower

geblasen *p/part of* **blasen**

geblieben *p/part of* **bleiben**

das **Geblök(e)** bleating

geblumt *Aust*, **geblümt** flowery

gebogen *p/part of* **biegen**

geboren *p/part of* **gebären;** born; (*eg* **~er Pole** Polish) by birth; **~e ...** née ...

geborgen *p/part of* **bergen;** *also* secure, safe (**vor** *dat* from) die **Geborgenheit** security

geborsten *p/part of* **bersten**

das **Gebot, -e** command; precept; dictates; bid; *bibl* commandment; (+*dat*) **zu ~(e) stehen** be at (s.o.'s) disposal

geboten *p/part of* **bieten, gebieten;** *also* necessary; due

Gebr. (= **Gebrüder**) Bros.

gebracht *p/part of* **bringen**

gebrannt *p/part of* **brennen**

gebraten *p/part of* **braten**

das **Gebräu, -e** brew

der **Gebrauch, ¨e** use; usage; custom; **~ machen von** make use of; **außer ~ kommen** fall into disuse; **im/in ~** in use

gebrauchen (*see also* **gebraucht**) use; **ich könnte … ~** I could do with; **zu nichts zu ~** useless

gebräuchlich usual, customary; (word) in current use

Gebrauchs– utility …; **die ~anweisung, -en** instructions (for use); **der ~artikel, -** article for everyday use; **g~fertig** ready for use; **der ~gegenstand, ¨e** article for everyday use; **die ~graphik** commercial art; **der ~graphiker, -** commercial artist; **die ~güter** *pl* consumer durables; **der ~wert, -e** utility value

gebraucht *p/part of* **brauchen, gebrauchen;** *also* second-hand, used; **der G~wagen, -** used car

gebrechen*: es gebricht mir an (*dat*) **I** lack

das **Gebrechen, -** infirmity

gebrechlich infirm; frail

gebrochen *p/part of* **brechen, gebrechen; ~ (Türkisch** *etc*) **sprechen** speak broken (Turkish *etc*)

die **Gebrüder** *pl comm* … Brothers

das **Gebrüll** roaring; bellowing

das **Gebrumm(e)** hum(ming); droning; growling

gebückt *p/part*; *also* stooping

die **Gebühr, -en** charge; fee; **nach ~** appropriately; **über ~** unduly; **zu ermäßigter ~** at a reduced rate

gebühren (+*dat*) be (s.o.'s) due; **sich ~** be fitting; **~d** due; proper

gebühren–: ~frei free of charge; **~pflichtig** for which a charge is made

gebührend due; proper

gebunden *p/part of* **binden;** *also* (price) fixed; *phys* latent; **~e Rede** verse

die **Geburt, -en** birth; **von ~** by birth; **das war eine schwere ~** *coll* that took some doing || **die ~en|kontrolle = die ~en|regelung** birth-control; **der ~en|rückgang, ¨e** drop in the birth-rate; **g~en|schwach** with a low birth-rate; **g~en|stark** with a high birth-rate; **die ~en|ziffer, -n** birth-rate

gebürtig: ~er (Ungar *etc*) (Hungarian *etc*) -born

Geburts– birth …; … of birth; native …; **das ~datum, -(t)en** date of birth; **der ~fehler, -** congenital defect; **das ~haus, ¨er** birthplace; **der ~helfer, -** obstetrician; **die ~helferin, -nen** obstetrician; midwife; **die ~hilfe** assistance at a birth; obstetrics; **der ~ort, -e** birthplace; **der ~tag, -e** birthday; date of birth (**ich habe G.** it's my birthday); **das ~tags|kind, -er** person whose birthday it is; **die ~urkunde, -n** birth certificate

das **Gebüsch, -e** bushes; undergrowth

der **Geck, -en** (*wk masc*) fop

geckenhaft foppish

gedacht *p/part of* **denken, gedenken;** *also* imaginary

das **Gedächtnis, -se** memory (*also comput*); **aus dem ~** from memory; **sich** *dat* **… ins ~ (zurück)rufen** call to mind; **zum ~ an** (*acc*) in memory of

Gedächtnis– memorial …; commemorative …; **der ~schwund** amnesia

gedämpft *p/part*; *also* (colours, light) subdued; (sound) muffled, (music) soft; **mit ~er Stimme** in a low voice

der **Gedanke** (*acc, dat* **-n**, *gen* **-ns**), **-n** idea; thought; **sich** *dat* **~n machen über** (*acc*) think about; worry about; **in ~n** lost in thought; (do) without thinking; in one's thoughts; **kein ~ (daran)!** not likely!

Gedanken– … of ideas/thought; **die ~freiheit** freedom of thought; **der ~gang, ¨e** train of thought; **das ~gut** (body of) ideas; **der ~leser, -** mind-reader; **g~los** unthinking; absent-minded; **der ~sprung, ¨e** mental leap; **der ~strich, -e** dash; **die ~übertragung** telepathy; **die ~verbindung, -en** association of ideas; **g~verloren** lost in thought; **g~voll** thoughtful; **die ~welt, -en** world of ideas/thought

gedanklich intellectual; of thought

die **Gedärme** *pl* intestines

das **Gedeck, -e** place (at table); set meal

gedeckt *p/part*; *also* (colours) subdued

Gedeih: auf ~ und Verderb for good or ill; (+*dat*) **auf ~ und Verderb ausgeliefert** completely at (s.o.'s) mercy

gedeihen (*p/t* **gedieh**, *p/part* **gediehen**) (*sn*) thrive, flourish; progress; **das Gedeihen** success

gedeihlich beneficial

Gedenk– commemorative …; memorial …; **die ~feier, -n** commemoration; **der ~tag, -e** commemoration day

gedenken* intend (to); (+*gen*) think of, remember; **das Gedenken** memory, remembrance

das **Gedicht, -e** poem; **… ist ein ~** *coll* … is heavenly

gediegen pure; solid; sound; *coll* odd

gedieh(en) *p/t* (*p/part*) *of* **gedeihen**

gedient *p/part*; **~er Soldat** man who has completed his military service
das **Gedränge** pushing; crowd; mêlée; **ins ~ kommen** get into difficulties; be pressed for time
gedrängt *p/part*; *also* compact; **~ voll** packed
gedrechselt [-ks-] *p/part*; *also* stilted
das **Gedröhn(e)** droning; booming
gedroschen *p/part of* **dreschen**
gedrückt *p/part*; *also* depressed
gedrungen *p/part of* **dringen;** *also* stocky
die **Geduld** patience
gedulden: sich ~ be patient
geduldig patient
Gedulds-: ~faden *coll* (**mir reißt der G.** my patience is exhausted); **die ~probe, -n** trial of patience; **das ~spiel, -e** puzzle
gedungen *p/part of* **dingen**
gedunsen bloated
gedurft *p/part of* **dürfen**
ge|ehrt *p/part*; **Sehr ~er Herr ...(!)/~e Frau ...(!)/~es Fräulein ...(!)** Dear Mr ... /Mrs ... /Miss ...; **Sehr ~e Herren(!)** Dear Sirs
ge|eicht *p/part*; **~ auf** (*acc*) expert in
ge|eignet *p/part*; *also* suitable
die **Geest, -en** sandy upland (on North Sea Coast)
gefächert diversified
die **Gefahr, -en** danger; risk; **~ laufen zu ...** run the risk of (+*ger*); **auf eigene ~** at one's own risk || **g~los** safe; **g~voll** dangerous
gefährden endanger; jeopardize; **gefährdet** *also* at risk
gefahren *p/part of* **fahren**
Gefahren- danger ...; **die ~quelle, -n** source of danger; **die ~zulage, -n** danger-money
gefährlich dangerous; unsafe; hazardous; **das ist nicht so ~** *coll* it's nothing to worry about
das **Gefährt, -e** conveyance
der **Gefährte, -n** (*wk masc*) companion
Gefall-: die ~sucht craving for admiration; **g~süchtig** craving admiration
das **Gefälle, -** slope; difference
gefallen[1]* (+*dat*) please; *usu expressed – with ind obj becoming subj – by* like (*eg* **das Bild gefällt mir** I like the picture, **er gefiel ihr** she liked him); **sich** *dat* **in einer Rolle ~** fancy oneself in a role; **sich** *dat* **... ~ lassen** put up with; **sich** *dat* **nichts ~ lassen** not put up with any nonsense; **das lasse ich mir ~!** that's just the job!
gefallen[2] *p/part of* **fallen, gefallen**
das **Gefallen** pleasure; **~ finden an** (*dat*) take pleasure in; take a liking to
der **Gefallen, -** favour; (+*dat*) **zu ~** to please
das **Gefallenen|denkmal, ⸚er** war memorial
gefällig pleasant; obliging; **... ~?** would you like (some) ...?; **hier ist was ~** *coll* things are getting lively; **~st** (*irritated*) would you mind ...?
die **Gefälligkeit, -en** favour; pleasantness; helpfulness
gefäll(s)t (*2nd,*) *3rd sing pres of* **gefallen**
gefangen *p/part of* **fangen;** *also* captured; captivated; **sich ~ geben** surrender; **der/die Gefangene** (*decl as adj*) prisoner || **~halten*** (*sep*) keep prisoner; keep in captivity; hold enthralled; **die G~nahme** capture; **~nehmen*** (*sep*) take prisoner; captivate
die **Gefangenschaft** captivity
das **Gefängnis, -se** prison; imprisonment; **die ~strafe, -n** prison sentence
gefärbt *p/part*; *also* biased
das **Gefasel** drivel
das **Gefäß, -e** vessel (*also anat*); container; *in compds med* vascular ...
gefaßt *p/part*; *also* composed; **~ auf** (*acc*) prepared for; **sich ~ machen auf** (*acc*) prepare oneself for
die **Gefaßtheit** composure
das **Gefecht, -e** battle; *fenc* bout; **außer ~ setzen** put out of action; **ins ~ führen** advance (as argument); **im Eifer des ~s** in the heat of the moment || **der ~s|kopf, ⸚e** warhead
gefedert sprung
gefeit: ~ gegen immune to
das **Gefieder, -** plumage
gefiedert feathered
die **Gefilde** *pl poet* fields
gefinkelt *Aust coll* crafty
das **Geflecht, -e** wicker-work; tangle; network
gefleckt spotted; speckled
geflissentlich studiously
geflochten *p/part of* **flechten**
geflogen *p/part of* **fliegen**
geflohen *p/part of* **fliehen**
geflossen *p/part of* **fließen**
das **Geflügel** poultry
geflügelt winged; **~es Wort** well-known quotation
das **Geflüster** whispering
gefochten *p/part of* **fechten**
das **Gefolge** retinue; **im ~** (+*gen*) in the wake of; **im ~ haben** bring in its train
die **Gefolgschaft, -en** allegiance; followers, following; *Nazi* work-force
gefragt *p/part*; *also* in demand
gefräßig voracious
der **Gefreite** (*decl as adj*) (army) lance-corporal, private 1st class *US*; (navy) ordinary seaman, seaman apprentice *US*; (air force) aircraftman, airman basic *US*
gefressen *p/part of* **fressen**
Gefrier- freezing ...; frozen ...; **das ~fach, ⸚er** freezing compartment; **der ~punkt, -e** freezing-point; **g~trocknen** (*usu infin and p/part* **g~getrocknet**) freeze-dry; **die ~truhe, -n** deep freeze
gefrieren* (*sn*) freeze

gefroren *p/part of* **frieren, gefrieren; das Gefrorene** (*decl as adj*) *SGer* ice-cream

^das **Gefüge, –** structure

gefügig compliant, submissive

^das **Gefühl, -e** feeling (**für** of); sense (of); **das höchste der ~e** *coll* the utmost; **im ~ haben** know instinctively; **mit gemischten ~en** with mixed feelings || **g~los** insensitive; unfeeling; numb; **g~voll** sensitive; (poem *etc*) sentimental

Gefühls– ... of emotion/the emotions; emotional ...; *anat* sensory ...; **g~arm** lacking in feeling; **g~betont** emotional; emotive (*also ling*); **die ~duselei** mawkishness; **g~duselig** *coll* mawkish; **g~geladen** emotionally-charged; **g~kalt** unfeeling; frigid; **das ~leben** emotional life; emotions; **g~mäßig** emotional, based on feeling; **der ~mensch, -en** (*wk masc*) emotional person; **der ~wert** sentimental value

gefüllt *p/part*; *also* stuffed; with a filling/soft centre

gefunden *p/part of* **finden**

gegangen *p/part of* **gehen**

gegeben *p/part of* **geben;** given (*also math*); **das ~e** the obvious thing (to do); **im ~en Fall** if the occasion should arise; **zu ~er Zeit** in due course || **~en|falls** if the occasion should arise; if necessary

^die **Gegebenheiten** *pl* circumstances; facts

gegen (+*acc*) against, *leg*, *sp* versus; (medicine) for; towards (midday *etc*, *SGer also* a place); (in exchange) for; compared with; (*of time, quantity*) about; **~ ... hin** towards

Gegen– counter–; opposite ...; rival ...; ... in return;

der ~angriff, -e counter-attack; **der ~besuch, -e** return visit; **der ~beweis, -e** proof to the contrary; **g~einander** against/towards one another; **die ~farbe, -n** complementary colour; **das ~gewicht, -e** counterbalance; **das ~gift, -e** antidote (**gegen** to); **die ~leistung, -en** service in return (**als G.** in return); **~licht (bei/im G.** against the light); **~liebe (auf wenig G. stoßen** meet with a cool reception); **das ~mittel, –** antidote (**gegen** to); **der ~papst, ¨-e** antipope; **die ~probe, -n** cross-check; **die ~reformation** the Counter-Reformation; **der ~satz, ¨-e** opposite; contrast; antithesis; (*pl*) differences (**im G. zu** unlike, in contrast with; **im G. stehen zu** conflict with; be in opposition to); **g~sätzlich** opposing; conflicting; contrasting; **der ~schlag, ¨-e** retaliation; **die ~seite, -n** opposite side; opposing side; **g~seitig** mutual; reciprocal; **die ~seitigkeit** reciprocity; **der ~spieler, –** opponent, antagonist; *sp* opposite number; **der ~stand, ¨-e** object; subject (*Aust also* = school subject); **g~ständlich** concrete; **g~stands|los** without foundation; irrelevant; *art* abstract; **die ~stimme, -n** vote against; **der ~stoß, ¨-e** counter-attack; **das ~stück, -e** counterpart; opposite; **das ~teil, -e** opposite (**im G.** on the contrary); **g~teilig** contrary; to the contrary; **g~über** *see separate entry*; **der ~verkehr** oncoming/two-way traffic; **die ~wart** presence; present (time); *gramm* present tense (**in G.** (+*gen*) in the presence of); **g~wärtig** present; (*adv*) at present (**... ist mir (nicht) g.** I (don't) recall ...); **~warts–** present-day ...; topical ...; contemporary ...; **g~warts|nah(e)** modern, of contemporary relevance; **der ~wert, -e** equivalent; **der ~wind, -e** head wind; **g~zeichnen** (*sep*) countersign; **die ~zeichnung, -en** countersignature; **der ~zug, ¨-e** counter-move; *rail* corresponding train in the other direction

^die **Gegend, -en** area; district; *anat* region; **aus/in dieser ~** from/in these parts; **in der ~** (+*gen*) in the vicinity of; **in die ~** *coll* all over the place

gegenüber 1 *prep* (+*dat*; *sometimes placed after noun, always after pronoun*) opposite, facing, (behaviour *etc*) towards, (say) to; vis-à-vis; in the face of; compared with; 2 *adv* opposite; **~ von** opposite; **das Gegen|über** person opposite

gegen|über– *sep pref*

gegen|überliegen* (+*dat*) be opposite, face; **sich** *dat pl* **~** face each other; **~d** opposite

gegen|übersehen*: sich ~ (+*dat*) be faced with

gegen|übersetzen (+*dat*) seat opposite; **sich ~** (+*dat*) sit down opposite

gegen|übersitzen* (+*dat*) sit opposite

gegen|überstehen* (+*dat*) face; be confronted/faced with; view (with hostility, scepticism, *etc*); be (helpless) in the face of; **sich** *dat pl* **~** face each other; (views) be opposed

gegen|überstellen (+*dat*) place opposite; confront with; compare with; contrast with; set against

^die **Gegen|überstellung, -en** *vbl noun*; *also* confrontation; comparison; contrast

gegen|übertreten* (*sn*) (+*dat*) face

gegessen *p/part of* **essen**

geglichen *p/part of* **gleichen**

geglitten *p/part of* **gleiten**

geglommen *p/part of* **glimmen**

geglückt *p/part*; *also* successful

^der **Gegner** [–e:–], **–** opponent; *mil* enemy

gegnerisch opposing; *mil* enemy

^die **Gegnerschaft** opposition

gegolten *p/part of* **gelten**

gegoren *p/part of* **gären**

gegossen *p/part of* **gießen**

gegr. (= **gegründet**) est.
gegraben *p/part of* **graben**
gegriffen *p/part of* **greifen**
Geh– walking …; **g~behindert** disabled; **die ~falte, –n** kick-pleat; **der ~rock, ⸚e** frock-coat; **der ~steig, –e** pavement, sidewalk *US*; **der ~weg, –e** pavement, sidewalk *US*; footpath
das **Gehabe** (affected) behaviour
gehaben: sich ~ *Aust* behave
das **Gehaben** conduct
gehabt *p/part of* **haben; wie ~** *coll* as usual
das **Gehackte** (*decl as adj*) mince, ground meat *US*
das **Gehalt, ⸚er** (*Aust also* **der**) salary
der **Gehalt, –e** (intellectual) content; (*eg* **~ an Alkohol** alcohol) content; **g~los** insubstantial; empty, superficial; **g~reich** = **g~voll** nutritious; rich in content
gehalten *p/part of* **halten;** *also* obliged (to)
Gehalts– salary …; **der ~empfänger, –** salaried person; **die ~erhöhung, –en** = **die ~zulage, –n** rise, raise *US*
das **Gehänge, –** festoon; pendant; sword-belt; *Aust* slope
gehangen *p/part of* **hängen** (*v/i*)
geharnischt sharply-worded; *hist* armour-clad
gehässig malicious
gehauen *p/part of* **hauen**
das **Gehäuse, –** case; (radio, TV) cabinet; (apple *etc*) core; *zool* shell; *footb coll* goal
das **Gehege, –** enclosure (in zoo *etc*); *hunt* preserve; (+*dat*) **ins ~ kommen** poach on (s.o.'s) preserve
geheim secret; **streng ~** top secret; **im ~en** in secret || **der G~dienst, –e** secret service; **~halten*** (*sep*) keep secret; **die G~rats|ecken** *pl coll* receding hair; **die G~schrift, –en** code; **die G~tinte, –n** invisible ink; **die G~tuerei** secretiveness
das **Geheimnis, –se** secret; mystery; **die ~krämerei** = **die ~tuerei** secretiveness; **g~tuerisch** secretive; **g~voll** mysterious
das **Geheiß** behest
geheißen *p/part of* **heißen**
gehemmt *p/part*; *also* inhibited; self-conscious
gehen (*p/t* **ging,** *p/part* **gegangen**) walk (kilometre *etc*); (*sn*) walk; go; (machine *etc*) work; (dough) rise; (*with infin of another verb*) go +*ger* (*eg* **einkaufen/schwimmen ~** go shopping/swimming); **es geht** it's all right; I can manage; so-so; (*with prep, eg* **es geht ins Gebirge/zum Strand**) I'm/we're *etc* off to …; **es geht nicht** it won't do; it's not possible; **so gut es geht** as best I *etc* can; **es geht mir (gut** *etc*) I'm (fine *etc*); **wie geht's (dir/Ihnen)?** how are you?; **laß es dir gut ~** take care of yourself; **es geht mir immer so** that always happens to me; I always feel like that; **das geht zu weit** that's going too far; **ach, geh!** *SGer* get away with you!; **geh mir (doch) mit …!** none of …!
~ an (*acc*) (inheritance) go to; get down to
~ auf (*acc*) (remark) be aimed at; (window *etc*) overlook; (+*dat*) **auf die Nerven ~** get on (s.o.'s) nerves; **auf die (50** *etc*) **~** be coming up to; **es geht auf …** it's nearly …
~ in (*acc*) go into (*also math*); **ins Kloster ~** enter a monastery/convent; **ins Bett/ins Büro/ins Kino/in die Kirche/ins Konzert/in die Oper/ins Theater ~** go to bed/to the office/to the cinema/to church/to a concert/to the opera/to the theatre; **in die Pilze/Himbeeren** *etc* **~** *coll* go mushrooming/raspberry *etc* -picking; **in die Hunderte/Tausende/Millionen ~** run into hundreds/thousands/millions; **in sich ~** search one's conscience
~ mit go out with; **mit der Zeit ~** move with the times
~ nach go/judge by; (window) face; *mus* go to (tune of …); **wo geht es nach …?** which is the way to …?; **wenn es nach mir ginge** if I had my way
~ über (*acc*) cross; go beyond; **… geht mir über alles** … means more to me than anything else; **nichts geht über …** there's nothing like …
~ um: es geht um … it concerns …, it's about …; … is *etc* at stake; **es geht mir um …** what matters to me is …; **es geht darum zu …** it's a matter of (+*ger*); **es geht mir darum zu …** my object is to …; **wenn es um … geht** when it comes to
~ unter (*acc*) mix with
vor sich ~ happen; go on
~ zu: zum Militär ~ join the army; **zum Film/Theater ~** go into films/on the stage
gehen|lassen* (*p/part usu* **~**; *sep*) leave alone; **sich ~** let oneself go; lose one's self-control
geheuer: nicht ~ eerie, spooky; suspicious; **mir ist nicht ganz ~** I have an uneasy feeling
das **Geheul** howling
der **Gehilfe, –n** (*wk masc*) assistant; helper
das **Gehirn, –e** brain; brains
Gehirn– brain …; cerebral …; **die ~erschütterung, –en** concussion; **die ~haut|entzündung, –en** meningitis; **der ~schlag, ⸚e** stroke; **die ~wäsche** brainwashing
gehoben *p/part of* **heben;** *also* elevated; (position) senior; **~e Stimmung** elation
das **Gehöft, –e** farmstead

gehọlfen *p/part of* **helfen**
^das^ **Gehọlz, -e** copse
^das^ **Gehọlze** *footb* rough play
^das^ **Gehör** hearing; ear (for music); **absolutes ~** perfect pitch; (+*dat*) **(kein) ~ schenken** (not) listen to; **sich** *dat* **~ verschaffen** make oneself heard; **nach dem ~** by ear; **zu ~ bringen** perform
Gehör- ... of hearing; *anat* auditory ...; **g~los** deaf; **der ~sinn** sense of hearing
gehọrchen (+*dat*) obey
gehören belong, go (somewhere); (+*dat*) belong to; **~ zu** belong to; be one/part of; **... gehört (ins Bett** *etc*/*SGer* **eingesperrt** *etc*) ... ought to be (in bed/locked up *etc*); **zu ... gehört ...** ... takes ..., ... calls for ...; **es gehört dazu** it's the done/normal thing; it's part of it; **es gehört schon etwas dazu** it takes some doing
sich ~ be proper
gehörig proper; *coll* good and proper; **~ zu** belonging to; part of
^das^ **Gehọ̈rn, -e** horns
gehọ̈rnt horned; **~er Ehemann** *coll* cuckold
gehorsam obedient
^der^ **Gehorsam** obedience
gehụpft *coll*: **das ist ~ wie gesprungen** it's six of one and half a dozen of the other
^der^ **Geier, -** vulture
^der^ **Geifer** slaver; venom, spite
geifern slaver; **~ gegen** rail against
^die^ **Geige, -n** violin; **die erste ~ spielen** *coll* call the tune
geigen *coll* play on the violin; (*v/i*) play the violin; (+*dat*) **die Meinung ~** give (s.o.) a piece of one's mind
^der^ **Geiger, -** violinist; **der ~zähler, -** Geiger counter
geil randy
^die^ **Geisel, -n** hostage; **die ~nahme, -n** taking of hostages
^der^ **Geiser, -** geyser
^die^ **Geiß, -en** *SGer* she-goat; **das ~blatt** honeysuckle; **der ~bock, ⸚e** *SGer* he-goat
^die^ **Geißel, -n** scourge; *SGer* whip
geißeln flagellate; scourge; lash out at
^der^ **Geißler, -** flagellant
^der^ **Geist, -er** mind; intellect; spirit (*also relig*); ghost; spirit (of comradeship, the age, *etc*); **wes ~es Kind** what sort of person; **im ~(e)** in one's imagination; in spirit/one's thoughts; **von allen guten ~ern verlassen sein** *coll* have taken leave of one's senses || **g~los** stupid; dull; **g~reich** witty; stimulating; **g~sprühend** sparkling; **g~tötend** soul-destroying; **g~voll** of high intellectual quality
Geister- ghost ...; **die ~beschwörung, -en** necromancy; exorcism; **der ~fahrer, -** driver going in the wrong direction (on autobahn *etc*); **~hand (wie von G.** as if by magic); **die ~stunde** witching hour; **die ~welt** spirit world
geisterhaft ghostly
geistern (*sn*) roam about like a ghost; **~ in** (*dat*) haunt (s.o.'s mind)
Geistes- mental ...; intellectual ...;
g~abwesend absent-minded; **der ~blitz, -e** brainwave; **die ~gegenwart** presence of mind; **g~gegenwärtig** quick-witted; (*adv*) with great presence of mind; **die ~geschichte** intellectual history; **g~gestört** mentally disturbed; **die ~größe, -n** intellectual greatness; great mind, genius; **die ~haltung, -en** attitude of mind; **g~krank** mentally ill; **die ~krankheit, -en** mental illness; **g~schwach** feeble-minded; **die ~verfassung, -en** state of mind; **g~verwandt** spiritually akin; **die ~wissenschaften** *pl* the humanities; **der ~zustand** mental state
geistig mental; intellectual; (being, bond, *etc*) spiritual; (beverage) alcoholic; **vor seinem ~en Auge** in one's mind's eye
geistlich religious; spiritual (*opp* temporal); ecclesiastical; **der Geistliche** (*decl as adj*) priest; clergyman; **die Geistliche** (*decl as adj*) woman priest
^die^ **Geistlichkeit** clergy
^der^ **Geiz** miserliness; **der ~hals, ⸚e = der ~kragen, -** miser, skinflint
geizen: ~ mit be sparing with; **mit Lob nicht ~** be unstinting in one's praise; **sie geizt nicht mit ihren Reizen** she doesn't hide her charms
geizig miserly
^das^ **Gejạmmer** moaning
gekạnnt *p/part of* **kennen**
^das^ **Geklạ̈ff** yapping
^das^ **Geklạpper** clatter(ing); rattling; chattering (of teeth)
^das^ **Geklịmper** tinkling (on piano), strumming; jingling; fluttering (of eyelashes *etc*)
^das^ **Geklịngel** ringing
^das^ **Geklịrr** clinking; clanking
geklọmmen *p/part of* **klimmen**
geklụngen *p/part of* **klingen**
geknịckt *p/part*; *also* crestfallen
geknịffen *p/part of* **kneifen**
gekọmmen *p/part of* **kommen**
gekọnnt *p/part of* **können;** *also* skilful
^das^ **Gekreisch(e)** screeching; squealing
^das^ **Gekrịtzel** scrawl
gekrọchen *p/part of* **kriechen**
^das^ **Gekröse, -** tripe
gekụ̈nstelt artificial; affected
^das^ **Gelạ̈chter** laughter; **in ~ ausbrechen** burst out laughing; **sich dem ~ aussetzen** make oneself a laughing-stock
gelạckmeiert *coll* bamboozled
geladen *p/part of* **laden**[1,2]; *coll* furious (**auf**

acc with)

das **Gelage, –** feast

das **Gelände, –** terrain; grounds; site; *in compds* cross-country ...; **die ~übung, –en** *mil* field exercise

das **Geländer, –** railing; banisters

gelang (gelänge) *p/t* (*subj*) *of* **gelingen**

gelangen (*sn*): **~ an** (*acc*)/**nach** get to; **in jmds. Besitz ~** come into s.o.'s possession; **~ zu** get to; achieve; arrive at; *the construction* **~** + **zu** + *vbl noun is sometimes employed as a substitute for the passive, eg* **zum Druck ~ = gedruckt werden** be printed, **zur Ausführung ~ = ausgeführt werden** be carried out

das **Gelaß, –(ss)e** *arch* (small) room

gelassen *p/part of* **lassen;** *also* calm; composed

die **Gelassenheit** calmness; composure

die **Gelatine** [ʒ–] gelatine

gelaufen *p/part of* **laufen**

geläufig common; familiar; fluent; **... ist mir nicht ~** I'm not familiar with ...

gelaunt (*eg* **gut ~**) in a (good *etc*) mood

das **Geläut** ringing; chimes

gelb yellow; (traffic light) amber, yellow *US*; **~ vor Neid** green with envy

gelb– yellow ...; (*with second colour-word attached*) yellowish–; **die G~sucht** jaundice; **~süchtig** suffering from jaundice

gelblich yellowish

das **Geld, –er** money; (*pl*) funds; **–geld** *also* ... fee; ... allowance; **bares ~** cash; **bei ~e** in the money; **zu ~ machen** turn into cash

Geld– money ...; cash ...; financial ...; monetary ...; **die ~aristokratie, –n** plutocracy; **der ~automat, –en** (*wk masc*) cash dispenser, automatic teller *US*; **der ~beutel, –** *SGer* purse; **die ~buße, –n** fine; **der ~einwurf, ⸚e** slot (for coin); **der ~geber, –** backer; **g~gierig** avaricious; **die ~mittel** *pl* funds; **der ~schrank, ⸚e** safe; **die ~strafe, –n** fine; **das ~stück, –e** coin; **der ~verdiener, –** breadwinner; **~verlegenheit (in G.** short of cash); **der ~wechsel** exchange of money („**G.**" 'bureau de change'); **der ~wechsel|automat, –en** (*wk masc*) change machine

geldlich financial

geleckt *p/part*; **wie ~** *coll* spruced up

das **Gelee** [ʒ–], **–s** (*also* **der**) jelly

gelegen *p/part of* **liegen;** *also* suitable; opportune; situated; **einsam ~** lonely; **mir ist viel/nichts ~ an** (*dat*) ... matter(s) a great deal/do(es) not matter to me; (+*dat*) **~ kommen** suit very well; come just at the right moment

die **Gelegenheit, –en** opportunity; occasion; *comm* bargain; **–gelegenheit** *also* ... facilities; **bei ~** when the opportunity arises

Gelegenheits– occasional ...; **die ~arbeit** casual work; **der ~arbeiter, –** casual labourer; **der ~kauf, ⸚e** bargain; chance buy

gelegentlich 1 *adj* occasional; (*adv*) occasionally, now and then; sometime; 2 *prep* (+*gen*) on the occasion of; during

gelehrig quick to learn

die **Gelehrsamkeit** erudition

gelehrt *p/part*; *also* learned; **der/die Gelehrte** (*decl as adj*) scholar

das **Geleise, – = Gleis**

das **Geleit, –e** escort; **freies ~** safe-conduct; (+*dat*) **das ~ geben** escort || **der ~schutz** escort; **das ~wort, –e** prefatory note; **der ~zug, ⸚e** convoy

geleiten escort

das **Gelenk, –e** joint; *in compds tech* articulated ...; **die ~entzündung, –en** arthritis

gelenkig supple; nimble

Gelenks– *Aust* = **Gelenk–**

gelernt *p/part*; *also* (worker) skilled; trained

gelesen *p/part of* **lesen**[1,2]

das **Gelichter** rabble

der **Geliebte** (*decl as adj*) lover; *arch* beloved

die **Geliebte** (*decl as adj*) mistress; *arch* beloved

geliefert *p/part*; *coll* done for

geliehen *p/part of* **leihen**

Gelier– [ʒ–]: **der ~zucker** preserving sugar

gelieren [ʒ–] gel

gelinde gentle; mild; **~ gesagt** to put it mildly; **da packte mich ~ Wut** *coll* I got pretty angry

gelingen (*p/t* **gelang** (*subj* **gelänge**), *p/part* **gelungen**) (*see also* **gelungen**) (*sn*) be successful; **... gelingt mir** I succeed with ...; **es gelingt mir zu ...** I succeed in (+*ger*); I manage to ...; **es gelingt mir nicht zu ...** I fail to ...; (+*dat*) **gut/schlecht ~** turn out well/badly; **... will mir nicht ~** I can't get ... right; **das Gelingen** success

gelitten *p/part of* **leiden**

gell shrill

gell? *SGer coll* = **gelt?**

gellen ring (out); (ears) ring; **~d** shrill

geloben vow; **das Gelobte Land** the Promised Land

das **Gelöbnis, –se** vow

gelockt *p/part*; *also* curly

gelogen *p/part of* **lügen**

gelöst *p/part*; *also* relaxed

die **Gelse, –n** *Aust* gnat

gelt? *SGer* won't you?/doesn't he?/isn't it? *etc*

gelten (**gilt(st)**, *p/t* **galt** (*subj* **gälte, gölte**), *p/part* **gegolten**) be worth; count for; (*v/i*) be valid; hold good; be in force; count; (+*dat*) be meant for; be for; **~ als** be regarded as; **~ für** apply to; be true of; *occ* be regarded as; **es gilt ...** ... is at stake; **es gilt zu ...** it is necessary to ..., we *etc* must ...;

the object is to ...; **es gilt!** agreed!; **jetzt gilt's!** this is it!; **was gilt's/gilt die Wette?** what do you bet?; ~ **lassen** accept

geltend valid; in force; (opinion *etc*) prevailing; ~ **machen** assert; bring to bear; **sich ~ machen** make itself felt

die **Geltung** validity; prestige; ~ **haben** be valid; **zur ~ bringen** bring to bear; show to advantage; **zur ~ kommen** be seen/heard to advantage || **das ~s|bedürfnis** need for recognition; **die ~s|sucht** craving for recognition

das **Gelübde, –** vow

gelungen *p/part of* **gelingen;** *also* successful; *coll* funny

das **Gelüst, –e** craving (**auf** *acc*/**nach** for)

gelüsten: mich gelüstet nach ... I crave for ...; **mich gelüstet zu ...** I have a strong desire to ...

das **Gemach, ⸚er** chamber; apartment

gemächlich leisurely

gemacht *p/part*; *also* contrived; ~ **für/zu** made for; **ein ~er Mann sein** be a made man

der **Gemahl, –e** husband; consort; **Ihr Herr ~** (*in respectful reference*) your husband, Mr ...

gemahlen *p/part of* **mahlen**

die **Gemahlin, –nen** wife; **Ihre Frau ~** (*in respectful reference*) your lady wife, Mrs ...

gemahnen: ~ **an** (*acc*) remind of

das **Gemälde, –** painting; portrayal, picture (of); **die ~galerie, –n** picture gallery

gemäß 1 *adj* appropriate (*following dat* to); 2 *prep* (+*dat*; *usu following the noun*) according to; in accordance with

---

-gemäß (*eg* **traditions~**) according to (tradition *etc*); *sometimes* = as + *p/part* (*eg* **erwartungs~** as expected, **wunsch~** as requested)

---

gemäßigt *p/part of* **mäßigen;** *also* moderate; *geog* (climate, zone) temperate

das **Gemäuer, –** masonry; ruins

das **Gemecker(e)** bleating; *coll* moaning, grousing

gemein mean; vulgar, coarse; common (*also bot, zool*); *math* vulgar; (*adv*) *coll* awfully; ~ **haben mit** have in common with; **nichts ~ haben wollen mit** want nothing to do with || **~gefährlich** dangerous to public health/safety; **das G~gut, ⸚er** common property; **~hin** generally; **die G~kosten** *pl* overheads; **~nützig** for the benefit of the community; non-profit-making, non-profit *US*; **der G~platz, ⸚e** commonplace; **der G~sinn** public spirit; **die G~sprache** standard language; **~verständlich** generally intelligible; popular (in presentation); **das G~wesen, –** community; commonwealth; **das G~wohl** public welfare

die **Gemeinde, –n** community; *admin* municipality; *eccles* parish; congregation; *arts* following (of artist *etc*); *in compds also* local ...; communal ...; municipal ...; **g~eigen** municipal; **die ~steuern** *pl* local tax

die **Gemeinheit, –en** meanness; vulgarity; mean trick

gemeinsam common; joint; shared; (friend) mutual; (*adv*) jointly; together; **~e Sache machen mit** make common cause with; ~ **haben** have in common

die **Gemeinsamkeit, –en** common element/feature; **zwischen ... gibt es viele ~en** ... have a great deal in common

die **Gemeinschaft, –en** community; association; **in ~ mit** jointly with

gemeinschaftlich common; joint; (*adv*) jointly; together

Gemeinschafts- *also* communal ...; shared ...; joint ...; party ...; co–; **die ~arbeit, –en** teamwork; joint effort; **die ~erziehung** coeducation; **die ~kunde** social studies; **die ~praxis, –(x)en** group practice; **der ~raum, ⸚e** common room; **die ~sauna, –s** mixed sauna; **die ~schule, –n** non-denominational school

das **Gemenge, –** mixture; jumble; throng

das **Gemengsel, –** mixture; hotchpotch

gemessen *p/part of* **messen;** *also* measured; (distance) respectful; **~en Schrittes** with measured tread

das **Gemetzel, –** massacre

gemieden *p/part of* **meiden**

das **Gemisch, –e** mixture

gemischt *p/part*; mixed; **mit ~en Gefühlen** with mixed feelings || **die G~bau|weise** composite construction; **~rassig** of mixed race; multi-racial

die **Gemme, –n** (engraved) gem (cameo *or* intaglio)

gemocht *p/part of* **mögen**

gemolken *p/part of* **melken**

das **Gemotze** *coll* carping

der **Gems|bock, ⸚e** chamois buck

die **Gemse, –n** chamois

das **Gemunkel** rumours; gossip

das **Gemurmel** murmur(ing); muttering

das **Gemüse, –** vegetables; **junges ~** *coll* (inexperienced) youngsters

Gemüse- vegetable ...; **der ~garten, ..gärten** kitchen garden; **der ~händler, –** greengrocer; **die ~konserven** *pl* canned vegetables

gemußt *p/part of* **müssen**

gemustert *p/part*; *also* patterned

das **Gemüt, –er** mind (referring to its emotional side); feeling; heart, soul; (*with adj*) disposition; soul (= person); **die ~er erregen** arouse strong feelings; **sich** *dat* **... zu ~e**

führen take to heart; *coll* treat oneself to || **g~los** unfeeling; **g~voll** warm-hearted

gemütlich cosy; leisurely; agreeable; convivial; (person) genial

die **Gemütlichkeit** cosiness; leisureliness; conviviality; **in aller ~** at one's leisure; **da hört doch die ~ auf!** that's the limit!

Gemüts–: g~arm lacking in warmth; **die ~art, –en** disposition; **die ~bewegung, –en** emotion; **g~krank** emotionally disturbed; **der ~mensch, –en** (*wk masc*) unflappable, good-natured person (**du bist** *etc* **ein G.!** you *etc* must be joking!); **~ruhe** *coll* (**in aller G.** calmly); **die ~verfassung, –en = der ~zustand, ⸚e** state of mind

das **Gen, –e** gene; **die ~technologie** genetic engineering

gen [–ɛ–] (+*acc*) *poet* towards

genannt *p/part of* **nennen;** *also* above-mentioned

genant [ʒe–] embarrassing

genas (genäse) *p/t* (*subj*) *of* **genesen**

genau exact; accurate; meticulous; detailed; (*adv*) exactly, just; right (in front of *etc*); (know) for certain; **~!** exactly!; **~ nehmen** take seriously; **es nicht sehr ~ nehmen mit** not be too particular about; **Genaueres** (*decl as adj*) further details; **~(e)stens = aufs ~(e)ste** minutely; down to the last detail || **~genommen** strictly speaking; **~so** just the same way; (*with adj/adv*) just as; **~so–** (*eg* **~sosehr**) just as (much *etc*)

die **Genauigkeit** exactness; accuracy; precision; meticulousness

der **Gendarm** [ʒan–], **–en** (*wk masc*) *Aust* rural policeman

die **Gendarmerie** [ʒan–] *Aust* rural police

der **Genealoge, –n** (*wk masc*) genealogist

die **Genealogie** genealogy

genealogisch genealogical

genehm convenient (*following dat* to); acceptable (to)

genehmigen approve; authorize; **sich** *dat* **einen ~** *joc* have a quick one

die **Genehmigung, –en** approval; authorization; permission; permit

geneigt *p/part*; *also* sloping; inclined; (*following dat*) well-disposed (towards)

die **Geneigtheit** inclination; goodwill

Genera *pl of* **Genus**

der **General, –e/⸚e** general; (air force) air chief marshal, general *US*

General– general ...; *postpositive* –general *in certain titles* (*eg* **der ~konsul** consul-general); **der ~direktor, –en** chairman, president *US*; **der ~gouverneur, –e** governor-general; **der ~inspekteur, –e** Chief of Defence Staff; **der ~intendant, –en** (*wk masc*) *theat* director; **der ~leutnant, –s** lieutenant-general; (air force) air marshal, lieutenant-general *US*; **der ~major, –e** major-general; (air force) air vice-marshal, major-general *US*; **die ~probe, –n** dress-rehearsal; **der ~sekretär, –e** secretary-general; **der ~staats|anwalt, ⸚e** chief public prosecutor; **der ~stab, ⸚e** general staff; **der ~streik, –s** general strike; **g~überholen** (*only infin and p/part* **g~überholt**) overhaul thoroughly

generalisieren generalize

die **Generalität, –en** the generals

die **Generation, –en** generation; **der ~s|konflikt, –e** *approx* = generation gap

der **Generator, –(or)en** generator

generell general

genesen (*p/t* **genas** (*subj* **genäse**), *p/part* **genesen**) (*sn*) recover; **der/die Genesende** (*decl as adj*) convalescent

die **Genesung** recovery

die **Genetik** [–ɪk] genetics

der **Genetiker, –** geneticist

genetisch genetic

Genf Geneva

Genfer (*indecl*) Genevan; **die ~ Konvention** the Geneva Convention; **der ~ See** Lake Geneva

genial brilliant

die **Genialität** brilliance; genius

das **Genick, –e** (nape of the) neck; (+*dat*) **das ~ brechen** *coll* be the ruin of; **sich** *dat* **das ~ brechen** break one's neck

das **Genie** [ʒe–], **–s** genius

Genien *pl of* **Genius**

genieren [ʒe–] bother; embarrass; **sich ~** be embarrassed

genierlich [ʒe–] bothersome; embarrassing

genießbar edible; drinkable; **nicht ~** *coll* in a foul mood

genießen (*p/t* **genoß** (*subj* **genösse**), *p/part* **genossen**) enjoy; eat *or* drink, consume; **nicht zu ~** *coll* in a foul mood

der **Genießer, –** pleasure-lover; gourmet

genießerisch showing great enjoyment; (*adv*) with great enjoyment; with relish

die **Genitalien** [–ĭən] *pl* genitals

der **Genitiv, –e** genitive

der **Genius, –(i)en** genius; *myth* guardian spirit

die **Genom|analyse** amniocentesis

genommen *p/part of* **nehmen**

genoß (genösse) *p/t* (*subj*) *of* **genießen**

der **Genosse, –n** (*wk masc*) comrade

genossen *p/part of* **genießen**

die **Genossenschaft, –en** co-operative

genossenschaftlich co-operative; (*adv*) as a co-operative

Genossenschafts– co-operative ...

der **Genozid, –e/–ien** [–ĭən] (*also* **das**) genocide

das **Genre** [ˈʒãːrə], **–s** genre

Gent Ghent

der **Gentleman** [ˈdʒɛnt|mən], **..men** [–mən]

gentleman; **g~like** [–laɪk] gentlemanly

Genua Genoa

der **Genuese, –n** (*wk masc*), **genuesisch** Genoese

genug enough; **~ haben von** have had enough of; **sich** *dat* **selbst ~ sein** not need the company of others; **damit nicht ~** that's not all; **nicht ~ (damit), daß ...** not content with (+*ger*) || **die G~tuung** satisfaction

Genüge: (+*dat*) **G. leisten/tun** satisfy; **zur ~** sufficiently; only too well

genügen be sufficient; (+*dat*) satisfy; **~d** sufficient; adequate

genügsam frugal; modest (in one's demands)

genuin genuine

das **Genus, –(n)era** *gramm* gender; *biol* genus

der **Genuß, ⸚(ss)e** pleasure; consumption (of); taking (of drugs); **in den ~ kommen von** receive (pension *etc*); get the benefit of; **mit ~** with relish/great enjoyment || **der ~mensch, –en** (*wk masc*) hedonist; **das ~mittel, –** stimulant (*eg* coffee, tobacco); **die ~sucht** pleasure-seeking

genüßlich pleasurable; (*adv*) with relish

der **Geograph, –en** (*wk masc*) geographer

die **Geographie** geography

geographisch geographical

der **Geologe, –n** (*wk masc*) geologist

die **Geologie** geology

geologisch geological

der **Geometer, –** surveyor

die **Geometrie** geometry

geometrisch geometric

die **Geopolitik** geopolitics

Georg ['geːɔrk] George

geozentrisch geocentric

das **Gepäck** luggage, baggage; **die ~abfertigung, –en** luggage/baggage counter/*aer* check-in; **die ~aufbewahrung, –en** left-luggage office, baggage room *US*; **die ~ausgabe, –n** baggage reclaim; **das ~netz, –e** luggage-rack, baggage rack *US*; **der ~schein, –e** luggage receipt, baggage check *US*; **der ~träger, –** porter; carrier (on bicycle); **der ~wagen, –** luggage-van, baggage car *US*

Gepäcks– *Aust* = **Gepäck–**

gepanzert armoured

der **Gepard** ['geː–], **–e** cheetah

gepfeffert *p/part*; peppered; *coll* spicy; (prices) steep; (questions) stiff, tough; (criticism) sharp

gepfiffen *p/part of* **pfeifen**

gepflegt *p/part*; *also* (appearance) tidy; well-kept/groomed, (skin *etc*) well cared-for; cultivated, refined; (wine *etc*) select

die **Gepflogenheit, –en** custom

das **Geplänkel, –** banter; *mil* skirmish

das **Geplapper** babbling; chatter

das **Geplärr(e)** bawling

das **Geplätscher** splashing; babbling

das **Geplauder** chatting

das **Gepolter** din; banging

das **Gepräge** character; stamp

das **Gepränge** pomp

gepriesen *p/part of* **preisen**

gepunktet dotted; spotted; polka-dot

gequält *p/part*; *also* (expression) pained; (smile) forced

das **Gequassel** *coll* blether

gequollen *p/part of* **quellen**

gerad–: ~linig straight; rectilinear; direct; (person) straight; (*adv*) in a straight line

gerade (*coll* **grade**) straight; upright; direct; (number) even; (person) straightforward; (*adv*) straight, right; exactly; just; at the moment; especially; ... of all ... (*eg* **~ heute** today of all days, **~ er** him of all people); *or conveyed by* ... happen(s) to ... (*eg* **damals war ich ~ in Hamburg** I happened to be in H. at the time); **das ist es ja ~!** that's just it!; **fünf ~ sein lassen** *coll* stretch a point; **~ erst** only just (*in time sense*); **~ noch** only just (= barely); just; **die Gerade** (*decl as adj*) *math* straight line; *sp* straight, straightaway *US*; **linke/rechte Gerade** *box* straight left/right || **~aus** straight ahead; **~biegen*** (*sep*) straighten out; **~halten*** (*sep*) hold straight (**sich g.** hold oneself upright; straighten up); **~heraus** *coll* straight out; **~machen** (*sep*) straighten; **~sitzen*** (*sep*) sit up straight; **~so** (= **genauso**); **~stehen*** (*sep*) stand up straight (**g. für** take responsibility for); **~wegs** directly; straight away; **~zu** positively, absolutely; nothing short of

geraden|wegs = geradewegs

gerädert *coll*: **wie ~** all in

die **Geradheit** straightforwardness

gerammelt *p/part*; **~ voll** *coll* packed

das **Gerangel** scrapping; wrangling

die **Geranie** [–ĭə], **–n** geranium

gerann *p/t of* **gerinnen**

gerannt *p/part of* **rennen**

der **Gerant** [ʒe'rant], **–en** (*wk masc*) *Swiss* manager

das **Geraschel** rustling

das **Gerassel** rattling; clanking

das **Gerät, –e** piece of equipment; appliance; tool; instrument; *rad*, *TV* set; *gym* piece of apparatus

Gerate–: ~wohl (aufs G. on the off-chance; at random)

geraten¹* (*sn*) turn out (well *etc*); *with prep*, *indicates a place s.o., sth. ends up in or a situation etc s.o., sth. gets into*:

~ an (*acc*) come across; come to; get

außer sich ~ be beside oneself

~ in (*acc*) find oneself in; get into; fall into (trap); get caught in (storm); fly into (rage); *often employed with*

nouns (*i*) *to express inception* (*eg* **in Bewegung** ~ begin to move, **ins Schleudern** ~ get into a skid, **in Wallung** ~ fly into a rage), (*ii*) = *passive* (*eg* **in Gefangenschaft/Vergessenheit** ~ get captured/forgotten)
~ **nach** take after
~ **unter** (*acc*) fall under (vehicle); come under (influence *etc*)
geraten² *p/part of* **raten, geraten;** *also* advisable
die **Gerätschaften** *pl* implements
geräuchert *p/part*; smoked; **das Geräucherte** (*decl as adj*) smoked meat
geraum: eine ~e Zeit a considerable time; **seit ~er Zeit** for some time; **vor ~er Zeit** some time ago
geräumig spacious
das **Geräusch, -e** noise; sound; **die ~kulisse, -n** background noise; *cin, TV, etc* sound effects; **g~los** silent; **der ~pegel, -** noise level; **g~voll** noisy
das **Geräusper** clearing of the throat
gerben tan
der **Gerber, -** tanner
die **Gerberei, -en** tannery; tanning
gerecht just; fair; **-gerecht** suitable for ..., tailored to ...; in accordance with ...; (+*dat*) ~ **werden** do justice to; live up to; fulfil; meet (demand *etc*) || **gerechter|weise** in all fairness
die **Gerechtigkeit** justice; fairness; (+*dat*) ~ **widerfahren/zuteil werden lassen** treat justly
das **Gerede** talk; gossip; **ins ~ bringen** get talked about; **ins ~ kommen** get oneself talked about
gereichen: (+*dat*) **zur Ehre** ~ do credit to; (+*dat*) **zum Nachteil** ~ be to (s.o.'s) disadvantage; (+*dat*) **zum Nutzen/Vorteil** ~ be to (s.o.'s) advantage
gereift *p/part*; *also* mature
gereizt *p/part*; *also* irritable; irritated
die **Gereiztheit** irritability; irritation
gereuen: ... gereut mich I regret ...
das **Gericht¹, -e** dish
das **Gericht², -e** court (of law); **das Jüngste/Letzte** ~ the Last Judgement; ~ **halten über** (*acc*) sit in judgement on; **scharf ins ~ gehen mit** take severely to task; **vor ~** in court; **vor ~ bringen** take to court; **zu ~ sitzen über** (*acc*) sit in judgement on
gerichtlich court; judicial; legal; forensic
Gerichts- court ...; legal ...; forensic ...; **der ~hof, ⸚e** (*in titles*) Court (of Justice); **die ~medizin** forensic medicine; **der ~saal, ..säle** courtroom; **das ~verfahren, -** court proceedings; **die ~verhandlung, -en** trial; hearing; **der ~vollzieher, -** bailiff
die **Gerichtsbarkeit** jurisdiction
gerieben *p/part of* **reiben;** *coll* crafty
gering small; slight; low; (quality *etc*) poor; **kein G~erer als ...** no less a person than ...; **nichts G~eres als ...** nothing less than ...; **nicht im ~sten** not in the least || **~achten** (*sep*) think little of; **~fügig** insignificant; slight; **~schätzen** (*sep*) think little of; have scant regard for; **~schätzig** contemptuous; **die G~schätzung** disdain, scorn
geringelt *p/part*; *also* curly; (horizontally) striped
geringsten|falls at the very least
gerinnen* (*sn*) curdle; coagulate, (blood) *also* clot
das **Gerinnsel, -** clot
das **Gerippe, -** skeleton; frame; (of essay *etc*) framework
gerippt ribbed
gerissen *p/part of* **reißen;** *coll* crafty
geritten *p/part of* **reiten**
der **Germane, -n** (*wk masc*) Teuton
germanisch Germanic; Teutonic
der **Germanist, -en** (*wk masc*) German scholar/student
die **Germanistik** [-ɪk] German studies
gern (*comp* **lieber,** *superl* **am liebsten**) gladly; *with verb indicating chosen activity etc, expressed by* ... like(s) (to do sth./doing sth., *eg* **sie liest** ~ she likes reading, **ich hätte es ~ gelesen** I would have liked to read it); *indicating a tendency, expressed by* ... tend(s) to ... (*eg* **Kakteen wachsen ~ auf trockenem Boden** cactuses tend to grow on dry soil); **von Herzen** ~ most gladly;
~ **geschehen!** don't mention it!; **das glaube ich** ~ I can well believe it; ~ **haben** like; **ich hätte ~ ...** I'd like ...; **es ~ haben, wenn ...** like it when ...; **du kannst ... ~ haben** you're welcome to ...; **... kann mich ~ haben!** ... can go to hell!; ~ **mögen** like; **ich möchte ~/'zu ~ ...** I'd like/love to ...; **etw. (nicht) ~ sehen** (not) like sth.; **es (nicht) ~ sehen, wenn ...** (not) like ... to ... (*eg* **er sieht es nicht ~, wenn man zu spät kommt** he doesn't like people to be late); ~ **gesehen** welcome; **ich hätte ~ ... gesprochen** I wonder if I might speak to ...?
gerne = gern; der G~groß, -e s.o. who likes to act the big guy
gerochen *p/part of* **riechen**
das **Geröll** boulders; scree
geronnen *p/part of* **rinnen, gerinnen**
die **Gerste** barley; **das ~n|korn, ⸚er** barleycorn; *med* sty
die **Gerte, -n** switch; *equest* crop; **gerten|schlank** willowy
der **Geruch, ⸚e** smell (**nach/von** of); sense of smell; reputation; **g~los** odourless; **g~tilgend** deodorant

Gerụchs– olfactory (nerve *etc*); **der ~sinn** sense of smell

das **Gerụcht, –e** rumour; **es geht das ~, daß …** it is rumoured that … || **der ~e|macher, –** rumour-monger; **g~weise** by hearsay (**g. verlautet, daß …** rumour has it that …)

gerufen *p/part of* **rufen**

geruhen deign (to)

geruhsam (evening *etc*) quiet

das **Gerụmpel** junk

gerụngen *p/part of* **ringen**

das **Gerụst, –e** scaffold(ing); framework, skeleton

gerụttelt *p/part*; **ein ~ Maß (an** *dat*/**von) …** a great deal of …; **~ voll** chock-full

das **ges, Ges** [–ɛ–] (*gen* –), – *mus* (the note) G flat; (*key*) **Ges** G flat major

gesạlzen *p/part of* **salzen;** salted; *coll* sharp; spicy; (price) steep

gesạmt entire; *in compds* complete …; total …; overall …, general …; **~deutsch** all-German; **die G~hoch|schule, –n** comprehensive university; **die G~schule, –n** comprehensive school; **das G~werk** complete works

gesạmthaft *Swiss* altogether

die **Gesạmtheit** totality; **die ~ der (Studenten** *etc*) all the (students *etc*); **in seiner/ihrer ~** in its entirety; as a whole

gesạndt *p/part of* **senden; der/die Gesandte** (*decl as adj*) envoy

die **Gesạndtschaft, –en** legation

der **Gesạng, ⸚e** song; singing; *liter* canto; book; **das ~buch, ⸚er** hymn-book; **der ~ver|ein, –e** choral society

Gesạngs– singing …; **das ~buch, ⸚er** *Aust* hymn-book; **der ~ver|ein, –e** *Aust* choral society

das **Gesäß, –e** buttocks

geschạffen *p/part of* **schaffen¹**

geschạfft *p/part of* **schaffen²;** *coll* worn out

das **Geschạ̈ft, –e** shop, store; business; deal, transaction; *coll* office; (*pl*) business; **~e machen mit** make money out of; = **ins ~ kommen mit** do business with || **g~e|halber** on business; **der ~e|macher, –** profiteer

geschạ̈ftig busy

geschạ̈ftlich business; (tone) business-like; (*adv*) on business

Geschạ̈fts– business …;

g~führend executive; *pol* caretaker; **der ~führer, –** manager; managing director; secretary (of club); **die ~führung, –en** management; **das ~jahr, –e** financial year; **die ~kosten** *pl* business expenses (**auf G.** on expenses); **die ~liste, –n** *Swiss* agenda; **der ~mann, ..leute** businessman; **g~mäßig** business-like; **die ~ordnung, –en** standing orders; **der ~reisende** (*decl as adj*) travelling salesman; **die ~stelle, –n** office; **die ~straße, –n** shopping street; **der ~träger, –** chargé d'affaires; **der ~verkehr** business dealings; **das ~viertel, –** business district; shopping centre; **die ~zeit, –en** business hours

geschah (geschähe) *p/t* (*subj*) *of* **geschehen**

geschẹckt (cow) spotted; (horse) piebald; skewbald

geschehen (geschieht, *p/t* **geschah** (*subj* **geschähe**), *p/part* **geschehen)** (*sn*) happen (*dat* to); be done; **ich wußte nicht, wie mir geschah** I didn't know what was happening to me; **das geschieht ihm recht** it serves him right; **es muß etwas ~** something must be done; **es ist um … geschehen …** is *etc* done for; that is the end of …

das **Geschehen** events

das **Geschehnis, –se** occurrence

gescheit clever; sensible; **du bist wohl nicht ganz ~!** you must be out of your mind!

das **Geschẹnk, –e** present; (+*dat*) **ein ~ machen** give (s.o.) a present || **die ~packung, –en** gift pack

die **Geschịchte, –n** story; history; *coll* affair; business; **~ machen** make history; **mach keine ~n!** don't be silly!; don't do anything silly!

geschịchtlich historical

Geschịchts– history …; historical …; **die ~klitterung, –en** falsification of history; **der ~schreiber, –** historian; **die ~schreibung** historiography

das **Geschịck¹, –e** fate, destiny

das **Geschịck²** = **die Geschịcklichkeit** skill; dexterity

geschịckt *p/part*; *also* skilful; dexterous

geschieden *p/part of* **scheiden;** *also* divorced; **~e Leute sein** be finished with each other; **der/die Geschiedene** (*decl as adj*) divorcee

geschieht *3rd sing pres of* **geschehen**

geschienen *p/part of* **scheinen**

das **Geschịrr, –e** crockery; dishes; (dinner/tea) service; harness; **sich ins ~ legen** buckle down to it || **die ~spül|maschine, –n** dishwasher; **das ~tuch, ⸚er** dish-cloth

geschịssen *p/part of* **scheißen**

geschlafen *p/part of* **schlafen**

geschlagen *p/part of* **schlagen;** *also* (hour *etc*) whole (*expressing disapproval*)

das **Geschlẹcht, –er** sex; race; family; generation; *gramm* gender; **das schöne ~** the fair sex

geschlẹchtlich sexual; (education) sex

Geschlẹchts– sexual …; sex …; **der ~akt, –e** sex act; **die ~krankheit, –en** venereal disease; **g~los** asexual; **g~reif** sexually mature; **die ~reife** sexual maturity; **die ~teile** *pl* genitals; **der ~verkehr** sexual intercourse; **das ~wort, ⸚er** *gramm* article

geschlịchen *p/part of* **schleichen**

geschlịffen *p/part of* **schleifen¹;** *also* (manners

etc) polished

geschlissen *p/part of* **schleißen**

geschlossen *p/part of* **schließen;** *also* closed; private; integrated; cohesive; *ling* close; (*adv*) unanimously; in a body; solidly; **in sich ~** self-contained; **~es Ganzes** unified whole; **~e Ortschaft** built-up area

die **Geschlossenheit** unity

das **Geschluchze** sobbing

geschlungen *p/part of* **schlingen[1,2]**

der **Geschmack, ¨-e**/*joc* **¨-er** taste; **~ finden an** (*dat*) come to like; **auf den ~ kommen** acquire a taste for sth.; **nach meinem ~** to my taste || **g~los** tasteless; in bad taste; **die ~losigkeit, -en** bad taste; tasteless remark/act; **~sache** (= **Geschmackssache**); **g~voll** tasteful

Geschmacks-: die ~richtung, -en flavour; taste (of era *etc*); **~sache** (**das ist G.** it's a matter of taste); **der ~sinn** sense of taste; **die ~ver|irrung, -en** lapse of taste

geschmalzen *p/part of* **schmalzen**

das **Geschmeide, -** *poet* jewellery

geschmeidig supple; lithe, lissom; flexible; adroit

das **Geschmier(e)** scribble; daub

geschmissen *p/part of* **schmeißen**

geschmolzen *p/part of* **schmelzen;** *also* molten

geschniegelt: ~ und gebügelt all spruced up

geschnitten *p/part of* **schneiden**

geschoben *p/part of* **schieben**

gescholten *p/part of* **schelten**

das **Geschöpf, -e** creature

geschoren *p/part of* **scheren**

das **Geschoß[1], -(ss)e** floor, storey

das **Geschoß[2], -(ss)e** missile; **die ~bahn, -en** trajectory

geschossen *p/part of* **schießen**

-geschossig -storey

geschraubt *p/part; also* stilted

das **Geschrei** shouting; cries; fuss

das **Geschreibsel** *coll* scribblings

geschrieben *p/part of* **schreiben**

geschrie(e)n *p/part of* **schreien**

geschritten *p/part of* **schreiten**

geschunden *p/part of* **schinden**

das **Geschütz, -e** (heavy) gun

das **Geschwader, -** *naut* squadron; *aer* wing, group *US*

das **Geschwafel** *coll* twaddle; waffle

das **Geschwätz** prattle; tittle-tattle

geschwätzig garrulous

geschweige: ~ (denn) let alone

geschwiegen *p/part of* **schweigen**

geschwind *esp SGer* quick

die **Geschwindigkeit, -en** speed; *phys* velocity; **mit einer ~ von** at a speed of || **die ~s|begrenzung, -en** speed limit; **der ~s|messer, -** speedometer

die **Geschwister** *pl* brother(s) and sister(s) (~ *also occurs as a neut sing in sociological etc terminology*, = sibling)

geschwisterlich brotherly *or* sisterly

geschwollen *p/part of* **schwellen** (*v/i*); *also* pompous

geschwommen *p/part of* **schwimmen**

geschworen *p/part of* **schwören;** *also* avowed; **der/die Geschworene** (*decl as adj*) juror; (*pl*) jury

die **Geschwulst, ¨-e** tumour

geschwunden *p/part of* **schwinden**

geschwungen *p/part of* **schwingen;** *also* curved

das **Geschwür, -e** ulcer; boil

gesegnet *p/part;* **einen ~en Appetit haben** have a healthy appetite; **einen ~en Schlaf haben** be a sound sleeper

gesehen *p/part of* **sehen**

das **Geselchte** (*decl as adj*) *SGer* smoked meat

der **Geselle, -n** (*wk masc*) fellow; journeyman

gesellen: sich ~ zu join

gesellig sociable; gregarious; convivial

die **Geselligkeit, -en** social life; sociability; gregariousness; social gathering

die **Gesellschaft, -en** society; company; party; *comm* company; *coll* crowd; **die ~** society; (*+dat*) **~ leisten** keep (s.o.) company

der **Gesellschafter, -** companion; *comm* partner

gesellschaftlich social

Gesellschafts- … of society; social …; **g~fähig** socially acceptable; presentable; **g~kritisch** critical of society; **der ~raum, ¨-e** reception room; **die ~reise, -n** conducted tour; **das ~spiel, -e** parlour game; **der ~tanz, ¨-e** ballroom dance/dancing

gesessen *p/part of* **sitzen**

das **Gesetz, -e** law; act (of parliament); **das ~buch, ¨-er** statute-book; **der ~entwurf, ¨-e** bill; **g~gebend** legislative; **der ~geber, -** legislator; **die ~gebung** legislation; **g~los** lawless; **die ~losigkeit** lawlessness; **g~mäßig** legal; in accordance with a natural law; **die ~mäßigkeit, -en** (physical *etc*) law; legality; **g~widrig** unlawful

Gesetzes- … of the law; **die ~kraft** force of law; **die ~vorlage, -n** bill

gesetzlich legal; statutory; (*adv*) legally; by law; **~ geschützt** registered

die **Gesetzlichkeit** legality

gesetzt *p/part; also* sober; sedate; **~ (den Fall), (daß) …** supposing …

ges. gesch. (= **gesetzlich geschützt**) regd.

gesichert *p/part; also* secure

das **Gesicht[1], -e** vision

das **Gesicht[2], -er** face; expression; look, appearance; **das Zweite ~** second sight; **ein anderes ~ bekommen** take on a different complexion; **das ~ verlieren/wahren** lose/save face; **sein wahres ~ zeigen** reveal one's true character; (*+dat*) **ins ~ sagen** say to (s.o.'s) face; **zu ~ bekommen** set eyes on

Gesichts– ... of the face; face ...; facial ...; **der ~ausdruck** expression; **die ~farbe, –n** complexion; **das ~feld, –er** field of vision; **der ~kreis, –e** (mental) horizon; **die ~maske, –n** mask; = **die ~packung, –en** face-pack; **der ~punkt, –e** point of view; **der ~sinn** sense of sight; **das ~wasser, ..wässer** face-lotion; **der ~winkel, –** visual angle; point of view; **die ~züge** *pl* features

das **Gesims, –e** ledge

das **Gesinde** *arch* servants; farm-labourers

das **Gesindel** rabble

gesinnt minded; (+*dat*) **freundlich/feindlich ~** well/ill-disposed towards

die **Gesinnung, –en** attitude; convictions; **der ~s|genosse, –n** (*wk masc*) like-minded person; **g~s|los** unprincipled; **der ~s|lump, –en** (*wk masc*) *coll* time-server; **die ~s|schnüffelei** prying into people's political beliefs; **der ~s|wandel, –** change of heart

gesittet well-behaved; civilized

die **Gesittung** civilized behaviour

das **Gesöff, –e** *coll* swill

gesoffen *p/part of* **saufen**

gesogen *p/part of* **saugen**

gesollt *p/part of* **sollen**

gesondert *p/part*; *also* separate

gesonnen *p/part of* **sinnen;** *also* disposed (to)

gesotten *occ p/part of* **sieden**

gespalten *p/part of* **spalten;** *also* cleft; (tongue) forked

das **Gespann, –e** team (of horses *etc*); *coll* pair

gespannt *p/part*; *also* taut; tense; strained; expectant, eager; **ich bin ~ auf** (*acc*) I can't wait to hear/see; **ich bin ~, ob ...** I wonder whether ...

das **Gespenst, –er** spectre; **~er sehen** *coll* imagine things

gespensterhaft = **gespenstisch** ghastly; eerie

gesperrt *p/part*; *print* letter-spaced (*eg* **g e s p e r r t**; *see p. lxviii*)

gespie(e)n *p/part of* **speien**

der **Gespiele, –n** (*wk masc*) playmate

gespielt *p/part*; *also* studied; a pretence

das **Gespinst, –e** spun yarn; tissue (of lies), web (of deceit)

gesplissen *p/part of* **spleißen**

gesponnen *p/part of* **spinnen**

das **Gespött** mockery; **zum ~ werden** become a laughing-stock

das **Gespräch, –e** conversation, talk; *tel* call; (*pl*) *pol* talks; **ins ~ kommen mit** get talking to; establish a dialogue with; **im ~ sein** be under discussion; be being talked about

gesprächig talkative

Gesprächs–: der ~partner, – person one/s.o. is talking to; someone to talk to; **der ~stoff, –e** topic(s) of conversation; **das ~thema, –(m)en** topic of conversation; **g~weise** in the course of conversation

gespreizt *p/part*; *also* affected

gesprenkelt *p/part*; *also* speckled

gespritzt *p/part*; **der Gespritzte** (*decl as adj*) *SGer* wine with soda water, spritzer

gesprochen *p/part of* **sprechen**

gesprossen *p/part of* **sprießen**

gesprungen *p/part of* **springen**

das **Gespür** feel (for sth.)

gest. (= **gestorben**) deceased

das **Gestade, –** *poet* shore

die **Gestalt, –en** shape; form; build; figure; *liter* character; **~ annehmen** take shape; **in ~** (+*gen*) in the form of || **g~los** amorphous

gestalten form, shape; create; arrange; organize; **künstlerisch** *etc* **~** give artistic *etc* form to; **interessanter** *etc* **~** make more interesting *etc*; **sich ~** turn out (in a certain way)

der **Gestalter, –** creator

gestalterisch creative

die **Gestaltung, –en** *vbl noun*; *also* creation; arrangement; organization; design

das **Gestammel** stammering

gestanden[1] *p/part of* **stehen;** *also* seasoned, experienced

gestanden[2] *p/part of* **gestehen**

geständig: ~ sein have confessed

das **Geständnis, –se** confession; **ein ~ ablegen** make a confession

der **Gestank** stink, stench

die **Gestapo** [ge'sta:po] (= **Geheime Staatspolizei:** *secret police in Third Reich*)

gestatten allow; **sich** *dat* **~ zu ...** take the liberty of (+*ger*); **~ Sie?** excuse me!; may I?

die **Geste** [–ɛ–, –e:–], **–n** gesture

gestehen* confess; **offen gestanden** quite frankly

die **Gestehungs|kosten** *pl comm* production costs

das **Gestein, –e** rock

das **Gestell, –e** frame; rack; stand; shelf; **langes ~** *coll* beanpole

gestellt *p/part*; *also* posed

gestelzt *p/part*; *also* stilted

gestern yesterday; **~ morgen/nachmittag/abend** yesterday morning/afternoon/evening; **~ in/vor (einer Woche** *etc*) (a week *etc*) yesterday, from yesterday/(a week *etc*) ago yesterday

gestiefelt in boots; **der G~e Kater** Puss in Boots; **~ und gespornt** *coll* ready to go

gestiegen *p/part of* **steigen**

die **Gestik** [–ɪk] gestures

gestikulieren gesticulate

das **Gestirn, –e** star

gestirnt starry

gestoben *p/part of* **stieben**

das **Gestöber, –** flurry

gestochen *p/part of* **stechen;** *also* precise

gestohlen *p/part of* **stehlen**

gestorben *p/part of* **sterben**
gestört *p/part; also* disturbed; **geistig ~** (mentally) disturbed
gestoßen *p/part of* **stoßen**
das **Gestotter** stuttering
das **Gesträuch, -e** bushes
gestreckt *p/part;* **in ~em Galopp** at full gallop
gestreift *p/part; also* striped
gestreßt [-ʃt-, -st-] under stress
gestrichelt *p/part;* (line) broken
gestrichen *p/part of* **streichen; ~ voll** full to the brim; **ein ~er Teelöffel (voll) ...** a level teaspoonful of ...
gestrig yesterday's; of yesterday
gestritten *p/part of* **streiten**
das **Gestrüpp, -e** undergrowth; maze, jungle (of)
das **Gestühl, -e** seats; pews
das **Gestümper** *coll* bungling; clumsy playing
gestunken *p/part of* **stinken**
das **Gestüt, -e** stud; **der ~hengst, -e** stud-horse
das **Gesuch, -e** application; petition
gesucht *p/part; also* sought-after; contrived
das **Gesumm(e)** hum(ming)
gesund (*comp, superl* ¨) healthy; well; sound; salutary; **wieder ~ werden** get better; **~ und munter** in fine fettle || **~beten** (*sep*) cure by prayer; **der G~beter, -** faith-healer; **~machen** (*sep*): **sich g.** *coll* make a pile (**an** *dat* out of); **~schrumpfen** (*sep*) *coll* streamline; **~stoßen*** (*sep*) *coll* (= **~machen**)
gesunden (*sn*) recover
die **Gesundheit** health; **bei guter/bester ~** in good health/the best of health; **~!** (*said to sneezer*) bless you!; **auf Ihre ~!** your health!
gesundheitlich (relating to) health; (*adv*) healthwise; **~er Zustand** state of health
Gesundheits- health ...; public health ...; **g~halber** for health reasons; **~rücksichten** (**aus G.** for health reasons); **g~schädlich** unhealthy; **das ~wesen** health service; **der ~zustand** state of health
die **Gesundung** recovery
gesungen *p/part of* **singen**
gesunken *p/part of* **sinken**
getan *p/part of* **tun**
das **Getier** animals; creature
getigert striped (like a tiger)
das **Getöse** din; crash; roar(ing)
getragen *p/part of* **tragen;** *also* stately
das **Getränk, -e** drink
das **Getratsch(e)** gossip
getrauen: sich ~ zu ... dare to ...
das **Getreide, -** grain; **die ~art, -en** cereal
getrennt *p/part; also* separate; (*adv*) *also* (live) apart; (sleep) in separate bedrooms; **mit ~er Post** under separate cover || **die G~schreibung** writing as two (or more) words
getreten *p/part of* **treten**
getreu loyal; true, faithful
das **Getriebe, -** (hustle and) bustle; *mech* gearbox; transmission; **die ~automatik** automatic transmission
getrieben *p/part of* **treiben**
getroffen *p/part of* **treffen**
getrogen *p/part of* **trügen**
getrost safely; confidently
getrunken *p/part of* **trinken**
das **Getto, -s** ghetto
das **Getue** fuss; affected behaviour
das **Getümmel** tumult; hurly-burly
getüpfelt *p/part; also* spotted
ge|übt *p/part; also* experienced; practised
das **Geviert, -e** square
das **Gewächs** [-ks], **-e** plant; wine; *med* growth; **das ~haus, ¨er** hothouse
gewachsen [-ks-] *p/part of* **wachsen[1]; (+*dat*) ~ sein** be equal to; be able to cope with
gewagt *p/part; also* daring; risqué
gewählt *p/part; also* choice, refined
gewahr: (+*acc/gen*) ~ werden become aware of; notice
die **Gewähr, g~leisten** (*insep*) guarantee; **die ~leistung, -en** *vbl noun; also* guarantee
gewahren catch sight of; notice
gewähren grant; give; afford; **~ lassen** let (s.o.) have his/her way
Gewährs-: der ~mann, ¨er/..leute source (of information)
Gewahrsam: in ~ in custody; **in ~ nehmen** take into custody/safe-keeping
die **Gewalt, -en** force; violence; authority; power; control; **höhere ~** act(s) of God; (+*dat*) **~ antun** do violence to; violate; **sich** *dat* **~ antun** force oneself; **in der ~ haben** be in control of; **mit ~** by force; **mit aller ~** with all one's might; at all costs || **die ~anwendung** use of force; **die ~herrschaft, -en** tyrannical rule; **g~los** non-violent; **die ~losigkeit** non-violence; **die ~maßnahme, -n** drastic measure; **der ~mensch, -en** (*wk masc*) brutal person; **die ~tat, -en** act of violence; **g~tätig** violent; **die ~tätigkeit, -en** violence; act of violence; **der ~verbrecher, -** violent criminal
die **Gewalten|teilung** separation of powers
gewaltig tremendous; powerful
gewaltsam violent; forcible; (*adv*) *also* by force
das **Gewand, ¨er** robe; *eccles* vestment
gewandt *p/part of* **wenden;** *also* agile; adroit; urbane
die **Gewandtheit** agility; adroitness; urbanity
gewann (gewänne) *p/t (subj) of* **gewinnen**
gewärtig: (+*gen*) ~ sein be prepared for
gewärtigen: zu ~ haben have to expect

[das] **Gewäsch** *coll* twaddle
gewaschen *p/part of* **waschen**
[das] **Gewässer, –** stretch of water; (*pl*) waters
[das] **Gewebe, –** fabric; web (of intrigue *etc*); *biol* tissue
geweckt *p/part*; *also* alert
[das] **Gewehr, –e** rifle; **~ ab!** order arms!; **das ~ über!** shoulder arms! || **der ~kolben, –** rifle-butt; **der ~lauf, ⸚e** rifle-barrel
[das] **Geweih, –e** antlers
gewellt *p/part*; *also* wavy; undulating; *tech* corrugated
[das] **Gewerbe, –** trade; *in compds also* industrial ...; **g~treibend** carrying on a trade
gewerblich commercial; industrial; business
gewerbs|mäßig professional; for profit
[die] **Gewerkschaft, –en** trade union
[der] **Gewerkschaftler, –** trade unionist
gewerkschaftlich trade union; **~ organisiert** unionized
Gewerkschafts– (trade) union ...
gewesen *p/part of* **sein**[1]; *esp Aust* former; **das Gewesene** (*decl as adj*) what is past
gewichen *p/part of* **weichen**[1]
gewichst [-ks-] *p/part*; *coll* crafty
[das] **Gewicht, –e** weight; **~ haben** carry weight; **~ legen auf** (*acc*) attach importance to; **nicht ins ~ fallen** be of no consequence || **das ~heben** weight-lifting; **der ~heber, –** weight-lifter
gewichten *stats* weight
gewichtig weighty
Gewichts– ... of weight; weight ...
gewieft *coll* cunning
gewiegt *coll* shrewd
[das] **Gewieher** neighing; *coll* guffaws
gewiesen *p/part of* **weisen**
gewillt prepared (to)
[das] **Gewimmel** throng; swarm
[das] **Gewinde, –** thread (of screw)
[der] **Gewinn, –e** profit; prize; winnings; **mit ~ verkaufen** sell at a profit || **die ~beteiligung** profit-sharing; **g~bringend** profitable; **die ~chancen** *pl* odds; **die ~liste, –n** list of winners; **das ~los, –e** winning ticket; **die ~spanne, –n** profit margin; **die ~sucht** greed for profit; **g~süchtig** greedy for profit
gewinnen (*p/t* **gewann** (*subj* **gewönne, gewänne**), *p/part* **gewonnen**) win; gain; acquire; *min* mine; (*v/i*) win; gain; improve (on acquaintance *etc*); **~ an** (*dat*) gain in; gain (height, speed); **~ aus** extract from; **~ für** win over to; **für sich ~** win over
gewinnend winning, engaging
[der] **Gewinner, –** winner
[der] **Gewinnler, –** profiteer
[die] **Gewinnung** *vbl noun*; *also* extraction
[das] **Gewirr, –e** tangle; maze; hubbub
gewiß certain, sure; (*before name, or* = unspecified, some) certain; (*adv*) certainly; (know) for certain; **aber ~!** but of course!
[das] **Gewissen** conscience; **auf dem ~ haben** be responsible for; have on one's conscience; **viel auf dem ~ haben** have a lot to answer for; **sich** *dat* **kein ~ machen aus** have no scruples about; (+*dat*) **ins ~ reden** reason with; **mit gutem ~** with a clear conscience || **g~los** unscrupulous
gewissenhaft conscientious
Gewissens– ... of conscience; **die ~bisse** *pl* pangs of conscience; guilty conscience; **die ~frage, –n** question of conscience; **die ~not, ⸚e** moral dilemma; **der ~zwang** moral constraint
gewisser|maßen so to speak; in a way
[die] **Gewißheit, –en** certainty
[das] **Gewitter, –** thunderstorm; (domestic) storm; **der ~regen, –** thundery shower; **die ~wolke, –n** thunder-cloud
gewittern: es gewittert it is thundering
gewittrig thundery
gewitzigt wiser (from experience)
gewitzt clever, smart
gewoben *p/part of* **weben**
gewogen *p/part of* **wägen, wiegen**[1]; *also* (*following dat*) well-disposed (to)
gewöhnen: ~ an (*acc*) accustom to; **sich ~ an** (*acc*) get used to; **gewöhnt an** used to
[die] **Gewohnheit, –en** habit; **aus ~** from force of habit; **zur ~ werden** become a habit
Gewohnheits– habitual ...; **g~mäßig** habitual; (*adv*) out of habit; **der ~mensch, –en** (*wk masc*) = **das ~tier, –e** *coll* creature of habit
gewöhnlich usual; ordinary; common; **für ~** usually; **wie ~** as usual
gewohnt usual; (+*acc*) **~ sein** be used to
[die] **Gewöhnung: ~ an** (*acc*) getting used to
[das] **Gewölbe, –** vault
gewölbt vaulted; domed; (road) cambered
[das] **Gewölk** (mass of) clouds
gewollt *p/part of* **wollen;** *also* contrived
gewönne *p/t subj*, **gewonnen** *p/part of* **gewinnen**
geworben *p/part of* **werben**
geworden *p/part of* **werden**
geworfen *p/part of* **werfen**
gewrungen *p/part of* **wringen**
[das] **Gewühl** (milling) crowd, throng
gewunden *p/part of* **winden**[1]; *also* winding; tortuous
gewürfelt *p/part*; *also* check(ed)
[das] **Gewürz, –e** spice; seasoning; **die ~gurke, –n** pickled gherkin; **das ~kraut, ⸚er** pot-herb; **die ~nelke, –n** clove
gewußt *p/part of* **wissen**
gez. (= **gezeichnet**) sgd.
gezackt jagged; serrated

gezahnt, gezähnt *p/part*; *also* toothed; serrated; *philat* perforated

das **Gezänk** squabbling

die **Gezeiten** *pl* tides; *in compds* tidal …

das **Gezeter** clamour

geziehen *p/part of* **zeihen**

gezielt *p/part*; *also* (measure *etc*) specific

geziemen: sich ~ be proper; **~d** fitting

geziert *p/part*; *also* affected

gezogen *p/part of* **ziehen**

das **Gezücht, -e** rabble

das **Gezwitscher** twittering

gezwungen *p/part of* **zwingen;** *also* forced; unnatural, stiff; **gezwungener|maßen** of necessity

GG = Grundgesetz

ggf. = gegebenenfalls

Ghana [g-] Ghana

der **Ghanese, -n** (*wk masc*), **ghanesisch** Ghanaian

der **Ghostwriter** ['goːstraętɐ], **-** ghostwriter; **~ sein für** ghost for

gib *imp sing*, **gib(s)t** (*2nd*,) *3rd sing pres of* **geben**

die **Gicht** gout

gichtisch gouty

der **Giebel, -** gable; (over window) pediment; **das ~dach, ⸚er** gabled roof

die **Gier** greed (**nach** for); craving (for)

gieren: ~ nach crave after

gierig greedy (**nach** for)

Gieß- casting …; foundry …; **der ~bach, ⸚e** (mountain) torrent; **die ~kanne, -n** watering-can

gießen (*p/t* **goß** (*subj* **gösse**), *p/part* **gegossen**) pour; water; *tech* cast; **es gießt (in Strömen)** it's pouring down

die **Gießerei, -en** foundry

das **Gift, -e** poison; venom; **darauf kannst du ~ nehmen** *coll* you can bet your life on it; **~ und Galle speien** be hopping mad

Gift- poison …; poisonous …; toxic …; poisoned …; **gift|grün** vivid green; **der ~mischer, -** preparer of poison; *joc* pharmacist; **die ~nudel, -n** *coll* vixen, shrew; **der ~pilz, -e** toadstool

giftig poisonous; toxic; venomous; **~ ansehen** look daggers at

der **Gigant, -en** (*wk masc*) giant

gigantisch gigantic

die **Gilde, -n** guild

gilt(st) (*2nd*,) *3rd sing pres of* **gelten**

der **Gimpel, -** bullfinch; *coll* ninny

der **Gin** [dʒɪn], **-s** gin

ging *p/t of* **gehen**

der **Ginster, -** *bot* broom

der **Gipfel, -** summit; pinnacle; **das ist der ~!** that beats everything! || **die ~konferenz, -en** summit conference; **der ~punkt, -e** pinnacle; **das ~treffen, -** summit (meeting)

gipfeln: ~ in (*dat*) culminate in

der **Gips, -e** plaster of Paris; *miner* gypsum; *med* plaster; **der ~abdruck, ⸚e** plaster cast; **das ~bein, -e** *coll* leg in plaster/a cast *US*; **der ~kopf, ⸚e** *coll* blockhead; **der ~verband, ⸚e** plaster cast

gipsen repair with plaster; plaster (wine); *coll* put in plaster/a cast *US*

der **Gipser, -** plasterer

die **Giraffe, -n** giraffe

girieren [ʒ-] endorse (cheque *etc*)

das **Girl** [gøːɐl, gœrl], **-s** chorus-girl; *coll* girl

die **Girlande, -n, mit ~n schmücken** festoon

der **Girlitz, -e** serin

das **Giro** [ʒ-], **-s** giro; endorsement (on cheque *etc*); **das ~konto, -(t)en** current account, checking account *US*

girren coo

das **gis, Gis** [-ɪ-] (*gen* **-**), **-** *mus* (the note) G sharp; (*key*) **Gis** G sharp major, **gis** G sharp minor

der **Gischt** (*also* **die**) spray

die **Gitarre, -n** guitar

der **Gitarrist, -en** (*wk masc*) guitarist

das **Gitter, -** bars; railing(s); grille; grating, grid; trellis; lattice; *elect, geog* grid; *phys* grating; lattice; **hinter ~n** *coll* behind bars || **das ~bett, -en** cot, crib *US*; **das ~fenster, -** barred window; **der ~mast, -en** pylon; **das ~netz, -e** *geog* grid; **der ~stab, ⸚e** bar

die **Glace** ['glasə], **-n** *Swiss* ice-cream

der **Glacé|handschuh** [-s-], **-e** kid glove

der **Gladiator, -(or)en** gladiator

die **Gladiole, -n** gladiolus

der **Glanz** sheen, lustre; gloss; radiance; splendour; **mit ~** *coll* brilliantly; (pass) with flying colours; **mit ~ und Gloria** *coll* (fail) spectacularly

Glanz- glossy …; brilliant …; **das ~leder** patent leather; **die ~leistung, -en** brilliant achievement; **g~los** dull; lacklustre; **die ~nummer, -n** star turn; **der ~punkt, -e** highlight; **das ~stück, -e** pièce de résistance; **g~voll** magnificent; brilliant; **die ~zeit, -en** heyday

glänzen shine (*also* = excel); be shiny; **durch seine Abwesenheit ~** *coll* be conspicuous by one's absence; **~d** shining; shiny; brilliant; splendid

das **Glas, ⸚er** glass (= material, vessel); jar; lens; binoculars; opera-glasses; **unter ~** behind/*hort* under glass || **der ~bläser, -** glass-blower; **die ~malerei, -en** (stained) glass painting; **die ~scheibe, -n** pane of glass; **g~weise** by the glass; **die ~wolle** glass wool

der **Glaser, -** glazier

die **Glaserei, -en** glazing; glazier's workshop

gläsern glass; glassy

glasieren glaze; *cul* ice

glasig glassy; *cul* transparent; (potatoes) waxy

^{die} **Glasur, -en** glaze; *cul* icing

glatt (*comp*, *superl also* ¨) smooth; (hair) straight; (cloth) plain; (road *etc*) slippery; (victory) clear; (break) clean; *coll* (lie *etc*) downright; (refusal) flat; (*adv*) smoothly; completely; *coll* straight (to s.o.'s face); flatly; simply; **das G~eis** (black) ice (**aufs G. führen** take for a ride); **~machen** (*sep*) smooth; *coll* settle; **~rasiert** clean-shaven; **~streichen*** (*sep*) smooth; smooth out; **~weg** [-vɛk] *coll* flatly; **~züngig** glib

die **Glätte** smoothness; slipperiness

glätten smooth; smooth out; *Swiss* iron; **sich ~** (sea) become calm

Glatz-: der ~kopf, ¨e bald head/*coll* person; **g~köpfig** bald

die **Glatze, -n** bald head; **eine ~ bekommen/haben** go/be bald

glaub-: ~würdig credible; (witness) reliable; **die G~würdigkeit** credibility; reliability

der **Glaube** (*acc*, *dat* **-n**, *gen* **-ns**) faith (**an** *acc* in); belief (in); (+*dat*) **~n schenken** give credence to

glauben believe (statement *etc*); think (that ...); (+*dat*) believe (s.o.'s story *etc*); (*v/i*) believe (**an** *acc* in); (+*dat*) believe (person); **ich glaube schon** I think so; **das glaube ich (gern)** I can well imagine; **nicht zu ~** incredible; **jmdn. ~ machen wollen, daß ...** try to make s.o. believe that ...; **dran ~ müssen** *coll* cop it

Glaubens- ... of faith; religious ...; **das ~bekenntnis, -se** creed; **der ~bruder, ..brüder** co-religionist; **der ~satz, ¨e** dogma

glaubhaft credible; plausible

die **Glaubhaftigkeit** credibility; plausibility

gläubig believing; religious; trusting; **-gläubig** believing in ...; **der/die Gläubige** (*decl as adj*) believer

der **Gläubiger, -** creditor

die **Gläubigkeit** faith; trust

glaublich: kaum ~ hardly credible

glazial *geol* glacial

gleich same; the same; equal; (+*dat*; *often following noun*) like; (*adv*) equally (fast *etc*); (treat *etc*) equally, the same; immediately, right away; in a minute; right (after, beside, *etc*); (*before num*) *not translated*; (*with interrog*) again (*eg* **wie heißt er doch ~?** what's his name again?); **-gleich** -like; **es ist mir ~** *coll* it's all the same to me; **ganz ~, ob** *etc* ... regardless of whether *etc* ...; **~ alt/groß/lang/schwer/viel** the same age/size/length/weight/amount; **~!** coming!; **bis ~!** see you later!; **das ~e** the same (thing) || **~altrig** of the same age; **~artig** of the same kind; similar; **~auf** *sp* level; **~bedeutend** synonymous; **~berechtigt** having equal rights; **die G~berechtigung** equal rights; equality; **~bleiben*** (*sep*; *sn*) stay the same; remain constant (**sich** *dat* **g.** stay the same; **das bleibt sich ~** it makes no difference); **~bleibend** constant; consistent; **~falls** likewise; too (**danke g.!** thank you, the same to you!); **~farbig** of the same colour; **~förmig** uniform; monotonous; **die G~förmigkeit** uniformity; monotony; **~ge|artet** similar; **~geschlechtlich** homosexual; **~gesinnt** like-minded; **~gestellt** *p/part*; *also* equal (*following dat* to), on a par (with); **das G~gewicht** balance; equilibrium (**aus dem G. bringen** throw off-balance); **~gültig** immaterial; indifferent (**das ist mir g.** it's all the same to me); **die G~gültigkeit** indifference; **der G~klang** harmony; **~kommen*** (*sep*; *sn*) (+*dat*) equal (**an** *dat* in); be tantamount to; **~laufend** parallel; *mech* synchronized; **~lautend** identically worded; **~machen** (*sep*) make equal, level (**dem Boden g.** raze to the ground); **die G~macherei** egalitarianism; **~macherisch** egalitarian; **das G~maß** evenness; symmetry; regularity; equanimity; **~mäßig** even; regular; **die G~mäßigkeit** evenness; regularity; **der G~mut** equanimity; **~mütig** serene; **~namig** of the same name; *math* with a common denominator; **~rangig** of equal rank/importance; (treatment) equal; **~schalten** (*sep*) *esp Nazi* bring into line; **die G~schaltung** *esp Nazi* bringing into line; **~schenklig** isosceles; **der G~schritt** marching in step (**G. halten** keep in step); **~sehen*** (*sep*) (+*dat*) resemble (**das sieht ihm ~!** that's just like him!); **~seitig** equilateral; **~setzen** (*sep*) equate; **die G~setzung** equation; **~stellen** (*sep*) (*see also* **gleichgestellt**) put on an equal footing; treat as equal(s); **der G~strom** direct current; **~tun*** (*sep*) (**es jmdm. g.** match s.o. (**an** *dat* in)); **~viel** nevertheless; no matter (whether *etc*); **~wertig** equivalent; equal; evenly-matched; **~wohl** nevertheless; **~zeitig** simultaneous; (*adv*) *also* at the same time; **die G~zeitigkeit** simultaneity; **~ziehen*** (*sep*) catch up (**mit** with)

gleichen (*p/t* **glich**, *p/part* **geglichen**) (+*dat*) resemble

gleicher-: ~maßen = ~weise equally

die **Gleichheit** equality; identity

das **Gleichnis, -se** parable; simile

gleichsam so to speak

die **Gleichung, -en** equation

das **Gleis, -e** track; **totes ~** siding; **der Zug läuft auf ~ (5** *etc*) **ein** the train is arriving on platform/track *US* (5 *etc*); **auf ein totes ~ schieben** put on ice; **aus dem ~ bringen** put off his/her stroke; upset; **aus dem ~**

springen jump the rails/track *US*; **ins rechte ~ bringen** straighten out
–gleisig –track
gleißen *poet* gleam
Gleit–: das ~boot, –e hydroplane; **der ~flug, ⸚e** glide; **das ~flugzeug, –e** glider; **der ~punkt, –e** *comput* floating point; **der ~schutz** anti-skid device
gleiten (*p/t* **glitt,** *p/part* **geglitten**) (*sn*) glide; slide; slip; **~ lassen +in** (*acc*) slip into; **+über** (*acc*) run (one's eye, finger) over; **~d** (scale) sliding; (working hours) flexible; *comput* floating
der **Gletscher, –** glacier; *in compds also* glacial ...; **die ~spalte, –n** crevasse
glich *p/t of* **gleichen**
das **Glied, –er** member; link; *anat* joint; limb; penis; *mil* rank; *bibl* generation; **an allen ~ern** (shake) all over || **die ~maßen** *pl* limbs; **der ~satz, ⸚e** subordinate clause
Glieder–: die ~puppe, –n jointed doll; **das ~reißen** *coll* = **die ~schmerzen** *pl* rheumatic pains
gliedern organize, structure; plan (essay); **~ in** (*acc*) divide into
die **Gliederung, –en** organization; division; structure; plan (of essay)
–gliedrig with ... limbs/joints/links/sections/members
Glimm–: der ~stengel, – *coll* 'fag'
glimmen (*p/t* **glomm/glimmte** (*subj* **glömme/glimmte**) *p/part* **geglommen/geglimmt**) glow
der **Glimmer, –** mica
glimmern glimmer
glimpflich lenient; **~ davonkommen** get off lightly
glitsch(er)ig slippery
glitt *p/t of* **gleiten**
glitzern glitter
global global; general
der **Globus, –se/Globen** globe
die **Glocke, –n** bell; (glass) cover; cloche (hat); **an die große ~ hängen** *coll* shout from the rooftops || **die ~n|blume, –n** campanula; **das ~n|geläut** peal of bells; **der ~n|schlag, ⸚e** stroke (of bell) (**mit dem G.** on the dot); **das ~n|spiel, –e** carillon, chimes; glockenspiel; **der ~n|turm, ⸚e** belfry
der **Glöckner, –** bell-ringer
glomm (glömme) *p/t* (*subj*) *of* **glimmen**
glor–: ~reich glorious
die **Glorie** [–ĭə], **–n** glory; = **der ~n|schein, –e** halo
glorifizieren glorify
die **Gloriole, –n** halo
glorios glorious
das **Glossar, –e** glossary
die **Glosse, –n** satirical commentary; sneering remark; *ling* gloss
glossieren write a satirical commentary on; sneer at; *ling* gloss
die **Glotz|augen** *pl coll* bulging eyes; **~ machen** goggle
glotzen *coll* stare, goggle
gluck: ~! cluck!; **~, ~!** glug, glug!
das **Glück** luck; (good) fortune; happiness; **~ haben** be lucky; **sein ~ versuchen** try one's luck (**bei** with); **ein ~, daß ...** it's a good thing ...; **viel ~!** good luck!; **auf gut ~** on the off-chance; at random; **ich kann von ~ sagen, daß ...** I can count myself lucky that ...; **zum ~** luckily || **g~bringend** lucky; **g~selig** blissful; **g~strahlend** radiant(ly happy); **g~verheißend** auspicious; **der ~wunsch, ⸚e** congratulations (**zu** on); good wishes
die **Glucke, –n** broody hen; mother-hen
glucken cluck; brood; *coll* sit around
glücken (*see also* **geglückt**) (*sn*) be a success, succeed; **ihm glückt alles** everything he does is a success; **es ist ihm geglückt zu ...** he succeeded in (+*ger*)
gluckern gurgle
glücklich happy; (chance *etc*) lucky; (*adv*) happily; safely; *coll* at last; **~e Reise!** bon voyage! || **glücklicher|weise** luckily
Glücks– lucky ...; der ~bringer, – mascot; talisman; **der ~fall, ⸚e** stroke of luck; **das ~gefühl** feeling of happiness; **die ~güter** *pl* the good things in life; **das ~kind, –er** lucky person; **der ~pilz, –e** *coll* lucky devil; **der ~ritter, –** adventurer; **~sache** (**das ist G.** it's a matter of luck); **das ~spiel, –e** game of chance; **der ~stern, –e** lucky star; **die ~strähne, –n** lucky streak; **der ~umstand, ⸚e** fortunate circumstance
glucksen chuckle; gurgle
Glüh–: die ~birne, –n electric light bulb; **der ~faden, ..fäden** filament; **die ~lampe, –n** electric light bulb; **der ~wein, –e** mulled wine; **das ~würmchen, –** glow-worm; firefly
glühen heat until red-hot; (*v/i*) glow; be aglow; **~ vor** (*dat*) be flushed with; burn with; **~d** glowing; red-hot; ardent; **~d heiß** scorching
die **Glukose** glucose
die **Glupsch|augen** *pl coll* bulging eyes
die **Glut, –en** embers; heat; (red) glow; ardour; **die ~hitze** scorching heat; **g~rot** fiery red
das **Glyzerin** glycerine
GmbH (= **Gesellschaft mit beschränkter Haftung**) Ltd.
die **Gnade** grace; mercy; favour; **~ für/vor Recht ergehen lassen** temper justice with mercy
gnaden: gnade dir/uns Gott! God help you/us!
Gnaden–: der ~akt, –e act of mercy; **das ~brot** keep (in old age); **die ~frist, –en**

respite; (... days' *etc*) grace; **der ~stoß, -̈e** coup de grâce

gnädig gracious; lenient; merciful; **G~e Frau, G~es Fräulein** Madam; **~ davonkommen** get off lightly

der **Gnom, -en** (*wk masc*) gnome

das **Gnu, -s** gnu

das **Goal** [goːl], **-s** *Aust, Swiss sp* goal

der **Gobelin** [gobəˈlɛ̃ː], **-s** Gobelin tapestry

der **Gockel, -** *esp SGer* cock

das **Go-in** [goːˈʔɪn], **-s** (demonstrators') disruption of a meeting (following unauthorized entry)

das **Gold** gold; **die ~ammer, -n** yellowhammer; **der ~barren, -** gold ingot; **der ~barsch, -e** ruff; **g~blond** golden; golden-haired; **der ~fisch, -e** goldfish; *joc* good catch; **das ~fisch|glas, -̈er** goldfish bowl; **g~gerändert** edged with gold; gold-rimmed; **der ~gräber, -** gold-digger; **die ~grube, -n** gold-mine; **das ~hähnchen, -** goldcrest; **g~haltig,** *Aust* **g~hältig** auriferous; **der ~junge, -n** (*wk masc*) *sp* golden boy; *coll* darling boy; **das ~kind, -er** *coll* darling; **der ~klumpen, -** gold nugget; **der ~lack** wallflower; **der ~rausch** gold-rush; **der ~regen, -** laburnum; **gọld|rịchtig** *coll* absolutely right; **der ~schmied, -e** goldsmith; **der ~schnitt** gilt edging; **das ~stück, -e** gold coin; *joc* (= person) gem; **~waage (jedes Wort auf die G. legen** weigh one's words; take everything too literally); **die ~währung** gold standard

golden gold; golden

goldig sweet, cute

das **Golf** golf

der **Golf, -e** gulf; (*in geographical names*: **der ~ von ...**) Gulf (of Aqaba, Corinth, *etc*), Bay (of Bengal, Biscay, Naples, *etc*)

Golf-: der ~platz, -̈e golf-course; **der ~schläger, -** golf-club; **der ~spieler, -** golfer; **die ~staaten** *pl* the Gulf States; **der ~strom** the Gulf Stream

die **Gondel, -n** gondola; cable-car

gondeln (*sn*) *coll* cruise (around)

der **Gong, -s** gong; *box* bell; **der ~schlag, -̈e** stroke of the gong

gongen sound the gong; **es gongt** the gong sounds

gönnen (+*dat*) not begrudge; allow

der **Gönner, -** patron; **die ~miene** patronizing air

gönnerhaft patronizing

die **Gonorrhöe** [gonɔˈrøː], **-n** [-ən] gonorrhoea

gor (göre) *p/t* (*subj*) *of* **gären**

das **Gör, -en, die Göre, -n** *NGer coll* kid; brat; (cheeky) young miss

gordisch: der ~e Knoten the Gordian knot

der **Gorịlla, -s** gorilla

die **Gosche, -n** *SGer vulg* 'gob'

goß (gösse) *p/t* (*subj*) *of* **gießen**

die **Gosse, -n** gutter

der **Gote, -n** (*wk masc*) Goth

Göteborg Gothenburg

die **Gotik** [-ɪk] Gothic (style)

gotisch, (*language*) **G~** Gothic

der **Gott, -̈er** god; *in exclamations frequently* heaven(s); **Gott** God; **~ und die Welt** everybody; **wie ~ in Frankreich leben** *coll* live like a king; **den lieben ~ einen guten Mann sein lassen** *coll* lead a happy-go-lucky life; **dem lieben ~ den Tag stehlen** *coll* idle away the time; **du bist wohl (total) von ~ verlassen** you must be out of your mind; **ach ~, ...** oh, (I can't complain *etc*); **ach (du lieber) ~! = o ~!** oh dear!; goodness!; **großer/mein ~!** good heavens!; **~ sei Dank!** thank heavens!; **um ~es willen!** for heaven's sake!; good heavens!; **weiß ~** heaven knows; **wollte ~, daß ...** would to God that ... || **~erbarmen** *coll* **(zum G.** pathetic(ally)); **g~ergeben** meek; **g~lo̲b** thank heavens; **g~los** godless; ungodly; **g~verlassen** godforsaken; **g~voll** *coll* divine

Götter- ... of the gods; divine ...; **die ~dämmerung** twilight of the gods; **der ~gatte, -n** (*wk masc*) *joc* lord and master; **die ~speise, -n** ambrosia; *cul* jelly

Gottes- ... of God; **die ~anbeterin, -nen** praying mantis; **der ~dienst, -e** (divine) service; **g~fürchtig** God-fearing; **das ~gnadentum** divine right of kings; **der ~lästerer, -** blasphemer; **die ~lästerung, -en** blasphemy

die **Gottheit, -en** deity; divinity

die **Göttin, -nen** goddess

göttlich divine

gotts|erbạ̈rmlich *coll* pitiful

der **Götze, -n** (*wk masc*) idol; **der ~n|dienst** idolatry

goutie̲ren [gu-] appreciate

die **Gouvernạnte** [gu-], **-n** governess

gouvernạntenhaft schoolmarmish

der **Gouverneur** [guvɛrˈnøːɐ], **-e** governor

das **Grab, -̈er** grave; tomb; **zu ~e tragen** bury; abandon (wish)

Grab- *also* burial ...; funeral ...; **der ~gesang, -̈e** dirge; **der ~hügel, -** burial mound; **die ~inschrift, -en** epitaph; **das ~mal, -̈er** tomb; monument; **die ~rede, -n** funeral oration; **die ~stätte, -n** burial-place; tomb; **der ~stein, -e** gravestone

grabbeln *NGer coll* grope about

graben (gräb(s)t, *p/t* **grub** (*subj* **grübe),** *p/part* **gegraben)** (*also v/i*) dig; **~ in** (*acc*) carve (initials *etc*) in; sink (teeth) into; **~ nach** dig for

sich ~ in (*acc*) (claws *etc*) sink into; imprint itself on (memory)

der **Graben,** *pl* **Gräben** ditch; moat; *mil* trench;

geol rift valley, graben
Grabes– sepulchral ...; **die ~stille** deathly hush
gräb(s)t (*2nd,*) *3rd sing pres of* **graben**
der **Grad, –e/**(*following num*) **–** degree; *mil* rank; **Vetter zweiten ~es** second cousin; **bis zu einem gewissen ~** to a certain extent; **in hohem ~(e)** to a great extent || **der ~messer, –** yardstick; **das ~netz, –e** (map) grid; **g~weise** by degrees
grade *coll* = **gerade**
graduell gradual; (difference) in degree
graduieren confer a degree on
der **Graf, –en** (*wk masc*) count; (*British*) earl
die **Graffiti** *pl* graffiti
Grafik(er) = **Graphik(er)**
die **Gräfin, –nen** countess
grafisch = **graphisch**
gräflich count's; earl's
die **Grafschaft, –en** county
das **Graham|brot** ['gra:ham–] (*type of*) wholemeal bread, graham bread *US*
der **Gral** the Grail; **der ~s|hüter, –** keeper of the Grail; custodian
gram: (+*dat***) ~ sein** bear (s.o.) ill will
der **Gram** grief; **g~erfüllt** = **g~voll** grief-stricken
grämen, sich ~ grieve
grämlich morose
das **Gramm, –e/**(*following num*) **–** gram(me)
die **Grammatik** [–ɪk], **–en** grammar
grammatikalisch grammatical
der **Grammatiker, –** grammarian
grammatisch grammatical
der **Granat, –e** garnet; **der ~apfel, ..äpfel** pomegranate; **das ~feuer** shell-fire; **der ~trichter, –** shell-crater; **der ~werfer, –** mortar
die **Granate, –n** shell; grenade
die **Grandezza** grandeur
grandios magnificent
der **Granit, –e** granite; **auf ~ beißen bei** *coll* not get anywhere with
grantig *SGer coll* grumpy
die **Grapefruit** ['gre:pfru:t], **–s** grapefruit
die **Graphik** [–ɪk], **–en** graphic arts; print
der **Graphiker, –** graphic artist
graphisch graphic; **~e Darstellung** graph
der **Graphit, –e** graphite
der **Graphologe, –n** (*wk masc*) graphologist
die **Graphologie** graphology
grapschen *coll* grab; **~ nach** make a grab at
das **Gras, ¨er** grass; **das ~ wachsen hören** read too much into things; **~ wachsen lassen über** (*acc*) let the dust settle on; **ins ~ beißen** *coll* bite the dust || **gras|grün** grass-green; **der ~halm, –e** blade of grass; **der ~hüpfer, –** *coll* grasshopper; **die ~mücke, –n** warbler; **die ~narbe, –n** turf; **die ~steppe, –n** prairie
grasen graze
grasig grassy
grassieren be rampant; be rife
gräßlich ghastly; awful
der **Grat, –e** ridge; dividing-line; **die ~wanderung, –en** hike along a mountain ridge; *pol etc* tightrope walk
die **Gräte, –n** fish-bone; **g~n|los** boneless; **das ~n|muster** herringbone (pattern); **der ~n|schritt** *ski* herringbone
die **Gratifikation, –en** bonus
gratis [–ɪs] free (of charge); **die G~probe, –n** free sample
die **Grätsche** [–ɛ:–], **–n** straddle
grätschen [–ɛ:–] straddle; (*v/i sn*) do a straddle
der **Gratulant, –en** (*wk masc*) well-wisher
die **Gratulation, –en** congratulations; **die ~s|cour** [–ku:ɐ], **–en** reception (held in s.o.'s honour)
gratulieren (+*dat*) congratulate (**zu** on); (+*dat*) **zum Geburtstag ~** wish (s.o.) many happy returns; **(ich) gratuliere!** congratulations!
grau grey; (past *etc*) dim and distant; **~e Haare bekommen** turn grey; **die ~e Substanz** grey matter; **~ in ~ malen** paint a gloomy picture of
grau– grey ...; (*with second colour-word attached*) greyish–; **das G~brot, –e** (loaf of) rye-bread; **G~bünden** the Grisons (*Swiss canton*); **die G~gans, ¨e** greylag goose; **~meliert** tinged with grey; greying; **der G~schimmel, –** grey (horse); **das G~tier, –e** *coll* donkey
das **Grauchen** [–ç–], **–** *coll* donkey
grauen[1] (day) dawn
grauen[2]**: mir graut vor** (*dat*) I dread
das **Grauen** horror; **g~erregend** horrifying; **g~voll** horrifying; *coll* dreadful
grauenhaft horrifying; *coll* dreadful
graulen: sich ~ *coll* be scared (**vor** *dat* of)
gräulich greyish
graupeln: es graupelt soft hail is falling
die **Graupeln** *pl* soft hail
die **Graupen** *pl* pearl-barley
der **Graus** *arch* horror; **o ~!** *joc* oh horror!
grausam cruel (**gegen/zu** to); *coll* dreadful
die **Grausamkeit, –en** cruelty; (act of) cruelty
grausen = **grauen**[2]
das **Grausen** horror; **da kann man das große ~ kriegen** *coll* it's enough to give you the creeps
grausig horrifying; *coll* dreadful
der **Graveur** [–'vø:ɐ], **–e** engraver
gravieren engrave
gravierend serious
die **Gravierung, –en** engraving
die **Gravitation** gravitation; *in compds* **~s–** gravitational ...
gravitätisch solemn

die **Gravur, –en** engraving
die **Grazie** [–ĭə], **–n** grace; *joc* charming young lady; (*pl*) Graces
grazil (delicately) slender
graziös graceful
Gregor Gregory
der **Greif, –e** (*or* **–en** (*wk masc*)) griffin
Greif– gripping ...; *zool* prehensile ...
greifbar tangible; available; ~ **nahe** within easy reach
greifen (*p/t* **griff,** *p/part* **gegriffen**) grasp; seize; *mus* strike (chord); (*v/i* wheel *etc*) grip; **zu hoch/niedrig gegriffen** (figure) too high/low; **zum Greifen nahe** within reach/one's grasp
~ **an** (*acc*) touch
hinter sich ~ **müssen** *sp* let in a goal
~ **in** (*acc*) dip into; **mächtig in die Tasten** ~ play with vigour
~ **nach** reach for; grab at; attempt to seize (power)
um sich ~ grope about; (fire, epidemic, *etc*) spread
~ **zu** reach for; take up (pen, arms); resort to; **zur Flasche** ~ take to drink
der **Greifer, –** *tech* grab
greinen *coll* whine
greis aged, very old; hoary
der **Greis, –e** old man; **das ~en|alter** extreme old age
greisenhaft senile
die **Greisin, –nen** old woman
grell glaring; shrill
das **Gremium, –(i)en** body; committee
Grenz– border ..., frontier ...; boundary ...; **der ~baum, ⸚e** (frontier) barrier; **der ~fall, ⸚e** borderline case; **der ~gänger, –** border crosser; **das ~gebiet, –e** border area; **die ~linie, –n** boundary; **der ~posten, –** border guard; **der ~schutz** border police; protection of the border; **die ~situation, –en** borderline situation; **der ~übergang, ⸚e** frontier crossing-point; = **der ~übertritt, –e** crossing of the border; **der ~wert, –e** *math, comput* limit
die **Grenze, –n** border; frontier; boundary; limit; dividing-line; **seine ~n kennen** know one's limitations; **keine ~n kennen** know no bounds; (+*dat*) **~n setzen** set limits to; **sich in ~n halten** be limited
grenzen: ~ an (*acc*) border on
grenzen|los boundless; infinite
der **Grenzer, –** *coll* border guard; customs official
Gretchen– ['greːtçən–]: **die ~frage** sixty-four-thousand-dollar question; **die ~frisur, –en** long blonde hair in plaits
der **Greuel, –** horror (**vor** *dat* of); abomination; (*pl*) atrocities; **... ist mir ein ~** I loathe ... || **die ~tat, –en** atrocity
greulich abominable; atrocious
der **Grieche, –n** (*wk masc*) Greek; **~n|land** Greece
griechisch, (*language*) **G~** Greek
grienen *NGer coll* smirk
Gries–: der ~gram, –e sourpuss; **g~grämig** grumpy
der **Grieß** semolina
griff *p/t of* **greifen**
der **Griff, –e** grip, *sp* hold, grip; handle; (*corresp to* **greifen: nach/zu**) reaching (for), (**in** *acc*) dipping (into); **falscher ~** false move; **einen guten ~ tun** make a good choice; **im ~ haben** have under control; have the knack of; **in den ~ bekommen** gain control of || **g~bereit** ready to hand; **das ~brett, –er** finger-board
der **Griffel, –** slate-pencil; *bot* style
griffig that grips well; (expression) handy
der **Grill, –s** grill; rotisserie; barbecue; *mot* grille
die **Grille, –n** cricket; whim; (*pl*) gloomy thoughts
grillen grill; barbecue
grillenhaft moody; whimsical
die **Grimasse, –n** grimace; **~n schneiden** pull faces
der **Grimm** wrath
grimmig furious; (humour *etc*) grim; (cold *etc*) severe
der **Grind, –e** scab
grindig scabby
grinsen, das Grinsen grin; smirk
grippal influenzal
die **Grippe, –n** influenza
der **Grips** *coll* grey matter
der **Grisly|bär** ['grɪsli–], **–en** (*wk masc*) grizzly bear
grob (*comp, superl* ⸚) coarse; rough; gross; **wir sind aus dem Gröbsten heraus** *coll* we're over the worst || **~körnig** coarse-grained; **~schlächtig** uncouth
die **Grobheit, –en** coarseness; roughness; coarse/rude remark
der **Grobian, –e** boor
gröblich gross
der **Grog** [grɔk], **–s** grog
groggy [–i] *box* groggy; *coll* all in
grölen *coll* bawl
der **Groll** grudge; resentment
grollen rumble; (+*dat*) bear a grudge against
Grönland Greenland
das **Gros** [groː] (*gen* **–** [–(s)]), **–** [–s] bulk, majority
der **Groschen** ['grɔʃŋ], **–** (*Austria*) groschen (*1/100 of a schilling*); (*E. & W. Germany*) *coll* 10-pfennig piece; (*in idioms*) penny; **der ~ ist gefallen** *coll* the penny has dropped || **der ~roman, –e** cheap novel
groß [–oː–] (*comp* **größer,** *superl* **größt../am größten**) big; tall; great; grown-up; grand;

(letter) capital; (*adv*) in style; *coll* (*with neg*) (very) much, particularly; *as coll particle*, *reinforces question* (*eg* **was soll man da ~ sagen?** what is there to say?); **die G~en Seen** the Great Lakes; **~ in** (*dat*) *coll* very good at; **~ und klein** young and old; **~ schreiben** (*cf* **großschreiben**) write with a capital letter; **~ werden** grow up; **im ~en und ganzen** on the whole; **größer..** *also* major

Groß– *also* large ...; large-scale ...; bulk ...; Greater ...; Grand ...;

g~angelegt large-scale; **g~artig** splendid; grand; **die ~aufnahme, –n** close-up; **~britannien** (Great) Britain; **der ~buch|stabe, –n** (*like* **Buchstabe**) capital letter; **das ~bürgertum** upper middle class; **g~deutsch** *hist* pan-German; **der ~einsatz, ⸚e** large-scale operation; **die ~eltern** *pl* grandparents; **die ~familie, –n** extended family; **g~flächig** large (in area); (face) broad; **das ~format** large size; **g~formatig** large-sized; **der ~handel** wholesale trade (**im G. kaufen/verkaufen** buy/sell wholesale); **der ~händler, –** wholesaler; **g~herzig** magnanimous; **der ~herzog, ⸚e** grand duke; **das ~herzogtum, ⸚er** grand duchy; **das ~hirn, –e** cerebrum; **der/die ~industrielle** (*decl as adj*) industrial magnate; **das ~kapital** big business; **die ~katze, –n** big cat; **g~kotzig** *coll* swaggering; **die ~macht, ⸚e** great power; **die ~manns|sucht** craving for prestige; **das ~maul, ⸚er** *coll* loudmouth; **g~mäulig** *coll* loud-mouthed; **die ~mut** magnanimity; **g~mütig** magnanimous; **die ~mutter, ..mütter** grandmother; **die ~offensive, –n** major offensive; **die ~packung, –en** economy pack; **der ~rat, ⸚e** *Swiss* member of a cantonal parliament; **der ~raum, ⸚e** larger area; area (= city with environs, *eg* **im G. Stuttgart** in the S. area); = **das ~raum|büro, –s** open-plan office; **das ~raum|flugzeug, –e** wide-bodied aircraft; **g~räumig** spacious; extensive; **der ~rechner, –** mainframe (computer); **das ~reine|machen** *coll* thorough cleaning; **g~schreiben*** (*sep*) (*cf* **groß schreiben** *at* **groß**) (**g~geschrieben werden** be stressed); **die ~schreibung** capitalization; **g~sprecherisch** boastful; **g~spurig** self-important; **die ~stadt, ⸚e** city; **der ~städter, –** city-dweller; **g~städtisch** (life *etc*) city; **der ~teil** greater part, bulk; large proportion; **der ~tuer, –** show-off; **g~tuerisch** boastful; **g~tun*: (sich) g.** (*sep*) brag (**mit** about); **der ~vater, ..väter** grandfather; **der ~verdiener, –** big earner; **das ~vieh** horses and cattle; **das ~wild** big game; **der ~wild|jäger, –** big-game hunter; **g~ziehen*** (*sep*) bring up; rear; **g~zügig** generous; broad-minded

die **Größe, –n** size; height; greatness; important figure; *astron* magnitude; *math, phys* quantity; *comput* (data) item; **unbekannte ~** unknown quantity || **die ~n|ordnung, –en** scale; magnitude; **der ~n|wahn** megalomania; **g~n|wahnsinnig** megalomaniac

großen|teils largely, for the most part

der **Grossist, –en** (*wk masc*) wholesaler

größt–: ~möglich greatest possible

größten|teils very largely

grotesk grotesque

die **Groteske, –n** *art* grotesque; *liter* grotesque tale

die **Grotte, –n** grotto

grub (grübe) *p/t* (*subj*) *of* **graben**

das **Grübchen, –** dimple

die **Grube, –n** pit (*also min*)

grübeln brood

Gruben– mine ...; pit ...; **der ~arbeiter, –** miner; **das ~gas** firedamp

der **Grübler, –** brooding person

grüblerisch pensive

grüezi! [–εtsi] *Swiss* hullo!

die **Gruft, ⸚e** (burial) vault; crypt

grün green; **die G~e Insel** the Emerald Isle; (+*dat*) **nicht ~ sein** *coll* have no time for; **sich ~ und blau/gelb ärgern** *coll* be hopping mad; **~ und blau schlagen** *coll* beat black and blue; **das ist dasselbe in G~** *coll* it's the same thing; **der/die Grüne** (*decl as adj*; *usu pl*) *pol* Green; **Grünes** (*decl as adj*) greenery; greens; green fodder; **im G~en/ins G~e** in/to the country

grün– green ...; (*with second colour-word attached*) greenish–; **die G~anlagen** *pl* (public) parks and gardens; **der G~donners|tag, –e** Maundy Thursday; **der G~fink, –en** (*wk masc*) greenfinch; **die G~fläche, –n** (grass-covered) open space; **der G~kohl** curly kale; **der G~schnabel, ..schnäbel** *coll* young whipper-snapper; greenhorn; **der G~span** verdigris; **der G~streifen, –** central reservation, median strip *US*; grass verge; **das G~zeug** *coll* (raw) green vegetables; herbs

der **Grund, ⸚e** ground; bottom; (back)ground; reason; *Aust* property; *poet* valley; **~ und Boden** land; **auf ~** (+*gen*) as a result of; on the basis of; **auf ~ geraten/laufen** run aground; (+*dat*) **auf den ~ gehen** get to the bottom of; **bis auf den ~** (drain) to the dregs; (raze) to the ground; **aus diesem ~** for this reason; **im ~e (genommen)** really, strictly speaking; **in ~ und Boden** utterly; outright; **von ~ auf/aus** completely

Grund– basic ...; **(grund–)** thoroughly ...; completely ...; extremely ...

der ~besitz land; land ownership; **das**

~**buch,** ¨**er** land register; **grund|falsch** utterly wrong; **die ~farbe, –n** primary/ground colour; **~festen (in seinen G. erschüttern** shake to its foundations); **die ~fläche, –n** area; *math* base; **die ~gebühr, –en** basic charge; **das ~gesetz** the Basic Law (*W. German constitution*); **der ~herr, –en** (*like* **Herr**) *hist* lord of the manor; **die ~lage, –n** basis; **g~legend** fundamental; **die ~linie, –n** *math*, *sp* base-line; **g~los** bottomless; groundless; (*adv*) without any reason; **die ~mauer, –n** foundation wall; **der ~pfeiler, –** supporting pillar/pier; keystone (of system *etc*); **der ~riß, –(ss)e** ground-plan; outline; **der ~satz,** ¨**e** principle; **g~sätzlich** fundamental; (*adv*) fundamentally; in/on principle; **die ~schule, –n** primary school; **der ~stein, –e** foundation-stone; foundation(s) (**zu** of); **die ~steuer, –n** property tax; **der ~stock** basis; **der ~stoff, –e** raw material; *chem* element; **das ~stück, –e** plot of land; **der ~stücks|makler, –** estate agent, realtor *US*; **die ~tendenz, –en** general trend; **grund|verschieden** totally different; **der ~vertrag** the General Relations Treaty (between E. and W. Germany); **das ~wasser** ground water; **die ~zahl, –en** cardinal number; *math* base; **der ~zug,** ¨**e** essential feature; (*pl*) essentials

gründen start; found; ~ **auf** (*acc*) base on; **sich ~ auf** (*acc*) be based on

der **Gründer, –** founder; **die ~jahre** *pl* = **die ~zeit** (*period of rapid industrial expansion following the Franco-Prussian War of 1870-71*)

grundieren prime

gründlich thorough

grünen turn green

grünlich greenish

der **Grünling, –e** greenfinch

grunzen grunt

die **Gruppe, –n** group; *mil* squad; **die ~n|arbeit** teamwork; **das ~n|bild, –er** group portrait; **der ~n|sex** group sex; **die ~n|therapie** group therapy; **g~n|weise** in groups

gruppieren, sich ~ group

die **Gruppierung, –en** grouping

der **Grus** (coal) slack; *geol* gravel

Grusel– horror …

gruselig creepy; spine-chilling

gruseln: mich/mir gruselt vor (*dat*) **… …** give(s) me the creeps

der **Gruß** [–u:–], ¨**e** greeting; *mil* salute; **mit freundlichen Grüßen/freundlichem ~** yours sincerely; **schöne Grüße an** (*acc*) (give) my regards to; **zum ~** in greeting

grüßen greet; *mil* salute; (*v/i*) say hullo; *mil* salute; **grüß dich!**, *SGer* **grüß Gott!** hullo!; **~ lassen** send (s.o.) one's regards; **grüß … von mir** give my regards to …

die **Grütze, –n** groats; *coll* brains

der **Gschaftlhuber, –** *SGer coll* busybody

das **Gspusi, –s** *SGer coll* sweetheart; love-affair

Guayana [gŭaj–] Guiana

der **Guayaner, –, guayanisch** Guianan

Guck–: die ~kasten|bühne, –n proscenium stage; **das ~loch,** ¨**er** peep-hole

gucken *coll* look; peep; **Fernsehen ~** watch television

Guerilla– [ge'rılja–]: **der ~kämpfer, –** guerilla; **der ~krieg, –e** guerilla war(fare)

der **Gugelhupf, –e** *SGer* (*type of cake baked in a fluted mould*)

die **Guillotine** [gijo–, gıljo–], **–n, guillotinieren** guillotine

Guinea [gi–] Guinea

der **Guineer, –, guineisch** Guinean

das **Gulasch, –e/–s** (*also* **der**) goulash; **die ~kanone, –n** *coll* field kitchen

der **Gulden, –** guilder

gülden *poet* golden

der **Gully** ['guli], **–s** (*also* **das**) drain

gültig valid; in force; (of coin) legal tender

die **Gültigkeit** validity; **~ haben** be valid/in force

das **Gummi** (*also* **der**), **–s** rubber; gum; **(der)** rubber (= eraser, *coll* condom); **das ~arabikum** gum arabic; **das ~band,** ¨**er** rubber band; elastic; **der ~baum,** ¨**e** gum-tree; rubber plant; **das ~höschen, –** plastic pants; **der ~knüppel, –** rubber truncheon; **die ~linse, –n** zoom lens; **der ~paragraph, –en** (*wk masc*) *coll* clause open to interpretation; **der ~schlauch,** ¨**e** inner tube; rubber hose; **der ~schuh, –e** galosh; **der ~stiefel, –** gumboot, rubber boot *US*; **der ~strumpf,** ¨**e** elastic stocking; **der ~überschuh, –e** galosh; **die ~zelle, –n** padded cell; **der ~zug,** ¨**e** elastic

gummieren gum

die **Gunst** favour; **zu jmds. ~en** in s.o.'s favour

günstig favourable; convenient

der **Günstling, –e** favourite; **die ~s|wirtschaft** favouritism

die **Gurgel, –n** throat

gurgeln gargle; gurgle

die **Gurke, –n** cucumber; gherkin; *coll* conk, schnozzle *US*

gurren coo

der **Gurt, –e** belt; strap; girth

der **Gürtel, –** belt; girdle; **den ~ enger schnallen** *coll* tighten one's belt || **die ~linie** waistline (**Schlag unter die G.** blow below the belt); **der ~reifen, –** radial(-ply) tyre; **die ~rose** shingles; **das ~tier, –e** armadillo

gürten gird; girth; **sich ~** gird oneself

der **Guru, –s** guru

der **Guß,** ¨**(ss)e** gush; downpour; *tech* casting; *cul* icing; **(wie) aus 'einem ~** all of a piece || **das ~eisen** cast iron; **g~eisern** cast-iron

Gustav Adolf Gustavus Adolphus
gustieren *Aust* taste, try
gustiös *Aust* appetizing
der **Gusto** *esp Aust* appetite; **nach jmds. ~** to s.o.'s taste
gut (*comp* **besser,** *superl* **best../am besten)** good; (*adv*) well; easily; (*eg* **~ zwei Pfund/drei Wochen)** a good (two pounds/three weeks *etc*); **~ und gern** easily; **sich** *dat* **... für ~ lassen** keep for best; **so ~ wie** as good as, virtually; **~!** all right!, O.K.!; **bloß ~, daß ...!** it's a good thing ...!; **also/nun ~!** all right then!; **schon ~!** that's all right!

(*with verbs*): **~ haben** (*cf* **guthaben**): **es ~ haben** be lucky; be well off; **du hast ~ lachen/reden** it's easy for you to laugh/talk; **ich kann nicht ~ ...** I can't very well ...; **so ~ ich kann** as best I can; **mach's ~!** cheerio!, so long!; **~ daran tun zu ...** do well to ...; (*with* **sein**) (+*dat*) **~ sein** be sweet on; **mir ist nicht ~** I don't feel well; **dafür/dazu bin ich mir zu ~** that's beneath me; **du bist ~!** you're a fine one!; you must be joking!; **das ist ~!** that's rich!; **wozu ist es ~?** what's it for?; what good is it?; **das ist alles ~ und schön, aber ...** that's all very well, but ...; **es ~ sein lassen** leave it at that;

das G~e (*decl as adj*) good; the good thing; **G~es tun** do good; **sein G~es haben** have its advantages; **des G~en zuviel** too much of a good thing; **des G~en zuviel tun** overdo it; **alles G~e!** all the best!; **im ~en** (*part*) amicably; **sich zum G~en wenden** change for the better
das **Gut, ⸗er** property; estate; (*pl*) goods; **–gut** (*collective*): (*i*) ... goods (*eg* **das Expreß~** express goods), (*ii*) *denotes material* (*eg* **das Streu~** grit for roads, **das Saat~** seed (*in collective sense*)), (*iii*) *with abstract concepts, sometimes* = body of ... (*eg* **das Gedanken~** body of ideas)
gut– well– (informed *etc*);

das G~achten, – (expert's) report; testimonial; **der G~achter, –, ~achtlich** expert; **~artig** good-natured; *med* benign; **~aussehend** good-looking; **gut|bürgerlich** solidly middle-class; (cooking) plain; **das G~dünken** discretion (**nach G.** at one's discretion); **~gehen*** (*sep; sn*) go well (**es geht mir gut** I'm fine; I'm doing fine); **~gehend** thriving; **~gelaunt** good-humoured; **~gemeint** well-meant; **~gesinnt** well-disposed (*following dat* towards); **~gläubig** trusting; **~haben*** (*sep*) (*cf* **es gut haben** *at* **gut**) have to one's credit; **das G~haben, –** *fin* credit; **~heißen*** (*sep*) approve; **~herzig** kind-hearted; **~machen** (*sep*) make up for; repay; **~mütig** good-natured; **~nachbarlich** neighbourly; **der G~schein, –e** voucher, coupon; gift token/certificate *US*; **~schreiben*** (*sep*) (+*dat*) credit to; **die G~schrift, –en** credit (item); credit note; **~situiert** well-to-do; **~tun*** (*sep*) (+*dat*) do (s.o.) good; **~verdienend** on a good salary; **~willig** willing
die **Güte** kindness; quality; **in ~** amicably; **(ach,) du liebe/meine ~!** good gracious! || **das ~zeichen, –** seal of quality
Güter– ... of goods/freight; goods ..., freight ...; **der ~bahnhof, ⸗e** goods/freight station; **die ~gemeinschaft** community of goods; **die ~trennung** separation of property; **der ~wagen, –** goods waggon, freight car *US*; **der ~zug, ⸗e** goods train, freight train *US*
gütig kind
gütlich amicable; **sich ~ tun an** (*dat*) feast on
Guts–: der ~besitzer, – = der ~herr, –en (*like* **Herr**) landowner; **der ~verwalter, –** steward
guttural guttural
Gymnasial– ... of a *Gymnasium*
der **Gymnasiast, –en** (*wk masc*) pupil at a *Gymnasium*
das **Gymnasium, –(i)en** *approx* = grammar school (*secondary school preparing pupils for university entrance*)
die **Gymnastik** [–ɪk] gymnastics; keep-fit exercises
der **Gymnastiker, –** gymnast
gymnastisch gymnastic
der **Gynäkologe, –n** (*wk masc*) gynaecologist
die **Gynäkologie** gynaecology
gynäkologisch gynaecological

H

[das] **H** [haː] (*gen*, *pl* **–**, *coll* [haːs]) H; **das h, H** *mus* (the note) B; (*key*) **H** B major, **h** B minor

h (*printed as* **h**, *for* hora; *eg* **8h** = (*and read as*) **8 Uhr**) o'clock

ha = Hektar

ha! ah!; aha!

[das] **Haar, –e** (*also pl denoting hair on head*) hair; **~e auf den Zähnen haben** (woman) be a tough customer; **kein gutes ~ lassen an** (*dat*) *coll* pull to pieces; **sich** *dat* **die ~e schneiden lassen** get one's hair cut; **sich** *dat* **keine grauen ~e wachsen lassen** *coll* not lose any sleep

in prepositional phrases:

an den ~en herbeiziehen *coll* drag in; **an den ~en herbeigezogen** *coll* rather far-fetched; **es hängt an einem ~** it's touch-and-go

auf: sich *dat pl* **aufs ~ gleichen** *coll* be as like as two peas in a pod

in: sich *dat pl* **in die ~e geraten** *coll* clash; **sich** *dat pl* **in den ~en liegen** *coll* be at loggerheads

um ein ~ *coll* very nearly; fractionally; **um kein/nicht um ein ~** *coll* not a whit; **um ein ~ hätte/wäre ...** *coll* ... came within an ace of (+*ger*)

Haar– hair ...; **die ~bürste, –n** hair-brush; **der ~festiger, –** setting lotion; **das ~garn** hair-cord; **haar|genau** *coll* very precise; (*adv*) *also* in great detail; **die ~klammer, –n** hair-grip, bobby pin *US*; **haar|klein** *coll* in minute detail; **die ~klemme, –n** hair-grip, bobby pin *US*; **der ~knoten, –** bun; **die ~nadel, –n** hairpin; **die ~nadel|kurve, –n** hairpin bend; **der ~riß, –(ss)e** hairline crack; **haar|scharf** *coll* very precise; (*adv*) by a hair's breadth; **der ~schnitt, –e** haircut; **die ~spalterei, –en** hair-splitting; **die ~spange, –n** hair-slide, barrette *US*; **die ~spitze, –n** end of a hair (**gespaltene ~spitzen** split ends); **h~sträubend** hair-raising; outrageous; **das ~teil, –e** hair-piece; **der ~trockner, –** hair-drier; **das ~wasch|mittel, –** shampoo; **das ~wasser, ..wässer** hair-lotion; **der ~wuchs** growth of hair

haaren: (sich) ~ lose its hair

Haares|breite: um ~ by a hair's breadth

haarig hairy; *coll* tricky; **–haarig** –haired

Hab: das ~ und Gut possessions || **die ~gier** greed; **h~gierig** greedy; **die ~seligkeiten** *pl* belongings; **die ~sucht** greed; **h~süchtig** greedy

[die] **Habe** possessions; **der ~nichts** (*gen* **–(es)**), **–e** have-not

haben (*pres* **habe, hast, hat, haben, habt, haben,** *subj 3rd sing* **habe;** *p/t* **hatte,** *subj* **hätte;** *p/part* **gehabt)** (*see also* **gehabt)**

1 have; have got; *coll* do (subject at school); **... hat etwas (Faszinierendes** *etc*) there is something (fascinating *etc*) about ...; **wir ~ ...** *also* it's ... (*eg* **wir ~ heute den 14. März** it's March 14th today, **~ wir noch August?** is it still August?); **ich habe heute Geburtstag** it's my birthday today; **es am Knie/an der Leber/auf der Brust** *etc* **~** *coll* have something wrong with one's knee/liver/chest *etc*; **was hast du/hat er** *etc***?** what's the matter with you/him *etc*?; **er hat/wir ~** *etc* **'s ja!** he/we *etc* can afford it; **da hast du's/~ wir's!** you see!; **zu ~** to be had, available; **noch zu ~** *coll* still single; **zu ~ sein für** be game for; **dafür bin ich nicht zu ~** (you can) count me out

an/auf sich ~ (*see* **an** 4, **auf** 4)

~ gegen: etwas/nichts ~ gegen have something/nothing against

hinter sich ~ (*see* **hinter**)

~ in (*dat*): **es im Halse/Knie ~** *coll* have a sore throat/bad knee; **in sich ~** (*see* **in** 2)

~ mit have (child) by; **es ~ mit** *coll* have a thing about; **etwas ~ mit** *coll* be carrying on with; **es nicht so sehr ~ mit** *coll* not be too particular about; **es mit (dem Herzen** *etc*) **~** *coll* have (heart *etc*) trouble

~ von get (sth.) from/out of; **er hat viel von seinem Vater** there's a good deal of his father in him; **das hat man davon** that's what comes of it

vor sich ~ (*see* **vor** 3)

woher hast du das? where did you get that?; who told you that?

2 (*as auxiliary*: + *p/part*) have + *p/part, or expressed by simple past* (*eg* **ich hab's gesehen** I've seen/I saw it, (*in past tense*, *forming pluperfect* had) **ich hatte es schon verkauft** I'd already sold it);

3 ~ + zu + *infin* have to ...; be required

to …; be (supposed) to …; **zu tun** ~ (*see* **tun** 3)

sich ~ *coll* make a fuss; **hab dich nicht so!** don't be so fussy!; don't make such a fuss!; **hat sich was!** some hopes!; **damit hat sich's!** that's that!

das **Haben** credit

habhaft: (+*gen*) ~ werden get hold of; apprehend

der **Habicht, -e** hawk; goshawk

die **Habilitation, -en** qualification to lecture at university

habilitieren: sich ~ qualify as a university lecturer

habituell habitual

der **Habitus** bearing; *med* disposition

hablich *Swiss* well-to-do

Habsburg [-a:-], **der Habsburger, -, habsburgisch** Hapsburg

hach! ah!; oh!

die **Hachse** [-ks-], **-n** *cul* knuckle; *coll* leg

Hack-: das ~beil, -e chopper; **der ~braten, -** meat loaf; **das ~brett, -er** chopping-board; *mus* dulcimer; **das ~fleisch** mince, ground meat *US*; **die ~frucht, ⸚e** root crop; **die ~ordnung, -en** pecking-order

die **Hacke**[1], **-n** hoe; pickaxe; *Aust* axe

die **Hacke**[2], **-n** heel; **die ~n zusammenschlagen** click one's heels

hacken (*see also* **Gehackte**) chop (*also cul*); hack; hoe; (*v/i*) hoe; peck (**nach** at)

der **Häcksel** (*also* **das**) chaff

der **Hader, hadern** quarrel

der **Hafen,** *pl* **Häfen** harbour; port; haven; **die ~anlagen** *pl* docks; **der ~arbeiter, -** docker, longshoreman *US*; **die ~stadt, ⸚e** port

der **Hafer** oats; **ihn sticht der** ~ *coll* he's feeling his oats || **der ~brei** porridge; **die ~flocken** *pl* porridge oats, oat flakes *US*; **der ~schleim** gruel

das **Haff, -e/-s** lagoon (on the Baltic)

die **Haft** custody; detention; **in ~ nehmen** take into custody

Haft-[1] … of detention; **Haft-**[2] adhesive …; **die ~anstalt, -en** prison; **der ~befehl, -e** warrant of arrest; **die ~fähigkeit** adhesion; **das ~glas, ⸚er** contact lens; **die ~pflicht** liability; **h~pflichtig** liable; **die ~pflicht|versicherung, -en** personal liability insurance; *mot* third-party insurance; **die ~schale, -n** contact lens

---

-haft (*forming adjectives indicating a quality*) *eg* **vorteil~** advantageous (**Vorteil** = advantage), **damen~** ladylike (**Dame** = lady), **greisen~** senile (**Greis** = old man), **episoden~** episodic (**Episode** = episode)

---

haftbar liable

haften[1]**: ~ für** be liable/responsible for

haften[2] stick (**an** *dat* to); cling (to); **~bleiben*** (*sep*; *sn*) stick (**an** *dat* to)

der **Häftling, -e** prisoner

die **Haftung**[1] liability

die **Haftung**[2] *phys* adhesion

der **Hag, -e** *poet* hedge; grove

Hage-: die ~butte, -n rose-hip; **der ~dorn, -e** hawthorn; **der ~stolz, -e** confirmed bachelor

der **Hagel** hail; **das ~korn, ⸚er** hailstone; **das ~wetter, -** hailstorm

hageln: es hagelt it is hailing; **es hagelte … …** came thick and fast; **~ auf** (*acc*) rain down on

hager lean

haha! haha!; aha!

der **Häher, -** jay

der **Hahn, ⸚e** cock; tap, faucet *US*; **~ im Korb sein** *coll* be the centre of female attention; **danach kräht kein** ~ *coll* nobody cares two hoots about it

das **Hähnchen, -** cockerel; *cul* chicken

Hahnen- cock's …; **der ~fuß** crowfoot; **der ~kamm, ⸚e** cockscomb; **der ~kampf, ⸚e** cock-fight(ing); **der ~schrei, -e** cock-crow; **der ~tritt** hound's-tooth check

der **Hahnrei, -e, zum ~ machen** cuckold

der **Hai, -e = der ~fisch, -e** shark

der **Hain, -e** *poet* grove; **die ~buche, -n** hornbeam

das **Häkchen, -** (small) hook; tick

Häkel-: die ~arbeit, -en crochet; piece of crochet work; **die ~nadel, -n** crochet-hook

häkeln crochet

haken hook (onto *etc* sth.); (*v/i*) be stuck

der **Haken, -** hook (*also box*); *coll* snag; **einen ~ schlagen** dart sideways (when fleeing) || **das ~kreuz, -e** swastika; **die ~nase, -n** hooked nose

halb half; (*in time phrases, referring to the following hour*) half past (*eg* ~ **12** = 11.30); (*adv*) half; **~ …, ~ …** half …, half …; **~ und ~** *coll* more or less; **~ und ~ machen** *coll* go halves; **mit ~em Herzen** half-heartedly; **auf ~er Höhe** half-way up; **es ist ~ so schlimm** it's not as bad as all that

halb- half-; semi-;

das H~blut half-caste; half-breed; **der H~edel|stein, -e** semi-precious stone; **~gar** half-done; **die H~geschwister** *pl* half-brothers and sisters; **der H~gott, ⸚er** demigod; **die H~insel, -n** peninsula; **das H~jahr, -e** half-year; **~jährig** six-month(-old); six months'; **~jährlich** half-yearly; **der H~kreis, -e** semi-circle; **die H~kugel, -n** hemisphere; **~lang** medium-length (**mach mal h.!** don't exaggerate!); **~laut** (voice) low; (*adv*) in an undertone; **das H~leinen** half-cloth; **der H~linke** (*decl as adj*) inside left; **~mast (auf h.** at half-mast); **der H~messer, –** radius; **der H~mond, –e** half-moon; crescent; **~offen** half-open; **~part (h. machen** go halves); **die H~pension** half-board; **der H~rechte** (*decl as adj*) inside right; **~rund** semicircular; **der H~schlaf** state between sleeping and waking **(im H.** half asleep); **der H~schuh, –e** shoe; **das H~schwer|gewicht** light-heavyweight class; **~seiden** half silk; *coll* rather dubious; 'queer'; **~staatlich** *EGer* partly state-controlled; **der H~starke** (*decl as adj*) young hooligan; **~stündig** half-hour; **~stündlich** half-hourly; (*adv*) half-hourly, every half hour; **der H~stürmer, –** inside forward; **~tags** (work) part-time; **H~tags–** part-time ...; **der H~ton, ̈–e** *mus* semitone; *art* half-tone; **die H~wahrheit, –en** half-truth; **~wegs** half-way; reasonably; fairly well; **die H~welt** demi-monde; **die H~welt|dame, –n** demi-mondaine; **die H~werts|zeit, –en** *phys* half-life; **~wüchsig** [–ks–], **der/die H~wüchsige** (*decl as adj*) adolescent; **die H~zeit, –en** *sp* half; half-time

halbe-halbe *coll*: **~ machen** go fifty-fifty

halber (*following gen*) on account of; for the sake of; *also* **–halber,** *eg* **umstände~** owing to circumstances, **abwechslungs~** for variety's sake

die **Halbheit, –en** half-measure

halbieren halve; *math, comput* bisect

die **Halde, –n** slope; *min* tip

half *p/t of* **helfen**

die **Hälfte, –n, zur ~** half; **um die ~** by half

das **Halfter, –** (*also* **der**) halter

die **Halfter, –n** (*also* **das,** *pl* **–**) holster

der **Hall, –e** (resonant) sound; echo

die **Halle, –n** hall; foyer; *rail* (station) concourse; *aer* hangar; *sp* indoor arena/*swim* pool; covered court

hallen resound; echo

Hallen– *sp* indoor ...; **das ~bad, ̈–er** indoor swimming-pool

die **Hallig, –en** (*small undyked island off western Schleswig-Holstein*)

hallo! ['halo, *if pleasantly surprised* ha'lo:] hullo!

der **Hallodri, –(s)** *SGer coll* happy-go-lucky character

die **Halluzination, –en** hallucination

halluzinieren hallucinate

der **Halm, –e** stalk; blade (of grass)

das **Halogen, –e** halogen

der **Hals, ̈–e** neck; throat; **~ über Kopf** *coll* in great haste; headlong; head over heels (in love); **am/auf dem ~ haben** *coll* be landed with; **aus vollem ~(e)** at the top of one's voice; **bis zum ~ in (Arbeit** *etc*) **stecken** be up to one's ears in (work *etc*); **in den falschen ~ bekommen** *coll* take the wrong way; **sich** *dat* **... vom ~(e) halten** *coll* keep at arm's length; **sich** *dat* **... vom ~(e) schaffen** *coll* get rid of; **bleib mir mit ... vom ~(e)** *coll* don't bother me with; **... hängt/wächst mir zum ~(e) heraus** *coll* I'm sick and tired of ... || **der ~abschneider, –** *coll* shark; **der ~ausschnitt, –e** neckline; **das ~band, ̈–er** (dog's) collar; *dated* necklace; **h~brecherisch** perilous; breakneck; **die ~entzündung, –en** sore throat; **die ~kette, –n** necklace; (dog's) chain; **der Hals-Nasen-Ohren-Arzt, ̈–e** ear, nose and throat specialist; **die ~schlag|ader, –n** carotid (artery); **die ~schmerzen** *pl* sore throat; **h~starrig** stubborn; **das ~tuch, ̈–er** scarf; neckerchief; **Hals- und Beinbruch!** good luck!; **die ~weite, –n** collar size; **der ~wirbel, –** cervical vertebra

–halsig –necked

halt *SGer* just, simply

der **Halt** hold; foothold; support; stop; **keinen (inneren) ~ haben** be unstable; **ohne ~** non-stop || **h~los** unstable; unrestrained; unfounded; **h~machen** (*sep*) stop **(vor nichts h.** stop at nothing)

hält *3rd sing pres of* **halten**

haltbar durable; (food) that keeps; tenable; *sp* stoppable; savable

die **Haltbarkeit** durability; tenability

Halte–: der ~griff, –e handle; **die ~schlaufe, –n** strap; **das ~signal, –e** stop signal; **die ~stelle, –n** (bus *etc*) stop; **das ~verbot, –e** no stopping (zone)

halten (hält(st), *p/t* **hielt,** *p/part* **gehalten)** (*see also* **gehalten**) hold; keep; maintain; treat; take (newspaper); make (speech); (*v/i*) hold; last, (food) keep; stop; **sich** *dat* **... ~** keep; **es so ~** do so; **halt!** stop!; wait a minute!; *mil* halt!; **in (Weiß** *etc*) **gehalten** in (white *etc*); **(zu allgemein** *etc*) **gehalten** expressed (in too general terms *etc*); **zum Halten bringen** bring to a halt

an sich ~ contain oneself

~ auf (*acc*) aim at; head for; attach importance to; **auf sich ~** take a pride in one's appearance; **... der/die (etwas) auf sich hält** self-respecting

~ für regard as; take for; think ... is *etc*

~ mit: es ~ mit agree with; be a great one for; handle (in a certain way); **wie hältst du's mit ...?** what is your attitude to ...?

~ von think of (*eg* **was hältst du von ...?** what do you think of ...?)

~ zu stand by

sich ~ carry oneself; keep one's balance; hold out; maintain one's position; do (well *etc*); (business) keep going; stay; keep; last; hold; **sich ~ an** (*acc*) stick to; ask, approach; **sich auf einem Posten ~** hold down a job; **sich ~ für** think one is; **sich links/rechts ~** keep left/right; **sich gut gehalten haben** *coll* (person) be well-preserved

[der] **Halter, –** holder; owner

–haltig, *Aust* **–hältig** containing ...

hältst *2nd sing pres of* **halten**

[die] **Haltung, –en** posture; attitude; composure; keeping; **~ annehmen** stand to attention; **~ bewahren** remain composed

[der] **Halunke, –n** (*wk masc*) scoundrel

Hameln Hamelin

hämisch malicious; **sich ~ freuen über** (*acc*) gloat over

[der] **Hammel, –** wether; *cul* mutton; *coll* ass; **~beine** *coll* ((+*dat*) **die H. langziehen** give (s.o.) a telling-off); **der ~braten, –** roast mutton; **das ~fleisch** mutton; **die ~keule, –n** leg of mutton; **das ~kotelett, –s** mutton chop; **der ~sprung, ⸚e** *parl* division

[der] **Hammer,** *pl* **Hämmer** hammer (*also anat, athl, mus*); **unter den ~ kommen** come under the hammer

hämmern hammer; beat (metal); *coll* hammer out (tune); (*v/i*) hammer; pound

[das] **Hämoglobin** haemoglobin

[die] **Hämorrhoiden** [–mɔro–] *pl* haemorrhoids

[der] **Hampel|mann, ⸚er** jumping-jack; *coll* spineless character

hampeln *coll* jump about

[der] **Hamster, –** hamster; **die ~backen** *pl coll* chubby cheeks

hamstern hoard

[die] **Hand, ⸚e** hand; **die öffentliche ~** the state; public funds; (+*dat*) **die ~ geben** shake hands with; **alle Hände voll zu tun haben** have one's hands full; **~ und Fuß haben** be sound; **~ legen an** (*acc*) lay hands on; **~ an sich legen** take one's own life; **letzte ~ legen an** (*acc*) put the finishing touches to; **~!** *sp* hands!; **~ aufs Herz** honestly; **Hände hoch!** hands up!

in prepositional phrases:

an ~ (+*gen*) with the aid of; (+*dat*) **an die ~ geben** furnish with; (+*dat*) **an die ~ gehen** lend (s.o.) a hand

auf der ~ liegen be obvious; **auf Händen tragen** spoil (adored woman)

aus erster/zweiter/dritter ~ first/second/third-hand; (+*dat*) **aus der ~ fressen** eat out of (s.o.'s) hand; **aus der ~ geben** part with; give up; **aus der ~ legen** put down

bei der ~ haben have to hand; have ready; **schnell bei der ~ sein mit** be ready with

in: (+*dat*) **in die Hände arbeiten** play into (s.o.'s) hands; **in die ~/Hände bekommen** get one's hands on; gain control of; **in die ~ nehmen** pick up; take in hand; **in die Hände klatschen** clap one's hands; **~ in ~** hand in hand

mit der ~ by hand; **sich mit Händen und Füßen wehren gegen** fight tooth and nail; **mit leeren Händen** empty-handed

unter den Händen haben have in hand

von: ... geht mir leicht von der ~ I find ... easy; **... ist nicht von der ~ zu weisen** ... cannot be denied; **von der ~ in den Mund leben** live from hand to mouth

zu Händen (von) ... for the attention of ...; **zur ~** at hand; **zur ~ haben** have to hand; have ready; (+*dat*) **zur ~ gehen** lend (s.o.) a hand

Hand– hand ...; manual ...; **der ~apparat, –e** reference works (assembled for research purposes); *tel* handset; **die ~arbeit, –en** manual work; needlework; knitting; hand-made article; **h~arbeiten** (*insep*) do needlework/knitting; **der ~arbeiter, –** manual worker; **die ~ausgabe, –n** concise edition; **die ~bewegung, –en** movement of the hand; gesture (**mit einer H. abtun** wave aside); **die ~bibliothek, –en** reference library; **die ~breit, –** hand's breadth; **die ~bremse, –n** handbrake; **das ~buch, ⸚er** handbook; manual; **die ~fertigkeit, –en** manual skill; **h~fest** sturdy; solid; flagrant; (scandal) tremendous; **die ~fläche, –n** palm of the hand; **h~ge|arbeitet** hand-made; **~gebrauch (für den/zum H.** for everyday use); **das ~gelenk, –e** wrist (**aus dem H.** *coll* with the greatest of ease; off the cuff); **h~gemalt** hand-painted; **h~gemein (h. werden** come to blows); **das ~gemenge, –** scuffle; **h~geschrieben** handwritten; **h~greiflich** obvious (**h. werden** become violent); **der ~griff, –e** handle; movement of the hand; chore; **die ~habe, –n** pretext (for intervening *etc*); **h~haben** (*insep*) handle; apply (method *etc*); administer (justice); **der ~karren, –** handcart; **h~kehr|um** *Swiss* all of a sudden; **der ~koffer, –** (small) suitcase; **der ~kuß, ⸚(ss)e** kiss on the hand (**mit H.** *coll* gladly); **der ~langer, –** labourer; dogsbody; stooge; **~langer|dienste (H. tun für** do (s.o.'s) dirty work); **die ~lese|kunst** palmistry; **das ~mehr** *Swiss* majority vote (by show of hands); **die ~reichung, –en** helping hand; recommendation; **der ~rücken, –** back of the hand; **die ~schelle, –n** handcuff; **der ~schlag** handshake (**mit H.** with a handshake; **keinen H. tun** not do a stroke); **das ~schreiben, –** handwritten letter; **die ~schrift, –en** hand(writing); manuscript; **h~schriftlich** handwritten; (sources *etc*) manuscript; (*adv*) by hand; in writing; **der ~schuh, –e** glove; **das ~spiel** handball; **der**

~streich, -e surprise attack; die ~tasche, -n handbag, purse *US*; der ~teller, - palm of the hand; das ~tuch, ¨-er towel (das H. werfen throw in the towel); der ~tuch|halter, - towel rail/rack *US*; ~umdrehen (im H. in no time); die ~voll, - handful; der ~wagen, - handcart; das ~werk, -e craft; trade ((+*dat*) das H. legen put a stop to (s.o.'s) game; sein H. verstehen know one's job; (+*dat*) ins H. pfuschen tread on (s.o.'s) toes); der ~werker, - workman; craftsman; h~werklich (skill *etc*) of a craftsman; das ~werks|zeug tools; tools of the trade; das ~wörter|buch, ¨-er concise dictionary; das ~zeichen, - signal, sign (made with the hand); show of hands; der ~zettel, - handbill

das **Händchen,** - little hand; ~ **halten** *coll* hold hands

Hände-: der ~druck, ¨-e handshake; das ~klatschen applause; h~ringend wringing one's hands

der **Handel** trade (**mit** in); business; deal; ~ **treiben mit** trade with; **aus dem ~ ziehen** withdraw; **im ~** on the market; **in den ~ bringen** put on the market

Händel Handel

die **Händel** *pl* quarrel

handeln act; trade; bargain (**um** over); ~ **mit** trade with; trade in, deal in; ~ **über** (*acc*)/**von** deal with; be about; **gehandelt werden** be sold; *fin* be quoted; **es handelt sich um** it is a question of; it is about; he/she/it is *or* they are; **das Handeln** *also* action

Handels- trade ...; trading ...; commercial ...;

der ~artikel, - commodity; die ~bank, -en merchant bank; die ~bilanz, -en balance of trade; h~einig (**h. werden mit** come to an agreement with); die ~flotte, -n merchant fleet; die ~gesellschaft, -en *comm* company; die ~kammer, -n chamber of commerce; die ~marine, -n merchant navy/marine *US*; die ~marke, -n trademark; die ~messe, -n trade fair; die ~niederlassung, -en branch; die ~organisation, -en trading organization (*EGer*: *state-owned company running shops, hotels, etc*); der ~platz, ¨-e trading centre; h~politisch relating to commercial policy; das ~recht commercial law; das ~schiff, -e merchant ship; die ~schule, -n commercial college; die ~straße, -n trade-route; h~üblich usual in the trade; standard; der ~vertreter, - commercial traveller; die ~vertretung, -en trade mission; die ~ware, -n commodity; (*pl*) merchandise („keine H." 'unsolicited gift'); der ~wert, -e market value

-händig -handed

das **Handikap** ['hɛndikɛp], **-s, handikapen** handicap (*also sp*)

händisch *Aust* manual

der **Händler,** - dealer

handlich handy; easy to handle

die **Handlung, -en** act(ion); plot (of play *etc*); **-handlung** ... shop, ... store; der/die ~s|bevollmächtigte (*decl as adj*) authorized agent; die ~s|freiheit freedom of action; der/die ~s|reisende (*decl as adj*) travelling salesman; die ~s|weise, -n conduct

hanebüchen [-y:-] outrageous

der **Hanf** hemp

der **Hänfling, -e** linnet

der **Hang,** ¨-e slope; propensity (**zu** to)

Hänge- hanging ...; die ~backen *pl* flabby cheeks; der ~bauch, ¨-e sagging paunch; die ~brücke, -n suspension bridge; der ~busen, - sagging bosom; die ~matte, -n hammock; die ~ohren *pl* lop-ears; das ~schloß, ¨-(ss)er padlock

Hangen: mit ~ und Bangen in fear and trembling

hängen hang (**an** *acc* on); **sich ~ an** (*acc*) hang on to; cling to; latch on to; set off in pursuit of

(*v/i*: *p/t* **hing,** *p/part* **gehangen**) hang; (curtain) be up; ~ **an** (*dat*) hang from/on; (trailer *etc*) be connected to; (mud *etc*) stick to; (eyes) be fixed on; be very attached to; *coll* be on (phone) (for hours *etc*); **den Kopf ~ lassen** hang one's head

Hängen *coll*: **mit ~ und Würgen** by the skin of one's teeth

hängen-: ~bleiben* (*sep*; *sn*) get caught (**an** *dat* on); get stuck; get bogged down; stick (in memory); *coll* have to repeat the year; ~lassen* (*p/part usu* ~**lassen;** *sep*) leave (hanging); let (sth.) hang down, (dog) put (tail) between its legs

der **Hänger,** - loose coat; (child's) loose dress; *coll* trailer

Hannover [-f-] Hanover

Hans-: der ~dampf (**H. in allen Gassen:** *highly active individual who tends to turn up everywhere and thinks he knows everything*); der ~wurst, -e buffoon

die **Hanse** *hist* the Hanseatic League; *in compds* Hanseatic ...

hänseln tease

die **Hantel, -n** dumb-bell

hantieren be busy; ~ **an** (*dat*) fiddle about with; ~ **mit** handle

hapern *coll*: **es hapert an** (*dat*) there is a shortage of; **es hapert mit** there are problems with

der **Happen,** - *coll* mouthful; bite (to eat)

happig *coll* (price *etc*) steep

das **Happy-End** ['hɛpi'ʔɛnt], **–s** happy ending

Harald Harold

das **Härchen, –** little hair

die **Hardware** [–wɛə] *comput* hardware

der **Harem** [–ɛm], **–s** harem

hären: ~es Gewand hair-shirt

die **Häresie, –(ie)n** heresy

der **Häretiker, –** heretic

häretisch heretical

die **Harfe, –n** harp

der **Harfenist, –en** (*wk masc*) harpist

die **Harke, –n, harken** *esp NGer* rake

der **Harlekin, –e** Harlequin

harm–: ~los harmless; innocent; (cold *etc*) slight; **die H~losigkeit** harmlessness; innocence

härmen: sich ~ grieve (**um** for)

die **Harmonie, –(ie)n** harmony

harmonieren (colours *etc*) harmonize

die **Harmonik** [–ɪk] harmonics

die **Harmonika, –s/–(k)en** harmonica; accordion; concertina

harmonisch harmonious; *math, mus* harmonic

harmonisieren harmonize

das **Harmonium, –(i)en** harmonium

der **Harn, –e** urine

der **Harnisch, –e** suit of armour; **in ~** up in arms; **in ~ bringen** get (s.o.'s) hackles up; **in ~ geraten** fly into a rage

die **Harpune, –n, harpunieren** harpoon

harren (*+gen*) await

harsch harsh; (snow) frozen

der **Harsch** frozen snow

hart (*comp, superl* ¨) hard; harsh; tough; (*adv*) hard; harshly; **~ bleiben** remain adamant; **~ an** (*dat*) close to; **es geht ~ auf ~** no one is pulling any punches || **die H~faser|platte, –n** hardboard; **~gekocht** hard-boiled; **das H~geld** coins; **~gesotten** (person) hard-boiled; hardened; **~herzig** hard-hearted; **das H~holz, ¨er** hardwood; **~näckig** obstinate; **die H~näckigkeit** obstinacy; **der H~platz, ¨e** hard court

die **Härte, –n** hardness; harshness, severity; toughness; hardship; **der ~fall, ¨e** case of hardship

härten harden; temper

das **Harz** [–aː–], **–e** resin; *mus* rosin

der **Harz** [–aː–] the Harz Mountains

harzig resinous

Hasard–: das ~spiel, –e game of chance; gamble (= risky undertaking)

der **Hasardeur** [–'døːʁ], **–e** gambler

das **Haschee, –s** *cul* hash

haschen[1] catch; **~ nach** (*dat*) grab at; strive after

haschen[2] *coll* smoke hash

das **Häschen** [–sç–], **–** young hare, leveret; bunny

haschieren mince (meat)

das **Haschisch** (*also* **der**) hashish

Haschmich *coll*: **einen ~ haben** have a screw loose

der **Hase, –n** (*wk masc*) hare; **alter ~** *coll* old hand; **falscher ~** meat loaf; **mein Name ist ~ (, ich weiß von nichts)** I know nothing about it; **sehen, wie der ~ läuft** *coll* see which way the wind blows

Hasel–: der ~busch, ¨e hazel; **die ~maus, ¨e** dormouse; **die ~nuß, ¨(ss)e** hazel-nut

Hasen– hare('s) ...; **der ~braten, –** roast hare; **der ~fuß, ¨e** *coll* = **das ~herz, –en** (*like* **Herz**) *coll* coward; **der ~pfeffer, –** *approx* = jugged hare; **h~rein** *coll* (**nicht ganz h.** rather fishy); **die ~scharte, –n** hare-lip

haspeln reel up; reel off; *coll* splutter out

der **Haß** (*gen* **Hasses**) hatred, hate (**auf** *acc*/**gegen** of, for); **h~erfüllt** full of hate; **die ~liebe** love-hate relationship

hassen hate; **~s|wert** hateful

häßlich ugly; (conduct *etc*) nasty

die **Häßlichkeit** ugliness; nastiness

hast *2nd sing pres of* **haben**

die **Hast** haste

haste *coll*: **~ was kannste** at full lick

hasten (*sn*) hasten

hastig hurried; hasty

hat *3rd sing pres of* **haben**

hätscheln fondle; pamper, coddle

hatschi! atishoo!, kerchoo! *US*

hatte (hätte) *p/t* (*subj*) *of* **haben**

der **Hattrick** ['hɛt–], **–s** *sp* hat-trick

hatzi! = hatschi!

Hau–: der ~degen, – old campaigner

die **Haube, –n** bonnet; (nurse's) cap; hair-dryer; cosy; *ornith* crest; *mot* bonnet, hood *US*; **unter die ~ bringen** *coll* marry off

Hauben– *ornith* crested ...

die **Haubitze, –n** howitzer

der **Hauch** breath; breath of air; waft; thin layer; touch, hint (of); aura; **hauch|dünn** extremely thin; wafer-thin; sheer; *sp* extremely narrow; **hauch|fein** extremely fine; **der ~laut, –e** aspirate; **hauch|zart** extremely delicate

hauchen breathe (words *etc*); **~ auf** (*acc*)/**gegen** breathe on

die **Haue, –n** *SGer* hoe

Haue *coll*: **~ bekommen** get a beating

hauen (*p/t* **haute/hieb**, *p/part* **gehauen**; *p/t is* **haute** *unless otherwise stated*) cut (steps *etc*), carve (statue); *coll* hit; knock (hole in sth.); fling (into corner *etc*); slam down (on table *etc*); (*v/i*): **~ auf** (*acc*) (*p/t* **hieb**, *coll* **haute**) hit out at; (*p/t also* **hieb**) *coll* bang on (table *etc*), thump (keys of piano); (*+dat*) **auf die Schulter ~** *coll* slap on the back; **um sich ~** (*p/t* **hieb**, *coll* **haute**) lay about one

sich ~ *coll* fling oneself; (*recip*) scrap

das **Häufchen, –** small pile; **wie ein ~ Elend dasitzen** *coll* sit there looking the very picture of misery

häufeln earth up

der **Haufen, –** heap, pile; crowd; *coll* heaps (of); **über den ~ werfen** *coll* upset (plan) || **h~weise** in heaps; piles of ...; in droves

häufen pile up; heap; **sich ~** accumulate, mount up; become more frequent; **gehäuft** (spoonful) heaped, heaping *US*

häufig frequent

die **Häufigkeit** frequency

die **Häufung, –en** accumulation

das **Haupt, ⸚er** head; *poet* peak; **an ~ und Gliedern** radically

Haupt– chief ...; main ...; principal ...;

h~amtlich full-time; (*adv*) (on a) full-time (basis); **der ~bahnhof, ⸚e** central station; **das ~buch, ⸚er** ledger; **der ~darsteller, –/die ~darstellerin, –nen** leading man/lady; **das ~fach, ⸚er** main subject, major *US* (**im H. studieren** study as one's main subject, major in *US*); **der ~gewinn, –e** first prize; **die ~leitung, –en** mains; **der ~mann, ..leute** captain; (air force) flight lieutenant, captain *US*; **die ~niederlassung, –en** head office; **die ~person, –en** central figure; **das ~quartier, –e** headquarters; **die ~sache** main thing (**in der H.** in the main; **H., ...** the main thing is ...); **h~sächlich** main, chief; (*adv*) mainly, chiefly; **der ~satz, ⸚e** *gramm* main clause; *mus* first subject; *phys etc* law (of ...); **die ~schlag|ader, –n** aorta; **der ~schlüssel, –** master key; **die ~schule, –n** (non-selective) secondary school; **der ~sitz, –e** head office; **die ~stadt, ⸚e** capital; **die ~straße, –n** main street; main road, highway *US*; **Haupt- und Staats|aktion** *coll* (**eine H. machen aus** make a song and dance about); **die ~verkehrs|zeit, –en** rush hour; **die ~versammlung, –en** general meeting (of shareholders); **die ~wache, –n** police headquarters; **das ~werk, –e** main factory; *arts* main work; **das ~wort, ⸚er** noun

das **Häuptel, –** *Aust* head (of lettuce *etc*); **der ~salat, –e** *Aust* lettuce

Hauptes|länge: um ~ überragen be head and shoulders above

der **Häuptling, –e** chieftain

hau ruck! heave-ho!

das **Haus, ⸚er** house (*also* = dynasty, *eg* **das ~ Habsburg** the House of Hapsburg; *also astrol, theat*); building; firm; *coll* (*with adj*) fellow; (+*dat*) **das ~ führen** keep house for; **ein großes ~ führen** entertain in style; **frei ~ liefern** deliver free of charge

in prepositional phrases:

aus gutem ~e from a good family

außer ~ essen eat out

ins ~ stehen *coll* be around the corner; **mit der Tür ins ~ fallen** *coll* blurt out what one has to say

nach ~e (go *etc*) home

von ~(e) aus originally; by nature; *or expressed by* ... was *etc* brought up to ... (*eg* **sie hat von ~e aus gute Manieren** she was brought up to have good manners)

zu ~e at home; (arrive) home; **zu ~e/wieder zu ~e sein** be in/back home; **zu ~e sein in** (*dat*) live in; be at home in; **sich wie zu ~e fühlen** feel at home

Haus– house ...; home ...; domestic ...;

die ~angestellte (*decl as adj*) domestic help; **die ~arbeit, –en** housework; *educ* homework; **der ~arzt, ⸚e** family doctor; **die ~aufgabe, –n** piece of homework; (*pl*) homework; **h~backen** homespun; pedestrian; **der ~besetzer, –** squatter; **der ~besorger, –** *Aust* caretaker, janitor; **das ~boot, –e** houseboat; **das ~buch, ⸚er** *EGer* register of residents; **h~eigen** belonging to the firm/hotel *etc*; private; **der ~flur, –e** hall; **die ~frau, –en** housewife; *SGer* landlady; **der ~freund, –e** friend of the family; *coll* (wife's) man-friend; **der ~friedens|bruch, ⸚e** trespass (in house/building); **die ~gehilfin, –nen** domestic help; **h~gemacht** home-made; **der ~halt, –e** household; housekeeping; *pol* budget; **–haushalt** (energy *etc*) balance (**den H. führen** keep house); **h~halten*** (*sep*) be economical (**h. mit** be economical with; husband); **die ~hälterin, –nen** housekeeper; **h~hälterisch** economical, thrifty; **~halts–** household ...; domestic ...; family ...; *pol* budget ...; (policy *etc*) budgetary; **das ~halts|geld** housekeeping (money); **der ~halts|plan, ⸚e** budget; **die ~haltung, –en** household; housekeeping; **der ~herr, –en** (*like* **Herr**) head of the household; host; *SGer* landlord; **haus|hoch** very high, (tree *etc*) towering, (waves) mountainous; (favourite) hot; (*adv*: win) hands down (**h. schlagen** trounce; (+*dat*) **h. überlegen sein** be head and shoulders above); **~macher–** home-made ...; **~macher|art** (**nach H.** made according to a traditional recipe); **die ~macht** power-base; **das ~mädchen, –** housemaid; **der ~mann, ⸚er** househusband; **die ~manns|kost** plain fare; **der ~meister, –** caretaker, janitor; *Swiss* house-owner; **das ~mittel, –** household remedy; **die ~mutter, ..mütter** housemother; **die ~ordnung, –en** rules for residents; **der ~putz, –e** spring cleaning; **der ~rat** household effects; **der**

~**schlüssel,** – front-door key; **der ~schuh, –e** slipper; **~segen** *coll* (**der H. hängt schief** they've fallen out); **~stand** (**einen H. gründen** set up house); **die ~suchung, –en** search of a house; **das ~tier, –e** domestic animal; pet; **die ~tür, –en** front door; **der ~vater, ..väter** housefather; **der ~wirt, –e** landlord; **die ~wirtschaft** housekeeping; **die ~wirtschafts|lehre** domestic science

das **Häuschen** [–sç–], – small house; cottage; *coll* toilet; **aus dem ~** *coll* beside oneself

hausen live (in primitive conditions); (**schlimm**) ~ wreak havoc

Häuser– ... of houses; **der ~block, –s** block (of houses); **der ~kampf, ⁼e** house-to-house fighting

hausieren: ~ mit peddle

der **Hausierer,** – hawker

häuslich domestic; family; domesticated; home-loving

die **Häuslichkeit** domesticity

die **Hausse** ['ho:s(ə)], **–n** boom (**an** *dat* in); (stock exchange) bull market

der **Haussier** [(h)o'sĭe:], **–s** (stock exchange) bull

die **Haut, ⁼e** skin; hide; peel; *coll* (*with adj*) soul; **seine ~ zu Markte tragen** risk one's neck; **aus der ~ fahren** *coll* fly off the handle; **bis auf die ~** to the skin; **ich möchte nicht in seiner ~ stecken** I shouldn't like to be in his shoes; **mit heiler ~ davonkommen** save one's skin; **mit ~ und Haar(en)** *coll* totally || **der ~arzt, ⁼e** dermatologist; **der ~ausschlag, ⁼e** rash; **haut|eng** skin-tight; **die ~farbe, –n** colour of the skin; complexion; **h~farben** flesh-coloured; **h~nah** close to the skin; very close; *coll* graphic; **die ~transplantation, –en** skin-graft

das **Häutchen,** – film; *anat, bot* membrane

häuten skin; **sich ~** shed its skin

die **Hautevolee** [o:tvo'le:] the upper crust

–häutig -skinned

Havanna Havana

die **Havarie, –(ie)n** *naut, aer, Aust mot* damage; accident

die **Haxe, –n** *SGer* = **Hachse**

Hbf. = **Hauptbahnhof**

h. c. (= **honoris causa**) honorary

he! hey!; **he?** eh?

das **Hearing** ['hi:–], **–s** *parl* hearing

die **Heb|amme, –n** midwife

Hebe– lifting ...; **der ~bock, ⁼e** jack; **die ~bühne, –n** hydraulic lift

der **Hebel,** – lever; **alle ~ in Bewegung setzen** move heaven and earth || **die ~kraft** leverage

heben (*p/t* **hob** (*subj* **höbe**), *p/part* **gehoben**) (*see also* **gehoben**) lift; raise; enhance; **sich ~** rise; (fog) lift; (bosom) heave; improve; *poet* begin; **einen ~** *coll* have a drink

der **Hebräer,** – Hebrew

hebräisch, (*language*) **H~** Hebrew

die **Hebriden** *pl* the Hebrides

die **Hebung, –en** *vbl noun*; *also* improvement; rise; *geog* elevation; *pros* stressed syllable, arsis

hecheln¹ hackle (flax); **~ über** (*acc*) *coll* gossip about

hecheln² pant

der **Hecht, –e** pike; **der ~sprung, ⁼e** *swim* pike-dive; *gym* long-fly; *footb* headlong dive

hechten (*sn*) dive full length

das **Heck, –e/–s** *naut* stern; *aer* tail; *mot* rear

Heck– *esp* rear ...; **die ~flosse, –n** tail fin; **die ~klappe, –n** tailgate; **der ~meck** *coll* rubbish; fuss; **die ~tür, –en** tailgate; **das ~tür|modell, –e** hatchback

die **Hecke, –n** hedge; **die ~n|braunelle, –n** hedge-sparrow; **die ~n|rose, –n** wild rose; **der ~n|schütze, –n** (*wk masc*) sniper

heda! hey there!

das **Heer, –e** army; host, army (of); *in compds* **~(es)–** *also* military ...; **der ~es|bericht, –e** military communiqué; **die ~es|leitung, –en** army command; **die ~scharen** *pl bibl* hosts; *coll* hosts (of)

die **Hefe, –n** yeast; dregs (of society)

das **Heft¹, –e** booklet; exercise-book; number, issue

das **Heft², –e** haft; hilt; handle; reins (of power)

Heft–: die ~klammer, –n staple; paper-clip; **die ~maschine, –n** stapler; **das ~pflaster,** – sticking-plaster; **die ~zwecke, –n** drawing-pin, thumbtack *US*

das **Heftchen,** – small book; cheap novel/magazine; book (of stamps *etc*)

heften *bookb* stitch; *dressm* tack; **~ an** (*acc*) clip/pin/staple to; **die Augen ~ auf** (*acc*) rivet one's gaze on; **sich an jmds. Fersen ~** dog s.o.'s heels

der **Hefter,** – file; stapler

heftig violent; (pain *etc*) acute; (rain) heavy; fierce; vehement; (person) quick-tempered; **~ werden** lose one's temper

die **Heftigkeit** violence; acuteness; heaviness; ferocity; vehemence; quick temper

die **Hegemonie, –(ie)n** hegemony

hegen tend; have, entertain (doubts, suspicion, *etc*); harbour (grudge); feel; **~ und pflegen** lavish care on

Hehl: kein(en) ~ machen aus make no secret of; **ohne ~** openly

der **Hehler,** – receiver (of stolen goods)

hehr lofty; sublime

hei! hey!

heiapopeia hushaby baby

der **Heide, –n** (*wk masc*) heathen, pagan

die **Heide, –n** heath; moorland; = **das ~kraut** heather

die **Heidel|beere, –n** bilberry

Heiden– heathen ..., pagan ...; *coll* tremendous ..., terrific ...; **~angst** *coll* (**eine H. haben** be scared stiff); **~geld** *coll* (**ein H.** (earn) a mint of money; (cost) a fortune); **h~mäßig** *coll* tremendous

das **Heidentum** heathendom, paganism; pagan world

heidnisch heathen, pagan

heikel delicate; tricky; *SGer* fussy

heil uninjured; undamaged; intact; (*adv*) safe and sound; safely; **wieder ~ sein** be healed; **wieder ~ werden** heal up

das **Heil** well-being; *relig* salvation; **sein ~ versuchen** try one's luck; **~ ...** (*dat*)! hail to ...!; **Ski ~/Weidmanns~** *etc*! good skiing/hunting *etc*!

Heil– healing ...; medicinal ...; medical ...; **die ~anstalt, –en** sanatorium, sanitarium *US*; mental home; **der ~butt, –e** halibut; **heil|froh** *coll* mightily relieved; **h~kräftig** medicinal; healing; **das ~kraut, ⸚er** medicinal herb; **die ~kunde** medical science; **h~los** unholy; terrible; **das ~mittel, –** remedy; medicine; **die ~pädagogik** remedial education; **der ~praktiker, –** unqualified practitioner of medicine (using natural remedies); **die ~quelle, –n** mineral spring; **die ~stätte, –n** sanatorium, sanitarium *US*; **das ~verfahren, –** (course of) treatment

der **Heiland** the Saviour

heilbar curable

heilen cure; heal; (*v/i sn*) heal

heilig holy; sacred; **der/die ~e** (+*name of saint*) St ...; **der H~e Abend** Christmas Eve; **das H~e Römische Reich Deutscher Nation** the Holy Roman Empire || **(der) H~abend** Christmas Eve; **~halten*** (*sep*) keep holy; hold sacred; **~sprechen*** (*sep*) canonize; **die H~sprechung, –en** canonization

der **Heilige** (*fem* **die ~**) (*decl as adj*) saint; **wunderlicher ~r** *coll* queer fish

heiligen hallow; sanctify; **der Zweck heiligt die Mittel** the end justifies the means

der **Heiligen|schein, –e** halo

die **Heiligkeit** holiness; sanctity

das **Heiligtum, ⸚er** shrine; (sacred) relic

Heils– ... of salvation; **die ~armee** the Salvation Army

heilsam salutary

heim home

das **Heim, –e** home; hostel; club-house

Heim– home ... (*also sp*); (**heim–** *sep pref*) ... home; **die ~arbeit, –en** work done at home; **der ~computer, –** home computer; **die ~fahrt, –en** journey home; **h~finden*** find one's way home; **h~führen** lead to the altar; **der ~gang** passing away; **h~gehen*** (*sn*) go home; pass away; **die ~kehr** homecoming; **h~kehren** (*sn*) return home; **der ~kehrer, –** returning prisoner-of-war; **h~leuchten** (+*dat*) *coll* give (s.o.) a piece of one's mind; **die ~reise, –n** journey home; **die ~stätte, –n** home; **h~suchen** strike, afflict; haunt; *joc* descend on; **die ~suchung, –en** affliction (**Mariä H.** the Visitation); **die ~tücke, –n** insidiousness; treachery; **h~tückisch** insidious; treacherous; **h~wärts** homewards; **der ~weg, –e** way home (**sich auf den H. machen** set out for home); **das ~weh** homesickness; nostalgia (**H. haben** be homesick (**nach** for)); **der ~werker, –** handyman; **h~zahlen** (+*dat*) pay back for

die **Heimat** home (= place, region where s.o., sth. comes from; *also bot*, *zool*); homeland; **in meiner ~** where I come from

Heimat– home ...; regional ...; **der ~film, –e** (*sentimental film with a rural setting*); **die ~kunde** study of local history and geography; **das ~land, ⸚er** homeland; **h~los** homeless; **das ~recht** right of domicile; **die ~stadt, ⸚e** home town; **der/die ~vertriebene** (*decl as adj*) displaced person (*esp* from the lost Eastern territories)

heimatlich native; of home/one's homeland; **das mutet mich ~ an** that reminds me of home

das **Heimchen, –** house-cricket

heimelig cosy

heimisch indigenous (**in** *dat* to); local; home; **~ werden** become acclimatized; **sich ~ fühlen** feel at home

heimlich secret; *Aust* cosy; (*adv*) secretly; in secret; **die H~tuerei** secretive behaviour; **~tun*** (*sep*) be secretive (**mit** about)

die **Heimlichkeit, –en** secrecy; (*pl*) secrets; **in aller ~** with great secrecy

der **Heini, –s** *coll* idiot; guy

Heinrich Henry

die **Heinzel|männchen** *pl folkl* brownies

die **Heirat, –en** marriage (= getting married)

heiraten marry; (*v/i*) get married, marry

Heirats– marriage ...; **die ~annonce, –n** advertisement for a marriage partner; **der ~antrag, ⸚e** (marriage) proposal ((+*dat*) **einen H. machen** propose to); **die ~anzeige, –n** announcement of marriage; advertisement for a marriage partner; **h~fähig** marriageable; **h~lustig** keen to marry; **der ~schwindler, –** confidence trickster who dupes women by promising marriage; **die ~urkunde, –n** marriage certificate; **die ~vermittlung, –en** marriage bureau

heischen demand; beg

heiser hoarse; husky

heiß hot; ardent; (wish) fervent; (battle *etc*) fierce, (argument) heated; *coll* on heat, in heat *US*; **mir ist ~** I'm hot; **~ machen** heat;

coll turn on; **sich** *dat* **die Köpfe ~ reden** argue hotly (about sth.); **~ und innig lieben** adore || **~blütig** hot-blooded; **~ersehnt** eagerly-awaited; **der H~hunger** ravenous appetite; **~hungrig** voracious; **H~luft–** hot air …; **der H~sporn, –e** hothead; **~umstritten** hotly-debated; **der H~wasser|bereiter, –** water heater

heißa(ssa)! hey!

heißen (*p/t* **hieß,** *p/part* **geheißen**) call (s.o. sth.); tell (to); (*v/i*) be called; mean; **ich heiße …** my name is …; **wie ~ Sie?** what is your name?; **wie heißt er mit Nachnamen?** what is his surname?; **wie heißt … auf (deutsch** *etc***)?** what is the (German *etc*) for …?; **es heißt, daß …** they say/(in Bible *etc*) it says that …; **es heißt** (+*infin*) we/you *etc* must …; **das heißt** that is; **das will (schon) etwas ~** that (really) means something; that's (really) saying something

---

–heit –ness, –ity, *etc*, *eg* **die Faul~** laziness, **die Gleich~** equality; *some nouns also function as countables* (*pl* **–en**), *eg* **die Schön~** beauty (*quality or woman*)

---

heiter cheerful; light-hearted; (sky *etc*) bright; 'merry'; **aus ~em Himmel** out of the blue; **das ist ja ~!** that's a fine state of affairs!; **das kann ja ~ werden!** that spells trouble

^die^ **Heiterkeit** cheerfulness; brightness; mirth, merriment

Heiz– heating …; **die ~anlage, –n** heating system; **die ~decke, –n** electric blanket; **das ~gerät, –e** heater; **das ~kissen, –** electric heating-pad; **der ~körper, –** radiator; **der ~lüfter, –** fan heater; **das ~material, –ien** fuel; **der ~ofen, ..öfen** (electric *etc*) heater; **die ~platte, –n** hot-plate; **die ~sonne, –n** (bowl-shaped) electric fire; **der ~strahler, –** (electric) wall-heater

heizbar heated; with heating

heizen heat; burn (fuel); (*v/i*) have the heating on; **(elektrisch/mit Öl** *etc***) ~** have (electric/oil *etc*) heating; **gut ~** give a good heat; **es wird geheizt** the heating is on

der **Heizer, –** boilerman; *naut* stoker; *rail* fireman

die **Heizung, –en** heating

das **Hektar** [*also* –'taːɐ], **–e**/(*following num*) **–** (*also* **der**) hectare

die **Hektik** [–ɪk] hectic activity/pace

hektisch hectic

der **Held, –en** (*wk masc*) hero; *in compds* **~en–** heroic …; hero's …; **der ~en|mut** valour

heldenhaft heroic

das **Heldentum** heroism

die **Heldin, –nen** heroine

Helena Helen (of Troy)

helfen (hilf(s)t, *p/t* **half** (*subj* **hülfe**), *p/part* **geholfen)** (+*dat*) help (**bei** with); **sich** *dat* **zu ~ wissen** know how to cope; **ich kann mir nicht ~** I can't help it; **ihm ist nicht zu ~** he's past help; **es hilft nichts** it's no use; **was hilft's?** what's the use?; **ich werde dir** *etc* **~!** I'll teach you *etc*!

der **Helfer, –** helper; **der ~s|helfer, –** accomplice

Helgoland Heligoland

hell bright (*also* = clever); light; pale; fair; clear; high(-pitched); (delight *etc*) sheer; **seine ~e Freude haben an** (*dat*) find great joy in; **in ~en Scharen** in vast numbers; **ein Helles** (*decl as adj*) *approx* = lager

hell– light …; **hell|auf (h. lachen** laugh out loud; **h. begeistert** extremely enthusiastic **(von** about)); **hell|blond** very fair; **das H~dunkel** chiaroscuro; **~häutig** fair-skinned; **~hörig** poorly sound-proofed **(h. sein für** have a keen ear for; **h. machen** make (s.o.) prick up his ears; **h. werden** prick up one's ears); **hellicht (am hellichten Tage** in broad daylight); **~sehen (h. können** be clairvoyant); **das H~sehen** clairvoyance; **der H~seher, –, ~seherisch** clairvoyant; **~sichtig** clear-sighted; **hell|wach** wide awake

helle *coll* (person) bright

die **Helle** brightness; lightness

der **Hellene, –n** (*wk masc*) Hellene

hellenisch Hellenic

der **Hellenismus** Hellenism

hellenistisch Hellenistic

der **Heller, –** heller (*former coin*); (*in idioms*) penny; farthing; **auf ~ und Pfennig** to the last farthing

die **Helligkeit** brightness; lightness; *astron* luminosity

der **Helm, –e** helmet

der **Helot, –en** (*wk masc*) helot

Helsinki ['hɛlz–] Helsinki

das **Hemd, –en** shirt; vest, undershirt *US*; **die ~bluse, –n** shirt-blouse, shirtwaist *US*; **das ~blusen|kleid, –er** shirt-waister; **die ~hose, –n** combinations

Hemds–: die ~ärmel *pl* shirt-sleeves **(in ~ärmeln** in one's shirt-sleeves); **h~ärmelig** in one's shirt-sleeves; *coll* casual

die **Hemisphäre, –n** hemisphere

Hemm–: der ~schuh, –e brake-shoe; hindrance

hemmen (*see also* **gehemmt**) hamper, hinder; check; inhibit (*also psych*)

das **Hemmnis, –se** hindrance

die **Hemmung, –en** *vbl noun*; *also* inhibition (*also psych*); check (*gen* on); **h~s|los** unrestrained; uninhibited

der **Hengst, –e** stallion

der **Henkel, –** handle

henken hang

der **Henker, –** hangman; executioner; *in ex-*

pletives = **Teufel; die ~s|mahlzeit, –en** last meal before execution/*joc* departure *etc*

die **Henne, –n** hen

her: das ist lange ~ that was a long time ago; **es ist (3 Jahre** *etc*) **~, daß/seit …** it's (3 years *etc*) since …; **~ zu mir!** come here!

hinter … (*dat*) **~** after; behind

~ mit …! = … ~! give me …!; **mit … ist es nicht weit ~** *coll* … is *etc* not up to much

neben … (*dat*) **~** beside

um … ~ around

von … ~ from; in terms of

vor … (*dat*) **~** in front of

---

her– *sep pref – general senses*:

(*i*) … here (*eg* **~locken** lure here);

(*ii*) = **herunter–** (*iii*);

(*iii*) *indicates movement* along *when used in conjunction with* **hinter, neben** *or* **vor** (*eg* **hinter … ~gehen** walk (along) behind)

---

herab [–ɛ–] down; (*following acc, eg* **den Hügel ~**) down (the hill *etc*); **von oben ~** from above; condescendingly

herab– *sep pref* … down

herabblicken: ~ auf (*acc*) look down on

herabhängen* (*like* **hängen** *v/i*) hang down; droop

herablassen* let down, lower; **sich ~ zu** condescend to give (answer); **sich (dazu) ~ zu …** condescend to …; **~d** condescending

die **Herablassung** condescension

herabsehen* look down; **~ auf** (*acc*) look down on

herabsetzen reduce; disparage; **~d** disparaging

die **Herabsetzung, –en** reduction; disparagement

herabsinken* (*sn*) sink (down); (night) fall; **~ zu** degenerate into

herabwürdigen treat degradingly

die **Herabwürdigung** degrading treatment

die **Heraldik** [–ɪk] heraldry

heraldisch heraldic

heran [–ɛ–] (*coll* **ran**): **bis an …** (*acc*) **~** right up to; **näher ~** closer; **nur ~!** come on!

heran– (*coll* **ran–**) *sep pref*: *indicates approach to s.o., sth.*

heranbilden train; **sich ~** develop

heranbringen*: ~ an (*acc*) bring close to; introduce to (problem)

heranführen bring up; **~ an** (*acc*) bring up to; introduce to; (*v/i*) lead up to

herangehen* (*sn*): **~ an** (*acc*) go up to; tackle; set about

herankommen* (*sn*) approach; **~ an** (*acc*) come close to; get at; get hold of; (*with neg*) touch (= equal); **die Dinge an sich ~ lassen** *coll* wait and see what happens

heranmachen: sich ~ an (*acc*) *coll* get down to; approach; make up to

herannahen (*sn*) draw near

heranreichen: ~ an (*acc*) reach; come up to the standard of; (*with neg*) touch (= equal)

heranreifen (*sn*) ripen; mature; **~ zu** grow into; **die Zeit für … ist herangereift** the time is ripe for

heranschleichen*: sich ~ an (*acc*) creep up on

herantragen* bring along; **~ an** (*acc*) approach with

herantrauen: sich ~ an (*acc*) dare to go near; dare to tackle

herantreten* (*sn*) come up; **~ an** (*acc*) come/go up to; approach (with request *etc*); (problem *etc*) confront

heranwachsen* [–ks–] (*sn*) grow up; **~ zu** grow into; **~d** (generation) rising

heranwagen: sich ~ an (*acc*) dare to go near; dare to tackle

heranwinken beckon over; hail (taxi)

heranziehen* pull over; call in; bring in; consult; rear (animals), cultivate (plants); train; (*v/i sn*) approach; **zum Vergleich ~** compare with this

herauf [–ɛ–] (*coll* **rauf**) up; (*following acc, eg* **die Treppe ~**) up (the stairs *etc*)

herauf– (*coll* **rauf–**) *sep pref* … up

herauf|arbeiten: sich ~ work one's way up

heraufbeschwören* bring about, cause (crisis *etc*); conjure up

heraufbitten* ask (to come) up

heraufdringen* (*sn*) rise up (from below)

heraufkommen* (*sn*) come up; rise; (storm) approach

heraufsetzen raise (prices *etc*)

heraufsteigen* (*sn*) climb up; rise; (day) dawn

heraufziehen* pull up; (*v/i sn*) approach; draw near

heraus [–ɛ–] (*coll* **raus**) out; **… ist ~** *coll* … is out; **es ist noch nicht ~, (wann** *etc*) **…** *coll* it's not yet known/decided (when *etc*) …; **aus … ~** out of; **aus sich ~** on one's own initiative; **von innen ~** from the inside; **~ damit!** out with it!

heraus– (*coll* **raus–**) *sep pref* … out; *with* **aus** = … out of …

heraus|arbeiten carve (from stone); bring out; *coll* make up (lost working-time); **sich ~ aus** extricate oneself from

herausbekommen* get out; get (… marks *etc*) change; find out; solve; **~ aus** get (information) out of

herausbilden: sich ~ develop, evolve

herausbitten* ask to come out

herausbringen* get out; bring out; put on (play); utter; *coll* find out; solve; **groß ~** give (s.o., sth.) a big build-up; launch with a great deal of publicity; splash (story)

herausdrücken squeeze out; stick out

herausfahren* drive out; *sp* achieve (by driving); (*v/i sn*, +*dat*) (remark) slip out; ~ **aus** drive out of; (*v/i sn*) drive out of, (train) pull out of; leap out of

herausfiltern filter out

herausfinden* pick out; find; find out; ~ **aus** find one's way out of; **sich** ~ **aus** find one's way out of; extricate oneself from

der **Herausforderer, –** challenger

herausfordern challenge; provoke; court (danger), tempt (fate); ~ **zu** challenge to (duel *etc*); (*v/i*) provoke; ~**d** challenging; provocative

die **Herausforderung, –en** challenge; provocation

herausfühlen sense

herausfüttern *coll* feed up

die **Herausgabe** handing over; return; publication

herausgeben* hand over; return; edit; publish; issue; (*v/i*) give change (**auf** *acc* for)

der **Herausgeber, –** editor; publisher

herausgehen* (*sn*) go out; (spot *etc*) come out; **aus sich** ~ come out of one's shell

herausgreifen* pick out

heraushaben* *coll* have got out; have found out/solved; have got the hang of; **den Bogen/Dreh** ~ have got the hang of it

heraushalten* hold out; ~ **aus** hold out of; keep out of; **sich** ~ **aus** stay out of

heraushängen hang out (flag *etc*) (**aus** of); (*v/i*: ~*, *like* **hängen** *v/i*) hang out (**aus** of)

heraushauen* (*p/t* **haute heraus**) chop down; carve (from stone); *coll* get (s.o.) out of a difficulty; *coll* get (better pay *etc*)

herausheben* lift out; single out; emphasize; **sich** ~ stand out

heraushelfen*: (+*dat*) ~ **aus** help out of

herausholen get out; *sp* achieve; gain; *coll* bring out; ~ **aus** *coll* get out of; **das Letzte** ~ **aus** get the utmost out of

heraushören hear (above other sounds); detect

herauskehren make a show of, parade; parade the fact that one is (the boss *etc*)

herauskommen* (*sn*) come out (*in var senses*); get out; come across; *coll* get out of practice; lose the rhythm; *coll cards* lead; **ganz groß** ~ *coll* be a big hit

~ **auf** (*acc*): **es kommt auf eins/dasselbe heraus** it comes to the same thing

~ **aus** come out of; get away from; get out of; **aus dem Lachen/Staunen nicht** ~ be unable to stop laughing/get over one's astonishment

~ **bei** come of; **was wird dabei ~?** what will come of it?

~ **mit** bring out; *coll* come out with

herauskramen dig out

herauskriegen *coll* = **herausbekommen**

herauskristallisieren: ~ **aus** extract from; *chem* crystallize out of; **sich** ~ crystallize, take shape; *chem* crystallize (out)

herauslassen* let out

herauslesen* pick out; ~ **aus** pick out from; gather from; read (meaning) into

herauslocken lure out; ~ **aus** coax out of

herauslösen: ~ **aus** detach from; take out of; hive off from

herauslügen*: **sich** ~ **aus** lie one's way out of

herausmachen *coll* get out (**aus** of); **sich gut** ~ do well; come on nicely

herausnehmen* take out; *sp* take off; ~ **aus** take out of; remove from (school); **den Gang** ~ put the car *etc* into neutral; **sich** *dat* **Freiheiten** ~ take liberties; **sich** *dat* **zuviel** ~ go too far

heraus|operieren remove by operation

herauspauken *coll* get (s.o.) out of a tight spot

herauspicken peck out; pick out

herausplatzen (*sn*) *coll* burst out laughing; ~ **mit** blurt out

herausputzen dress up; decorate; **sich** ~ dress up

herausragen = **hervorragen**

herausreden: **sich** ~ **aus** talk one's way out of; **du willst dich nur** ~ you're just making excuses

herausreißen* tear out; pull out; *coll* get (s.o.) out of a tight spot; *coll* make up for; ~ **aus** tear out of; pull out of; tear away from; shake out of

herausrücken move out; *coll* hand over; fork out; (*v/i sn*) move out; ~ **mit** (*sn*) *coll* come out with; hand over; fork out; **mit der Sprache** ~ come out with it

herausrufen* call out; *theat etc* call back; ~ **aus** call out of (meeting *etc*)

herausschälen take out; single out, isolate; **sich** ~ emerge; become apparent; **sich** ~ **aus** peel off (clothes)

herausschinden (*p/part* **herausgeschunden**) *coll* wangle (time off); make (money) (**aus** out of); gain (advantage) (from)

herausschlagen* knock out; *coll* = **herausschinden;** ~ **aus** strike (sparks) out of; *coll* make (money) out of; (*v/i sn*: flames) leap out of

herausschmuggeln smuggle out

herausschneiden* cut out

herausschrauben unscrew

heraußen *SGer* out here

herausspringen* (*sn*) leap out (**aus** of); pop out (of); protrude (from); (piece) come out (of); ~ **für** *coll* be in it for; **es wird nicht viel dabei** ~ *coll* there isn't much to be got out of it; **wieviel springt für mich dabei**

heraus? *coll* how much do I get out of it?
herausspritzen (*sn if v/i*) squirt out
herausstellen put out; emphasize; highlight; *sp* send off; **klar ~** set out clearly; **sich ~** (innocence *etc*) be proved; **sich ~ als** prove to be; **es stellte sich heraus, daß ...** it turned out that ...
herausstrecken put out, stick out
herausstreichen* delete (**aus** from); praise
herausströmen (*sn*) stream out (**aus** of)
heraussuchen [–uː–] pick out
heraustreten* (*sn*) step out (**aus** of); protrude
herauswachsen* [–ks–] (*sn*): **~ aus** grow out of; **~ lassen** let (hair) grow out
herauswagen: sich ~ dare to come out
herauswinden*: sich ~ aus wriggle out of
herauswirtschaften make (profit) (**aus** from); obtain (from)
herauswollen* want to get out; **mit der Sprache nicht ~** *coll* not want to come out with it
herausziehen* pull out (*also mil*); (*v/i sn*) move out; **~ aus** pull out of; extract from; *coll* drag out of; (*v/i sn*) move out of
herb tart; tangy; (wine) dry; (loss *etc*) bitter; (beauty) austere; (words) harsh
herbei– [–ɛ–] *sep pref* ... along; ... up (to speaker *etc*)
herbei|eilen (*sn*) hurry over; rush to the scene
herbeiführen bring about; cause
herbeilassen*: sich ~ zu ... condescend to ...
herbeilaufen* (*sn*) come running up
herbeireden talk oneself into (crisis *etc*)
herbeirennen* (*sn*) come running up
herbeirufen* call over; call; summon (help)
herbeischaffen bring; get; produce (evidence)
herbeisehnen long for (to come)
herbeiwinken beckon over; hail (taxi)
herbeiwünschen long for; wish (s.o.) would come
herbeiziehen* pull up (chair)
herbeizitieren summon
herbekommen* get hold of; get (s.o.) to come (here)
herbemühen trouble to come (here); **sich ~** take the trouble to come (here)
die **Herberge, –n** lodging; hostel; **der Herbergs|vater, ..väter** hostel warden
herbestellen send for, ask to come; order
herbitten* ask to come (here)
herbringen* (*see also* **hergebracht**) bring (here)
der **Herbst, –e** autumn, fall *US*; *in compds also* autumnal ...; **die ~zeit|lose** (*decl as adj*) meadow saffron
herbsteln: es herbstelt autumn is on its way
herbstlich autumn; autumnal
der **Herd** [–eː–], **–e** cooker, stove; home; centre, seat (of unrest *etc*); *geol, med* focus; **am heimischen ~** at home
die **Herde** [–eː–], **–n** herd; flock (of sheep); **der ~n|mensch, –en** (*wk masc*) person who follows the crowd; **das ~n|tier, –e** gregarious animal
herein [–ɛ–] (*coll* **rein**) in; **~!** come in!; **hier ~!** this way!; **von draußen ~** from outside
herein– (*coll* **rein–**) *sep pref* ... in
hereinbitten* ask (to come) in
hereinbrechen* (*sn*) set in; (night) fall; **~ über** (*acc*) (calamity) overtake
hereinbringen* bring in; *coll* make up for
hereinfallen* (*sn*) *coll* be taken in; **~ auf** (*acc*) be taken in by; fall for
hereinfliegen* (*sn*) fly in; *coll* = **hereinfallen**
hereinführen show in
hereinholen bring in; *coll* make up for
hereinkommen* (*sn*) come in
hereinlassen* let in, admit
hereinlegen *coll* take in
hereinplatzen (*sn*) *coll* barge in
hereinrasseln (*sn*) *coll* be taken in; get into a mess
hereinregnen: es regnet herein the rain is coming in
hereinreiten* (*coll exc v/i*) get (s.o.) into a mess; (*v/i sn*) ride in
hereinrufen* call in
hereinschauen drop in (**bei** on); *SGer* look in
hereinschmuggeln smuggle in
hereinschneien (*coll* person: *sn*) blow in; **es schneit herein** the snow is coming in
hereinspazieren (*sn*) *coll* walk in; **(nur) hereinspaziert!** walk up!
hereinstecken: den Kopf zur Tür ~ put one's head in at the door
hereinwagen: sich ~ dare to come in
hereinziehen* pull in; (*sn*) march in; **es zieht herein** there is a draught
herfahren* drive here; (*v/i sn*) drive/come here; **hinter/neben/vor ...** (*dat*) **~** (*sn*) drive (along) behind/beside/in front of
die **Herfahrt, –en** journey here
herfallen* (*sn*): **~ über** (*acc*) attack; pounce on
herfinden* find one's way here
der **Hergang** course of events; details (of what happened)
hergeben* hand over; give up; lose (son *etc* in war); **wieder ~** give back; **seinen Namen ~ für/zu** lend one's name to; **sein Letztes ~** give everything one has; (athlete *etc*) give all one has got; **einiges/nichts/viel/wenig ~** have something/nothing/much/little to offer; **gib her!** give it to me!
sich ~ für/zu lend one's name to, be a party to
hergebracht *p/part*; *also* traditional; customary

hergehen* (*sn*): **hinter/neben/vor ...** (*dat*) ~ walk (along) behind/beside/in front of; **es geht heiß her** *coll* things are getting heated; **es geht hoch her** *coll* everyone is in high spirits; **es geht über ...** (*acc*) **her** *coll* a lot of ... is used up; (person) is pulled to pieces
herhaben* *coll*: **wo hat er** *etc* **... her?** where did he *etc* get ... from?
herhalten* hold out (plate *etc*); ~ **müssen** have to do/serve; be the scapegoat; take the rap
herholen fetch; **weit hergeholt** far-fetched
herhören: alle mal ~! everybody listen!
der **Hering, –e** herring; tent-peg
herinnen *SGer* in here
herkommen* (*sn*) come (here); (*with* **wo**) come from; ~ **von** come from; **das Herkommen** tradition; origin
herkömmlich traditional; conventional
Herkules [–ɛs] Hercules; **die ~arbeit, –en** Herculean task
herkulisch Herculean
die **Herkunft, ⸚e** origin; **das ~s|land, ⸚er** country of origin
herlaufen* (*sn*): **hinter/neben/vor ...** (*dat*) ~ run after/beside/ahead of
herleiten: ~ **aus** deduce from; derive from; ~ **von** derive from; **sich ~ aus/von** be derived from
hermachen *coll*: **viel/wenig/nichts ~** look very/not look very/not look at all impressive; **viel/wenig/nichts ~ von** make a great fuss/little fuss/no fuss over
sich ~ über (*acc*) get stuck into; lay into
der **Hermaphrodit, –en** (*wk masc*) hermaphrodite
das **Hermelin, –e** *zool* ermine
der **Hermelin, –e** ermine (fur)
hermetisch hermetic
hermüssen* have to come (here); **... muß her** I/we must have ...
hernach afterwards
hernehmen* get; **wo soll ich ... ~?** where am I supposed to get ... from?
hernieder down
heroben *SGer* up here
Herodes [–ɛs] Herod
das **Heroin** heroin
heroisch heroic
der **Heroismus** heroism
der **Herold, –e** herald
der **Heros** [–ɔs], **–(o)en** hero
herplappern rattle off
der **Herr** (*acc, gen and dat sing* **–n**), **–en** (gentle)man; master; (*before surname*) Mr, (*before other titles*) *usually not translated* (*eg* ~ **Dr. X** Dr X, ~ **Ober!** waiter!); **der ~** the Lord; **mein ~, der ~** sir; **meine ~en** gentlemen; **Alter ~** (*graduate member of a* Verbindung); **der alte ~** *coll* my old man; (+*gen*) ~ **werden** master; bring under control; ~ **werden über** (*acc*) master ‖ **der ~gott** the Lord (**Herrgott noch mal!** for heaven's sake!); **~gotts|frühe** (**in aller H.** at the crack of dawn)
das **Herrchen, –** (dog's) master
herreichen (+*dat*) pass to
die **Herreise, –n** journey here
Herren– (gentle)man's ...; men's ...; **die ~bekanntschaft, –en** gentleman friend; **der ~besuch, –e** male visitor(s); **das ~leben** life of luxury (**ein H. führen** live like a lord); **h~los** ownerless; stray; **~sitz** (**im H. reiten** ride astride); **der ~schnitt, –e** shingle (=haircut); **das ~volk** master race
herrichten prepare; **(neu) ~** do up
die **Herrin, –nen** mistress
herrisch imperious
herrje! (*also* **herrjemine!** [–ne]) my goodness!; **ach ~!** oh dear!
herrlich splendid
die **Herrlichkeit, –en** splendour
Herrsch–: die ~sucht domineering nature; **h~süchtig** domineering
die **Herrschaft, –en** power; rule; control; master and mistress (of the house); *hist* estate; (*pl*) ladies and gentlemen; **meine ~en!** ladies and gentlemen!
herrschaftlich belonging to a person of rank; grand
herrschen rule; be rife; prevail; be (*eg* **überall herrschte große Aufregung** there was great excitement everywhere, **es herrschte schlechtes Wetter** the weather was bad); ~ **über** (*acc*) rule (over)
der **Herrscher, –** ruler; *in compds* ruling ...; **der ~blick, –e** imperious look
herrühren: ~ **von** come from; be due to
hersagen recite (mechanically)
herstammen: ~ **von** come from; be descended from; **wo stammt ... her?** where does ... come from?
herstellen produce; establish; put here; **hergestellt in** (*dat*) made in
der **Hersteller, –** manufacturer
die **Herstellung** manufacture; establishment; *in compds* **~s–** production ...; manufacturing ...; **das ~s|land, ⸚er** country of manufacture
herüben *SGer* over here
herüber [–ɛ–] (*coll* **rüber**) over here; across
herüber– (*coll* **rüber–**) *sep pref* ... over, ... across
herüberbitten* ask (to come) over/across
herüberbringen* bring over/across
herüberfahren* drive over/across; (*v/i sn*) come over/across; drive over/across
herüberholen bring over/across
herüberkommen* (*sn*) come over/across
herüberreichen pass over/across; (*v/i*) reach

over/across

herüberretten bring across to safety; keep alive (tradition *etc*); **sich ~** (tradition *etc*) survive (**in** *acc* down to)

herüberschaffen get over/across

herübertragen* carry over/across

herüberziehen* pull over/across; (*v/i sn*) come over/across; move over/across; **zu sich ~** pull over/across towards one; win over

herum [–ɛ–] (*coll* **rum**): **um ... ~** (a)round; *coll* (*of amount, time*) round about, around; **links/rechts ~** round to the left/right; **... ist ~ ...** is over; (news *etc*) has got around

herum– (*coll* **rum–**) *sep pref*: (*i*) ... round (*eg* **~reichen** pass round); (*ii*) ... around, ... about (*eg* **~kriechen** creep around/about); *with* **an** (*dat*) = ... around/about with ... (*eg* **an etw. ~fingern** fiddle around/about with sth.); *with* **um** = ... round ... (*eg* **um etw. ~laufen** run round sth.)

herum|albern *coll* fool around

herum|ärgern: sich ~ mit *coll* keep struggling with

herumbasteln *coll*: **~ an** (*dat*) tinker about with

herumbekommen* *coll* get round (person); get through (time)

herumbringen* *coll* spread around; = **herumbekommen**

herumdoktern *coll*: **~ an** (*dat*) attempt to treat; tinker about with

herumdrehen turn (key); turn over; *coll* 'turn round'; **~ an** (*dat*) twiddle; **sich ~** turn round; turn over; turn (in grave, on own axis); (+*dat*) **das Wort im Mund(e) ~** twist (s.o.'s) words

herumdrücken: sich ~ *coll* hang about; **sich ~ um** dodge

herumdrucksen *coll* hum and haw

herum|experimentieren experiment

herumfahren* drive around; (*v/i sn*) drive around; travel around; spin round; **~ um** (*sn*) drive round; travel round; **mit den Händen in der Luft ~** wave one's hands about in the air

herumfingern *coll*: **~ an** (*dat*) fiddle about with

herumflegeln: sich ~ *coll* lounge about

herumfragen *coll* ask around

herumfuchteln *coll*: **~ mit** wave about

herumführen show round; lead round; **~ in** (*dat*) show round; **~ um** lead round; run (road *etc*) round; (*v/i* road *etc*) go round

herumfummeln *coll*: **~ an** (*dat*) fumble with; fiddle about with

herumgehen* (*sn*) go/walk round; be passed round; (news) get around; (time *etc*) pass; **~ um** go/walk round; avoid; **~ lassen** circulate

herumhacken *coll*: **~ auf** (*dat*) get at

herumhängen* (*like* **hängen** *v/i*) *coll* hang around

herumhantieren *coll* potter about

herumhorchen *coll* keep one's ears open

herumirren (*sn*) wander about

herumkommandieren *coll* order about

herumkommen* (*sn*) come/get round; get around; **mit den Armen ~** get one's arms round it; **~ um** come/get round (corner); get out of, dodge; get round (difficulty *etc*); (*with neg*) get away from (fact)

herumkriegen *coll* get round (person); get through (time)

herumlaufen* (*sn*) go around; run around; **~ um** run round

herumlungern *coll* loaf about

herummäkeln *coll*: **~ an** (*dat*) find fault with

herummurksen *coll*: **~ an** (*dat*) fiddle about with

herumnörgeln *coll*: **~ an** (*dat*) nag at

herumplagen: sich ~ mit *coll* struggle with

herumrätseln [–ɛː–]: **~ an** (*dat*) puzzle over

herumreden: ~ um avoid (issue *etc*)

herumreichen pass round

herumreißen* swing round

herumreiten* (*sn*) ride about; **~ auf** (*dat*) *coll* harp on; keep on at; **~ um** ride round

herumscharwenzeln (*p/part* **herumscharwenzelt**) (*sn*) *coll*: **~ um** dance attendance on

herumschlagen*: ~ um wrap round; **sich ~ mit** *coll* scrap with; battle with, wrestle with

herumschleppen *coll* lug around; drag around; **~ in** (*dat*) drag round (town *etc*); **mit sich ~** carry around with one; go around with (cold *etc*); have on one's mind

herumsitzen* sit around; **~ um** sit round

herumsprechen*: sich ~ get around; **es hat sich herumgesprochen, daß ...** word has got around that ...

herumstehen* stand around; **~ um** stand round

herumstochern: ~ in (*dat*) poke about in; pick at (food)

herumstreichen* (*sn*) roam around; prowl around

herumstreiten*: sich ~ *coll* quarrel

herumtanzen (*sn*) dance around; **~ um** dance round; (+*dat*) **auf dem Kopf/der Nase ~** *coll* do as one pleases with

herumtollen (*sn*) romp about

herumtragen* carry around; *coll* spread; **mit sich ~** carry around with one; be considering (plan *etc*); have on one's mind

herumtreiben* drive around; **sich ~** *coll* knock about; hang around

der **Herumtreiber, –** *coll* tramp; vagabond

herumwerfen* throw around; swing round; turn (head) round sharply; **mit dem Geld ~** *coll* throw one's money around; **sich (im Bett) ~** toss and turn
herumwirtschaften *coll* potter about
herumwühlen: ~ in (*dat*) grub about in; rummage about in
herumwurs(ch)teln *coll*: **~ an** (*dat*) fiddle about with
herumzeigen show round
herumziehen* pull around; (*v/i sn*) move around; travel around; **in der Welt ~** roam the world; **~ mit** (*sn*) knock about with; **~ um** (*sn*) go round
 sich ~ um (fence *etc*) run round
herumziehend itinerant
herunten *SGer* down here
herunter [–ɛ–] (*coll* **runter**) down; (*following acc, eg* **die Straße ~**) down (the street *etc*); **... ist ~** ... is down; ... is off; *coll* ... is run down; **von ... ~** down from
herunter– (*coll* **runter–**) *sep pref*: (*i*) ... down; (*ii*) *indicates removal* ... off; (*iii*) *indicates monotonous delivery or performance*
herunterbekommen* get down; get off
herunterbeten *coll* rattle off
herunterbitten* ask (to come) down
herunterbrennen* (*sn*) burn down
herunterbringen* bring down; ruin; *coll* get (food) down
herunterdrücken press down; bring down
herunterfallen* (*sn*) fall down; **~ von** fall off
heruntergehen* (*sn*) go down; drop; **~ auf** (*acc*) go down to; slow down to; **~ mit** lower; **~ von** get off
heruntergekommen *p/part*; *also* dilapidated; run-down; down-and-out; **sittlich ~** depraved
herunterhandeln beat down; **vom Preis ~** get (sth.) knocked off the price
herunterhängen* (*like* **hängen** *v/i*) hang down; **schlaff ~** droop
herunterhauen* (*p/t only* **haute herunter**) *coll* toss off; **jmdm. eine ~** give s.o. a clout
herunterholen bring down (*also* = shoot down)
herunterklappen turn down; close (lid)
herunterkommen* (*sn*) (*see also* **heruntergekommen**) come down; *coll* become run-down; go downhill; **~ von** *coll* improve on (mark)
herunterlassen* let down; lower
herunterleiern *coll* drone out
heruntermachen *coll* run down; give (s.o.) a dressing-down
herunternehmen* take down; take off; **~ von** take down from; take off
herunterprasseln (*sn*) *coll* pelt down
herunterputzen *coll* come down on
herunterrasseln *coll* rattle off
herunterreißen* pull down; pull off
herunterschalten *mot* change down, shift down *US* (**in** *acc* into)
herunterschlucken swallow
herunterschrauben turn down (lamp); moderate; **sich ~** *aer* spiral downwards
heruntersehen* look down; **~ an** (*dat*) look (s.o.) up and down; **~ auf** (*acc*) look down on
heruntersetzen reduce; belittle, disparage
herunterspielen perform mechanically; play down
heruntertransformieren *elect* step down
herunterwirtschaften ruin by bad management
herunterwürgen choke down
herunterziehen* pull down; drag down (to one's own level); (*v/i sn*) move down; **sich ~ bis zu** (road) run down to
hervor [–ɛ–]: **aus ... ~** out of; **hinter/unter ...** (*dat*) **~** (out) from behind/under
hervor– *sep pref* ... out (towards speaker *etc*); *with* **aus** = ... out of ...; *with* **hinter** (*dat*)/**unter** (*dat*) = ... (out) from behind/under ...
hervorbrechen* (*sn*) burst out; **~ aus** burst out of; break through (cloud); (s.o.'s anger) explode
hervorbringen* produce; utter
hervordringen* (*sn*): **~ aus** issue from
hervorgehen* (*sn*): **~ aus** come from; emerge from; *or expressed – with prep obj becoming subj – by* produce (*eg* **viele bedeutende Künstler sind aus dieser Stadt hervorgegangen** this city has produced many major artists); **daraus geht hervor, daß ...** this shows that ...; **als Sieger ~** emerge victorious
hervorheben* stress, emphasize
hervorholen get out
hervorkehren make a show of, parade; parade the fact that one is (the boss *etc*)
hervorkommen* (*sn*) come out (**aus** of, **hinter** *dat* from behind, **unter** *dat* from under)
hervorlocken lure out (**aus** of, **hinter** *dat* from behind, **unter** *dat* from under)
hervorquellen* (*sn*) well up (**aus** in); pour out (of); bulge (out of)
hervorragen protrude; stand out; **~ aus** protrude from; tower above; **~d** protruding; outstanding
hervorrufen* cause, give rise to; arouse; evoke; call to (s.o.) to come out, *theat* recall
hervorstechen* stick out; stand out; **~d** striking
hervorstehen* stick out; protrude
hervortreten* (*sn*) step out, (sun, moon)

emerge (**hinter** *dat* from behind); protrude; stand out; become apparent; **~ als** make a name for oneself as; **~ mit** bring out

hervortun*: sich ~ distinguish oneself; show off

hervorwagen: sich ~ dare to come out (**aus** of)

hervorzaubern conjure up

hervorziehen* pull out (**aus** of)

der **Herweg** way here; **auf dem ~** on the way here

das **Herz** (*gen* **–ens,** *dat* **–en**), **–en** heart; *cards* hearts, (card: *pl* –) heart; (+*dat*) **das ~ brechen** break (s.o.'s) heart; **sich** *dat* **ein ~ fassen** pluck up courage; **sein ~ hängen an** (*acc*) set one's heart on; **ein ~ und eine Seele sein** be the best of friends; **schweren ~ens** with a heavy heart; **mein ~(chen)** darling

in prepositional phrases:

an: ... liegt mir sehr am ~en I am very concerned about ...; (+*dat*) **ans ~ legen** urge on; entrust to; (+*dat*) **ans ~ wachsen** become very dear to

auf dem ~en haben have on one's mind; **auf ~ und Nieren prüfen** examine thoroughly; **Hand aufs ~!** honestly!

aus tiefstem ~en from the bottom of one's heart; (+*dat*) **aus dem ~en sprechen** voice (s.o.'s) innermost thoughts

in sein/ins ~ schließen grow very fond of

mit ganzem ~en wholeheartedly; **mit halbem ~en** half-heartedly

nach: ein Mann nach meinem ~en a man after my own heart

über: es nicht übers ~ bringen zu ... not have the heart to ...

um: es wird mir leicht/schwer ums ~ I feel very relieved/sad

von: sich *dat* **... vom ~en reden** get off one's chest; **von (ganzem) ~en** with all one's heart; **von ~en gern** most gladly

zu: (+*dat*) **zu ~en gehen** touch deeply; **sich** *dat* **... zu ~en nehmen** take to heart

Herz– heart ...; *med* cardiac ...; *cards* ... of hearts; **der ~anfall, ¨–e** heart-attack; **h~bewegend** deeply moving; **h~erfrischend** refreshing; **h~ergreifend** deeply moving; **h~erquickend** refreshing; **der ~fehler, –** heart defect; **der ~infarkt, –e** cardiac infarction; **die ~kammer, –n** ventricle; **das ~klopfen** palpitations (of the heart) (**mit H.** with a pounding heart); **h~krank** suffering from heart trouble; **die ~krankheit, –en** heart disease; **h~los** heartless; **die ~losigkeit** heartlessness; **der ~schlag, ¨–e** heart-beat; heart failure; **die ~schwäche** weak heart; **der ~spender, –** heart-donor; **die ~transplantation, –en** heart-transplant; **h~zerreißend** heart-rending

herzeigen show (to s.o.); **zeig her!** let me see!

Herzens–: die ~angelegenheit, –en matter near to one's heart; **der ~brecher, –** lady-killer; **~grund** (**aus H.** from the bottom of one's heart); **h~gut** very kind; **die ~güte** great kindness; **~lust** (**nach H.** to one's heart's content); **die ~sache, –n** matter near to one's heart; **der ~wunsch, ¨–e** fondest wish

herzhaft hearty; tasty

herziehen* pull over; (*v/i sn*) move here; **hinter/neben/vor ...** (*dat*) **~** (*sn*) march (along) behind/beside/in front of; **hinter sich ~** pull along; **~ über** (*acc*) (*sn*) *coll* pull to pieces

herzig sweet; **–herzig** –hearted

herzlich warm, cordial; heartfelt; warm-hearted; (*adv*) *also* thoroughly (boring *etc*); **~ gern!** with the greatest of pleasure!; **~ wenig** precious little; **~en Dank!** thank you very much!; **mit ~en Grüßen** kind regards; **~st** yours affectionately

der **Herzog, ¨–e** duke

die **Herzogin, –nen** duchess

herzoglich ducal; (the) duke's

das **Herzogtum, ¨–er** duchy

herzu– [–ɛ–] *sep pref* ... up (to speaker *etc*)

der **Hesse, –n** (*wk masc*) Hessian

Hessen Hesse

hessisch Hessian

heterogen heterogeneous

heterosexuell heterosexual

Hetz– inflammatory ...; **die ~jagd, –en** hunt (with hounds); rush

die **Hetze** rush; agitation

hetzen hunt (with hounds); rush; (*v/i*) rush; stir up hatred; (*sn*) race; **~ auf** (*acc*) set (dog *etc*) on; **~ gegen** stir up feeling against; **~ zu** agitate for; **zu Tode ~** hunt/hound to death; flog (expression) to death; **mit allen Hunden gehetzt sein** *coll* know all the tricks; **sich ~** rush

die **Hetzerei, –en** rush; agitation

das **Heu** hay; **der ~boden, ..böden** hay-loft; **die ~gabel, –n** pitch-fork; **der ~schnupfen** hay-fever; **die ~schrecke, –n** grasshopper; locust

die **Heuchelei, –en** hypocrisy

heucheln feign; (*v/i*) dissemble, sham

der **Heuchler, –** hypocrite

heuchlerisch hypocritical

heuer *SGer* this year

heuern *naut* sign on

heulen howl; (engine) whine; (siren) wail; **... ist zum Heulen** *coll* ... is enough to make you weep

heureka! eureka!

heurig *SGer* this year's; (summer *etc*) this; **der Heurige** (*decl as adj*) *Aust* new wine

heute today (*also* = nowadays); **~ morgen/nachmittag/abend** this morning/afternoon/evening; **~ nacht** last night; tonight; **~ in/vor (einer Woche** *etc*) (a week *etc*) today, from today/(a week *etc*) ago today; **von ~ auf morgen** overnight; **noch ~** to this day; this very day; **~ ist (Ausverkauf** *etc*) there's a (sale *etc*) today

heutig today's; present-day; **bis auf den ~en Tag** to this day; **mit dem ~en Tag** as of today

heutzutage nowadays

die **Hexe, -n** witch; **alte ~** old hag; **kleine ~** minx

hexen conjure up; (*v/i*) perform magic

Hexen-: die ~jagd, -en witch-hunt; **der ~kessel, -** pandemonium; **der ~meister, -** sorcerer; **der ~schuß, ⸚(ss)e** lumbago; **die ~verfolgung, -en** witch-hunt

die **Hexerei, -en** magic; witchcraft

hg (= Hektogramm) hg; **hg. (= herausgegeben), Hg. (= Herausgeber)** ed.

das **Hickhack** *coll* bickering

hie: ~ und da here and there; now and then

hieb *p/t of* **hauen**

der **Hieb, -e** blow; lash; cut; gash; dig (**auf** *acc* at); (*pl*) thrashing; **einen ~ haben** *coll* have a screw loose; **auf den ersten ~** at the first attempt; **auf 'einen ~** *coll* in one go || **hieb- und stich|fest** (argument *etc*) watertight; (alibi) cast-iron

hielt *p/t of* **halten**

hier here; **~ und da** here and there; now and then; **~ (spricht) ...** *tel* (this is) ... speaking; **~ ist ...** *rad* this is ...

hier- + *prep*: ... this (*eg* **~für** for *etc* this); *for the full range of possible translations of the prepositional element see the preposition concerned* (*eg* **für**) *or – where appropriate – the relevant verb or adjective entry* (*eg for* **hierauf gehen wir nicht ein** we won't go into this *see* **eingehen auf** go into)

hieran (*emph* **hieran;** *see* **hier-**) on/to/in/by *etc* this

die **Hierarchie** [-ie-, -ç-], **-(ie)n** hierarchy

hierarchisch [-ie-, -ç-] hierarchical

hierauf (*emph* **hierauf;** *see* **hier-**) on *etc* this; after this; then

hieraus (*emph* **hieraus;** *see* **hier-**) out of/from *etc* this

hier|behalten* (*sep*) keep here

hierbei (*emph* **hierbei**) here; in this connection; on this occasion; in doing so

hier|bleiben* (*sep; sn*) stay here

hierdurch (*emph* **hierdurch;** *see* **hier-**) through here; through/because of *etc* this; hereby

hierfür (*emph* **hierfür;** *see* **hier-**) for *etc* this

hiergegen (*emph* **hiergegen;** *see* **hier-**) against/compared with *etc* this

hierher (*emph* **hierher**) here (= to this place); **bis ~** this far

hierher- *sep pref* ... here (*eg* **~stellen** put here); **~gehören** belong here; be relevant (**nicht h.** be irrelevant)

hierherum (*emph* **hierherum**) round this way; *coll* hereabouts

hierhin (*emph* **hierhin**) here (= to this place); **bis ~** this far; up to this point

hierin (*emph* **hierin;** *see* **hier-**) in this; here, on this point

hier|lassen* (*sep*) leave here

hiermit (*emph* **hiermit;** *see* **hier-**) with this; herewith; hereby

hiernach (*emph* **hiernach;** *see* **hier-**) after/according to *etc* this

die **Hieroglyphe** [-ie-], **-n** hieroglyph

hieroglyphisch [-ie-] hieroglyphic

hier|sein* (*sep; sn*) be here; **das Hiersein** being here; presence; stay

hierüber (*emph* **hierüber;** *see* **hier-**) over/about *etc* this

hierum (*emph* **hierum;** *see* **hier-**) round/about this

hierunter (*emph* **hierunter;** *see* **hier-**) under/by *etc* this; among these

hiervon (*emph* **hiervon;** *see* **hier-**) of/from *etc* this

hiervor (*emph* **hiervor;** *see* **hier-**) in front of *etc* this

hierzu (*emph* **hierzu;** *see* **hier-**) for/to/with regard to/in addition to *etc* this; **vgl. ~ ...** cf. ...

hierzulande in this country/these parts

hiesig local

hieß *p/t of* **heißen**

hieven *naut, coll* heave

Hi-fi- ['haefi-, -'fae] hi-fi ...; **die ~-Anlage, -n** hi-fi (system)

high [hae] *coll* 'high'; **das H~life** [-laef] (*gen* -(s)) high life (**H. machen** *coll* live it up)

hihi! hee-hee!

hijacken ['haedʒɛkŋ] hijack

der **Hijacker** [-ɐ], **-** hijacker

hilf *imp sing of* **helfen**

hilf-: ~los helpless; **die H~losigkeit** helplessness; **~reich** helpful

die **Hilfe, -n** help; aid; assistance; (*pl*) aids (*also equest*); **Erste ~** first aid; (+*dat*) **~ leisten** help; **mit ~** (+*gen*) with the help/aid of; (+*dat*) **zu ~ kommen** come to (s.o.'s) aid; **zu ~ nehmen** make use of; **(zu) ~!** help! || **h~flehend** imploring; **die ~leistung, -en** help, assistance; **der ~ruf, -e** cry for help; **die ~stellung, -en** help; *gym* support; **h~suchend** seeking help; imploring

Hilfs- auxiliary ...; assistant ...; relief ...; **die ~aktion, -en** relief operation; campaign; **der ~arbeiter, -** labourer; unskilled worker; **h~bedürftig** in need of help; needy; **h~bereit** helpful; **die ~bereitschaft** helpfulness; **die ~kraft, ⸚e** assistant; **das ~mittel, –** aid; (*pl*) resources; aid; **die ~quelle, –n** (financial) source; (*usu pl*) source; resource; **das ~verb, –en** auxiliary (verb); **das ~werk, –e** welfare organization

hilf(s)t (*2nd*,) *3rd sing pres of* **helfen**

der **Himalaja** (*gen* –(s)) the Himalayas

Himbeer– raspberry ...

die **Himbeere, –n** raspberry

der **Himmel, –** sky; heaven; canopy; **am ~** in the sky; **im ~** in heaven; **in den ~ heben** praise to the skies; **in den ~ kommen** go to heaven; **unter freiem ~** out in the open; **weiß der ~!** heaven knows!; **du lieber ~! = Gott im ~!** good heavens!; **um ~s willen!** for heaven's sake!; good heavens! || **himmel|angst (mir ist/wird h. I** am/get scared to death); **das ~bett, –en** four-poster; **himmel|blau** sky-blue; **~fahrt** (*no art*) Ascension Day (**Christi H.** the Ascension; **Mariä H.** the Assumption); **das ~fahrts|kommando, –s** *coll* suicide mission/squad; **die ~fahrts|nase, –n** *coll* snub nose; **Himmel|herrgott (H. nochmal!** damn it all!); **himmel|hoch** towering; **das ~reich** the Kingdom of Heaven; **der ~schlüssel, –** primrose; **h~schreiend** outrageous; **himmel|weit** *coll* (**ein h~weiter Unterschied** a world of difference; **h~weit verschieden** poles apart)

Himmels– ... of heaven/the sky; heavenly ...; celestial ...; **der ~körper, –** celestial body; **die ~richtung, –en** direction; point of the compass; **die ~schrift** sky-writing; **der ~spion, –e** spy satellite; **der ~stürmer, –** starry-eyed idealist

himmlisch heavenly; (patience) infinite

hin [-ɪ-]: **ich bin ~** *coll* I'm all in; **... ist ~** *coll* ... has had it; ... is lost; ... has gone; ... has kicked the bucket; **ich bin von ... (ganz) ~** *coll* I'm crazy about; **bis zu ... ist es noch lange ~** ... is *etc* a long way off; **wo ist ... ~?** where has ... gone?; **nichts wie ~!** what are we waiting for?

an ... (*dat*) **~** along

auf ... (*acc*) **~** in response to; at (request *etc*); on the basis of; (examine *etc*) for

bis ~ zu (*see* **bis**)

durch ... ~ across; over (years *etc*)

gegen ... ~ towards

... ~, ... her *coll* ... or no ... (*eg* **Freundschaft ~, Freundschaft her** friendship or no friendship); **~ und her** to and fro; **das Hin und Her** toing and froing; **nach langem Hin und Her** after much deliberation/discussion; **das ist ~ wie her** *coll* it makes no difference

nach ... ~ towards; in (direction)

über ... (*acc*) **~** over; across

~ und wieder now and then; **~ und zurück** there and back; **einmal** (**München** *etc*) **~ und zurück** a return/round trip *US* to (Munich *etc*)

vor sich ~ to oneself

zu ... ~ towards

---

hin– *sep pref – general senses*:

(*i*) ... there (*eg* **~schicken** send there, **~gehen** go there); *with modal auxiliary, translated by* go (there) (*eg* **~dürfen** be allowed to go (there), **ich muß hin** I must go (there));

(*ii*) ... down (*eg* **~knien** kneel down);

(*iii*) ... along (*eg* **~gleiten** glide along);

(*iv*) *indicates casualness* (*eg* **~kritzeln** scribble down)

---

hinab down

hinab– *sep pref* ... down

hinan up

hinan– *sep pref* ... up

hin|arbeiten: ~ auf (*acc*) work towards; work for (examination)

hinauf (*coll* **rauf**) up; (*following acc, eg* **den Fluß ~**) up (the river *etc*)

hinauf– (*coll* **rauf–**) *sep pref* ... up; ... upstairs

hinauf|arbeiten: sich ~ work one's way up

hinaufbringen* take up; **sich ~** *Aust* rise in the world

hinaufdienen: sich ~ work one's way up

hinaufgehen* (*sn*) go/walk up; go/walk upstairs; **~ in** (*acc*) go up into; *mot* change up into, shift into *US*; **~ mit** put up (price)

hinaufkommen* (*sn*) come up; get up

hinaufschrauben push up (prices); step up; **sich ~** spiral upwards

hinaufsteigen* (*sn*) climb up

hinauftransformieren *elect* step up

hinauftreiben* drive (cattle) up; push up (prices)

hinaufziehen* pull up; (*v/i sn*) go up; move up (**in** *acc* to); **sich ~** pull oneself up

hinaus (*coll* **raus**) out; **auf ...** (*acc*) **~** out to (sea); for (years *etc*) ahead; **über ...** (*acc*) **~** beyond; past; over and above; **zu ... ~** out of (door, window)

hinaus– (*coll* **raus–**) *sep pref* ... out; *with* **über** (*acc*) = ... beyond ... (*eg* **über etw. ~gelangen** get beyond sth.); *with* **zu** = ... out of ... (*eg* **zum Fenster ~steigen** climb out of the window)

hinausbefördern transport out of (area *etc*); *coll* eject

hinausbegleiten show out

hinausbugsieren *coll* bundle out

hinaus|ekeln *coll* drive out (**aus** of)

hinausfahren* drive out (**aus** of); (*v/i sn*) go/drive/ride out; (train) pull out; (ship) put to sea; ~ **über** (*acc*) (*sn*) go beyond
hinausfliegen* fly out; (*v/i sn*) fly out; *coll* be thrown out
hinausgehen* (*sn*) go out
~ **auf** (*acc*) go out onto; (room *etc*) overlook
~ **in** (*acc*) go out into; (door) open onto
~ **nach** face (south *etc*)
~ **über** (*acc*) go beyond; exceed
~ **zu** go out by; (road *etc*) go out to
hinausjagen chase out; (*v/i sn*) race out
hinauskommen* (*sn*) come out; get out
~ **auf** (*acc*) be tantamount to; **es kommt auf eins/dasselbe hinaus** it comes to the same thing
~ **aus** get out of
~ **über** (*acc*) get beyond
hinauskomplimentieren show out with great courtesy; show (s.o.) the door
hinauslaufen* (*sn*) run out; ~ **auf** (*acc*) run out into/onto; amount to; **es läuft auf eins/dasselbe hinaus** it comes to the same thing; **es wird darauf ~, daß ...** the upshot will be that ...
hinauslehnen: sich ~ lean out (**zu** of); **„nicht ~!“** 'do not lean out of the window'
hinausschieben* push out; put off (**auf** *acc* until)
hinausschießen* (*sn*) shoot out (**zu** of)
hinausschmeißen* *coll* chuck out; **das Geld zum Fenster** ~ chuck one's money down the drain
hinausschmuggeln smuggle out
hinaussetzen put out(side); *coll* turn out; **sich in den Garten** ~ sit out in the garden
hinaussollen* be supposed to go/get out; **wo soll das noch hinaus?** where will it all end?
hinaustragen* carry out; **in alle Welt** ~ broadcast (news *etc*) throughout the world; ~ **über** (*acc*) carry beyond
hinaustreten* (*sn*) step out (**aus** of)
hinauswachsen* [–ks–] (*sn*): ~ **über** (*acc*) grow taller than; outgrow; surpass; **über sich (selbst)** ~ surpass oneself
hinauswagen: sich ~ dare to go out
hinausweisen* order out (**aus** of); ~ **auf** (*acc*) point out to (sea)
hinauswerfen* throw out (**aus** of); **das Geld zum Fenster** ~ throw one's money down the drain; **hinausgeworfenes Geld** money down the drain
hinauswollen* want to go/get out; ~ **auf** (*acc*) be after; be driving at; **hoch** ~ have great ambitions; **zu hoch** ~ set one's sights too high
hinausziehen* pull out; protract; put off; (*v/i sn*) go out; move out; **sich** ~ drag on; be delayed
hinauszögern put off; **sich** ~ be delayed
hinbekommen* *coll* = **hinkriegen**
hinbiegen* *coll* manage; lick (person) into shape
hinblättern *coll* fork out
Hinblick: im ~ **auf** (*acc*) in view of; with regard to
hinbringen* take there; pass (time); *coll* get done; ~ **zu** take to
hindenken *coll*: **wo denkst du hin!** what *are* you thinking of!
hinderlich that gets in the way; (be, prove) a hindrance; (+*dat*) ~ **sein** get in (s.o.'s) way; be a hindrance to
hindern hinder; hamper; ~ **an** (*dat*) prevent from (+*ger*)
das **Hindernis, –se** obstacle (**für** to); *athl* hurdle; **der ~lauf, ¨–e** *athl*, **das ~rennen, –** *horse rac* steeplechase
hindeuten: ~ **auf** (*acc*) point to; (circumstance *etc*) suggest; **alles deutet darauf hin, daß ...** all the indications are that ...
das **Hindi** (*gen* –) Hindi
die **Hindin, –nen** *poet* hind
der **Hindu** (*gen* –(s)), –(s) Hindu; *in compds* Hindu ...
der **Hinduismus** Hinduism
hindurch (*following noun – usu qualified by* **ganz** – *in acc*) throughout, all ... (*eg* **den ganzen Sommer** ~ throughout the summer, all summer); **durch ...** ~ through; **den ganzen Tag/die ganze Nacht** ~ all day/night (long); **die ganze Zeit** ~ all the time
hindurch– *sep pref* ... through; *with* **durch** = ... through ...
hin|eilen (*sn*) hurry there; hurry along; ~ **zu** hurry to
hinein (*coll* **rein**) in; **in ...** (*acc*) ~ into; **bis in ...** (*acc*) ~ right into; **bis tief in ...** ~ well into; **da** ~ in there; ~ **mit dir/euch!** in you go!
hinein– (*coll* **rein–**) *sep pref* ... in
hinein|arbeiten: ~ **in** (*acc*) work into; **sich** ~ **in** (*acc*) get into
hineinbekommen* get in
hineinbringen* take in; get in; ~ **in** (*acc*) take into; introduce into
hineindenken*: sich in jmdn./jmds. Lage ~ put oneself in s.o.'s position
hineindeuten: ~ **in** (*acc*) read into
hineinfahren* drive in; (*v/i sn*) go/drive/ride in; ~ **in** (*acc*) drive into; (*v/i sn*) go/drive/ride into; slip into; **mit der Hand** ~ **in** (*acc*) (*sn*) slip one's hand into
hineinfallen* (*sn*) fall in; ~ **in** (*acc*) fall into; **sich** ~ **lassen in** (*acc*) drop into
hineinfinden*: sich ~ **in** (*acc*) get used to
hineinfressen*: in sich ~ wolf down; bottle up (anger *etc*), swallow (disappointment *etc*); **sich** ~ **in** (*acc*) eat its way into; (rust

etc) eat into
hineingeboren: ~ in (*acc*) born into
hineingeheimnissen: etwas ~ in (*acc*) see a hidden meaning in
hineingehen* (*sn*) go in; **~ in** (*acc*) go into, enter; **in (den Saal** *etc*) **gehen ... hinein** (the hall *etc*) holds ...
hineingeraten* (*sn*): **~ in** (*acc*) get into; get caught in (storm)
hineingrätschen [-ɛː-] (*sn*) *footb* carry out a sliding tackle
hineingreifen*: ~ in (*acc*) put one's hand in
hinein|interpretieren: ~ in (*acc*) read into
hineinknien: sich ~ in (*acc*) *coll* buckle down to
hineinkommen* (*sn*) come in; get in; **~ in** (*acc*) enter; get into; get caught in (storm); *coll* go (= belong) in
hineinlachen: in sich ~ chuckle to oneself
hineinlegen put in; **~ in** (*acc*) put into; read into
hineinleuchten: ~ in (*acc*) shine into; throw light on; **mit einer Lampe ~ in** shine a light into
hineinmischen: sich ~ in (*acc*) interfere in
hineinpassen: ~ in (*acc*) fit into; (*v/i*) fit into; fit in with
hineinreden: ~ in (*acc*) interfere in; **sich** *dat* **nicht ~ lassen** brook no interference; **sich ~ in** (*acc*) talk oneself into
hineinriechen* *coll*: **~ in** (*acc*) take a look at
hineinschlingen*: in sich ~ wolf down
hineinschlittern (*sn*): **~ in** (*acc*) slide into; drift into
hineinschlüpfen (*sn*) slip in; **~ in** (*acc*) slip into
hineinschmuggeln smuggle in
hineinspielen be a factor; **~ in** (*acc*) enter into; **sich ~ in** (*acc*) play one's way into
hineinstecken put in; **~ in** (*acc*) put in(to); **den Kopf zur Tür ~** put one's head in at the door
hineinstehlen*: sich ~ in (*acc*) steal into
hineinsteigern: sich ~ in (*acc*) work oneself up into; be obsessed with (problem *etc*)
hineinstopfen stuff in; **~ in** (*acc*) stuff into; **in sich ~** *coll* stuff oneself with
hineintragen* carry in; **~ in** (*acc*) carry into; introduce into
hineintun* put in; **einen Blick ~ in** (*acc*) take a look in; take a look at (newspaper)
hineinversetzen: sich in jmdn./jmds. Lage ~ put oneself in s.o.'s position; **sich in ...** (*acc*) **hineinversetzt fühlen** imagine one is in
hineinwachsen* [-ks-] (*sn*): **~ in** (*acc*) grow into; get the feel of
hineinwagen: sich ~ dare to go in
hineinwerfen* throw in; **~ in** (*acc*) throw into; cast (glance) into; **sich ~ in** (*acc*) throw oneself into
hineinwirken: ... wirkt in ... (*acc*) **hinein** the influence of ... extends to ...
hineinziehen* pull in; drag in; **~ in** (*acc*) pull into; drag into (*also* dispute *etc*); (*v/i sn*) make one's/its way into; move into
hineinzwängen: ~ in (*acc*), **sich ~ in** (*acc*) squeeze into
hinfahren* drive there; (*v/i sn*) go there; drive there; **~ an** (*dat*) (*sn*) go/drive along; **~ über** (*acc*) (*sn*) go/drive across; **mit der Hand ~ über** (*acc*) run one's hand over; **~ zu** drive to; (*v/i sn*) go/drive to
die **Hinfahrt, -en** journey there; outward journey
hinfällig frail; invalid; **~ machen** render invalid
die **Hinfälligkeit** frailty; invalidity
hinfinden* = sich ~ find one's way there
hinflegeln: sich ~ *coll* loll about
hinfliegen* fly there; (*v/i sn*) fly there; *coll* come a cropper; **~ über** (*acc*) (*sn*) fly over/across
der **Hinflug, ⸚e** outward flight
hinfort henceforth
hinführen take there; lead there; **~ an** (*dat*) (road *etc*) run along; **~ zu** take to; lead to; (*v/i* road *etc*) lead to; **wo soll das ~?** where will it all end?
hing *p/t of* **hängen** (*v/i*)
die **Hingabe** devotion; dedication; sacrifice (of)
hingeben* give up; sacrifice; **sich ~** (+*dat*) devote/dedicate oneself to; abandon oneself to; give oneself to
hingebungs|voll devoted; dedicated
hingegen on the other hand
hingegossen *coll*: **wie ~ daliegen** recline gracefully
hingehen* (*sn*) go (there); (time) pass; **~ zu** go to; **~ lassen** overlook, let pass
hingehören belong (somewhere)
Hinhalte-: die ~taktik delaying tactics
hinhalten* hold out; put off, stall; *mil* hold off; **den Kopf ~** take the rap (**für** for)
hinhauchen breathe (words)
hinhauen* (*p/t* **haute hin**) *coll* chuck down; toss off; chuck up; (*v/i*) work; be all right; do (= be adequate); (*sn*) fall down; **sich ~** hit the hay; flop down
hinhören listen
hinken (walk with a) limp; (comparison) be inapt; (*sn*) limp (along)
hinknien (*sn*) **= sich ~** kneel down
hinkommen* (*sn*) get there; *coll* go, belong; *coll* manage (**mit** on); *coll* be right; **es wird schon ~** *coll* it'll be all right; **wo ist ... hingekommen?** where has ... got to?; **wo kämen wir hin, wenn ...?** where would we be if ...?
hinkriegen *coll* manage (to do); **wieder ~** put

right; **das hast du prima hingekriegt** you made a grand job of that
Hinkunft *Aust*: **in ~** in future
hinlangen *coll* make a grab at s.o./sth.; help oneself; be enough
hinlänglich sufficient, adequate
hinlegen put down; put to bed; *coll* execute brilliantly; **sich ~** lie down
hinlenken: ~ auf (*acc*) draw (attention) to; turn (conversation) to; **~ zu** steer to; turn (steps) towards
hinlümmeln: sich ~ *coll* loll about
hinmachen *coll* put up; destroy; ruin; *vulg* do in; (*v/i*) do one's/its business; (*sn*) go there
hinmorden massacre
die **Hinnahme** acceptance
hinnehmen* accept, take; **als selbstverständlich ~** take for granted
hinpassen *coll* fit in
hinreichen (+*dat*) pass to; (*v/i*) be enough; **~d** sufficient
die **Hinreise, -n** journey there, outward journey
hinreisen (*sn*) go there, travel there
hinreißen* thrill; **~ zu** provoke (s.o.'s admiration *etc*); **sich ~ lassen** let oneself be carried away (**von** by); +**zu** make (remark *etc*) in the heat of the moment; **hingerissen von** in raptures over; **~d** enchanting; captivating; thrilling; **~d schön** ravishing(ly beautiful)
hinrichten execute
die **Hinrichtung, -en** execution
hinscheiden* (*sn*) pass away
hinschieben* (+ *dat*) push over to
der **Hinschied** *Swiss* decease
hinschlachten slaughter
hinschlagen* strike, hit; (*sn*) *coll* fall down (heavily)
hinschleppen carry (there); drag (there); **sich ~** drag oneself along; drag on
hinschmeißen* *coll* fling down; chuck up; toss off; (+*dat*) chuck to
hinschmieren *coll* scribble; daub
hinschreiben* write down (one's name *etc*); write down without thinking; (*v/i*) *coll* write (to them)
hinsehen* look; **~ zu** look towards; **bei genauerem Hinsehen** on closer examination
hinsetzen put down; seat; sit (child); **sich ~** sit down
Hinsicht: in (**dieser** *etc*) **~** in (this *etc*) respect; **in** (**finanzieller** *etc*) **~** from a (financial *etc*) point of view, ...ly (*eg* financially); **in gewisser ~** in a way; **in ~ auf** (*acc*) with regard to
hinsichtlich (+*gen*) with regard to
hinsitzen* (*sn*) *Aust*, *Swiss* sit down
das **Hinspiel** *sp* first leg

hinstellen put down; put; **~ als** make out to be; hold up as (example); **sich ~** stand (there); **sich gerade ~** stand up straight; **sich ~ als** make oneself out to be
hinsteuern: ~ auf (*acc*) (*sn*) aim at; **~ zu** steer towards; (*v/i sn*) steer towards; head for
hinstrecken hold out; *poet* lay low; **sich ~** stretch out; extend
hint|an- *sep pref*: **~setzen** put last; **~stehen*** take second place; **~stellen** put last
hinten at the back; behind; **~ in** (*dat*) at/in the back of; **nach ~** to the back; backwards; *coll* at the back (of house); **~ und vorn(e) bedienen** *coll* wait on hand and foot; **von ~** from behind/the back; (spell *etc*) backwards || **~herum** round the back; *coll* in a roundabout way; under the counter; behind his/her *etc* back; **~nach** *esp SGer* afterwards; **~über** backwards
hinter (+*acc*, *indicating direction*) behind; (+*dat*, *indicating location*) behind; after
  ~ ... (*dat*) **her** behind; after (*eg* **sie sind ~ seinem Geld her** they're after his money)
  ~ ... (*dat*) **hervor** from behind
  ~ sich haben have behind one; have covered (distance); have completed; have been through; have had (illness); **~ sich lassen** leave behind
hinter.. (*see also* **hinterst..**) back; rear; (end) far
hinter- *sep* (*stressed*) *and insep* (*unstressed*) *pref*
Hinter- back ...; rear ...; *zool* hind ...
die **Hinter|achse, -n** rear axle
die **Hinterbacke, -n** buttock
der **Hinterbänkler, -** back-bencher
das **Hinterbein, -e** hind leg; **sich auf die ~e setzen/stellen** get up on its hind legs; *coll* kick up a fuss; *coll* pull one's socks up
der **Hinterbliebene** (*fem* **die ~**) (*decl as adj*) surviving dependant; **die ~n** *pl* the bereaved
hinterbringen* (+ *dat of pers*) inform (secretly) of
das **Hinterdeck, -s** after-deck
hinterdrein- = hinterher-
hinter|einander one after/behind another; in a row; running, in succession; **~schalten** (*sep*) *elect* connect in series
hinterfragen subject (institution, opinion, *etc*) to critical scrutiny
der **Hintergaumen|laut, -e** velar
der **Hintergedanke, -n** (*like* **Gedanke**) ulterior motive
hintergehen* deceive
der **Hintergrund, ⸚e** background; *theat* backdrop; (*pl*) background; **auf/vor dem ~** (+*gen*) against the background of; **sich im ~ halten** stay in the background; **in den ~**

treten recede into the background

hintergründig cryptic; enigmatic

hinterhaken *coll* follow it up

der **Hinterhalt, –e, aus dem ~ überfallen** ambush; **im ~ haben** *coll* have in reserve

hinterhältig underhand

die **Hinterhand** *zool* hind quarters; *cards* youngest hand; **in der ~ haben** *coll* have up one's sleeve

das **Hinterhaus, ⸚er** back of the house

hinterher afterwards; behind; **~gehen*** (*sep*; *sn*) walk behind; **~hinken** (*sep*; *sn*) limp behind; be behind (**mit** with) (**h. hinter** (*dat*) lag behind); **~kleckern** (*sep*; *sn*) *coll* lag behind (**h. mit** be behind with); **~kommen*** (*sep*; *sn*) follow (behind); come after; **~laufen*** (*sep*; *sn*) run after him/her *etc*; (+*dat*) *coll* chase (girl *etc*); **~sein*** (*sep*; *sn*) *coll* lag behind; (+*dat*) be after (**h., daß ...** see to it that ...)

der **Hinterhof, ⸚e** backyard

Hinter|indien Indochina

der **Hinterkopf, ⸚e** back of the head

der **Hinterlader, –** *mil* breech-loader

das **Hinterland** hinterland

hinterlassen* leave behind; leave (message, impression, *etc*); (+*dat*) leave to

die **Hinterlassenschaft, –en** estate (of deceased person); heritage; legacy (of war *etc*)

hinterlegen deposit (**bei** with); leave (with)

der **Hinterleib, –er** abdomen (of insect)

die **Hinterlist** guile

hinterlistig deceitful; underhand

hinterm *coll* = **hinter dem**

der **Hintermann, ⸚er** person behind; man behind (operation *etc*); (journalist's) source

die **Hintermannschaft, –en** *sp* defence

hintern *coll* = **hinter den**

der **Hintern, –** *coll* backside; (+*dat*) **in den ~ kriechen** suck up to

das **Hinterrad, ⸚er** rear wheel; **der ~antrieb** rear wheel drive; **die ~aufhängung, –en** rear suspension

hinterrücks from behind; behind s.o.'s back

hinters *coll* = **hinter das**

die **Hinterseite, –n** back

der **Hintersinn** deeper meaning

hintersinnig with a deeper meaning

hinterst.. rearmost; (row) last

das **Hinterteil, –e** *zool* hind quarters; *coll* backside

Hintertreffen: ins ~ geraten fall behind; take a back seat

hintertreiben* foil; prevent

die **Hintertreppe, –n** backstairs; **der ~n|roman, –e** trashy novel

Hintertupfingen *coll* the back of beyond

die **Hintertür, –en** back door; = **das Hintertürchen, –** loophole

der **Hinterwäldler, –** backwoodsman

hinterwäldlerisch backwoods

hinterziehen* evade

die **Hinterziehung, –en** evasion

das **Hinterzimmer, –** back room

der **Hinterzungen|vokal, –e** back vowel

hintragen* carry there; **~ zu** take to

hinträumen: vor sich ~ day-dream

hintreten* (*sn*) step; **~ vor** (*acc*) approach (about sth.)

hintun* *coll* put (somewhere)

hinüber (*coll* **rüber**) across; over; **über ...** (*acc*) **~** across; **... ist ~** *coll* ... has had it; ... is done for; ... is well away (= drunk); (food) is off

hinüber– (*coll* **rüber–**) *sep pref* ... across; ... over

hinüberfahren* drive across/over; (*v/i sn*) drive across/over; travel across/over; **~ nach** (*sn*) cross over to; **~ über** (*acc*) (*sn*) cross

hinübergehen* (*sn*) go across/over; walk across/over; cross over (**auf** *acc* to); pass on; **~ über** (*acc*) cross

hinüberretten take across to safety; **in die Gegenwart ~** keep alive (tradition *etc*); **sich ~** get to safety; **sich in die Gegenwart ~** survive down to the present day

hinüberwagen: sich ~ dare to go across

hinüberwechseln [–ks–] (*also sn*): **~ auf** (*acc*) cross over to; **~ in** (*acc*)/**zu** switch to

hin- und her– *sep pref* ... to and fro

Hin- und Rück– ... there and back

hinunter (*coll* **runter**) down; (*following acc*, *eg* **die Straße ~**) down (the street *etc*)

hinunter– (*coll* **runter–**) *sep pref* ... down

hinunterbringen* take down; *coll* get down

hinunterfahren* drive down; (*v/i sn*) go/drive/ride down

hinuntergehen* (*sn*) go down

hinunterlassen* let down, lower

hinunterschlingen* bolt

hinunterschlucken swallow; gulp down (anger, tears)

hinunterspülen wash down; flush down

hinunterstürzen hurl down; gulp down; (*v/i sn*) fall (from a height); race down; **sich ~ von** throw oneself from

hinuntertransformieren *elect* step down

hinunterwagen: sich ~ dare to go down

hinunterwürgen choke down (food); choke back (anger, tears)

hinwagen: sich ~ dare to go there

der **Hinweg, –e** way there; **auf dem ~** on the way there

hinweg away; **über ...** (*acc*) **~** over; across; for (years *etc*); in spite of (difficulties); **ich bin über ... ~** I am past (age); I have got over

hinweg– *sep pref* ... away; *with* **über** (*acc*) = ... across ...; ... over ...

hinwegbringen*: ~ über (*acc*) help (s.o.) get over; help (s.o.) get through
hinwegfegen sweep away; **~ über** (*acc*) (*sn*) sweep across/over
hinweggehen* (*sn*): **~ über** (*acc*) pass over; disregard
hinweghelfen*: (+*dat*) **~ über** (*acc*) help (s.o.) over; help (s.o.) get over; help (s.o.) get through
hinweghören: ~ über (*acc*) ignore (remark)
hinwegkommen* (*sn*): **~ über** (*acc*) get over; get through; disregard
hinwegsehen*: ~ über (*acc*) see over; ignore, overlook
hinwegsetzen: ~ über (*acc*) (*usu sn*) clear; **sich ~ über** (*acc*) ignore
hinwegtäuschen: ~ über (*acc*) mislead about; blind to; (*v/i*) disguise; **darüber ~, daß ...** disguise the fact that ...; **sich ~ über** (*acc*) blind oneself to
hinwegtrösten [–øː–]: **~ über** (*acc*) console for; make up for
der **Hinweis, –e** reference (**auf** *acc* to); indication; hint; comment; (*pl*) information (concerning crime *etc*); **mit dem ~ auf** (*acc*) referring to; **mit dem ~, (daß) ...** pointing out that ...
hinweisen*: ~ auf (*acc*) point out to; (*v/i*) point to; point out; refer to; **darauf ~, daß ...** point out that ...; **~d** *gramm* demonstrative
hinwenden*: ~ zu turn (head *etc*) towards; **sich ~ zu** turn towards
die **Hinwendung: ~ zu** turning to
hinwerfen* throw down; dash off; drop (remark); *coll* drop; chuck up; (+*dat*) throw to; **sich ~** throw oneself down
hinwieder(um) on the other hand; in turn
hinwirken: ~ auf (*acc*) endeavour to bring about
Hinz: ~ und Kunz *coll* every Tom, Dick and Harry
hinzaubern rustle up
hinziehen* drag out; (*v/i sn*) move there; **~ an** (*dat*) (*sn*) move across (sky); **~ über** (*acc*) (*sn*) move across (plain *etc*); **~ zu** draw to; (*v/i sn*) move towards; **es zieht mich zu ... hin** I am drawn to; **sich hingezogen fühlen zu** feel drawn to
sich ~ extend; drag on; be delayed; **sich ~ an** (*dat*) run along
hinzielen: ~ auf (*acc*) aim at; be driving at
hinzu in addition
hinzu– *sep pref* = '*in addition*'
hinzufügen add (*dat* to); append (to)
die **Hinzufügung, –en** addition
hinzugesellen: sich ~ zu join
hinzukommen* (*sn*) come along; supervene; be added; **~ zu** join; be added to; **kommt noch etwas hinzu?** will there be anything else (, sir/madam)?; **hinzu kommt/kommen ...** in addition there is/are ...; **hinzu kommt, daß ...** added to which ...
hinzurechnen add on
hinzusetzen add; **sich ~ zu** sit down with
hinzutreten* (*sn*) come along; supervene; be added; **~ zu** join; be added to
hinzutun* *coll* add
hinzuzählen add on
hinzuziehen* call in
Hiob ['hiːɔp] Job; **die ~s|botschaft, –en** bad news
hipp, hipp, hurra! hip, hip, hurrah!
Hippokrates [–ɛs] Hippocrates
hippokratisch Hippocratic
das **Hirn, –e** brains (*also cul*); *anat* brain; *in compds also* cerebral ...; **das ~gespinst, –e** fantasy; figment of the imagination; **die ~haut|entzündung, –en** meningitis; **h~los** brainless; **die ~schale, –n** cranium; **h~verbrannt** hare-brained
Hiroshima [*also* –'roːʃi–] Hiroshima
der **Hirsch, –e** (red) deer; stag; *cul* venison; **das ~horn** horn; **der ~käfer, –** stag-beetle; **das ~kalb, ⸚er** (male) fawn; **die ~kuh, ⸚e** hind; **das ~leder** deerskin
die **Hirse** millet
der **Hirt, –en** (*wk masc*) herdsman; shepherd; *in compds* **~en–** shepherd's ...; pastoral ...
die **Hirtin, –nen** herdswoman; shepherdess
das **his, His** [–ɪ–] (*gen* –), – *mus* (the note) B sharp; (*key*) **His** B sharp major, **his** B sharp minor
der **Hispanist, –en** (*wk masc*) Hispanicist
die **Hispanistik** [–ɪk] Spanish studies
hissen hoist (flag, sail)
das **Histörchen, –** little story; anecdote
der **Historiker, –** historian
historisch historical; historic
der **Hit** [–ɪ–] (*gen* –(s)), **–s** *mus etc* hit; **die ~liste, –n** top twenty *etc*
Hitler–: der ~gruß, ⸚e Hitler salute; **die ~zeit** the Nazi era
Hitz–: der ~kopf, ⸚e hothead; **h~köpfig** hot-headed; **der ~schlag, ⸚e** heat-stroke
die **Hitze** heat; hot spell; **fliegende ~** hot flushes/flashes *US*; **in ~ geraten** get heated || **h~beständig** heat-resistant; **h~frei (wir** *etc* **haben h.** the school is closed because of the hot weather); **der ~schild, –e** heat-shield; **die ~welle, –n** heat-wave
hitzig hot-tempered; heated; *zool* on/in heat
die **HJ** *Nazi* = **Hitlerjugend**
hl = **Hektoliter; hl.** (= **heilige ...**) St
hm! h'm!
die **H-Milch** (= **haltbare Milch**) U.H.T. milk
die **HO** *EGer* = **Handelsorganisation;** *also* state-owned shop
ho! oh!
hob (höbe) *p/t* (*subj*) *of* **heben**

^das^ **Hobby** [–i], **–s** hobby

^der^ **Hobel, –** *carp* plane; *cul* slicer; **die ~bank, ⸚e** carpenter's bench; **die ~späne** *pl* shavings

hobeln *carp* plane; *cul* slice

hoch [–oː–] (*attrib* **hoh..**; *comp* **höher,** *superl* **höchst../am höchsten)** (*see also* **höchst)** high, (tree *etc*) tall; (age *etc*) great; (amount) large; (loss, penalty) heavy; distinguished; high-ranking; (favourite) hot; (*adv*) highly; (*eg* **drei Treppen ~** three floors) up; *math* to the power of; **(vier** *etc***) Mann ~** *coll* (four *etc*) of us/them *etc*; **das hohe C** top C; **~ und niedrig** rich and poor; **~ und heilig** *coll* (promise) faithfully; **das ist mir zu ~** *coll* it's beyond me; **wenn es ~ kommt** at most; **~ hinauswollen** (*see* **hinauswollen**); **höhere Schule = Gymnasium; für Höheres/zu Höherem bestimmt** destined for higher things

^das^ **Hoch** [–oː–], **–s** cheer; *meteor* high; **ein dreifaches ~ ausbringen auf** (*acc*) give three cheers for

hoch– 1 *sep pref*, *esp* … up, *with* **an** (*dat*) = … up …; 2 highly …;

~achten think highly of; **die H~achtung** esteem (**mit vorzüglicher H.** yours faithfully); **~achtungs|voll** yours faithfully; **das H~amt, ⸚er** *RC* High Mass; **~arbeiten: sich h.** work one's way up; **~aufgeschossen** lanky; **die H~bahn, –en** elevated railway/railroad *US*; **der H~bau** structural engineering; **der H~betrieb** great activity; rush; **~bringen*** bring/take up; get back on his/her/its feet; *coll* get (s.o.'s) back up; **die H~burg, –en** stronghold (of faith, party, *etc*); **~busig** high-bosomed; **~deutsch,** (*language*) **H~deutsch** High (= *standard*) German; **~dotiert** highly-paid; **der H~druck** high pressure (*also meteor*) **(mit/unter H.** (work) flat out); **die H~ebene, –n** plateau; **~entwickelt** highly-developed; **~fahrend** high-handed; **~favorisiert** much-fancied; **die H~finanz** high finance; **~fliegend** high-flown; **die H~form** top form; **die H~frequenz** *phys* high frequency; **die H~garage, –n** multi-storey car park, multistory parking garage *US*; **das H~gebirge, –** high mountains; **das H~gefühl** elation; **~gehen*** (*sn*) go up; rise; (sea) run high; *coll* blow up; blow one's top; be 'busted' **(h. lassen** *coll* blow up; (police) 'bust'); **der H~genuß, ⸚(ss)e** great delight; real treat; **~geschlossen** high-necked; **~gespannt** (expectations) great; *elect* high-voltage; *tech* high-pressure; **~gesteckt** *p/part*; *also* (aim) ambitious; **~gestellt** *p/part*; *also* high-ranking; *print* superior; **~gestochen** *coll* high-flown; stuck-up; **~gewachsen** tall; **~gezüchtet** thoroughbred; pedigree; highly refined; **der H~glanz** high polish **(auf H. bringen** polish until it gleams; make spick and span); **~gradig** extreme; utter; **~hackig** high-heeled; **~halten*** hold up; uphold; **das H~haus, ⸚er** multi-storey building; **~heben*** lift up; raise (arm, hand); **~herrschaftlich** very grand; **~herzig** magnanimous; **~interessant** most interesting; **~jagen** start (animal); get (s.o.) out of bed; *mot* race (engine); **~kant** on end; **~karätig** high-carat; first-rate; **~klappen** tip up; fold up; turn up; lift; **~kommen*** (*sn*) *coll* come up; get up; get ahead; **die H~konjunktur, –en** boom; **~krempeln** roll up; **das H~land, ⸚er** uplands; Highlands; **~leben (h. lassen** give three cheers for; **… lebe hoch!** three cheers for …!); **H~leistungs–** high-performance …; heavy-duty …; **~modern** ultra-modern; **der H~mut** arrogance; **~mütig** arrogant, haughty; **~näsig** *coll* snooty; **~nehmen*** lift/pick up; *coll* pull (s.o.'s) leg; *coll* fleece; *coll* pick up (criminal); **der H~ofen, ..öfen** blast-furnace; **~prozentig** highly-concentrated; (spirits) high-proof; **~qualifiziert** highly-qualified; **~rappeln: sich h.** *coll* struggle to one's feet; recover; **~rechnen** *stats* project; **die H~rechnung, –en** *stats* projection; **~rot** bright red; **der H~ruf, –e** cheer; **die H~saison** high season; **~schätzen** think highly of; **~schnellen** (*sn*) leap up; shoot up; **~schrauben** raise by screwing; push up (prices); pitch high; **~schrecken** (*like* **aufschrecken;** *sn if v/i*) (= **aufschrecken**); **H~schul–** university …; higher education …; **die H~schule, –n** university *or institution of university status, eg academy of music, agricultural college*; **die H~schul|reife** university entrance qualification; **das H~schul|wesen** higher education; **H~see–** deep-sea …; **der H~sicherheits|trakt, –e** maximum security wing; **der H~sitz, –e** raised hide/blind *US*; **der H~sommer, –** midsummer; **die H~spannung** great suspense/tension; *elect* high tension; **~spielen** play up; **die H~sprache, –n** standard language; **~sprachlich** standard; (*adv*) in the standard language; **der H~sprung, ⸚e** high jump; **die H~stapelei, –en** imposture; confidence trick; **der H~stapler, –** impostor; confidence-trickster; **~stecken** (*see also* **~gesteckt**) put up (hair); **~stehend** of high standing; superior (**geistig h.** of high intellect); **~steigen*** (*sn*) climb up; rise **(h. in** (*dat*) well up in); **~stellen** (*see also* **~gestellt**) put up; turn up; **~stilisieren (h. zu** build up into); **die H~stimmung** high spirits; **die H~straße, –n** flyover, overpass *US*; **H~touren** [–tuː–] **(auf H.** at full speed;

(work) flat out; **auf H. bringen** make (s.o.) work/(sth.) go flat out); **~tourig** [–tu:–] high-revving; **~trabend** high-flown; **~transformieren** *elect* step up; **~treiben*** push up (prices); **der H~- und Tiefbau** building and civil engineering; **der H~verrat** high treason; **der H~verräter, –** traitor; **~verräterisch** treasonable; **das H~wasser, –** high water; flood(s); **~werfen*** throw up; toss (coin); **~wertig** high-grade; high-quality; highly nutritious; **~willkommen** most welcome; **H~würden** (Reverend) Father; **die H~zahl, –en** *math* exponent; **Hochzeit** *see separate entry*; **~ziehen*** pull up; raise (eyebrows); run up (flag); *aer* put into a steep climb **(sich h. an** (*dat*) pull oneself up)

höchst [–øːç–] 1 *adj* **höchst..** (*superl of* **hoch**) highest/tallest *etc*; maximum; top; utmost; supreme; 2 *adv* highly, extremely, most; **~e Zeit** high time; **aufs ~e** extremely

Höchst– maximum ...; top ...; highest ...; **die ~leistung, –en** maximum output; *sp* best performance; **~maß (ein H. an** (*dat*) a maximum amount of); **höchst|persönlich** in person; **höchst|wahrscheinlich** most probably; **h~zulässig** maximum permissible

höchstens [–øːç–] at most; except

die **Hochzeit** [–ɔ–], **–en** wedding; **die ~s|reise, –n** honeymoon; **der ~s|tag, –e** wedding day/anniversary

die **Hocke, –n** squatting position; *ski* crouch; **in die ~ gehen** squat down

hocken (*sn in SGer exc* **sich ~**) crouch; *coll* sit; perch; **sich ~** squat down

der **Hocker, –** stool

der **Höcker, –** hump; bump

höck(e)rig hump-backed; bumpy

das **Hockey** ['hɔki, -ke] hockey; **der ~schläger, –** hockey-stick

die **Hoden** *pl* testicles; **der ~sack, ⸚e** scrotum

Hoek van Holland ['hʊk fan 'hɔlant] the Hook of Holland

der **Hof, ⸚e** yard; courtyard; (school) playground; farm; court (of king *etc*); (*in names*, *eg* **Bayrischer ~**) Inn; *astron* halo; **am/bei ~(e)** at court; (+*dat*) **den ~ machen** court || **die ~dame, –n** lady-in-waiting; **h~fähig** presentable at court; socially acceptable; **h~halten*** (*sep*) hold court; **der ~lieferant, –en** (*wk masc*) purveyor to the court; **der ~meister, –** *hist* private tutor; **der ~narr, –en** (*wk masc*) *hist* court jester; **die ~schranze, –n** *hist* (obsequious) courtier

die **Hoffart** *arch* haughtiness

hoffärtig *arch* haughty

hoffen hope; **~ auf** (*acc*) hope for; put one's hope in; **das will ich ~!** I should hope so!; **das will ich nicht ~** I hope not; **es bleibt zu ~, daß ...** it is to be hoped that ...

hoffentlich it is to be hoped; I hope (so)

die **Hoffnung, –en** hope (**auf** *acc* of); **guter ~** expecting; (+*dat*) **~(en) machen** raise (s.o.'s) hopes || **der ~s|lauf, ⸚e** repêchage; **h~s|los** hopeless; **die ~s|losigkeit** hopelessness; **der ~s|schimmer, –** glimmer of hope; **h~s|voll** hopeful; promising

hofieren court

höfisch courtly

höflich polite; courteous; **~st** respectfully

die **Höflichkeit, –en** politeness; courtesy; polite remark; **die ~s|floskel, –n** polite phrase

der **Höfling, –e** courtier; sycophant (at court)

hoh.. *see* **hoch**

die **Höhe, –n** height; hill; size; level; rate; amount; *astron*, *geog*, *math* altitude; *mus* pitch; **das ist (doch) die ~!** that's the limit!; **auf der ~** *coll* up to the mark; up to date; **auf der ~** (+*gen*) level with; off; at the height of (one's fame *etc*); **auf gleicher ~** level; **in die ~** (shoot *etc*) up; **in die ~ gehen** (prices *etc*) go up; *coll* hit the roof; **in ~ von** to the tune of; (prize *etc*) of; at the rate of; **in voller ~** in full || **der ~punkt, –e** climax (*also* = orgasm); peak; highlight

Hohe– (*decl with adj endings*): **das ~lied** the Song of Songs; **der ~priester,** *pl* **die Hohenpriester** high priest

die **Hoheit, –en** sovereignty; majesty; (*title*) Highness; **das ~s|gebiet, –e** (sovereign) territory; **die ~s|gewässer** *pl* territorial waters; **h~s|voll** majestic; **das ~s|zeichen, –** national emblem

Höhen– altitude ...; mountain ...; **die ~flosse, –n** tailplane; **der ~flug, ⸚e** high-altitude flight; flight of fancy; **der ~messer, –** altimeter; **die ~sonne, –n** mountain sun; sun-ray lamp/treatment; **die ~strahlung** cosmic radiation; **der ~unterschied, –e** difference in height/altitude; **der ~zug, ⸚e** mountain range

höher *see* **hoch**

hohl hollow; **~äugig** hollow-eyed; **der H~kopf, ⸚e** numskull; **~köpfig** empty-headed; **das H~maß, –e** measure of capacity; **der H~raum, ⸚e** cavity; **der H~saum, ⸚e** hemstitch; **~wangig** hollow-cheeked; **der H~weg, –e** defile

die **Höhle, –n** cave; den; hovel; *anat* socket (of eye); **der ~n|bewohner, –** cave-dweller; **der ~n|forscher, –** speleologist; **die ~n|forschung** speleology; **der ~n|mensch, –en** (*wk masc*) cave-man

die **Höhlung, –en** hollow; cavity

der **Hohn** scorn; **das ~gelächter** scornful laughter; **h~lachend** with a scornful laugh; **h~sprechen*** (*sep*) (+*dat*) make a mockery of

höhnen mock; (*v/i*) jeer

höhnisch derisive
hoho! oho!
hoi! ooh!; hey!
der **Hokuspokus** hocus-pocus; fooling about; **~, ...!** hey presto, ...!
hold *poet* sweet; (+*dat*) **~ sein** be fond of; (fortune *etc*) smile on
holen get; fetch; draw (breath); win; **sich** *dat* **... ~** get; win; *coll* catch (cold *etc*); **hol('s** *etc*) **der Teufel!** to hell with ...!; **~ lassen** send for
holla! hey!
Holland Holland
der **Holländer, –** Dutchman; **die ~** the Dutch
die **Holländerin, –nen** Dutchwoman
holländisch, (*language*) **H~** Dutch
die **Hölle** hell; (+*dat*) **die ~ heiß machen** *coll* give (s.o.) hell
Höllen– ... of hell; infernal ...; *coll* tremendous ...; **~angst** *coll* (**eine H. haben** be scared stiff); **die ~qual** torments of hell (**~qualen ausstehen** suffer agonies)
höllisch infernal; *coll* hellish, infernal; tremendous; (*adv*: hurt) like hell
holp(e)rig bumpy; jerky
holpern (*sn if indicating direction*) jolt; (in reading) stumble
holterdiepolter bumpety-bump; helter-skelter
der **Holunder, –** elder; **die ~beere, –n** elderberry
das **Holz, ⸚er** wood; timber; *mus* woodwind; (*pl* –) skittle; **~ sägen** saw wood; *coll* snore || **der ~apfel, ..äpfel** crab-apple; **das ~bein, –e** wooden leg; **das ~blas|instrument, –e** woodwind instrument; **der ~fäller, –** woodcutter; **die ~faser|platte, –n** fibreboard; **der ~hammer, ..hämmer** mallet; **die ~hammer|methode** sledge-hammer method; **die ~kohle** charcoal; **der ~kopf, ⸚e** *coll* blockhead; **die ~pantine, –n** clog; **die ~plastik, –en** wood-carving; **das ~scheit, –e** log; **der ~schnitt, –e** woodcut; **die ~schnitzerei, –en** wood-carving; **der ~schuh, –e** wooden shoe; **die ~späne** *pl* wood shavings; **die ~span|platte, –n** chipboard, particle board *US*; **~weg** *coll* (**auf dem H.** on the wrong track); **die ~wolle** wood-wool; **der ~wurm, ⸚er** woodworm
holzen *footb coll* play rough
hölzern wooden
holzig woody; stringy
Homer Homer
homerisch Homeric
homogen homogeneous
homogenisieren homogenize
die **Homogenität** homogeneity
das **Homonym, –e** homonym
der **Homöopath, –en** (*wk masc*) homoeopath
die **Homöopathie** homoeopathy
homöopathisch homoeopathic
die **Homosexualität** homosexuality
homosexuell, der Homosexuelle (*decl as adj*) homosexual
Hongkong ['hɔŋkɔŋ] Hong Kong
der **Honig** honey; (+*dat*) **~ um den Bart/ums Maul schmieren** *coll* butter up || **~lecken** *coll* (**das ist kein H.** it's no picnic); **honig|süß** as sweet as honey; honeyed; **die ~wabe, –n** honeycomb
die **Honneurs** [ɔ'nøːɐs]: **die ~ machen** welcome the guests
das **Honorar, –e** fee; royalty
die **Honoratioren** [–ts–] *pl* dignitaries
honorieren pay a fee for; pay (s.o.) a fee; reward; *fin* honour (cheque)
honorig *coll* respectable
der **Hopfen, –** hop; hops; **bei ... ist ~ und Malz verloren** *coll* ... is *etc* a dead loss || **die ~stange, –n** hop-pole; *coll* 'beanpole'
hopp! quick!
hoppeln (*sn*) lollop
hoppla! whoops!
hops *coll* kaput; lost; **~gehen*** (*sep*; *sn*) *coll* go west; get nabbed; kick the bucket; **~nehmen*** (*sep*) *coll* nab
der **Hops, –e** *coll* jump
hopsa(sa)! upsadaisy!
hopsen (*sn*) *coll* jump; hop
der **Hopser, –** *coll* (little) jump
Hör– hearing ...; *anat* auditory ...; **der ~apparat, –e** hearing-aid; **die ~folge, –n** radio series/serial; **der ~funk** sound radio; **das ~gerät, –e** hearing-aid; **die ~muschel, –n** ear-piece; **das ~rohr, –e** ear-trumpet; *med* stethoscope; **der ~saal, ..säle** lecture-hall; **das ~spiel, –e** radio play; **~weite** (**außer/in H.** out of/within earshot)
Horaz Horace
hörbar audible
die **Hörbarkeit** audibility
Horch–: das ~gerät, –e *mil* sound-detector; **der ~posten, –** *mil* listening-post
horchen listen (**auf** *acc* for); eavesdrop
die **Horde**[1], **–n** horde
die **Horde**[2], **–n** rack
horden|weise in hordes
hören (*p/part* **gehört,** (*after dependent infin*) **hören**) (*also v/i*) hear; listen to; **~, wie jmd./etw. ...** hear s.o./sth. (do *or* doing sth.) (*see* **wie** 2); **gut/schlecht ~** have good/poor hearing; **ich kann ... nicht ~** I can't hear; I can't bear to hear; **das läßt sich ~** that sounds all right; **das läßt sich eher ~** that sounds more like it; **laß ~!** come on – tell us!; **~ Sie mal!** listen!; look here!; **hört, hört!** come, come!; **nie gehört!** never heard of him/it *etc*!; **mir vergeht Hören und Sehen** I don't know whether I'm coming or going
~ an (*dat*) hear from, tell by/from

~ **auf** (*acc*) listen to, heed; answer to (name)
~ **bei** attend ...'s lectures; study under
~ **von** hear about; hear from; **ich lasse von mir** ~ I'll be in touch; **er hat (schon lange) nichts mehr von sich** ~ **lassen** we *etc* haven't heard from him (for a long time)

Hören|sagen: vom ~ by hearsay

der **Hörer, –** listener; *univ* student (attending lecture-course); *tel* receiver; (*pl*) headphones

die **Hörerschaft** audience

hörig in bondage; (*following dat*) in bondage (to); (sexually) dependent (on); **sich** *dat* ... ~ **machen** enslave (nation); make (sexually) dependent on oneself; **der/die Hörige** (*decl as adj*) bondsman/woman

die **Hörigkeit** bondage; (sexual) dependence

der **Horizont, –e** horizon; (mental) outlook; **am** ~ on the horizon; **das geht über meinen** ~ that's beyond me

horizontal, die Horizontale, –n horizontal

das **Hormon, –e** hormone; **der ~haushalt, –e** hormone balance

hormonal = **hormonell** hormone; hormonal

das **Horn, ⸚er** horn; *mus* horn; French horn; bugle; *mot* horn, hooter; *coll* bump (on head); **sich** *dat* **die Hörner abstoßen** *coll* sow one's wild oats; (+*dat*) **Hörner aufsetzen** *coll* cuckold; **ins gleiche ~ blasen/stoßen/tuten** *coll* say the same thing || **die ~brille, –n** horn-rimmed glasses; **die ~haut, ⸚e** horny skin; cornea; **der ~ochse, –n** (*wk masc*) *coll* blockhead; **das ~vieh** horned cattle; (*pl* **~viecher**) *coll* blockhead

Hornberger: wie das ~ Schießen ausgehen/enden come to nothing

das **Hörnchen, –** little horn; croissant

hornig horny

die **Hornisse, –n** hornet

der **Hornist, –en** (*wk masc*) horn player; bugler

das **Horoskop, –e** horoscope; (+*dat*) **das ~ stellen** cast (s.o.'s) horoscope

horrend horrendous

der **Horror** horror (**vor** *dat* of)

der **Horst, –e** eyrie; *aer* airfield, airbase *US*

der **Hort, –e** stronghold (of); refuge; day-home for schoolchildren after school; *poet* hoard; treasure

horten hoard; stockpile

die **Hortensie** [–ĭə], **–n** hydrangea

das **Höschen** [–sç–], **–** panties; (child's) pants, panties *US*

die **Hose, –n** (*also pl*) trousers; breeches; trunks; underpants; panties; **die ~n anhaben** *coll* wear the trousers; **die ~n (gestrichen) voll haben** *coll* be in a blue funk || **der ~n|anzug, ⸚e** trouser-suit, pantsuit *US*; **der ~n|boden, ..böden** seat (of trousers); **der ~n|bund, ⸚e** waistband; **der ~n|matz, ⸚e** *coll* little chap; **der ~n|rock, ⸚e** divided skirt; **der ~n|schlitz, –e** fly (of trousers); **der ~n|träger, –** braces, suspenders *US*

der **Hospitant, –en** (*wk masc*) person sitting in on a lecture *etc*

hospitieren sit in on a lecture *etc*

das **Hospiz, –e** hospice; private hotel (run by religious organization)

die **Hostess** (*or* **–ß**) [–ɔ–], **–(ss)en** hostess (at exhibition *etc*)

die **Hostie** [–ĭə], **–n** *RC* host

das **Hotel, –s** hotel; ~ **garni** hotel providing bed and breakfast || **der ~page, –n** (*wk masc*) page-boy, bellboy *US*

der **Hotelier** [–'lĭe:], **–s** hotelier

die **Hotellerie** hotel industry

das **Hottehü, –s** (*baby-talk*) gee-gee

der **Hottentotte, –n** (*wk masc*) Hottentot

das **Hovercraft** ['ho:vɐkra:ft], **–s** hovercraft

HR = Hessischer Rundfunk

hrsg. (= herausgegeben), Hrsg. (= Herausgeber) ed.

Hs(s). (= Handschrift(en)) MS(S).

hu! ugh!; ooh!; (*to scare*) boo!

hü! gee-up!

der **Hub, ⸚e** *mech* lift; stroke; **der ~raum** cubic capacity; **der ~schrauber, –** helicopter

hüben on this side; ~ **und/wie drüben** on either side

hübsch pretty; handsome; nice; *coll* (sum *etc*) tidy; **sich ~ machen** make oneself look pretty

huch! ooh!

Hucke *coll*: (+*dat*) **die ~ voll hauen** *coll* give (s.o.) a sound thrashing; (+*dat*) **die ~ voll lügen** *coll* tell (s.o.) a pack of lies || **h~pack** piggyback; **der ~pack|verkehr** motorail, piggyback service *US*

der **Huf, –e** hoof; **das ~eisen, –** horseshoe; **der ~lattich** coltsfoot; **das ~tier, –e** hoofed animal

Hüft– hip ...; **das ~gelenk, –e** hip-joint; **der ~gürtel, – = der ~halter, –** girdle

die **Hüfte, –n** hip

der **Hügel, –** hill; mound; **das ~grab, ⸚er** *archaeol* barrow; **das ~land, ⸚er** hilly country

hüg(e)lig hilly

der **Hugenotte, –n** (*wk masc*) Huguenot

das **Huhn, ⸚er** chicken; **dummes** ~ *coll* silly goose; **verrücktes** ~ *coll* queer fish

das **Hühnchen, –** young chicken; **ein ~ zu rupfen haben mit** *coll* have a bone to pick with

Hühner– chicken ...; poultry ...; **das ~auge, –n** corn (on foot); **die ~brühe, –n** chicken broth; **das ~ei, –er** hen's egg; **der ~habicht, –e** goshawk; **die ~pest** fowl-pest; **der ~stall, ⸚e** chicken-coop; **die ~zucht** poultry-farming

huhu! yoo-hoo!; **huhu!** ooh!

hui! [huɪ] whoosh!; ooh!; **im Hui** *coll* before you can/could say Jack Robinson

die **Huld** *arch* grace; favour; **h~voll** *arch* gracious

huldigen (+*dat*) pay homage to; subscribe to (view); indulge in

die **Huldigung, –en** homage

hülfe *p/t subj of* **helfen**

die **Hülle, –n** cover; wrapping; case; (record) sleeve; *poet* cloak (of night *etc*); **sterbliche ~** mortal remains; **die ~n fallen lassen** peel off; **in ~ und Fülle** in abundance; galore

hüllen: ~ in (*acc*) wrap in; **in Nebel gehüllt** shrouded in mist; **sich in Schweigen ~** keep silence

hüllen|los unclothed

die **Hülse, –n** pod; husk; case; **die ~n|frucht, ⸚e** legume

human humane; (superior *etc*) decent

der **Humanismus** humanism

der **Humanist, –en** (*wk masc*) humanist

humanistisch humanistic; (education) classical

humanitär humanitarian

die **Humanität** humanity (= quality)

die **Hummel, –n** bumble-bee; **wilde ~** tomboy

der **Hummer, –** lobster

der **Humor** humour; sense of homour; **h~los** humourless

die **Humoreske, –n** humorous sketch; *mus* humoresque

humorig humorous

der **Humorist, –en** (*wk masc*) humorist

humoristisch humorous

humpeln (walk with a) limp; (*sn*) hobble

der **Humpen, –** tankard

der **Hund, –e** dog; *coll* (*often with adj*) dog; devil; **junger ~** puppy; **auf den ~ kommen** *coll* = **vor die ~e gehen** *coll* go to the dogs; **damit kann man keinen ~ hinter dem Ofen hervorlocken** *coll* that won't tempt anybody

Hunde– dog ...; dog's ...; **die ~arbeit** *coll* drudgery; **hunde|elend** *coll* miserable; **die ~hütte, –n** kennel; **hunde|kalt** *coll* freezing cold; **das ~leben** *coll* dog's life; **hunde|müde** *coll* dog-tired; **die ~rasse, –n** breed of dog; **das ~wetter** *coll* foul weather

hundert (a) hundred

das **Hundert, –e**/(*following* **einige** *etc*) **–(e)** *or before noun* **–** (*gen pl* **–er** *if case not otherwise indicated*) hundred; **zu ~en** in their hundreds

hundert– hundred ...; **~fach** hundredfold; (*adv*) a hundred times; **die H~jahr|feier, –n** centenary; **~mal** a hundred times; **~prozentig** (a) hundred per cent; (alcohol) pure; *coll* out-and-out; (*adv*) *coll* a hundred per cent; absolutely; for sure

der **Hunderter, –** hundred; *coll* hundred-mark *etc* note; **h~lei** (*indecl*) a hundred different (things)

die **Hundertschaft, –en** unit of a hundred men

hundertst.. hundredth; **vom H~en ins Tausendste kommen** *coll* ramble on

hundertstel: ein ~ ... a hundredth of a ...

das **Hundertstel, –** hundredth

die **Hündin, –nen** bitch

hündisch servile; (devotion) dog-like

hunds–: hunds|gemein *coll* rotten, mean; **hunds|miserabel** *coll* wretched; **die H~tage** *pl* dog-days

der **Hüne, –n** (*wk masc*) giant (of a man); **das ~n|grab, ⸚er** megalithic grave

hünenhaft gigantic

der **Hunger** hunger (**nach** for); **~ haben** be hungry || **der ~leider, –** *coll* starveling; **der ~lohn, ⸚e** pittance; **der ~streik, –s** hunger-strike; **der ~tod** starvation; **~tuch** *coll* (**am H. nagen** be on the breadline)

hungern starve, go hungry; starve oneself; **~ nach** hunger for; **mich hungert** I feel hungry; **~ lassen** starve

die **Hungers|not, ⸚e** famine

hungrig hungry (**nach** for)

der **Hunne, –n** (*wk masc*) Hun

Hup–: das ~konzert, –e chorus of (car) horns; **das ~signal, –e** hoot, honk

die **Hupe, –n** *mot* horn

hupen *mot* honk, hoot

hüpfen (*sn*) hop; gambol; bounce; **vor Freude ~** jump for joy; **Hüpfen spielen** play hopscotch

die **Hürde, –n** hurdle (*also sp*); (sheep) pen; **der ~n|lauf, ⸚e** hurdles; **der ~n|läufer, –** hurdler

die **Hure, –n, huren** whore

die **Hurerei, –en** whoring

hurra: ~! hurrah!, hooray!; **der H~patriotismus** jingoism

der **Husar, –en** (*wk masc*) *hist* hussar; **der ~en|ritt, –e** daring venture; **das ~en|stück, –e** daring coup

husch! shoo!; whoosh!

huschen (*sn*) dart, (mice *etc*) scurry; (smile *etc*) flit

hüsteln [–yː–] cough slightly

husten [–uː–] cough (up); (*v/i*) cough; **~ auf** (*acc*) *coll* not give a damn for; **dem** *etc* **werde ich was ~!** he *etc* can get lost!

der **Husten** [–uː–] cough; **der ~anfall, ⸚e** coughing fit; **das ~bonbon, –s** (*also* **der**) cough-drop; **das ~mittel, –** cough medicine; **der ~reiz** tickle in the throat; **der ~saft, ⸚e** cough-mixture

der **Hut, ⸚e** hat; **den ~ nehmen (müssen)** *coll* (have to) go; **~ ab vor ... (*dat*)!** I take off my hat to ...!; **unter einen ~ bringen** *coll* reconcile

die **Hut** (*in phrases*) care; protection; **auf der ~** on one's guard (**vor** *dat* against)

Hut–: der ~macher, – hatter; milliner; **die ~nadel, –n** hat-pin; **~schnur** *coll* (**das geht mir über die H.** that's beyond a joke)
hüten look after; tend; guard (secret); watch (one's tongue); **sich ~ vor** (*dat*) be on one's guard against; **sich ~ zu …** take care not to …; **das Bett/Zimmer ~** stay in bed/one's room; **ich werde mich ~!** not likely!
die **Hütte, –n** hut; cabin; *tech* iron and steel works; glassworks; *naut* poop; **das ~n|kombinat, –e** *EGer* iron and steel combine; **die ~n|kunde** metallurgy; **das ~n|werk, –e** (= ~ *tech*)
hutz(e)lig shrivelled; wizened
die **Hyäne, –n** hyena
die **Hyazinthe, –n** hyacinth
hybrid hybrid
der **Hydrant, –en** (*wk masc*) hydrant
das **Hydrat, –e** hydrate
die **Hydraulik** [–ɪk] hydraulics; hydraulic system
hydraulisch hydraulic
hydrieren hydrogenate
die **Hygiene** hygiene
hygienisch hygienic
die **Hymne, –n** hymn; anthem
hyper– hyper–; **~modern** ultramodern; **~sensibel** hypersensitive
die **Hyperbel, –n** hyperbole; *math* hyperbola
die **Hypnose, –n** hypnosis
hypnotisch hypnotic
der **Hypnotiseur** [–'zøːɐ], **–e** hypnotist
hypnotisieren hypnotize
der **Hypnotismus** hypnotism
der **Hypochonder** [–x–], **–** hypochondriac
die **Hypochondrie** [–x–] hypochondria
hypochondrisch [–x–] hypochondriac
die **Hypothek, –en** mortgage; burden
die **Hypothese, –n** hypothesis
hypothetisch hypothetical
die **Hysterie, –(ie)n** hysteria
hysterisch hysterical

I

^das^ **I** [iː] (*gen, pl* –, *coll* [iːs]) I
i! ugh! (*see* **i bewahre, i wo**)
i. = **in, im**
Ia (= **eins a**) A1
i. A. (= **im Auftrag**) p.p.
iah! hee-haw!
^der^ **Iberer, –, iberisch** Iberian
i bewahre! good heavens, no!
^der^ **Ibis** [–ɪs], **–se** ibis
IC– = **Inter-City-**
ich (*see p. xxvi*) I; ~ **bin's!** it's me!; **mir nichts, dir nichts** (*see* **mir**); **das Ich** (*gen* –(**s**)), –(**s**) self; *psych* ego; **zweites Ich** alter ego || ~**bezogen** self-centred; **die I~form** first person (singular); **der I~-Laut, –e** 'soft' *ch*; **die I~sucht** egoism; ~**süchtig** egoistic
ideal ideal
^das^ **Ideal, –e** ideal
Ideal– ideal ...; **der** ~**fall, ⸚e** ideal case (**im I.** ideally)
idealisieren idealize
^der^ **Idealismus, –(m)en** idealism
^der^ **Idealist, –en** (*wk masc*) idealist
idealistisch idealistic
^die^ **Idee, –(ee)n** idea; **fixe** ~ obsession; **eine** ~ ... *coll* a fraction (higher *etc*); a touch of (salt *etc*); **keine** ~! not a bit!
ideell non-material; spiritual; (content *etc*) intellectual; (reason *etc*) idealistic
Ideen– ... of ideas; **i~arm** unimaginative; **i~reich** imaginative
ident *Aust* identical
identifizieren identify; **sich** ~ **mit** identify (oneself) with
^die^ **Identifizierung, –en** identification
identisch identical
^die^ **Identität, –en** identity
^der^ **Ideologe, –n** (*wk masc*) ideologist
^die^ **Ideologie, –(ie)n** ideology
ideologisch ideological
^das^ **Idiom, –e** idiom
^die^ **Idiomatik** [–ɪk] idioms
idiomatisch idiomatic
^der^ **Idiot, –en** (*wk masc*) idiot; **der** ~**en|hang, ⸚e** *coll* nursery slope; **i~en|sicher** fool-proof
^die^ **Idiotie, –(ie)n** idiocy
^das^ **Idiotikon** [–ɔn], **–(k)en/–(k)a** dialect dictionary
idiotisch idiotic
^das^ **Idol, –e** idol
^das^ **Idyll, –e** idyll
^die^ **Idylle, –n** *liter* idyll
idyllisch idyllic

–ieren –ate, –ize, *eg* **imprägnieren** impregnate, **oxydieren** oxidize; *sometimes the English equivalent has no suffix, eg* **importieren** import

---

–ig –y, –ous, *etc*, *eg* **sandig** sandy (**Sand** = sand), **wässerig** watery (**Wasser** = water), **mutig** courageous (**Mut** = courage)

IG (= **Industriegewerkschaft**) industrial trade union
^der^ **Igel, –** hedgehog
igitt(igitt)! ugh!
^der^ **Iglu** ['iː–], **–s** (*also* **das**) igloo
^der^ **Ignorant, –en** (*wk masc*) ignoramus
^die^ **Ignoranz** ignorance
ignorieren ignore
ihm (*dat of* **er, es**: *see p. xxvi*) (to/for) him/it
ihn (*acc of* **er**: *see p. xxvi*) him; it
ihnen (*dat of* **sie** 2: *see p. xxvi*) (to/for) them
Ihnen (*dat of* **Sie**: *see p. xxvi*) (to/for) you
ihr 1 *pron* (*see p. xxvi*; *in correspondence*: **I~**) you (*familiar pl*); 2 *pron* (*dat of* **sie** 1: *see p. xxvi*) (to/for) her/it; 3 *poss adj* (*corresp to* **sie**: *see p. xxiii*) her; its; their; ~**er**/~**e**/~**(e)s** (*see p. xxviii*; *also* **der/die/das** ~**e**) hers; its; theirs
Ihr 1 *pron* (*in correspondence*): *see* **ihr** 1; 2 *poss adj* (*corresp to* **Sie**: *see p. xxiii*) your; ~**er**/~**e**/~**(e)s** (*see p. xxviii*; *also* **der/die/das** ~**e**) yours; **das** ~**e** *also* what is yours/hers/its/theirs; **das** ~**e tun** do your/her/its/their bit
ihrer (*gen of* **sie**: *see p. xxvi*) of her/it/them; ~**seits** for her/its/their part; on her/its/their part
Ihrer (*gen of* **Sie**: *see p. xxvi*) of you; ~**seits** for/on your part
ihres|gleichen people like her(self)/them(selves); ..., **die** ~ **sucht** unparalleled ...
Ihres|gleichen people like you (*or* yourself/selves)
ihret–: ~**wegen** because of her/it/them; = (**um**) ~**willen** for her/its/their sake
Ihret–: ~**wegen** because of you; = (**um**) ~**willen** for your sake
ihrige/Ihrige: der/die/das ~ = **der/die/das ihre/Ihre** (*at* **ihr, Ihr**)

die **Ikone, –n** icon
die **Ilias** ['i:lĭas] the Iliad
illegal illegal
die **Illegalität** illegality
illegitim illegitimate
illoyal ['ɪlŏaja:l] disloyal
die **Illoyalität** [ɪlŏaja–] disloyalty
die **Illumination, –en** illumination
illuminieren illuminate
die **Illusion, –en** illusion; **sich** *dat* **~en machen** delude oneself
illusionär illusory
illusions|los without illusions
illusorisch illusory; futile
illuster illustrious
die **Illustration, –en** illustration
illustrieren illustrate; **die Illustrierte** (*decl as adj*) illustrated (magazine)
der **Iltis** [–ɪs] (*gen* **–ses**), **–se** polecat
im [ɪm] = **in dem; ~** + *infin noun* = *Engl pres/part* (*eg* **etw. ~ Stehen tun** do sth. standing up)
das **Image** ['ɪmɪtʃ] (*gen* **–(s)**), **–s** image (of product, politician, *etc*)
imaginär imaginary
das **i-Männchen** ['i:–], – *coll* beginner (at primary school)
der **Imbiß, –(ss)e** snack; **die ~halle, –n** = **die ~stube, –n** snack-bar
Imitat–, –imitat imitation ...
die **Imitation, –en** imitation
imitieren imitate; **imitiert** (jewellery *etc*) imitation
der **Imker, –** bee-keeper
die **Imkerei** bee-keeping
immanent immanent, inherent (*following dat* in)
die **Immatrikulation, –en** matriculation
immatrikulieren, sich ~ matriculate
immens immense
immer always; all the time; (two *etc*) at a time; (*generalizing*) –ever (*eg* **wann (auch) ~** whenever); (*followed by comp*, *eg* **~ größer**) ...er and ...er; more and more ...; *as emotive particle*, *used to exhort* (*eg* **~ langsam!** easy does it!, **(nur) ~ zu!** keep it up!); **~ mehr** more and more; **~ noch** = **noch ~** still; even now; **~, wenn ...** whenever ..., every time ...; **~ wieder** again and again; *or conveyed by* keep(s) on (+*ger*); **auf/für ~** for ever; **schon ~** always || **immer|fort** continually; **~grün** evergreen; **immer|hin** after all; at least; all the same; **immer|während** perpetual; **immer|zu** *coll* all the time
die **Immobilien** [–ĭən] *pl* real estate, immovables
immun immune (**gegen** to); **das I~system, –e** immune system
immunisieren immunize
die **Immunität** immunity
der **Imperativ, –e** *gramm* imperative; **kategorischer ~** categorical imperative
das **Imperfekt, –e** imperfect (tense)
der **Imperialismus** imperialism
der **Imperialist, –en** (*wk masc*), **imperialistisch** imperialist
das **Imperium, –(i)en** empire
impertinent impertinent
die **Impertinenz, –en** impertinence
Impf– vaccination ... ; **der ~schein, –e** vaccination certificate; **der ~stoff, –e** vaccine; **der ~zwang** compulsory vaccination
impfen vaccinate
der **Impfling, –e** person (to be) vaccinated
die **Impfung, –en** vaccination
das **Implantat, –e** *med* implant
die **Implikation, –en** implication
implizieren imply
implizite [–te] implicitly
die **Imponderabilien** [–ĭən] *pl* imponderables
Imponier–: das ~gehabe showing-off; *zool* display
imponieren (+*dat*) impress; **~d** impressive
der **Import, –e** import (of); (country's) imports; (*pl*) imports; *in compds* import ...
der **Importeur** [–'tø:ɐ], **–e** importer
importieren import
imposant imposing
impotent impotent
die **Impotenz** impotence
imprägnieren impregnate; waterproof
die **Impression, –en** impression (of)
der **Impressionist, –en** (*wk masc*) impressionist
impressionistisch impressionist
das **Impressum, –(ss)en** (publisher's) imprint; *journ* masthead
die **Improvisation, –en** improvisation
improvisatorisch improvisatory
improvisieren improvise; **improvisiert** improvised; impromptu
der **Impuls, –e** impulse; impetus; *elect* pulse; *phys* impulse; momentum
impulsiv impulsive
die **Impulsivität** impulsiveness
imstande: ~ zu ... capable of (+*ger*); **... ist** *etc* **~ und ...** ... is *etc* quite capable of (+*ger*)
in[1] [ɪn] (*see also* **im**) **1** (+*acc*, *indicating movement*) in(to); **~ die Kirche/Schule/Oper gehen** go to church/school/the opera; **~s Kino/Theater gehen** go to the cinema/theatre;
2 (+*dat*) (*indicating place*) in; at; (*indicating time*) in (... weeks *etc*); at (age); (*distributive*) a, an (*eg* **zweimal ~ der Woche** twice a week); **waren Sie schon ~ (Deutschland** *etc*)? have you been to (Germany *etc*)?; (**heute** *etc*) **~ 8 Tagen** *etc* a week *etc* (from) (today *etc*); **es ~ sich haben** *coll* have a lot of kick in it; be pretty

tough; (person) be quite a guy/girl
in[2] [ɪn] *coll* 'in'

-in [–ɪn] (*pl* **–nen**) *forming nouns denoting females (often with mutation of stem-vowel where possible)* female ...; woman ...; –woman; –ess; she–; *eg* **die Arbeiterin** (female/woman) worker, **die Ärztin** (woman) doctor (**Arzt** = male doctor), **die Französin** Frenchwoman (**Franzose** = Frenchman), **die Russin** Russian (woman) (**Russe** = (male) Russian), **die Gräfin** countess (**Graf** = count, earl), **die Füchsin** vixen (**Fuchs** = fox), **die Hündin** bitch (**der Hund** = dog)

---

in|adäquat inappropriate
in|aktiv inactive; *med* quiescent, inactive; *phys* inert
die **In|angriff|nahme** starting; tackling
die **In|anspruch|nahme** demands (*gen* on); utilization
der **Inbegriff** embodiment, personification; quintessence
inbegriffen included
Inbetrieb–: die ~nahme inauguration; = **die ~setzung** putting into operation
die **Inbrunst** fervour
inbrünstig fervent
indem by (+*ger*) (*eg* **sie erreichte das Fenster, ~ sie auf den Stuhl stieg** she reached the window by climbing on the chair); while, as, *or conveyed by pres/part* (*eg* **~ sie auf das Fenster zeigte, sagte sie ...** pointing to the window she said ...)
der **Inder, –** Indian
indes(sen) 1 *adv* however; meanwhile; 2 *conj* while
der **Index** (*gen* **–(es)**), **–e/Indizes** [–eːs] index (*also econ, math – pl* **Indizes**); *in compds* index ...; *econ* index-linked ...
indexieren *econ* index
die **Indexierung, –en** *econ* indexation
der **Indian, –e** *Aust* turkey
der **Indianer, –, indianisch** (Red) Indian
Indien [–ĭən] India
indifferent indifferent (*also chem, phys*)
die **Indifferenz** indifference (*also chem, phys*)
indigniert indignant
die **Indikation, –en** *med* indication; **medizinische/soziale ~** medical/social grounds (for abortion)
der **Indikativ, –e** indicative (mood)
indirekt indirect
indisch Indian; **der I~e Ozean** the Indian Ocean; **indisch–** Indo–
indiskret indiscreet
die **Indiskretion, –en** indiscretion
indiskutabel out of the question; (taste *etc*) impossible
indisponiert indisposed
der **Individualist, –en** (*wk masc*) individualist
individualistisch individualistic
die **Individualität, –en** individuality; individual personality
individuell individual; personal; **das ist ~ verschieden** it varies from person to person
das **Individuum, –(du)en** individual
das **Indiz, –ien** [–ĭən] indication, sign (**für** of); (*pl*) circumstantial evidence; **der ~ien|beweis, –e** (piece of) circumstantial evidence
Indizes *pl of* **Index**
Indo–: Indochina Indo-China; **indogermanisch** Indo-European
die **Indoktrination, –en** indoctrination
indoktrinieren indoctrinate
Indonesien [–ĭən] Indonesia
der **Indonesier** [–ĭɐ], **–, indonesisch** Indonesian
das **Indossament, –e** *fin* endorsement
indossieren *fin* endorse
die **Induktion, –en** *elect, philos* induction
der **Indus** (*gen* **–**) the Indus
industrialisieren industrialize
die **Industrialisierung** industrialization
die **Industrie, –(ie)n** industry; *Swiss* (small) factory; **in der ~** in industry
Industrie– industrial ...; **das ~gebiet, –e** industrial area; **der ~kapitän, –e** captain of industry; **die ~nation, –en** industrialized nation; **der ~zweig, –e** branch of industry
industriell industrial; **der/die Industrielle** (*decl as adj*) industrialist
induzieren *elect, philos* induce
in|einander (*also sep pref* **in|einander–**) in(to) one another; **~fließen*** (*sn*) flow into one another; merge; **~fügen** fit into one another; **~greifen*** mesh; interlock
infam shameful, disgraceful; *coll* dreadful
die **Infamie, –(ie)n** shamefulness; shameful act
die **Infanterie** [–t(ə)r–], **–n** [–ən] infantry
der **Infanterist, –en** (*wk masc*) infantryman
infantil infantile
der **Infarkt, –e** infarction
der **Infekt, –e** infection
die **Infektion, –en** infection; *in compds* **~s–** ... of infection; infectious ...
infektiös [–ts–] infectious
infernalisch infernal
das **Inferno** inferno
die **Infiltration, –en** infiltration
infiltrieren infiltrate
der **Infinitiv, –e** infinitive
infizieren infect; **sich ~** become infected
in flagranti (catch) in the act
die **Inflation, –en** inflation
inflationär = **inflationistisch** inflationary
die **Inflations|rate, –n** rate of inflation
infolge (+*gen*) as a result of; owing to; **infolge|dessen** as a result
der **Informant, –en** (*wk masc*) informant

die **Informatik** [-ɪk] computer science
der **Informatiker, –** computer scientist
die **Information, –en** (piece of) information; (*pl*) information; **zu Ihrer ~** for your information
informativ informative
informieren inform (**über** *acc* about); **falsch ~** misinform; **sich ~** inform oneself (**über** *acc* about)
infra–: ~rot infra-red; **die I~struktur, –en** infrastructure
die **Infusion, –en** *med* infusion, drip
Ing. = Ingenieur
der **Ingenieur** [ɪnʒe'nǐøːɐ], **–e** engineer; **die ~schule, –n** college of engineering
ingeniös ingenious
das **Ingenium, –(i)en** genius
die **Ingredienz(i)en** *pl* ingredients
der **Ingwer** ginger
Inh. (= **Inhaber**) prop.
der **Inhaber, –** proprietor; holder; occupant; bearer (of cheque, passport)
inhaftieren arrest
inhalieren inhale
der **Inhalt, –e** contents; content, subject-matter; meaning; *math* area; volume; **zum ~ haben** be about
inhaltlich as regards content
Inhalts–: die ~angabe, –n synopsis; summary; **i~leer = i~los** empty; meaningless; **i~schwer** significant; **das ~verzeichnis, –se** list of contents
inhärent inherent
inhuman inhuman; inhumane
die **Initiale** [–ts–], **–n** initial (letter)
die **Initiative** [–tsǐa–], **–n** initiative; **aus eigener ~** on one's own initiative
der **Initiator** [–ts–], **–(or)en** initiator
initiieren [–ts–] initiate
die **Injektion, –en** injection
injizieren inject
der **Inka** (*gen* –(s)), **–(s)** Inca
inkl. = inklusive
inklusive inclusive (*gen* of)
inkognito, das Inkognito, –s incognito
inkonsequent inconsistent
die **Inkonsequenz, –en** inconsistency
das **Inkraft|treten** coming into force
die **Inkubation, –en** incubation; **die ~s|zeit, –en** incubation period
das **Inland** home country; interior (of country); **im ~** at home; inland; **im In- und Ausland** at home and abroad
inländisch home, domestic
Inlands– home ..., domestic ...; *post etc* inland ..., domestic ... *US*
der **Inlaut, –e** *ling* medial sound; **im ~** in medial position
das **Inlett, –s/–e** (bed) ticking
inliegend *esp Aust* enclosed
inmitten (+*gen*) in the midst of
in natura in the flesh; (payment) in kind
inne– *sep pref*; **~haben*** hold (position *etc*); possess; **~halten*** stop, pause; **~werden*** (*sn*) (+*gen*) become aware of; **~wohnen** (+*dat*) be inherent in
innen inside; **nach ~** inwards; **von ~** from inside
Innen– internal ...; interior ...; inner ...; inside ...; indoor ...; **der ~architekt, –en** (*wk masc*) interior designer; **der ~hof, ⸚e** inner courtyard; quadrangle; **das ~leben** inner life; **der ~minister, –** minister of the interior; (*of U.K.*) Home Secretary; (*of U.S.A.*) Secretary of the Interior; **das ~ministerium, –(i)en** ministry of the interior; (*of U.K.*) Home Office; (*of U.S.A.*) Department of the Interior; **die ~politik** home affairs; domestic policy; **i~politisch** domestic; relating to home affairs; **der ~raum, ⸚e** interior; room inside; *sp* central area (inside track); (*pl*) inner rooms; **die ~seite, –n** inside; **die ~stadt, ⸚e** town/city centre; **die ~welt** inner life
inner.. (*see also* **innerst..**) inner; inside; internal (*also med*, *pol*); (calm *etc*) inner, inward; **das Innere** (*decl as adj*; **des/dem I~(e)n**) inside; interior (*also geog*); heart; **Minister des I~en = Innenminister**
inner– intra–; (*eg* **~parteilich**) within (the party *etc*); **~betrieblich** within the company, internal; **~deutsch** within Germany; domestic (relating to Germany); (relations *etc*) inter-German; **~halb** (*usu* + *gen*) within; inside
die **Innereien** *pl* entrails
innerlich internal; inner, inward; introspective; (*adv*) inwardly
die **Innerlichkeit** inwardness; introspectiveness; depth of feeling
innerst.. innermost; **das Innerste** (*decl as adj*) innermost being; **bis ins I~e treffen** cut to the quick
innert *Swiss* (+*gen/dat*) within
innig close; heartfelt; (*adv*: love) dearly
die **Innigkeit** closeness; warmth (of feeling)
Innozenz Innocence (*popes' name*)
die **Innung, –en** guild
in|offiziell unofficial
in|operabel *med* inoperable
in petto *coll*: **~ haben** have up one's sleeve
in praxi in practice
in puncto as regards
die **Inquisition** the Inquisition
der **Inquisitor, –(or)en** inquisitor
inquisitorisch inquisitorial
ins = in das
der **Insasse, –n** (*wk masc*) occupant; inmate
insbesondere in particular
die **Inschrift, –en** inscription

^das^ **Insekt, –en** insect; **i~en|fressend** insectivorous; **die ~en|kunde** entomology
^das^ **Insektizid, –e** insecticide
^die^ **Insel, –n** island; (*in geographical names*) Isle (*eg* **die ~ Man** the Isle of Man); **der ~bewohner, –** islander
^das^ **Inserat, –e** advertisement
^der^ **Inserent, –en** (*wk masc*) advertiser
inserieren (*also v/i*) advertise
insgeheim secretly, in secret
insgesamt in all, altogether
^der^ **Insider** ['ɪnsaɐ̯dɐ], – insider
^die^ **Insignien** [–ĭən] *pl* insignia
inskribieren *Aust univ* enrol for; (*v/i*) enrol
^die^ **Inskription, –en** *Aust univ* enrolment
insofern 1 *adv* in this respect; 2 *conj* (**insofern**) if; **~ als …** insofar as …; in that …
insonderheit especially
insoweit (insoweit) = insofern
in spe [… 'speː]: (*eg* **Schwiegersohn**) ~ prospective (son-in-law *etc*)
^der^ **Inspekteur** [–'tøːɐ], **–e** chief of staff
^die^ **Inspektion, –en** inspection; offices of the inspectorate; *mot* service; **zur ~ bringen** take in for a service || **die ~s|reise, –n** tour of inspection
^der^ **Inspektor, –(or)en** inspector
^die^ **Inspiration, –en** inspiration
inspirieren inspire
^der^ **Inspizient, –en** (*wk masc*) *theat* stage-manager; *rad*, *TV* production manager
inspizieren inspect
^der^ **Installateur** [–'tøːɐ], **–e** plumber; fitter
^die^ **Installation, –en** installation; plumbing
installieren install; **sich ~** install oneself
instand: ~ halten maintain; **~ setzen** repair; renovate; enable (to) || **die I~haltung** upkeep; **die I~setzung** repair; renovation
inständig earnest; insistent; **~ bitten** implore
^die^ **Instanz, –en** authority; *leg* court; **erste/zweite/dritte ~** first/second/third instance || **der ~en|weg** official channels; *leg* stages of appeal (**auf dem I.** through official channels/*leg* the various stages of appeal)
^der^ **Instinkt, –e** instinct; **i~mäßig** instinctive
instinktiv instinctive
^das^ **Institut, –e** institute; *leg* institution
^die^ **Institution, –en** institution
institutionalisieren institutionalize
institutionell institutional
instruieren instruct; brief
^der^ **Instrukteur** [–'tøːɐ], **–e** instructor
^die^ **Instruktion, –en** instruction
instruktiv instructive
^das^ **Instrument, –e** instrument (*also mus*)
instrumental *mus* instrumental
^das^ **Instrumentarium, –(i)en** instruments (*also mus*); apparatus; (administrative) machinery
^die^ **Instrumentation, –en** instrumentation; orchestration
Instrumenten– instrument …
instrumentieren orchestrate, score
^der^ **Insulaner, –** islander
^das^ **Insulin** insulin
inszenatorisch directing; as a director
inszenieren *theat* stage, *cin* direct; stage-manage (protest *etc*)
^die^ **Inszenierung, –en** *theat* production; *cin* direction
intakt intact
^die^ **Intarsien** [–ĭən] *pl* marquetry
integer of integrity; honest
integral integral; **die I~rechnung** integral calculus
^die^ **Integration, –en** integration
integrieren integrate (*also math*) (**in** *acc* into); **~d** integral
^die^ **Integrität** integrity
^der^ **Intellekt** intellect
intellektuell, der/die Intellektuelle (*decl as adj*) intellectual
intelligent intelligent
^die^ **Intelligenz** intelligence; intelligentsia; **der ~quotient, –en** (*wk masc*) intelligence quotient, I.Q.
^die^ **Intelligenzija** intelligentsia
^der^ **Intelligenzler, –** egghead
^der^ **Intendant, –en** (*wk masc*) *theat*, *rad*, *TV* director
^die^ **Intendanz, –en** *theat*, *rad*, *TV* directorship (of theatre *etc*); director's office
intendieren intend; have as its object
^die^ **Intensität** intensity
intensiv intense; intensive; **der I~kurs, –e** crash course; **die I~station, –en** intensive care unit
intensivieren intensify
^die^ **Intensivierung** intensification
^die^ **Intention, –en** intention
^der^ **Intercity-Zug** [–'sɪti–], **¨–e** inter-city express
interdependent interdependent
^die^ **Interdependenz** interdependence
^das^ **Interdikt, –e** interdict
interdisziplinär inter-disciplinary
interessant [–t(ə)r–] interesting; *comm* attractive; **sich ~ machen** attract attention || **interessanter|weise** interestingly enough
^das^ **Interesse** [–t(ə)r–], **–n** interest (**an** *dat*/**für** in); **~ haben an** (*dat*) be interested in || **i~los** uninterested; **die ~losigkeit** lack of interest
Interessen–: die ~gemeinschaft, –en group of people *etc* with common interests; *comm* syndicate; **die ~gruppe, –n = der ~verband, ¨–e** pressure-group; *parl* lobby
^der^ **Interessent** [–t(ə)r–], **–en** (*wk masc*) interested person
interessieren [–t(ə)r–] interest (**für** in); (*v/i*)

be of interest; **sich ~ für** be interested in; **interessiert** interested; (*adv*) with interest; (**politisch** *etc*) **interessiert** interested in (politics *etc*); **interessiert sein an** (*dat*) be interested/have an interest in

die **Interferenz, –en** *ling, phys* interference

interfraktionell inter-party

das **Interieur** [ɛ̃te'rĭøːɐ], **–s/–e** interior (*also art*)

Interims– interim ...; provisional ...

interkonfessionell interdenominational

interkontinental inter-continental

das **Intermezzo, –s/Intermezzi** intermezzo; (amusing) incident

intern internal; domestic; **–intern** (*eg* **partei~**) within (the party *etc*)

das **Internat, –e** boarding-school; **der ~s|schüler, –** boarder

international international

die **Internationale, –n** *pol* Internationale; **die ~** *mus* the Internationale

internieren intern; **der/die Internierte** (*decl as adj*) internee

die **Internierung, –en** internment

der **Internist, –en** (*wk masc*) internist

interplanetar(isch) interplanetary

der **Interpret, –en** (*wk masc*) interpreter (of) (*also arts*)

die **Interpretation, –en** interpretation (*also arts*)

interpretatorisch interpretative (*also arts*)

interpretieren interpret (*also arts*); **falsch ~** misinterpret

interpunktieren punctuate

die **Interpunktion** punctuation; **das ~s|zeichen, –** punctuation mark

das **Interrogativ|pronomen, –/–(m)ina** interrogative pronoun

das **Intervall, –e** interval (*also mus*); **das ~training, –s** interval training

intervenieren intervene

die **Intervention, –en** intervention

das **Interview** [–vjuː], **–s, interviewen** [–'vjuː–] (*p/part* **interviewt**) interview

der **Interviewer** [–'vjuːɐ], **–** interviewer

die **Inthronisation, –en** enthronement

inthronisieren enthrone

intim intimate; **die I~sphäre** privacy; private life; **der I~verkehr** intimacy (= sex)

die **Intimität, –en** intimacy

der **Intimus, –(m)i** closest friend

intolerant intolerant

die **Intoleranz** intolerance

die **Intonation, –en** intonation

intonieren begin to sing/play; give (note)

intransitiv intransitive

das **Intra|uterin|pessar, –e** intra-uterine device

intravenös intravenous

intrigant scheming

der **Intrigant, –en** (*wk masc*) schemer

die **Intrige, –n, intrigieren** intrigue

introvertiert introvert

die **Introvertiertheit** introversion

die **Intuition, –en** intuition

intuitiv intuitive

intus *coll*: **~ haben** have (food, drink) inside one; have got into one's head; **einen ~ haben** have had a few

der **Invalide, –n** (*wk masc*) invalid

die **Invalidität** disablement

die **Invasion, –en** invasion

die **Invektive, –n** invective

das **Inventar, –e** equipment; inventory; **lebendes ~** livestock; **totes ~** furniture and equipment; **zum ~ gehören** *coll* be part of the furniture

inventarisieren make an inventory of

die **Inventur, –en** stocktaking; **~ machen** take stock

die **Inversion, –en** inversion

investieren invest (**in** *acc* in)

die **Investition, –en** investment

der **Investor, –(or)en** investor

inwendig *coll*: **in- und auswendig kennen** know inside out

inwiefern = **inwieweit** to what extent; in what way

der **Inzest, –e** incest

inzestuös incestuous

die **Inzucht** inbreeding

inzwischen in the meantime; (by) now

das **IOK** (= **Internationales Olympisches Komitee**) I.O.C.

das **Ion, –en** ion; *in compds* **~en–** ion ...; ionic ...

ionisch Ionic; Ionian

ionisieren ionize

die **Ionosphäre** ionosphere

i. R. (= **im Ruhestand**) retd.

der **Irak** (*gen* **–(s)**; *also without art*) Iraq

der **Iraker, –, irakisch** Iraqi

der **Iran** (*gen* **–(s)**; *also without art*) Iran

der **Iraner, –, iranisch** Iranian

irden earthen(ware)

irdisch earthly; worldly

der **Ire, –n** (*wk masc*) Irishman; **die ~n** the Irish

irgend possibly; at all; **~ etwas** something; anything; **~ jemand** someone; anyone || **irgend|ein** some (... or other); any; **irgend|einer** someone; anyone; **irgend|einmal** sometime; **irgend|wann** sometime (or other); **irgend|was** *coll* something; anything; **irgend|welch** any; **irgend|wer** *coll* someone; anyone; **irgend|wie** somehow (or other); anyhow; **irgend|wo** somewhere (or other); anywhere; **irgend|woher** from somewhere (or other); **irgend|wohin** (go *etc*) somewhere (or other)

die **Irin, –nen** Irishwoman

die **Iris** [–ɪs], **–** *anat, bot* iris

irisch, (*language*) **I~** Irish; **die I~e See** the Irish Sea

irisieren be iridescent; **~d** iridescent

Irland Ireland

die **Ironie, –(ie)n** irony

ironisch ironic(al)

ironisieren treat ironically

irr = irre

Irr–: die ~fahrt, –en wandering; **der ~garten, ..gärten** maze; **der ~glaube** (*like* **Glaube**) mistaken belief; **die ~lehre, –n** false doctrine; **das ~licht, –er** will-o'-the-wisp; **der ~sinn** madness; **i~sinnig** mad; *coll* terrific; **der ~weg, –e** wrong track; mistake (**auf ~wege geraten** go astray); **der ~wisch, –e** will-o'-the-wisp

irrational irrational

irre mad, crazy; confused; (price *etc*) crazy; (*adv*) *coll* terrifically; **~ werden an** (*dat*) begin to have one's doubts about; lose faith in; **wie ~** *coll* like mad; **der/die Irre** (*decl as adj*) madman/woman

Irre: in die ~ führen mislead; **in die ~ gehen** get lost; be mistaken

irre–: ~führen (*sep*) mislead; **~führend** misleading; **~gehen*** (*sep*; *sn*) get lost; be mistaken; **~leiten** (*sep*) misdirect; mislead; **~machen** (*sep*) disconcert (**i. an** (*dat*) make (s.o.) have doubts about); **~reden** (*sep*) rave; **das I~sein** insanity

irreal unreal

irrelevant irrelevant

die **Irrelevanz, –en** irrelevance

irren be mistaken; (*sn*) wander; **sich ~** be mistaken; **sich ~ in** (*dat*) be wrong about; get (date *etc*) wrong; **sich ~ um** be … out

Irren–: die ~anstalt, –en lunatic asylum; **das ~haus, ⸚er** lunatic asylum; *coll* madhouse

irreversibel irreversible

irrig erroneous; **irriger|weise** mistakenly

irritieren irritate; confuse, muddle

der **Irrtum, ⸚er** mistake; **im ~** in error; **~!** wrong!

irrtümlich mistaken; = **irrtümlicher|weise** by mistake

–isch –ic(al), –ian, –ish, –ese, *etc*, *eg* **historisch** historic(al), **vegetarisch** vegetarian, **türkisch** Turkish, **japanisch** Japanese

---

der **Ischias** [–as] (*also* **das**) sciatica; **der ~nerv, –en** sciatic nerve

der **Islam** [ɪs'laːm, 'ɪslam] (*gen* **–(s)**) Islam

islamisch Islamic

Island ['iːs–] Iceland

der **Isländer, –** Icelander

isländisch, (*language*) **I~** Icelandic

die **Isobare, –n** isobar

die **Isolation, –en** isolation; *elect etc* insulation; **die ~s|haft** solitary confinement

der **Isolationismus** isolationism

der **Isolator, –(or)en** insulator

Isolier– *elect etc* insulating …; **das ~band, ⸚er** insulating tape; **die ~station, –en** isolation ward

isolieren isolate; *elect etc* insulate; **sich ~** isolate oneself

die **Isoliertheit** isolation

die **Isolierung, –en = Isolation**

das **Isotop, –e** isotope

Israel ['ɪsraɛl] Israel

der **Israeli, –s, israelisch** Israeli

der **Israelit, –en** (*wk masc*), **israelitisch** Israelite

iß *imp sing*, **ißt** *2nd/3rd sing pres of* **essen**

ist *3rd sing pres of* **sein**[1]

Ist– actual …; **die ~-Stärke, –n** effective strength

der **Isthmus, –(m)en** isthmus

die **„Iswestija"** 'Izvestia'

der **Itaker** ['iːta–], **–** *coll* Eyetie, Wop *US*

Italien [–ĭən] Italy

der **Italiener, –, italienisch** Italian; **italienisch–** Italo–; (dictionary) Italian–

I-Tüpfelchen ['iː–], *Aust* **I-Tüpferl: bis aufs ~** down to the smallest detail

das **IUP, –(s)** (**= Intrauterinpessar**) I.U.D.

i. V. (**= in Vertretung**) p.p.

Iwan ['iːvaːn] Ivan; **der ~, –s** *coll* Russky; (*collectively*: **der ~**) the Russkies

i wo! good heavens, no!

J

das **J** [jɔt, *Aust* jeː] (*gen*, *pl* **–**, *coll* [jɔts, *Aust* jeːs]) J

ja yes (, I do/we have *etc*); even (*eg* **kritische, ~ brutale Worte** critical, even brutal words); indeed; (*as emotive particle*) after all; of course; just; *or not translated* (*eg* **du weißt ~, wie das ist** you know how it is); *or* = *initial* ah/oh/why, ... (*eg* **da bist du ~!** ah, there you are!); (*stressed particle*) be sure to ..., do ... (*eg* **schreib '~ recht bald!** do write soon!); **~, ...** (*in reply*) *also* well, ...; **... '~ nicht** don't ... whatever you do; **~?** really?; *tel* hullo?; (*appended*) isn't it?, won't he?, *etc*; O.K.?; **aber ~!** (why,) of course!; **wenn ~** if so || **~ja** yes – all *right*!; **der J~sager, –** yes-man; **die J~stimme, –n** vote in favour; *parl* aye, yea *US*; **~wohl** yes (indeed); yes sir; **das J~wort, –e** consent (to marry s.o.) ((+*dat*) **das J. geben** agree to marry)

die **Jacht, –en** yacht

die **Jacke, –n** jacket; cardigan; **das ist ~ wie Hose** *coll* it's as broad as it's long || **das ~n|kleid, –er** two-piece

das **Jackett** [ʒ–], **–s** jacket

der **Jade** ['jaːdə] (*also* **die**) jade

die **Jagd** [jaːkt], **–en** hunt; hunting; pursuit (**auf** *acc* of), chase (after); = **~revier; die ~ nach (dem Glück** *etc*) the pursuit of (happiness *etc*); **~ machen auf** (*acc*) hunt; **auf die ~ gehen** go hunting (**nach** for)

Jagd– hunting ...; **die ~beute, –n** *hunt* bag; **der ~bomber, –** fighter-bomber; **der ~flieger, –** fighter pilot; **das ~flugzeug, –e** *aer* fighter; **das ~gewehr, –e** hunting-rifle; **das ~horn, ⸚er** hunting-horn; **der ~hund, –e** gun dog; **das ~revier, –e** shoot (= land used for shooting over); **der ~schein, –e** game licence (**den/einen J. haben** *joc* be certified); **das ~springen** show-jumping; **die ~staffel, –n** fighter squadron; **der ~stock, ⸚e** shooting-stick; **das ~wesen** hunting; **das ~wild** game; **die ~wurst, ⸚e** (*kind of smoked sausage*); **die ~zeit, –en** hunting/shooting-season

jagen hunt; chase; (*v/i*) hunt, go hunting; (*sn*) race; **~ aus** chase/drive out of; **~ in** (*acc*) drive into; **~ nach** chase (happiness *etc*); **sich** *dat* **eine Kugel durch den Kopf ~** *coll* blow one's brains out; **in die Luft ~** *coll* blow up
sich ~ chase one another; (events *etc*) follow each other in rapid succession

der **Jäger, –** hunter; sportsman (with a gun); *mil* rifleman; *aer* fighter; **das ~latein** tall stories of hunting exploits; **das ~schnitzel, –** escalope chasseur

der **Jaguar, –e** jaguar

jäh sudden; sheer; **der J~zorn** violent temper; sudden rage; **~zornig** hot-tempered

jählings suddenly; steeply

das **Jahr, –e** year; **alle ~e** every year; **das ganze ~ hindurch/über** all the year round; **~ für ~** year after year; **im ~e (1949** *etc*) in (1949 *etc*); **in den besten ~en** in one's prime; **in die ~e kommen** be getting on in years; **nach/seit/vor ~ und Tag** after many years/for years/many years ago; **übers ~** in a year's time || **j~aus (j., j~ein** year in, year out); **das ~buch, ⸚er** year-book; almanac; **der ~gang, ⸚e** vintage; year's issues, (of periodical) volume; those born in ... (*eg* **der J. 1987**); *educ* year (**er ist mein J.** he was born the same year as I was); **das ~hundert, –e** century; **j~hunderte|alt** centuries-old; **j~hunderte|lang** lasting for centuries; (*adv*) for centuries; **die ~hundert|feier, –n** centenary; **die ~hundert|wende** turn of the century; **der ~markt, ⸚e** fair; **das ~tausend, –e** millennium; **das ~zehnt, –e** decade; **j~zehnte|lang** lasting for decades; (*adv*) for decades

jahre|lang years of ...; (*adv*) for years, (take) years

jähren: heute jährt sich der Tag (unserer Begegnung *etc*) it's a year ago today that (we met *etc*); **heute jährt sich ... zum (fünften** *etc*) **Mal** today is the (fifth *etc*) anniversary of

Jahres– annual ...; year's ...; **das ~ende** end of the year; **die ~feier, –n** anniversary; **~frist (binnen/nach/seit J.** within/after/for a year); **die ~rente, –n** annuity; **der ~tag, –e** anniversary; **der ~wechsel, –** New Year; **die ~zahl, –en** date; **die ~zeit, –en** season; **j~zeitlich** seasonal

–jährig -year-old; -year; ... years of

jährlich annual; **–jährlich** -yearly; (*adv*) every ... years

der **Jährling, –e** yearling

jaja *see* **ja**

Jakob [–ɔp] James; *bibl* Jacob
der **Jakobiner, –** *hist* Jacobin
die **Jalousie** [ʒalu–], **–(ie)n** Venetian blind; *tech* louvre
Jalta Yalta
jambisch iambic
der **Jambus, –(b)en** iamb
der **Jammer** misery; lamentation; **es ist ein ~, daß ...** it's a crying shame that ...; **es ist ein ~ zu ...** it's heart-breaking to ... || **das ~geschrei** lamentation; **die ~gestalt, –en** pathetic figure; **der ~lappen, –** *coll* sissy; **jammer|schade** *coll* (**es ist j., daß ...** it's a crying shame that ...); **das ~tal** vale of tears; **j~voll** wretched; pitiful
jämmerlich wretched; pitiful
jammern moan; **~ nach** moan for; **~ über** (*acc*) bemoan; moan about; **~ um** bemoan; **... jammert mich** I feel sorry for ...; ... makes me feel sorry
der **Jangtse** [–ə] (*gen* –(s)) the Yangtze
der **Janker, –** (*South German and Austrian traditional-style jacket*)
der **Jänner, –** *Aust*, **der Januar** ['ja–] (*gen* –(s)), **–e** January; **im ~** in January
Japan ['ja:pan] Japan
der **Japaner, –** Japanese
japanisch, (*language*) **J~** Japanese
der **Japse, –n** (*wk masc*) *coll* Jap
japsen *coll* pant
der **Jargon** [ʒar'gɔ̃:], **–s** jargon; slang
der **Jasmin, –e** jasmine
der **Jaspis** [–ɪs] (*gen* –(ses)), **–se** jasper
jäten, Unkraut ~ weed
die **Jauche, –n** liquid manure; *coll* swill
jauchzen jubilate; **vor Freude ~** shout for joy
der **Jauchzer, –** joyful cry
jaulen howl
die **Jause, –n** *Aust* snack; **die ~n|station, –en** *Aust* snack-bar
jausnen *Aust* have a snack
der **Jazz** [dʒɛs] (*gen* –) jazz; **der ~tanz** jazz-dancing
Jb. = Jahrbuch
je[1] 1 *adv* ever; (*followed by numeral*) each; at a time; 2 *prep* (+*acc*) per; **~ ..., ~/desto ...** the ... the ...; **~ nach** according to, depending on; **~ nachdem** (*see* **nachdem**)
je[2]: **ach/o ~!** oh dear!
die **Jeans** [dʒi:ns] *pl* jeans; **der ~anzug, ⸗e** denim suit; **die ~jacke, –n** denim jacket; **der ~stoff, –e** denim
jeden|falls anyway; at any rate; at least
jeder/jede/jedes (*see p. xviii*) 1 *adj* every; each; any; all; either; 2 *pron* each (one); (**jeder**) everyone; anyone; **jeder einzelne von uns** each one of us; **ein jeder** everyone
jeder–: ~lei (*indecl*) every kind of; **~mann** everyone; anyone; **~zeit** at any time
jedes|mal every time; always; **~, wenn ...** whenever ..., every time ...
jedoch however
jedwed.. any; every
der **Jeep** [dʒi:p], **–s** jeep
jeglich.. any; every; all
jeher ['je:he:ɐ]: **seit/von ~** always
jein *joc* yes and no
das **Jelänger|jelieber, –** honeysuckle
jemals ever
jemand (*acc* **–(en)**, *gen* **–(e)s**, *dat* **–(em)**) someone; anyone
jen–: ~seitig on the other side; **~seits** (+ *gen*) on the other side of; beyond (**j. von** on the other side of); **das J~seits** the hereafter (**ins J. befördern** *coll* send to kingdom come)
Jenaer Glas (*trade-mark*) Pyrex
jener/jene/jenes (*see p. xviii*) 1 *adj* that; (*pl*) those; 2 *pron* that one; the former; (*pl*) those; the former
Jeremia(s) Jeremiah
Jerusalem [–ɛm] Jerusalem
Jesaja Isaiah
der **Jesuit, –en** (*wk masc*) Jesuit
jesuitisch Jesuitical
Jesus (Christus) (*gen* **Jesu (Christi)**) Jesus (Christ)
der **Jet** [dʒɛt] (*gen* –(s)), **–s** jet (aircraft)
der **Jett** [dʒɛt] (*also* **das**) *miner* jet
jetten [dʒ–] (*sn*) *coll* jet
jetzig present
jetzt now; **bis ~** until now; **~, da/wo ...** now that ...; **eben ~** just now; **noch ~** even now; **~ oder nie!** now or never!; **~ schon** already; (by) now; **von ~ an** from now on || **die J~zeit** modern times
jeweilig (obtaining) at the time; particular; respective
jeweils each time; in each case; (one *etc*) at a time; each
Jg. (= **Jahrgang,** *of periodical*) vol.
Jh. (= **Jahrhundert**) c(ent).
jiddisch, (*language*) **J~** Yiddish
der **Job** [dʒɔp], **–s** *coll* job
jobben [dʒ–] *coll* take a temporary job
das **Joch, –e** yoke; *geog* (mountain) pass; **das ~bein, –e** cheek-bone
der **Jockei** ['dʒɔke, –ki], **–s** jockey
das **Jod** iodine
jodeln yodel
der **Jodler, –** yodel; yodeller
joggen [dʒ–] jog
der **Jogger, –** jogger
das **Jogging** [dʒ–] jogging
der **Joghurt** ['jo:gurt] (*gen* –(s)), **–(s)** (*also* **das**) yoghurt
Johann (*name of kings*), **Johannes** [–əs] (*saints, popes*) John
Johanna Joanna; Jane; **die heilige ~** St Joan
die **Johannis|beere, –n: (rote) ~** redcurrant;

schwarze ~ blackcurrant

johlen bawl

der **Joker** [j–, dʒ–], – *cards* joker

Jokohama Yokohama

die **Jolle, –n** jolly-boat, dinghy

Jonas [–as] Jonah

der **Jongleur** [ʒɔ̃'gløːɐ], **–e** juggler

jonglieren [ʒɔ̃g–], **~ mit** juggle

die **Joppe, –n** (*kind of men's jacket*)

Jordanien [–ĭən] Jordan

der **Jordanier** [–ĭɐ], **–, jordanisch** Jordanian

Josef Joseph

Josua Joshua

das **Jota** (*gen* **–(s)**), **–s** iota; **kein/nicht ein ~** not one iota

der **Journalismus** [ʒʊr–] journalism

der **Journalist** [ʒʊr–], **–en** (*wk masc*) journalist

die **Journalistik** [ʒʊr–, –ɪk] journalism (= subject of study)

journalistisch [ʒʊr–] journalistic

jovial affable (in a patronizing way)

die **Jovialität** affability

die **JP** *EGer* = **Junge Pioniere**

der **Jubel** jubilation, rejoicing; cheering; **~, Trubel, Heiterkeit** great merriment; noisy goings-on || **die ~hochzeit, –en** special wedding anniversary (*eg* golden wedding); **~jahre** *coll* (**alle J. (einmal)** once in a blue moon); **das ~paar, –e** couple celebrating a special wedding anniversary (*eg* golden wedding)

jubeln jubilate; cheer; **zu früh ~** count one's chickens before they're hatched

der **Jubilar, –e** person celebrating an anniversary

das **Jubiläum, –(ä)en** jubilee; anniversary

jubilieren jubilate; (bird) carol

juchhe!, juchhei(rassa)! whoopee!

der **Juchten** (*also* **das**) Russia leather

Juck–: das ~pulver, – itching powder; **der ~reiz** itching; itch

jucken make (s.o.) itch; *coll* tempt; (*v/i*) itch; **es juckt mich am (Rücken** *etc*) **= mir/mich juckt (der Rücken** *etc*) my (back *etc*) itches; **es juckt mich zu ...** *coll* I'm itching to ...; **sich ~** *coll* scratch oneself

der **Jude, –n** (*wk masc*) Jew; **der Ewige ~** the Wandering Jew

jüdeln speak with a Jewish accent

Juden– ... of the Jews; Jewish ...; **der ~stern, –e** Star of David

das **Judentum** Judaism; Jewry; Jewishness

die **Jüdin, –nen** Jewess

jüdisch Jewish; **jüdisch–** Judaeo–

das **Judo** (*gen* **–(s)**) judo

die **Jugend** youth; young people; **von ~ auf** from one's youth || **das ~alter** youth; adolescence; **das ~amt, ⸚er** youth welfare office; **j~frei** (film) approved for young people; **der ~freund, –e** friend of one's youth; *EGer* member of the F.D.J.; **die ~fürsorge** youth welfare; **das ~gericht, –e** juvenile court; **die ~herberge, –n** youth hostel; **die ~jahre** *pl* early years, youth; **die ~kriminalität** juvenile delinquency; **die ~liebe, –n** love/sweetheart of one's youth; **die ~pflege** youth welfare; **der ~richter, –** juvenile court magistrate; **der ~schutz** protection of children and young people; **der ~stil** art nouveau; Jugendstil; **die ~straf|anstalt, –en** reform school; **die ~weihe, –n** *esp Nazi*, *EGer* youth initiation ceremony (*in E. Germany = ceremony in which 14-year-olds pledge themselves to work for Socialism*); **der ~werk|hof, ⸚e** *EGer* reform school; **die ~zeit** youth, younger days

jugendlich youthful; **der/die Jugendliche** (*decl as adj*) young person; (**der**) youth

der **Jugoslawe, –n** (*wk masc*) Yugoslav

Jugoslawien [–ĭən] Yugoslavia

jugoslawisch Yugoslav

der **Juli** ['juːli, *to avoid confusion with* **Juni** *on telephone etc* ju'lae] (*gen* **–(s)**), **–s** July; **im ~** in July

der **Jumbo(-Jet)** ['jʊmbo(dʒɛt)], **–s** jumbo (jet)

jung (*comp, superl* ⸚; *see also* **jüngst**) young; (wine) new; *geog* young, *ling* recent; **~ und alt** young and old; **von ~ auf** from childhood; **jünger..** younger; youngish; recent; later; **jüngst..** youngest; latest; (most) recent; **das Jüngste Gericht** the Last Judgement; **der Jüngste Tag** Doomsday; **das Junge** (*decl as adj*) young animal; cub; nestling; (*pl*) young

Jung– young ...; junior ...; neo–; **der ~brunnen** fountain of youth; **der ~filmer, –** young film-maker; **die ~frau, –en** virgin; *astron*, *astrol* Virgo; **j~fräulich** virginal; maidenly; (snow, *phys* neutron, *etc*) virgin; **die ~fräulichkeit** virginity; **der ~geselle, –n** (*wk masc*) bachelor; **die ~gesellin, –nen** bachelor-girl; **die ~stein|zeit** the Neolithic; **j~stein|zeitlich** Neolithic; **j~verheiratet** newly-wed; **der ~vogel, ..vögel** fledgeling

der **Junge, –n** (*wk masc*) (*coll pl* **–ns, Jungs**) boy; **~, ~!** boy (oh boy)!; **schwerer ~** *coll* thug

jungen have young

jungenhaft boyish

der **Jünger, –** disciple

die **Jungfer, –n** spinster; old maid; *in compds* **~n–** maiden (flight, voyage, speech); **das ~n|häutchen, –** hymen

die **Jungfernschaft** virginity

der **Jüngling, –e** youth

jüngst (*see also* **jung**) recently

der **Juni** (*gen* **–(s)**), **–s** June; **im ~** in June

der **Junior, –(or)en** junior partner (*usu* son of the proprietor); *sp* junior; **der ~chef, –s** son of the proprietor

der **Junker, –** *hist* junker (*member of the Prussian*

landed aristocracy)

das **Junktim** [–ɪm], **–s** package (deal)

die **Junta** [x–, j–], **–(t)en** junta

Jupiter *myth* Jupiter; **der** ~ (*gen* **–s**) *astron* Jupiter; **die ~lampe, –n** klieg light

Jura (*no art*) law (= subject of study); **~ studieren** read for the Bar

der **Jura** (*gen* **–(s)**) the Jura (Mountains); (*gen* **–s**) *geol* the Jurassic

juridisch *Aust* = **juristisch**

die **Jurisprudenz** jurisprudence

der **Jurist, –en** (*wk masc*) lawyer; law student

juristisch legal; juridical

die **Jury** [ʒy'riː, 'ʒyːri], **–s** (contest) judges; (exhibition) selection committee

Jus (*no art*) *Aust* = **Jura**

der **Juso, –s** = **Jungsozialist**

just just; precisely

justieren *tech* adjust; *print* justify

der **Justitiar** [–ts–], **–e** legal adviser

die **Justiz** (administration of) justice; judiciary; **der ~irrtum, ⸚er** miscarriage of justice; **der ~minister, –** minister of justice; **das ~ministerium, –(i)en** ministry of justice; **der ~mord, –e** judicial murder

die **Jute** jute

Jütland Jutland

das **Juwel, –en** (*also* **der**) jewel, gem; (*pl*) jewellery; (*pl* **–e**; = prized person/thing) jewel, gem

der **Juwelier, –e** jeweller; **das ~geschäft, –e** jeweller's (shop); **die ~waren** *pl* jewellery

der **Jux, –e** *coll* lark; **sich** *dat* **einen ~ machen mit** play a joke on; **aus ~** for a lark

j. w. d., jwd [jɔtveː'deː] *joc* (= **janz weit draußen**) out in the wilds

K

das **K** [kaː] (*gen, pl* –, *coll* [kaːs]) K
das **Kabarett, –e/–s** (satirical) cabaret
der **Kabarettist, –en** (*wk masc*) artiste in a (satirical) cabaret
kabbeln: sich ~ *coll* squabble
das **Kabel, –** *tech* cable; *elect* cable; lead; **das ~fern|sehen** cable television
der **Kabeljau, –e/–s** cod
kabeln cable
die **Kabine, –n** cabin; booth; cubicle; (cable-) car; **der ~n|roller, –** bubble-car
das **Kabinett, –e** small room (*esp* for exhibitions); *pol* cabinet; **das ~stück, –e** master-stroke; **der ~wein, –e** cabinet wine
Kabinetts– *pol* cabinet ...
der **Kabis** [–ɪs] (*gen* –) *Swiss* cabbage
das **Kabrio** (*gen* –(s)), **–s** *coll* = **das Kabriolett, –s** *mot* convertible
die **Kachel, –n** (glazed) tile; **der ~ofen, ..öfen** tiled stove
kacheln tile
die **Kacke** *vulg*, **kacken** *vulg* shit
der **Kadaver, –** carcass; **der ~gehorsam** blind obedience
die **Kadenz, –en** cadence; cadenza
der **Kader, –** cadre; member of a cadre; *sp* squad; **die ~abteilung, –en** *EGer* personnel department; **der ~leiter, –** *EGer* personnel officer
der **Kadett, –en** (*wk masc*) cadet; **ihr ~en!** *coll* you rascals!
der **Kadi, –s** *coll* 'beak'; **vor den ~ bringen** take to court; **zum ~ laufen** go to court
der **Käfer, –** beetle; *coll* 'chick'
das **Kaff, –s/–e** *coll* 'dump'
der **Kaffee** ['kafe, *esp Aust* ka'feː], **–s** coffee; **das ist kalter ~** *coll* that's old hat || **das ~haus, ⸚er** *Aust* café; **die ~kanne, –n** coffee-pot; **der ~klatsch, –e** *coll* (women's) coffee party, coffee klatsch *US*; **die ~maschine, –n** coffee-maker; **die ~mühle, –n** coffee-grinder; **der ~satz** coffee-grounds
der **Kaffer**[1], **–** *coll* idiot
der **Kaffer**[2], **–n** (*wk masc*) Kaffir
der **Käfig, –e** cage
kafkaesk Kafkaesque
der **Kaftan** [–an], **–e** caftan
kahl bald; (room *etc*) bare; barren; **der K~fraß** defoliation by insects; **~fressen*** (*sep*) strip bare; **~geschoren** shorn; **der K~kopf, ⸚e** bald head; bald person; **~köpfig** bald-headed; **der K~schlag, ⸚e** clearing; deforestation; axing (**an** *dat* of); **~schlagen*** (*sep*) clear
der **Kahn, ⸚e** (small) boat; barge; *coll* bed; 'jug'; (*pl*) *coll* clodhoppers
der **Kai, –e/–s** quay
Kairo Cairo
der **Kaiser, –** emperor; *in compds* imperial ...; **das ~reich, –e** empire; **der ~schmarren, –** *Aust* (*type of pancake with raisins, torn into small pieces while frying*); **der ~schnitt, –e** Caesarean (section)
die **Kaiserin, –nen** empress
kaiserlich imperial
das **Kaisertum** empire
der **Kajak** [–ak], **–s** kayak
die **Kajüte, –n** cabin
der **Kakadu** ['ka–], **–s** cockatoo
der **Kakao** cocoa; **durch den ~ ziehen** *coll* make fun of
der **Kakerlak** [–ak], **–en** (*also wk masc*) cockroach
die **Kaktee** [–ə], **–n** = **der Kaktus, –(t)een**/*coll* **–se** cactus
die **Kalamität, –en** difficulty; predicament
der **Kalauer, –** corny pun/joke
das **Kalb, ⸚er** calf; *coll* silly goose; **das ~fleisch** veal
kalben calve
kalbern *coll* fool about
Kalbs– calf's ...; veal ...; ... of veal; **der ~braten, –** roast veal; **die ~hachse, –n** knuckle of veal; **das ~leder** calf(skin); **das ~schnitzel, –** veal escalope
das **Kaleidoskop, –e** kaleidoscope
der **Kalender, –** calendar; diary (for appointments *etc*); **das ~jahr, –e** calendar year
das **Kali** potash; **der ~salpeter** saltpetre; **das ~salz** potassium salt
das **Kaliber, –** calibre
kalibrieren calibrate
der **Kalif, –en** (*wk masc*) caliph
das **Kalifat, –e** caliphate
Kalifornien [–ĭən] California
der **Kalifornier** [–ĭɐ], **–, kalifornisch** Californian
das **Kalium** potassium
der **Kalk** lime; *physiol* calcium; **gebrannter ~** quicklime; **gelöschter ~** slaked lime || **k~haltig** limy; **der ~ofen, ..öfen** limekiln; **der ~stein** limestone
kalken whitewash; *agr* lime

^der^ **Kalkül, -e** (*also* **das**) calculation; *math* calculus
^die^ **Kalkulation, -en** calculation; estimate
kalkulieren calculate
Kalkutta Calcutta
^der^ **Kalligraph, -en** (*wk masc*) calligrapher
^die^ **Kalligraphie** calligraphy
^die^ **Kalorie, -(ie)n** calorie; **k~n|arm** low-calorie; **k~n|bewußt** calorie-conscious
kalt (*comp, superl* ¨) cold; **mir ist ~** I feel cold || **~bleiben*** (*sep*; *sn*) remain unmoved; **der K~blüter, -** cold-blooded animal; **~blütig** cold-blooded; cool-headed; **die K~front, -en** cold front; **~herzig** cold-hearted; **~lächelnd** *coll* as cool as you please; **~lassen*** (*sep*) leave cold; **~machen** (*sep*) *coll* bump off; **~schnäuzig** *coll* cool; (*adv*) coolly, as cool as you please; **der K~start, -s** cold start (**beim K.** when starting from cold); **~stellen** (*sep*) (*cf* **kalt stellen** *at* **stellen**) *coll* relegate to a position without influence
^die^ **Kälte** cold; coldness; **der ~schauer, -** cold shiver; **die ~welle, -n** cold spell
^der^ **Kalvarien|berg** [-ĭən-] Calvary
^der^ **Kalvinismus** Calvinism
^der^ **Kalvinist, -en** (*wk masc*), **kalvinistisch** Calvinist
^das^ **Kalzium** calcium
kam *p/t of* **kommen**
Kambodscha [-dʒ-] Cambodia
käme *p/t subj of* **kommen**
^die^ **Kamee** [-ə], **-n** cameo
^das^ **Kamel, -e** camel; *coll* silly ass; **das ~haar** camel-hair
^die^ **Kamelie** [-ĭə], **-n** camellia
Kamellen *pl coll*: **alte/olle ~** old stories
^die^ **Kamera** ['ka-], **-s** camera; **die ~führung** camera-work; **der ~mann, ¨er/..leute** cameraman
^der^ **Kamerad, -en** (*wk masc*) comrade; companion; mate
^die^ **Kameradschaft** comradeship; companionship
kameradschaftlich comradely
Kamerun Cameroon
^die^ **Kamille** camomile; **der ~n|tee, -s** camomile tea
^der^ **Kamin, -e** fireplace; *SGer, mount* chimney
^der^ **Kamm, ¨e** comb (*also* of cock); crest (of wave, horse); (mountain) ridge; *cul* neck; spare rib; **alle/alles über einen ~ scheren** lump everyone/everything together || **das ~garn, -e** worsted; **das ~stück, -e** *cul* neck; spare rib
kämmen comb; **sich ~** comb one's hair
^die^ **Kammer, -n** (small) room; chamber (*also parl, tech*); *anat* ventricle; **-kammer** (*in titles of professional organizations, eg* **die Anwalts~** Bar Association) || **der ~diener, -** valet; **die ~musik** chamber music; **der ~sänger, -, der ~schau|spieler, -** (*titles conferred on singers and actors of distinction*); **die ~spiele** *pl* intimate theatre; **der ~ton** concert pitch
Kämmerlein: im stillen ~ on one's own
^die^ **Kampagne** [-'panjə], **-n** campaign; drive
^der^ **Kämpe, -n** (*wk masc*) *poet* warrior
^der^ **Kampf, ¨e** fight (**um** for); struggle (for); battle (for); *mil* fighting, *pl* fighting; *sp* contest; **innere Kämpfe** inner conflicts; **~ auf Leben und Tod** life-and-death struggle; (+*dat*) **den ~ ansagen** declare war on; **„~ (dem Krebs** *etc*)!" 'fight (cancer *etc*)!'
Kampf- fighting ...; battle ...; combat ...;
die ~bahn, -en arena; **k~bereit** ready for action; **k~fähig** *mil* fit for action; *box* fit to fight; **der ~flieger, -** bomber/fighter pilot; **das ~flugzeug, -e** warplane; **der ~geist** fighting spirit; **das ~gericht, -e** *sp* judges; **die ~gruppe, -n** task-force; *EGer* unit of the workers' militia; **die ~handlungen** *pl mil* action (**an K. teilnehmen** see action); **k~los** without a fight; **k~lustig** eager to fight; **die ~maßnahmen** *pl* militant action; **das ~mittel, -** weapon; **der ~platz, ¨e** battleground; *sp* arena; **der ~richter, -** *sp* judge; referee; umpire; **der ~stoff, -e** warfare agent; **k~unfähig** *mil* unfit for active service; out of action; *box* unable to fight (**k. machen** put out of action); **der ~wagen, -** chariot
kämpfen fight; struggle; **~ gegen** fight (against); battle against; **~ mit** fight (with); battle with; fight back (tears); **~ um** fight for; struggle for
^der^ **Kampfer** camphor
^der^ **Kämpfer, -** fighter; **alter ~** old campaigner || **die ~natur, -en** fighter (by nature)
kämpferisch fighting
kampieren camp; camp out; *coll* kip down
Kanada ['ka-] Canada
^der^ **Kanadier** [-ĭɐ], **-, kanadisch** Canadian
^die^ **Kanaille** [-'naljə], **-n** *coll* scoundrel; rabble
^der^ **Kanake, -n** (*wk masc*) South Sea Islander, Kanaka; *coll* wog
^der^ **Kanal, ¨e** channel (*also comput, TV*); canal (*also anat*); drain; sewer; **der ~** the Channel; **den ~ voll haben** *coll* be 'canned'; have had a bellyful || **die ~inseln** *pl* the Channel Islands
^die^ **Kanalisation, -en** sewerage (system); canalization
kanalisieren canalize; provide with sewerage; channel (energy *etc*)
^der^ **Kanari, -** *SGer coll* canary
kanarien- [-ĭən-]: **~gelb, der K~vogel, ..vögel** canary
Kanarisch: die ~en Inseln *pl* the Canary Islands

Kandare: an die ~ nehmen take in hand
der **Kandelaber, –** candelabra
der **Kandidat, –en** (*wk masc*) candidate; *EGer* candidate member (of Communist Party)
die **Kandidatur, –en** candidature, candidacy
kandidieren stand, run *US* (**für** for)
kandieren candy
der **Kandis** [–ɪs] = **der ~zucker** sugar-candy
die **Kanditen** *pl Aust* candied fruit; sweets, candies *US*
das **Känguruh, –s** kangaroo
das **Kanin** coney
das **Kaninchen, –** rabbit; **der ~stall, ⸚e** rabbit-hutch
der **Kanister, –** can
kann *1st/3rd sing pres of* **können**
die **Kanne, –n** jug; pot; can
kannelieren *archit* flute
der **Kannibale, –n** (*wk masc*) cannibal
kannibalisch cannibal; bestial
der **Kannibalismus** cannibalism
kannst *2nd sing pres of* **können**
kannte *p/t of* **kennen**
der **Kanon** [–ɔn], **–s** canon (*also mus*)
die **Kanonade, –n** cannonade; tirade
die **Kanone, –n** gun; *hist* cannon; *coll* ace; **unter aller ~** *coll* incredibly bad || **das ~n|boot, –e** gunboat; **das ~n|futter** *coll* cannon-fodder; **die ~n|kugel, –n** cannon-ball
der **Kanonier, –e** gunner
kanonisch canonical; (law) canon
Kanossa|gang: einen ~ antreten eat humble pie
Kant–: ~haken *coll* (**beim K. nehmen** give (s.o.) a good talking-to)
die **Kantate, –n** cantata
die **Kante, –n** edge; **auf die hohe ~ legen** *coll* put by for a rainy day
kanten tilt; *ski* edge
der **Kanten, –** *NGer* crust
der **Kanter|sieg, –e** *sp* easy victory, walkover
kantig angular; squared; **–kantig** -sided
die **Kantine, –n** canteen
der **Kanton, –e** canton
kantonal cantonal
der **Kantonist, –en** (*wk masc*) *coll*: **unsicherer ~** unreliable fellow
der **Kantönli|geist** *Swiss* parochialism
Kantons– *Swiss* cantonal …
der **Kantor, –(or)en** choirmaster and organist
das **Kanu** ['ka:nu, ka'nu:], **–s, ~ fahren** canoe
die **Kanüle, –n** cannula
der **Kanute, –n** (*wk masc*) canoeist
die **Kanzel, –n** *eccles* pulpit; *aer* cockpit; *hunt* raised hide/blind *US*
die **Kanzlei, –en** *SGer* office; *hist* chancellery; **der ~stil** officialese
der **Kanzler, –** chancellor
das **Kaolin, –e** kaolin
das **Kap** [–a–], **–s** *geog* cape; **das ~ der Guten Hoffnung** the Cape of Good Hope; **~ Hoorn** Cape Horn || **~stadt** Cape Town
der **Kapaun, –e** capon
die **Kapazität, –en** capacity; (= person) authority
Kapee *coll*: **schwer von ~** slow on the uptake
Kapell–: der ~meister, – conductor; band leader
die **Kapelle, –n** chapel; *mus* band
die **Kaper, –n** *bot*, *cul* caper
Kaper–: das ~schiff, –e privateer
kapern *naut* seize (ship); **sich** *dat* **… ~** *coll* nab
kapieren *coll* understand; **kapiert?** got it?
Kapillar– capillary …; **das ~gefäß, –e** capillary
kapital major
das **Kapital, –e/–ien** [–ĭən] capital; (of quality *etc*) asset; **~ schlagen aus** capitalize on || **die ~flucht** flight of capital; **k~intensiv** capital-intensive; **der ~verkehr** movement of capital; **das ~verbrechen, –** serious crime
das **Kapitälchen, –** small capital
der **Kapitalismus** capitalism
der **Kapitalist, –en** (*wk masc*), **kapitalistisch** capitalist
der **Kapitän, –e** *naut*, *aer*, *sp* captain; **~ zur See** (naval) captain; **der ~leutnant, –s** *naut* lieutenant
das **Kapitel, –** chapter
das **Kapitell, –e** *archit* capital
das **Kapitol** (*gen* **–s**) the Capitol
die **Kapitulation, –en** capitulation, surrender
kapitulieren capitulate (**vor** *dat* in the face of)
der **Kaplan, ⸚e** *RC* curate; chaplain
die **Kappe, –n** cap; toe-cap; cap, top (of bottle *etc*); **auf seine (eigene) ~ nehmen** *coll* take responsibility for
kappen caponize (cockerel); pollard (tree), cut back (branches); prune, cut back (expenditure *etc*); *naut* cut
der **Kappes** (*gen* **–**) *NGer coll* rubbish
das **Käppi, –s** *coll* small cap; képi
die **Kaprice** [–sə], **–n** caprice
die **Kapriole, –n** capriole; caper
kaprizieren: sich ~ auf (*acc*) be dead set on
kapriziös capricious
die **Kapsel, –n** capsule (*also bot*, *space*); case
kaputt *coll* bust, kaput; smashed up; on the blink; on the rocks; dead beat; **~fahren*** (*sep*) *coll* drive into the ground; wreck (car); **~gehen*** (*sep*; *sn*) *coll* break; break down; fall to bits; go on the blink; go bust; be ruined (**an** *dat* by); **~lachen** (*sep*): **sich k.** *coll* laugh oneself silly; **~machen** (*sep*) *coll* break; smash; ruin (**sich k.** wear oneself out); **~schlagen*** (*sep*) *coll* smash
die **Kapuze, –n** hood; *eccles* cowl
der **Kapuziner, –** Capuchin; **die ~kresse** nas-

turtium

Kar–: der ~freitag, –e Good Friday; **die ~woche, –n** Holy Week

der **Karabiner, –** carbine

Karacho *coll*: **mit ~** at full tilt

die **Karaffe, –n** carafe; decanter

die **Karambolage** [–ʒə], **–n** *bill* cannon, carom *US*; *mot coll* smash; pile-up

karambolieren *bill* cannon, carom *US*

der **Karamel** caramel

die **Karamelle, –n** caramel (toffee)

das **Karat, –e/**(*following num*) **–** carat

das **Karate** (*gen* **–(s)**) karate

–karätig –carat

Karatschi Karachi

die **Karawane, –n** caravan (in desert)

das **Karbid, –e** carbide

Karbol– carbolic ...

die **Karbonade, –n** *esp Aust* chop, cutlet

der **Karbunkel, –** carbuncle

der **Kardinal, ⸚e** cardinal; *in compds* cardinal ...; **die ~zahl, –en** cardinal number

das **Kardiogramm, –e** cardiogram

die **Karenz, –en = die ~zeit, –en** waiting period

der **Karfiol** *esp Aust* cauliflower

der **Karfunkel, –** carbuncle (stone); *coll* carbuncle; **der ~stein, –e** carbuncle (stone)

karg meagre; scant; **~ sein mit** be sparing of

kargen: (nicht) ~ mit be (un)sparing of

kärglich meagre

die **Karibik** [–ɪk] the Caribbean

karibisch Caribbean

kariert check(ed); (paper) squared; **red nicht so ~!** don't talk such nonsense

die **Karies** [–ɛs] caries

die **Karikatur, –en** cartoon; caricature

der **Karikaturist, –en** (*wk masc*) cartoonist; caricaturist

karikieren caricature

kariös carious

karitativ charitable; (*adv*: work) for charity

Karl Charles; **~ der Große** Charlemagne

der **Karmeliter, –** Carmelite

Karmeliter– Carmelite ...

karmesin(rot) crimson

der **Karneval** [–nəval], **–s/–e** (Shrovetide) carnival

karnevalistisch carnival

das **Karnickel, –** *coll* rabbit; scapegoat

Kärnten Carinthia (*Austrian province*)

der **Kärntner, –, kärntnerisch** Carinthian

das **Karo, –s** square; (pattern) check; *cards* diamonds, (card: *pl* –) diamond; *in compds* check ...; *cards* ... of diamonds; **das ~hemd, –en** check shirt

der **Karolinger, –, karolingisch** Carolingian

die **Karosse, –n** state-coach

die **Karosserie, –(ie)n** body(work)

die **Karotte, –n** carrot

die **Karpaten** *pl* the Carpathians

der **Karpfen, –** carp

die **Karre, –n** cart; barrow; *coll* old crate; **die ~ aus dem Dreck ziehen** *coll* set things to rights

das **Karree, –s** square; *Aust cul* loin

karren cart

der **Karren, –** cart; barrow; *coll* old crate; **den ~ aus dem Dreck ziehen** *coll* set things to rights; **vor seinen ~ spannen** make use of (for one's own purposes)

die **Karriere** [–'rĭeːrə, –ɛː–], **–n** career; *equest* full gallop; **~ machen** get ahead || **die ~frau, –en** career woman; **der ~macher, –** careerist

kart. = kartoniert

der **Kartäuser, –** Carthusian

Kartäuser– Carthusian ...

die **Karte, –n** card (*also cards*); ticket; map; menu; **nach der ~ essen** eat à la carte; **seine ~n aufdecken** put one's cards on the table; (+*dat*) **die ~n legen** tell (s.o.'s) fortune from the cards; **~n spielen** play cards; **alles auf 'eine ~ setzen** put all one's eggs in one basket; **auf die falsche ~ setzen** back the wrong horse

die **Kartei, –en** card index, card file; **die ~karte, –n** index-card; **der ~schrank, ⸚e** filing-cabinet

das **Kartell, –e** cartel

Karten– map ...; card ...; **der ~brief, –e** letter-card; **das ~haus, ⸚er** house of cards; **das ~kunst|stück, –e** card-trick; **die ~legerin, –nen** fortune-teller; **das ~spiel, –e** card-game; card-playing; pack of cards; **der ~verkauf** sale of tickets; ticket office; **der ~vorverkauf** advance booking (office)

Karthago Carthage

die **Kartoffel, –n** potato; *coll* conk, schnozzle *US*; hole (in sock *etc*); **der ~brei, –e** mashed potatoes; **der ~käfer, –** Colorado beetle; **das ~mus** mashed potatoes; **der ~puffer, –** potato fritter; **das ~püree, –s** mashed potatoes; **der ~salat, –e** potato salad; **der ~schäler, –** potato-peeler

der **Kartograph, –en** (*wk masc*) cartographer

die **Kartographie** cartography

der **Karton** [–'tɔŋ], **–s** cardboard; cardboard box; *art* cartoon (for tapestry *etc*)

kartoniert (bound) in paper boards

die **Kartothek, –en** card index

die **Kartusche, –n** cartridge; *archit etc* cartouche

das **Karussell, –s/–e** roundabout, merry-go-round

der **Karzer, –** *hist* (students') lock-up; detention

karzinogen carcinogenic

das **Karzinom, –e** carcinoma

die **Kaschemme, –n** low dive

kaschieren conceal; *tech* laminate

Kaschmir Kashmir

der **Kaschmir, –e** cashmere

^der^ **Käse** cheese; *coll* nonsense; **das ~blatt, ⸚er** *coll* local rag; **die ~glocke, –n** cheese-cover; **der ~kuchen, –** cheesecake; **die ~stange, –n** cheese-straw

^die^ **Kasematte, –n** casemate

^die^ **Kaserne, –n** barracks; **der ~n|hof, ⸚e** barrack square

kasernieren quarter in barracks

käsig cheesy; *coll* pale

^das^ **Kasino, –s** casino; *mil* officers' mess

^die^ **Kaskade, –n** cascade

^die^ **Kasko|versicherung, –en** comprehensive insurance

^das^ **Kasperle|theater, –** Punch and Judy show

Kaspisch: das ~e Meer the Caspian Sea

^die^ **Kassa, –(ss)en** *Aust* = **Kasse**

^der^ **Kassandra|ruf, –e** prophecy of doom

^die^ **Kasse, –n** cash-box; till, cash-register; cash-desk; check-out; ticket-office, *cin*, *theat* box-office; cashier's office; cash, funds; (= **Kranken~**) health insurance scheme; (= **Spar~**) savings bank; **~ machen** balance the cash; **getrennte ~ machen** go Dutch; **gegen/per ~** for cash; **gut bei ~** *coll* 'flush'; **knapp bei ~** *coll* short of cash; **zur ~ bitten** *coll* ask to pay up

^das^ **Kasseler** cured pork loin

Kassen–: der ~arzt, ⸚e doctor (treating *Krankenkasse* patients); **der ~bestand, ⸚e** cash balance; **der ~schlager, –** big seller; *cin*, *theat* box-office hit; **der ~schrank, ⸚e** safe; **der ~sturz, ⸚e** *coll* cashing-up (**K. machen** cash up; check one's money); **der ~wart, –e** treasurer; **der ~zettel, –** sales slip

^die^ **Kasserolle, –n** stew-pan

^die^ **Kassette, –n** case; box; cassette; **der ~n|-recorder, –** cassette recorder

^der^ **Kassier, –e** *SGer* = **Kassierer**

kassieren[1] collect (payment); *coll* pocket; take away; pick up; win (praise *etc*); receive; **darf ich ~, bitte?** would you like to pay now?

kassieren[2] *leg* quash

^der^ **Kassierer, –** cashier; treasurer

^das^ **Kaßler** = **Kasseler**

^die^ **Kastagnetten** [–anj–] *pl* castanets

^die^ **Kastanie** [–ĭə], **–n** chestnut; = **der ~n|baum, ⸚e** chestnut tree; **kastanien|braun** chestnut

^die^ **Kaste, –n** caste

kasteien (*p/part* **kasteit**): **sich ~** mortify the flesh

^das^ **Kastell, –e** Roman fort; (*esp in S. Europe*) castle

^der^ **Kasten,** *pl* **Kästen** box (*also gym*); case; crate; *SGer* cupboard; *coll* 'crate'; 'tub'; barn (of a place); *coll sp* goal; *coll mil* cooler; **was auf dem ~ haben** *coll* be brainy

Kastilien [–ĭən] Castile

^der^ **Kastilier** [–ĭɐ], **–** Castilian

kastilisch, (*language*) **K~** Castilian

^der^ **Kastrat, –en** (*wk masc*) eunuch; *mus* castrato

^die^ **Kastration, –en** castration

kastrieren castrate

^der^ **Kasus, –** [–uːs] *gramm* case

^die^ **Katakombe, –n** catacomb

^der^ **Katalane, –n** (*wk masc*) Catalan

katalanisch, (*language*) **K~** Catalan

^der^ **Katalog, –e, katalogisieren** catalogue

Katalonien [–ĭən] Catalonia

^der^ **Katalysator, –(or)en** catalyst; *mot* catalytic convertor

^die^ **Katalyse, –n** catalysis

katalytisch catalytic

^der^ **Katamaran, –e** catamaran

^das^ **Katapult, –e** (*also* **der**) catapult

katapultieren catapult; **sich ~** *aer* eject

^der^ **Katarakt, –e** cataract

^der^ **Katarrh** [–'tar], **–e** catarrh

^der^ **Kataster, –** (*also* **das**) land-register

katastrophal catastrophic; disastrous

^die^ **Katastrophe, –n** catastrophe; disaster; **das ~n|gebiet, –e** disaster area

^die^ **Kate, –n** *NGer* (farm-labourer's) cottage

^der^ **Katechismus** [–ç–], **–(m)en** catechism

^die^ **Kategorie, –(ie)n** category

kategorisch categorical

kategorisieren categorize

^der^ **Kater, –** tomcat; *coll* hangover; **der Gestiefelte ~** Puss in Boots

Katharina Catherine

^das^ **Katheder, –** (*also* **der**) teacher's desk; *univ* lectern

^die^ **Kathedrale, –n** cathedral (*esp* in England, France, Spain)

^der^ **Katheter, –** catheter

^die^ **Kathode, –n** cathode

^der^ **Katholik, –en** (*wk masc*), **katholisch** Catholic

^der^ **Katholizismus** Catholicism

^der^ **Kattun, –e** calico

Katz *coll*: **~ und Maus spielen mit** play cat and mouse with; **für die ~ sein** be a waste of time || **k~balgen** (*insep*): **sich k.** *coll* scuffle playfully; **k~buckeln** (*insep*) *coll* bow and scrape (**vor** *dat* to)

^das^ **Kätzchen, –** kitten; *bot* catkin

^die^ **Katze, –n** cat; **die ~ aus dem Sack lassen** let the cat out of the bag; **die ~ im Sack kaufen** buy a pig in a poke; **wie die ~ um den heißen Brei gehen** beat about the bush

Katzen– cat …; cat's …; **das ~auge, –n** cat's eye; *cycl* reflector; **k~freundlich** over-friendly; **der ~jammer, –** *coll* hangover; the blues; **die ~musik** caterwauling; **der ~sprung** *coll* stone's throw; **der ~tisch, –e** *joc* children's table; **die ~wäsche** *coll* 'cat's lick'

katzenhaft cat-like, feline

Kau– chewing …; **der ~gummi, –s** (*also* **das**) chewing-gum das **Kauder|welsch** (*gen* –(s)) gibberish; (linguistic) hotchpotch

kauen chew; bite (fingernails); (*v/i*) chew; **~ an** (*dat*) chew (on); bite (fingernails)

kauern crouch; **sich ~** crouch down

der **Kauf, ⸚e** buying, purchase; buy; **in ~ nehmen** accept || **das ~haus, ⸚er** department store; **die ~kraft** purchasing power; **k~kräftig** with money to spend; **k~lustig** keen to buy; **der ~mann, ..leute** businessman; trader; merchant; **k~männisch** commercial (**k~männischer Angestellter** clerk); **der ~preis, –e** purchase price; **der ~vertrag, ⸚e** bill of sale; **der ~wert, –e** market value; **der ~zwang** obligation to buy (**kein/ohne K.** no/without obligation)

kaufen buy; (*v/i*) shop (**bei** at); **sich** *dat* **... ~** *coll* give (s.o.) a piece of one's mind; **dafür kann ich mir nichts ~** it's no use to me

der **Käufer, –** buyer; shopper

käuflich for sale; venal; (*adv*: acquire) by purchase; **~es Mädchen** prostitute

der **Kaukasier** [–ĭɐ], **–, kaukasisch** Caucasian

der **Kaukasus** the Caucasus

die **Kaul|quappe, –n** tadpole

kaum hardly, scarcely; **~ daß ...** hardly ... when ..., no sooner ... than ...; **~ noch** hardly ... any more/left; **(wohl) ~** hardly; I doubt it

kausal causal

die **Kausalität, –en** causality

die **Kautel, –en** proviso

die **Kaution, –en** security; deposit (on rented accommodation); *leg* bail; **~ stellen** stand bail; **gegen ~** on bail

der **Kautschuk** [–ʊk], **–e** (india)rubber

der **Kauz, ⸚e** (*popular name for various small owls, eg* tawny owl); **komischer ~** *coll* queer bird

kauzig quaint

der **Kavalier, –e** gentleman; beau; **das ~s|delikt, –e** trivial offence

die **Kavalkade, –n** cavalcade

die **Kavallerie, –(ie)n** cavalry

der **Kavallerist, –en** (*wk masc*) cavalryman

der **Kaviar, –e** caviar

keck saucy; pert

der **Keeper** ['ki:pɐ], **–** *Aust footb* goalkeeper

der **Kegel, –** skittle; *geol, math* cone; *in compds mech* conical ...; taper(ed) ...; bevel ...; **die ~bahn, –en** skittle/bowling-alley; **der ~bruder, ..brüder** *coll* (fellow) skittle-player; (fellow) bowler; **k~förmig** conical; **das ~spiel, –e** skittles; tenpin bowling; game of skittles/tenpin bowling

kegeln play skittles; (tenpin bowling) bowl

der **Kegler** [–e:–], **–** skittle-player; bowler

Kehl–: der ~kopf, ⸚e larynx; **die ~kopf|entzündung, –en** laryngitis; **der ~kopf|krebs** cancer of the throat; **der ~laut, –e** guttural

die **Kehle, –n** throat; **aus voller ~** at the top of one's voice; **ich habe ... in die falsche ~ bekommen** (food) went down the wrong way; I took (remark) the wrong way

kehlig throaty; guttural

die **Kehlung, –en** groove

Kehr–: die ~maschine, –n carpet/street-sweeper; **der ~reim, –e** refrain; **die ~seite, –n** reverse; drawback; other side; *coll* back; backside (**die K. der Medaille** the other side of the coin)

die **Kehre, –n** sharp (*esp* hairpin) bend; *gym* swing with half turn

kehren[1] turn; (+*dat*) **den Rücken ~** turn one's back on; **kehrt!** about turn!; **in sich gekehrt** withdrawn; **sich nicht ~ an** (*dat*) take no notice of

kehren[2] *SGer* sweep

der **Kehricht** (*also* **das**) sweepings; *Swiss* refuse, garbage *US*; **der ~abfuhr|wagen, –** *Swiss* dust-cart, garbage truck *US*; **die ~schaufel, –n** dustpan

kehrt–: ~machen (*sep*) turn on one's heel; do an about-turn; **die K~wendung, –en** about-turn; *mil* about-face, about-turn

keifen scold

der **Keil, –e** wedge; *dressm* gusset; *mil* V-formation; **der ~riemen, –** fan-belt; **die ~schrift** cuneiform

Keile *coll*: **~ bekommen** get a thrashing

der **Keiler, –** wild boar

die **Keilerei, –en** *coll* brawl

der **Keim, –e** germ; embryo; young shoot; seeds (of); **im ~ ersticken** nip in the bud || **die ~drüse, –n** gonad; **k~frei** sterile; **k~tötend** antiseptic; **die ~zelle, –n** germ-cell

der **Keimling, –e** embryo; young shoot

keimen germinate; sprout; (hope *etc*) arise

kein not a/any; no; (*pl*) less than (*eg* **~e fünf Tage** less than five days); **~er** nobody; **~er/~e/~(e)s** not one; not any, none; **~er/~e/~(e)s von beiden** neither (of them); **~e(r) von euch/uns beiden** neither of you/us || **~mal** not once

keinerlei (*indecl*) no ... at all

keines–: ~falls under no circumstances; **~wegs** not at all

–keit, –igkeit –ness, –ity, *etc, eg* **die Einsamkeit** loneliness (**einsam** = lonely), **die Ewigkeit** eternity (**ewig** = eternal), **die Hoffnungslosigkeit** hopelessness (**hoffnungslos** = hopeless), **die Genauigkeit** accuracy, precision (**genau** = accurate, precise); *some nouns also function as countables* (*pl* **–en**), *eg* **die Unzulänglichkeit** inadequacy

---

der **Keks** [–e:–], **–e** biscuit, cookie *US*; **die ~dose,**

-n biscuit tin, cookie jar *US*

[der] **Kelch, -e** goblet; cup (of sorrow *etc*); *eccles* chalice; *bot* calyx

[die] **Kelle, -n** ladle; trowel; *rail* baton (with disc) used to give the signal for departure

[der] **Keller, -** cellar; basement; **die ~assel, -n** wood-louse; **das ~geschoß, -(ss)e** basement; **die ~wohnung, -en** basement flat/apartment *US*

[die] **Kellerei, -en** wine-cellars

[der] **Kellner, -** waiter

[die] **Kellnerin, -nen** waitress

kellnern *coll* work as a waiter

[der] **Kelte, -n** (*wk masc*) Celt

[die] **Kelter, -n** press, *esp* wine-press

keltern press (*esp* grapes)

keltisch Celtic

Kenia Kenya

[der] **Kenianer, -, kenianisch** Kenyan

Kenn-: der ~satz, ⸚e *comput* label; **das ~wort, ⸚er** code-word; password; *comm* reference; **die ~zahl, -en** code number; *tel* code; *math* characteristic; **das ~zeichen, -** characteristic; hallmark; mark, sign; *mot* registration number, license number *US*; *comput* flag; **k~zeichnen** (*insep*) mark; characterize; **k~zeichnend** characteristic (**für** of); **die ~ziffer, -n** code/reference number; *math* characteristic

kennen (*p/t* **kannte** (*subj rare* **kennte**), *p/part* **gekannt**) know (= be acquainted with); **~ an** (*dat*) recognize by; **..., da kenne ich nichts** *coll* ... and nothing can stop me

sich ~ know oneself/(*recip*) one another; **wir ~ uns schon** we've met; **sich nicht mehr ~ vor** (*dat*) be beside oneself with

kennen|lernen (*sep*) get/come to know; meet

[der] **Kenner, -** connoisseur; expert; **der ~blick, -e** expert eye

kennerhaft = kennerisch like a connoisseur

kenntlich recognizable (**an** *dat* by); **~ machen** identify

[die] **Kenntnis, -se** knowledge; (*pl*) knowledge (**in** *dat* of: subject; *also* **-kenntnisse,** *eg* **Deutschkenntnisse** knowledge of German); **fremdsprachliche ~se** a knowledge of foreign languages; **in ~ setzen von** apprise of; **zur ~ nehmen** take note of || **~nahme** (**zur K.** for information; **zur freundlichen K.** with compliments); **k~reich** knowledgeable

kentern (*sn*) capsize

[die] **Keramik** [-ɪk], **-en** ceramics; pottery; piece of pottery

keramisch ceramic

Kerb-: ~holz *coll* (**viel auf dem K. haben** have a lot to answer for); **das ~tier, -e** insect

[die] **Kerbe, -n** notch; **in die gleiche ~ hauen** *coll* take the same line

[der] **Kerbel** chervil

kerben notch

[der] **Kerker, -** dungeon; *Aust hist* imprisonment

[der] **Kerl, -e** *coll* fellow, guy; character; **ein ganzer ~** a real man; (*either sex*) **guter ~** good sort, **lieber ~** dear

[der] **Kern, -e** stone; kernel; pip; nucleus (*also astron, biol, phys*); centre (of town); core, heart (of problem *etc*); essence

Kern- central ...; core ...; *phys* nuclear ...; **der ~beißer, -** hawfinch; **die ~energie** nuclear energy; **die ~frage, -n** central issue/question; **das ~gehäuse, -** core (of fruit); **kern|gesund** in perfect health; **das ~kraft|werk, -e** nuclear power station; **k~los** seedless; **das ~obst** pomes; **die ~physik** nuclear physics; **der ~reaktor, -en** nuclear reactor; **die ~seife** washing-soap; **die ~spaltung** nuclear fission; **das ~stück, -e** main item; centrepiece; central element, core; **die ~truppe, -n** crack troops; **die ~waffen** *pl* nuclear weapons; **der ~waffen|versuch, -e** nuclear test

kernig robust; pithy

[das] **Kerosin** kerosene

[die] **Kerze, -n** candle; *mot* plug; *footb* skyer; **kerzen|gerade** dead straight; (*adv*) bolt upright; **der ~n|halter, -** candlestick; **das ~n|licht** candlelight (**bei K.** by candlelight); **der ~n|schein** candlelight

keß (-ss-) *coll* saucy

[der] **Kessel, -** kettle; boiler; cauldron; *geog* basin; *mil* pocket; **die ~pauke, -n** kettle-drum; **der ~stein** scale; **das ~treiben, -** witch-hunt; *hunt* circular beat

[die] **Kette, -n** chain (*also* of shops, hotels, *etc*); necklace; line; series; *mot* track; *text* warp; *aer* flight; **an die ~ legen** chain up

ketten: ~ an (*acc*) chain to

Ketten- chain ...; **das ~fahrzeug, -e** tracked vehicle; **das ~gebirge, -** mountain range; **das ~glied, -er** link (in chain); **das ~hemd, -en** coat of chain mail; **der ~hund, -e** watchdog; **der ~laden, ..läden** chain store; **das ~rad, ⸚er** sprocket; **der ~raucher, -** chain-smoker; **die ~reaktion, -en** chain reaction; **die ~säge, -n** chain-saw

[der] **Ketzer, -** heretic

[die] **Ketzerei, -en** heresy

ketzerisch heretical

Keuch-: der ~husten, - whooping-cough

keuchen pant

[die] **Keule, -n** club; *cul* leg

keusch chaste

[die] **Keuschheit** chastity

kfm. = kaufmännisch

[das] **Kfz** [ka:ʔɛf'tsɛt], **-(s)** (= **Kraftfahrzeug**) motor vehicle

kg = Kilogramm

[die] **KG, -(s) = Kommanditgesellschaft,** *EGer*

Konsumgenossenschaft

der **KGB** the K.G.B.

kgl. = königlich

das **Khaki** [k–] khaki (= colour)

der **Khaki** [k–] khaki (= material)

Khartum [k–] Khartoum

der **Kibbuz, –e/Kibbuzim** kibbutz

kichern giggle; titter

kicken *coll* kick; (*v/i*) play football; **~ für** (footballer) play for

der **Kicker, –** *coll* footballer

kidnappen ['kɪtnɛpn̩] kidnap

der **Kidnapper** ['kɪtnɛpɐ], – kidnapper

das **Kidnapping** ['kɪtnɛpɪŋ], **–s** kidnap(ping)

der **Kiebitz, –e** lapwing

der **Kiefer, –** jaw

die **Kiefer, –n** pine; **das ~n|holz** pine(wood)

Kieker *coll*: **auf dem ~ haben** have it in for

der **Kiel[1], –e** quill

der **Kiel[2], –e** keel; **die ~linie** line ahead; **k~oben** bottom up; **das ~wasser** wake (**in jmds. K. segeln** follow in s.o.'s wake)

die **Kieme, –n** gill

Kien *coll esp Berlin*: **auf dem ~** on the ball

der **Kies** gravel; *miner* (*esp* **–kies,** *eg* **der Eisen~** iron) pyrites; *coll* 'dough'

der **Kiesel, –** pebble; **die ~säure** silicic acid; **der ~stein, –e** pebble

Kiew ['kiːɛf] Kiev

kikeriki! cock-a-doodle-doo!

der **Kilimandscharo** [–dʒ–] (*gen* **–(s)**) Mount Kilimanjaro

killekille! (*baby-talk*) tickle, tickle!

killen *coll* bump off

der **Killer, –** *coll* killer; hit-man

das **Kilo, –(s)** kilo

das **Kilogramm, –e/**(*following num*) **–** kilogram

das **Kilohertz, –** kilohertz

der **Kilometer, –** kilometre; **der ~stand** mileage; **der ~zähler, –** mileometer, odometer *US*

das **Kilowatt, –** kilowatt

die **Kimme, –n** backsight

das **Kind, –er** child; baby; **ein ~ bekommen** have a baby; **das ~ beim rechten Namen nennen** call a spade a spade; **sich lieb ~ machen bei** *coll* worm one's way into (s.o.'s) favour; **mit ~ und Kegel** with the whole family; **von ~ auf** from childhood; **~er!** *also* folks!; = **~er, ~er!** good heavens!

Kinder– … of/for children; child …; child's …; children's …;

die ~arbeit child labour; **der ~arzt, ⸚e** paediatrician; **das ~bett, –en** child's bed; cot, crib *US*; **der ~garten, ..gärten** nursery school, kindergarten; **die ~gärtnerin, –nen** nursery-school teacher; **das ~geld** child allowance; **die ~heil|kunde** paediatrics; **der ~hort, –e** day nursery; **die ~krankheit, –en** children's illness; teething troubles; **der ~laden, ..läden** (anti-authoritarian) play-group; **die ~lähmung** poliomyelitis; **kinder|leicht** child's play; **k~lieb** fond of children; **k~los** childless; **das ~mädchen, –** nursemaid; **k~reich** (family) large; **der ~schreck** *coll* bogey-man; **der ~schuh, –e** child's shoe (**noch in den ~schuhen stecken** be still in its infancy); **das ~spiel, –e** children's game (**ein K. sein** be child's play); **die ~stube** upbringing; **der ~wagen, –** pram, baby carriage *US*

die **Kinderei, –en** childish behaviour

Kindes– … of a child; **das ~alter** childhood; **~beinen** (**von K. an** from early childhood); **die ~mißhandlung, –en** child abuse

kindhaft childlike

die **Kindheit** childhood

kindisch childish

kindlich childlike; child's, of a child; (*adv*) like a child

der **Kinds|kopf, ⸚e** *coll* big kid

die **Kinetik** [–ɪk] kinetics

kinetisch kinetic

die **Kinkerlitzchen** *pl coll* knicknacks; **mach keine ~!** none of your tricks!

das **Kinn, –e** chin; **der ~haken, –** hook to the chin; **die ~lade, –n** jawbone

das **Kino, –s** cinema, movie theater *US*; **ins ~ gehen** go to the cinema/movies *US* || **der ~besucher, –** cinemagoer

der **Kintopp** [–iː–], **–s/⸚e** (*also* **das**) *coll* 'pictures', 'flicks' (*refers esp to cinema viewed purely as entertainment*)

der **Kiosk, –e** kiosk

das **Kipferl, –n** *Aust* croissant

Kipp– tipping …; tilting …

die **Kippe[1], –n** tip; *gym* upstart; **auf der ~ stehen** be precariously balanced; hang in the balance

die **Kippe[2], –n** *coll* fag-end, butt *US*

kippelig *coll* wobbly

kippeln *coll* wobble

kippen tip; tilt; (*v/i sn*) tip over; overturn; **einen ~** *coll* have a drink

der **Kipper, –** dump truck

Kirch–: der ~gang going to church; **der ~gänger, –** churchgoer; **der ~hof, ⸚e** churchyard; **das ~spiel, –e** parish; **der ~tag, –e** *Aust* fair; **der ~turm, ⸚e** steeple; **die ~turm|politik** parish-pump politics; **die ~weih, –en** fair

die **Kirche, –n** church; **die ~ im Dorf lassen** *coll* not get carried away

Kirchen– church …; ecclesiastical …; **der ~diener, –** sexton; **das ~lied, –er** hymn

kirchlich church; ecclesiastical; by the church; (*adv*) in church

die **Kirmes** [–ɛs, –əs], **–sen** fair

kirre *coll*, **~ machen** tame

der **Kirsch, –** kirsch; *in compds* cherry …; **das ~wasser, –** kirsch

die **Kirsche, -n** cherry; **mit ... ist nicht gut ~n essen** *coll* ... is not an easy person to get on with

das **Kissen, -** cushion; pillow; sachet; **der ~bezug, ⸚e** pillowcase; cushion-cover; **die ~schlacht, -en** pillow-fight

die **Kiste, -n** box; crate (*also coll* = car, plane); packing-case; *coll* business

der **Kitsch** kitsch

kitschig kitschy

der **Kitt, -e** putty; (adhesive) cement

das **Kittchen, -** *coll* 'clink'

der **Kittel, -** (white) coat; overall; smock; *Aust* skirt

kitten putty; cement; patch up (friendship *etc*)

das **Kitz, -e** kid; fawn

der **Kitzel** tickle; titillation; itch (to do sth.)

kitz(e)lig ticklish

kitzeln tickle; **es kitzelt mich zu ...** I'm itching to ...

der **Kitzler, -** clitoris

klacks! splosh!

der **Klacks, -e** *coll* dollop

die **Kladde, -n** rough book

kladderadatsch! crash-bang-wallop!

der **Kladderadatsch, -e** *coll* fiasco; scandal

klaffen gape; **~d** gaping; (contradiction) blatant

kläffen yelp

klagbar actionable

die **Klage, -n** complaint; lament(ation); *leg* action; **eine ~ erheben gegen** bring an action against || **das ~lied, -er** lament; **die ~mauer** the Wailing Wall; **~weg (auf dem K.** by bringing an action)

klagen (*Aust in 1st sense*) sue; (*v/i*) complain; wail; **~ auf** (*acc*) sue for; **~ gegen** sue; **~ über** (*acc*) complain about/of; **~ um** lament, mourn; (+*dat*) **sein Leid ~** pour out one's sorrow to

der **Kläger, -** plaintiff; petitioner

kläglich pitiful; miserable; despicable

der **Klamauk** *coll* row; ballyhoo

klamm numb; clammy; cold and damp

die **Klamm, -en** gorge

klamm|heimlich *coll* on the quiet

die **Klammer, -n** clothes peg, clothespin *US*; clip; paper-clip; staple; *dent* brace; *build* cramp; *print etc*, *math* bracket; **~ auf/zu** open/close brackets; **in ~n** in brackets

klammern: ~ an (*acc*) clip to; peg on, pin on *US* (clothes-line); **sich ~ an** (*acc*) cling to

die **Klamotten** *pl coll* things (= clothes); junk

der **Klang, ⸚e** sound; ring; **einen guten ~ haben** have a good tone/reputation || **die ~farbe, -n** tone colour, timbre; **die ~fülle** sonority; **k~los** toneless; **k~voll** sonorous; (name) famous

klang (klänge) *p/t* (*subj*) *of* **klingen**

klanglich tonal; **~ gut sein** have a good tone

Klapp- folding ...; **das ~messer, -** jack-knife; **das ~rad, ⸚er** folding bicycle; **das ~verdeck, -e** folding hood/top *US*

die **Klappe, -n** flap; (hinged) lid; *anat*, *mus* valve; *Aust tel* extension; *coll* 'trap'; **die ~ halten** *coll* shut one's trap; **in die ~ gehen** *coll* hit the hay

klappen (shutter *etc*) bang (**gegen** against); *coll* work (out); go well; **nach oben** *etc* **~** fold/tip up *etc*; turn up *etc* (collar)

der **Klappen|text, -e** blurb

die **Klapper, -n** rattle; **die ~kiste, -n** *coll* bone-shaker; **die ~schlange, -n** rattlesnake; **der ~storch, ⸚e** (*baby-talk*) stork (that brings babies)

klapp(e)rig shaky; rickety

klappern (*sn if indicating direction*) rattle; clatter; **~ mit** clatter; *coll* flutter (eyelids); **er klappert mit den Zähnen** his teeth are chattering

der **Klaps, -e** smack; **einen ~ haben** *coll* have a screw loose || **die ~mühle, -n** *coll* loony-bin

klar clear; **sich** *dat* **im ~en sein über** (*acc*) realize; be clear about; **(na,) ~!** of course!; **alles ~?** all set? || **~denkend** clear-thinking; **~kommen*** (*sep*; *sn*) *coll* (**k. mit** be able to cope with); **~legen** (*sep*) explain (*dat* to); **~machen** (*sep*) make clear (*dat* to); *naut* make ready (**sich** *dat* **... k.** realize; get clear in one's own mind); **~sehen*** (*sep*) *coll* see clearly (**k. in** (*dat*) be clear about); **K~sicht-** transparent ...; **~stellen** (*sep*) clarify; make clear; **die K~stellung, -en** clarification; **der K~text** plain text (**im K.** in clear; in plain English); **~werden*** (*sep*; *sn*) (+*dat*) become clear to (**sich** *dat* **k. über** (*acc*) get clear in one's own mind)

die **Klär|anlage, -n** sewage plant

klären clear; treat (sewage); clarify; (*v/i*) *sp* clear (the ball); **sich ~** clear; become clear

die **Klarheit** clarity; **sich** *dat* **~ verschaffen über** (*acc*) become clear about

die **Klarinette, -n** clarinet

die **Klärung** treatment (of sewage); clarification

klasse (*indecl*) *coll* terrific

die **Klasse, -n** class (*also biol*, *pol*); grade; **... erster/zweiter ~** first/second-class ...; **erster/zweiter ~ reisen** travel first/second class; **(große) ~** *coll* terrific

das **Klassement** [-ə'mã:], **-s** *sp* final positions

Klassen- class ...; **k~bewußt** class-conscious; **das ~bewußt|sein** class-consciousness; **der ~kampf, ⸚e** class struggle; **k~los** classless; **das ~zimmer, -** class-room

die **Klassifikation, -en** classification

klassifizieren classify

die **Klassifizierung, -en** classification

-klassig -class

die **Klassik** [-ɪk] classical age; classicism

der **Klassiker, -** classic (author)

klassisch classical; classic

der **Klassizismus** neoclassicism

klatsch! splash!; smack!

der **Klatsch, -e** splash; smack; *coll* gossip; **die ~base, -n** *coll* gossip; **der ~kolumnist, -en** (*wk masc*) gossip columnist; **der ~mohn, -e** poppy; **klatsch|naß** *coll* soaking wet; **die ~spalte, -n** gossip column; **die ~tante, -n** *coll* gossip

klatschen clap; *coll* gossip; (*also sn*) splash; **Beifall ~** applaud; **~ auf** (*acc*) slap onto; (+*dat*) **auf das Bein** *etc* **~** slap (s.o.'s) leg *etc*; **in die Hände ~** clap one's hands

die **Klaue, -n** claw; *coll* 'paw'; *coll* scrawl; (*pl*) *coll* clutches

klauen *coll* 'pinch'

die **Klause, -n** (monk's) cell; den

die **Klausel, -n** clause (of contract)

Klausenburg Cluj

der **Klausner, -** recluse

die **Klausur, -en** seclusion; *eccles* enclosure (in monastery, convent); *univ* = **die ~arbeit, -en** examination (paper)

die **Klaviatur, -en** keyboard

das **Klavichord** [-k-], **-e** clavichord

das **Klavier, -e** piano; **~ spielen** play the piano || **der ~auszug, ⸚e** piano score/arrangement; **das ~konzert, -e** piano recital/concerto; **das ~stück, -e** composition for the piano

Kleb(e)- adhesive ...; **die ~folie, -n** adhesive film; **der Kleb|stoff, -e** glue; **der ~streifen, -** adhesive tape

kleben stick; (*v/i*) stick; *coll* be sticky; *coll* buy insurance stamps; **~ an** (*dat*) stick to; cling to; **an seinen Händen klebt Blut** he has blood on his hands; **jmdm. eine ~** *coll* give s.o. a slap in the face || **~bleiben*** (*sep*; *sn*) stick (**an** *dat* to); *coll* be stuck; have to repeat a year

klebrig sticky

Klecker-: die ~beträge *pl coll* piddling amounts; **k~weise** *coll* in dribs and drabs

kleckern *coll* spill (food *etc*); (*v/i*) spill food/paint *etc*; proceed by fits and starts; come in in dribs and drabs; (*sn*: paint *etc*) spill

der **Klecks, -e** spot; blob; blot

klecksen blot; *coll* daub

der **Klee** clover; **über den grünen ~ loben** praise to the skies || **das ~blatt, ⸚er** clover-leaf; trio

der **Kleiber, -** nuthatch

das **Kleid, -er** dress; (*pl*) clothes

kleiden dress, clothe; suit; **in Worte ~** put into words; **sich ~** dress

Kleider- clothes ...; **die ~ablage, -n** cloakroom; hall-stand; **der ~bügel, -** coat-hanger; **der ~kasten, ..kästen** *SGer* wardrobe; **die ~puppe, -n** tailor's dummy; **der ~schrank, ⸚e** wardrobe

kleidsam becoming

die **Kleidung** clothing; **das ~s|stück, -e** garment

die **Kleie, -n** bran

klein little; small; short; petty; minor; **~es Geld** (small) change; **~e Leute** ordinary folk; **ein ~ wenig** a little bit; **sich ~ machen** stoop; **~ und häßlich machen** *coll* make (s.o.) feel small; **~ (und häßlich) werden** *coll* be deflated; **von ~ auf** from childhood; **bis ins ~ste** down to the last detail

Klein- small ...; micro-;

die ~arbeit detailed work (**in mühevoller K.** with painstaking attention to detail); **~asien** Asia Minor; **der ~bürger, -, k~bürgerlich** petit bourgeois; **das ~bürgertum** petite bourgeoisie; **der ~bus, -se** minibus; **die ~familie, -n** nuclear family; **der ~garten, ..gärten** allotment, garden plot *US*; **das ~gedruckte** (*decl as adj*) small print; **das ~geld** (small) change; **k~gläubig** of little faith; faint-hearted; **k~hacken** (*sep*) chop up; **das ~hirn, -e** cerebellum; **das ~holz** firewood (**K. machen aus** *coll* smash to pieces; make mincemeat of); **~kaliber-** small-bore ...; **k~kariert** *coll* petty; small-time; **das ~kind, -er** small child, infant; **der ~kram** *coll* odds and ends; trivialities; **der ~krieg, -e** guerrilla war(fare); running battle; **k~kriegen** (*sep*) *coll* smash; get through (money); wear down (person) (**nicht k~zukriegen** irrepressible); **k~laut** subdued; **k~mütig** faint-hearted; **das ~od** ['klaeno:t], **-ien** [-'no:dɪən] gem, jewel; (*pl* **-e**) treasure, gem; **k~schneiden*** (*sep*) chop up; **die ~schreibung** spelling with a small initial letter; **der ~staat, -en** small state; **die ~staaterei** particularism; **der ~städter, -, k~städtisch** provincial; **das ~vieh** small livestock; **k~weis** *Aust* little by little

die **Kleinigkeit, -en** trifle; minor detail; *coll* bite (to eat); (a) little something; **der ~s|krämer, -** pedant

kleinlich petty; mean

Kleinst- very small ...; miniature ...; **das ~kind, -er** infant (aged 0–2); **k~möglich** smallest possible

der **Kleister, -, kleistern** paste

Klemens ['kle:məns] Clement

die **Klemme, -n** clip; clamp (*also med*); (*in idioms*) tight spot

klemmen wedge; stick (in position); (*v/i*) jam; **sich** *dat* **... ~** catch (finger in door *etc*); **sich ~ hinter** (*acc*) *coll* get stuck into; get onto

der **Klempner, -** plumber

die **Klempnerei, -en** plumber's workshop; plumbing

Kleopatra Cleopatra
der **Klepper, –** old nag
der **Kleptomane, –n** (*wk masc*) kleptomaniac
die **Kleptomanie** kleptomania
der **Kleriker, –** *RC* cleric
der **Klerus** *RC* clergy
das **Klett|band** Velcro
die **Klette, –n** burr
Kletter– climbing ...; **das ~gerüst, –e** climbing-frame; **die ~pflanze, –n** creeper
klettern (*sn*) climb; **~ auf** (*acc*) climb
klicken click
der **Klient, –en** (*wk masc*) (lawyer's) client
die **Klientel** [–iɛn–], **–en** clientele
das **Klima, –s/Klimate** climate; **die ~anlage, –n** air-conditioning (**mit K.** air-conditioned); **der ~wechsel, –** change of climate
das **Klimakterium** menopause, climacteric
klimatisch climatic
klimatisieren air-condition
der **Klimbim** *coll* junk; fuss, to-do
Klimm–: der ~zug, ⸚e pull-up
klimmen (*p/t* **klomm** (*subj* **klömme**), *p/part* **geklommen**) (*sn*) (*esp in compds*) climb
der **Klimper|kasten, ..kästen** *coll* old joanna
klimpern: ~ auf (*dat*) *coll* strum/tinkle on; **~ mit** jingle; *coll* flutter (eyelids *etc*)
die **Klinge, –n** blade
die **Klingel, –n** bell; **der ~beutel, –** *eccles* collection-bag; **der ~knopf, ⸚e** bell-push; **der ~zug, ⸚e** bell-pull
klingeling! ting-a-ling!
klingeln ring; **es klingelt** the doorbell rings; the bell rings; **aus dem Bett ~** wake by ringing the doorbell/phoning; **~ nach** ring for
klingen (*p/t* **klang** (*subj* **klänge**), *p/part* **geklungen**) ring; sound
der **Klingklang** tinkling
die **Klinik** [–ɪk], **–en** clinic; (university) hospital
klinisch clinical; **~ tot** clinically dead
die **Klinke, –n** door-handle
der **Klinker, –** clinker brick
klipp *coll*: **~ und klar** quite openly
die **Klippe, –n** rock (in sea); hurdle, obstacle
der **Klips, –e** clip; clip-on ear-ring
klirren jangle; tinkle; clank; clink; **~ mit** clank, rattle; jangle; **~d** (frost) severe
das **Klischee, –s** cliché; *print* block; **die ~vorstellung, –en** stereotype(d idea)
klischeehaft hackneyed
das **Klistier, –e** enema
die **Klitoris** [–ɪs] **–/Klitorides** [–e:s] clitoris
klitsch: ~, klatsch! splash! || **klitsch|naß** *coll* soaking wet
klitzeklein *coll* teeny-weeny
das **Klo, –s** *coll* loo, john *US*; **aufs ~ gehen** go to the loo/john *US* || **das ~papier** loo paper
die **Kloake, –n** sewer; *zool* cloaca
der **Kloben, –** log
klobig hefty; clumsy

klomm (klömme) *p/t* (*subj*) *of* **klimmen**
der **Klon, –e, klonen** clone
klönen *NGer coll* have a natter
Klopf–: k~fest anti-knock; **der ~käfer, –** death-watch beetle; **das ~zeichen, –** knock
klopfen knock (into wall *etc*); beat; (*v/i*) knock; (heart) beat; *mot* knock; **(+*dat*) auf die Finger ~** give (s.o.) a rap on the knuckles; (+*dat*) **auf die Schulter** *etc* **~** pat/tap on the shoulder *etc*; **es klopft** there is a knock at the door
der **Klopfer, –** (carpet) beater; knocker
der **Klöppel, –** bobbin; clapper (of bell); **die ~spitze, –n** bobbin-lace
klöppeln make bobbin-lace
der **Klops, –e** meat-ball
das **Klosett, –s** *coll* toilet
der **Kloß** [–o:–], **⸚e** dumpling; **einen ~ im Hals haben** have a lump in one's throat
das **Kloster** [–o:–], *pl* **Klöster** monastery; convent
klösterlich [–ø:–] monastic; cloistered
der **Klotz, ⸚e** block; *coll* oaf; (+*dat*) **ein ~ am Bein sein** *coll* be a millstone round (s.o.'s) neck; **schlafen wie ein ~** sleep like a log
klotzig massive
der **Klub** [–ʊp], **–s** club; **die ~jacke, –n** blazer; **der ~sessel, –** (upholstered) armchair
die **Kluft**[1], **⸚e** cleft; chasm; gulf (between parties *etc*)
die **Kluft**[2], **–en** *coll* outfit; uniform
klug (*comp*, *superl* ⸚) clever; intelligent; sensible; **nicht ~ werden aus** be unable to figure out || **der K~scheißer, –** *vulg* = **der K~schnacker, –** *coll* wise guy
kluger|weise wisely
die **Klugheit** cleverness; intelligence; good sense
Klump–: der ~fuß, ⸚e club-foot; **k~füßig** club-footed
klumpen turn lumpy
der **Klumpen, –** lump; clod; nugget; clot
klumpig lumpy
der **Klüngel, –** clique
der **Klüver** [–v–], **–** jib
km (= **Kilometer**) km.; **km²** (= **Quadratkilometer**) sq.km.; **km/h** k.p.h.
knabbern nibble (**an** *dat* at)
der **Knabe, –n** (*wk masc*) (*now chiefly in official style*, *coll phrases such as* **alter ~** old boy *or compounds* (**~n–** boy's ...; boys' ...) boy; **das ~n|kraut** (wild) orchid
knabenhaft boyish
knack! crack!
der **Knack, –e** crack(ing sound); **der ~laut, –e** glottal stop; **die ~wurst, ⸚e** (*type of frankfurter that makes a cracking sound when bitten into*)
das **Knäckebrot** crispbread, knäckebröd *US*
knacken crack; squash (lice *etc*); *coll* crack (safe), break into (car); (*v/i*) crack; crackle; (*sn*) snap; **~ mit** crack (one's fingers)

der **Knacker, –** *coll* = **Knackwurst; alter ~** old fogey

knackig *coll* crisp; crunchy; (girl) dishy

knacks! crack!

der **Knacks, –e** crack; **einen ~ haben** *coll* be cracked; be dicky; (marriage) be in a shaky state; (person) be 'cracked'

knacksen *coll* crack; (*sn*) snap

der **Knall, –e** crack; bang; **einen ~ haben** *coll* be crazy; **~ und Fall** *coll* all of a sudden; on the spot || **das ~bonbon, –s** (*also* **der**) (Christmas) cracker; **der ~effekt, –e** *coll* big surprise; **knall|eng** *coll* skin-tight; **die ~erbse, –n** torpedo (= firework); **der ~frosch, ⸚e** jumping jack; **knall|gelb** *coll* bright yellow; **knall|grün** *coll* bright green; **knall|hart** *coll* as hard as nails; brutal; (*adv*) without batting an eyelid; **knall|heiß** *coll* blazing hot; **der ~kopf, ⸚e** *coll* blockhead; **der ~körper, –** fire-cracker; **knall|rot** *coll* bright red

knallen slam (into net *etc*); slam down (on table *etc*); *coll* put (bullet into sth.); (*v/i*) bang; crack; pop; *coll* beat down; (colour) glare; **~ gegen** (*sn*) bang against; **~ mit** slam; click (one's heels); crack (whip); **jmdm. eine ~** *coll* clout s.o.

knallig *coll* (colour) loud

knapp meagre; scarce, in short supply; (garment) tight; (majority *etc*) narrow; barely (*eg* **~e fünf Minuten** barely five minutes); concise, terse; (*adv*) just; barely; **~ werden** run short; **~ bei Kasse** *coll* short of cash; **mit ~er Not** only just; **mit ~er Not davonkommen** have a close shave; **und nicht zu ~!** and how! || **k~halten*** (*sep*) keep short

die **Knappheit** scarcity, shortage (**an** *dat* of); conciseness

knapsen *coll*: **~ mit** economize on; **mit dem Geld ~** economize

die **Knarre, –n** rattle; *coll* shooter

knarren creak; **~d** (voice) grating

der **Knast, ⸚e/–e** *coll* 'clink'

knattern (gunfire, machine-gun) crackle; (motor-cycle *etc*) bang away; (flag) flap

das **Knäuel, –** (*also* **der**) ball (of wool); cluster, knot (of people); tangle; bundle of fluff

der **Knauf, ⸚e** knob; pommel

der **Knauser, –** *coll* skinflint

knauserig *coll* stingy

knausern *coll*: **~ mit** be stingy/sparing with

die **Knaus-Ogino-Methode** rhythm method

Knautsch–: die ~zone, –n crumple zone

knautschen *coll* crumple

der **Knebel, –** gag; toggle

knebeln gag (*also* press *etc*)

der **Knecht, –e** farm-labourer; slave (*gen* of, to); *arch* servant

knechten subjugate, enslave

knechtisch slavish; servile

die **Knechtschaft** servitude

Kneif–: die ~zange, –n pincers; pliers

kneifen (*p/t* **kniff,** *p/part* **gekniffen**) pinch; (*v/i*) *coll* back out; **~ vor** (*dat*) *coll* duck; **den Schwanz zwischen die Beine ~** (dog) put its tail between its legs

der **Kneifer, –** pince-nez

Kneip–: die ~tour, –en *coll* pub-crawl

die **Kneipe, –n** *coll* pub, saloon *US*

Knet–: die ~masse, –n modelling clay

kneten knead; work

der **Knick, –e** (sharp) bend; kink; crease; crack

das **Knickebein** advocaat filling

knicken (*see also* **geknickt**) crease; snap; crush (pride *etc*); (*v/i sn*) snap

die **Knickerbocker** *pl* plus-fours

knick(e)rig *coll* stingy

knickern *coll* be stingy

der **Knicks, –e, knicksen** curtsey

das **Knie, –** [–iːə] knee; (sharp) bend (in river); *tech* elbow; **in die ~ gehen** sink to one's knees; submit; **übers ~ brechen** rush || **die ~beuge, –n** knee-bend; **der ~fall, ⸚e** falling on one's knees; capitulation (**vor** *dat* to) (**einen K. tun** go down on one's knees); **k~fällig** on bended knee; **k~frei** that shows the knees; **k~lang** knee-length; **die ~scheibe, –n** knee-cap; **der ~schützer, –** knee pad; **der ~strumpf, ⸚e** knee-length sock; **k~weich (k. werden** turn weak-kneed)

knien [–iː(ə)–] (*sn in SGer exc* **sich ~**) kneel; **sich ~ in** (*acc*) *coll* knuckle down to

kniff *p/t of* **kneifen**

der **Kniff, –e** pinch; crease; trick

kniff(e)lig fiddly; tricky

kniffen make a fold/crease in

der **Knigge** (*title of work on etiquette*)

der **Knilch, –e** *coll* (unpleasant) type

knipsen *coll* punch (ticket); flick (switch); *phot* snap; **~ mit** snap (one's fingers)

der **Knirps, –e** little fellow; (*trade-mark*) telescopic umbrella

knirschen crunch; (brakes *etc*) grind; **mit den Zähnen ~** grind/gnash one's teeth

knistern rustle; (fire) crackle; **~ mit** rustle

die **Knittel|verse** *pl* (*verse form – used eg in Goethe's 'Faust' – employing rhyming couplets, each line containing four stresses and an irregular number of unstressed syllables*)

der **Knitter, –** crease; **k~frei** crease-resistant

knittern (*also v/i*) crease; crinkle

der **Knobel|becher, –** dice-cup; *mil coll* army boot

knobeln decide sth. by means of dice *etc*; **~ an** (*dat*) puzzle over

der **Knoblauch** [–oːp–, –oːb–] garlic

der **Knöchel, –** ankle; knuckle; **k~lang** ankle-length

der **Knochen, –** bone; **bis auf/in die ~** through and through, to the core || **die ~arbeit** *coll* back-breaking work; **der ~bau** bone structure; **der ~bruch, ¨e** (bone) fracture; **knochen|dürr** *coll* skinny; **das ~gerüst, –e** skeleton; **das ~mark** bone-marrow; **das ~mehl** bone-meal; **knochen|trocken** *coll* bone-dry

knöchern bone; bony

knochig bony; **–knochig** -boned

knockout [nɔk'ʔaot]: **~ schlagen** knock out

der **Knockout** [nɔk'ʔaot] (*gen* –(s)), **–s** knock-out

der **Knödel, –** *SGer* dumpling

die **Knolle, –n** tuber; corm; **die ~n|nase, –n** bulbous nose

knollig bulbous; tuberous

der **Knopf, ¨e** button; (push-)button; knob; *coll* (*with adj*) (little) fellow; **das ~loch, ¨er** buttonhole

knöpfen button (up)

knorke *dated coll* smashing

der **Knorpel, –** gristle; *anat* cartilage

knorp(e)lig gristly; *anat* cartilaginous

knorrig gnarled; knotty; gruff

die **Knospe, –n, knospen** bud

knoten knot; tie a knot in

der **Knoten, –** knot (*also naut*); (= hairstyle) bun; *med* lump; *bot* node; **der ~punkt, –e** junction

knotig knotty; gnarled

das **Know-how** [no:'hao] (*gen* –(s)) know-how

der **Knuff, ¨e** *coll*, **knuffen** *coll* poke; nudge

der **Knülch, –e** *coll* (unpleasant) type

knüllen crumple

der **Knüller, –** *coll* hit; sensation

knüpfen tie; knot; form (friendship); **~ an** (*acc*) tie to; attach (condition) to; have (expectations) of; put (question) following; **enger ~** strengthen (bonds); **sich ~ an** (*acc*) be associated with

der **Knüppel, –** club; truncheon; *aer* control-stick; **(+*dat*) einen ~ zwischen die Beine werfen** put a spoke in (s.o.'s) wheel || **knüppel|dick** *coll* (**k. haben** be sick and tired of; **... hat's k. hinter den Ohren** there are no flies on ...; **es kam k.** it was one thing after another; **k~dick(e) voll** jam-packed; absolutely plastered)

knurren growl; (stomach) rumble

knurrig grumpy

knusp(e)rig crisp; crunchy; (girl) scrumptious

knuspern crunch

der **Knust** [–u:–], **–e/¨e** *NGer* crust

Knut Canute

die **Knute, –n** knout; **unter der ~** (+*gen*) under the heel of

Knutsch– [–u:–]: **der ~fleck, –e** *coll* love-bite

knutschen [–u:–] *coll* neck with; (*v/i*) = **sich ~** neck

k. o. [ka:'ʔo:] knocked out; *coll* all in; **~ schlagen** knock out || **der K.-o.-Schlag, ¨e** knockout (blow)

koalieren: ~ mit form a coalition with

die **Koalition, –en** coalition

das **Kobalt** cobalt; **k~blau** cobalt blue

der **Kobold, –e** imp

Kobolz: ~ schießen do a somersault

die **Kobra, –s** cobra

der **Koch, ¨e** cook

Koch– cooking ...; **der ~apfel, ..äpfel** cooking-apple; **das ~buch, ¨er** cookery-book, cookbook *US*; **k~echt** (= **k~fest**); **die ~ecke, –n** cooking area; **k~fest** that may be boiled; (colour) fast; **die ~gelegenheit, –en** cooking facilities; **der ~herd, –e** stove; **die ~kunst, ¨e** culinary art; **der ~löffel, –** wooden spoon; **die ~nische, –n** kitchenette; **die ~platte, –n** hotplate; **der ~topf, ¨e** saucepan; (cooking-)pot

kochen cook; boil; make (tea, coffee); (*v/i*) boil; **vor Wut ~** *coll* fume; **zum Kochen bringen** bring to the boil; **~d heiß** boiling hot

der **Kocher, –** (small) stove

der **Köcher, –** quiver

die **Köchin, –nen** (female) cook

der **Kode** [ko:t], **–s** code

das **Kodein** codeine

der **Köder, –** bait; lure

ködern lure; entice

der **Kodex** (*gen* –(es)), **–e/Kodizes** [–e:s] codex; (moral) code; *leg hist* codex

kodifizieren codify

das **Kodizill, –e** codicil

die **Koedukation** co-education

der **Koeffizient, –en** (*wk masc*) coefficient

die **Koexistenz** co-existence

das **Koffein** caffeine; **k~frei** decaffeinated

der **Koffer, –** suitcase; trunk; case; *mil coll* heavy shell; *in compds* portable ...; **der ~kuli, –s** (luggage) trolley; **der ~raum, ¨e** *mot* boot, trunk *US*

der **Kognak** ['kɔnjak], **–s** brandy, cognac; **der ~schwenker, –** brandy glass

kohärent coherent

die **Kohäsion** cohesion

der **Kohl** cabbage; *coll* nonsense; **~dampf** *coll* (**K. schieben** be starving); **der ~kopf, ¨e** cabbage; **die ~meise, –n** great tit; **kohl|raben|schwarz** jet/pitch-black; **der ~rabi** (*gen* –(s)), –(s) kohlrabi; **kohl|schwarz** jet/pitch-black; black as coal; **die ~sprosse, –n** *Aust* Brussels sprout; **der ~weißling, –e** cabbage white

die **Kohle, –n** coal; charcoal; (*pl*) *coll* 'dough'; *in compds* coal ...; carbon ...; **das ~hydrat, –e** carbohydrate; **das ~papier** carbon paper

kohlen[1] carbonize, char; *naut* take on coal
kohlen[2] *coll* fib
Kohlen– coal ...; **das ~dioxyd** carbon dioxide; **das ~hydrat, –e** carbohydrate; **das ~(monoxyd** carbon monoxide; **der ~pott** *coll* the Ruhr; **k~sauer** ... carbonate; **die ~säure** carbonic acid; **der ~stoff** carbon; **der ~wasser|stoff** hydrocarbon
die **Kohorte, –n** cohort
koitieren copulate
der **Koitus, –** [–uːs]/**–se** coitus
die **Koje, –n** bunk; (exhibition) stand
das **Kokain** cocaine
die **Kokerei, –en** coking; coking plant
kokett coquettish
die **Koketterie, –(ie)n** coquettishness; coquetry
kokettieren: ~ mit flirt with; toy with
der **Kokolores** [–əs] (*gen* –) *coll* rubbish; palaver
der **Kokon** [–'kõː], **–s** cocoon
Kokos– [–ɔs–] coconut ...; **die ~nuß, ⸚(ss)e** coconut; **die ~palme, –n** coconut tree; **die ~raspeln** *pl* dessicated coconut
der **Koks**[1], **–e** coke; *coll* rubbish; *coll* 'dough'
der **Koks**[2] *coll* 'coke'
die **Kola|nuß, ⸚(ss)e** cola nut
der **Kolben, –** (rifle) butt; *bot* cob; *chem* flask; *mech* piston; plunger; *coll* conk, schnozzle *US*; **der ~hub, ⸚e** piston-stroke
die **Kolchose** [–ç–], **–n** collective farm (in U.S.S.R.)
der **Kolibri, –s** humming-bird
die **Kolik** [–ɪk], **–en** colic
der **Kolk|rabe, –n** (*wk masc*) raven
kollabieren (*sn*) *med* collapse
der **Kollaborateur** [–'tøːɐ], **–e** collaborator (with enemy)
die **Kollaboration, –en** collaboration (with enemy)
kollaborieren collaborate (with enemy)
der **Kollaps, –e** *med* collapse
das **Kolleg, –s** lecture-course; **die ~mappe, –n** document case
der **Kollege, –n** (*wk masc*) colleague
kollegial helpful; (*adv*) like a good colleague
die **Kollegialität** helpfulness (as a colleague); spirit of co-operation among colleagues
das **Kollegium, –(i)en** (teaching) staff; board
die **Kollekte, –n** *eccles* collection
die **Kollektion, –en** collection (*also fash*); selection
kollektiv, das Kollektiv, –e/–s collective
Kollektiv– collective ...; **die ~wirtschaft, –en** collective farm/economy
kollektivieren collectivize
die **Kollektivierung, –en** collectivization
das **Kollektivum, –(v)a/–(v)en** *gramm* collective
der **Koller, –** *coll* tantrum
kollern (turkey) gobble; (stomach) rumble
kollidieren clash, conflict; (*sn*) collide
das **Kollier** [–'lĭeː], **–s** necklace
die **Kollision, –en** collision; clash, conflict
das **Kolloquium, –(i)en** colloquium; *Aust univ* examination
Köln Cologne
Kölnisch: ~ Wasser = das Kölnisch|wasser eau de Cologne
Kolonial– colonial ...; **die ~waren** *pl dated* groceries; **der ~waren|händler, –** *dated* grocer
der **Kolonialismus** colonialism
die **Kolonie, –(ie)n** colony (*also biol*)
die **Kolonisation, –en** colonization; settling
der **Kolonisator, –(or)en** colonizer
kolonisieren colonize; settle
der **Kolonist, –en** (*wk masc*) colonist; settler
die **Kolonnade, –n** colonnade
die **Kolonne, –n** column (*also* of figures); gang (of workmen); line (of traffic); *mil* convoy; **fünfte ~** fifth column
die **Koloratur, –en** coloratura
kolorieren colour
das **Kolorit, –e** colouring; atmosphere, flavour; *mus* (tone-)colour
der **Koloß, –(ss)e** colossus
kolossal colossal; *coll* tremendous
das **Kolosseum** (*gen* **–s**) the Coliseum
die **Kolportage** [–ʒə], **–n** trashy literature; rumour-mongering
der **Kolporteur** [–'tøːɐ], **–e** rumour-monger
kolportieren circulate (rumour)
der **Kolumbianer, –, kolumbianisch** Colombian
Kolumbien [–ĭən] Colombia
der **Kolumbier** [–ĭɐ], **–, kolumbisch** Colombian
Kolumbus Columbus; **das Ei des ~** (*see* **Ei**)
die **Kolumne, –n** (newspaper) column
der **Kolumnist, –en** (*wk masc*) columnist
das **Koma, –s/–ta** coma; **im ~ liegen** be in a coma
komatös comatose
der **Kombi, –s** *coll* = **der ~wagen, –** estate car, station wagon *US*
das **Kombinat, –e** combine (in Communist states)
die **Kombination, –en** combination (*also* for lock); conjecture; deduction; overalls, *aer* flying suit; *chess, sp* combination; *sp* (combined) move; **das ~s|schloß, ⸚(ss)er** combination lock
kombinatorisch deductive
die **Kombine** [kɔm'baen], **–s** *EGer* combine harvester
kombinieren combine; (*v/i*) deduce
die **Kombüse, –n** *naut* galley
der **Komet, –en** (*wk masc*) comet
kometenhaft meteoric
der **Komfort** [–'foːɐ] comfort; luxury; amenities
komfortabel [–fɔr–] comfortable; luxurious
die **Komik** [–ɪk] comedy; comic effect; comic element; **die Situation entbehrt nicht einer gewissen ~** the situation is not without its funny side

der **Komiker, –** comedian
komisch funny; comic; **komischer|weise** funnily enough
das **Komitee, –s** committee
das **Komma, –s/–ta** comma; *math* decimal point (*eg* **fünf ~ acht (5,8)** five point eight (5·8))
der **Kommandant, –en** (*wk masc*) *mil* commanding officer; commandant
die **Kommandantur, –en** *mil* headquarters
der **Kommandeur** [–'døːɐ], **–e** *mil* commander
kommandieren command (army *etc*); order (to a place); *coll* order about
die **Kommandit|gesellschaft, –en** limited partnership
das **Kommando, –s** command; squad; **das ~ führen** be in command; **auf ~** on command; to order || **die ~brücke, –n** *naut* bridge; **die ~kapsel, –n** command module
kommen (*p/t* **kam** (*subj* **käme**), *p/part* **gekommen**) (*sn*) come; go; get; turn out; happen; (+*dat*) (idea) occur to; *coll* be (cheeky, rude) to; **ange(rast** *etc*) **~** come ...ing (*eg* tearing) along (*see the relevant simple verb*, *eg* **rasen**); **komme, was da wolle** come what may; **wie kommt das?** why is that?; **das kommt, weil ...** that's because ...; **'daher kommt es, daß ...** that's why ...; **ich komme schon!** coming!; **so darfst du mir nicht ~!** don't try that on me!; **~ lassen** send for; order
  ~ an (*acc*) come to; get to; get hold of; (property *etc*) pass to
  ~ auf (*acc*) come onto; get onto; go on (bill), go into (account); hit on; think of; come down to, be handed down to; (conversation) come round to; *coll* make, get; cost; **auf ... kommt/~ ...** for every ... there is/are ...; **nichts ~ lassen auf** refuse to have anything said against; **auf den Geschmack ~** acquire a taste for sth.; **wie kommst du 'da drauf?** what gave you *that* idea?
  ~ hinter (*acc*) find out; get to the bottom of; **~ hinter** (*dat*) come after
  ~ in (*acc*) come into; get into; go into (hospital *etc*), go to (heaven, prison); **ins (Stottern** *etc*) **~** begin to (stutter *etc*)
  ~ mit come by (*eg* **mit dem Auto/Bus ~** come by car/bus); have (request), come up with (suggestion); **komm mir nicht mit ...!** spare me ...!, don't give me ...!
  ~ über (*acc*) pass (s.o.'s lips); come over
  ~ um be deprived of, lose; get out of
  ~ unter (*acc*) get under; get run over by; come under (heading); mix with
  ~ von come from; be the result of; **das kommt davon!** serves you/her *etc* right!; **das kommt davon, wenn ...** that's what happens when ...; that's what comes of (+*ger*)
  ~ zu come to; get to; come and see; get around to; come by; **es kam zu ...** ... came about; there was/were ...; **zu ... kommt ...** on top of ... there is ...; **zu nichts ~** not get around to anything; not get anywhere; **zu sich ~** come round; recover; sort oneself out; **wie komme ich zu ...?** could you tell me the way to ...?; **wie komme ich dazu?** why should I?; **wie ~ Sie dazu?** how dare you!
das **Kommen** coming, arrival; **im ~** on the way in
kommend coming; next
der **Kommentar, –e** comment; commentary; **kein ~!** no comment
der **Kommentator, –(or)en** commentator
kommentieren comment on; annotate
der **Kommers, –e** ceremonial drinking-session of students in a *Verbindung*
der **Kommerz** commerce
kommerzialisieren commercialize
kommerziell commercial
der **Kommilitone, –n** (*wk masc*) fellow-student
der **Kommiß** *coll* army; **beim ~** in the army
der **Kommissar** (*Aust*, *Swiss* **–är**), **–e** commissioner; (police) superintendent
das **Kommissariat, –e** commissionership; office of superintendent; commissioner's/superintendent's office; *Aust* police-station
kommissarisch temporary
die **Kommission, –en** commission; **in ~** on sale or return
der **Kommissionär, –e** commission agent
die **Kommode, –n** chest of drawers
kommunal local; municipal; **die K~verwaltung** local government
die **Kommune, –n** municipality; commune
die **Kommunikation, –en** communication; connection; **das ~s|mittel, –** means of communication
die **Kommunion, –en** *RC* communion
das **Kommuniqué** [–my–], **–s** communiqué
der **Kommunismus** Communism
der **Kommunist, –en** (*wk masc*), **kommunistisch** Communist
kommunizieren communicate; *RC* receive Holy Communion
der **Komödiant, –en** (*wk masc*) play-actor; *hist* player
komödiantisch (talent *etc*) acting
die **Komödie** [–ĭə], **–n** comedy; play-acting
der **Kompagnon** [–panjɔ̃ː], **–s** *comm* partner
kompakt compact
die **Kompanie, –(ie)n** *mil* company; **der ~chef, –s** company commander
die **Komparatistik** [–ɪk] comparative literature
der **Komparativ, –e** *gramm* comparative
der **Komparse, –n** (*wk masc*) *cin* extra; *theat*

supernumerary

die **Komparserie, –(ie)n** *cin* extras; *theat* supernumeraries

der **Kompaß, –(ss)e** compass

kompatibel *tech* compatible

das **Kompendium, –(i)en** compendium

die **Kompensation, –en** compensation

kompensatorisch compensatory

kompensieren compensate for, offset

kompetent competent; responsible

die **Kompetenz, –en** authority; competence; responsibility

die **Kompilation, –en** compilation (from other works); scissors-and-paste job

kompilieren compile (from other works)

komplementär complementary

das **Komplet** [kɔ̃'ple:] (*gen* –(s)), **–s** dress with matching coat/jacket

komplett complete; *Aust* full (up)

komplex, der Komplex, –e complex

die **Komplexität** complexity

die **Komplikation, –en** complication (*also med*)

das **Kompliment, –e** compliment; (+*dat*) **ein ~ machen** pay (s.o.) a compliment

der **Komplize, –n** (*wk masc*) accomplice

komplizieren complicate; **kompliziert** complicated

das **Komplott, –e** plot

die **Komponente, –n** component; element

komponieren *esp arts* (*mus also v/i*) compose

der **Komponist, –en** (*wk masc*) composer

die **Komposition, –en** *esp arts* composition

kompositorisch compositional

das **Kompositum, –(t)a** compound (word)

der **Kompost** [*also* 'kɔm–] compost; **der ~haufen, –** compost heap

das **Kompott, –e** stewed fruit; **–kompott** stewed …

die **Kompresse, –n** compress

die **Kompression, –en** compression

der **Kompressor, –(or)en** compressor

komprimieren compress; condense

der **Kompromiß, –(ss)e** compromise; **k~bereit** willing to compromise; **k~los** uncompromising

kompromittieren compromise; **sich ~** compromise oneself

die **Komteß, –(ss)en = die Komtesse, –n** countess (= count's daughter)

Kondens–: die ~milch condensed milk; **der ~streifen, –** vapour-trail; **das ~wasser** condensation (on window *etc*)

die **Kondensation, –en** *chem, phys* condensation

der **Kondensator, –(or)en** condenser

kondensieren condense (*also phys*); (*v/i, also sn*) *phys* condense

die **Kondition, –en** condition (= shape s.o. is in); (*pl*) *comm* conditions, terms

konditional *gramm* conditional

konditionell *sp* as regards fitness

Konditions–: die ~schwäche lack of condition; **das ~training** fitness training

der **Konditor, –(or)en** pastry-cook

die **Konditorei, –en** cake-shop (*usu* with café); **die ~waren** *pl* cakes and pastries

Kondolenz– … of condolence

kondolieren (+*dat*) offer one's condolences to

das **Kondom, –e** (*also* **der**) condom

der **Kondor, –e** condor

der **Kondukteur** [–'tø:ɐ], **–e** *Swiss* conductor, *rail* guard, conductor *US*

das **Konfekt** confectionery

die **Konfektion** (manufacture of) ready-to-wear clothing; (ready-to-wear) clothing industry

der **Konfektionär, –e** manufacturer of ready-to-wear clothing

konfektionieren manufacture

Konfektions– ready-to-wear …

die **Konferenz, –en** meeting; conference

konferieren compère; (*v/i*) confer

die **Konfession, –en** (religious) denomination; *theol* confession of faith; **k~s|los** non-denominational; **die ~s|schule, –n** denominational school

konfessionell denominational

das **Konfetti** (*gen* –(s)) confetti

der **Konfident, –en** (*wk masc*) *Aust* police informer

der **Konfirmand, –en** (*wk masc*) *Prot* candidate for confirmation

die **Konfirmation, –en** *Prot* confirmation

konfirmieren *Prot* confirm

die **Konfiskation, –en** confiscation

konfiskatorisch confiscatory

konfiszieren confiscate

die **Konfitüre, –n** jam

der **Konflikt, –e** conflict; **in ~ geraten mit** come into conflict with || **die ~kommission, –en** *EGer* disputes tribunal (*dealing with industrial and other disputes as well as certain minor misdemeanours*)

die **Konföderation, –en** confederation

konföderieren: sich ~ confederate

konform concurring; **~ gehen mit** agree with

der **Konformismus** conformity

der **Konformist, –en** (*wk masc*), **konformistisch** conformist

die **Konfrontation, –en** confrontation

konfrontieren: ~ mit confront with

konfus confused

Konfuzius Confucius

kongenial congenial, kindred; (translation) that perfectly matches the original

das **Konglomerat, –e** conglomeration; *geol* conglomerate

der **Kongo** (*gen* –(s)) the Congo

der **Kongolese, –n** (*wk masc*), **kongolesisch** Congolese

der **Kongreß, –(ss)e** congress

kongruent concurring; *math* congruent

die **Kongruenz, –en** agreement; *gramm*, *math* congruence

der **König, –e** king (*also cards, chess*); **das ~reich** [–ɪk–], **–e** kingdom

die **Königin, –nen** queen; **die ~mutter, ..mütter** queen mother

königlich [–ɪk–] royal; regal; **sich ~ amüsieren** *coll* have the time of one's life

Königs– king's ...; royal ...; **der ~macher, –** kingmaker; **der ~tiger, –** Bengal tiger; **k~treu** royalist

Königsberg Kaliningrad, *hist* Königsberg

das **Königtum** monarchy

konisch conical

die **Konjugation, –en** conjugation

konjugieren conjugate

die **Konjunktion, –en** *astron*, *gramm* conjunction

der **Konjunktiv, –e** subjunctive (mood)

die **Konjunktur, –en** economic situation; boom; **steigende ~** business revival; **rückläufige ~** recession; **~ haben** enjoy a boom

Konjunktur– economic ...; **k~bedingt** due to economic factors; **der ~ritter, –** opportunist; **der ~zyklus, –(l)en** trade cycle

konjunkturell economic

konkav concave

das **Konklave, –n** conclave

das **Konkordat, –e** concordat

konkret concrete

konkretisieren put in concrete terms

die **Konkubine, –n** concubine

der **Konkurrent, –en** (*wk masc*) competitor, rival

die **Konkurrenz, –en** competition; competitors, (the) competition; (+*dat*) **~ machen** compete with || **k~fähig** competitive; **der ~kampf, ⸚e** competition (in industry *etc*); **k~los** without competition

konkurrenzieren *Aust*, *Swiss* compete with

konkurrieren compete

der **Konkurs, –e** bankruptcy; **~ anmelden** declare oneself bankrupt || **der ~verwalter, –** official receiver

können (*pres* **kann, kannst, kann, können, könnt, können,** *subj* **könne** *etc*; *p/t* **konnte,** *subj* **könnte;** *p/part* **gekonnt,** (*after dependent infin*) **können**) (*see p. xlvii*; *see also* **gekonnt**) be able to, (I *etc*) can (*also* = may); manage to; (*ellipt*) be able to do; know, (be able to) speak (German *etc*); be able to go (home, to ..., *etc*); **ich kann nicht mehr** I can't go on/take any more; **ich kann nichts dafür** I can't help it; it's not my fault; **ich kann nicht umhin zu ...** I can't help (+ *ger*); **(das) kann sein** it's possible; **das kann nicht sein** that can't be true; **du kannst** *etc* **mich mal!** to hell with you *etc*!; **mir/uns kann keiner!** they can't touch me/us!; **das will gekonnt sein** you have to have the knack;

konnte could, was able to; managed to; **könnte** could (*ie* potentially), would be able to; **... konnte** + *p/part* + **werden:** *expressed by* it was possible to + *infin*; they managed to + *infin* (*eg* **der Verbrecher konnte gefaßt werden** they managed to catch the criminal);

habe ... ~ have been/was able to; **hätte ... ~** would have been able to, could have + *p/part*

das **Können** ability; skill

der **Könner, –** expert

der **Konnex, –e** connection; contact

konnte (könnte) *p/t* (*subj*) *of* **können**

der **Konsens, –e** agreement, consensus; assent

konsequent consistent; logical; single-minded; **~ decken** *sp* mark closely

die **Konsequenz, –en** consequence; (logical) conclusion; consistency; determination; **die ~en ziehen** act accordingly; take appropriate action

konservativ conservative

der **Konservator, –(or)en** (*wk masc*) curator

das **Konservatorium, –(i)en** conservatoire

die **Konserve, –n** can; *med* unit of stored blood; (*pl*) preserved food; canned food; **Musik aus der ~** *coll* canned music || **die ~n|büchse, –n = die ~n|dose, –n** can

konservieren preserve

die **Konservierung, –en** preservation; **das ~s|mittel, –** preservative

das **Konsistorium, –(i)en** consistory

die **Konsole, –n** *archit*, *comput* console

konsolidieren consolidate

die **Konsolidierung, –en** consolidation

der **Konsonant, –en** (*wk masc*) consonant

konsonantisch consonantal

die **Konsorten** *pl coll* gang

das **Konsortium** [–ts–], **–(i)en** consortium

der **Konspekt, –e** *EGer* synopsis, summary

die **Konspiration, –en** conspiracy

konspirativ conspiratorial

konspirieren conspire

konstant constant

die **Konstante, –n** (*or decl as adj*) constant factor; *math*, *phys* constant

Konstantin Constantine

Konstantinopel Constantinople

Konstanz Constance

konstatieren establish; state

die **Konstellation, –en** (political *etc*) situation; combination of circumstances; *astron*, *astrol* constellation

konsterniert dismayed

konstituieren constitute; **sich ~** be established; **~d** (assembly) constituent

die **Konstitution, –en** *pol*, *med* constitution

konstitutionell constitutional

konstruieren construct; fabricate; *tech* design; *gramm*, *math* construct; **kon-**

struiert *also* contrived
der **Konstrukteur** [–'tø:ɐ], **–e** *tech* designer
die **Konstruktion, –en** construction; *tech* design; structure; *gramm, math* construction; **der ~s|fehler, –** design fault
konstruktiv constructive
der **Konsul** [–ʊl], **–n** consul
konsularisch consular
das **Konsulat, –e** consulate
die **Konsultation, –en** consultation
konsultieren consult
der **Konsum¹** ['kɔn–], **–s** co-op
der **Konsum²** consumption; **die ~genossenschaft, –en** co-operative society; **die ~gesellschaft** consumer society; **die ~güter** *pl* consumer goods; **der ~terror** (in the consumer society) intense commercial pressures to which the consumer is subjected
die **Konsumation, –en** *Aust, Swiss* meal (taken in restaurant)
der **Konsument, –en** (*wk masc*) consumer
konsumieren consume
der **Kontakt, –e** contact; (*pl*) *mot* points; **in ~ stehen mit** be in contact with || **k~arm (k. sein** not make friends easily); **der ~bereichs|be|amte** (*decl as adj*) policeman who patrols his beat on foot; **k~freudig** sociable; **die ~linsen** *pl* contact lenses; **der ~mann, ⸚er** contact; **die ~person, –en** *med* contact; **die ~schalen** *pl* contact lenses
Konten *pl of* **Konto**
Konter– counter–
der **Konter|admiral, –e** rear-admiral
die **Konterbande** contraband
das **Konterfei, –e/–s** *arch* likeness
kontern (*also v/i*) counter
die **Konterrevolution, –en** counter-revolution
der **Kontext** [*also* –'tɛkst], **–e** context
der **Kontinent** [*also* –'nɛnt], **–e** continent
Kontinental– continental ...
das **Kontingent, –e** quota; *mil* contingent
kontingentieren apply quotas to
kontinuierlich continuous
die **Kontinuität** continuity
das **Konto, –(t)en** account; **... geht auf mein ~** I am responsible for ... || **der ~auszug, ⸚e** bank statement; **der ~stand, ⸚e** state of an account
das **Kontor, –e** branch office (abroad); *EGer* marketing board; *arch* office
der **Kontorist, –en** (*wk masc*) clerk
kontra (+*acc*) versus; (+*dat*) **Kontra geben** *coll* stand up to
der **Kontrabaß, ⸚(ss)e** double-bass
kontradiktorisch contradictory
der **Kontrahent, –en** (*wk masc*) opponent; *leg* contracting party
der **Kontrakt, –e** contract
kontraktlich contractual
der **Kontrapunkt, –e** counterpoint
kontrapunktisch contrapuntal
konträr contrary
der **Kontrast, –e** contrast; **die ~farbe, –n** contrasting colour; **k~reich** full of contrast
kontrastieren: ~ mit contrast with
kontrastiv *ling* contrastive
Kontroll– check ...; control ...; **der ~abschnitt, –e** counterfoil, stub; **die Kontrollampe, –n** pilot-light; indicator lamp; *mot* warning light; **die ~gruppe, –n** *med etc* control; **die ~karte, –n** time-card; **der ~punkt, –e** checkpoint; *mot sp* control; **der ~turm, ⸚e** control-tower; **die ~uhr, –en** time-clock
die **Kontrolle, –n** check; supervision; control; **die ~ verlieren über** (*acc*) lose control of; **außer ~ geraten** get out of control; **unter ~ haben/halten** have/keep under control
der **Kontrolleur** [–'lø:ɐ], **–e** inspector
kontrollieren check; inspect; supervise; control
der **Kontrollor, –e** *Aust* inspector
kontrovers controversial
die **Kontroverse, –n** dispute
die **Kontur, –en** contour
konturieren outline
die **Konvention, –en** convention
konventionell conventional
konvergent convergent
die **Konvergenz, –en** convergence
konvergieren converge
die **Konversation, –en** conversation; **das ~s|lexikon, –(k)a** encyclopaedia
die **Konversion, –en** conversion
der **Konverter, –** *comput, nucl tech, etc* converter
konvertierbar *fin* convertible
konvertieren *fin* convert (**in** *acc* into); **~ zu** (*also sn*) become a convert to
der **Konvertit, –en** (*wk masc*) convert
konvex convex
das **Konvikt, –e** seminary; *Aust* (Catholic) boarding-school
der **Konvoi, –s** convoy
das **Konvolut, –e** bundle (of papers)
konzedieren (+*dat*) grant
das **Konzentrat, –e** condensation (of sth.); *chem* concentrate
die **Konzentration, –en** concentration; **das ~s|lager, –** concentration camp; **die ~s|schwäche** lack of concentration
konzentrieren concentrate (*also chem*) (**auf** *acc*); **sich ~** concentrate (**auf** *acc* on); be concentrated (on); **konzentriert** concentrated (*also chem*); (*adv*) intently; with concentration
konzentrisch concentric
das **Konzept, –e** (rough) draft; plan, programme; **aus dem ~ bringen** put off his/her stride; **aus dem ~ kommen** lose the thread; (+*dat*) **nicht ins ~ passen** not suit (s.o.'s) book ||

das ~papier rough paper
die **Konzeption, –en** conception (*also biol*)
der **Konzern, –e** combine
das **Konzert, –e** concert; concerto; **ins ~ gehen** go to a concert || **der ~besucher, –** concert-goer; **der ~meister, –** leader (of orchestra)
konzertieren give a concert; **konzertiert** concerted
die **Konzession, –en** concession (*also min*); licence (to carry on a trade)
konzessionieren license
konzessiv *gramm* concessive
das **Konzil, –e/–ien** [–ĭən] *eccles* council
konziliant obliging, accommodating
die **Konzilianz** accommodating attitude
konzipieren draft; conceive
der **Koog,** *pl* **Köge** *NGer* polder
die **Ko|operation, –en** co-operation
ko|operativ, die Ko|operative, –n co-operative
ko|operieren co-operate
die **Ko|ordinate, –n** co-ordinate
die **Ko|ordination, –en** co-ordination
ko|ordinieren co-ordinate
Kopenhagen Copenhagen
der **Köper, –** twill
der **Kopf, ⸚e** head (*also* of cabbage, hammer, pin, *etc*); mind; heading, (of letter) head; (of pipe) bowl; (*with adj*) (capable *etc*) person; thinker; *pl* minds, brains; figures; **seinen ~ durchsetzen** get one's way; **~ und Kragen riskieren** risk one's neck; **seinen ~ verlieren** lose one's head; **~ hoch!** chin up!
in prepositional phrases:
~ an ~ shoulder to shoulder; neck and neck; (+*dat*) **an den ~ werfen** hurl (insults) at
auf den ~ hauen *coll* blow (money); **auf den ~ stellen** *coll* turn upside-down; stand (facts) on their heads; **er ist nicht auf den ~ gefallen** *coll* he wasn't born yesterday
aus dem ~ from memory; **sich** *dat* **... aus dem ~ schlagen** put out of one's mind; **... will mir nicht aus dem ~** *coll* I can't get ... out of my mind
durch den ~ gehen lassen think over
im ~ haben have in one's head; remember, carry in one's head; **nichts als ... im ~ haben** have on the brain; **sich** *dat* **... in den ~ setzen** set one's mind on; **... will mir nicht in den ~** *coll* I can't get ... into my head
pro ~ per head
über: (+*dat*) **über den ~ wachsen** outgrow; (thing) get on top of; **über jmds. ~ hinweg** over s.o.'s head
von ~ bis Fuß from top to toe
vor den ~ stoßen *coll* offend; **wie vor den ~ geschlagen** *coll* dumbfounded
zu: (+*dat*) **zu ~(e) steigen** go to (s.o.'s) head
Kopf–: das ~-an-~-Rennen, – neck-and-neck race; **die ~arbeit** brainwork; **der ~bahnhof, ⸚e** *rail* terminus; **der ~ball, ⸚e** header; **die ~bedeckung, –en** headgear; **das ~ende, –n** head (of bed, table); **das ~geld, –er** reward; **die ~haut, ⸚e** scalp; **der ~hörer, –** headphones; **der ~jäger, –** head-hunter; **das ~kissen, –** pillow; **der ~kissen|bezug, ⸚e** pillowcase; **~länge (um eine K.** by a head); **k~lastig** top-heavy; **k~los** headless; panicky; (*adv*) in a panic (**k. werden** lose one's head); **die ~losigkeit** panic; **das ~nicken** nod; **k~rechnen** (*only infin*) do mental arithmetic; **das ~rechnen** mental arithmetic; **der ~salat, –e** lettuce; **k~scheu** *coll* (**k. machen** intimidate; **k. werden** be intimidated); **die ~schmerzen** *pl* headache; **die ~schuppen** *pl* dandruff; **das ~schütteln** shake of the head; **k~schüttelnd** shaking one's head; **das ~spiel** heading (ball); **der ~sprung, ⸚e** *swim* header; **der ~stand, ⸚e** headstand; **k~stehen*** (*sep*) *coll* be beside oneself/bewildered; be in a state of turmoil; (world) be upside-down; **das ~stein|pflaster, –** cobblestones; **die ~stimme, –n** falsetto; **der ~stoß, ⸚e** *box* butt; *footb* header; **die ~stütze, –n** headrest; **das ~tuch, ⸚er** headscarf; **k~über** headlong; **das ~weh** *coll* headache; **die ~zahl, –en** number of persons; **~zerbrechen** *coll* ((+*dat*) **K. bereiten/machen** be a headache for; **sich** *dat* **K. machen über** (*acc*) worry about)
das **Köpfchen, –** little head; *coll* brains
köpfeln *Aust footb* head
köpfen behead; *footb* head
–köpfig -headed; -man; (*eg* **vier)~e Familie** family of (four *etc*)
die **Kopie, –(ie)n, kopieren** copy; duplicate; *phot* print
Kopier–: das ~gerät, –e photocopier; **der ~stift, –e** indelible pencil
der **Kopilot, –en** (*wk masc*) co-pilot
das **Koppel, –** *mil* (leather) belt
die **Koppel, –n** paddock; *hunt* pack (of hounds); leash
koppeln couple; link
die **Kopplung, –en** coupling; **das ~s|manöver, –** *space* docking
die **Koproduktion, –en** co-production
der **Koproduzent, –en** (*wk masc*) co-producer
kopulieren copulate
die **Koralle, –n** coral
der **Koran** the Koran
der **Korb, ⸚e** basket; **einen ~ bekommen** be turned down; (+*dat*) **einen ~ geben** turn

down

Korb– basket ...; wicker ...; **der ~ball** (*type of basketball*); **der ~blütler, –** *bot* composite; **das ~geflecht** wickerwork; **der ~sessel, – = der ~stuhl, ⸚e** wicker chair; **die ~waren** *pl* wickerwork

das **Körbchen, –** little basket; cup (of bra)

der **Kord = der ~samt** corduroy

die **Kordel, –n** cord (of dressing-gown *etc*)

die **Kordilleren** [–lj–] *pl* the Cordilleras

der **Kordon** [–'dɔ̃:], **–s** cordon

Korea Korea

der **Koreaner, –** Korean

koreanisch, (*language*) **K~** Korean

Korfu Corfu

Korinth Corinth

die **Korinthe, –n** currant

der **Kork** cork (= substance)

der **Korken, –** cork; stopper; **der ~zieher, –** corkscrew

der **Kormoran, –e** cormorant

das **Korn**[1], **⸚er** grain (*also phot*); corn, grain

das **Korn**[2], **–e** front sight; **aufs ~ nehmen** take aim at; *coll* attack (abuse *etc*)

der **Korn, –** *coll* schnapps (made from corn)

Korn–: die ~blume, –n cornflower; **korn|blumen|blau** cornflower blue; *coll* drunk as a lord; **der ~brannt|wein, –e** schnapps (made from corn); **die ~kammer, –n** granary

das **Körnchen, –** (small) grain; granule

körnen grain; granulate

das **Kornett, –e/–s** cornet

körnig granular; grainy

die **Korona, –(n)en** *astron* corona; *coll* crowd (of *esp* young people)

der **Körper, –** body; **am ganzen ~** all over (one's body)

Körper– body ...; ... of the body; bodily ...; physical ...; **der ~bau** build; **k~behindert** physically handicapped; **der/die ~behinderte** (*decl as adj*) disabled person; **der ~geruch** body odour; **die ~haltung, –en** posture; **die ~kultur** *EGer* physical education; **die ~pflege** personal hygiene; **die ~sprache** body language; **der ~teil, –e** part of the body

körperlich physical; (punishment) corporal

die **Körperschaft, –en** body; corporation; **die ~s|steuer, –n** corporation tax

der **Korporal, –e** *Swiss*/**⸚e** *Aust*: *Aust*, *Swiss* corporal

die **Korporation, –en** students' association

das **Korps** [ko:ɐ] (*gen* **–** [–(s)]), **–** [–s] *mil etc* corps; *univ* duelling corps; **der ~geist** esprit de corps

korpulent corpulent

die **Korpulenz** corpulence

der **Korpus, –se** *joc* body

das **Korpuskel, –n** corpuscle

korrekt correct

das **Korrektiv, –e** corrective

der **Korrektor, –(or)en** proof-reader

die **Korrektur, –en** correction; *print* proof-reading; proof; **die ~flüssigkeit, –en** correcting fluid

der **Korrespondent, –en** (*wk masc*) *journ*, *comm* correspondent

die **Korrespondenz, –en** correspondence

korrespondieren: ~ mit correspond with (*also* = match)

der **Korridor, –e** corridor (*also pol*)

korrigieren correct

korrodieren (*sn if v/i*) corrode

die **Korrosion, –en** corrosion

korrumpieren corrupt; **korrumpiert** corrupt

korrupt corrupt

die **Korruption, –en** corruption

die **Korsage** [–ʒə], **–n** strapless bodice

der **Korsar, –en** (*wk masc*) corsair

der **Korse, –n** (*wk masc*) Corsican

das **Korsett, –e/–s** corset; **die ~stange, –n** stay

Korsika Corsica

korsisch Corsican

der **Korso, –s** procession

das **Kortison** cortisone

die **Korvette, –n** corvette; **der ~n|kapitän, –e** lieutenant-commander

die **Koryphäe** [–ə], **–n** eminent authority

der **Kosak, –en** (*wk masc*) Cossack

koscher [–o:–] kosher

Kose–: die ~form, –en pet form; **der ~name, –n** (*like* **Name**) pet name; **das ~wort, ⸚er** term of endearment

kosen *poet*: **~ mit** caress

die **Kosmetik** [–ɪk] beauty culture; **chirurgische ~** cosmetic surgery || **der ~koffer, –** vanity-case

die **Kosmetika** *pl* cosmetics

die **Kosmetikerin, –nen** cosmetician

kosmetisch cosmetic

kosmisch cosmic

der **Kosmonaut, –en** (*wk masc*) cosmonaut

der **Kosmopolit, –en** (*wk masc*), **kosmopolitisch** cosmopolitan

der **Kosmos** [–ɔs] cosmos

die **Kost** food, fare; diet; **~ und Logis** [–'ʒi:] board and lodging || **das ~geld** board; **die ~probe, –n** taste; sample; **k~spielig** costly, expensive; **~ver|ächter** *coll* (**kein K. sein** like good food; fancy the girls)

kostbar precious, valuable

die **Kostbarkeit, –en** preciousness, great value; precious object

kosten[1] cost; take (time, effort, *etc*); **koste es, was es wolle** cost what it may; **sich** *acc/dat* **... etwas/(1000 Mark** *etc*) **~ lassen** *coll* spend a lot/(1000 marks *etc*) on

kosten[2] taste, sample; taste (happiness *etc*)

die **Kosten** *pl* cost(s); **die ~ tragen** bear the

cost(s); **auf ~** (+*gen*) at the expense of; **auf jmds. ~ gehen** be at s.o.'s expense; **auf seine ~ kommen** be well satisfied || **der ~anschlag, ⸚e** estimate; **der ~aufwand** outlay; **k~los** free of charge; **der ~punkt** matter of the cost; *coll* cost; **der ~vor|anschlag, ⸚e** estimate

köstlich delicious; delightful; priceless

die **Köstlichkeit, –en** deliciousness *etc*; delicacy; (literary) gem

das **Kostüm, –e** (woman's) suit; fancy-dress; *theat* costume; **das ~fest, –e** fancy-dress ball

kostümieren: sich ~ dress up; **kostümiert** in costume

der **Kot** excrement; droppings; mud; **der ~flügel, –** wing, fender *US*

der **Kotau, –s** kowtow; **~ machen** kowtow (**vor** *dat* to)

das **Kotelett** [kɔtl–], **–s** chop; cutlet

die **Koteletten** [kɔtl–] *pl* sideboards, sideburns

der **Köter, –** *coll* cur

kotig filthy

die **Kotze**[1], **–n** *SGer* woollen cape/blanket

die **Kotze**[2] *vulg* puke

kotzen *vulg* puke; **... ist zum Kotzen! ...** is enough to make you puke!

die **KPD/KPÖ/KPdSU = Kommunistische Partei Deutschlands/Österreichs/der Sowjetunion**

die **Krabbe, –n** shrimp; crab; *joc* tot; young thing

krabb(e)lig *coll* ticklish

krabbeln *coll* tickle; (*v/i sn*) crawl

krach! crash!

der **Krach, –s/–e/***coll* **⸚e** crash; row, racket; *coll* row, bust-up; *coll fin* crash; **~ machen** make a racket; *coll* = **~ schlagen** kick up a row

krachen crash; creak; crack; (*sn*) split; (ice) crack; *coll* (bank *etc*) crash; **~ gegen** (*sn*) crash into; **sich ~** *coll* have a row; **... daß es nur so kracht** *coll* with a bang; with a vengeance

krächzen caw; croak

der **Kräcker, –** cracker

das **Krad, ⸚er** *esp mil* = **Kraftrad**

kraft (+*gen*) by virtue of

die **Kraft, ⸚e** strength; energy; power; force (*also phys*); worker, employee, *pl* staff, personnel; **aus eigener ~** by one's own efforts; **außer ~ setzen** cancel; **außer ~ treten** become invalid; **wieder bei Kräften sein** have got one's strength back; **in ~** in force; **in ~ treten** come into force; **nach (besten) Kräften** to the best of one's ability; **(wieder) zu Kräften kommen** recover one's strength || **der ~akt, –e** strong-man act; **der ~aufwand** (expenditure of) effort; **der ~ausdruck, ⸚e** swear-word; (*pl*) strong language; **die ~brühe, –n** consommé; **der ~fahrer, –** motorist; **das ~fahrzeug, –e** motor vehicle; **der ~fahrzeug|brief, –e** registration book/certificate *US*; **die ~fahrzeug|steuer, –n** road tax, automobile tax *US*; **k~los** weak; **der ~meier, –** *coll* muscle-man; tough guy; **der ~mensch, –en** (*wk masc*) muscle-man; **die ~post** post-bus (service); **die ~probe, –n** trial of strength; **das ~rad, ⸚er** motor-cycle; **der ~stoff, –e** fuel; **k~strotzend** bursting with energy; **die ~übertragung, –en** (power) transmission; **k~voll** powerful; forceful; **der ~wagen, –** motor vehicle (with more than two wheels); **das ~werk, –e** power station

Kräfte–... of forces/energy; **das ~spiel** interplay of forces; **das ~verhältnis, –se** relative strength

kräftig strong; forceful; vigorous; (swig *etc*) big; nourishing; **~e Ausdrücke** strong language

kräftigen strengthen

der **Kragen, –/***SGer also* **Krägen** collar; **es geht ihm an den ~** *coll* he's in for it || **der ~knopf, ⸚e** collar stud; **die ~nummer, –n** = **die ~weite, –n** collar size

die **Krähe, –n, krähen** crow

Krähen–: die ~füße *pl* crow's-feet; scrawl; **das ~nest, –er** crow's-nest

Krakau Cracow

der **Krake, –n** (*wk masc*) octopus

der **Krakeel** *coll* row

krakeelen (*p/part* **krakeelt**) *coll* kick up a racket

die **Krakelei, –en** *coll* scrawl

krakelig *coll* spidery

krakeln *coll* scrawl

der **Kral, –e** kraal

die **Kralle, –n** claw; talon

krallen shape like a claw; *coll* 'pinch'; nab; **~ in** (*acc*) dig (fingers *etc*) into; **sich ~ an** (*acc*) cling to; **sich ~ in** (*acc*) dig one's fingers into; (nails) dig into

der **Kram** *coll* junk; things; business; **mach deinen ~ alleine!** you can jolly well do it yourself!; (+*dat*) **nicht in den ~ passen** not suit (s.o.'s) book || **der ~laden, ..läden** small shop selling a wide assortment of cheap goods

kramen *coll* rummage about (**nach** for)

der **Krämer, –** petty-minded person; *arch* small shopkeeper; **die ~seele, –n** petty-minded person

die **Krampe, –n** (U-shaped) staple

der **Krampen, –** (U-shaped) staple; *Aust* pick-axe

der **Krampf, ⸚e** cramp; spasm; convulsion; **... ist ~** *coll* **...** is forced/unnatural; **einen ~ bekommen** get cramp || **die ~ader, –n** varicose vein; **k~artig** convulsive

krampfhaft convulsive; frantic; forced

[der] **Kran, ⸚e** crane

[der] **Kranich, –e** *ornith* crane

krank (*comp, superl* ⸚) sick, ill; ailing; **~ machen** *coll* get on (s.o.'s) nerves; **sich ~ melden** report sick; **~ schreiben** give (s.o.) a medical certificate; **~ werden** fall ill; **der/die Kranke** (*decl as adj*) sick person; patient || **~feiern** (*sep*) *coll* stay away from work (on the pretext of being ill); **~lachen** (*sep*): **sich k.** *coll* laugh oneself silly; **~machen** (*sep*) *coll* (= **~feiern**)

kränkeln be in poor health; **~d** ailing

kranken: ~ an (*dat*) suffer from (lack *etc*)

kränken wound, hurt

Kranken–: der ~bericht, –e medical report; **das ~bett, –en** sick-bed; **das ~geld, –er** sickness benefit; **die ~geschichte, –n** medical history; **die ~gymnastik** physiotherapy; **die ~gymnastin, –nen** physiotherapist; **das ~haus, ⸚er** hospital (**im/ins K.** in/(in)to (the *US*) hospital); **die ~kasse, –n** health insurance scheme; **das ~lager, –** sick-bed; **die ~pflege** nursing; **der ~pfleger, –** male nurse; **der ~saal, ..säle** ward; **der ~schein, –e** health insurance certificate (entitling patient to treatment); **die ~schwester, –n** nurse; **~stand** *Aust* (**im K. sein** be off sick); **die ~versicherung, –en** health insurance; **der ~wagen, –** ambulance; **das ~zimmer, –** sick-room

krankhaft diseased; morbid; pathological

[die] **Krankheit, –en** illness; disease; **das ~s|bild, –er** syndrome; **der ~s|erreger, –** germ; **die ~s|erscheinung, –en** symptom; **k~s|halber** owing to illness; **der ~s|überträger, –** carrier (of disease)

kränklich sickly

[die] **Kränkung, –en** *vbl noun*; *also* insult

[der] **Kranz, ⸚e** garland; wreath; circle, ring; **das ~gefäß, –e** coronary artery

[das] **Kränzchen, –** small garland/wreath; (women's) coffee *etc* circle

[der] **Krapfen, –** *esp SGer* doughnut

kraß (–ss–) crass; glaring; blatant

[der] **Krater, –** crater

Kratz–: die ~bürste, –n *coll* prickly woman; **k~bürstig** *coll* prickly; **das ~eisen, –** (shoe-)scraper

[die] **Krätze** scabies

kratzen (*also v/i*) scratch; scrape

[der] **Kratzer, –** scraper; *coll* scratch

kratzig *coll* scratchy, prickly; (voice) rasping

[das] **Kraul = der ~stil** *swim* crawl

kraulen[1] fondle; stroke (one's beard); **unter dem Kinn ~** chuck under the chin

kraulen[2] *swim* do the crawl; (*sn*) swim (somewhere) doing the crawl

kraus crinkly; frizzy; wrinkled; (ideas *etc*) muddled; **~ ziehen** knit (one's brow); screw up (one's nose) || **der K~kopf, ⸚e** frizzy head; frizzy-headed person

[die] **Krause, –n** ruff; ruffle

kräuseln curl; crimp; pucker (lips), screw up (nose); (wind) ruffle; *dressm* gather; **sich ~** curl; (smoke) curl up; (water) ripple

[das] **Kraut, ⸚er** herb; (of turnips *etc*) tops; *SGer* cabbage; sauerkraut; *coll* tobacco; **wie ~ und Rüben** *coll* higgledy-piggledy; **gegen ... ist kein ~ gewachsen** *coll* nothing can be done about; **ins ~ schießen** get out of hand

Kräuter– herb ...; herbal ...

[der] **Krawall, –e** riot; *coll* din, racket

[die] **Krawatte, –n** tie; **die ~n|nadel, –n** tie-pin

kraxeln (*sn*) *esp SGer coll* clamber

[die] **Kreation, –en** *fash* creation

kreativ creative

[die] **Kreativität** creativity

[die] **Kreatur, –en** creature (*also* = tool of s.o.)

kreatürlich animal

[der] **Krebs** [–e:ps], **–e** crab; crayfish, crawfish *US*; *med* cancer; *bot* canker; *astron, astrol* Cancer; **k~artig** crablike; *med* cancerous; **k~erregend** carcinogenic; **das ~geschwür, –e** cancerous ulcer; cancer, canker (in society); **k~krank** suffering from cancer; **krebs|rot** as red as a lobster; **der ~schaden, ..schäden** chief ill; **das ~tier, –e** crustacean

[die] **Kredenz, –en** *arch exc Aust* sideboard

kredenzen (*p/part* **kredenzt**) (+*dat*) proffer

[der] **Kredit, –e** credit; loan; **auf ~** on credit || **k~fähig** creditworthy; **der ~geber, –** creditor; **der ~hai, –e** *coll* loan shark; **die ~karte, –n** credit-card

kreditieren (+*dat*) credit to; give (s.o. sth.) in the form of a credit

kregel *NGer coll* lively

[die] **Kreide** chalk; **(tief) in der ~ sein/stehen bei** *coll* be (deep) in debt to || **kreide|bleich** as white as a sheet

kreidig chalky

kreieren [kre–] *fash, theat* create

[der] **Kreis, –e** circle; (administrative) district; sphere; *elect* circuit; **weite ~e der Bevölkerung** wide sections of the population; **seine ~e ziehen** circle; **(weite) ~e ziehen** have (wide) repercussions

Kreis– *also* circular ...; *math* ... of a circle; **die ~bahn, –en** orbit; **k~förmig** circular; (*adv*) in a circle; **der ~lauf** circulation; cycle; **~lauf–** circulatory ...; **kreis|rund** circular; **die ~säge, –n** circular saw; *coll* boater; **die ~stadt, ⸚e** chief town of a *Landkreis*; **der ~verkehr** roundabout traffic, rotary traffic *US*

kreischen screech; shriek

[der] **Kreisel, –** spinning-top; *tech* gyroscope

kreisen (*also sn*) circle; circulate; **~ um** circle round; revolve around

[der] **Kreiß|saal, ..säle** labour ward

[die] **Krem, –s** cream (filling)

das **Krematorium, –(i)en** crematorium
der **Kreml** [–eː–, –ɛ–] (*gen* –(s)) the Kremlin
die **Krempe, –n** brim
der **Krempel** *coll* junk
der **Kren** *Aust* horseradish
der **Kreole, –n** (*wk masc*), **kreolisch** Creole
krepieren (*sn*) explode; *coll* (animal) die; *vulg* kick the bucket; die a miserable death
der **Krepp, –s/–e** crêpe; **die ~sohle, –n** crêpe sole
die **Kresse, –n** cress
Kreta Crete
Krethi: ~ und Plethi *coll* every Tom, Dick and Harry
der **Kretin** [–'tɛ̃ː], **–s** cretin
kreuz: ~ und quer this way and that; criss-cross
das **Kreuz, –e** cross; small of the back; *mot* intersection; *cards* clubs, (card: *pl* –) club; *mus* sharp; **es ist ein ~ mit ...** *coll* ... is *etc* a big problem; **drei ~e machen hinter** (*dat*) wish (s.o.) good riddance; **aufs ~ legen** throw flat on his/her back; *coll* take for a ride; *vulg* 'lay'; **über ~** crosswise (one on top of the other); **zu ~e kriechen** eat humble pie
Kreuz– cross ...; *cards* ... of clubs; **(kreuz–)** *coll* awfully ...; **der ~fahrer, –** crusader; **die ~fahrt, –en** cruise; *hist* crusade; **das ~feuer** crossfire (**im K. stehen** be under fire from all sides); **der ~gang, ⸗e** cloister; **k~lahm** *coll* (**ich bin k.** my back aches); **die ~otter, –n** adder; **der ~ritter, –** crusader; **die ~schmerzen** *pl* pains in the small of the back; **kreuz|unglücklich** *coll* absolutely miserable; **das ~verhör, –e** cross-examination (**ins K. nehmen** cross-examine); **der ~weg, –e** crossroads; *relig* way of the Cross; **k~weise** crosswise; **das ~wort|rätsel, –** crossword (puzzle); **der ~zug, ⸗e** crusade
kreuzen cross (*also biol*); (*v/i, also sn*) cruise; tack; **sich ~** cross, intersect; (letters) cross; (interests *etc*) clash; **ihre Blicke kreuzten sich** their eyes met
der **Kreuzer, –** cruiser; *hist* kreutzer
kreuzigen crucify
die **Kreuzigung, –en** crucifixion
die **Kreuzung, –en** cross-roads, intersection; *biol* crossing; cross
kribb(e)lig *coll* edgy
kribbeln: es kribbelt mir auf der Haut/in der Nase *etc* my skin/nose *etc* is itching; **es kribbelt (und krabbelt) von** the place is swarming with
krickeln *coll* scrawl
das **Kricket** [–ət] cricket; **der ~spieler, –** cricketer
Kriech–: die ~spur, –en crawler lane, creeper lane *US*; trail (of snail *etc*); **das ~tier, –e** reptile
kriechen (*p/t* **kroch** (*subj* **kröche**), *p/part* **gekrochen**) (*sn*) creep; crawl; **~ vor** (*dat*) (*also sn*) *coll* crawl to
der **Kriecher, –** crawler
kriecherisch bootlicking
der **Krieg, –e** war; warfare; **der kalte ~** the Cold War; (+*dat*) **den ~ erklären** *mil*/**ansagen** declare war on; **~ führen** wage war (**mit/gegen** against) || **k~führend** warring, belligerent; **die ~führung** warfare; conduct of the war
kriegen *coll* = **bekommen** (*a*)
der **Krieger, –** warrior; **das ~denkmal, ⸗er** war memorial; **die ~witwe, –n** war widow
kriegerisch warlike
Kriegs– ... of war; war ...; wartime ...; **der ~beginn** start of the war; **das ~beil, –e** tomahawk (**das K. begraben** bury the hatchet); **die ~bemalung, –en** war-paint; **k~beschädigt** war-disabled; **der ~dienst|verweigerer, –** conscientious objector; **das ~ende** end of the war; **die ~erklärung, –en** declaration of war (**an** *acc* on); **~fuß** (**auf K. stehen mit** be at daggers drawn with); **der/die ~gefangene** (*decl as adj*) prisoner of war; **das ~gericht, –e** court-martial (**vor ein K. stellen** court-martial); **der ~gewinnler, –** war profiteer; **die ~marine, –n** navy; **k~müde** war-weary; **~pfad** (**auf dem K.** on the warpath); **der ~rat** council of war; **das ~recht** conventions of war; martial law; **der ~schau|platz, ⸗e** theatre of war; **das ~schiff, –e** warship; **die ~schuld** war guilt; **das ~verbrechen, –** war crime; **der ~verbrecher, –** war criminal; **k~versehrt** war-disabled; **das ~ziel, –e** war aim; **der ~zustand** state of war (**im K.** at war)
die **Krim** [–ɪ–] Crimea; **der ~krieg** the Crimean War
der **Krimi** [–ɪ–], **–s** *coll* crime novel; thriller
Kriminal– criminal ...; crime ...; **der ~be|amte** (*decl as adj*) detective; **der ~kommissar, –e** detective superintendent; **die ~polizei** criminal investigation department; **der ~roman, –e** detective novel
der **Kriminale** (*decl as adj*) *coll* detective
kriminalisieren drive to crime; make out to be criminal
der **Kriminalist, –en** (*wk masc*) detective; criminologist
die **Kriminalistik** [–ɪk] criminology
kriminalistisch criminological
die **Kriminalität** crime (*collect*); crime-rate
kriminell, der/die Kriminelle (*decl as adj*) criminal
der **Krimskrams** *coll* odds and ends; junk
der **Kringel, –** (small) ring; ring-shaped biscuit
kringelig curly; **sich ~ lachen** *coll* double up (with laughter)
kringeln: sich ~ curl; **sich (vor Lachen) ~** *coll*

double up (with laughter)

die **Krinoline, –n** crinoline

die **Kripo = Kriminalpolizei**

die **Krippe, –n** crib; crèche; **das ~n|spiel, –e** nativity play; **der ~n|tod** cot death, crib death *US*

die **Krise, –n** crisis

kriseln: es kriselt there is a crisis looming

Krisen– crisis ...; **k~n|fest** stable; **der ~n|herd, –e** trouble-spot

das **Kristall** crystal (glass)

der **Kristall, –e** crystal

Kristall–: kristall|klar crystal-clear; **die ~nacht** the Night of the Broken Glass (*pogrom of 9-10 November 1938*)

kristallen crystal; crystalline

kristallisieren, sich ~ crystallize

das **Kriterium, –(i)en** criterion

die **Kritik, –en** criticism (**an** *dat* of); notice, review; (the) critics; **~ üben an** (*dat*) criticize; **unter aller ~** beneath contempt || **die ~fähigkeit** critical faculty; **k~los** uncritical

der **Kritiker, –** critic

kritisch critical

kritisieren criticize

die **Krittelei, –en** fault-finding

kritteln find fault (**an** *dat* with)

die **Kritzelei, –en** scribble; scribbling

kritz(e)lig *coll* scrawly

kritzeln scribble

der **Kroate, –n** (*wk masc*) Croat

Kroatien [–tsĭən] Croatia

kroatisch Croatian

kroch (kröche) *p/t* (*subj*) *of* **kriechen**

das **Krocket** [*also* 'krɔkət] croquet

der **Krokant** cracknel

die **Krokette, –n** croquette

das **Kroko** crocodile leather

das **Krokodil, –e** crocodile; **die ~s|tränen** *pl* crocodile tears

der **Krokus, –(se)** crocus

Kron– crown ...; **der ~leuchter, –** chandelier; **der ~prinz, –en** (*wk masc*) crown prince; **der ~zeuge, –n** (*wk masc*) person who turns King's/Queen's/*US* State's evidence

die **Krone, –n** crown; coronet; crown (of tooth, tree), crest (of wave); (Czech) crown, (Danish, Norwegian) krone, (Icelandic, Swedish) krona; *bot* corolla; **das setzt allem die ~ auf!** *coll* that beats everything!; **einen in der ~ haben** *coll* have had a drop too much

krönen crown

die **Krönung, –en** coronation; culmination

der **Kropf, ⸚e** *med* goitre; *zool* crop

das **Kropp|zeug** *coll* riff-raff; junk

kroß (–ss–) *NGer* crisp

Krösus, (= wealthy man) **der ~, –se** Croesus

die **Kröte, –n** toad; (*pl*) *coll* pennies; **kleine ~** *coll* little scamp

Krück–: der ~stock, ⸚e walking-stick

die **Krücke, –n** crutch; crook (of umbrella handle); *coll* (= person) washout

der **Krug, ⸚e** jug; beer-mug; *NGer* inn

die **Kruke, –n** *NGer* stone jug

die **Krume, –n** crumb; *agr* top-soil

der **Krümel, –** crumb

krümelig crumbly

krümeln make crumbs; (cake *etc*) crumble

krumm (*comp, superl* ⸚) bent; crooked (*also* = dishonest); (*adv*: walk) with a stoop; **~e Finger machen** *coll* be light-fingered; **einen ~en Rücken machen** stoop; bow and scrape || **~beinig** bow-legged; **~lachen** (*sep*): **sich k.** *coll* laugh oneself silly; **~legen** (*sep*): **sich k.** *coll* pinch and scrape; **~nehmen*** (*sep*) *coll* take amiss; **der K~säbel, –** scimitar; **der K~stab, ⸚e** crozier

krümmen bend; (cat) arch; **sich ~** bend; (river *etc*) wind; writhe; double up

die **Krümmung, –en** *vbl noun*; *also* bend, curve; *math, phys, med* curvature

krumpfen pre-shrink

der **Krüppel, –, zum ~ machen** cripple

krüpp(e)lig crippled; (growth) stunted

die **Kruste, –n** crust; *med* scab; **das ~n|tier, –e** crustacean

krustig crusty

die **Krux = Crux**

das **Kruzifix** [*also* –'fɪks], **–e** crucifix

Kruzitürken! *SGer* damnation!; heavens!

die **Krypta, –(t)en** crypt

die **KSZE** (= **Konferenz über Sicherheit und Zusammenarbeit in Europa**) Conference on Security and Co-operation in Europe

Kuba Cuba

der **Kubaner, –, kubanisch** Cuban

der **Kübel, –** tub; bucket

Kubik (*no art*) *mot* c.c.; *in compds* cubic ...; **die ~wurzel, –n** cube root

kubisch cubic

der **Kubismus** cubism

der **Kubist, –en** (*wk masc*), **kubistisch** cubist

der **Kubus, –(b)en** *math* cube

die **Küche, –n** kitchen; cooking, cuisine; kitchen furniture and fittings; **kalte ~** cold dishes

der **Kuchen** [–u:–], **–** cake; **das ~blech, –e** baking-sheet; **die ~form, –en** cake-tin; **die ~gabel, –n** pastry-fork; **der ~teig, –e** cake mixture

Küchen– kitchen ...; **das ~gerät, –e** kitchen utensil(s); **das ~kraut, ⸚er** pot-herb; **das ~latein** dog Latin; **die ~maschine, –n** (electric) kitchen appliance; mixer; **der ~meister, –** chef; **die ~schabe, –n** cockroach

kucken *NGer* = **gucken**

kuckuck! cuckoo!

[der] **Kuckuck, -e** cuckoo; **hol dich der ~!** get lost!; **(das) weiß der ~!** heaven (only) knows!; **zum ~ (noch mal)!** hell's bells! || **die ~s|uhr, -en** cuckoo-clock

[der] **Kuddelmuddel** (*also* **das**) *coll* muddle

[die] **Kufe, -n** runner (of sledge *etc*); *aer* skid

[die] **Kugel, -n** bullet; ball; sphere; *athl* shot; **die ~ stoßen** put the shot; **eine ruhige ~ schieben** *coll* have a cushy job; **sich** *dat* **eine ~ durch den Kopf jagen** *coll* blow one's brains out

Kugel– *also* spherical ...; **k~förmig** spherical; **das ~gelenk, -e** *anat*, *mech* ball-and-socket joint; **der ~hagel** hail of bullets; **die ~kopf(schreib)maschine, -n** golf-ball typewriter; **das ~lager, -** ball-bearing; **kugel|rund** as round as a ball; *coll* tubby; **der ~schreiber, -** ball-point (pen); **k~sicher** bullet-proof; **das ~stoßen** shot-put

kug(e)lig spherical; **sich ~ lachen** *coll* double up (with laughter)

kugeln (*sn*) roll; **sich ~** roll about; *coll* double up (with laughter); **... ist zum Kugeln** *coll* ... is hilarious

[die] **Kuh, ⸗e** cow; **heilige ~** sacred cow || **das ~dorf, ⸗er** *coll* one-horse town; **der ~fladen, -** cow-pat; **der ~handel, ..händel** *coll* (piece of) horse-trading; **~haut** *coll* (**auf keine K. gehen** be beyond belief); **die ~milch** cow's milk; **die ~pocken** *pl* cow-pox; **der ~stall, ⸗e** cow-shed

kühl cool; **mir wird ~** I feel chilly

Kühl– *tech* cooling ...; **die ~anlage, -n** cold-storage plant; *rail* cooling unit; **das ~mittel, -** coolant; **der ~raum, ⸗e** cold-storage room; **das ~schiff, -e** refrigerator ship; **der ~schrank, ⸗e** refrigerator; **die ~tasche, -n** cool bag; **die ~truhe, -n** freezer; **der ~turm, ⸗e** cooling-tower

[die] **Kühle** cool(ness); coolness (of manner *etc*)

kühlen cool; chill; refrigerate

[der] **Kühler, -** cooler; ice-bucket; *chem* condenser; *mot* radiator; *coll* = **die ~haube, -n** bonnet, hood *US*

kühn bold

kujonieren *coll* harass, bully

k. u. k. ['kaːʔʊnt'kaː] (= **kaiserlich und königlich**) Austro-Hungarian

[das] **Küken, -** chick; *coll* little girl

[der] **Kukuruz** ['kukurʊts] (*gen* **-(es)**) *esp Aust* maize

kulant obliging; (terms *etc*) generous

[die] **Kulanz** willingness to oblige; generosity

[der] **Kuli**[1], **-s** coolie

[der] **Kuli**[2], **-s** *coll* ball-point (pen)

kulinarisch culinary

[die] **Kulisse, -n** flat, piece of scenery, *pl* scenery; backdrop; **das ist alles nur ~** that's only a façade; **hinter den ~n** behind the scenes || **der ~n|schieber, -** scene-shifter

[die] **Kuller|augen** *pl coll* big round eyes

kullern (*sn if v/i*) *coll* roll

[die] **Kulmination, -en** culmination (*also astron*)

kulminieren culminate (*also astron*) (**in** *dat* in)

[der] **Kult, -e** cult; worship; **(einen) ~ treiben mit** make a cult of

Kult– *also* ... of worship; ritual ...; **die ~stätte, -n** place of worship

kultisch ritual

kultivieren cultivate; **kultiviert** cultured, sophisticated; civilized

[die] **Kultivierung** cultivation

[die] **Kultur, -en** culture; civilization; *agr* cultivation; *biol*, *med* culture; **(keine) ~ haben** be (un)cultured; **in ~ nehmen** bring under cultivation

Kultur– ... of culture/civilization; culture ...; cultural ...; *agr* cultivated ...; **der ~banause, -n** (*wk masc*) *coll* philistine; **die ~beilage, -n** arts supplement; **der ~beutel, -** toilet bag; **k~fähig** cultivable; **der ~film, -e** documentary (film); **die ~geographie** human geography; **die ~geschichte, -n** cultural history; history of civilization; **das ~gut, ⸗er** thing of cultural value; (*collect*) cultural heritage/wealth; **die ~hoheit** cultural and educational autonomy; **k~los** uncultured; **der ~raum, ⸗e** area with a common culture; *EGer* room (in factory) for cultural functions; **die ~revolution** *Chinese hist* the Cultural Revolution; **der ~schock, -s** culture shock; **die ~sprache, -n** civilized/literary language; **der ~träger, -** person who/thing that contributes to the transmission of cultural values; **das ~volk, ⸗er** civilized nation; **das ~zentrum, -(r)en** cultural centre; arts centre

kulturell cultural

Kultus–: die ~gemeinde, -n religious community; **der ~minister, -** minister of education and the arts; **das ~ministerium, -(i)en** ministry of education and the arts

[der] **Kümmel, -** caraway; = **der ~brannt|wein** kümmel; **der ~türke, -n** (*wk masc*) *coll* Turk

kümmeln *coll*: **einen ~** have a drink

[der] **Kummer** grief, sorrow; distress; (+*dat*) **~ bereiten/machen** cause (s.o.) worry· grieve || **k~voll** sorrowful

kümmerlich meagre; miserable

[der] **Kümmerling, -e** stunted plant/animal; *coll* weakling

kümmern concern; **was kümmert mich das?** what's that to me?; **das kümmert mich nicht** that doesn't bother me

sich ~ um look after; see to; bother about

[der] **Kumpan, -e** *coll* pal

[der] **Kumpel, -/***coll* **-s** miner; *coll* (work-)mate

kumulieren accumulate

kund–: die K~gabe announcement; **~geben*** (*sep*) announce; **die K~gebung, –en** (political) rally; manifestation; **~machen** (*sep*) *esp Aust* promulgate; **die K~machung, –en** *SGer* (official) announcement; **~tun*** (*sep*) make known

kündbar terminable; redeemable

der **Kunde, –n** (*wk masc*) customer; *coll* (nasty *etc*) customer

die **Kunde** news, tidings; **–kunde** '*study of …*', *eg* **die Völker~** ethnology, **die Meeres~** oceanography, **die Stil~** stylistics, **die England~** *approx* = British Life and Institutions

Kunden–: der ~dienst after-sales service; **der ~kreis, –e** clientele

künden: ~ von tell of; bear witness to

kundig well-informed; expert; (+*gen*) **~ sein** have a knowledge of (language *etc*), (*eg* **des Lesens**) be able to (read *etc*)

kündigen cancel; terminate; *fin* foreclose; *coll or Aust* give (s.o.) notice; (*v/i*) give in one's notice; (+*dat*) give (s.o.) his/her notice; give (s.o.) notice to quit; (+*dat*) **die Stellung/Wohnung ~** give (s.o.) notice; (+*dat*) **die Freundschaft ~** break with; (+*dat*) **den Gehorsam ~** refuse to obey

die **Kündigung, –en** notice; cancellation; termination; notice to quit; *fin* foreclosure; **die ~s|frist, –en** (period of) notice; **der ~s|termin, –e** last day for giving notice

die **Kundschaft**[1], **–en** clientele, customers; *Aust* customer

die **Kundschaft**[2], **–en** reconnaissance; *arch* news

der **Kundschafter, –** *mil etc* scout

künftig future; … to come; (*adv*) = **künftig|hin** in future

kungeln *coll* do a secret deal

die **Kunst, ⸚e** art; skill; **die schönen Künste** the fine arts; **die ~ zu …** the art of (+*ger*); **das ist keine ~** *coll* there's nothing to it; **was macht die ~?** *coll* how's tricks?; **mit seiner ~ am/zu Ende sein** be at one's wits' end; **nach allen Regeln der ~** in textbook fashion; *coll* good and proper

Kunst– art …; artificial …, synthetic …; **das ~druck|papier** art paper; **der ~dünger, –** artificial fertilizer; **die ~faser, –n** man-made fibre; **der ~fehler, –** *med* professional error; **k~fertig** skilful; **die ~fertigkeit, –en** skill; **der ~flug, ⸚e** aerobatics; **die ~form, –en** art-form; **der ~freund, –e** art-lover; **der ~gegenstand, ⸚e** objet d'art; **k~gerecht** expert; **die ~geschichte, –n** history of art; **das ~gewerbe, –** arts and crafts; **der ~griff, –e** trick; **der ~händler, –** art dealer; **die ~handlung, –en** art dealer's shop; **das ~leder** imitation leather; **das ~lied, –er** (*opp* **Volkslied**) lied; **k~los** plain, unsophisticated; **die ~pause, –n** (rhetorical) pause; *joc* (awkward) pause; **der ~reiter, –** trick rider; **die ~richtung, –en** *arts* school; **der ~sammler, –** art-collector; **die ~seide** rayon; **der ~sinn** artistic sense; **der ~stoff, –e** synthetic material; (*pl*) plastics; **~stoff–** plastic …; plastics …; **k~stopfen** (*only infin and p/part* **k~gestopft**) repair by invisible mending; **das ~stück, –e** feat; trick, stunt (**K.!** no wonder!; **das ist kein K.** there's nothing to it); **der ~tischler, –** cabinet-maker; **k~verständig** with an appreciation of art; **k~voll** artistic; elaborate; **das ~werk, –e** work of art

der **Künstler, –** artist; artiste; past master; **der ~name, –n** (*like* **Name**) pseudonym; *theat* stage-name

künstlerisch artistic

das **Künstlertum** artistic nature; artistry

künstlich artificial; forced

kunterbunt *coll* motley; full of variety; chaotic; **~ durcheinander** higgledy-piggledy; **das Kunterbunt** jumble

das **Kupee, –s** *Aust rail* compartment

das **Kupfer** copper; **das ~geld** coppers; **der ~stich, –e** copperplate engraving (= process, print)

kupfern copper

kupieren dock (tail)

der **Kupon** [–'põ:], **–s** = **Coupon**

die **Kuppe, –n** rounded peak; tip (of finger)

die **Kuppel, –n** cupola, dome

die **Kuppelei, –en** matchmaking; *leg* procuring

kuppeln couple; join; (*v/i*) matchmake; *mot* engage the clutch

der **Kuppler, –** matchmaker; *leg* procurer

die **Kupplung, –en** *mech* coupling; *mot* clutch; **die ~s|scheibe, –n** clutch-plate; **das ~s|seil, –e** clutch cable

die **Kur, –en** cure (*esp* at a health resort); (course of) treatment; **eine ~ machen** take a cure

die **Kür, –en** = **die ~übung, –en** *gym* voluntary exercises; *skat* free skating

Kur– spa …; *hist* Electorate of …; **der ~fürst, –en** (*wk masc*) *hist* elector; **das ~fürstentum, ⸚er** *hist* electorate; **der ~gast, ⸚e** visitor to a spa; **der ~ort, –e** health resort; spa; **der ~pfuscher, –** quack; **die ~taxe, –n** visitors' tax (at health resort, spa)

Kuratel: unter ~ stehen be under close supervision; **unter ~ stellen** keep a close watch on

der **Kurator, –(or)en** keeper, curator; trustee

das **Kuratorium, –(i)en** committee; board of trustees

die **Kurbel, –n** crank; handle; **das ~gehäuse, –** crankcase; **die ~welle, –n** crankshaft

kurbeln wind up; *cin coll* shoot (film)

[der] **Kürbis** [–ɪs], **–se** pumpkin; *coll* 'nut'
küren choose; elect; **~ zu** choose as; elect (s.o. chairman *etc*)
[die] **Kurie** [–ĭə] the Curia
[der] **Kurier, –e** courier
kurieren cure (**von** of)
kurios curious, odd
[die] **Kuriosität, –en** curio, curiosity; oddness
[das] **Kuriosum, –(s)a** curious fact; curiosity
[der] **Kurs, –e** *aer, naut, educ* course; *pol* line; *fin* rate of exchange; (share) price; **den ~ ändern/halten** change/hold course; **~ nehmen auf** (*acc*) set course for; **außer ~ setzen** withdraw from circulation; **hoch im ~ stehen** be at a premium/highly thought of || **die ~änderung, –en** change of course; **das ~buch, ⸚er** *rail* timetable; **die ~notierung, –en** market quotation; **der ~wagen, –** through coach; **der ~wert, –e** market value
[der] **Kürschner, –** furrier
kursieren circulate
[der] **Kursist, –en** (*wk masc*) *EGer* participant in a course
kursiv italic; (*adv*) in italics; **die K~schrift, –en** italics
kursorisch cursory
[der] **Kursus,** *pl* **Kurse** course (of instruction)
[die] **Kurtisane, –n** courtesan
[die] **Kurve, –n** curve; bend; corner; (*pl*) *coll* (female) curves; **eine ~ fliegen** *aer* bank; **die ~ kratzen** *coll* slip away; **die ~ kriegen** *coll* manage it; **eine ~ machen** (road) bend; **die ~ raushaben/weghaben** *coll* have got the hang of it; **in der ~** when cornering
kurven (*sn*) *aer* circle; **~ durch** *coll* drive/ride around
Kurven–: das ~fahren *mot* cornering; **k~reich** winding; *coll* curvaceous; **die ~vorgabe, –n** *sp* stagger
kurz (*comp, superl* ⸚) short; brief; (*adv*) briefly; for a moment/short time; just, shortly (before, after), just (above, outside, *etc*); **~ angebunden** curt; **~ gesagt** in short; **~ und bündig** terse; (*adv*) straight out; **~ und gut** in short; **~ und klein schlagen** smash to pieces; **über ~ oder lang** sooner or later; **zu ~ kommen** get a raw deal; (thing) suffer; **binnen ~em** before long; **seit ~em** for a short time; of late; **(bis) vor ~em** (until) recently; **der Kurze** (*decl as adj*) *coll* short (circuit); **den kürzeren ziehen** lose out || **die K~arbeit** short-time; **~arbeiten** (*sep*) work short-time; **~ärm(e)lig** short-sleeved; **~atmig** short-winded; **die K~fassung, –en** abridged version; **der K~film, –e** short (film); **~fristig** short-term; (*adv*) in the short term; at short notice; **~gefaßt** concise; **die K~geschichte, –n** short story; **~geschnitten** close-cropped; **K~haar–, ~haarig** short-haired; **~halten*** (*sep*) keep short; **~lebig** short-lived; **die K~meldung, –en** news flash; **die K~nachrichten** *pl* news in brief; **die K~park|zone, –n** short-term parking zone; **~schließen*** (*sep*) short-circuit; **der K~schluß, ⸚(ss)e** short-circuit; misconception; **die K~schluß|handlung, –en** sudden irrational action; **die K~schrift, –en** shorthand; **~sichtig** short-sighted; **das K~strecken|flugzeug, –e** short-haul aircraft; **der K~strecken|lauf, ⸚e** sprint; **der K~strecken|läufer, –** sprinter; **~treten*** (*sep*) *coll* economize; take things easy; **~um** in short; **die K~waren** *pl* haberdashery, notions *US*; **~weg** *coll* without further ado; **~weilig** entertaining; **die K~welle, –n** short wave; **K~wellen–** short-wave …
[die] **Kürze** shortness; brevity; **in ~** shortly
[das] **Kürzel, –** shorthand symbol; abbreviation
kürzen shorten; abridge; cut; *dressm* take up; *math* cancel
kurzer|hand without further ado; on the spot
kürzlich recently
[die] **Kürzung, –en** *vbl noun*; *also* abridgement; reduction, cut (*gen* in); *math* cancellation
kuschelig snug
kuscheln: sich ~ an (*acc*) cuddle up to; **sich ~ in** (*acc*) snuggle up in
kuschen knuckle under (**vor** *dat* to); **= sich ~** (dog) lie down
[die] **Kusine, –n** (female) cousin
[der] **Kuß, ⸚(ss)e** kiss; **k~echt** kiss-proof; **~hand** ((+*dat*) **eine K. zuwerfen** blow (s.o.) a kiss; **mit K. nehmen** *coll* be only too glad to take)
küssen, sich ~ kiss
[die] **Küste, –n** coast; *in compds* **~n–** coastal …; **die ~n|fischerei** inshore fishing; **die ~n|schiffahrt** coastal shipping; **der ~n|strich, –e** stretch of coast; littoral; **die ~n|wacht** coastguard
[der] **Küster, –** sexton
[der] **Kustos** [–ɔs], **–(od)en** curator
kutan cutaneous
Kutsch–: der ~bock, ⸚e coach-box
[die] **Kutsche, –n** (horse-drawn) coach; *coll* jalopy
[der] **Kutscher, –** coachman
kutschieren (*sn if v/i*) drive (in a coach); *coll* drive
[die] **Kutte, –n** (monk's) habit
[die] **Kutteln** *pl SGer* tripe
[der] **Kutter, –** cutter
[das] **Kuvert** [–'veːɐ, –'vɛːɐ], **–s** envelope; cover (at table)
[die] **Kuvertüre, –n** chocolate coating
k.v. (**= kriegsverwendungsfähig**) fit for war service
KV (**= Köchelverzeichnis**) K.

die **Kybernetik** [–ɪk] cybernetics
kyrillisch Cyrillic
Kyros [–ɔs] Cyrus

das **KZ, –(s) = Konzentrationslager**
der **KZler** [kaːˈtsɛtlɐ], – *coll* concentration camp detainee

L

^das^ **L** [ɛl] (*gen, pl* –, *coll* [ɛls]) L
l = **Liter**
labb(e)rig *coll* wishy-washy; slack
laben refresh; **sich ~ an** (*dat*) refresh oneself with; feast one's eyes on
labil unstable; (health) delicate
^die^ **Labilität** instability; delicateness
^das^ **Labor, –s** laboratory
^der^ **Laborant, –en** (*wk masc*) laboratory assistant
^das^ **Laboratorium, –(i)en** laboratory
laborieren: ~ an (*dat*) toil over; fight (flu *etc*)
^das^ **Labsal, –e** refreshment; treat (for the eyes), balm
^das^ **Labyrinth, –e** maze; labyrinth (*also anat*)
labyrinthisch labyrinthine
Lach– laughing ...; **das ~gas** laughing gas; **der ~krampf, ⸚e** paroxysm of laughter; **die ~salve, –n** outburst of laughter
^die^ **Lache[1], –n** puddle; pool
^die^ **Lache[2], –n** *coll* laugh
lächeln smile (**über** *acc* at); **das Lächeln** smile
lachen laugh (**über** *acc* at); (sun *etc*) smile brightly, (+*dat*: fortune) smile on; **daß ich nicht lache!** don't make me laugh!; **es wäre gelacht, wenn ...** it would be ridiculous if ...; **das Lachen** laughter; **... ist zum Lachen** ... is ridiculous; **mir ist nicht zum Lachen** I'm not in a laughing mood; **zum Lachen bringen** make (s.o.) laugh
^der^ **Lacher, –** laugher; *coll* laugh
lächerlich ridiculous; **~ machen** make (s.o.) look silly; **sich ~ machen** make a fool of oneself; **ins Lächerliche ziehen** ridicule
^die^ **Lächerlichkeit, –en** absurdity; triviality; **der ~ preisgeben** make a laughing-stock of
lachhaft ridiculous, laughable
^der^ **Lachs** [–ks], **–e** salmon; **l~farben** salmon-(pink); **die ~forelle, –n** salmon trout; **der ~schinken** (*rolled, mild-cured, smoked loin of pork*)
^der^ **Lack, –e** varnish; lacquer; *mot* paint; **der ~affe, –n** (*wk masc*) *coll* fop; **das ~leder, –** patent leather; **l~meiern** (*see* **gelackmeiert**); **der ~schuh, –e** patent-leather shoe
^die^ **Lacke, –n** *Aust* = **Lache[1]**
lackieren lacquer; varnish; *mot* spray; *coll* dupe
^das^ **Lackmus** [–ʊs] (*also* **der**) litmus; **das ~papier** litmus paper
Lade– loading ...; load ...; *elect* charging ...; **das ~gerät, –e** (battery) charger; **die ~hemmung, –en** jamming (of gun) (**L. haben** jam; *coll* have a mental block); **der ~raum, ⸚e** hold
laden[1] (**läd(s)t,** *p/t* **lud** (*subj* **lüde**), *p/part* **geladen**) (*see also* **geladen**) load; *elect* charge; **auf sich ~** take upon oneself; incur; **geladen mit** charged with (tension *etc*); **schwer geladen haben** *coll* be 'tanked up'
laden[2] (*like* **laden[1]**) invite; *leg* summon
^der^ **Laden,** *pl* **Läden** shop, store *US*; shutter; *coll* business; **der ~dieb, –e** shoplifter; **der ~dieb|stahl, ⸚e** shoplifting; **der ~hüter, –** unsaleable article; **der ~inhaber, –** shopkeeper, storekeeper *US*; **der ~preis, –e** retail price; **der ~schluß** closing-time; **die ~straße, –n** shopping street; **der ~tisch, –e** counter; **die ~tochter, ..töchter** *Swiss* salesgirl
lädieren *coll* damage; **lädiert aussehen** look the worse for wear
läd(s)t (*2nd,*) *3rd sing pres of* **laden[1,2]**
^die^ **Ladung[1], –en** *vbl noun*; *also* load; cargo; *elect* charge
^die^ **Ladung[2], –en** *vbl noun*; *leg* summons
^die^ **Lafette, –n** gun-carriage
^der^ **Laffe, –n** (*wk masc*) *coll* fop
lag (läge) *p/t* (*subj*) *of* **liegen**
^die^ **Lage, –n** situation; position; site; layer; *mus* position; register; *coll* round (of drinks); (*pl, eg* **400 m ~n**) *swim* medley; **in der ~ zu ...** in a position to ..., able to ...; **nach ~ der Dinge** in the circumstances || **die ~besprechung, –en** review of the situation; **die ~n|staffel, –n** *swim* medley relay; **l~n|weise** in layers
^das^ **Lager, –** camp (*also* = party, side); bed; store(house); *geol* stratum; *mech* bearing; **am/nicht am ~** in/out of stock; **auf ~ haben** have in stock; *coll* have on tap || **der ~bestand, ⸚e** stock; **das ~feuer, –** camp fire; **das ~haus, ⸚er** warehouse; **die ~stätte, –n** *geol* deposit
^der^ **Lagerist, –en** (*wk masc*) storeman
lagern store; lay down; (*v/i*) be stored; lie; *mil* camp; **hoch/kühl ~** keep in a raised position/cool place; **ähnlich/anders/(schwierig** *etc*) **gelagert** similar/different/(difficult *etc*); **sich ~** settle down
^die^ **Lagerung** storage
^die^ **Lagune, –n** lagoon

lahm lame; *coll* stiff; *coll* dull; (excuse) lame; **~legen** (*sep*) bring to a halt; paralyse (industry *etc*)
lahmen be lame (**auf** *dat* in)
lähmen paralyse
die **Lähmung, -en** *vbl noun*; *also* paralysis
der **Laib, -e** *esp SGer* loaf
Laibach Ljubljana
der **Laich, -e, laichen** spawn
der **Laie, -n** (*wk masc*) layman; *in compds* **~n-** lay ...; *arts* amateur ...
laienhaft amateurish; (opinion *etc*) lay
der **Lakai, -en** (*wk masc*) lackey
die **Lake, -n** brine
das **Laken, -** sheet
lakonisch laconic
die **Lakritze, -n** liquorice
lallen mumble; babble
das **Lama, -s** llama
die **Lamelle, -n** slat (of Venetian blind); *bot* lamella, gill; *tech* plate; *elect* bar
lamentieren *coll* moan
das **Lamento, -s** *coll* moaning
das **Lametta** tinsel; *coll* 'gongs', 'fruit salad' *US*
laminieren laminate
das **Lamm, ⸚er** lamb; **der ~braten, -** roast lamb; **das ~fell, -e** lambskin; **das ~fleisch** lamb; **lamm|fromm** *coll* as meek as a lamb; **die ~s|geduld** *coll* patience of Job; **die ~wolle** lamb's wool
lammen lamb
das **Lämmerne** (*decl as adj*) *Aust cul* lamb
die **Lampe, -n** lamp; light; **das ~n|fieber** stage-fright; **der ~n|schirm, -e** lampshade
der **Lampion** [lam'pĩɔ̃:], **-s** Chinese lantern
lancieren [lãs-] launch; put out (story)
das **Land, ⸚er**/*poet* **-e** land; country; Land (*constituent state of the Federal Republic of Germany*); **~ sehen** see land; see the light at the end of the tunnel; **an ~** ashore; **an ~ gehen** go ashore; **an ~ ziehen** pull ashore; land (fish, *coll* contract, *etc*); **aufs ~/auf dem ~e** (in)to/in the country; **außer ~es** out of the country; **ins ~ gehen** (years *etc*) pass; **aus aller Herren Länder(n)** from all over the globe
Land- country ...; rural ...; land ...;
der ~adel landed aristocracy; **der ~arbeiter, -** agricultural worker; **l~auf (l., l~ab** all over the country); **l~aus (l., l~ein** far and wide); **l~einwärts** inland; **die ~enge, -n** isthmus; **das ~erziehungs|heim, -e** country boarding-school; **der ~film** *EGer* mobile cinema; **die ~flucht** migration from the country to the towns; **der ~friedens|bruch, ⸚e** breach of the peace; **das ~gericht, -e** district court; **das ~gut, ⸚er** estate; **die ~karte, -n** map; **der ~kreis, -e** rural district; **die ~kriegs|ordnung** (**Haager L.** Hague Convention); **l~läufig** popular; widely-held; **die ~maschinen** *pl* agricultural machinery; **die ~nahme** acquisition of territory; colonization, settlement; **die ~plage, -n** plague (of insects); *coll* menace, pest; **die ~pomeranze, -n** *coll* country wench; **der ~rat, ⸚e** Landrat (*chief administrative officer of a Landkreis*); **die ~ratte, -n** *coll* landlubber; **der ~regen, -** continuous rain; **der ~sitz, -e** country seat; **die ~spitze, -n** headland; **die ~straße, -n** country road; **der ~streicher, -** tramp; **der ~strich, -e** tract of land; district; **der ~tag, -e** Landtag (*parliament of a Land*; *in Austria*: *provincial parliament*); **der ~weg, -e** country lane (**auf dem L.** by land, overland); **der ~wirt, -e** farmer; **die ~wirtschaft, -en** agriculture, farming; farm; **l~wirtschaftlich** agricultural; **~wirtschafts-** agricultural ...; **die ~zunge, -n** spit
der **Landauer, -** landau
Lande- landing ...; **die ~bahn, -en** runway; **der ~kopf, ⸚e** beach-head; **die ~rechte** *pl* landing rights
landen land (*also box*); (*v/i sn*) land; *coll* end up; **nicht ~ bei** *coll* not get anywhere with
Länder-: der ~kampf, ⸚e international (match); **die ~kunde** regional geography; **das ~spiel, -e** international (match)
die **Ländereien** *pl* estates, lands
Landes- ... of a/the country/land, national ...; of a Land, (*Austria*) provincial ...; regional ...; **~ebene** (**auf L.** at regional level); **der ~haupt|mann, ⸚er** chief executive (of Austrian province); **der ~herr, -en** (*like* **Herr**) *hist* ruler; **die ~kunde** area studies; **die ~liste, -n** regional list (in parliamentary elections); **die ~regierung, -en** government of a Land; **die ~sprache, -n** language (of the country); **der ~teil, -e** part of the country; **die ~tracht, -en** national costume; **l~üblich** customary (in a country); **der ~verrat** treason; **der ~verräter, -** traitor
der **Ländler, -** *SGer* ländler (*waltz-like country dance*)
ländlich country; rural; **ländlich-sittlich** countrified
Lands-: der ~knecht, -e *hist* lansquenet, mercenary; **der ~mann, ..leute, die ~männin, -nen** compatriot (**was für ein ~mann/eine ~männin sind Sie?** where do you hail from?)
die **Landschaft, -en** countryside; landscape (*also art*); scenery; region; *pol etc* scene
landschaftlich scenic; regional
Landschafts- landscape ...; **das ~schutz|gebiet, -e** nature reserve
der **Landser, -** *mil coll* private
die **Landung, -en** landing; **das ~s|boot, -e**

landing-craft; **die ~s|brücke, -n** landing-stage

lang[1] (*comp, superl* ¨) long; tall; (*time*: *following acc, eg* **ein Jahr ~, monate~**) for (a year, months, *etc*); **längere Zeit** for some time; **~ und breit** at great length; **seit ~em** for a long time now; **die Zeit wird mir ~** time is hanging heavy on my hands

lang[2] *coll* = **entlang**

lang– long …; **~ärm(e)lig** long-sleeved; **~atmig** long-winded; **~beinig** long-legged; **~ersehnt** longed-for; **der L~finger, –** *coll* thief; pickpocket; **~fristig** long-term; (*adv*) in/for the long term; **~gezogen** sustained; **~haarig** long-haired; **~jährig** of many years' standing; long-standing; (many) years of …; **der L~lauf, ¨e** cross-country skiing; **~lebig** long-lasting/lived; **~legen** (*sep*): **sich l.** *coll* have a lie-down; **~mütig** patient; **der L~schläfer, –** late riser; **die L~spiel|platte, -n** long-playing record; **L~strecken–** long-distance/range …; **der L~streckler, –** long-distance runner; **~weilen** (*insep*) bore (**sich l.** be bored); **~weilig** boring; *coll* slow; **die L~welle, -n** long wave; **~wierig** lengthy; long-drawn-out; **L~zeit–** long-term …

lange (*comp* **länger**, *superl* **am längsten**) for a long time; (*with* how *or neg*) long; **es ist schon ~ her, daß …** it's a long time since …; **~ nicht** nowhere near; **schon ~ nicht mehr** not for a long time; **nicht mehr ~** not much longer; **so ~, bis …** until (such time as) …; **wie ~ noch?** how much longer?

Lange–: die ~weile (*1st element is sometimes inflected*) boredom

die **Länge, -n** length (*also sp*); longueur; *geog* longitude; **(30°** *etc*) **östlicher/westlicher ~** longitude (30° *etc*) east/west; **in die ~ ziehen** stretch; spin out; **sich in die ~ ziehen** drag on; **der ~ nach** lengthwise; = **l~lang** *coll* full length

langen *coll* (+*dat*) pass to; (*v/i*) be enough; **jmdm. eine ~** fetch s.o. one; **jetzt langt's mir aber!** I've just about had enough!

~ bis an (*acc*)/**auf** (*acc*)/**zu** reach

~ in (*acc*) put one's hand in

~ mit manage on

~ nach reach for

Längen–: der ~grad, -e degree of longitude; **der ~kreis, -e** meridian; **das ~maß, -e** linear measure

länger|fristig longer-term; (*adv*) in the longer term

länglich oblong; longish; **länglich|rund** oval

längs lengthwise; (+*gen*) along

Längs– longitudinal …; **die ~seite, -n** long side; **l~seits** *naut* alongside

langsam slow; gradual; (*adv*) slowly; gradually, *or expressed by* … begin(s) to … (*eg* **sie wurden ~ müde** they were beginning to feel tired); **~er fahren/gehen** slow down; **es wird ~ Zeit, daß …** it's about time that …; **das wird mir ~ zuviel!** I've just about had enough!; **immer schön ~!** take it easy!

längst long ago; for a long time; **~ nicht** nowhere near

die **Languste, -n** spiny lobster

die **Lanze, -n** lance; spear; **eine ~ brechen für** take up the cudgels for

die **Lanzette, -n** lancet

Laos ['la:ɔs] Laos

der **Laote, -n** (*wk masc*), **laotisch** Laotian

lapidar terse, pithy

Lapp–: ~land Lapland; **der ~länder, –, l~ländisch** Lapp

die **Lappalie** [-ĭə], **-n** trifle

der **Lappe, -n** (*wk masc*) Lapp

der **Lappen, –** rag; cloth; *anat* lobe; (+*dat*) **durch die ~ gehen** *coll* give (s.o.) the slip || **der ~taucher, –** grebe

läppern *coll*: **es läppert sich** it mounts up

lappig *coll* limp

lappisch Lapp

läppisch silly

der **Lapsus, –** [-u:s] slip; **der ~ linguae** […ˈlɪŋgŭɛ] slip of the tongue

die **Lärche, -n** larch

large [-ʒ] *Swiss* (treatment) generous

das **Larifari** *coll* nonsense

der **Lärm** (*gen usu* **-s**) noise; **viel ~ um nichts** much ado about nothing; **viel ~ machen um** make a big fuss about; **~ schlagen** kick up a fuss || **die ~bekämpfung** noise abatement; **die ~belästigung, -en** noise pollution

lärmen make a noise; **~d** noisy

lärmig *Swiss* noisy

larmoyant [-mŏaj-] lachrymose

das **Lärvchen, –** *coll*: **hübsches ~** pretty face

die **Larve** [-fə], **-n** mask; *zool* larva

las *p/t of* **lesen**[1,2]

lasch *coll* feeble, (handshake) limp; wishy-washy

die **Lasche, -n** flap; tongue (of shoe); *rail* fishplate

läse *p/t subj of* **lesen**[1,2]

der **Laser** ['le:zɐ], **–** laser; **der ~strahl, -en** laser beam

lasieren glaze (painting)

lassen (*2nd/3rd sing pres* **läßt**, *p/t* **ließ**, *p/part* **gelassen**, (*after dependent infin*) **lassen**) (*see also* **gelassen**)

1 (*a*) leave (in a place, state); let (into room, out of tyre, *etc*), run (water into bath *etc*); stop (doing sth.); not do; *coll* lose (at cards *etc*); spend (in shop *etc*); **laß das!** stop it!; **laß mich** *etc*! leave me *etc* alone!; **laß man/nur …** say what you like …; don't worry (, **I'll do it** *etc*); **tu, was du**

nicht ~ kannst if you must, you must; **sich nicht zu ~ wissen** be beside oneself (**vor** *dat* with);

(*b*) (+*dat*) let (s.o.) have; **sich** *dat* **Zeit ~** take one's time; **das muß man ihm ~** you've got to hand it to him;

~ bei: alles beim alten ~ leave things as they are; **es dabei ~** leave it at that

hinter sich ~ leave behind one; **weit hinter sich ~** leave far behind

~ von give up

2 (+*infin*) (*a*) let (*eg* **er ließ das Feuer ausgehen/hat das Feuer ausgehen ~** he let the fire go out, **man ließ mich nicht zur Rede kommen** they didn't let me speak); **laß(t) uns ...!** let's ...!; **etw. sein ~** not do sth.; stop (+*ger*); **laß das sein!** stop it!;

(*b*) (*causation*) (*i*, = '*get s.o., sth. to do sth.*') have/make + *infin* (*eg* **Schiller läßt Don Carlos sagen: ...** Schiller has D.C. say: ..., **er ließ es verschwinden** he made it disappear); (*ii*, = '*get sth. done*') have +*p/part* (*eg* **ich ließ ihn verhaften** I had him arrested; (*with dat refl*) **er ließ sich** *dat* **ein Haus bauen** he had a house built, **ich habe mir die Haare schneiden ~** I've had my hair cut);

(*c*) (*with refl pron*): **sich** + *infin* + ~ (*i*, *said of person*) (let oneself) be + *p/part* (*eg* **sich beeinflussen ~** (let oneself) be influenced); have oneself + *p/part* (*eg* **sich rasieren ~** have oneself shaved); **ich lasse mich nicht (einschüchtern** *etc*) I won't be (browbeaten *etc*); (*ii*, *said of thing*: **... läßt sich ...**) ... can be + *p/part* (*eg* **es läßt sich vermeiden** it can be avoided, **Prousts Werke ~ sich zwar zusammenfassen, aber ...** Proust's works *can* be summarized, but ..., **wir wollen sehen, was sich tun läßt** let's see what can be done); *sometimes translated by an originally transitive verb with passive force* (*eg* **seine Stimme läßt sich gut aufnehmen** his voice records well, **Kricketausdrücke wie „backward short leg" ~ sich schlecht ins Deutsche übersetzen** cricketing terms such as 'backward short leg' do not translate well into German); **sich leicht/schwer (übersetzen** *etc*) ~ be easy/hard to (translate *etc*); **das läßt sich hören/trinken** that sounds all right/that's not a bad drink

lässig casual; nonchalant

läßlich (sin) venial

[die] **Last, -en** load; burden; (*pl*) charges; **unter der ~** (+*gen*) under the weight of; **zu ~en** (+*gen*) to the detriment of; **zu ~en gehen von** be chargeable to; be to the disadvantage of; (+*dat*) **zur ~ fallen** be a burden to; (+*dat*) **zur ~ legen** lay at (s.o.'s) door || **das ~auto, -s** lorry, truck; **der ~kahn, ⸗e** barge; **der ~kraft|wagen, -** lorry, truck; **die ~schrift, -en** debit item; **das ~tier, -e** pack-animal; **der ~träger, -** porter (on expedition *etc*); **der ~wagen, -** lorry, truck; **der ~wagen|fahrer, -** lorry/truck driver; **der ~zug, ⸗e** lorry/truck with trailer

lasten: ~ auf (*dat*) weigh on; (responsibility) rest on; **auf dem Haus lastet eine Hypothek** the house is encumbered with a mortgage

[das] **Laster, -** vice; **langes ~** *joc* lanky fellow/girl

[der] **Laster, -** lorry, truck

Läster-: das ~maul, ⸗er *coll* backbiter; **die ~zunge, -n** *coll* vicious tongue

lasterhaft depraved

lästerlich blasphemous

lästern blaspheme against; **~ über** (*acc*) run down

[das] **Lastex** (*gen* **-**) (*trade-mark*) stretch nylon

lästig annoying; a nuisance; (+*dat*) **~ fallen** be a nuisance to

last not least ['la:st ...] last but not least

[die] **Lasur, -en** glaze; **der ~stein, -e** lapis lazuli

lasziv lascivious

[die] **Laszivität** lasciviousness

[das] **Latein** Latin; **mit seinem ~ am Ende sein** be at one's wits' end || **~amerika** Latin America; **l~amerikanisch** Latin-American

lateinisch Latin; (character *etc*) Roman

latent latent

[die] **Latenz** latency

[die] **Laterne, -n** lantern (*also archit*); street-light; **der ~n|pfahl, ⸗e** lamp-post

[die] **Latrine, -n** latrine

[die] **Latsche, -n = die ~n|kiefer, -n** dwarf-pine

latschen [-a:-] (*sn*) *coll* shuffle

[der] **Latschen** [-a:-], **-** *coll* slipper; old shoe

[die] **Latte, -n** slat; lath; *sp* (cross)bar; **lange ~** *coll* lanky fellow/girl || **der ~n|zaun, ⸗e** paling

[der] **Latz, ⸗e** flap; bib; **die ~hose, -n** dungarees

[das] **Lätzchen, -** bib

lau mild; = **~warm** lukewarm

[das] **Laub** foliage; leaves; **der ~baum, ⸗e** deciduous tree; **der ~frosch, ⸗e** tree-frog; **die ~säge, -n** fret-saw; **der ~wald, ⸗er** deciduous forest; **das ~werk** foliage (*also art*)

[die] **Laube, -n** summerhouse; arbour; (*pl*) arcade; **der ~n|gang, ⸗e** arcade; pergola

[der] **Lauch, -e** leek

[die] **Laudatio, -(o)nes** [-e:s] eulogy

Lauer: auf der ~ liegen lie in wait

lauern lie in wait, lurk; **~ auf** (*acc*) lie in wait for; *coll* wait (impatiently) for; **~d** lurking; (glance) furtive

[der] **Lauf, ⸗e** course (of river, events, *etc*; *also astron*); run (*also mus*); race; running (of machine); barrel (of gun); *hunt* leg; (+*dat*) **freien ~ lassen** let (sth.) take its course; give free rein to; **seinen ~ nehmen** take its

course; **im ~(e)** (+*gen*) in the course of; **in vollem ~** at full speed || **die ~bahn, -en** career; *athl* track; **der ~bursche, -n** (*wk masc*) errand-boy; **die ~disziplin, -en** track event; **~feuer (wie ein L.** like wildfire); **das ~gitter, -** play-pen; **die ~katze, -n** *tech* crab; **der ~kran, ¨-e** travelling crane; **die ~kundschaft, -en** occasional custom; **die ~masche, -n** (in stocking *etc*) ladder, run; **~paß** *coll* ((+*dat*) **den L. geben** send packing); **~schritt (im L.** at the double); **der ~stall, ¨-e** play-pen; **der ~steg, -e** catwalk; **die ~zeit, -en** running-time; life (of machine); period of validity; *cin* run; *fin* term; *athl* time

laufen (läuf(s)t, *p/t* **lief,** *p/part* **gelaufen)** (*also sn*) *sp* set (record), clock (time); (*sn*) walk (distance); (car *etc*) do; (*v/i sn*) run; walk; (nose, tap, tears, *etc*) run; (engine *etc*) run, go, (radio *etc*) be on, (clock) work; (film) be showing, (TV programme) be shown; (path *etc*) run; (contract *etc*) run, be valid; be in progress/under consideration; *coll* sell (well *etc*); **~ auf** (*acc*) (*sn*) be in (s.o.'s name); **gelaufen kommen** come running; **die Sache ist gelaufen** *coll* it's all settled; **~ lassen** (*cf* **laufenlassen**) run (water, engine, *horse rac* racehorse); let slide || **~lassen*** (*p/part usu* **~lassen;** *sep*) (*cf* **laufen lassen** *at* **laufen**) let go

laufend current; regular; (*adv*) constantly; **~e Nummer** serial number; **am ~en Band** *coll* continually; **auf dem ~en** up-to-date; **auf dem ~en halten** keep (s.o.) informed (**über** *acc* about); **sich auf dem ~en halten** keep track (**über** *acc* of)

der **Läufer, -** runner (*also* = rug); *footb* half-back; *chess* bishop

die **Lauferei, -en** *coll* running about

läufig on heat

läuf(s)t (*2nd,*) *3rd sing pres of* **laufen**

die **Lauge, -n** soapy water; *chem* lye

die **Laune, -n** mood; whim; (*pl*) quirks (of fate); vagaries; **(bei/in) guter/schlechter ~** in a good/bad mood; **nicht bei ~** in a bad mood

launenhaft moody; capricious

launig humorous

launisch moody

die **Laus, ¨-e** louse; **ihm ist eine ~ über die Leber gelaufen** *coll* something's rubbed him up the wrong way || **der ~bub, -en** (*wk masc*) scamp

lauschen listen (attentively); eavesdrop; (+*dat*) listen to; **~ auf** (*acc*) listen (out) for

der **Lauscher, -** eavesdropper

lauschig secluded

Lause-: der ~bengel, - *coll* = **der ~junge, -n** (*wk masc*) *coll* young rascal

lausen delouse; *coll* 'clean out'; **ich denke, mich laust der Affe!** *coll* you could have knocked me down with a feather!

lausig *coll* lousy, rotten; awful

laut[1] (+*gen/dat*; +*dat* – *eg* **~ Berichten** – *when gen pl form not distinctive*) according to

laut[2] loud (*also* colour); noisy; (*adv*: say) out loud, (read, think) aloud; **~er sprechen** speak up; **~er stellen** turn up; **~ werden** become known; be voiced; **~ werden lassen** divulge; **es wurden Stimmen ~, daß ...** people were beginning to say that ...

der **Laut, -e** sound; **l~hals** at the top of one's voice; **die ~lehre** phonetics; phonology; **l~los** noiseless; silent; **l~malend** onomatopoeic; **die ~malerei** onomatopoeia; **die ~schrift, -en** phonetic transcription; **der ~sprecher, -** loudspeaker; **die ~sprecher|anlage, -n** public address system; **die ~sprecher|box, -en** (stereo) loudspeaker; **l~stark** noisy; vociferous; **die ~stärke, -n** volume

lautbar: ~ werden become known

die **Laute, -n** lute

Läute-: das ~werk, -e bell

lauten read; (wording) run; **~ auf** (*acc*) be in (s.o.'s name); (charge, verdict) be

läuten (*also v/i*) ring; (+*dat*) = **~ nach** ring for; **es läutet** the bell is/bells are ringing; there is a ring at the door; **ich habe davon etwas ~ hören** *coll* I've heard a rumour about that

lauter (gold *etc*) pure; honest; (*indecl*) sheer; nothing but

die **Lauterkeit** honesty

läutern purify; reform (person, character)

die **Läuterung, -en** purification; reformation

lautlich phonetic

die **Lautung, -en** pronunciation

lau|warm *see* **lau**

die **Lava, -(v)en** lava

das **Lavabo** (*gen* -(s)), **-s** *Swiss* wash-basin

der **Lavendel, -** lavender

lavieren *coll* manoeuvre

die **Lawine, -n** avalanche

lax lax

die **Laxheit, -en** laxness, laxity

das **Layout** [leːˈʔaot], **-s** layout

der **Layouter** [leːˈʔaotɐ], **-** layout man

das **Lazarett, -e** military hospital; **das ~schiff, -e** hospital ship

der **Lazarus, -se** *coll*: **(armer) ~** poor devil

die **LDPD** *EGer* = **Liberal-Demokratische Partei Deutschlands**

-le *diminutive suffix*: *see* **-erl**

leasen [-iːz-] *comm* lease

das **Leasing** [-iːz-], **-s** *comm* leasing

Leb-: der ~kuchen, - gingerbread; **l~los** lifeless; **~tag** *coll* (**mein** *etc* **L.** (in) all my *etc* life); **~zeiten (zu jmds. L.** in s.o.'s lifetime; **schon zu L.** (a legend *etc*) in s.o.'s own lifetime)

Lebe–: die ~dame, –n good-time girl; **das ~hoch, –s** three cheers; **der ~mann, ⸗er** fast liver; **das ~wesen, –** living creature; **das ~wohl, –e/–s** farewell

leben (*see also* **lebend**) live (**von** on); be alive; (+*dat*) live for; **hier lebt es sich gut/läßt es sich (gut)** ~ life is good here; ~ **und** ~ **lassen** live and let live; **es lebe ...!** long live ...!; ... for ever!; **lebe wohl!** farewell!

die **Leben, –** life; **sein ~ lassen** lose one's life (for s.o., sth.); **sich** *dat* **das ~ nehmen** take one's own life; **das nackte ~ retten** escape with one's life; **am ~** alive; **am ~ bleiben** stay alive; survive; **für sein ~ gern (jäten** *etc*) *coll* love (weeding *etc*); **ins ~ rufen** bring into being; **nach dem ~ zeichnen** draw from life; **ums ~ kommen** die; be killed; **zeit meines** *etc* **~s** all my *etc* life || **l~spendend** life-giving; **l~sprühend** sparkling with life

lebend living; alive; **~es Inventar** livestock || **~gebärend** viviparous

lebendig living; lively; **bei ~em Leibe** (burnt *etc*) alive; ~ **werden** come to life; ~ **werden lassen** bring to life

Lebens– ... of life/living; life ...; vital ...;

der ~abend old age; **das ~alter, –** age; **die ~art, –en** way of life; manners; **l~bejahend** positive; **die ~bejahung** positive attitude to life; **die ~beschreibung, –en** biography; **die ~dauer** life-span; *tech* working life; **l~echt** true to life; **das ~ende** end of (s.o.'s) life; **die ~er|innerungen** *pl* memoirs; **die ~erwartung** life expectancy; **l~fähig** capable of living; viable; **die ~form, –en** way of life; *biol* life-form; **l~fremd** out of touch with life; **die ~freude** joie de vivre; **l~froh** merry; **die ~gefahr, –en** danger (to life) (**in L.** in danger of one's life; dangerously ill); **l~gefährlich** highly dangerous; critical; **das ~gefühl** feeling for life (**ein neues L. haben** feel a new person); **~geister (jmds. L. wecken** put new life into s.o.); **l~groß** life-size; **~größe (in L.** life-size); **die ~haltung, –en** standard of living; **die ~haltungs|kosten** *pl* cost of living; **der ~inhalt, –e** purpose in life; **das ~jahr, –e** year (of s.o.'s life); **der ~kampf, ⸗e** struggle for existence; **die ~kraft, ⸗e** vitality; vital force; **der ~künstler, –** person who makes the best of life; **die ~lage, –n** situation (in life); **l~lang** life-long; (*adv*) all one's life; **l~länglich** (sentence) life; **der ~lauf, ⸗e** curriculum vitae, résumé *US*; **die ~lüge, –n** self-deception (on which s.o.'s life is founded) (**mit einer L. leben** live a lie); **die ~lust** zest for life; **l~lustig** with a zest for life; **die ~mittel** *pl* food; **das ~mittel|geschäft, –e** grocer's (shop), grocery store *US*; **l~müde** weary of life; **der ~mut** courage to face life; **l~nah** true to life; **l~notwendig** vital; **die ~qualität** quality of life; **der ~raum** *biol* biotope; *pol* lebensraum; **der ~standard, –s** standard of living; **die ~stellung, –en** permanent post; **l~tüchtig** able to cope with life; **der ~unterhalt** livelihood; **die ~versicherung, –en** life insurance; **l~wahr** true to life; **der ~wandel** (way of) life, (moral) conduct; **der ~weg** life; journey through life; **die ~weise, –n** way of life; **das ~werk, –e** life's work; **l~wert** worth living; **l~wichtig** vital; **der ~wille** (*like* **Wille**) will to live; **das ~zeichen, –** sign of life; **die ~zeit** life(time) (**auf L.** for life; **Mitglied auf L.** life member)

die **Leber, –n** liver; **frisch/frei von der ~ weg reden** *coll* speak frankly

Leber– liver ...; **die ~entzündung, –en** hepatitis; **der ~fleck, –e** mole; **der ~käs(e)** *SGer* (*type of*) meat loaf; **die ~pastete, –n** liver pâté; **der ~tran** cod-liver oil; **die ~wurst, ⸗e** liver-sausage (**die beleidigte/gekränkte L. spielen** *coll* go into a huff)

lebhaft lively; vivid; (trading *etc*) brisk

die **Lebhaftigkeit** liveliness; vividness; briskness

lechzen: ~ nach yearn for; thirst for

leck leaky; **~ sein** leak

das **Leck, –s** leak

lecken[1] leak

lecken[2] lick; ~ **an** (*dat*) lick (stamp, spoon, *etc*); **leck mich (am Arsch)!** *vulg* to hell with you!

lecker delicious; (girl) fetching; **~, ~!** yum-yum! || **der L~bissen, –** delicacy; treat; **das L~maul, ⸗er** *coll* person with a sweet tooth

die **Leckereien** *pl* goodies

das **Leder, –** leather; *footb* ball; **vom ~ ziehen** let fly (**gegen** at) || **die ~hose, –n** leather shorts; **die ~waren** *pl* leather goods

ledern leather; (meat *etc*) leathery

ledig single, unmarried; (+*gen*) free of

lediglich [-ɪk-] merely, only

Lee *naut*: **in ~** on the leeward; **nach ~** to leeward

leer empty (**an** *dat* of); blank; vacant; **–leer** *esp* –less; **mit ~en Händen** empty-handed; ~ **laufen** (*cf* **leerlaufen**) (factory *etc*) be idle; (engine) idle; ~ **machen** empty; **ins L~e greifen** clutch at thin air; **ins L~e starren** stare into space || **~gefegt (wie l.** deserted); **das L~gewicht, –e** unladen weight; **das L~gut** empties; **der L~lauf** idling (of engine); wasted effort (**im L.** in neutral; **im L. fahren** coast); **~laufen*** (*sep*; *sn*) (*cf* **leer laufen** *at* **leer**) run dry; **~stehend** vacant; **die L~taste, –n** space-bar; **das L~zimmer, –** unfurnished room

die **Leere** emptiness; void; vacuum

leeren, sich ~ empty
die **Leerung, –en** emptying; *post* collection
die **Lefze, –n** (dog's) lip
legal legal
legalisieren legalize; *leg* authenticate
die **Legalität** legality
die **Legasthenie** dyslexia
der **Legastheniker, –, legasthenisch** dyslexic
das **Legat, –e** legacy
der **Legat, –en** (*wk masc*) legate
die **Lege|henne, –n** layer
legen lay; put, place (somewhere); lay (egg; *also v/i*); set (hair); fold (washing); lay (carpet, cable, track, *etc*); *sp* bring down; **sich ~** lie down; (dust *etc*) settle; (noise, excitement, *etc*) die down, subside, (pain) ease; **sich ~ auf** (*acc*) lie on; (snow *etc*) settle on; affect (throat *etc*); **sich in die Sonne ~** lie in the sun; **sich schlafen ~** go to bed
legendär legendary
die **Legende, –n** legend
leger [–'ʒɛːɐ, –'ʒɛːɐ] casual
legieren *tech* alloy; *cul* thicken
die **Legierung, –en** *vbl noun*; *also* alloy
die **Legion, –en** legion; **... ist ~** ... is legion
der **Legionär, –e** legionnaire; *hist* legionary; **die ~s|krankheit** legionnaires' disease
die **Legislative, –n** legislature
die **Legislatur|periode, –n** legislative period
legitim legitimate
die **Legitimation, –en** justification; identification (papers); *leg* legitimation (of child)
legitimieren justify; authorize (to); *leg* legitimize; **sich ~** prove one's identity
die **Legitimität** legitimacy
der **Leguan, –e** iguana
das **Lehen, –** *hist* fief; *in compds* **~s–** feudal ...; **das ~s|wesen** feudalism
der **Lehm, –e** loam; clay; **die ~hütte, –n** mud hut
lehmig loamy; clayey
Lehn–: der ~sessel, – = der ~stuhl, ⸚e armchair; **die ~übersetzung, –en** loan-translation; **das ~wort, ⸚er** (fully assimilated) loanword (*eg* **Pilz** < *Latin* boletus)
die **Lehne, –n** back (of chair); arm-rest; *SGer* slope
lehnen: ~ an (*acc*) lean (sth.) against; **~ an** (*dat*) lean against; **sich ~ an** (*acc*)**/aus/über** (*acc*) lean against/out of/across
Lehns– *hist* feudal ...; **der ~herr, –en** (*like* **Herr**) liege lord; **der ~mann, ⸚er/..leute** vassal; **das ~wesen** feudalism
Lehr– teaching ...; educational ...; *liter* didactic ...; **das ~amt, ⸚er** teaching post; teaching; **das ~buch, ⸚er** textbook; **das ~fach, ⸚er** subject; **der ~gang, ⸚e** course; **~geld** (**L. zahlen** learn the hard way); **das ~jahr, –e** year of apprenticeship; (*pl*) apprenticeship; **der ~junge, –n** (*wk masc*) apprentice; **das ~kombinat, –e** *EGer* (residential) industrial training centre; **der ~körper, –** (teaching) staff; **die ~kraft, ⸚e** teacher; **das ~mädchen, –** (girl) apprentice; **die ~meinung, –en** received opinion; **die ~mittel** *pl* teaching aids; **der ~plan, ⸚e** curriculum; syllabus; **das ~programm, –e** teaching programme; **l~reich** instructive; **der ~satz, ⸚e** theorem; **der ~stuhl, ⸚e** *univ* chair (**für** of); **der ~vertrag, ⸚e** indentures; **die ~zeit, –en** apprenticeship
die **Lehre¹, –n** teaching(s); doctrine; science; theory; lesson (drawn from experience); moral; advice; apprenticeship; **–lehre** '*science/theory of ...*' (*eg* **die Farben~** chromatics, **die Sprach~** grammar); **in die ~ geben bei** apprentice to; **in die ~ gehen bei** be apprenticed to; learn one's art from
die **Lehre², –n** *tech* gauge
lehren (*univ also v/i*) teach; **jmdn. (lesen/das Lesen** *etc*) **~** teach s.o. to (read *etc*)
der **Lehrer, –** teacher; **das ~zimmer, –** staff room
lehrhaft didactic; schoolmasterish
der **Lehrling, –e** apprentice
–lei *see* **–erlei**
der **Leib, –er** body; stomach; **am ganzen ~(e)** all over; **am eigenen ~(e) erleben** experience for oneself; (+*dat*) **(wie) auf den ~ geschrieben/geschnitten** tailor-made for; **gut bei ~e** *coll* well-fed; **mit ~ und Seele** heart and soul; (+*dat*) **vom ~e bleiben** keep away from; **+mit** *coll* not pester with; **sich** *dat* **... vom ~e halten** keep at bay; **sich** *dat* **... vom ~e schaffen** get rid of; (+*dat*) **zu ~e gehen/rücken** tackle (task *etc*) || **der ~arzt, ⸚e** personal physician; **der/die ~eigene** (*decl as adj*) serf; **die ~eigenschaft** bondage; serfdom; **die ~garde, –n** bodyguard; **das ~gericht, –e** favourite dish; **die ~rente, –n** life-annuity; **die ~schmerzen** *pl* abdominal pains; **die ~speise, –n** favourite dish; **die ~wache, –n** bodyguard; **der ~wächter, –** bodyguard; **die ~wäsche** underclothes
das **Leibchen, –** *Aust, Swiss* vest, undershirt *US*; *sp* shirt
leiben: wie er/sie leibt und lebt to the life
Leibes–: die ~erziehung physical education; **~kräften (aus L.** with all one's might); **die ~übungen** *pl* physical education; **der ~umfang** girth; **die ~visitation, –en** body search
leibhaftig [*also* 'laep–] personified; (*adv*) in person
leiblich bodily, physical; (parents *etc*) own
die **Leiche, –n** corpse, (dead) body; *SGer* funeral; **~ im Keller** skeleton in the cupboard; **über ~n gehen** stick at nothing || **die ~n|bitter|miene, –n** *coll* woebegone look; **leichen|blaß** deathly pale; **der ~n|fledderer, –** person who robs the dead; **die ~n|frau, –en** layer-out; **die ~n|halle, –n**

mortuary; **die ~n|öffnung, -en** autopsy; **die ~n|rede, -n** funeral oration; **die ~n|schau, -en** post-mortem; **der ~n|schmaus, ⸚e** funeral meal; **das ~n|tuch, ⸚er** shroud; **die ~n|verbrennung, -en** cremation; **der ~n|wagen, -** hearse; **der ~n|zug, ⸚e** funeral procession

der **Leichnam, -e** body, corpse

leicht light; easy, (duties *etc*) light; slight, (wind *etc*) light; (cigar) mild; loose (= immoral); (*adv*) lightly; slightly; easily, (~ ...bar/...lich, *eg* ~ **faßbar**) easy to (grasp *etc*); **das ist ~ möglich** that's quite possible; **~en Herzens** with a light heart; **es ist/wird mir ~er (ums Herz)** I feel relieved; **es ~ haben** have an easy time of it; **so ~ wieder nicht** not ... again in a hurry; **es ist mir ein ~es zu ...** it is easy for me to ... || **der L~athlet, -en** (*wk masc*) (track and field) athlete; **die L~athletik** (track and field) athletics; **die L~bau|weise** lightweight construction; **~bekleidet** scantily-clad; **~fallen*** (*sep*; *sn*) (+*dat*) come easy to; **~fertig** frivolous; thoughtless; rash; **die L~fertigkeit** frivolity; thoughtlessness; rashness; **~füßig** light-footed, nimble; **das L~gewicht** lightweight class; **der L~gewichtler, -** lightweight; **~gläubig** credulous; gullible; **die L~gläubigkeit** credulity; gullibility; **~herzig** light-hearted; **leicht|hin** lightly; casually; **~lebig** easy-going; **~machen** (*sep*) (+*dat*) make easy for (**es sich** *dat* **l.** make things easy for oneself; take the easy way out); **~nehmen*** (*sep*) take lightly; **der L~sinn** rashness; recklessness; carelessness; **~sinnig** rash; reckless; careless; **~tun*** (*sep*): **sich** *acc/dat* **l. mit** *coll* find easy; **~verständlich** easily understood

die **Leichtigkeit** lightness; ease; **mit ~** easily

leid: (+*acc*) **~ sein** be sick of; **es tut mir ~** I'm sorry; **... tut mir ~** I'm sorry for ...; **... kann einem ~ tun** you can't help feeling sorry for ...

das **Leid** sorrow, grief; suffering; harm; **l~geprüft** sorely-tried; **der/die ~tragende** (*decl as adj*) mourner; person to suffer; **~wesen (zu jmds. L.** to s.o.'s regret)

die **Leide|form** passive (voice)

leiden (*p/t* **litt**, *p/part* **gelitten**) suffer; allow; (*v/i*) suffer (**an** *dat*/**unter** *dat* from); **(gut) ~ können/mögen** like; **~d** ailing; (glance *etc*) long-suffering; **der/die Leidende** (*decl as adj*) sufferer; **gut/wohl gelitten** popular (**bei** with)

Leiden Leyden

das **Leiden, -** suffering; *med* complaint; ailment; **der ~s|gefährte, -n** (*wk masc*) fellow-sufferer; **die ~s|geschichte, -n** tale of woe; *bibl* the Passion; **die ~s|miene, -n** long-suffering expression

die **Leidenschaft, -en** passion

leidenschaftlich passionate; impassioned; **~ gern (essen** *etc*) adore (eating *etc*)

leidenschafts|los dispassionate

leider unfortunately; I'm afraid; **~ Gottes!** unfortunately; **~ ja/nicht!** I'm afraid so/not!

leidig disagreeable; tiresome

leidlich reasonable; (*adv*) reasonably

die **Leier, -n** lyre; *astron* Lyra; **die alte ~** *coll* the same old story || **der ~kasten, ..kästen** barrel-organ; **der ~kasten|mann, ⸚er** organ-grinder; **der ~schwanz, ⸚e** lyre-bird

leiern *coll* wind; drone out

Leih-: die ~bibliothek, -en lending library; **die ~gabe, -n** loan (= loaned work *etc*); **die ~gebühr, -en** hire/lending charge; **das ~haus, ⸚er** pawnshop; **die ~mutter, ..mütter** surrogate mother; **der ~schein, -e** pawn ticket; borrowing slip; **der ~wagen, -** hire(d) car, rented car *US*; **l~weise** on loan

leihen (*p/t* **lieh**, *p/part* **geliehen**) (+*dat*) lend; (*also* + **sich** *dat*) borrow

der **Leim, -e** glue; (+*dat*) **auf den ~ gehen** *coll* fall for (s.o.'s) tricks; **aus dem ~ gehen** *coll* fall apart; lose one's figure || **die ~farbe, -n** distemper

leimen glue; *coll* take in

leimig gluey

der **Lein, -e** flax; **das ~öl** linseed oil; **der ~samen** linseed; **die ~wand, ⸚e** canvas; *cin etc* screen (**über die L. laufen** be screened)

-lein (*pl* -) *chiefly poet*: *diminutive suffix* (*making noun neuter and causing stem-vowel to be mutated where possible*) little ..., *eg* **das Bäch~** little stream, brooklet (**Bach** = stream)

---

die **Leine, -n** (fishing-, washing-, *naut*) line; lead, leash; **~ ziehen** *coll* clear out

leinen linen

das **Leinen, -** linen; **in ~ gebunden** cloth-bound

leise soft; quiet; faint; light, gentle; slight; **mit ~r Stimme** in a low voice; **~r stellen** turn down || **der L~treter, -** *coll* pussyfoot

die **Leiste, -n** strip (of metal, wood, *etc*); border; skirting, baseboard *US*; *text* selvedge; *anat* groin; *mount* spur

leisten achieve; do (*also mot*, of engine); give (assistance *etc*); offer (resistance); take (oath); make (payment); **sich** *dat* **... ~** treat oneself to; get up to; **sich** *dat* **... ~ können** be able to afford

der **Leisten, -** last; **alles über einen ~ schlagen** *coll* measure everything by the same yardstick || **der ~bruch, ⸚e** hernia

die **Leistung, -en** achievement; performance; standard; output, *mech* power; service (rendered); payment; (*pl*) performance; contributions; (insurance *etc*) benefits; **der ~s|druck** pressure to do well; **l~s|fähig** efficient; *mech* powerful; *fin* able to pay; **die ~s|fähigkeit** efficiency; capacity; *mech* power; *fin* ability to pay; **die ~s|gesellschaft** *approx* = meritocracy; **die ~s|prämie, –n** *esp EGer* productivity bonus; **der ~s|sport** competitive sport; **das ~s|vermögen** (= **~sfähigkeit**); **die ~s|zulage, –n** productivity bonus

Leit– leading ...; guiding ...; guide ...; **der ~artikel, –** leading article, editorial *US*; **der ~artikler, –** leader-writer, editorialist *US*; **das ~bild, –er** model; **der ~faden, ..fäden** guide, manual; **l~fähig** conductive; **die ~fähigkeit** conductivity; **der ~gedanke, –n** (*like* **Gedanke**) central idea; **der ~hammel, –** bell-wether; *coll* leader; **die ~linie, –n** guide-line; *mot* broken white line; **das ~motiv, –e** leitmotif; **die ~planke, –n** crash-barrier, guardrail *US*; **der ~satz, ⸚e** basic/guiding principle; **die ~schiene, –n** *rail* guardrail; *Aust mot* crash-barrier, guardrail *US*; **der ~spruch, ⸚e** motto; **der ~stern, –e** lodestar; guiding star; **die ~währung, –en** reserve currency; **das ~werk, –e** *aer* tail (unit)

leiten lead; pipe (gas, oil); route; divert; forward (to authorities *etc*); run (business *etc*), be in charge of (project *etc*), lead (discussion *etc*), chair (meeting), *sp* referee; guide; *phys* conduct; **sich ~ lassen von** be guided by; **~d** leading; guiding; senior; (post) managerial; *phys* conductive

der **Leiter, –** leader; manager; head; (artistic *etc*) director; *phys* conductor

die **Leiter, –n** ladder

die **Leitung, –en** *vbl noun*; *also* management; direction; leadership; chairmanship; guidance; (= persons) management; *tech* pipe; cable; wire; *tel* line; *phys* conduction; **eine lange ~ haben** *coll* be slow on the uptake; **unter der ~ von** under the direction of; *mus* conducted by || **das ~s|netz, –e** mains system; *elect* grid; **das ~s|wasser** tap-water

die **Lektion, –en** lesson

der **Lektor, –(or)en** publisher's reader; *univ* foreign language assistant

die **Lektüre, –n** reading; reading-matter

Lemberg Lvov

die **Lende, –n** loin; *in compds* **~n–** *anat* lumbar ...; **der ~n|braten, –** roast loin; **l~n|lahm** stiff; *coll* (excuse) lame; **der ~n|schurz, –e** loin-cloth

Leningrad ['leːniːngraːt] Leningrad

Lenk– steering ...; **das ~rad, ⸚er** steering-wheel; **die ~säule, –n** steering-column; **die ~stange, –n** handlebars

lenkbar steerable; (child) manageable

lenken steer; guide; direct; control (economy *etc*); **~ auf** (*acc*) draw (attention) to; steer (conversation) onto; divert (suspicion) to; **auf sich ~** attract (attention)

der **Lenker, –** driver (of vehicle; *in Aust, Swiss usage often without a following gen phrase*); *cycl, mot cycl* handlebars

die **Lenkung, –en** *vbl noun*; *also* direction; control; *mot* steering

der **Lenz, –e** *poet* spring; **sich** *dat* **einen (schönen) ~ machen** *coll* take things easy; **er/sie zählt (20** *etc*) **~e** he is a youth/she is a girl of (20 *etc*) summers

Leo Leo

der **Leopard, –en** (*wk masc*) leopard

die **Lepra** [–eː–] leprosy; **der/die ~kranke** (*decl as adj*) leper

lepros [–e–], **leprös** leprous

die **Lerche, –n** lark

Lern– learning ...; **die ~begierde** eagerness to learn; **l~begierig** eager to learn; **die ~maschine, –n** teaching-machine; **die ~mittel** *pl* school books (and other materials); **die ~mittel|freiheit** free provision of school books *etc*; **die ~schwester, –n** student nurse

lernen (*see also* **gelernt**) learn (**von** from); *coll* (*eg* **Schneider ~**) train to be (a tailor *etc*); (*v/i*) learn; train; study; **~ aus** learn from (books, experience, *etc*); **das lernt sich leicht** that's easy to learn

die **Les|art, –en** reading; variant

lesbar legible; readable

die **Lesbe, –n** *coll* Lesbian

die **Lesbierin** [–ĭə–], **–nen, lesbisch** Lesbian

die **Lese, –n** grape harvest

Lese– reading ...; *comput* read ...; **das ~buch, ⸚er** reader; **die ~probe, –n** extract (from book); *theat* reading; **die ~ratte, –n** *coll* bookworm; **der ~saal, ..säle** reading-room; **der ~stoff, –e** reading matter; **das ~zeichen, –** bookmark

lesen[1] (*2nd/3rd sing pres* **liest**, *p/t* **las** (*subj* **läse**), *p/part* **gelesen**) read (*also parl, comput*); (*v/i*) read; *univ* lecture (**über** *acc* on); **sich (gut** *etc*) **~** (book *etc*) read (well *etc*); **sich in den Schlaf ~** read oneself to sleep

lesen[2] (*like* **lesen**[1]) pick; sort

lesens|wert worth reading

der **Leser, –** reader; **der ~brief, –e** reader's letter; **der ~kreis, –e** readership; **die ~zuschrift, –en** reader's letter

leserlich legible

die **Leserschaft** readership

die **Lesung, –en** reading (*also parl*); *eccles* lesson

die **Lethargie** lethargy

lethargisch lethargic

der **Lette, –n** (*wk masc*) Latvian

die **Letter, –n** (printed) letter; *print* type

lettisch, (*language*) **L~** Latvian

Lettland Latvia

letzt.. last; final; ultimate; extreme; (mysteries) deepest; (news *etc*) latest; (days *etc*) last few; **als ~es** last of all; **als ~er/~e/~es** last, *or conveyed by* ... is *etc* the last to ...; **in ~er Zeit** of late; **bis ins ~e** down to the last detail; (know) inside out; **das ist das L~e!** that's the limit!; **sein L~es (her)-geben** give one's all; **~er..** latter

Letzt: zu guter ~ finally

letzt– last ...; **letzt|endlich** in the end; **~genannt** last-named; **letzt|hin** recently; **~malig** final, last; **~mals** for the last time

letzte|mal: das ~ the last time

letzten|mal: zum ~ for the last time

letztens recently; lastly

letztlich ultimately; finally

der **Leu, –en** (*wk masc*) *poet* lion

Leucht– luminous ...; fluorescent ...; illuminated ...; **das ~feuer, –** beacon; **der ~käfer, –** glow-worm; **die ~kraft** luminosity; **die ~kugel, –n** flare; **die ~pistole, –n** Very pistol; **die ~rakete, –n** flare; **die ~reklame, –n** neon sign(s); **die ~röhre, –n** fluorescent tube; **die ~schrift** neon writing; **das ~spur|geschoß, –(ss)e** tracer bullet; **~stoff–** fluorescent ...; **der ~turm, ⸚e** lighthouse; **das ~ziffer|blatt, ⸚er** luminous dial

die **Leuchte, –n** light; *coll* luminary

leuchten shine a light; shine; glow; **~des Beispiel** shining example

der **Leuchter, –** candlestick

leugnen deny; (*v/i*) deny everything; **es ist nicht zu ~/läßt sich nicht ~, daß ...** there's no denying that ...

die **Leukämie, –(ie)n** leukaemia

das **Leukoplast** (*trade-mark*) sticking plaster, adhesive tape *US*

der **Leumund** reputation

leut–: ~selig affable

die **Leutchen** *pl coll* folk; folks

die **Leute** *pl* people; workers, people, staff, *mil* men; **–leute** (*i*) ... people (*eg* **Zirkus~** circus people); (*ii*) *forms plural of certain nouns ending in* **–mann** (*eg* **See~** seamen, *pl of* **Seemann** seaman); **kleine ~** ordinary people; **die ~** (*generalizing*) people; **unter die ~ bringen** spread around; **unter die ~ kommen** (get out and) meet people; (news) get out || **der ~schinder, –** slavedriver (= employer *etc*)

der **Leutnant, –s** second lieutenant; (air force) pilot officer, second lieutenant *US*; **~ zur See** acting sub-lieutenant, ensign *US*

der **Level** ['lɛvḷ], **–s** level

die **Leviten** *coll*: (+*dat*) **die ~ lesen** read (s.o.) the riot act

die **Levkoje** [lɛf–], **–n** *bot* stock

die **Lexik** [–ɪk] lexis

lexikalisch lexical

der **Lexikograph, –en** (*wk masc*) lexicographer

die **Lexikographie** lexicography

lexikographisch lexicographical

das **Lexikon** [–ɔn], **–(k)a** encyclopaedia; *dated* dictionary

die **Liaison** [liɛ'zɔ̃ː], **–s** liaison

der **Libanese, –n** (*wk masc*), **libanesisch** Lebanese

der **Libanon** ['liːbanɔn] (*gen* **–(s)**) the Lebanon

die **Libelle, –n** dragonfly; *tech* spirit-level

liberal liberal; **der/die Liberale** (*decl as adj*) liberal

liberalisieren liberalize

der **Liberalismus** liberalism

der **Libero, –s** *footb* sweeper

libidinös libidinous

die **Libido** libido

der **Librettist, –en** (*wk masc*) librettist

das **Libretto, –s/–(tt)i** libretto

Libyen Libya

der **Libyer, –, libysch** Libyan

–lich *forming adjectives* (*often with mutation of the stem-vowel*):

(*i*) *signifying 'characteristic of', 'pertaining to' or indicating periodic recurrence, eg* **mensch~** human (**Mensch** = man), **münd~** oral (**Mund** = mouth), **täg~** daily (**Tag** = day);

(*ii*) –ish (*esp with colour words*), *eg* **bläu~** bluish (**blau** = blue), **ält~** oldish (**alt** = old);

(*iii*) (*added to verb stems*) –able, –ible, *eg* **erhält~** obtainable (**erhalten** = obtain), **unglaub~** incredible (**glauben** = believe)

---

licht light; bright; sparse; (moment) lucid; **~e Höhe** headroom

das **Licht, –er** light; candle; **~ machen** put on the light; **mir geht ein ~ auf** I'm beginning to see the light; **ans ~ kommen** come to light; (+*dat*) **aus dem ~ gehen** get out of (s.o.'s) light; **bei ~** in daylight; **bei ~(e) besehen** on closer examination; **hinters ~ führen** lead up the garden path; (+*dat*) **im ~ stehen** stand in (s.o.'s) light; **ins rechte ~ rücken** show in a favourable light || **l~beständig** non-fading; **das ~bild, –er** passport photograph; **der ~bilder|vortrag, ⸚e** illustrated talk; **der ~blick, –e** ray of hope; bright spot; **der ~bogen, –** *elect* arc; **l~durchlässig** translucent; **l~echt** light-fast, non-fading; **l~empfindlich** sensitive to light; photosensitive; **die ~empfindlichkeit** sensitivity to light; *phot* speed; **die ~hupe, –n** headlight flasher; **der ~kegel, –** beam (from headlight *etc*); **das ~jahr, –e** light year; **die ~maschine, –n** dynamo, generator *US*; **~meß (Mariä L.** Candlemas); **die ~pause, –n** blueprint; **die ~reklame, –n** neon advertising; **der ~satz** filmsetting, photocomposition *US*; **der ~schein, –e** gleam of light; **l~scheu** shunning light; shady; **die ~schranke, –n** photoelectric beam; **die ~seite, –n** bright side; **l~stark** *phot* fast; **l~undurchlässig** opaque

lichten[1] thin (out); **sich ~** thin; clear

lichten[2]**: den Anker ~** weigh anchor

lichter–: lichter|loh (l. brennen be ablaze); **das L~meer** sea of lights

die **Lichtung, –en** clearing

das **Lid, –er** eyelid; **der ~schatten, –** eyeshadow; **der ~strich, –e** line drawn along the eyelid

lieb (*see also* **lieber**) dear; nice; kind; (guest) welcome; **das ist mir ~ so** that's how I like it; **(mehr** *etc*) **als mir ~ ist** (more *etc*) than I would like; **es wäre mir ~, wenn …** I should be glad if …; **… ist** *etc* **mir ~er** I prefer … (**als** to); **es wäre mir ~er, wenn …** I should prefer it if …; **sei so ~ und …** be an angel and …; **am ~sten würde ich …** most of all I should like to …; **du ~e Zeit!** good heavens!; **den ~en langen Tag** all day long; **L~ste(r)** darling || **~äugeln** (*insep*) (**l. mit** have one's eye on; toy with (idea); *pol* flirt with); **~gewinnen*** (*sep*) grow fond of; **~geworden** cherished; **~haben*** (*sep*) be fond of; **der L~haber, –** lover; enthusiast; collector; *in compds* collector's …; **die L~haberei, –en** hobby; **~kosen** [*also* 'liːp–] (*insep*; *p/part* **~kost, ge~kost** [–'liːp–]) caress; **~los** unkind; unloving; (*adv*: cooked *etc*) any old how; **die L~losigkeit, –en** unkindness; **der L~reiz** charm; **~reizend** charming

das **Liebchen, –** *arch* sweetheart

die **Liebe** love (**zu** for, of); sex, love-making; **~ machen** *coll* make love; **tu mir die ~ (an) und …** do me a favour and …; **aus ~ zu** out of love for; **mit ~** lovingly || **l~bedürftig** needing much affection; **die ~dienerei** obsequiousness; **l~voll** loving

die **Liebelei, –en** flirtation

lieben love; make love to; **es ~ zu …** love (+*ger*); **sich ~** love one another; make love; **ich würde ~d gern …** I should love to …; **die Liebenden** *pl* lovers || **~lernen** (*sep*) come to love

liebens–: ~wert lovable; endearing; **~würdig** kind; **liebens|würdiger|weise** kindly; **die L~würdigkeit** kindness

lieber (*comp of* **lieb** (*see above*), **gern**) sooner, rather; better; *or conveyed by* prefer (*eg* **ich trinke ~ Tee als Kaffee** I prefer tea to coffee, **sie bleibt ~ zu Hause** she prefers to stay at home); **~ haben/mögen** prefer (**als** to); **… hätte ~ (warten** *etc*) **sollen** … would have done better to (wait *etc*)

Liebes– love …; … of love; amorous …; **der ~akt, –e** sex act; **die ~beziehung, –en** (sexual) relationship; **der ~brief, –e** love-letter; **der ~dienst, –e** favour ((+*dat*) **einen L. erweisen** do (s.o.) a favour); **die ~erklärung, –en** declaration of love; **die ~heirat, –en** love-match; **l~krank** lovesick; **der ~kummer** lovesickness (**L. haben** be lovesick); **das ~leben** love-life; **~müh(e) (das ist vergebliche/verlorene L.** that is futile); **das ~paar, –e** (pair of) lovers; **der ~roman, –e** romantic novel; **das ~verhältnis, –se** love-affair

lieblich delightful; (scent *etc*) sweet; (wine) mild

der **Liebling, –e** darling; *in compds* **~s–** favourite …; **der ~s|platz, ⸚e** favourite haunt

die **Liebschaft, –en** affair

das **Lied, –er** song; lied; *liter* lay; **das alte ~** *coll* the same old story; **ich weiß ein ~ davon zu singen** I could tell you a thing or two about that

Lieder– song …; **der ~abend, –e** song-recital

liederlich slovenly; dissolute; loose

lief *p/t of* **laufen**

Liefer– delivery …; **die ~firma, –(m)en** suppliers; **der ~schein, –e** delivery note; **der ~termin, –e** delivery date; **der ~wagen, –** van, delivery truck *US*

der **Lieferant, –en** (*wk masc*) supplier

lieferbar available

liefern (*see also* **geliefert**) deliver; supply; provide; put up (fight); yield; (+*dat of pers*) supply with

die **Lieferung, –en** delivery; supply; instalment (of work)

die **Liege, –n** divan; couch; **der ~platz, ⸚e** berth; **der ~sitz, –e** reclining seat; **der ~stuhl, ⸚e** deck-chair; **der ~stütz, –e** press-up; **der ~wagen, –** couchette car; **die ~wiese, –n** lawn for sunbathing

liegen (*p/t* **lag** (*subj* **läge**), *p/part* **gelegen**) (*see also* **gelegen**) (*sn in SGer*) lie; be situated; be; *mot* hold the road; (+*dat*, *often with neg*) suit; appeal to, be (s.o.'s) cup of tea; **so wie die Dinge ~** the way things are; **~ haben** have (in a specified place); have (work) to do

~ an (*dat*) be (situated) by/on; be due to; **mir liegt viel/nichts an …** … matter(s) a lot/do(es)n't matter to me; **mir liegt daran zu …** I'm anxious to …; **daran liegt's** that's the reason (for it); **es liegt daran, daß …** it's because …; **woran liegt das?** why is that?

~ auf (*dat*) lie on; (customs duty, stress, *etc*) be on; *med*, *sp* be in (ward, 5th *etc* place); **auf seinem Gesicht lag ein Ausdruck (der Erwartung** *etc*) there was a look of (expectancy *etc*) in his face

~ **bei** be (situated) near; (average age *etc*) be about; (damage *etc*) be of the order of/on the order of *US*; (decision, responsibility) lie with, rest with, (power *etc*) reside in; **das liegt ganz bei dir** it's entirely up to you

~ **hinter** (*dat*) lie behind; be behind

~ **in** (*dat*) lie in; be (situated) in; be in (s.o.'s interest, nature, *etc*); **in jmds. Absicht** ~ be s.o.'s intention; **in der Familie** ~ run in the family

~ **nach** (room *etc*) face (east *etc*)

~ **über** (*dat*) lie above/over; be (situated) above/over; (haze *etc*) hang over, lie over; be above (the average *etc*)

~ **unter** (*dat*) lie below/under; be (situated) below/under; be below (the average *etc*)

~ **vor** (*dat*) lie/be (situated) in front of/outside; be ahead of

liegen–: ~bleiben* (*sep*; *sn*) remain lying; stay in bed; be left (behind); remain unsold; remain unfinished; not get done; *mot* break down; **~lassen*** (*p/part usu* **~lassen;** *sep*) leave (behind); leave (work) unattended to (**alles liegen- und stehenlassen** drop everything; **links l.** *coll* cold-shoulder)

liegend lying; situated (in specified place); *art* reclining; *mech* horizontal

^die^ **Liegenschaften** *pl* property

lieh *p/t of* **leihen**

lies *imp sing of* **lesen**

ließ *p/t of* **lassen**

liest *2nd/3rd sing pres of* **lesen**[1,2]

^der^ **Lift, –e/–s** lift, elevator *US*

liften lift; **sich ~ lassen** have a face-lift

^das^ **Lifting, –s** face-lift

^die^ **Liga, –(g)en** league

^die^ **Ligatur, –en** *med*, *mus*, *print* ligature

^der^ **Liguster, –** privet

liieren: sich ~ mit join forces with; enter into a liaison with; **liiert sein mit** be (closely) associated with; have a liaison with

^der^ **Likör, –e** liqueur

lila (*indecl*) lilac; purple

^die^ **Lilie** [–ĭə], **–n** lily

Liliput– ['liːlipʊt–] miniature ...

^der^ **Liliputaner, –** midget

^das^ **Limit** ['lɪmɪt], **–s** limit; *fin* ceiling

limitieren limit; *fin* put a ceiling on

^die^ **Limo, –(s)** *coll* = **Limonade**

^die^ **Limonade, –n** soft drink

^die^ **Limousine** [–mu–], **–n** saloon, sedan *US*

lind[1] gentle; mild

lind[2] (*indecl*) lime green

lind–: lind|grün lime green; **der L~wurm, ¨–er** *myth* (wingless) dragon

^die^ **Linde, –n** lime-tree

lindern alleviate

^die^ **Linderung** alleviation

^das^ **Lineal, –e** ruler

linear linear

–ling (*pl* **–e**):

(*i*) *used pejoratively to refer to individuals*, *eg* **der Primitiv~** primitive person, **der Dichter~** poetaster (**Dichter** = poet);

(*ii*) *used of persons undergoing something*, *eg* **der Prüf~** examinee (**prüfen** = examine), **der Anlern~** trainee (**anlernen** = train);

(*iii*) **der Zwilling** twin, **der Drilling** triplet, **der Vierling** quadruplet, *etc*

---

^der^ **Linguist, –en** (*wk masc*) linguist (= expert in linguistics)

^die^ **Linguistik** [–ɪk] linguistics

^die^ **Linie** [–ĭə], **–n** line (*also geneal*, *mil*, *pol*); (bus *etc*) route, line *US*; **auf die (schlanke) ~ achten** watch one's figure; **auf der ganzen ~** all along the line; **in erster ~** first and foremost, primarily; **in zweiter ~** secondarily || **das ~n|blatt, ¨–er** ruled sheet (supplied with writing-pad); **der ~n|bus, –se** public service bus; **der ~n|dienst** regular service; **der ~n|flug, ¨–e** scheduled flight; **die ~n|führung** lines; route; **das ~n|netz, –e** network of routes; **das ~n|papier** ruled paper; **der ~n|richter, –** linesman; **das ~n|schiff, –e** liner; **l~n|treu** faithful to the party line (**l. sein** toe the party line); **der ~n|verkehr** regular service

lin(i)ieren rule (paper)

link.. left; *pol* left-wing; **~e Seite** left(-hand) side; reverse (of fabric); **die Linke** (*decl as adj*) left; left hand; *box* left; *pol* (the) Left; **zur L~en** on the left

linkisch gauche

links on the left; inside out; *coll* left-handed; **nach/von ~** to/from the left; **~ liegenlassen** *coll* cold-shoulder; **~ stricken** purl

Links– left ...; left-hand ...; *pol* left-wing ...; **der ~außen, –** outside left; **l~gerichtet** leftist; **der ~händer, –** left-handed person; **l~händig** left-handed; **l~herum** round to the left; **der/die ~intellektuelle** (*decl as adj*) left-wing intellectual; **die ~kurve, –n** left-hand bend; **l~radikal** extreme left-wing; **l~rheinisch** on the left of the Rhine; **l~stehend** leftist; **l~um!** left turn/face *US*!; **der ~verkehr** driving on the left

Linnésch Linnaean

Linol–: der ~schnitt, –e linocut

^das^ **Linoleum** linoleum

^der^ **Linon** [–'nɔ̃ː] (*gen* –(s)), **–s** *text* lawn

^die^ **Linse, –n** *phys* lens; *bot*, *cul* lentil

linsen *coll* peep

Linsen–: das ~gericht, –e lentil dish; **die**

~suppe, –n lentil soup

die **Lippe, –n** lip; *bot* labium; **an jmds. ~n hängen** hang on s.o.'s every word; **über die ~n bringen** bring oneself to say || **das ~n|bekenntnis, –se** lip-service; **der ~n|laut, –e** labial; **der ~n|stift, –e** lipstick

–lippig -lipped

die **Liquidation, –en** elimination; liquidation (*also comm*)

liquidieren do away with, eliminate; liquidate (person); *comm* liquidate, wind up (firm); (*v/i*) *comm* go into liquidation

lispeln lisp; whisper

Lissabon [–ɔn] Lisbon

die **List, –en** cunning; trick, ruse

die **Liste, –n** list (*also comput*); **schwarze ~** black list; **auf die schwarze ~ setzen** blacklist

listig cunning, crafty

die **Litanei, –en** litany; *coll* catalogue (of complaints *etc*)

Litauen [–ɪ–] Lithuania

der **Litauer** [–ɪ–], – Lithuanian

litauisch [–ɪ–], (*language*) **L~** Lithuanian

der **Liter, –** (*also* **das**) litre

Literar–: der ~historiker, – literary historian; **l~historisch** relating to literary history

literarisch literary

der **Literat, –en** (*wk masc*) littérateur; literary hack

die **Literatur, –en** literature; *in compds* ... of literature; literary ...

die **Litfaß|säule** [–ɪ–], **–n** advertising pillar

der **Lithograph** [li–], **–en** (*wk masc*) lithographer

die **Lithographie** [li–], **–(ie)n** lithography; lithograph

lithographieren [li–] lithograph

lithographisch [li–] lithographical

litt *p/t of* **leiden**

die **Liturgie, –(ie)n** liturgy

liturgisch liturgical

die **Litze, –n** cord; braid

live [laef] *rad*, *TV* live; **die L~-Sendung, –en** live broadcast

Livius Livy

die **Livree, –(ee)n** livery

livriert liveried

die **Lizenz, –en** licence; **in ~ herstellen** manufacture under licence || **der ~inhaber, –** licensee; **der ~spieler, –** *footb* professional player

der **Lkw, LKW** ['ɛlkaːveː, ɛlkaː'veː], **–(s)** (= **Lastkraftwagen**) lorry, truck

das **Lob** praise; **über jedes ~ erhaben** beyond praise; **zu jmds. ~** to s.o.'s credit || **der ~gesang, ⸚e** song of praise; **die ~hudelei, –en** fulsome praise; **l~hudeln** (*insep*) (*also* +*dat*) heap fulsome praise on; **das ~lied, –er** song of praise (**ein L. anstimmen auf** (*acc*) sing the praises of); **die ~rede, –n** eulogy (**auf** *acc* of); **der ~redner, –** eulogist

die **Lobby** [–i], **–s/Lobbies** *parl* lobby

loben praise; **das lobe ich mir!** that's what I like! || **~s|wert** praiseworthy

löblich *esp iron* laudable

das **Loch, ⸚er** hole (*also golf*); *bill* pocket; *coll* 'clink'; *coll* 'hole', 'dump'; **schwarzes ~** black hole; **saufen wie ein ~** *coll* drink like a fish; (+*dat*) **ein ~/Löcher in den Bauch fragen** *coll* bombard with questions; **sich** *dat* **ein ~/Löcher in den Bauch reden** *coll* talk till one is blue in the face; **auf dem letzten ~ pfeifen** *coll* be on one's last legs/beam-ends || **die ~karte, –n** punched card; **der ~streifen, –** punched tape

lochen punch (tape *etc*); punch a hole/holes in

der **Locher, –** punch; punch operator

löcherig full of holes

löchern *coll* pester (with questions)

Lock–: das ~mittel, – bait, lure; **der ~ruf, –e** call (*esp* of bird); **der ~spitzel, –** agent provocateur; **der ~vogel, ..vögel** decoy; stool-pigeon

die **Locke, –n** curl; **~n haben** have curly hair

locken[1] lure; tempt

locken[2] curl (hair); **sich ~** curl

Locken–: der ~kopf, ⸚e curly head; **der ~wickler, –** curler

locker loose; slack; light (in texture); (posture *etc*) relaxed; **~lassen*** (*sep*) *coll* (**nicht l.** not give up); **~machen** (*sep*) *coll* fork out

lockern loosen; slacken; break up (soil); relax; **sich ~** work loose; slacken; relax; ease; become freer/less close

die **Lockerungs|übung, –en** limbering-up exercise

lockig curly; **–lockig** with ... locks/curls

der **Loden, –** loden

lodern blaze; (*also sn*: flames) leap up

der **Löffel, –** spoon; spoonful; *hunt* ear (of hare, rabbit); **der ~bagger, –** shovel dredger; **das ~biskuit, –s** (*also* **der**) sponge finger; **l~weise** by the spoonful

löffeln spoon up

der **Löffler, –** spoonbill

log *p/t of* **lügen**

Log– ['lɔk–]: **das ~buch, ⸚er** log-book

der **Logarithmus, –(m)en** logarithm

die **Loge** [–ʒə], **–n** (porter's, masonic) lodge; *theat* box

löge *p/t subj of* **lügen**

logieren [–ʒ–] stay (**bei** with); lodge (with)

die **Logik** [–ɪk] logic

das **Logis** [–'ʒiː] (*gen* – [–(s)]), – [–s] lodgings; *naut* crew's quarters

logisch logical; *coll* natural; **das ist doch ~!** it's obvious! || **logischer|weise** logically

die **Lohe, –n** flames, blaze

lohen blaze

der **Lohn, ¨-e** wage(s); reward; **der ~empfänger, -** wage-earner; **l~intensiv** wage-intensive; **die Lohn-Preis-Spirale, -n** wage-price spiral; **die ~steuer, -n** income tax (on earned income); **der ~stopp, -s** wage freeze; **der ~streifen, -** pay slip; **die ~tüte, -n** pay packet/envelope *US*

lohnen be worth (effort, visit, *etc*); (+*dat of pers*) reward for; **sich ~** be worthwhile; pay; **~d** worthwhile; rewarding

die **Löhnung, -en** *mil* pay

die **Loipe, -n** *ski* marked course (for cross-country races)

die **Lok** [-ɔ-], **-s** (= **Lokomotive**) locomotive; **der ~führer, -** engine-driver, engineer *US*

lokal local

das **Lokal, -e** pub, bar; restaurant; premises

Lokal- local ...; **das ~kolorit** local colour; **der ~patriotismus** local patriotism; **der ~termin, -e** *leg* visit to the scene of the crime

lokalisieren localize; locate; **~ auf** (*acc*) limit to

die **Lokalität, -en** locality; *coll* cloakroom, washroom *US*

Lokomotiv-: der ~führer, - engine-driver, engineer *US*; **der ~schuppen, -** engine-shed

die **Lokomotive, -n** locomotive

der **Lokus, -se** *coll* toilet

die **Lombardei** Lombardy

der **Longdrink, -s** long drink

der **Look** [luk], **-s** *fash* look (*esp in compds*)

der **Looping** ['lu:pɪŋ], **-s** (*also* **das**) looping the loop; **einen ~ drehen** loop the loop

der **Lorbeer** [-ɔ-] laurel; laurel wreath; *cul* bay-leaf; **~en** *pl* laurels (= honour); **(sich) auf seinen ~en ausruhen** *coll* rest on one's laurels || **das ~blatt, ¨-er** bay-leaf

die **Lore, -n** *min etc* truck

los loose; **es ist etwas ~** something's up; there's something going on; **hier ist nichts ~** there's nothing doing here; **mit ... ist etwas ~** there's something wrong with ...; **mit ... ist nicht viel ~** ... is *etc* not up to much; **was ist ~?** what's up?; **was ist hier ~?** what's going on here?; **was ist mit ... ~?** what's the matter with ...?; (+*acc*) **~ sein** *coll* be rid of; have lost/spent; **~!** come on!; go on!; **auf die Plätze, fertig, ~!** on your marks, get set, go!

das **Los, -e** lot; lottery-ticket; **das Große ~ ziehen** win first prize; hit the jackpot; **durch das ~ entscheiden** decide by drawing lots

---

los- *sep pref – general senses*:

(*i*) ... off (*eg* **~marschieren** march off);

(*ii*) *with* **auf** (*acc*), *indicates direction* ... for ..., ... towards ... (*eg* **auf etw. ~fahren** head for) *or vigorous activity directed at someone or something* (*eg* **auf etw. ~hämmern** pound away at sth.);

(*iii*) *indicates separation* un- (*eg* **~ketten** unchain);

(*iv*) *indicates beginning of action* (*eg* **~brüllen** start roaring)

-los -less (*eg* **hoffnungs~** hopeless); without ... (*eg* **widerstands~** without resistance)

---

lösbar soluble (*also chem*)

losbekommen* *coll* get off

losbinden* untie

losbrechen* break off; (*v/i sn*) break off; (gunfire *etc*) break out; (storm) break

Lösch- fire-extinguishing/fighting ...; **das ~blatt, ¨-er** sheet of blotting-paper; **der ~kalk** slaked lime; **der ~kopf, ¨-e** erasing head; **das ~papier** blotting-paper

löschen[1] put out, extinguish; slake (lime); quench (thirst); erase (tape, sth. from blackboard or tape); erase, wipe out (memory); cancel, delete (entry); liquidate (debt), redeem (mortgage); blot (ink)

löschen[2] *naut* unload

der **Löscher, -** blotter; fire-extinguisher

losdonnern *coll* start to roar; (*v/i sn*) roar off

losdrücken pull the trigger

lose loose; **~ verkaufen** sell loose || **L~blatt-** loose-leaf ...

das **Löse|geld, -er** ransom

los|eisen *coll*: **~ aus** get (s.o.) out of; **~ bei** get (money) out of; **~ von** get (s.o.) away from; **sich ~ von** get away from

losen draw lots (**um** for)

lösen (*see also* **gelöst**) remove; undo; take off (brake); loosen (cough, s.o.'s tongue); dissolve; cancel (contract), break off (engagement *etc*); solve; buy (ticket)

sich ~ come off; come undone; come/work loose; (cough) loosen; dissolve; solve/resolve itself; (tension *etc*) ease; **sich ~ von** come off; break away from; break with; free oneself of

losfahren* (*sn*) set off; drive off; **~ auf** (*acc*) head for; go for

losgehen* (*sn*) set off; (gun *etc*) go off; *coll* come off/undone; *coll* start; **~ auf** (*acc*) make for; go for; **jetzt geht's los!** it's starting!; here we go!; this is it!; **wann geht's los?** when does it/do we *etc* start?; **der Schuß ging nach hinten los** the gun backfired; the plan backfired on him/us *etc*

loshaben* *coll*: **etwas/nichts ~ in** (*dat*) be good/no good at

loshaken unhook

loshämmern: ~ auf (*acc*) pound away at

loskaufen ransom

loskommen* (*sn*) get away; ~ **von** get away from; get off (ground); kick (addiction); **gut** ~ get a good start

loskriegen *coll* get off; get rid of

loslachen burst out laughing; **laut** ~ laugh out loud

loslassen* let go of; release, let go; *coll* come out with (joke, remark, *etc*); send off; ~ **auf** (*acc*) set (dog) on; let loose on; **nicht** ~ (memory *etc*) haunt

loslegen *coll* get cracking; fire away; let rip

löslich soluble; **–löslich** soluble in …

die **Löslichkeit** solubility

loslösen detach (**von** from); **sich** ~ come off; **sich** ~ **von** come off; break away from

losmachen untie; (*v/i*) *naut* cast off; *coll* get a move on; **sich** ~ free oneself; get loose; **sich** ~ **von** get away from; free oneself of

losplatzen (*sn*) *coll* burst out; burst out laughing

losreißen* tear off, rip off; **sich** ~ break loose (**von** from); tear oneself away (from)

losrennen* (*sn*) run off

der **Löß, –(ss)e** loess

lossagen: sich ~ **von** renounce; break with

die **Lossagung, –en** renunciation; break (with)

losschießen* begin firing; *coll* start talking; (*sn*) shoot off; ~ **auf** (*acc*) (*sn*) race up to; **schieß los!** fire away!

losschlagen* knock off; *coll* dispose of; (*v/i*) *mil etc* attack; ~ **auf** (*acc*) hit out at

losschrauben unscrew

lossprechen*: ~ **von** release from; *eccles* absolve from

lossteuern (*sn*): ~ **auf** (*acc*) head for; aim at

losstürmen (*sn*) charge off; ~ **auf** (*acc*) rush towards; make a rush for

lostrennen take off (button *etc*); separate

die **Losung[1], –en** slogan, watchword; *mil* password

die **Losung[2], –en** *hunt* droppings

die **Lösung, –en** *vbl noun*; *also* solution (*also chem*) (*gen* to); **das ~s|mittel, –** solvent

loswerden* (*sn*) get rid of; *coll* dispose of; lose; spend

losziehen* (*sn*) *coll* set out; ~ **mit** go off with; ~ **gegen** run down

das **Lot, –e** plumb-line, *naut* (sounding) lead; *math* perpendicular; *tech* solder; **im** ~ plumb; all right; **(wieder) ins** ~ **bringen** put right || **l~recht** perpendicular

Löt– soldering …; **der ~kolben, –** soldering iron; **die ~lampe, –n** blow-lamp, blowtorch *US*

loten plumb

löten solder

Lothringen [–oː–] Lorraine

der **Lotos** [–ɔs], **–** lotus

der **Lotse** [–oː–], **–n** (*wk masc*) *naut* pilot

lotsen [–oː–] guide; *naut* pilot; *coll* drag (along) (to party *etc*); (+*dat*) **das Geld aus der Tasche** ~ *coll* persuade to part with his *etc* money

Lotter–: das ~leben dissolute life; **die ~wirtschaft** *coll* chaos

die **Lotterie, –(ie)n** lottery

lott(e)rig *coll* slovenly

das **Lotto, –s** (state) lottery; lotto

der **Louis** ['luːi] (*gen* – [–(s)]), – [–s] *coll* pimp

der **Löwe, –n** (*wk masc*) lion; *astron*, *astrol* Leo

Löwen Louvain

Löwen– lion's …; **der ~anteil** lion's share; **der ~bändiger, –** lion-tamer; **das ~maul** = **das ~mäulchen, –** snapdragon; **der ~zahn** dandelion

die **Löwin, –nen** lioness

loyal [lŏaj–] loyal; fair

die **Loyalität** [lŏaj–] loyalty; fairness

die **LP, –(s)** L.P.

die **LPG, –(s)** *EGer* (= **Landwirtschaftliche Produktionsgenossenschaft**) agricultural co-operative

lt. (= **laut**) according to

der **Luchs** [–ks], **–e** lynx

die **Lücke, –n** gap; loophole; **der ~n|büßer, –** stopgap; **l~n|los** without a gap; complete; unbroken

lückenhaft full of gaps; incomplete

lud (lüde) *p/t* (*subj*) *of* **laden[1,2]**

das **Luder, –** 'bitch'; *hunt* bait; **armes/dummes** ~ poor/silly creature; **kleines** ~ little devil || **das ~leben** dissolute life

Ludwig Ludwig; Louis

der **Luffa|schwamm, ⸚e** loofah

die **Luft, ⸚e** air; breeze; **es ist dicke** ~ the atmosphere is tense; **die ~ ist rein** *coll* the coast is clear; **tief** ~ **holen** take a deep breath; (+*dat*) ~ **machen** *coll* give vent to; **an die** ~ **setzen** *coll* chuck out; fire; **aus der** ~ **gegriffen** pure fabrication; **in die** ~ **gehen** blow up, explode; *coll* blow one's top; **in die** ~ **sprengen** blow up; **in der** ~ **hängen** *coll* be up in the air; be in limbo

Luft– air …; aerial …; pneumatic …; **der ~angriff, –e** air-raid; **Luft-Boden–** air-to-surface …; **die ~brücke, –n** airlift (**über eine L. herein-/hineinbringen** airlift); **l~dicht** airtight; **der ~druck** air/atmospheric pressure; (from explosion) blast; **der ~druck|messer, –** barometer; **die ~fahrt** aviation; **l~gekühlt** air-cooled; **das ~gewehr, –e** air-rifle; **die ~herrschaft** air supremacy; **das ~kissen|fahrzeug, –e** hovercraft; **die ~klappe, –n** air-valve; *mot* choke; **der ~krieg, –e** aerial warfare; **der ~kur|ort, –e** (climatic) health resort; **die ~lande|truppen** *pl* airborne troops; **l~leer (l~leerer Raum** vacuum; **im ~leeren Raum** in a vacuum); **~linie (in der L.** as the crow flies); **das ~loch, ⸚er** airpocket; **Lụft-Lụft–** air-to-air ...; **die ~matratze, –n** air-mattress; **die ~parade, –n** fly-past, flyover *US*; **der ~pirat, –en** (*wk masc*) hijacker; **die ~post** airmail (**mit/per L.** (by) airmail); **der ~post|brief, –e** airmail letter; **der ~post|leicht|brief, –e** aerogramme; **der ~raum** air-space; **die ~röhre, –n** windpipe; **der ~röhren|schnitt, –e** tracheotomy; **der ~sack, ⸚e** *mot* air bag; *ornith* air sac; **das ~schiff, –e** airship; **die ~schlange, –n** streamer; **die ~schlösser** *pl* castles in the air; **der ~schutz** anti-aircraft defence; **~schutz–** air-raid ...; **die ~spiegelung, –en** mirage; **der ~sprung, ⸚e** leap in the air (**vor Freude einen L. machen** jump for joy); **die ~stewardeß, –(ss)en** air-hostess; **die ~streit|kräfte** *pl* air force; **die ~verkehrs|gesellschaft, –en** airline; **die ~waffe, –n** air force; **der ~weg, –e** air route; (*pl*) respiratory channels (**auf dem L.** by air); **der ~zug, ⸚e** draught

lüften air; lift (hat *etc*); reveal (secret)

luftig airy; (clothing) light

der **Luftikus, –se** *coll* happy-go-lucky fellow

die **Lüftung** airing; ventilation

Lug: ~ und Trug lies and deception

die **Lüge, –n** lie; (+*acc*) **~n strafen** give the lie to

lugen peep

lügen (*p/t* **log** (*subj* **löge**), *p/part* **gelogen**) (tell a) lie; **das ist gelogen** that's a lie

Lügen–: der ~detektor, –en lie-detector; **die ~geschichte, –n** cock-and-bull story; **das ~gespinst, –e** tissue of lies; **das ~maul, ⸚er** *coll* liar

lügenhaft untrue

der **Lügner, –** liar

lügnerisch untrue; lying

Lukas [–as] Luke

die **Luke, –n** skylight; hatch

lukrati̱v lucrative

Lukre̱z Lucretius

lukụllisch epicurean

der **Lulatsch, –e** *coll*: **(langer) ~** beanpole

lullen: in den Schlaf ~ sing to sleep

der **Lümmel, –** lout

lümmeln: sich ~ sprawl

der **Lump, –en** (*wk masc*) scoundrel

lumpen *coll*: **sich nicht ~ lassen** be generous

der **Lumpen, –** rag; **das ~gesindel = das ~pack** rabble; **das ~proletariat** lumpenproletariat; **der ~sammler, –** rag-and-bone man; *joc* last bus/train *etc*

die **Lumpere̱i, –en** shabby trick; *coll* trifle

lumpig mean; *coll* paltry

das **Lunch|paket** ['lan(t)ʃ–], **–e** packed lunch

die **Lunge, –n** lungs; lung; **auf ~ rauchen** inhale

Lungen– lung ...; pulmonary ...; **die ~entzündung, –en** pneumonia; **der ~flügel, –** lung; **l~krank** suffering from tuberculosis; **der ~krebs** lung cancer

lungern loaf about

Lunte *coll*: **~ riechen** smell a rat; sense danger

die **Lupe, –n** magnifying-glass; **unter die ~ nehmen** *coll* scrutinize || **l~n|rein** flawless; impeccable

lüpfen lift

die **Lupi̱ne, –n** lupin

der **Lurch, –e** amphibian

die **Lust, ⸚e** pleasure (**an** *dat* in); desire; **~ bekommen zu ...** feel like (+*ger*); **~ haben auf** (*acc*)/**zu** feel like; **~ haben zu ...** feel like (+*ger*); **keine ~ haben** not feel like it; (+*dat*) **die ~ verderben an** (*dat*) put off; **mit ~ und Liebe** with great enthusiasm; **nach ~ und Laune** just as the fancy takes one || **das ~gefühl, –e** feeling of pleasure; **l~los** unenthusiastic; *comm* slack; **der ~molch, –e** *coll* (old) lecher; **der ~mord, –e** sex murder; **der ~mörder, –** sex killer; **das ~objekt, –e** sex object; **das ~spiel, –e** comedy; **l~wandeln** (*insep*; *sn*) promenade

die **Lustbarkeit, –en** *dated* (public) entertainment

der **Lüster, –** chandelier; *cer*, *text* lustre

lüstern lustful; greedy (**nach** for)

lustig jolly, merry; gay; amusing, funny; **das kann ja ~ werden!** *iron* that'll be fun!; **sich ~ machen über** (*acc*) make fun of

der **Lüstling, –e** lecher

der **Luthera̱ner** [lʊtə–], **–, lutherisch** ['lʊtə–] Lutheran

lutschen, ~ an (*dat*) suck

der **Lutscher, –** lollipop, Popsicle *US*; *coll* teat, nipple *US* (of bottle); dummy, pacifier *US*

Lüttich Liège

Luv *naut*: **in/nach ~** to windward

Luxemburg Luxembourg

luxuri̱ö̱s luxurious

der **Luxus** luxury; *in compds also* de luxe ...; **der ~artikel, –** luxury article/*pl* goods; **die ~ausführung, –en** de luxe model; **das ~weibchen, –** pampered female

Luzẹrn Lucerne

Luzifer [–ɛr] Lucifer

Lymph– lymphatic ...

die **Lymphe** lymph

Lynch– ['lʏnç–]: **die ~justiz** lynch-law

lynchen ['lʏnçn̩] lynch

Lyon [liɔ̃ː] Lyons

die **Lyra, –(r)en** lyre

die **Lyrik** [–ɪk] lyric poetry

der **Lyriker, –** lyric poet, lyricist

lyrisch lyrical

M

[das] **M** [ɛm] (*gen, pl* –, *coll* [ɛms]) M
M *EGer* = **Mark**
m (= **Meter**) m.; **m²** (= **Quadratmeter**) sq.m.; **m³** (= **Kubikmeter**) cu.m.
MA. = **Mittelalter; M.A.** = **Magister Artium** (*see* **Magister**)
[der] **Mäander, –** *art, geog* meander
[die] **Maas** the Meuse
[der] **Maat, –e(n)** *naut* petty officer, petty officer 1st class *US*
Mach–: die ~art, –en style; type; **das ~werk, –e** (poor *etc*) effort; **die ~-Zahl, –en** Mach number
machbar feasible
[die] **Mache** sham; **in der ~ haben** *coll* be working on; = **in die ~ nehmen** *coll* go for (verbally); work over
machen (*see also* **gemacht**) do; make; go on (journey); take (examination); put (comma *etc*); go ('miaow' *etc*); come to (specified total); (+*adj*) make one (tired *etc*)/one look (old *etc*); *coll* play the part of; act as; (+*dat*; *see also* **Angst, Mut,** *etc*) make (trouble, work) for; cause (s.o. pain *etc*), give (s.o. pleasure *etc*); (*v/i*) *coll* go (to a place); **das macht (das Wetter** *etc*) it's (the weather *etc*); **(das) macht nichts** *coll* it doesn't matter; **... macht mir nichts** *coll* I don't mind ...; **da ist nichts zu ~/kann man nichts ~** *coll* there's nothing one can do about it; **was macht ...?** what is ... doing?; how is ... doing?; how is ... coming along?; *math* what is (8 divided by 2 *etc*)?; **was macht das?** what does that come to?; **mach doch/schon!** hurry up!; **mach's gut!** all the best!; **mach, daß du fortkommst!** get out of here!; **~ lassen** have (sth.) done/made/ seen to; **laß mich nur ~!** *coll* just leave it to me!
~ **auf** *coll*: **auf (Künstler** *etc*) **~** play the (artist *etc*); **auf (gelehrt** *etc*) **~** play the (scholar *etc*)
~ **aus** make (object) from/out of; make (film-star *etc*) of; **etwas aus sich zu ~ wissen** know how to make the most of oneself; **sich** *dat* **nichts ~ aus** not let (sth.) bother one; not care for; **sich** *dat* **wenig ~ aus** not care much for
~ **in** (*dat*) *coll* be in (specified line of business, *eg* **sie macht in Computern** she's in computers); be into (culture *etc*); make a show of; **ins Bett/in die Hose(n) ~** wet the bed/oneself; make a mess in the bed/one's pants
~ **mit** do (sth.) with
~ **von: sich** *dat* **einen Begriff/eine Vorstellung ~ von** form an idea of
~ **zu** make (s.o./sth. sth., *eg* s.o. one's wife, Berlin the capital); turn into; **sich** *dat* **... zum Freund/Feind ~** make a friend/an enemy of
sich ~ come on; look (nice *etc*) (in a certain position); **sich ~ an** (*acc*) get down to; **sich an die Arbeit ~** set to work; **sich auf den Weg ~** set off; **sich ~ hinter** (*acc*) *coll* get down to; **sich ~ zu** make oneself (spokesman *etc*); **sich gut ~ zu** go well with
[die] **Machenschaften** *pl* machinations
[der] **Macher, –** *coll* man of action
machiavellistisch [–k–] Machiavellian
[die] **Macht, ⸚e** power; force; **an der ~** in power; **an die ~ kommen** come into power; **mit aller ~** with all one's might || **der ~bereich, –e** sphere of influence; **die ~ergreifung, –en** (*esp* Hitler's) seizure of power; **die ~gier** lust for power; **die ~haber** *pl* (despotic) rulers; **m~los** powerless; impotent; **das ~mittel, –** instrument of power; **die ~probe, –n** trial of strength; **die ~stellung, –en** position of power; **die ~übernahme** takeover; **m~voll** powerful; **die ~vollkommenheit** absolute power (**aus eigener M.** on one's own authority); **~wort** (**ein M. sprechen** put one's foot down)
mächtig powerful; mighty; huge; *coll* tremendous; (*adv*) *coll* tremendously; **seiner selbst/seiner Sinne nicht ~ sein** not be in control of oneself; **einer Sprache ~ sein** have a command of a language
Macke *coll*: **eine ~ haben** have a screw loose
Madagaskar Madagascar
[der] **Madagasse, –n** (*wk masc*), **madagassisch** Madagascan
[das] **Mädchen, –** girl; maid; **leichtes ~** loose woman; **~ für alles** *coll* maid of all work || **der ~handel** white-slave traffic; **der ~händler, –** white-slaver; **der ~name, –n** (*like* **Name**) girl's/maiden name
mädchenhaft girlish
[die] **Made, –n** maggot
[das] **Mädel, –**/*NGer* **–s** *coll* lass
madig maggoty; **~ machen** *coll* run down;

(+*dat*) put off

die **Madonna, –(nn)en** madonna

mag *1st/3rd sing pres of* **mögen**

das **Magazin, –e** storeroom; (in gun) magazine; (illustrated) magazine

der **Magaziner, –** *Swiss* storeman

der **Magazineur** [–'nøːɐ], **–e** *Aust* storekeeper

die **Magd** [maːkt], **⸚e** farm-girl; maid; *poet* maid(en)

der **Magen,** *pl* **Mägen** stomach; **mit leerem ~** on an empty stomach; **... liegt mir im ~** *coll* I can't stomach (person); (+*dat*) **(schwer) im ~ liegen** lie heavy on (s.o.'s) stomach; *coll* prey on (s.o.'s) mind

Magen– stomach ...; gastric ...; **der ~bitter, –** bitters; **der Magen-Darm-Katarrh, –e** gastroenteritis; **die ~grube, –n** pit of the stomach; **der ~krebs** cancer of the stomach; **die ~säure** gastric acid; **die ~schleim|haut, ⸚e** lining of the stomach; **die ~schleim|haut|entzündung, –en** gastritis; **die ~schmerzen** *pl* stomach-ache; **die ~verstimmung, –en** stomach upset

mager lean; (diet) low-fat; (soil) poor; meagre; **die M~milch** skimmed milk; **die M~sucht** anorexia

die **Magie** magic

der **Magier** [–ĭɐ], **–** magician

magisch magic; magical; **~es Auge** magic eye

der **Magister, –** (*for* **~ Artium**: *degree in Arts, equivalent to the* Diplom *in other faculties*)

der **Magistrat, –e** municipal authority

der **Magnat, –en** (*wk masc*) magnate

das **Magnesium** magnesium

der **Magnet, –e** (*or* **–en** (*wk masc*)) magnet; *in compds* magnetic ...; **das ~band, ⸚er** magnetic tape; **der ~zünder, –** magneto

magnetisch magnetic

magnetisieren magnetize

der **Magnetismus** magnetism

die **Magnolie** [–ĭə], **–n** magnolia

magst *2nd sing pres of* **mögen**

mäh! baa!

Mäh–: der ~drescher, – combine harvester; **die ~maschine, –n** mower

das **Mahagoni** mahogany

der **Maharadscha, –s** maharajah

mähen[1] mow; reap (corn)

mähen[2] bleat

das **Mahl, –e/⸚er** meal, repast

Mahl–: der ~stein, –e millstone; **der ~zahn, ⸚e** molar; **die ~zeit, –en** meal; feed (of baby) **(gesegnete) M.!** enjoy your meal; **M.!** (*greeting used around lunchtime, esp at work*) hullo!; 'bye!; **(prost) M.!** that's just great!; heaven help us!; not a hope!

mahlen (*p/part* **gemahlen**) grind; (*v/i*: *mot* wheels) spin

Mahn–: der ~brief, –e reminder (to pay); **das ~mal, –e** monument

die **Mähne, –n** mane

mahnen remind (**an** *acc* of); admonish; send a reminder to; **~ zu** urge on

die **Mahnung, –en** reminder; admonition

die **Mähre, –n** jade

Mähren Moravia

der **Mai** (*gen* **–(e)s/–**), **–e** May; **im ~** in May || **der ~baum, ⸚e** maypole; **die ~feier, –n** May Day celebrations; **das ~glöckchen, –** lily of the valley; **der ~käfer, –** cockchafer

die **Maid, –en** *poet* maiden

Mailand Milan

der **Mailänder, –, mailändisch** Milanese

die **Main|linie** (*River Main as 'boundary' between N. and S. Germany*)

der **Mais** maize, corn *US*; **der ~kolben, –** corn-cob; corn on the cob; **die ~stärke** cornflour, cornstarch *US*

die **Majestät, –en** majesty

majestätisch majestic

der **Major, –e** major; (air force) squadron-leader, major *US*

der **Majoran, –e** marjoram

majorisieren outvote

der **Majorz** *Swiss* first-past-the-post system

makaber macabre

der **Makel, –** blemish; stigma; stain (on character); **m~los** perfect, flawless; immaculate; impeccable; untarnished

mäkeln: ~ an (*dat*) find fault with

das **Make-up** [meːk'ʔap], **–s** make-up; foundation; face-lift (given to building *etc*)

die **Makkaroni** *pl* macaroni

der **Makler, –** broker; estate agent, real estate agent *US*; **ehrlicher ~** honest broker

die **Makrele, –n** mackerel

Makro– macro–

die **Makrone, –n** macaroon

die **Makulatur, –en** waste paper; *print* spoiled sheets

mal[1] *coll* = **einmal**

mal[2] *math* times

das **Mal**[1], **–e** mark; monument; *sp* base

das **Mal**[2], **–e** time (= occasion); **dies(es) eine ~** just this once; **mit einem ~e** suddenly; **von ~ zu ~** (better *etc*) each time; **zum (ersten** *etc*) **~** for the (first *etc*) time

Mal– painting ...; **das ~buch, ⸚er** colouring-book; **der ~kasten, ..kästen** paint-box; **m~nehmen*** (*sep*) multiply (**mit** by); **das ~zeichen, –** multiplication sign

–mal ... times

der **Malaie, –n** (*wk masc*) Malay(an)

malaiisch Malay; Malayan; (*language*) **M~** Malay

die **Malaria** malaria

Malaysia [–'laẹ–] Malaysia

der **Malaysier** [–'laẹzĭɐ], **–, malaysisch** [–'laẹ–] Malaysian

malen paint; write laboriously; **sich ~ lassen**

have one's portrait painted

der **Maler, –** painter

die **Malerei, –en** painting (= art, picture)

malerisch picturesque; as a painter

das **Malheur** [ma'lø:ʁ], **–s/–e** *coll* mishap

–malig (done/occurring) ... times, *or simply rendered by the appropriate numeral* (*with noun in pl*), *eg* **nach zweimaligem Tiebreak** after two tiebreaks

maliziös malicious

Mallorca [ma'lɔrka, ma(l)'jɔrka] Majorca

malochen *coll* slave away

Malta Malta

der **Malteser, –, maltesisch** Maltese

malträtieren ill-treat

die **Malve, –n** mallow; **m~n|farbig** mauve

das **Malz** malt; **das ~bonbon, –s** (*also* **der**) malt lozenge

die **Mama** ['ma–], **–s** *coll* = **die Mami, –s** *coll* mummy, mommy *US*

das **Mammut, –e/–s** mammoth; *in compds* mammoth ...; marathon ...

mampfen *coll* munch

man¹ [–a–] (*acc* **einen,** *dat* **einem;** *see p. xxx*) one; you; people; they; we; *or translated by passive* (*eg* **~ hat gesagt, daß ...** it has been said that ...); *with subjunctive, expresses an instruction* (*eg* **~ nehme ...** take ...)

man² [–a–] *NGer coll* just (*eg* **er soll's ~ versuchen** just let him try), *or left untranslated* (*eg* **mach du ~** you do it)

das **Management** ['mɛnɪdʒmənt], **–s** management

managen ['mɛnɪdʒn̩] (*p/part* **gemanagt**) manage (pop-star *etc*); *coll* fix

der **Manager** ['mɛnɪdʒʁ], **–** manager; **die ~krankheit** stress disease

die **Managerin** ['mɛnɪdʒ–], **–nen** manageress

manch.. (*uninflected* **manch**) many a; **~e** *pl* some; **~er** many a person; **~es** some things; a number of things; **~ einer** many a person || **~mal** sometimes

mancher–: ~lei (*indecl*) 1 *adj* various (kinds of); 2 *pron* various things; **~orts** in various places

der **Manchester** [man'ʃɛstʁ] corduroy

der **Mandant, –en** (*wk masc*) *leg* client

die **Mandarine, –n** mandarin (orange)

das **Mandat, –e** mandate; *parl* seat; *leg* brief; **sein ~ niederlegen** resign one's seat

der **Mandatar, –e** *Aust* member of parliament

die **Mandel, –n** almond; *anat* tonsil; **die ~entzündung, –en** tonsillitis

die **Mandoline, –n** mandoline

die **Mandschurei** Manchuria

die **Manege** [–ʒə], **–n** (circus) ring

das **Mangan** manganese

der **Mangel,** *pl* **Mängel** lack (**an** *dat* of); shortage (of); deficiency (of); fault, defect

die **Mangel, –n** mangle; **durch die ~ drehen** *coll* put through the mill

Mangel–: die ~krankheit, –en deficiency disease; **~ware** (**M. sein** be in short supply)

mangelhaft inadequate; poor

mangeln¹ mangle

mangeln²: mir mangelt ... I lack ...; **es mangelt an** (*dat*) there is a lack of; **es mangelt mir an** (*dat*) I lack; I am lacking in; **~d** (a) lack of (*eg* **seine ~de Entschlußkraft** his lack of determination)

mangels (+*gen*) for lack of

die **Manie, –(ie)n** mania

die **Manier** manner (*also art*); affectation; **die ~en** *pl* manners; **das ist keine ~** *coll* that's no way to behave

manieriert affected, mannered

der **Manierismus** *arts* mannerism

der **Manierist, –en** (*wk masc*) *arts* mannerist

manierlich well-behaved

das **Manifest, –e** manifesto; *naut* manifest

der **Manifestant, –en** (*wk masc*) *Aust, Swiss* demonstrator

manifestieren manifest, demonstrate; **sich ~** manifest itself

die **Maniküre, –n** manicure; manicurist

maniküren (*p/part* **manikürt**) manicure

die **Manipulation, –en** manipulation

manipulieren manipulate

manisch manic; **manisch-depressiv** manic-depressive

das **Manko, –s** drawback; shortcoming; *comm* deficit

der **Mann, ⸚er/**(*following num also*) **–** man; husband; *naut* hand; **die ~en** *pl hist or joc* men; **seinen ~ stehen** hold one's own; **~s genug** man enough; **an den ~ bringen** *coll* find a buyer/husband for; **bis zum letzten ~** to the last man; **~ für ~** one after another; **mit ~ und Maus** with all hands; **wie 'ein ~** as one man || **die ~deckung** man-to-man marking; **das ~loch, ⸚er** manhole; **das ~weib, –er** masculine woman

mannbar marriageable

das **Männchen, –** little man; *zool* male; **–männchen** male ...; **~ machen** sit up on its hind-legs; (dog) sit up and beg; **~ malen** doodle

das **Mannequin** ['manəkɛ̃], **–s** (fashion) model

Männer– man's ...; men's ...; male ...; **m~mordend** man-eating; **~sache** (**... ist M.** ... is a man's business); **die ~stimme, –n** male voice; **die ~welt** the menfolk

das **Mannes|alter** manhood; **im besten ~** in the prime of one's life

mannhaft manly; (*adv*: bear) like a man

mannig–: ~fach = **~faltig** various; diverse; **die M~faltigkeit** variety; diversity

männlich male; masculine (*also gramm, pros*)

die **Männlichkeit** manliness; masculinity

Manns–: das ~bild, –er *coll esp SGer* man; **manns|hoch** as high/tall as a man; **m~toll** man-mad

die **Mannschaft, –en** *sp etc* team; *naut* crew; (*pl*) *mil* men

das **Manöver, –** manoeuvre; **im ~** on manoeuvres

manövrier–: ~fähig manoeuvrable

manövrieren (*also v/i*) manoeuvre

die **Mansarde, –n** attic; **das ~n|fenster, –** dormer-window

manschen *coll* mess about

die **Manschette, –n** cuff; frill; *tech* collar; **~n haben** *coll* be scared stiff (**vor** *dat* of) || **der ~n|knopf, ⸚e** cuff-link

der **Mantel,** *pl* **Mäntel** coat; mantle (of snow *etc*); *tech* casing (of tyre *etc*); jacket; sheath (of cable); *geol* mantle; **den ~ nach dem Wind(e) drehen/hängen** *coll* trim one's sails to the wind || **der ~tarif, –e** collective agreement (on working conditions)

manuell manual

das **Manuskript, –e** manuscript; *print* copy

die **Mappe, –n** briefcase; satchel; folder

die **Mär, –en** *arch* tale; fairy-tale (= lie)

Marathon– [–ɔn–]: **der ~lauf, ⸚e** marathon; **der ~läufer, –** marathon runner

das **Märchen, –** fairy-tale; **der ~prinz, –en** (*wk masc*) Prince Charming

märchenhaft (elements *etc*) fairy-tale; fabulous

der **Marder, –** marten

Margarete Margaret

die **Margarine, –n** margarine

die **Marge** [–ʒə], **–n** *comm* margin

die **Margerite, –n** marguerite

Maria Mary; **~ Stuart** [... 'ʃtu:art] Mary Queen of Scots; **~ Theresia** Maria Theresa

die **Marie** *coll* 'dough'; **dicke ~** bulging wallet

Marien– *esp* ... of the Virgin Mary; **der ~käfer, –** ladybird, ladybug *US*

das **Marihuana** marijuana

die **Marille, –n** *Aust* apricot

die **Marinade, –n** marinade

die **Marine** navy; *in compds* naval ...; **marine|blau** navy-blue

marinieren marinate

die **Marionette, –n** puppet; *in compds* **~n–** puppet ...

das **Mark** (bone) marrow; *bot* pith; (+*dat*) **durch ~ und Bein gehen** (scream *etc*) go right through; **bis ins ~ treffen** cut to the quick

die **Mark¹, –** (E. or W. German) mark (**M** *and* **DM** *respectively*); **die Deutsche ~** the deutschmark

die **Mark², –en** *hist* borderland; (*pl*) marches

Mark–: m~erschütternd blood-curdling; **der ~graf, –en** (*wk masc*) *hist* margrave; **der ~stein, –e** landmark (in history); **das ~stück, –e** one-mark piece

markant striking

Mark Anton Mark Antony; **Mark Aurel** Marcus Aurelius

die **Marke, –n** brand; make; postage stamp; token; disc; coupon; mark (showing level *etc*); **komische ~** *coll* odd character

märken *Aust* mark (laundry)

Marken–: der ~artikel, – branded article; **die ~butter** best-quality butter; **m~frei** unrationed; **der ~name, –n** (*like* **Name**) brand-name

der **Marketender, –** *hist* sutler

das **Marketing** ['markətɪŋ] marketing

markieren mark; accentuate; *Aust* punch (ticket); *sp* mark (opponent); score; *theat* walk through (part); *coll* feign; act (the hero *etc*)

markig powerful; vigorous

die **Markise, –n** awning; *jewel* marquise

der **Markt, ⸚e** market (*also comm*); market-place; **auf den ~ bringen** market || **der ~anteil, –e** share of the market; **die ~forschung** market research; **m~gängig** marketable; **m~gerecht** geared to market requirements; **die ~kräfte** *pl* market forces; **die ~lücke, –n** gap in the market; **der ~platz, ⸚e** market-place; **der ~schreier, –** barker; **m~schreierisch** (**m~schreierische Reklame** advertising ballyhoo); **die ~wirtschaft** (**freie/soziale M.** free/social market economy)

Markus Mark

die **Marmelade, –n** jam

der **Marmor, –e** marble

marmoriert marbled

marmorn marble

der **Marodeur** [–'dø:ɐ], **–e** marauder

marodieren maraud

der **Marokkaner, –, marokkanisch** Moroccan

Marokko Morocco

die **Marone, –n** sweet chestnut

die **Marotte, –n** quirk

der **Marquis** [–'ki:] (*gen* **–** [–(s)]), **–** [–s] marquess, marquis

die **Marquise** [–'ki:zə], **–n** marchioness; marquise

Mars (*gen* **–**) *myth*, **der ~** *astron* Mars || **der ~bewohner, – = der ~mensch, –en** (*wk masc*) Martian

marsch! off you go!; *mil* march!

der **Marsch, ⸚e** march (*also mus*); (long) walk; (+*dat*) **den ~ blasen** *coll* haul over the coals; **sich in ~ setzen** move/*mil* march off

die **Marsch, –en** (*low-lying alluvial land protected by dykes*)

Marsch– marching ...; **der ~befehl, –e** marching orders; **m~bereit** ready to march/*coll* go; **der ~flug|körper, –** cruise missile; **die ~richtung, –en** direction of march; line of approach, tactics; **die**

~route, -n route of march; line of approach, tactics

^der^ **Marschall, ⸗e** marshal

marschieren (*sn*) march (**auf** *acc* on); walk

Marseille [–'sɛːj] Marseilles

^die^ **Marter, -n** torment

^das^ **Marterl, -n** *SGer* roadside shrine (marking site of accident)

martern torture; torment

martialisch [–ts–] martial

Martins–: das ~fest Martinmas; **das ~horn, ⸗er** (ambulance *etc*) siren

^der^ **Märtyrer, -** martyr; **zum ~ machen** make a martyr of

^das^ **Märtyrertum** martyrdom

^das^ **Martyrium, -(i)en** martyrdom

^der^ **Marxismus** Marxism

^der^ **Marxist, -en** (*wk masc*), **marxistisch** Marxist

^der^ **März** (*gen* **-(es)**), **-e** March; **im ~** in March

^das^ **Märzen(bier)** (*type of strong beer*)

^das^ **Marzipan, -e** marzipan

^die^ **Masche, -n** mesh; stitch; (stocking) ladder, run; *Aust* bow; *coll* ploy, trick; gimmick; craze; **linke ~** purl; **rechte ~** plain; **die ~ raushaben** *coll* have got the knack || **der ~n|draht** wire netting; **m~n|fest** run-proof

-maschig -meshed

maschin–: ~schreiben* *Aust*: *see* **maschineschreiben; ~schriftlich** *Aust* typewritten

^die^ **Maschine, -n** machine; typewriter; sewing-machine; aircraft; *coll* fat woman; (*pl*) machinery; **auf/mit der ~ schreiben** type (sth.) || **m~geschrieben** *p/part*; *also* typewritten; **m~schreiben*** (*Aust* **maschin-**) (*sep*: **ich schreibe Maschine;** *p/part* **m~geschrieben** (*Aust* **maschin-**)) type

maschinell mechanical; (*adv*) *also* by machine; **~ bearbeiten** machine; **~ lesbar** machine-readable

Maschinen–: der ~bau mechanical engineering; machine construction; **der ~bauer, -** mechanical engineer; **das ~gewehr, -e** machine-gun (**mit dem M. beschießen/erschießen** machine-gun); **m~lesbar** machine-readable; **das ~öl** machine-oil; **die ~pistole, -n** submachine gun; **der ~schaden, ..schäden** mechanical fault; *aer etc* engine trouble; **der ~schlosser, -** fitter; **die ~schrift** typescript (**in M.** typewritten); **m~schriftlich** typewritten

^die^ **Maschinerie, -(ie)n** machinery

^der^ **Maschinist, -en** (*wk masc*) machine-operator; *naut* (ship's) engineer

^die^ **Maser, -n** vein (in wood *etc*)

maserig grained

^die^ **Masern** *pl* measles

^die^ **Maserung, -en** grain (of wood *etc*)

^die^ **Maske, -n** mask; masked person, masker; *theat* make-up; (+*dat*) **die ~ vom Gesicht reißen** unmask; **unter der ~** (+*gen*) under the guise of || **der ~n|ball, ⸗e** masked ball; **der ~n|bildner, -** make-up artist; **das ~n|kostüm, -e** fancy dress

^die^ **Maskerade, -n** disguise; *arch* masquerade

maskieren mask; disguise, mask (intentions *etc*); **sich ~ als** dress up as

^das^ **Maskottchen, -** mascot

^das^ **Maskulinum** [*also* –'liː–], **-(n)a** masculine (noun)

^der^ **Masochismus** [–x–] masochism

^der^ **Masochist** [–x–], **-en** (*wk masc*) masochist

masochistisch [–x–] masochistic

maß *p/t of* **messen**

^das^ **Maß** [–aː–], **-e** (*see also* **Maßen**) measure; measurement; degree, measure (**an** *dat* of); moderation; **das rechte ~ halten** practise moderation; (+*dat*) **~ nehmen** take (s.o.'s) measurements; **das ~ ist voll** enough is enough; **um das ~ vollzumachen** to cap it all; **in dem ~e, wie ...** as ...; **in (gewissem** *etc*) **~e** to a (certain *etc*) extent/degree; **in besonderem ~e** especially; **in hohem ~e** to a high degree; **in reichem/vollem/zunehmendem ~e** amply/fully/increasingly; **mit zweierlei ~ messen** apply a double standard; **nach ~** made to measure

^die^ **Maß** [–aː–], **-(e)/**(*following num*) **-** *SGer* tankardful (= 1 litre) of beer

Maß– *esp* made-to-measure ...; **~arbeit (das war M.** that was perfect timing/a perfect fit/beautifully judged); **die ~einheit, -en** unit of measurement; **~gabe (nach M.** (+*gen*) in accordance with); **m~gebend** = **m~geblich** authoritative; leading; decisive; (circles) influential (**m. beteiligt sein an** (*dat*) play a key role in); **m~geschneidert** tailor-made; **m~halten*** (*sep*) practise moderation; **der ~krug, ⸗e** *SGer* (one-litre) beer mug; **m~los** immoderate; inordinate; excessive; (exaggeration) gross; (*adv*) extremely; grossly; **die ~nahme, -n** measure, step (**~nahmen ergreifen/treffen** take steps); **m~regeln** (*insep*) reprimand; discipline; **der ~schneider, -** bespoke tailor, custom tailor *US*; **der ~stab, ⸗e** standard; criterion; *geog* scale; **m~stab(s)|gerecht** = **m~stab(s)|getreu** scale; to scale; **m~voll** moderate

^die^ **Massage** [–ʒə], **-n** massage; **der ~salon, -s** massage-parlour

^das^ **Massaker, -, massakrieren** massacre

^die^ **Masse, -n** mass (*also phys*); crowd; *cul* mixture; *leg* estate; (*pl*) (the) masses; **eine ~ ...** *coll* masses of ...; **in ~n** in droves

mäße *p/t subj of* **messen**

Maßen: mit ~ in moderation; **über alle/die ~** beyond measure

-maßen *forming adverbs* (*with level stress*), *eg* **erklärtermaßen** avowedly, **folgender-**

maßen as follows
Massen– mass ...; **der ~artikel,** – mass-produced article; **die ~medien** *pl* mass media; **die ~produktion** mass production; **die ~szene, –n** crowd scene; **die ~tier|haltung** factory farming; **m~weise** in vast numbers
massenhaft in vast numbers; (*adv*) *coll* masses of
der **Masseur** [–'søːɐ], **–e** masseur
die **Masseuse** [–'søːzə], **–n** masseuse
massieren[1] *mil* mass
massieren[2] massage
massig massive; (*adv*) *coll* masses of
mäßig moderate; mediocre; (*adv*) in moderation; ~ **leben** lead a life of moderation

---

–mäßig *forming adjectives*:
(*i*) = '*in accordance with*', *eg* **verfassungs~** constitutional (**Verfassung** = constitution), **gewohnheits~** habitual (**Gewohnheit** = habit);
(*ii*) in terms of, as regards, '–wise', *eg* **qualitäts~** in terms of/as regards quality, 'quality-wise';
(*iii*) = '*in the nature of*', *eg* **behelfs~** makeshift (**Behelf** = makeshift), **roboter~** robot-like, like a robot;
(*iv*) (*adverbial*) *denotes manner*, *eg* **kartei~** (record *etc*) on index-cards (**Kartei** = card-index), **zahlen~** (express) in figures (**Zahl** = figure)

---

mäßigen (*see also* **gemäßigt**) moderate; check; slacken (speed); **sich** ~ restrain oneself; (storm *etc*) die down
die **Mäßigkeit** moderation, restraint
die **Mäßigung** *vbl noun*; *also* moderation
massiv (gold, chocolate, *etc*) solid; solidly-built; (attack, resistance) heavy; (verbal attack) vehement, (threat) grave; ~ **werden** *coll* cut up rough
das **Massiv, –e** massif
der **Mast, –e(n)** mast; pole; *elect* pylon
die **Mast, –en** fattening; *in compds also* fattened ...; **der ~darm, ⸚e** rectum
mästen fatten
–mastig –masted
der **Matador, –e** matador; *sp etc* star
das **Match** [mɛtʃ], **–s/–e** match; **der ~ball, ⸚e** match-point; **der ~beutel, –** = **der ~sack, ⸚e** duffel bag
das **Material, –ien** [–ĭən] material; materials; *leg* evidence; **rollendes** ~ rolling stock
der **Materialismus** materialism
der **Materialist, –en** (*wk masc*) materialist
materialistisch materialistic
die **Materie** [–ĭə], **–n** subject-matter; *phys* matter
materiell material; financial; materialistic

die **Mathe** ['matə] *coll* maths, math *US*
die **Mathematik** mathematics
der **Mathematiker, –** mathematician
mathematisch mathematical
die **Matinee, –(ee)n** morning performance
der **Matjes|hering** ['matjəs–], **–e** salted young herring
die **Matratze, –n** mattress
die **Mätresse, –n** *hist* mistress
matriarchalisch [–ç–] matriarchal
das **Matriarchat** [–ç–], **–e** matriarchy
die **Matrikel, –n** *esp univ* register; *Aust* = **Personenstandsregister**
die **Matrize, –n** stencil; *print* matrix
die **Matrone, –n** matron (= older woman)
matronenhaft matronly
der **Matrose, –n** (*wk masc*) sailor
der **Matsch** mush; slush; mud
matschen *coll* splash about
matschig *coll* mushy; slushy; muddy
matt weak, feeble; weary; dull; dim; matt; frosted; *chess* mate; ~ **setzen** checkmate || **das M~glas** frosted glass; **die M~scheibe, –n** *phot* focusing screen; *TV coll* 'the box', 'the tube' *US* (**M. haben** *coll* have a mental block)
die **Matte**[1], **–n** mat
die **Matte**[2], **–n** *Aust, Swiss* alpine meadow
Matthäi *coll*: **bei ... ist ~ am letzten ...** is broke/on his *etc* last legs
Matthäus Matthew
mattieren give a matt finish to; frost (glass)
die **Mattigkeit** weariness
die **Matura** *Aust, Swiss* = **Abitur**
der **Maturand, –en** (*wk masc*) *Swiss* = **der Maturant, –en** (*wk masc*) *Aust* candidate for the *Matura*
maturieren *Aust, Swiss* take the *Matura*
der **Matz, ⸚e** *coll* little fellow
das **Mätzchen, –** little fellow; (*pl*) *coll* antics; ~ **machen** fool around; **mach keine ~!** no monkey-business!
die **Mauer, –n** wall (*also footb*); **das ~blümchen, –** *coll* wallflower (at dance); **der ~segler, –** swift; **das ~werk** masonry; walls
mauern build (in stone or brick); (*v/i*) lay bricks; stonewall; *sp* play a defensive game
das **Maul, ⸚er** (animal's) mouth; *coll* 'trap'; (evil *etc*) tongue; *in idioms often* = **Mund; das ~ aufreißen** *coll* talk big; **halt's ~!** shut up! || **~affen** *coll* (**M. feilhalten** stand gaping); **der ~beer|baum, ⸚e** mulberry tree; **die ~beere, –n** mulberry; **der ~esel, –** mule; **m~faul** *coll* too lazy to speak; **der ~held, –en** (*wk masc*) *coll* loud-mouth; **der ~korb, ⸚e** muzzle ((+*dat*) **einen M. anlegen** muzzle); **die ~schelle, –n** *coll* slap in the face; **das ~tier, –e** mule; **die Maul- und Klauen|seuche** foot-and-mouth disease; **das ~werk** *coll* mouth; **der ~wurf, ⸚e**

mole; **der ~wurfs|haufen, –** molehill
maulen *coll* grumble
der **Maure, –n** (*wk masc*) Moor
der **Maurer, –** bricklayer; **die ~arbeit** bricklaying
maurisch Moorish
die **Maus, ⸚e** mouse; (*term of endearment*) sweetie; (*pl*) *coll* 'dough'; **weiße ~** *coll* traffic cop; **weiße Mäuse sehen** *coll* see pink elephants || **die ~falle, –n** *Aust* mousetrap; **maus|grau** mouse-grey
mauscheln *coll* talk Yiddish; mumble; do shady deals; cheat
das **Mäuschen** [–sç–], **–** little mouse; (*term of endearment*) sweetie; **mäuschen|still** *coll* dead quiet
Mause–: die ~falle, –n mousetrap; **das ~loch, ⸚er** mousehole; **mause|tot** *coll* as dead as a doornail
Mäuse– mouse ...; **~melken** *coll* **(... ist zum M. ...** is enough to drive you up the wall**)**
mausen *coll* 'pinch'
die **Mauser** moult; **in der ~** moulting
mausern: sich ~ moult; *coll* blossom out (**zu** into)
mausig *coll*: **sich ~ machen** get uppish
das **Mausoleum, –(ee)n** mausoleum
die **Maut, –en** *Aust* toll
maximal maximum; (*adv*) at the most; *in compds* **M~–** maximum ...
die **Maxime, –n** maxim
maximieren maximize
das **Maximum, –(m)a** maximum (**an** *dat* of)
die **Mayonnaise** [majɔ'nɛːzə], **–n** mayonnaise
Mazedonien [–ĭən] Macedonia
der **Mazedonier** [–ĭɐ], **–, mazedonisch** Macedonian
der **Mäzen, –e** patron (of the arts)
das **Mäzenatentum** patronage (of the arts)
die **Mazurka** [–z–], **–(k)en/–s** mazurka
Md. = Milliarde(n)
MdB [ɛmdeː'beː] **= Mitglied des Bundestages**
MdL [ɛmdeː'ʔɛl] **= Mitglied des Landtages**
MdV [ɛmdeː'faʊ̯] *EGer* **= Mitglied der Volkskammer**
m. E. (= meines Erachtens) in my opinion
die **Mechanik** [–ç–, –ɪk], **–en** mechanics; mechanism
der **Mechaniker** [–ç–], **–** mechanic
der **Mechanisator** [–ç–], **–(or)en** *EGer agr* machine servicer
mechanisch [–ç–] mechanical
mechanisieren [–ç–] mechanize
die **Mechanisierung** mechanization
der **Mechanismus** [–ç–], **–(m)en** mechanism
Mecheln Malines
der **Meckerer, –** *coll* grumbler
meckern bleat; *coll* moan
die **Medaille** [–'daljə], **–n** medal; **der ~n|gewinner, –** medallist; **der ~n|spiegel, –** medal table; **m~n|verdächtig** a medal prospect
das **Medaillon** [–dal'jɔ̃ː], **–s** medallion; locket
der **Mediävist, –en** (*wk masc*) medievalist
die **Mediävistik** [–ɪk] medieval studies
Medien *pl of* **Medium**
das **Medikament, –e** medicine
medikamentös medicinal
der **Medikus, –se/Medizi** *joc* medico
medioker mediocre
die **Meditation, –en** meditation
mediterran Mediterranean
meditieren meditate
das **Medium, –(i)en** medium
die **Medizin, –en** medicine; *coll* medicine (taken); **der ~ball, ⸚e** medicine ball; **der ~mann, ⸚er** medicine man; **der ~student, –en** (*wk masc*) medical student
Medizinal–: der ~assistent, –en (*wk masc*) houseman, intern *US*; **der ~rat, ⸚e** medical officer of health
der **Mediziner, –** medical man/student
medizinisch medical; medicinal; medicated
das **Meer, –e** sea; ocean; **am ~** by the sea, at the seaside || **der ~busen, –** gulf, bay; **die ~enge, –n** straits; **die ~jungfrau, –en** mermaid; **der ~rettich, –e** horseradish; **das ~schweinchen, –** guinea-pig
Meeres– sea ...; marine ...; **der ~arm, –e** inlet; **die ~kunde** oceanography; **der ~spiegel** sea-level (**über dem M.** above sea-level)
das **Meeting** [–iː–], **–s** meeting; *sp* meeting, meet *US*
Mega– mega-
das **Megahertz, –** megahertz
Megalith– megalithic ...
das **Megaphon, –e** megaphone
die **Megatonne, –n** megaton
das **Mehl** flour; meal; powder; **die ~schwitze, –n** roux; **die ~speise, –n** dessert (containing flour); *Aust* dessert; cake; **der ~tau** mildew
mehlig floury; mealy
mehr (*indecl*) more; **~ (Künstler** *etc*) **als (Gelehrter** *etc*) more of (an artist *etc*) than (a scholar *etc*)
immer ~ more and more
kaum ~ hardly ... any more
kein ... ~ no more ...; no ... left; no longer (a child *etc*)
nicht ~ no longer, not ... any more; **nicht ~ lange** not much longer
nichts ~ nothing more; **es ist nichts ~ da** there's nothing left
nie ~ never again, not ... ever again
noch ~ even more
nur ~ *SGer* **= nur noch** (*see* **nur**)
~ oder minder/weniger more or less; to a greater or lesser degree
um so ~ all the more; **um so ~ als ...** the more so as ...

~ **und** ~ more and more; **und andere(s)** ~ and so on

[das] **Mehr** increase; *Swiss* majority; **ein** ~ **an** (*dat*) an increase in, more

Mehr– multi–; poly–; multiple …; additional …; (**mehr–**, *eg* **m~schichtig**) consisting of several (layers *etc*)

die ~**arbeit** extra work; **m~deutig** ambiguous; (word *etc*) with several meanings; **m~fach** multiple; repeated; (*adv*) several times (**in m~facher Hinsicht** in several ways; **ein** ~**faches** several times as much); ~**fach–** multiple …; **m~farbig,** *Aust* **m~färbig** multi-coloured; **das** ~**gewicht** excess weight; **m~jährig** several years'; lasting several years; **m~malig** repeated; **m~mals** several times; **das** ~**parteien|system** multi-party system; **m~silbig** polysyllabic; **m~sprachig** polyglot, multilingual; **m~stimmig** for several voices (**m~stimmiges Lied** part-song); **m~stöckig** multi-storey; **die** ~**stufen|rakete, –n** multi-stage rocket; **m~stufig** multi-stage; **m~stündig** several hours'; lasting several hours; **m~tägig** several days'; lasting several days; **die** ~**wert|steuer** value-added tax; **m~wöchig** several weeks'; lasting several weeks; **die** ~**zahl** majority; *gramm* plural; ~**zweck–** multipurpose …; **das** ~**zweck|kampf|flugzeug, –e** multirole combat aircraft

mehren increase; **sich** ~ multiply

mehrere several; ~**s** several things

mehrer|lei (*indecl*) 1 *adj* several (kinds of); 2 *pron* several things

[die] **Mehrheit, –en** majority; **mit knapper** ~ by a bare majority

mehrheitlich by a majority

Mehrheits– majority …; **der** ~**beschluß, ⸗(ss)e** majority decision; **das** ~**wahl|recht** first-past-the-post system

[die] **Mehrung** increase

meiden (*p/t* **mied,** *p/part* **gemieden**) avoid

[die] **Meile, –n** mile; **der** ~**n|stein, –e** milestone; **m~n|weit** miles and miles of; (*adv*) for miles (**m. entfernt** miles away)

[der] **Meiler, –** charcoal pile; (atomic) pile

mein (*see p. xxxiii*) my; ~**er**/~**e**/~**(e)s** (*see p. xxviii*; *also* **der/die/das** ~**e**) mine; **das M~e** what is mine; **das M~e tun** do my bit; **die M~en** my family

[der] **Mein|eid, –e** perjury; **einen** ~ **leisten** perjure oneself

meinen mean (**mit** by); think (= believe); say; **ich möchte** ~ I would think; **man sollte** ~ one would have thought; **das will ich** ~**!** I should think so!; **ich meine nur** it was just a thought; **es ernst** ~ be serious; **es gut** ~ mean well; **es nicht böse** ~ mean no harm

meiner (*gen of* **ich:** *see p. xxvi*) of me; ~**seits** for/on my part

meines|gleichen people like me/myself

meinet–: ~**wegen** because of me; for my sake; as far as I'm concerned; (*citing possible instance*) let's say (**m.!** I don't mind); (**um**) ~**willen** for my sake

meinige: der/die/das ~ = **der/die/das meine** (*at* **mein**)

[die] **Meinung, –en** opinion; **die öffentliche** ~ public opinion; **der** ~ **sein, daß …** be of the opinion that …; **'einer** ~ **sein** be of the same opinion; (+*dat*) **gehörig/gründlich die** ~ **sagen** *coll* give (s.o.) a piece of one's mind; **nach meiner** ~ = **meiner** ~ **nach** in my opinion || **die** ~**s|äußerung, –en** expression of opinion; **der** ~**s|austausch** exchange of views; **die** ~**s|bildung** forming of public opinion; **der** ~**s|forscher, –** pollster; **die** ~**s|forschung** public opinion research; **die** ~**s|freiheit** freedom of speech; **die** ~**s|umfrage, –n** opinion poll; **die** ~**s|verschiedenheit, –en** difference of opinion

[die] **Meise, –n** tit(mouse); **eine** ~ **haben** *coll* be crazy

[der] **Meißel, –, meißeln** chisel

Meiß(e)ner: ~ **Porzellan** Dresden china

meist mostly; usually; **der/die/das** ~**e …** most (of the) …; **das** ~**e** most (of it); **die** ~**en** most (people); **am** ~**en** most (of all)

meist– most …; **der/die M~bietende** (*decl as adj*) highest bidder; **das M~gebot, –e** highest bid; ~**gekauft** best-selling; ~**gelesen** most widely read; ~**gesucht** most wanted

meisten–: ~**teils** mostly

meistens mostly; usually

[der] **Meister, –** master; *sp* champion(s); **seinen** ~ **finden** meet one's match; **ein** ~ **in …** (*dat*) **sein** be a past master at || **das** ~**stück, –e** masterpiece; master stroke; **das** ~**werk, –e** masterpiece

meisterhaft masterly; (*adv*) in a masterly fashion

meistern master

[die] **Meisterschaft, –en** mastery; *sp* championship

Mekka *geog* Mecca; **das** ~ (*gen* **–s**), **–s** Mecca (**für** of)

[die] **Melancholie** [–ŋk–] melancholy

[der] **Melancholiker** [–ŋk–], **–** melancholy person

melancholisch [–ŋk–] melancholy

[die] **Melange** [–'lã:ʒə], **–n** mixture; *Aust* [–'lã:ʒ] white coffee

[die] **Melasse, –n** molasses

Melde– registration …; **der** ~**fahrer, –** dispatch rider; **die** ~**pflicht** obligation to register with/notify the authorities; **m~pflichtig** (disease) notifiable; **der** ~**schluß** closing date (for entries); **der** ~**zettel, –** *Aust* registration form

melden report (*dat*/**bei** to); announce (visitor); enter (**zu** for); **nichts zu ~ haben** *coll* have no say

sich ~ report; register; volunteer; enter (one's name); get in touch; let s.o. know; put one's hand up; (baby) cry (because it wants something); make itself felt; (winter) set in; (stomach) begin to complain; *tel* answer; **sich ~ auf** (*acc*) answer (advertisement); **sich ~ bei** report to; register with; go to see; get in touch with; **sich ~ zu** report for; volunteer for; enrol for; enter (one's name) for; **sich freiwillig ~** volunteer; **sich krank ~** report sick; **sich zu Wort ~** ask to speak; **wir ~ uns wieder um 22 Uhr mit Nachrichten** we'll be back with the news at 10 o'clock

die **Meldung, -en** *vbl noun*; *also* report; news item; announcement; entry (for contest *etc*); **~ machen** report

meliert flecked; **grau ~** (hair) streaked with grey

Melk- milking ...

melken (*p/part* **gemolken**) milk; **~de Kuh** milch cow

die **Melodie, -(ie)n** melody; tune

die **Melodik** [-ık] melodics; melodiousness

melodisch melodic; melodious

das **Melodrama, -(m)en** melodrama

melodramatisch melodramatic

die **Melone, -n** melon; *coll* bowler, derby *US*

der **Meltau** [-e:-] honeydew

die **Membran, -en** = **die Membrane, -n** *anat* membrane; *chem*, *phys*, *tech* diaphragm

die **Memme, -n** *coll* cissy

die **Memoiren** [-'mŏa:-] *pl* memoirs

das **Memorandum, -(d)en/-(d)a** memorandum

memorieren memorize

die **Menage** [-ʒə], **-n** cruet-stand; *Aust mil* [-ʒ] rations

die **Menge, -n** quantity; crowd; *math* set; **eine ~** *coll* a lot (of); **jede ~** *coll* masses (of); **... die ~** *coll* plenty of ...

mengen mix

Mengen- ... of quantity; *comm* bulk ...; **die ~lehre** *math* set theory; **m~mäßig** quantitative; **der ~preis, -e** bulk price

die **Mensa, -(s)en** (students') refectory, commons *US*

der **Mensch, -en** (*wk masc*) human (being); person, *pl* people; *sometimes expressed by* human (*adj*) (*eg* **~ bleiben** stay human, **er ist auch nur ein ~** he's only human); **der ~** man (= species); **der moderne ~** modern man; **die ~en** man(kind); people; **kein ~** no-one; not a soul; **jeder ~** everyone; **unter die ~en kommen** mix with people; **~!** gosh!; (*addressing s.o.*) hey!; **~ Meier!** heavens above!; **„~, ärgere dich nicht"** ludo || **die ~werdung** incarnation

Menschen- human ...;

der ~affe, -n (*wk masc*) anthropoid (ape); **m~ähnlich** man-like; **das ~alter** generation; lifetime; **die ~ansammlung, -en** crowd; **m~arm** sparsely-populated; **der ~feind, -e** misanthropist; **m~feindlich** misanthropic; **der ~fresser, -** cannibal; **die ~fresserei** cannibalism; **der ~freund, -e** philanthropist; **m~freundlich** philanthropic; **~gedenken** (**seit M.** within living memory; since time immemorial); **das ~geschlecht** human race; **der ~handel** slave trade; **der ~haß** misanthropy; **der ~kenner, -** good judge of character; **die ~kenntnis** knowledge of human nature; **m~leer** deserted; **die ~liebe** philanthropy; **die ~menge, -n** crowd; **menschen|möglich** humanly possible (**das m~mögliche tun** do all that is humanly possible); **das ~opfer, -** human sacrifice; (*pl*) fatalities; **die ~rechte** *pl* human rights; **m~scheu** retiring; **der ~schlag** breed of men; **die ~seele, -n** human soul (**keine M.** not a soul); **der ~sohn** the Son of Man; **m~unwürdig** unfit for/unworthy of human beings; unfit for human habitation; **~verstand** (**der gesunde M.** common sense); **m~würdig** fit for/worthy of human beings; fit for human habitation

Menschens|kind! heavens above!

das **Menschentum** humanity

die **Menschheit** mankind, humanity

menschlich human; humane

die **Menschlichkeit** humanity

die **Menstruation, -en** menstruation

menstruieren menstruate

die **Mensur, -en** students' duel

die **Mentalität, -en** mentality

das **Menthol** menthol

der **Mentor, -(or)en** mentor; tutor

das **Menü, -s** set meal; *comput* menu; **der ~laden, ..läden** *EGer* shop selling ready-to-eat meals

das **Menuett, -e** minuet

mephistophelisch Mephistophelian

Meran Merano

der **Mergel, -** marl

der **Meridian, -e** meridian

die **Meriten** *pl* merits

Merk-: das ~blatt, ⸚er leaflet; instruction sheet; **das ~mal, -e** characteristic, feature; **m~würdig** curious, odd; **merk|würdiger|weise** oddly enough; **die ~würdigkeit, -en** oddness; oddity

merkbar perceptible, noticeable; **leicht/schwer ~** easy/hard to remember

merken notice; realize; **sich** *dat* **... ~** remember; make a mental note of; **~ an** (*dat*) tell by; **jmdn.** (**seine Enttäuschung** *etc*) **~ lassen** let s.o. see, show (one's disap-

pointment *etc*); **sich** *dat* **nichts ~ lassen** *coll* not let on; **merke: ...** note: ...
merklich noticeable; distinct
Merkur *myth*, **der ~** (*gen* **–s**) *astron* Mercury
meschugge *coll* crazy
der **Mesner** ['mɛs–], – *RC* sexton
Mesopotamien [–ĭən] Mesopotamia
der **Mesopotamier** [–ĭɐ], –, **mesopotamisch** Mesopotamian
Meß– measuring ...; *RC* mass ...; **das ~band, ⸚er** tape-measure; **das ~buch, ⸚er** *RC* missal; **der ~diener, –** *RC* server; **das ~gerät, –e = das ~instrument, –e** measuring instrument; gauge; **der ~stab, ⸚e** *mot* dipstick; **das ~tisch|blatt, ⸚er** *approx* = ordnance survey map
meßbar measurable
die **Messe**[1], **–n** *RC*, *mus* mass; **die ~ lesen** say mass
die **Messe**[2], **–n** *mil* mess
die **Messe**[3], **–n** (trade) fair; **das ~gelände, –** showground; **der ~stand, ⸚e** stand (at fair)
messen (*2nd/3rd sing pres* **mißt**, *p/t* **maß** [–aː–] (*subj* **mäße**), *p/part* **gemessen**) (*see also* **gemessen**) measure; take (time, s.o.'s temperature, *etc*); judge (distance *etc*); (*v/i*) measure; stand (6 *etc* foot); **mit Blicken ~** size up; **seine Kraft/seinen Verstand ~ an** (*dat*) pit one's strength/wits against; **gemessen an** (*dat*) compared with
sich ~ mit compete with; **sich nicht ~ können mit** be no match for
das **Messer, –** knife; (cut-throat) razor; *tech* blade; **ans ~ liefern** hand over (treacherously) || **messer|scharf** razor-sharp; trenchant; **die ~spitze, –n** knife-point; *cul* pinch; **die ~stecherei, –en** knife fight; **der ~stich, –e** stab (with a knife); stab wound
messianisch Messianic
der **Messias** [–as] (*gen* –) Messiah
das **Messing** brass
die **Messung, –en** measurement
der **Mestize, –n** (*wk masc*) mestizo
der **Met** mead
der **Metabolismus** metabolism
das **Metall, –e** metal; *in compds also* metallic ...; **der ~arbeiter, –** metalworker; **der ~detektor, –en** metal detector; **die ~säge, –n** hacksaw; **die ~waren** *pl* hardware
metallen metal; metallic
der **Metaller, –** metalworker
metallisch metallic
der **Metallurg, –en** (*wk masc*) metallurgist
die **Metallurgie** metallurgy
metallurgisch metallurgical
die **Metamorphose, –n** metamorphosis
die **Metapher, –n** metaphor
die **Metaphorik** [–ɪk] imagery; use of imagery
metaphorisch metaphorical
die **Metaphysik** metaphysics
metaphysisch metaphysical
der **Meteor, –e** meteor
der **Meteorit, –e** (*or* **–en** (*wk masc*)) meteorite
der **Meteorologe, –n** (*wk masc*) meteorologist; *rad*, *TV* weatherman
die **Meteorologie** meteorology
meteorologisch meteorological
der **Meter, –** (*also* **das**) metre; **das ~maß, –e** tape-measure; **die ~ware, –n** goods sold by the metre; **m~weise** by the metre
das **Methan(gas)** methane
die **Methode, –n** method
die **Methodik** [–ɪk] methodology
methodisch methodical; (difficulties *etc*) of method
Methusalem [–ɛm] Methuselah
das **Metier** [–'tĭeː], **–s** job
Metren *pl of* **Metrum**
die **Metrik** [–ɪk] metrics
metrisch metric; *pros* metrical
das **Metronom, –e** metronome
die **Metropole, –n** metropolis
das **Metrum, –(r)en** *pros* metre
Mett–: die ~wurst, ⸚e ((*smoked*) *sausage containing minced beef or pork*)
die **Mette, –n** midnight mass; matins
die **Metzelei, –en** massacre
der **Metzger, –** *esp SGer* butcher
die **Metzgerei, –en** *esp SGer* butcher's (shop)
Meuchel–: der ~mord, –e (treacherous) murder; **der ~mörder, –** (treacherous) murderer
meuchlerisch treacherous; murderous
meuchlings treacherously
die **Meute, –n** pack (of hounds); mob
die **Meuterei, –en** mutiny; (prison) riot
der **Meuterer, –** mutineer; (prison) rioter
meutern mutiny; (prisoners) riot; *coll* rebel; **~d** mutinous; rioting
der **Mexikaner, –, mexikanisch** Mexican
Mexiko Mexico; **~ City** Mexico City
MEZ = Mitteleuropäische Zeit
mg = Milligramm; das MG, –(s) = Maschinengewehr
MHz = Megahertz
Mi. (= Mittwoch) Wed.
miau! miaow!
miauen miaow
mich (*acc of* **ich:** *p. xxvi*) me; (*refl*) myself
Michel *coll*: **der deutsche ~** (*stereotype of the honest, hard-working but politically naïve German*)
Michelangelo [mike'landʒelo] Michelangelo
mick(e)rig *coll* measly; puny
Mickymaus Mickey Mouse
die **Midlife-crisis** ['mɪdlaef kraesɪs] midlife crisis
mied *p/t of* **meiden**
das **Mieder, –** bodice; foundation garment; **die ~hose, –n** pantie-girdle
der **Mief** *coll* fug

miefen *coll* pong; **hier mieft's** there's a fug/pong in here

die **Miene, –n** expression, face; **~ machen zu …** make as if to …; **gute ~ zum bösen Spiel machen** put a bold face on it; **keine ~ verziehen** not turn a hair || **das ~n|spiel** play of features

mies *coll* rotten; **~machen** (*sep*) *coll* run down; **der M~macher, –** *coll* fault-finder; **die M~muschel, –n** (edible) mussel

Miese–: der ~peter, – *coll* sourpuss; **m~pet(e)rig** *coll* grumpy

Miet– rent …; rented …; hired …; **das ~auto, –s** hire(d) car, rented car *US*; **m~frei** rent-free; **der ~preis, –e** rent; **das ~verhältnis, –se** tenancy; **der ~vertrag, ⸚e** lease; **der ~wagen, –** hire(d) car, rented car *US*; **der ~wucher** charging of exorbitant rents; **der ~zins, –e** *SGer* rent

die **Miete[1], –n** rent; **zur ~ wohnen** live in rented accommodation

die **Miete[2], –n** *agr* pit

mieten rent; hire

der **Mieter, –** tenant; lodger; **der ~schutz** protection of tenants

Miets–: das ~haus, ⸚er block of (rented) flats, apartment house *US*; **die ~kaserne, –n** *coll* (big, unsightly) tenement-house

die **Mieze, –n** *coll* pussy; 'chick'; **die ~katze, –n** *coll* pussycat

die **Migräne, –n** migraine

Mikro– micro–

die **Mikrobe, –n** microbe

der **Mikro|film, –e** microfilm; **das ~lese|gerät, –e** microfilm reader

das **Mikrophon, –e** microphone

der **Mikro|prozessor, –en** microprocessor

das **Mikroskop, –e** microscope

mikroskopisch microscopic; (*adv*: examine) under the microscope

die **Mikro|wellen** *pl* microwaves; **der ~herd, –e** microwave oven

der **Milan, –e** kite (= bird)

die **Milbe, –n** mite

die **Milch** milk; *zool* soft roe; **dicke ~** curdled milk || **die ~bar, –s** milk-bar; **die ~flasche, –n** milk-bottle; baby's bottle; **das ~geschäft, –e** dairy; **das ~glas** frosted glass; **der ~händler, –** dairyman; **das ~mädchen, –** dairymaid; **die ~mädchen|rechnung, –en** *coll* naïve, illusory expectation; **der ~mann, ⸚er** milkman; **das ~mix|getränk, –e** milk-shake; **das ~pulver, –** powdered milk; **der ~reis** rice pudding; **die ~säure** lactic acid; **die ~straße** the Milky Way; **die ~tüte, –n** milk carton; **die ~wirtschaft** dairy-farming; **der ~zahn, ⸚e** milk tooth

milchig milky

mild mild; gentle; lenient; **~e gesagt/gesprochen** to put it mildly || **~tätig** charitable

die **Milde** mildness; gentleness; leniency; **~ walten lassen** be lenient

mildern alleviate; moderate; tone down; mitigate; **~de Umstände** extenuating circumstances

das **Milieu** [mi'liø:], **–s** environment; (social) background; *biol* medium

militant militant

die **Militanz** militancy

das **Militär** army; **beim ~ sein** be in the army; **zum ~ gehen** join the army

der **Militär, –s** (army) officer

Militär– military …; **der ~arzt, ⸚e** (army) medical officer; **der ~dienst** military service; **m~pflichtig** liable for military service; **das ~wesen** military affairs

militärisch military

militarisieren militarize

der **Militarismus** militarism

der **Militarist, –en** (*wk masc*) militarist

militaristisch militaristic

die **Military** ['mɪlɪtəri], **–s** *equest* three-day event

die **Miliz, –en** militia; **der ~soldat, –en** (*wk masc*) militiaman

Mill. = **Million(en)**

der **Milliardär, –e** multi-millionaire

die **Milliarde, –n** thousand million, billion

das **Milligramm, –e**/(*following num*) **–** milligramme

der **Millimeter, –** millimetre; **das ~papier** graph paper

die **Million, –en** million

der **Millionär, –e** millionaire

millionst.. millionth

millionstel: ein ~ … a millionth of a …

das **Millionstel, –** millionth

die **Milz, –en** spleen; **der ~brand** anthrax

der **Mime, –n** (*wk masc*) *arch* Thespian

mimen *coll* act (the innocent *etc*); feign

die **Mimik** [-ɪk] (changing) facial expression and gestures

die **Mimikry** ['mɪmikri] disguise, camouflage; *zool* mimicry

mimisch mimic

die **Mimose, –n** mimosa; highly sensitive person

mimosenhaft highly sensitive

das **Minarett, –e** minaret

minder 1 *adj* **minder..** lesser; inferior; 2 *adv* less; *in compds* **minder–** less …; **~bemittelt** of limited means (**geistig m.** *coll* not very bright); **~jährig** under age; **der/die M~jährige** (*decl as adj*) minor; **~wertig** inferior; **die M~wertigkeit** inferiority; **der M~wertigkeits|komplex, –e** inferiority complex; **M~zahl** (**in der M.** in the minority)

die **Minderheit, –en** minority

mindern, sich ~ diminish; lessen

mindest.. least; **nicht im ~en** not in the least; **zum ~en** at least
Mindest– minimum ...; lowest ...; **das ~maß** minimum (**an** *dat* of)
die **Mine, –n** lead (in pencil); refill (for pen); *mil, min* mine; **das ~n|feld, –er** minefield; **der ~n|leger, –** mine-layer; **das ~n|such|boot, –e = der ~n|sucher, –** minesweeper; **das ~n|such|gerät, –e** mine-detector
das **Mineral, –e/–ien** [–ĭən] mineral; **das ~öl** mineral oil; **die ~öl|gesellschaft, –en** oil company; **die ~quelle, –n** mineral spring; **das ~wasser, ..wässer** mineral water
mineralisch mineral
der **Mineraloge, –n** (*wk masc*) mineralogist
die **Mineralogie** mineralogy
mineralogisch mineralogical
Mini– mini–; **der ~car, –s** minicab; **das ~golf** miniature golf; **der ~kini, –s** topless swimsuit; **der ~rock, ⸚e** miniskirt
die **Miniatur, –en** miniature; *in compds* miniature ...
minimal minimal; *in compds* **M~–** minimum ...
das **Minimum, –(m)a** minimum (**an** *dat* of)
der **Minister, –** minister; **der ~präsident, –en** (*wk masc*) prime minister; **der ~rat** the Council of Ministers
Ministerial–: der ~be|amte (*decl as adj*) ministry official; **der ~direktor, –en** head of a government department
ministeriell ministerial
das **Ministerium, –(i)en** ministry
der **Ministrant, –en** (*wk masc*) *RC* server
ministrieren *RC* serve
Minna *coll*: **grüne ~** Black Maria
die **Minne** *liter* courtly love; **der ~sang** courtly love-poetry; **der ~sänger, –** minnesinger
minoisch Minoan
die **Minorität, –en** minority
minus minus
das **Minus, –** deficit; drawback; **der ~pol, –e** negative pole; **das ~zeichen, –** minus sign
die **Minute, –n** minute; **auf die ~** to the minute; **in letzter ~** at the last moment || **m~n|lang** lasting several minutes; (*adv*) for several minutes; **der ~n|zeiger, –** minute-hand
–minutig –minute
–minütlich every ... minutes
minuziös meticulous
die **Minze, –n** mint
Mio. = Millionen
mir (*dat of* **ich**: *see p. xxvi*) (to/for) me/myself; (*ethic dative*) *not translated* (*eg* **daß du ~ gut aufpaßt!** mind you pay attention/take care now); **~ nichts, dir nichts** without so much as a by-your-leave; just like that; **von ~ aus!** I don't mind
die **Mirabelle, –n** mirabelle (plum)
der **Misanthrop, –en** (*wk masc*) misanthropist
die **Misanthropie** misanthropy
misanthropisch misanthropic
Misch– mixing ...; mixed ...; **die ~batterie, –n** mixer tap; **die ~ehe, –n** mixed marriage; **der ~masch, –e** *coll* hotchpotch; **das ~pult, –e** *cin, TV, etc* mixing desk, mixer; **der ~wald, ⸚er** mixed forest
mischen (*see also* **gemischt**) mix; blend; *comput* merge; *cards* shuffle
sich ~ mix; **sich ~ in** (*acc*) meddle in; butt into; **in (jmds. Freude** *etc*) **mischt sich ...** (s.o.'s joy *etc*) is mingled with ...; **sich ~ unter** (*acc*) mingle with
der **Mischling, –e** half-caste, half-breed; *biol* hybrid
die **Mischung, –en** *vbl noun*; *also* mixture; blend; assortment
miserabel rotten; wretched
die **Misere, –n** wretched state of affairs; mess; plight
die **Mispel, –n** medlar
miß *imp sing of* **messen**
Miß Miss (*in titles of beauty queens, eg* **~ Australien**); **die ~wahl, –en** beauty contest
miß– *insep pref* (*unstressed exc in* **~verstehen**)
miß|achten disregard; hold in contempt
die **Miß|achtung** disregard; contempt
das **Missale, –n/Missalien** [–ĭən] *RC* missal
das **Mißbehagen** unease
die **Mißbildung, –en** deformity
mißbilligen disapprove of
die **Mißbilligung** disapproval
der **Mißbrauch, ⸚e** misuse; improper use; abuse; **~ treiben mit** abuse (power *etc*)
mißbrauchen misuse; abuse; assault (sexually)
mißbräuchlich (use) improper
mißdeuten misinterpret
die **Mißdeutung, –en** misinterpretation
Misse–: die ~tat, –en *arch* misdeed; **der ~täter, –** *arch* culprit; wrongdoer
missen do without; miss (experience)
der **Miß|erfolg, –e** failure
die **Miß|ernte, –n** crop failure
mißfallen* (+*dat*) displease
das **Mißfallen** displeasure; **jmds. ~ erregen** incur s.o.'s displeasure
mißgebildet misshapen
die **Mißgeburt, –en** freak; washout
das **Mißgeschick, –e** misfortune; mishap
mißgestaltet misshapen
mißgestimmt ill-humoured
mißglücken (*sn*) fail; **... ist mir mißglückt** my ... was a failure; **mißglückt** unsuccessful
mißgönnen (+*dat*) begrudge
der **Mißgriff, –e** mistake
die **Mißgunst** resentment (at s.o.'s success)
mißgünstig resentful
mißhandeln ill-treat

die **Mißhandlung, -en** ill-treatment; cruelty (to child)

die **Mißhelligkeit, -en** disagreement

das **Missingsch** (*form of High German containing Low German elements*)

die **Mission, -en** mission (*also eccles, pol*)

der **Missionar** (*Aust* **-är**), **-e** missionary

missionieren proselytize; (*v/i*) do missionary work

der **Mißklang, ⸚e** discord (*also mus*); discordant note

Mißkredit: in ~ bringen bring into disrepute; **in ~ geraten** fall into disrepute

mißlang (mißlänge) *p/t* (*subj*) *of* **mißlingen**

mißlich awkward

mißliebig unpopular; (elements) undesirable

mißlingen (*p/t* **mißlang** (*subj* **mißlänge**), *p/part* **mißlungen**) (*see also* **mißlungen**) (*sn*) fail

das **Mißlingen** failure

mißlungen *p/part of* **mißlingen;** *also* unsuccessful, abortive

der **Mißmut** moroseness

mißmutig disgruntled, morose

mißraten* (*sn*) go wrong, be a failure; (child) turn out badly; **mißraten** (that is) a failure; wayward

der **Mißstand, ⸚e** bad state of affairs; abuse

die **Mißstimmung, -en** discord; bad mood

mißt *2nd/3rd sing pres of* **messen**

der **Mißton, ⸚e** discordant note

mißtönend discordant

mißtrauen (+*dat*) mistrust

das **Mißtrauen** mistrust; **der ~s|antrag, ⸚e** motion of no confidence; **das ~s|votum, -(t)en** vote of no confidence

mißtrauisch distrustful (**auf** *acc* of); suspicious (of)

das **Mißvergnügen** displeasure

mißvergnügt displeased

das **Mißverhältnis, -se** disproportion; discrepancy; **im ~ stehen zu** be out of proportion to

mißverständlich ambiguous; that can be misunderstood

das **Mißverständnis, -se** misunderstanding, misapprehension

mißverstehen* (*insep exc* **mißzuverstehen**) misunderstand; **nicht mißzuverstehend** unequivocal

die **Mißwirtschaft** mismanagement, maladministration

der **Mist** manure; manure heap; *coll* rubbish; **~ machen** *coll* make a mess of things; **so ein ~!** damn it!; **das ist nicht auf meinem ~ gewachsen** *coll* I didn't think that up myself

Mist- manure ...; dung ...; *coll* lousy ...; **das ~beet, -e** hotbed; **die ~gabel, -n** pitchfork; **der ~haufen, -** dung-heap; **der ~käfer, -** dung-beetle; **der ~kübel, -** *Aust* dustbin, trash can *US*; **das ~stück, -e** *vulg* 'bastard'; 'bitch'; **das ~vieh, ..viecher** *vulg* wretched beast; 'bastard'; 'bitch'; **das ~wetter** *coll* rotten weather

die **Mistel, -n** mistletoe

mistig mucky; *coll* rotten

mit [-ɪ-] **1** *prep* (+*dat*) (*a*) (*in various senses*) with;

(*b*) (*indicating means*) with; by; in (ink *etc*); *also used with certain verbs denoting a physical action where English has a transitive verb* (*eg* **~ der Zunge schnalzen** click one's tongue, **~ dem Schwanz wedeln** wag its tail, **~ der Peitsche knallen** crack the whip);

(*c*) (*indicating speed*) at (... kilometres per hour);

(*d*) (*indicating time*) at (daybreak, the stroke of ..., *etc*); with (*eg* **~ einsetzendem Winter** with the onset of winter); at the age of; *Aust* as of;

das ~ ... the business about ...; the bit about ...; **du** *etc* **~ ...** you *etc* and ...; **was ist ~ ...?** what's the matter with ...?; what about ...?; **wie wäre es ~ ...?** how about ...?

2 *adv* (*a*) (along) with s.o.; also, too, as well (*eg* **es liegt ~ daran, daß ...** it is also due to the fact that ...); *or translated by* help to (*eg* **sie haben das ~ aufgebaut** they helped to build it up); **ich war ~ (dabei)** I was there too; **es gehört ~ dazu** it's part of it; **ich kann das nicht ~ ansehen** I can't bear to watch it; **die Kosten sind ~ berechnet** the costs are included;

(*b*) (*followed by superl*) *coll* one of the ...; among the ... (*eg* **~ der Beste, ~ am besten** one of the best, **~ am wichtigsten sind ...** among the most important are ...)

---

mit- *sep pref – general senses*:

(*i*) *indicates participation* (*eg* **~helfen** lend a hand, **~spielen** join in, play in a team *etc*, **~verdienen** go out to work as well); *with modal auxiliary eg* **~dürfen** = go/come along (with s.o.) (*eg* **darf ich mit?** can I come along with you?);

(*ii*) *indicates inclusion* (*eg* **~rechnen** count, include)

Mit- co-; joint ...; fellow ...

die **Mit|arbeit** co-operation, collaboration; **unter ~ von** in collaboration with

mit|arbeiten: ~ an (*dat*) work on; collaborate on

der **Mit|arbeiter, -** collaborator; contributor; assistant; colleague; member of staff

mitbekommen* be given, get; catch (what is said)

der **Mitbesitzer, -** co-owner

mitbestimmen have a say in; help to

decide/determine; (*v/i*) have a say (**in** *dat* in)
die **Mitbestimmung** co-determination; **das ~s|recht** right of co-determination
der **Mitbewerber, –** rival; *sp* fellow competitor
mitbringen* bring with one; bring (along); have (qualifications *etc*); (+*dat*) bring
das **Mitbringsel, –** (little) present
der **Mitbürger, –** fellow citizen
mit|einander with one another; together; **das Mit|einander** living/working together
mit|empfinden* feel (s.o. else's pain *etc*); share
der **Mit|erbe, –n** (*wk masc*) co-heir
mit|erleben witness; experience (along with others)
der **Mit|esser, –** blackhead
Mitfahr–: die ~gelegenheit, –en lift (*usu* with costs shared)
mitfahren* (*sn*) go with s.o.; get a lift; **~ lassen** give (s.o.) a lift
der **Mitfahrer, –** passenger (in car); **die ~zentrale, –n** agency arranging lifts in private cars
mitfühlen feel (s.o. else's pain *etc*); share; **~d** sympathetic
mitführen carry (with one); (river) carry
mitgeben* (+*dat*) give (to take with him/her); give (s.o. education *etc*)
das **Mitgefühl** sympathy; **~ haben mit** feel for
mitgehen* (*sn*) go/come along (with s.o.); **~ mit** (audience) respond to; **mit der Zeit ~** move with the times; **~ heißen/lassen** *coll* walk off with
mitgenommen *p/part*; *also* worn-out; battered, the worse for wear
die **Mitgift, –en** dowry
das **Mitglied, –er** member; **~ werden (bei)** join || *in compds* **~s–** membership ...; **das ~s|land, ¨–er** member country
die **Mitgliedschaft, –en** membership
mithaben* have with one
mithalten* keep up (**mit** with); hold one's own
mithelfen* help, lend a hand
der **Mitherausgeber, –** co-editor
die **Mithilfe** assistance; **unter ~** (+*gen*) with the aid of
mithin thus
mithören overhear; listen in to; monitor; listen to (concert *etc*); (*v/i*) listen in
der **Mit|inhaber, –** co-owner
der **Mitkämpfer, –** comrade-in-arms
mitklingen* resonate (with sth. else); **in (jmds. Worten** *etc*) **klingt ... mit** there is a note of ... in (s.o.'s words *etc*)
mitkommen* (*sn*) come (with s.o.); keep up; **~ mit** (manage to) catch; **da komme ich nicht mit** *coll* it's beyond me
mitkönnen* *coll* be able to come/go (with s.o.); **~ mit** be able to keep up with; **da kann ich nicht mehr mit** it's beyond me
mitkriegen *coll* be given, get; catch (what is said)
mitlachen join in the laughter
mitlaufen* (*sn*) run (along) (with s.o.); be carried out at the same time
der **Mitläufer, –** non-active member (of party); fellow-traveller
der **Mitlaut, –e** consonant
das **Mitleid** compassion, pity (**mit** for); sympathy (for); **~ haben mit** feel pity for || **m~erregend** pitiful; **m~(s)|los** pitiless
Mitleidenschaft: in ~ ziehen affect
mitleidig sympathetic; pitying
mitmachen take part in; join in; take (course); follow (fashion); go/live through; (*v/i*) join in; take part; go along (with sth.); **~ bei** join in; take part in; **nicht mehr ~** *coll* (heart *etc*) give out
der **Mitmensch, –en** (*wk masc*) fellow-man
mitmenschlich (contacts *etc*) human
mitmischen *coll* be in on sth.; hold one's own; **~ bei/in** (*dat*) be involved in
die **Mitnahme** taking along
mitnehmen* (*see also* **mitgenommen**) take along; take; give (s.o.) a lift; take it out of; *coll* take in (en route); **~ aus** get out of (lecture *etc*); **sehr ~** take a lot out of
mitnichten *arch* not at all
mitprägen help to shape
die **Mitra, –(r)en** mitre
mitrechnen include; count; **... nicht mitgerechnet** not counting ...
mitreden join in (the conversation); have a say (**bei** in); **du kannst hier gar nicht ~** you don't know anything about it
mitreisen (*sn*) travel with s.o.; **der/die Mitreisende** (*decl as adj*) fellow passenger/traveller
mitreißen* sweep away; drag along; fire with enthusiasm; **~d** rousing, stirring
mitsammen *esp Aust* together
mitsamt (+*dat*) together with
mitschicken send (along) with s.o.; send (with letter)
mitschleppen *coll* take (heavy suitcase *etc*) along; drag (person) along
mitschneiden* *rad*, *TV*, *etc* record
mitschreiben* take down; *educ* take (test); (*v/i*) take notes
die **Mitschuld** complicity (**an** *dat* in)
mitschuldig: ~ sein an (*dat*) be a party to (crime); **der/die Mitschuldige** (*decl as adj*) accomplice
der **Mitschüler, –** schoolmate; classmate
mitschwingen* resonate (with sth. else); **ein Ton von ... schwingt in jmds. Worten** *etc* **mit** there is a note of ... in s.o.'s words *etc*
mitspielen join in; play (in team); (thing) play

a part, be a factor; *coll* play along; ~ **in** (*dat*) be in (film, play); play in (orchestra, team); (+*dat*) **übel** ~ give (s.o.) a rough time

der **Mitspieler, –** player; *sp* team-mate; *theat etc* fellow-actor

die **Mitsprache** [–a:–] say; **das ~recht** right to a say (in a matter)

mitsprechen* say (together with others); (*v/i*) have a say; (thing) play a part

mitstenographieren [–ʃt–] take down in shorthand

Mitt–, *eg* **der ~(fünfziger)/die ~(fünfzigerin)** man in his/woman in her mid-(fifties *etc*); **m~schiffs** amidships; **der ~sommer** midsummer; **der ~woch, –e** Wednesday; **m~wochs** on Wednesdays

mittag: gestern/heute/morgen ~ at midday yesterday/today/tomorrow

der **Mittag, –e** noon, midday; ~ **machen** *coll* have one's lunch-break; **zu ~ essen** have lunch || **das ~essen, –** lunch

mittäglich midday

mittags at midday/noon

Mittags– midday ..., noon ...; lunch ...; **die ~pause, –n** lunch-hour; **der ~schlaf** afternoon nap; **der ~tisch, –e** lunch table; midday meal

der **Mittäter, –** accomplice

die **Mittäterschaft** complicity

die **Mitte** middle; centre (*also pol*); ~ **(Dezember** *etc*) in the middle of; ~ **(Fünfzig/der Fünfziger** *etc*) **sein** be in one's mid-(fifties *etc*); **die goldene ~** the golden mean; **aus/in unserer ~** from/in our midst; **in der ~** in the middle/centre; halfway, midway

mitteilen (+*dat of pers*) inform of; communicate to; **sich ~** (+*dat*) confide in; communicate itself to

mitteilsam communicative

die **Mitteilung, –en** communication; (official) announcement

das **Mittel, –** means; *med* remedy; cure; medicine; *math* average, mean; *chem* agent; *phys* medium; (*pl*) funds; means, resources; ~ **zum Zweck** means to an end

Mittel– middle ...; central ...; medium ...; medium-sized ...; intermediate ...;

das ~alter the Middle Ages; **m~alterlich** medieval; **der ~bau, –ten** central block; *univ* non-professorial staff; **~deutschland** *geog* Central Germany; *pol* (*postwar W. German usage*) East Germany; **das ~ding** cross (between); **m~fristig** medium-range/term; **m~groß** medium-sized; of medium height; **m~hoch|deutsch, ~hoch|deutsch** Middle High German; **m~ländisch** Mediterranean; **der ~läufer, –** centre-half; **m~los** destitute; **das ~maß** average (standard); **m~mäßig** mediocre; average, middling; **das ~meer** the Mediterranean; **der ~meer|raum** the Mediterranean (region); **m~prächtig** *joc* tolerable; fair to middling; **der ~punkt, –e** centre; focal point; centre of attention; **die ~punkt|schule, –n** central school (serving rural area); **das ~schiff, –e** nave; **die ~schule, –n** (non-classical) secondary school; **der ~stand** middle classes; **m~ständisch** middle-class; **~strecken–** medium-haul/range ...; *athl* middle-distance ...; **der ~streckler, –** middle-distance runner; **der ~streifen, –** central reservation, median strip *US*; **der ~stürmer, –** centre-forward; **der ~weg, –e** middle path/course (**der goldene M.** the golden mean); **die ~welle, –n** medium wave; **der ~wert, –e** *math* mean; **das ~wort, ⸚er** participle

mittelbar indirect

mittels (*usu*+*gen*) by means of

Mittels–: der ~mann, ⸚er/..leute = die ~person, –en intermediary, go-between

mitten: ~ auf (*dat*) in the middle of; **~ durch** through the middle of; **~ in** (*acc/dat*) into/in the middle of; **~ in der Luft** in mid-air; **~ unter uns** in our midst || **~drịn** in the middle (of it) (**m. sein zu ...** be in the middle of (+*ger*)); **~dụrch** through the middle

Mitter–: die ~nacht, m~nächtlich midnight; **m~nachts** at midnight

der **Mittler, –** mediator

mittler.. middle; medium; medium-sized; **~en Alters** middle-aged; **~e Reife** (*see* **Reife**); **der M~e Westen** the Midwest (of U.S.A.) || **~we̲ile** in the meantime

mit|ụnter occasionally

mitverantwortlich jointly responsible

mitverdienen go out to work as well

die **Mitvergangenheit** *Aust* imperfect (tense)

die **Mitwelt** the people around one; one's contemporaries

mitwirken (factor *etc*) play a part; **es wirkten mit: ...** those taking part were ...

~ an (*dat*) assist in; participate in

~ bei assist in; participate in; (factor) play a part in

~ in (*dat*) *theat etc* be in; *mus* play in

der **Mitwirkende** (*fem* **die ~**) (*decl as adj*) performer; (*pl*) *theat* cast

die **Mitwirkung** co-operation; participation; assistance; **unter ~** (+*gen*) with the co-operation/participation of

der **Mitwisser, –** person who has knowledge of a crime *etc*

mitzählen count, include; (*v/i*) count

mitziehen* pull along; (*v/i*) *coll* follow suit; go along with sth.; *athl* stay with s.o.; (*sn*) march along

Mix–: der ~becher, – cocktail shaker; **das**

~gerät, –e (electric) mixer; **das ~getränk, –e** mixed drink
mixen mix (*esp* drinks, *cin etc* sounds)
der **Mixer, –** (electric) mixer; barman; *cin etc* mixer
die **Mixtur, –en** *pharm* mixture
mm (= **Millimeter**) mm.
Mo. (= **Montag**) Mon.
die **Möbel** *pl* furniture; **das ~stück, –e** piece of furniture; **der ~tischler, –** cabinet-maker; **der ~wagen, –** removal van, moving van *US*
mobil mobile; *mil* mobilized; *coll* lively; **~ machen** mobilize || **die M~machung, –en** mobilization
das **Mobile** ['mo:bilə], **–s** *art* mobile
das **Mobiliar** furnishings
die **Mobilien** [–ĭən] *pl* movables
mobilisieren mobilize (*also mil*)
die **Mobilität** mobility
möblieren furnish; **möbliert wohnen** live in furnished accommodation
Moçambique [mosam'bi:k] Mozambique
mochte (möchte) *p/t* (*subj*) *of* **mögen**
Möchte|gern– would-be …
die **Modalität, –en** modality; (*pl*) procedure
die **Mode** fashion; **(große) ~ sein** be (all) the fashion; **aus der ~ kommen** go out of fashion; **in ~ kommen** come into fashion; **mit der ~ gehen** follow the fashion
Mode– fashion …; fashionable …; **m~bewußt** fashion-conscious; **die ~schau, –en** fashion show; **der ~schmuck** costume jewellery; **der ~schöpfer, –** couturier; **das ~wort, ⸚er** vogue-word; **der ~zeichner, –** fashion designer; **die ~zeitung, –en** fashion magazine
das **Modell, –e** model (*also art, phot*); **~ stehen** pose (*dat* for) || **die ~eisen|bahn, –en** model railway/railroad *US*; **der ~versuch, –e** pilot scheme
Modellier– modelling …; **die ~masse, –n** modelling clay
modellieren model
Moden– = **Mode–**
der **Moder** decaying matter; **der ~geruch, ⸚e** musty smell
der **Moderator, –(or)en** (*wk masc*) *rad, TV* presenter
moderieren *rad, TV* present
mod(e)rig musty
modern (*also sn*) rot
modern modern; fashionable; progressive
die **Moderne** modern times; modern art/literature/music
modernisieren modernize
die **Modernisierung** modernization
die **Modernität** modernity
modifizieren modify
modisch fashionable
die **Modistin, –nen** milliner
das **Modul, –e** *comput etc* module
die **Modulation, –en** modulation
modulieren modulate
der **Modus, –(d)i** manner; mode; *gramm* mood
das **Mofa, –s** (= **Motorfahrrad**) (smaller-capacity) moped
mogeln *coll* cheat
mögen (*pres* **mag, magst, mag, mögen, mögt, mögen,** *subj* **möge** *etc*; *p/t* **mochte,** *subj* **möchte;** *p/part* **gemocht,** (*after dependent infin*) **mögen**) (*see p. xlvii*)
1 (gern) ~ like; **nicht ~** dislike; **lieber ~** prefer; **möchte (gern)** would like; (*ellipt*) would like to go (back, home, to …, *etc*);
2 *as auxiliary*: (*a*) (I *etc*) may, (*in question*) can; *may express estimate of time, quantity, etc* (*eg* **sie mochte etwa 30 sein** she would have been about 30); *frequently used in concessive clauses* (*eg* **was ich auch tun mag** whatever I may do, **mochte ich mich hierin auch geirrt haben** mistaken though I might have been about this); **(das) mag sein** that may be so;
(*b*) like/want to (*esp with neg, eg* **ich mag/mochte nicht weggehen** I don't/didn't want to leave); **möchte (gern)** would like to; **möchte lieber** would rather;
(*c*) **möge …** (*expressing wish*) may …; … **möge …** (*or with inversion*: **möge …**) let … (*eg* **das möge dir zur Warnung dienen** let that be a warning to you); **(sag ihm,) er möge/möchte …** ask him to …
möglich (*see also* **möglichst**) possible (*also* **–möglich,** *eg* **best~/größt~** best/largest possible); **alle ~en …** all kinds of …; **das ist gut/leicht ~** that's quite possible; **ist denn so was ~?** would you believe it?; **nicht ~!** never!; **alles ~e** all kinds of things; **alles M~e tun** do everything possible
möglicher|weise possibly
die **Möglichkeit, –en** possibility; opportunity, chance; (possible) way; (*pl*) potential; facilities; **–möglichkeit** possible …; **es gibt keine andere ~** there is no alternative/other way; **keine andere ~ haben (als zu …)** have no alternative (but to …); **nach ~** as far as possible; if possible; **ist das die ~?** would you believe it!
möglichst if possible; as … as possible; **sein ~es tun** do all one can
Mohammed ['mo:hamɛt] Mohammed
der **Mohammedaner, –, mohammedanisch** Mohammedan
der **Mohn** poppy; poppy-seed; **die ~blume, –n** poppy
der **Mohr, –en** (*wk masc*) *arch* blackamoor; **die ~rübe, –n** carrot
die **Möhre, –n** carrot
der **Mohren|kopf, ⸚e** (*chocolate-coated, cream-*

filled round cake)
mokant mocking
mokieren: sich ~ über (*acc*) poke fun at
der **Mokka, –s** mocha
der **Molch, –e** newt
die **Mole, –n** *naut* mole
das **Molekül, –e** molecule
molekular molecular
die **Molke** whey
die **Molkerei, –en** dairy
das **Moll** *mus* minor (key); **–Moll** ... minor (*eg* **a-Moll** A minor)
mollig *coll* cosy, snug; (woman) plump
der **Moloch** [–x], **–e** Moloch
der **Molotow|cocktail** ['mo:lotɔf–], **–s** Molotov cocktail
das **Molybdän** molybdenum
das **Moment, –e** factor; element; *phys* moment
der **Moment, –e** moment; **jeden ~** any moment; **~ (mal)!** just a minute!; **im ~** at the moment || **die ~aufnahme, –n** snapshot
momentan momentary; present; (*adv*) momentarily; at the moment
der **Monarch** [–ç], **–en** (*wk masc*) monarch
die **Monarchie** [–ç–], **–(ie)n** monarchy
monarchisch [–ç–] monarchic(al)
der **Monarchist** [–ç–], **–en** (*wk masc*), **monarchistisch** monarchist
der **Monat** [–at], **–e** month; **m~e|lang** months of; lasting for months; (*adv*) for months
–monatig –month; –month-old
monatlich monthly; **–monatlich** –monthly; (*adv*) every ... months
Monats– ... of the month; monthly ...; **die ~blutung, –en** menstruation; **die ~karte, –n** (monthly) season ticket; **die ~schrift, –en** monthly; **der ~wechsel, –** monthly allowance
der **Mönch, –e** monk
mönchisch monastic; monkish
Mönchs– monk's ...; monastic ...
das **Mönch(s)tum** monasticism
der **Mond** [–o:–], **–e** moon; **hinter dem ~ leben** *coll* be behind the times; **in den ~ gucken** *coll* be left empty-handed
Mond– lunar ...; moon ...; **die ~fähre, –n** lunar module; **die ~finsternis, –se** eclipse of the moon; **m~hell** moonlit; **der ~schein** moonlight; **die ~sichel, –n** crescent moon; **m~süchtig (m. sein** sleepwalk); **der/die ~süchtige** (*decl as adj*) sleepwalker, somnambulist
mondän highly elegant/fashionable
monetär monetary
die **Moneten** *pl coll* 'dough'
der **Mongole, –n** (*wk masc*) Mongol
die **Mongolei** Mongolia
mongolisch Mongol(ian)
mongoloid [–o'i:t] Mongoloid; *med* mongoloid
monieren complain about; *comm* make a complaint about; **~, daß ...** complain that ...
Mono– mono–
monochrom [–kr–] monochrome
monocolor *Aust* single-party
monogam monogamous
die **Monogamie** monogamy
das **Monogramm, –e** monogram
die **Monographie, –(ie)n** monograph
das **Monokel, –** monocle
die **Monokultur** ['mɔ–], **–en** monoculture
der **Monolog, –e** monologue
das **Monopol, –e** monopoly (**auf** *acc* of)
monopolisieren monopolize
monoton monotonous
die **Monotonie** monotony
das **Monster, –** monster; *in compds* mammoth ...; **der ~film, –e** mammoth epic
monströs monstrous
das **Monstrum, –(r)en** monster; monstrosity
der **Monsun, –e** monsoon
der **Montag** [–o:–], **–e** Monday; **blauen ~ machen** *coll* take Monday off
die **Montage** [–ʒə], **–n** assembly; installation; *arts* montage; *cin* editing; **der ~bau** construction method using prefabricated units; **das ~werk, –e** assembly plant
montags on Mondays
Montan–: die ~industrie coal and steel industry; **die ~union** the European Coal and Steel Community
der **Montblanc** [mɔ̃'blã:] (*gen* **–(s)**) Mont Blanc
der **Monteur** [–'tø:ɐ], **–e** fitter; mechanic
montieren install; assemble; fit (**an/auf** *acc* to); *arts* put together (collage *etc*); *cin* edit
die **Montur, –en** *esp Aust* uniform; *coll* rig-out
das **Monument, –e** monument
monumental monumental
das **Moor, –e** bog; **das ~bad, ⸗er** mud-bath; **das ~huhn, ⸗er** grouse
moorig boggy
das **Moos, –e** moss; *coll* 'dough'
moosig mossy
der **Mop** [–ɔ–], **–s** mop
das **Moped** [–ɛt], **–s** moped
moppen mop
der **Mops, ⸗e** pug; *coll* roly-poly; (*pl*) *coll* 'dough'; **mops|fidel** *coll* chirpy
mopsen *coll* 'pinch'; **sich ~** be bored
die **Moral** morals; morality; moral (of story); morale; **doppelte ~** double standard
Moral– moral ...; **der ~apostel, –** moralizer; **die ~pauke, –n** *coll* homily; **der ~prediger, –** moralizer; **die ~predigt, –en** *coll* homily
moralin|sauer *coll* priggish
moralisch moral
moralisieren moralize
der **Moralist, –en** (*wk masc*) moralist
moralistisch moralistic

[die] **Moräne, –n** moraine
[der] **Morast, –e/⸚e** morass; mire
morastig boggy
[das] **Moratorium, –(i)en** moratorium
morbid sickly; degenerate
[die] **Morchel, –n** morel
[der] **Mord, –e** murder (**an** *dat* of); **der ~anschlag, ⸚e** assassination attempt; **die ~kommission, –en** murder squad; **der ~versuch, –e** attempted murder
morden (commit) murder
[der] **Mörder, –** murderer; **~grube (aus seinem Herzen keine M. machen** speak frankly)
[die] **Mörderin, –nen** murderess
mörderisch murderous; *coll* dreadful; (speed) breakneck
Mords– *coll* tremendous ...; fantastic ...; **~hunger** *coll* (**einen M. haben** be starving); **der ~kerl, –e** *coll* hell of a guy; huge fellow; **m~mäßig** *coll* tremendous
[die] **Morelle, –n** morello cherry
morgen tomorrow; **~ früh/abend** tomorrow morning/evening; **gestern/heute ~** yesterday/this morning; **~ in/vor (acht Tagen** *etc*) (a week *etc*) tomorrow, from tomorrow/(a week *etc*) ago tomorrow
[der] **Morgen, –** morning; (measurement) *approx* = acre; **guten ~!** good morning!; **am ~** in the morning || **die ~dämmerung** dawn; **~frühe (in der M.** early in the morning); **das ~grauen** dawn; **das ~land** *arch* the Orient; **der ~mantel, ..mäntel = der ~rock, ⸚e** dressing-gown; **das ~rot = die ~röte** red sky (at sunrise); dawn (of age *etc*)
morgendlich morning
morgens in the morning; in the morning(s)
morgig tomorrow's
[die] **Moritat, –en** (*usu* gruesome) street-ballad
[das] **Morphium** morphine
morsch rotten; brittle
[das] **Morse|alphabet** ['mɔrzə–] Morse code
morsen ['mɔrzn̩] send in Morse; (*v/i*) send a message in Morse
[der] **Mörser, –** mortar (*also mil*)
[der] **Mörtel, –** *build* mortar
[das] **Mosaik, –e(n)** mosaic
mosaisch Mosaic
[die] **Moschee, –(e)n** mosque
[der] **Moschus** musk; **der ~ochse, –n** (*wk masc*) musk-ox
[die] **Möse, –n** *vulg* cunt
[der] **Mosel, – = der ~wein, –e** Moselle (wine)
[die] **Mosel** the Moselle
Moses [–ɛs] Moses; **die fünf Bücher Mose** the Pentateuch; **das erste/zweite/dritte/vierte/fünfte Buch Mose** Genesis/Exodus/Leviticus/Numbers/Deuteronomy
Moskau Moscow
[der] **Moskauer, –** Muscovite
[der] **Moskito, –s** mosquito
[der] **Moslem** [–ɛm], **–s** Moslem
[der] **Most** (unfermented) fruit-juice; must; *SGer* fruit wine; cider
[der] **Mostrich** *NGer* mustard
[das] **Motel, –s** motel
[die] **Motette, –n** motet
[die] **Motion, –en** *Swiss parl* motion (in writing)
[der] **Motionär, –e** *Swiss parl* proposer of a motion
[das] **Motiv, –e** motive; *arts* motif; theme; (of painting *etc*) subject
[die] **Motivation, –en** motivation
motivieren account for; motivate; **~ mit** give as the reason for
[die] **Motivierung, –en** motivation
[das] **Moto-Cross** (*gen* –) motocross
[der] **Motor, –(or)en** engine; motor; driving force; **das ~boot, –e** motor-boat; **die ~haube, –n** bonnet, hood *US*; **das ~rad, ⸚er** motorcycle (**M. fahren** motorcycle); **der ~rad|fahrer, –** motorcyclist; **der ~roller, –** motor-scooter; **der ~schaden, ..schäden** engine trouble; **der ~sport** motor sport
[das] **Motoren|öl, –e** engine oil
–motorig –engined
motorisch *physiol* motor
motorisieren motorize; fit with an engine
[die] **Motte, –n** moth; **du kriegst die ~n!** well, I'm blowed! || **m~n|echt = m~n|fest** moth-proof; **~n|kiste (aus der M.** ancient; **aus der M. hervorholen** dig out); **die ~n|kugel, –n** mothball; **m~n|zerfressen** moth-eaten
[das] **Motto, –s** motto
motzen *coll* beef
mouillieren [muj–] palatalize
moussieren [mʊ–] effervesce; sparkle
[die] **Möwe, –n** seagull
[die] **MP, –s = Maschinenpistole**
Mrd. = Milliarde(n)
[die] **M + S-Reifen** ['ɛmʔʊnt'ʔɛs–] *pl* (= **Matsch- und Schneereifen**) snow tyres
[die] **MTA, –s** (= **medizinisch-technische Assistentin**) medical laboratory technician
[die] **MTS, –** *EGer hist* (= **Maschinen-Traktoren-Station**) agricultural machinery centre
[die] **Mücke, –n** gnat; mosquito; **aus einer ~ einen Elefanten machen** *coll* make a mountain out of a molehill
[der] **Muckefuck** *coll* ersatz coffee
[die] **Mucken** *pl coll* moods; **(seine) ~ haben** be moody; (car *etc*) be temperamental; **die Sache hat ihre ~** there are snags
mucken *coll* grumble; **ohne zu ~** without a murmur
Mucks *coll*: **keinen ~ sagen/tun** not say a word/make a sound || **mucks|mäuschen|still** *coll* quiet as a mouse
mucksen *coll*: **sich nicht ~** not stir; not make a sound

müde tired; **–müde** weary of ...; –weary; (+*gen*) **~ werden** tire of; **es ~ sein zu ...** be tired of (+*ger*)

die **Müdigkeit** tiredness; fatigue

der **Muff**[1], **–e** muff

der **Muff**[2] *NGer* musty smell

die **Muffe, –n** *tech* sleeve

der **Muffel, –** *coll* old misery; **–muffel** *coll* (*person who is not a fan of something, eg* **der Party~** person who dislikes parties, **der Ehe~** person who is not keen on marrying)

muff(e)lig *coll* grumpy

muffeln *coll* mutter; (*v/i*) munch; be grumpy

muffig musty; *coll* grumpy

muh! moo!; **die Muh|kuh, ⸚e** (*baby-talk*) moo-cow

die **Mühe, –n** effort; trouble; **verlorene ~** a waste of effort/time; **der ~ wert** worth the trouble, worthwhile; **sich** *dat* **~ geben** take trouble (**mit** over); **alle ~ haben zu ...** be hard put to it to ...; **sich** *dat* **die ~ machen zu ...** take the trouble to ...; **mit Müh und Not** with great difficulty; only just || **m~los** effortless; easy; **m~voll** laborious; arduous

muhen moo

mühen: sich ~ take pains (to)

Mühl– mill ...; **das ~rad, ⸚er** mill-wheel; **der ~stein, –e** mill-stone

die **Mühle, –n** mill; (coffee) grinder; (administrative) machinery; *coll* 'crate'

die **Mühsal, –e** toil

mühsam arduous; (*adv*) with difficulty

mühselig arduous

der **Mulatte, –n** (*wk masc*) mulatto

die **Mulde, –n** hollow

das **Muli, –(s)** *SGer* mule

der **Mull** muslin; *med* gauze

der **Müll** refuse, garbage *US*; (industrial) waste; **die ~abfuhr** refuse collection, garbage collection *US*; dustmen, garbage men *US*; **der ~ablade|platz, ⸚e** rubbish dump; **der ~eimer, –** dustbin, garbage can *US*; **der ~haufen, –** rubbish heap, garbage heap *US*; **der ~kutscher, –** *coll* dustman, garbage man *US*; **die ~schaufel, –n** dustpan; **der ~schlucker, –** waste disposal unit, garbage chute *US*; **die ~tonne, –n** dustbin, garbage can *US*; **die ~verbrennungs|anlage, –n** incinerator; **der ~wagen, –** dustcart, garbage truck *US*

der **Müller, –** miller

mulmig rotten; *coll* dodgy; (feeling) funny; **mir wird ~** *coll* I feel funny

der **Multi, –s** *coll* multinational

multi– multi–

multipel multiple

die **Multiplikation, –en** multiplication

der **Multiplikator, –(or)en** multiplier

multiplizieren multiply

die **Mumie** [–ĭə], **–n** mummy

mumifizieren mummify

der **Mumm** *coll*: **~ (in den Knochen)** guts; muscle

der **Mummel|greis, –e** *coll* doddering old man

der **Mummenschanz** masquerade

der **Mumpitz** *coll* hooey

der **Mumps** (*gen* –) mumps

München Munich

der **Mund, ⸚er** mouth; **~ und Nase aufsperren** *coll* gape (with astonishment); **den ~ halten** *coll* keep one's mouth shut; **halt den ~!** shut up!; (+*dat*) **den ~ verbieten** order to be silent; **sich** *dat* **den ~ verbrennen** burn one's mouth; *coll* put one's foot in it; **den ~ voll nehmen** *coll* brag

in prepositional phrases:

an jmds. ~(e) hängen hang on s.o.'s lips

auf: nicht auf den ~ gefallen sein *coll* never be at a loss for words

in: (ständig) im ~(e) führen be constantly talking about; **in aller ~e sein** be on everyone's lips; (+*dat*) **in den ~ legen** put (words) in (s.o.'s) mouth; **in den ~ nehmen** put in one's mouth; use (word, expression)

mit offenem/vollem ~ with one's mouth open/full

nach: (+*dat*) **nach dem ~(e) reden** say what (s.o.) wants to hear

über: (+*dat*) **über den ~ fahren** *coll* jump down (s.o.'s) throat

Mund– ... of the mouth; mouth ...; oral ...; **die ~art, –en** dialect; **m~artlich** dialectal; **m~faul** *coll* too lazy to open one's mouth; **m~gerecht** ready to eat ((+*dat*) **m. machen** make palatable for); **der ~geruch** bad breath; **die ~harmonika, –s** mouth-organ; **das ~stück, –e** mouthpiece; tip (of cigarette); **m~tot** (**m. machen** muzzle); **der ~voll, –** mouthful; **das ~wasser, ..wässer** mouth-wash; **das ~werk** *coll* mouth (**ein böses/großes/loses M. haben** have a vicious tongue/a big mouth/an unbridled tongue; **ein freches M. haben** be cheeky; **ein gutes M. haben** have the gift of the gab); **der ~winkel, –** corner of the mouth; **die ~-zu-~-Be|atmung** mouth-to-mouth resuscitation

das **Mündel, –** ward

munden (+*dat*) taste delicious; **sich** *dat* **... ~ lassen** eat with relish

münden (*also sn*): **~ auf** (*acc*) lead into (square); **~ in** (*acc*) flow into; lead into; (discussions *etc*) lead to

mündig of age; responsible, mature; **~ werden** come of age

die **Mündigkeit** majority; maturity

mündlich oral; verbal

die **Mündung, –en** mouth (of river); estuary; muzzle (of gun)

der **Mungo, –s** mongoose

die **Munition, -en** ammunition; **die ~s|fabrik, -en** munitions factory
munkeln: man munkelt von people are talking about; **man munkelt, daß ...** rumour has it that ...
das **Münster, -** cathedral (*esp* in S. Germany)
munter lively; merry, cheerful; awake
Münz- coin ...; coin-operated ...; monetary ...; **der ~automat, -en** (*wk masc*) slot machine; **der ~fern|sprecher, -** pay phone; **die ~kunde** numismatics; **die ~stätte, -n** mint; **der ~tank, -s** coin-operated pump; **der ~wechsler, -** change machine
die **Münze, -n** coin; mint; **für bare ~ nehmen** take at its face value; (+*dat*) **in/mit gleicher ~ heimzahlen** pay back in his/her own coin for; **in/mit klingender ~** in hard cash
münzen mint; **gemünzt sein auf** (*acc*) be aimed at
mürbe crumbly; (meat) tender; **~ machen** wear down; **~ sein/werden** be worn down || **der M~teig** short pastry
der **Murks** *coll* botch-up; **~ machen** make a mess of things
murksen *coll* bungle things; fiddle about
die **Murmel, -n** (child's) marble; **das ~tier, -e** marmot
murmeln murmur; mumble; mutter
murren grumble (**über** *acc* about)
mürrisch surly
das **Mus, -e** purée
die **Muschel, -n** mussel; shell; *Aust* basin; (lavatory) bowl, pan; *tel* ear-piece; mouthpiece
die **Muschi, -s** *coll* pussy
die **Muse, -n** Muse; **die leichte ~** light entertainment
museal (treasures *etc*) museum; antiquated
das **Museum, -(ee)n** museum; **das ~s|stück, -e** museum piece
das **Musical** ['mjuːzɪkl̩], **-s** musical
die **Musik** music; *coll* band; **~ machen** make music || **der ~automat, -en** (*wk masc*) musical box, music box *US*; = **die ~box, -en** juke-box; **die ~hoch|schule, -n** academy of music; **das ~instrument, -e** musical instrument; **die ~kapelle, -n** band; **das ~stück, -e** piece of music; **die ~truhe, -n** radiogram, radio-phonograph *US*; **die ~wissenschaft** musicology
die **Musikalien** [-ĭən] *pl* (printed) music; **die ~handlung, -en** music shop/store *US*
musikalisch musical
die **Musikalität** musicality
der **Musikant, -en** (*wk masc*) (street *etc*) musician; **der ~en|knochen, -** funnybone, crazy bone *US*
der **Musiker, -** musician
der **Musikus, -(i)zi** *joc* musician
musisch artistic
musizieren make music

der **Muskat** nutmeg; **die ~blüte, -n** mace; **die ~nuß, ⸚(ss)e** nutmeg
der **Muskel, -n** muscle; *in compds also* muscular ...; **der ~kater, -** stiff muscles (**M. haben** be stiff); **die ~kraft** physical strength; **der ~protz, -e** (*or* **-en** (*wk masc*)) *coll* muscleman; **der ~riß, -(ss)e** torn muscle (**sich** *dat* **einen M. zuziehen** tear a muscle); **der ~schwund** muscular atrophy; **die ~zerrung, -en** pulled muscle
die **Muskete, -n** musket
der **Musketier, -e** musketeer
die **Muskulatur, -en** muscular system
muskulös muscular
das **Müsli, -s** muesli
das **Muß** necessity; must; *in compds* mandatory ...; **die ~heirat, -en** *coll* shotgun wedding
die **Muße** leisure; **mit ~** in a leisurely fashion
der **Musselin, -e** muslin
müssen (*pres* **muß, mußt, muß, müssen, müßt, müssen,** *subj* **müsse** *etc*; *p/t* **mußte,** *subj* **müßte;** *p/part* **gemußt,** (*after dependent infin*) **müssen**) (*see p. xlvii*) have to, (I *etc*) must; be obliged to; be bound to; (*ellipt*) have to go (home, to ..., *etc*); (*emotive*: *of unwelcome occurrence*) (I *etc*) *would* have to; **nicht ~** not have to; (*in 2nd pers*) *NGer* must not; **... muß (erneuert** *etc*) **werden** ... needs (+*ger*, *eg* renewing); **ich muß mal** *coll* I need to go to the loo/bathroom *US*; **ich muß schon sagen!** well, I *must* say!; **muß das sein?** is that really necessary?; **wenn es sein muß** if it's really necessary; if you/he *etc* must;
mußte had to; was obliged to; was bound to; **müßte** would have to; ought to, should; would be bound to; *may also express a wish* (*eg* **reich müßte man sein!** wouldn't it be nice to be rich!);
habe ... ~ (have) had to; **hätte ... ~** would have had to; would have been bound to; ought to/should have +*p/part*
müßig idle; **der M~gang** idleness; **der M~gänger, -** idler
Mussorgski Mussorgsky
das **Muster, -** pattern; sample; specimen; model (**an** *dat* of); *in compds* model ...; perfect ...; *comm* ... of samples; **das ~beispiel, -e** perfect example (**für** of); **das ~buch, ⸚er** pattern book; **m~gültig** exemplary
musterhaft exemplary
mustern scrutinize; *mil* inspect; give (s.o.) his/her medical; **von oben bis unten ~** look up and down
die **Musterung, -en** pattern; *mil* inspection; medical (examination)
der **Mut** courage; **frohen/guten ~es sein** be in good spirits; **~ fassen** pluck up courage; (+*dat*) **~ machen** encourage; (+*dat*) **~**

nehmen discourage; **den ~ verlieren** lose heart; **nur ~!** never say die! || **m~los** despondent; **die ~losigkeit** despondency; **m~maßen** (*insep*) surmise; **m~maßlich** probable; suspected; putative; **die ~maßung, –en** conjecture; **der ~wille** (*like* **Wille**) wilfulness; wantonness; **m~willig** wilful; wanton

die **Mutation, –en** breaking of the voice; *biol* mutation

mutieren (voice) break; *biol* mutate; **er hat schon mutiert** his voice has broken

mutig brave

die **Mutter**[1], **–n** *tech* nut

die **Mutter**[2], *pl* **Mütter** mother; *in compds also* maternal ...; parent ...; **der ~boden, ..böden** topsoil; **der ~kuchen, –** placenta; **das ~land, ⸚er** mother country; **der ~leib** womb; **das ~mal, –e** birthmark; mole; **das ~schaf, –e** ewe; **mutter|seelen|allein** all alone; **das ~söhnchen, –** mother's darling; **die ~sprache, –n** native language; **~stelle** (**M. vertreten bei** be like a mother to); **der ~tag, –e** Mother's Day; **der ~witz** native wit

die **Mütter|beratungs|stelle, –n** child welfare clinic

Mütterchen mother; **das ~, –: altes ~** little old woman

mütterlich maternal; motherly; **~er|seits** on one's/the mother's side

die **Mutterschaft** motherhood; **der ~s|urlaub** maternity leave

die **Mutti, –s** *coll* mum(my), mom(my) *US*

die **Mütze, –n** cap; **der ~n|schirm, –e** peak (of cap)

m. W. = meines Wissens

MwSt. (= **Mehrwertsteuer**) V.A.T. (value-added tax)

Mykenä Mycenae

die **Myriaden** *pl* myriads

die **Myrrhe** ['mʏrə], **–n** myrrh

die **Myrte, –n** myrtle

das **Mysterien|spiel** [–ĭən–], **–e** mystery play

mysteriös mysterious

das **Mysterium, –(i)en** mystery

mystifizieren mysticize

die **Mystik** [–ɪk] mysticism

der **Mystiker, –** mystic

mystisch mystic(al); mysterious

der **Mystizismus** mysticism

mythisch mythical

die **Mythologie, –(ie)n** mythology

mythologisch mythological

der **Mythos** [–ɔs], **–(th)en** myth (= traditional story); legend (= legendary figure *etc*)

Mz. (= **Mehrzahl**) pl.

N

das **N** [ɛn] (*gen, pl* –, *coll* [ɛns]) N
N (= **Nord(en)**) N.
na! well!; ~, ~! now, now!; ~ **also!** what did I tell you!; ~ **gut!** all right then!; ~ **ja!** oh well; ~ **'so was!** fancy that!; ~ **'und?** so what?; ~ **und 'ob!** I'll say!
die **Nabe, –n** hub
der **Nabel, –** navel; *in compds* umbilical ...; **die ~schau** contemplation of one's navel; **die ~schnur, ⸚e** umbilical cord
nach [–aː–] (+*dat*) (*a*) (*indicating direction*) towards; ...wards (*eg* ~ **Osten** eastwards); (*followed by name of country or place*) to, (leave) for; (throw) at;
(*b*) (long, reach, search, send, *etc*) for; **mir ist ~ ...** I feel like ...;
(*c*) (*indicating time, sequence*) after; (... minutes) past; ~ **Ihnen!** after you!;
(*d*) *Aust* (widow) of;
(*e*) (smell, taste) of; **es sieht ~ ... aus** it looks like (rain, sabotage, *etc*);
(*f*) (*other senses – often following noun*) in accordance with; according to; by (weight); on (points); (arrange, judge, *etc*) by; to judge by, from; in (s.o.'s opinion); to (s.o.'s taste); (paint, draw) from (life *etc*); after (Rubens *etc*); (dance) to; *sometimes a phrase with ~ is rendered by an adverb* (*eg* **dem Alphabet ~** alphabetically); **wenn es ~ mir ginge** if I had my way
~ **... hin** towards; in (direction)
je ~ according to, depending on
~ **und ~** little by little, gradually
~ **wie vor** still; *or conveyed by* ... continue(s) to ...; **... ist** *etc* ~ **wie vor ... ...** continue(s) to be ..., ... remain(s) ...
~ **... zu** towards

---

nach–[1] *sep pref – general senses*:
(*i*) (+*dat*) ... after ... (*eg* **jmdm. etw. ~werfen** throw sth. after s.o.); ... for ... (**jmdm. ~trauern** mourn for s.o.);
(*ii*) *indicates something done in addition* re–; ... in addition; add ...; *or subsequently* ... later (*eg* **~drucken** reprint, **~füllen** refill, **~salzen** add more salt to, **~zahlen** pay in addition/later); *or in imitation* (*eg* **(jmdm.) etw. ~sprechen** repeat sth. (after s.o.), **~äffen** ape);
(*iii*) *indicates continuation* (*eg* **~wirken** continue to have an effect);
(*iv*) *indicates investigation* (*eg* **~fragen** make enquiries, **~schlagen** look up)

---

nach–[2] (*prefixed to adj*) post– (*eg* **~klassisch** post-classical); **Nach–** re–; after–; additional ...; post–
nach|äffen ape; mimic
nach|ahmen imitate; mimic; **~s|wert** worthy of imitation; exemplary
der **Nach|ahmer, –** imitator
die **Nach|ahmung, –en** imitation
nach|arbeiten make up (lost working time); reproduce, copy; *tech* finish (by hand *etc*); (*v/i*, +*dat*) take as a model
nach|arten [–aː–] (*sn*) (+*dat*) take after
der **Nachbar** ['nax–] (*acc, dat* **–(n)**, *gen* **–n**), **–n** neighbour; *in compds* neighbouring ...; **das ~haus, ⸚er** neighbouring house (**im N.** next door)
nachbarlich neighbouring; neighbourly
die **Nachbarschaft** neighbourhood; neighbours; vicinity
die **Nachbars|leute** *pl* neighbours
nachbauen reconstruct
nachbehandeln give (sth.) further treatment; *med* give (s.o.) after-care
nachbessern touch up
nachbestellen reorder; order another .../some more ...
die **Nachbestellung, –en** *vbl noun*; *also* repeat order
nachbeten repeat (uncritically)
der **Nachbeter, –** person who repeats s.o.'s words, parrot
nachbilden reproduce; (+*dat*) model on
die **Nachbildung, –en** *vbl noun*; *also* reproduction
nachblicken (+*dat*) follow with one's eyes; gaze after
nachbohren rebore; redrill; (*v/i*) *coll* probe
nachdatieren antedate
nachdem after; now that; once; *SGer* since (*causal*); **je ~** it depends; **je ~, (wie** *etc*) **...** depending on (how *etc*) ...
nachdenken* think (**über** *acc* about); **das Nachdenken** thought, reflection
nachdenklich thoughtful, pensive
nachdichten write a free translation of
die **Nachdichtung, –en** *vbl noun*; *also* free translation

nachdrängen (*also sn*) push from behind
nachdrehen *cin* reshoot
der **Nachdruck, -e** stress, emphasis; reproduction; reprinting; reprint; (+*dat*) ~ **verleihen** underline; **mit** ~ forcefully; emphatically
nachdrucken reprint
nachdrücklich emphatic; (*adv*: advise *etc*) strongly
nachdunkeln (*sn*) grow darker
nach|eifern (+*dat*) emulate
nach|eilen (*sn*) (+*dat*) hurry after
nach|einander one after another; in succession; **das Nach|einander** succession
nach|eiszeitlich post-glacial
nach|empfinden* feel (by empathy); ... (*dat*) **nachempfunden** modelled on
der **Nachen, -** *poet* (small) boat
nach|erzählen retell (in one's own words)
Nachf. = Nachfolger
der **Nachfahre, -n** (*wk masc*) descendant
nachfahren* (*also sn*) go over (with pencil *etc*); (*sn*) (+*dat*) follow (in car *etc*)
nachfassen *coll* ask further questions (in the hope of eliciting a satisfactory answer)
die **Nachfeier, -n** extra celebration (after main festivities); celebration held at a later date
die **Nachfolge** succession; **jmds.** ~ **antreten** succeed s.o.
nachfolgen (*sn*) (+*dat*) follow; succeed; **~d** following; **im ~den** below
der **Nachfolger, -** successor
nachforschen (+*dat*) enquire into; investigate
die **Nachforschungen** *pl* enquiries; investigations
die **Nachfrage, -n** enquiry; *comm* demand (**nach** for)
nachfragen enquire
nachfühlen feel (by empathy); understand
nachfüllen refill; top up
Nachgang: im ~ zu further to
nachgeben* (+*dat*) give (s.o.) another helping of; (*v/i*) give in; give way; (thing) give (way); *fin* ease; (+*dat*) give in to, yield to; indulge
nachgeboren born later
die **Nachgebühr, -en** postage due
die **Nachgeburt** [-u:-], **-en** afterbirth
nachgehen* (*sn*) (clock) be slow; (+*dat*) follow; pursue; go about (one's business, work); look into, investigate; (words *etc*) linger in (s.o.'s) mind
nachgelassen *p/part*; *also* posthumous
nachgemacht *p/part*; *also* imitation; counterfeit
nachgerade positively
nachgeraten* (*sn*) (+*dat*) take after
der **Nachgeschmack** aftertaste; **einen bitteren ~ hinterlassen** leave a nasty taste in the mouth
nachgestellt *p/part*; *gramm* postpositive
nachgiebig compliant; indulgent; (material) pliant
nachgießen* refill (glass *etc*); add more ...; (*v/i*, +*dat*) refill (s.o.'s) glass *etc*
nachgrübeln: ~ über (*acc*) ponder (over); brood over
nachhaken *footb* trip an opponent from behind; *coll* probe
der **Nachhall** reverberation; echo
nachhallen reverberate; echo
nachhalten* last
nachhaltig lasting; **~ beeinflussen** have a lasting influence on
nachhängen* (*like* **hängen** *v/i*) (+*dat*) dwell on; give oneself up to (one's thoughts); (reputation) cling to; **~ in** (*dat*) *coll* lag behind in
der **Nachhause|weg** way home
nachhelfen* help; (+*dat*) help; refresh (s.o.'s memory)
nachher afterwards; later; **bis ~!** see you later!
die **Nachhilfe** help; *educ* coaching; **die ~stunde, -n** private lesson; (*pl*) = **der ~unterricht** coaching
nachhinein: im ~ afterwards; after the event
nachhinken (*sn*) lag behind; (+*dat*) hobble after
der **Nachhol|bedarf** desire to catch up (on things missed); need to make up lost ground
nachholen make up for; catch up on; fetch later
die **Nachhut, -en** *mil* rearguard
nach|impfen revaccinate; reinoculate; give (s.o.) a booster
die **Nach|impfung, -en** revaccination; reinoculation; booster
nachjagen (*sn*) (+*dat*) chase after
der **Nachklang, ¨-e** lingering sound; lingering impression
nachklingen* go on sounding; **~ in** (*dat*) linger in (s.o.'s) mind
der **Nachkomme, -n** (*wk masc*) descendant
nachkommen* (*sn*) follow (later); keep up (**mit** with); (+*dat*) follow; comply with; fulfil (duty *etc*); **~ lassen** send for
die **Nachkommenschaft** descendants
der **Nachkömmling, -e** late addition (to family)
Nachkriegs- postwar ...; **die ~zeit** post-war period
nachladen* reload
der **Nachlaß, -(ss)e/¨-(ss)e** (price) reduction; (deceased's) estate; **literarischer ~** literary remains
nachlassen* (*see also* **nachgelassen**) slacken; (*v/i*) ease (off); abate, (rain *etc*) let up; wear off; (hearing *etc*) deteriorate; wane; (standard) go down; (business) become slack; **vom Preis ~** knock off the price

nachlässig careless; sloppy; casual
nachlaufen* (*sn*) (+*dat*) run after; chase (girl *etc*)
nachleben (+*dat*) model one's life on (s.o. else's); live by
die **Nachlese** *agr* gleaning; gleanings; *liter* additional selection
nachlesen* read up; *agr* glean; ~ **über** (*acc*) read up
nachliefern supply later/in addition
nachlösen: (eine Fahrkarte) ~ buy a ticket on the train/on arrival
nachmachen (*see also* **nachgemacht**) imitate; copy; counterfeit; do later
nachmalen copy (picture); touch up (colours)
nachmessen* remeasure
nachmittag: gestern/heute/morgen ~ yesterday/this/tomorrow afternoon
der **Nachmittag, -e** afternoon; **am** ~ in the afternoon
nachmittäglich afternoon
nachmittags in the afternoon; in the afternoon(s)
Nachmittags- afternoon ...; **das ~schläfchen, -** afternoon nap; **die ~vorstellung, -en** matinée
Nachnahme: per ~ schicken send C.O.D. || **die ~sendung, -en** C.O.D. parcel
der **Nachname, -n** (*like* **Name**) surname
nachnehmen* collect (amount) on delivery; **sich** *dat* **...** ~ help oneself to some more ...
nachplappern *coll* repeat parrot-fashion
das **Nachporto, -s** postage due
nachprüfen check (out); *educ* re-examine; examine at a later date
die **Nachprüfung, -en** check; verification; *educ* re-examination; resit, retest *US*; later examination
nachrechnen check; work it out
die **Nachrede, -n** epilogue; **üble** ~ defamation
nachreden (+*dat*) say about; repeat (what s.o. says)
nachreisen (*sn*) (+*dat*) follow
nachrennen* (*sn*) (+*dat*) *coll* = **nachlaufen**
die **Nachricht, -en** (piece of) news; message; (*pl*) *rad*, *TV* news; ~ **bekommen/erhalten von** hear from; (+*dat*) ~ **geben** send word to; **~en hören** listen to the news; **in den ~en** on the news || **die ~en|agentur, -en** = **das ~en|büro, -s** news agency; **der ~en|dienst, -e** news service; *mil* intelligence (service); **der ~en|satellit, -en** (*wk masc*) communications satellite; **die ~en|sendung, -en** news (broadcast), newscast; **die ~en|sperre, -n** news blackout; **der ~en|sprecher, -** newsreader, newscaster; **die ~en|technik** telecommunications; **das ~en|wesen** communications
nachrücken (*sn*) move up (**auf** *acc* into); (+*dat*) *mil* march after
der **Nachruf, -e** obituary
nachrufen* (+*dat*) shout after
der **Nachruhm** posthumous fame
nachsagen repeat; (+*dat*) say after; say about; (+*dat*) **Gutes/Übles** ~ speak well/ill of; **ihm wird (Stolz** *etc*) **nachgesagt** he is said to be (proud *etc*); **man sagt ihm nach, daß er ...** he is said to ...
die **Nachsaison** [-zɛzɔ̃:] late season
nachsalzen add more salt to
der **Nachsatz, ⸚e** additional paragraph
nachschauen *esp SGer* = **nachsehen** (*exc* +*dat*, = overlook)
nachschicken send on (*dat* to); forward (mail) (to)
Nachschlage-: das ~werk, -e reference work
nachschlagen* look up; (+*dat*) (*sn*) take after; ~ **in** (*dat*) look up in; (*v/i*) consult
nachschleichen* (*sn*) (+*dat*) sneak after
nachschleifen[1]* (*like* **schleifen[1]**) regrind; resharpen
nachschleifen[2] trail behind
der **Nachschlüssel, -** duplicate key
nachschreiben* take down; *educ* do (test) later
nachschreien* (+*dat*) shout after
die **Nachschrift, -en** postscript; (lecture) notes
der **Nachschub** *mil* supply (**an** *dat* of); fresh supplies; **der ~weg, -e** *mil* supply route
nachschütten put on/pour out more
nachsehen* look up; (have a) look at; check; (+*dat*) overlook (s.o.'s mistakes *etc*); (*v/i*) have a look; (+*dat*) gaze after; watch (s.o., sth.) go
das **Nachsehen: das ~ haben** be left empty-handed
nachsenden* send on (*dat* to); forward (mail) (to); **„bitte ~!"** 'please forward'
nachsetzen (+*dat*) pursue
die **Nachsicht** leniency; forbearance; ~ **haben mit** be lenient with
nachsichtig lenient; forbearing
die **Nachsilbe, -n** suffix
nachsingen* sing (after s.o.)
nachsinnen* (+*dat*/**über** *acc*) muse on; ponder
nachsitzen: ~ müssen be kept in
der **Nachsommer, -** Indian summer
die **Nachsorge** after-care
der **Nachspann, -e** credit titles, credits
die **Nachspeise, -n** dessert
das **Nachspiel, -e** sequel; consequences; repercussions; *mus* postlude; *theat* epilogue
nachspielen play (scene, tune) (after seeing/hearing it performed by s.o. else); re-enact; *theat* stage (subsequently); ~ **lassen** *sp* add on (injury time)
nachspionieren (+*dat*) spy on
nachsprechen* repeat (*dat* after)

nachspüren (+*dat*) trail; investigate; probe

nächst [–ɛ:ç–] 1 *prep* (+*dat*) next to; 2 *adj* **nächst..** (*superl of* **nah(e)**) next; nearest; closest; (days *etc*) next few; **der/die/das ~e beste** the first ... that comes along/that one comes across; **der Nächste** (*decl as adj*) fellow being; **der ~e, bitte!** next, please!; **am ~en** closest, nearest; **fürs ~e** for the time being

nächst– next ...; **~best** the first ... that comes along/that one comes across; **~folgend** next; **~liegend** nearest; obvious; **das N~liegende** the obvious thing to do

nächste–: das ~mal (the) next time; next

nachstehen* (+*dat*) take second place to; be inferior to (**an** *dat* in); (+*dat*) **nicht ~ an** (*dat*) be (s.o.'s) equal in; **~d** following; (*adv*) = **im ~den** below

nachsteigen* (*sn*) (+*dat*) *coll* chase (girl *etc*)

nachstellen (*see also* **nachgestellt**) put (clock) back; *tech* adjust; (+*dat*) *gramm* place after; (*v/i*, +*dat*) pursue; *coll* chase (girl *etc*)

die **Nachstellung, –en** *vbl noun*; *tech* adjustment; *gramm* postposition; (*pl*) pursuit

die **Nächsten|liebe** charity (= love of one's neighbour)

nächstens [–ɛ:ç–] before long, soon

nachstreben (+*dat*) emulate; aspire to

nachstürzen (*sn*) (+*dat*) rush after

nachsuchen [–u:–] search; **~ um** request

nacht (*eg* **Freitag ~** Friday) night; **heute ~** last night; tonight; **gestern ~** the night before last

die **Nacht, ¨–e** night; *SGer* evening; **die Heilige ~** night of Christmas Eve; **sich** *dat* **die ~ um die Ohren schlagen** *coll* stay up all night; **bei ~ = des ~s** at night; **bei ~ und Nebel** in the dead of night; **die ganze ~ durch** all night long; **bis tief in die ~** far into the night; **in der ~ zum (Dienstag** *etc*) on (Monday *etc*) night; **über ~** overnight || **n~blind** night-blind; **der ~dienst** night-duty/service; **die ~eule, –n** *coll* night-owl; **der ~falter, –** moth; **das ~hemd, –en** nightshirt; nightdress; **der ~klub, –s** night-club; **das ~lager, –** place where one stays the night; **das ~leben** night life; **das ~lokal, –e** night-club; **das ~mahl, ¨–er** *Aust* evening meal; **n~mahlen** (*insep*) *Aust* have one's evening meal; **die ~mütze, –n** nightcap; **der ~schatten, –** nightshade; **n~schlafend** (**bei/zu n~schlafender Zeit** in the middle of the night); **der ~schwärmer, –** moth; *coll* night-owl; **der ~strom** off-peak electricity; **der ~tisch, –e** bedside table; **der ~topf, ¨–e** chamber-pot; **die ~-und-Nebel-Aktion, –en** cloak and dagger operation; **der ~wächter, –** nightwatchman; *coll* sleepyhead; **n~wandeln** (*insep*; *also sn*) walk in one's sleep; **der ~wandler, –** sleepwalker; **n~wandlerisch** (**mit n~wandlerischer Sicherheit** with instinctive assurance)

nachtanken get some more petrol/gasoline *US*

nächte–: ~lang night after night

der **Nachteil, –e** disadvantage; **im ~** at a disadvantage; **zum ~** (+*gen*) to the detriment of; **sich zu seinem ~ verändern** change for the worse

nachteilig disadvantageous; detrimental; unfavourable

nächtens *poet* by night

die **Nachtigall, –en** nightingale

nächtigen spend the night; *Aust* stay (overnight)

die **Nächtigung, –en** *Aust* overnight stay

der **Nachtisch, –e** dessert

nächtlich night; nocturnal; of the/at night

der **Nachtrag, ¨–e** supplement; addendum

nachtragen* add; (+*dat*) carry after; hold against; **~d** vindictive

nachträglich later; subsequent; belated; additional; (*adv*) later; subsequently

nachtrauern (+*dat*) mourn for (one's lost youth *etc*)

nachts at night; **~über** during the night

nachtun*: es jmdm. ~ do the same as s.o.

die **Nach|untersuchung** [–u:–], **–en** *med* check-up

nachvollziehen* follow (train of thought); re-enact

nachwachsen* [–ks–] (*sn*) grow again

die **Nachwahl, –en** by-election, special election *US*

die **Nachwehen** *pl* painful aftermath; *med* after-pains

nachweinen (+*dat*) = **nachtrauern;** (+*dat*) **keine Träne ~** not shed any tears over

der **Nachweis, –e** proof; *chem etc* detection; **–nachweis** *also* ... agency

nachweisbar provable; demonstrable

nachweisen* prove, establish; *chem etc* detect; (+*dat*) prove that (s.o.) has committed/made; give (s.o.) information about (vacant post *etc*); **man konnte ihm nichts ~** they were unable to prove anything against him

nachweislich demonstrable

die **Nachwelt** posterity

nachwerfen* (+*dat*) throw after

nachwiegen* (*like* **wiegen**[1]) re-weigh

der **Nachwinter, –** wintry spell (in spring)

nachwirken continue to have an effect

die **Nachwirkung, –en** after-effect; (*pl*) aftermath

das **Nachwort, –e** postscript (to book)

der **Nachwuchs** [–ks] new blood/generation/recruits; *coll* offspring; *in compds* young ..., up-and-coming ...; **die ~kraft, ¨–e** young man/woman (starting career)

nachzahlen pay extra/later

nachzählen check (by counting); re-count

die **Nachzahlung, –en** additional payment; back-payment

nachzeichnen copy; trace (history)

nachziehen* tighten; drag behind one; go over (line *etc*), pencil (eyebrows); grow more ...; (*v/i*) *chess* make the next move; *coll* follow suit; (+*dat*) (*sn*) follow; move to the same place as

der **Nachzügler, –** straggler; late addition (to family)

der **Nackedei, –e/–s** *joc* naked child; naked person

der **Nacken, –** (nape of the) neck; (+*dat*) **im ~ sitzen** breathe down (s.o.'s) neck || **der ~schlag, ⸗e** blow (= sudden misfortune)

nackend *coll* = **nackig** *coll* naked

–nackig -necked

nackt naked; bare; (truth) naked, (reality) stark; *art* nude; (*adv*) in the nude

Nackt– nude ...; **der ~frosch, ⸗e** *joc* naked child; **die ~kultur** nudism; **die ~schnecke, –n** slug

die **Nacktheit** nakedness, nudity; bareness

die **Nadel, –n** needle (*var senses*); pin; brooch; **wie auf ~n sitzen** be on tenterhooks || **der ~baum, ⸗e** conifer; **das ~kissen, –** pincushion; **das ~öhr, –e** eye of a needle; **der ~stich, –e** pinprick; *needlew* stitch; **der ~streifen|anzug, ⸗e** pinstripe suit; **der ~wald, ⸗er** coniferous forest

nadeln shed its needles

Nage–: das ~tier, –e rodent

der **Nagel,** *pl* **Nägel** nail (*also anat*); tack; **den ~ auf den Kopf treffen** hit the nail on the head; **an den ~ hängen** *sp* hang up; *coll* give up; (+*dat*) **auf den Nägeln brennen** *coll* be extremely urgent; **sich** *dat* **... unter den ~ reißen/ritzen** *coll* help oneself to || **die ~bürste, –n** nail-brush; **die ~feile, –n** nail-file; **die ~haut, ⸗e** cuticle; **der ~lack, –e** nail-varnish; **der ~lack|entferner, –** nail-varnish remover; **nagel|neu** *coll* brand-new; **die ~probe, –n** acid test; **die ~schere, –n** nail-scissors

nageln nail (**an/auf** (*acc*) (on)to)

nagen gnaw; nibble; **~ an** (*dat*) gnaw at; nibble at; eat into; undermine (health); prey on; **~d** gnawing; (doubts) nagging

der **Nager, –** rodent

Nah– close ...; near ...; **die ~aufnahme, –n** close-up; **der ~kampf, ⸗e** close combat; *box* infighting; **~ost** (*in prep phrases*) Middle East; **~ost–, n~östlich** Middle East(ern); **der ~schnell|verkehr** local medium-fast train service; **der ~verkehr** local service; **der ~verkehrs|zug, ⸗e** local train; **n~verwandt** closely-related; **das ~ziel, –e** immediate objective

Näh– sewing ...; **das ~garn, –e** thread; **der ~kasten, ..kästen** work-box; **die ~maschine, –n** sewing-machine; **die ~nadel, –n** needle

nah(e) (*comp* **näher,** *superl* **nächst../am nächsten**) 1 *adj* close; near; (end *etc*) approaching, (future) near; (*following dat*) close to; on the verge of; **–nah(e)** close to ...; **der Nahe Osten** the Middle East; **~ an** (*acc/dat*)/**bei** near, close to; **~ daran zu ...** on the point of (+*ger*); (+*dat*) **zu ~ treten** offend; 2 (**nahe**) *prep* (+*dat*) close to, near

die **Nähe** closeness, proximity; **aus der/nächster ~** from close/very close to; **in der ~** close by; (+*gen*) near

nahe–: nahe|bei nearby; **~bringen*** (*sep*) (+*dat*) bring close to; teach to appreciate; **~gehen*** (*sep*; *sn*) (+*dat*) affect deeply; **~gelegen** *p/part*; *also* nearby; **~kommen*** (*sep*; *sn*) (+*dat*) get close to; come close to; **~legen** (*sep*) (+*dat*) suggest to; **~liegen*** (*sep*) seem likely; (idea) suggest itself (**die Annahme liegt nahe, daß ...** it seems reasonable to assume that ...); **~liegend** natural; (reasons) obvious; **~stehen*** (*sep*) (+*dat*) be close to (person); *pol* sympathize with; **~stehend** close; **~zu** nearly; virtually

nahen (*sn*) approach

nähen sew; stitch (*also med*); make (dress *etc*)

näher (*comp of* **nah(e)**) nearer, closer; more detailed; (vicinity) immediate; (*adv*) nearer, closer; more closely; in greater detail; **Näheres** (*decl as adj*) further particulars || **~bringen*** (*sep*) (+*dat of pers*) deepen (s.o.'s) understanding of; **~kommen*** (*sep*; *sn*) (+*dat*) get closer to; **~liegen*** (*sep*) be more natural (**es liegt ~ zu ... als zu ...** it seems better to ... than to ...); **~liegend** *comp of* **naheliegend; ~stehen*** (*sep*) (+*dat*) be closer to

die **Näherei, –en** sewing; piece of sewing

die **Näherin, –nen** seamstress

nähern: sich ~ approach; **sich ~** (+*dat*) approach; **sich seinem Ende ~** draw to a close

nahm (nähme) *p/t* (*subj*) *of* **nehmen**

Nähr– nutrient ...; **der ~boden, ..böden** breeding-ground; *biol* culture-medium; **die ~creme, –s** nourishing cream; **die ~mittel** *pl* cereal products; **der ~stoff, –e** nutrient; **der ~wert, –e** nutritional value

nähren feed; nurture; (*v/i*) be nourishing; **sich ~ von** live on; live by

nahrhaft nourishing, nutritious

die **Nahrung** food; nourishment; **feste ~** solids; (+*dat*) **~ geben** strengthen (suspicion *etc*) || **das ~s|mittel, –** foodstuff

die **Naht, ⸗e** seam; *tech* join; *anat, med* suture;

aus den/allen Nähten platzen *coll* be bursting at the seams || **n~los** seamless; (transition) smooth; (*adv*) imperceptibly; **die ~stelle, –n** join; place where (East and West *etc*) meet

naiv naïve; **~e Malerei** naïve painting

die **Naivität** naïvety

die **Najade, –n** naiad

der **Name** (*acc*, *dat* **–n**, *gen* **–ns**), **–n** name; **sich** *dat* **einen ~n machen** make a name for oneself; **auf jmds. ~n** in s.o.'s name; **die Dinge/das Kind beim rechten ~n nennen** call a spade a spade; **im ~n** (+*gen*) on behalf of; in the name of; **mit ~n ...** by the name of ...; **dem ~n nach** by name; in name

Namen– ... of names; **n~los** unnamed; anonymous; unknown; unspeakable

namens by the name of; (+*gen*) on behalf of

Namens–: die ~änderung, –en change of name; **das ~schild, –er** name-plate; **der ~tag, –e** name-day; **der ~vetter, –n** namesake; **der ~zug, ¨–e** signature; monogram

namentlich (calling *etc*) by name; (*adv*) especially; (call *etc*) by name

namhaft noted; considerable; **~ machen** name

nämlich 1 *adj arch* same; 2 *adv* namely; (*by way of explanation*) as ...; you see; *or left untranslated* (*eg* **ich verstand ihn nicht, er war ~ Chinese** I didn't understand him: he was Chinese)

nannte *p/t of* **nennen**

nanu! well, well!

der **Napf, ¨–e** bowl; **der ~kuchen, –** (*type of cake baked in a fluted mould*)

die **Narbe, –n** scar; *bot* stigma

narbig scarred

die **Narkose, –n** anaesthetic; **in ~** under anaesthetic

das **Narkotikum, –(k)a, narkotisch** narcotic

narkotisieren anaesthetize

der **Narr, –en** (*wk masc*) fool; *hist* jester; **–narr** ... fan; **einen ~en gefressen haben an** (*dat*) *coll* dote on; **zum ~en haben/halten** make a fool of

narren fool

Narren–: die ~freiheit freedom from restraint (at carnival time); free rein; **das ~haus, ¨–er** madhouse; **n~sicher** foolproof

die **Narrheit, –en** folly; foolish thing (to do)

die **Närrin, –nen** fool

närrisch foolish; crazy; **~ auf** (*acc*) crazy about; **~ verliebt in** (*acc*) madly in love with

die **Narzisse, –n** narcissus

der **Narzißmus** narcissism

narzißtisch narcissistic

Nas–: das ~horn, ¨–er rhinoceros; **n~lang** *coll* (= **naselang**)

nasal nasal; **der N~laut, –e** nasal (sound)

naschen eat (*esp* sweet things; *also v/i*); **~ an** (*dat*) nibble at

naschhaft sweet-toothed

die **Nase, –n** nose (*also aer*); (+*dat*) **eine lange ~ machen** *coll* thumb one's nose at; **seine ~ stecken in** (*acc*) *coll* poke one's nose into; **die ~ voll haben von** *coll* be sick of; **an der ~ herumführen** *coll* lead by the nose; **auf die ~ fallen** *coll* come a cropper; (+*dat*) **auf die ~ binden** *coll* tell (unnecessarily); **auf der ~ liegen** *coll* be laid up; (+*dat*) **aus der ~ ziehen** *coll* worm out of; **pro ~** *coll* per head; (+*dat*) **unter die ~ reiben** *coll* rub in || **n~lang** *coll* (**alle n.** all the time); **n~weis** saucy

näseln speak through one's nose; **~d** nasal

Nasen– ... of the nose; nose ...; nasal ...; **das ~bluten** nose-bleed; **der ~flügel, –** side of the nose; **~länge** (**um eine N.** by a nose); **das ~loch, ¨–er** nostril; **der ~rücken, –** bridge of the nose; **die ~spitze, –n** tip of the nose; **der ~stüber, –** flick on the nose

–nasig –nosed

naß (**–ss–**; *comp*, *superl also* **¨–**) wet; **(sich) ~ machen** wet (oneself); **durch und durch ~** wet through

das **Naß** water; liquid

naß–: ~kalt cold and wet

der **Nassauer, –** *coll* sponger

nassauern *coll* sponge (**bei** off, on)

die **Nässe** wetness; wet

nässen wet; (*v/i* wound) weep

die **Nation, –en** nation

national (*in compds* **N~–**) national; **die N~hymne, –n** national anthem; **der N~rat, ¨–e** (member of the) National Council (*representative assembly in Austria, Switzerland*); **der N~sozialismus** National Socialism; **der N~sozialist, –en** (*wk masc*), **~sozialistisch** National Socialist; **der N~spieler, –** *sp* international; **der N~staat, –en** nation-state

das **Nationale, –** *Aust* particulars

nationalisieren nationalize; naturalize

die **Nationalisierung, –en** nationalization; naturalization

der **Nationalismus** nationalism

der **Nationalist, –en** (*wk masc*) nationalist

nationalistisch nationalistic

die **Nationalität, –en** nationality

die **NATO** ['na:to] NATO

das **Natrium** sodium

das **Natron** [–ɔn] sodium bicarbonate

die **Natter, –n** snake (of the family *Colubridae*, *eg* grass snake)

die **Natur, –en** nature; countryside; disposition, nature; constitution; nature (of things, *eg* **Fragen allgemeiner ~** questions of a general nature); (serious *etc*) person; **~ sein** (hair *etc*) be natural; **nach der ~** (draw *etc*) from nature; **von ~** by nature; **von ~ aus** by nature; naturally (blonde *etc*); (+*dat*) **zur zweiten ~ werden** become second nature to

Natur– ... of nature; natural ...; nature ...; **n~belassen** unadulterated; **die ~erscheinung, –en** natural phenomenon; **n~farben** natural-coloured; **der ~forscher, –** naturalist; **der ~freund, –e** nature-lover; **n~gegeben** natural; **n~gemäß** natural; (*adv*) naturally; by its very nature; **das ~gesetz, –e** law of nature; **n~getreu** faithful, lifelike; **die ~heil|kunde** nature cure, naturopathy; **die ~katastrophe, –n** natural disaster; **die ~kunde** natural history; **der ~mensch, –en** (*wk masc*) child of nature; **n~rein** unadulterated, natural; **die ~schätze** *pl* natural resources; **der ~schutz** nature conservancy (**unter N. stehen** be a protected species); **das ~schutz|gebiet, –e** nature reserve; **das ~talent, –e** natural talent; natural; **das ~volk, ¨–er** primitive people; **n~widrig** unnatural; **die ~wissenschaften** *pl* natural sciences; **der ~wissenschaftler, –** scientist; **n~wissenschaftlich** scientific; **der ~zustand** natural state

die **Naturalien** [–ĭən] *pl* natural produce; natural history specimens; **in ~** (pay) in kind

naturalisieren naturalize (*also* animal, plant)

die **Naturalisierung, –en** naturalization

der **Naturalismus** naturalism

naturalistisch naturalistic

das **Naturell, –e** disposition

natürlich natural; (*adv*) naturally; of course, naturally; **natürlicher|weise** naturally

'nauf *SGer coll* = **hinauf**

'naus *SGer coll* = **hinaus**

die **Nautik** [–ɪk] nautical science, navigation

nautisch nautical

die **Navigation** navigation

navigieren navigate

der **Nazi, –s** Nazi

der **Nazismus** Nazism

nazistisch Nazi

n. Br. = nördlicher Breite, *eg* **20° ~** latitude 20° north

n. Chr. (**= nach Christus**) A.D.

die **NDPD** *EGer* = **National-Demokratische Partei Deutschlands**

der **NDR = Norddeutscher Rundfunk**

'ne *coll* = **eine**

Neapel Naples

der **Nebel, –** fog; mist; *astron* = **der ~fleck, –e** nebula; **das ~horn, ¨–er** foghorn; **der ~schein|werfer, –** fog lamp

nebelhaft nebulous

neben (+*acc*) (sit down *etc*) beside, next to; (+*dat*) (be seated *etc*) beside, next to; apart from; compared with; **~ ...** (*dat*) **her** beside

Neben– secondary ...; additional ...; supplementary ...; side ...;

n~an next door; in the next room; **der ~anschluß, ¨–(ss)e** *tel* extension; **n~bei** incidentally; on the side; in addition; **der ~beruf, –e** second job (**im N.** as a sideline); **n~beruflich** (work) extra; (*adv*) as a sideline; **die ~beschäftigung, –en** second job; **der ~buhler, –** rival; **n~einander** next to one another; side by side; at the same time; **das ~einander** existence side by side; juxtaposition; **n~einander|stellen** (*sep*) place side by side; juxtapose; **der ~eingang, ¨–e** side entrance; **das ~fach, ¨–er** subsidiary subject, minor *US*; **der ~fluß, ¨–(ss)e** tributary; **das ~gebäude, –** annexe; **das ~geräusch, –e** background noise; **n~her** in addition; **n~her–** *sep pref* ... alongside; **der ~mann, ¨–er** neighbour (in row *etc*); **das ~produkt, –e** by-product; **die ~rolle, –n** supporting role; (in politics *etc*) minor role (**eine N. spielen für** not be important to); **die ~sache, –n** minor matter (**... ist N. ...** is unimportant); **n~sächlich** unimportant; **der ~satz, ¨–e** subordinate clause; **die ~stelle, –n** branch office; *tel* extension; **die ~straße, –n** side-street; by-road; **die ~strecke, –n** branch-line; **der ~tisch, –e** next table; **der ~winkel, –** adjacent angle; **die ~wirkung, –en** side-effect; **das ~zimmer, –** adjoining room

neblig [–eː–] foggy; misty

nebst [–eː–] (+*dat*) (together) with

das **Necessaire** [nesɛ'sɛːɐ], **–s** toilet-bag

necken tease (**mit** about)

die **Neckerei, –en** teasing; teasing remark

neckisch teasing; saucy

nee *coll* no

der **Neffe, –n** (*wk masc*) nephew

die **Negation, –en** negation; *gramm* negative

negativ negative (*also elect*, *math*, *etc*)

das **Negativ, –e** *phot* negative

der **Neger, –** Negro; **der ~kuß, ¨–(ss)e** chocolate marshmallow

die **Negerin, –nen** Negress

negieren deny; reject (view); *gramm* negate

das **Negligé** [–ʒ–], **–s** negligee

nehmen (**nimm(s)t,** *p/t* **nahm** (*subj* **nähme**), *p/part* **genommen**) take (*also mil*); be on, take (drugs, the pill); use (hammer, oil, *etc*); charge (for sth.); (+*dat*) take (away) from; rob (s.o.) of, deprive (s.o.) of; **sich** *dat* **... ~** help oneself to; engage (lawyer); take (husband, wife, hotel room, one's own life, *etc*); **sich** *dat* **Zeit ~** take one's time; **sich** *dat* **die Zeit ~ für** make time for; **ernst/wörtlich ~** take seriously/literally; **sich** *dat* **... frei ~** take (day *etc*) off; **man**

nehme ... (in recipe) take ...; **wie man's nimmt** it depends on how you look at it; **zu ~ wissen** know how to handle (person); **es sich** *dat* **nicht ~ lassen zu ...** insist on (+*ger*); **hart im Nehmen sein** be able to take setbacks/disappointments *etc* in one's stride; *box* be able to take a lot of punishment

an sich ~ take; take charge of

auf sich ~ take upon oneself; make (sacrifice)

in die Hand ~ pick up; take in hand

zu sich ~ take in(to one's home); take (food)

die **Nehrung, –en** *geog* spit

der **Neid** envy; **der ~hammel, –** *coll* envious person; **n~los** ungrudging

neiden (+*dat*) envy (s.o. sth.)

neidisch envious (**auf** *acc* of)

die **Neige, –n** dregs; **zur ~ gehen** draw to a close; (sun) go down; run low

neigen (*see also* **geneigt**) incline; tilt; bend (one's body); bow (one's head); **~ zu** be inclined to; tend towards; be susceptible to; **dazu ~ zu ...** tend to ...

sich ~ bend; bow; slope; tilt; (ship) list; draw to a close

die **Neigung, –en** incline; inclination; list (of ship); tendency, inclination; affection (**zu** for); **der ~s|winkel, –** angle of inclination

nein no (, I don't/we haven't *etc*); (*intensifying*) indeed; even; **~, ...!** (*surprise*) my, ...!; **~, 'so was!** well I never!; **aber ~!** certainly not! || **die N~stimme, –n** vote against; *parl* no, nay *US*

'nein *SGer coll* = **hinein**

der **Nektar** nectar

die **Nektarine, –n** nectarine

die **Nelke, –n** carnation; *cul* clove

'nen *coll* = **einen**

Nenn–: die ~form, –en infinitive; **der ~wert, –e** nominal value (**zum N.** at par)

nennen (*p/t* **nannte** (*subj rare* **nennte**), *p/part* **genannt**) call; name (**nach** after); mention; **sich ~** call oneself; be called; **genannt ...** known as ... || **~s|wert** worth mentioning; appreciable

der **Nenner, –** denominator; **auf einen (gemeinsamen) ~ bringen** reconcile (interests, opinions)

Neo– neo–

das **Neolithikum** the Neolithic

neolithisch Neolithic

der **Neologismus, –(m)en** neologism

das **Neon** [–ɔn] neon; **die ~reklame** neon sign

der **Nepp** *coll* daylight robbery; **das ~lokal, –e** *coll* clip-joint

neppen *coll* 'fleece'

Neptun *myth*, **der ~** (*gen* **–s**) *astron* Neptune

der **Nerv** [–f], **–en** nerve (*also bot*); **der hat (viel-leicht) ~en!** *coll* he's got a nerve!; (+*dat*) **auf die ~en gehen** get on (s.o.'s) nerves; **ich bin mit den ~en fertig/herunter** my nerves are worn to a frazzle || **n~tötend** nerve-racking

nerven [–f–] *coll* get on (s.o.'s) nerves

Nerven– [–f–] nerve ...; nervous ...; **der ~arzt, ⸗e** neurologist; **n~aufreibend** nerve-racking; **das ~bündel, –** *coll* bundle of nerves; **die ~heil|anstalt, –en** mental hospital; **der ~kitzel, –** thrill; **n~krank** suffering from a nervous disorder; **die ~krankheit, –en** nervous disorder; **der ~krieg, –e** war of nerves; **das ~leiden, –** nervous disorder; **die ~säge, –n** *coll* pain in the neck; **die ~schmerzen** *pl* neuralgia; **n~stärkend (n~stärkendes Mittel** nerve tonic); **das ~system, –e** nervous system; **der ~zusammenbruch, ⸗e** nervous breakdown

nervig [–v–] sinewy

nervlich [–f–] (strain *etc*) nervous

nervös [–v–] nervous; **~ machen** make nervous; get on (s.o.'s) nerves

die **Nervosität** [–v–] nervousness

der **Nerz, –e** mink

die **Nessel, –n** nettle; **sich in die ~n setzen** *coll* get into hot water

das **Nest, –er** nest; hideout; *coll* bed; *coll* 'hole', 'dump'; **sein eigenes ~ beschmutzen** foul one's own nest || **das ~häkchen, –** baby of the family; **die ~wärme** warmth and security of home

nesteln: ~ an (*dat*) fiddle with

der **Nestor, –(or)en** doyen

nett nice

die **Nettigkeit, –en** niceness; (*pl*) kind words

netto *comm* net

das **Netz, –e** net; web; (luggage) rack; string bag; netting; *rail etc* network, system; *rad*, *TV* network; *elect* mains; grid; *geog* grid (on map); (+*dat*) **ins ~ gehen** walk into (s.o.'s) trap; **ins ~ schlagen** net (ball); **~!** let! || **der ~anschluß, ⸗(ss)e** mains connection; **die ~haut, ⸗e** retina; **das ~hemd, –en** string vest; **die ~karte, –n** (*ticket permitting unlimited travel within a specified area for a specified period*); **das ~werk, –e** network

netzen moisten

neu new; (*adv*) newly; recently; re– (*eg* **~ anordnen** rearrange, **~ beziehen** re-cover); **~er..** newer; more recent; (history, literature, *etc*) recent; **die ~eren Sprachen** modern languages; **in ~erer Zeit** in recent times; **~est..** newest; most recent; latest; **in ~ester Zeit** very recently; **was gibt's N~es?** what's new?; **aufs ~e = von ~em** afresh; **das N~este** the latest; the latest news; **das N~este vom N~en** the very latest thing; **seit ~estem** since a short while ago; just recently

neu– new ..., (*with p/part*) newly ...; re–; neo–;

der N~ankömmling, –e newcomer; **die N~anschaffung, –en** new acquisition; **~artig** new; new type of; novel; **die N~bau|wohnung, –en** flat/apartment *US* in a new (or relatively new) building; **die N~bildung, –en** formation of (a) new ...; new formation; *ling* neologism; **N~–Delhi** [–li] New Delhi; **N~england** New England; **die N~erscheinung, –en** new publication; **N~fund|land** Newfoundland; **der N~fund|länder, –** Newfoundland (= dog); **~gebacken** fresh-baked; *coll* (husband *etc*) brand-new; **~geboren** newborn (**sich wie n. fühlen** feel a new man/woman); **die N~gier(de)** curiosity; **~gierig** curious (**auf** *acc* about) (**n. sein, ob ...** wonder whether ...); **die N~gliederung, –en** restructuring; **N~griechisch** modern Greek; **~hoch|deutsch, N~hoch|deutsch** New High German; **das N~jahr** [*also* –'jaːɐ] New Year's Day; **das N~land** virgin territory; new ground (**N. betreten** break new ground); **die N~land|gewinnung** land reclamation; **~modisch** new-fangled; **der N~mond** new moon; **die N~ordnung, –en** reorganization; **der N~philologe, –n** (*wk masc*) modern linguist; **die N~philologie** (study of) modern languages; **die N~regelung, –en** revision; **~reich, der/die N~reiche** (*decl as adj*) nouveau riche; **N~schottland** Nova Scotia; **N~see|land** New Zealand; **der N~see|länder, –** New Zealander; **~see|ländisch** New Zealand; **der N~sprachler, –** modern linguist; **~sprachlich** modern language; **N~süd|wales** New South Wales; **~vermählt** newly-wed; **die N~verteilung, –en** redistribution; **der N~wert, –e** value when new; **die N~zeit** the modern era; **~zeitlich** modern

Neuenburg Neuchâtel

neuerdings recently, of late; *SGer* again

[der] **Neuerer, –** innovator

neuerlich new; (*adv*) recently, of late

[die] **Neuerung, –en** innovation

neuestens of late

[die] **Neuheit, –en** newness; novelty; new thing, innovation (on market)

[die] **Neuigkeit, –en** (piece of) news; (*pl*) news

neulich the other day

[der] **Neuling, –e** novice

neun, die Neun, –en nine; **das N~auge, –n** lamprey; **~mal|klug** *coll* smart-alecky; **der/die N~mal|kluge** (*decl as adj*) smart aleck

neunt: zu ~ (*see* **zu** 1 (*i*)); **neunt..** ninth

neuntel: ein ~ ... a ninth of a ...

[das] **Neuntel, –** ninth

neuntens ninthly

neunzehn nineteen

neunzehnt.., das Neunzehntel, – nineteenth

neunzig ninety

neunziger: die ~ Jahre the nineties; **der Neunziger, –** nonagenarian; (*pl*) nineties

neunzigst.., das Neunzigstel, – ninetieth

[die] **Neuralgie, –(ie)n** neuralgia

neuralgisch neuralgic; **~er Punkt** trouble spot; thing s.o. is highly touchy about

[der] **Neurologe, –n** (*wk masc*) neurologist

[die] **Neurologie** neurology

neurologisch neurological

[die] **Neurose, –n** neurosis

[der] **Neurotiker, –, neurotisch** neurotic

neutral neutral

neutralisieren neutralize (*also chem*); *sp* suspend (race)

[die] **Neutralität** neutrality

[das] **Neutron** [–ɔn], **–(on)en** neutron; **die Neutronen|bombe, –n** neutron bomb

[das] **Neutrum, –(r)a** neuter (noun)

N.F. (= **Neue Folge**) N.S.

nicht not; no (better, fewer, *etc*); (*in command, followed by infin, eg* **~ berühren!**) do not/don't (touch *etc*); **~ (doch)!** don't!; **..., ~ (wahr)?** ..., isn't he/doesn't she/can't you *etc*?; **ich ~** not me, I haven't/won't *etc*; **auch ~** not ... either, (*following pers pron, eg* **ich auch ~**) neither can/did/would *etc* (I *etc*); **~, daß ...** not that ...; **~ einmal** not even; **~ mehr** no longer, not ... any more; **wenn ... ~** if ... not; unless ...; **wo ~** if not

Nicht– (*eg* **der ~angriffspakt, ~schwimmer**) non– (aggression pact, swimmer, *etc*); (*eg* **die ~beachtung** +*gen*) failure to (observe *etc*), non– (observance *etc*) of; **der ~kämpfer, –** non-combatant; **n~krieg|führend** neutral; **n~pakt|gebunden** *EGer* non-aligned; **der ~raucher, –** non-smoker; *rail* = **das ~raucher|abteil, –e** no-smoking compartment; **n~rostend** rust-proof; (steel) stainless; **das ~vorhanden|sein** absence; **die ~weiter|verbreitung** non-proliferation; **das ~wissen** ignorance; **~zutreffendes** („**N. bitte streichen!**" 'please delete where inapplicable')

[die] **Nichte, –n** niece

nichtig trivial, trifling; *leg* invalid, void; **für ~ erklären** declare (null and) void

[die] **Nichtigkeit, –en** triviality; trivial matter/remark; *leg* invalidity

nichts nothing; not ... anything/a thing; **~ (Neues** *etc*) nothing (new *etc*); **~ sein** *coll* be no good; **das ist ~ für ...** it's not (right) for ... ; **mit ... ist es ~ ...** is *etc* off; **~ (anderes) als** nothing but; **~ da!** *coll* nothing doing!; **~ dergleichen** nothing like that; **für**

~ **und wieder** ~ for/over nothing at all; **mir** ~, **dir** ~ (*see* **mir**); **weiter** ~ nothing else; **wie** ~ in no time; ~ **wie (hin/raus** *etc*)! *coll* let's get (over there/out of here *etc*) quick!; **das Nichts** nothingness; void; trifle; (*pl* **–e**) nonentity; **vor dem Nichts stehen** be faced with ruin || **~ahnend** unsuspecting; **~desto|weniger** nonetheless; **der N~könner, –** bungler; **der N~nutz, –e, ~nutzig** good-for-nothing; **~sagend** meaningless; empty; **der N~tuer, –** idler; **~tuerisch** idle; **das N~tun** inactivity, idleness; **~würdig** despicable

das **Nickel** nickel

nicken nod; *coll* doze

das **Nickerchen, –** *coll* snooze

der **Nicki, –s** velour pullover

nie never; ~ **mehr** never again; not ... ever again; **fast** ~ hardly ever; **noch** ~ never before; ~ **und nimmer** never ever

nieder 1 *adv* down; 2 *adj* **nieder..** (birth *etc*) low; low-ranking; base; *biol* lower; ~ **mit ...!** down with ...!

nieder– *sep pref* ... down

Nieder– Lower ...

niederbeugen bow; **sich** ~ bend down

niederbrennen* (*sn if v/i*) burn down

niederbrüllen shout down

niederdeutsch, N~ Low German

niederdrücken (*see also* **niedergedrückt**) press down; depress; **~d** depressing

die **Niederfrequenz, –en** *phys* low frequency

der **Niedergang** decline

niedergedrückt *p/part*; *also* depressed

niedergehen* (*sn*) come down; (storm) break; *box* go down

niedergeschlagen *p/part*; *also* dejected

die **Niedergeschlagenheit** dejection

niederhalten* keep down; repress; oppress (people)

niederkämpfen overcome; fight back (tears)

niederknallen *coll* shoot down

niederknien (*sn*) kneel down

niederknüppeln club down

niederkommen* (*sn*) *arch* give birth (**mit** to)

die **Niederkunft, ⸚e** *arch* confinement

die **Niederlage, –n** defeat (*also sp*); *comm* depot; *arch* branch

die **Niederlande** *pl* the Netherlands

der **Niederländer, –** Dutchman; **die** ~ the Dutch

die **Niederländerin, –nen** Dutchwoman

niederländisch, (*language*) **N~** Dutch

niederlassen*: sich ~ sit down, (bird) alight; settle (down); **sich** ~ **als** set up as; **die niedergelassenen Ärzte** general practitioners

die **Niederlassung, –en** settlement; setting up a practice; settlement (= place); *comm* branch

niederlegen put down; lay (wreath); lay down (arms); put to bed; resign (office); set down (in writing); **die Arbeit** ~ down tools; **sich** ~ lie down

niedermachen slaughter

niedermähen mow down

niedermetzeln slaughter

Nieder|österreich Lower Austria

niederprasseln (*sn*): ~ **auf** (*acc*) beat down on; **Fragen prasseln auf ... nieder** ... is *etc* bombarded with questions

niederreißen* pull down; break down (barrier)

Niedersachsen Lower Saxony

niederschießen* shoot down; (*v/i sn*) swoop down (**auf** *acc* on)

der **Niederschlag, ⸚e** sediment; fall-out; *chem* precipitate; *mus* downbeat; *box* knockdown; knock-out; (*esp pl*) rainfall; precipitation; **seinen** ~ **finden in** (*dat*) be reflected in

niederschlagen* (*see also* **niedergeschlagen**) knock down; (rain) beat down; lower (eyes, glance); crush (revolt *etc*); *chem* precipitate; *leg* dismiss (case)

sich ~ settle (**an** *dat* on); *chem* precipitate; **sich** ~ **in** (*dat*) be reflected in

niederschlags–: ~arm with low rainfall; **~frei** dry; **~reich** with high rainfall

niederschmettern strike down; (news) shatter; **~d** shattering

niederschreiben* write down

niederschreien* shout down

die **Niederschrift, –en** writing down; (written) record

niedersetzen put down; **sich** ~ sit down

niedersinken* (*sn*) sink down; ~ **in** (*acc*) sink into

die **Niederspannung, –en** *elect* low tension

niederstampfen trample down

niederstimmen vote down

niederstoßen* knock down (*Aust also mot*); (*v/i sn*) swoop down (**auf** *acc* on)

niederstrecken bring down; **sich** ~ lie down

niedertourig [–tu:–] low-revving

die **Niedertracht** baseness; base act

niederträchtig base, vile

die **Niederträchtigkeit, –en** baseness; base act

niedertreten* tread down; wear down

die **Niederung, –en** low ground; (*pl*) darker side (of life); depths

niederwalzen flatten; crush

niederwerfen* put down (revolt); defeat; (illness) lay low; (news) shatter; **sich** ~ throw oneself down (**vor** *dat* at (s.o.'s) feet)

niederzwingen* force to the ground; force into submission; conquer (emotion)

niedlich sweet, cute

niedrig low; base; **~gesinnt** low-minded; **~stehend** backward; **das N~wasser** low water

die **Niedrigkeit, –en** lowness; baseness; base act
niemals = nie
niemand (*acc* –(en), *gen* –(e)s, *dat* –(em)) nobody, no one; not … anybody/anyone; ~ **anders** nobody else; ~ **anders als** nobody but; **ein Niemand** a nobody || **das N~s|land** no-man's-land
die **Niere, –n** kidney; **künstliche** ~ kidney machine
Nieren– kidney …; renal …
Nies–: das ~pulver, – sneezing-powder; **die ~wurz** hellebore
Niesel–: der ~regen drizzle
nieseln: es nieselt it is drizzling
niesen sneeze
niet–: niet- und nagel|fest *coll* (**alles mitnehmen, was nicht n. ist** strip the place bare)
die **Niete**[1], **–n** rivet
die **Niete**[2], **–n** blank (in lottery); *coll* washout
nieten rivet
die **Nieten|hose, –n** jeans (with studs)
der **Niger** (*gen* –(s)) the Niger
Nigeria Nigeria
der **Nigerianer, –, nigerianisch** Nigerian
der **Nihilismus** nihilism
der **Nihilist, –en** (*wk masc*) nihilist
nihilistisch nihilistic
Nikolaus Nicholas; St Nicholas' Day; **der** ~ St Nicholas || **der ~tag** St Nicholas' Day (*Dec. 6th*)
das **Nikotin** nicotine
der **Nil** (*gen* –(s)) the Nile; **das ~pferd, –e** hippopotamus
der **Nimbus** aura; mystique; *art* halo
nimm *imp sing of* **nehmen**
nimmer *arch* never; *SGer* no longer; not again; **~mehr** *SGer* never again; **nimmer|müde** untiring; **~satt** insatiable; **der N~satt, –e** glutton; **N~wiedersehen** *coll* (**auf N.** for good; never to be seen again)
nimm(s)t (*2nd,*) *3rd sing pres of* **nehmen**
Nimwegen [–ɪ–] Nijmegen
Ninive [–ve] Nineveh
der **Nippel, –** *mech* nipple
nippen sip; ~ **an** (*dat*) sip (at); sip from
die **Nippes** *pl* = **die Nipp|sachen** *pl* knick-knacks
nirgends = nirgend|wo nowhere
das **Nirwana** (*gen* –(s)) nirvana
die **Nische** [–iː–], **–n** niche; recess
die **Nisse, –n** nit
Nist– nesting …; **der ~kasten, ..kästen** nesting-box
nisten nest
das **Nitrat, –e** nitrate
das **Nitrit, –e** nitrite
das **Nitroglyzerin** nitroglycerine
das **Niveau** [–'voː], **–s** level; standard; ~ **haben** be of a high standard; have class; **mit/von** ~ of a high standard || **n~los** mediocre; **n~voll** high-class

nivellieren level out (differences *etc*); (*v/i*) *surv* level
nix *coll* = **nichts**
die **Nixe, –n** water-nymph
Nizza Nice
n. J./n. M. (= **nächsten Jahres/Monats**) of next year/month
NN = Normal-Null; N. N. (= *nomen nescio*) name not known
NO (= **Nordost(en)**) N.E.
nobel noble; grand, posh; *coll* generous
der **Nobel|preis, –e** Nobel prize; **der ~träger, –** Nobel prizewinner
die **Noblesse** nobility, nobleness
noch 1 *adv* still; yet; only (yesterday *etc*), as late as (*eg* ~ **im 14. Jahrhundert** as late as the 14th century); *often left untranslated when indicating a future action* (*eg* **ich sage ihm** ~ **Bescheid** I'll let him know) *or used for emphasis in expressions of time* (*eg* ~ **am selben Abend** that same evening, ~ **ehe ich antworten konnte** before I could answer); (*indicating addition*) as well, (*followed by number*) another (*eg* ~ **zwei Monate** another two months), (*with interrog*, *eg* what) else; (*indicating sth. remaining – with* **haben**) (any/some) … left (*eg* **hast du** ~ **Geld?** have you any money left?); (+*comp*, *eg* ~ **besser**) even (better *etc*); *limiting a positive statement, not translated* (*eg* **das ist** ~ **billig** that's cheap); (*as emotive particle, indicating attempt to recollect*) again (*eg* **wie hieß er ~?** what was his name again?); 2 *conj* nor
doch ~ (*see* **doch**)
~ **ein** another; ~ **einmal**/*coll* **mal** (once) again, once more; ~ **einmal**/*coll* **mal so** twice as; ~ **eins** another one; one other thing
~ **etwas**/*coll* **was** (*see* **etwas**)
~ **immer = immer** ~ still (*emphatic*)
~ **kein** not a/any … yet; not, less than
~ + **…mal** (*eg* **dreimal** three) more times (*see also* ~ **einmal** *above*)
~ **nicht/nichts** not/nothing yet
~ **nie** never (before); **wie** ~ **nie** as never before
~ **niemand** nobody … yet
nur ~ (*see* **nur**)
~ **so** however (small *etc*); **und wenn …** ~ **so …** no matter how (much) …, however (much) …
~ **und** ~ *coll* interminably; (*also following noun*) heaps and heaps of …
noch–: ~malig further; renewed; re–; **~mals** (once) again; re–
der **Nocken, –** cam; **die ~welle, –n** camshaft
das **Nockerl, –n** *Aust* small dumpling
das **Nocturne** [–'tʏrn], **–s** (*also* **die**) nocturne
das **NOK = Nationales Olympisches Komitee**

^der^ **Nomade, –n** (*wk masc*) nomad; *in compds* **~n–** nomadic …
nomadenhaft = nomadisch nomadic
nomadisieren lead a nomadic life; **~d** nomadic
^das^ **Nomen, –(m)ina** noun
Nominal– *fin, gramm* nominal …
^der^ **Nominativ, –e** nominative
nominell nominal
nominieren nominate; *sp* name
^die^ **Nominierung, –en** nomination; *sp* naming
Nonchalance [nɔ̃ʃa'lã:s] nonchalance
nonchalant [nɔ̃ʃa'lã:, –'lant (*attrib always thus*)] nonchalant
^die^ **None, –n** *mus* ninth
^die^ **Nonne, –n** nun; **das ~n|kloster, ..klöster** convent
^der^ **Nonsens** [–zɛns] (*gen* **–(es)**) nonsense
Nonstop– [–st–, –ʃt–] non-stop …
^die^ **Noppe, –n** burl
Nord north; *in compds* north …; northern …; **~amerika** North America; **das ~kap** the North Cape; **der ~länder, –, n~ländisch** Scandinavian; **das ~licht, –er** northern lights; *SGer esp pej* North German (politician *etc*); **der ~-Ostsee|kanal** the Kiel Canal; **der ~pol** the North Pole; **~polar–** Arctic …; **Nordrhein-Westfalen** North Rhine-Westphalia; **die ~see** the North Sea; **der ~stern** the Polar Star; **das Nord-Süd-Gefälle** North-South divide; **n~wärts** northwards
^der^ **Norden** north
nordisch Nordic; *hist* Norse
nördlich 1 *adj* northern; northerly; (*adv*) (to the) north (**von** of); 2 *prep* (+*gen*) (to the) north of
^die^ **Nörgelei, –en** grumbling
nörgeln grumble (**an** *dat* about)
^der^ **Nörgler, –** grumbler
^die^ **Norm, –en** norm; standard; *econ* quota; **n~widrig** non-standard
normal normal
Normal– standard …; normal …; **~fall (im N.** as a rule); **das ~null** sea-level; **die ~spur, –en** standard gauge; **der ~verbraucher, –** average consumer; middlebrow
normaler|weise normally
normalisieren normalize; **sich ~** return to normal
^die^ **Normalität** normality
^die^ **Normandie** Normandy
^der^ **Normanne, –n** (*wk masc*), **normannisch** Norman
normativ normative
^das^ **Normativ, –e** *EGer econ* norm
normen standardize
^der^ **Normen|ausschuß** standards board
normieren standardize; *comput* scale

Norwegen ['nɔr–] Norway
^der^ **Norweger** ['nɔr–], **–** Norwegian
norwegisch ['nɔr–], (*language*) **N~** Norwegian
^die^ **Nostalgie** nostalgia
nostalgisch nostalgic
not: ~ tun/sein be necessary; **mir tut … not** I need …
^die^ **Not, ⸚e** need; poverty; distress; difficulty; necessity; **–not** lack of …; **wenn ~ am Mann ist** if the need arises; **seine (liebe) ~ haben mit** have no end of trouble with; **~ leiden** suffer hardship; **mit knapper ~** only just; **zur ~** if need be; at a pinch, in a pinch *US*
Not– emergency …; temporary …;
der ~ausgang, ⸚e emergency exit; **der ~behelf, –e** stopgap; **die ~bremse, –n** emergency brake; *rail* communication cord, emergency brake *US*; **~durft (seine N. verrichten** relieve oneself); **n~dürftig** scanty; rough-and-ready; **der ~fall, ⸚e** emergency (**im N.** if necessary); **n~falls** if necessary; **n~gedrungen** of necessity; **der ~groschen, –** nest-egg; **die ~lage, –n** plight; **n~landen** (*insep exc* **n~zulanden,** *p/part* **n~gelandet**) (*sn*) make an emergency landing; **die ~landung, –en** emergency landing; **n~leidend** needy; **die ~lösung, –en** temporary solution; **die ~lüge, –n** white lie; **der ~ruf, –e** emergency call/number; **die ~ruf|säule, –n** emergency telephone; **die ~rutsche, –n** emergency chute; **das ~signal, –e** distress signal; **der ~sitz, –e** folding seat (on train *etc*); **der ~stand, ⸚e** (state of) emergency; crisis; **das ~stands|gebiet, –e** distressed area; **n~wassern** (*insep exc* **n~zuwassern,** *p/part* **n~gewassert**) (*sn*) *aer* ditch; **die ~wehr** self-defence; **n~wendig** necessary; (*adv*: need) urgently (**das ~wendigste** the essentials); **not|wendiger|weise** necessarily; **die ~wendigkeit, –en** necessity; **die ~zeiten** *pl* times of need; **die ~zucht, n~züchtigen** (*insep*) *leg* rape
^die^ **Notabeln** *pl* notables
^der^ **Notar, –e** notary (public)
^das^ **Notariat, –e** notary's office
notariell notarial; **~ beglaubigt** attested by a notary, notarized *US*
^die^ **Note, –n** note (*mus, pol; also* = banknote); (personal *etc*) touch; character; *educ* mark; (*pl*) (sheet) music; **ganze ~** semibreve, whole note *US*; **halbe ~** minim, half note *US*; **nach ~n** from music; *coll* (thrash) soundly; **(wie) nach ~n** *coll* like clockwork
Noten–: der ~austausch exchange of notes; **die ~bank, –en** issuing bank; **das ~blatt, ⸚er** sheet of music; **das ~pult, –e** music-stand; **der ~schlüssel, –** clef; **der ~ständer,**

– music-stand; **der ~wechsel, –** exchange of notes

notieren note down, make a note of; *mus* write down in musical notation; *fin* quote (**mit** at); (*v/i*) *fin* be quoted (**mit** at)

die **Notierung, –en** *vbl noun*; *mus* notation; *fin* quotation

nötig necessary; **~ brauchen** need badly; **(bitter) ~ haben** need (badly); **es nicht ~ haben zu …** not need to …; **wenn ~** if necessary; **das Nötigste** (*decl as adj*) the bare essentials

nötigen compel (to); press (to); **lassen Sie sich nicht ~!** don't wait to be asked

nötigen|falls if necessary

die **Nötigung, –en** compulsion; *leg* coercion

die **Notiz, –en** note; (news) item; **sich** *dat* **~en machen** take notes; **~ nehmen von** pay attention to; **keine ~ nehmen von** take no notice of || **der ~block, –s** note-pad; **das ~buch, ⸚er** note-book

notorisch notorious

der **Nougat** ['nu:gat], **–s** (*also* **das**) nougat

Nova *pl of* **Novum**

die **Nova, –(v)ä** nova

die **Novelle, –n** *liter* novella; *parl* amendment

der **Novellist, –en** (*wk masc*) writer of novellas

die **Novellistik** [–ɪk] art of the novella; (*collect*) the novella

der **November** (*gen* **–(s)**), **–** November; **im ~** in November

die **Novität, –en** novelty; new publication/play

der **Novize, –n** (*wk masc*) novice

das **Novum, –(v)a** novelty; something new

Nowgorod ['nɔfgorɔt] Novgorod

Nowossibirsk [novɔ–] Novosibirsk

Nr. (= **Nummer**) No.

NS– (= **nationalsozialistisch**) Nazi; **die NS-Zeit** the Nazi era

die **NSDAP** *hist* = **Nationalsozialistische Deutsche Arbeiterpartei** (*title of Nazi party*)

N. T. (= **Neues Testament**) N.T.

Nu: im ~ in a flash

die **Nuance** [ny'ã:sə], **–n** nuance; shade

nuancieren [nyãs–] shade off (colours); express/portray with great subtlety; **nuanciert** nuanced; subtle

'nüber *SGer coll* = **hinüber**

nüchtern sober; matter-of-fact; (room, facts, *etc*) bare, plain; (food) insipid; (*adv*: take) on an empty stomach; **auf ~en Magen** on an empty stomach

die **Nüchternheit** soberness, sobriety; matter-of-fact outlook; bareness, plainness; insipidness

die **Nudel, –n** noodle, *pl* (*general sense*) pasta; *coll* (odd) character; (fat) creature; **das ~holz, ⸚er** rolling-pin; **die ~suppe, –n** noodle soup

nudeln cram (goose); **(wie) genudelt** *coll* full to bursting

der **Nudismus** nudism

der **Nudist, –en** (*wk masc*) nudist

nuklear nuclear; **~er Winter** nuclear winter

null nought, zero; *sp* nil, *tennis* love; *tel* O; **~ und nichtig** null and void; **~ Fehler/Punkte** no mistakes/points; **~ Uhr** 12 midnight

die **Null, –en** nought, zero; *coll* washout; **gleich ~ sein** (chances *etc*) be nil; **in ~ Komma nichts** *coll* in no time

null–: null|acht|fünfzehn (08/15) (*also* **Nullachtfünfzehn–**) *coll* nondescript, run-of-the-mill; **der N~punkt, –e** zero (**den N. erreichen = auf dem N. ankommen** reach rock-bottom); **der N~tarif** free admission/travel; **das N~wachstum** zero growth

die **Nulpe, –n** *coll* 'drip'

das **Numerale, –(l)ien** [–ĭən] *gramm* numeral

numerieren number

die **Numerierung, –en** numbering

die **Numerik** [–ɪk] *tech* numerical control

numerisch numerical

der **Numerus, –(r)i** *gramm* number; *math* antilogarithm; **~ clausus** restricted entry (to university course *etc*)

die **Numismatik** [–ɪk] numismatics

der **Numismatiker, –** numismatist

die **Nummer, –n** number; size (of garment); issue, number (of magazine *etc*); number, item (in cabaret *etc*), act (in circus); *coll* (*with adj*) character; **alte ~** back number; **eine gute ~ haben bei** *coll* be in (s.o.'s) good books; **auf ~ Sicher gehen** *coll* play safe; **auf ~ Sicher sein/sitzen** *coll* be behind bars || **das ~n|konto, –(t)en** numbered account; **die ~n|scheibe, –n** *tel* dial; **das ~n|schild, –er** number-plate, license plate *US*

nun 1 *conj arch* now that; 2 *adv* now; (*as emotive particle*) well (then); **~?** well?; **~, ~!** come now!; **~, da …** now that …; **~ denn!** right then!; **~ einmal**/*coll* **mal** just (**das ist ~ (ein)mal so** that's the way it is); **~ erst** only now; **~ gut!** all right then!; **~ ja** oh, well; **von ~ an** from now on; **~, wo …** now that … || **~mehr** now; from now on

'nunter *SGer coll* = **hinunter**

der **Nuntius** [–ts–], **–(i)en** nuncio

nur 1 *adv* only; just; (*as emotive particle*) just; possibly (*eg* **sobald ich ~ kann** as soon as I possibly can); (how, why, *etc*) -ever; *or rendered by emphasis* (*eg* **was soll ich ~ mit dir anstellen?** what *am* I to do with you?); (*in command*) just (*eg* **stell dir ~ vor!** just imagine!, **~ Geduld!** just be patient!), do … (**kommen Sie ~ herein!** do come in!), *or – esp with a negative – left untranslated* (*eg* **~ keine Ausreden!** no excuses!, **~ nicht so laut!** not so loud!); 2 *conj* only; however

auch ~ even; **ohne auch ~ zu ...** without so much as (+*ger*)

~ daß ... only ...; except that ...

~ mehr *SGer* = **~ noch** (*exc* + *comp*)

~ nicht (*see also* **~** *in a command with a negative*, *at* 1 *above*) **alle, ~ ... nicht** everyone except ...; **alles, ~ nicht ...** anything/everything except ...; **~ 'das nicht** anything but that

~ noch only (... now); now only; only ... left/more; **~ noch** (+*comp*) only ... even (worse *etc*)

~ so *coll* fairly; just; **... daß es ~ so (krachte** *etc*) ... with a tremendous (bang *etc*); (*replying*) **(ach,) ~ so!** no special reason; **ich hab's ~ so gesagt** I didn't really mean it; **ich tue ~ so** I'm just pretending

wenn ... ~ ...! if only ...!

~ zu! go ahead!

Nürnberg Nuremberg

nuscheln (*also v/i*) *coll* mumble

die **Nuß, ⸚(ss)e** nut; **eine harte ~** *coll* a hard nut to crack || **der ~baum, ⸚e** walnut tree; = **das ~baum|holz** walnut; **der ~knacker, –** nutcracker

die **Nüstern** *pl* nostrils (of horse *etc*)

die **Nute, –n, nuten** *tech* groove; rabbet

der **Nutria, –s** nutria (= fur)

die **Nutria, –s** coypu

die **Nutte, –n** tart

nutz *SGer* = **nütze**

Nutz *arch*: **zu ~ und Frommen** (+*gen*) for the benefit of

Nutz– (*refers to things in respect of their practical or commercial usefulness to man*, *esp as food or material*); **die ~anwendung, –en** practical application; moral; **n~bringend** profitable; **der ~effekt, –e** efficiency, effectiveness; **das ~fahrzeug, –e** commercial vehicle; **die ~fläche, –n** agricultural land; usable floor-space; **der ~garten, ..gärten** kitchen-garden; **das ~holz** timber; **die ~last, –en** payload; **die ~leistung, –en** effective output; **n~los** useless; (*adv*) *also* needlessly; **die ~losigkeit** uselessness; **der ~nießer, –** beneficiary; *leg* usufructuary

nutzbar utilizable; **~ machen** cultivate (soil); utilize; harness

nütze: zu etwas ~ of use; **zu wenig/nichts ~** little/no use

nützen (nutzen) use, make use of; (*v/i*, +*dat*) be of use to; **etwas/nichts/wenig ~** be some/no/little use (*dat* to); **was nützt ...?** what's the good of ...?

der **Nutzen** use; benefit; profit; **~ ziehen aus** benefit from; **von ~** of use (*following dat* to); **zum ~** (+*gen*) for the benefit of

nützlich useful; **sich ~ machen** make oneself useful

die **Nutzung** use; utilization

n. u. Z. *EGer* (= **nach unserer Zeitrechnung**) A.D.

die **NVA** *EGer* = **Nationale Volksarmee** (*E. German armed forces*)

NW (= **Nordwest(en)**) N.W.

das **Nylon** ['nae̯lɔn] (*gen* **–(s)**) nylon

die **Nymphe, –n** nymph

die **Nymphomanie** nymphomania

die **Nymphomanin, –nen, nymphomanisch** nymphomaniac

O

[das] **O** [oː] (*gen, pl* –, *coll* [oːs]) O
O (= **Ost(en)**) E.
o ...! (*eg* **o nein!**) oh ...!
o. ä. (= **oder ähnliche(s)**) etc.
[der] **ÖAMTC** = **Österreichischer Automobil-, Motorrad- und Touring-Club** (*Austrian motoring organization*)
[die] **Oase, –n** oasis
ob[1] [ɔp] *conj* whether, if; (look *etc*) to see if; (*elliptical use*) I wonder if ...?; perhaps ...?; *or translated by direct question* (*eg* ~ **er Deutscher sei?** was he German?, ~ **ich einen Kaffee wünsche?** would I like a coffee?); ~ **...,** ~ **...** whether ... or ...; **und '~ (...)!** you bet (...)!
ob[2] *prep* 1 (+*gen*) on account of; 2 (+*dat*; *Swiss or in place-names*) above
[der] **OB, –(s)** = **Oberbürgermeister**
Obacht ['oːbaxt] *esp SGer*: ~ **geben** take care; +**auf** (*acc*) pay attention to; keep an eye on; **gib ~!** watch out!
[die] **ÖBB** = **Österreichische Bundesbahnen**
[das] **Obdach** shelter; **o~los** homeless; **die ~losigkeit** homelessness
[die] **Obduktion** [ɔp–], **–en** autopsy
obduzieren [ɔp–] perform an autopsy on
[die] **O-Beine** *pl* bow-legs
o-beinig bow-legged
[der] **Obelisk, –en** (*wk masc*) obelisk
oben above; upstairs; up (in the north *etc*); at the top; on top; on the surface; ~ **an** (*dat*) at the top of; ~ **auf** (*dat*) on top of; **bis ~ (hin)** to the top; **die da ~** *coll* the powers that be; **dort/hier ~** up there/here; **nach ~** up(wards); to the top/surface; upstairs; ~ **ohne** topless; **von ~** from above/the top/upstairs; **von ~ bis unten** from top to bottom; (eye) up and down; **von ~ herab** (treat *etc*) condescendingly; **weiter ~** further up || **~an** at the top (**auf** *dat* of); **~auf** on top/the surface (**wieder o. sein** be one's old self again); **~drauf** *coll* on top; **~drein** what is more; into the bargain; **~erwähnt** = **~genannt** above-mentioned; **~gesteuert** (valve) overhead; (engine) overhead-valve; **~hin** casually; superficially; **~hinaus** *coll* (**o. wollen** have great ambitions); **Oben-ohne-** topless ...
ober *Aust* (+*dat*) above
ober.. upper; top; **der O~e See** Lake Superior; **die ~en Zehntausend** high society; **der Obere** (*decl as adj*) *eccles* superior; **die O~en** *pl* people at the top; bosses
[der] **Ober, –** waiter; **Herr ~!** waiter!
Ober– upper ..., *geog* Upper ...; senior ...; chief ...; head ...; *for* **~prima, ~sekunda,** *etc see* **Prima, Sekunda,** *etc*
der ~bau superstructure; *rail* permanent way, roadway *US*; **der ~befehl** supreme command; **der ~befehls|haber, –** commander-in-chief; **der ~begriff, –e** generic term; **die ~bekleidung** outer garments; **das ~bett, –en** quilt; **der ~bürger|meister, –** mayor (of major city); **o~faul** *coll* very fishy; **die ~fläche, –n** surface (**an der O.** on the surface); **o~flächlich** superficial; **die ~flächlichkeit** superficiality; **o~halb** (+*gen*) above; **die ~hand** upper hand (**die O. gewinnen** gain the upper hand (**über** *acc* over)); **das ~haupt, ¨er** head; chief; **das ~haus** upper house; (*U.K.*) the House of Lords; **die ~haut** epidermis; **das ~hemd, –en** shirt; **die ~herrschaft** = **die ~hoheit** supremacy, sovereignty; **o~irdisch** above ground; **~italien** Northern Italy; **der ~kellner, –** head waiter; **das ~kommando, –s** supreme command; **der ~körper, –** upper part of the body (**mit nacktem O.** stripped to the waist); **das ~land** uplands; **das ~landes|gericht, –e** appeal court (of a *Land*); **der ~lauf, ¨e** upper reaches; **das ~leder, –** upper (of shoe); **der ~leutnant, –e** (army) lieutenant, first lieutenant *US*; (navy) sub-lieutenant, lieutenant junior grade *US*; (air force) flying officer, first lieutenant *US*; **das ~licht, –er** skylight; light from above; **die ~lippe, –n** upper lip; **der ~meister, –** (police) sergeant; **~österreich** Upper Austria; **der ~schenkel, –** thigh; **die ~schicht, –en** top layer; upper class (**geistige O.** intelligentsia); **die ~schule, –n** grammar school; *EGer* high school (for all age-groups); **die ~seite, –n** top (side); **die ~stimme, –n** soprano; treble; **der ~stock, ¨e** upper floor; **der ~studien|direktor, –en** headmaster (of a *Gymnasium*); **der ~studien|rat, ¨e** senior master (in a *Gymnasium*); **die ~stufe, –n** upper school; *univ* advanced level; **das ~teil, –e** (bikini, pyjama, *etc*) top; **die ~töne** *pl mus* overtones; **~wasser** (**O.**

haben/bekommen be in/get into a strong position); **die ~weite, –n** chest/bust measurement; bust

[die] **Oberin, –nen** *med* (hospital) matron; *eccles* mother superior

[das] **Obers** *Aust* cream

[der] **Oberst, –en** (*also wk masc*) colonel; (air force) group captain, colonel *US*; **der ~leutnant, –e** lieutenant-colonel; (air force) wing commander, lieutenant-colonel *US*

oberst.. top; highest; supreme; **das O~e zuunterst kehren** turn everything upside down

obgleich although

[die] **Obhut** care; **in jmds. ~ geben** entrust to s.o.'s care; **in (seine) ~ nehmen** take charge of

obig above(-mentioned)

[das] **Objekt** [ɔp–], **–e** object (*also gramm*); *Aust* building; *EGer* state-run establishment; *esp comm* property; publication; **der ~träger, –** (microscope) slide

objektiv [ɔp–] objective

[das] **Objektiv** [ɔp–], **–e** lens

objektivieren [ɔp–] objectify

[die] **Objektivität** [ɔp–] objectivity

[die] **Oblate, –n** wafer; *eccles* host

obliegen* (*usu insep exc* **obzuliegen,** *p/part* **obgelegen**) (+*dat*) be incumbent on; *arch* apply oneself to

[die] **Obliegenheit** ['ɔp–], **–en** duty

obligat (swimming-pool *etc*) statutory, obligatory; *mus* obbligato

[die] **Obligation, –en** obligation; *fin* bond

obligatorisch compulsory; obligatory

[der] **Obmann, ⸚er/..leute** chairman (of group); foreman (of jury)

[die] **Oboe** [–ə], **–n** oboe

[der] **Oboist, –en** (*wk masc*) oboist

[der] **Obolus, –(se)** (small) contribution

[die] **Obrigkeit, –en** (the) authorities; **der ~s|staat, –en** authoritarian state; **o~s|staatlich** authoritarian

[der] **Obrist, –en** (*wk masc*) colonel (in military junta)

obschon although

[das] **Observatorium** [ɔp–], **–(i)en** observatory

obskur [ɔp–] obscure; dubious

[die] **Obsorge** *Aust* care

[das] **Obst** [o:pst] fruit (*collect*); **der ~bau** fruit-growing; **der ~baum, ⸚e** fruit-tree; **der ~garten, ..gärten** orchard; **der ~händler, –** fruiterer, fruit dealer *US*; **der ~saft, ⸚e** fruit-juice

[die] **Obstruktion, –en** *pol* filibuster; obstruction

obszön [ɔps–] obscene

[die] **Obszönität** [ɔps–], **–en** obscenity

[der] **Obus, –se** (= **Oberleitungsbus**) trolleybus

obwaltend prevailing

obwohl = **obzwar** although

och! oh!

[der] **Ochse** [–ks–], **–n** (*wk masc*) ox; bullock; *coll* blockhead; **dastehen wie der Ochs vorm Berg** *coll* not have the faintest idea what to do

ochsen [–ks–] (*also v/i*) *coll* cram

Ochsen– ox ...; **die ~schwanz|suppe, –n** oxtail soup; **die ~tour** *coll* hard grind; **die ~zunge, –n** ox-tongue

[der] **Ocker, –** (*also* **das**), **o~farben** ochre

od. = **oder**

Öd–: das ~land barren land

[die] **Ode, –n** ode

öde bleak, desolate; dreary

[die] **Öde, –n** wasteland; bleakness; dreariness

[der] **Odem** *poet* breath

[das] **Ödem, –e** oedema

oder or; **..., ~?** ..., does(n't) it/must(n't) we/have(n't) they *etc*?; **~ aber** or else

[die] **Oder** the Oder

Ödipus Oedipus; **der ~komplex** Oedipus complex

[die] **Odyssee** the Odyssey; **die ~, –(ee)n** odyssey

Odysseus [–ɔ͜ʏs] Odysseus

[das] **Œuvre** ['ø:vrə], **–s** oeuvre

OEZ = **Osteuropäische Zeit**

[der] **Ofen,** *pl* **Öfen** stove; heater; oven, stove; *tech* furnace; **das ~rohr, –e** stovepipe

offen open (*also ling*); frank; vacant; **Tag der ~en Tür** open day/house *US;* **~ haben** *coll* be open; **das Haar ~ tragen** wear one's hair loose; **~ gesagt/gestanden** quite frankly || **~bleiben*** (*sep*; *sn*) be left open; **~halten*** (*sep*) keep open; **~herzig** open-hearted; *joc* (dress) revealing; **~kundig** obvious; **~lassen*** (*sep*) leave open; **~legen** (*sep*) disclose; **~sichtlich** obvious; **~stehen*** (*sep*) be open/undone; (payment) be outstanding; (+*dat*) be open to (**es steht mir offen zu ...** I am free to ...); **~stehend** open; outstanding

offenbar obvious; (*adv*) apparently

offenbaren (*insep*; *p/part* **offenbart**) reveal; **sich ~** be revealed; (+*dat*) be revealed to; unbosom oneself to; *relig* (God) reveal himself to; **sich ~ als** show oneself to be

[die] **Offenbarung, –en** revelation (*also relig*)

[die] **Offenheit** openness, frankness

offensiv *mil* offensive; *sp* attacking

[die] **Offensive, –n** offensive; **die ~ ergreifen** take the offensive

öffentlich public; (secret, session, *etc*) open; (*adv*) in public, publicly; **die ~e Hand** the state; the public purse

[die] **Öffentlichkeit** the public; public nature (of proceedings); **in aller ~** publicly || **die ~s|arbeit** public relations

offerieren *comm etc* offer

[die] **Offerte, –n** *comm etc* offer; tender

offiziell, der/die Offizielle (*decl as adj*) official

[der] **Offizier, –e** officer; **der ~s|anwärter, –** officer cadet; **das ~s|kasino, –s** officers' mess
offiziös semi-official
öffnen open; undo; (*v/i*) answer the door; (+*dat*) open the door to; **sich ~** open; open out
[der] **Öffner, –** opener
[die] **Öffnung, –en** opening; hole; *phot* aperture; **die ~s|zeiten** *pl* hours of opening
oft (*comp, superl* ⸗) often; **öfter** *also* = **des öfteren** quite often || **~mals** often
[das] **OG, –(s)** *EGer* = **Oberstes Gericht**
[der] **ÖGB** = **Österreichischer Gewerkschaftsbund**
oh! oh!
[die] **OHG, –(s)** (= **Offene Handelsgesellschaft**) general partnership
[das] **Ohm** (*gen* –(s)), – ohm
Ohn–: die ~macht, –en faint; impotence (**in O. fallen** faint); **o~mächtig** unconscious; powerless; helpless (**o. werden** faint)
ohne (+*acc*) without; not counting; but for; **~ daß ...** without (s.o., sth.) (+*ger*); **~ zu ...** without (+*ger*); **~ mich!** count me out!; **nicht (so) ~** *coll* not bad at all; not that easy; not without danger; **~ weiteres** easily; readily; without further ado/thinking twice about it; just like that; **nicht ~ weiteres** not ... automatically/just like that; **oben ~** topless || **~dies** anyway; **~einander** without each other; **~gleichen** (*pred or after noun*) unparalleled (**er/sie singt** *etc* **o.** his/her singing *etc* is unequalled); **~hin** anyway; as it is; **~weiters** *Aust* = **ohne weiteres** (*see* **ohne**)
oho! hey!
[das] **Ohr, –en** ear; **ganz ~ sein** be all ears; **mir klingen die ~en** my ears are burning
in prepositional phrases:
auf: taub auf einem ~ deaf in one ear; **sich aufs ~ legen** *coll* take a nap
hinter: sich *dat* **... hinter die ~en schreiben** *coll* take to heart; **noch naß/noch nicht trocken hinter den ~en** still wet behind the ears
in: (+*dat*) **in den ~en liegen** *coll* keep on at
übers ~ hauen *coll* take for a ride; **bis über die ~en** *coll* head over heels (in love); up to one's ears (in debt)
um: sich *dat* **die Nacht um die ~en schlagen** *coll* stay up all night; **sich** *dat* **den Wind um die ~en wehen lassen** *coll* see a bit of the world; **viel um die ~en haben** *coll* have a lot on one's plate
zu: es ist mir zu ~en gekommen it has come to my attention
Ohr–: die ~feige, –n slap (in the face); box on the ears; **o~feigen** (*insep*) box (s.o.'s) ears; **das ~läppchen, –** ear-lobe; **die ~muschel, –n** outer ear; **der ~ring, –e** earring; **der ~wurm, ⸗er** earwig; *coll* catchy hit
[das] **Öhr, –e** eye (of needle)
Ohren– ear ...; **der ~arzt, ⸗e** ear specialist; **o~betäubend** deafening; **der ~schmalz** earwax; **der ~schmaus** treat for the ears; **die ~schmerzen** *pl* earache; **der ~schützer, –** ear-muff
–ohrig –eared
o. J. (= **ohne Jahr**) no date
oje! = **ojemine!** [–ne] oh dear!
o.k., okay [o'keː] *coll* O.K., okay
okkult occult
[der] **Okkultismus** occultism
[der] **Okkupant, –en** (*wk masc*) *mil* occupier
[die] **Okkupation, –en** *mil* occupation
okkupieren *mil* occupy
Öko– eco–; **das ~system, –e** ecosystem
[der] **Ökologe, –n** (*wk masc*) ecologist
[die] **Ökologie** ecology
ökologisch ecological
[der] **Ökonom, –en** (*wk masc*) *esp EGer* economist; *Aust* farmer
[die] **Ökonomie, –(ie)n** economy (in use of sth.); economics; *Aust* farm
ökonomisch economic; economical
[die] **Oktan|zahl, –en** octane rating
[das] **Oktav** octavo
[die] **Oktave, –n** *mus* octave
[der] **Oktober** (*gen* –(s)), – October; **im ~** in October || **das ~fest** (*Munich beer festival*)
okulieren graft
ökumenisch ecumenical
[der] **Okzident** the Occident
ö. L. = **östliche Länge,** *eg* **20° ~** longitude 20° east
[das] **Öl, –e** oil; **der ~baum, ⸗e** olive tree; **der ~berg** the Mount of Olives; **die ~farbe, –n** oil paint; (*pl*) oils; **das ~feld, –er** oil-field; **das ~gemälde, –** oil painting; **~götze** *coll* (**wie ein Ö.** like a stuffed dummy); **der ~hafen, ..häfen** tanker terminal; **die ~heizung, –en** oil-fired central heating; **der ~meß|stab, ⸗e** dipstick; **die ~pest** oil pollution; **die ~sardine, –n** sardine (in oil); **der ~stand** oil level; **der ~stands|anzeiger, –** oil gauge; **der ~teppich, –e** oil slick; **die ~wanne, –n** sump, oil pan *US*; **der ~wechsel, –** oil change; **das ~zeug** oilskins; **der ~zweig, –e** olive-branch
[der] **Oldtimer** ['oːlttaęmɐ], – veteran/vintage car; vintage aircraft, steamer, *etc*; *sp* veteran
ölen oil; lubricate; **wie geölt** *coll* like clockwork
[das] **OLG, –(s)** = **Oberlandesgericht**
ölig oily
[die] **Oligarchie** [–ç–], –(ie)n oligarchy
Olim [–ɪm] *joc*: **seit ~s Zeiten** for donkey's years; **zu ~s Zeiten** donkey's years ago
oliv (*indecl*) = **oliv|grün** olive(-green)

die **Olive, –n** olive; **das ~n|öl** olive oil
oll *NGer coll* old; **mein O~er/meine O~e** my old man/woman
die **Ölung, –en** oiling; lubrication; **die Letzte ~** Extreme Unction
der **Olymp** (*gen* **–s**) (Mount) Olympus; *theat coll* the gods
Olympia (*gen* **–s;** *no art*) the Olympics; *in compds* Olympic ...; **der ~sieger, –** Olympic champion
die **Olympiade, –n** Olympics; *EGer* contest
der **Olympionike, –n** (*wk masc*) Olympic competitor
olympisch Olympic
die **Oma, –s** *coll* granny
das **Omelett** [ɔm(ə)–], **–e/–s** omelette
das **Omen, –/Omina** omen
ominös ominous; dubious
der **Omnibus** (*gen* **–ses**), **–se** bus; coach; **der ~bahnhof, ⸚e** bus/coach station
die **Onanie** masturbation
onanieren masturbate
das **Ondit** [ɔ̃'diː], **–s** rumour
der **Onkel, –** uncle; (*said by or to child*) man; gentleman; **die ~ehe, –n** *coll* (*cohabitation of a widow with a man to whom she is not married, to avoid losing her pension*)
onkelhaft avuncular
die **ÖNORM, –EN** (= **Österreichische Norm**) Austrian Standard
der **OP, –(s)** = **Operationssaal**
der **Opa, –s** *coll* grandpa
der **Opal, –e** opal
die **OPEC** ['oːpɛk] OPEC
die **Oper, –n** opera; opera-house; opera company; **in die ~ gehen** go to the opera
der **Operateur** [–'tøːɐ], **–e** (operating) surgeon
die **Operation, –en** operation (*also comput*); **der ~s|saal, ..säle** operating theatre/room *US*
operativ *med* surgical; *mil* operational
der **Operator, –(or)en** *comput* operator
die **Operette, –n** operetta
operieren operate on; (*v/i*) operate (*also med*); **~ mit** employ (term *etc*); **sich ~ lassen** have an operation
Opern– opera ...; operatic ...; **das ~glas, ⸚er** opera glasses; **der ~text, –e** libretto
das **Opfer, –** sacrifice; victim; **ein ~ bringen** make a sacrifice; (+*dat*) **zum ~ fallen** fall victim to
Opfer– ... of sacrifice; sacrificial ...; **o~bereit** self-sacrificing; **die ~bereitschaft** spirit of self-sacrifice; **die ~gabe, –n** offering; **das ~lamm, ⸚er** sacrificial lamb; innocent victim; **der ~mut** spirit of self-sacrifice; **der ~stock, ⸚e** offertory-box; **o~willig** self-sacrificing
opfern sacrifice (*dat* to); **sich ~** sacrifice one's life; make sacrifices
das **Opiat, –e** opiate
das **Opium** opium
opponieren: ~ gegen oppose
opportun opportune
der **Opportunismus** opportunism
der **Opportunist, –en** (*wk masc*) opportunist
opportunistisch opportunistic
die **Opposition, –en** opposition (*also parl*)
oppositionell opposed to the government *etc*; *parl* opposition
optieren: ~ für opt for
die **Optik** [–ɪk] optics; optical system; visual effect; perspective, view
der **Optiker, –** optician
optimal optimum
optimieren optimize
der **Optimismus** optimism
der **Optimist, –en** (*wk masc*) optimist
optimistisch optimistic
die **Option, –en** option (*also comm*)
optisch optical; visual; **~e Täuschung** optical illusion
das **Orakel, –** oracle
orakelhaft oracular
orakeln (*p/part* **orakelt**) prophesy (enigmatically)
orange [o'rãːʒə] (*indecl*) orange
das **Orange** [o'rãːʒə], **–** orange (colour)
die **Orange** [o'rãːʒə], **–n** orange (= fruit)
orange–: ~farben orange
die **Orangeade** [orã'ʒaːdə], **–n** orangeade
das **Orangeat** [orã'ʒaːt] candied orange peel
Orangen–: die ~limonade, –n orangeade; **die ~marmelade, –n** marmalade; **die ~schale, –n** orange peel
der **Orang-Utan** [–an], **–s** orang-outang
Oranien [–ĭən] *hist* Orange
der **Oranje** (*gen* **–(s)**) the Orange (River); **der ~frei|staat** the Orange Free State
das **Oratorium, –(i)en** oratorio
der **Orbit** [–ɪt], **–s** *space* orbit
Orbital– *space* orbital ...
das **Orchester** [–k–], **–** orchestra; *theat* = **der ~graben, ..gräben** orchestra (pit)
orchestrieren [–k–] orchestrate
die **Orchidee** [–çi'deː(ə)], **–(ee)n** orchid
der **Orden, –** *mil* decoration; *eccles* order; **die ~s|tracht, –en** habit (of an order)
ordentlich tidy; neat; orderly; decent, respectable; (member, professor) full; (achievement *etc*) reasonable; *coll* (meal *etc*) proper; (*adv*) *coll* really; heartily
die **Order, –n** *comm, mil* order
die **Ordinal|zahl, –en** ordinal number
ordinär vulgar; ordinary
der **Ordinarius, –(i)en** (full) professor
die **Ordination, –en** *eccles* ordination; *Aust* (doctor's) consulting room; surgery, office hours *US*
ordnen put in order; order, arrange; **alphabetisch/chronologisch ~** put into alpha-

betical/chronological order; **sich ~** form up

der **Ordner, –** file; (at meeting) steward

die **Ordnung, –en** order (*also biol*); **~ machen/schaffen** tidy up; put things in order; **in ~** all right; in order; **... ist** *etc* **nicht in ~** there's something wrong with ...; **in ~ bringen** fix; sort out; **geht in ~!** O.K.!; **zur ~ rufen** call to order || **o~s|gemäß** proper, in accordance with regulations; (*adv*) correctly; duly; **der ~s|hüter, –** *joc* guardian of the law; **die ~s|liebe** love of order; **die ~s|strafe, –n** fine; **o~s|widrig** against regulations; **die ~s|widrigkeit, –en** infringement; **die ~s|zahl, –en** ordinal/*phys* atomic number

die **Ordonnanz, –en** orderly

der **ORF** = **Österreichischer Rundfunk**

das **Organ, –e** organ (of body); voice; (= publication) organ, mouthpiece; body, authority; organ, instrument; **ein ~ haben für** have a feeling for; **die bewaffneten ~e** *EGer* the armed forces || **die ~bank, –en** transplant bank; **die ~spende, –n** donation of an organ; **der ~spender, –** donor (of an organ); **die ~spender|karte, –n** donor card

die **Organisation, –en** organization

der **Organisator, –(or)en** organizer

organisatorisch organizational

organisch organic (*also chem, med*)

organisieren organize; *coll* get hold of (*esp* by dubious means); **sich ~** organize

der **Organismus, –(m)en** organism

der **Organist, –en** (*wk masc*) organist

der **Orgasmus, –(m)en** orgasm

orgastisch orgasmic

die **Orgel, –n** *mus* organ; **die ~pfeife, –n** organ-pipe (**dastehen wie die ~pfeifen** *coll* stand in order of height)

die **Orgie** [–ĭə], **–n** orgy

der **Orient** ['oː–] the Middle East

der **Orientale, –n** (*wk masc*) person from the Middle East

orientalisch Middle Eastern

der **Orientalist, –en** (*wk masc*) specialist in Middle Eastern studies

die **Orientalistik** [–ɪk] Middle Eastern studies

orientieren orientate; **~ auf** (*acc*) *EGer* direct towards; (*v/i*) draw attention to; aim at; **~ über** (*acc*) inform about

sich ~ orientate oneself; find one's bearings; **sich ~ an** (*dat*) find one's bearings by; follow; **sich ~ auf** (*acc*) *EGer* concentrate on; **sich ~ nach** take as a model; **sich ~ über** (*acc*) inform oneself about

die **Orientierung, –en** *vbl noun*; *also* orientation; **~ auf** (*acc*) *EGer* concentration on; **zu Ihrer ~** for your guidance || **der ~s|sinn** sense of direction

original original; (**~** *or* **~-**, *eg* **~ indisch/~-indisch, ~ Schweizer**) genuine

das **Original, –e** original; (= person) character

Original– original ...; **die ~abfüllung, –en** estate-bottled wine

die **Originalität** originality; genuineness

originär original

originell (artist, idea, *etc*) original

der **Orkan, –e** hurricane; storm (of applause *etc*)

das **Ornament, –e** ornament

die **Ornamentik** [–ɪk] ornamentation

der **Ornat, –e** robes; *eccles* vestments

der **Ornithologe, –n** (*wk masc*) ornithologist

die **Ornithologie** ornithology

ornithologisch ornithological

der **Ort, –e** place, (of crime) scene; place, (small) town *or* village; (*pl* **⸚er**) *astron* position; *math* locus; **höheren ~(e)s** by/to a higher authority; **am ~** in the place; locally; **an ~ und Stelle** on the spot; in its proper place/their proper places; (arrive) at one's destination; **vor ~** on the spot; *min* at the coalface

das **Örtchen, –** little place; *coll* loo, john *US*

orten *aer, naut* locate

orthodox orthodox

die **Orthodoxie** orthodoxy

die **Orthographie** orthography

orthographisch orthographic(al)

der **Orthopäde, –n** (*wk masc*) orthopaedist

die **Orthopädie** orthopaedics

orthopädisch orthopaedic

örtlich local

die **Örtlichkeit, –en** locality

Orts– local ...; **o~ansässig** resident; **o~fremd** non-resident (**o. sein** be a stranger (to the locality)); **das ~gespräch, –e** *tel* local call; **o~kundig** familiar with the locality; **der ~name, –n** (*like* **Name**) place-name; **die ~netz|kenn|zahl, –en** dialling code; **der ~sinn** sense of direction; **o~üblich** local; customary (in the place concerned); **der ~verkehr** local traffic/mail/*tel* calls; **die ~zeit** local time; **der ~zuschlag, ⸚e** local allowance

die **Ortschaft, –en** (small) town; village

die **Öse, –n** eye (on clothing)

Oskar *coll*: **frech wie ~** as bold as brass

Oslo ['ɔslo] Oslo

der **Osmane, –n** (*wk masc*), **osmanisch** Ottoman

die **Osmose, –n** osmosis

Ost east; *in compds* east ...; eastern ...; **der ~block** the Eastern bloc; **Ost|indien** the East Indies; **die ~mark**[1] *hist* Austria (1938–45); **die ~mark**[2], **–** *coll* East German mark; **~rom** the Byzantine Empire; **o~römisch** Byzantine; **die ~see** the Baltic; **o~wärts** eastwards

der **Osten** east

Ostende [ɔstˀ–] Ostend

ostentativ pointed; ostentatious

Oster– ['oː–] Easter ...; **das ~ei, –er** Easter egg; **die ~glocke, –n** daffodil; **der ~hase, –n** (*wk masc*) Easter rabbit (which, according to myth, brings Easter eggs); **die ~insel** Easter Island; **der ~montag, –e** Easter Monday; **der ~sonntag, –e** Easter Sunday

österlich ['øː–] Easter

das **Ostern** ['oː–] (*esp Aust, Swiss* **die ~** *pl*) Easter (*~ usu occurs without article*; *treated as sing* (*eg* **~ fällt dieses Jahr früh** Easter is early this year), *as sing or pl following adj* (*eg* **nächste(s) ~** next Easter), *as pl in* **frohe/fröhliche ~!** happy Easter!, **weiße ~** a white Easter); **zu**/*SGer* **an ~** at Easter

Österreich ['øː–] Austria

der **Österreicher, –** Austrian

österreichisch Austrian; **österreichisch-ungarisch** Austro-Hungarian

ostisch (race) alpine

östlich 1 *adj* eastern; easterly; (*adv*) (to the) east (**von** of); 2 *prep* (*+gen*) (to the) east of

das **Östrogen, –e** oestrogen

oszillieren oscillate

der **Otter, –** otter

die **Otter, –n** adder

der **Output** ['aʊtpʊt], **–s** *comput* output

die **Ouvertüre** [u–], **–n** *mus* overture

oval oval

die **Ovation, –en** ovation

der **Overall** ['oːvərɔːl], **–s** overalls; jump suit

Ovid Ovid

die **ÖVP = Österreichische Volkspartei**

die **Ovulation, –en** ovulation

das **Oxyd, –e** oxide

die **Oxydation, –en** oxidation

oxydieren (*also sn if v/i*) oxidize

das **Oxymoron** [–ɔn], **–(r)a** oxymoron

der **Ozean, –e** ocean

Ozeanien [–ĭən] Oceania

ozeanisch oceanic

die **Ozeanographie** oceanography

der **Ozelot** [–ɔt], **–e** ocelot

das **Ozon** ozone; **die ~schicht** ozone layer

P

^das^ **P** [peː] (*gen, pl* –, *coll* [peːs]) P
paar: ein ~ a few; **alle ~** every few; **die ~** the few
^das^ **Paar, –e**/(*following num*) – couple; pair
Paar–: der ~hufer, – cloven-hoofed animal; **der ~lauf** pair-skating; **ein p~mal** a few times; **p~weise** in pairs
paaren mate; *sp* match; **sich ~** mate; **sich ~ mit** be combined with; **gepaart mit** coupled with
paarig in pairs
^die^ **Paarung, –en** mating; *sp* match; **die ~s|zeit, –en** mating season
^die^ **Pacht, –en** lease; rent; **in ~ geben** let out on lease; **in ~ nehmen** lease || **der ~brief, –e** lease; **das ~geld, –er** rent; **der ~vertrag, ⸚e** lease
pachten lease
^der^ **Pächter, –** leaseholder; tenant farmer
^das^ **Pack** rabble
^der^ **Pack, –e/⸚e** bundle; pile
Pack– packing ...; **das ~eis** pack-ice; **der ~esel, –** pack-ass; drudge; **das ~papier** wrapping-paper; **das ~tier, –e** pack animal; **der ~wagen, –** luggage van, baggage car *US*
^das^ **Päckchen, –** packet, pack; *post* packet
packeln *Aust coll* do a deal
packen pack; grab; hold spellbound; (panic *etc*) seize (*esp pass*); **sich ~** *coll* clear out; **~d** gripping
^der^ **Packen, –** bundle; pile
^der^ **Packer, –** packer
^die^ **Packung, –en** packet, pack; box (of chocolates); *med*, *cosmetics* pack; *sp coll* thrashing
^der^ **Pädagoge, –n** (*wk masc*) educationalist; educator
^die^ **Pädagogik** [–ɪk] education (= subject of study)
pädagogisch educational; **P~e Hochschule** college of education (for primary school teachers)
^das^ **Paddel, –** paddle; **das ~boot, –e** canoe
paddeln (*also sn*; *if indicating direction or distance travelled, only sn*) paddle; dog-paddle
paff! bang!
paffen puff (away) at; (*v/i*) puff; puff away
^der^ **Page** [–ʒə], **–n** (*wk masc*) page(-boy); *hist* page; **die ~n|frisur, –en** page-boy (= hair-style)
paginieren paginate
^die^ **Pagode, –n** pagoda
pah! pah!, bah!
^die^ **Paillette** [pa'jɛtə], **–n** sequin
^die^ **Pak** [–a–], **–s** (= **Panzerabwehrkanone**) anti-tank gun
^das^ **Paket, –e** package (*also pol etc*); packet; *post* parcel; **die ~annahme, –n** parcels counter; **die ~karte, –n** dispatch note; **die ~post** parcel post
Pakistan ['paːkɪstaːn] Pakistan
^der^ **Pakistani** (*gen* –(s)), –(s), **pakistanisch** Pakistani
^der^ **Pakt, –e** pact
paktieren: ~ mit make a pact with
^das^ **Palais** [–'lɛː] (*gen* – [–(s)]), – [–s] palace
paläo– palaeo–
^das^ **Paläolithikum** the Palaeolithic
paläolithisch Palaeolithic
^der^ **Palast, ⸚e** palace; **p~artig** palatial; **die ~revolution, –en** palace revolution
Palästina Palestine
^der^ **Palästinenser, –, palästinensisch** Palestinian
palatal palatal
^die^ **Palatschinke** [–tʃ–], **–n** *Aust* pancake filled with jam
^das^ **Palaver, –, palavern** (*p/part* **palavert**) palaver
palen *NGer* shell (peas)
^der^ **Paletot** ['paləto], **–s** *arch* greatcoat
^die^ **Palette, –n** palette; range; *tech* pallet
^die^ **Palisade, –n** palisade
^der^ **Palisander = das ~holz** rosewood
Palm–: das ~kätzchen, – catkin; **das ~öl** palm-oil; **der ~sonntag, –e** Palm Sunday; **der ~wedel, –** palm-leaf
^die^ **Palme, –n** palm; **auf die ~ bringen** *coll* drive up the wall
^das^ **Palmin** (*trade-mark*) coconut fat
^die^ **Pampelmuse, –n** grapefruit
^das^ **Pamphlet, –e** polemical pamphlet
pampig *esp NGer* mushy; *coll* cheeky
Pan [–aː–] Pan
pan– [–a–] pan–
^das^ **Pandschab** [–'dʒaːp] (*gen* **–s**) the Punjab
^das^ **Paneel, –e** panel; panelling
päng! bang!
^das^ **Panier, –e** slogan; *arch* banner; **das ~mehl** *cul* breadcrumbs
panieren coat with breadcrumbs
^die^ **Panik** [–ɪk], **–en** panic; **in ~ geraten** panic; **in**

~ **versetzen** panic; **von ~ ergriffen** panic-stricken

panisch: ~e Angst panic; **in ~er Flucht davonstürzen** flee in panic

das **Pankreas** [–as], **–(a)ten** pancreas

die **Panne, –n** breakdown; puncture; *coll* slip-up; **eine ~ haben** have a breakdown/puncture || **der ~n|dienst** breakdown service

das **Panoptikum, –(k)en** waxworks; collection of curiosities

das **Panorama, –(m)en** panorama; *in compds* panoramic …

panschen adulterate; water down; (*v/i*) *coll* splash about

der **Panther, –** panther

die **Pantine, –n** *NGer* clog

der **Pantoffel, –n** slipper; **unter dem ~ stehen** *coll* be hen-pecked || **der ~held, –en** (*wk masc*) *coll* hen-pecked husband

die **Pantolette, –n** mule (= shoe)

der **Pantomime, –n** (*wk masc*) mime (= artist)

die **Pantomime, –n** mime

pantomimisch in mime; **~ darstellen** mime

pantschen = panschen

der **Panzer, –** *mil* tank; armour-plating; *hist* armour; *zool* armour; shell; *in compds also* armoured …; anti-tank …; **die ~abwehr|kanone, –n** anti-tank gun; **die ~faust, ⸚e** bazooka; **das ~glas** bullet-proof glass; **das ~hemd, –en** coat of mail; **der ~schrank, ⸚e** safe; **der ~turm, ⸚e** tank turret; **der ~wagen, –** armoured car; **die ~weste, –n** bullet-proof vest

panzern armour-plate; **sich ~ gegen** arm oneself against

der **Papa, –s** *coll* daddy

der **Papagei, –en** parrot; **der ~(en)|taucher, –** puffin

die **Papeterie, –(ie)n** *Swiss* stationery; stationer's

das **Papier, –e** paper; (*pl*) papers; *fin* securities; **auf dem ~** on paper; **zu ~ bringen** put down on paper || **der ~bogen, –** sheet of paper; **das ~deutsch** officialese; **die ~fabrik, –en** paper-mill; **das ~geschäft, –e** stationer's, stationery store *US*; **der ~korb, ⸚e** wastepaper basket; **der ~krieg** *coll* red tape; **das ~maché** [papĭema'ʃeː] papier-mâché; **die ~schlange, –n** streamer; **das ~taschen|tuch, ⸚er** paper handkerchief, tissue; **die ~waren** *pl* stationery

papieren paper; bookish

Papp– cardboard …; **der ~becher, –** paper cup; **der ~deckel, –** piece of cardboard; **der ~karton, –s** cardboard box; **das ~maché** [–ʃ–] papier-mâché; **der ~schnee** sticky snow

die **Pappe, –n** cardboard; **nicht von ~** *coll* not to be underestimated; quite something

die **Pappel, –n** poplar

pappen *coll* (snow *etc*) stick (to sth.); **~ an/auf** (*acc*) stick (sticker *etc*) on

Pappen–: ~heimer *coll* (**ich kenne meine P.** I know you/these people (*ie* what you/they are like)); **~stiel** *coll* (**für einen P.** for a song; **… ist kein P.** … is not to be sneezed at; **keinen P. wert** not worth a brass farthing)

papperlapapp! stuff and nonsense!

pappig *coll* sticky

der **Paprika, –(s)** paprika; = **die ~schote, –n** (green/red) pepper

paprizieren *Aust* flavour with paprika

der **Papst** [–aː–], **⸚e** pope

päpstlich [–ɛː–] papal

das **Papsttum** papacy

der **Papyrus, –(r)i** papyrus

die **Parabel, –n** parable; *math* parabola

die **Parabol|antenne, –n** satellite dish

parabolisch parabolic (*also math*)

die **Parade, –n** *mil* parade; review; *footb etc* save; *fenc* parry; *equest* halt; **die ~ abnehmen** take the salute || **das ~beispiel, –e** textbook example; **das ~pferd, –e** show horse; *coll* showpiece; star performer; **der ~schritt** goose-step; **das ~stück, –e** showpiece; **die ~uniform, –en** dress uniform

der **Paradeiser, –** *Aust* tomato

paradieren *mil* parade; **~ mit** flaunt

das **Paradies, –e** paradise; **der ~vogel, ..vögel** bird of paradise

paradiesisch paradisiacal; heavenly, blissful

das **Paradigma, –(m)en** paradigm

paradox paradoxical; **paradoxer|weise** paradoxically

das **Paradox, –e** paradox

die **Paradoxie, –(ie)n** paradoxical nature; paradox

das **Paradoxon** [–ɔn], **–(x)a** paradox

das **Paraffin, –e** paraffin

der **Paragraph, –en** (*wk masc*) *leg etc* section; article; paragraph; **der ~en|reiter, –** stickler for the rules

Paraguay [–'gŭaːi] Paraguay

der **Paraguayer** [–'gŭaːjɐ], **–, paraguayisch** Paraguayan

parallel parallel (**zu** to)

die **Parallele, –n** parallel (line); parallel (**zu** to)

die **Parallelität, –en** parallelism

das **Parallelogramm, –e** parallelogram

die **Paralyse, –n** paralysis

der **Paralytiker, –, paralytisch** paralytic

der **Parameter, –** parameter

paramilitärisch paramilitary

die **Paranoia** paranoia

paranoid [–o'iːt] paranoid

der **Paranoiker, –, paranoisch** paranoiac

die **Para|nuß, ⸚(ss)e** Brazil nut

paraphieren initial (treaty *etc*)

die **Paraphrase, –n** paraphrase (*also mus*)

der **Parasit, –en** (*wk masc*) parasite

parasitär = parasitisch parasitic
parat ready; ~ **halten** keep ready; be ready with (excuse *etc*)
das **Pärchen, –** (loving) couple
der **Parcours** [–'kuːɐ] (*gen* – [–(s)]), – [–s] (show-jumping) course
pardon! [–'dɔ̃ː] sorry!; excuse me!; **keinen Pardon geben** show no mercy
die **Parenthese, –n** parenthesis
parenthetisch parenthetical
die **Parforce|jagd** [–'fɔrs–], **–en** riding to hounds
das **Parfüm, –s/–e** perfume
die **Parfümerie, –(ie)n** perfumery
parfümieren perfume; **sich ~** put perfume on
der **Paria, –s** pariah
parieren[1] *coll* obey, do what one is told
parieren[2] parry (question *etc*); *fenc* parry, *footb* deflect; *equest* rein in
Paris Paris
der **Pariser, –** Parisian
Pariser (*indecl*), **pariserisch** Parisian
die **Parität, –en** parity (*also fin*)
paritätisch with equal representation
der **Park, –s** park; **–park** fleet of …
Park– park …; parking …; **die ~anlage, –n** (public) park; **das ~(hoch)haus, ⸚er** multi-storey car park, parking garage *US*; **die ~landschaft, –en** parkland; **das ~licht, –er** parking light; **die ~lücke, –n** parking space; **der ~platz, ⸚e** parking space; car park, parking lot *US*; **die ~scheibe, –n** parking disc; **die ~uhr, –en** parking meter; **das ~verbot, –e** parking ban; no parking; **das ~verbots|schild, –er** 'no parking' sign
der **Parka, –s** (*also* **die**) parka
parken park; (*v/i*) park; (car) be parked
das **Parkett, –e** parquet flooring; (diplomatic *etc*) circles; *theat* stalls, parquet *US*
parkieren *Swiss* park
das **Parlament, –e** parliament; **ins ~ gewählt werden** be elected to parliament
der **Parlamentär, –e** truce negotiator
der **Parlamentarier** [–ĭɐ], – parliamentarian
parlamentarisch parliamentary
der **Parlamentarismus** parliamentarianism
Parlaments– … of parliament; parliamentary …; **die ~ferien** *pl* recess
der **Parnaß** (*gen* –(ss)es) Parnassus
die **Parodie, –(ie)n** parody (**auf** *acc* of)
parodieren parody
parodistisch parodistic
die **Parole, –n** slogan; *mil* password
Paroli: (+*dat*) **~ bieten** stand up to
der **Part, –e** *mus*, *theat* part
die **Parte, –n** *Aust* = **der ~zettel, –** *Aust* announcement of (s.o.'s) death
die **Partei, –en** (political) party; tenant(s); *leg* party; *sp* side; **~ ergreifen/nehmen für/gegen** take sides with/against || **der ~apparat, –e** party machine; **das ~chinesisch** *coll* party jargon; **die ~führung** party leadership; **der ~gänger, –** party supporter; **der ~genosse, –n** (*wk masc*) *Nazi* party member; **p~intern** within the party; **die ~linie** party line; **p~los** independent; **die ~nahme** taking sides; **die ~politik** party politics; **p~politisch** party political; **der ~tag, –e** party conference/convention
der **Parteien|verkehr** *Aust* office hours
parteiisch partisan
parteilich *pol* party; *EGer* in accordance with Party doctrine
die **Parteilichkeit** partiality
das **Parterre** [–'tɛr], **–s** ground floor; *theat* rear stalls, parterre *US*
der **Parthenon** [–ɔn] the Parthenon
die **Partie, –(ie)n** part (*also mus*, *theat*); (good *etc*) match; *sp*, *games* game; *comm* lot; *arch* excursion; **mit von der ~ sein** *coll* be in on it
partiell [–ts–] partial
das **Partikel, –** *phys* particle
die **Partikel, –n** *gramm* particle
der **Partisan, –en** (*also wk masc*) *mil* partisan
die **Partitur, –en** *mus* score
das **Partizip, –ien** [–ĭən] participle; **~ Präsens/Perfekt** present/past participle
partizipieren: ~ an (*dat*) participate in
der **Partner, –** partner; *cin* co-star; **als jmds. ~ spielen** play opposite s.o. || **die ~stadt, ⸚e** twin town; **der ~tausch** wife-swapping
die **Partnerschaft, –en** partnership
partnerschaftlich based on partnership; (*adv*) as partners
partout [–'tuː] *coll* absolutely; simply; at all costs
die **Party** ['paːɐti], **–s/Parties** party
die **Parzelle, –n** plot (of land)
parzellieren parcel out
der **Pascha, –s** pasha; *coll* lord and master
die **Paspel, –n** piping
der **Paß, ⸚(ss)e** passport; *geog*, *sp* pass; **das ~bild, –er** passport photograph; **die ~form** fit; **der ~gang** amble (of quadruped); **die ~kontrolle, –n** passport control; **die ~stelle, –n** passport office
passabel passable; presentable
die **Passage** [–ʒə], **–n** passage (*var senses*); arcade
der **Passagier** [–'ʒiːɐ], **–e** passenger; **blinder ~** stowaway
das **Passah = das ~fest, –e** Passover
der **Passant, –en** (*wk masc*) passer-by; pedestrian
der **Passat, –e = der ~wind, –e** trade-wind
passé passé; out of fashion
passen[1] fit; be convenient; (+*dat*) fit; (time *etc*) suit, *or expressed – with ind obj becoming subj – by* like (*eg* **es ist mir ganz egal, ob es ihm paßt oder nicht** I don't care whether he likes it or not); **das könnte dir so ~!**

you'd like that, wouldn't you?
~ **auf** (*acc*) (lid, description, *etc*) fit
~ **in** (*acc*) fit into; fit in with
~ **zu** go with; be suited to; match; **zueinander** ~ be suited (to each other)
passen² *cards etc* pass
passen³ *footb* pass
passend suitable; apt; (shoes *etc*) to match; **es ~ haben** have the exact money
Passier–: der ~schein, –e pass
passierbar passable
passieren pass; pass over, cross; pass through; *cul* strain; (*v/i*) pass; (*sn*) happen (*dat* to); **die Zensur ~** pass the censor
die **Passion, –en** passion; **die ~ (Christi)** the Passion (of Christ)
passioniert enthusiastic
Passions–: die ~frucht, ⸗e passion fruit; **das ~spiel, –e** Passion play; **die ~woche, –n** Holy Week
passiv passive; *comm* (balance of trade) adverse
das **Passiv** *gramm* passive (voice)
Passiv– *comm* debit ...; **das ~rauchen** passive smoking
die **Passiva** *pl comm* liabilities
passivisch *gramm* passive
die **Passivität** passivity
der **Passus, –** [–u:s] passage (in book *etc*)
Past–: die ~milch *Swiss* pasteurized milk
die **Paste, –n** paste
das **Pastell, –e** pastel (drawing); *in compds* pastel ...; **p~farben** pastel; **der ~ton, ⸗e** pastel shade
die **Pastete, –n** pâté; pie; vol-au-vent
pasteurisieren [–ø–] pasteurize
die **Pastille, –n** pastille
der **Pastor, –(or)en** *esp Prot* pastor
pastoral pastoral; solemn
die **Pastorale, –n** (*also* **das**, *pl* **–s**) *arts* pastoral; *mus* pastorale; **„Die ~"** 'The Pastoral Symphony'
der **Pate, –n** (*wk masc*) godfather, sponsor; **~ stehen bei** stand godfather to; help bring about; play a part in || **der ~n|betrieb, –e** *EGer* sponsoring enterprise; **das ~n|kind, –er** godchild; **der ~n|onkel, –** godfather; **die ~n|tante, –n** godmother
die **Patenschaft, –en** sponsorship; **die ~ übernehmen für** sponsor; adopt
patent *coll* splendid; (method *etc*) ingenious
das **Patent, –e** patent; *Swiss* permit, licence; *mil* commission; *naut* (master's) certificate; **das ~amt, ⸗er** patent office; **der ~inhaber, –** patentee; **die ~lösung, –en = das ~rezept, –e** ready-made solution
patentieren patent
der **Pater, –/Patres** [–e:s] *RC* Father
pathetisch emotional; histrionic
der **Pathologe, –n** (*wk masc*) pathologist
die **Pathologie** pathology
pathologisch pathological
das **Pathos** [–ɔs] emotionalism; emotion (in s.o.'s voice)
die **Patience** [pa'sĭã:s], **–n** *cards* patience, solitaire *US*; **~n/eine ~ legen** play patience
der **Patient** [–ts–], **–en** (*wk masc*) patient
die **Patin, –nen** godmother
die **Patina** ['pa:–] patina; **~ ansetzen** become coated with a patina
Patres *pl of* **Pater**
der **Patriarch** [–ç], **–en** (*wk masc*) patriarch
das **Patriarchat** [–ç–], **–e** patriarchy
patriarchalisch [–ç–] patriarchal
der **Patriot, –en** (*wk masc*) patriot
patriotisch patriotic
der **Patriotismus** patriotism
der **Patrizier** [–ĭɐ], **–**, **patrizisch** patrician
der **Patron, –e** patron saint; *arch* patron; **frecher ~** *coll* cheeky beggar; **übler ~** *coll* nasty piece of work
das **Patronat, –e** patronage
die **Patrone, –n** cartridge; **die ~n|hülse, –n** cartridge case
die **Patrouille** [–'trʊljə], **–n**, **patrouillieren** [–trʊlj–] (*also sn*) patrol
patsch! splash!; smack!
Patsche *coll*: (+*dat*) **aus der ~ helfen** help out of a tight corner; **in der ~ sitzen** be in a fix
patsch(e)–: patsch(e)|naß *coll* soaking wet
patschen *coll* splash (about); (*sn*) splash (through puddles *etc*); **~ auf** (*acc*) smack
das **Patt, –s** stalemate
die **Patte, –n** flap (on pocket)
patzen *coll* boob, goof *US*
der **Patzer, –** *coll* boob, goof *US*; bungler
patzig *coll* impudent
die **Pauke, –n** kettledrum; **auf die ~ hauen** *coll* blow one's own trumpet; paint the town red
pauken (*coll in 1st sense*) cram (*also v/i*); (*v/i*) beat the drum; *univ* fight a duel
Paul Paul
Paulus (St) Paul
Paus–: die ~backen *pl* chubby cheeks; **p~bäckig** chubby-cheeked; **das ~papier** tracing-paper
pauschal flat-rate; (sum) lump; all-in; (statement) blanket, sweeping; (*adv*) across the board; at a flat rate; (paid) in a lump sum; lumped together; (condemn *etc*) wholesale; **die P~gebühr, –en** flat rate; **der P~preis, –e** flat rate; all-in price; **die P~reise, –n** package tour; **die P~summe, –n** lump sum; **das P~urteil, –e** sweeping statement
die **Pauschale, –n** flat rate
die **Pause¹, –n** break; pause; (at school) break, recess *US*; *mus* rest; *theat* interval, intermission *esp US*; **eine ~ einlegen** take a

break

die **Pause²**, **–n** tracing; (photo)copy

pausen trace

pausen–: ~**los** incessant, non-stop; **das P~zeichen, –** *mus* rest; *rad* call sign

pausieren take a break

der **Pavian** ['paː–], **–e** baboon

der **Pavillon** [–vɪl'jɔ̃ː], **–s** pavilion

der **Pazifik** [–ɪk] the Pacific

pazifisch Pacific; **der P~e Ozean** the Pacific Ocean

der **Pazifismus** pacifism

der **Pazifist, –en** (*wk masc*), **pazifistisch** pacifist

der **PC, –(s)** (= **Personalcomputer**) p.c.

das **Pech** pitch; *coll* bad luck; ~ **haben** *coll* be unlucky || **pech(raben)schwarz** pitch/jet-black; **die** ~**strähne, –n** *coll* run of bad luck; **der** ~**vogel, ..vögel** *coll* unlucky person

das **Pedal, –e** pedal

der **Pedant, –en** (*wk masc*) pedant

die **Pedanterie** pedantry

pedantisch pedantic

die **Pediküre, –n** chiropody; chiropodist

pediküren (*p/part* **pedikürt**) give (s.o.) a pedicure

die **Peepshow** ['piːpʃoː], **–s** peep-show

der **Pegel, –** water-gauge; level; **der** ~**stand, ¨–e** water-level

Peil– *rad* direction-finding ...; *naut* sounding ...

peilen take a bearing on; *naut* sound; **die Lage** ~ *coll* see how the land lies; **über den Daumen** ~ *coll* estimate roughly

die **Pein** agony; torment

peinigen torture; torment

der **Peiniger, –** tormentor

peinlich embarrassing; awkward; meticulous; ~ **berührt** embarrassed; ~ **genau** very thorough; meticulous

die **Peitsche, –n** whip

peitschen whip; lash; ~ **an** (*acc*)/**gegen** (*also sn*) lash against

Peitschen–: der ~**hieb, –e** whiplash; **der** ~**knall, –e** crack of a whip

der **Pekinese, –n** (*wk masc*) pekinese

Peking Peking, Beijing

pekuniär pecuniary

der **Pelikan, –e** pelican

die **Pelerine, –n** cape

Pell–: die ~**kartoffeln** *pl* potatoes boiled in their jackets

die **Pelle, –n** *NGer* (sausage *etc*) skin; (+*dat*) **nicht von der** ~ **gehen** *coll* = (+*dat*) **auf der** ~ **liegen/sitzen** *coll* not leave in peace; (+*dat*) **auf die** ~ **rücken** *coll* crowd; pester

pellen *NGer* peel; shell; **sich** ~ peel; **wie aus dem Ei gepellt** *coll* spick and span

der **Peloponnes** (*gen* **–(es)**) the Peloponnese

der **Pelz, –e** fur; fur coat; (+*dat*) **auf den** ~ **rücken** crowd; pester || **der** ~**händler, –** furrier; **der** ~**jäger, –** trapper; **der** ~**mantel, ..mäntel** fur coat; **das** ~**tier, –e** fur-bearing animal; **der** ~**tier|jäger, –** trapper

pelzig furry; (tongue) furred

das **Pendant** [pã'dãː], **–s** counterpart (**zu** of)

das **Pendel, –** pendulum; **die** ~**tür, –en** swing-door; **die** ~**uhr, –en** pendulum clock; **der** ~**verkehr** commuter traffic; shuttle service

pendeln swing (to and fro); fluctuate; *box* weave; (*usu sn*) commute; (bus *etc*) operate a shuttle service

die **Pendenz, –en** *Swiss* outstanding matter

der **Pendler, –** commuter

penetrant penetrating, pungent; importunate

die **Penetranz** pungency; importunate nature

peng! bang!

penibel meticulous

der **Penis** [–ɪs] (*gen* **–**), **–se/Penes** [–eːs] penis

das **Penizillin** penicillin

Penn–: der ~ **bruder, ..brüder** *coll* tramp

der **Pennäler, –** *coll* pupil at a *Gymnasium*

pennen *coll* kip

Pensa *pl of* **Pensum**

die **Pension** [paŋ–], **–en** (civil servant's) pension; boarding-house; **halbe/volle** ~ half/full board; ~ **beziehen** draw a pension; **in** ~ **gehen** retire

der **Pensionär** [paŋ–], **–e** pensioner; boarding-house guest

das **Pensionat** [paŋ–], **–e** (*esp* girls') boarding school

pensionieren [paŋ–] pension off; **sich** ~ **lassen** retire; **pensioniert** retired

die **Pensionierung, –en** pensioning off; retirement

der **Pensionist** [pɛn–], **–en** (*wk masc*) *Aust* pensioner

Pensions–: p~berechtigt entitled to a pension; **die** ~**kasse, –n** pension fund; **p~reif** ready for retirement

das **Pensum, –(s)en/–(s)a** (allotted) task; *educ* material (to be covered)

die **Peperoni** *pl* chillies

das **Pepita** (*also* **der**) shepherd's check

per by (rail *etc*); *comm* per; *comm* by (date)

perennierend perennial

perfekt perfect; settled; ~ **machen** clinch

das **Perfekt, –e** perfect (tense)

die **Perfektion** perfection

perfektionieren perfect

der **Perfektionismus** perfectionism

der **Perfektionist, –en** (*wk masc*), **perfektionistisch** perfectionist

perfid(e) perfidious

die **Perfidie, –(ie)n** perfidy

die **Perforation, –en** perforation

perforieren perforate

^das^ **Pergament, –e** parchment; **das ~papier** greaseproof paper
Perikles [–ɛs] Pericles
^die^ **Periode, –n** period (*also physiol*); *elect* cycle; **das ~n|system** periodic table
periodisch periodic; *math* recurring
peripher peripheral
^die^ **Peripherie, –(ie)n** periphery; outskirts
^das^ **Periskop, –e** periscope
Perl– pearl ...; **das ~huhn, ⸗er** guinea-fowl; **das ~mutt, die ~mutter, p~muttern** mother-of-pearl
^die^ **Perle, –n** pearl; bead; (dew)drop; bubble
perlen sparkle; (*sn*) trickle, (tear) roll; **der Schweiß perlte ihm von der Stirn** his face was covered with beads of sweat; **~des Lachen** rippling laughter
Perlen– pearl ...
^das^ **Perlon** [–ɔn] (*trade-mark*) *approx* = nylon
perlustrieren *Aust* search (suspect *etc*)
permanent permanent
^die^ **Permanenz** permanence; **in ~** continuously
^der^ **Perpendikel, –** (*also* **das**) pendulum
perplex dumbfounded
^der^ **Perron** [–'rɔ̃ː], **–s** *arch exc Swiss rail* platform
^die^ **Persenning, –e(n)** tarpaulin
^der^ **Perser, –** Persian; = **der ~teppich, –e** Persian carpet
^der^ **Persianer, –** Persian lamb (coat)
Persien [–ĭən] Persia
^die^ **Persiflage** [–ʒə], **–n** spoof (**auf** *acc* of)
persiflieren do a spoof of
persisch, (*language*) **P~** Persian; **der P~e Golf** the Persian Gulf
^die^ **Person, –en** person (*also gramm*); *liter* character; *coll* female; **ich für meine ~** I personally; **in eigener ~** in person, personally; **... in einer ~** ... rolled into one; **... ist (der Geiz** *etc*) **in ~** ... is (avarice *etc*) personified; **pro ~** per person
^das^ **Personal** staff; personnel; *in compds also* personal ...; **der ~ausweis, –e** identity card; **der ~computer, –** personal computer; **das ~pronomen, –/..(m)ina** personal pronoun; **die ~union, –en** personal union
^die^ **Personalien** [–ĭən] *pl* (personal) particulars
personell personnel; in terms of personnel
Personen– personal ...; passenger ...; **die ~beschreibung, –en** (personal) description; **der ~kraft|wagen, –** motor-car; **der ~kult, –e** personality cult; **der ~schaden, ..schäden** injury to persons; **das ~stands|-register, –** register of births, marriages and deaths/burials *US*; **der ~wagen, –** motor-car; *rail* carriage, passenger car *US*; **der ~zug, ⸗e** slow train
personifizieren personify
^die^ **Personifizierung, –en** personification
persönlich personal; (*adv*) personally; in person
^die^ **Persönlichkeit, –en** personality; figure
Persons–: die ~beschreibung, –en *Aust* (personal) description
Perspektiv– ** *EGer*: **der ~plan, ⸗e long-term plan; **die ~planung** long-term planning
^die^ **Perspektive, –n** perspective; angle, point of view; prospect
perspektivisch perspective; in perspective
Peru Peru
^der^ **Peruaner, –, peruanisch** Peruvian
^die^ **Perücke, –n** wig
pervers perverted
^die^ **Perversion, –en** perversion
^die^ **Perversität, –en** perversion; pervertedness
pervertieren pervert; (*v/i sn*) become perverted
pesen (*sn*) *coll* dash
^das^ **Pessar, –e** pessary
^der^ **Pessimismus** pessimism
^der^ **Pessimist, –en** (*wk masc*) pessimist
pessimistisch pessimistic
^die^ **Pest** plague; **wie die ~ hassen** *coll* hate like poison
^das^ **Pestizid, –e** pesticide
Peter Peter; (+*dat*) **den Schwarzen ~ zuschieben** pass the buck to || **der ~wagen, –** *coll* patrol-car
Peters–: die ~kirche St Peter's; **der ~platz** St Peter's Square
^die^ **Petersilie** [–ĭə] parsley
^die^ **Petition, –en** petition
Petrarca Petrarch
^der^ **Petrodollar, –s** petrodollar
^das^ **Petroleum** paraffin (oil), kerosene *US*
Petrus Peter
^das^ **Petschaft** ['pɛt–], **–e** seal
^die^ **Petunie** [–ĭə], **–n** petunia
^die^ **Petze, –n** *coll* telltale, sneak
petzen *coll* tell tales
Pf = Pfennig
^der^ **Pfad, –e** path; **der ~finder, –** boy scout; **die ~finderin, –nen** girl guide/scout *US*
^der^ **Pfaffe, –n** (*wk masc*) *pej* cleric
^der^ **Pfahl, ⸗e** stake; post; pile; **der ~bau, –ten** pile dwelling; **die ~wurzel, –n** tap-root
pfählen impale; *hort* stake
^die^ **Pfalz** the Palatinate
^der^ **Pfälzer, –** inhabitant/wine of the Palatinate
pfälzisch of the Palatinate
^das^ **Pfand, ⸗er** pledge; security; deposit (on bottle *etc*); *games* forfeit; **der ~brief, –e** bond; **das ~haus, ⸗er** pawnshop; **die ~leihe, –n** pawnshop; pawnbroking; **der ~leiher, –** pawnbroker; **der ~schein, –e** pawn-ticket
pfänden *leg* distrain upon
^die^ **Pfändung, –en** *leg* distraint
Pfann–: der ~kuchen, – pancake (**Berliner P.** doughnut)
^die^ **Pfanne, –n** (frying-)pan; *anat* socket; **in die ~**

hauen *coll* make mincemeat of
Pfarr–: der ~bezirk, –e parish; **das ~haus, ⸚er** parsonage; **die ~kirche, –n** parish church
die **Pfarrei, –en** parish; parsonage
der **Pfarrer, –** parson; priest; minister
der **Pfau, –en** peacock; **die ~en|henne, –n** peahen
Pfd. (= **Pfund**) pound (*weight*)
der **Pfeffer** pepper; **das ~korn, ⸚er** peppercorn; **der ~kuchen, –** gingerbread; **das ~minz, –e** peppermint (= sweet, candy *US*); **der ~minz, –e** crème de menthe; **~minz–** peppermint ...; **der ~minz|likör, –e** crème de menthe; **die ~mühle, –n** pepper-mill
pfefferig peppery
pfeffern (*see also* **gepfeffert**) pepper; *coll* fling
der **Pfefferoni** (*gen* –), – *Aust* chilli
Pfeif–: das ~konzert, –e chorus of whistles; **der ~ton, ⸚e** whistle
die **Pfeife, –n** pipe; whistle; **nach jmds. ~ tanzen** dance to s.o.'s tune
pfeifen (*p/t* **pfiff,** *p/part* **gepfiffen**) (*also v/i*) whistle; **~ auf** (*acc*) *coll* not give a damn about; **ich werd' ihm** *etc* **was ~!** he's *etc* got another think coming!; **~der Atem** wheezing
der **Pfeifer, –** piper
der **Pfeil, –e** arrow; dart; **~ und Bogen** bow and arrow; **alle seine ~e verschossen haben** have run out of arguments || **der ~flügel, –** sweptback wing; **p~förmig** arrow-shaped; *aer* sweptback; **pfeil|schnell** as quick as lightning
der **Pfeiler, –** pillar; (of bridge) pier
der **Pfennig, –e**/(*following num*) – (E. or W. German) pfennig (*1/100 of a mark*); (*in idioms*) penny, cent; **der ~absatz, ⸚e** stiletto heel; **der ~fuchser** [-ks-], – *coll* skinflint
der **Pferch, –e** (sheep-)pen
pferchen: ~ in (*acc*) cram into
das **Pferd** [-eː-], **–e** horse (*also gym*); *chess* knight; **zu ~e** on horseback; **das ~ beim Schwanz aufzäumen** *coll* put the cart before the horse; **wie ein ~ arbeiten** *coll* work like a Trojan
Pferde– horse ...; horse's ...; horse-drawn ...; **die ~äpfel** *pl* horse manure; **der ~fuß, ⸚e** cloven hoof; *coll* hidden snag; **die ~kur, –en** *coll* drastic treatment; **die ~länge, –n** *horse rac* length; **die ~renn|bahn, –en** race-course; **das ~rennen, –** horse-race; horse-racing; **der ~schwanz, ⸚e** horse's tail; (= hair-style) pony-tail; **die ~stärke, –n** horsepower
pfiff *p/t of* **pfeifen**
der **Pfiff, –e** whistle; *coll* style; **letzter ~** finishing touch
der **Pfifferling, –e** chanterelle; **keinen ~ wert** *coll* not worth a brass farthing

pfiffig clever, smart
Pfingst–: die ~ferien *pl* Whitsun holidays; **das ~fest** Whitsun; **der Pfingst|montag, –e** Whit Monday; **die ~rose, –n** peony; **der Pfingst|sonntag, –e** Whit Sunday; **die ~woche** Whit week
das **Pfingsten** (*esp Aust, Swiss* **die ~** *pl*) Whitsun (*~ usu occurs without article*; *treated as sing* (*eg* **~ fällt dieses Jahr früh** Whitsun is early this year), *as sing or pl following adj* (*eg* **nächste(s) ~** next Whitsun), *as pl in* **frohe/fröhliche ~!** happy Whitsun!); **zu/** *SGer* **an ~** at Whitsun
pfingstlich Whitsun
der **Pfirsich, –e** peach
die **Pflanze, –n** plant
pflanzen plant; *Aust coll* kid; **sich ~** *coll* plant oneself
Pflanzen– plant ..., vegetable ...; **das ~fett, –e** vegetable fat; **p~fressend** herbivorous; **der ~fresser, –** herbivore; **die ~kunde** botany; **das ~öl, –e** vegetable oil; **das ~reich** vegetable kingdom; **das ~schutz|mittel, –** pesticide
pflanzlich vegetable
der **Pflänzling, –e** seedling
die **Pflanzung, –en** planting; plantation
das **Pflaster, –** road surface; cobblestones; *med* plaster; **heißes/teures ~** *coll* dangerous/pricey place || **der ~maler, –** pavement artist, sidewalk artist *US*; **p~müde** *coll* dead on one's feet; **der ~stein, –e** paving-stone; cobblestone
pflastern pave; cobble
die **Pflaume, –n** plum; *coll* twit; **der ~n|baum, ⸚e** plum-tree; **der ~n|kern, –e** plum-stone
die **Pflege** care; maintenance; cultivation (of good relations *etc*); **in ~ geben** have (s.o., sth.) looked after; foster out; **in ~ nehmen** look after; foster || **p~bedürftig** in need of care; **die ~eltern** *pl* foster parents; **das ~heim, –e** nursing-home; **das ~kind, –er** foster-child; **p~leicht** easy-care; easy to look after; **die ~mutter, ..mütter** foster-mother; **der ~vater, ..väter** foster-father
pflegen (*see also* **gepflegt**) (*a*) look after; tend; cultivate, foster (friendship *etc*); **Kontakt ~ mit** maintain contact with; **sich ~** take trouble over one's appearance;
(*b*) **~ zu** + *infin* be in the habit of (+*ger*); (thing) tend to; **... pflegte zu ...** ... would ..., ... used to ...; **wie es (so) zu gehen pflegt** as usually happens
der **Pfleger, –** (male) nurse; keeper (at zoo); *leg* guardian
die **Pflegerin, –nen** nurse
pflegerisch nursing
pfleglich careful
der **Pflegling, –e** foster-child
die **Pflicht, –en** duty; *sp* compulsory exercises;

–pflicht *also* (*eg* **die Unterhalts~, Wahl~**) obligation to (pay maintenance, vote, *etc*), (*eg* **die Schul~**) compulsory (education *etc*); **~ und Schuldigkeit** bounden duty; **es ist seine verdammte ~ und Schuldigkeit zu …** *coll* he'll damn well have to …; **… ist ~** … is compulsory; **es sich** *dat* **zur ~ machen zu …** make it one's business to …

Pflicht– … of duty; compulsory …; **p~bewußt** dutiful; conscientious; **das ~bewußt|sein** sense of duty; **der ~eifer** zeal (in performing one's duty); **das ~gefühl** sense of duty; **p~gemäß** in accordance with one's duty; **p~schuldig** due; **p~vergessen** neglectful of one's duty, remiss; **p~versichert** compulsorily insured

–pflichtig = '*subject to …*', '*requiring …*', '*required to …*', *eg* **zoll~** dutiable, **rezept~** available on prescription, **unterhalts~** required to pay maintenance, **schul~** required to attend school

der **Pflock, ⸚e** (tent- *etc*) peg; stake (for tethering animals)

pflücken pick (berries, flowers, *etc*)

der **Pflug, ⸚e** plough; **die ~schar, –en** ploughshare

pflügen (*also v/i*) plough

die **Pforte, –n** gate; entrance; (*in geog names*) Gap

der **Pförtner, –** porter; gatekeeper; doorkeeper; *anat* pylorus

der **Pfosten, –** post

die **Pfote, –n** paw; *coll* scrawl

der **Pfriem, –e** awl

der **Pfropf, –e** = **Pfropfen**; *in compds* grafting …; **das ~reis, –e** graft

pfropfen cork; *hort* graft; **~ in** (*acc*) cram into; **gepfropft voll** crammed full

der **Pfropfen, –** stopper; cork; bung; plug; *med* clot

die **Pfründe, –n** sinecure; *RC* living, benefice

der **Pfuhl, –e** (dirty) pool; sink (of iniquity)

pfui! [–uɪ] hey! (*displeasure*); ugh!; **~ über …** (*acc*)! shame on …! || **der Pfui|ruf, –e** boo

das **Pfund, –e**/(*following num*) – pound (*as weight = 500 grams*); **p~weise** by the pound

–pfündig -pound

Pfunds– *coll* 'great' …

der **Pfusch** *coll* botch-up

pfuschen *coll* bungle sth., make a mess of things; (*+dat*) **ins Handwerk ~** meddle in (s.o.'s) affairs

der **Pfuscher, –** *coll* botcher

die **Pfuscherei, –en** bungling; botch-up

die **Pfütze, –n** puddle

der **Pg, –(s)** *Nazi* = **Parteigenosse**

die **PGH, –(s)** *EGer* = **Produktionsgenossenschaft des Handwerks** (*craftsmen's production co-operative*)

die **PH, –(s)** = **Pädagogische Hochschule**

die **Phalanx** ['faː–], **–(an)gen** phalanx

phallisch phallic

der **Phallus, –(ll)en/–(ll)i** phallus

das **Phänomen, –e** phenomenon

phänomenal phenomenal

die **Phantasie, –(ie)n** imagination; fantasy; **schmutzige ~** dirty mind || **das ~gebilde, –** figment of the imagination; **p~los** unimaginative; **p~voll** imaginative

phantasieren fantasize (**von** about); *mus* improvise; *med* be delirious

der **Phantast, –en** (*wk masc*) dreamer

die **Phantasterei, –en** fantasy; fantastic notion

die **Phantastik** [–ɪk] fantastic quality

phantastisch fantastic; fanciful

das **Phantom, –e** phantom; **das ~bild, –er** identikit

der **Pharao, –(o)nen** Pharaoh; *in compds* **~(o)nen–** … of the Pharaohs

der **Pharisäer, –** Pharisee; pharisee, hypocrite

das **Pharisäertum** pharisaism, hypocrisy

pharisäisch Pharisaic; pharisaic(al)

der **Pharmakologe, –n** (*wk masc*) pharmacologist

die **Pharmakologie** pharmacology

pharmakologisch pharmacological

der **Pharmazeut, –en** (*wk masc*) pharmacist

pharmazeutisch pharmaceutical

die **Pharmazie** pharmacy, pharmaceutics

die **Phase, –n** phase; *in compds* **~n–** phase …

–phasig -phase

der **Philanthrop, –en** (*wk masc*) philanthropist

philanthropisch philanthropical

die **Philatelie** philately

der **Philatelist, –en** (*wk masc*) philatelist

die **Philharmonie, –(ie)n** (*in titles*) Philharmonic (Orchestra); Philharmonic Hall

der **Philharmoniker, –** member of a philharmonic orchestra; (*pl, in titles*) Philharmonic (Orchestra)

philharmonisch philharmonic

Philipp ['fiː–] Philip

die **Philippinen** *pl* the Philippines

philippinisch Philippine

der **Philister, –** Philistine; philistine

philisterhaft philistine

das **Philistertum** philistinism

der **Philologe, –n** (*wk masc*) teacher/student of language and literature

die **Philologie** study of language and literature

philologisch relating to the study of language and literature

der **Philosoph, –en** (*wk masc*) philosopher

die **Philosophie** philosophy

philosophieren philosophize

philosophisch philosophical; **~e Fakultät** faculty of arts

die **Phiole, –n** phial

das **Phlegma** phlegm; phlegmatic nature

der **Phlegmatiker, –** phlegmatic person
phlegmatisch phlegmatic
die **Phobie, –(ie)n** phobia
das **Phonem, –e** phoneme
die **Phonetik** [–ɪk] phonetics
der **Phonetiker, –** phonetician
phonetisch phonetic
der **Phönix, –e** phoenix
Phönizien [–ĭən] Phoenicia
der **Phönizier** [–ĭɐ], **–, phönizisch** Phoenician
die **Phonotypistin, –nen** audiotypist
das **Phosphat, –e** phosphate
der **Phosphor** phosphorus; **die ~säure** phosphoric acid
die **Phosphoreszenz** phosphorescence
phosphoreszieren phosphoresce; **~d** phosphorescent
phosphorig (acid) phosphorous
das **Photo, –s** photo; **ein ~ machen** take a photo || **der ~apparat, –e** camera; **p~elektrisch** photoelectric; **die ~kopie, –(ie)n, p~kopieren** photocopy; **das ~kopier|gerät, –e** photocopier; **die ~synthese** photosynthesis; **die ~zelle, –n** photoelectric cell
photogen photogenic
der **Photograph, –en** (*wk masc*) photographer
die **Photographie, –(ie)n** photography; photograph
photographieren photograph; **sich ~ lassen** have one's picture taken; photograph (well *etc*)
photographisch photographic
die **Phrase, –n** (empty) phrase; *ling*, *mus* phrase; **~n dreschen** *coll* churn out clichés || **der ~n|drescher, –** *coll* phrasemonger
phrasieren *mus* phrase
die **Physik** physics
physikalisch physical; physics
der **Physiker, –** physicist
die **Physiognomie, –(ie)n** physiognomy
physiognomisch physiognomical
der **Physiologe, –n** (*wk masc*) physiologist
die **Physiologie** physiology
physiologisch physiological
der **Physiotherapeut, –en** (*wk masc*) physiotherapist
die **Physiotherapie** physiotherapy
die **Physis** [–ɪs] physique
physisch (strength *etc*) physical
der **Pianist, –en** (*wk masc*) pianist
picheln *coll* booze
die **Picke, –n** pick-axe
der **Pickel**[1], **–** pimple
der **Pickel**[2], **–** pick(-axe); ice-axe
die **Pickel|haube, –n** (Prussian) spiked helmet
pick(e)lig pimply
picken[1] (*also v/i*) peck; **~ an** (*dat*) peck at
picken[2] *Aust* stick (into album *etc*); (*v/i*) stick (**an** *dat* to)
das **Pickerl, –n** *Aust coll* sticker

das **Picknick, –e/–s** picnic; **(ein) ~ machen** have a picnic
picknicken picnic
das **Pidgin-Englisch** ['pɪdʒɪn–] pidgin English
der **Piefke, –s** *Aust coll* Kraut (*esp* = N. German)
piek– *coll*: **~fein** posh; **~sauber** spotless
piek(s)en *coll* prick
Piemont [pie–] Piedmont
der **Piep** cheep; **einen ~ haben** *coll* have a screw loose; **keinen ~ sagen** *coll* not say a word || **p~egal** *coll* (= **piepe**); **der ~matz, –e/⸚e** (*baby talk*) dicky-bird
piepe *coll*: **das ist mir ~** I couldn't care less
piepen squeak; cheep; bleep; **bei dir piept's wohl?** are you crazy?; **... ist zum Piepen** *coll* ... is a scream
die **Piepen** *pl coll* 'dough'
der **Pieper, –** pipit
der **Pieps, –e** *coll* = **Piep; piepsen = piepen**
der **Piepser, –** *coll* cheep; bleeper
piepsig *coll* squeaky
der **Pier, –e/–s** pier, jetty
piesacken *coll* torment; pester
die **Pietät** reverence; respect; **p~los** disrespectful; **p~voll** reverent
piff, paff! bang, bang!
das **Pigment, –e** pigment
Pik *coll*: **einen ~ haben auf** (*acc*) have a down on
das **Pik, –s** *cards* spades, (card: *pl* –) spade; *in compds* ... of spades
pikant piquant; risqué
die **Pikanterie, –(ie)n** piquancy; suggestive remark; racy story
pikaresk picaresque
die **Pike, –n** *hist* pike; **von der ~ auf dienen** *coll* (start at the bottom and) work one's way up
der **Pikee, –s** piqué
piken *coll* prick
das **Pikett, –e** *Swiss* stand-by squad; **auf ~** on stand-by
pikiert piqued
piksen [–iː–] *coll* prick
der **Pilger, –** pilgrim; **die ~fahrt, –en** pilgrimage
pilgern (*sn*) make a pilgrimage; *coll* make one's way (on foot)
die **Pille, –n** pill; **die ~ nehmen** be on the pill || **der ~n|dreher, –** scarab
der **Pilot, –en** (*wk masc*) *aer* pilot; *mot rac* driver
Pilot– pilot ...; experimental ...; **das ~projekt, –e** pilot scheme; **die ~studie, –n** pilot study
pilotieren *aer* pilot; *mot rac* drive
das **Pils, –** Pilsener
Pilsen Plzen
das **Pils(e)ner, –** Pilsener
der **Pilz, –e** mushroom; toadstool; fungus; **wie ~e aus dem Boden schießen** mushroom
der **Pimmel, –** *coll* willie

pimp(e)lig *coll* namby-pamby
pingelig *coll* fussy
der **Pinguin** [–uiːn], **–e** penguin
die **Pinie** [–ĭə], **–n** stone-pine
pink shocking pink
der **Pinkel,** – *coll*: **feiner/vornehmer** ~ swell
pinkeln *coll* piddle, pee
die **Pinke(pinke)** *coll* 'dough'
die **Pinne, –n** tiller
der **Pinscher,** – pinscher; *coll* pipsqueak
der **Pinsel,** – (paint-)brush; *coll* ninny; **die ~führung** brushwork; **der ~strich, –e** brush-stroke
pinseln *med* paint; *coll* write (laboriously); (*also v/i*) paint; daub
die **Pinte, –n** *esp Swiss* pub, saloon *US*
das **Pin-up-Girl** [pɪn'ʔapgœrl], **–s** pin-up (girl)
die **Pinzette, –n** tweezers
der **Pionier, –e** pioneer; *mil* engineer; **(Junger) ~** *EGer* Young Pioneer || **die ~arbeit** pioneering work
die **Pipeline** ['paeplaen], **–s** pipeline
die **Pipette, –n** pipette
das **Pipi** (*baby talk*), **~ machen** wee-wee
der **Pirat, –en** (*wk masc*) pirate; **der ~en|sender,** – pirate radio station
die **Piraterie** piracy
Piräus Piraeus
der **Pirol, –e** oriole; golden oriole
die **Pirouette** [–ru–], **–n, eine ~ drehen** pirouette
die **Pirsch** deer-stalking; **auf (die) ~ gehen** go stalking
pirschen stalk
pissen *vulg* piss
die **Pistazie** [–ĭə], **–n** pistachio
die **Piste, –n** *sp* track; *ski* run, piste; *aer* runway
die **Pistole, –n** pistol; (*+dat*) **die ~ auf die Brust setzen** hold a pistol to (s.o.'s) head; **mit vorgehaltener ~** at gunpoint
pitsch, patsch! pitter-patter; **pitsch(e)|naß** *coll* soaking wet
pittoresk picturesque
Pius Pius
die **Pizza, –s** pizza
Pkt(e). = Punkt(e)
der **Pkw, PKW** ['peːkaːveː, peːkaː'veː], **–(s)** (= **Personenkraftwagen**) motor-car
placieren [–ts–] = **plazieren**
placken: sich ~ *coll* slave away
die **Plackerei** *coll* drudgery
pladdern *NGer coll* (rain) pelt down
plädieren: ~ auf (*acc*) *leg* put the case for; **~ für** argue in favour of; *leg* put the case for
das **Plädoyer** [–dŏa'jeː], **–s** plea; *leg* summing-up
der **Plafond** [–'fɔ̃ː], **–s** *Aust* ceiling
die **Plage, –n** nuisance; scourge; **seine ~ haben mit** have a lot of trouble with || **der ~geist, –er** *coll* pest
plagen torment; trouble; pester; **sich ~** slave away; **sich ~ mit** struggle with; be troubled with (cough *etc*)
das **Plagiat, –e** plagiarism
der **Plagiator, –(or)en** plagiarist
plagiieren (*also v/i*) plagiarize
das **Plaid** [pleːt], **–s** tartan travelling-rug/lap robe *US*
das **Plakat, –e** poster; placard
plakatieren advertise (with posters)
plakativ (effect *etc*) bold
die **Plakette, –n** badge; plaque
der **Plan, ⸚e** plan; map; schedule; **Pläne schmieden** make plans; **auf den ~ rufen/treten** bring/appear on the scene; **nach ~ verlaufen** go according to plan || **die ~erfüllung** *EGer* fulfilment of the economic plan; **die ~kommission** *EGer* planning commission; **p~los** haphazard, unsystematic; **p~mäßig** planned; systematic; scheduled; as planned/scheduled; **das ~soll** *EGer* production target; **die ~stelle, –n** established post; **p~voll** systematic; **der ~wagen,** – covered wagon; **die ~wirtschaft, –en** planned economy; **das ~ziel, –e** *econ etc* target
die **Plane, –n** tarpaulin; awning
planen plan
der **Planer,** – planner
der **Planet, –en** (*wk masc*) planet
planetarisch planetary
das **Planetarium, –(i)en** planetarium
Planeten– planetary ...
Planier–: die ~raupe, –n bulldozer
planieren *tech* planish; *civ eng* level
die **Planke, –n** plank, board
die **Plänkelei, –en** banter
plänkeln engage in banter
das **Plankton** [–ɔn] plankton
das **Plansch|becken,** – paddling-pool
planschen splash about
die **Plantage** [–ʒə], **–n** plantation
die **Planung, –en** planning
das **Plapper|maul, ⸚er** *coll* chatterbox
plappern *coll* chatter
plärren *coll* howl, bawl; (radio *etc*) blare
das **Plasma, –(m)en** plasma
der **Plast, –e** *EGer* plastic; *in compds* plastic ...
die **Plaste, –n** *EGer coll* plastic
das **Plastik** [–ɪk] plastic
die **Plastik** [–ɪk], **–en** sculpture (= art, work); vividness; *med* plastic surgery
Plastik– plastic ...; **die ~tüte, –n** plastic bag
das **Plastilin** plasticine
plastisch graphic; plastic (*also med*)
die **Plastizität** plasticity; vividness
die **Platane, –n** plane-tree
das **Plateau** [–'toː], **–s** plateau; **die ~sohle, –n** platform sole
das **Platin** ['plaːtiːn] platinum; **p~blond** platinum blonde
die **Platitüde, –n** platitude

Plato, Platon [-ɔn] Plato
platonisch, *philos* **P~** Platonic
platsch! splash!
platschen splash
plätschern splash (about); babble; **~ an** (*acc*) (*sn*) (waves) lap against
platt flat; trite; *coll* flabbergasted; **einen P~en haben** *coll* have a flat tyre
das **Platt** (*gen* -(s)) Low German
platt-: ~deutsch, P~deutsch Low German; **der P~fisch, -e** flatfish; **die P~form, -en** platform; basis; **der P~fuß, ⸚e** flat foot/*coll* tyre; **~füßig** flat-footed
Plätt- *NGer* ironing ...
die **Platte, -n** plate (used for serving); (gramophone) record, disc; hotplate; sheet (of metal, plywood, *etc*); (rock) ledge; slab; tile; (table-)top; leaf (of table); *Aust* gang; *comput* disc; *dent, phot, print* plate; **kalte ~** selected cold meats
plätten *NGer* iron
Platten- record ...; *comput* disc ...; *elect* plate ...; **der ~see** Lake Balaton; **der ~spieler, -** record-player; **der ~teller, -** turntable; **der ~wechsler, -** record-changer
die **Plattheit, -en** flatness; platitude
plattieren *tech* plate
der **Platz, ⸚e** place (*also sp*); seat; square; room, space; *sp* ground; **~ behalten** remain seated; **~ greifen** (custom *etc*) spread; (+*dat*) **~ machen** make way for; **~ nehmen** take a seat; **den ~ tauschen mit** change places with; **fehl/nicht am ~(e)** out of place; **an seinem ~** (of thing) in place; **auf die Plätze!** on your marks!; **vom ~ stellen/verweisen** *sp* send off; **~!** (to dog) sit!; **~ da!** out of the way! || **die ~angst** agoraphobia; *coll* claustrophobia; **der ~anweiser, -** usher; **die ~anweiserin, -nen** usherette; **die ~karte, -n** seat reservation, reserved seat ticket *US*; **das ~konzert, -e** open-air concert; **der ~mangel** lack of space; **die ~patrone, -n** blank; **p~raubend** space-consuming; **der ~regen, -** cloudburst; **p~sparend** space-saving; **der ~verweis, -e** *sp* sending-off
das **Plätzchen, -** spot, little place; biscuit, cookie *US*
platzen (*sn*) burst; split; explode; *coll* fall through; (cheque) bounce; **~ vor** (*dat*) be bursting with; **vor Lachen ~** split one's sides laughing
Plauder-: das ~stündchen, - chat; **die ~tasche, -n** *coll* chatterbox
die **Plauderei, -en** chat; *journ* causerie
plaudern chat
der **Plausch** *coll*, **plauschen** *coll* chat
plausibel plausible; (+*dat*) **~ machen** put across to
Play- ['ple:-]: **das ~back** [-bɛk] playback; (singer's) miming; **der ~boy, -s** playboy; **das ~girl, -s** good-time girl
das **Plazet** [-ɛt], **-s** approval
plazieren place; land (blow); **sich ~** *sp* finish (**unter** *dat* among); **sich nicht ~ können** be unplaced
der **Plebejer, -, plebejisch** plebeian
das **Plebiszit, -e** plebiscite
pleite *coll* broke; bust; **~ gehen** go bust
die **Pleite, -n** *coll* bankruptcy; washout; **~ machen** go bust
plemplem *coll* batty
die **Plenar|sitzung, -en** plenary session
das **Plenum** plenary session
der **Pleonasmus, -(m)en** pleonasm
pleonastisch pleonastic
Pleuel-: das ~lager, - connecting-rod bearing; **die ~stange, -n** connecting-rod
das **Plexi|glas** (*trade-mark*) Perspex, Plexiglas *US*
Plinius Pliny
das **Plissee, -s** pleating; **der ~rock, ⸚e** pleated skirt
plissieren pleat
die **Plombe, -n** lead seal; *dent* filling
plombieren seal; *dent* fill
die **Plötze, -n** roach
plötzlich sudden; (*adv*) suddenly, all of a sudden; **ein bißchen/etwas ~!** look sharp!
plump clumsy; crude; **plump-vertraulich** over-familiar
plumps! bump!; plop!
der **Plumps, -e** *coll* thud; plop; **das ~klo, -s** *coll* earth-closet
plumpsen (*sn*) *coll* thud; plop
der **Plunder** junk
der **Plünderer, -** looter
plündern loot, plunder; ransack; *coll* raid (larder *etc*), strip (tree)
der **Plural, -e** plural
der **Pluralismus** pluralism
pluralistisch pluralistic
plus [-ʊs] plus
das **Plus** [-ʊs], **-** plus; profit; surplus; advantage; **der ~pol, -e** positive pole; **der ~punkt, -e** point (for team *etc*); advantage; point in s.o.'s favour; **das ~quamperfekt, -e** pluperfect (tense); **das ~zeichen, -** plus sign
der **Plüsch** [-y:-], **-e** plush; **das ~tier, -e** soft toy
plustern [-u:-]: **sich/die Federn ~** ruffle up its feathers
Pluto *myth*, **der ~** (*gen* -) *astron* Pluto
der **Plutokrat, -en** (*wk masc*) plutocrat
die **Plutokratie, -(ie)n** plutocracy
plutokratisch plutocratic
das **Plutonium** plutonium
PLZ = Postleitzahl
der **Pneu** [pnɔø, *Swiss* pnø:], **-s** *esp Aust, Swiss* tyre
pneumatisch pneumatic

der **Po**[1] (*gen* –(s)) the (River) Po
der **Po**[2], **–s** *coll* bottom
der **Pöbel** rabble, mob; **die ~herrschaft** mob rule
pöbelhaft uncouth
pochen knock; pound; throb; **~ auf** (*acc*) insist on; boast of; **es pocht** there is a knock at the door
pochieren [pɔʃ–] poach (egg)
die **Pocke, –n** pustule; (*pl*) smallpox; **die ~n|narbe, –n** pock-mark
das **Podest, –e** (*also* **der**) (low) rostrum
der **Podex, –e** *coll* posterior
das **Podium, –(i)en** rostrum; platform; **das ~s|gespräch, –e** panel discussion
die **Poesie** poetry; **p~los** pedestrian
der **Poet, –en** (*wk masc*) poet
die **Poetik** [–ɪk] poetics
poetisch poetic
das **Pogrom, –e** (*also* **der**) pogrom
die **Pointe** ['põɛ̃:tə], **–n** punch-line; *liter* climax (of novella)
pointieren [põɛ̃t–] emphasize; **pointiert** pithy
der **Pokal, –e** goblet; *sp* cup; **das ~end|spiel, –e** cup-final; **der ~sieger, –** cup-winner; **das ~spiel, –e** cup-tie
Pökel–: das ~fleisch salt meat; **der ~hering, –e** salt herring
pökeln pickle, salt; cure
das **Poker** *cards* poker; **das ~gesicht, –er** poker face
pokern play poker; **hoch ~** play for high stakes
der **Pol, –e** *astron*, *geog*, *phys* pole; **ruhender ~** calming influence
der **Polack, –en** (*wk masc*) *coll* Polack
polar polar; (views *etc*) opposite
Polar– polar ...; **der ~fuchs, ¨–e** arctic fox; **der ~kreis, –e** polar circle (**der nördliche/südliche P.** the Arctic/Antarctic Circle); **das ~licht** the polar lights; **der ~stern** the Pole Star
polarisieren, sich ~ polarize
die **Polarität, –en** polarity
der **Pole, –n** (*wk masc*) Pole
die **Polemik** [–ɪk], **–en** controversy; polemics; polemic
der **Polemiker, –** polemicist
polemisch polemical
polemisieren: ~ gegen polemicize against
Polen Poland; **noch ist ~ nicht verloren** all is not yet lost
die **Polente** *coll* the 'fuzz'
die **Police** [–sə], **–n** (insurance) policy
der **Polier, –e** *build* foreman
polieren polish
die **Poliklinik** [–ɪk], **–en** outpatients' department
Polit– political ...; **das ~büro** Politburo
die **Politesse, –n** (female) traffic warden, meter maid *US*
die **Politik** politics; policy
der **Politiker, –** politician
das **Politikum, –(k)a** political issue/matter
politisch political; **–politisch** (*eg* **handels~**) relating to (commercial *etc*) policy
politisieren politicize; make politically aware; (*v/i*) talk politics
die **Politisierung** *vbl noun*; *also* politicization
der **Politologe, –n** (*wk masc*) political scientist
die **Politologie** political science
die **Politur, –en** polish; polishing
die **Polizei** police; **der ~be|amte** (*decl as adj*) police officer; **der ~kommissar, –e** superintendent; **das ~kommissariat, –e** *Aust* = **der ~posten, –** *Swiss* police station; **der ~präsident, –en** (*wk masc*) chief constable, chief of police *US*; **das ~präsidium, –(i)en** police headquarters; **das ~revier, –e** police station; police district/precinct *US*; **der ~staat, –en** police state; **die ~stunde** closing time; **die ~wache, –n** police station
polizeilich police; (*adv*) by/(register) with the police; **~ verboten** against the law
der **Polizist, –en** (*wk masc*) policeman
die **Polizistin, –nen** policewoman
die **Polizze, –n** *Aust* (insurance) policy
die **Polka, –s** polka
der **Pollen, –** pollen
polnisch, (*language*) **P~** Polish
das **Polo** polo; **das ~hemd, –en** sports shirt
die **Polonäse, –n** polonaise
das **Polster, –** cushion (of chair *etc*); pad(ding); (financial) reserves; *coll* layer of fat
der **Polster, –/Pölster** *Aust* cushion; pillow; = **(das) Polster**
Polster– upholstered ...; padded ...; **die ~möbel** *pl* upholstered furniture; **der ~sessel, –** easy chair
der **Polsterer, –** upholsterer
polstern upholster; pad
die **Polsterung, –en** *vbl noun*; *also* upholstery
Polter–: der ~abend, –e eve-of-wedding party (with ritual breaking of crockery to bring the couple good luck); **der ~geist, –er** poltergeist
poltern bang about; make a racket; bluster; *coll* celebrate on the eve of a wedding (with a *Polterabend*); (*sn*) clatter
das **Polyäthylen** polythene, polyethylene
das **Polyeder, –** polyhedron
der **Polyester, –** polyester
polygam polygamous
die **Polygamie** polygamy
polyglott polyglot
das **Polygon, –e** polygon
Polynesien [–ĭən] Polynesia
der **Polynesier** [–ĭɐ], **–, polynesisch** Polynesian
der **Polyp, –en** (*wk masc*) polyp; *coll* cop(per); (*pl*) adenoids
polyphon polyphonic
das **Polystyrol, –e** polystyrene

das **Polytechnikum** [–ç–], **–(k)a** advanced technical college
polytechnisch [–ç–] polytechnic
die **Pomade, –n** hair-cream
pomadig (hair) slicked-down; *coll* sluggish
die **Pomeranze, –n** bitter orange
der **Pommer, –n** (*wk masc*) Pomeranian
Pommern Pomerania
pommersch Pomeranian
die **Pommes frites** [pɔm'frɪt(s)] *pl* chips, French fries *US*
der **Pomp** pomp
Pompeji Pompeii
Pompejus Pompey
pompös grandiose
das **Pontifikat, –e** (*also* **der**) pontificate
Pontius [–ts–] *coll*: **von ~ zu Pilatus** from pillar to post
der **Ponton** [pɔn'tɔ̃ː], **–s** pontoon
das **Pony** ['pɔni], **–s** pony
der **Pony** ['pɔni], **–s** = **die ~frisur, –en** fringe, bangs *US*
der **Pool** [–uː–], **–s** *econ* pool
der **Pop** [–ɔ–] *art* pop-art; *mus* pop; *in compds* pop …
der **Popanz, –e** bogey, bugbear; puppet
der **Popel, –** *coll* bogey (in nose); nobody
pop(e)lig *coll* measly; stingy
der **Popelin, die Popeline** poplin
popeln *coll*: **(in der Nase) ~** pick one's nose
der **Popo, –s** *coll* bottom
poppig *coll* pop; jazzy
populär popular; **~wissenschaftlich** (magazine *etc*) popular science
popularisieren popularize
die **Popularität** popularity
die **Pore, –n** pore
porig porous
der **Porno, –s** *coll* pornographic film/book; *in compds* pornographic …
die **Pornographie** pornography
pornographisch pornographic
porös porous
der **Porree, –s** leeks
Port–: der ~wein, –e port
das **Portal, –e** portal
Porte– [pɔrt–]: **das ~feuille** [–(ə)'føːj], **–s** *pol, fin* portfolio; *arch* wallet; **das ~monnaie** [–mɔ'neː], **–s** purse
der **Portier** [–'tieː], **–s** doorman
die **Portiere** [–'tieːrə, –ɛː–], **–n** door curtain
portieren *Swiss pol* put up (for election)
die **Portion, –en** portion, helping; *coll* amount
das **Porto, –s** postage; **p~frei** postage paid
das **Porträt** [–'trɛː], **–s** portrait
porträtieren paint a portrait of; portray; **sich ~ lassen** have one's portrait painted
Portugal ['pɔrtugal] Portugal
der **Portugiese, –n** (*wk masc*) Portuguese
portugiesisch, (*language*) **P~** Portuguese

das **Porzellan** porcelain; china; **Meißner ~** Dresden china
die **Posaune, –n** trombone
posaunen (*p/part* **posaunt**) *coll*: **in alle Welt ~** shout from the rooftops
der **Posaunist, –en** (*wk masc*) trombonist
die **Pose, –n** pose
Posen Poznan.
posieren pose; play-act
die **Position, –en** position; *comm* item; **die ~s|lichter** *pl* navigation lights
positiv positive (*also elect, math, etc*)
das **Positivum, –(v)a** positive aspect
die **Positur, –en** posture; **sich in ~ setzen/stellen/werfen** strike a pose
die **Posse, –n** farce
der **Possen, –** prank; **~ reißen** lark about || **der ~reißer, –** clown, buffoon
possenhaft farcical
possessiv *gramm* possessive; **das P~pronomen, –/..(m)ina** possessive pronoun
possierlich comical
die **Post** post, mail; post-office; *hist* mail-coach; *arch* news; **mit der ~** by post/mail; **mit getrennter ~** under separate cover
Post– post …, mail …; postal …;
das ~amt, ⸚er post office; **die ~anweisung, –en** money order (delivered by post); **der ~bote, –n** (*wk masc*) postman, mailman *US*; **das ~fach, ⸚er** P.O. box; **die ~karte, –n** postcard; **die ~kutsche, –n** mail-coach; **p~lagernd** poste restante; **die ~leit|zahl, –en** post code, zip code *US*; **das ~scheck|konto, –(t)en** Post Office giro account, postal check account *US*; **das ~schließ|fach, ⸚er** P.O. box; **die ~spar|kasse, –n** Post Office savings bank, postal savings bank *US*; **der ~stempel, –** postmark; **p~wendend** by return (of post), by return mail *US*; **das ~wert|zeichen, –** postage stamp; **das ~wesen** postal system; **die ~wurf|sendung, –en** household delivery; **der ~zug, ⸚e** mail train; **die ~zustellung, –en** postal delivery
postalisch postal
das **Postament, –e** pedestal
der **Posten, –** post, position; *mil* sentry; *comm* item; lot; **~ stehen** be on sentry-duty; **auf dem ~ sein** *coll* be in good shape; be on the ball; **nicht ganz auf dem ~ sein** *coll* be a bit under the weather; **auf verlorenem ~ stehen** be fighting a losing battle
das **Poster** ['pɔstɐ], **–** (*also* **der**) poster
postieren post (sentry *etc*); **sich ~** station oneself
der **Postler, –** *SGer coll*, **der Pöstler, –** *Swiss coll* post-office employee
das **Postskriptum, –(t)a** postscript
das **Postulat, –e** demand; *philos* postulate
postulieren demand; *philos* postulate

postum posthumous

Potemkinsch: ~e Dörfer façade

potent potent

der **Potentat, –en** (*wk masc*) potentate

das **Potential** [–ts–], **–e, potentiell** [–ts–] potential

die **Potenz, –en** power (*also math*); *physiol* potency; **zweite ~** square; **dritte ~** cube; **in die (vierte** *etc*) **~ erheben** raise to the power of (four *etc*); **in höchster ~** *coll* to the highest degree

potenzieren increase; *math* raise to a power

das **Potpourri** ['pɔtpʊri], **–s** medley

Pott–: die ~asche potash; **pott|häßlich** *coll* ugly as sin; **der ~wal, –e** sperm whale

poussieren [pu–] *dated coll* flirt

power *coll* poor; wretched

prä– pre–

die **Präambel, –n** preamble (*gen* to)

die **Pracht** splendour; magnificence; **es ist eine wahre ~, wie ...** *coll* it's really marvellous the way ...; **... daß es eine ~ ist** *coll* marvellously

Pracht– magnificent ...; **die ~ausgabe, –n** de luxe edition; **das ~exemplar, –e** splendid specimen; **der ~kerl, –e** *coll* great guy; **die ~straße, –n** boulevard; **das ~stück, –e** splendid specimen; **p~voll** magnificent

prächtig splendid, magnificent

prädestinieren predestine

das **Prädikat, –e** rating, *educ* grade, mark; grade (awarded); title (of nobility); *gramm* predicate

der **Präfekt, –en** (*wk masc*) prefect

die **Präferenz, –en** *econ* preference; **der ~zoll, ¨–e** preferential duty

das **Präfix, –e** prefix

Prag Prague

prägen mint; emboss; coin (expression); mould, shape; **~ auf** (*acc*) imprint (animal) on; (+*dat*) **sich ins Gedächtnis ~** engrave itself on (s.o.'s) memory

die **Pragmatik** [–ɪk] pragmatism (in politics *etc*)

der **Pragmatiker, –** pragmatist

pragmatisch pragmatic

pragmatisieren *Aust* appoint to the permanent staff

prägnant succinct; pithy

die **Prägung, –en** *vbl noun*; *also* character; style (*eg* **... alter/deutscher ~** old/German-style ...); (= word *etc*) coinage

prähistorisch prehistoric

Prahl–: der ~hans (*gen* **–es**), **¨–e** *coll* braggart; **die ~sucht** boastfulness

prahlen boast (**mit** about)

der **Prahler, –** boaster

die **Prahlerei, –en** boasting

prahlerisch boastful

das **Präjudiz, –e/–ien** [–ĭən] prejudice; *leg* precedent

präjudizieren prejudice

die **Praktik** [–ɪk], **–en** practice; (*pl*) (sharp) practices

praktikabel practicable

der **Praktikant, –en** (*wk masc*) student undergoing practical training, trainee

der **Praktiker, –** practical man

das **Praktikum, –(k)a** practical training

praktisch practical; (*adv*) practically; in practice; **~er Arzt** general practitioner

praktizieren put into practice; (*v/i*) (doctor *etc*) practise; *Aust* do one's practical training; **~ in** (*acc*) *coll* slip into (pocket *etc*)

der **Prälat, –en** (*wk masc*) prelate

die **Präliminarien** [–ĭən] *pl* preliminaries

die **Praline, –n, das Praliné, –s,** *Aust*, *Swiss* **das Pralinee, –s** chocolate

prall bulging; (breasts, sails, *etc*) full; (sunshine) blazing; **~ sitzen** cling to (s.o.'s) figure; **~ gefüllt** filled to bursting || **prall|voll** full to bursting; bulging

der **Prall, –e** impact

prallen: ~ auf (*acc*) (sun) beat down on; (*sn*) crash into; **~ gegen** (*sn*) bump/crash into; bounce against; (waves) beat against

die **Prämie** [–ĭə], **–n** bonus; (insurance) premium; (lottery) prize; **das ~n|sparen** Government savings scheme (with bonuses)

präm(i)ieren award a prize to; award a bonus for; **prämiiert werden** be awarded a prize

die **Prämisse, –n** premise

prangen be resplendent; be boldly displayed

der **Pranger, –** *hist*, **an den ~ stellen** pillory

die **Pranke, –n** (tiger's *etc*) paw

das **Präparat, –e** preparation; *biol*, *med* specimen

präparieren prepare; *biol*, *med* dissect; preserve; **sich ~** prepare (for lesson)

die **Präposition, –en** preposition

präpositional prepositional

präpotent *Aust* arrogant

die **Präpotenz** *Aust* arrogance

die **Prärie, –(ie)n** prairie

das **Präsens** [–ɛns] (*gen* **–**) present (tense)

präsent present; (+*dat*) **nicht ~ sein** (name *etc*) escape

das **Präsent, –e** present

der **Präsentator, –(or)en** *TV* presenter

Präsentier–: ~teller *coll* **(wie auf dem P. sitzen** be exposed to the gaze of all and sundry)

präsentieren present; (+*dat of pers*) present with; **sich ~** present oneself; **präsentiert das Gewehr!** present arms!

die **Präsenz** presence; **die ~bibliothek, –en** reference library; **der ~dienst** *Aust* military service; **die ~stärke** effective strength

das **Präservativ, –e** (contraceptive) sheath

der **Präses** [–ɛs] (*gen* **–**), *pl* **Präsides** [–eːs]/**Präsiden** *Prot* head (of synod)

der **Präsident, –en** (*wk masc*) president; *in*

compds ~**en**– presidential ...
die **Präsidentschaft** presidency
präsidial presidential
präsidieren (+*dat*) preside over
das **Präsidium, –(i)en** chairmanship; committee; (police) headquarters; *pol* (in Communist countries) praesidium
prasseln beat down; (fire *etc*) crackle; ~ **auf** (*acc*) (*sn*) beat down on; ~ **gegen** (*sn*) beat against; ~**d** (applause) thunderous
prassen live in luxury
der **Prätendent, –en** (*wk masc*) pretender
prätentiös [–ts–] pretentious
das **Präteritum, –(t)a** preterite
präventiv preventive; *in compds* **P~–** preventive ...
die **„Prawda"** 'Pravda'
die **Praxis, –(x)en** practice; (practical) experience; *leg, med* practice; *leg* (lawyer's) office, *med* surgery, doctor's office *US*; **in der** ~ in practice; **in die** ~ **umsetzen** put into practice || **p~nah(e)** based on practical experience
der **Präzedenz|fall, ¨–e** precedent
präzis(e) precise
präzisieren state more precisely
die **Präzision** precision; **die** ~**s|arbeit, –en** precision work
predigen (*also v/i*) preach
der **Prediger, –** preacher
die **Predigt, –en** sermon
der **Preis, –e** price; prize; *poet* praise; **der Große** ~ **von (Italien** *etc*) the (Italian *etc*) Grand Prix; **im** ~ (go up/down) in price; **um jeden** ~ at all costs; **um keinen** ~ not at any price; **unterm** ~ cut-price || **der** ~**anstieg, –e** price rise; **das** ~**ausschreiben, –** competition; **die** ~**bindung** retail price maintenance, fair trade *US*; **die** ~**erhöhung, –en** price rise; **die** ~**frage, –n** question of price; question set for a competition; *coll* sixty-four thousand dollar question; **die** ~**gabe** abandoning; surrender; giving away; **p~geben*** (*sep*) abandon; surrender; give away; (+*dat*) expose to; **p~gekrönt** prize-winning; (stallion *etc*) prize; **das** ~**gericht, –e** jury (for competition); **p~günstig** inexpensive; **die** ~**kontrolle, –n** price control; **die** ~**lage, –n** price range (**in jeder P.** at all prices); **die** ~**liste, –n** price-list; **das** ~**rätsel, –** prize competition; **der** ~**richter, –** judge (in competition); **das** ~**schild, –er** price-tag; **der** ~**schlager, –** bargain offer; **die** ~**senkung, –en** price cut; **die** ~**steigerung, –en** price rise; **der** ~**stopp, –s** price freeze; **der** ~**sturz, ¨–e** sudden drop in prices; **der** ~**träger, –** prizewinner; **der** ~**treiber, –** person who forces up prices; **p~wert** inexpensive; (that is) good value (**p~wertes Angebot** bargain)
die **Preisel|beere, –n** cranberry
preisen (*p/t* **pries,** *p/part* **gepriesen**) praise; **sich glücklich** ~ count oneself lucky
preislich price; (*also adv*) in price
prekär awkward; precarious
Prell–: der ~**bock, ¨–e** scapegoat; *rail* buffer, bumper *US*; **der** ~**schuß, ¨–(ss)e** ricochet
prellen bruise; *coll* cheat (**um** out of); **die Zeche** ~ leave without paying the bill
die **Prellung, –en** bruise
der **Premier** [prəˈmĭeː], **–s** premier; **der** ~**minister, –** prime minister
die **Premiere** [prəˈmĭeːrə, –ɛː–], **–n** première
der **Presbyterianer, –, presbyterianisch** Presbyterian
preschen (*sn*) dash
Preß–: das ~**glas** pressed glass; **die** ~**luft** compressed air; **der** ~**luft|bohrer, –** pneumatic drill
Preßburg Bratislava
die **Presse, –n** press; *coll* (= school) crammer; **eine gute** *etc* ~ **haben** have a good *etc* press || **die** ~**freiheit** freedom of the press; **die** ~**konferenz, –en** press conference; **die** ~**stelle, –n** press office; **die** ~**stimmen** *pl* press comment; **das** ~**wesen** journalism
pressen press
pressieren *SGer coll* be pressing; **mir pressiert es** I'm in a hurry
die **Pression, –en** pressure (brought to bear)
die **Pressure-group** [ˈprɛʃəgruːp], **–s** pressure group
das **Prestige** [–ʒə] prestige; **der** ~**verlust, –e** loss of prestige
die **Pretiosen** [–ts–] *pl* valuables
der **Preuße, –n** (*wk masc*) Prussian; **so schnell schießen die** ~**n nicht** *coll* these things take time
Preußen Prussia
preußisch Prussian
preziös precious, affected
prickeln tingle; bubble; ~**d** *also* piquant; thrilling; titillating; ~**der Reiz** thrill
der **Priel, –e** channel (in mud-flats)
der **Priem, –e** plug of tobacco
priemen chew tobacco
pries *p/t of* **preisen**
der **Priester, –** priest; **die** ~**weihe, –n** ordination
die **Priesterin, –nen** priestess
priesterlich priestly
die **Priesterschaft** priesthood
Prim–: die ~**zahl, –en** prime number
prima (*indecl*) *comm* first-class; *coll* 'great'
die **Prima, –(m)en** (*eighth* **(Unter~)** *and ninth* **(Ober~)** *years of the* Gymnasium)
die **Primadonna, –(nn)en** prima donna
der **Primaner, –** pupil in the *Prima*
Primar–: die ~**schule, –n** *Swiss* primary school
primär primary

der **Primas** [–as], **–se/Primaten** *eccles* primate; *mus* leader (of gypsy band)
das **Primat, –e** (*also* **der**) primacy
der **Primat, –en** (*wk masc*) *zool* primate
die **Primel, –n** primula; primrose
primitiv primitive; crude
die **Primitivität** primitiveness; crudity
der **Primitivling, –e** *coll* primitive person
der **Primus, –se/Primi** top pupil in the class
die **Printe, –n** (*oblong-shaped gingerbread biscuit/cookie US*)
der **Prinz, –en** (*wk masc*) prince; **der ~gemahl, –e** prince consort
die **Prinzessin, –nen** princess
das **Prinzip, –ien** [–ĭən] principle; **aus ~** on principle; as a matter of principle; **im ~** in principle; **Mann mit ~ien** man of principle
prinzipiell (*also adv*) on/in principle
Prinzipien– [–ĭən–]: **die ~frage, –n** matter of principle; **p~los** unprincipled; **der ~reiter, –** person who sticks inflexibly to his principles
der **Prior, –(or)en** prior
die **Priorität, –en** priority; (*pl*) *comm* preference shares, preferred stock *US*
die **Prise, –n** pinch (of snuff *etc*)
das **Prisma, –(m)en** prism
prismatisch prismatic
die **Pritsche, –n** plank bed; platform (of truck); **der ~n|wagen, –** platform truck
privat private; (*adv*) privately, in private; *in compds* **P~–** private ...; **der P~dozent, –en** (*wk masc*) (non-salaried) university lecturer; **das P~leben** private life; privacy; **die P~sphäre** privacy
privatim [–ɪm] privately; in confidence
privatisieren privatize, transfer to private ownership; (*v/i*) live on private means
das **Privileg, –ien** [–ĭən] privilege
privilegiert privileged
pro (+*acc*) per; **das Pro und Kontra** the pros and cons
probat tried
die **Probe, –n** test; sample; *mus*, *theat* rehearsal; **die ~ aufs Exempel machen** put it to the test; **auf ~** (employ) on a trial basis; **auf die ~ stellen** (put to the) test; tax (patience); **zur ~** on trial
Probe– test ...; trial ...; specimen ...; probationary ...; **p~fahren** (*only infin and p/part* **p~gefahren**) test-drive; (*v/i sn*) go for a test-drive; **die ~fahrt, –en** test-drive; **das ~stück, –e** specimen; sample; **p~weise** on a trial basis; **die ~zeit, –en** probationary/trial period
proben (*also v/i*) rehearse
probieren try; try (out); try, taste
das **Problem, –e** problem; **p~los** problem-free; (*adv*) without any problems; **p~orientiert** *comput* problem-oriented; **die ~stellung, –en** formulation of a problem; problem
die **Problematik** [–ɪk] problematic nature; problems
problematisch problematic
pro domo on one's own behalf
das **Produkt, –e** product; (*pl*) *agr* produce
die **Produktion, –en** production; **der ~s|ausfall, ⸗e** loss of production; **die ~s|genossenschaft, –en** *EGer* co-operative; **die ~s|mittel** *pl* means of production
produktiv productive (*also ling*)
die **Produktivität** productivity
der **Produzent, –en** (*wk masc*) producer (*also cin*)
produzieren produce; *coll* create (noise *etc*); trot out (excuse); **sich ~** show off
profan secular; mundane
professionell professional
der **Professionist, –en** (*wk masc*) *Aust* craftsman
der **Professor, –(or)en** professor; *Aust* teacher at a *Gymnasium*
professoral professorial
die **Professur, –en** (university) chair
der **Profi, –s** *coll* pro
das **Profil, –e** profile; (of tyre, sole of shoe) tread; image; personality; *tech* section; **im ~** in profile
profilieren: sich ~ make one's mark; **profiliert** clear-cut; distinguished
der **Profit, –e** profit; **mit ~** at a profit || **die ~gier** greed for profit
profitabel profitable
profitieren profit (**von** from)
pro forma for form's sake
profund profound
die **Prognose, –n** prognosis; forecast (*also meteor*)
prognostizieren prognosticate, predict
das **Programm, –e** programme; (publisher's) list; *TV* channel; *comput* program; **p~gemäß** according to plan; **die ~gestaltung** programme planning; **das ~heft, –e** programme
die **Programmatik** [–ɪk] declared aims
programmatisch programmatic
Programmier–: die ~sprache, –n programming language
programmieren *comput* program; **programmiert auf** (*acc*) conditioned to; **programmierter Unterricht** programmed instruction
der **Programmierer, –** *comput* programmer
die **Programmierung** *comput* programming
progressiv progressive; (tax) graduated
das **Projekt, –e** project, scheme
projektieren project (road *etc*)
die **Projektion, –en** projection (*also geog*, *math*)
der **Projektor, –(or)en** projector
projizieren project (*also psych*) (**auf** *acc* onto)

^die **Proklamation, –en** proclamation
proklamieren proclaim
Prokofjew [–ɛf] Prokofiev
^das **Prokrustes|bett** [–ɛs–] Procrustean bed
^die **Prokura, –(r)en** power of attorney
^der **Prokurist, –en** (*wk masc*) attorney
^der **Prolet, –en** (*wk masc*) *coll* prole
^das **Proletariat, –e** proletariat
^der **Proletarier** [–ĭɐ], –, **proletarisch** proletarian
proletarisieren proletarianize
proletenhaft plebeian
^der **Prolog, –e** prologue
^die **Promenade, –n** promenade; **die ~n|mischung, –en** *joc* mongrel
promenieren (*sn if indicating direction*) take a stroll
^das **Promille** [–ə], – thousandth; *coll* alcohol level (of blood); **die ~grenze, –n** maximum permitted alcohol level
prominent prominent; **der/die Prominente** (*decl as adj*) V.I.P.
^die **Prominenz** (*collect*) prominent figures
^die **Promiskuität** promiscuity
^die **Promotion, –en** conferment of/obtaining a doctorate
promovieren obtain a doctorate
prompt prompt
^das **Pronomen, –/Pronomina** pronoun
prononciert [–ɔ̃s–] staunch; pronounced
^die **Propaganda** propaganda
^der **Propagandist, –en** (*wk masc*) *pol* propagandist; *comm* demonstrator
propagandistisch propagandistic
propagieren advocate; propagate
^das **Propan|gas** propane gas
^der **Propeller, –** propeller; **die ~turbine, –n** turboprop
proper [–ɔ–] *coll* tidy, neat
^der **Prophet, –en** (*wk masc*) prophet
^die **Prophetie, –(ie)n** prophecy
prophetisch prophetic
prophezeien (*p/part* **prophezeit**) prophesy; predict
^die **Prophezeiung, –en** prophecy; prediction
^die **Proportion, –en** proportion
proportional proportional, proportionate
proportioniert: gut ~ well-proportioned
^der **Proporz, –e** proportional distribution of posts (in accordance with the number of votes cast or on the basis of denominational, regional, *etc* representation); *Aust, Swiss* = **die ~wahl** *Aust, Swiss* proportional representation
proppen|voll *coll* chock-full
^der **Propst** [–oː–], **⸚e** provost
^die **Prosa** prose
^der **Prosaiker, –** prosaic person; *arch* prose writer
prosaisch prosaic
^der **Prosaist, –en** (*wk masc*) prose-writer

prosit [–zɪt]: **~!** cheers!; (*to sneezer*) bless you!; **~ Neujahr!** a happy New Year to you!; **das Prosit, –s** toast
^der **Prospekt, –e** brochure; prospectus; *art* perspective view; *theat* backdrop
prosperieren prosper
^die **Prosperität** prosperity
prost! [–oː–] = **prosit!** (*see also* **Mahlzeit**)
^die **Prostata** [–ɔ–], **–(t)ae** [–tɛː] prostate gland
prostituieren: sich ~ prostitute oneself; **die Prostituierte** (*decl as adj*) prostitute
^die **Prostitution** prostitution
^das **Proszenium, –(i)en** proscenium
protegieren [–ʒ–] favour, pull strings for
^das **Protein, –e** protein
^die **Protektion** patronage
^das **Protektorat, –e** patronage; *pol* protectorate
^der **Protest, –e** protest; **~ erheben** make a protest (**gegen** against)
^der **Protestant, –en** (*wk masc*), **protestantisch** Protestant
^der **Protestantismus** Protestantism
protestieren protest
^die **Prothese, –n** artificial limb; *dent* dentures; **–prothese** artificial …
^das **Protokoll, –e** minutes; record; (diplomatic) protocol; *comput* printout; **(das) ~ führen** take the minutes; **zu ~ geben** make (statement) || **der ~chef, –s** chief of protocol; **der ~führer, –** person who takes the minutes
protokollarisch on record; minuted; (rules *etc*) of protocol; (*adv*) in the minutes; as regards protocol
protokollieren take down; record; (*v/i*) take the minutes
^das **Proton** [–ɔn], **–(on)en** proton
^das **Protoplasma** protoplasm
^der **Prototyp, –en** archetype; *tech* prototype
^das **Protozoon** [–ɔn], **–(o)en** protozoon
^der **Protz, –e** (*or* **–en** (*wk masc*)) *coll* show-off
protzen *coll* show off; **~ mit** show off, flaunt
protzig *coll* showy
^die **Provence** [prɔ'vɑ̃ːs] Provence
^die **Provenienz, –en** provenance
^der **Provenzale** [provɛnts–, –vɑ̃s–], **–n** (*wk masc*), **provenzalisch** Provençal
^der **Proviant** provisions (for journey)
^die **Provinz, –en** province; **die ~** the provinces
Provinz– provincial …
provinziell provincial
^der **Provinzler, –** (narrow-minded) provincial
provinzlerisch (outlook *etc*) provincial
^die **Provision, –en** *comm* commission; **auf ~** on commission
provisorisch provisional
^das **Provisorium, –(i)en** temporary arrangement
provokant provocative
^der **Provokateur** [–'tøːɐ], **–e** agent provocateur
^die **Provokation, –en** provocation
provokatorisch provocative

provozieren provoke; ~**d** provocative
die **Prozedur, -en** procedure (*also comput*); rigmarole
das **Prozent, -e**/(*following num*) – per cent; (*pl*) *coll* percentage; discount; **der ~satz, ⸚e** percentage
-prozentig ... per cent
prozentual, *Aust* **prozentuell** percentage; (*adv*) in percentage terms; as a percentage; **~ beteiligt sein an** (*dat*) receive a percentage of
der **Prozeß, -(ss)e** process; *leg* trial; lawsuit; (+*dat*) **den ~ machen** bring an action against; **kurzen ~ machen mit** *coll* make short work of
prozessieren go to court; **~ gegen** bring an action against
die **Prozession, -en** *eccles* procession
der **Prozessor, -(or)en** *comput* processor
prüde prudish
die **Prüderie** prudery, prudishness
Prüf- testing ...; test ...; **der ~stein, -e** touchstone; **die ~stelle, -n** testing-station
prüfen check (**auf** *acc* for); test (for); inspect; examine; scrutinize; (fate *etc*) try; *comm* audit; *educ* examine (**in** *dat* in); **sich ~** search one's heart; **geprüft** qualified; **schwer geprüft** sorely-tried
prüfend (glance) searching
der **Prüfer, -** examiner
der **Prüfling, -e** examinee
die **Prüfung, -en** examination; inspection; check; trial, ordeal; **die ~s|kommission, -en** board of examiners
der **Prügel, -** club; (*pl*) beating; **der ~knabe, -n** (*wk masc*) whipping-boy, scapegoat; **die ~strafe, -n** corporal punishment
die **Prügelei, -en** fight
prügeln beat; **sich ~ (mit)** fight
der **Prunk** splendour; pomp; **das ~gemach, ⸚er** stateroom; **das ~stück, -e** showpiece; **die ~sucht** love of ostentation; **p~voll** magnificent
prunken be resplendent; **~ mit** flaunt
prusten [-uː-] splutter; snort
PS (= **Pferdestärke**) h.p., (= **Postskriptum**) P.S.
der **Psalm, -en** psalm
der **Psalter, -** psalter
pseudo- pseudo-
das **Pseudonym, -e** pseudonym
pst! sh!
die **Psyche** [-çə], **-n** psyche; *Aust arch* dressing-table
der **Psychiater** [-ç-], **-** psychiatrist
die **Psychiatrie** [-ç-] psychiatry
psychiatrieren [-ç-] *Aust* give (s.o.) a psychiatric examination
psychiatrisch [-ç-] psychiatric
psychisch [-ç-] psychological; mental; psychic
die **Psycho|analyse** [-ç-] psychoanalysis
der **Psycho|analytiker** [-ç-], **-** psychoanalyst
psycho|analytisch [-ç-] psychoanalytical
der **Psychologe** [-ç-], **-n** (*wk masc*) psychologist
die **Psychologie** [-ç-] psychology
psychologisch [-ç-] psychological
der **Psychopath** [-ç-], **-en** (*wk masc*) psychopath
psychopathisch [-ç-] psychopathic
die **Psychose** [-ç-], **-n** psychosis
der **Psychotherapeut** [-ç-], **-en** (*wk masc*) psychotherapist
die **Psychotherapie** [-ç-] psychotherapy
psychotisch [-ç-] psychotic
ptolemäisch Ptolemaic
Ptolemäus Ptolemy
pubertär pubertal; adolescent
die **Pubertät** puberty
pubertieren reach the age of puberty
die **Publicity** [pa'blɪsɪti] publicity
die **Public relations** ['pablɪk rɪ'leːʃəns] *pl* public relations
publik public; **~ werden** become public knowledge
die **Publikation, -en** publication
das **Publikum** public; audience; readership; clientele; *sp* crowd; **p~s|wirksam** with public appeal
publizieren publish
der **Publizist, -en** (*wk masc*) (*esp* political) journalist
die **Publizistik** [-ɪk] journalism; study of the mass media
publizistisch journalistic
die **Publizität** publicity (= state of being widely known)
der **Pudding, -s** blancmange; instant whip
der **Pudel, -** poodle; **des ~s Kern** the crux of the matter; **wie ein begossener ~ dastehen** *coll* look sheepish || **die ~mütze, -n** bobble-cap; **pudel|nackt** *coll* stark naked; **pudel|naß** *coll* soaking wet; **pudel|wohl** *coll* (**sich p. fühlen** feel great)
der **Puder, -** (face, talcum, *etc*) powder; **die ~dose, -n** compact; **die ~quaste, -n** powder-puff; **der ~zucker** icing sugar, confectioner's sugar *US*
puderig powdery
pudern powder; **sich ~** powder oneself
puff! bang!
der **Puff**[1], **-e** pouffe; (upholstered) linen-basket
der **Puff**[2], **⸚e** *coll* thump; nudge; dig (in ribs)
der **Puff**[3], **-s** (*also* **das**) *coll* whorehouse
Puff-: der ~ärmel, - puff(ed) sleeve; **der ~mais** popcorn; **die ~mutter, ..mütter** *coll* madam; **die ~otter, -n** puff-adder; **der ~reis** puffed rice
puffen[1] (*sn if indicating locomotion*) puff
puffen[2] *coll* thump; nudge; dig (in ribs)
der **Puffer**[1], **-** potato pancake

der **Puffer²,** – *rail* buffer, bumper *US*; *comput* buffer; **der ~staat, -en** buffer state; **die ~zone, -n** buffer zone

puh! phew!; ugh!

der **Pulk, -s** group, bunch

die **Pulle, -n** *coll* bottle

der **Pulli, -s** *coll* = **der Pullover** [pʊ'loːvɐ], – pullover

Pullman- [-man-]: **die ~kappe, -n** *Aust* beret; **der ~wagen,** – Pullman car

der **Pullunder** [pʊ'lʊndɐ], – tank top

der **Puls, -e** pulse; **die ~ader, -n** artery; **der ~schlag, ⸗e** pulse-beat

der **Pulsar, -e** pulsar

pulsen, pulsieren pulsate; throb

das **Pult, -e** lectern; desk

das **Pulver** [-f-, -v-], – powder; **sein ~ verschossen haben** have shot one's bolt || **das ~faß, ⸗(ss)er** powder keg (**(wie) auf einem P. sitzen** be sitting on top of a volcano); **der ~kaffee** instant coffee; **der ~schnee** powder snow

pulv(e)rig [-f-, -v-] powdery

pulverisieren pulverize

der **Puma, -s** puma

der **Pummel,** – *coll* = **das Pummelchen,** – *coll* roly-poly

pumm(e)lig *coll* chubby

der **Pump** *coll* credit; **auf ~** on tick

die **Pumpe, -n** pump

pumpen pump; (+*dat*) *coll* lend; (*also* + **sich** *dat*) *coll* borrow (**bei/von** from)

der **Pumpen|schwengel,** – pump-handle

pumpern *Aust coll* thump

der **Pumpernickel** ⁻ pumpernickel (*Westphalian rye-bread*)

der **Pumps** [-œ-] (*gen* -), – court-shoe, pump *US*

der **Punching|ball** ['pantʃ-], ⸗e punchball, punching bag *US*

der **Punkt, -e** point; dot; item (on agenda *etc*); *gramm* full stop, period *esp US*; *print* point; ~/*Aust, Swiss* **p~** (**12** *etc*) **Uhr** at (12 *etc*) o'clock sharp; **den toten ~ überwinden** break the deadlock; get one's second wind; **auf einem toten ~ ankommen** reach deadlock; **wunder ~** sore point; **in diesem ~** on this point; **nach ~en** on points || **p~gleich** *sp* level (on points); **die ~gleichheit** level score; **die ~niederlage, -n** points defeat; **der ~richter,** – *sp* judge; **die ~schrift** Braille; **p~schweißen** (*only infin and p/part* **p~geschweißt**) spot-weld; **der ~sieg, -e** points win; **das ~spiel, -e** league match; **der ~streik, -s** selective strike; **die ~wertung, -en** points system; **die ~zahl** score

punktieren dot; prick out (pattern); *med* puncture; **punktierte Linie** dotted line

die **Punktion, -en** *med* puncture

pünktlich punctual; *arch* meticulous; (*adv*) punctually; on time

die **Pünktlichkeit** punctuality; *arch* meticulousness

punktuell relating to a specific point/specific points; selective

Punktum: und damit ~! and that's that!

der **Punsch, -e** (hot) punch

die **Punze, -n, punzen** *tech* punch

der **Pup, -e** *coll* rude noise

pupen *coll* make a rude noise

die **Pupille, -n** pupil (of eye)

die **Puppe, -n** doll (*also coll* = girl); puppet; dummy; *zool* pupa, chrysalis; **bis in die ~n** *coll* till all hours

Puppen- doll's ...; puppet ...; **das ~haus, ⸗er** doll's house, dollhouse *US*; **das ~spiel, -e** puppet show; **der ~spieler,** – puppeteer; **das ~stadium** chrysalid stage

der **Pups** [-uː-], **-e** *coll* = **Pup**

pupsen [-uː-] *coll* = **pupen**

pur pure; sheer; (drink) neat

das **Püree, -s** purée; mashed potatoes

pürieren liquidize

der **Purismus** purism

der **Purist, -en** (*wk masc*), **puristisch** purist

der **Puritaner,** – Puritan

puritanisch Puritan; puritanical

der **Puritanismus** Puritanism

der **Purpur, p~farben = p~rot** crimson

purpurn crimson

der **Purzel|baum, ⸗e** somersault; **einen ~ machen/schießen/schlagen** do a somersault

purzeln (*sn*) tumble

Puschkin [-iːn] Pushkin

pusselig *coll* fussy

pusseln *coll* fuss about; **~ an** (*dat*) fiddle about with

die **Puste** [-uː-] *coll* puff; **außer ~** puffed; **mir geht die ~ aus** I'm running out of puff/steam || **die ~blume, -n** *coll* dandelion; **~kuchen** *coll* (**(ja,) P.!** some hopes!); **das ~rohr, -e** *coll* pea-shooter

die **Pustel, -n** pustule

pusten [-uː-] *coll* blow; (*v/i*) blow; be breathalysed; puff

die **Pute, -n** turkey (hen); **dumme ~** *coll* silly creature

der **Puter,** – turkey (cock); **puter|rot** as red as a beetroot

der **Putsch, -e** putsch; **der ~versuch, -e** attempted coup

putschen revolt

der **Putschist, -en** (*wk masc*) rebel

die **Putte, -n** putto

der **Putz** finery; *build* plaster; **die ~frau, -en** cleaner; **der ~lappen,** – cloth; **die ~macherin, -nen** milliner; **das ~mittel,** – cleanser, cleansing agent; **der ~teufel,** – *coll* woman obsessed with housework; **das ~zeug** cleaning things

putzen clean; trim (wick); groom (horse); *dated* decorate; *Aust* dry-clean; *build* plaster; **sich** *dat* **die Nase ~** blow one's nose; **sich** *dat* **die Zähne ~** clean one's teeth; **sich ~** dress up; (bird) preen itself, (cat) wash

die **Putzerei, –en** *Aust* dry cleaners

putzig cute; funny, odd

puzzeln ['paz–] do a jigsaw/jigsaws

das **Puzzle** ['pazl], **–s = das ~spiel, –e** jigsaw (puzzle); **der ~stein, –e** jigsaw piece

der **Pygmäe, –n** (*wk masc*) pygmy

der **Pyjama** [–dʒ–], **–s** (pair of) pyjamas, pajamas *US*

die **Pyramide, –n** pyramid

die **Pyrenäen** *pl* the Pyrenees; **die ~halb|insel** the Iberian Peninsula

pyrenäisch Pyrenean

der **Pyrrhus|sieg** ['pʏrʊs–], **–e** Pyrrhic victory

Pythagoras [–as] Pythagoras

pythagoräisch *Aust*, **pythagoreisch** Pythagorean

der **Python** [–ɔn], **–s/Pythonen = die ~schlange, –n** python

Q

^das^ **Q** [kuː, *Aust* kveː] (*gen, pl* –, *coll* [kuːs, *Aust* kveːs]) Q; **q...** (= **Quadrat–**) sq. (*eg* **qm** sq. m.), *now officially replaced by* ² (*eg* **m²**)
quabb(e)lig *coll* flabby; wobbly; (frog) slimy
quabbeln *coll* wobble
Quack–: der ~salber, – quack; **die ~salberei** quackery
^der^ **Quader, –** cuboid; = **der ~stein, –e** ashlar
^der^ **Quadrant, –en** (*wk masc*) quadrant
^das^ **Quadrat, –e** square; (**... Meter** *etc*) **im ~** ... square; **ins ~ erheben** square; (**drei** *etc*) **zum ~** ... squared
Quadrat– square (metre, mile, *etc*); **die ~latschen** *pl coll* clodhoppers; **der ~schädel, –** *coll* big square head; pigheaded person; **die ~wurzel, –n** square root
quadratisch square; *math* quadratic
^die^ **Quadratur, –en** quadrature; squaring (of circle)
quadrieren square
^die^ **Quadrille** [ka'drɪljə], **–n** quadrille
quak! quack!; croak!
quaken quack; croak
quäken squawk; screech
^der^ **Quäker, –** Quaker
^die^ **Qual, –en** agony; anguish; **unter großen ~en** in agony || **q~voll** agonizing
Quäl–: der ~geist, –er *coll* pest
quälen (*see also* **gequält**) torment; torture; pester; **sich ~** torment oneself; struggle; **~d** agonizing; excruciating
^die^ **Quälerei, –en** torture; agony, torment; drudgery
quälerisch tormenting
^die^ **Qualifikation, –en** qualification; *sp* qualifying contest/match/round; *in compds* **~s–** *sp* qualifying ...
qualifizieren qualify (**zu** for, as); **~ als** describe as; **sich ~** qualify (*also sp*) (**zu** as)
^die^ **Qualität, –en** quality (*also ling*); **die ~s|ware, –n** quality product; (*pl*) quality goods; **der ~s|wein, –e** quality wine
qualitativ qualitative; (*adv*) in quality
^die^ **Qualle, –n** jellyfish
^der^ **Qualm** (thick) smoke
qualmen (*coll in 1st sense*) puff away at; (*v/i*) (give off) smoke; *coll* (person) smoke; **es qualmt** there is smoke
qualmig smoky
^das^ **Quant, –en** quantum; *in compds* **~en–** quantum ...

^die^ **Quantität, –en** quantity (*also ling*)
quantitativ quantitative; (*adv*) in quantity
^das^ **Quantum, –(t)en** quantity; share, quota
^die^ **Quappe, –n** tadpole
^die^ **Quarantäne** [ka–], **–n** quarantine; **in ~** in quarantine; **unter ~ stellen** quarantine
^der^ **Quark** quark (*type of low-fat soft cheese*); *coll* rubbish; trifle; **die ~speise, –n** quark dessert
^das^ **Quart** quarto
^die^ **Quarta, –(t)en** (*third year of the* Gymnasium)
^das^ **Quartal, –e** quarter (of year); **der ~s|säufer, –** *coll* periodic heavy drinker
^der^ **Quartaner, –** pupil in the *Quarta*
quartär Quaternary; **das Quartär** the Quaternary
^die^ **Quarte, –n** *mus* fourth
^das^ **Quartett, –e** quartet
^das^ **Quartier, –e** accommodation, *mil* quarters, billet; *Aust dated, Swiss* part (of town)
^der^ **Quarz** [–aː–], **–e** quartz
^der^ **Quasar, –e** quasar
quasi virtually; *in compds* quasi–
Quassel–: die ~strippe, –n *coll* chatterbox; phone
quasseln *coll* chatter, jabber
^die^ **Quaste, –n** tassel
^die^ **Quästur, –en** *univ* bursary
^der^ **Quatsch** *coll* nonsense; rubbish; **~ machen** mess about; go wrong; **mach keinen ~!** don't be daft!; don't do anything silly! || **der ~kopf, ⸚e** *coll* windbag; **quatsch|naß** *coll* soaking wet
quatschen¹ *coll* talk nonsense; chat; talk (= reveal a secret); **Unsinn ~** talk nonsense
quatschen² *coll* squelch
Queck–: das ~silber mercury; **q~silb(e)rig** fidgety, restless
^die^ **Quecke, –n** couch-grass
^der^ **Quell, –e** *poet* = **Quelle; das ~wasser** spring water
^die^ **Quelle, –n** spring; source; **an der ~ sitzen** *coll* have direct access (to goods, information); **aus amtlicher/zuverlässiger ~** from an official/a reliable source
quellen (quill(s)t, *p/t* **quoll** (*subj* **quölle**), *p/part* **gequollen**) (*sn*) (peas, wood, *etc*) swell; **~ aus** pour from; well from; bulge out over; (eyes) pop out of; **~ durch** pour through
^die^ **Quellen|angabe, –n** citing of sources; (*pl*)

works consulted

der **Queller, –** glasswort

queng(e)lig *coll* whining

quengeln *coll* whine

das **Quentchen, –** little bit

quer crosswise; diagonally; at right angles (**zu** to); **~ durch/über** (*acc*) (right) through/across

Quer– cross ...; transverse ...;

der ~balken, – cross-beam; transom; **q~feld|ein, der ~feld|einlauf, ⸚e** cross-country; **die ~frage, –n** interposed question; **q~gehen*** (*sep*; *sn*) *coll* go wrong; **der ~kopf, ⸚e** *coll* awkward customer; **q~köpfig** *coll* wrong-headed; **die ~latte, –n** crossbar; **q~legen** (*sep*): **sich q.** *coll* be awkward; **das ~ruder, –** aileron; **q~schießen*** (*sep*) *coll* throw a spanner in the works/a monkey wrench into things *US*; **das ~schiff, –e** transept; **der ~schläger, –** ricocheting bullet *etc*; **der ~schnitt, –e** cross-section (**durch** of); **q~schnitt(s)|gelähmt** paraplegic; **die ~schnitt(s)|lähmung** paraplegia; **der ~schuß, ⸚(ss)e** *coll* spanner in the works, monkey wrench *US*; **die ~straße, –n** road/street crossing another; (first *etc*) turning; **der ~treiber, –** *coll* awkward customer (who tries to thwart others' plans); **die ~verbindung, –en** connection, link; **der ~verweis, –e** cross-reference

Quere: (+*dat*) **in die ~ kommen** *coll* cross (s.o.'s) path; get in (s.o.'s) way; **der ~ nach** across; widthwise

die **Querelen** *pl* squabbles

queren cross

der **Querulant, –en** (*wk masc*) grumbler

querulieren grumble

Quetsch–: die ~kommode, –n *coll* squeeze-box; **die ~wunde, –n** bruise

quetschen squeeze; crush, squash; **~ in** (*acc*) squeeze into; **sich ~** catch one's finger *etc* (in door *etc*); squeeze (into *etc* sth.)

die **Quetschung, –en** bruise

das **Queue** [kø:], **–s** *bill* cue

quick|lebendig *coll* very lively; sprightly

quiek! squeak!

quiek(s)en squeal; squeak; **... ist zum Quieken** *coll* ... is a scream

der **Quiekser, –** *coll* squeal; squeak

quietsch– *coll*: **~fidel = ~vergnügt** as happy as a sandboy

quietschen squeal; squeak

quill *imp sing*, **quill(s)t** (*2nd,*) *3rd sing pres of* **quellen**

die **Quinta, –(t)en** (*second year of the* Gymnasium)

der **Quintaner, –** pupil in the *Quinta*

die **Quinte, –n** *mus* fifth

die **Quintessenz, –en** essence

das **Quintett, –e** quintet

der **Quirl, –e** whisk (with star-shaped head); *bot* whorl; *coll* live wire

quirlen whisk; (*v/i*) (*sn if indicating direction*) swirl

quirlig *coll* very lively

der **Quisling, –e** quisling

quitt quits

die **Quitte, –n** quince

quittieren receipt; sign for; **~ mit** receive with; greet with; **den Dienst ~** resign

die **Quittung, –en** receipt (**für/über** *acc* for); penalty (for); what you *etc* get (for); **gegen ~** on production of a receipt

Quivive [ki'vi:f] *coll*: **auf dem ~** on the alert

das **Quiz** [kvɪs] (*gen* –), **–** quiz; **der ~master** [–ma:stɐ], **–** quizmaster

quoll (quölle) *p/t* (*subj*) *of* **quellen**

die **Quote, –n** quota; proportion; (accident, failure, *etc*) rate

der **Quotient** [–ts–], **–en** (*wk masc*) quotient

R

^das^ **R** [ɛr] (*gen, pl* –, *coll* [ɛrs]) R
^der^ **Rabạtt, –e** discount; **die ~marke, –n** trading stamp
^die^ **Rabạtte, –n** (flower) border
^der^ **Rabạtz** *coll* din
^der^ **Rabauke, –n** (*wk masc*) *coll* hooligan
^der^ **Rabbiner, –** rabbi
^der^ **Rabe, –n** (*wk masc*) raven
Raben–: die ~eltern *pl coll* uncaring parents; **die ~krähe, –n** carrion crow; **raben|schwạrz** jet-black
rabiat rough; wild
Rach–: die ~gier thirst for revenge; **r~gierig** eager for revenge; vengeful; **die ~sucht** thirst for revenge; **r~süchtig** eager for revenge; vengeful
^die^ **Rache** revenge; **der ~akt, –e** act of revenge; **der ~engel, –** avenging angel
^der^ **Rachen, –** throat; jaws (of animal); **die ~höhle, –n** pharynx; **der ~katarrh, –e** pharyngitis
rächen avenge (**an** *dat* on); **sich ~** take revenge (**an** *dat* on); **... rächt sich** the penalty is paid for ...; **es wird sich ~, daß du ...** you'll pay for (*+ger*)
^die^ **Rachitis** [–'xiːtɪs] rickets
Rachmaninow [–ɔf] Rachmaninov
^der^ **Racker, –** *coll* scamp
^das^ **Rad, ⸚er** wheel; bicycle; **ein ~ schlagen** do a cartwheel; (peacock) spread its tail; **unter die Räder kommen** *coll* go to the dogs || **der ~dampfer, –** paddle-steamer; **r~fahren*** (*sep*: **ich fahre Rad**; *p/part* **radgefahren**) (*sn*) cycle; *coll* crawl to one's superiors and bully one's subordinates; **der ~fahrer, –** cyclist; *coll* person who crawls to his superiors and bullies his subordinates; **die ~kappe, –n** hub-cap; **der ~kranz, ⸚e** wheel-rim; **die ~renn|bahn, –en** cycle track; **das ~rennen, –** cycle race; cycle racing; **der ~renn|fahrer, –** racing cyclist; **der ~sport** cycling; **der ~stand** wheelbase; **die ~tour, –en = die ~wanderung, –en** cycling tour; **der ~wechsel, –** wheel-change; **der ~weg, –e** cycle track
^der^ **Radar** (*also* **das**) radar; **die ~falle, –n** speed trap; **der ~schirm, –e** radar screen
^der^ **Radau** *coll* din; **der ~bruder, ..brüder** *coll* = **der ~macher, –** *coll* hooligan
^das^ **Rädchen, –** small wheel; *dressm* tracing wheel; *cul* pastry wheel; **nur ein ~ im Getriebe sein** be just a cog in the machine
rade|brechen (*insep*) speak (language) very badly; (*eg* **Englisch ~**) speak broken (English *etc*)
radeln (*also sn*; *if indicating direction or distance travelled, only sn*) *coll* cycle
^der^ **Rädels|führer, –** ringleader
Räder– wheeled ...; **das ~werk** works, mechanism; wheels (of government *etc*)
–räd(e)rig –wheel(ed)
rädern (*see also* **gerädert**) *hist* break on the wheel
^der^ **Radi, –** *SGer* radish
radial radial
Radien *pl of* **Radius**
Radier–: der ~gummi, –s eraser
radieren erase; *art* etch
^der^ **Radierer, –** etcher; *coll* eraser
^die^ **Radierung, –en** etching
^das^ **Radieschen** [–sç–], **–** radish
radikal radical; drastic; (denial) categorical; **der/die Radikale** (*decl as adj*) radical || **der R~en|erlaß** ban on the employment by the (W. German) state of persons regarded as radicals; **die R~kur, –en** drastic remedy
radikalisieren radicalize
^der^ **Radikalịsmus** radicalism
^das^ **Radio, –s** radio; **~ hören** listen to the radio; **im ~** on the radio || **der ~apparat, –e** radio set
radio|aktiv radioactive
^die^ **Radio|aktivität** radioactivity
^die^ **Radio|astronomie** radioastronomy
^der^ **Radiologe, –n** (*wk masc*) radiologist
^die^ **Radiologie** radiology
^das^ **Radioteleskop, –e** radiotelescope
^die^ **Radiotherapie** radiotherapy
^das^ **Radium** radium
^der^ **Radius, –(d)ien** [–ĭən] radius
^der^ **Radler, –** cyclist; = **die ~maß, –** *SGer* shandy
–rädrig *see* **–räd(e)rig**
^der^ **Radscha** ['raːdʒa], **–s** rajah
Raff–: die ~gier greed; **r~gierig** grasping
Raffael [–aɛl] Raphael
raffen snatch up; gather (material); gather up (dress *etc*); amass; **an sich ~** snatch up
^die^ **Raffinade, –n** refined sugar
^das^ **Raffinement** [–ə'mãː], **–s** refinement; cunning
^die^ **Raffinerie, –(ie)n** refinery
^die^ **Raffinẹsse, –n** refinement; cunning

raffinieren refine (sugar *etc*); **raffiniert** *also* cunning; ingenious; sophisticated

die **Raffiniertheit** cunning; ingenuity; sophistication

der **Raffke, –s** *coll* money-grubber

Rage [–ʒə] *coll*: **in ~ bringen** infuriate; **in ~ kommen** fly into a rage

ragen rise, tower up

das **Ragout** [ra'gu:], **–s** ragout

die **Rahe, –n** *naut* yard

der **Rahm** *esp SGer* cream

rahmen frame

der **Rahmen, –** frame; framework; setting; context; scope; **den ~ sprengen von** be beyond the scope of; **aus dem ~ fallen** be out of the ordinary; be out of place; (person) misbehave; **im ~** (+*gen*) in (the course of); within the framework of; in the context of; as part of, under (scheme); **im ~ des Möglichen** within the bounds of possibility; **in kleinerem/größerem ~** on a small/large scale

Rahmen–: das ~gesetz, –e (*law providing a framework for subsequent detailed legislation*); **der ~sucher, –** viewfinder

rahmig *esp SGer* creamy

der **Rain, –e** grassy strip (beside lane or between fields)

die **Rakete, –n** rocket; = **das ~n|geschoß, –(ss)e** missile; **die ~n|technik** rocketry; **der ~n|werfer, –** rocket-launcher

die **Rallye** ['rali, 'rɛli], **–s** *sp* rally

Ramm–: der ~bock, ⸚e ram; **r~dösig** *coll* dizzy

die **Ramme, –n** pile-driver

rammen ram; **~ in** (*acc*) drive into (ground *etc*)

die **Rampe, –n** ramp; *theat* apron, forestage; **das ~n|licht, –er** footlights (**im R. stehen** be in the limelight)

ramponieren *coll* knock about; **ramponiert** *also* (reputation) tarnished

der **Ramsch** *coll* junk

ramschen *coll* buy up cheaply

Ramses [–zɛs] Ram(e)ses

ran [–a–] *coll* = **heran; ~gehen*** (*sep*; *sn*) *coll* (= **herangehen; r. wie Blücher** go at it hammer and tongs); **~halten*** (*sep*): **sich r.** *coll* get a move on; get stuck in

die **Ranch** [rɛntʃ], **–(e)s** ranch

der **Rand, ⸚er** edge; margin; rim; brim; brink; ring (round eyes *etc*); border; **halt den ~!** hold your tongue!; **am ~** in the margin; **am ~e** in passing; marginally; on the sidelines; +*gen* on the edge/outskirts of; on the verge/brink of; on the fringe(s) of (society *etc*); **das versteht sich am ~e** that goes without saying; **außer ~ und Band geraten** get out of hand, go wild; **zu ~e kommen mit** cope with

Rand– *also* marginal ...; peripheral ...; **der ~auslöser, –** margin release; **die ~bemerkung, –en** marginal note; passing remark; **die ~erscheinung, –en** phenomenon/occurrence *etc* of peripheral importance; **die ~figur, –en** minor figure; **das ~gebiet, –e** frontier area; outskirts; peripheral subject; **r~los** rimless; **die ~siedlung, –en** suburban housing estate/development *US*; **der ~steller, –** margin stop; **der ~streifen, –** verge; hard shoulder

randalieren go on the rampage; **~d** on the rampage

der **Randalierer, –** hooligan

die **Rande, –n** *Swiss* beetroot, beet *US*

–ränd(e)rig -edged; -rimmed; -brimmed

rändern border, edge

–randig = **–ränd(e)rig**

rang (ränge) *p/t* (*subj*) *of* **ringen**

der **Rang, ⸚e** rank; status; (lottery) class; *theat* circle; (*pl*) *sp* terraces; **erster/zweiter ~** *theat* dress/upper circle; (+*dat*) **den ~ ablaufen** outstrip; **... von ~** eminent ... || **r~höchst** highest-ranking; **die ~liste, –n** *mil* (army *etc*) list; *sp* rankings; **r~mäßig** according to rank; (*adv*) according to rank; (higher, lower) in rank (**r. stehen über** (*dat*)/**unter** (*dat*) rank above/below); **die ~ordnung, –en** hierarchy; order of precedence/rank; **die ~stufe, –n** rank; **der ~unterschied, –e** difference in rank

die **Range, –n** urchin; tomboy

rangeln *coll* scrap; **~ um** wrangle over; **sich ~** sprawl

Rangier– [raŋʒ–]: **der ~bahnhof, ⸚e** marshalling yard; **die ~lokomotive, –n** shunter, switcher *US*

rangieren [raŋʒ–] *rail* shunt; (*v/i*) rank; come (before *etc*)

–rangig -rate

Rangun Rangoon

rank: ~ (und schlank) slender

die **Ranke, –n** tendril; shoot

die **Ränke** *pl* intrigues; **~ schmieden** intrigue || **der ~schmied, –e** schemer; **r~voll** scheming

ranken put out tendrils; **sich ~ an** (*dat*) climb up; **sich ~ um** entwine itself around; (legend) have grown up around

das **Ranken|gewächs, –e** climbing plant

rann (ränne) *p/t* (*subj*) *of* **rinnen**

rannte *p/t of* **rennen**

der **Ranzen, –** satchel; *coll* belly

ranzig rancid

rapid(e) rapid

der **Rappe, –n** (*wk masc*) black horse

Rappel *coll*: **einen ~ haben** be crazy; **einen ~ bekommen** get one of one's crazy moods

rappelig *coll* crazy; jumpy

rappeln *coll* rattle; *Aust* be crazy; **bei ...**

rappelt's ... is *etc* crazy
der **Rappen, –** (Swiss) centime (*1/100 of a franc*)
der **Rapport** [–'pɔrt], **–e** report; *psych* rapport
der **Raps, –e** *bot* rape
rar rare; **sich ~ machen** *coll* make oneself scarce
die **Rarität, –en** rarity
rasant *phys* (trajectory) flat; *coll* (development *etc*) rapid, (career *etc*) meteoric; (car) very fast; (speed *etc*) terrific; *coll* (woman) smashing
die **Rasanz** *phys* flatness (of trajectory); *coll* terrific speed
rasch quick; hasty
rascheln, ~ mit rustle
rasen rave; go wild; (storm) rage; (*sn*) tear, race; **~ gegen** (*sn*) hurtle into; **~d** furious; raging; terrific; thunderous; excruciating, (headache) splitting; (jealousy) intense; (*adv*) *coll* madly (in love *etc*); **~d machen** infuriate; **... ist zum R~dwerden** ... is infuriating
der **Rasen, –** grass; turf; lawn; **der ~mäher, –** lawn-mower; **der ~platz, ⸚e** lawn; *sp* grass court; (grass) pitch
die **Raserei** rage; raving; mad rush, *mot* senseless speeding
Rasier– shaving ...; **der ~apparat, –e** razor; **die ~klinge, –n** razor-blade; **das ~messer, –** cut-throat razor, straight razor *US*; **das ~wasser, –/..wässer** after-shave
rasieren, sich ~ shave
Räson [–'zɔ̃ː]: **zur ~ bringen/kommen** bring to/see reason
die **Raspel, –n** rasp; *cul* grater
raspeln rasp; *cul* grate
die **Rasse, –n** race; breed; **sie hat ~** she's a spirited girl/woman
Rasse– pedigree ...; thoroughbred ...; **r~rein** pure-bred; thoroughbred
die **Rassel, –n** rattle; **die ~bande, –n** *coll* bunch of little monkeys
rasseln (*sn if indicating motion*) rattle; **~ durch** (*sn*) *coll* flunk; **~ mit** rattle (keys *etc*)
Rassen– racial ...; **die ~hygiene** eugenics; **die ~kreuzung, –en** cross-breeding; **die ~mischung** miscegenation; **die ~schranke, –n** racial barrier; colour-bar; **die ~trennung** racial segregation
rassig spirited; (car) sleek; (face *etc*) striking
rassisch racial
der **Rassismus** racism
der **Rassist, –en** (*wk masc*), **rassistisch** racist
die **Rast, –en** rest; **~ machen** stop for a rest/to eat || **das ~haus, ⸚er** (*esp* motorway) restaurant; **r~los** restless; untiring; **der ~platz, ⸚e** (motorway) lay-by; **die ~stätte, –n** (motorway) restaurant
rasten rest (on journey)
das **Raster, –** *TV* raster
der **Raster, –** framework; *print, phot* screen
die **Rasur, –en** shave; erasure
der **Rat**[1] (piece of) advice; **~ schaffen** find a way; **~ wissen** know what to do; **sich** *dat* **keinen ~ mehr wissen** be at one's wits' end; **da ist guter ~ teuer** it's hard to know what to do; **zu ~e ziehen** consult
der **Rat**[2], **⸚e** council; *hist* soviet; **–rat** ... council; (*denoting person*) ... councillor; *or used in titles indicating a senior official*
Rat–: der ~geber, – adviser; **das ~haus, ⸚er** town hall, city hall *US*; **r~los** helpless; at a loss; **die ~losigkeit** helplessness; **der ~schlag, ⸚e** (piece of) advice; **der/die R~suchende** (*decl as adj*) person seeking advice
rät *3rd sing pres of* **raten**
die **Rate, –n** instalment; rate; **auf ~n** in instalments
Rate–: das ~spiel, –e guessing-game
Räte– *hist* soviet ...
raten (rät(st), *p/t* **riet,** *p/part* **geraten)** (*see also* **geraten**) guess; solve (puzzle); (*v/i*, +*dat*) advise; (+*dat*) **~ zu** recommend (doctor *etc*) to; advise (s.o. to do/be sth., *eg* **jmdm. zur Flucht/Geduld ~** advise s.o. to flee/be patient; *also with ind obj understood, eg* **zur Vorsicht ~** advise caution); (+*dat*) **~ zu ...** advise to ...; **laß dir ~!** take my advice; **was ~ Sie mir?** what would you advise?; **das möchte ich dir auch geraten haben!** you better had!
Raten–: der ~kauf, ⸚e hire-purchase, installment plan *US*; **r~weise** in instalments; **die ~zahlung, –en** payment by instalments; payment of an instalment
ratifizieren ratify
die **Ratifizierung, –en** ratification
die **Ration, –en** ration
rational rational
rationalisieren rationalize; streamline
die **Rationalisierung, –en** rationalization
rationell efficient
rationieren ration
Rats–: der ~herr, –en (*like* **Herr**) councillor; **der ~keller, –** (*restaurant in the cellar of the Rathaus*); **die ~sitzung, –en** council meeting
ratsam advisable
ratsch! rip!
die **Ratsche** [–aː–], **–n** *SGer* rattle; chatterbox
ratschen [–aː–] *SGer* swing a rattle; chatter
das **Rätsel** [–ɛː–], **–** riddle; puzzle; mystery, riddle; (+*dat*) **~ aufgeben** baffle || **das ~raten** solving puzzles/riddles; speculation
rätselhaft mysterious, puzzling; **es ist mir ~, wie ...** it's a mystery to me how ...
rätseln [–ɛː–] puzzle; speculate
rätst *2nd sing pres of* **raten**
die **Ratte, –n** rat; **der ~n|fänger, –** rat-catcher

(**der R. von Hameln** the Pied Piper of Hamelin); **der ~n|schwanz, ¨-e** rat's tail; *coll* string (of questions *etc*); (*pl*) *coll* bunches

rattern (*sn if indicating motion*) rattle, clatter

die **Ratze, -n** *coll* rat; **ratze|kahl** *coll* (**alles r. aufessen** eat every scrap)

ratzen *coll* kip

der **Raub** robbery; abduction; loot; prey; **auf ~ ausgehen** go robbing; (animal) go on the prowl

Raub-: der ~bau over-exploitation (**an** *dat* of) (**R. am Fischbestand** overfishing; **R. treiben mit** over-exploit; ruin (one's health)); **der ~fisch, -e** predatory fish; **die ~gier** rapaciousness; **r~gierig** rapacious; **der ~mord, -e** murder committed in the course of a robbery; **die ~möwe, -n** skua; **der ~ritter, -** robber-knight; **das ~tier, -e** beast of prey; **der ~überfall, ¨-e** robbery; **der ~vogel, ..vögel** bird of prey; **der ~zug, ¨-e** foray

rauben steal; abduct; (+*dat of pers*) rob of

der **Räuber, -** robber; **die ~geschichte, -n** story about robbers; *coll* tall story; **die ~höhle, -n** robbers' den; **die ~pistole, -n** tall story; **das ~zivil** *joc* scruffy old clothes

räuberisch rapacious; predatory

räubern thieve

der **Rauch** smoke; **die ~fahne, -n** trail of smoke; **der ~fang, ¨-e** chimney hood; *Aust* chimney; **das ~fleisch** smoked meat; **das ~glas** smoked glass; **die ~säule, -n** column of smoke; **die ~schwalbe, -n** swallow; **die ~waren¹** *pl* tobacco products; **die ~waren²** *pl* furs; **die ~wolke, -n** cloud of smoke

rauchen (*also v/i*) smoke

der **Raucher, -** smoker; *rail* = **das ~abteil, -e** smoking compartment

Räucher- smoked ...; **die ~kammer, -n** smokehouse; **das ~stäbchen, -** joss-stick

räuchern smoke (meat *etc*); (*v/i*) burn incense

rauchig smoky

die **Räude** mange

räudig mangy

rauf *coll* = **herauf, hinauf**

Rauf-: der ~bold, -e ruffian; **r~lustig** pugnacious

die **Raufe, -n** hay-rack

raufen pull (flax); (*v/i*) = **sich ~** fight; **sich** *dat* **die Haare ~** tear one's hair (in despair *etc*)

die **Rauferei, -en** scrap

rauh rough; rugged; raw; harsh; hoarse; husky; (throat) sore; **... in ~en Mengen** *coll* heaps of ... || **das R~bein, -e** *coll* rough diamond; **die R~faser** woodchip; **der R~haar|dackel, -** wire-haired dachshund; **~haarig** wire-haired; **der R~putz** roughcast; **der R~reif** hoar-frost

die **Rauheit** roughness *etc* (*see* **rauh**)

der **Raum, ¨-e** room, space; area; (political *etc*) sphere; room, scope; (in building) room; *space* space; **der ~ (Köln** *etc*) the (Cologne *etc*) area; (+*dat*) **~ geben** entertain (idea)

Raum- *esp* space ...;

der ~anzug, ¨-e spacesuit; **die ~fähre, -n** space shuttle; **die ~fahrt** space travel; **~fahrt-** space ...; **das ~fahrzeug, -e** spacecraft; **die ~gestaltung** interior design; **der ~inhalt, -e** volume; **die ~kapsel, -n** space capsule; **der ~klang** stereophonic sound; **die ~lehre** geometry; **der ~mangel** lack of space; **die ~pflegerin, -nen** cleaner; **das ~schiff, -e** spaceship; **die ~sonde, -n** space probe; **r~sparend** space-saving; **die ~station, -en** space station; **der ~teiler, -** room-divider; **der ~ton** stereophonic sound; **der ~transporter, -** space shuttle

räumen clear; clear (away), remove; vacate; **aus dem Weg ~** get rid of; remove (difficulty)

räumlich spatial; three-dimensional; (*adv*) from the point of view of space

die **Räumlichkeiten** *pl* premises; rooms

der **Räumungs|verkauf, ¨-e** clearance sale

raunen whisper

raunzen *SGer coll* grumble

die **Raupe, -n** caterpillar; **das ~n|fahrzeug, -e** tracked vehicle; **der ~n|schlepper, -** caterpillar tractor

raus *coll* = **heraus, hinaus; nach vorne/hinten ~** at the front/back (of house); **~!** get out! || **~fliegen*** (*sep*; *sn*) *coll* be chucked out; **~schmeißen*** (*sep*) *coll* chuck out; **der R~schmeißer, -** *coll* bouncer; **der R~schmiß, -(ss)e** *coll* chucking-out

der **Rausch, ¨-e** intoxication; ecstasy; **sich** *dat* **einen ~ antrinken** get drunk; **im ~** while drunk || **das ~gift, -e** drug; **der ~gift|handel** traffic in drugs; **der ~gift|händler, -** drug trafficker; **die ~gift|sucht** drug addiction; **r~gift|süchtig** addicted to drugs; **der/die ~gift|süchtige** (*decl as adj*) drug addict; **das ~gold** gold foil

rauschen roar; rustle; (brook) murmur; swish; hiss; (*sn*) sweep (through room *etc*); (boat *etc*) sweep along; (water) pour noisily; **~d** (applause) resounding; (celebrations) magnificent

rauschhaft ecstatic

räuspern: sich ~ clear one's throat

die **Raute, -n** *math* rhombus; *bot* rue

der **Rayon** [rɛˈjɔː, *Aust usu* raˈjoːn], **-s** *Aust*, *Swiss* district; *Aust* department (of store)

die **Razzia, -(i)en** (police) raid

rd. (= **rund**) approx.

das **Reagens** [-ɛns] (*gen* -), **-(ẹn)zien** [-ĭən] reagent

das **Reagẹnz|glas, ¨-er** test-tube

reagieren react; ~ **auf** (*acc*) react to; respond to

[die] **Reaktion, –en** reaction (*also chem*) (**auf** *acc* to); response (to); *pol* reactionary elements/forces

reaktionär, der Reaktionär, –e reactionary

Reaktions– reaction ...; **die ~fähigkeit** ability to react; reactions; *chem* reactivity; **r~schnell** with fast reactions (**r. sein** have fast reactions); **das ~vermögen** ability to react; reactions; **die ~zeit, –en** reaction time

reaktivieren reactivate; recall (to post); *med* restore to use

[der] **Reaktor, –(or)en** reactor

real real; (assets) tangible; in real terms; realistic; **das R~büro, –s** *Aust* estate agency, real-estate agency *US*; **das R~einkommen, –** real income; **das R~gymnasium, –(i)en** *Aust* grammar school (with emphasis on the sciences); **die R~kanzlei, –en** *Aust* estate agency, real-estate agency *US*; **die R~politik** realpolitik; **die R~schule, –n** (non-classical) secondary school

[die] **Realien** [–ĭən] *pl* facts

realisieren carry out; realize (*also fin*)

[die] **Realisierung** *vbl noun*; *also* realization

[der] **Realismus** realism

[der] **Realist, –en** (*wk masc*) realist

[die] **Realistik** [–ɪk] *arts* realism

realistisch realistic

[die] **Realität, –en** reality; (*pl*) *Aust* real estate

realiter [–ɐ] in reality

Reb–: das ~huhn, ⸚er partridge; **der ~stock, ⸚e** vine

[die] **Rebe, –n** vine

[der] **Rebell, –en** (*wk masc*) rebel

rebellieren rebel

[die] **Rebellion, –en** rebellion

rebellisch rebellious

[das] **Rechaud** [reˈʃoː], **–s** (*also* **der**) plate-warmer; tea/coffee-warmer

rechen, der Rechen, – *esp SGer* rake

Rechen–: die ~anlage, –n computer; **die ~aufgabe, –n** arithmetical problem; **der ~fehler, –** miscalculation; **die ~maschine, –n** calculator; **der ~schieber, – = der ~stab, ⸚e** slide-rule; **die ~tabelle, –n** ready-reckoner; **die ~zeit, –en** computer time; **das ~zentrum, –(r)en** computer centre

Rechenschaft: ~ ablegen über (*acc*) account for; (+*dat*) **~ schuldig sein** have to account to; **zur ~ ziehen** call to account || **der ~s|bericht, –e** (chairman's) report

[die] **Recherchen** [reˈʃɛrʃn̩] *pl* investigations, inquiries

recherchieren [reʃɛrʃ–] investigate

rechnen calculate, work out; allow (amount *etc*); (*v/i*) calculate; *coll* economize; **... nicht gerechnet** not counting ...; **rund gerechnet** around

~ **auf** (*acc*) reckon on

~ **mit** expect; reckon on/with; **mit ... wird gerechnet** ... is *etc* expected

~ **unter** (*acc*) count among

~ **zu** count among; (*v/i*) be counted among

[das] **Rechnen** arithmetic

[der] **Rechner, –** computer; calculator; **ein guter ~ sein** be good at figures || **r~abhängig** *comput* on-line; **r~unabhängig** *comput* off-line

rechnerisch arithmetical

[die] **Rechnung, –en** bill; calculation; **alte ~** *also* old score; **die ~ geht nicht auf** the sum doesn't work out; things do not work out as planned; (+*dat*) **~ tragen** take into account; **auf ~** on account; **in ~ stellen** take into account; (+*dat*) charge for

Rechnungs–: die ~einheit, –en unit of account; **der ~hof, ⸚e** audit office; **das ~jahr, –e** financial year, fiscal year *US*; **der ~prüfer, –** auditor; **die ~prüfung, –en** audit; **das ~wesen** accountancy

recht (*see also* **recht..**) right; proper; (*adv*) properly; aright; (*as intensifier*) quite; pretty; very; **~ und billig** right and proper; **das geht nicht mit ~en Dingen zu** there's something funny about it; **erst '~** (*see* **erst**); **nicht so ~** not really; **nach dem Rechten sehen** make sure that everything's all right;

(*with verbs*): **~ behalten** be (= prove to be) right; (+*dat*) **~ geben** have to admit (s.o.) is right, agree with; (event *etc*) prove right; **gehe ich ~ in der Annahme, daß ...?** am I right in thinking that ...?; **es geschieht ihm ~** it serves him right; **~ haben** be right; **es jmdm. ~ machen** please s.o.; **ich kann ihm nichts ~ machen** I can't do a thing right for him; **~ daran tun zu ...** be right to ...; (**~ sein**): **das ist mir ~** it's all right with me; **so ist es ~!** that's the idea!; **mir soll's ~ sein** it's all right with me; **alles, was ~ ist** *coll* say what you like; fair's fair

[das] **Recht, –e** right (**auf** *acc* to); (person's) rights; law; justice; **das ~ des Stärkeren** the law of the jungle; **~ sprechen** dispense justice; **alle ~e vorbehalten** all rights reserved; **im ~ sein** be in the right; **mit ~** rightly; **von ~s wegen** as of right; *coll* by rights; **zu ~** rightly; **zu ~ bestehen** (claim *etc*) be well-founded; **zu seinem ~ kommen** get what is due to one; come into one's own; have its place

recht.. right (*opp* left); *pol* right-wing; **die Rechte** (*decl as adj*) right; right hand; *box* right; *pol* (the) Right; **zur R~en** on the right

Recht–: das ~eck, –e rectangle; **r~eckig** rectangular; **r~fertigen** (*insep*) justify; **die ~fertigung, –en** justification (**zu seiner R.** (say) in one's defence); **r~gläubig** orthodox; **die ~haberei** dogmatism; **r~haberisch** dogmatic, opinionated; **r~los** without rights; **r~mäßig** lawful; legitimate; rightful; **r~schaffen** decent, honest; (*adv*) really; **~schreib–** spelling ...; **die ~schreibung** spelling; **die ~sprechung** administration of justice; jurisdiction; **r~winklig** right-angled; **r~zeitig** timely; in time; (*adv*) in time; on time

rechten: ~ mit argue with

rechtlich legal

rechts on the right; **nach/von ~** to/from the right

Rechts– ... of law; legal ...; right-hand ...; ... to the right; clockwise ...; *pol* right-wing ...;

der ~anwalt, ⸚e lawyer; **der ~außen, –** outside right; **der ~beistand, ⸚e** legal adviser; **das ~empfinden = das ~gefühl** sense of justice; **der/die ~gelehrte** (*decl as adj*) jurist; **r~gültig** legally valid; **die ~gültigkeit** legal validity; **r~herum** round to the right; **r~kräftig** having the force of law; (judgement) final; **die ~kurve, –n** right-hand bend; **das ~mittel, –** *leg* appeal; **die ~pflege** administration of justice; **r~radikal** extreme right-wing; **r~rheinisch** on the right of the Rhine; **der ~spruch, ⸚e** verdict; **der ~staat, –en** state based on the rule of law; **der ~streit, –e** lawsuit; **r~um!** right turn/face *US*!; **r~verbindlich** legally binding; **der ~verkehr** driving on the right; **der ~weg** recourse to the law (**den R. beschreiten** go to court; **auf dem R.** in court); **das ~wesen** legal system; **r~widrig** illegal; **die ~wissenschaft** jurisprudence

das **Reck, –e** horizontal bar

der **Recke, –n** (*wk masc*) *poet* warrior

recken stretch; crane (one's neck); **sich ~** stretch (oneself)

der **Recorder** [re'kɔrdɐ], – (cassette) recorder

das **Recycling** [ri'saẹklɪŋ] recycling

red–: ~selig talkative

der **Redakteur** [–'tøːɐ], **–e** editor

die **Redaktion, –en** editorial offices/staff; editing

redaktionell editorial

der **Redaktions|schluß** (copy) deadline

der **Redaktor, –(or)en** *Swiss* editor

die **Rede, –n** speech (*also ling*); talk, conversation; (*pl*) words; **der langen ~ kurzer Sinn** the long and the short of it; **nicht der ~ wert** not worth mentioning; (+*dat*) **~ und Antwort stehen** explain oneself to; **die ~ bringen auf** (*acc*) turn the conversation to; **eine ~ halten** make a speech (**vor** *dat* to); (+*dat*) **in die ~ fallen** cut short; **es ist die ~ von** there is talk of; we're *etc* talking about; **von ... kann keine ~ sein** ... is *etc* out of the question; **zur ~ stellen** call to account || **der ~fluß** flow of words; **die ~freiheit** free speech; **r~gewandt** eloquent; **die ~gewandtheit** eloquence; **der ~schwall** torrent of words; **die ~weise, –n** way of speaking; **die ~wendung, –en** phrase, expression

reden talk; say (words); (*v/i*) talk, speak (**mit** to, **von** about); speak, make a speech; **du hast gut ~** it's easy for you to talk; **mit sich ~ lassen** be open to persuasion; **nicht mit sich ~ lassen** be adamant; **von sich ~ machen** get talked about; be in the news

Redens: viel ~ machen von make a great fuss about || **die ~art, –en** saying; (empty) phrase; (*pl*) words; talk (**das ist nur so eine R.** that's just a manner of speaking)

die **Rederei, –en** *coll* talk; gossip

redigieren edit

redlich honest

die **Redlichkeit** honesty

der **Redner, –** speaker; orator; **die ~bühne, –n** rostrum

rednerisch oratorical

die **Reduktion, –en** reduction (*also chem*)

reduzieren reduce (*also chem*) (**auf** *acc* to); **sich ~** diminish

die **Reede, –n** roadstead

der **Reeder, –** shipowner

die **Reederei, –en** shipping line

reell honest, (firm) solid; (price *etc*) fair, reasonable; (chance, *math* number) real

der **REFA-Fachmann** ['reːfa–], *pl* **-Fachleute** time and motion expert

das **Referat, –e** report; *univ* paper; *admin* section (within department)

der **Referendar, –e** trainee (in civil service); student teacher; *leg* articled clerk

das **Referendum, –(d)en/–(d)a** referendum

der **Referent, –en** (*wk masc*) speaker; expert; head of section; **persönlicher ~** personal assistant

die **Referenz, –en** reference; **als ~** (give) as a referee

referieren: ~ über (*acc*) report on; *univ* read a paper on

reffen *naut* reef

reflektieren reflect; **~ auf** (*acc*) *coll* have one's eye on; **~ über** (*acc*) reflect on

der **Reflektor, –(or)en** reflector

reflektorisch *physiol* reflex

der **Reflex, –e** reflection; *physiol* reflex; **die ~bewegung, –en** reflex action

die **Reflexion, –en** *phys* reflection; (*pl*) reflections

reflexiv *gramm* reflexive; **das R~pronomen, –/..(m)ina** reflexive pronoun

die **Reform, –en** reform; **r~bedürftig** in need of reform; **der ~eifer** reforming zeal; **das ~haus, ⸚er** health food shop; **die ~kost**

health food
die **Reformation** the Reformation
der **Reformator, –(or)en** reformer
reformatorisch reformative
der **Reformer, –** reformer
reformieren reform
der **Refrain** [rə'frɛ̃:], **–s** refrain
das **Refugium, –(i)en** refuge
reg–: ~los motionless
das **Regal, –e** (set of) shelves
die **Regatta, –(tt)en** regatta
Reg.-Bez. = Regierungsbezirk
rege lively; alert; active; busy; *comm* brisk
die **Regel, –n** rule; *physiol* period; **in der ~** as a rule; **es sich** *dat* **zur ~ machen zu ...** make it a rule to ...; **zur ~ werden** become a habit/the rule || **~fall (im R.** as a rule); **r~los** disorderly; irregular; **r~mäßig** regular (*also gramm*); **die ~mäßigkeit** regularity; **r~recht** proper, real; downright; **die ~studien|zeit, –en** *univ* period within which s.o.'s studies must be completed; **r~widrig** against the rules; irregular
regeln regulate; control; settle; **sich ~** sort itself out
die **Regelung, –en** regulation; control; settlement; management (of affairs); arrangement (made)
regen move (finger *etc*); **sich ~** move, stir; (conscience *etc*) stir
der **Regen** rain; shower (of bullets *etc*); **saurer ~** acid rain || **der ~bogen, –** rainbow; **die ~bogen|haut, ⸚e** *anat* iris; **der ~guß, ⸚(ss)e** downpour; **die ~haut, ⸚e** plastic raincoat; **der ~mantel, ..mäntel** raincoat; **der ~messer, –** rain-gauge; **r~naß** wet from the rain; **der ~pfeifer, –** plover; **der ~schauer, –** shower of rain; **der ~schirm, –e** umbrella; **der ~tag, –e** rainy day; **der ~tropfen, –** raindrop; **der ~wald, ⸚er** rain-forest; **das ~wetter** wet weather; **die ~wolke, –n** rain cloud; **der ~wurm, ⸚er** earthworm; **die ~zeit, –en** rainy season, rains
die **Regeneration** regeneration
regenerieren, sich ~ regenerate
der **Regent, –en** (*wk masc*) sovereign; regent
die **Regentschaft, –en** reign; regency
die **Regie** [re'ʒi:], **–(ie)n** management; *cin* direction; *theat etc* production, direction *US*; **~ führen bei** *cin* direct; *theat etc* produce; **in eigener ~** on one's own; **unter der ~ von** directed/*theat etc* produced by || **der ~fehler, –** slip-up (in arrangements)
regieren govern (*also gramm*), rule; (*v/i*) govern; (monarch) reign
die **Regierung, –en** government; rule; reign; **die ~ antreten** take office || **der ~s|bezirk, –e** administrative district; **der ~s|chef, –s** head of government; **der ~s|direktor, –en** (*senior official in the W. German civil service*); **r~s|fähig** capable of governing; (majority) working; **die ~s|form, –en** form of government; **die ~s|partei, –en** governing party; **der ~s|präsident, –en** (*wk masc*) chief administrative officer (of a *Regierungsbezirk*); **der ~s|rat, ⸚e** (*official in the W. German civil service ranking below* Regierungsdirektor; (*Switzerland*) *executive council of a canton*); **der ~s|sprecher, –** government spokesman; **die ~s|umbildung, –en** cabinet reshuffle; **der ~s|wechsel, –** change of government; **die ~s|zeit, –en** rule; term of office
das **Regime** [re'ʒi:m], **–** [–ə]/**–s** [–s] régime
das **Regiment, –e**/*mil* **–er** rule; *mil* regiment; **das ~ führen** be in charge; **ein strenges ~ führen** rule with a rod of iron
Regiments– regimental ...
die **Region, –en** region
regional regional; **der R~fonds** (E.C.) Regional Fund
der **Regisseur** [reʒi'sø:ɐ], **–e** *cin* director; *theat etc* producer, director *US*
das **Register, –** register; index; *mus* register; (of organ) stop, register; **alle ~ ziehen** pull out all the stops || **die ~tonne, –n** register ton
die **Registratur, –en** registration; filing department; filing-cabinet
Registrier–: die ~kasse, –n cash register
registrieren record; register; note
die **Registrierung** recording; registration
das **Reglement** [reglə'mã:], **–s** regulations
reglementieren [regləmen–] regulate; regiment
die **Reglementierung, –en** regulation; regimentation
der **Regler, –** regulator; *mech* governor
regnen [–e:–]: **es regnet** it is raining; **es regnete ...** there was a flood of (complaints *etc*); **es regnet Bindfäden** *coll* it's raining cats and dogs
regnerisch rainy
der **Regreß, –(ss)e** *leg* recourse; **~ nehmen auf** (*acc*) have recourse against
regsam lively, alert
regulär regular; normal
regulieren regulate
die **Regung, –en** movement; feeling, stirring (of pity *etc*); impulse; **r~s|los** motionless
das **Reh, –e** roe (deer); **der ~bock, ⸚e** roebuck; **der ~braten, –** roast venison; **r~braun = r~farben** light brown; **das ~kitz, –e** fawn; **das ~leder** deerskin; **das ~wild** roe deer (*collect*)
rehabilitieren rehabilitate, clear (s.o.'s) name; (after illness *etc*) rehabilitate; **sich ~** clear one's name
die **Rehabilitierung, –en** rehabilitation
Reib–: das ~eisen, – grater

reiben (*p/t* **rieb,** *p/part* **gerieben**) (*see also* **gerieben**) rub; grate; (*v/i*) rub, chafe; **sich ~ an** (*dat*) rub oneself against; not get on with; **sich (aneinander) ~** rub each other up the wrong way

die **Reibereien** *pl coll* friction

die **Reibung, -en** *vbl noun*; *phys* friction; **r~s|los** frictionless; smooth, trouble-free; (*adv*) smoothly, without a hitch

reich rich (**an** *dat* in); (experience, knowledge, selection, *etc*) wide; **-reich** full of ...; rich in ...; with a high ... content

das **Reich, -e** empire; realm; kingdom; **das Deutsche ~** the German Empire; **das Heilige Römische ~ Deutscher Nation** the Holy Roman Empire; **das Dritte ~** the Third Reich

reich-: ~haltig rich; (selection) wide; (programme) varied; **die R~weite** range; reach (*also box*); scope (**außer R.** out of range/reach; **in R.** within range/reach)

reichen (+*dat*) hand to; serve (refreshments) to; hold out (one's hand) to; offer; (*v/i*) reach, extend; (voice) carry; be sufficient; be long enough; (provisions *etc*) last; **~ bis an** (*acc*)/**zu** come up to; (voice) carry to; **~ mit** *coll* manage on; **... reicht von ... bis hin zu** ranges from ... to; **so weit das Auge reicht** as far as the eye can see; **mir reicht's!** I've had enough!

reichlich ample; generous; (hour *etc*) good; (*adv*) *also* plenty of; a good (100 marks *etc*); (*as intensifier*) *coll* pretty; **~ vorhanden sein** abound

Reichs- imperial ...; Imperial ...; (1918–45) German ..., (*esp with reference to Third Reich*) Reich ...; **der ~apfel** imperial orb; **die (Deutsche) ~bahn** (*since 1949 in E. Germany*) German State Railways; **der/die ~deutsche** (*decl as adj*) German national (in Third Reich); **die ~insignien** *pl* = **die ~kleinodien** *pl* imperial regalia; **der ~tag** *hist* the Imperial Diet; (1871–1945) the Reichstag (*German parliament*); **die ~wehr** (*German armed forces, 1921–35*)

der **Reichtum, ⸚er** wealth; richness; wealth (**an** *dat* of), abundance (of); (*pl*) riches

reif ripe; mature; **-reif** ready for ...; **~ für** ready for

der **Reif**[1] hoar-frost

der **Reif**[2]**, -e** hoop; *poet* circlet; bangle; ring

die **Reife** ripeness; maturity; **mittlere ~** school-leaving certificate (taken at a *Mittelschule, Realschule*) || **die ~prüfung, -en** (= **Abitur**); **das ~zeugnis, -se** *Abitur* certificate

reifen[1] (*sn*) (*see also* **gereift**) ripen; mature

reifen[2]**: es hat gereift** there is a hoar-frost

der **Reifen, -** tyre; hoop; bangle; **der ~defekt, -e** = **die ~panne, -n** puncture; **der ~wechsel, -** tyre change

reiflich: nach ~er Überlegung after careful consideration; **sich** *dat* **... ~ überlegen** consider carefully

der **Reigen, -** round dance; **den ~ eröffnen** lead off

reih-: ~um in turn (**r. gehen** be passed round; **r. gehen lassen** pass round)

die **Reihe, -n** row; series (*also comput, math, mus*); number (of); **an die ~ kommen** be next; **ich bin an der ~** it's my turn; **die ~ ist an** (*dat*) it's ...'s turn; **aus der ~ tanzen** *coll* step out of line; **in Reih und Glied stehen** be lined up; **in den eigenen ~n** in one's own ranks; **der ~ nach** in turn

reihen tack (seam *etc*); **auf eine Schnur ~** string; **sich ~ an** (*acc*) follow (*eg* **Erfolg reihte sich an Erfolg** success followed success)

Reihen-: die ~folge, -n order; sequence (**alphabetische R.** alphabetical order); **das ~haus, ⸚er** terraced house, row house *US*; **die ~untersuchung, -en** mass screening; **r~weise** in rows; in large numbers

der **Reiher, -** heron

-reihig with ... rows; *tail*-breasted

der **Reim, -e** rhyme; **sich** *dat* **einen ~ machen auf** (*acc*) make sense of || **das ~lexikon, -(k)a** rhyming dictionary; **r~los** unrhymed; **das ~paar, -e** rhyming couplet; **der ~schmied, -e** versifier; **das ~wort, ⸚er** rhyme

reimen rhyme (**auf** *acc* with); **sich ~** rhyme (**auf** *acc* with); **das reimt sich nicht** it doesn't make sense

rein[1] pure (*also opp* applied); sheer; clean; (skin, conscience) clear; (*adv*) purely; *coll* absolutely; **die Luft ist ~** the coast is clear; **im ~en sein mit** have come to grips with; **mit sich (selbst) im ~en sein** be at one with oneself; **ins ~e bringen** clear up, sort out; **ins ~e kommen mit** sort things out with; come to grips with; **mit sich (selbst) ins ~e kommen** sort things out in one's own mind; **ins ~e schreiben** make a fair copy of

rein[2] *coll* = **herein, hinein**

rein-: der R~erlös, -e = **der R~ertrag, ⸚e** net proceeds; **der R~fall, ⸚e** *coll* flop; **~fallen*** (*sep*; *sn*) *coll* (= **hereinfallen, hineinfallen**); **der R~gewinn, -e** net profit; **die R~kultur, -en** pure culture (**... in R.** *coll* pure (kitsch *etc*)); **~legen** (*sep*) *coll* (= **hereinlegen, hineinlegen**); **die R~mache|frau, -en** cleaner, cleaning woman; **~rassig** pedigree; thoroughbred; **die R~schrift, -en** fair copy; **rein|seiden** pure silk; **das R~vermögen, -** net assets; **~waschen*** (*sep*) clear (**von** of); **~weg** *coll* absolutely; **~wollen** pure wool

reine-: die R~mache|frau, -en (= **Reinmachefrau**); **~weg** (= **reinweg**)

die **Reine|claude** [rɛːnəˈkloːdə], **-n** greengage

Reineke Fuchs Reynard the Fox

die **Reinheit** purity; cleanness

reinigen clean; purify; **chemisch ~** dry-clean; **die Atmosphäre ~** clear the air; **sich ~ von** clear oneself of

die **Reinigung, -en** cleaning; purification; = **die ~s|anstalt, -en** dry cleaners; **die ~s|creme, -s** cleansing cream; **das ~s|mittel, -** cleaning agent

reinlich (house *etc*) clean; (habitually) clean; clear-cut

die **Reinlichkeit** cleanliness

das **Reis, -er** twig; *hort* graft

der **Reis** rice; **das ~feld, -er** paddy-field; **das ~korn, ⸚er** grain of rice; **das ~papier** rice-paper

die **Reise, -n** journey; trip; *naut* voyage; (*pl*) travels; **eine ~ machen** go on a journey; **glückliche/gute ~!** bon voyage!; **auf ~n** away (on a trip); **viel auf ~n sein** do a lot of travelling; **auf ~n gehen** go away

Reise– travel ...; travelling ...; portable ...;
das ~andenken, - souvenir; **die ~apotheke, -n** first-aid kit; **der ~bericht, -e** account of one's journey; travelogue; **das ~büro, -s** travel agency; **die ~decke, -n** travelling-rug; **r~fertig** ready to leave; **das ~fieber** excitement before going on a journey; **der ~führer, -** guide; guide-book; **das ~gepäck** luggage, baggage; **die ~geschwindigkeit, -en** cruising speed; **die ~gesellschaft, -en** tour operator; party of tourists; **der ~koffer, -** suitcase; **der ~leiter, -** courier; **die ~lektüre** reading-matter for the journey; **die ~lust** wanderlust; **der ~onkel, -** *coll* keen traveller; **der ~paß, ⸚(ss)e** passport; **die ~pläne** *pl* plans for a journey; **der ~prospekt, -e** travel brochure; **die ~route, -n** itinerary; **der ~scheck, -s** traveller's cheque; **die ~tante, -n** *coll* keen traveller; **die ~tasche, -n** holdall; **das ~unternehmen, -** tour operator; **die ~unterbrechung, -en** stopover; **der ~verkehr** holiday traffic; **die ~vorbereitungen** *pl* preparations for a/the journey; **die ~zeit, -en** tourist season; travelling time; **das ~ziel, -e** destination

reisen (*sn*) travel; **der/die Reisende** (*decl as adj*) traveller; passenger; *comm* travelling salesman

die **Reiserei** *coll* (constant) travelling about

das **Reisig** brushwood

Reiß–: ~aus *coll* (**R. nehmen** take to one's heels); **das ~brett, -er** drawing-board; **die ~leine, -n** rip-cord; **der ~nagel, ..nägel** drawing-pin, thumbtack *US*; **die ~schiene, -n** T-square; **der ~verschluß, ⸚(ss)e** zip(fastener), zipper *US*; **der ~wolf, ⸚e** shredder; **der ~zahn, ⸚e** fang; **das ~zeug** drawing instruments; **die ~zwecke, -n** drawing-pin, thumbtack *US*

reißen (*p/t* **riß**, *p/part* **gerissen**) (*see also* **gerissen**) tear, rip; pull (to one side *etc*); (animal) kill; crack (joke); *athl* knock off; *weightlift* snatch; (*v/i sn*) tear, rip; break; crack; **~ an** (*dat*) tug at; **an sich ~** seize; monopolize (conversation); **~ aus** tear (page) out of; snatch from/out of; take out of (context); **zu Boden ~** pull to the ground
sich ~ cut oneself (**an** *dat* on); **sich ~ um** *coll* scramble for

das **Reißen** *vbl noun*; *weightlift* snatch; *coll* rheumatism

reißend searing; (torrent) raging; **~en Absatz finden** sell like hot cakes

der **Reißer, -** *coll* sensational novel/film *etc*; *comm* big seller

reißerisch sensational

Reit– riding ...; **die ~bahn, -en** arena; **die ~hose, -n** riding-breeches; **der ~knecht, -e** groom; **die ~kunst** horsemanship; **der ~sport** riding (as sport); **das ~turnier, -e** horse-show; **der ~weg, -e** bridle-path

reiten (*p/t* **ritt**, *p/part* **geritten**) (*also sn if v/i; if indicating direction or distance travelled, only sn*) ride

der **Reiter, -** rider; *mil* cavalryman; *in compds* equestrian ...; *mil* cavalry ...

der **Reiz, -e** charm; appeal, attraction; *physiol* stimulus; (*pl*) charms; **keinen ~ haben für** not appeal to || **der ~husten, -** dry cough; **das ~klima, -s/-te** invigorating climate; **r~los** unappealing; **das ~mittel, -** stimulant; **die ~überflutung, -en** constant exposure to stimuli; **r~voll** delightful; appealing; **die ~wäsche** *coll* sexy underwear

reizbar irritable

die **Reizbarkeit** irritability

reizen (*see also* **gereizt**) stimulate; (smoke *etc*) irritate; tickle (palate); appeal to; provoke; tease (animal); arouse (curiosity *etc*); (*also v/i*) *cards* bid; **~ zu** rouse to (anger); **zum Widerspruch ~** provoke into contradicting s.o./one; (*v/i*) invite contradiction; **mich reizt (die Gefahr** *etc*) I get a thrill out of (danger *etc*); **es reizt mich zu ...** I feel tempted to ...; I get a thrill out of (+*ger*); **~d** delightful; charming

rekapitulieren recapitulate

rekeln: sich ~ stretch; sprawl

die **Reklamation, -en** *comm* complaint; *sp* appeal

die **Reklame, -n** advertising, publicity; advertisement; **~ machen für** advertise; publicize; **~ machen mit** *coll* show off

reklamieren make a complaint about (lost parcel *etc*); claim; *sp* appeal for (off-side *etc*); (*v/i*) complain, make a complaint

rekommandieren *Aust* register (letter *etc*)

rekonstruieren reconstruct

die **Rekonstruktion, –en** reconstruction
der **Rekonvaleszent, –en** (*wk masc*) convalescent
die **Rekonvaleszenz** convalescence
der **Rekord, –e** record; **die ~ernte, –n** bumper crop; **der ~inhaber, –** record-holder; **die ~zeit, –en** record time
der **Rekordler, –** *coll* record-holder
der **Rekrut, –en** (*wk masc*) recruit
rekrutieren recruit; **sich ~ aus** be drawn from
die **Rekrutierung, –en** recruitment
die **Rektion, –en** *gramm* government
der **Rektor, –(or)en** headmaster, principal *esp US*; *univ* vice-chancellor, president *US*
das **Rektorat, –e** headmaster's *etc* office (*see* **Rektor**); headmastership, principalship *esp US*, *univ* vice-chancellorship, presidency *US*
das **Relais** [rə'lɛː] (*gen* – [–(s)]), – [–s] *elect* relay
die **Relation, –en** relation; **in keiner ~ stehen zu** bear no relation to
relativ [*also* 'reː–] relative; (majority) simple; (*adv*) relatively; fairly; reasonably || **das R~pronomen, –/–(m)ina** relative pronoun; **der R~satz, ⸚e** relative clause
relativieren relativize, make relative; qualify
die **Relativität** relativity
relegieren expel; *univ* send down
relevant relevant
die **Relevanz** relevance
das **Relief** [re'li̯ɛf], **–s/–e** *art, geog* relief
die **Religion, –en** religion; *in compds* **~s–** … of religion; religious …; **der ~s|unterricht** religious instruction
religiös religious
die **Religiosität** religiousness
das **Relikt, –e** relic; *biol, geol* relict
die **Reling, –s** *naut* rail
die **Reliquie** [–i̯ə], **–n** *eccles* relic
die **Reminiszenz, –en** reminiscence
remis [rə'miː] *chess, sp* drawn; (*adv*: end) in a draw; **das Remis** (*gen* – [–(s)]), – [–s]/ **–en** [–zn̩] *chess, sp* draw
die **Remise** [rə–], **–n** *Aust* (tram *etc*) depot, carbarn *US*
das **Remmidemmi** *coll* racket
die **Remoulade** [remu–], **–n** = **die ~n|soße, –n** rémoulade
rempeln *coll* jostle; barge into
das **Ren** [–ɛ–, –eː–], **–s** [rɛns]/**–e** ['reːnə] = **das ~tier, –e** reindeer
die **Renaissance** [rənɛ'sãːs], **–n** renaissance; revival; **die ~** *hist* the Renaissance
das **Rendezvous** [rãde'vuː] (*gen* – [–(s)]), – [–s] rendezvous (*also space*)
die **Rendite, –n** *fin* return (on investment)
der **Renegat, –en** (*wk masc*) renegade
die **Reneklode, –n** greengage
renitent recalcitrant
die **Renitenz** recalcitrance
Renn– race …; racing …; **die ~bahn, –en** race-track; racecourse; **der ~fahrer, –** racing driver/cyclist/motorcyclist; **das ~pferd, –e** racehorse; **der ~platz, ⸚e** racecourse; **der ~sport** racing; **der ~stall, ⸚e** racing stable; *mot rac* équipe; **die ~strecke, –n** race-track; course; **die ~ver|anstaltung, –en** race-meeting; **der ~wagen, –** racing-car
rennen (*p/t* **rannte** (*subj rare* **rennte**), *p/part* **gerannt**) (+*dat*) run (knife *etc*) into; (*v/i sn*) run; *sp* race; **~ gegen** (*sn*) bump into; **zu Boden ~** knock down
das **Rennen, –** running; *sp* racing; race; **totes ~** dead heat; **das ~ machen** win; come out on top
der **Renner, –** (good) racehorse; *comm* winner
das **Renommee** [re–], **–s** reputation
Renommier– [re–] prestige …
renommieren [re–] boast (**mit** about); **renommiert** noted; of repute
renovieren renovate; redecorate
die **Renovierung, –en** renovation; redecoration
rentabel profitable; viable
die **Rentabilität** profitability; viability
die **Rente, –n** pension; annuity; income (from investment *etc*); **die ~n|versicherung, –en** pension scheme
rentieren: sich ~ pay; be worthwhile
der **Rentner, –** pensioner
re|organisieren reorganize
reparabel repairable
die **Reparationen** *pl* reparations
die **Reparatur, –en** repair; **in ~** being repaired; **in ~ geben** have repaired || **r~bedürftig** in need of repair; **die ~werk|statt, ⸚en** repair shop; garage
reparieren repair; **nicht mehr zu ~** beyond repair
das **Repertoire** [repɛr'tŏaːɐ], **–s** repertoire
repetieren revise, review *US*; (*v/i*) repeat a class
der **Repetitor, –(or)en** (*wk masc*) coach (for examination)
das **Repetitorium, –(i)en** revision course/manual, review course/manual *US*
der **Report** [re–], **–e** report
die **Reportage** [repɔr'taːʒə], **–n** report (in media)
der **Reporter** [re'pɔrtɐ], **–** reporter
der **Repräsentant** [re–], **–en** (*wk masc*) representative; **das ~en|haus** the House of Representatives
die **Repräsentanz** representation
die **Repräsentation** representation; (official) entertaining
repräsentativ representative (**für** of); distinguished-looking; imposing; in keeping with one's position; (duties) social
repräsentieren represent; (*v/i*) perform official social duties, entertain
die **Repressalien** [–i̯ən] *pl* reprisals

[die] **Repression, –en** repression
repressiv repressive
[der] **Reprint** [re–], **–s** reprint
[die] **Reprise, –n** *cin, theat* revival; *mus* recapitulation
reprivatisieren denationalize
[die] **Reprivatisierung, –en** denationalization
[die] **Reproduktion, –en** reproduction
reproduzieren reproduce
[das] **Reptil, –ien** [–ĭən] reptile
[die] **Republik, –en** republic; (*in names of countries, eg* ~ **Südafrika**) Republic of; **die ~flucht** *EGer* illegal emigration (from E. Germany)
[der] **Republikaner, –, republikanisch** republican
[das] **Requiem** ['reːkviɛm], **–s** requiem
requirieren requisition
[das] **Requisit, –en** piece of equipment; (*pl*) *theat* properties
resch *Aust* crisp; vivacious
[das] **Reservat, –e** (Indian *etc*) reservation; reserve
[die] **Reservation, –en** (Indian *etc*) reservation
[die] **Reserve, –n** reserve (supply) (**an** *dat* of); reserve (= reticence); (*pl*) *mil* reserves; **in ~** in reserve
Reserve– reserve ...; spare ...; **die ~bank, ⸚e** substitutes' bench; **das ~rad, ⸚er** spare wheel
reservieren reserve, book; **reserviert** reserved (*also* = reticent)
[die] **Reserviertheit** reserve
[der] **Reservist, –en** (*wk masc*) reservist
[das] **Reservoir** [rezɛr'vŏaːɐ], **–e** reservoir; pool (of talent *etc*)
[die] **Residenz, –en** residence (of prince *etc*)
[die] **Resignation** resignation (= being resigned)
resignieren give up; **resigniert** resigned; (*adv*) resignedly; with resignation
[die] **Resistenz, –en** resistance (**gegen** to)
resolut resolute
[die] **Resolution, –en** *pol etc* resolution
[die] **Resonanz, –en** resonance; response (**auf** *acc* to); **der ~boden, ..böden** sounding-board
[das] **Resopal** (*trade-mark*) Formica
resorbieren absorb
[die] **Resorption, –en** absorption
resozialisieren rehabilitate
[die] **Resozialisierung, –en** rehabilitation
resp. = respektive
[der] **Respekt (vor** *dat* for); **r~los** disrespectful, irreverent; **r~voll** respectful
respektabel respectable
respektieren respect
respektive or; and ... respectively
[die] **Respekts|person, –en** person commanding respect
[das] **Ressentiment** [rɛsãti'mãː], **–s** resentment
[das] **Ressort** [rɛ'soːɐ], **–s** department; **das ist (nicht) mein ~** that's (outside) my province || **r~mäßig** departmental

[die] **Ressourcen** [rɛ'sʊrsn̩] *pl* resources
[der] **Rest, –e/***comm* **–er** remains; remainder (*also math*); rest; vestige; *text* remnant; *chem* residue; group; (*pl*) left-overs; remains (of building *etc*); **der letzte ~** the last bit; (+*dat*) **den ~ geben** *coll* finish off
Rest– remaining ...; residual ...; *prefixed to the name of a country that has suffered territorial losses* (*as in* **~deutschland**), *it refers to the part which is left*; **der ~betrag, ⸚e** balance; **r~los** complete, total; **der ~posten, –** remainder (of stock); **die ~summe, –n** balance; **das ~volk, ⸚er** remnant of a people
[das] **Restaurant** [–to'rãː], **–s** restaurant
[die] **Restauration[1], –en** restoration (*also pol*)
[die] **Restauration[2]** [–tor–], **–en** *Aust* restaurant
restaurativ aimed at restoring the old order
[der] **Restaurator, –(or)en** *art* restorer
restaurieren restore (*also pol*)
restlich rest of the ..., remaining
restriktiv restrictive
[das] **Resultat, –e** result; **r~los** without result
resultieren: ~ aus result from, be the result of
[das] **Resümee, –s** summary, résumé
resümieren sum up
[die] **Retorte, –n** *chem* retort; **aus der ~** synthetic; (baby) test-tube || **das ~n|baby, –s** test-tube baby
retour [re'tuːɐ] *Aust* back; **das R~billett, –e/–s** *Swiss* return ticket, roundtrip ticket *US*; **der R~gang** *Aust* reverse gear; **die R~karte, –n** *Aust* return ticket, roundtrip ticket *US*; **die R~kutsche, –n** *coll* retort (in same terms); **das R~spiel, –e** *Aust, Swiss* return match
retournieren [–tur–] *esp Aust* return
retrospektiv [re–], **die Retrospektive, –n** retrospective
retten rescue **(aus/vor** *dat* from); save (from); salvage; **bist du noch zu ~?** have you taken leave of your senses?
sich ~ escape (**vor** *dat* from); **sich ~ in** (*acc*) take refuge in; **sich nicht mehr ~ können/zu ~ wissen vor** (*dat*) be swamped with; **rette sich, wer kann!** it's every man for himself!
[der] **Retter, –** rescuer; *theol* saviour
[der] **Rettich, –e** radish
[die] **Rettung, –en** rescue; salvation; *Aust* ambulance (service); **die ~s|aktion, –en** rescue operation; **die ~s|boje, –n** lifebuoy; **das ~s|boot, –e** lifeboat; **das ~s|floß, ⸚e** life-raft; **der ~s|gürtel, –** lifebelt; **r~s|los** hopeless (**... ist r. verloren** there is no hope for ...); **der ~s|ring, –e** lifebelt; **das ~s|schwimmen** life-saving; **der ~s|schwimmer, –** life-saver; lifeguard; **der ~s|wagen, –** ambulance

[die] **Retusche, –n** retouching
retuschieren retouch
reu–: ~mütig remorseful; rueful
[die] **Reue** repentance; remorse; **r~voll** repentant; remorseful
reuen: ... reut mich I regret ...
reuig penitent
[die] **Reuse, –n** fish-trap
reüssieren succeed
[die] **Revanche** [re'vã:ʃ(ə)], **–n** revenge; *sp* = **das ~spiel, –e** return match
revanchieren [revãʃ–]: **sich ~** get one's own back; return s.o.'s hospitality/kindness; **sich ~ für** get one's own back for; repay; return (invitation)
[der] **Revanchismus** [revãʃ–] revanchism
[der] **Revanchist** [revãʃ–], **–en** (*wk masc*), **revanchistisch** revanchist
Reverenz [reve–]: (+*dat*) **seine ~ erweisen** show one's respect for
[das] **Revers** [–'vɛ:ɐ] (*gen* – [–(s)]), – [–s] lapel
reversieren *Aust mot* reverse
revidieren revise; check; *comm* audit
[das] **Revier, –e** territory (of individual, animal, *etc*); (police) district, precinct *US*; police-station; *hunt* shoot; *mil* sick-bay
[das] **Revirement** [revirə'mã:], **–s** *pol* reshuffle
[die] **Revision, –en** revision (of opinion *etc*); checking; *comm* audit; *leg* appeal (on point of law)
[der] **Revisionismus** revisionism
[der] **Revisionist, –en** (*wk masc*), **revisionistisch** revisionist
[der] **Revisor, –(or)en** (*wk masc*) auditor; press-reader
[die] **Revolte, –n, revoltieren** revolt
[die] **Revolution, –en** revolution
revolutionär, der Revolutionär, –e revolutionary
revolutionieren revolutionize
Revolutions– revolutionary ...
[der] **Revoluzzer, –** would-be revolutionary
[der] **Revolver** [re'vɔlvɐ], – revolver; **das ~blatt, ⸚er** *coll* scandal-sheet; **der ~held, –en** (*wk masc*) *coll* gunslinger
[die] **Revue** [rə'vy:], **–n** [–ən] revue; **~ passieren lassen** pass in review || **das ~girl, –s** chorus-girl
[der] **Rezensent, –en** (*wk masc*) reviewer
rezensieren review
[die] **Rezension, –en** review; recension (of text)
[das] **Rezept, –e** *cul* recipe; *med* prescription; **~ für** recipe for (long life *etc*); **~ gegen** remedy for; **auf ~** on prescription || **r~pflichtig** available on prescription
[die] **Rezeption, –en** reception; reception (desk)
[der] **Rezeptor, –(or)en** receptor
[die] **Rezeptur, –en** dispensing; dispensary; formula
[die] **Rezession, –en** recession
rezessiv recessive
reziprok reciprocal
[die] **Rezitation, –en** recitation
[das] **Rezitativ, –e** recitative
[der] **Rezitator, –(or)en** reciter
rezitieren recite
[das] **R-Gespräch, –e** transferred charge call, collect call *US*
[der] **RGW** *EGer* (= **Rat für Gegenseitige Wirtschaftshilfe**) COMECON
[der] **Rhabarber** rhubarb
[die] **Rhapsodie, –(ie)n** rhapsody
[der] **Rhein** (*gen* **–s**) the Rhine; **r~ab(wärts)/auf(wärts)** down/up the Rhine; **das ~land** the Rhineland; **der ~länder, –** Rhinelander; **r~ländisch** Rhineland; **Rheinland-Pfalz** Rhineland-Palatinate; **der ~wein, –e** Rhine wine, hock
rheinisch Rhenish; Rhine
Rhesus– rhesus ...
[die] **Rhetorik** [–ɪk] rhetoric
[der] **Rhetoriker, –** rhetorician
rhetorisch rhetorical
[das] **Rheuma** rheumatism
[der] **Rheumatiker, –, rheumatisch** rheumatic
[das] **Rhinozeros** [–ɔs] (*gen* **–(ses)**), **–se** rhinoceros; *coll* ass
[das] **Rhododendron** [–ɔn], **–(r)en** (*also* **der**) rhododendron
Rhodos ['rɔdɔs] Rhodes
[die] **Rhone** [–ə] the Rhône
[die] **Rhythmik** ['rʏtmɪk] rhythmics; rhythm
rhythmisch ['rʏt–] rhythmic(al)
[der] **Rhythmus** ['rʏt–], **–(m)en** rhythm
[der] **RIAS** ['ri:as] = **Rundfunksender im amerikanischen Sektor**
[die] **Ribisel, –n** *Aust* redcurrant; blackcurrant
Richt– guiding ...; *rad* directional ...; *hist* executioner's (sword *etc*); **der ~block, ⸚e** *hist* block (used in execution); **das ~fest, –e** topping-out; **die ~geschwindigkeit, –en** recommended speed(-limit); **die ~linien** *pl* guidelines; **der ~platz, ⸚e** place of execution; **der ~preis, –e** recommended price; **die ~schnur, –en** guide-line; guiding principle
richten judge; *arch* execute; *esp SGer* prepare; make (bed); lay (table); do (one's hair); fix; (*v/i*) judge
~ an (*acc*) address to; put (question) to
~ auf (*acc*) aim at; direct towards
~ über (*acc*) sit in judgement on
sich ~ auf (*acc*)/**gegen** be directed towards/against; **sich ~ nach** go by; be guided by; comply with; fit in with; depend on; *gramm* agree with; **richt't euch!** *mil* right dress!
[der] **Richter, –** judge; **sich zum ~ aufwerfen** set oneself up in judgement || **der ~stuhl** *leg* (the) Bench; *bibl* judgement-seat

richterlich judicial

richtig right; correct; real; proper; (*adv*, *as intensifier*) *coll* really; ~ **sein** *coll* be O.K.; ~**!** that's right!; **so ist's** ~**!** that's the stuff!; **und** ~**, …** and sure enough …; **du bist mir der R~e!** you're a fine one! || ~**gehend** (clock) accurate; real; (*adv*) really; ~**liegen*** (*sep*) *coll* say/do the right thing; ~**machen** (*sep*) *coll* settle (bill); ~**stellen** (*sep*) correct; **die R~stellung, -en** correction

die **Richtigkeit** correctness; **das hat/damit hat es seine** ~ that's correct

die **Richtung, -en** direction; line (of thought *etc*); *arts*, *pol* trend; movement; **die** ~ **ändern** change direction; **in dieser** ~ in this direction; **in** ~ (*followed by place-name*), **in** ~ **auf** (*acc*) in the direction of; **nach allen** ~**en** in all directions || **der** ~**s|wechsel, -** change of direction; **r~weisend** pointing the way (**r. sein für** point the way for)

die **Ricke, -n** doe

rieb *p/t of* **reiben**

Riech- olfactory …; **das** ~**salz** smelling salts

riechen (*p/t* **roch** (*subj* **röche**), *p/part* **gerochen**) (*also v/i*) smell; ~ **an** (*dat*) smell, sniff at; ~ **nach** smell of; *coll* smack of; **es riecht nach …** there's a smell of …; **ich kann … nicht** ~ I can't smell; I can't stand the smell of; *coll* I can't stand; **das konnte ich doch nicht** ~**!** *coll* how was I to know?

der **Riecher, -** *coll* conk, schnozzle *US*; nose (for sth.)

das **Ried, -e** reeds; marsh; **das** ~**gras, ¨-er** sedge

rief *p/t of* **rufen**

die **Riege, -n** team (of politicians *etc*); *gym* squad

der **Riegel, -** bolt; bar (of chocolate, soap); (+*dat*) **einen** ~ **vorschieben** put a stop to

der **Riemen**[1], **-** strap; belt (*also mech*); **den** ~ **enger schnallen** *coll* tighten one's belt; **sich am** ~ **reißen** *coll* pull oneself together

der **Riemen**[2], **-** *naut* oar

der **Riese, -n** (*wk masc*) giant

die **Riesel|felder** *pl* sewage farm

rieseln drizzle; (snow) fall gently; (*sn*) trickle; **ein Schauder rieselte mir über den Rücken** a shiver ran down my spine

Riesen- giant … (*also bot*, *zool*); gigantic …; tremendous …; **riesen|groß** enormous; **das** ~**rad, ¨-er** Ferris wheel; **die** ~**schlange, -n** constrictor (*eg* python, boa)

riesig gigantic; (*adv*) *coll* tremendously

die **Riesin, -nen** giantess

riet *p/t of* **raten**

das **Riff, -e** reef

rigoros rigorous

das **Rigorosum, -(s)a** viva voce (for doctorate)

die **Rikscha, -s** rickshaw

die **Rille, -n** groove

Rimski-Korsakow [-ɔf] Rimsky-Korsakov

rin [-ɪ-] *coll* = **herein, hinein**

das **Rind, -er** ox; cow; beef; (*pl*) cattle; **das** ~**fleisch** beef; **das** ~**vieh** cattle; *coll* (*pl* ~**viecher**) ass

die **Rinde, -n** bark; crust; rind; *anat* cortex

Rinder- beef …; cattle …; **der** ~**braten, -** roast beef; **das** ~**filet, -s** fillet of beef; **die** ~**herde, -n** herd of cattle; **die** ~**roulade, -n** beef olives, roulade of beef *US*; **die** ~**zucht** cattle-farming

Rinds- *SGer* = **Rinder-**

der **Ring, -e** ring (*also astron*, *sp*); ring-road, beltway *US*; circle (of poets *etc*), ring (of criminals *etc*); circle, cycle; *in compds also* circular …; **die** ~**bahn, -en** circular railway, belt line *US*; **das** ~**buch, ¨-er** loose-leaf file; **die** ~**drossel, -n** ring-ouzel; **r~förmig** ring-shaped; *chem* cyclic; *astron* annular; **der** ~**kampf, ¨-e** wrestling match; wrestling; **der** ~**kämpfer, -** wrestler; **der** ~**richter, -** *box* referee; **die** ~**sendung, -en** *rad* hook-up; **die** ~**straße, -n** ring-road, beltway *US*

der **Ringel, -** small ring; ringlet; **die** ~**blume, -n** marigold; **die** ~**locke, -n** ringlet; **die** ~**natter, -n** grass-snake; **der** ~**pie(t)z, -e** *coll* 'hop'; **der** ~**pulli, -s** *coll* striped polo jumper; **der** ~**reihen, -** ring-a-ring o' roses, ring-around-a-rosy *US*; **die** ~**socke, -n** striped sock; **das** ~**spiel, -e** *Aust* merry-go-round; **die** ~**taube, -n** ring-dove

ringeln (*see also* **geringelt**) curl; **sich** ~ curl; coil

ringen (*p/t* **rang** (*subj* **ränge**), *p/part* **gerungen**) wring (one's hands); (*v/i*) wrestle

~ **aus** wrest from

~ **mit** wrestle with; fight back (tears)

~ **nach** struggle for (breath)/to gain (composure)/to find (words)

~ **um** fight for (recognition, s.o.'s life, *etc*); struggle to find (words)

das **Ringen** struggle; *sp* wrestling

der **Ringer, -** wrestler

rings all around; ~ **im Kreis(e)** in a circle; (look) all around; ~ **um** around || **rings|(her)um** all around

Rinn-: der ~**stein, -e** gutter

die **Rinne, -n** channel; gutter

rinnen (*p/t* **rann** (*subj* **ränne, rönne**), *p/part* **geronnen**) (*sn*) run, flow

das **Rinnsal, -e** rivulet; trickle

der **Rio de la Plata** (*gen* **- - - -**) the River Plate, the Río de la Plata *US*

das **Rippchen, -** (*esp* pork) rib

die **Rippe, -n** rib (*also archit*, *bot*); *mech* fin; *in compds* ~**n-** *also* ribbed …; *anat* costal …; **die** ~**n|fell|entzündung, -en** pleurisy; **der** ~**n|speer** (*also* **das**) (lightly cured) spare rib of pork; **der** ~**n|stoß, ¨-e** dig in the ribs; **das** ~**n|stück, -e** *cul* rib der **Rips, –e** rep

rips, raps! rip!

das **Risiko, –s/Risiken** risk; **auf eigenes ~** at one's own risk || **r~reich** high-risk

riskant risky

riskieren risk; venture; **ein Auge ~** *coll* steal a glance at s.o.

riß (risse) *p/t* (*subj*) *of* **reißen**

der **Riß, –(ss)e** tear (in paper *etc*); crack; rift; **–riß** torn (ligament *etc*); **... hat einen ~ bekommen** a rift has developed in ... || **die ~wunde, –n** laceration

rissig cracked; chapped

der **Rist, –e** instep; back of the hand; *zool* withers

Riten *pl of* **Ritus**

ritsch, ratsch! rip!

ritt *p/t of* **reiten**

der **Ritt, –e** ride; **einen ~ machen** go for a ride; **auf einen/in einem ~** *coll* at one go || **der ~meister, –** *hist* captain of horse

der **Ritter, –** knight; **arme ~** *pl* (*bread soaked in milk with egg and then fried*); **fahrender ~** knight errant; **zum ~ schlagen** knight || **der ~roman, –e** romance; **der ~schlag, ⸚e** accolade; **der ~sporn, –e** larkspur; **der ~stand** knighthood; **die ~zeit** the Age of Chivalry

ritterlich chivalrous

das **Rittertum** chivalry

rittlings: ~ auf (*dat*) astride

das **Ritual, –e/–ien** [–ĭən], **rituell** ritual

der **Ritus, –(t)en** rite

der **Ritz, –e** scratch; crack, chink

die **Ritze, –n** crack, chink

ritzen scratch

der **Rivale, –n** (*wk masc*) rival

rivalisieren: ~ mit compete with; **~d** rival, competing

die **Rivalität, –en** rivalry

das **Rizinus|öl** castor oil

RM *hist* = **Reichsmark**

die **Robbe, –n** seal; **der ~n|fang** sealing

robben (*also sn*; *if indicating direction or distance covered, only sn*) crawl (using elbows)

die **Robe, –n** robe; (evening) gown

roboten ['rɔbɔtn̩] *coll* slave away

der **Roboter** ['rɔbɔtɐ], **–** robot

roboterhaft robot-like

robust robust; sturdy

roch (röche) *p/t* (*subj*) *of* **riechen**

die **Rochade** [–x–, –ʃ–], **–n** *chess* castling; *sp* change of position

röcheln breathe stertorously; give the death-rattle; **das Röcheln** death rattle

der **Rochen, –** *zool* ray

rochieren [–x–, –ʃ–] *chess* castle; *sp* (*also sn*) change positions

der **Rock[1], ⸚e** skirt; *dated* (men's) jacket

der **Rock[2]** (*gen* –(s)) rock (music)

Rock–: der ~schoß, ⸚e coat-tail; **~zipfel** *coll* (**an Mutters R. hängen** be tied to one's mother's apron-strings)

Rodel–: die ~bahn, –en toboggan-run; **der ~schlitten, –** toboggan; **der ~sport** tobogganing

rodeln (*also sn*; *if indicating direction or distance travelled, only sn*) toboggan

roden clear (forest)

der **Rogen, –** roe

der **Roggen** rye; **das ~brot, –e** rye bread

roh raw; rough; crude (= unprocessed); (manners *etc*) rough; **~e Gewalt** brute force; **... ist im ~en fertig** the rough draft/sketch *etc* of ... is complete || **der R~bau, –ten** shell (of building) (**das Haus ist im R. fertig** the shell of the house is complete); **das R~eisen** pig-iron; **der R~ertrag, ⸚e** gross yield; **das R~gewicht, –e** gross weight; **die R~kost** uncooked fruit and vegetables; **das R~öl** crude oil; **der R~stoff, –e** raw material; **der R~zucker** unrefined sugar

die **Roheit, –en** rawness; roughness

der **Rohling, –e** brute; *tech* blank

das **Rohr, –e** pipe; tube; cane; reed(s); (gun) barrel; *esp Aust* oven; **die ~ammer, –n** reed-bunting; **das ~blatt, ⸚er** *mus* reed; **der ~bruch, ⸚e** burst pipe; **die ~dommel, –n** bittern; **die ~leitung, –en** pipe; pipeline; **die ~post** pneumatic dispatch; **der ~stock, ⸚e** cane; **der ~stuhl, ⸚e** cane chair; **der ~zucker** cane sugar

die **Röhre, –n** tube; oven; *rad*, *TV* valve, tube *US*; *TV coll* 'the box', 'the tube' *US*; **in die ~ gucken** *coll* watch the box/tube *US*; be left out

röhren *hunt* (stag) bell

das **Rokoko** ['rɔkoko] rococo; rococo period

Roll–: der Rolladen, –/..läden (rolling) shutter; roll-top; **die ~bahn, –en** runway; taxiway; **der ~film, –e** roll film; **der ~kragen, –, der ~kragen|pullover, –** polo-neck, turtleneck *US*; **der ~mops, ⸚e** roll-mop (herring); **der ~schreib|tisch, –e** roll-top desk; **der ~schuh, –e** roller-skate (**R. laufen** roller-skate); **der ~schuh|läufer, –** roller-skater; **der ~sitz, –e** *row* sliding seat; **der ~splitt** loose chippings; **der ~stuhl, ⸚e** wheel-chair; **die ~treppe, –n** escalator

die **Rolle[1], –n** roll; coil; reel; spool; scroll; roller; castor; pulley; *aer*, *gym* roll

die **Rolle[2], –n** role (*also sociol*); *cin*, *theat* part; **eine ~ spielen** play a part (**bei** in); be a factor (in); **... spielt keine ~** ... doesn't matter (**bei** to); (money *etc*) is no object; **aus der ~ fallen** forget oneself; **sich in jmds. ~ versetzen** put oneself in s.o.'s place

rollen roll; roll up; *cul* roll out; (*v/i*) (thunder, guns) rumble; (ship) roll; (*sn*) roll (along);

aer taxi; **das R ~** roll one's r's; **~ mit** roll (one's eyes); **sich ~** curl up; **den Stein ins Rollen bringen** set the ball rolling; **ins Rollen kommen** start to move; get under way

Rollen– role ...; *mech etc* roller ...; **die ~besetzung, –en** casting; **das ~fach, ⸚er** type of role; **r~förmig** cylindrical; **das ~lager, –** roller bearing; **das ~spiel** role-playing; **der ~tausch** exchange of roles; *sociol* role-reversal

der **Roller, –** scooter (*also mot*); *Aust* roller-blind

rollern (*also sn*; *if indicating direction or distance travelled, only sn*) ride one's scooter

das **Rollo, –s** roller-blind

Rom Rome

der **Roman, –e** novel; **der ~schrift|steller, –** novelist

der **Romancier** [romã'sie:], **–s** novelist

der **Romane, –n** (*wk masc*) Latin

die **Romania** (*territory in which the Romance languages are spoken*)

die **Romanik** [–ɪk] Romanesque; Romanesque period

romanisch Romance; *arts* Romanesque

der **Romanist, –en** (*wk masc*) Romance scholar; student of Romance languages and literature

die **Romanistik** [–ɪk] Romance studies

die **Romantik** [–ɪk] romance; *arts* Romanticism

der **Romantiker, –, romantisch** romantic; *arts* Romantic

romantisieren romanticize

die **Romanze, –n** romance (*also liter, mus*)

der **Römer**[1], **–** (*type of wine-glass with green or brown stem*)

der **Römer**[2], **–** Roman; **die ~straße, –n** Roman road; **das ~reich** the Roman Empire

römisch Roman; **römisch-katholisch** Roman Catholic

röm.-kath. (**= römisch-katholisch**) R.C.

das **Rommé** rummy

das **Rondell, –e** round tower; circular flower-bed

rönne *p/t subj of* **rinnen**

röntgen, die R~aufnahme, –n X-ray; **die R~assistentin, –nen** radiographer; **die R~strahlen** *pl* X-rays; **die R~therapie** radiotherapy

röntgenisieren *Aust* X-ray

der **Röntgenologe, –n** (*wk masc*) radiologist

die **Röntgenologie** radiology

röntgenologisch radiological

rosa (*indecl*) pink; **~rot** deep pink

die **Rose, –n** rose; **er ist nicht auf ~n gebettet** his life is not a bed of roses || **die ~n|knospe, –n** rosebud; **der ~n|kohl** Brussels sprouts; **der ~n|kranz, ⸚e** garland of roses; *RC* rosary (**den R. beten** tell one's beads); **der ~n|montag, –e** Shrove Monday; **der ~n|stock, ⸚e** rose (tree)

der **Rosé, –s = der ~wein, –e** rosé

die **Rosette, –n** rosette

rosig rosy

die **Rosine, –n** raisin; **große ~n im Kopf haben** *coll* have big ideas

der **Rosmarin** [–o:–] rosemary

das **Roß, –(ss)e** *poet* steed; *coll* fathead; (*pl* ⸚(ss)er) *SGer* horse; **auf dem hohen ~ sitzen** *coll* be on one's high horse

Roß– horse ...; **das ~haar** horsehair; **die ~kastanie, –n** horse-chestnut; **die ~kur, –en** *coll* drastic cure

der **Rössel|sprung, ⸚e** *chess* knight's move

der **Rost**[1] rust

der **Rost**[2], **–e** grill; grating; *cul* grill

Rost–: der ~braten, – roast; **die ~brat|wurst, ⸚e** grilled sausage; **r~frei** rustproof; stainless; **der ~schutz** rust-proofing

Röst– [–œ–, –ø:–]: **das ~brot** toast; **die ~kastanien** *pl* roast chestnuts

rosten (*also sn*) rust

rösten [–œ–, –ø:–] grill; roast; toast

rostig rusty

rot (*also* ⸚ *exc fig*) red (*also pol*); **das R~e Kreuz** the Red Cross; **das R~e Meer** the Red Sea; **~ werden** go red

rot– red ...; (*with second colour-word attached*) reddish–; **der R~armist, –en** (*wk masc*) soldier in the Red Army; **~bäckig** rosy-cheeked; **der R~barsch, –e** rosefish; **R~bart (Kaiser R.** (Emperor Frederick I) Barbarossa); **~blond** sandy; sandy-haired; strawberry blonde; **der R~fuchs, ⸚e** red fox; chestnut (horse); *coll* redhead; **~glühend** red-hot; **die R~glut** red heat; **~haarig** red-haired; **die R~haut, ⸚e** redskin; **der R~hirsch, –e** red deer; **R~käppchen** Little Red Riding Hood; **das R~kehlchen, –** robin (redbreast); **der R~kohl = das R~kraut** *SGer* red cabbage; **das R~licht** red light; **der R~schimmel, –** roan; **der R~schwanz, ⸚e = das R~schwänzchen, –** redstart; **~sehen*** (*sep*) *coll* see red; **der R~stift, –e** red pencil (**dem R. zum Opfer fallen** be scrapped); **der R~wein, –e** red wine; **das R~welsch** thieves' cant; **das R~wild** red deer

die **Rotation, –en** rotation

die **Röte** red(ness); blush; **die ~ stieg ihm ins Gesicht** his face reddened

die **Röteln** *pl* German measles

röten, sich ~ redden

rotieren rotate

rötlich reddish; ruddy

der **Rotor, –(or)en** rotor

die **Rotte, –n** gang; pack (of wolves); *mil* pair of aircraft/ships (operating together)

Rotterdam Rotterdam

die **Rotunde, –n** rotunda

der **Rotz** *vulg* snot; **der ~junge, –n** (*wk masc*) *vulg* cheeky little devil; **die ~nase, –n** *vulg* snotty nose; cheeky little devil

rotzig *vulg* snotty

[die] **Roulade** [ru–], **–n** (beef *etc*) olives, roulade *US*

[das] **Rouleau** [ru'loː], **–s** roller-blind

[das] **Roulett** [ru–], **–e/–s, das Roulette** [–'lɛt], **–s** roulette; **russisches ~** Russian roulette

[die] **Route** ['ruːtə], **–n** route

[die] **Routine** [ru–] experience; routine; *in compds* routine ...; **r~mäßig** routine; (*adv*) as a matter of routine; **die ~sache, –n** routine matter

[der] **Routinier** [ruti'nĭeː], **–s** old hand

routiniert [ru–] experienced; practised

[der] **Rowdy** ['raodi], **–s** hooligan; rowdy

[das] **Rowdytum** hooliganism; rowdyism

[der] **Royalismus** [rŏaja–] royalism

[der] **Royalist** [rŏaja–], **–en** (*wk masc*), **royalistisch** royalist

Rp. *Swiss* = **Rappen**

rubbeln *NGer coll* rub; rub down

[die] **Rübe, –n** turnip; beet; *coll* 'nut'; **freche ~** *coll* cheeky monkey; **gelbe ~** *SGer* carrot; **rote ~** beetroot, beet *US*

[der] **Rubel, –** rouble

[der] **Rüben|zucker** beet sugar

rüber *coll* = **herüber, hinüber**

[der] **Rubikon** [–ɔn] (*gen* –(s)) the Rubicon

[der] **Rubin, –e, r~rot** ruby

[die] **Rubrik, –en** heading; category; *journ* section

ruch– [–uː–]: **~los** infamous

ruchbar [–uː–]: **~ werden** get abroad

[der] **Ruck, –e** jerk; jolt; *pol* shift; **sich** *dat* **einen ~ geben** *coll* make an effort; **in einem ~** *coll* in one go; **mit einem ~** with a jerk; *coll* suddenly; **ruck, zuck** (*see separate entry*) || **r~artig** jerky; **der ~sack, ¨–e** rucksack; **r~weise** by fits and starts

Rück– back ...; rear ...; return ...; re–; (*Note: vbl nouns corresponding to verbs with the prefix* **zurück–** *are sometimes formed with* **Rück–**; *if not listed below, see under* **zurück–**);

die ~antwort, –en reply (**Telegramm mit R.** reply-paid telegram); **die ~besinnung** (**R. auf** (*acc*) calling to mind); **r~bezüglich** reflexive; **die ~bildung, –en** *biol* degeneration; *ling* back-formation; **die ~blende, –n** flashback; **der ~blick, –e** look back (**auf** *acc* at) (**im R.** in retrospect); **r~blickend** retrospective; (*adv*) in retrospect; **r~erstatten** (*only infin and p/part* **r~erstattet**) refund; **die ~erstattung, –en** refunding; refund; **die ~fahr|karte, –n** = **der ~fahr|schein, –e** return ticket, roundtrip ticket *US*; **die ~fahrt, –en** return journey; **der ~fall, ¨–e** relapse (*also med*) (**in** *acc* into); *leg* repetition of an offence; **r~fällig** (**r. werden** relapse; *leg* relapse into crime); **der ~flug, ¨–e** return flight; **die ~frage, –n** further enquiry (**R. halten bei** check with); **r~fragen** (*only infin and p/part* **r~gefragt**) enquire (**r. bei** check with); **die ~führung** return, repatriation; tracing back (**auf** *acc* to); **die ~gabe** return; **der ~gang** decline (*gen* in); drop (in); **r~gängig** (**r. machen** cancel; revoke); **r~gebildet** *biol* vestigial; **die ~gewinnung** recovery; reclamation; **die ~gliederung** reincorporation; **das ~grat, –e** backbone (*also* = mainstay), spine ((+*dat*) **das R. brechen** break (person); (+*dat*) **das R. stärken/steifen** give (s.o.) moral support; **kein R. haben** be spineless; **R. zeigen** show strength of character); **der ~griff** recourse (**auf** *acc* to); falling back (on); **der ~halt** backing; **r~halt|los** unreserved; (frankness *etc*) absolute; (*adv*) unreservedly, without reservation; **die ~hand** *sp* backhand; **die ~kehr** return; **r~koppeln** (*only infin and p/part* **r~gekoppelt**) feed back; **die ~kopp(e)lung** feedback; **die ~lage, –n** savings; (*pl*) *comm* reserves; **der ~lauf** rewind (of tape); *mech* return travel; **r~läufig** declining; downward; (index) reverse; **das ~licht, –er** tail-light; **der ~marsch, ¨–e** march back; retreat; **die ~nahme** taking back; withdrawal; **das ~porto, –s** return postage; **der ~prall** rebound; **die ~reise, –n** return journey; **die ~schau, –en** review (**auf** *acc* of) (**R. halten auf** (*acc*) look back on); **der ~schlag, ¨–e** rebound; recoil; setback; *Swiss* deficit; *med* relapse; *biol* throwback; **der ~schluß, ¨–(ss)e** conclusion, inference (**~schlüsse ziehen auf** (*acc*) draw conclusions about); **der ~schritt, –e** retrograde step; **r~schrittlich** retrograde; reactionary; **die ~seite, –n** back; reverse (of coin *etc*) (**siehe R.** see over(leaf)); **die ~sicht, –en** consideration (**auf** *acc* for); (*pl*) (financial *etc*) considerations (**keine R. kennen** be ruthless; **R. nehmen auf** (*acc*) show consideration for; consider; **aus R. auf** (*acc*) out of consideration for; **mit R. auf** (*acc*) in view of; out of consideration for; **ohne R. auf** (*acc*) regardless of); **die ~sicht|nahme** consideration; **r~sichts|los** inconsiderate, *mot* reckless; ruthless; **die ~sichts|losigkeit** lack of consideration, *mot* recklessness; ruthlessness; **r~sichts|voll** considerate; **der ~siedler, –** repatriate; **die ~siedlung, –en** repatriation; **der ~sitz, –e** back seat; **der ~spiegel, –** rear-view mirror; **das ~spiel, –e** return match; **die ~sprache, –n** consultation (**R. nehmen mit** confer with); **r~spulen** (*only infin and p/part* **r~gespult**) rewind; **der ~stand, ¨–e** remains, *chem* residue; arrears; backlog (**den R. aufholen** catch up; close the gap; **im R. sein** be behind (**mit** with); **mit (0:8**

etc) **im R. sein** be (8 *etc*) goals *etc* down; **in R. geraten** fall behind); **r~ständig** backward; antiquated; (amount) outstanding; **der ~stau, -e/-s** *mot* tailback; **der ~stoß, ¨-e** recoil; *phys* repulsion; **der ~strahler, -** reflector; **die ~strahlung** reflection; **die ~taste, -n** back-spacer; **der ~tritt, -e** resignation; **die ~tritt|bremse, -n** back-pedal brake, coaster brake *US*; **r~übersetzen** (*only infin and p/part* **r~übersetzt**) translate back (into the original language); **r~vergüten** (*only infin and p/part* **r~vergütet**) refund; **die ~vergütung, -en** refunding; refund; **r~versichern** (*only infin and p/part* **r~versichert**) reinsure (**sich r.** reinsure; cover oneself; **sich r. bei** check with (as a safeguard)); **die ~versicherung, -en** reinsurance; **r~verweisen** (*only infin and p/part* **r~verwiesen**) refer back; **die ~wand, ¨-e** back wall; (of wardrobe *etc*) back; **der ~wanderer, -** returning emigrant; **r~wärtig** back; rear; **r~wärts** backwards; *SGer* at the back (**r. fahren** back); **~wärts-** backward ...; reverse ...; **der ~wärts|gang, ¨-e** reverse gear (**im R. fahren** reverse); **r~wärts|gehen*** (*sep*; *sn*) *coll* (**es geht rückwärts mit ...** ... is *etc* going downhill); **der ~weg** way back ((+*dat*) **den R. abschneiden** cut off (s.o.'s) retreat; **auf dem R.** on the way back); **r~wirkend** retrospective (**r. von** retroactively from; (pay) backdated to); **die ~wirkung, -en** repercussion (**auf** *acc* on); retroactive force (**mit R. von** retroactively from; (pay) backdated to); **die ~zahlung, -en** repayment; **der ~zieher, -** *footb* overhead kick; *coll* backtracking (**einen R. machen** *coll* backtrack); **der ~zug, ¨-e** retreat (**den R. antreten** beat a retreat); **das ~zugs|gefecht, -e** rearguard action

rucken jolt

rücken (*sn if v/i*) move; **~ an** (*dat*) move (hands of clock); pull at; **ins rechte Licht ~** show in a favourable light; **nicht von der Stelle ~** not budge

der **Rücken, -** back (*also* of chair); bridge (of nose); spine (of book); *geog* ridge; *cul* saddle; (+*dat*) **den ~ decken** back up; **sich** *dat* **den ~ decken** cover oneself; (+*dat*) **den ~ kehren** turn one's back on; (+*dat*) **den ~ stärken/steifen** give (s.o.) moral support

in prepositional phrases:

~ an ~ back to back

auf dem ~ haben *coll* have reached the age of; **auf seinen ~ geht viel** *coll* he can take a lot

hinter jmds. ~ behind s.o.'s back

im ~ (+*gen*) to the rear of; **im ~ haben** have behind one/*mil* in one's rear; *coll* have (rich father *etc*) behind one; (+*dat*) **in den ~ fallen** stab in the back

mit dem ~ zur Wand stehen have one's back to the wall

über: es lief mir kalt über den ~ a cold shiver ran down my spine

Rücken- back ...; *anat* dorsal ...; **der ~ausschnitt, -e** (low *etc*) back (**mit tiefem R.** (dress) low-backed); **die ~deckung** backing, support; **r~frei** backless; **die ~lage** supine position (**in der R.** on one's back); **die ~lehne, -n** back (of chair); **das ~mark** spinal cord; **die ~schmerzen** *pl* backache; **r~schwimmen** (*only infin*) do the backstroke; **das ~schwimmen** backstroke; **die ~stärkung** (moral) support; **das ~stück, -e** *cul* chine; saddle; **der ~wind** tail wind

rücklings backwards; from behind

ruck, zuck *coll* in no time; **ruck, zuck!** make it snappy!

rüde coarse; rough

der **Rüde, -n** (*wk masc*) (male) dog; dog fox/wolf; *hunt* hound

das **Rudel, -** pack; herd; *coll* swarm (of people)

das **Ruder, -** oar; *aer, naut* rudder; **am ~** at the helm; **ans ~ kommen** come to power; **sich in die ~ legen** row hard; *coll* put one's back into it

Ruder- rowing ...; **das ~blatt, ¨-er** (oar) blade; **das ~boot, -e** rowing-boat, rowboat *US*; **die ~pinne, -n** tiller; **der ~sport** rowing

der **Ruderer, -** oarsman

rudern row; (*v/i also sn*; *if indicating direction or distance travelled, only sn*) row; (*sn*) (duck *etc*) paddle; **~ mit** wave (one's arms) about

das **Rudiment, -e** remnant; *biol* vestige

rudimentär rudimentary

der **Ruf, -e** call (*also ornith*); shout; cry; reputation; *univ* offer of a chair; **~ (22 33 44** *etc*) tel.: ...; **in schlechten ~ bringen** bring into disrepute; **... von ~** ... of repute || **der ~mord, -e** character assassination; **der ~name, -n** (*like* **Name**) Christian name by which s.o. is usually known; **die ~nummer, -n** telephone number; **die ~säule, -n** telephone (for taxis); emergency telephone; **~weite** (**außer/in R.** out of/within earshot); **das ~zeichen, -** *rad* call-sign; *tel* ringing tone; *Aust* exclamation mark/point *US*

rufen (*p/t* **rief**, *p/part* **gerufen**) (*also v/i*) call; cry; **sich** *dat* **... ins Gedächtnis ~** recall; **~ nach** call for; **um Hilfe ~** call for help; **zu sich ~** send for; **wie gerufen kommen** come just at the right moment; **~ lassen** send for

der **Rüffel, -** *coll* telling-off

das **Rugby** ['rakbi] rugby

die **Rüge, -n** reprimand

rügen reprimand; reprehend

[die] **Ruhe** rest; peace; quiet; composure; **die ~ vor dem Sturm** the lull before the storm; **~ und Ordnung** law and order; **die ~ bewahren** keep calm; **keine ~ finden** find no peace; (+*dat*) **keine ~ lassen** give (s.o.) no peace; **die ~ weghaben** *coll* be unflappable; **~!** silence!, quiet!; **angenehme ~!** sleep well!

in prepositional phrases:

aus: sich nicht aus der ~ bringen lassen remain unperturbed

in ~ (work *etc*) in peace; **in aller ~** calmly; as if one had all the time in the world; **in ~ lassen** leave in peace

mit: immer mit der ~! take it easy!

zur ~ kommen get some peace; settle down; (wheel *etc*) come to rest; **nicht zur ~ kommen lassen** give (s.o.) no peace; **sich zur ~ begeben/setzen** retire (to bed/from work)

Ruhe–: r~bedürftig in need of quiet/rest; **das ~gehalt, ⸗er** pension; **die ~lage, –n** resting position (**in R.** at rest); **r~los** restless; (times) unsettled; **die ~losigkeit** restlessness; **die ~pause, –n** break; **der ~platz, ⸗e** resting-place; **der ~stand** retirement (**im R.** retired; **in den R. treten/versetzen** retire); **der ~ständler, –** retired person; **die ~stätte, –n** (**letzte R.** final resting-place); **die ~störung, –en** disturbance of the peace; **der ~tag, –e** rest day; day off

ruhen rest; (production *etc*) have stopped, be at a standstill; be in abeyance; **~ auf** (*dat*) rest on; **„hier ruht ..."** 'here lies ...' || **~lassen*** (*p/part usu* **~lassen;** *sep*) let rest

ruhig quiet; calm; (hand) steady; (conscience) clear; (*as emotive particle*) (*with imp, or 2nd pers of* **können**) by all means + *imp*; go ahead and + *imp*; (*with* **dürfen, können**) safely (*eg* **man kann ~ sagen, daß ...** one may safely say that ...), *or expressed by* it's quite all right for ... to ...; (*with* **können**) jolly well (*eg* **sie kann ~ warten** she can jolly well wait), *or expressed by* it wouldn't hurt ... to ... (*eg* **du könntest dir ~ mal die Haare schneiden lassen** it wouldn't hurt you to have your hair cut); **das dürfen Sie mir ~ glauben** believe you me

[der] **Ruhm** fame; glory; **jmds. ~es voll sein** be full of praise for s.o.; **sich mit ~ bedecken** cover oneself with glory || **r~los** inglorious; **r~reich** glorious

rühmen praise; **sich ~** (+*gen*) boast of; **sich ~ zu ...** be proud to ...; **ohne mich ~ zu wollen** without wishing to boast || **r~s|wert** praiseworthy

[das] **Ruhmes|blatt** glorious chapter

rühmlich praiseworthy, laudable

[die] **Ruhr** dysentery

Ruhr–: das ~gebiet the Ruhr

Rühr–: das ~ei, –er scrambled eggs; **der ~löffel, –** mixing spoon; **die ~maschine, –n** mixer; **das ~mich|nicht|an, –** *bot* touch-me-not; **r~selig** (over-)sentimental; tear-jerking; **die ~seligkeit** (over-)sentimentality; **der ~teig, –e** sponge mixture

rühren stir; move (arm, wing, *etc*); (emotionally) move, touch; **~ an** (*acc*) touch; touch on; **~ von** come from; **das rührt daher, daß ...** that is due to the fact that ...; **zu Tränen ~** move to tears; **keinen Finger ~** *coll* not lift a finger

sich ~ stir; move; **rührt euch!** *mil* at ease!

rührend touching; moving; **das ist ~ von Ihnen** that's very kind of you

rührig active

[die] **Rührung** emotion; **vor ~ nicht sprechen können** be too deeply moved to speak

[der] **Ruin** ruin; **vor dem ~ stehen** be on the verge of ruin; **jmds. ~ sein** be the ruin(ation) of s.o.

[die] **Ruine, –n** ruin(s) (of building); *coll* (= person) wreck

ruinenhaft ruined

ruinieren ruin; **sich ~** ruin oneself

ruinös ruinous

rülpsen *coll*, **der Rülpser, –** *coll* belch

rum [–ʊ–] *coll* = **herum**

[der] **Rum** [–ʊ–], **–s** rum

[der] **Rumäne, –n** (*wk masc*) Rumanian

Rumänien [–ĭən] Rumania

rumänisch, (*language*) **R~** Rumanian

[die] **Rumba, –s** (*coll* **der**) rumba

[der] **Rummel** *coll* hurly-burly; ballyhoo; *NGer* funfair; **der ganze ~** the whole bag of tricks || **der ~platz, ⸗e** *coll* fairground

[das] **Rummy** ['rœmi, 'ra–] *Aust* rummy

rumoren (*p/part* **rumort**) *coll* make a noise; **in jmds. Kopf ~** (thought) occupy s.o.'s mind; **es rumort in meinem Magen** my stomach is rumbling; **es rumort im Volk** there is growing unrest among the people

Rumpel–: die ~kammer, –n lumber-room; **~stilzchen** Rumpelstiltskin

rumpeln (*sn if indicating motion*) rumble

[der] **Rumpf, ⸗e** trunk; torso; *aer* fuselage; *naut* hull

rümpfen: die Nase ~ turn up one's nose (**über** *acc* at)

[das] **Rumpsteak** ['rumpste:k], **–s** rump steak

rums! bang!

[der] **Run** [ran], **–s** run (**auf** *acc* on)

rund round; circular; plump; (flavour, sound) full; (*adv*) about, roughly; **~ um** around || **der R~bau, –ten** rotunda; **der R~blick, –e** panoramic view; **der R~bogen, –/..bögen** round arch; **der**

R~brief, -e circular; **der R~erlaß, -(ss)e** official directive (in form of circular); **~erneuern** (*only infin and p/part* **~erneuert**) retread, remould; **die R~fahrt, -en** (circular) tour (**durch** of); **die R~frage, -n** survey; **der R~funk** radio; broadcasting (**im R.** on the radio); **die R~funk|anstalt, -en** radio station; **der R~gang, ⸚e** round; walk (**durch** round); tour (of building *etc*); *archit* circular gallery; **~gehen*** (*sn*) *coll* (**es geht rund** it's all go); **rund|heraus** *coll* straight out, flatly; **rund|herum** all around; **die R~reise, -n** (circular) tour (**durch** of); **die R~schau** (*in titles*) Review; **das R~schreiben, -** circular; **die R~strecke, -n** *sp* circuit; **das R~tisch|gespräch, -e** *EGer* round-table conference; **rund|um** all around; totally; **rund|weg** flatly

die **Runde, -n** walk (round garden *etc*); round(s); circle (of people); round (of drinks, talks); *sp* round; lap; **die ~ machen** do one's rounds; circulate; be passed around; **in die ~** all around; **über die ~n bringen** *coll* bring (person) through; manage; **über die ~n kommen** *coll* get by

runden round; **sich ~** become round

rundlich roundish; plump

die **Rundung, -en** *vbl noun*; *also* curve; (*pl*) (female) curves

die **Rune, -n** rune; *in compds* **~n–** runic ...

die **Runkel|rübe, -n** mangel-wurzel

runter *coll* = **herunter, hinunter**

die **Runzel, -n** wrinkle

runz(e)lig wrinkled

runzeln: die Stirn ~ frown; **sich ~** wrinkle

der **Rüpel, -** lout

rüpelhaft loutish

rupfen pull up; pluck; *coll* fleece

der **Rupfen, -** hessian

die **Rupie** [-ĭə], **-n** rupee

ruppig uncouth, (reply *etc*) gruff; scruffy

Ruprecht Rupert

die **Rüsche** [-y:-], **-n** frill

der **Ruß** [-u:-] soot; **die ~flocke, -n** smut

der **Russe, -n** (*wk masc*) Russian

der **Rüssel, -** trunk; snout; proboscis; **der ~käfer, -** weevil

rußen [-u:-] smoke; (stove) form soot

rußig [-u:-] sooty

russisch, (*language*) **R~** Russian; **~e Eier** egg mayonnaise

russisch– Russo–; (dictionary) Russian–

Rußland Russia

Rüst–: die ~kammer, -n armoury; **das ~zeug** know-how

rüsten arm; **(sich) ~ zu** prepare for

die **Rüster** [-y:-], **-n** elm

rüstig spry

rustikal rustic

die **Rüstung, -en** armament; *hist* (suit of) armour; **der ~s|wett|lauf** arms race

die **Rute, -n** switch; rod; birch (for chastisement); *hunt* tail; **der ~n|gänger, -** water-diviner

der **Rutsch, -e** slip, slide; *pol* swing; *coll* jaunt; **auf einen ~** *coll* in one go; **guten ~ (ins neue Jahr)!** Happy New Year! || **die ~bahn, -en** chute; slide; **r~fest** non-slip; *mot* non-skid; **die ~gefahr** danger of skidding; **die ~partie, -n** *coll* slip; slide

die **Rutsche, -n** chute; slide

rutschen (*sn*) slide; slip; *mot* skid; *coll* move up; *coll* (food) go down; **~ nach** *coll* slip off to; **auf den Knien gerutscht kommen** *coll* go down on bended knee

rutschig slippery

rütteln (*see also* **gerüttelt**) shake; (*v/i*) shake; rattle; jolt; *ornith* hover; **~ an** (*dat*) shake by (arm *etc*); (*v/i*) rattle; shake (foundations *etc*); tamper with

S

^das^ **S** [ɛs] (*gen, pl* –) S
S (= **Süd(en)**) S.; *Aust* = **Schilling; S.** (= **Seite**) p.
s. (= **siehe**) see
's *coll, poet* = **es**
^die^ **SA** *Nazi* (= **Sturmabteilung**) Stormtroopers;
Sa. (= **Samstag**) Sat.
Sä–: der ~mann, ¨er sower; **die ~maschine, –n** seed-drill
^der^ **Saal,** *pl* **Säle** hall; (large) room; **die ~tochter, ..töchter** *Swiss* waitress
^das^ **Saar|land** the Saar(land)
^die^ **Saat, –en** seed (*collect*); young crops; = **die ~bestellung, –en** sowing; **das ~gut** seed; **die ~krähe, –n** rook
^der^ **Sabbat** [–at], **–e** sabbath
^das^ **Sabber|lätzchen, –** *coll* bib
sabbern *coll* dribble; prattle
^der^ **Säbel, –** sabre; **die ~beine** *pl coll* bow legs; **s~beinig** bow-legged; **das ~rasseln, s~rasselnd** sabre-rattling
säbeln *coll* hack
^die^ **Sabotage** [–ʒə], **–n** sabotage
^der^ **Saboteur** [–'tøːɐ], **–e** saboteur
sabotieren sabotage
^das^ **Sac(c)harin** [zaxa–] saccharin
Sach–: der ~be|arbeiter, – employee/official responsible for a particular field; **das ~buch, ¨er** non-fiction book (presenting subject in popular style); **s~dienlich** (information) relevant; **die ~frage, –n** question of fact; **das ~gebiet, –e** area; **s~gemäß** = **s~gerecht** proper, appropriate; **der ~katalog, –e** subject catalogue; **der ~kenner, –** expert; **die ~kenntnis, –se** = **die ~kunde** expertise; expert knowledge; **s~kundig, der/die ~kundige** (*decl as adj*) expert; **die ~lage** situation; state of affairs; **die ~leistung, –en** payment in kind; **das ~register, –** subject-index; **der ~schaden, ..schäden** damage to property; **der ~verhalt, –e** facts (of the case); **der ~verstand** expertise; expert knowledge; **s~verständig, der/die ~verständige** (*decl as adj*) expert; **der ~walter, –** trustee; agent; advocate (of sth.); **der ~wert, –e** real value; (*pl*) material assets; **das ~wörter|buch, ¨er** specialist dictionary; **die ~zwänge** *pl* force of circumstances
^die^ **Sache, –n** thing; matter; affair; cause (fought for); *leg* case; (*pl*) things; **seine ~ verstehen** know what one is about; **seiner ~ sicher sein** be sure of oneself; **es ist ~** (+*gen*) it is up to/a matter for; **die ~ ist die, daß ...** the thing is ...; **das ist so eine ~** *coll* it's rather tricky; **~n gibt's (, die gibt's gar nicht)!** would you believe it!; **mach keine ~n!** you're joking!; don't do anything silly!
in prepositional phrases:
bei: ich bin bei der ~ my mind is on the job *etc*; **bei der ~ bleiben** stick to the point
in ~n ... in the matter/*leg* case of ...; **in eigener ~** on one's own behalf
mit: die ~ mit ... the business about ...; the ... business; **mit (160** *etc*) **~n fahren** *coll* do (100 *etc*) m.p.h.
zur ~! to come to the point; **das gehört nicht zur ~** that's irrelevant; **zur ~ kommen** get to the point; **das tut nichts zur ~** that makes no difference
^das^ **Sächelchen, –** *coll* little thing
^die^ **Sacher|torte, –n** (*kind of chocolate cake*)
sachlich objective; matter-of-fact; factual; (style) functional
^die^ **Sachlichkeit** objectivity; functionalism
sächlich neuter
^der^ **Sachse** [–ks–], **–n** (*wk masc*) Saxon
sächseln [–ks–] speak with a Saxon accent
Sachsen [–ks–] Saxony
sächsisch [–ks–] Saxon
sacht(e) gentle; **sachte, sachte!** easy does it!
^der^ **Sack, ¨e** sack; *bot, zool* sac; *coll* (lazy *etc*) bastard; *SGer coll* trouser pocket; **mit ~ und Pack** *coll* bag and baggage; **in den ~ hauen** *coll* chuck it in; **in den ~ stecken** *coll* put in the shade || **der ~bahnhof, ¨e** terminus; **die ~gasse, –n** dead end; impasse; **das ~hüpfen** sack-race; **das ~leinen** = **die ~lein|wand** sacking; **die ~pfeife, –n** bagpipe; **das ~tuch, ¨er** *SGer* handkerchief
sacken (*sn*) sink
^der^ **Sadismus** sadism
^der^ **Sadist, –en** (*wk masc*) sadist
sadistisch sadistic
säen sow; **dünn gesät** thin on the ground
^die^ **Safari, –s** safari
^der^ **Safe** [seːf], **–s** (*also* **das**) safe
^der^ **Saffian** [–a(ː)n] morocco
^der^ **Safran** [–a(ː)n] saffron
^der^ **Saft, ¨e** juice; *Aust cul* gravy; *bot* sap; **ohne ~ und Kraft** *coll* feeble; wishy-washy || **der**

~laden, ..läden *coll* crummy joint; s~reich juicy; s~- und kraft|los feeble; wishy-washy

saftig juicy; lush; *coll* spicy; hefty; (letter) that really lets s.o. have it

die **Saga, –s** saga

die **Sage, –n** legend; **es geht die ~, daß ...** the story goes that ...

die **Säge, –n** saw; **der ~bock, ⸚e** saw-horse; **das ~mehl** sawdust; **das ~messer, –** serrated knife; **die ~späne** *pl* sawdust; **das ~werk, –e** sawmill

sagen say; (+*dat*) say to; tell; mean (something) to; **etwas zu ~ haben** have a say/something to say; **nichts zu ~ haben** have no say/nothing to say; (fact *etc*) be of no importance; **auf alles etwas zu ~ wissen** have an answer for everything; **das sagt sich leicht** it's easy to say; **es ist nicht zu ~** you wouldn't believe it; **sage und schreibe** *coll* believe it or not; **~ wir** let's say; **gesagt, getan** no sooner said than done; **unter uns gesagt** between you and me; **wie gesagt** as I was saying; **~ Sie/sag mal!** tell me; **was Sie nicht ~!** you don't say!

~ lassen: (+*dat*) **~ lassen, daß ...** send (s.o.) word that ...; **sich** *dat* **... ~ lassen** be told; **er läßt sich nichts ~** he won't listen to reason; **laß dir das gesagt sein** you mark my words

Sagen: das ~ haben be the boss

sägen saw; (*v/i*) saw; *coll* snore

sagenhaft legendary; *coll* fabulous

sah (sähe) *p/t* (*subj*) *of* **sehen**

die **Sahara** ['za:hara, za'ha:ra] the Sahara

die **Sahne** cream; **das ~bonbon, –s** (*also* **der**) toffee; **die ~torte, –n** cream gateau

sahnig creamy

die **Saison** [zɛ'zɔ̃:], **–s** season; *in compds* seasonal ...; **s~bedingt** seasonal

saisonal [zɛzo–] seasonal

der **Saisonnier** [zɛzɔ'nĭe:], **–s** *Swiss* seasonal worker

die **Saite, –n** *mus*, *sp* string; **eine ~ anschlagen in** (*dat*) strike a chord in; **andere ~n aufziehen** *coll* take a tougher line || **das ~n|instrument, –e** stringed instrument

–saitig –stringed

der **Sakko, –s** (*also* **das**) sports jacket

sakral (art *etc*) religious

das **Sakrament, –e** sacrament

das **Sakrileg, –e** sacrilege

die **Sakristei, –en** vestry

sakrosankt sacrosanct

säkular secular

säkularisieren secularize

der **Salamander, –** salamander

die **Salami, –(s)** salami; **die ~taktik** (*policy of step-by-step achievement of one's aims*)

das **Salär, –e** *Swiss*, **salarieren** *Swiss* pay

der **Salat, –e** salad; lettuce; **da haben wir den ~!** now we're in a fine mess! || **die ~soße, –n** salad-dressing

salbadern hold forth in an unctuous manner

die **Salbe, –n** ointment

der **Salbei** [*also* –'baе̯] (*also* **die**) sage

salben rub with ointment; anoint

die **Salbung, –en** *vbl noun*; *also* anointment; **s~s|voll** unctuous

saldieren *comm* balance; *Aust* confirm payment of

der **Saldo, –s/Salden/Saldi** *comm* balance; **der ~übertrag, ⸚e** balance carried forward

Säle *pl of* **Saal**

die **Saline, –n** saltworks

der **Salmiak** [*also* 'zal–] sal ammoniac; **der ~geist** liquid ammonia

die **Salmonellen** *pl* salmonellae

Salomon ['za:lomɔn] Solomon

salomonisch Solomonic

der **Salon** [za'lɔ̃:], **–s** drawing-room, *naut* saloon; (hairdresser's *etc*) salon; exhibition (room); *hist* salon; **s~fähig** socially acceptable; **der ~löwe, –n** (*wk masc*) lounge lizard

salopp casual; (speech) slovenly

der **Salpeter** saltpetre; **die ~säure** nitric acid

salpetrig nitrous

der **Salto, –s/Salti** somersault

der **Salut, –e** (gun) salute

salutieren salute

die **Salve, –n** (gun) salute; salvo; volley

die **Salweide, –n** sallow

das **Salz, –e** salt; *in compds* salt ...; salted ...; **das ~faß, ⸚(ss)er** salt-cellar; **die ~kartoffeln** *pl* boiled potatoes; **die ~lösung, –en** saline solution; **die ~säure** hydrochloric acid; **die ~stange, –n** salt stick; **das ~wasser** salt water; brine

salzen (*p/part* **gesalzen**) (*see also* **gesalzen**) salt

salzig salty

der **Samariter, –** Samaritan

die **Samba, –s** (*also* **der**) samba

der **Sambesi** (*gen* **–(s)**) the Zambezi

Sambia Zambia

der **Sambier** [–ĭɐ], **–, sambisch** Zambian

der **Samen, –** seed; *biol* sperm, semen; *in compds biol* seminal ...; **der ~erguß, ⸚(ss)e** ejaculation; **der ~händler, –** seed merchant; **das ~korn, ⸚er** seed; **der ~leiter, –** vas deferens; **die ~zelle, –n** sperm cell

die **Sämereien** *pl* seeds

sämig (soup *etc*) thick

der **Sämling, –e** seedling

Sammel–: der ~band, ⸚e omnibus (volume); **das ~becken, –** reservoir; rallying point; **der ~begriff, –e** collective term; **die ~bestellung, –en** joint order; **die ~büchse, –n** collecting-box; **der ~fahr|schein, –e**

group ticket; multiple ticket (for several journeys); **die ~mappe, -n** file; **der ~platz, ⸚e** assembly point; **die ~stelle, -n** collecting point; assembly point; **das ~surium, -(i)en** *coll* conglomeration

sammeln collect; gather; gain (experience); **sich ~** gather, (water *etc*) collect; collect one's thoughts; *phys* converge

der **Sammler, -** collector; *elect* accumulator

die **Sammlung, -en** *vbl noun*; *also* collection; composure

der **Samowar, -e** samovar

der **Samstag, -e** Saturday

samstags on Saturdays

samt (+*dat*) together with; **~ und sonders** each and every one

der **Samt, -e, samten** velvet

samtig velvety

sämtlich all; (works) complete

das **Sanatorium, -(i)en** sanatorium

der **Sand, -e** sand; **im ~e verlaufen** fizzle out; (+*dat*) **~ in die Augen streuen** *coll* pull the wool over (s.o.'s) eyes || **die ~bank, ⸚e** sandbank; **die ~burg, -en** sand-castle; **der ~kasten, ..kästen** sandpit, sandbox *US*; **der ~kuchen, -** Madeira cake, pound cake *US*; **das ~männchen** sandman; **das ~papier** sandpaper; **der ~sack, ⸚e** sandbag; *box* (heavy) punch-bag, punching bag *US*; **der ~stein, -e** sandstone; **s~strahlen** (*only infin and p/part* **gesandstrahlt**) sandblast; **der ~strand, ⸚e** sandy beach; **der ~sturm, ⸚e** sandstorm; **die ~torte, -n** Madeira cake, pound cake *US*; **die ~uhr, -en** hour-glass

die **Sandale, -n** sandal

die **Sandalette, -n** (woman's) sandal (with heel)

sandig sandy

sandte *p/t of* **senden**

das **Sandwich** ['sɛntvɪtʃ] (*gen* **-(e)s**), **-(e)s** sandwich; **der ~wecken, -** *Aust* French loaf

sanft gentle; soft; (sleep *etc*) peaceful; **die S~mut** gentleness; **~mütig** gentle; meek

die **Sänfte, -n** sedan chair

sang (sänge) *p/t* (*subj*) *of* **singen**

Sang: mit ~ und Klang *coll* (fail) spectacularly || **sang- und klanglos** quietly, without any fuss

der **Sänger, -** singer; *in compds* choral ...

der **Sanguiniker** [-ŭ-], **-** sanguine person

sanguinisch [-ŭ-] sanguine

sanieren redevelop (district); rehabilitate, renovate; *comm* reorganize (on a sound financial basis)

sanitär sanitary; **~e Anlagen** sanitation

die **Sanität, -en** *Aust, Swiss*: *mil* medical service; *coll* ambulance

der **Sanitäter, -** first-aid attendant; *mil* (medical) orderly

Sanitäts- medical ...; **die ~wache, -n** first-aid post; **der ~wagen, -** ambulance

sank (sänke) *p/t* (*subj*) *of* **sinken**

Sankt Saint, St; **der ~-Lorenz-Strom** the St Lawrence River

die **Sanktion, -en, sanktionieren** sanction

sann (sänne) *p/t* (*subj*) *of* **sinnen**

Sansibar Zanzibar

das **Sanskrit** [-ɪt] Sanskrit

der **Saphir** ['zaːfiːɐ], **-e** [za'fiːrə] sapphire

der **Sarazene, -n** (*wk masc*), **sarazenisch** Saracen

die **Sardelle, -n** anchovy

die **Sardine, -n** sardine

Sardinien [-ĭən] Sardinia

der **Sardinier** [-ĭɐ], **-, sardinisch** Sardinian

sardonisch sardonic

der **Sarg, ⸚e** coffin

der **Sarkasmus** sarcasm

sarkastisch sarcastic

der **Sarkophag, -e** sarcophagus

saß (säße) *p/t* (*subj*) *of* **sitzen**

der **Satan** [-an], **-e** Satan; *coll* devil

satanisch satanic

der **Satellit, -en** (*wk masc*) satellite; **das ~en|fernsehen** satellite television; **der ~en|staat, -en** satellite (state)

der **Satin** [za'tɛ̃ː], **-s** satin

die **Satire, -n** satire

der **Satiriker, -** satirist

satirisch satirical

satt full (= replete); (colour) rich; **~ bekommen/kriegen** *coll* grow tired of; **~ haben/sein** be fed up with; **nicht ~ werden zu ...** not tire of (+*ger*); **~ machen** be filling; **sich ~ essen** eat one's fill (**an** *dat* of); **sich nicht ~ hören/sehen können an** (*dat*) not tire of hearing/seeing

der **Sattel,** *pl* **Sättel** saddle; *geog* col, saddle; **aus dem ~ heben** unsaddle; oust || **s~fest (s. in** (*dat*) well-versed in); **der ~gurt, -e** girth; **der ~schlepper, -** tractor (of articulated lorry), truck tractor *US*; **die ~tasche, -n** saddlebag (*also cycl*)

satteln saddle; **gesattelt für** ready for

sättigen satisfy; *chem, phys, comm* saturate; **sich ~** satisfy one's appetite; **~d** filling

die **Sättigung, -en** *vbl noun*; *chem, phys, comm* saturation

der **Sattler, -** saddler

sattsam: ~ bekannt all too familiar

saturieren satiate

Saturn *myth*, **der ~** (*gen* **-s**) *astron* Saturn

der **Satyr, -e** (*or* **-n** (*wk masc*)) satyr

der **Satz, ⸚e** leap; set; sediment, (coffee) grounds; proposition, *math* theorem; rate; *gramm* sentence; clause; *mus* movement; *print* setting; *comput* record; *sp* set; **mit einem ~** with one bound; **einen ~ machen** leap || **der ~ball, ⸚e** set point; **der ~bau** sentence construction; **der ~gegenstand, ⸚e** *gramm* subject; **die ~lehre** syntax; **s~weise** sentence by sentence; in sets; **das**

~zeichen, – punctuation mark

die **Satzung, –en** statutes; **s~s|gemäß** according to the statutes

die **Sau, ¨–e** sow; *vulg* dirty pig; **unter aller ~** *coll* lousy; **zur ~ machen** *coll* 'take apart'

Sau– *vulg esp* lousy ...; (**sau–**) *vulg* damn ..., bloody ...; **die ~bohne, –n** broad bean; **sau|dumm** *coll* damn stupid; **der ~kerl, –e** *vulg* swine; **s~mäßig** *vulg* lousy; **der ~stall, ¨–e** *vulg* pigsty; **sau|wohl** *coll* (**sich s. fühlen** feel great)

sauber clean; neat; clear-cut; (accent *etc*) faultless; (character *etc*) decent; *iron* fine; *SGer* pretty || **~halten*** (*sep*) keep clean; **~machen** (*sep*) clean

die **Sauberkeit** cleanness; neatness; decency

säuberlich neatly

säubern clean; clear (**von** of); *pol* purge (of)

die **Säuberung, –en** *vbl noun*; *also* clean-up; *pol* purge; **die ~s|aktion, –en** *mil* mopping-up operation; *pol* purge

die **Sauce** ['zoːsə], **–n** gravy; sauce

die **Sauciere** [zo'sĭeːrə, –ɛː–], **–n** sauce-boat

Saudi–: **der ~araber, –** Saudi Arabian; **~-Arabien** Saudi Arabia; **s~arabisch** Saudi (Arabian)

sauer sour; acid; (work) hard; *cul* pickled; *coll* cross (**auf** *acc* with); **–sauer** *chem* –ate (*eg* **schwefel~** ... sulphate); **saurer Regen** acid rain; **... wird mir ~** I find ... hard; **sich** *dat* **... ~ erworben/verdient haben** have worked hard for; (+*dat*) **das Leben ~ machen** make life miserable for; **gib ihm Saures!** let him have it! || **der S~ampfer** sorrel; **der S~braten, –** (*beef marinated in vinegar and braised*); **die S~kirsche, –n** morello cherry; **das S~kraut** sauerkraut; **der S~stoff** oxygen; **die S~stoff|flasche, –n** oxygen cylinder; **das S~stoff|gerät, –e** oxygen apparatus; **das S~stoff|zelt, –e** oxygen tent; **der S~teig** leaven; **der S~topf, ¨–e** *coll* sourpuss; **~töpfisch** *coll* peevish

die **Sauerei, –en** *vulg* mess; scandal, disgrace; (*pl*) filthy jokes

säuerlich sourish, slightly sour; (face *etc*) sour

säuern ferment (cabbage); *cul* make sour by adding lemon juice or vinegar; (*v/i*, *also sn*) turn sour

Sauf– drinking ...; **der ~bruder, ..brüder** *coll* boozer; drinking-companion; **das ~gelage, –** *coll* binge

saufen (**säuf(s)t**, *p/t* **soff** (*subj* **söffe**), *p/part* **gesoffen**) (animal) drink; *coll* booze; **wie ein Loch ~** *vulg* drink like a fish

der **Säufer, –** *coll* boozer

die **Sauferei, –en** *coll* boozing; binge

Saug– suction ...; **s~fähig** absorbent; **die ~flasche, –n** feeding bottle; **der ~heber, –** siphon; **der ~napf, ¨–e** *zool* sucker; **die ~pumpe, –n** suction pump

Säuge–: **das ~tier, –e** mammal

saugen (*p/t* **sog/saugte** (*subj* **söge/saugte**), *p/part* **gesogen/gesaugt**; *in compounds the weak forms tend to predominate*), **~ an** (*dat*) suck

säugen suckle

der **Sauger, –** teat, nipple *US* (on baby's bottle); dummy, pacifier *US*

der **Säuger, –** mammal

der **Säugling, –e** baby; **das ~s|alter** babyhood; **die ~s|sterblichkeit** infant mortality

säuisch *vulg* filthy

die **Säule, –n** pillar; column; **der ~n|gang, ¨–e** colonnade

der **Saum, ¨–e** hem; edge (of forest *etc*); **der ~pfad, –e** mule-track; **s~selig** dilatory

säumen[1] hem; line

säumen[2] (*usu with neg*) delay

säumig tardy

die **Sauna, –s/Saunen** sauna

saur.. = sauer..

Saure–: **die ~gurken|zeit** *coll* dead season

die **Säure, –n** acid; sourness; acidity; **der ~gehalt** acidity

der **Saurier** [–ĭɐ], **–** saurian

Saus: **in ~ und Braus leben** live it up

säuseln (person) purr; (*v/i* wind, leaves) rustle

sausen (wind) whistle; (ears, head) buzz; (*sn*) hurtle; (arrow *etc*) whizz; *coll* dash; **~ durch** (*sn*) *coll* fail (examination); **es saust mir in den Ohren** my ears are buzzing || **~lassen*** (*p/part usu* **~lassen**; *sep*) *coll* give (sth.) a miss; drop (girl-friend *etc*)

die **Savanne, –n** savannah

Savoyen Savoy

das **Saxophon, –e** saxophone

der **Saxophonist, –en** (*wk masc*) saxophonist

die **S-Bahn, –en** (= **Schnellbahn**) suburban railway/railroad *US*

die **SBB** (= **Schweizerische Bundesbahnen**) Swiss Federal Railways

s. Br. = **südlicher Breite**, *eg* **20° ~** latitude 20° south

die **SBZ** *hist* (= **Sowjetische Besatzungszone**) Soviet Zone of Occupation

---

–sch (*see p. lxvi, (iii) (b)*) –ian (*eg* **Freud~** Freudian, **Wagner~** Wagnerian); ...'s (*eg* **das Ohm~e Gesetz** Ohm's Law, **der Halley~e Komet** Halley's Comet)

---

die **Schabe, –n** cockroach

schaben scrape

der **Schaber, –** scraper

der **Schabernack, –e** prank; (+*dat*) **einen ~ spielen** play a prank on

schäbig shabby; mean

die **Schablone, –n** stencil, *tech* template; (set)

routine; cliché; **nach ~** according to a set routine
schablonenhaft stereotyped
das **Schach** chess; (+*dat*) **~ bieten** stand up to; *chess* check; **in ~ halten** keep in check; keep covered; **~ (dem König)!** check! || **das ~brett, -er** chess-board; **die ~figur, -en** chessman; pawn (= manipulated person); **schach|matt** checkmated; *coll* dead beat (**s. setzen** checkmate; **s.!** checkmate!); **das ~spiel, -e** chess; chess-playing; game of chess; chess set; **der ~zug, ¨-e** move (in chess; *also* = manoeuvre)
der **Schacher** haggling
der **Schächer, -** *bibl* thief
schachern haggle (**um** over)
der **Schacht, ¨-e** shaft
die **Schachtel, -n** box; packet, pack *US* (of cigarettes); **alte ~** *coll* old frump || **der ~halm, -e** *bot* horse-tail; **der ~satz, ¨-e** involved sentence
Schad-: s~los (sich s. halten an (*dat*) make good one's loss at the expense of; make up for a missed meal *etc* by having); **der ~stoff, -e** harmful substance
schade: wie ~! what a pity!; **(es ist) ~, daß ...** it's a pity ...; **es ist ~ um** it's a pity about; **zu ~ für** too good for; wasted on
der **Schädel, -** skull; *coll* head; *in compds also* cranial ...; **der ~bruch, ¨-e** fractured skull
schaden (+*dat*) harm; damage; **das schadet nichts** it doesn't matter; **das schadet ihm** *etc* **gar nichts!** it'll do him *etc* good!
der **Schaden,** *pl* **Schäden** damage; injury; harm; (mechanical) defect; **~ nehmen** (health *etc*) suffer; = **zu ~ kommen** be hurt; **zum ~** (+*gen*) to the detriment of || **der ~ersatz** compensation, damages; **der ~freiheits|-rabatt, -e** no-claim bonus; **die ~freude** gloating, schadenfreude; **s~froh** gloating
der **Schadens|ersatz** compensation, damages
schadhaft damaged; defective
schädigen, die Schädigung, -en harm; damage
schädlich harmful; **~ für** injurious to
der **Schädling, -e** pest; **die ~s|bekämpfung** pest control; **das ~s|bekämpfungs|mittel, -** pesticide
das **Schaf, -e** sheep; *coll* ninny; **der ~bock, ¨-e** ram; **das ~fell, -e** sheepskin; **die ~garbe, -n** yarrow; **die ~herde, -n** flock of sheep; **der ~pelz, -e** sheepskin (coat)
das **Schäfchen, -** lamb; (*pl*) fleecy clouds; **sein ~ ins trockene bringen** *coll* feather one's nest
der **Schäfer, -** shepherd; *in compds liter* pastoral ...; **der ~hund, -e** sheepdog (**deutscher S.** Alsatian, German shepherd; **schottischer S.** collie); **das ~stündchen, -** lovers' rendezvous
die **Schäferin, -nen** shepherdess

schaffen[1] (*p/t* **schuf** (*subj* **schüfe**), *p/part* **geschaffen**) create; make (room *etc*), establish (order); **wie geschaffen für** made for
schaffen[2] make (room *etc*), establish (order); manage (to do); do, get done; pass (examination); take, get (to a place); *coll* finish off; (*v/i*) *SGer* work; (+*dat*) **zu ~ machen** give (s.o.) trouble; **sich** *dat* **zu ~ machen** busy oneself (**an** *dat* with); **etwas/nichts zu ~ haben mit** have something/nothing to do with; **das wäre geschafft!** that's that (finished)!
das **Schaffen** work (of artist)
schaffend creative
Schaffens-: der ~drang; creative urge, **die ~kraft** creativity
der **Schaffner, -** conductor (on bus *etc*); *rail* guard, conductor *US*
die **Schaffnerin, -nen** conductress
die **Schaffung** creation (of)
das **Schafott, -e** *hist* scaffold
Schafs-: der ~käse, - sheep's milk cheese; **der ~kopf, ¨-e** *coll* blockhead; **der ~pelz, -e** (= **Schafpelz**)
der **Schaft, ¨-e** shaft; stock (of rifle); leg (of boot); **der ~stiefel, -** high boot; jackboot

---

-schaft (*pl* **-en**):
(*i*) *group of persons*, *eg* **die Studenten~** student body;
(*ii*) *role or office* -ship *etc*, *eg* **die Urheber~** authorship, **die Vater~** paternity (**Vater** = father), **die Präsident~** presidency;
(*iii*) *state*, *eg* **die Bereit~** readiness (**bereit** = ready), **die Feind~** hostility (**Feind** = enemy)

---

der **Schah, -s** Shah
der **Schakal, -e** jackal
der **Schäker, -** joker; flirt
schäkern: ~ mit jest with (in teasing fashion); flirt with
schal flat; stale; (life) empty, (joke) stale
der **Schal, -s** scarf
die **Schale**[1], **-n** shell (*also phys*); skin; peel; husk; **sich in ~ werfen** *coll* put on one's glad rags
die **Schale**[2], **-n** (shallow) dish; pan (of scales); cup (of bra); *esp Aust* cup
Schalen-: der ~sitz, -e bucket seat
schälen shell; peel; skin; husk; **sich ~** peel; **sich aus den Kleidern ~** peel off
der **Schalk, -e/¨-e** rascal
schalkhaft mischievous, roguish
der **Schall** sound; **der ~dämpfer, -** silencer (on gun); *mot* silencer, muffler *US*; **s~dicht** sound-proof; **die Schallehre** acoustics; **die ~geschwindigkeit** speed of sound; **die ~mauer** sound-barrier; **die ~platte, -n**

record; ~**platten–** record ...; **die ~welle, –n** sound-wave

schallen (*p/t occ* **scholl**) resound, echo; ring out; ~**des Gelächter** peals of laughter

die **Schalmei, –en** shawm

die **Schalotte, –n** shallot

schalt *p/t of* **schelten**

Schalt–: das ~bild, –er circuit diagram; **das ~brett, –er** switchboard, control panel; **der ~hebel, –** *elect* switch lever; *mot* gear-lever, gearshift *US*; **das ~jahr, –e** leap year; **der ~knüppel, –** gear-lever, gearshift *US*; **das ~pult, –e** control panel; **die ~stelle, –n** nerve-centre; **die ~tafel, –n** switchboard, control panel

schalten switch; switch on; (*v/i*) change gear, shift gear *US*; *coll* catch on; react; **~ auf** (*acc*) (*also v/i*) switch to; **~ in** (*acc*) change into, shift into *US* (gear); **~ und walten** have a free hand; **~ und walten lassen** give (s.o.) a free hand

der **Schalter, –** (counter) position, *rail* ticket-window; *elect* switch; **der ~be|amte** (*decl as adj*) counter clerk; *rail* ticket clerk/agent *US*

die **Schaltung, –en** *vbl noun*; *mot* gear change, gearshift *US*; *elect* circuit

die **Schaluppe, –n** sloop

die **Scham** shame; private parts || **das ~bein, –e** pubic bone; **das ~gefühl** sense of shame; **die ~haare** *pl* pubic hair; **die ~lippen** *pl* labia; **s~los** shameless; brazen, barefaced; **s~rot** blushing (**s. werden** blush with shame); **die ~röte** blush

schämen: sich ~ be ashamed (*gen*/**wegen** of); **schäme dich!** shame on you!

schamhaft bashful; modest

der **Schamott** *coll* junk

die **Schamotte** fire-clay

schampunieren shampoo

der **Schampus** *coll* bubbly

Schand–: der ~fleck, –e stain *etc* that spoils the appearance of sth.; blot (on landscape); eyesore; disgrace (of family *etc*); **das ~geld** ridiculous price; **das ~maul, ¨er** *coll* evil tongue; backbiter; **die ~tat, –en** infamous deed (**zu jeder S. bereit** *joc* game for anything)

schandbar shameful; *coll* awful

die **Schande,** (+*dat*) **~ machen** disgrace

schänden dishonour; desecrate; ravish

schändlich shameful; *coll* awful

Schanghai [*also* –'haẹ] Shanghai

schanghaien (*p/part* **schanghait**) shanghai

die **Schank, –en** *Aust* bar; **die ~erlaubnis, –se** (publican's) licence, excise license *US*; **der ~tisch, –e** bar; **die ~wirtschaft, –en** pub, saloon *US*

der **Schanker, –** chancre

die **Schanze, –n** *ski* ski-jump; *mil* earthworks

die **Schar**[1], **–en** crowd; band; flock; **in ~en** in droves; **in ~en kommen** flock (to a place)

die **Schar**[2], **–en** ploughshare

die **Scharade, –n** charade

scharen: um sich ~ gather round one; **sich ~ um** gather round

scharen|weise in droves

scharf (*comp, superl* ¨) sharp; keen; highly-seasoned, (curry *etc*) hot; (vinegar, alcohol, *etc*) strong; (solution) caustic; pungent; shrill; cutting; (protest *etc*) strong; severe, tough; (dog) fierce; (ride) hard; (ammunition) live; *coll* randy; **~e Sachen** *coll* the hard stuff; hot stuff; **~ eingestellt** in focus; **~ machen** sharpen; arm (bomb *etc*); *coll* 'turn on'; **~ schießen** shoot with live ammunition; **~ sein auf** (*acc*) *coll* be very keen on || **der S~blick** perspicacity; **~kantig** sharp-edged; **~machen** (*sep*) *coll* stir up; **der S~macher, –** *coll* agitator; **der S~richter, –** executioner; **der S~schütze, –n** (*wk masc*) marksman; **~sichtig** sharp-sighted; perspicacious; **der S~sinn** acumen; **~sinnig** astute

die **Schärfe, –n** (*see* **scharf**) sharpness; keenness; causticity; pungency; strength; severity, toughness; ferocity; *phot* definition; (+*dat*) **die ~ nehmen** take the edge off

schärfen sharpen

der **Scharlach** scarlet; *med* scarlet fever; **scharlach|rot** scarlet

der **Scharlatan** [–an], **–e** charlatan

die **Scharlatanerie, –(ie)n** charlatanism

das **Scharmützel, –** *arch*, **scharmützeln** (*p/part* **scharmützelt**) *arch* skirmish

das **Scharnier, –e** hinge

die **Schärpe, –n** sash

scharren scrape; scratch; **~ mit** shuffle (one's feet); **mit dem Huf ~** paw the ground

die **Scharte, –n** notch; *geog* wind gap; *hist* embrasure; **eine ~ (wieder) auswetzen** *coll* make amends

die **Scharteke, –n** *coll* tattered old book; old frump

schartig jagged

scharwenzeln (*p/part* **scharwenzelt**) (*also sn*): **~ um** dance attendance on

der **Schaschlik** [–ɪk], **–s** (*also* **das**) kebab

schassen *coll* chuck out

Schatt–: die ~seite, –n *Aust, Swiss* (= **Schattenseite**)

der **Schatten, –** shadow; shade; **nur noch ein ~ seiner selbst sein** be only a shadow of one's former self; **einen ~ werfen auf** (*acc*) cast a shadow on; **in den ~ stellen** overshadow, eclipse || **das ~dasein** shadowy existence; **das ~kabinett, –e** shadow cabinet; **der ~riß, –(ss)e** silhouette; **die ~seite, –n** shady side; dark side; drawback

schattenhaft shadowy

schattieren shade
die Schattierung, –en shade; shading
schattig shady
die Schatulle, –n casket
der Schatz, ¨–e treasure; (treasured) possession; wealth (an *dat* of: experience, knowledge, *etc*); sweetheart; darling; (*pl*) (art *etc*) treasures; (natural) resources; (mein) ~ darling || das ~amt Treasury; der ~gräber, – treasure-hunter; der ~kanzler, – Chancellor of the Exchequer; der ~meister, – treasurer
Schätz–: der ~wert, –e estimated value
das Schätzchen, – darling
schätzen estimate (auf *acc* at); reckon (that ...); appreciate; value; think highly of; sich glücklich ~ count oneself lucky; zu ~ wissen appreciate || ~lernen (*sep*) come to appreciate; ~s|wert estimable
die Schätzung, –en estimation; estimate; valuation || s~s|weise at a rough estimate
die Schau, –en show; (mystical) vision; eine ~ abziehen *coll* put on a show; (+*dat*) die ~ stehlen *coll* steal the show from; aus (historischer *etc*) ~ from a (historical *etc*) viewpoint; zur ~ stellen exhibit; parade; zur ~ tragen display
Schau– *esp* show ...; *sp* exhibition ...;
das ~bild, –er diagram; die ~bude, –n booth (at fair); das ~fenster, – shop-window; der ~fenster|bummel, – window-shopping; das ~geschäft show business; der ~kasten, ..kästen showcase; s~lustig curious; der/die ~lustige (*decl as adj*) (curious) onlooker; der ~platz, ¨–e scene (of); *liter* setting; der ~prozeß, –(ss)e show trial; das ~spiel, –e play; spectacle; der ~spieler, – actor; die ~spielerei acting; play-acting; die ~spielerin, –nen actress; s~spielerisch acting; s~spielern (*insep*) play-act; das ~spiel|haus, ¨–er theatre; die ~spiel|kunst dramatic art; der ~steller, – showman; die ~tafel, –n (illustrated) chart
der Schauder, – shudder; shiver; thrill; s~erregend horrifying
schauderhaft horrible; *coll* dreadful, ghastly
schaudern shudder; shiver; mich/mir schaudert I shudder; I shiver
schauen *esp SGer* look at (pictures *etc*), see (film *etc*), watch (television); *poet* behold; (*v/i*) look (in a certain direction); look (sad *etc*); ~ auf (*acc*) look at; pay attention to; ~ nach see to; schau, schau! well, what do you know!
der Schauer, – shudder; shiver; thrill; shower; die ~geschichte, –n horror story; der ~mann, ..leute docker, longshoreman *US*; der ~roman, –e horror story
schauerlich horrible; *coll* ghastly
schauern = schaudern
die Schaufel, –n shovel; scoop; *tech* paddle; blade (of turbine *etc*); das ~rad, ¨–er paddle-wheel
schaufeln shovel; dig (ditch *etc*)
die Schaukel, –n swing; das ~pferd, –e rocking-horse; der ~stuhl, ¨–e rocking-chair
schaukeln rock (baby *etc*); (*v/i*) swing; rock; wir werden das Kind/die Sache schon ~ *coll* we'll manage it somehow
der Schaum, ¨–e foam; froth; lather; ~ schlagen *coll* talk a lot of hot air || das ~bad, ¨–er bubble-bath; s~gebremst low-sud; der ~gummi foam rubber; der ~schläger, – *coll* boaster; die ~schlägerei, –en *coll* hot air; der ~stoff, –e foam plastic; der ~wein, –e sparkling wine
schäumen foam; froth; lather; bubble; vor Wut ~ foam with rage
schaumig foamy; frothy; lathery
schaurig gruesome; *coll* dreadful, ghastly
der Scheck, –s cheque, check *US* (über *acc* for); das ~buch, ¨–er = das ~heft, –e cheque-book, check book *US*; die ~karte, –n cheque (guarantee) card
der Schecke, –n (*wk masc*), die Schecke, –n piebald; skewbald; spotted ox *or* cow
scheckig piebald; skewbald; spotted
scheel envious; suspicious
der Scheffel, – bushel; sein Licht unter den ~ stellen hide one's light under a bushel; in ~n = s~weise in large quantities
scheffeln *coll* rake in
die Scheibe, –n slice; disc; pane, *mot* window; *sp* target; *ice hock* puck; sich *dat* eine ~ abschneiden von *coll* take a leaf out of (s.o.'s) book || die ~n|bremse, –n disc-brake; der ~n|honig comb honey (S.! sugar!); ~n|kleister (S.! sugar!); das ~n|schießen target shooting; die ~n|wasch|anlage, –n windscreen washer, windshield washer *US*; der ~n|wischer, – windscreen wiper, windshield wiper *US*
der Scheich, –e/–s sheik
das Scheichtum, ¨–er sheikhdom
die Scheide, –n sheath; border; *anat* vagina; die ~wand, ¨–e partition; ~weg (am S. stehen be at the crossroads)
scheiden (*p/t* schied, *p/part* geschieden) (*see also* geschieden) separate; divorce; dissolve (marriage); (*v/i sn*) part; depart; aus dem Amt ~ resign one's post; sich ~ lassen get divorced; sich ~ lassen von divorce
sich ~ (opinions) diverge
Scheiden– vaginal ...
die Scheidung, –en separation; divorce; die ~ einreichen file a petition for divorce; in ~ leben be getting a divorce || der ~s|grund, ¨–e grounds for divorce; die ~s|klage, –n petition for divorce; der ~s|prozeß, –e divorce proceedings

der **Schein**[1], **–e** banknote; certificate

der **Schein**[2] light; glow; gleam; appearance(s); **das ist alles nur ~** it's all a sham; **den ~ wahren** keep up appearances; **dem ~ nach** on the face of it; **nur zum ~ tun** only pretend to do

Schein– pseudo–; sham ...; **s~heilig** hypocritical (**s. tun** act the innocent); **die ~heiligkeit** hypocrisy; **die ~schwangerschaft, –en** phantom pregnancy; **der ~tod** suspended animation; **s~tot** in a state of suspended animation; **der ~werfer, –** searchlight; floodlight; *theat* spotlight; *mot* headlight

scheinbar apparent; (*adv*) apparently (but not in reality; *coll* = it would seem)

scheinen (*p/t* **schien,** *p/part* **geschienen**) shine; seem, appear; **scheint's** *coll* apparently; **mir scheint, (daß) ...** it seems to me that ...; **wie es scheint** it would seem

Scheiß– *vulg* shit ...; bloody ..., goddam ... *US*; **der ~dreck** *vulg* crap; bloody business, goddam business *US* (**das geht dich einen S. an** it's none of your bloody business/goddam business *US*); **s~egal** *vulg* (**das ist mir s.** I don't give a fuck); **s~freundlich** *coll* pretending to be ever so friendly; **der ~kerl, –e** *vulg* 'shit'

die **Scheiße** *vulg* shit, crap

scheißen (*p/t* **schiß,** *p/part* **geschissen**) *vulg* shit; **~ auf** (*acc*) not give a shit about

der **Scheißer, –** *vulg* 'shit'

das **Scheit, –e** log

der **Scheitel, –** crown, top (of the head); parting, part *US*; *math* apex, vertex; **vom ~ bis zur Sohle** from top to toe || **der ~punkt, –e** *math* apex, vertex; *astron* zenith

scheiteln part (hair)

der **Scheiter|haufen, –** funeral pyre; *hist* stake

scheitern (*sn*) fail; founder; *arch* (ship) be wrecked; **~ an** (*dat*) fail because of; founder because of; *sp* be beaten by; **das Scheitern** failure; *arch* (ship)wreck

die **Schelde** the Scheldt

der **Schelf, –e** (*also* **das**) *geol* shelf

Schell–: der ~fisch, –e haddock

die **Schelle**[1], **–n** (small) bell

die **Schelle**[2], **–n** *tech* clamp

schellen ring (bell); **es schellt** there is a ring at the door

der **Schelm, –e** rascal; *arch* scoundrel || **der ~en|roman, –e** picaresque novel; **der ~en|streich, –e** = **das ~en|stück, –e** prank

die **Schelmerei, –en** prank; roguishness

schelmisch roguish

Schelt–: das ~wort, –e term of abuse

die **Schelte, –n** scolding

schelten (**schilt(st),** *p/t* **schalt** (*subj* **schölte**), *p/part* **gescholten**) scold; call (s.o. sth.)

das **Schema, –s/Schemata** scheme; diagram; pattern; **nach ~ F** *coll* mechanically; according to a set pattern/routine

schematisch schematic, diagrammatic; mechanical

schematisieren schematize

der **Schemel, –** stool

der **Schemen, –** shadowy figure/object; phantom

schemenhaft shadowy

Schenk– = **Schank–**

die **Schenke, –n** (small) inn

der **Schenkel, –** thigh; *math* side (of angle)

schenken (+*dat*) give (as a present); let off (punishment); **sich** *dat* **... ~** skip; **das ist (fast/halb) geschenkt** that's dirt cheap; **geschenkt bekommen** get as a present

die **Schenkung, –en** *leg* gift

scheppern *coll*, **~ mit** clatter

die **Scherbe, –n** fragment; *archaeol* potsherd; **in ~n gehen** shatter

die **Schere, –n** scissors; shears; *zool* claw (of lobster *etc*); *gym*, *wrestl* scissors

scheren[1] (*p/t* **schor** (*subj* **schöre**), *p/part* **geschoren**) crop; clip; shear (sheep)

scheren[2]: **das schert mich nicht** I don't care; **was schert mich das?** what's that to me?; **sich ~** *coll* get, go (somewhere: *usu with imp*, *eg* **scher dich ins Bett!** get to bed!, **scher dich zum Teufel!** go to blazes!); **sich nicht ~ um** *coll* not care about

die **Schererei, –en** (*usu pl*) *coll* trouble

das **Scherflein, –** small contribution

der **Scherge, –n** (*wk masc*) myrmidon

der **Scherz, –e** joke; **seinen ~ treiben mit** make fun of; **aus/im/zum ~ sagen** say in fun; **~ beiseite** joking apart || **s~weise** in fun; **das ~wort, –e** quip

scherzen joke; **damit ist nicht zu ~** it's no laughing matter

scherzhaft jocular

schesen (*sn*) *esp NGer coll* dash

scheu shy; timid; **~ werden** (horse) shy, take fright

die **Scheu** shyness; timidity; awe; **die ~klappen** *pl* blinkers

scheuchen shoo; scare away

scheuen shun; avoid; (*v/i*) shy; **keine Mühe ~** spare no effort; **sich ~ vor** (*dat*) be afraid of; shrink from; **sich ~ zu ...** shrink from (+*ger*)

die **Scheuer, –n** *SGer* barn

Scheuer–: die ~bürste, –n scrubbing-brush; **der ~lappen, –** floorcloth; **der ~sand** scouring powder; **das ~tuch, ¨er** floorcloth

scheuern scour; scrub; chafe; **~ an** (*dat*) chafe; **sich ~ an** (*dat*) rub against; (+*dat*) **eine ~** *coll* give (s.o.) a clout

die **Scheune, –n** barn; **~n|drescher** *coll* (**wie ein S. essen** eat like a horse); **das ~n|tor, –e** barn door

das **Scheusal, –e** monster (= person)

scheußlich hideous; atrocious; *coll* dreadful

der **Schi, –er** = **Ski**

die **Schicht, –en** layer; film (of dust *etc*); (social) class; shift; *geol* stratum; *in compds also* laminated ...; **die ~arbeit** shift work; **s~weise** in layers/shifts

die **Schichte, –n** *Aust* = **Schicht** (*exc 3rd, 4th senses*)

schichten stack; layer

–schichtig -layer; -ply

die **Schichtung, –en** *vbl noun*; *also* lamination; *geol* stratification

schick smart; **(es ist) ~, daß ...** *coll* it's great that ...

der **Schick** chic

schicken send; **~ nach** send for; **sich ~** be seemly; **sich ~ in** (*acc*) resign oneself to

die **Schickeria** smart set

schicklich proper; becoming

die **Schicklichkeit** propriety

das **Schicksal, –e** fate; destiny

schicksalhaft fateful

Schicksals–: der ~gefährte, –n (*wk masc*) fellow-sufferer; **der ~schlag, ⸚e** blow; **s~schwer** fateful

Schiebe– sliding ...; **das ~dach, ⸚er** sunshine roof; **die ~tür, –en** sliding door

schieben (*p/t* **schob** (*subj* **schöbe**), *p/part* **geschoben**) push; *coll* traffic in; 'push' (drugs); (*v/i sn*) shuffle; **~ auf** (*acc*) put (blame) on; **~ mit** *coll* traffic in; 'push' (drugs); **von sich ~** push away/off; reject

der **Schieber, –** slide; (baby's) pusher; bed-pan; *coll* racketeer; **das ~geschäft, –e** *coll* racket

die **Schiebung, –en** racket; fiddle; rigging

schied *p/t of* **scheiden**

Schieds–: das ~gericht, –e court of arbitration; *sp* judges; **der ~richter, –** arbitrator; *sp* judge; referee; umpire; **s~richtern** (*insep*) arbitrate; *sp* referee; umpire; **der ~spruch, ⸚e** award; **das ~verfahren, –** arbitration

schief crooked; leaning; distorted; *phys* (plane) inclined; *math* oblique; **auf die ~e Ebene geraten** go astray; **ein ~es Gesicht/einen ~en Mund ziehen** *coll* pull a (wry) face; **~ ansehen** look askance at || **~gehen*** (*sep*; *sn*) go wrong; **~gewickelt** *coll* mistaken; **~lachen** (*sep*): **sich s.** *coll* double up with laughter; **~liegen*** (*sep*) *coll* be wrong; **~treten*** (*sep*) wear down (heels); **~wink(e)lig** oblique

der **Schiefer, –** slate; *esp Aust* splinter; **der ~bruch, ⸚e** slate quarry; **das ~öl** shale oil; **die ~tafel, –n** slate (for writing); **der ~ton, –e** shale

schielen squint; **~ auf** (*acc*) *coll* steal a glance at; **~ nach** *coll* steal a glance at; have one's eye on

schien *p/t of* **scheinen**

das **Schien|bein, –e** shin

die **Schiene, –n** *rail etc* rail; *med* splint

schienen put in a splint/splints

Schienen– rail ...; track ...; **der ~bus, –se** diesel rail-car; **der ~strang, ⸚e** section of track

schier[1] pure; sheer

schier[2] almost; virtually

der **Schierling, –e** hemlock

Schieß– shooting ...; **der ~befehl, –e** order to shoot; **die ~bude, –n** shooting-gallery; **die ~buden|figur, –en** target figure; *coll* ludicrous figure; **~hund** *coll* (**aufpassen wie ein S.** watch like a hawk); **der ~platz, ⸚e** firing-range; **das ~pulver** gunpowder; **der ~stand, ⸚e** rifle-range

schießen (*p/t* **schoß** [-ɔ-] (*subj* **schösse**), *p/part* **geschossen**) shoot; fire; *sp* score; *coll* take (picture); (*v/i*) shoot (**auf** *acc* at); (*sn*) shoot (round corner *etc*); shoot up; (blood) rush; flash (through s.o.'s mind); *Aust* fade; **... ist zum Schießen** *coll* ... is a scream || **~lassen*** (*p/part usu* **~lassen;** *sep*) *coll* drop, forget

die **Schießerei, –en** gunfight, shoot-out; shooting

das **Schiff, –e** ship; *archit* nave; aisle; **die Schiffahrt** shipping; **die Schiffahrts|straße, –n** = **der Schiffahrts|weg, –e** shipping lane; **der ~bau** shipbuilding; **der ~bruch, ⸚e** shipwreck (**S. erleiden** be shipwrecked; fail); **s~brüchig** shipwrecked

schiffbar navigable

das **Schiffchen, –** little boat; shuttle (on loom, sewing-machine); *mil* forage-cap

schiffen *vulg* piss

der **Schiffer, –** boatman; skipper

Schiffs– ship's ...; **der ~junge, –n** (*wk masc*) cabin boy; **die ~ladung, –en** cargo; **der ~rumpf, ⸚e** hull

die **Schikane, –n** harassment; *mot rac* chicane; **mit allen ~n** *coll* with all the trimmings

schikanieren harass; victimize

schikanös harassing

das **Schild, –er** sign; name-plate; label; tag; peak (of cap)

der **Schild, –e** shield; **auf den ~ erheben** choose as leader; **im ~e führen** *coll* be up to

Schild–: der ~bürger, – idiot, person who commits a foolish act; **der ~bürger|streich, –e** foolish act; **die ~drüse, –n** thyroid gland; **die ~kröte, –n** tortoise; turtle; **das ~patt** tortoiseshell

Schilder–: das ~haus, ⸚er sentry-box; **der ~maler, –** sign-painter; **der ~wald, ⸚er** jungle of traffic signs

schildern describe; depict, portray

die **Schilderung, –en** description; depiction, portrayal

das **Schilf, –e** reed; reeds; **das ~rohr** reed

die **Schiller|locke, –n** (*puff-pastry cone filled with*

cream; *strip of smoked dogfish*)
schillern shimmer; **~d** iridescent; ambiguous; enigmatic
der **Schilling, –e**/(*following num*) – (*Austria*) schilling
schilt *imp sing, 3rd sing pres*, **schiltst** *2nd sing pres of* **schelten**
der **Schimmel, –** white horse; mould; mildew
schimmelig mouldy; mildewy
schimmeln (*also sn*) go mouldy
der **Schimmer** glimmer; gleam; shimmer; hint (of smile); **keinen blassen ~ haben von** *coll* not have a clue about
schimmern glimmer; gleam; shimmer
der **Schimpanse, –n** (*wk masc*) chimpanzee
Schimpf: mit ~ und Schande in disgrace
Schimpf–: die ~kanonade, –n tirade; **der ~name, –n** (*like* Name) abusive name; **das ~wort, –e/⸚er** term of abuse; swear-word
schimpfen grumble (loudly) (**auf** *acc*/**über** *acc* about); call (s.o. sth.); **~ mit** give (s.o.) a telling-off
schimpflich disgraceful; ignominious
Schind–: ~luder *coll* (**S. treiben mit** treat abominably; abuse)
die **Schindel, –n** shingle
schinden (*p/part* **geschunden**) ill-treat; sweat (labour); *mot coll* flog (engine); **sich ~** *coll* slave away (**mit** at); **Eindruck ~ wollen** *coll* try to impress; **Zeit ~** *coll* play for time
der **Schinder, –** slave-driver (= employer *etc*)
die **Schinderei, –en** grind
der **Schinken, –** ham; *coll* fat tome; film *etc* of little artistic merit
die **Schippe, –n** shovel; **eine ~ machen** *joc* pout; **auf die ~ nehmen** *coll* pull (s.o.'s) leg
schippen shovel
schippern (*sn*) *coll* sail
der **Schirm, –e** umbrella; sunshade; shade; screen; peak (of cap); *mil* shield; **die ~bild|aufnahme, –n** X-ray; **der ~herr, –en** (*like* **Herr**) patron; **die ~herrschaft, –en** patronage (**unter der S. von** under the auspices of); **die ~mütze, –n** peaked cap; **der ~ständer, –** umbrella stand
der **Schirokko, –s** sirocco
das **Schisma, –(m)en** schism
schiß (schisse) *p/t* (*subj*) *of* **scheißen**
der **Schiß** *vulg* shit; **~ haben/kriegen** be in/get into a funk
schizoid [ʃitso'iːt] schizoid
schizophren [ʃi–] schizophrenic; contradictory
die **Schizophrenie** [ʃi–] schizophrenia; contradictoriness
schlabb(e)rig *coll* floppy; (soup *etc*) watery
schlabbern *coll* slurp; (*v/i*) slobber
die **Schlacht, –en** battle; **die ~ bei ...** the Battle of ...; (+*dat*) **eine ~ liefern** do battle with || **das ~feld, –er** battlefield; **das ~haus, ⸚er** = **der ~hof, ⸚e** slaughterhouse; **der ~plan, ⸚e** battle-plan; plan of action; **der ~ruf, –e** battle-cry; **das ~schiff, –e** battleship; **das ~vieh** animals for slaughter
schlachten slaughter
der **Schlachten|bummler, –** *sp* supporter, fan (accompanying team to away match)
der **Schlachter, –** *NGer* butcher
die **Schlachterei, –en** *NGer* butcher's
die **Schlächterei, –en** butchery, slaughter
die **Schlacke, –n** clinker; *geol*, *metall* slag; (*pl*) *physiol* waste products
der **Schlaf** sleep; **einen leichten ~ haben** be a light sleeper; **in den ~ singen** sing to sleep; **in tiefem ~ liegen** be fast asleep
Schlaf– *esp* sleeping ...;
der ~anzug, ⸚e pyjamas; **die ~gelegenheit, –en** sleeping accommodation; **die ~krankheit** sleeping sickness; **s~los** sleepless; **die ~losigkeit** insomnia; **das ~mittel, –** sleeping drug/pill; **die ~mütze, –n** *coll* sleepyhead; **der ~raum, ⸚e** dormitory; **der ~rock, ⸚e** dressing-gown; **der ~saal, ..säle** dormitory; **der ~sack, ⸚e** sleeping-bag; **die ~tablette, –n** sleeping-pill; **s~trunken** drowsy; **der ~wagen, –** *rail* sleeper; **s~wandeln** (*insep*; *also sn*) walk in one's sleep; **der ~wandler, –** sleepwalker; **das ~zimmer, –** bedroom; bedroom suite; **der ~zimmer|blick, –e** *coll*: *approx* = come-hither look
das **Schläfchen, –** snooze
die **Schläfe, –n** temple
schlafen (schläf(s)t, *p/t* **schlief,** *p/part* **geschlafen)** sleep; be asleep; *coll* not pay attention; **~ mit** sleep with; **darüber ~** sleep on it; **~ gehen** go to bed
die **Schlafens|zeit** bedtime
der **Schläfer, –** sleeper
schlaff slack; limp; flabby; (person) listless
Schlafittchen *coll*: **am/beim ~ nehmen** collar
schläfrig sleepy
schläf(s)t (*2nd*,) *3rd sing pres of* **schlafen**
der **Schlag, ⸚e** blow; punch; slap; stroke (*also* of lightning, *sp*, *med coll*); beat; type (of person); song (of bird); carriage-door; *elect* shock; *coll* helping; (*pl*) a thrashing; **~**/*Aust* **s~** (**6** *etc*) *coll* at (6 *etc*) o'clock sharp; **ich dachte, mich rührt der ~** *coll* you could have knocked me down with a feather; **auf 'einen ~** all at once; in one go; **~ auf ~** in quick succession; **~ ins Kontor** *coll* nasty surprise; **~ ins Wasser** flop; **mit 'einem ~** all at once; in one go; **mit ~** *Aust* with whipped cream
Schlag– *tech* impact ...;
die ~ader, –n artery; **der ~anfall, ⸚e** stroke; **s~artig** sudden; (*adv*) all of a sudden; **der ~ball, ⸚e** rounders; rounders ball; **der ~baum, ⸚e** barrier; **s~fertig** quick-

witted; **das ~instrument, -e** percussion instrument; **die ~kraft** force (of argument *etc*); *box* punching power; *mil* striking power; **s~kräftig** powerful; forceful; **~licht (ein S. werfen auf** (*acc*) highlight); **das ~loch, ⸚er** pothole; **der ~mann, ⸚er** *row* stroke; **das ~obers** *Aust* whipped cream; **der ~ring, -e** knuckleduster; **die ~sahne** whipped cream; **die ~seite** *naut* list (**S. haben** *naut* list; *joc* be sloshed); **das ~wort, -e** catchword, slogan; (*pl* **⸚er**) (catalogue) heading; **die ~zeile, -n** headline (**~zeilen machen** hit the headlines); **das ~zeug** percussion; **der ~zeuger, -** drummer; percussionist

schlagbar *sp* beatable

schlagen (schläg(s)t, *p/t* **schlug** (*subj* **schlüge**), *p/part* **geschlagen)** (*see also* **geschlagen**) strike, hit; beat; knock (unconscious *etc*); fell; describe (circle *etc*); build (bridge); fight (battle); *mil*, *sp*, *etc* beat, defeat, *chess* take; *cul* beat; whisk; whip (cream); (*v/i*) beat; (clock) strike; (bird) sing; **ein geschlagener Mann** a broken man; **sich geschlagen geben** throw in one's hand

~ **an** (*acc*) fix to; nail to; (*v/i* rain, waves) beat against

~ **auf** (*acc*) add to (price); (*v/i sn*) affect (part of body); **mit der Faust auf den Tisch ~** bang the table (with one's fist); **mit dem Hammer auf den Nagel ~** hit the nail with the hammer

~ **aus** knock out of (s.o.'s hand); make (money *etc*) out of; (*v/i*, *also sn*) (flames) leap from; (smoke) pour from

~ **gegen** (rain, waves) beat against; **mit dem Kopf ~ gegen** (*sn*) hit one's head against

~ **in** (*acc*) knock into; knock (hole) in; sink (claws *etc*) in; wrap in; *cul* break (egg) into; (*v/i*) (*also sn*) (lightning) strike; (*sn*) (grenade *etc*) hit; (+*dat*) **ins Gesicht ~** hit/punch/slap in the face

~ **mit** beat (wings)

~ **nach** hit out at; (*sn*) take after

~ **über** (*acc*) cover with; throw (bridge) across

~ **um** wrap round; **um sich ~** wrap round oneself; (*v/i*) lash out

~ **zu** add to; **zum Ritter ~** knight

sich ~ fight (**um** over); **sich auf jmds. Seite ~** side with s.o.; **sich ~ zu** go over to

schlagend convincing; *univ* duelling

[der] **Schlager, -** hit; best-seller; *mus* pop song; **der ~sänger, -** pop singer

[der] **Schläger, -** tough; *sp* club; bat; mallet; stick; racket; batsman; **der ~typ, -en** tough

[die] **Schlägerei, -en** brawl

schlägern *Aust* fell (tree)

schlaksig [-a-] *coll* gangling

[der] **Schlamassel** (*also* **das**) *coll* mess

[der] **Schlamm** mud; sludge; **das ~bad, ⸚er** mud-bath; **die ~packung, -en** mud pack

schlammig muddy; sludgy

[die] **Schlampe, -n** *coll* slattern, slut

schlampen *coll* be slovenly

[die] **Schlamperei** *coll* slovenliness; slovenly work

schlampig *coll* slovenly, sloppy

schlang (schlänge) *p/t* (*subj*) *of* **schlingen[1,2]**

[die] **Schlange, -n** snake; queue, line *US*; **~ stehen** queue, stand in line *US*

[die] **Schlängel|linie, -n** wavy line

schlängeln: sich ~ weave one's way; wind (its way)

Schlangen- snake ...; snake's ...; **der ~beschwörer, -** snake-charmer; **der ~biß, -(ss)e** snake-bite; **das ~gift** (snake's) venom; **das ~leder** snakeskin; **die ~linie, -n** wiggly line; **der ~mensch, -en** (*wk masc*) contortionist

schlank slim; **die ~e Linie** one's figure/waistline || **~weg** *coll* flatly

[die] **Schlankheits|kur, -en** diet; **eine ~ machen** slim

schlapp slack; limp; weary, worn-out, (after illness) run-down; *coll* lifeless; **der S~hut, ⸚e** slouch-hat; **~machen** (*sep*) *coll* flake out; **die S~ohren** *pl* floppy ears; **der S~schwanz, ⸚e** *coll* sissy

[die] **Schlappe, -n** *coll* setback, reverse

[der] **Schlappen, -** *coll* slipper

[das] **Schlaraffen|land** Cockaigne, imaginary land of idleness and luxury

schlau cunning, crafty; *coll* clever; **nicht ~ werden aus** *coll* be unable to make head or tail of || **der S~berger, -** *coll* = **der S~kopf, ⸚e** *coll* = **der S~meier, -** *coll* clever person

[der] **Schlauch, ⸚e** hose; tube (of tyre); (wine *etc*) skin; *coll* long and narrow room; **... ist ein ~** *coll* ... is a slog || **das ~boot, -e** rubber dinghy; **s~los** tubeless

schlauchen *coll* wear out

[die] **Schläue** cunning, craftiness

[die] **Schlaufe, -n** loop

[die] **Schlauheit** cunning, craftiness

[der] **Schlawiner, -** *coll* rogue

schlecht bad; poor (in quality); (*adv*) badly; not very well; hardly, (afford) ill; not really; **~ in** (*dat*) poor at (subject); **~ zu sprechen sein auf** (*acc*) not have a good word to say for; **mir ist/wird ~** I feel sick; **heute geht es ~** today isn't very convenient; **~ hören/sehen** have poor hearing/eyesight; **~ werden** go bad/off; **(gar) nicht ~** not bad; **~ und recht = mehr ~ als recht** after a fashion || **~gehen*** (*sep*; *sn*) (**es geht ihm ~** he's in a bad way/having a hard time of it); ~gelaunt in a bad mood; ~hin simply; absolutely; as such; ~machen (*sep*) run down; das S~wetter bad weather; die S~wetter|periode, –n spell of bad weather

schlechter|dings simply

die **Schlechtigkeit, –en** badness; bad deed

schlecken *esp SGer* lick; (*v/i*) eat sweets/candies *US*; ~ **an** (*dat*) lick

der **Schlegel, –** drumstick; mallet; *SGer cul* leg

die **Schlehe, –n** sloe

Schleich–: der ~handel illicit trading (**mit** in); **der ~weg, –e** secret path (**auf ~wegen** by surreptitious means); **die ~werbung** plug (for product *etc*)

schleichen (*p/t* **schlich,** *p/part* **geschlichen**) (*sn*) creep; steal; **sich ~** steal (into, out of, *etc* sth.); **~d** (inflation *etc*) creeping; (disease) insidious

die **Schleie, –n** tench

der **Schleier, –** veil; haze; film; **die ~eule, –n** barn-owl

schleierhaft *coll* a mystery (to s.o.)

Schleif– grinding ...; **das ~papier** abrasive paper; **der ~stein, –e** grindstone

die **Schleife, –n** bow; bow-tie; S-bend, (in river) horseshoe bend; loop (*also comput*)

schleifen[1] (*p/t* **schliff,** *p/part* **geschliffen**) (*see also* **geschliffen**) grind, sharpen; polish; cut (glass *etc*); *mil coll* drill hard

schleifen[2] drag; *mil* raze (to the ground); (*v/i, also sn*) (dress *etc*) trail (along); ~ **an** (*dat*) rub on/against; ~ **lassen** trail (on ground); *mot* slip (clutch); **die Zügel ~ lassen** relax discipline

der **Schleifer, –** grinder

der **Schleim, –e** slime; *physiol* mucus; phlegm; *in compds* mucous ...; **die ~haut, ⸚e** mucous membrane; **der ~scheißer, –** *vulg* boot-licker

schleimig slimy; *physiol* mucous

der **Schlemm, –e** *cards* slam

schlemmen feast

der **Schlemmer, –** gourmand

schlendern (*sn*) stroll, saunter

der **Schlendrian** *coll* same old (careless, inefficient) way of working; jog-trot

der **Schlenker, –, einen ~ machen** swerve

schlenkern, ~ mit swing, dangle

Schlepp: im ~ haben have in tow; **in ~ nehmen** take in tow

Schlepp– towing ...; **der ~dampfer, –** tugboat; **der ~kahn, ⸚e** (towed) barge; **der ~lift, –e** ski tow; **das ~netz, –e** trawl; **das ~tau, –e** tow-rope (**ins S. nehmen** take in tow); **der ~zug, ⸚e** train of barges

die **Schleppe, –n** train (of dress)

schleppen tow; drag; lug; *coll* wear again and again; **sich ~** drag oneself (along); drag on; **~d** (gait) shuffling; sluggish; slow

der **Schlepper, –** tug(boat); tractor

Schlesien [–ĭən] Silesia

der **Schlesier** [–ĭɐ], **–, schlesisch** Silesian

die **Schleuder, –n** catapult, slingshot *US*; spin-dryer, dryer *US*; = **die ~maschine, –n** centrifuge; extractor; **der ~preis, –e** give-away price; **der ~sitz, –e** ejector seat

schleudern hurl; spin-dry, dry *US*; centrifuge; extract (honey); (*v/i, also sn*) skid

schleunig prompt, speedy; **~st** at once; in great haste

die **Schleuse, –n** lock; sluice; *space* decompression chamber

schleusen pass (ship) through a lock; smuggle (abroad *etc*); ~ **durch** steer through (customs *etc*)

schlich *p/t of* **schleichen**

die **Schliche** *pl* tricks; (+*dat*) **auf die ~ kommen** *coll* rumble

schlicht simple; plain; modest; **der S~hobel, –** smoothing-plane

schlichten settle (dispute); *tech* dress; smooth; (*v/i*) mediate; arbitrate

der **Schlichter, –** mediator; arbitrator

die **Schlichtheit** simplicity; plainness

die **Schlichtung, –en** settlement; arbitration

der **Schlick, –e** silt

schlief *p/t of* **schlafen**

die **Schliere, –n** streak

Schließ–: das ~fach, ⸚er P.O. box; safe-deposit box; (luggage) locker; **der ~muskel, –n** sphincter; **der ~tag, –e** *EGer* weekday when a shop/restaurant is closed

die **Schließe, –n** fastening; clasp

schließen (*p/t* **schloß** (*subj* **schlösse**), *p/part* **geschlossen**) (*see also* **geschlossen**) close, shut; close down; close, conclude (letter *etc*); conclude (treaty *etc*), make (peace); (*v/i*) close, shut; close down; close, conclude; **Freundschaft ~ mit** make friends with; **die Ehe ~ mit** marry

~ **an** (*acc*) chain to; add (remark) to

~ **auf** (*acc*): **aus ... auf ... ~** infer from; **~ lassen auf** suggest; point to; **von sich auf andere ~** judge others by one's own standards

~ **aus** infer from

~ **in** (*acc*) lock up in; **in die Arme ~** take into one's arms; **ins Herz ~** grow very fond of; **in sich** *dat* **~** contain, include

sich ~ close, shut; (wound) close; **an ...** (*acc*) **schloß sich ...** ... was/were followed by ...

schließlich in the end, finally; after all; **~ und endlich** at long last; after all

die **Schließung, –en** *vbl noun*; *also* closure (of factory *etc*); conclusion

schliff *p/t of* **schleifen**[1]

der **Schliff, –e** cutting (of gem *etc*); cut; polish, refinement; (+*dat*) **den letzten ~ geben** put the finishing touches to

schlimm bad; **ist es ~, wenn ...?** would you mind very much if ...?; **es ist halb so ~** it's not as bad as all that; **es ist nicht so ~** it doesn't matter || **~sten|falls** at worst

Schling–: das ~gewächs, –e = die ~pflanze, –n climber

die **Schlinge, –n** loop; noose; snare; *med* sling

der **Schlingel, –** rascal

schlingen[1] (*p/t* **schlang** (*subj* **schlänge**), *p/part* **geschlungen**) tie (knot); **~ um** wind around; wrap around; **sich ~ um** twine around; coil around

schlingen[2] (*p/t* **schlang** (*subj* **schlänge**), *p/part* **geschlungen**) (*also v/i*) bolt (one's food)

schlingern *naut* roll; (*sn*) lurch (in a certain direction)

der **Schlips, –e** tie; (+*dat*) **auf den ~ treten** *coll* tread on (s.o.'s) toes; **sich auf den ~ getreten fühlen** *coll* be put out

Schlitt–: der ~schuh, –e, S. laufen skate; **die ~schuh|bahn, –en** ice-rink; **der ~schuh|läufer, –** skater

schlitteln (*sn*) *Swiss* toboggan

der **Schlitten, –** sledge, sled *US*; sleigh; *coll* 'bus'; **~ fahren** go tobogganing; **+mit** *coll* haul over the coals || **die ~fahrt, –en** sleigh-ride; **der ~hund, –e** husky

die **Schlitter|bahn, –en** slide

schlittern slide (on ice); (*sn*) slide, slip; *mot* skid

der **Schlitz, –e** slit; slot; flies; vent (in jacket); **die ~augen** *pl* slanting eyes; **s~äugig** slant-eyed

schlitzen slit

schlohweiß (hair) snow-white

schloß (schlösse) *p/t* (*subj*) *of* **schließen**

das **Schloß**[1], **¨(ss)er** castle; palace; country mansion; château

das **Schloß**[2], **¨(ss)er** lock; padlock; **hinter ~ und Riegel** behind bars; **ins ~ fallen** slam shut; **unter ~ und Riegel** under lock and key || **~hund** *coll* (**heulen wie ein S.** cry one's eyes out)

der **Schlosser, –** fitter; locksmith

die **Schlosserei, –en** metalwork; metalwork shop

der **Schlot, –e** chimney; *naut*, *rail* funnel; *geol* chimney, vent; *coll* slob; **rauchen wie ein ~** *coll* smoke like a chimney || **der ~baron, –e** *coll* industrial tycoon

schlott(e)rig trembling; (hanging) loose

schlottern tremble; hang loose

die **Schlucht, –en** ravine

schluchzen, der Schluchzer, – sob

der **Schluck, –e** gulp; sip; drop (of ...); **der ~auf** hiccups; **die ~beschwerden** *pl* difficulty in swallowing; **die ~impfung, –en** oral vaccination; **s~weise** in sips

schlucken swallow; *coll* swallow up; (car *etc*) guzzle; *coll* swallow (insult *etc*)

der **Schlucken** hiccups

der **Schlucker, –** *coll*: **armer ~** poor devil

schlud(e)rig *coll* sloppy

schludern *coll* do sloppy work

schlug (schlüge) *p/t* (*subj*) *of* **schlagen**

der **Schlummer** slumber; **die ~rolle, –n** bolster

schlummern slumber; lie dormant; **~d** latent (*also med*), dormant

der **Schlund, ¨e** gullet, pharynx; abyss; mouth (of cave); jaws (of hell)

Schlupf–: das ~loch, ¨er hole (in wall *etc*); hiding-place; loophole; **der ~winkel, –** hiding-place

schlüpfen (*sn*) slip; hatch (out); **~ in** (*acc*) slip into (coat *etc*)

der **Schlüpfer, –** panties

schlüpfrig slippery; indecent, lewd

schlurfen (*sn*) shuffle

schlürfen slurp; sip

der **Schluß, ¨(ss)e** end; ending, conclusion; conclusion (reached); end, rear; **~ machen** finish, stop; call it a day; break it off; *coll* do away with oneself; **+mit** stop (smoking *etc*); put an end to; finish with; **einen ~ ziehen aus** draw a conclusion from; **mit ... ist ~** ... is *etc* over/finished; ... has *etc* had it; **am ~** at the end (*gen* of); in the end; **gegen ~** towards the end (*gen* of); **zum ~** in the end, finally; in conclusion; (+*gen*) at the end of; **~ damit/jetzt!** that's enough!; **~ mit ...!** stop ...!; **(und damit) ~!** and that's that!

Schluß– final ...; closing ...; **der ~ball, ¨e** end-of-term ball; **s~endlich** *Aust*, *Swiss* ultimately; **s~folgern** (*insep*) conclude, deduce (**aus** from); **die ~folgerung, –en** conclusion; **der ~läufer, –** *athl* anchor man; **das ~licht, –er** tail-light; *coll* back marker (**das S. bilden** bring up the rear); **~punkt (einen S. setzen unter** (*acc*) close (matter) once and for all); **~strich (einen S. ziehen unter** (*acc*) close (matter) once and for all); **der ~verkauf, ¨e** (end-of-season) sale

der **Schlüssel, –** key (**zu** to); spanner, wrench *US*; cipher, *comput* code; ratio (of distribution); *mus* clef; *in compds* key ...; **das ~bein, –e** collar-bone; **die ~blume, –n** cowslip; **der ~bund, –e** bunch of keys; **s~fertig** ready for occupation; **die ~industrie, –n** key industry; **das ~kind, –er** latch-key child; **das ~loch, ¨er** keyhole; **der ~ring, –e** key-ring; **der ~roman, –e** roman à clef; **die ~stellung, –en** key position

schlüssig conclusive; **sich** *dat* **~ sein** have made up one's mind; **sich** *dat* **~ werden** make up one's mind

die **Schmach** [–a:–] ignominy; **s~voll** ignominious

Schmacht–: der ~fetzen, – *coll* tear-jerker; **der ~lappen, –** *coll* lovesick swain; **die**

~locke, –n *coll* kiss-curl
schmachten languish; ~ **nach** pine for; **~d** yearning; languishing
schmächtig slight
schmackhaft palatable, tasty; (+*dat*) ~ **machen** make palatable to
Schmäh–: die ~rede, –n diatribe; (*pl*) invective; **die ~schrift, –en** defamatory piece of writing; lampoon
schmähen revile
schmählich humiliating; ignominious
die **Schmähung, –en** abuse
schmal (*comp, superl also* ¨) narrow; slender; (lips *etc*) thin; meagre; **der S~film, –e** cine-film; **die S~film|kamera, –s** cine-camera; **S~hans** *coll* (**bei ... ist S. Küchenmeister** ... have little to eat); **die S~spur, –en** narrow gauge; **S~spur–** narrow-gauge ...; small-time ...
schmälern diminish; detract from
das **Schmalz, –e** dripping; lard
der **Schmalz** *coll* schmaltz
schmalzig *coll* schmaltzy, mushy
das **Schmankerl, –n** *SGer coll* delicacy
schmarotzen (*p/part* **schmarotzt**): ~ **auf** (*dat*)/**in** (*dat*) *biol* be parasitic on; ~ **bei** sponge on
der **Schmarotzer, –** sponger; *biol* parasite; *in compds* parasitic ...
das **Schmarotzertum** parasitism
der **Schmarren, –** *SGer cul* (*type of pancake, torn into small pieces while frying*); *coll* rubbish; **das geht dich einen ~ an!** that's none of your business!
der **Schmatz, –e** *coll* smacker (= kiss)
schmatzen eat noisily; **mit den Lippen ~** smack one's lips
schmauchen puff away at; (*v/i*) puff away
der **Schmaus, ¨e** *now joc* spread
schmausen *now joc* feast on; (*v/i*) feast
schmecken taste; *SGer* smell; (*v/i*) taste; taste good; ~ **nach** taste of; smack of; **... schmeckt mir** I like ...; **das schmeckt!** it's delicious!; **schmeckt's?** do you like it?; **es sich** *dat* ~ **lassen** tuck in; **laß es dir (gut) ~!** I hope you enjoy it
die **Schmeichelei, –en** flattery; (*pl*) flattering remarks
schmeichelhaft flattering
schmeicheln be flattering; (+*dat*) flatter; **sich geschmeichelt fühlen** feel flattered
der **Schmeichler, –** flatterer
schmeichlerisch flattering
Schmeiß–: die ~fliege, –n bluebottle
schmeißen (*p/t* **schmiß**, *p/part* **geschmissen**) *coll* fling; stand (round of drinks), throw (party); 'screw up' (performance *etc*); **den Laden/die Sache ~** manage it; ~ **mit** chuck; **um sich ~ mit** chuck (one's money *etc*) about; bandy about
der **Schmelz, –e** *poet* bloom (of youth); mellowness (of voice *etc*); *cer* glaze; *dent* enamel; **die ~hütte, –n** smelting works; **der ~käse, –** processed cheese, process cheese *US*; **der ~ofen, ..öfen** smelting furnace; **der ~punkt, –e** melting-point; **der ~tiegel, –** crucible; melting-pot; **das ~wasser, –** melted snow and ice
schmelzen (*2nd/3rd sing pres* **schmilzt**, *p/t* **schmolz** (*subj* **schmölze**), *p/part* **geschmolzen**) melt; *tech* smelt; (*v/i sn*) melt
die **Schmelzerei, –en** smelting works
der **Schmer|bauch, ¨e** *coll* paunch
der **Schmerz, –en** pain; grief; **–schmerzen** *pl* -ache; **~en haben** be in pain; have a pain (in one's leg *etc*); **mit ~en** (realize) sadly; *coll* (await) impatiently || **s~empfindlich** sensitive to pain; **s~frei** free of pain; painless; **s~los** painless; **das ~mittel, –** painkiller; **s~stillend** pain-killing
schmerzen hurt (physically); hurt, pain; (*v/i*) hurt; ache; **~d** painful
Schmerzens–: das ~geld, –er damages; **der ~schrei, –e** cry of pain
schmerzhaft painful
schmerzlich (experience *etc*) painful
der **Schmetter|ball, ¨e** *sp* smash
der **Schmetterling, –e** butterfly; **der ~s|stil** butterfly stroke
schmettern hurl, fling; slam; bellow (song); (bird) warble; (trumpet) blare out; *sp* smash; (*v/i* trumpet) blare (out); **einen ~** *coll* knock back a drink
der **Schmied, –e** (black)smith
die **Schmiede, –n** forge; **das ~eisen** wrought iron; **s~eisern** wrought-iron
schmieden forge; hatch (plot); **Reime ~** versify
schmiegen: sich ~ an (*acc*) snuggle up to; (garment) hug
schmiegsam supple; flexible
Schmier– lubricating ...; **der ~fink, –en** (*wk masc*) *coll* graffiti writer; muckraker; (= child) scrawler; messy creature; **das ~geld, –er** *coll* slush money; **das ~heft, –e** jotter; **das ~mittel, –** lubricant; **das ~papier** rough paper; **die ~seife, –n** soft soap
die **Schmiere, –n** *coll* grease; lubricant; smeary mess; *theat* third-rate company; ~ **stehen** *coll* keep a look-out
schmieren grease; oil; spread (slice of bread *etc*); scrawl (slogan); scribble (article, play, *etc*); *coll* (*esp* child) scrawl; *coll* grease (s.o.'s) palm; (*v/i*) (pen *etc*) smudge; *coll* give a bribe/bribes; ~ **auf** (*acc*) spread on; rub on; **wie geschmiert** *coll* like clockwork, without a hitch; (+*dat*) **eine ~** *coll* clout
schmierig greasy; (café *etc*) grotty; (person) smarmy, oily; (joke *etc*) dirty
die **Schmierung, –en** lubrication

schmilz *imp sing*, **schmilzt** *2nd/3rd sing pres of* **schmelzen**
die **Schminke, -n** make-up
schminken make up; **sich ~** make oneself up
der **Schmirgel** emery; **das ~papier** emery paper
schmirgeln rub down, sand
schmiß (schmisse) *p/t (subj) of* **schmeißen**
der **Schmiß, -(ss)e** *univ* (duelling) scar; *coll* pep; **~ haben** *coll* have plenty of go; (music) go with a swing
schmissig *coll* spirited
der **Schmöker, -** *coll* (fat/old) book (providing light reading)
schmökern *coll* bury oneself in a book; browse
Schmoll-: der ~mund pout; **~winkel** *coll* (**im S. sitzen** have the sulks)
schmollen sulk
schmolz (schmölze) *p/t (subj) of* **schmelzen**
der **Schmor|braten, -** pot roast
schmoren braise; (*v/i*) braise; *coll* swelter; **(im eigenen Saft) ~ lassen** *coll* let (s.o.) stew in his/her own juice
der **Schmu** *coll* cheating; **~ machen** cheat
schmuck *dated* neat; smart
der **Schmuck** jewellery; decoration; **das ~kästchen, -** jewel-case; **s~los** plain; **die ~sachen** *pl* jewellery; **das ~stück, -e** piece of jewellery; gem (of collection *etc*)
schmücken decorate; embellish; **sich ~** adorn oneself
schmudd(e)lig *coll* mucky
der **Schmuggel** smuggling; **die ~ware, -n** contraband
schmuggeln smuggle
der **Schmuggler, -** smuggler
schmunzeln smile to oneself
der **Schmus** *coll* nonsense; blarney
schmusen *coll*, **~ mit** cuddle
der **Schmutz** dirt; smut; **in den ~ ziehen** drag in the mud || **der ~fink, -en** (*wk masc*) *coll* dirty fellow; mucky pup; **der ~fleck, -e** dirty mark
schmutzen get dirty
schmutzig dirty; **~e Wäsche (vor anderen Leuten) waschen** wash one's dirty linen in public; **sich ~ machen** get dirty
der **Schnabel,** *pl* **Schnäbel** beak; spout; *coll* mouth; **reden, wie einem der ~ gewachsen ist** *coll* say just what one thinks || **das ~tier, -e** platypus
schnäbeln: (sich) ~ bill and coo
schnabulieren *coll* eat with relish
der **Schnack, -s/⸚e** *NGer coll* chat; idle talk
das **Schnadahüpfl, -** *SGer* (*humorous Alpine ditty*)
die **Schnake, -n** daddy-long-legs; *SGer* gnat
die **Schnalle, -n** buckle; *Aust* door-handle
schnallen: ~ auf (*acc*) strap to; **den Gürtel/Riemen enger ~** tighten one's belt (*also* = economize)
schnalzen: ~ mit click; snap; crack (whip)
Schnapp-: das ~schloß, ⸚(ss)er spring lock; **der ~schuß, ⸚(ss)e** snapshot
schnappen (dog *etc*) snatch; grab (one's hat *etc*); *coll* catch (crook *etc*); (*v/i sn*) fly up; **~ nach** snatch at, (animal) snap at; gasp for; **ins Schloß ~** (*sn*) click shut
der **Schnaps, ⸚e** schnapps; **der ~bruder, ..brüder** *coll* boozer; **die ~idee, -n** *coll* crackpot idea; **die ~leiche, -n** *coll* drunk
schnarchen snore
der **Schnarcher, -** snorer; snore
die **Schnarre, -n** rattle
schnarren rasp (out); (*v/i*) buzz; creak; **~d** (voice) rasping
die **Schnatter|gans, ⸚e** *coll* chatterbox
schnattern (goose *etc*) cackle; *coll* chatter
schnauben snort; **sich** *dat* **die Nase ~** *esp NGer* blow one's nose
schnaufen puff, pant
der **Schnaufer, -** *coll* breath
das **Schnauferl, -** *SGer coll* veteran car
der **Schnauz, ⸚e** *Swiss* moustache; **der ~bart, ⸚e** handlebar moustache
die **Schnauze, -n** snout, (of dog) muzzle; spout; *coll* nose (of car, aircraft, *etc*); *vulg* 'trap'; **halt die ~!** shut your trap!; **die ~ voll haben** *coll* be sick and tired of it; **frei nach ~** *coll* as the fancy takes one
schnauzen *coll* bawl
der **Schnauzer, -** schnauzer; *coll* = **Schnauzbart**
die **Schnecke, -n** snail; slug; *anat* cochlea; *cul* Chelsea bun; *mech* worm; *mus* scroll (on violin); **zur ~ machen** *coll* make mincemeat of
Schnecken- snail's ...; *mech* worm ...; **s~förmig** spiral; **das ~gehäuse, - = das ~haus, ⸚er** snail-shell; **~tempo** *coll* (**im S.** at a snail's pace)
der **Schnee** snow; **das war schon im Jahre ~** *Aust coll* that was donkey's years ago; **zu ~ schlagen** *cul* beat until stiff || **der ~ball, ⸚e** snowball; **das ~ball|system** pyramid selling; **s~bedeckt** snow-covered; **der ~besen, -** whisk; **s~blind** snow-blind; **die ~decke, -n** blanket of snow; **der ~fall, ⸚e** fall of snow; **die ~flocke, -n** snow-flake; **die ~fräse, -n** rotary snow-plough; **das ~gestöber, -** snowstorm; **das ~glöckchen, -** snowdrop; **die ~grenze, -n** snow-line; **die ~kette, -n** snow chain; **~könig** *coll* (**sich freuen wie ein S.** be as pleased as Punch); **der ~mann, ⸚er** snowman; **der ~mensch, -en** (*wk masc*) Abominable Snowman; **der ~pflug, ⸚e** snow-plough (*also ski*); **der ~regen, -** sleet; **der ~schläger, -** whisk; **die ~schmelze, -n** thaw; **der ~schuh, -e** snow-shoe; **der ~sturm, ⸚e** snowstorm; **die ~verwehung, -en = die ~wehe, -n**

snowdrift; **schnee|weiß** snow-white; **~wittchen** Snow White
schneeig snowy
der **Schneid** *coll* guts; **der ~brenner, –** oxy-acetylene cutter
die **Schneide, –n** cutting-edge; **auf des Messers ~ stehen** hang in the balance; **es steht auf des Messers ~, ob ...** it's touch and go whether ...
Schneide– cutting ...; **der ~zahn, ¨–e** incisor
schneiden (*p/t* **schnitt,** *p/part* **geschnitten**) cut (*also* = ignore); slice; pull (face); (road *etc*) cross; *med* operate on; lance; *dressm* cut out; *cin etc* cut, edit; *sp* put spin on, slice; *mot* cut (corner); cut in on; **der Wind schneidet** the wind is biting; **sich** *dat* **die Haare ~ lassen** have one's hair cut
  sich ~ cut oneself (**an** *dat* on); (*recip*) intersect; **sich** *dat* **in den Finger ~** cut one's finger
schneidend cutting; (cold, wind) biting; (pain) sharp; (voice) piercing; (remark *etc*) cutting, (irony) biting
der **Schneider, –** tailor; **aus dem ~** *coll* out of the wood(s *US*) || **die ~puppe, –n** tailor's dummy; **~sitz** (**im S.** cross-legged)
die **Schneiderei, –en** tailor's/dressmaker's workshop; tailoring; dressmaking
die **Schneiderin, –nen** dressmaker
schneidern make (clothes)
schneidig dashing
schneien: es schneit it is snowing; (+*dat*) **ins Haus ~** (*sn*) *coll* breeze in
die **Schneise, –n** passage cut through a forest; *aer* lane
schnell fast; quick; **das geht ~** it doesn't/won't take long; **das ging aber ~!** that was quick!; **so ~ nicht** not ... in a hurry; **(mach) ~!** quick!
Schnell– *esp* high-speed ...; express ...; **die ~bau|weise** construction with prefabricated components; **das ~boot, –e** speedboat; *mil* motor torpedo boat; **schnellebig** (times) fast-moving; (fashion) short-lived; **der ~gang** overdrive; **die ~gast|stätte, –n** cafeteria; **der ~hefter, –** (loose-leaf) file; **der ~imbiß, –(ss)e** snack-bar; **der ~kurs, –e** crash-course; **die ~straße, –n** expressway; **das ~verfahren, –** rapid method; *leg* summary proceedings (**im S.** summarily); **der ~zug, ¨–e** (**D-Zug**) express train
die **Schnelle, –n** rapid; **auf die ~** *coll* in a hurry; (visit) very briefly
schnellen (*sn*) shoot
die **Schnelligkeit** speed
schnellst–: ~möglich fastest possible
schnellstens as quickly as possible
die **Schnepfe, –n** snipe; *coll* street-walker
schneuzen *SGer*: **sich** *dat* **die Nase ~ = sich ~** blow one's nose
der **Schnickschnack** *coll* tittle-tattle; knick-knacks
schnieke *Berlin coll* snazzy
Schnippchen *coll*: (+*dat*) **ein ~ schlagen** outwit
der **Schnippel, –** (*also* **das**) *coll* scrap
schnippeln *coll* snip; **~ an** (*dat*) snip at
schnippen flick; **~ mit** snap (one's fingers)
schnippisch saucy
schnipp, schnapp! snip, snip!
der **Schnipsel, –** (*also* **das**) *coll* scrap
schnipseln *coll* = **schnippeln**
schnipsen *coll* = **schnippen**
schnitt *p/t of* **schneiden**
der **Schnitt, –e** cut, *med* incision; cutting, *cin* editing; shape (of eyes *etc*), *tail* cut; edge (of book); *fash* pattern; *tech* (microscopic *etc*) section; *math* intersection; *coll* average; **im ~** on average || **die ~blumen** *pl* cut flowers; **die ~bohne, –n** French bean, kidney bean *US*; **s~fest** (tomato) firm; **die ~fläche, –n** section; **der ~lauch** chives; **das ~muster, –** *fash* pattern; **der ~punkt, –e** intersection (*also math*); **die ~stelle, –n** *comput* interface; **die ~wunde, –n** cut
die **Schnitte, –n** slice; open sandwich
schnittig stylish, sleek
Schnitz–: die ~arbeit, –en (wood-)carving; **die ~kunst** (art of) (wood-)carving
das **Schnitzel**[1]**, –** escalope; schnitzel
das **Schnitzel**[2]**, –** (*also* **der**) scrap, shred; **die ~jagd, –en** paper-chase
schnitzeln *cul* shred
schnitzen (*also v/i*) carve
der **Schnitzer, –** carver; *coll* blunder
die **Schnitzerei, –en** (wood-)carving
schnodd(e)rig *coll* brash
schnöde disdainful; base, despicable
der **Schnorchel, –** snorkel
der **Schnörkel, –** flourish (in writing or speech); (ornamental design) scroll
schnörkelig full of flourishes
schnorren *coll* cadge (**bei** from)
der **Schnösel, –** *coll* young pup
Schnuckelchen: mein ~ sweetie(-pie)
schnuckelig *coll* cute
schnüffeln sniff; *coll* snoop; **~ an** (*dat*) sniff (at)
der **Schnüffler, –** *coll* snooper
der **Schnuller, –** dummy, pacifier *US*
die **Schnulze, –n** *coll* mushy song/film *etc*
Schnupf–: der ~tabak, –e snuff
schnupfen sniff (cocaine *etc*); (*v/i*) take snuff
der **Schnupfen, –** cold (in the head)
schnuppe *coll*: **das ist mir ~** I couldn't care less
schnuppern (*also v/i*) sniff; **~ an** (*dat*) sniff (at)
die **Schnur, ¨–e** string; cord; braid; *elect* flex, cord *US*; **~ springen** *Aust* skip, skip/jump rope

US || **schnur|gerade** dead straight; **s~los** cordless; **schnur|stracks** straight

Schnür–: der ~boden, ..böden *theat* grid; **der ~schuh, –e** laced shoe; **der ~senkel, –** (shoe)lace

Schnürchen *coll*: **wie am ~** like clockwork

schnüren lace; tie up

Schnürl– *Aust*: **der ~regen, –** continuous rain; **der ~samt, –e** corduroy

Schnurr–: der ~bart, ¨–e moustache; **die ~haare** *pl zool* whiskers

schnurren purr; whirr, hum

schnurrig droll

schnurz(egal) *coll*: **das ist mir ~** I couldn't care less

die **Schnute, –n** *coll* mouth; **eine ~ machen/ziehen** pout

schob (schöbe) *p/t* (*subj*) *of* **schieben**

der **Schober, –** *SGer* stack (of hay *etc*)

der **Schock, –s** shock (*also med*); **unter ~ stehen** be in a state of shock || **die ~therapie** shock therapy

schocken *med* give (s.o.) an electric shock; *coll* shock

schockieren shock, scandalize; **~d** shocking

schofel(ig) *coll* mean

der **Schöffe, –n** (*wk masc*) lay assessor; **das ~n|gericht, –e** district court (with judge and two lay assessors)

Schoko– chocolate ...

die **Schokolade, –n, schokoladen** chocolate

scholl (schölle) *occ p/t* (*subj*) *of* **schallen**

die **Scholle[1], –n** plaice

die **Scholle[2], –n** clod (of earth); ice-floe; **heimatliche ~** native soil

schölte *p/t subj of* **schelten**

schon (*a*) already; (by) now; (*in questions*) already; yet; *sometimes expressed by* be beginning to (*in a developing situation, eg* **die Leute werden ~ aufmerksam** people are beginning to notice); *often not translated* (*eg* **es wird ~ spät** it's getting late, **werden Sie ~ bedient?** are you being served?, **da sind wir ~!** here we are!); (*in time phrases*) as early as (*eg* **~ 1912/im Mittelalter** as early as 1912/the Middle Ages); only (*eg* **~ nach zwei Tagen** after only two days);

(*b*) (*emphasis*) very (*eg* **~ der Name** the very name); ... alone (*eg* **~ das Hotel kostete 180 Mark** the hotel alone cost 180 marks, **~ deshalb** for this reason alone); even (*eg* **~ diese kleine Portion war zuviel** even this small portion was too much); as it is (*eg* **das ist ~ teuer genug** that's dear enough as it is);

(*c*) (*as emotive particle, expressing scepticism, impatience, confidence, reassurance, etc*) *usually not translated, being conveyed by an inflexion of the voice or by emphasis* (*eg* **was ändert das ~?** what difference does that make?, **mach ~!** get a move on!, **ich schaffe das ~** I'll manage, **ich muß ~ sagen!** well, I *must* say!, **wenn ich ~ gehen muß** if I have to go, (*concessive nuance*) **das ist ~ wahr, aber ...** that is true, but ...); *in emphatic use* = quite, really, certainly (*eg* **das war ~ ein Erlebnis/~ erstaunlich** it was quite an experience/quite extraordinary); *when used to make a reply to a question or negative statement, rendered by English personal pronoun + auxiliary verb* (do, have, will, *etc*) (*eg* **„Das kann man einfach nicht machen!" – „Zu Hause ~!"** 'You simply can't do that!' – 'You can at home!', **„Ob man in Deutschland darauf Rücksicht nimmt?" – „Im Süden ~"** 'Do they take that into consideration in Germany?' – 'They do in the South'); **(ja,) ~** (*indicating qualified assent*) yes ...; **das ~, aber ...** yes I do/she has/they will *etc*, but ...

~ damals even then; already

~ (ein)mal before; now and again; (*in questions*) ever

... ~ gar nicht let alone ...

~ immer all along; always

~ jetzt already

~ noch yet (= eventually)

~ weil ... if only because ...

schön beautiful, lovely; handsome; fine; nice; *iron* fine, nice; (*adv*) beautifully; nicely; (*with adj/adv*) nice and ...; *coll* pretty (stupid *etc*); **ganz ~** *coll* quite a; (*adv*) ever so, jolly (cold *etc*); quite a lot; pretty hard; **das ist alles ~ und gut, aber ...** that's all very well, but ...; **~!** right!; **das wäre ja noch ~er!** certainly not!; **die Schöne** (*decl as adj*) beauty, belle; **das S~e daran ist ...** the beauty of it is ...

Schon–: die ~frist, –en period of grace; **die ~kost** light diet; **die ~zeit, –en** close season

schön–: ~färben (*sep*) whitewash; **die S~färberei, –en** whitewash; **der S~geist, –er** aesthete; **~geistig** aesthetic (**~geistige Literatur** belles-lettres); **~machen** (*sep*) (dog) sit up and beg (**sich s.** spruce oneself up); **die S~tuerei, –en** flattery; **~tun*** (*sep*) (+*dat*) flatter; **die S~wetter|periode, –n** spell of fine weather

schonen take care of; go/be easy on; spare; save; (soap *etc*) be kind to; **sich ~** look after oneself; **~d** considerate; gentle; (+*dat*) **~d beibringen** break gently to

der **Schoner[1], –** *naut* schooner

der **Schoner[2], –** antimacassar

die **Schönheit, –en** beauty; **die ~s|farm, –en** beauty farm; **der ~s|fehler, –** blemish; flaw; **der ~s|fleck, –e** beauty-spot; **die ~s|königin, –nen** beauty queen; **die ~s|operation, –en** cosmetic surgery; **das ~s|-**

pflästerchen, – beauty-spot; **der ~s|sinn** sense of beauty

die **Schonung, –en** *vbl noun*; *also* rest; mercy; *for* plantation of young trees; **mit ~ behandeln** treat with care || **s~s|los** merciless; unsparing; (frankness) brutal

der **Schopf, ⸗e** (shock of) hair; **die Gelegenheit beim ~(e) fassen** seize the opportunity with both hands

Schöpf–: die ~kelle, –n = der ~löffel, – ladle

schöpfen scoop; ladle; draw (breath); summon up; find (hope *etc*)

der **Schöpfer, –** creator; *rel* Creator; *in compds* creative ...

schöpferisch creative

die **Schöpfung, –en** creation; work

der **Schoppen, –** (*approx* half-pint) glass of *usu* wine

schor (schöre) *p/t* (*subj*) *of* **scheren**

der **Schorf, –e** scab

schorfig scabby

die **Schorle, –n** wine with mineral water, spritzer

der **Schorn|stein, –e** chimney; *naut*, *rail* funnel; **in den ~ schreiben** *coll* say goodbye to (money) || **der ~feger, –** chimney-sweep

schoß (schösse) *p/t* (*subj*) *of* **schießen**

der **Schoß¹, ⸗(ss)e** shoot

der **Schoß²** [–o:–], **⸗e** lap; bosom (of family *etc*); *poet* womb; *tail* coat-tail

die **Schoß** [–o:–], **–en** *Aust* skirt

Schoß– [–o:–]: **der ~hund, –e** lap-dog; **das ~kind, –er** pet

das **Schößchen** [–ø:–], **–** peplum

der **Schößling, –e** shoot

die **Schote, –n** pod

das **Schott, –en** *naut* bulkhead

der **Schotte, –n** (*wk masc*) Scot, Scotsman

der **Schotten, –** tartan (= fabric); **das ~karo, –s** tartan (= pattern); **der ~rock, ⸗e** kilt

der **Schotter, –** gravel; road-metal; *rail* ballast

die **Schottin, –nen** Scotswoman

schottisch Scottish, Scots; (whisky) Scotch

Schottland Scotland

schraffieren hatch (drawing *etc*)

die **Schraffierung, –en** *vbl noun*; *also* = **die Schraffur, –en** hatching

schräg sloping; slanting; diagonal; (*adv*) at an angle; diagonally; **~e Musik** hot music; **~ gegenüber** diagonally opposite || **das S~band** bias binding; **der S~strich, –e** oblique

die **Schräge, –n** slant; slope

schrak (schräke) *p/t* (*subj*) *of* **schrecken** (*in v/i compds*)

die **Schramme, –n** scratch

die **Schrammel|musik** (*type of popular Viennese music*)

schrammen scratch

der **Schrank, ⸗e** cupboard; wardrobe; cabinet; *coll* hulk (of a man); **das ~bett, –en** fold-away bed, Murphy bed *US*; **der ~koffer, –** wardrobe trunk; **die ~wand, ⸗e** wall-unit

die **Schranke, –n** barrier; *rail* gate; (*pl*) limits; **sich in ~n halten** restrain oneself; **in die ~n (ver)weisen** put in his/her place; **vor den ~n des Gerichts** before the court

der **Schranken, –** *Aust rail* gate; **s~los** boundless; unrestrained; **der ~wärter, –** *rail* gate-keeper, gateman *US*

das **Schrapnell, –e/–s** shrapnel

Schraub–: der ~deckel, – screw-on lid; **der ~stock, ⸗e** vice; **der ~verschluß, ⸗(ss)e** screw-cap

die **Schraube, –n** screw (*also aer*, *naut*); bolt; *gym* twist; **alte ~** *coll* old bag; **~ ohne Ende** vicious spiral

schrauben (*see also* **geschraubt**) screw; **in die Höhe ~** push up (prices); **sich in die Höhe ~** spiral upwards

Schrauben– screw ...; **die ~mutter, –n** nut; **der ~schlüssel, –** spanner, wrench *US*; **der ~zieher, –** screwdriver

der **Schreber|garten, ..gärten** allotment, garden plot *US*

der **Schreck, –e** fright, scare; **einen ~ bekommen** get a fright; **ach du ~!** good grief! || **das ~gespenst, –er** nightmare (of war *etc*); bogeyman; **der ~schuß, ⸗(ss)e** warning shot; **die ~sekunde, –n** moment of shock (in which s.o. is unable to react)

schrecken frighten, scare; **aus dem Schlaf ~** startle out of his/her sleep; (*v/i*) start from one's sleep

der **Schrecken, –** fright; (= person) terror (of); (*pl*) horrors; **in ~ versetzen** terrify; **zu jmds. ~** to s.o.'s dismay || **s~erregend** terrifying

Schreckens– ... of terror; terrible ...; **schreckens|bleich** as white as a sheet; **die ~herrschaft, –en** reign of terror

schreckhaft easily startled; jumpy

schrecklich terrible

der **Schrei, –e** cry, shout; **der letzte ~** *coll* the latest thing || **der ~hals, ⸗e** *coll* howling child; **der ~krampf, ⸗e** screaming fit

Schreib– writing ...; **die ~arbeit, –en** clerical work; **der ~bedarf** writing materials; **der ~block, –s** writing-pad; **s~faul (s. sein** be a poor correspondent); **der ~fehler, –** spelling mistake; slip of the pen; **die ~kraft, ⸗e** typist; **die ~maschine, –n** typewriter; **das ~maschinen|papier** typing paper; **das ~papier** notepaper; **die ~schrift, –en** script; **der ~tisch, –e** desk; **das ~verfahren, –** *comput* recording mode; **die ~waren** *pl* stationery; **der ~waren|händler, –** stationer; **die ~waren|handlung, –en** stationer's, stationery store *US*; **die ~weise, –n** spelling; style; *comput*, *math* notation; **das ~zeug** writing materials

schreiben (*p/t* **schrieb,** *p/part* **geschrieben)** write (*also comput*) (+*dat*/**an** *acc* to) (*also v/i*); spell; do (test); ~ **an** (*dat*) be writing; ~ **auf** (*acc*) answer (advertisement); *comm* credit to; put on (bill); **auf/mit der Maschine** ~ type; **falsch** ~ misspell
sich ~ be spelt; spell one's name; (*recip*) write to each other, correspond

das **Schreiben, –** writing; letter; **auf Ihr ~ vom …** in reply to your letter of …

der **Schreiber, –** writer; *Swiss* secretary; *hist* scribe; *coll* something to write with

die **Schreiberei, –en** (irksome) paperwork; writing

der **Schreiberling, –e** pen-pusher; hack

die **Schreibung, –en** spelling

schreien (*p/t* **schrie,** *p/part* **geschrie(e)n)** shout; (*v/i*) shout; scream; cry out; (donkey) bray, (monkey, owl, *etc*) screech, (baby, gull) cry; ~ **nach** shout for; cry for; (thing) be crying out for; **… ist zum Schreien** *coll* … is a scream; **~d** glaring

der **Schrein, –e** shrine

der **Schreiner, –** *esp SGer* joiner; cabinet-maker

die **Schreinerei, –en** *esp SGer* joiner's workshop; joinery

schreinern *esp SGer* make (piece of furniture); (*v/i*) do carpentry

schreiten (*p/t* **schritt,** *p/part* **geschritten)** (*sn*) stride; ~ **zu** adopt (measures); proceed to; **zur Tat** ~ take action, act

schrie *p/t of* **schreien**

schrieb *p/t of* **schreiben**

der **Schrieb, –e** *coll* letter

die **Schrift, –en** writing; script; treatise; tract; paper; *print* type(-face); (*pl*) writings; works; *Swiss* papers; **die (Heilige)** ~ the (Holy) Scriptures || **das ~bild, –er** (appearance of) writing; *print* (type-)face; **das ~deutsch** (standard) written German; *Swiss* (Swiss) standard German; **der ~führer, –** secretary; **der ~gelehrte** (*decl as adj*) *bibl* scribe; **der ~grad, –e** type-size; **die ~leitung, –en** editorial staff; editorship; **die ~rolle, –n** scroll; **der ~satz, ⸚e** *print* forme; *leg* written statement; **der ~setzer, –** compositor; **die ~sprache, –n** (standard) written language; **der ~steller, –** author, writer; **die ~stellerei** writing; **s~stellerisch** literary; (*adv*) as a writer; **s~stellern** (*insep*) write; **das ~stück, –e** document; **der ~verkehr = der ~wechsel** correspondence; **das ~zeichen, –** character; **der ~zug, ⸚e** stroke (of handwriting)

schriftlich written; (*adv*) in writing

das **Schrifttum** literature

schrill shrill

schrillen sound/ring shrilly

schritt *p/t of* **schreiten**

der **Schritt, –e/**(*following num*) **–** step (*also* = measure); stride; footstep; gait, walk, *equest* walk; pace (= distance); *tail* crotch; **gemessenen ~es** with measured tread; ~ **halten mit** keep up with/abreast of; **einen ~ machen/tun** take a step; **auf ~ und Tritt** at every turn; (+*dat*) **auf ~ und Tritt folgen** dog (s.o.'s) footsteps; **aus dem ~ kommen** get out of step; ~ **für** ~ step by step; **im ~** at walking pace; *equest* at a walk || **der ~macher, –** pacemaker (*also med, sp*); **s~weise** gradual; phased; (*adv*) gradually; step by step

schroff sheer, steep; abrupt; (contrast) sharp

schröpfen *coll* fleece

der **Schrot** (*also* **das**) coarsely ground grain; (small) shot; **Mann von echtem ~ und Korn** man of solid character || **das ~brot** wholemeal bread, whole-wheat bread *US*; **die ~büchse, –n = die ~flinte, –n** shotgun

schroten grind coarsely

der **Schrott** scrap metal; **zu ~ fahren** wreck || **der ~händler, –** scrap merchant; **s~reif** ready for the scrap-heap

schrubben scrub

der **Schrubber, –** (long-handled) scrubbing-brush

die **Schrulle, –n** odd idea; quirk; crone

schrullenhaft = schrullig cranky

Schrumpf–: der ~kopf, ⸚e shrunken head

schrumpfen (*sn*) shrink; shrivel; dwindle

der **Schrund, ⸚e** *esp Aust, Swiss* crevice; crevasse

der **Schub, ⸚e** push; batch (*also comput*); *aer, mech, phys* thrust; *med* bout; **das ~fach, ⸚er** drawer; **die ~karre, –n = der ~karren, –** wheelbarrow; **die ~kraft** *mech, phys* thrust; **die ~lade, –n** drawer; **s~ladisieren** *Swiss* shelve (plan *etc*); **der ~lad|kasten, ..kästen** *Aust* chest of drawers; **s~weise** in batches

der **Schubs** [–ʊ–], **–e** *coll*, **schubsen** *coll* shove

schüchtern shy; timid; diffident

schuf (schüfe) *p/t* (*subj*) *of* **schaffen**[1]

der **Schuft, –e** scoundrel

schuften *coll* slave

die **Schufterei** *coll* grind

der **Schuh, –e** shoe; **wo drückt der ~?** *coll* what's the trouble?; (+*dat*) **in die ~e schieben** *coll* blame on || **der ~anzieher, –** shoehorn; **die ~bürste, –n** shoe-brush; **die ~creme, –s** shoe-polish; **der ~löffel, –** shoehorn; **der ~macher, –** shoemaker; **der ~plattler, –** (*type of Bavarian and Tyrolean folk-dance, in which the male performers rhythmically slap their thighs, knees and the soles of their feet*); **der ~putzer, –** bootblack; **der ~spanner, –** shoe-tree; **das ~werk = das ~zeug** *coll* footwear

Schuko– (= **Schutzkontakt–**) *elect* safety …

Schul– school …;
der ~abgänger, – school-leaver; **die**

~arbeit, -en schoolwork; *Aust* test; (*pl*) = **die ~aufgaben** *pl* homework; **die ~ausbildung** education; **die ~bank, ⸚e** school desk (**die S. drücken** *coll* be at school); **das ~beispiel, -e** classic example (**für** of); **der ~besuch** attendance at school; **der ~dienst** schoolteaching; **s~frei** (**s~freier Tag** school holiday; **s. haben** have a holiday); **der ~funk** broadcasting for schools; **das ~geld** school fees; **der ~hof, ⸚e** (school) playground; **der ~junge, -n** (*wk masc*) schoolboy; **der ~kamerad, -en** (*wk masc*) schoolmate; **das ~kind, -er** schoolchild; **das ~mädchen, -** schoolgirl; **die ~mappe, -n** schoolbag; **die ~medizin** orthodox medicine; **der ~meister, -** pedant; *now esp joc* schoolmaster; **s~meisterlich** pedantic; **s~meistern** (*insep*) lecture; **die ~pflicht** compulsory school attendance; **s~pflichtig** of school age; **der ~sack, ⸚e** *Swiss* satchel; **das ~schiff, -e** training ship; **der ~schluß** end of school; **die ~stunde, -n** period; **die ~tasche, -n** schoolbag; **der ~typ, -en** type of school; **der ~weg, -e** way to and from school; **die ~weisheit** book-learning; **das ~wesen** educational system; **die ~zeit** schooldays; **das ~zeugnis, -se** (school) report, report card *US*

schuld: **~ haben/sein** be to blame (**an** *dat* for); **ich bin ~ (daran)** I'm to blame, it's my fault; (+*dat*) **~ geben** blame

^die^ **Schuld, -en** debt; blame; guilt; **... ist meine ~** ... is my fault; (+*dat*) **die ~ geben** put the blame on (**an** *dat* for); **in ~en geraten** get into debt; **in jmds. ~ sein/stehen** be in s.o.'s debt || **das ~bekenntnis, -se** confession of guilt; **s~bewußt** (expression *etc*) guilty; **das ~bewußt|sein = das ~gefühl, -e** feeling of guilt; **s~los** innocent; **die ~losigkeit** innocence; **der ~schein, -e** I.O.U., promissory note; **die ~verschreibung, -en** debenture (bond)

schulden (+*dat*) owe

schulden|frei free from debt

schuldhaft culpable

schuldig guilty (*gen* of); due; (+*dat*) **~ sein** owe; (+*dat*) **die Antwort ~ bleiben** not have an answer; **keine Antwort ~ bleiben** never be at a loss for an answer; (+*dat*) **nichts ~ bleiben** give as good as one gets; **sich ...** (*gen*) **~ machen** be guilty of; **~ sprechen** find guilty; **der/die Schuldige** (*decl as adj*) culprit || **die S~sprechung, -en** conviction

^die^ **Schuldigkeit** duty

^der^ **Schuldner, -** debtor

^die^ **Schule, -n** school (*also arts*, *philos*, *etc*); **~ machen** (example) be imitated; **aus der ~ plaudern** tell tales out of school; **in der ~** at school; **in die/zur ~ gehen** go to school; **in die ~ gehen bei** learn much from

schulen train

^der^ **Schüler, -** schoolboy; pupil; disciple, *arts* pupil; **der ~lotse, -n** (*wk masc*) older pupil acting as a road-crossing warden; **die ~mitverwaltung** pupils' participation in the planning of school activities *etc*

^die^ **Schülerin, -nen** schoolgirl; (girl) pupil

schulisch school; at school; scholastic

^die^ **Schulter, -n** shoulder; **~ an ~** shoulder to shoulder; **auf die leichte ~ nehmen** make light of; **über die ~ ansehen** look down on || **das ~blatt, ⸚er** shoulder-blade; **s~frei** strapless; **s~lang** shoulder-length; **die ~tasche, -n** shoulder-bag

-schult(e)rig -shouldered

schultern shoulder

^die^ **Schulung, -en** training

schummeln *coll* cheat

schumm(e)rig *NGer coll* dusky; dimly-lit

^der^ **Schund** junk; trash; **die ~literatur** trashy literature; **der ~roman, -e** trashy novel

schunkeln sway to and fro with arms linked (in time to the music)

^die^ **Schuppe, -n** *bot*, *zool* scale; (*pl*) dandruff

schuppen scale; **sich ~** (skin) flake

^der^ **Schuppen, -** shed; *coll* unsightly building

schuppig scaly

^die^ **Schur, -en** shearing; clip; **die ~wolle** fleece-wool (**reine S.** pure new wool)

schüren poke (fire); stir up, foment

schürfen graze (knee *etc*); *min* mine; **~ nach** prospect for; **sich ~** graze oneself

schurigeln *coll* bully

^der^ **Schurke, -n** (*wk masc*) rogue, scoundrel

^die^ **Schurkerei, -en** rascally trick

schurkisch rascally

^der^ **Schurz, -e** (workman's) apron; loin-cloth; **das ~fell, -e** leather apron

^die^ **Schürze, -n** apron

schürzen tuck up; **die Lippen ~** purse one's lips

Schürzen-: **~band** ((+*dat*) **am S. hängen** be tied to (s.o.'s) apron-strings); **der ~jäger, -** *coll* wolf

^der^ **Schuß, ⸚(ss)e** shot, (*pl also - following num*) round (of ammunition); bullet wound; dash (of); *sp* shot, *footb* shot (at goal), kick; *ski* schuss; *text* weft, woof; **(im) ~ fahren** schuss; **(gut) in ~** *coll* in good shape; **weit vom ~** *coll* well out of harm's way; miles from anywhere; **zum ~ kommen** get a shot in; get a chance

Schuß- ... of fire; firing ...; **s~bereit** ready to fire/*phot coll* shoot; **der ~faden, ..fäden** weft thread; **die ~fahrt, -en** schuss; **s~fest** bullet-proof; **die ~linie** line of fire (**in die S. geraten** come under fire); **die ~verletzung, -en** bullet wound; **die ~waffe, -n** firearm; **die ~weite** range (of fire) (**außer S.** out of range; **in S.** within range); **die ~wunde, -n** bullet wound

der **Schussel, -** *coll*, **die ~, -n** *coll* scatterbrain

die **Schüssel, -n** bowl; dish

schusselig *coll* scatterbrained

der **Schuster** [-u:-], **-** shoemaker; **auf ~s Rappen** *coll* on Shanks's pony

der **Schutt** rubble; *geol* debris; **„~ abladen verboten!"** 'no dumping'; **in ~ und Asche legen** reduce to ashes; **in ~ und Asche liegen** be in ruins || **der ~ablade|platz, ⸚e** refuse dump; **der ~haufen, -** heap of rubble

Schütt-: das ~gut, ⸚er bulk goods; **der ~stein, -e** *Swiss* sink

Schüttel-: der ~frost shivering fit; **der ~reim, -e** (*humorous couplet in which the initial letters of the rhyming words or syllables are interchanged*)

schütteln shake; **den Kopf/mit dem Kopf ~** shake one's head; **sich ~** shake; (dog) shake itself; **sich ~ vor** (*dat*) shudder with (disgust); shake with (laughter)

schütten pour; tip; **es schüttet** *coll* it's pouring with rain

schütter (hair, beard) sparse

der **Schutz** protection (**vor** *dat* from); shelter (from); **im/unter dem ~** (+*gen*) under cover of; **in ~ nehmen** defend; **zum ~** (+*gen*) for the protection of

Schutz- *esp* protective …;

der/die ~befohlene (*decl as adj*) charge; ward; **das ~blech, -e** *cycl* mudguard, fender *US*; *tech* guard; **der ~brief, -e** safe-conduct; **die ~brille, -n** protective goggles; **der ~engel, -** guardian angel; **das ~gebiet, -e** nature reserve; *pol* protectorate; **die ~gebühr, -en** (nominal) charge; (*also pl*) *coll* protection money; **die ~haft** protective custody; **der/die ~heilige** (*decl as adj*) patron saint; **der ~helm, -e** safety helmet; **der ~herr, -en** (*like* **Herr**) patron; **die ~hülle, -n** protective covering; dust-jacket; **die ~impfung, -en** vaccination; **s~los** defenceless; unprotected; **der ~mann, ⸚er/..leute** *dated* policeman; **die ~marke, -n** trade-mark; **die ~maßnahme, -n** precaution; **das ~mittel, -** means of protection; **das ~netz, -e** safety-net; **der ~patron, -e** patron saint; **der ~umschlag, ⸚e** dust-jacket; **die ~vorrichtung, -en** *tech* guard; **der ~wall, ⸚e** defensive wall; **der ~weg, -e** *Aust* pedestrian crossing

der **Schütze, -n** (*wk masc*) marksman; rifleman; *astron*, *astrol* Sagittarius

schützen protect (**vor** *dat*/**gegen** from, against); shelter (from); shield (from); safeguard; (*v/i*) give protection (**vor** *dat*/**gegen** from, against); **sich ~** protect oneself (**vor** *dat*/**gegen** from, against); **gesetzlich geschützt** registered

Schützen-: das ~fest, -e fair (held in connection with a shooting match); **der ~graben, ..gräben** *mil* trench; **die ~hilfe** *coll* support, backing; **das ~loch, ⸚er** *mil* foxhole; **der ~ver|ein, -e** rifle club

der **Schützling, -e** protégé(e); charge

schwabbelig *coll* flabby; wobbly

schwabbeln *coll* wobble

der **Schwabe, -n** (*wk masc*) Swabian

schwäbeln speak Swabian dialect/with a Swabian accent

Schwaben Swabia; **der ~streich, -e** foolish action, folly

schwäbisch Swabian

schwach (*comp*, *superl* ⸚) weak (*also gramm*); faint; poor; **~ in** (*dat*) poor at; **das ~e Geschlecht** the weaker sex; **~e Seite** (s.o.'s) weak point; **mir wird ~** I feel faint; **nur nicht ~ werden!** don't weaken! || **der S~kopf, ⸚e** idiot; **~köpfig** brainless; **der S~sinn** feeble-mindedness; **~sinnig** feeble-minded; **die S~stelle, -n** weak point; **der S~strom** low-voltage current

die **Schwäche, -n** weakness (*also* = soft spot); faintness; **der ~zustand, ⸚e** debility

schwächen weaken

die **Schwachheit, -en** weakness; **bilde dir nur keine ~en ein!** don't kid yourself!

schwächlich delicate

der **Schwächling, -e** weakling

der **Schwaden, -** (*usu pl*) cloud

die **Schwadron, -en** *hist* troop of cavalry

der **Schwadroneur** [-'nø:ɐ], **-e** blusterer

schwadronieren bluster

schwafeln *coll* talk drivel; waffle

der **Schwager,** *pl* **Schwäger** brother-in-law; *hist* coachman

die **Schwägerin, -nen** sister-in-law

die **Schwalbe, -n** swallow; **die ~n|nester|suppe, -n** bird's nest soup; **der ~n|schwanz, ⸚e** *ent* swallowtail; *carp* dovetail

der **Schwall, -e** flood, torrent (of words)

schwamm (schwämme) *p/t* (*subj*) *of* **schwimmen**

der **Schwamm, ⸚e** sponge; dry rot; *SGer* mushroom; **~ drüber!** (let's) forget it!

schwammig spongy; flabby; (concept *etc*) woolly

der **Schwan, ⸚e** swan

schwand (schwände) *p/t* (*subj*) *of* **schwinden**

schwanen *coll*: **mir schwant, daß …** I have a hunch that …; **mir schwant nichts Gutes** I fear the worst

Schwanen-: der ~gesang, ⸚e swan-song; **„~see"** 'Swan Lake'

schwang (schwänge) *p/t* (*subj*) *of* **schwingen**

schwanger pregnant

schwängern make pregnant; **geschwängert mit** impregnated with die **Schwangerschaft, -en** pregnancy; **der ~s|streifen, -** stretch-mark; **die ~s|unterbrechung, -en** termination of pregnancy

schwank *poet* swaying; unsteady

der **Schwank, ¨-e** *hist* comical tale; farce

schwanken sway; rock, shake; oscillate; fluctuate, vary; waver, vacillate; (*sn*) totter, stagger; **~d** *also* unsteady

die **Schwankung, -en** *vbl noun*; *also* fluctuation, variation (*gen* in); oscillation

der **Schwanz, ¨-e** tail (*also* of aircraft, kite, comet, *etc*); tail end; *vulg* 'prick'; **kein ~** *coll* not a living soul; **einen ~ machen** *coll* fail part of an exam; **den ~ einziehen** *coll* climb down; (+*dat*) **auf den ~ treten** *coll* tread on (s.o.'s) toes

schwänzeln wag its tail; (*sn*) *coll* mince; **~ um** (*also sn*) *coll* suck up to

schwänzen *coll* cut (class *etc*); **(die Schule) ~** play truant

-schwänzig -tailed

schwappen splash about; (*sn*) splash

der **Schwarm, ¨-e** swarm; *coll* heart-throb; **der ~geist, -er** visionary; zealot

schwärmen (*also sn in 1st sense*) swarm; **~ für** adore; be crazy about; **~ von** enthuse over; **ins Schwärmen kommen** go into raptures

der **Schwärmer, -** dreamer; *ent* hawk-moth

die **Schwärmerei, -en** enthusiasm; infatuation, 'crush'

schwärmerisch enthusiastic; gushing

die **Schwarte, -n** rind; *hunt* hide, skin; *coll* old book, tome

schwarz (*comp*, *superl* ¨) black; *coll* dirty; *coll* illegal; *coll* Catholic; (*adv*) *coll* on the black market; illegally; **~ von Menschen** crowded with people; **~ auf weiß** in black and white; **das S~e Brett** the notice-board/bulletin board *US*; **~es Loch** black hole; **das S~e Meer** the Black Sea; **mir wird ~ vor den Augen** I black out; **sich ~ ärgern** be hopping mad; **der/die Schwarze** (*decl as adj*) black; dark-haired person; *coll* Catholic; **ins S~e treffen** hit the bull's-eye || **S~afrika** Black Africa; **die S~arbeit** illicit work; moonlighting; **~arbeiten** (*sep*) do illicit work; moonlight; **das S~brot, -e** black bread; **~fahren*** (*sep*; *sn*) drive without a licence; travel without paying; **der S~fahrer, -** person who drives without a licence; fare-dodger; **~haarig** black-haired; **der S~handel** black market **(mit** in); **der S~händler, -** black marketeer; **~hören** (*sep*) listen to the radio without a licence; **der S~hörer, -** *rad* licence-dodger; **~sehen*** (*sep*) be pessimistic **(für** about); *TV* view without a licence; **der S~seher, -** pessimist; *TV* licence-dodger; **die S~seherei** pessimism; **der S~sender, -** *rad*, *TV* pirate station; **der S~wald** the Black Forest; **S~wälder** (*indecl*) Black Forest; **schwarz|weiß** black and white; **S~weiß-** black-and-white ...; **die S~wurzel, -n** salsify

die **Schwärze** blackness; *print* printer's ink

schwärzen blacken

schwärzlich blackish

der **Schwatz, -e** *coll* chat

schwatzen, *SGer* **schwätzen** chat; chatter; prattle; **dummes Zeug ~** talk rubbish

der **Schwätzer, -** gas-bag; chatterbox

schwatzhaft garrulous

Schwebe: in der ~ in the balance, undecided; **sich in der ~ halten** (balloon) float in the air || **die ~bahn, -en** suspension railway; **der ~balken, - = der ~baum, ¨-e** *gym* beam; **der ~zustand** state of suspense

schweben float; hover; hang, be suspended; be (in danger); *leg* be pending; (*sn*) float; glide; **... schwebt mir vor Augen** I see ... in my mind's eye; (+*dat*) **auf der Zunge ~** be on the tip of (s.o.'s) tongue

der **Schwede, -n** (*wk masc*) Swede

Schweden Sweden

schwedisch, (*language*) **S~** Swedish; **hinter ~en Gardinen** *coll* behind bars

der **Schwefel** sulphur; **s~sauer** ... sulphate; **die ~säure** sulphuric acid; **der ~wasser|stoff** hydrogen sulphide

schwef(e)lig sulphurous

schwefeln sulphurize

der **Schweif, -e** tail (*also astron*)

schweifen *tech* curve; (*v/i sn*) roam

Schweige-: das ~geld, -er hush-money; **der ~marsch, ¨-e** silent protest march; **die ~pflicht** professional secrecy

schweigen (*p/t* **schwieg,** *p/part* **geschwiegen**) be silent; (music, noise) stop; **~ auf** (*acc*) make no reply to; **~ zu** keep silent about; make no reply to; **ganz zu ~ von** not to mention

das **Schweigen, zum ~ bringen** silence

schweigend silent; (*adv*) *also* in silence

schweigsam taciturn

die **Schweigsamkeit** taciturnity

das **Schwein, -e** pig; *coll* swine; little pig; **armes ~** *coll* poor wretch; **kein ~** *coll* nobody; **~ haben** *coll* be dead lucky || **der ~igel, -** *coll* dirty pig; **s~igeln** (*insep*) *coll* make a mess; tell dirty jokes

Schweine- pig ...; *cul* pork ...; **der ~braten, -** roast pork; **die ~bucht** the Bay of Pigs; **das ~fleisch** pork; **der ~hund, -e** *coll* swine (**der innere S.** one's weaker self); **das ~kotelett, -s** pork chop; **das ~schmalz** dripping; lard; **der ~stall, ¨-e** pigsty

die **Schweinerei, -en** *coll* filthy mess; dirty trick; scandal; dirty joke; indecent act

schweinisch *coll* filthy

Schweins– pig's …; *esp SGer cul* pork …; **das ~leder, s~ledern** pigskin

der **Schweiß** sweat; *in compds tech* welding …; **das ~band, ⸚er** sweat-band; **das ~blatt, ⸚er** dress-shield; **der ~brenner, –** welding-torch; **die ~drüse, –n** sweat gland; **die ~füße** *pl* sweaty feet; **s~gebadet** bathed in perspiration; **die ~naht, ⸚e** weld

schweißen weld

die **Schweiz** Switzerland

der **Schweizer, –** Swiss; dairyman; Swiss Guard; **die ~** the Swiss

Schweizer (*indecl*) Swiss; **~ Käse** Swiss cheese || **s~deutsch, ~deutsch** Swiss German

schweizerisch Swiss

schwelen smoulder

schwelgen feast; **~ in** (*dat*) feast on; indulge in; revel in

die **Schwelgerei, –en** feasting; indulgence; revelling

schwelgerisch sumptuous; self-indulgent

Schwell–: der ~körper, – erectile tissue

die **Schwelle, –n** threshold (*also* of era *etc*, *physiol*, *psych*); *rail* sleeper, tie *US*

schwellen swell (sails); (*v/i*: **schwill(s)t,** *p/t* **schwoll** (*subj* **schwölle**), *p/part* **geschwollen)** (*sn*) swell

die **Schwellung, –en** swelling

Schwemm– alluvial …

die **Schwemme, –n** watering-place; glut (**an** *dat* of); *Aust* bargains department

schwemmen water (cattle *etc*); wash (ashore *etc*); *esp Aust* rinse

der **Schwengel, –** clapper; handle (of pump)

der **Schwenk, –s** swing; *cin* pan; **der ~arm, –e** swivel arm

schwenkbar swivelling

schwenken swing; swivel; wave; rinse; *cin* pan; (*v/i sn*) swing; *cin* pan; *mil* wheel

die **Schwenkung, –en** *vbl noun*; *also* swing; *mil* wheel; *pol etc* change of direction

schwer heavy; difficult; hard; serious, (punishment *etc*) severe, (disappointment) great; (food *etc*) rich; (*adv*) heavily; very (much); badly; seriously (ill *etc*); (work) hard; (offend) deeply; with difficulty; hardly; (**1 Kilo** *etc*) **~** weighing (1 kilo *etc*); (**10 Millionen** *etc*) **~ sein** *coll* be worth (10 million *etc*); **~ …bar/…lich** (*eg* **~ faßbar**) hard to (grasp *etc*); **nur ~** only with difficulty; *or conveyed by* … find(s) it hard to …, … have/has difficulty in (+*ger*); **~ von Begriff** *coll* slow on the uptake; **~es Geld** *coll* a tidy sum; **~er Junge** *coll* crook; **es ~ haben** have a hard time of it

Schwer– heavy …; (**schwer–**) heavily …; seriously …; hard– (earned *etc*); hard to …;

s~behindert severely disabled; **s~erziehbar** (child) maladjusted; **s~fallen*** (*sep*; *sn*) (+*dat*) be hard for; **s~fällig** clumsy; ponderous; slow; **das ~gewicht** main emphasis; *sp* heavyweight class; **der ~gewichtler, –** heavyweight; **s~hörig** hard of hearing; **die ~industrie** heavy industry; **die ~kraft** gravity; **s~krank** seriously ill; **s~machen** (*sep*) (+*dat*) make difficult for; **das ~metall, –e** heavy metal; **die ~mut, s~mütig** melancholy; **s~nehmen*** (*sep*) take to heart; **der ~punkt, –e** centre of gravity; focal point; main emphasis; key point; (political *etc*) centre; **s~punkt|mäßig** concentrating on key areas; **s~reich** *coll* extremely rich; **s~tun*** (*sep*): **sich s. mit** *coll* make heavy weather of; **der ~verbrecher, –** dangerous criminal; **s~verdaulich** hard to digest, heavy; **s~verständlich** difficult to understand; **der ~wasser|reaktor, –en** heavy-water reactor; **s~wiegend** weighty

die **Schwere** heaviness; weight; severity; seriousness; *phys* gravity; **s~los** weightless; **die ~losigkeit** weightlessness; **der ~nöter, –** *coll* ladykiller

schwerlich hardly, scarcely

das **Schwert** [–eː–], **–er** sword; *naut* centreboard; **der ~fisch, –e** swordfish; **die ~lilie, –n** iris; **der ~wal, –e** killer whale

die **Schwester, –n** sister; *med* nurse; *eccles* nun

schwesterlich sisterly

die **Schwestern|tracht, –en** nurse's uniform; nun's habit

schwieg *p/t of* **schweigen**

Schwieger–: die ~eltern *pl* parents-in-law; **die ~mutter, ..mütter** mother-in-law; **der ~sohn, ⸚e** son-in-law; **die ~tochter, ..töchter** daughter-in-law; **der ~vater, ..väter** father-in-law

die **Schwiele, –n** callus

schwielig callused

schwierig difficult

die **Schwierigkeit, –en** difficulty; (*pl*) difficulties; trouble; (+*dat*) **~en machen** make things difficult for; **in ~en geraten** get into difficulties/trouble

schwill *imp sing*, **schwill(s)t** (*2nd*,) *3rd sing pres of* **schwellen** (*v/i*)

Schwimm– swimming …; floating …; **das ~bad, ⸚er** (public) swimming-pool; **das ~bassin, –s = das ~becken, –** swimming-pool; **die ~blase, –n** air-bladder; **s~fähig** buoyant; **die ~fähigkeit** buoyancy; **die ~halle, –n** indoor swimming-pool; **die ~haut, ⸚e** web; **das ~kissen, –** water-wings; **der ~lehrer, –** swimming instructor; **der ~sport** swimming; **die ~weste, –n** life-jacket

schwimmen (*p/t* **schwamm** (*subj* **schwömme, schwämme**), *p/part* **geschwommen**) (*also* *sn*) swim (record); (*v/i*, *also sn*; *if indicating direction or distance swum*, *only sn*) swim; float; *coll* be awash; *coll* flounder; **im Geld ~** *coll* be rolling in money

^der^ **Schwimmer, –** swimmer; *tech*, *fish* float

Schwind–: die ~sucht consumption; **s~süchtig** consumptive

^der^ **Schwindel** dizziness; vertigo; *coll* swindle; trick; **der ganze ~** *coll* the whole caboodle || **s~erregend** (height) dizzy; staggering; **das ~gefühl, –e** feeling of dizziness

schwind(e)lig dizzy; **ich bin/mir ist ~** I feel dizzy

schwindeln (head) reel; *coll* fib; **mir schwindelt** I feel dizzy; **~d** (height) dizzy

schwinden (*p/t* **schwand** (*subj* **schwände**), *p/part* **geschwunden**) (*sn*) dwindle; fade; vanish; **im Schwinden** on the wane

^der^ **Schwindler, –** swindler; fraud

Schwing–: die ~tür, –en swing door

^die^ **Schwinge, –n** *poet* pinion

schwingen (*p/t* **schwang** (*subj* **schwänge**), *p/part* **geschwungen**) (*see also* **geschwungen**) swing; brandish; wave (hat *etc*); *coll* make (speech); (*v/i*) swing; oscillate; vibrate; (tone) linger; (*sn*) *ski* swing

sich ~ swing oneself (onto *etc* sth.); **sich ~ über** (*acc*) (bridge) span

^der^ **Schwinger, –** *box* swing

^die^ **Schwingung, –en** oscillation; vibration

Schwipp– *coll*: **der ~schwager, ..schwäger** brother/sister-in-law's brother; sister-in-law's husband; **die ~schwägerin, –nen** brother/sister-in-law's sister; brother-in-law's wife

schwịpp, schwạpp! splish-splash!

Schwips *coll*: **einen ~ haben** be tipsy

schwirren (*sn*) whirr; whizz; buzz; **mir schwirrt der Kopf** my head is in a whirl

Schwitz–: das ~bad, ¨–er Turkish bath

schwitzen sweat; stream with condensation

^der^ **Schwof, –e** *coll* 'hop'

schwofen *coll* dance

schwoll (schwölle) *p/t* (*subj*) *of* **schwellen** (*v/i*)

schwömme *p/t subj of* **schwimmen**

schwören (*p/t* **schwor** (*subj* **schwüre**), *p/part* **geschworen**) swear; **~ auf** (*acc*) swear by

schwul *coll* 'gay'

schwül sultry, close; oppressive; sensuous

^die^ **Schwüle** sultriness, closeness; oppressive atmosphere; sensuousness

Schwulitạ̈ten *coll*: **in ~** in a jam; **in ~ geraten** get into a fix

^der^ **Schwulst** bombast

schwulstig (lips) thick; *Aust* bombastic

schwülstig bombastic

schwummerig *coll* dizzy; uneasy; **mir wird ~** I feel dizzy/uneasy

^der^ **Schwund** decrease (*gen* in), dwindling (of); shrinkage; *med* atrophy; *rad* fading

^der^ **Schwung, ¨–e** swing, *ski* turn; verve, zest; momentum; sweep; *coll* (whole) lot (of); bunch (of people); **in ~ bringen** *coll* get (s.o., sth.) going/moving; **in ~ kommen** *coll* get going || **die ~kraft** centrifugal force; **s~los** lifeless; **das ~rad, ¨–er** flywheel; **s~voll** lively, spirited; sweeping

schwunghaft (trade) brisk

schwụpp(diwụpp)! in a flash

^der^ **Schwur, ¨–e** oath; vow; **einen ~ leisten** take an oath || **das ~gericht, –e** (*court, composed of judges and jury, dealing with serious crimes*)

schwüre *p/t subj of* **schwören**

^das^ **Schwyzer|dütsch** [–iː–] Swiss German (dialects)

^die^ **Science-fiction** ['sa̯eəns'fɪkʃn̩] science fiction

s. d. (**= siehe dies**) q.v.

sechs [–ks] six; **die Sechs, –en** six (*also = sixth and lowest grade* – **'ungenügend'** – *in marking scale*) || **das S~eck, –e** hexagon; **~eckig** hexagonal

^der^ **Sechsling, –e** sextuplet

sechst: zu ~ (*see* **zu** 1 (*i*)); **sechst..** sixth

sechstel: ein ~ ... a sixth of a ...

^das^ **Sechstel, –** sixth

sechstens sixthly

sechzehn [–ç–] sixteen

sechzehnt.. sixteenth

^das^ **Sechzehntel, –** sixteenth; **die ~note, –n** semiquaver, sixteenth note *US*

sechzig [–ç–] sixty

sechziger: die ~ Jahre the sixties; **der Sechziger, –** sexagenarian; (*pl*) sixties

sechzigst.., das Sechzigstel, – sixtieth

^die^ **SED** (**= Sozialistische Einheitspartei Deutschlands**) Socialist Unity Party of Germany

^der^ **See, –n** [–ən] lake; (*in geographical names*) **–see** (*eg* **der Ontario~**) Lake (Ontario *etc*)

^die^ **See, –n** [–ən] sea; **an der ~** by the sea(side); **an die ~ fahren** go to the seaside; **auf ~** at sea; **auf hoher ~** on the high seas; **in ~ stechen** put to sea; **zur ~ gehen** go to sea; **Kapitän zur ~** naval captain

See– sea ...; marine ...; maritime ...; naval ...;

das ~bad, ¨–er seaside resort; **der ~bär, –en** (*wk masc*) sea-dog; **der ~-Elefant, –en** (*wk masc*) sea-elephant; **s~fahrend** seafaring; **der ~fahrer, –** seafarer; **die ~fahrt, –en** voyage; seafaring; **s~fest** seaworthy; not subject to sea-sickness (**s. werden** find one's sea-legs); **der ~fisch, –e** salt-water fish; **der ~fracht|brief, –e** bill of lading; **der ~gang** (rough *etc*) sea; **der ~hund, –e** seal; **der ~igel, –** sea-urchin; **die ~jung|frau, –en** mermaid; **die ~karte, –n** *naut* chart; **s~klar** ready to sail; **s~krank** sea-sick; **die ~krankheit** sea-sickness; **der ~löwe, –n** (*wk masc*) sea-lion; **die ~macht, ¨–e** naval power; **der ~mann, ..leute** seaman; **s~männisch** nautical; **~manns–** nautical ...; sailor's ...; sailors' ...; **die ~meile, –n** nautical mile; **die ~not** distress at sea; **das ~pferdchen, –** sea-horse; **der ~räuber, –** pirate; **die ~räuberei** piracy; **die ~reise, –n** voyage; **die ~rose, –n** water-lily; **die ~schwalbe, –n** tern; **der ~stern, –e** starfish; **s~tüchtig** seaworthy; **der ~vogel, ..vögel** seabird; **s~wärts** towards the sea; **der ~weg, –e** sea-route (**auf dem S.** by sea); **die ~zunge, –n** sole

Seel–: die ~sorge pastoral care; **der ~sorger, –** pastor; **s~sorgerisch** pastoral

die **Seele, –n** soul; **eine ~ von Mensch/einem Menschen** a perfect dear; (+*dat*) **auf die ~ binden** impress on; (+*dat*) **auf der ~ liegen** weigh heavily on; **aus tiefster ~** utterly; from the bottom of one's heart; (+*dat*) **aus der ~ sprechen** express exactly what (s.o.) feels; **in der/tiefster ~** deeply; **mit/von ganzer ~** with all one's heart; **sich** *dat* **... von der ~ reden** get off one's chest

Seelen– ... of the/one's soul; ... of souls; ... of mind; **das ~amt, ⸚er** requiem (mass); **der ~frieden** peace of mind; **die ~größe** magnanimity; **seelen|gut** kind-hearted; **das ~leben** inner life; **s~los** soulless; **die ~massage** *coll* gentle persuasion; **die ~messe, –n** requiem mass; **die ~qual, –en** mental anguish; **die ~ruhe** composure (**in aller S.** calmly); **seelen|ruhig** calmly; **s~verwandt** (**s. sein** be kindred spirits); **die ~verwandtschaft** affinity; **s~voll** soulful; **die ~wanderung, –en** transmigration of souls; **der ~wärmer, –** *joc* woolly; pick-me-up

seelisch mental; emotional

das **Segel, –** sail; **die ~ streichen** strike sail; give in; **mit vollen ~n** under full sail

Segel– sailing ...; **das ~boot, –e** sailing-boat, sailboat *US*; **s~fliegen** (*only infin*) glide; **das ~fliegen** gliding; **der ~flieger, –** glider pilot; **das ~flug|zeug, –e** glider; **das ~schiff, –e** sailing-ship; **der ~sport** yachting, sailing; **das ~tuch** canvas

segeln (*also sn*; *if indicating direction*, *only sn*) sail; **~ durch** (*sn*) sail through; *coll* fail

der **Segen** blessing (*also* = boon); **der ganze ~** *coll* the (whole) lot; **seinen ~ geben zu** *coll* give one's blessing to; **zum ~ der Menschheit** for the benefit of mankind || **s~s|reich** beneficial

der **Segler, –** yachtsman; sailing ship; *aer* glider; *ornith* swift

das **Segment, –e** segment

segnen [–eː–] (*see also* **gesegnet**) bless

die **Segnung, –en** (*usu pl*) blessing

Seh– *esp* visual ...; **der ~fehler, –** sight defect; **die ~kraft** (eye)sight; **der ~nerv, –en** optic nerve; **das ~rohr, –e** periscope; **die ~schwäche** poor eyesight; **der ~test, –s** eye-test; **das ~vermögen** (eye)sight

sehen (sieh(s)t, *p/t* **sah** (*subj* **sähe**), *p/part* **gesehen,** (*after dependent infin*) **sehen)** see; (*v/i*) see; look; **~, wie jmd./etw. ...** see s.o./sth. (do *or* doing sth.) (*see* **wie** 2); (*eg* **historisch**) **gesehen** from a (historical *etc*) point of view; **gut/schlecht ~** have good/poor eyesight; **ich kann ... nicht ~** I can't see; I can't stand the sight of; **zu ~ bekommen** (get to) see; **~ lassen** show; **sich ~ lassen** put in an appearance; show one's face; **sich ~ lassen können** cut a good figure; (thing) be quite impressive; be quite a respectable performance/score *etc*; **+mit** need not be ashamed of; **siehe** see; **und siehe da!** lo and behold!; **siehst du (wohl)!** you see!; **~ Sie (mal)** you see; **da sieht man's mal** it just shows; **mal ~!** I'll/we'll see; **und hast du nicht gesehen, ...** *coll* and before you could say Jack Robinson ...; **vom Sehen (her)** by sight

~ auf (*acc*) be particular about; (room *etc*) look out on; face

~ nach see to; see how ... is *etc*; look at (clock, watch); (room *etc*) look out on; face

sich ~ see oneself (in mirror *etc*); find oneself (in situation; *esp with p/part*, *eg* **sich mit ... konfrontiert ~** find oneself confronted with); (*recip*) meet, see each other

sehens–: ~wert worth seeing; **die S~würdigkeit, –en** object/place of interest; (*pl*) sights

der **Seher, –** prophet, seer

seherisch prophetic

Sehn–: die ~sucht, ⸚e longing (**nach** for); **s~süchtig** longing; wistful

die **Sehne, –n** *anat* tendon; *mus* string (of bow); *math* chord

sehnen: sich ~ nach long for; **das Sehnen** longing

die **Sehnen|zerrung, –en** pulled tendon

sehnig sinewy; (meat) stringy

sehnlich ardent; (wish) heartfelt

sehr very; (*with verb*) (very) much, a lot; **so ~** so much; **wie ~ ...** how much ...; however much ...; **zu ~** too much

sei *imp sing*, *1st/3rd sing pres subj of* **sein**[1]

seicht shallow

seid *imp pl*, *2nd pl pres of* **sein**[1]

die **Seide, –n** silk

das **Seidel, –** beer-mug; **der ~bast, –e** daphne

seiden silk

Seiden– silk ...; silky ...; **das ~papier** tissue-paper; **die ~raupe, –n** silkworm; **der ~schwanz, ⸚e** waxwing; **die S~straße** the Silk Road; **seiden|weich** soft as silk

seidig silky

die **Seife, –n** soap

Seifen– soap ...; **die ~blase, –n** soap-bubble;

die ~lauge soap-suds; **die ~oper, -n** soap opera; **der ~schaum** lather
seifig soapy
seihen strain
das **Seil, -e** rope; cable; **die ~bahn, -en** cable railway; **s~hüpfen** (*only infin and p/part* **s~gehüpft**) = **s~springen** (*only infin and p/part* **s~gesprungen**) skip, skip/jump rope *US*; **s~tanzen** (*only infin and p/part* **s~getanzt**) walk the tightrope; **der ~tänzer, -** tightrope-walker
die **Seilschaft, -en** *mount* roped party
sein[1] (*pres* **bin, bist, ist, sind, seid, sind,** *subj* **sei, sei(e)st, sei, seien, seiet, seien;** *p/t* **war,** *subj* **wäre;** *p/part* **gewesen** (*see also* **gewesen**) (*sn*)
1 (*a*) be; (*followed by infin or adv phr of place*) *coll* have gone (*eg* **er ist in die Stadt** he's gone into town, **sie sind einkaufen** they've gone shopping);
ich bin's it's me; **ich war's nicht!** it wasn't me!; **es ist/sind** (*esp of presence in a specified place*) there is/are; **ist irgend etwas?** is something wrong?; **wir** *etc* **sind (drei** *etc*) there are (three *etc*) of us *etc*; **waren Sie schon in ...** (*dat*)? have you been to ...?; **kann sein** maybe; **muß das ~?** is that really necessary?; **es hat nicht ~ sollen** it wasn't to be;
sei es ..., sei es ... whether ... or ...; **es sei denn, (daß) ...** unless ...; **wie dem auch sei** be that as it may; **sei's drum!** I don't mind!;
wenn ... nicht wäre *etc* if it weren't for ...; **was wäre, wenn ...?** what if ...?; **wie wäre es mit ...?** how about ...?; **wie wäre es, wenn ...?** how about (+*ger*)?; **das wär's (für heute)** that's it (for today); **da wären wir nun endlich!** here we are at last!;
(*b*) (+*dat*): **mir ist (kalt/schwindelig** *etc*) I feel (cold/dizzy *etc*); **mir ist/es ist mir (so), als (ob) ...** I feel as if ... (*eg* **es war mir, als ob mir der Kopf platzte** I felt as if my head were bursting); I have the feeling that ...; **ist dir was?** is something the matter with you?;
2 (*as auxiliary* (+*p/part*) *with intransitive verbs indicating change of place or state and with* **bleiben, sein, werden**) have + *p/part*, *or expressed by simple past* (*eg* **ich bin nach Wien geflogen** I've flown/I flew to Vienna, (*in past tense, forming pluperfect* had) **er war Priester geblieben/gewesen** he'd remained/been a priest);
3 *with* **zu** + *infin* (*eg* **die Tür ist geschlossen zu halten**): *see* **zu** 2(*b*)
sein[2] (*corresp to* **er, es:** *see p. xxxiii*) his; its; one's; **~er/~e/~(e)s** (*see p. xxviii*; *also* **der/die/das ~e**) his; its; **das S~e** what is his/its; what is one's own; **das S~e tun** do one's bit; **die S~en** his/one's family

das **Sein** being; existence; **-sein** (*eg* **das Alt~**) being (old *etc*); **~ und Schein** appearance and reality
sein-: ~lassen* (*p/part* **~lassen;** *sep*) stop (doing); drop
die **Seine** ['sɛːnə] the Seine
seiner (*gen of* **er, es:** *see p. xxvi*) of him/it; **~seits** for/on his/its part; **~zeit** at that time; *Aust dated* in due course; **~zeitig** at that time; then
seines|gleichen people like him(self)/oneself; **wie ~ behandeln** treat as an equal; **..., der/das ~ sucht** unparalleled ...
seinet-: ~wegen because of him; = **(um) ~willen** for his sake
seinige: der/die/das ~ = **der/die/das seine** (*at* **sein**[2])
die **Seismik** [-ɪk] seismology
seismisch seismic
der **Seismograph, -en** (*wk masc*) seismograph
der **Seismologe, -n** (*wk masc*) seismologist
die **Seismologie** seismology
seismologisch seismological
seit 1 *prep* (+*dat*) since (point of time); for (period); *here Ger pres tense = Eng perfect* (*eg* **ich wohne hier ~ 1982/~ Jahren** I've lived here since 1982/for years); **2** *conj* (ever) since; **~ damals** since then; **~ kurzem** for a short time; of late; **~ langem** for a long time now; **~ ... nicht mehr** not for/since
seit-: ~dem 1 *conj* (ever) since; **2** *adv* since (then); ever since; **~her** (= **~dem** 2); **~wärts** sideways; on one side
die **Seite, -n** side; page; side, facet (of character); aspect (of case *etc*); angle; **obere ~** top; **untere ~** bottom; **vordere ~** front; **hintere ~** back; **jmds. starke ~** s.o.'s strong point; **jmds. schwache ~** s.o.'s weak spot; **die ~n wechseln** *sp* change ends
in prepositional phrases:
an jmds. ~ at s.o.'s side; **~ an ~** side by side
auf die ~ schaffen *coll* bump off; help oneself to; **auf die ~ legen** put aside; **auf jmds. ~ sein/stehen** be on s.o.'s side; **auf der einen ~ ..., auf der anderen ~ ...** on the one hand ..., on the other hand ...
nach allen ~n in all directions
von der ~ ansehen give (s.o.) a sidelong glance; look askance at; (+*dat*) **nicht von der ~ gehen/weichen** never leave (s.o.'s) side; **von (kirchlicher** *etc*) **~** on the part of (the Church *etc*); **von (offizieller** *etc*) **~** from (official *etc*) sources; **von allen ~n** from all sides/quarters
zur ~ (step, take) aside; (look *etc*) to one side; *theat* aside; (+*dat*) **zur ~ stehen**

give (s.o.) support

seiten: auf/von ~ (+*gen*) on the part of

Seiten– side ...; *esp tech* lateral ...;

der ~blick, –e sidelong glance; **das ~gewehr, –e** bayonet; **der ~hieb, –e** jibe, sideswipe; **s~lang** several pages long; **die ~lehne, –n** arm (of chair); **die ~linie, –n** *geneal* collateral branch; *rail* branch-line; *tennis* side, *footb etc* touch-line; **das ~ruder, –** *aer* rudder; **das ~schiff, –e** aisle; **der ~schlitz, –e** side-split; **der ~sprung, ¨–e** extra-marital escapade; **das ~stechen = die ~stiche** *pl* stitch (in the side); **die ~straße, –n** side-road/street; **s~verkehrt** the wrong way round; **der ~wechsel, –** change of ends; **der ~weg, –e** byway; **der ~wind, –e** cross-wind; **die ~zahl, –en** page-number; number of pages

seitens (+*gen*) on the part of

–seitig –sided; –page; –lateral

seitlich side; lateral; (*adv*) at/from the side; (+*gen*) at the side of; **~er Wind** cross-wind

Sek. (= **Sekunde**) sec.

sekkant *Aust coll* tiresome

sekkieren *Aust coll* torment; badger, pester

das **Sekret, –e** secretion

der **Sekretär, –e** secretary; (= writing-desk) bureau, secretaire; *ornith* secretary-bird

das **Sekretariat, –e** (administrative) office(s); secretariat

die **Sekretärin, –nen** secretary

der **Sekt, –e** champagne

die **Sekte, –n** sect

der **Sektierer, –, sektiererisch** sectarian

die **Sektion, –en** section; *EGer univ* school of studies; *med* autopsy

der **Sektor, –(or)en** sector (*also math*); field

die **Sekunda, –(d)en** (*sixth* **(Unter~)** *and seventh* **(Ober~)** *years of the* Gymnasium)

der **Sekundaner, –** pupil in the *Sekunda*

der **Sekundant, –en** (*wk masc*) second (in duel, *box, etc*)

Sekundar–: die ~schule, –n *Swiss* secondary school

sekundär (*in compds* **S~–**) secondary

die **Sekunde, –n** second (*also mus*); **~n|schnelle (in S.** within seconds); **der ~n|zeiger, –** second hand

sekundieren (+*dat*) second (*also box etc*)

selb.. (*following coalesced prep + art, eg* **im ~en Augenblick**) same; **selbständig, die Selbständigkeit:** *see separate entries*

selber *coll* = **selbst** 1

selbst 1 *pron* myself; yourself; himself/herself; itself; oneself; ourselves; yourselves; themselves; 2 *adv* even; **von ~** on my/your/one's/its *etc* own; of my/your/one's/its *etc* own accord; **das Selbst** self

Selbst– self–; automatic ...; **(selbst–,** *also*) home– (brewed *etc*);

die ~achtung self-esteem; **die ~anklage, –n** self-reproach; **die ~bedienung** self-service; **die ~befriedigung** masturbation; **die ~beherrschung** self-control; **die ~besinnung** self-examination; **die ~bestätigung** boost for one's ego; **das ~bestimmungs|recht** right of self-determination; **die ~beteiligung** excess (on insurance policy); **s~bewußt** self-assured; **das ~bewußt|sein** self-assurance; **das ~bildnis, –se** self-portrait; **die ~disziplin** self-discipline; **der ~erhaltungs|trieb** instinct of self-preservation; **die ~erkenntnis** self-knowledge; **der ~fahrer, –** driver of a self-drive car; **s~gefällig** self-satisfied, complacent, smug; **das ~gefühl** self-esteem; ego; **s~gemacht** home-made; **s~gerecht** self-righteous; **das ~gespräch, –e** soliloquy; **s~gezogen** home-grown; **s~herrlich** high-handed; **die ~hilfe** self-help; **s~klebend** self-adhesive; **die ~kosten** *pl* prime cost; **der ~kosten|preis, –e** cost price; **die ~kritik** self-criticism; **die ~lade|pistole, –n** automatic (pistol); **der ~laut, –e** vowel; **s~los** unselfish; **das ~mitleid** self-pity; **der ~mord, –e, der ~mörder, –** suicide; **s~mörderisch** suicidal; **s~quälerisch** self-tormenting; **s~redend** naturally, of course; **s~sicher** self-assured; **die ~sicherheit** self-assurance; **das ~studium** private study; **die ~sucht** egoism; **s~süchtig** egoistic; **s~tätig** automatic; **das ~tor, –e** own goal; **s~tragend (s~tragender Aufbau** monocoque); **die ~überwindung** willpower; effort; **s~vergessen** lost in thought; **s~verständlich** self-evident; natural; a matter of course; (*adv*) naturally; of course **(das ist doch s.** that goes without saying; but of course; **als s. annehmen = für s. halten** take for granted); **die ~verständlichkeit, –en** matter of course; self-evident truth; matter-of-course manner; **das ~verständnis** self-image; **das ~vertrauen** self-confidence; **die ~verwaltung** autonomy, self-government; **der ~wähl|fern|dienst** automatic long-distance dialling; (*in U.K.*) S.T.D.; **das ~wert|gefühl** self-esteem, ego; **s~zufrieden** self-satisfied; **die ~zufriedenheit** self-satisfaction; **der ~zweck** end in itself

selb|ständig independent; self-employed; (*adv*) independently, on one's own; (think) for oneself; **sich ~ machen** set up on one's own; *coll* come off; go off on its own

die **Selb|ständigkeit** independence

selbstisch selfish

selchen (*see also* **geselcht**) *SGer cul* smoke

die **Selektion, –en** selection (*also biol*)

selektiv selective

das **Selen** selenium

selfmade ['sɛlfmeːt] (*in compds* **S–**) *coll* home-made; **der S~man** [–mɛn], **..men** self-made man

selig blissful; overjoyed; *rel* blessed; *arch* late (= deceased); *coll* 'merry'; **~sprechen*** (*sep*) beatify; **die S~sprechung, –en** beatification

die **Seligkeit, –en** bliss (*also rel*)

der **Sellerie, –(s)** celery; celeriac

selten rare; (*adv*) rarely, seldom; exceptionally; **nicht ~** not infrequently

die **Seltenheit, –en** rarity; **der ~s|wert** rarity value

das **Selters** (*gen* –) = **das ~wasser** soda-water

seltsam strange; **seltsamer|weise** strangely enough

die **Seltsamkeit, –en** strangeness; oddity

die **Semantik** [–ɪk] semantics

semantisch semantic

das **Semester, –** semester (= term of six months); (**erstes** *etc*) **~** student in (first *etc*) semester || **die ~ferien** *pl* vacation

–semestrig –semester

das **Semifinale, –(s)** semi-final

das **Semikolon** [–ɔn], **–s/–(l)a** semicolon

das **Seminar, –e** *univ* department; seminar; *eccles* seminary

der **Semit, –en** (*wk masc*) Semite

semitisch Semitic

die **Semmel, –n** *esp SGer* roll; **wie warme ~n weggehen** *coll* sell like hot cakes

der **Senat, –e** senate (*in Bremen, Hamburg and W. Berlin: title of the city's executive*)

der **Senator, –(or)en** senator

Sende– transmitting ...; broadcasting ...; **die ~folge, –n** programme; **der ~leiter, –** producer; **die ~pause, –n** interval; **der ~raum, ⸚e** (broadcasting) studio; **die ~reihe, –n** series (of broadcasts); **der ~schluß** close-down

senden (*p/t* **sandte**/*occ* **sendete** (*rare subj* **sendete**), *p/part* **gesandt**/*occ* **gesendet**) send; (*p/t* **sendete**, *p/part* **gesendet**) broadcast; transmit (signal *etc*)

der **Sender, –** (broadcasting) station; transmitter

die **Sendung, –en** consignment; parcel *etc* sent; (historic *etc*) mission; *rad, TV* broadcasting (of); broadcast; programme; **das ~s|bewußt|sein** sense of mission

der **Senf, –e** mustard; **seinen ~ dazugeben** *coll* stick one's oar in || **das ~korn, ⸚er** mustard-seed

sengen singe; (*v/i*) scorch

senil senile

die **Senilität** senility

der **Senior, –(or)en** *comm* senior partner; *sp* senior (player); (*pl*) senior citizens

Senk–: das ~blei, –e plummet; **der ~fuß, ⸚e** fallen arches; **die ~grube, –n** cesspit; **s~recht** vertical; *math* perpendicular (**immer schön s. bleiben!** keep your end up!; **das einzig ~rechte** *coll* the only thing to do); **die ~rechte** (*decl as adj*) perpendicular; **der ~recht|starter, –** V.T.O.L. aircraft, jump-jet; high-flyer

die **Senke, –n** hollow, depression

senken lower; dip; bow (head); **sich ~** sink; sag; subside; drop

die **Senkung, –en** *vbl noun*; *also* subsidence; *med* blood sedimentation; *pros* unstressed syllable, thesis

der **Senn, –e** *SGer* Alpine cowherd and dairyman

die **Senne, –n** *SGer* Alpine pasture

die **Sennerin, –nen** *SGer* Alpine dairymaid

die **Sensation, –en** sensation

sensationell sensational

Sensations– sensational ...; **s~lüstern** sensation-seeking; **die ~mache** sensationalism

die **Sense, –n** scythe; (**jetzt ist**) **~!** that's enough!

sensibel sensitive

die **Sensibilität** sensitivity

sensitiv hyper-sensitive

der **Sensor, –(or)en** sensor

die **Sentenz, –en** aphorism

sentimental sentimental

die **Sentimentalität, –en** sentimentality

separat separate; self-contained

der **Separatismus** separatism

der **Separatist, –en** (*wk masc*), **separatistisch** separatist

separiert *Aust* self-contained; separate

die **Sepsis** [–ɪs], **–(s)en** sepsis

der **September** (*gen* **–(s)**), **–** September; **im ~** in September

das **Septett, –e** septet

die **Septime, –n** *mus* seventh

septisch septic

sequentiell [–ts–] *comput* sequential

die **Sequenz, –en** sequence (*also comput*)

Sera *pl of* **Serum**

das **Serail** [–'raːj], **–s** seraglio

der **Serbe, –n** (*wk masc*) Serb

serbeln *Swiss* wilt

Serbien [–ĭən] Serbia

serbisch Serbian

Serbokroatisch Serbo-Croat(ian)

Seren *pl of* **Serum**

die **Serenade, –n** serenade

die **Serie** [–ĭə], **–n** series; *bill* break; **in ~ herstellen** mass-produce

seriell *comput, mus* serial

Serien– series ...; standard ...; serial ... (*also comput*); **die ~herstellung** mass production; **s~mäßig** mass-produced; standard (**s. herstellen** mass-produce); **die ~produktion** mass production

seriös serious; respectable; reputable

die **Seriosität** seriousness; respectability; reputableness

der **Sermon, –e** *coll* lecture, talking-to; long-winded speech
die **Serpentine, –n** winding road; hairpin bend
das **Serum, –(r)en/–(r)a** serum
das **Service** [zɛr'viːs] (*gen* –(s) [–(əs)]), – [–(ə)] (dinner *etc*) service
der **Service** ['søːɐvɪs] (*gen* –) service (to customers)
Servier–: der ~tisch, –e serving-table; **die ~tochter, ..töchter** *Swiss* waitress; **der ~vorschlag, ⸚e** serving suggestion; **der ~wagen, –** trolley, tea cart *US*
servieren serve (food, drink); (*v/i*) serve (*also tennis*); (+*dat*) *footb* pass the ball to
die **Serviererin, –nen** waitress
die **Serviette, –n** napkin
servil servile
die **Servilität** servility
Servus! *esp Aust* hullo!; 'bye!
der **Sesam** [–am], **–s** sesame; **~, öffne dich!** open, Sesame!
der **Sessel, –** armchair; *Aust* chair; **der ~lift, –e** chair-lift
seßhaft settled; resident; **~ werden = sich ~ machen** settle
das **Set** [sɛt], **–s** set; place-mat
der **Setter** ['sɛtɐ], **–** setter
Setz–: der ~kasten, ..kästen *print* case; **die ~maschine, –n** typesetting machine; **der ~teich, –e** fish-pond (for breeding)
setzen (*see also* **gesetzt**) put; set; *hort* plant; *naut* hoist; *games* move (piece); *sp* seed; *print* set, compose; (+*dat*) erect (memorial) to; set (s.o. deadline *etc*); **~ auf** (*acc*) put on; sit on; pin (hopes) on, put (trust) in; (*v/i*) bank on; back; **~ über** (*acc*) ferry across (river); (*v/i, also sn*) jump (over); cross; **es setzt Hiebe/Prügel/Schläge/was** *coll* you *etc* 'll get a thrashing
sich ~ sit down; (insect, dust, *etc*) settle; **sich ~ zu** join
der **Setzer, –** compositor
die **Setzerei, –en** composing room
der **Setzling, –e** seedling; young fish (for breeding)
die **Seuche, –n** epidemic; **das ~n|gebiet, –e** infected area; **der ~n|herd, –e** centre of an/the epidemic
seufzen sigh
der **Seufzer, –** sigh; **einen ~ ausstoßen** heave a sigh || **die ~brücke** the Bridge of Sighs
Sevilla [ze'vɪlja] Seville
der **Sex** [s–] (*gen* –(es)) sex; = **der ~-Appeal** [...əpiːl] sex-appeal; **die ~bombe, –n** sexpot; **das ~symbol, –e** sex symbol
der **Sexismus** sexism
der **Sexist, –en** (*wk masc*), **sexistisch** sexist
die **Sexta, –(t)en** (*first year of the* Gymnasium)
der **Sextaner, –** pupil in the *Sexta*
der **Sextant, –en** (*wk masc*) sextant
die **Sexte, –n** *mus* sixth
das **Sextett, –e** sextet
Sexual– sex ...; sexual ...; **die ~kunde** sex education; **das ~objekt, –e** sex object
die **Sexualität** sexuality
sexuell sexual
der **Sexus** (*gen* –) sexuality
sexy ['sɛksi] (*indecl, usu pred or adv*) *coll* sexy
die **Seychellen** [zeʃ–] *pl* the Seychelles
die **Sezession, –en** secession
Sezier– dissecting ...
sezieren dissect
das **Shampoo** [ʃam'puː], **–s** shampoo
die **Shorts** [ʃoːɐts, ʃɔrts] *pl* shorts
die **Show** [ʃoː], **–s** show; **das ~busineß** [–bɪznɪs] = **das ~geschäft** show business; **der ~master** [–maːstɐ], **–** compère, master of ceremonies *US*
Siam ['ziːam] Siam; **die ~katze, –n** Siamese cat
der **Siamese, –n** (*wk masc*), **siamesisch** Siamese
Sibirien [–ĭən] Siberia
der **Sibirier** [–ĭɐ], **–, sibirisch** Siberian
sich *refl pron* (*acc and dat*) (*see p. xxviii*)

1 (*a*) (*acc*) himself; herself; itself; oneself; yourself; (*pl*) yourselves; themselves; (*recip*) each other, one another; *often not translated, the reflexive or reciprocal sense being implied by the English intransitive verb* (*eg* **~ waschen** wash (*ie* oneself), **~ schlagen** fight (*ie* one another)); (*b*) (*dat*) (to/for) himself/herself/itself/oneself/yourself; (*pl*) (to/for) yourselves/themselves; (*recip*) (to/for) each other/one another;

2 (*giving passive meaning to active verbs*): (*i*) (*English has passive, eg* **seine Befürchtungen bestätigten ~** his fears were confirmed); (*ii*) (*English has transitive verb used intransitively with passive force, eg* **es liest/trägt ~ gut** it reads/wears well, **ob es ~ auch in Neuseeland verkauft?** will it sell in New Zealand too?; *with* **leicht, schwer** *the reflexive verb is translated by* be (easy, hard) to + *infin*, *eg* **es singt ~ leicht/schwer** it's easy/hard to sing, **das sagt ~ leicht** that's easy to say);

3 (*impersonal constructions with intransitive verb* + **gut, leicht,** *etc*: *eg* **hier fährt/schläft es ~ gut** this is a good road for driving on/a good place to sleep, **es schreibt ~ so schwer mit einem ausgetrockneten Filzstift** it's so hard writing with a dried-out felt pen)

Sich– *forming part of verbal nouns corresponding to reflexive verbs* (*eg* **das S~ausweinen** having a good cry (*cf* **sich ausweinen**), **das S~umgewöhnenmüssen** having to adapt, necessity of adaptation (*cf*

sich umgewöhnen + müssen))

[die] **Sichel, –n** sickle; crescent

sicher sure, certain; secure; safe (**vor** *dat* from); (hand) steady, sure; self-assured; (income, job) steady; (*adv*) safely; no doubt, doubtless; I expect; I'm sure; ... is *etc* sure to ...; **–sicher** –proof; sure of ...; (**sich** *dat*) ... (*gen*) ~ **sein** be sure of; ... **ist mir** ~ I am certain to get ...; (**aber**) ~! certainly!, of course! || ~**gehen*** (*sep*; *sn*) play safe (**um** ~**zugehen** to be on the safe side); ~**stellen** (*sep*) ensure, guarantee; impound

[die] **Sicherheit, –en** safety; security; certainty; sureness; self-assurance; *fin* security; **in** ~ safe; **in** ~ **bringen** get (s.o., sth.) to safety; put out of harm's way; **in** ~ **wiegen** lull (s.o.) into a false sense of security; **mit** ~ for certain || **der** ~**s|abstand, ⸚e** safe distance (between vehicles); **der** ~**s|gurt, –e** safety-belt; seat-belt; **s**~**s|halber** for safety's sake; as a precaution, to be on the safe side; **die** ~**s|nadel, –n** safety-pin; **der** ~**s|rat** the Security Council (of U.N.); **das** ~**s|ventil, –e** safety-valve

sicherlich I'm sure; no doubt, doubtless

sichern (*see also* **gesichert**) secure; safeguard; guarantee; ensure; (+*dat*) secure for; **sich** ~ *mount* secure oneself; **sich** ~ **gegen/vor** (*dat*) guard against

[die] **Sicherung, –en** *vbl noun*; *also* safeguard; safety-catch (on gun); *elect* fuse

[die] **Sicht** visibility; view (of sth.; *also* = angle on sth.); **auf** ~ *comm* at sight; *aer* (fly) visually; **auf kurze/lange** ~ in the short/long term; **aus meiner** ~ from my point of view; **außer** ~ out of sight; **in** ~ in sight; **in** ~ **kommen** come into sight; **in** (**deutscher** *etc*) ~ in the (German *etc*) view || **das** ~**gerät, –e** visual display unit, V.D.U.; **die** ~**marke, –n** cursor; **die** ~**verhältnisse** *pl* visibility; **der** ~**vermerk, –e** visa; **der** ~**wechsel, –** sight draft; **die** ~**weite, –n** range of vision (**außer/in S.** out of/within sight)

sichtbar visible; ~ **machen** show

sichten sight; sift through

sichtlich evident, visible

sickern (*sn*) seep; trickle

sie (*see p. xxvi*) (*nom/acc*) 1 (*referring to fem noun*) she/her; it; 2 they/them

Sie (*see p. xxvi*) (*nom/acc*) you; **eine** ~ *coll* a she

[das] **Sieb, –e** sieve; strainer; **der** ~**druck, –e** silk-screen printing/print

sieben[1] sieve, sift; screen; sift through

sieben[2], **die Sieben, –(en)** seven; **S**~**bürgen** Transylvania; **das S**~**eck, –e** heptagon; ~**eckig** heptagonal; **die S**~**meilen|stiefel** *pl* seven-league boots; **die S**~**sachen** *pl* belongings, things; **der S**~**schläfer, –** dormouse

sieb(en)t: zu ~ (*see* **zu** 1(*i*)); **sieb(en)t..** seventh

sieb(en)tel: ein ~ ... a seventh of a ...

[das] **Sieb(en)tel, –** seventh

sieb(en)tens seventhly

siebzehn seventeen; **S**~ **und Vier** pontoon

siebzehnt.., das Siebzehntel, – seventeenth

siebzig seventy

siebziger: die ~ **Jahre** the seventies; **der Siebziger, –** septuagenarian; (*pl*) seventies

siebzigst.., das Siebzigstel, – seventieth

siech *arch* infirm

[das] **Siechtum** lingering illness

Siede– boiling ...; **der** ~**punkt, –e** boiling-point

siedeln settle (in a place)

sieden (*p/t* **siedete**/*occ* **sott** (*subj* **siedete**/*occ* **sötte**), *p/part* **gesiedet**/*occ* **gesotten**) (water *etc*) boil; ~**d heiß** boiling hot

[der] **Siedler, –** settler; **die** ~**stelle, –n** homestead

[die] **Siedlung, –en** settlement; housing-estate, housing development *US*

[der] **Sieg, –e** victory; win(ning); **den** ~ **davontragen** carry the day || **s**~**reich** victorious

[das] **Siegel, –** seal; **der** ~**lack** sealing-wax; **der** ~**ring, –e** signet ring

siegen be victorious; win

[der] **Sieger, –** victor; winner; **die** ~**ehrung, –en** victory ceremony; **der** ~**kranz, ⸚e** victor's wreath; **die** ~**macht, ⸚e** victorious power; **die** ~**mannschaft, –en** winning team

Sieges– ... of victory; victory ...; triumphal ...; **s**~**bewußt** confident of victory; **das** ~**podest, –e** victory rostrum; **der** ~**rausch** exhilaration (of a victor/winner) (**im S.** in the first flush of victory); **s**~**sicher** confident of victory; **das** ~**tor, –e** triumphal arch; *sp* winning goal; **der** ~**zug, ⸚e** triumphal procession; triumphant progress

sieghaft confident of success

sieh (**siehe**) *imp sing*, **sieh(s)t** (*2nd*,) *3rd sing pres of* **sehen**

[das] **Siel, –e** sluice

Sielen: in den ~ **sterben** die in harness

siezen address as 'Sie'

[das] **Sigel, –** logogram

Signa *pl of* **Signum**

[das] **Signal, –e** signal; *in compds* signal(ling) ...

signalisieren signal; indicate

[die] **Signatar|macht, ⸚e** signatory (power)

[die] **Signatur, –en** signature; shelf-mark; (map) symbol

signieren sign

[das] **Signum, –(n)a** initials; monogram; sign

[die] **Silbe, –n** syllable; **mit keiner** ~ **erwähnen** not breathe a word of

[das] **Silber** silver; **der** ~**blick** *coll* (slight) squint; **das** ~**fischchen, –** silverfish; **s**~**haltig** argentiferous; **silber|hell** silvery; **die** ~**hochzeit, –en** silver wedding; **der** ~**löwe,**

–n (*wk masc*) puma; **das ~papier** tinfoil; **der ~schmied, –e** silversmith; **der ~streifen (S. am Horizont** ray of hope)

^der **Silberling, –e** *bibl* piece of silver

silbern silver; silvery

–silbig –syllabled, –syllabic

silbrig silvery

^die **Silhouette** [zilu'ɛtə], **–n** silhouette

^das **Silikat, –e** silicate

^das **Silikon, –e** silicone

^das **Silizium** silicon

^der **Silo, –s** (*also* **das**) silo; **das ~futter** silage

^der **Silvester, –** (*also* **das**; *usu no art*) = **der ~abend, –e** New Year's Eve

Simbabwe [–və] Zimbabwe

^der **Simbabwer, –, simbabwisch** Zimbabwean

^der **Simili|stein, –e** imitation stone

simpel simple; simplistic; simple-minded

simplifizieren simplify

^der **Sims, –e** (*also* **das**) ledge; sill; mantelpiece

Simson [–ɔn] Samson

^der **Simulant, –en** (*wk masc*) malingerer

simulieren feign; *tech* simulate; (*v/i*) sham

simultan (*in compds* **S~–**) simultaneous

sind *1st/3rd pl pres of* **sein**[1]

^die **Sinfonie, –(ie)n** symphony

^der **Sinfoniker, –** member of a symphony orchestra; (*pl, in titles*) Symphony Orchestra

sinfonisch symphonic

Sing–: die ~drossel, –n song-thrush; **der ~sang** monotonous singing; (of speech) singsong; **das ~spiel, –e** singspiel; **die ~stimme, –n** vocal part; singing voice; **der ~vogel, ..vögel** songbird

Singapur [–ŋg–] Singapore

singen (*p/t* **sang** (*subj* **sänge**), *p/part* **gesungen**) sing; (*v/i*) sing; *coll* 'squeal'

^das **Single** [sɪŋl] (*gen* –(s)), **–(s)** *sp* singles

^der **Single** [sɪŋl] (*gen* –(s)), **–s** single (person)

^die **Single** [sɪŋl], **–(s)** single (= record)

^der **Singular, –e** singular

singulär unusual; unique

sinken (*p/t* **sank** (*subj* **sänke**), *p/part* **gesunken**) (*sn*) sink; go down; (price *etc*) drop, fall; diminish; **~ lassen** let (one's hands *etc*) drop; **den Mut ~ lassen** lose heart

^der **Sinn, –e** sense (= faculty); meaning, sense; point; mind; (*pl*) (sexual) desire; **~ für** sense of; appreciation of; **'eines ~es sein mit** see eye to eye with; **einen ~ ergeben** make sense; **es hat keinen/wenig ~** it's no use/not much use; **es hat keinen/wenig ~ zu ...** there's no point/not much point in (+*ger*)

in prepositional phrases:

aus: sich *dat* **... aus dem ~ schlagen** put out of one's mind; **... will mir nicht aus dem ~** I can't get ... out of my mind

bei: nicht bei ~en out of one's mind

im ~e (+*gen*) in accordance with; **in meinem ~e** in accordance with my wishes; **in diesem ~e** in this sense; to this effect; **im wahrsten ~e des Wortes** in the fullest sense of the word; **im ~ haben** have in mind; **nichts im ~ haben mit** have no time for; (+*dat*) **in den ~ kommen** occur to

nach meinem ~ to my liking; **dem ~e nach** according to the spirit (of sth.)

ohne ~ und Verstand without rhyme or reason

von ~en out of one's mind

Sinn–: das ~bild, –er symbol; **s~bildlich** symbolic (**für** of); **s~entstellend** distorting (the sense); **s~fällig** clear; **die ~gebung, –en** significance; interpretation; **das ~gedicht, –e** epigram; **der ~gehalt, –e** significance; **s~gemäß** giving the gist (of sth.); mutatis mutandis (**s. wiedergeben** give the gist of); **s~getreu** faithful (in rendering sense of original); **s~los** senseless; meaningless; (rage) blind (**s. betrunken** dead drunk); **s~reich** ingenious; **der ~spruch, ⸚e** maxim; **s~verwandt** synonymous; **s~voll** meaningful; sensible; **s~widrig** absurd

sinnen (*p/t* **sann** (*subj* **sänne**), *p/part* **gesonnen**) (*see also* **gesonnen**) ponder; **~ auf** (*acc*) plan, plot; **all sein Sinnen und Trachten** his every thought

Sinnen– sensual ...; **der ~mensch, –en** (*wk masc*) sensuous person; **die ~welt** material world

Sinnes– sensory ...; **die ~änderung, –en** change of mind; **das ~organ, –e** sense organ; **die ~täuschung, –en** hallucination; **der ~wandel, –** change of mind

sinnieren ruminate (**über** *acc* about, over)

sinnig *usu iron* (idea *etc*) clever; **sinniger|weise** *iron* incongruously

sinnlich sensuous; sensual; (perception) sensory

^die **Sinnlichkeit** sensuousness; sensuality

^der **Sinologe, –n** (*wk masc*) Sinologist

^die **Sinologie** Sinology

^die **Sint|flut** the Flood; deluge, flood (of)

^der **Sinus, –** [–uːs]/**–se** *anat* sinus; *math* sine

^der **Siphon** ['ziːfɔ̃], **–s** siphon; *Aust* soda (water); *tech* trap

^die **Sippe, –n** (wider) family; *coll* 'tribe'

^die **Sippschaft, –en** *coll* 'tribe'; bunch

^die **Sirene, –n** siren (*also tech*)

^der **Sirup** [–ʊp], **–e** syrup; treacle, molasses *US*; thickened fruit-juice

^der **Sisal** [–al] sisal

sistieren suspend; *esp leg* detain

^die **Sisyphus|arbeit, –en** Sisyphean task

^die **Sitte, –n** custom; (*usu pl*) manners; morals; **... ist ~ ...** is customary/the custom

Sitten– ... of morals; moral ...; **das ~bild, –er** *art* genre piece; *liter* picture of society; **die ~lehre** ethics; **s~los** immoral; **die ~losigkeit** immorality; **die ~polizei** vice squad; **s~streng** puritanical; **der ~strolch, –e** (sexual) molester; **s~widrig** immoral

der **Sittich, –e** parakeet

sittlich moral

die **Sittlichkeit** morality; **das ~s|delikt, –e** sexual offence; **das ~s|verbrechen, –** sex crime; **der ~s|verbrecher, –** sex offender

sittsam demure; well-mannered

die **Situation, –en** situation; **die ~s|komik** funny side of a situation; situation comedy

situiert: gut/schlecht ~ well/badly off

der **Sitz, –e** seat (*also parl*); headquarters; fit (of garment); **einen guten ~ haben** be a good fit || **das ~bad, ⸚er** hip-bath; **~fleisch** *coll* (**S. haben** be able to sit still for a long time; be in no hurry to go; **kein S. haben** be unable to sit still/stick at anything); **die ~garnitur, –en** suite; **die ~gelegenheit, –en** seat; something to sit on; **der ~gurt, –e** seat-belt; **die ~ordnung, –en** seating plan; **der ~platz, ⸚e** seat; **der ~streik, –s** sit-down strike

sitzen (*p/t* **saß** [–aː–] (*subj* **säße**), *p/part* **gesessen**) (*sn in SGer*) sit; (ancient tribe *etc*) live (in a certain place); (garment, *tech*) fit; be (*esp* = be situated); *Swiss* sit down; *coll* 'do time'; *coll* stick (in s.o.'s memory); *coll* tell; hit home; (+*dat*) sit for; **~ bleiben** (*cf* **sitzenbleiben**) remain seated; **~ lassen** (*cf* **sitzenlassen**) let sit; **einen ~ haben** *coll* be tipsy

~ **auf** (*dat*) sit on; be perched on

~ **bei** sit next to; sit over; be having (breakfast *etc*)

~ **in** (*dat*) sit in; sit on (committee *etc*), *parl etc* have a seat in

~ **über** (*dat*) pore over

sitzen–: ~bleiben* (*sep*; *sn*) (*cf* **sitzen bleiben** *at* **sitzen**) *coll* be left on the shelf; (pupil) have to repeat the year (**s. auf** (*dat*) be stuck with); **~lassen*** (*p/part usu* **~lassen;** *sep*) (*cf* **sitzen lassen** *at* **sitzen**) *coll* jilt; walk out on; stand up; leave in the lurch; keep down (pupil) (**auf sich s.** take lying down)

sitzend sitting; sedentary

–sitzig with ... seats

die **Sitzung, –en** meeting; session; *art*, *parl* sitting

Sixtinisch: die ~e Kapelle the Sistine Chapel

der **Sizilianer, –, sizilianisch** Sicilian

Sizilien [–ǐən] Sicily

die **Skala, –(l)en** scale (*also mus*); range; gamut

der **Skalp, –e** scalp

das **Skalpell, –e** scalpel

skalpieren scalp

der **Skandal, –e** scandal; **die ~presse** gutter press; **s~umwittert** surrounded by scandal

skandalös scandalous

skandieren *pros* scan

Skandinavien [–ǐən] Scandinavia

der **Skandinavier** [–ǐɐ], – **skandinavisch** Scandinavian

der **Skarabäus, –(ä)en** scarab

der **Skat** skat (*German card-game for three players*)

das **Skateboard** ['skeːtbɔːt], **–s** skateboard

das **Skelett, –e** skeleton

die **Skepsis** [–ɪs] scepticism

der **Skeptiker, –** sceptic

skeptisch sceptical

der **Sketch** (*gen* **–(es)**), **–e** *theat* sketch

der **Ski** [ʃiː], **–er, ~ fahren/laufen** ski || **der ~fahrer, –** skier; **das ~haserl, –(n)** *coll* girl skier; **die ~hose, –n** ski pants; **der ~läufer, –** skier; **der ~lehrer, –** skiing instructor; **der ~lift, –e** ski-lift; **die ~piste, –n** ski-run; **der ~sport** skiing; **der ~stock, ⸚e** ski stick

die **Skizze, –n** sketch; *liter etc* draft; sketch; vignette; **das ~n|buch, ⸚er** sketch-book

skizzenhaft roughly sketched; (*also adv*) in broad outline

skizzieren sketch; outline

der **Sklave, –n** (*wk masc*) slave; **die ~n|arbeit** slave-labour; slavery (= hard work); **der ~n|handel** slave-trade; **der ~n|händler, –** slave-trader, slaver

die **Sklaverei** slavery

sklavisch slavish

die **Sklerose, –n** sclerosis; **multiple ~** multiple sclerosis

der **Skonto, –s** (*also* **das**) discount

der **Skooter** ['skuːtɐ], – dodgem car

der **Skorbut** scurvy

der **Skorpion, –e** scorpion; *astron*, *astrol* Scorpio

der **Skrupel, –** (*usu pl*) scruple; **s~los** unscrupulous; (*adv*) unscrupulously; without scruple; **die ~losigkeit** unscrupulousness

die **Skulptur, –en** sculpture (= piece of work, art)

skurril droll

die **Skurrilität, –en** drollery; droll act/idea *etc*

die **S-Kurve, –n** double bend

der **Slalom** [–ɔm], **–s** slalom

der **Slawe, –n** (*wk masc*) Slav

slawisch Slav, Slav(on)ic

der **Slawist, –en** (*wk masc*) Slavicist

die **Slawistik** [–ɪk] Slavonic studies

der **Sling|pumps, –** slingback

der **Slip, –s** briefs; **die ~-Einlage, –n** pantyliner

der **Slipper, –** casual shoe, *pl* casuals

der **Slogan** ['sloːgn̩], **–s** slogan

der **Slowake, –n** (*wk masc*) Slovak

die **Slowakei** Slovakia

slowakisch Slovak(ian)

der **Slowene, –n** (*wk masc*) Slovene

Slowenien [–ǐən] Slovenia

slowenisch, (*language***) S~** Slovene

die **Slums** [slams] *pl* slums
der **Smaragd** [–kt], **–e, s~grün** emerald
der **Smog** [–ɔk] (*gen* –(s)), –s smog
der **Smoking** [–o:–], **–s** dinner-jacket; **das ~hemd, –en** dress-shirt
der **Snob** [–ɔp], **–s** snob
der **Snobismus** [–ɔ–], **–(m)en** snobbery
snobistisch [–ɔ–] snobbish
SO (= **Südost(en)**) S.E.; **s. o.** (= **siehe oben**) see above; **So.** (= **Sonntag**) Sun.
so 1 *adv* like this/that; (in) this/that way; thus; this/that is how/the way; so much; (*quoting person etc*) according to; (*followed by adj or adv*) so; that; *coll* without having to pay/being invited/practising/an umbrella/a prescription *etc*; *left untranslated when used – optionally – after a subordinate clause* (*eg* **was deine Bedenken anlangt, (~) ...** as regards your misgivings, ...); *often employed to suggest vagueness or a casual attitude* (*eg* **~ gegen acht** about eight (o'clock), **sie trägt ~ eine Art Toga** she wears some sort of toga, **jeder hat ~ seine Geheimnisse** everyone has his little secrets, **ich habe ~ ein Gefühl** I have this feeling), *or to introduce a command* (*eg* **~ 'komm doch!** oh, (do) come on!);
es ist ~, daß ... it is a fact that ...; **ich will (mal) nicht ~ sein** I'll be generous; I don't want to be a spoilsport; **~ ist das nicht!** don't get me wrong!; well, I wouldn't say that!; **~ ist das Leben** that's life; **~ ist das nun mal** that's how it is; **~!** right!; that's that!; there!; I see!; **~?** oh?; really?; is she/are you/did they *etc*?; **~ ~!** well, well!
2 *conj* (*a*) (*followed by adj or adv*) however, ... as ..., ... though ... (*eg* **~ wertvoll solche Hinweise sind** however valuable/valuable as/valuable though such hints are); as ... as (*eg* **~ schnell ich konnte** as fast as I could); (*b*) *arch* if;
ach ~! (oh,) I see!
auch ~ anyway; as it is; **~ ... auch** however (rich *etc*), (rich *etc*) as/though
~ daß ... so (= with the result) that ...; **~, daß ...** in such a way that ...; so much that ...
~ ein such a; that kind of; a ... like that; **~ ein ...!** what a ...!; what (weather)!; **~ einer/eine/ein(e)s** one like that; (*masc*, *fem*) someone/a person like him/her; that kind of person
~ etwas something/a thing like that; such a thing; that kind of thing; **(na/nein,) '~ etwas!** well, I never!, would you believe it!
~ lala *coll* so-so
nur ~ (*see* **nur**)
oder ~ or so; or something/some such thing; **~ oder ~** one way or the other; either way
~ sehr (*cf* **sosehr**) so much
und ~ and the like; **~ und ~** in such and such a way; **~ und ~ oft** time and again; **und ~ weiter** and so on
~ was *coll* = **~ etwas**
~ wie ... (*cf* **sowie**) the way ...; like ...; as ...; **~ ... wie ... as ... as ...**; **~ wie ich ... kenne** if I know ...; **~ wie die Dinge liegen** the way things are
sobald as soon as, the moment
die **Socke, –n** sock; **sich auf die ~n machen** *coll* make tracks; **von den ~n** *coll* flabbergasted
der **Sockel, –** base; pedestal, plinth; *elect* socket
Sod–: das ~brennen heartburn
die **Soda** (*also* **das**) soda; **das ~wasser** soda-water
sodann then
sodaß *Aust* = **so daß** (*see* **so**)
die **Sode, –n** *esp NGer* sod
so|eben just (now)
das **Sofa, –s** sofa
sofern provided (that); **~ ... nicht** unless
Sofia ['zɔfia, 'zo:–] Sofia
soff (söffe) *p/t* (*subj*) *of* **saufen**
sofort immediately; *in compds* **S~–** immediate ...; instant ...; **die S~hilfe** emergency relief
sofortig immediate
Soft– [s–]: **das ~-Eis, –** soft ice-cream; **die ~ware** [–wɛə] *comput* software
sog (söge) *p/t* (*subj*) *of* **saugen**
der **Sog, –e** suction; pull
sog. = sogenannt
sogar even
sogenannt so-called
sogleich immediately
sohin *Aust* thus, hence
die **Sohle, –n** sole; bottom (of river *etc*), floor (of valley); *min* level; floor
sohlen sole
der **Sohn, ¨–e** son; **der verlorene ~** the Prodigal Son
soigniert [sõanj–] well-groomed
die **Soiree** [sõa–], **–(ee)n** soirée
Soja– soya ...; **die ~bohne, –n** soya-bean, soybean
Sokrates ['zo:kratɛs] Socrates
sokratisch Socratic
Sol–: das ~bad, ¨–er brine bath; salt-water spa; **das ~ei, –er** pickled egg
solange 1 *conj* as long as; **2** *adv coll* in the meantime; **ich warte ~** I'll wait (for you)
solar (*in compds* **S~–**) solar
das **Solarium, –(i)en** solarium
solch.. (*uninflected* **solch**) such, ... like that; **ein ~er/eine ~e/ein ~es** such a, a ... like that; **als ~er/~e/~es** as such; **es gibt ~e (Sänger** *etc*) **und ~e** there are (singers *etc*) and (singers); **~e, die ...** those who ... ||

~**erlei** 1 *adj* (*indecl*) that kind of; such; 2 *pron* such things

der **Sold, –e** (soldier's) pay

der **Soldat, –en** (*wk masc*) soldier; **einfacher ~** private; ~ **werden** join up

Soldaten– soldiers' …; army …; military …

die **Soldateska, –(k)en** (undisciplined) soldiery

soldatisch soldierly; military

der **Söldner, –** mercenary

die **Sole, –n** brine

Soli *pl of* **Solo**

solidarisch: ~ **handeln** make common cause; **sich ~ erklären mit** declare one's solidarity with

solidarisieren: sich ~ mit show one's solidarity with

die **Solidarität** solidarity

solide solid; sound; respectable; (firm) reliable

der **Solist, –en** (*wk masc*) soloist

das **Soll** (*gen* –(s)), –(s) *comm* debit; *econ* quota; target; *in compds also* nominal …; **die ~-Stärke, –n** required strength

sollen (*pres* **soll, sollst, soll, sollen, sollt, sollen**, *subj* **solle** *etc*; *p/t* **sollte**, *subj* **sollte**; *p/part* **gesollt**, (*after dependent infin*) **sollen**) (*see p. xlvii*) be to; be said/supposed to; be intended to; (*ellipt*) be (supposed) to go (home, to …, *etc*)/to do; (*esp in 1st-person questions*) shall, should; *with interrogatives, expressed by* to + *infin* (*eg* **ich weiß nicht, was ich tun soll** I don't know what to do); (*voicing a threat, challenge, etc*) let … (*eg* **die soll es nur versuchen!** just let her try!);

du sollst nicht (töten *etc*) *bibl* thou shalt not (kill *etc*); **es soll nicht wieder vorkommen** it won't happen again; **was soll …?** what is the meaning of …?; **was soll das heißen?** what's that supposed to mean?; **was soll ich hier?** what am I doing here?; **was soll's?** what the heck!;

sollte should, ought to; was to; was said/supposed to; would, was to (= was destined to); (*conditional*: **sollte …**) if … should/were to, should …; **sollte …?** *also* (*possibility*) could …?; **… sollte lieber … it** would be better if …; **man sollte annehmen/meinen, daß …** one would think that …;

es hat nicht ~ sein it was not to be; **hätte … ~** should/ought to have + *p/part*

der **Söller, –** *hist* balcony

das **Solo, –s/Soli** *mus* solo

somit therefore

der **Sommer, –** summer; **die ~frische, –n** *dated* summer holiday/vacation *US*; summer resort; **der ~frischler, –** *dated* (summer) holidaymaker/vacationist *US*; **der ~schluß|verkauf, ⸚e** summer sale; **die ~sprosse, –n** freckle; **s~sprossig** freckled; **die ~zeit** summertime; summer time, daylight saving time *US*

sommerlich summer; summery

sommers in summer

die **Sonate, –n** sonata

die **Sonde, –n** *med*, *space* probe

Sonder– special …; **das ~angebot, –e** special offer; **der ~ausschuß, ⸚(ss)e** select committee; **der ~druck, –e** off-print; **sonder|gleichen** (*after noun*) unparalleled; **die ~marke, –n** special issue; **das ~recht, –e** privilege; **die ~schule, –n** special school

sonderbar odd, strange; **sonderbarer|weise** oddly/strangely enough

sonderlich odd; (*with neg*) particular, special; (*adv*) *Aust*, *Swiss* particularly; **nicht ~** not particularly

der **Sonderling, –e** eccentric

sondern[1] (*see also* **gesondert**) separate (**von** from)

sondern[2]**: nicht …, ~ …** not … but …; **nicht nur …, ~ auch** not only … but also

sondieren sound out; *med* probe

das **Sondierungs|gespräch, –e** exploratory talk

das **Sonett, –e** sonnet

der **Song** [s–], **–s** pop-song; (satirical) ballad

Sonn–: der ~abend, –e *esp NGer* Saturday; **s~abends** *esp NGer* on Saturdays; **der ~tag, –e** Sunday; **s~täglich** Sunday; (*adv*: dressed up) in one's Sunday best; **s~tags** on Sundays; **der ~tags|fahrer, –** Sunday driver; **das ~tags|kind, –er** person born on a Sunday; lucky person; **der ~tags|maler, –** Sunday painter; **der ~tags|staat** Sunday best; **s~verbrannt** *Aust*, *Swiss* sunburnt; **die ~tags|zeitung, –en** Sunday paper

die **Sonne, –n** sun

sonnen: sich ~ bask (in the sun); **sich ~ in** (*dat*) bask in (s.o.'s favour *etc*)

Sonnen– sun …; solar …;

der ~aufgang, ⸚e sunrise; **s~baden** (*usu only infin and p/part* **s~gebadet**) sunbathe; **die ~bank, ⸚e** sunbed; **die ~blende, –n** *mot* sun-visor; *phot* lens hood; **die ~blume, –n** sunflower; **der ~brand, ⸚e** sunburn; **die ~bräune** sun-tan; **die ~brille, –n** sunglasses; **das ~dach, ⸚er** sun-blind, awning; **die ~energie** solar energy; **die ~finsternis, –se** eclipse of the sun; **der ~fleck, –e** sunspot; **s~gebräunt** sun-tanned; **die ~hitze** heat of the sun; **sonnen|klar** *coll* as plain as a pikestaff; **der ~kollektor, –en** solar panel; **das ~öl, –e** sun-tan lotion; **der ~schein** sunshine; **der ~schirm, –e** sunshade; parasol; **das ~segel, –** awning; **die ~seite, –n** sunny side; **der ~stand, ⸚e** position of the sun; **der ~stich, –e** sunstroke; **der ~strahl, –en** ray of sunlight; **das ~sys-**

tem the solar system; **die ~uhr, –en** sundial; **der ~untergang, ⸚e** sunset, sundown; **s~verbrannt** sunburnt; **die ~wende, –n** solstice

sonnig sunny

sonor sonorous

sonst otherwise; in other respects/ways; usually; formerly, *or expressed by* ... used to ...; (*with pron*, *adv*) else (*eg* **~ niemand/nichts** nobody/nothing else, **wer/wo ~?** who/where else?); **~ noch Fragen?** any other questions?; **~ noch etwas?** is that all?, anything else? || **~was** *coll* anything; (try) everything; **~wie** *coll* in some/any other way; **~wo(hin)** *coll* somewhere/anywhere else

sonstig other

so|oft whenever

der **Sophist, –en** (*wk masc*) sophist

die **Sophisterei, –en** sophistry

Sophokles ['zo:foklɛs] Sophocles

der **Sopran, –e** soprano (*also* = voice); treble (*also* = voice)

die **Sopranistin, –nen** soprano

der **Sorbe, –n** (*wk masc*) Sorb

sorbisch Sorbian

Sorg–: die ~falt care (taken); **s~fältig** careful; **s~los** carefree; careless; **die ~losigkeit** carefree manner; unconcern

die **Sorge, –n** worry; care; (+*dat*) **~n machen** worry; **sich** *dat* **~n machen** worry (**um** about); **~ tragen für** see to; take care of; **in ~ sein** be worried (**um** about); **mit ~** with concern; **keine ~!** don't you worry! || **das ~recht** custody (of child)

sorgen: ~ für take care of; provide; **dafür ~, daß ...** ensure that ...; **sich ~** worry (**um** about)

sorgen–: ~frei carefree; **das S~kind, –er** problem child; headache (= problem); **~los** carefree; **~voll** worried

sorgsam careful

Sorrent Sorrento

die **Sorte, –n** type, sort; variety (of apples *etc*); *comm* grade; (*pl*) *fin* foreign currency

Sortier– *comput* sort ...; **die ~maschine, –n** sorter (*also comput*)

sortieren sort (*also comput*); grade

der **Sortierer, –** sorter

das **Sortiment, –e** assortment (**an** *dat* of); = **der ~s|buch|handel** retail book trade

sosehr: ~ (... auch) however much; much as

soso *coll* so-so; **~!** well, well!; really!

die **Soße, –n** gravy; sauce

sott (sötte) *occ p/t* (*subj*) *of* **sieden**

das **Soufflé** [su–, zu–], **–s** soufflé

der **Souffleur** [zu'flø:ɐ], **–e, die Souffleuse** [–'flø:zə], **–n** *theat* prompter

soufflieren [zu–] *theat* prompt

der **Sound** [saont], **–s** *mus* sound

so|und|so *coll*: **~ breit/groß/hoch/lang** of such-and-such a width/size/height/length; (**Seite** *etc*) **~** (page *etc*) so-and-so, such-and-such; **~ oft** umpteen times; **~ viel** so much (unspecified)

das **Souper** [su'pe:, z–], **–s** (formal) dinner

soupieren [su–, zu–] dine

die **Soutane** [zu–], **–n** (priest's) cassock

das **Souterrain** [sutɛ'rɛ̃:, z–], **–s** basement

das **Souvenir** [suvə–, z–], **–s** souvenir

souverän [zuvə–] masterly; *pol* sovereign; (*adv*) in masterly fashion; **~ sein** be on top of things; **die Lage ~ beherrschen** be in full command of the situation

der **Souverän** [zuvə–], **–e** sovereign; *Swiss* electorate

die **Souveränität** [zuvə–] mastery; *pol* sovereignty

soviel 1 *conj* as far as; as much as; 2 *pron* so much; **~ ... auch** however much; **~ wie** as much as

soweit 1 *conj* so far as; insofar as; if; 2 *adv* by and large; **~ sein** be ready; have got that far/to that stage; **es ist ~** it's time; the time has come; we have reached that stage; **wenn es ~ ist** when the time comes

sowenig: ~ ... auch however little; **~ wie** as little as; no more than

sowie as well as; as soon as

sowieso anyway; as it is; **das ~!** that goes without saying

der **Sowjet** [zɔ'vjɛt, 'zɔ–], **–s** soviet; **der Oberste ~** the Supreme Soviet; **die Sowjets** ['zɔ–] *pl* the Soviets

Sowjet– [*also* 'zɔ–] Soviet ...; **der ~bürger, – = der ~mensch, –en** (*wk masc*) Soviet citizen; **die ~union** the Soviet Union

sowjetisch [zɔ–] Soviet

sowohl: ~ ... als auch ... both ... and ...

der **Sozi, –s** *coll, freq pej* = **Sozialdemokrat**

sozial social; **~ denken** be socially minded

Sozial– social ...; welfare ...;

die ~abgaben *pl* social security contributions; **die ~arbeit** social work; **der ~arbeiter, –** social worker; **der ~demokrat, –en** (*wk masc*) social democrat; **s~demokratisch** social democratic; **die ~fürsorge** *esp EGer* welfare; **die ~kritik** social criticism; **die ~leistungen** *pl* social security payments; **die ~partner** *pl*: *approx* = the two sides of industry; **die ~politik** social policy; **das ~produkt, –e** national product; **der ~staat, –en** welfare state; **die ~versicherung** social security; **die ~wissenschaften** *pl* social sciences; **die ~wohnung, –en** *approx* = *U.K.* council flat

sozialisieren *econ* nationalize; *psych*, *sociol* socialize

der **Sozialismus** socialism

der **Sozialist, –en** (*wk masc*), **sozialistisch**

socialist
^der^ **Soziologe, –n** (*wk masc*) sociologist
^die^ **Soziologie** sociology
soziologisch sociological
sozioökonomisch socio-economic
^der^ **Sozius, –se** pillion passenger; *comm* partner; = **der ~sitz, –e** pillion
sozusagen so to speak, as it were
^der^ **Spachtel, –** putty-knife; **die ~masse, –n** filler
spachteln smooth (surface); (*v/i*) *coll* tuck in
^der^ **Spagat**[1], **–e** (*also* **das**) the splits; **~ machen** do the splits
^der^ **Spagat**[2], **–e** *SGer* string
^die^ **Spaghetti** [ʃpa'gɛti] *pl* spaghetti
Späh–: der ~trupp, –s reconnaissance patrol
spähen peer; **~ nach** look out for
^der^ **Späher, –** *mil* scout
^das^ **Spalier, –e** lane (formed by two lines of persons); *hort* trellis; **~ stehen** form a lane
^der^ **Spalt, –e** crack; chink; split (in organization *etc*); *in compds phys* fission ...
spaltbar *phys* fissionable; fissile
^die^ **Spalte, –n** crack; fissure; crevice; crevasse; *Aust* slice; *print* column
spalten (*p/part* **gespalten**) (*see also* **gespalten**), **sich ~** split (*also phys*)
–spaltig –column
^die^ **Spaltung, –en** splitting; *phys* fission; *pol etc* split (*gen* in)
^der^ **Span, ⸚e** (wood) shaving; filing; **das ~ferkel, –** sucking pig
^die^ **Spange, –n** buckle; bangle; (hair) slide, barrette *US*; *dent* brace
^der^ **Spaniel** ['ʃpaːnĭɛl], **–s** spaniel
Spanien [–ĭən] Spain
^der^ **Spanier** [–ĭɐ], **–** Spaniard; **die ~** the Spanish
spanisch, (*language*) **S~** Spanish; (+*dat*) **~ vorkommen** *coll* seem funny to
spanisch– Hispano–; (dictionary) Spanish–
spann (spänne) *p/t* (*subj*) *of* **spinnen**
^der^ **Spann, –e** instep; **der ~beton** pre-stressed concrete; **die ~kraft** vigour, energy; **die ~weite, –n** span; range
^die^ **Spanne, –n** space of time; *comm* margin
spannen (*see also* **gespannt**) stretch, tauten; tense (muscles); put up (washing-line); cock (gun), string (bow), *phot* set (shutter); (*v/i*) be too tight; **~ in** (*acc*) put in (typewriter, vice); **~ vor** (*acc*) harness to; **zu hoch ~** pitch too high
sich ~ tauten; (muscle) tense; **sich ~ über** (*acc*) span; stretch across
spannend exciting; thrilling
^der^ **Spanner, –** press; shoe-tree; *coll* peeping Tom
^die^ **Spannung, –en** tension; suspense; excitement; *mech* stress; *elect* tension, voltage; **s~s|geladen** charged; full of suspense; **der ~s|messer, –** voltmeter
Spar– savings ...; economy ...; **das ~buch, ⸚er** savings-book; **die ~büchse, –n** money-box; **die ~einlage, –n** savings deposit; **die ~flamme, –n** low flame; **die ~kasse, –n** (communal) savings-bank; **das ~konto, –(t)en** savings account; **der ~pfennig, –e** nest-egg; **das ~schweinchen, –** piggy-bank; **der ~vertrag, ⸚e** savings agreement
sparen save; **sich** *dat* **... ~** spare oneself (trouble *etc*); (*v/i*) save; economize; **~ an** (*dat*) economize on; **~ auf** (*acc*)/**für** save (up) for; **~ mit** be sparing with; **nicht ~ mit** not be sparing/be unstinting with; **... kannst du dir ~!** I can do without ...!
^der^ **Sparer, –** saver
^der^ **Spargel, –** asparagus
spärlich sparse; scanty; meagre; poor
^der^ **Sparren, –** rafter
sparsam economical; thrifty, frugal
^die^ **Sparsamkeit** economy; thrift, frugality
^der^ **Spartaner, –, spartanisch** Spartan
^die^ **Sparte, –n** branch; section
^der^ **Spaß** [–aː–], **⸚e** joke; lark; fun; **~ haben an** (*dat*) enjoy; **er macht nur ~** he's only joking; **... macht (viel) ~** ... is (great) fun; **... macht mir ~** I enjoy ...; **sich** *dat* **einen ~ daraus machen zu ...** take pleasure in (+*ger*); **seinen ~ treiben mit** make fun of; **keinen ~ verstehen** have no sense of humour; be unable to take a joke; (about money matters) be very particular; **aus/zum ~** for fun; = **im ~** (say) in fun; **~ beiseite!** joking apart; **viel ~!** have fun! || **der ~macher, –** joker; **der ~verderber, –** spoilsport; **der ~vogel, ..vögel** joker
spaßen joke; **mit ... ist nicht zu ~** ... is *etc* not to be trifled with/no joking matter
spaßes|halber for fun
spaßhaft = **spaßig** funny
^der^ **Spastiker** [ʃp–, sp–], **–, spastisch** spastic
spät late; **zu ~ kommen** be late; **wie ~ ist es?** what's the time?; **bis ~er!** see you later! || **der S~entwickler, –** late developer; **der ~herbst, –e** late autumn; **die S~lese, –n** late vintage; **der ~sommer, –** late summer; **die S~verkaufs|stelle, –n** *EGer* shop that stays open late; **das S~werk, –e** late work; **die S~zeit** late period; **die S~zündung, –en** retarded ignition (**S. haben** *joc* be slow on the uptake)
^der^ **Spatel, –** *med* spatula
^der^ **Spaten, –** spade
späterhin later on, subsequently
spätestens at the latest
^der^ **Spatz, –en** (*wk masc*) sparrow; **die ~en pfeifen es von allen Dächern** *coll* it's all over the town
^die^ **Spätzle** *pl SGer* (*Swabian pasta speciality*)
Spazier–: die ~fahrt, –en ride; **der ~gang, ⸚e** walk (**einen S. machen** go for a walk); **der ~gänger, –** walker; **der ~stock, ⸚e**

walking-stick; **der ~weg, -e** footpath, walk
spazieren (*sn*) stroll; **~fahren*** (*sep*) take for a drive/(baby) for a walk; (*v/i sn*) go for a drive; **~führen** (*sep*) take for a walk; **~gehen*** (*sep*; *sn*) go for a walk
die **SPD = Sozialdemokratische Partei Deutschlands**
der **Specht, -e** woodpecker
der **Speck, -e** smoked bacon fat; blubber; *coll* flab, fat; ~ **ansetzen** *coll* put on weight; **ran an den ~!** let's get weaving! || **der ~bauch, ⸚e** *coll* paunch; **die ~schwarte, -n** bacon rind; **die ~seite, -n** side of bacon
speckig greasy
spedieren dispatch
der **Spediteur** [–'tøːɐ], **-e** furniture remover, mover *US*; carrier
die **Spedition, -en** carriage (of goods); furniture remover, moving company *US*; haulage contractor; dispatch department (of store)
speditiv *Swiss* expeditious
der **Speer, -e** spear; *athl* javelin
spei-: spei|übel *coll* (**mir ist s.** I think I'm going to be sick)
die **Speiche, -n** spoke; *anat* radius
der **Speichel** saliva; **die ~drüse, -n** salivary gland; **der ~fluß** salivation; **der ~lecker, -** bootlicker; **die ~leckerei** bootlicking
das **Speichen|rad, ⸚er** spoked wheel; *mot* wire wheel
der **Speicher, -** granary, silo; warehouse; reservoir; *esp SGer* attic, loft; *comput* store, memory; *in compds* storage ...; *comput* memory ...; **die ~heizung, -en** storage heater
speichern store (*also comput*)
die **Speicherung** storage (*also comput*)
speien (*p/t* **spie**, *p/part* **gespie(e)n**) spit; (volcano) spew; (*v/i*) spit; vomit
der **Speis** *SGer* mortar
die **Speise, -n** food; dish; dessert; **das ~eis** ice-cream; **das ~fett, -e** cooking-fat; **die ~kammer, -n** pantry; **die ~karte, -n** menu; **das ~öl, -e** salad-oil; **die ~reste** *pl* left-overs; **die ~röhre, -n** gullet; **der ~saal, ..säle** dining-hall, (hotel *etc*) dining-room; **der ~wagen, -** dining-car; **das ~zimmer, -** dining-room; dining-room suite
speisen feed (*also tech*); (*v/i*) dine; **sich ~ aus** draw on
der **Spektakel** *coll* racket; row
spektakulär spectacular
die **Spektral|farben** [ʃp–, sp–] *pl* colours of the spectrum
das **Spektrum** [ʃp–, sp–], **-(r)en/-(r)a** spectrum
der **Spekulant, -en** (*wk masc*) speculator
die **Spekulation, -en** speculation (*also fin*)
der **Spekulatius** [–ts–], **-** (*kind of spiced biscuit/cookie US*)

spekulieren speculate (*also fin*: **mit** in); **~ auf** (*acc*) *coll* have hopes of
die **Spelunke, -n** *coll* dive
die **Spelze, -n** husk
spendabel *coll* generous
die **Spende, -n** donation
spenden donate, give; afford (shade), give (warmth, comfort); bestow (praise); *eccles* administer; **Beifall ~** applaud
der **Spender, -** donor
Spendier-: ~hosen *coll* (**die S. anhaben** be in a generous mood)
spendieren *coll* pay for (round); (+*dat*) *coll* treat to
der **Spengler, -** *esp SGer* plumber
der **Sperber, -** sparrow-hawk
Sperenzchen *coll*: **~ machen** be difficult
der **Sperling, -e** sparrow
Sperr-: sperr|angel|weit *coll* (**s. offen** wide open); **der ~ballon, -s** barrage balloon; **der ~druck** letter-spacing (*see p. lxviii*); **das ~feuer, -** barrage; **das ~gebiet, -e** prohibited area; **das ~gut** bulky goods; **das ~holz** plywood; **das ~konto, -(t)en** blocked account; **der ~müll** bulky refuse; **der ~sitz, -e** (circus) front seat; (cinema) seat in the back stalls; **die ~stunde, -n** closing time; *mil* curfew
die **Sperre, -n** barrier (*also rail*); ban, *comm* embargo, *sp* ban, suspension; **eine ~ haben** *coll* have a mental block
sperren (*see also* **gesperrt**) block (*also sp* = obstruct); close (street *etc*: **für** to); disconnect, cut off (gas, telephone, *etc*); *esp Aust* close (shop *etc*); *comm* block, freeze; stop (cheque); *sp* ban, suspend; *comput* inhibit; *print* space; (*v/i*) (door, window) stick; **~ in** (*acc*) shut in; **sich ~ gegen** baulk at, jib at
sperrig bulky; unwieldy
die **Sperrung, -en** *vbl noun*; *sp* suspension; *print* letter-spacing
die **Spesen** *pl* expenses; **das ~konto, -(t)en** expense account
die **Spezereien** *pl arch* spices
der **Spezi, -s** *SGer coll* pal
Spezial- special ...; specialized ...; **das ~geschäft, -e** specialist shop
spezialisieren: sich ~ specialize (**auf** *acc* in); **spezialisiert auf** (*acc*) specializing in
der **Spezialist, -en** (*wk masc*) specialist (**für** in)
das **Spezialistentum** specialization
die **Spezialität, -en** speciality, specialty; favourite dish
speziell special; specialized; specific; **auf dein Spezielles!** here's to you!
die **Spezies** ['ʃpeːtsĭɛs, sp–], **-** [–ĭeːs] species
die **Spezifikation, -en** specification; itemization
spezifisch specific
spezifizieren specify; itemize
die **Spezifizierung, -en** specification; itemization

die **Sphäre, –n** sphere
sphärisch spherical
das **Sphäroid** [–o'iːt], **–e** spheroid
die **Sphinx, –e** sphinx
Spick–: der ~aal, –e *NGer* smoked eel; **die ~gans, ⸚e** *NGer* smoked breast of goose; **die ~nadel, –n** larding-needle
spicken lard; **mit Fehlern gespickt** riddled with errors
spie *p/t of* **speien**
der **Spiegel, –** mirror; surface (of sea *etc*); (silk) lapel, *mil* tab; *med* level; **im ~** (+*gen*) as seen by; as reflected in || **das ~bild, –er** reflection; mirror image; **spiegel|blank** shining; **das ~ei, –er** fried egg; **die ~fechterei, –en** shadow-boxing; bluff; **spiegel|glatt** as smooth as glass/a millpond; **s~gleich** symmetrical; **die ~reflex|kamera, –s** reflex camera; **die ~schrift** mirror-writing
spiegeln reflect; (*v/i*) shine; reflect the light; **sich ~ in** (*dat*) be reflected in
die **Spiegelung, –en** reflection
das **Spiel, –e** game; play(ing), *mus* playing, *theat* acting, *sp* play; gambling; play (of waves, light and shade, *etc*), (inter)play (of forces); quirk (of fate); *mech* play; *theat* play (*esp* of simple type); *sp* game; match; *cards* pack, deck *US*; **wie steht das ~?** what's the score?; **ein falsches ~ treiben mit** play false; **gewonnenes ~ haben** be home and dry; **leichtes ~ haben mit** have no difficulty with; **auf dem ~ stehen** be at stake; **aufs ~ setzen** risk; **aus dem ~ lassen** leave out of it; **im ~** *sp* in play; **(mit) im ~** involved, at work; **ins ~ bringen** bring into play; introduce; **ins ~ kommen** come in(to play)
Spiel– playing ...; play ...; gambling ...;
die ~art, –en variety; **der ~automat, –en** (*wk masc*) gambling-machine; one-armed bandit; **der ~ball, ⸚e** ball; plaything (of fortune *etc*); *sp* game point; **die ~bank, –en** casino; **die ~dose, –n** musical box, music box *US*; **s~fähig** fit to play; **das ~feld, –er** *sp* field, ground; **der ~film, –e** (feature) film; **die ~folge, –n** programme; **der ~führer, –** *sp* captain; **der ~gefährte, –n** (*wk masc*) playmate; **die ~hölle, –n** gambling den; **die ~karte, –n** playing-card; **die ~klasse, –n** *sp* division; **der ~leiter, –** *cin* director, *theat etc* producer, director *US*; *TV* compère, master of ceremonies *US*; quizmaster; **der ~mann, ..leute** bandsman; *hist* minstrel; **die ~marke, –n** chip; **der ~meister, –** *EGer TV* (= **~leiter** *TV*); **der ~plan, ⸚e** *theat* programme; **der ~platz, ⸚e** playground; **der ~raum** latitude, leeway; scope; *mech* play, clearance; **die ~regeln** *pl* rules; **die ~sachen** *pl* toys; **der ~stand, ⸚e** score; **die ~theorie** game(s) theory; **die ~uhr, –en** musical box, music box *US*; **das ~verbot, –e** *sp* ban, suspension (**S. haben** be banned); **der ~verderber, –** spoilsport; **die ~waren** *pl* toys; **die ~weise, –n** style of play; **die ~wiese, –n** playground; play area; **die ~zeit, –en** *sp* playing-time; *cin*, *theat* run; *theat* season; **das ~zeug, –e** toy; (*collect*) toys; **~zeug–** toy ...; **das ~zimmer, –** playroom
spielen (*see also* **gespielt**) play; *theat etc* play; perform; (*v/i*) play; gamble; (play, film) be on; (radio) be on; (gem) glitter; **(Klavier** *etc*) **~** play the (piano *etc*); **was wird hier gespielt?** what's going on?; **~ lassen** use; bring into play
~ gegen play
~ in (*dat*) be set in; **ins (Grünliche** *etc*) **~** have a (greenish *etc*) tinge
~ mit play with; toy with
~ um play for; (smile) play on
~ vor (*dat*) play to
spielend easily; (win) hands down; **mit ~er Leichtigkeit** with the greatest of ease
der **Spieler, –** player; gambler
die **Spielerei, –en** playing about; diversion; child's play; (*pl*) gadgets
spielerisch playful; *sp* playing; as a player; *theat* acting; **mit ~er Leichtigkeit** with the greatest of ease
der **Spieß, –e** spear; *cul* spit; *mil coll* sergeant-major; **wie am ~ schreien** *coll* scream one's head off; **den ~ umdrehen/umkehren** turn the tables **(gegen** on) || **der ~bürger, –, s~bürgerlich** (petit) bourgeois; **der ~geselle, –n** (*wk masc*) accomplice; crony; **~ruten (S. laufen** run the gauntlet)
spießen: ~ auf (*acc*) stick on (nail *etc*); **sich ~** *Aust* get stuck; make no progress
der **Spießer, –, spießig** (petit) bourgeois
die **Spikes** [ʃpaeks, sp–] *pl athl* spikes; *mot* studs; = **die ~reifen** *pl* studded tyres
spinal spinal; **~e Kinderlähmung** poliomyelitis
der **Spinat** spinach
der **Spind, –e** (*also* **das**) *esp mil* locker
die **Spindel, –n** spindle; **spindel|dürr** spindly
das **Spinett, –e** spinet
Spinn– spinning ...; **das ~rad, ⸚er** spinning-wheel
die **Spinne, –n** spider; **pfui ~!** ugh! || **spinne|feind** *coll* ((+*dat*) **s. sein** hate like poison)
spinnen (*p/t* **spann** (*subj* **spönne, spänne**), *p/part* **gesponnen**) spin; (*v/i*) *coll* be crazy
das **Spinnen|gewebe, –** cobweb
der **Spinner, –** spinner; *coll* crazy character
die **Spinnerei, –en** spinning-mill; *coll* crazy idea
spintisieren *coll* brood
der **Spion, –e** spy; window-mirror (for watching the street); peep-hole

die **Spionage** [–ʒə] espionage; *in compds* spy ...; **die ~abwehr** counter-espionage

spionieren spy; pry, snoop

Spiral– spiral ...

die **Spirale, –n** spiral; *med* coil

spiralig spiral

der **Spiritismus** [ʃp–, sp–] spiritualism

der **Spiritist** [ʃp–, sp–], **–en** (*wk masc*), **spiritistisch** spiritualist

die **Spirituosen** [ʃp–, sp–] *pl* spirits

der **Spiritus, –se** spirit; **der ~kocher, –** spirit-stove

das **Spital, ⸚er** *Aust, Swiss* hospital

spitz pointed; sharp; (remark) pointed, barbed, (tongue) sharp; *math* acute; *coll* peaky; **mit ~en Fingern anfassen** pick up gingerly; **~e Klammer** angle bracket; **~ zulaufen** taper

der **Spitz, –e** spitz

Spitz– pointed ...; **der ~bart, ⸚e** goatee (beard); **s~bekommen*** (*sep*) *coll* get wise to; **der ~bube, –n** (*wk masc*) rogue; scamp; **s~bübisch** roguish; **s~findig** hair-splitting; **die ~hacke, –n** pickaxe; **die ~kehre, –n** *ski* kick turn; **s~kriegen** (*sep*) *coll* get wise to; **die ~maus, ⸚e** shrew; **der ~name, –n** (*like* **Name**) nickname; **s~wink(e)lig** acute-angled

Spitzbergen Spitsbergen

die **Spitze**[1], **–n** point; tip; top; peak; head (of column *etc*); leadership (of organization); (cigar/cigarette) holder; jibe, dig (**gegen** at); *sp* lead; *coll* top speed; (*pl*) leaders; top people; **~ sein** *coll* be the tops; (+*dat*) **die ~ bieten** defy; (+*dat*) **die ~ nehmen** take the sting out of; **an der ~** at the head/top; *sp* in the lead; **auf die ~ treiben** carry to extremes

die **Spitze**[2], **–n** lace; (*pl*) lace

der **Spitzel, –** informer

spitzeln act as an informer

spitzen sharpen; purse (one's lips); **die Ohren ~** prick up its ears/one's ears; **(sich) ~ auf** (*acc*) *coll* look forward to; be after (post)

Spitzen– top ...; peak ...; top-class/quality; leading ...; *text* lace ...; **die ~gruppe, –n** leading group, leaders; **die ~leistung, –en** first-class/peak performance; *tech* maximum output; **der ~reiter, –** *sp etc* leader; *mus* number one

der **Spitzer, –** sharpener

der **Spleen** [ʃpliːn], **–e/–s** eccentricity; crazy idea; obsession

spleenig ['ʃpliː–] eccentric, cranky

spleißen (*p/t* **spliß**, *p/part* **gesplissen**) *naut* splice

splendid [sp–] generous

spliß *p/t of* **spleißen**

der **Splitt, –e** chippings

der **Splitter, –** splinter; *bibl* mote; **splitter|faser|nackt** stark naked; **s~frei** shatter-proof; **die ~gruppe, –n** splinter group; **splitter|nackt** stark naked; **die ~partei, –en** splinter party

splitt(e)rig splintered; liable to splinter

splittern (*also sn*) splinter

die **SPÖ = Sozialistische Partei Österreichs**

spönne *p/t subj of* **spinnen**

sponsern ['ʃpɔnzɐn] *sp etc*, **der Sponsor** [–zɐ], **–s** *sp etc* sponsor

spontan spontaneous

die **Spontaneität** [–ei–] spontaneity

sporadisch sporadic

die **Spore, –n** spore

der **Sporn**, *pl* **Sporen** spur; **s~streichs** post-haste

spornen spur (horse); spur on

der **Sport** sport; hobby; **~ treiben** go in for sport

Sport– sports ...; sporting ...; **die ~art, –en** sport; **die ~artikel** *pl* sports goods; **der ~flieger, –** amateur pilot; **der ~freund, –e** sports enthusiast; **das ~hemd, –en** sports shirt, sport shirt *US*; **die ~hoch|schule, –n** college of physical education; **die ~kleidung** sportswear; **der ~lehrer, –** P.E. teacher; **der ~platz, ⸚e** sports ground; **der ~taucher, –** skin-diver; **der ~ver|ein, –e** sports club; **der ~wagen, –** push-chair, stroller *US*; *mot* sports car

der **Sportler, –** sportsman

die **Sportlerin, –nen** sportswoman

sportlich sporting (*also* = sportsmanlike); athletic; sporty; (wear) casual

der **Sports|mann, ⸚er/..leute** sportsman

Spot– ['spɔt–] *comm* spot (market, price, *etc*)

der **Spott** mockery, ridicule; **(seinen) ~ treiben mit** make fun of

Spott– *esp* satirical ...; **spott|billig** *coll* dirt-cheap; **die ~figur, –en** figure of fun; **~geld (für/um ein S.** dirt-cheap); **die ~lust** delight in mocking others; **der ~name, –n** (*like* **Name**) (derisive) nickname; **der ~preis, –e** ridiculously low price

spötteln: ~ über (*acc*) poke gentle fun at

spotten: ~ über (*acc*) make fun of, mock; **jeder Beschreibung ~** beggar description

der **Spötter, –** scoffer

spöttisch mocking; derisive

sprach *p/t of* **sprechen**

Sprach– [–aː–] linguistic ...; language ...; speech ...;

s~begabt good at languages; **der ~fehler, –** speech impediment; **der ~führer, –** phrase-book; **das ~gebiet, –e** (= **~raum**); **der ~gebrauch** usage; **das ~gefühl** feeling for a language; **s~gewandt** articulate; **die ~heil|kunde** speech therapy; **das ~kabinett, –e** *EGer* language laboratory; **s~kundig** proficient in languages; **das ~labor, –s** language laboratory; **die ~lehre** grammar; **s~los** speechless; **der ~raum, ⸚e**

speech area; (English *etc*) –speaking countries; **das ~rohr, –e** megaphone; mouthpiece (of); **die ~wissenschaft** linguistics; **der ~wissenschaftler, –** linguist(ician); **s~wissenschaftlich** linguistic

die **Sprache** [–aː–], **–n** language (*also comput*); speech; **in (holländischer** *etc*) **~** in (Dutch *etc*); **die ~ bringen auf** (*acc*) bring the conversation round to; **heraus mit der ~!** out with it!; **zur ~ bringen** broach, bring up; **zur ~ kommen** come up (for discussion)

spräche *p/t subj of* **sprechen**

Sprachen– language ...

–sprachig [–aː–] –speaking; –language; in ... languages

sprachlich [–aː–] linguistic

sprang (spränge) *p/t* (*subj*) *of* **springen**

der **Spray** [spreː], **–s** (*also* **das**) spray; **die ~dose, –n** aerosol, spray

sprayen ['spreːən] spray; lacquer (hair)

Sprech– speech ...; speaking ...; **die ~anlage, –n** intercom; entryphone, intercom *US*; **die ~blase, –n** balloon; **der ~chor, ⸚e** chorus of voices; **der ~funk** radiotelephony; **das ~funk|gerät, –e** radiotelephone; walkie-talkie; **der ~gesang** sprechgesang; **die ~stunde, –n** office hours; consultation hours; (doctor's) surgery, office hours *US*; **die ~stunden|hilfe, –n** (doctor's) receptionist; **der ~unterricht** elocution lessons; **die ~weise, –n** way of speaking, diction; **die ~werk|zeuge** *pl* organs of speech; **das ~zimmer, –** consulting-room

sprechen (sprich(s)t, *p/t* **sprach** [–aː–] (*subj* **spräche** [–ɛː–]), *p/part* **gesprochen)** speak; say; speak to; (*v/i*) speak, talk; **ich hätte gern ... gesprochen** I wonder if I might speak to ...?; **sprich** (*in parenthesis*) that is to say; pronounced; **(allgemein** *etc*) **gesprochen** (generally *etc*) speaking; **(nicht) zu ~ sein** (not) be available; **zum Sprechen bringen** get (s.o.) to talk

auf (*acc*): **zu ~ kommen auf** get to talking about; **schlecht/nicht gut zu ~ sein auf** be ill-disposed towards

aus ... spricht ... there is an expression of ... in (s.o.'s eyes); (s.o.'s words *etc*) express ...

~ für speak for; speak in favour of; point to; bespeak; **für sich ~** speak for itself/themselves; **das spricht für ihn** that's a point in his favour; **vieles spricht dafür** there is a lot to be said for it; **alles/nichts spricht dafür, daß ...** there is every/no reason to suppose that ...

~ gegen argue against; militate against; (appearances) be against

~ mit speak to, talk to

~ über (*acc*) speak/talk about

~ von speak/talk about

~ vor (*dat*) address

~ zu speak to; address

sprechend expressive; (glance) telling; (similarity) striking; **–sprechend** –speaking; (+*dat*) **~ ähnlich sehen** be the image of

der **Sprecher, –** speaker; spokesman; *rad*, *TV* announcer

die **Spreize, –n** *gym* straddle

spreizen (*see also* **gespreizt)** spread (out); splay; **sich ~** make a show of reluctance; put on airs

Spreng– *esp* explosive ...; **die ~arbeiten** *pl* blasting; **die ~kapsel, –n** detonator; **das ~kommando, –s** bomb-disposal squad; demolition squad; **der ~kopf, ⸚e** warhead; **der ~körper, –** explosive device; **die ~ladung, –en** explosive charge; **der ~meister, –** explosives expert; **der ~stoff, –e** explosive; **der ~wagen, –** water-cart

der **Sprengel, –** parish; *Aust* district

sprengen[1] blow up; blast; burst (one's bonds); break (bank); break up (meeting); **den Rahmen ~ von** go beyond the scope of

sprengen[2] sprinkle

sprengen[3] (*sn*) gallop

der **Sprenkel, –** spot, speckle

sprenkeln (*see also* **gesprenkelt)** sprinkle; speckle

die **Spreu** chaff

sprich *imp sing of* **sprechen**

Sprich–: das ~wort, ⸚er proverb; **s~wörtlich** proverbial

sprich(s)t (*2nd*,) *3rd sing pres of* **sprechen**

sprießen (*p/t* **sproß** (*subj* **sprösse**), *p/part* **gesprossen**) (*sn*) sprout

Spring–: der ~bock, ⸚e springbok; **der ~brunnen, –** fountain; **die ~flut, –en** spring-tide; **die ~form, –en** cake-release tin; **der ~ins|feld, –e** harum-scarum; **die ~maus, ⸚e** jerboa; **das ~pferd, –e** show-jumper; **das ~reiten** show-jumping; **der ~reiter, –** show-jumper; **das ~seil, –e** skipping-rope, jump rope *US*

springen (*p/t* **sprang** (*subj* **spränge**), *p/part* **gesprungen**) (*sn*) jump; leap; skip; bounce; crack; (bud *etc*) burst; gush; (spark) fly; *SGer coll* nip, pop; *sp* jump; vault; dive; **aus dem Gleis/den Schienen ~** jump the rails; **~ lassen** *coll* stand (round); **der ~de Punkt** the crux of the matter

der **Springer, –** jumper; *chess* knight

der **Sprint, –s, sprinten** (*sn*) sprint

der **Sprinter, –** sprinter

der **Sprit** [–ɪ–] *coll* 'juice'

Spritz– spray ...; **der ~guß** injection moulding; *metall* die-casting; **der ~kuchen, –** (*ring-shaped cake made of dough and fried in deep fat*, = cruller *US*); **der ~lack, –e**

spray paint; **die ~pistole, -n** spray-gun; **die ~tour, -en** 'spin'

die **Spritze, -n** syringe; *med* injection; *coll* injection (of money)

spritzen spray; squirt; splash; mix with mineral/soda water; *cul* pipe; *med* inject; (*v/i, also sn*) squirt; spurt; splash; (fat) spit; (*sn*) *coll* dash

der **Spritzer, -** splash; dash (of)

spritzig (wine) piquant; witty; sparkling; (car) nippy

spröde brittle; (skin) chapped; (voice) rough; (person, manner) reserved; (subject *etc*) difficult, intractable

die **Sprödigkeit** brittleness; roughness; reserve; intractability

sproß (sprösse) *p/t* (*subj*) *of* **sprießen**

der **Sproß, -(ss)e** shoot; scion

die **Sprosse, -n** rung

sprossen (*sn*) sprout

Sprossen-: der ~kohl *Aust* (Brussels) sprouts; **die ~wand, ¨-e** wall bars

der **Sprößling, -e** *joc* offspring

die **Sprotte, -n** sprat

der **Spruch, ¨-e** saying; aphorism; (from Bible) quotation; *leg* verdict; *coll* patter; (*pl*) *coll* empty talk; **Sprüche machen** *coll* talk big || **das ~band, ¨-er** banner; **s~reif** ripe for decision

der **Sprudel, -** (effervescent) mineral water; fizzy drink

sprudeln (*Aust in 1st sense*) whisk; (*v/i*) effervesce; bubble; **~ aus** (*sn*) bubble from; **~ vor** (*dat*) bubble over with; **~d** effervescent

der **Sprudler, -** *Aust* whisk

Sprüh-: die ~dose, -n spray, aerosol; **der ~regen** drizzle

sprühen spray; emit (sparks); (*v/i, sn if indicating motion*) spray; (spark) fly; **~ vor** (*dat*) sparkle with; **es sprüht** it is drizzling; **~d** sparkling, scintillating

der **Sprung, ¨-e** jump; leap; crack; *comput* jump, branch; *sp* jump; vault; dive; **nur ein ~** *coll* only a stone's throw; **~ ins Ungewisse** leap in the dark; **einen ~ haben** be cracked; **den ~ wagen** take the plunge; **keine großen Sprünge machen können** *coll* not be able to do much (on one's income); **auf einen ~ vorbeikommen** *coll* drop in (for a minute) (**bei** on); **immer auf dem ~ sein** *coll* be always in a hurry; **auf dem ~ sein zu ...** be on the point of (+*ger*); (+*dat*) **auf die Sprünge helfen** *coll* help to get started; (+*dat*) **auf die Sprünge kommen** *coll* rumble || **das ~brett, -er** springboard; stepping-stone (to sth.); **die ~feder, -n** spring; **die ~grube, -n** *athl* pit; die ~schanze, -n ski-jump; **das ~tuch, ¨-er** jumping-sheet, life net *US*; **der ~turm, ¨-e** diving-platform

sprunghaft erratic; disjointed; abrupt; (*adv*) by leaps and bounds

die **SPS = Sozialdemokratische Partei der Schweiz**

Spuck-: der ~napf, ¨-e spittoon

die **Spucke** *coll* spit; **mir bleibt die ~ weg** I'm speechless

spucken (*also v/i*) spit; **große Bogen/Töne ~** *coll* talk big

der **Spuk** ghostly apparition/goings-on; *coll* nightmare (of Fascism *etc*); *coll* racket; fuss; **die ~geschichte, -n** ghost story

spuken (ghost) walk; **~ in** (*dat*) haunt; **hier spukt es** this place is haunted

spukhaft ghostly

Spül-: der ~automat, -en (*wk masc*) dishwasher; **das ~becken, -** (kitchen) sink; **der ~kasten, ..kästen** cistern; **der ~lappen, -** dishcloth; **die ~maschine, -n** dishwasher; **das ~mittel, -** washing-up liquid, dishwashing liquid *US*; **der ~stein, -e** (kitchen) sink; **der ~tisch, -e** sink unit; **das ~wasser** dishwater

die **Spule, -n** spool, reel; bobbin; *elect* coil

die **Spüle, -n** (kitchen) sink

spulen wind onto a spool/reel/bobbin

spülen rinse; wash (wound); flush (toilet); (waves *etc*) wash (ashore, overboard, *etc*); (*v/i*) rinse; flush the toilet; **(das Geschirr) ~** wash up, do the dishes *US*

der **Spüler, -** dishwasher

der **Spund[1], ¨-e** bung; *carp* tongue

der **Spund[2], -e** *coll*: **junger ~** young pup

die **Spur, -en** track (*also comput*); trace, sign; trail; (traffic) lane; touch (of salt *etc*); *rail* gauge; *mot* track; **keine/nicht die ~** *coll* not in the slightest; (+*dat*) **auf die ~ kommen** get onto; get to the bottom of || **s~los** without trace (**... ist nicht s. an ...** (*dat*) **vorübergegangen** ... has left its mark on); **die ~weite, -n** *rail* gauge; *mot* track

Spür-: der ~hund, -e tracker-dog; *coll* sleuth; **die ~nase, -n** nose (for sth.); **der ~sinn** (dog's) nose (= sense of smell); instinct, flair

spürbar perceptible

spuren *coll* toe the line; do as one is told

spüren feel; sense; **zu ~ bekommen** feel the effect/full force of; get a taste of

das **Spuren|element, -e** trace element

-spurig -lane; *rail* -gauge

der **Spurt, -s** *sp* spurt, sprint

spurten (*also sn*) *sp* spurt, sprint; (*sn*) *coll* sprint, dash

die **SRG = Schweizerische Radio- und Fernsehgesellschaft** (*Swiss broadcasting corporation*)

Sri Lanka Sri Lanka

der **Srilanker, -, srilankisch** Sri Lankan

die **SS** *Nazi* (**= Schutzstaffel**) the S.S.

der **SSD** = **Staatssicherheitsdienst** (*E. German secret police*)
st! sh!; pst!
St. (= **Sankt**) St., (= **Stück**) piece, (= **Stunde**) hour
der **Staat, –en** state; *zool* colony; *coll* finery; **„Der ~"** 'The Republic' (Plato); **~ machen** *coll* make a show
Staaten– ... of states; **der ~bund, ⸚e** confederation; **s~los** stateless
staatlich state; national; (*adv*) by the state; state-(approved *etc*)
Staats– ... of (the) state; state ...; national ...; government ...; public ...;
der ~akt, –e state occasion; **~aktion** *coll* (**eine S. machen aus** make a song and dance about); **der/die ~angehörige** (*decl as adj*) national; subject; **die ~angehörigkeit, –en** nationality; **der ~anwalt, ⸚e** public prosecutor; **der ~besuch, –e** state visit; **der ~bürger, –** citizen; **die ~bürger|kunde** civics; **der ~chef, –s** head of state; **der ~dienst** civil service; **s~eigen** state-owned; **das ~examen, –/–(m)ina** state examination (*approx* = degree); **s~feindlich** subversive; **die ~form, –en** form of government; **die ~gewalt** authority of the state; (the) authorities; **die ~kasse, –n** public purse, treasury; **die ~kirche, –n** established church; **der ~mann, ⸚er** statesman; **s~männisch** statesmanlike; **das ~oberhaupt, ⸚er** head of state; **die ~prüfung, –en** (= **~examen**); **die ~räson** [–zõ] reasons of State; **der ~rat** Council of State; **das ~recht** constitutional law; **der ~säckel, –** *coll* the nation's coffers; **der ~sekretär, –e** *approx* = permanent secretary; **der ~streich, –e** coup (d'état); **das ~verbrechen, –** political crime; **der ~vertrag, ⸚e** treaty; (*Austria*: **der S.**) the State Treaty; **das ~wesen** polity
der **Stab**[1]**, ⸚e** staff (*also mil*)
der **Stab**[2]**, ⸚e** rod; wand; bar (of cage *etc*); *athl, mus* baton; *athl* pole; *eccles* crosier; **den ~ brechen über** (*acc*) condemn || **der ~hoch|sprung** pole-vault; **der ~reim, –e** alliteration
stabil sturdy, robust; stable
der **Stabilisator, –(or)en** stabilizer
stabilisieren, sich ~ stabilize
die **Stabilität** stability
stach (stäche) *p/t* (*subj*) *of* **stechen**
der **Stachel, –n** quill, spine (of porcupine); spine (of hedgehog, cactus); sting (of bee *etc*); barb (on barbed wire); goad; (+*dat*) **den ~ nehmen** take the sting out of || **die ~beere, –n** gooseberry; **der ~draht** barbed wire; **der ~draht|verhau, –e** barbed-wire entanglement; **das ~schwein, –e** porcupine
stach(e)lig prickly

der **Stadel, –** *SGer* barn; shed
das **Stadion** [–ɔn], **–(i)en** stadium
das **Stadium, –(i)en** stage; phase
die **Stadt** [–t], **⸚e** [–ɛːt–] town; city; *in compds also* urban ...; municipal ...; **s~bekannt** known all over the town; **der ~bewohner, –** town/city-dweller; **das ~bild, –er** appearance of a/the town/city; townscape; **der ~direktor, –en** town/city manager; **die ~gemeinde, –n** municipality; **das ~gespräch, –e** talk of the town; *tel* local call; **die ~mitte** town/city centre; **der ~plan, ⸚e** street map; **der ~rand, ⸚er** outskirts; **der ~rat, ⸚e** town/city council; town/city councillor; **die ~rund|fahrt, –en** sightseeing tour of the town/city; **der ~staat, –en** city-state; **der ~teil, –e** district; **der/die ~ver|ordnete** (*decl as adj*) town/city councillor; **das ~zentrum, –(r)en** town/city centre
Städte– [–ɛːt–] ... of towns/cities; **der ~bau** town planning, city planning *US*
der **Städter** [–ɛːt–], **–** town/city-dweller
städtisch [–ɛːt–] town *or* city; municipal; urban
die **Stafette, –n** *hist* courier
die **Staffage** [–ʒə], **–n** window-dressing; *art* figures in a landscape
die **Staffel, –n** *aer* squadron; *sp* relay team; = **der ~lauf, ⸚e** relay (race)
die **Staffelei, –en** easel
staffeln grade, graduate; stagger; *mil* echelon
das **Stag, –e(n)** *naut* stay
die **Stagnation** stagnation
stagnieren stagnate; **~d** stagnant
stahl (stähle) *p/t* (*subj*) *of* **stehlen**
der **Stahl, ⸚e** steel; **der ~beton** reinforced concrete; **stahl|blau** steel-blue; **das ~blech, –e** steel sheet; sheet steel; **stahl|hart** as hard as steel; steely; **die ~kammer, –n** strong-room; **die ~(rohr)möbel** *pl* tubular furniture; **das ~werk, –e** steel works
stählen: (sich) ~ toughen (oneself)
stählern steel; steely, (nerves) of steel, (will) of iron
stak (stäke) *p/t* (*subj*) *of* **stecken** (*v/i*)
staken pole; punt; (*v/i sn*) pole; punt; *coll* stalk
staksen [–aː–] (*sn*) *coll* stalk
staksig [–aː–] *coll* gawky
der **Stalagmit** [ʃt–, st–], **–e** (*or* **–en** (*wk masc*)) stalagmite
der **Stalaktit** [ʃt–, st–], **–e** (*or* **–en** (*wk masc*)) stalactite
die **Stalin|orgel** [ˈʃtaːliːn–], **–n** *coll* (Soviet) multiple rocket-launcher (in 2nd World War)
der **Stall, ⸚e** stable; cowshed; pigsty; hutch; *horse/mot rac* stable; *coll* 'hole'; **der ~knecht, –e** stable-lad
die **Stallungen** *pl* stables

[der] **Stamm, ¨e** (tree) trunk; tribe; (family) line; (**~ von Kunden/Arbeitern**/*sp* **~ der Mannschaft**) regular customers/workforce/ team-members; *gramm* stem; *bot*, *zool* strain; *in compds* regular ...; ancestral ...; **die ~aktie, –n** ordinary share; **der ~baum, ¨e** family tree; pedigree; **das ~buch, ¨er** family record; herd-book; **der ~gast, ¨e** regular customer; **der ~halter, –** son and heir; **die ~kneipe, –n** 'local'; **der ~kunde, –n** (*wk masc*) regular customer; **das ~lokal, –e** 'local'; favourite restaurant; **die ~tafel, –n** genealogical table; **der ~tisch, –e** table reserved for regulars; (meeting of a) group of regulars (in pub); **~tisch–** *approx* = armchair ...; **s~verwandt** related; *ling* cognate

stammeln (*also v/i*) stammer

stammen: ~ aus come from; be from; date from; **~ von** come from; be by; **... stammt von (meiner Tante** *etc*) ... belonged to

Stammes– ... of a/the tribe; tribal ...

stämmig sturdy; stocky

stampfen stamp; pound; crush; mash; (*v/i*) stamp; (ship) pitch; (*sn*) tramp; **aus dem Boden/der Erde ~** conjure up from nowhere; **~ mit** stamp (one's foot)

[die] **Stampiglie** [–'pɪljə], **–n** *Aust* rubber-stamp; stamp

stand *p/t of* **stehen**

[der] **Stand, ¨e** standing position; (taxi) rank, stand; stall; stand; state, *sp* score; level, (meter *etc*) reading; class, *hist* estate; profession; *Swiss* canton; **einen schweren ~ haben bei** have a hard time of it with; **auf den neuesten ~ bringen** bring up to date; **„~ (Mai 1990** *etc*)" 'as at ...' || **das ~bild, –er** statue; **s~fest** steady; steadfast; **das ~gericht, –e** drumhead court-martial; **s~halten*** (*sep*) stand firm; (+*dat*) stand up to, withstand; bear (scrutiny); **das ~licht, –er** parking light; **der ~ort, –e** position (*also aer*, *naut*); site; location; *mil* garrison; *bot* habitat; **die ~pauke, –n** *coll* lecture ((+*dat*) **eine S. halten** *coll* lecture); **der ~platz, ¨e** position; (taxi) rank, stand; **der ~punkt, –e** point of view, standpoint (**auf dem S. stehen, daß ...** take the view that ...; **vom S. (+***gen***) aus** from the point of view of, in terms of); **s~rechtlich** (shoot) by order of a court-martial; **s~sicher** stable; **die ~uhr, –en** grandfather clock

[der] **Standard** ['ʃtandart], **–s** standard (*EGer also = industrial etc standard*)

Standard– standard ...; **das ~werk, –e** standard work

standardisieren standardize

[die] **Standardisierung** standardization

[die] **Standarte, –n** *mil*, *pol* standard; *Nazi* (*unit of the S.A. or S.S.*)

[das] **Ständchen, –**, (+*dat*) **ein ~ bringen** serenade

stände *p/t subj of* **stehen**

Stände–: der ~rat, ¨e (member of) the Council of States (*second chamber of the Swiss legislature, composed of representatives of the cantons*)

[der] **Stander, –** pennant

[der] **Ständer, –** stand; rack

Standes– *esp* class ...; **das ~amt, ¨er** registry office; **s~amtlich** (marriage) civil; **der ~be|amte** (*decl as adj*) registrar; **das ~bewußt|sein** status-consciousness; **s~gemäß** (*also adv*) in keeping with one's status/rank

standhaft steadfast; staunch

[die] **Standhaftigkeit** steadfastness; staunchness

ständig permanent; constant; (committee) standing; (*adv*) constantly, always, forever

[die] **Stange, –n** pole; rod; bar; perch; stick (of dynamite, sealing-wax, *etc*), carton (of cigarettes); **eine ~ Geld** *coll* a tidy sum; (+*dat*) **die ~ halten** *coll* stick up for; **bei der ~ bleiben** *coll* stick at it; **von der ~** off the peg || **die ~n|bohne, –n** runner bean; **der ~n|spargel** asparagus spears

stank (stänke) *p/t* (*subj*) *of* **stinken**

[der] **Stänkerer, –** *coll* troublemaker

stänkern *coll* stir things up

[das] **Stanniol(papier)** tinfoil

stante pede ['ʃtantə 'peːdə] *joc* right away

[die] **Stanze[1], –n** *tech* punch; die

[die] **Stanze[2], –n** *liter* ottava rima

stanzen punch (*also comput*); stamp; press (machine part *etc*)

[der] **Stapel, –** stack, pile; *naut* stocks; *comput* stack; batch; pack; **vom ~ lassen** launch; *coll* deliver (speech), come out with; **vom ~ laufen** be launched || **der ~lauf, ¨e** launch

stapeln pile up, stack; **sich ~** pile up

[die] **Stapfe, –n** footprint

stapfen (*sn*) trudge

[der] **Stapfen, –** footprint

[der] **Star[1], –e** starling

[der] **Star[2], –e** *med*: **grauer ~** cataract; **grüner ~** glaucoma

[der] **Star[3]** [st–], **–s** *cin etc* star; **die ~allüren** *pl* airs and graces (of a star)

starb *p/t of* **sterben**

stark (*comp*, *superl* ¨) strong (*also gramm*); powerful; thick, (person *euph*) large; (interest *etc*) great, (pain *etc*) severe, (demand, rain, traffic, smoker, *etc*) heavy, (competition) stiff, (applause) loud, (temperature, wind) high, (storm) violent; (*adv*) very much, a lot; greatly; strongly; heavily; (*with adj*) very; **für die stärkere Dame** for the fuller figure; **(800** *etc*) **Seiten ~** (800 *etc*) pages long; **das ist ~/ein ~es**

Stück! that's a bit much!; **sich ~ machen für** *coll* stand up for || **~leibig** corpulent; **der S~strom** power current

[die] **Stärke, -n** strength; power; severity; heaviness; violence (of storm); thickness; strong point; *chem* starch; **das ~mehl** cornflour, cornstarch *US*

stärken strengthen; fortify; boost; starch; **~des Mittel** tonic; **sich ~** fortify oneself

[die] **Stärkung, -en** *vbl noun*; *also* refreshment; **das ~s|mittel, -** tonic

[das] **Starlet** ['staːɐlɛt], **-s** starlet

starr stiff; rigid; (gaze) fixed; **~ ansehen** stare at || **der S~kopf, ⸚e** stubborn person; **~köpfig** stubborn; **der S~krampf, ⸚e** tetanus; **der S~sinn** obstinacy; **~sinnig** stubborn

starren stare (**auf** *acc* at); **~ von** bristle with; = **~ vor** (*dat*) be covered with

[der] **Start, -s** *sp* start; participation; *aer* take-off, *space* launch; *in compds also* starting ...; **die ~bahn, -en** runway; **s~berechtigt** eligible to compete; **s~bereit** ready to start; *aer* ready for take-off, *space* ready for lift-off; **der ~block, ⸚e** starting-block; **die ~erlaubnis** *sp* permission to compete; *aer* take-off clearance; **die ~hilfe** help (to get started); **die ~hilfe|kabel** *pl* jump leads, jumper cables *US*; **die ~rakete, -n** booster rocket; **die ~rampe, -n** launching-pad; **das ~verbot, -e** *aer* grounding; *sp* ban, suspension (**S. haben** *aer* be grounded; *sp* be suspended); **das ~zeichen, -** starting signal

starten start (motor), *space* launch; launch (campaign *etc*); (*v/i sn*) set out (**zu** for); *aer* take off (**nach** for); *sp* start; compete

[der] **Stasi** *EGer* = **Staatssicherheitsdienst**

[die] **Statik** [-ɪk] statics

[die] **Station, -en** stop; stage (of s.o.'s life *etc*); *meteor etc* station; *med* ward; **freie ~** free board and lodging; **~ machen** stop off

stationär *tech* stationary; *med* (treatment) as an in-patient; **~ behandelter Patient** in-patient

stationieren *mil* station, base

statisch static

[der] **Statist, -en** (*wk masc*) *cin* extra; *theat* supernumerary; **die ~en|rolle, -n** walk-on part

[die] **Statisterie** *cin* extras; *theat* supernumeraries

[die] **Statistik** [-ɪk], **-en** statistics; set of statistics

[der] **Statistiker, -** statistician

statistisch statistical

[das] **Stativ, -e** *phot* tripod

statt (*usu* + *gen*) instead of; **~ zu ...** instead of (+*ger*); **~ dessen** instead

Statt: an Eides ~ in lieu of an oath; **an jmds. ~** in s.o.'s place; **an Kindes ~ annehmen** adopt

statt-: ~finden* (*sep*) take place; **~geben*** (*sep*) (+*dat*) accede to; **der S~halter, -** *hist* governor

[die] **Stätte, -n** place; site

statthaft permitted

stattlich imposing; impressive; considerable

[die] **Statue** [-ŭə], **-n** statue

statuenhaft statuesque

[die] **Statuette, -n** statuette

statuieren: ein Exempel ~ an (*dat*) make an example of

[die] **Statur, -en** build

[der] **Status** [ʃt-, st-], **-** [-uːs] state; status (*also leg*); **der Status quo** (*gen* **- -**) status quo; **das ~symbol, -e** status symbol

[das] **Statut, -en** statute

[der] **Stau, -e/-s** build-up (of water *etc*); *mot* tailback; **der ~damm, ⸚e** dam; **der ~see, -n** reservoir; **das ~strahl|trieb|werk, -e** ramjet (engine); **das ~werk, -e** dam

[der] **Staub** dust; *bot* pollen; **~ saugen** vacuum-clean; **~ wischen** dust; **(viel) ~ aufwirbeln** *coll* cause (quite) a stir; **sich aus dem ~(e) machen** *coll* take to one's heels || **der ~beutel, -** anther; **das ~blatt, ⸚er = das ~gefäß, -e** stamen; **das ~korn, ⸚er** speck of dust; **der ~lappen, -** duster; **die ~lunge, -n** pneumoconiosis; **s~saugen** (*insep exc* **s~zusaugen,** *p/part* **s~gesaugt)** vacuum-clean; **der ~sauger, -** vacuum cleaner; **das ~tuch, ⸚er** duster; **die ~wolke, -n** cloud of dust

stauben be dusty; make dust; **es staubt** it is dusty

stäuben: ~ auf (*acc*) sprinkle on

staubig dusty

[die] **Staude, -n** herbaceous perennial; *SGer* shrub

stauen dam (up); *med* stop the flow of; **sich ~** accumulate; pile up; (traffic) come to a standstill; (anger) build up

[der] **Staufer, -, staufisch** Hohenstaufen

staunen be amazed (**über** *acc* at); **~d** amazed; wondering; (*adv*) in amazement

[das] **Staunen** amazement; **in ~ (ver)setzen** amaze || **s~s|wert** amazing

[die] **Staupe, -n** *vet* distemper

[die] **Stauung, -en** *vbl noun*; *also* build-up (of water *etc*); *med* congestion; *mot* tailback

Std(e). (= **Stunde**) hr.

[das] **Steak** [steːk], **-s** steak

[das] **Stearin, -e** stearin

Stech-: die ~fliege, -n stable-fly; **der ~ginster** gorse; **der ~heber, -** pipette; **die ~karte, -n** clocking-in card; **die ~mücke, -n** gnat, mosquito; **die ~palme, -n** holly; **der ~rüssel, -** proboscis; **der ~schritt, -e** goose-step; **die ~uhr, -en** time-clock; **der ~zirkel, -** dividers

stechen (stich(s)t, *p/t* **stach** [-aː-] (*subj* **stäche** [-ɛː-]), *p/part* **gestochen)** (*see also* **gestochen**) prick; stab; cut (turf *etc*); (insect) sting, (gnat) bite; pierce (holes); *cards* take; *art* engrave; (*v/i*) prick; stab (**nach** at); (insect) sting, (gnat) bite; (sun) beat down; **die Kontrolluhr ~** clock in/out; (**Herz** *etc*) **sticht** (hearts *etc*) are trumps; **es sticht mich/mir in der Seite** *etc* I feel a sharp pain in my side *etc*; **es wird gestochen** *sp* there is a play-off/jump-off/shoot-off; **in See ~** put to sea; (+*dat*) **ins Auge/in die Augen ~** catch (s.o.'s) eye; **ins (Grüne** *etc*) **~** have a tinge of (green *etc*); **~d** penetrating; (pain) sharp; **das Stechen** *also* sharp pain; *sp* play-off; jump-off

Steck–: der ~brief, –e 'wanted' notice; description; **die ~dose, –n** *elect* socket, outlet *US*; **die ~nadel, –n** pin; **die ~rübe, –n** swede, rutabaga *US*; **der ~schuß, ⸚(ss)e** shot-wound (with missile lodged in body); **die ~zwiebel, –n** bulb

stecken put, stick (in, out of, *etc* sth.); tuck (in, under sth.); pin up (hem); (*v/i*: *p/t* **steckte**/*lit* **stak** (*subj* **steckte**/*lit* **stäke**)) be (in a certain place, state, *etc*); be stuck; (key) be in the lock; **jmdm./sich** *dat* **ein Ziel ~** set s.o./oneself a task; **~ an** (*acc*) pin to; put on (finger); **~ hinter** (*dat*) be behind; **~ in** (*acc*) *also* put (money *etc*) into

[der] **Stecken, –** *esp SGer* stick

stecken–: ~bleiben* (*sep*; *sn*) get stuck; **~lassen*** (*p/part usu* **~lassen;** *sep*) leave (in a certain place); leave (key) in the lock; **das S~pferd, –e** hobby-horse; hobby

[der] **Stecker, –** *elect* plug

[der] **Steckling, –e** *hort* cutting

[der] **Steepler** ['sti:plɐ], **–** steeplechaser

[der] **Steg, –e** footbridge; jetty; (on ski pants *etc*) strap (under foot); (of spectacles, *mus*) bridge; *arch* path; **~reif (aus dem S.** impromptu; off the cuff; **aus dem S. reden** ad-lib); *in compds* impromptu ...; improvised ...

Steh– stand-up ...; **das ~auf|männchen, –** tumbler (= toy); indomitable character; **der ~kragen, –** stand-up collar; **die ~lampe, –n** standard lamp, floor lamp *US*; **die ~leiter, –n** step-ladder; **der ~platz, ⸚e** space to stand, *theat* space in the standing-room; *theat* standing-room ticket; (*pl*) standing-room; **das ~vermögen** staying-power, stamina

stehen (*p/t* **stand** (*subj* **stände, stünde**), *p/part* **gestanden**) (*see also* **gestanden**) (*sn in SGer*) stand; be (in a certain position, state, *etc*); (clock *etc*) have stopped; *coll* be finished; (+*dat*) suit; **gut/schlecht ~** be going/doing well/badly; **es steht (1:1 [eins zu eins]** *etc*) the score is (1-1 *etc*); **wie steht's?** how are things?; **wie steht es/das Spiel?** what's the score?; (**hier** *etc*) **steht ...** it says (here *etc*) ...; **es steht zu erwarten/fürchten/hoffen, daß ...** it is to be expected/feared/hoped that ...; **~ bleiben** (*cf* **stehenbleiben**) remain standing; **~ haben** have (in a certain place); **~ und fallen mit** stand or fall by; **zum Stehen bringen/kommen** bring/come to a standstill; **im Stehen** standing up

~ auf (*acc*) *coll* 'dig'; **~ auf** (*dat*) read; indicate; be at; **auf ... steht ...** the penalty for ... is ...; *gramm* ... takes ...; **auf dem Standpunkt ~, daß ...** take the view that ...

~ bei: es steht (ganz) bei ... zu ... it's (entirely) up to ... to ...

~ bis: ... steht mir bis hier (oben) *coll* I'm sick to the teeth of ...

~ für stand for

~ hinter (*dat*) come after; back, be behind

~ mit *gramm* take; **es steht gut/schlecht mit/um ...** ... is *etc* in good shape/a bad way; things look good/bad for ...; **wie steht es mit ...?** how is *etc* ...?; what about ...?

~ über (*dat*) be above

~ um (*see* **~ mit**)

~ unter (*dat*) be under (influence, direction, *etc*)

~ vor (*dat*) be faced with; be on the brink of; be about to take (examination); be approaching (completion); *coll* be stiff with

~ zu stand by; **wie ~ Sie zu ...?** what are your views on ...?; **zur Diskussion ~** be under discussion

sich gut/schlecht ~ be well/badly off; **+mit** get on well/badly with; **sich müde ~** tire oneself out with standing

stehen–: ~bleiben* (*sep*; *sn*) (*cf* **stehen bleiben** *at* **stehen**) stop; come to a standstill; (time) stand still; be left, remain; get left behind (**wo sind wir stehengeblieben?** where did we get to?); **~lassen*** (*p/part usu* **~lassen;** *sep*) leave; leave standing; leave behind; *cul* let stand (**sich** *dat* **einen Bart s.** grow a beard; **alles ~- und liegenlassen** drop everything)

stehend standing; stationary; stagnant; **~en Fußes** right away; **~e Redewendung** set phrase

[der] **Steher, –** *sp* stayer

stehlen (stiehl(s)t, *p/t* **stahl** (*subj* **stähle**), *p/part* **gestohlen**) steal (*dat* from); **sich ~ aus/in** (*acc*) steal out of/into; **... kann mir gestohlen bleiben** *coll* to hell with ...!

[die] **Steiermark** Styria

steif stiff (**vor** *dat* with); rigid (with); starched; **~ und fest** *coll* stubbornly || **~halten*** (*sep*) *coll* (**die Ohren s.** keep one's chin up)

[die] **Steife, –n** stiffness; *tech* brace
steifen stiffen; starch; (+*dat*) **den Nacken ~** back up
Steig–: der ~bügel, – stirrup; **das ~eisen, –** crampon
steigen (*p/t* **stieg,** *p/part* **gestiegen**) (*sn*) climb; rise; (horse) rear; (price *etc*) rise, increase; *coll* (party *etc*) be held; **einen Drachen ~ lassen** fly a kite; **im Steigen begriffen** rising, on the increase
~ **auf** (*acc*) climb; get on(to); rise to; **auf die Bremse ~** *coll* jam on the brakes
~ **aus** get out of; get off (bus *etc*)
~ **in** (*acc*) get in(to); get on(to) (bus *etc*); go down to (cellar); (blood) rush to (s.o.'s face, head); *coll* put on (one's clothes); *coll* sit (exam)
~ **von** get off; climb down from; dismount from
[der] **Steiger, –** *min* overseer
steigern increase; heighten, intensify; enhance; *gramm* compare; (*v/i*) bid (**um** for); **sich ~** increase; be heightened/intensified; improve one's performance, (performance) improve; **sich ~ in** (*acc*) work oneself up into
[die] **Steigerung, –en** *vbl noun*; *also* increase; intensification; enhancement; *Swiss* auction; *gramm* comparison
[die] **Steigung, –en** gradient; slope, incline
steil steep; sheer; (rise *etc*) rapid; **der S~hang, ⸚e** steep slope; *geol* escarpment; **die S~küste, –n** cliffs; **der S~paß, ⸚(ss)e** through pass
[der] **Stein, –e** stone (*also jewel, med*); *games* piece; **~ des Anstoßes** cause of annoyance; bone of contention; **einen ~ im Brett haben bei** *coll* be in (s.o.'s) good books; **mir fällt ein ~ vom Herzen** that's a load off my mind
Stein– stone ...; stony ...;
der ~adler, – golden eagle; **stein|alt** as old as the hills; **der ~bock, ⸚e** ibex; *astron*, *astrol* Capricorn; **der ~bruch, ⸚e** quarry; **der ~butt, –e** turbot; **der ~druck, –e** lithograph; lithography; **~erweichen (zum S. weinen** cry heart-rendingly); **der ~garten, ..gärten** rockery; **das ~gut** earthenware; **stein|hart** rock-hard; **der ~kauz, ⸚e** little owl; **die ~kohle, –n** coal; **der ~metz, –en** (*wk masc*) stonemason; **der ~pilz, –e** edible boletus, cep; **stein|reich** *coll* rolling in money; **das ~salz** rock salt; **der ~schlag, ⸚e** rockfall, falling rocks; **der ~wurf, ⸚e** throwing of a stone; stone's throw; **die ~zeit** the Stone Age; **s~zeitlich** Stone Age
steinern stone; stony, (heart) of stone
steinig stony
steinigen stone
[der] **Steirer, –, steirisch** Styrian
[der] **Steiß, –e** coccyx; *coll* backside; **das ~bein, –e** coccyx; **die ~geburt, –en** breech birth
Stell–: das ~dich|ein (*gen* –(s)), –(s) *dated* rendezvous; **s~vertretend** deputy; vice–; acting; vicarious (**s. für** on behalf of); **der ~vertreter, –** deputy; proxy; **~vertretung (die S. übernehmen für** deputize for); **das ~werk, –e** signal-box, signal tower *US*
[die] **Stellage** [–ʒə], **–n** rack
[die] **Stelle, –n** place (*in var senses*); spot; patch; passage (of text, *also mus*); job; authority (= official body); *math, comput* digit; *math* (decimal) place; **–stelle** ... bureau; ... office; **freie ~** vacancy
in prepositional phrases:
an ~ (+*gen*) in place of; **an dieser ~** here; **an Ihrer ~** in your place, if I were you; **an (erster** *etc*) **~** in the (first *etc*) place; in (first *etc*) position; **an erster ~ stehen** come first; **an jmds. ~ treten/an die ~ treten von** take s.o.'s place/the place of
auf der ~ immediately; instantaneously; **auf der ~ treten** mark time; make no progress
von: nicht von der ~ bekommen be unable to move; **nicht von der ~ kommen** be unable to move; make no progress
zur ~ there; on the spot
stellen (*see also* **gestellt**) put; place; stand; set (**auf** *acc* at; for); provide (labour *etc*), produce (witness); make (application, diagnosis, *etc*); catch; *parl etc* move; (+*dat*) put (question) to; set (s.o. deadline, task, *etc*); cast (s.o.'s horoscope); **~ vor** (*acc*) confront with; **kalt/warm ~** keep (sth.) cool/warm; **höher/niedriger ~,** *rad etc* **lauter/leiser ~** turn up/down; **gut/schlecht gestellt** well/badly off; **auf sich (selbst) gestellt sein** have to fend for oneself
sich ~ stand (in a certain position); give oneself up; *mil* report for military service; (*with adj*) pretend to be; (+*dat*) give oneself up to; agree to meet (press); face (up to); **sich ~ gegen** oppose; **sich ~ hinter** (*acc*) back; **sich gut ~ mit** get on good terms with; **sich ~ vor** (*acc*) protect
Stellen–: das ~angebot, –e job offer; **s~los** unemployed, jobless; **der ~markt** job market; **der ~nachweis, –e = die ~vermittlung, –en** job centre; **s~weise** in places; **der ~wert, –e** significance; standing; rating; *comput, math* place value
stellig *Aust*: **~ machen** trace; **–stellig** –figure; –place
[die] **Stellung, –en** position (*also* = post, *mil*); **~ nehmen +für/gegen** come out in favour of/against; **+zu** comment on; **in ~ bringen** bring into position || **die ~nahme, –n** comment (**zu** on); statement (on); **der**

~s|krieg, –e trench warfare; s~s|los unemployed

Stelz–: der ~fuß, ¨–e peg-leg (*also* = person)

die **Stelze, –n** stilt; (*pl*) *coll* 'pins'

stelzen (*see also* **gestelzt**) (*sn*) stalk

Stemm–: der ~bogen, –/..bögen *ski* stem-turn; **das ~eisen, –** chisel

stemmen lift (weight) above one's head; chisel; (*v/i*) *ski* stem; **~ auf** (*acc*) prop (elbows) on; **~ gegen** press (foot *etc*) against; **die Arme in die Seite(n) ~** place one's hands on one's hips; **die Arme in die Seite(n) gestemmt** with arms akimbo; **sich ~ gegen** apply one's weight against; set one's face against

der **Stempel, –** (rubber-)stamp; die; stamp (= mark stamped), (on gold, silver) hallmark, *post* postmark; *min* prop; *bot* pistil; (+*dat*) **seinen ~ aufdrücken** leave one's/its mark on || **das ~geld, –er** *coll* dole; **das ~kissen, –** ink-pad

stempeln stamp; hallmark; *post* frank; **~ zu** brand (as); **~ gehen** *coll* be/go on the dole

der **Stengel, –** stalk, stem

das **Stenogramm, –e** shorthand text

der **Stenograph, –en** (*wk masc*) shorthand writer

die **Stenographie** shorthand

stenographieren take down in shorthand; (*v/i*) do shorthand

die **Stenotypistin, –nen** shorthand typist

die **Stentor|stimme, –n** stentorian voice

der **Step** [ʃtɛp, st–], **–s = der ~tanz, ¨–e** tap-dance; **der ~tänzer, –** tap-dancer

Stephan ['ʃtɛfan] Stephen

Stepp–: die ~decke, –n quilt; **der ~stich, –e** back-stitch

die **Steppe, –n** steppe

steppen[1] [ʃt–, st–] tap-dance

steppen[2] machine-stitch; quilt

Steppen– steppe ...; **der ~wolf, ¨–e** coyote

Sterbe– ... of death; death ...; **das ~bett, –en** deathbed; **der ~fall, ¨–e** death; **das ~geld, –er** funeral allowance (paid by insurance company); **die ~hilfe, –n** euthanasia; = **~geld; die ~sakramente** *pl* last rites; **die ~urkunde, –n** death-certificate

sterben (stirb(s)t, *p/t* **starb** (*subj* **stürbe**), *p/part* **gestorben)** (*sn*) die **(an** *dat* of: illness *etc*, from: wound); **~ vor** (*dat*) die of (hunger, grief, *coll* shame, *etc*); **als (Held** *etc*) **~** die (a hero *etc*); **eines (natürlichen** *etc*) **Todes ~** die a (natural *etc*) death; **im Sterben liegen** be dying; **zum Sterben langweilig** *coll* deadly boring || **sterbens|krank** dangerously ill; **sterbens|langweilig** *coll* deadly boring; **Sterbens|wörtchen** *coll* **(kein S.** not a word)

sterblich mortal; (*adv*) *coll* awfully; desperately (in love); **~e Hülle** mortal remains; **der/die Sterbliche** (*decl as adj*) mortal

die **Sterblichkeit** mortality; **die ~s|ziffer, –n** death-rate

Stereo– [ʃt–, st–] stereo ...; **die ~anlage, –n** stereo system; **die ~box, –en** stereo speaker

stereophon stereophonic

stereotyp stereotyped; (smile) forced

steril sterile

die **Sterilisation, –en** sterilization

sterilisieren sterilize

die **Sterilität** sterility

der **Stern, –e** star; **das ~bild, –er** *astron* constellation; *astrol* sign of the zodiac; **der ~deuter, –** astrologer; **die ~deutung** astrology; **die ~fahrt, –en** rally (in which participants, starting from different points, converge on one location); **stern|hagel|voll** *coll* blind drunk; **s~hell** starlit; **die ~kunde** astronomy; **der ~marsch, ¨–e** *esp pol* (*march in which participants, starting from different points, converge on one location*); **die ~schnuppe, –n** shooting-star; **die ~stunde, –n** great moment; **die ~warte, –n** observatory

das **Sternchen, –** little star; *cin* starlet; *print* asterisk

Sternen– starry ...; **das ~banner** the Stars and Stripes

der **Sterz, –e** plough-handle; *ornith* tail

stet constant

das **Stethoskop** [ʃt–, st–], **–e** stethoscope

stetig steady, constant

stets [–eː–] always

Stettin Szczecin, *hist* Stettin

das **Steuer, –** *mot* steering-wheel; *naut* helm; *aer* controls; **am ~** at the wheel/*naut* helm/*aer* controls

die **Steuer, –n** tax

Steuer– tax ...; *comput*, *tech* control ...

der ~berater, – tax consultant; accountant; **das ~bord** starboard; **s~bord(s)** to starboard; **die ~erklärung, –en** income-tax return; **s~frei** tax-free; **die ~hinterziehung, –en** tax evasion; **der ~knüppel, –** control stick; **der ~mann, ¨–er/..leute** helmsman; *row* cox; **das ~paradies, –e** tax haven; **s~pflichtig** taxable; liable to pay tax; **das ~pult, –e** control panel; **das ~rad, ¨–er** (steering-)wheel; **die ~ver|anlagung, –en** tax assessment; **das ~wesen** tax system; **der ~zahler, –** taxpayer

steuerlich tax; (*adv*) for taxation purposes; from the tax point of view

steuern steer, *mot rac* drive, *aer* pilot; *econ*, *tech*, *etc* control; (*v/i*, +*dat*) curb; **~ nach** (*sn*) head for

die **Steuerung, –en** *vbl noun*; *also* steering (mechanism); *aer*, *mot* controls; *comput* control

[der] **Steven, –** *naut* stem; stern

[der] **Steward** ['stju:ɐt], **–s** *aer, naut* steward

[die] **Stewardeß** ['stju:ɐ–, *also* –'dɛs], **–(ss)en** *aer, naut* stewardess

[das] **StGB** [ɛste:ge:'be:] = **Strafgesetzbuch**

stibitzen *coll* 'pinch'

stich *imp sing of* **stechen**

[der] **Stich, –e** prick; stab; stab-wound; (of insect) sting; bite; shooting pain; *needlew* stitch; *art* engraving; *cards* trick; **es gab mir einen ~ (ins Herz)** I was cut to the quick; **einen ~ haben** be slightly off; *coll* have a screw loose; **einen ~ ins (Grüne** *etc*) **haben** have a touch of (green *etc*); **~ halten** hold water; **einen ~ machen** take a trick; **im ~ lassen** abandon (thing); leave in the lurch, let down, (memory) fail || **die ~flamme, –n** jet of flame; **s~halten*** (*sep*: **es hält ~,** *p/part* **s~gehalten)** *Aust* hold water; **s~haltig,** *Aust* **s~hältig** sound (**s. sein** hold water); **die ~probe, –n** random sample; spot check; **der ~tag, –e** appointed day/date; **die ~wahl, –en** final ballot; **das ~wort, ⸚er** word (given in dictionary); (*pl, referring to number*) entries; (*pl* **–e**) cue (*also theat*); (*usu pl*) key word

[der] **Stichel, –** graver

[die] **Stichelei, –en** sewing (with small stitches); gibing; gibe

sticheln sew (with small stitches); gibe (**gegen** at)

[der] **Stichling, –e** stickleback

stich(s)t (*2nd,*) *3rd sing pres of* **stechen**

Stick– embroidery ...; **der ~stoff** nitrogen; **s~stoff|haltig** nitrogenous

sticken (*also v/i*) embroider

[die] **Stickerei, –en** embroidery

stickig stuffy

stieben (*p/t* **stob/stiebte** (*subj* **stöbe/stiebte**), *p/part* **gestoben/gestiebt**) (*also sn*) (sparks) fly; (snow *etc*) fly about; (*sn*) flee; scatter

Stief– step–; **das ~kind, –er** stepchild; poor relation; **das ~mütterchen, –** pansy; **s~mütterlich** (**s. behandeln** treat unkindly; neglect)

[der] **Stiefel, –** boot

[die] **Stiefelette, –n** bootee

stiefeln (*see also* **gestiefelt**) (*sn*) *coll* hoof it

stieg *p/t of* **steigen**

[die] **Stiege, –n** narrow stairs, *SGer* stairs; crate; **das ~n|haus, ⸚er** *SGer* staircase

[der] **Stieglitz** [–g–], **–e** goldfinch

stiehl *imp sing,* **stiehl(s)t** (*2nd,*) *3rd sing pres of* **stehlen**

[der] **Stiel, –e** handle; stem (of glass); *bot* stalk; **~augen** *coll* (**S. machen** goggle)

stier (glance) vacant; *Aust coll* broke

[der] **Stier, –e** bull; *astron, astrol* Taurus; **der ~kampf, ⸚e** bullfight; **der ~kämpfer, –** bullfighter

stieren stare (vacantly) (**auf** *acc* at)

[der] **Stiesel, –** *coll* oaf

stieß *p/t of* **stoßen**

[das] **Stift, –e** (religious) foundation; seminary

[der] **Stift**[1], **–e** pencil; crayon; tack; pin; peg

[der] **Stift**[2], **–e** *coll* apprentice

stiften donate; found; cause; make (peace); **~gehen*** (*sep; sn*) *coll* make oneself scarce

[der] **Stifter, –** donor; founder

[die] **Stiftung, –en** *vbl noun*; *also* foundation; donation

[das] **Stigma** [ʃt–, st–], **–ta/Stigmen** stigma

[der] **Stil, –e** style; **im großen ~ leben** live in style

Stil– ... of style; stylistic ...; **die ~blüte, –n** howler; **der ~bruch, ⸚e** stylistic inconsistency; **das ~gefühl** sense of style; **die ~kunde** stylistics; **s~los** lacking in style; **das ~mittel, –** stylistic device; **die ~möbel** *pl* period furniture; **die ~richtung, –en** style; **s~voll** stylish

[das] **Stilett, –e** stiletto

stilisieren stylize

[der] **Stilist, –en** (*wk masc*) stylist

[die] **Stilistik** [–ɪk], **–en** stylistics; handbook on style

stilistisch stylistic

still quiet; silent; still; (*adv*: hold, lie, *etc*) still; **der S~e Ozean** the Pacific Ocean; **es ist ~ geworden um ...** you don't hear anything about ... any more; **im ~en** secretly; inwardly || **das Stilleben, –** still life; **stillegen** (*sep*) close down; **die Stillegung, –en** closure; **das S~geld, –er** *EGer* nursing mothers' allowance; **~halten*** (*sep*) keep still; not object; **stilliegen*** (*sep*) lie idle; **~schweigen*** (*sep*) be silent; keep quiet (about sth.); **das S~schweigen** silence; **~schweigend** silent; tacit; (*adv*) tacitly; in silence (**s. dulden** connive at); **~sitzen*** (*sep*) sit still; **der S~stand** standstill (**zum S. bringen/kommen** bring/come to a standstill; stop); **~stehen*** (*sep*) stop; lie idle; be at a standstill, (time) stand still; *mil* stand to attention (**~gestanden!** attention!); **~vergnügt** quietly content

[die] **Stille** quiet; silence; stillness; **in aller ~** quietly

stillen breast-feed; quench; satisfy (hunger, curiosity, *etc*); staunch (blood); relieve (pain)

Stimm– vocal ...; *pol* voting ...; **die ~abgabe, –n** voting, casting of one's vote; **die ~bänder** *pl* vocal cords; **s~berechtigt** entitled to vote; **die ~bildung** voice production/training; **der ~bruch** (= **~wechsel**); **der ~bürger, –** *Swiss* citizen entitled to vote; **die ~enthaltung, –en** abstention; **die ~gabel, –n** tuning-fork; **s~gewaltig** with a powerful voice; **die ~lage, –n** *mus* register; **s~los** unvoiced;

das ~recht (right to) vote; **der ~wechsel, –** breaking of the voice (**er ist im S.** his voice is breaking); **der ~zettel, –** ballot-paper

die **Stimme, –n** voice; *pol* vote; *mus* part; **gut bei ~** in good voice; **mit (leiser** *etc*) **~** in a (low *etc*) voice

stimmen make (s.o.) (feel) (sad *etc*); *mus* tune; (*v/i* thing) be right; **nicht ~** be wrong; **~ für/gegen** vote for/against; **(das) stimmt!** that's right!; **stimmt das?** is that so?; **da stimmt etwas nicht** there's something wrong here; **bei dir stimmt's wohl nicht?** you must be crazy!; **(fröhlich** *etc*) **gestimmt** in a (cheerful *etc*) mood

Stimmen– ... of votes; **das ~gewirr** babble of voices; **die ~mehrheit** majority

stimmhaft voiced

–stimmig -part, for ... voices

stimmlich vocal

die **Stimmung, –en** atmosphere; mood; (public) sentiment; *mus* pitch; tuning; **~ machen für/gegen** whip up support for/feeling against; **in ~ kommen** liven up; **in ~ sein** be in good spirits || **die ~s|kanone, –n** *coll* life and soul of the party; **die ~s|mache** *coll* propaganda; **s~s|voll** full of atmosphere

das **Stimulans, –(an)zien** [–ĭən] stimulant

stimulieren stimulate

Stink–: die ~bombe, –n stink-bomb; **stink|faul** *coll* bone-idle; **stink|langweilig** *coll* as dull as ditchwater; **die ~laune, –n** *coll* foul mood; **stink|reich** *coll* stinking rich; **das ~tier, –e** skunk; **stink|vornehm** *coll* frightfully posh; **die ~wut** *coll* filthy temper

stinken (*p/t* **stank** (*subj* **stänke**), *p/part* **gestunken**) stink (**nach** of); *coll* be fishy; **... stinkt mir** *coll* I'm sick of ...; **~d faul** *coll* bone-idle

stinkig *coll* stinking

der **Stipendiat, –en** (*wk masc*) recipient of a grant

das **Stipendium, –(i)en** (student) grant

Stipp–: die ~visite, –n *coll* flying visit

stippen *NGer*: **~ in** (*acc*) dip into

stirb *imp sing*, **stirb(s)t** (*2nd*,) *3rd sing pres of* **sterben**

die **Stirn, –en** forehead; (*+dat*) **die ~ bieten** stand up to; **die ~ haben zu ...** have the impudence to ... || **das ~band, ⸚er** headband; **die ~falte, –n** wrinkle (on forehead); **das ~runzeln** frown; **s~runzelnd** with a frown; **die ~seite, –n** front

–stirnig -browed

stob (stöbe) *p/t* (*subj*) *of* **stieben**

stöbern: ~ in (*dat*) rummage in (**nach** for)

stochern: ~ in (*dat*) pick at; poke about in; pick (teeth)

der **Stock¹**, (*only following num*) – storey, floor; **im (ersten** *etc*) **~** on the (first *etc*/second *etc US*) floor

der **Stock²**, **⸚e** stick; cane; stump (with roots); hive; *hist* stocks; *SGer* offertory-box; *geol* massif; **am ~ gehen** walk with a stick; *coll* be hard up/in bad shape

Stock– (Englishman *etc*) through and through; **(stock–)** thoroughly ...; **stock|betrunken** dead drunk; **stock|blind** as blind as a bat; **stock|dunkel** pitch-dark; **die ~ente, –n** mallard; **stock|finster** pitch-dark; **der ~fisch, –e** dried cod *etc*; *coll* dry old stick; **der ~fleck, –e(n)** spot of mildew; fox-mark; **der ~schnupfen** persistent cold; **stock|steif** stiff as a poker; **stock|taub** stone-deaf; **das ~werk, –e** (= **Stock¹**)

der **Stöckel|schuh, –e** stiletto-heeled shoe, spike-heeled shoe *US*

stocken falter; (traffic *etc*) be held up; (conversation) flag; (heart) miss a beat; develop fox-marks; (*also sn*) *SGer* curdle; **ins Stocken geraten/kommen** come to a standstill; begin to flag

Stockholm [ʃt–, *also* ˈʃtɔk–] Stockholm

–stöckig -storey(ed)

die **Stockung, –en** *vbl noun*; *also* hold-up; congestion

der **Stoff, –e** material, fabric; subject-matter; *chem* substance; *phys* matter; *coll* 'dope'; **die ~bahn, –en** length of material; **der ~rest, –e** *text* remnant; **das ~tier, –e** soft toy; **der ~wechsel** metabolism; **~wechsel–** metabolic ...

der **Stoffel, –** *coll* oaf

stoff(e)lig *coll* oafish

stofflich as regards the subject-matter

stöhnen groan, moan

der **Stoiker** [ˈʃtoːi–, st–], **–, stoisch** stoic; *philos* Stoic

der **Stoizismus** [ʃtoi–, st–] stoicism; *philos* Stoicism

die **Stola** [ʃt–, st–], **–(l)en** stole

der **Stollen, –** stud (on boot); *min* gallery; *cul* fruit loaf (eaten at Christmas)

Stolper–: der ~draht, ⸚e trip-wire; **der ~stein, –e** stumbling-block

stolpern (*sn*) stumble, trip (**über** *acc* over)

stolz proud (**auf** *acc* of); imposing

der **Stolz** pride (**auf** *acc* in); **seinen ~ dareinsetzen zu ...** make it a point of honour to ...; **jmds. ganzer ~ sein** be s.o.'s pride and joy

stolzieren (*sn*) strut

Stopf– darning ...

stopfen stuff; fill; plug; darn; *mus* mute; (*v/i*) constipate; *coll* stuff oneself; **~ in** (*acc*) stuff into; (*+dat*) **den Mund ~** shut up; **gestopft voll** *coll* jam-packed

der **Stopp, –s** stop; ban (**für** on); (wage *etc*) freeze; **der ~ball, ⸚e** dropshot; **das ~licht, –er** stop-light; **das ~schild, –er** stop sign; **die ~straße, –n** minor road, stop street *US*; **die ~uhr, –en** stop-watch

die **Stoppel, –n** stubble; **der ~bart, ⸚e** stubbly

beard, stubble; **der ~zieher, -** *Aust* corkscrew

stoppelig stubbly

stoppen stop, halt; *sp* time; *sp* trap (ball); (*v/i*) stop, pull up

der **Stopper, -** timekeeper; *footb* centre-half

der **Stöpsel, -** plug; stopper; *coll* little fellow

der **Stör, -e** sturgeon

Stör- disruptive ...; **die ~aktion, -en** (organized) disruption; **der ~fall, ⸚e** nuclear accident; **das ~geräusch, -e** *rad*, *TV* interference; **der ~sender, -** jamming transmitter

der **Storch, ⸚e** stork

storchen (*sn*) *joc* stride stiffly

der **Store** [stoːɐ], **-s** net curtain

stören (*see also* **gestört**) disturb; disrupt; bother; *rad* jam; (*v/i*) be disturbing; **stört es (Sie), wenn ich ...?** do you mind if I ...?; **sich ~ an** (*dat*) be bothered by; **~d** disturbing

der **Stören|fried, -e** troublemaker

stornieren *comm* cancel; reverse

der **Storno, -(n)i** (*also* **das**) *comm* cancellation; reversal

störrisch stubborn

die **Störung, -en** disturbance; disruption; hold-up; interruption; *tech* fault, malfunction; *rad* interference; jamming; *meteor* disturbance; *med* disorder; **s~s|frei** trouble-free; *rad* free from interference

die **Story** ['stɔːri], **-s** story

der **Stoß** [-oː-], **⸚e** push; punch; kick; nudge, dig; butt; thrust, stab; blow (**in** *acc* on: trumpet *etc*); impact; shock; bump, jolt; pile (of sth.); *mil* thrust; *med* intensive course of drugs; *fenc* thrust, *athl* put, *swim* stroke || **der ~dämpfer, -** shock-absorber; **s~fest** shock-proof; **das ~gebet, -e** quick prayer; **die ~kraft, ⸚e** impact; **der ~seufzer, -** deep sigh; **die ~stange, -n** bumper (**S. an S.** bumper to bumper); **der ~trupp, -s** raiding party; **der ~verkehr** rush-hour traffic; **s~weise** by fits and starts, spasmodically; in piles; **der ~zahn, ⸚e** tusk; **die ~zeit, -en** rush-hour; peak period

der **Stößel, -** pestle; *mech* tappet

stoßen (*2nd/3rd sing pres* **stößt**, *p/t* **stieß**, *p/part* **gestoßen**) push; punch; kick; nudge, dig; butt; thrust; *cul* pound (with pestle); *athl* put (shot); (*v/i*) butt; **sich** *dat* **den Kopf ~** bump one's head (**an** *dat* on)

~ an (*acc*) adjoin; (*sn*) bump into

~ auf (*acc*) (*sn*) come across; meet with, come up against; **auf Erdöl ~** strike oil

~ gegen (*sn*) bump into

von sich ~ push away; reject

~ zu (*sn*) join; join up with

sich ~ bump oneself; **sich ~ an** (*dat*) bump oneself on; bump one's ...; take exception to

stottern (*also v/i*) stutter; *mot coll* splutter; **auf Stottern** *coll* on the never-never/the cuff *US*

das **Stövchen, -** tea/coffee-pot warmer

die **StPO** [ɛsteːpeː'ʔoː] = **Strafprozeßordnung**

Str. (= **Straße**) St.

stracks immediately

Straf- ... of punishment/a sentence; penal ...; criminal ...; punitive ...; *sp* penalty ...;

die ~anstalt, -en prison; **der ~antrag, ⸚e** *leg* action; sentence proposed by the state prosecutor; **die ~arbeit, -en** *educ* imposition; **der ~aufschub, ⸚e** reprieve; **die ~aussetzung, -en** suspension of sentence (**bedingte S.** suspended sentence); **der/die ~entlassene** (*decl as adj*) released prisoner; **der ~erlaß, ⸚(ss)e** remission (of sentence); **s~fällig** (**s. werden** commit a criminal offence); **s~frei** (**s. ausgehen** get off scot-free); **die ~freiheit** immunity from prosecution; **der/die ~gefangene** (*decl as adj*) prisoner; **das ~gericht, -e** criminal court; (divine) judgement; **das ~gesetz|buch, ⸚er** penal code; **die ~kammer, -n** division of court dealing with criminal cases; **die ~kolonie, -n** penal settlement; **das ~mandat, -e** ticket (for traffic offence); **s~mildernd** mitigating; **das ~porto** postage due; **die ~predigt, -en** severe lecture ((*+dat*) **eine S. halten** give (s.o.) a severe lecture); **der ~prozeß, -(ss)e** criminal proceedings; **die ~prozeß|ordnung** code of criminal procedure; **der ~raum, ⸚e** penalty area; **das ~recht** criminal law; **s~rechtlich** criminal; (problem *etc*) of criminal law (**s. verfolgen** prosecute); **das ~register, -** criminal records; **die ~sache, -n** criminal case; **der ~stoß, ⸚e** *footb* penalty (kick); *hock* penalty (shot); **die ~tat, -en** criminal offence; **das ~verfahren, -** criminal proceedings; **s~versetzen** (*only infin and p/part* **s~versetzt**) transfer for disciplinary reasons; **der ~verteidiger, -** defence counsel; **der ~vollzug** execution of a sentence; **s~weise** as a punishment; **der ~zettel, -** *coll* ticket (for traffic offence)

strafbar punishable; **... ist ~** ... is an offence; **sich ~ machen** commit an offence

die **Strafe, -n** punishment; *leg* penalty; fine; sentence; *sp* penalty; **... ist eine ~** *coll* ... is a pain in the neck; **bei ~** (prohibit) by law; **+von** under penalty of; **zur ~** as a punishment

strafen punish

straff taut; tight; (breasts) firm; (bearing) upright; (organization) tight, (discipline) strict; concise; **~ anziehen** tighten

straffen tighten; tighten up (organization

etc); **sich** ~ straighten oneself; tighten
sträflich criminal (= unpardonable)
der **Sträfling, –e** convict
der **Strahl, –en** ray (*also phys*); beam; jet; *in compds aer* jet ...; **das ~trieb|werk, –e** jet engine
strahlen shine; gleam; (stove *etc*) radiate warmth; beam; be radiant (**vor** *dat* with); *phys* radiate; **~d** radiant; brilliant; shining; beaming
Strahlen– radiation ...; ray ...; **die ~behandlung, –en** radiotherapy; **das ~bündel, –** pencil of rays; **s~förmig** radial; **die ~krankheit** radiation sickness; **die ~therapie** radiotherapy
–strahlig -jet
die **Strahlung, –en** radiation; **die ~s|wärme** radiant heat
die **Strähne, –n** strand (of hair)
strähnig in strands
stramm tight; taut; upright, erect; strapping; sturdy; *coll* hard, strenuous; **S~er Max** (*open sandwich with boiled ham and fried egg*) || **~stehen*** (*sep*) stand to attention; **~ziehen*** (*sep*) *coll* tighten ((+*dat*) **die Hosen s.** give (child) a spanking)
das **Strampel|höschen, –** rompers
strampeln (baby) kick (and wave its arms about); *coll* put one's back into it; (*sn*) *coll* pedal
der **Strand, ⸚e** beach; shore; **am ~** on the beach || **das ~bad, ⸚er** open-air swimming-pool (by lake or river); bathing beach; **das ~gut** flotsam and jetsam; **der ~korb, ⸚e** wicker beach chair; **der ~läufer, –** sandpiper
stranden (*sn*) run aground, be stranded; fail; **gestrandet** stranded
der **Strang, ⸚e** rope; hank, skein; *rail* track; *anat* bundle; *liter* strand; **wenn alle Stränge reißen** *coll* if the worst comes to the worst; **an einem ~ ziehen** pull together; **über die Stränge schlagen** *coll* kick over the traces
strangulieren strangle
strapaz–: ~fähig *Aust* = **strapazierfähig**
die **Strapaze, –n** (physical) strain
strapazier–: ~fähig hard-wearing
strapazieren be hard on (clothing *etc*); strain; try (patience *etc*); take a lot out of
strapaziös wearing
der **Straps, –e** suspender, garter *US*; suspender belt, garter belt *US*
straß|auf: ~, straßab all over the town
Straßburg [-aː-] Strasbourg
die **Straße, –n** road; street; (*in geographical names*) Strait(s); **auf der ~** in the street; **auf die ~ setzen** *coll* turn out; sack || **der ~n|anzug, ⸚e** lounge-suit, business suit *US*; **die ~n|arbeiten** *pl* road works/work *US*; **die ~n|bahn, –en** tram, streetcar *US*; tramway, streetcar line *US*; **das ~n|bild, –er** street scene; **die ~n|ecke, –n** street corner; **der ~n|feger, –** roadsweeper; **die ~n|karte, –n** road-map; **der ~n|kehrer, –** roadsweeper; **die ~n|lage** road-holding; **das ~n|mädchen, –** street-walker; **der ~n|raub** mugging; **die ~n|schäden** *pl* damage to the road; **die ~n|seite, –n** side of the road/street; **die ~n|sperre, –n** road-block; **die ~n|verkehrs|ordnung** traffic regulations; **die ~n|verkehrs-Zulassungs-Ordnung** motor vehicle licensing regulations; **der ~n|zustand** road conditions
der **Stratege, –n** (*wk masc*) strategist
die **Strategie, –(ie)n** strategy
strategisch strategic
die **Stratosphäre** stratosphere
stratosphärisch stratospheric
sträuben ruffle up; **sich ~** (hair) stand on end; (animal's fur, hair) bristle; **sich ~ gegen** resist; **sich ~ zu ...** jib at (+*ger*)
der **Strauch, ⸚er** shrub, bush; **das ~werk** shrubbery
straucheln (*sn*) trip up; go astray
der **Strauß**[1], **–e** ostrich
der **Strauß**[2], **⸚e** bunch (of flowers); bouquet
Straußen– ostrich ...
Strawinski [ʃt-, st-] Stravinsky
die **Strebe, –n** brace, strut; **der ~bogen, –** flying buttress; **der ~pfeiler, –** buttress
streben: ~ nach strive after; aspire to; (plant) seek; **~ zu** (plant) seek; (*sn*) make for; push towards; **in die Höhe ~** (*sn*) soar aloft; **danach ~ zu ...** strive/aspire to ...; **das Streben** striving; endeavour
der **Streber, –** pusher; *educ* swot, grind *US*
strebsam keen to get ahead
Streck–: der ~muskel, –n extensor (muscle); **der ~verband, ⸚e** *med* traction bandage
die **Strecke, –n** stretch; distance (*also sp*); route; passage (of book); *rail* section (of line); *min* gallery; *math* segment of line; **auf der ~ bleiben** not make it; fall by the wayside; **zur ~ bringen** hunt down; *hunt* bag, kill
strecken (*see also* **gestreckt**) stretch; crane (one's neck); stick (head *etc*) (out of, through, *etc* sth.); eke out; make (sth.) go further; thin (liquid); *comput* unwind; **die Waffen ~** surrender; **von sich ~** stretch out (one's legs); **zu Boden ~** floor; **sich ~** stretch (oneself)
Strecken–: die ~führung, –en route; **das ~netz, –e** *aer, rail* network (of routes); **der ~wärter, –** linesman, trackwalker *US*; **s~weise** in places
der **Streich, –e** blow; prank; (+*dat*) **einen ~ spielen** play a trick/(memory) play tricks on
Streich– *mus* string ...; **s~fertig** ready to apply/spread; **das ~holz, ⸚er** match; **die ~holz|schachtel, –n** matchbox; **das**

~**instrument, –e** stringed instrument; (*pl*) strings; **der ~käse, –** cheese spread; **die ~musik** music for strings

streicheln stroke; caress

streichen (*p/t* **strich,** *p/part* **gestrichen**) stroke; spread (jam *etc*); paint; cross out, delete; cancel; *mus* play (violin); **~ aus** delete from, cross off; **~ über** (*acc*) (*sn*) (bird, wind) sweep across; **mit der Hand ~ über** (*acc*) stroke; **~ um** (*sn*) prowl around; **sich ~ lassen** spread; **gestrichen** *also* (spoonful) level; **„frisch gestrichen!"** 'wet paint'; **gestrichen voll** full to the brim

^die^ **Streichung, –en** *vbl noun*; *also* deletion; cut; cancellation

Streif–: das ~band, ̈–er wrapper; **die ~band|zeitung, –en** mailed newspaper; **~licht (ein S./~lichter werfen auf** (*acc*) throw light on); **der ~schuß, ̈–(ss)e** grazing shot; **der ~zug, ̈–e** ramble; brief survey **(durch** of)

^die^ **Streife, –n** patrol

streifen (*see also* **gestreift**) touch (lightly), brush against; (car) scrape, (bullet) graze; touch on; (*sn*) wander, roam; **~ an** (*acc*) verge on; **mit einem Blick ~** glance at; **~ über** (*acc*) slip over; **von der Hand/den Beinen ~** slip off

^der^ **Streifen, –** strip; stripe; streak; tape; *cin coll* film, movie; **weißer ~** *mot* white line || **der ~dienst** patrol duty; **der ~locher, –** tape punch; **das ~muster, –** striped pattern; **der ~wagen, –** patrol-car

streifig streaky

^der^ **Streik, –s** strike; **wilder ~** wildcat strike; **in den ~ treten** go on strike || **der ~brecher, –** strike-breaker; **das ~geld** strike pay; **der ~posten, –** picket; **das ~recht** right to strike

streiken (be/go on) strike; *coll* go on strike (= refuse); *coll* conk out

^der^ **Streikende** (*fem* **die ~**) (*decl as adj*) striker

^der^ **Streit, –e** quarrel; argument; dispute; **~ haben** quarrel; **im ~ liegen mit** be at loggerheads with; **in ~ geraten** fall out || **die ~axt, ̈–e** battle-axe; **der ~fall, ̈–e** dispute; **die ~frage, –n** controversial question, point at issue; **das ~gespräch, –e** debate; disputation; **der ~hahn, ̈–e** *coll* = **der ~hammel, –** *coll* squabbler; **die ~kräfte** *pl* (armed) forces; **die ~lust** pugnacity; **s~lustig** pugnacious; **die ~macht, ̈–e** forces; **der ~punkt, –e** point at issue; **das ~roß, –(ss)e** warhorse; **die ~schrift, –en** polemical pamphlet; **die ~sucht** quarrelsomeness; **s~süchtig** quarrelsome

streitbar contentious; *arch* valiant

streiten (*p/t* **stritt,** *p/part* **gestritten**) quarrel; argue; **~ für/gegen** fight for/against; **sich ~** quarrel; argue; **darüber läßt sich ~** it's a debatable point

^die^ **Streiterei, –en** (continual) quarrelling

streitig: (+*dat*) **~ machen** dispute (s.o.'s right *etc*); (+*dat*) **den Rang ~ machen** challenge (s.o.'s) position

^die^ **Streitigkeiten** *pl* quarrels

streng strict; severe; stern; stringent; austere; (taste) sharp; **~ geheim** top secret || **~genommen** strictly speaking; **~gläubig** (Catholic *etc*) strict

^die^ **Strenge** strictness; severity; sternness; stringency; austerity; sharpness

strengstens strictly

^der^ **Streß** [ʃt–, st–] (*gen* **..sses**) *med* stress

^die^ **Streu** bed of straw; *agr* litter; **das ~gut** grit (for roads); **der ~zucker** granulated sugar

streuen strew; scatter (*also phys*); spread; sprinkle; grit *or* salt (road)

^der^ **Streuer, –** pepper-pot; salt-cellar

streunen (*also sn*) roam about; **~d** stray

^die^ **Streusel** *pl* crumble topping; **der ~kuchen, –** (*type of cake baked with a crumble topping*)

^die^ **Streuung, –en** *vbl noun*; *phys* scattering; *stats* scatter, dispersion

strich *p/t of* **streichen**

^der^ **Strich, –e** stroke; line; dash; tract (of land); (compass) point; *mus* bowing; *text* nap; **auf den ~ gehen** *coll* walk the streets; **gegen den ~** (brush) the wrong way; **es geht mir gegen den ~** *coll* it goes against the grain; **nach ~ und Faden** *coll* good and proper; **einen ~ machen unter** (*acc*) forget (the past *etc*); (+*dat*) **einen ~ durch die Rechnung machen** *coll* upset (s.o.'s) plans || **der ~code, –s** bar code; **der ~junge, –n** (*wk masc*) *coll* male prostitute; **das ~mädchen, –** *coll* street-walker; **das ~männchen, –** matchstick man; **der ~punkt, –e** semicolon; **der ~regen, –** local shower; **s~weise** *esp meteor* in some areas

stricheln, *Aust* **strichlieren** sketch in; hatch; **gestrichelt** (line) broken

^der^ **Strick, –e** rope; cord; *joc* young rascal; **wenn alle ~e reißen** *coll* if the worst comes to the worst; (+*dat*) **einen ~ drehen aus** use against

Strick– knitting ...; knitted ...; **die ~arbeit, –en** knitting; **die ~jacke, –n** cardigan; **die ~leiter, –n** rope-ladder; **die ~nadel, –n** knitting-needle; **die ~waren** *pl* knitwear; **das ~zeug** knitting

stricken (*also v/i*) knit

^der^ **Striegel, –** currycomb

striegeln groom, curry

^der^ **Striemen, –** weal

strikt strict

^der^ **Strip** [strɪp, ʃt–], **–s** *coll* strip

^die^ **Strippe, –n** *coll* string; cord; phone

strippen [st–, ʃt–] *coll* do a striptease, strip

^die^ **Stripperin, –nen** *coll* stripper

der **Striptease** ['strɪptiːs, ʃt–] (*gen* –) (*also* **das**) striptease; **die ~tänzerin, –nen** stripper

stritt *p/t of* **streiten**

strittig at issue; contentious

das **Stroh** straw; **leeres ~ dreschen** *coll* talk a lot of hot air || **stroh|blond** flaxen-haired; (hair) flaxen; **die ~blume, –n** immortelle; **das ~dach, ¨er** thatched roof; **das ~feuer** flash in the pan; **s~gedeckt** thatched; **stroh|gelb** straw-coloured; **der ~halm, –e** straw; (drinking-)straw (**sich an einen S. klammern** clutch at a straw); **der ~kopf, ¨e** *coll* numskull; **der ~mann, ¨er** front (man); *cards* dummy; **stroh|trocken** extremely dry; **die ~witwe, –n** grass-widow; **der ~witwer, –** grass-widower

strohig (hair) like straw; (vegetable) tough

der **Strolch, –e** vagabond; *coll* (young) rascal

strolchen (*sn*) roam about

der **Strom, ¨e** (large) river; current; stream (of); flood (of); *elect* electricity; current; **gegen den/mit dem ~ schwimmen** swim against/with the current; go against/with the tide; **es regnet in Strömen** it's pouring with rain; **unter ~ stehen** be live || **s~ab(wärts)** downstream; **s~auf(wärts)** upstream; **s~führend** *elect* live; **das ~gebiet, –e** (river) basin; **der ~kreis, –e** (electrical) circuit; **die ~linien|form, –en** streamlining; **s~linien|förmig** streamlined; **das ~netz, –e** mains; **die ~schiene, –n** conductor rail; **die ~schnelle, –n** (*usu pl*) rapid; **die ~sperre, –n** power cut; **die ~stärke, –n** current; amperage; **der ~zähler, –** electricity meter

strömen (*sn*) stream, pour

der **Stromer, –** *coll* tramp

stromern (*sn*) *coll* roam about

die **Strömung, –en** current; trend

die **Strophe, –n** stanza

–strophig of ... stanzas

strophisch stanzaic

strotzen: ~ von/vor (*dat*) be full of/bursting with; be bristling with; **von Schmutz ~** be covered with dirt

Strubbel–: der ~kopf, ¨e shock of tousled hair; tousle-headed person

strubbelig *coll* tousled

der **Strudel, –** whirlpool; whirl (of events *etc*); *SGer cul* strudel

strudeln whirl, swirl, eddy

die **Struktur, –en** structure; *text* texture; *in compds* structural ...

strukturell structural

strukturieren structure

der **Strumpf, ¨e** sock; stocking; **das ~band, ¨er** garter; = **der ~halter, –** suspender, garter *US*; **der ~halter|gürtel, –** suspender belt, garter belt *US*; **die ~hose, –n** tights, panty hose *esp US*; **die ~maske, –n** head stocking; **die ~waren** *pl* hosiery

der **Strunk, ¨e** stalk; (tree-)stump

struppig unkempt; shaggy

das **Strychnin** [–ç–] strychnine

der **Stubben, –** *NGer* tree-stump

die **Stube, –n** *reg* room; *educ* dormitory; *mil* barrack-room; **gute ~** parlour || **~n|arrest** (**S. haben** not be allowed out (as punishment)); **die ~n|fliege, –n** house-fly; **der ~n|gelehrte** (*decl as adj*) bookish person; **der ~n|hocker, –** *coll* stay-at-home; **s~n|rein** house-trained, housebroken *US*; *joc* (joke) clean

die **Stubs|nase** [–ʊps–], **–n** turned-up nose

der **Stuck** stucco

das **Stück, –e/**(*following num*) **–** piece; bit; lump (of sugar), bar (of soap); passage (from book); *theat* play; *mus* piece; *coll* (cheeky *etc*) beggar; **zehn** *etc* **~ (von ...)** ten *etc* (of ...); **(20 Pfennig** *etc*) **das ~** each; **ein ~** *also* (accompany *etc*) a little way; **das ist ein starkes ~!** that's a bit much!; **große ~e halten auf** (*acc*) think highly of; **am/im ~** unsliced; **aus freien ~en** of one's own free will; **~ für ~** piece by piece; **in ~e** (smash *etc*) to pieces; **sich in ~e reißen lassen für** *coll* do anything for || **die ~arbeit** piecework; **das ~gut, ¨er** *rail* (separately despatched) item of freight; **der ~lohn** piece-rate; **der ~preis, –e** unit price; **s~weise** piece by piece, piecemeal; *comm* by the piece; **~werk** (**S. sein/bleiben** be/remain incomplete)

Stücke–: der ~schreiber, – playwright

stückeln piece together

stucken *Aust coll* cram

der **Student, –en** (*wk masc*) (university *etc*) student; *Aust arch*, *Swiss* pupil (at a *Gymnasium*); **das ~en|futter** mixed nuts and raisins; **das ~en|heim, –e** hall of residence, dormitory *US*

die **Studentenschaft, –en** student body

studentisch student

die **Studie** [–ĭə], **–n** essay; *art* study

Studien [–ĭən] *pl of* **Studie, Studium;** *in compds* ... of study; study ...; university ...; **der ~assessor, –en** probationary teacher (at a *Gymnasium*); **der ~gang, ¨e** course (of studies); **s~halber** for the purpose of study; **der ~platz, ¨e** (university *etc*) place; **der ~rat, ¨e** teacher (at a *Gymnasium*); **der ~referendar, –e** trainee teacher (at a *Gymnasium*); **die ~reise, –n** study trip

Studier–: das ~zimmer, – study

studieren study; (*v/i*) study; go to university/college; **studiert** *coll* university/college-educated

der **Studierende** (*fem* **die ~**) (*decl as adj*) student

das **Studio, –s** studio

das **Studium, –(i)en** study (of); (university *etc*)

studies; **nach dem ~** after graduating

die **Stufe, -n** step; stage (of rocket, development, *etc*); grade; tier; level (*also comput*); *mus* degree; **auf gleicher ~ stehen mit** be on a par with

stufen grade; layer (hair)

Stufen- graduated ...; **der ~barren, -** asymmetric bars; **s~förmig** stepped; gradual; (*adv*) in steps/tiers; gradually; **die ~leiter, -n** ladder (of success *etc*); **die ~rakete, -n** multi-stage rocket; **s~weise** gradual; (*adv*) step by step, in stages

stufig: ~ schneiden layer (hair); **-stufig** -stage; -tier; with ... steps

der **Stuhl, ⸚e** chair; *med* stool; bowel movement; **der Heilige ~** the Holy See; **sich zwischen zwei Stühle setzen** fall between two stools || **der ~gang** bowel movement; **die ~lehne, -n** back of a chair

der **Stuka** [-u:-, -ʊ-], **-s** (= **Sturzkampfbomber**) dive-bomber

die **Stukkatur, -en** stucco(-work)

die **Stulle, -n** *NGer* slice of bread and butter

die **Stulpe, -n** (turned-back) cuff; top (of boot)

stülpen: ~ auf (*acc*) place on; clap (hat) on; **nach oben/unten ~** turn up/down; **~ über** (*acc*) place over

stumm dumb; mute; silent; (role) non-speaking; *ling* mute; **~ vor** (*dat*) speechless with || **der S~film, -e** silent film

der **Stummel, -** stub; stump; (cigarette) end, butt; **der ~schwanz, ⸚e** docked tail

der **Stumpen, -** cheroot

der **Stümper, -** botcher, bungler

die **Stümperei, -en** botching, bungling; botched job

stümperhaft botched, bungled; bungling

stümpern bungle things

stumpf blunt; (nose) snub; (hair, colour, *etc*) dull; apathetic; *pros* masculine; *math* obtuse; **~ gegen** indifferent to

der **Stumpf, ⸚e** stump; **mit ~ und Stiel** root and branch

stumpf-: der S~sinn apathy; tedium, tediousness; **~sinnig** apathetic; tedious

die **Stunde, -n** hour; moment; *educ* lesson, period; **~n nehmen** take lessons (**bei** from); **die ~ Null** new beginning (after a catastrophe *etc*, *esp* with reference to Germany after the collapse of the Third Reich); **in der/pro ~** per hour; **von ~ zu ~** hourly; **zu jeder ~** at any time

stünde *p/t subj of* **stehen**

stunden (+*dat*) allow (s.o.) time to pay

Stunden-: das ~buch, ⸚er book of hours; **das ~geld, -er** tuition fee; **die ~geschwindigkeit** average speed per hour; **das ~glas, ⸚er** hour-glass; **die ~kilometer** *pl* kilometres per hour; **s~lang** lasting for hours; (*adv*) for hours; **der ~lohn, ⸚e** hourly wage; **der ~plan, ⸚e** (school) timetable, schedule *US*; **der ~schlag, ⸚e** striking of the hour (**mit dem S.** (**12** *etc*) on the stroke of (12 *etc*)); **s~weise** by the hour; part-time; **der ~zeiger, -** hour-hand

-stündig -hour

stündlich hourly; (*adv*) every hour, hourly; hour by hour; **-stündlich** every ... hours

die **Stundung, -en** deferment of payment

der **Stunk** *coll* row; **~ machen** kick up a stink

stupend stupendous

stupid stupid; tedious, monotonous

die **Stupidität** stupidity; tedium, monotony

der **Stups** *coll* [-ʊ-], **-e** nudge; **die ~nase, -n** *coll* turned-up nose

stupsen [-ʊ-] *coll* nudge

stur *coll* stubborn, pigheaded

stürbe *p/t subj of* **sterben**

der **Sturm, ⸚e** gale, storm, *meteor* strong gale (= *Beaufort scale 9*); storm (of protest *etc*); rush (**auf** *acc* for), *fin* run (on); *mil* assault; *sp* forward line; **~ und Drang** *liter* Storm and Stress; **~ im Wasserglas** storm in a teacup, tempest in a teapot *US*; **~ laufen gegen** be up in arms against; **~ läuten** keep one's finger on the doorbell; **im ~ erobern** take by storm || **der ~angriff, -e** *mil* assault; **die ~flut, -en** storm tide; **s~frei** *coll* (**s~freie Bude** (*room where one can freely entertain members of the opposite sex*)); **die ~laterne, -n** hurricane lamp; **~schritt** (**im S.** at the double, on the double *US*); **die ~schwalbe, -n** storm(y) petrel; **die ~warnung, -en** gale warning

stürmen storm (*also mil*); (*v/i*) (wind) rage; *sp* attack; play in the forward line; *mil* charge; (*sn*) charge; **es stürmt** it is blowing a gale

der **Stürmer, -** *sp* forward, striker

stürmisch stormy, (sea, crossing, *etc*) rough; turbulent; gales of (laughter), tumultuous; vehement; passionate; (progress *etc*) rapid

der **Sturz**[1], **-e** *archit* lintel

der **Sturz**[2], **⸚e** fall; plunge; drop, fall (*gen* in); *pol* fall; overthrow; *SGer* glass cover; **der ~bach, ⸚e** torrent; **der ~flug, ⸚e** nose-dive; **der ~helm, -e** crash-helmet; **das ~kampf|flugzeug, -e** dive-bomber; **der ~regen, -** downpour; **die ~see, -n = die ~welle, -n** breaker

stürzen turn upside down, *cul* turn out; *pol* bring down; overthrow; (*v/i sn*) fall; plunge; rush, dash; **~ in** (*acc*) hurl into; plunge into; (*v/i sn*) burst into (room); **~ über** (*acc*) put (lid) on

sich ~ auf (*acc*) pounce on; pitch into; **sich ~ aus** leap from; **sich ~ in** (*acc*) fall on (sword); throw oneself into (*also* task *etc*); plunge into; **sich ~ von** leap from

der **Stuß** (*gen* **Stusses**) *coll* nonsense

[die] **Stute, -n** mare
Stutz-: der ~bart, ⸚e trimmed beard; **der ~flügel, -** baby grand; **die ~uhr, -en** mantelpiece clock
Stütz- supporting ...; **die ~mauer, -n** retaining wall; **der ~punkt, -e** base (*also mil*); *tech* fulcrum
[die] **Stütze, -n** support; help; mainstay
stutzen[1] dock (tail); trim, clip; prune
stutzen[2] stop short
[der] **Stutzen, -** carbine; leg-warmer, *SGer* footless sock, *footb* sock; *tech* connecting piece
stützen support (physically); shore up; support, back up; *EGer econ* peg; **die Ellenbogen auf den Tisch ~** prop one's elbows on the table; **den Kopf in die Hände ~** hold one's head in one's hands; **sich ~ auf** (*acc*) lean on; draw on; be based on
[der] **Stutzer, -** fop, dandy
stutzerhaft foppish
stutzig: ~ machen make (s.o.) wonder; **~ werden** begin to wonder
[das] **Styling** ['stae-] styling
[das] **Styropor** (*trade-mark*) polystyrene
[die] **SU** (= **Sowjetunion**) the U.S.S.R.
s. u. (= **siehe unten**) see below
[die] **Suada** ['zŭaː-], **-(d)en** torrent of words; eloquence
[das] **Suaheli** [zŭ-] (*gen* **-(s)**) Swahili
sub|altern [zʊp-] subordinate; obsequious
[der] **Subbotnik** [-ɪk], **-(s)** *EGer* subbotnik (*voluntary unpaid work – esp on Saturdays – on Soviet model*)
[das] **Subjekt** [zʊp-], **-e** *gramm, philos* subject; *coll* (shady *etc*) customer
subjektiv [zʊp-] subjective
[die] **Subjektivität** [zʊp-] subjectivity
[der] **Subkontinent** ['zʊp-], **-e** subcontinent
[die] **Subkultur** ['zʊp-], **-en** subculture
subkutan [zʊp-] subcutaneous
sublim highly subtle
sublimieren sublimate
[der] **Subskribent** [zʊp-], **-en** (*wk masc*) subscriber (to book)
subskribieren [zʊp-] subscribe to (book)
[die] **Subskription** [zʊp-], **-en** subscription (to book)
[das] **Substantiv** ['zʊp-], **-e** noun
substantivieren [zʊp-] substantivize
substantivisch [zʊp-] substantival
[die] **Substanz** [zʊp-], **-en** substance (*also chem*); assets, capital
[das] **Substrat** [zʊp-], **-e** substratum
subsumieren: ~ unter (*acc/dat*) subsume under
subtil [zʊp-] subtle
[die] **Subtilität** [zʊp-], **-en** subtlety
subtrahieren [zʊp-] subtract
[die] **Subtraktion** [zʊp-], **-en** subtraction
[die] **Subtropen** ['zʊp-] *pl* subtropics
subtropisch ['zʊp-] subtropical
[die] **Subvention** [zʊp-], **-en** subsidy
subventionieren [zʊp-] subsidize
[die] **Subversion** [zʊp-] subversion
subversiv [zʊp-] subversive
Such- [-uː-] search ... (*also comput*); **die ~aktion, -en** (large-scale) search; **der ~dienst, -e** tracing service; **das ~gerät, -e** detector; **der ~hund, -e** sniffer dog; **der ~trupp, -s** search-party
[die] **Suche** [-uː-] search (**nach** for); **auf der ~ sein nach** be looking for
suchen [-uː-] (*see also* **gesucht**) look for; seek; endeavour (to); **~ nach** look for; search for; **was suchst du hier?** what are you doing here?; **du hast hier nichts zu ~** you've no business to be here; **„... gesucht"** 'wanted: ...'
[der] **Sucher, -** viewfinder
[die] **Sucht, ⸚e** addiction (**nach** to); craving (for); mania (for)
süchtig addicted (**nach** to); **-süchtig** addicted to ...; obsessed with ...; **~ werden** become an addict; **der/die Süchtige** (*decl as adj*) addict
[der] **Sud, -e** vegetable *etc* water; (meat) juice
Süd south; *in compds* south ...; southern ...; **~afrika** South Africa; **der ~afrikaner, -, s~afrikanisch** South African; **~amerika** South America; **der ~amerikaner, -, s~amerikanisch** South American; **die ~früchte** *pl* Mediterranean and tropical fruit; **der ~länder, -** Latin; **s~ländisch** Mediterranean; Latin; **~ost|asien** South-East Asia; **der ~pol** the South Pole; **~polar-** Antarctic ...; **die ~see** the South Seas; **die ~staaten** *pl* the Southern States, the South (of U.S.A.); **der ~staatler, -** Southerner (in U.S.A.); **~tirol** South Tyrol; **s~wärts** southwards; **der ~wein, -e** Mediterranean wine; **der ~wester, -** sou'wester
[der] **Sudan** (*gen* **-(s)**) the Sudan
[der] **Sudanese, -n** (*wk masc*), **sudanesisch** Sudanese
sudeln *coll* scrawl; do slovenly work
[der] **Süden** south
[die] **Sudeten** *pl* the Sudeten Mountains; **das ~land** the Sudetenland
südlich 1 *adj* southern; southerly; (*adv*) (to the) south (**von** of); 2 *prep* (+*gen*) (to the) south of
Sues ['zuːɛs] Suez; **der ~kanal** the Suez Canal
[der] **Suff** *coll* boozing; **dem ~ verfallen** hit the bottle; **im ~** while under the influence
[der] **Süffel, -** *coll* tippler
süffeln *coll* tipple
süffig (wine) very palatable
süffisant self-satisfied; superior

^das^ **Suffix, –e** suffix
suggerieren (thing) suggest, hint at; (+*dat*) insinuate (idea *etc*) into (s.o.'s) mind
^die^ **Suggestion, –en** *psych* suggestion
suggestiv exercising an influence (by means of suggestion); **die S~frage, –n** leading question
suhlen: sich ~ in (*dat*) wallow in
^die^ **Sühne** atonement; **der ~termin, –e** conciliation hearing
sühnen atone for
^die^ **Suite** ['svi:tə, 'sŭi:–], **–n** suite (*also mus*)
^das^ **Sujet** [sy'ʒe:], **–s** subject (of work of art)
^die^ **Sukkade, –n** candied peel
sukzessiv gradual
^das^ **Sulfat, –e** sulphate
^das^ **Sulfid, –e** sulphide
^das^ **Sulfonamid, –e** sulphonamide
^der^ **Sultan, –e** sultan
^die^ **Sultanine, –n** sultana (= raisin)
^die^ **Sulz, –en** *SGer* brawn
Sülz–: das ~kotelett, –s pork chop in aspic
^die^ **Sülze, –n** brawn
^der^ **Sumerer, –, sumerisch** Sumerian
summ! buzz!
Summ–: der ~ton, ⸚e buzz(ing sound)
summarisch summary
^die^ **Summe, –n** sum, amount; total; sum (total) (of s.o.'s knowledge *etc*)
summen hum; (*v/i*) hum; buzz
^der^ **Summer, –** buzzer
summieren sum up; **sich ~** add up
^der^ **Sumpf, ⸚e** bog, marsh, swamp; **das ~fieber** malaria; **das ~huhn, ⸚er** crake; **das ~land** marshland
sumpfen *coll* live it up
sumpfig marshy
Sums *coll*: **einen großen ~ machen** kick up a great fuss (**um** about)
Sünd–: die ~flut (= **Sintflut**); **sünd|teuer** wickedly expensive
^die^ **Sünde, –n** sin
Sünden– ... of (s.o.'s) sins; **der ~bock, ⸚e** scapegoat; **der ~fall** the Fall; **~geld** *coll* (**ein S.** a mint of money); **der ~pfuhl, –e** sink of iniquity; **das ~register, –** *coll* list of (s.o.'s) misdemeanours
^der^ **Sünder, –** sinner
sündhaft sinful; *coll* (price) wicked; **~ teuer** *coll* wickedly expensive
sündig sinful
sündigen sin; *joc* indulge
^das^ **Super** high-octane petrol/gasoline *US*
Super– super ...; (**super–**) ultra–; **der ~intendent, –en** (*wk masc*) *Prot* superintendent; **s~klug** *coll* clever-clever; **die ~macht, ⸚e** super-power; **der ~markt, ⸚e** supermarket; **s~modern** ultramodern; **die ~nova, –(v)ä** supernova; **der ~star, –s** superstar

^der^ **Superlativ, –e** superlative
^die^ **Suppe, –n** soup; **die ~ auslöffeln** *coll* face the music || **die ~n|schüssel, –n** tureen; **der ~n|würfel, –** stock cube
^der^ **Supra|leiter, –** superconductor
^der^ **Supremat, –e** (*also* **das**) = **die Suprematie, –(ie)n** supremacy
Surf– ['sø:ɐf–, 'sœrf–]: **das ~brett, –er** surfboard; sailboard, surfboard *US*
surfen ['sø:ɐ–, 'sœr–] go surfing/windsurfing
^der^ **Surfer, –** surfer; windsurfer
^das^ **Surfing** ['sø:ɐ–, 'sœr–] surfing; windsurfing
^der^ **Surrealismus** surrealism
surrealistisch surrealist
surren buzz; hum; whirr; (*sn, indicating direction*) buzz; whirr
^das^ **Surrogat, –e** substitute
suspekt suspect
suspendieren suspend (**von** from)
süß [–y:–] sweet; **das S~holz** liquorice (= plant) (**S. raspeln** *coll* turn on the charm); **der S~most, –e** unfermented fruit-juice; **süß-sauer** sour-sweet; (smile) forced; **die S~speise, –n** sweet, dessert; **der S~stoff, –e** artificial sweetener; **die S~waren** *pl* confectionery; **das ~waren|geschäft, –e** sweet shop, candy store *US*; **das S~wasser** fresh water; **S~wasser–** freshwater ...
^die^ **Süße** sweetness
süßen sweeten; sugar
^die^ **Süßigkeiten** *pl* sweets, candy *US*
süßlich sweetish; sickly (sweet); mawkish; sugary
^die^ **SVP = Schweizerische Volkspartei**
SW (= **Südwest(en)**) S.W.
^der^ **Swimmingpool** ['svɪmɪŋpu:l], **–s** (private) swimming-pool
^die^ **Sylphe, –n** sylph
^die^ **Symbiose, –n** symbiosis
symbiotisch symbiotic
^das^ **Symbol, –e** symbol (**für** of); **s~trächtig** rich in symbolism
symbolhaft symbolic
^die^ **Symbolik** [–ɪk] symbolism
symbolisch symbolic (**für** of)
symbolisieren symbolize
^die^ **Symmetrie, –(ie)n** symmetry
symmetrisch symmetrical
^die^ **Sympathie, –(ie)n** liking; sympathy; (+*dat*) **~ entgegenbringen** be sympathetic towards
^der^ **Sympathisant, –en** (*wk masc*) *esp pol* sympathizer
sympathisch likeable, appealing; *anat* sympathetic; **... ist mir ~** I like ...; **~ finden** take to
sympathisieren: ~ mit *esp pol* sympathize with
Symphonie *etc* = **Sinfonie** *etc*
^das^ **Symposion** [–ɔn, *also* –'po:–], **–(i)en = das**

Symposium [*also* –'po:–], **–(i)en** symposium

das **Symptom, –e** symptom (**für** of)

symptomatisch symptomatic (**für** of)

die **Synagoge, –n** synagogue

synchron [–kr–] synchronous (*also comput*); **~ sein mit** *cin* synchronize with || **das S~getriebe, –** synchromesh; **das S~schwimmen** synchronized swimming

die **Synchronisation** [–kr–], **–en** synchronization; *cin* dubbing

synchronisieren [–kr–] synchronize; *cin* dub

das **Syndikat, –e** syndicate

der **Syndikus, –(i)zi** company lawyer, corporation lawyer *US*

das **Syndrom, –e** syndrome

die **Synkope, –n** *mus* syncopation

synkopieren *mus* syncopate

synkopisch *mus* syncopated

die **Synode, –n** synod

synonym synonymous

das **Synonym, –e** synonym

die **Synopse, –n** synopsis

syntaktisch syntactic

die **Syntax** syntax

die **Synthese, –n** synthesis

die **Synthetics** *pl* synthetics

synthetisch synthetic; *text* man-made

die **Syphilis** ['zy:filɪs] syphilis

Syrien [–ĭən] Syria

der **Syr(i)er, –, syrisch** Syrian

das **System, –e** system; method; **~ bringen in** (*acc*) systematize || **die ~analyse, –n** systems analysis; **der ~analytiker, –** systems analyst; **s~los** unsystematic

die **Systematik** [–ɪk], **–en** system; *biol* systematics

systematisch systematic

systematisieren systematize

das **Szenario** [sts–], **–s** scenario (= imagined events)

die **Szene** [sts–], **–n** scene (*var senses incl theat*); (+*dat*) **eine ~ machen** make a scene; **hinter der ~** behind the scenes; *theat* backstage; **in ~ setzen** stage; **sich in ~ setzen** play to the gallery || **der ~n|wechsel, –** scene-change

die **Szenerie** [sts–], **–(ie)n** scenery

szenisch [sts–] *theat* scenic

das **Szepter** [sts–], **–** sceptre

Szylla [sts–]: **zwischen ~ und Charybdis** [ça'rʏpdɪs, ka–] between the devil and the deep blue sea

T

das **T** [teː] (*gen, pl* –, *coll* [teːs]) T; **t** (= **Tonne** metric ton) t.

der **Tabak** ['taːbak], **–e** tobacco; **der ~händler, –** tobacconist; **der ~laden, ..läden** tobacconist's, tobacco store *US*; **die Tabak|trafik, –en** *Aust* tobacconist's, tobacco store *US* (also selling stamps, newspapers, *etc*); **die ~waren** *pl* tobacco products

tabellarisch tabular; in tabular form

tabellarisieren tabulate

die **Tabelle, –n** table; chart; *sp* league table; **~n|form (in T.** in tabular form); **der ~n|führer, –** league leaders

tabellieren *comput* tabulate

das **Tabernakel, –** (*also* **der**) *RC* tabernacle

das **Tablett, –s** tray

die **Tablette, –n** tablet, pill

tabu, das Tabu, –s, tabu(is)ieren taboo

tabula rasa: ~ machen make a clean sweep (**mit** of)

tachinieren [–x–] *Aust coll* loaf about

der **Tachinierer, –** *Aust coll* loafer

der **Tacho** [–x–], **–s** *coll* speedo

der **Tachometer** [–x–], **–** (*also* **das**) speedometer

der **Tadel, –** reprimand, rebuke; censure; *educ* black mark; **öffentlicher ~** *EGer leg* public reprimand || **t~los** perfect; flawless

tadeln reprimand, rebuke; censure; **etwas zu ~ finden/haben an** (*dat*) find fault with; **~d** reproachful || **~s|wert** reprehensible

die **Tafel, –n** bar (of chocolate *etc*); tablet, plaque; panel; (black)board; (notice-) board, *Swiss* road-sign; plate (in book); (festively-laid) table; (festive) meal; **die ~ aufheben** (host) rise from table || **der ~berg** Table Mountain; **das ~land, ⸚er** tableland; **die ~runde, –n** company at table; *liter* Round Table; **das ~wasser, ..wässer** table-water; **der ~wein, –e** table wine

tafeln feast

täfeln panel

die **Täfelung, –en** panelling

der **Taft, –e** taffeta

der **Tag, –e** day; (*pl*) *coll* (menstrual) period; **–tag** *also* … assembly; … convention; **der ~ X** D-Day; **~ (der Arbeit/Republik** *etc*) (Labour/Republic *etc*) Day; **den ganzen ~** all day long; **acht ~e** a week; **alle ~e** every day; **dieser ~e** in the next few days; the other day; **eines ~es** one day, one of these days; **guten ~!** good morning/afternoon!; how do you do?; (*abbreviated as*) **~!** [tax] *coll* hullo!, hi!; **sich** *dat* **einen guten ~ machen** *coll* have a nice day; **jeden ~** every day; any day now; **es ist/wird ~** it's light/getting light; **jetzt wird's ~!** whatever next!

in prepositional phrases:

am ~(e) by day; by daylight; **zweimal** *etc* **am ~(e)** twice *etc* a day; **an diesem ~(e)** on that day; **am folgenden/vorigen ~(e)** the following/previous day; **am hellichten ~e** in broad daylight; **früh/spät am ~(e)** early/late in the day; **an den ~ bringen/kommen** bring/come to light; **an den ~ legen** display (interest *etc*)

auf den ~ (genau) to the day; **auf meine/seine** *etc* **alten ~e** at my/his *etc* time of life

bei ~(e) by day; by daylight

~ für ~ day after day

in diesen ~en in the last/next few days; **(heute/Montag** *etc*) **in acht/vierzehn ~en** a week/fortnight (today/on Monday *etc*), (today/Monday *etc*) week/fortnight; **in den ~ hinein leben** live from day to day; **bis in unsere ~e** up to the present day

über ~e *min* above ground

um: einen ~ um den anderen every other day; **~ um ~** day after day

unter ~e *min* underground

von ~ zu ~ from day to day; (be getting better *etc*) every day

Tag– (*SGer* = **Tage–** *in* **~bau** *etc*): **t~aus (t., t~ein** day in, day out); **der ~dienst** day duty; **der ~falter, –** butterfly; **tag|hell** as bright as day; **der ~raum, ⸚e** *SGer* day-room; **die ~schicht, –en** day shift; **tag|täglich** daily; (*adv*) day after day; **der ~traum, ⸚e** day-dream; **die Tag|und|nacht|gleiche, –n** equinox; **die ~wache, –n** *Aust*, *Swiss* reveille

Tage–: **der ~bau** open-cast mining; **das ~blatt, ⸚er** (*in titles of newspapers*) Daily News; **das ~buch, ⸚er** diary; journal; **der ~dieb, –e** idler; **das ~geld, –er** daily allowance; **t~lang** lasting for days; (*adv*) for days (on end); **der ~lohn, ⸚e** day's pay; **der**

~löhner, – day-labourer; **die ~reise, –n** day's journey; **t~weise** on a daily basis; **das ~werk** day's work

tagen[1] meet; *leg, parl* sit

tagen[2] **: es tagt** dawn is breaking

Tages– daily ...; day ...; day's ...; ... of the day;

der ~anbruch daybreak; **der ~bericht, –e** news bulletin; **die ~decke, –n** bedspread; **das ~gericht, –e** plat du jour; **das ~gespräch, –e** topic of the day; **das ~grauen** daybreak; **die ~karte, –n** day ticket; menu of the day; **die ~kasse, –n** box-office (for advance bookings); day's takings; **das ~licht** daylight (**ans T. kommen** come to light); **die ~mutter, ..mütter** child-minder; **die ~ordnung, –en** agenda (**an der T. sein** be the order of the day; **auf der T. stehen** be on the agenda; **zur T. übergehen** get down to business); **der ~raum, ¨–e** day-room; **der ~satz, ¨–e** daily rate; **die ~schau, –en** TV news; **die ~zeit, –en** time of day; **die ~zeitung, –en** daily (newspaper)

–tägig –day; –day-old

täglich daily; (*adv*) every day, daily; **–täglich** every ... days

tags: ~ darauf/zuvor the day after/before || **~über** during the day

die **Tagung, –en** conference; **der ~s|ort, –e** venue of a/the conference

der **Taifun, –e** typhoon

die **Taille** ['taljə], **–n** waist; **die ~n|weite, –n** waist measurement

tailliert [ta'jiːɐt] waisted

die **Takelage** [takə'laːʒə], **–n** *naut* rigging

takeln *naut* rig

die **Takelung, –en = das Takel|werk, –e** *naut* rigging

der **Takt, –e** tact; *mus* time; *mus* bar, *pros* foot; *mech* stroke; *tech* phase (of automated production); **den ~ angeben** beat time; call the tune; **(den) ~ halten** keep time; **aus dem ~ bringen** make (s.o.) lose the beat; put off his/her stroke; **aus dem ~ kommen** lose the beat; be put off one's stroke; **im ~** in time || **die ~frequenz, –en** *comput* clock rate; **das ~gefühl** tact; **der ~impuls, –e** *comput* clock pulse; **t~los** tactless; **die ~losigkeit, –en** tactlessness; indiscretion; **der ~stock, ¨–e** (conductor's) baton; **die ~straße, –n** assembly line; **der ~strich, –e** *mus* bar(-line); **t~voll** tactful

taktieren manoeuvre (tactically)

die **Taktik** [–ɪk], **–en** tactics

der **Taktiker, –** tactician

taktisch tactical

das **Tal, ¨–er** valley; **zu ~** down into the valley || **t~ab(wärts)** down into the valley; downstream; **t~auf(wärts)** up the valley; upstream; **die ~enge, –n** defile; **die ~fahrt, –en** descent; *econ* downward trend; **der ~kessel, –** *geog* basin; **die ~sohle, –n** valley bottom; *econ* trough; **die ~sperre, –n** dam (erected across valley)

der **Talar, –e** *univ* gown; *eccles* cassock; *leg* robe

das **Talent, –e** talent (**zu** for); talented person; (*pl*) talent (*collect*); **t~los** untalented; **der ~sucher, –** talent scout

talentiert talented

der **Taler, –** thaler (*former coin*)

der **Talg, –e** tallow; *cul* suet; **die ~drüse, –n** sebaceous gland

der **Talisman** ['taːlɪsman], **–e** talisman

der **Talk** talc(um)

das **Talmi** pinchbeck

der **Talmud** the Talmud

talmudisch Talmudic

die **Talschaft, –en** *Aust, Swiss* inhabitants of a valley

der **Tambour** [–buːɐ], **–e** drummer; **der ~major, –e** drum major

das **Tamburin** [*also* –'riːn], **–e** tambourine

der **Tampon** ['tampɔn, tam'poːn], **–s, tamponieren** tampon

das **Tamtam, –s** tom-tom; *coll* ballyhoo

die **TAN** *EGer* (= **technisch begründete Arbeitsnorm**) work norm based on technical criteria

der **Tand** baubles; frippery

tändeln play about; **~ mit** dally with

das **Tandem** [–ɛm], **–s** tandem

der **Tandler, –** *Aust* second-hand dealer

der **Tang, –e** seaweed

die **Tangente, –n** ring-road, belt *US*; *math* tangent

Tanger ['taŋɐ] Tangier

tangieren affect; *math* be tangent to

der **Tango, –s** tango

der **Tank, –s** tank (= container); **die ~säule, –n** petrol pump, gasoline pump *US*; **das ~schiff, –e** tanker; **die ~stelle, –n** filling-station; **der ~wagen, –** tanker; *rail* tank-car; **der ~wart, –e** petrol pump attendant, gas station attendant *US*

tanken *mot* fill up with; put in (... litres); *coll* soak up (sun, culture), get (fresh air); (*v/i*) *mot* fill up; get petrol/gasoline *US*; *aer, mot rac* refuel; **neue Kräfte ~** *coll* build up one's strength again; **zuviel getankt haben** *coll* have had one too many

der **Tanker, –** *naut* tanker

die **Tanne, –n** fir(-tree); **der ~n|baum, ¨–e** Christmas tree; *coll* fir-tree; **die ~n|meise, –n** coal-tit; **der ~n|wald, ¨–er** pine forest; **der ~n|zapfen, –** fir-cone

Tansania Tanzania

der **Tansanier** [–ǐɐ], **–, tansanisch** Tanzanian

die **Tantalus|qualen** *pl* torments of Tantalus; **~ ausstehen** be tantalized; (+*dat*) **~ bereiten** tantalize

^die^ **Tante, –n** aunt; *coll* (old *etc*) woman; (*said by or to child*) lady; **der ~-Emma-Laden, ..Läden** *coll* corner shop

tantenhaft old-maidish

^die^ **Tantieme** [–'tĭe:–], **–n** royalty; percentage of profits

^der^ **Tanz, ⸚e** dance; *coll* row; scene; **einen ~ aufführen** *coll* make a song and dance; **zum ~ auffordern** ask to dance

Tanz– dance ...; dancing ...; **die ~bar, –s** bar with dancing; **~bein** *coll* (**das T. schwingen** shake a leg); **das ~café, –s** café with dancing; **die ~fläche, –n** dance-floor; **die ~kapelle, –n** dance-band; **das ~lokal, –e** dance-hall; **der ~saal, ..säle** dance-hall; ballroom; **die ~schule, –n** school of dancing; **der ~sport** (competition) ballroom-dancing; **die ~stunde, –n** dancing-class; **der ~tee, –s** thé dansant

tänzeln (horse) prance; (*sn*) skip, trip

tanzen (*also v/i: sn if indicating direction*) dance; **~ gehen** go dancing; **nach jmds. Pfeife ~** dance to s.o.'s tune

^der^ **Tänzer, –** dancer; dancing-partner

tänzerisch dancing; dance-like

^der^ **Taper|greis, –e** *coll* old dodderer

tap(e)rig *coll* doddery

Tapet *coll*: **aufs ~ bringen** bring up (topic)

^die^ **Tapete, –n** wallpaper; **der ~n|wechsel, –** *coll* change of surroundings

tapezieren paper; *Aust* upholster

^der^ **Tapezierer, –** paperhanger; *Aust* upholsterer

tapfer brave

^die^ **Tapferkeit** bravery

^die^ **Tapisserie, –(ie)n** tapestry

tappen (*sn exc* **~ nach, im dunkeln ~**) walk with faltering steps; (bear) lumber; **~ in** (*acc*) blunder into; **~ nach** grope about for; **im dunkeln ~** grope in the dark; (police *etc*) be in the dark

täppisch clumsy

tapsen (*sn as at* **tappen**) *coll* = **tappen**

tapsig *coll* clumsy

^die^ **Tara, –(r)en** *comm* tare

^die^ **Tarantel, –n** tarantula

Tarent Taranto

^der^ **Tarif, –e** rate; tariff; scale of charges; wage scale; salary scale; **die ~autonomie** free collective bargaining; **der ~lohn, ⸚e** standard wage; **die ~verhandlungen** *pl* pay negotiations; **der ~vertrag, ⸚e** agreement on pay and working conditions

tariflich in accordance with/relating to the tariff/pay agreement

Tarn– camouflage ...; **die ~kappe, –n** magic cloak (bestowing invisibility on the wearer)

tarnen, die Tarnung, –en camouflage; disguise

^das^ **Tarock** (*also* **der**) tarot

^die^ **Tartan|bahn** [–tan–], **–en** tartan track

^die^ **Tasche, –n** pocket; bag; (+*dat*) **auf der ~ liegen** *coll* live off; **in die eigene ~ arbeiten** line one's pockets; **(tief) in die ~ greifen** *coll* dig deep into one's pocket; **in die ~ stecken** *coll* run rings round; **in der ~ haben** *coll* have in the bag || **das ~n|buch, ⸚er** paperback; **der ~n|dieb, –e** pickpocket; **das ~n|format** pocket size; **das ~n|geld** pocket-money; **die ~n|lampe, –n** torch, flashlight *US*; **das ~n|messer, –** pocket-knife; **der ~n|rechner, –** pocket calculator; **der ~n|spieler, –** conjurer; **das ~n|tuch, ⸚er** handkerchief; **die ~n|uhr, –en** pocket-watch

^die^ **Tasse, –n** cup; *Aust* tray; **trübe ~** *coll* wet blanket; **nicht alle ~n im Schrank haben** *coll* not be quite right in the head

Tast–: das ~organ, –e tactile organ; **der ~sinn** sense of touch

^die^ **Tastatur, –en** keyboard

^die^ **Taste, –n** key (on keyboard); push-button

tasten *tech* key (radio message *etc*); keyboard (text); (*v/i*) feel one's way; **~ nach** feel for; **sich ~** feel one's way; **~d** tentative

Tasten–: das ~instrument, –e keyboard instrument; **das ~telefon, –e** push-button telephone

^der^ **Taster, –** keyboard operator; *zool* feeler

tat (täte) *p/t* (*subj*) *of* **tun**

^die^ **Tat, –en** act; deed; feat; **Mann der ~** man of action; **auf frischer ~ ertappen** catch in the act; **in die ~ umsetzen** put into effect; **in der ~** indeed; actually; sure enough || **der ~bestand, ⸚e** state of affairs; *leg* facts (of the case); **die ~kraft** energy, vigour; **t~kräftig** energetic; **der ~ort, –e** scene of the crime; **die ~sache, –n** fact (**vollendete T.** fait accompli; **T. bleibt/ist, daß ...** the fact remains/is, ...; **T.!** it's true!); **der ~sachen|bericht, –e** documentary report; **t~sächlich** actual; (*adv*) actually, really, in (point of) fact; sure enough (**t~sächlich!** so it is/they are *etc*!; **t~sächlich?** is that so?); **der ~verdacht** suspicion (of having committed a crime); **die ~zeit, –en** time of the crime

^das^ **Tatar** (*gen* **–(s)**) = **das ~beefsteak** steak tartare

^der^ **Tatar, –en** (*wk masc*), **tatarisch** Tartar

Taten–: der ~drang zest for action; **t~los** (**t. herumstehen** stand idly by; **t. zusehen** watch (without doing anything to help))

^der^ **Täter, –** culprit

^die^ **Täterschaft** guilt

tätig active; **~ sein** work; **~ sein in** (*dat*) work in; be in (insurance *etc*)

tätigen effect; make (purchase *etc*)

^die^ **Tätigkeit, –en** activity; work; **außer ~ setzen** stop; **in ~ setzen** activate; set in motion; **in**

~ **treten** come into operation; (volcano) become active || **die ~s|form** *gramm* active (voice)

tätlich violent; ~ **werden gegen** assault

die **Tätlichkeiten** *pl* violence

tätowieren tattoo

die **Tätowierung, -en** *vbl noun*; *also* tattoo

tätscheln pat

tatschen *coll*: ~ **auf** (*acc*) paw

Tatterich *coll*: **den/einen ~ bekommen/haben** get/have the shakes

tatt(e)rig *coll* doddery; shaky

die **Tatze, -n** paw

das **Tau, -e** rope

der **Tau** dew

Tau-: **tau|frisch** dewy; fresh; **der ~tropfen, -** dew-drop; **das ~wetter** thaw (*also pol*) (**es ist/wir haben T.** it is thawing); **das ~ziehen** tug-of-war

taub deaf (**auf** *dat* in); (limb) numb; (nut) empty; ~ **gegen** deaf to; **sich ~ stellen** pretend not to hear; +**gegen** turn a deaf ear to || **~stumm** deaf and dumb; **der/die T~stumme** (*decl as adj*) deaf-mute

die **Taube, -n** pigeon; dove; **der ~n|schlag, ⸚e** dovecote

Tauch- diving ...; *tech* immersion ...; dip ...; dipping ...; **das ~boot, -e** submarine (for short dives); **t~fähig** submersible; able to dive; **das ~gerät, -e** diving apparatus; aqualung; **der ~kolben, -** plunger; **die ~kugel, -n** bathysphere; **der ~sieder, -** mini-boiler; **~station** (**auf T. gehen** *naut* dive; *coll* make oneself scarce)

tauchen dip; give (s.o.) a ducking; immerse; (*v/i*: *also sn*; *if indicating direction or distance travelled, only sn*) dive (**nach** for); *naut* submerge; ~ **in** (*acc*) dip in(to); (*v/i sn*) dive into; disappear into; (sun) dip into (sea); **in Licht getaucht** bathed in light; ~ **unter** (*acc*) (*sn*) (sun) dip below (horizon)

der **Taucher, -** diver (*also ornith*); *in compds* diving ...; **der ~anzug, ⸚e** diving-suit

tauen[1]: **es taut** the dew is falling

tauen[2] (*also sn if v/i, exc* **es taut**) thaw; **es taut** it is thawing

Tauf- baptismal ...; **das ~becken, -** font; **das ~kleid, -er** christening robe; **der ~name, -n** (*like* **Name**) Christian name; **der ~pate, -n** (*wk masc*) godfather; **die ~patin, -nen** godmother; **der ~schein, -e** certificate of baptism; **der ~stein, -e** font

die **Taufe, -n** baptism; christening; *naut* launching ceremony; **die ~ empfangen** be christened; **aus der ~ heben** launch

taufen baptize; christen; **auf den Namen ... ~** christen (s.o.) ...

Täufer: Johannes der ~ John the Baptist

der **Täufling, -e** child/person to be baptized

Tauge-: **der ~nichts** (*gen* **-(es)**), **-e** good-for-nothing

taugen: ~ **für/zu** be suitable for; be suited to; **... taugt nicht zum ...** ... is not cut out to be a ...; **etwas/nichts/nicht viel ~** be some/no/not much good

tauglich suitable; *mil* fit (for service); ~ **für/zu** suitable for; suited to

die **Tauglichkeit** suitability; *mil* fitness (for service)

der **Taumel** giddiness, dizziness; frenzy

taum(e)lig giddy, dizzy

taumeln (*also sn*; *if indicating direction, only sn*) stagger; **~d** *also* ecstatic

der **Tausch, -e** exchange; **im ~ für/gegen** in exchange for || **das ~geschäft, -e** exchange, swap; barter; **der ~handel** barter (**T. treiben** barter)

tauschen exchange, swap (**gegen** for); barter (for); **die Plätze ~** change places; **ich möchte nicht mit ... ~** I wouldn't like to change places with

täuschen deceive; betray (trust); (*v/i*) be deceptive; **sich ~** be mistaken (**in** *dat* about); **~d** deceptive; (resemblance) striking; (+*dat*) **~d ähnlich sehen** look remarkably like

die **Täuschung, -en** deception; illusion; **das ~s|manöver, -** ploy

tausend (a) thousand; ~ **Dank!** thanks a million!; ~ **und aber ~** thousands and thousands of

das **Tausend, -e/-** (*for use of pl forms incl gen* **-er** *cf* **Hundert**) thousand; **zu ~en** in their thousands

tausend- thousand ...; **der T~füß(l)er, -** centipede; millipede; **~mal** a thousand times (**ich bitte t. um Entschuldigung** a thousand apologies); **der T~sas(s)a, -(s)** *coll* hell of a guy; **das T~schönchen, -** daisy; **tausend|und|ein** a thousand and one („**T~undeine Nacht**" 'The Arabian Nights')

der **Tausender, -** thousand; *coll* thousand-mark *etc* note; **t~lei** (*indecl*) a thousand different (things)

tausendstel: ein ~ ... a thousandth of a ...

das **Tausendstel, -** thousandth

tausendst.. thousandth

die **Tautologie, -(ie)n** tautology

tautologisch tautological

Tax-: **der ~preis, -e** estimated price; **der ~wert, -e** estimated value

der **Taxameter, -** taximeter

der **Taxator, -(or)en** valuer

die **Taxe**[1], **-n** (fixed) charge; tax; scale of charges; valuation

die **Taxe**[2], **-n** taxi

das **Taxi, -s** taxi; **der ~fahrer, -** taxi-driver; **der ~stand, ⸚e** taxi-rank, taxi stand *US*

taxieren assess (**auf** *acc* at); estimate (at); *coll* size up

[der] **Taxler, –** *Aust coll* cabby

[der] **Taxus, –** yew

[die] **Tb(c)** [teː'beː, teːbeː'tseː] (= **Tuberkulose**) T.B.; **~-krank** suffering from T.B.

[das] **Teak|holz** ['tiːk–] teak

[das] **Team** [tiːm], **–s** team; **die ~arbeit** = **das ~work** [–wøːɐk] teamwork

[die] **Technik** ['teçnɪk], **–en** technology, *univ* engineering; technique; technical department; *Aust* technological university; *mech* mechanics; equipment, machinery

[der] **Techniker** [–ç–], **–** engineer; technician

[das] **Technikum** [–ç–], **–(k)a** technical college

technisch [–ç–] technical; technological; **–technisch** (*eg* **fahr~**) in terms of/relating to (driving *etc*) technique; **~e Disziplin** *athl* field event; **T~e Hochschule/Universität** technological university

technisieren [–ç–] mechanize

[die] **Technisierung** [–ç–], **–en** mechanization

[der] **Technokrat** [–ç–], **–en** (*wk masc*) technocrat

[der] **Technologe** [–ç–], **–n** (*wk masc*) technologist

[die] **Technologie** [–ç–], **–(ie)n** technology

technologisch [–ç–] technological

[das] **Techtelmechtel, –** *coll* flirtation

[der] **Teckel, –** dachshund

[der] **Teddy** [–i], **–s** = **der ~bär, –en** (*wk masc*) teddy (bear)

[der] **TEE** (*gen* **–(s)**), **–(s)** (= **Trans-Europ-Express**) Trans-European Express

[der] **Tee, –s** tea; tea-party; **abwarten und ~ trinken** wait and see || **der ~beutel, –** tea-bag; **das ~-Ei, –er** tea-infuser, tea-ball; **die ~kanne, –n** teapot; **der ~löffel, –** teaspoon; **die ~pause, –n** tea-break; **die ~rose, –n** tea-rose; **das ~sieb, –e** tea-strainer; **die ~tasse, –n** tea-cup; **der ~wagen, –** tea-trolley; **der ~wärmer, –** tea-cosy; **die ~wurst, ⸚e** (*type of*) smoked sausage spread

[der] **Teenager** ['tiːneːdʒɐ], **–** teenage girl; (*pl*) teenagers; teenage girls

[der] **Teer, –e** tar; **die ~pappe, –n** tar paper

teeren tar

teerig tarry

Teheran ['teːhəraːn, –'raːn] Teh(e)ran

[der] **Teich, –e** pond

[der] **Teig, –e** dough; pastry; batter; **die ~waren** *pl* pasta

teigig doughy

[das] **Teil, –e** part; component; (spare) part; share; **ein gut ~** a good deal (of); a good many; *see also next entry*

[der] **Teil, –e** part; section; share; *leg* party; **~ sein von** be part of; **der größte ~** the bulk; **zu gleichen ~en** in equal shares; **zum ~** partly, in part; **zum größten ~** for the most part, mostly;

(*also neut*) **sich** *dat* **sein(en) ~ denken** *coll* have one's own thoughts (about sth.); **sein(en) ~ tun** do one's bit; **sein(en) ~ weghaben** *coll* have got what was coming to one; **ich für mein(en) ~** I for my part

Teil– partial ...; **(teil–)** partly ...; **der ~betrag, ⸚e** part of an amount; instalment; **t~entrahmt** semi-skimmed; **das ~gebiet, –e** part (of territory); branch (of subject); **die ~habe** participation, share (**an** *dat* in); **t~haben*** (*sep*) (**t. an** (*dat*) share in; participate in; **t. lassen an** (*dat*) share with); **der ~haber, –** *comm* partner (**stiller T.** sleeping partner, silent partner *US*); **die ~haberschaft, –en** *comm* partnership; **die ~nahme** participation (**an** *dat* in), (refuse *etc*) to participate, *leg* complicity; interest (in); sympathy; **t~nahms|los** indifferent, apathetic; listless; **die ~nahms|losigkeit** indifference, apathy; listlessness; **t~nahms|voll** sympathetic; **t~nehmen*** (*sep*) (**t. an** *dat* take part in, participate in; fight in; share in); **t~nehmend** participating; sympathetic; **der ~nehmer, –** participant; *sp* competitor; *tel* subscriber; **die ~nehmer|zahl, –en** number of participants/*tel* subscribers; attendance; **die ~strecke, –n** section; stage; **der ~strich, –e** graduation mark; **das ~stück, –e** part; section; **t~weise** partial; (*adv*) partly; in parts; in some cases; **die ~zahlung, –en** instalment (**auf T.** on hire-purchase/the installment plan *US*); **die ~zeit|arbeit** part-time work

teilbar divisible

[das] **Teilchen, –** *phys* particle

teilen divide (*also math*) (**in** *acc* into); share; (*v/i*) share; **sich ~** divide; (curtain) part; split up; (opinions) differ; **sich ~ in** (*acc*) divide into; share (costs *etc*); **geteilter Meinung sein** disagree

[der] **Teiler, –** *math* divisor

teilhaftig: (+*gen*) **~ werden** receive; be blessed with

–teilig -part; -piece

teils partly; **~, ~** (*in reply*) yes and no; so-so; **~ ..., ~ ...** partly ..., partly ...; some ..., some ...

[die] **Teilung, –en** division (*also math*); **~ der Gewalten** separation of powers

[der] **Teint** [tɛ̃ː], **–s** complexion

[der] **Telebrief, –e** fax

[das] **Telefon, –e** telephone; **~ haben** be on the phone; **ans ~ gehen** answer the phone

Telefon– [*also* 'teː–] telephone ...; **das ~buch, ⸚er** telephone directory; **das ~gespräch, –e** telephone call/conversation; **die ~nummer, –n** telephone number; **die ~seel|sorge** *approx* = the Samaritans; **die ~zelle, –n** telephone booth; **die ~zentrale, –n** switchboard

[das] **Telefonat, –e** telephone call

telefonieren telephone, make a telephone call; be on the phone; ~ **mit** speak to on the telephone
telefonisch telephone; (*adv*) by telephone
der **Telefonist, –en** (*wk masc*) telephone operator, telephonist
telegen telegenic
das **Telegramm, –e** telegram; **der ~stil** telegraphic style
der **Telegraph, –en** (*wk masc*) telegraph; *in compds* **~en–** telegraph ...; **der ~en|mast, –e(n)** telegraph pole
die **Telegraphie** telegraphy
telegraphieren telegraph, wire
telegraphisch telegraphic; (*adv*) by telegram
das **Telekolleg** *approx* = Open University
das **Tele|objektiv, –e** telephoto lens
die **Telepathie** telepathy
telepathisch telepathic
Telephon *etc* = **Telefon** *etc*
das **Teleskop, –e** telescope
teleskopisch telescopic
das **Telex, –(e)** telex
telexen, *Swiss* **telexieren** telex
der **Teller, –** plate; *ski* basket; **der ~wäscher, –** dish-washer
der **Tempel, –** temple
die **Tempera|farbe, –n** tempera
das **Temperament, –e** temperament; vivaciousness, high spirits; **sein ~ geht mit ihm durch** his temper runs away with him || **t~los** spiritless; **t~voll** spirited; vivacious
die **Temperatur, –en** temperature (*also med*); **jmds. ~ messen** take s.o.'s temperature
Temperatur– ... in temperature; **der ~regler, –** thermostat
temperieren heat moderately; keep (feelings) in check; **gut temperiert** (wine) at the right temperature; = **angenehm temperiert** (room) pleasantly warm
das **Tempo** speed; pace; (*pl* **Tempi**) *mus* tempo; ~(, ~)! step on it! || **das ~limit, –s** speed limit; **das ~taschen|tuch, ⸚er** (*trade-mark*) *cf* Kleenex
temporal *gramm* temporal
temporär temporary
das **Tempus, –(p)ora** *gramm* tense
die **Tendenz, –en** tendency (**zu** towards); trend (*also fin*); slant; **die ~ haben zu ...** tend to ..., have a tendency to ...
Tendenz– *liter* (drama, novel, literature) with a (political, social, *etc*) message; **die ~wende, –n** change of direction
tendenziell according to tendency
tendenziös tendentious; slanted
tendieren tend (*also fin*); (*eg* **nach links ~**) show a (leftward *etc*) tendency; ~ **zu** tend towards; tend to have; **dazu ~ zu ...** tend to ...
Teneriffa Tenerife

die **Tenne, –n** threshing-floor
das **Tennis** [–ɪs] (*gen* –) tennis; **der ~crack, –s** top tennis player; **der ~platz, ⸚e** tennis court; **der ~schläger, –** tennis racket
der **Tenor**[1] tenor (of sth.)
der **Tenor**[2], **⸚e** *mus* tenor
der **Tentakel, –** (*also* **das**) tentacle
das **Tenü, –s** *Swiss* garb
der **Teppich, –e** carpet; **auf dem ~ bleiben** *coll* be reasonable; **unter den ~ kehren** sweep under the carpet || **der ~boden, ..böden** wall-to-wall carpeting; **die ~kehr|maschine, –n** carpet-sweeper; **der ~klopfer, –** carpet-beater
Terenz Terence
der **Termin, –e** (appointed) date; deadline; appointment; *leg* hearing; **letzter ~** deadline; closing date
Termin– *comm* forward ...; **t~gemäß** = **t~gerecht** on schedule; **der ~kalender, –** (appointments) diary
das **Terminal** ['tøːɐminəl, 'tœr–], **–s** (*see also next entry*) *comput* terminal
der **Terminal** ['tøːɐminəl, 'tœr–], **–s** (*also* **das**) (air, container) terminal
die **Terminologie, –(ie)n** terminology
terminologisch terminological
der **Terminus, –(n)i** term; ~ **technicus** [–ç–], **–(n)i –(c)i** [–tsi] technical term
die **Termite, –n** termite
das **Terpentin** turpentine; = **das ~öl** (oil of) turpentine, turps
das **Terrain** [–'rɛ̃ː], **–s** terrain; **das ~ sondieren** see how the land lies; *mil* spy out the land
die **Terrakotta, –(tt)en** terracotta
die **Terrasse, –n** terrace; patio; **t~n|förmig** (**t. angelegt** terraced)
terrassieren terrace
der **Terrier** [–iɐ], **–** terrier
die **Terrine, –n** tureen
territorial (*in compds* **T~–**) territorial
das **Territorium, –(i)en** territory; *EGer* (administrative) area
der **Terror** terrorism; *in compds* terrorist ...; **der ~akt, –e** terrorist act
terrorisieren terrorize
der **Terrorismus** terrorism
der **Terrorist, –en** (*wk masc*), **terroristisch** terrorist
die **Tertia** [–ts–], **–(i)en** (*fourth* (**Unter~**) *and fifth* (**Ober~**) *years of the* Gymnasium)
der **Tertianer** [–ts–], **–** pupil in the *Tertia*
tertiär [–ts–] tertiary; *geol* Tertiary; **das Tertiär** the Tertiary
die **Terz, –en** *mus* third; *fenc* tierce
das **Terzett, –e** (vocal) trio
Tesa– (*trade-mark*): **~film** (*no art*) Sellotape, Scotch tape *US* (**mit T. ankleben** sellotape, scotch-tape *US*); **~krepp** (*no art*) masking tape

das **Tessin** Ticino
der **Test, –s/–e** test; **das ~bild, –er** *TV* test card/pattern *US*; **die ~person, –en** subject; **der ~pilot, –en** (*wk masc*) test pilot; **die ~reihe, –n** series of tests
das **Testament, –e** will; (political *etc*) legacy; *bibl* Testament
testamentarisch testamentary; (*also adv*) in one's will
Testaments–: die ~er|öffnung, –en reading of the will; **der ~vollstrecker, –** executor
testen test (**auf** *acc* for)
das **Tetra|eder, –** tetrahedron
teuer dear, expensive; (price) high; (friend *etc*) dear; (*adv*: buy, sell) at a high price; **wie ~ ist ...?** what does ... cost?; **teurer werden** go up (in price); (+*acc*) **~ zu stehen kommen** cost (s.o.) a lot; cost (s.o.) dear
die **Teuerung, –en** rise in prices; **die ~s|rate, –n** rate of price increases
der **Teufel, –** devil; **dort ist der ~ los** *coll* all hell's broken loose; **hol ihn der ~!** damn him!; **den ~ werde ich tun!** I'm damned if I will!; **weiß der ~, ...** *coll* God only knows ...; **den ~ an die Wand malen** tempt providence; **des ~s sein** *coll* be off one's head; **wie der ~** *coll* like blazes; **pfui ~!** ugh!; **~ noch mal!** damn it!; **auf ~ komm raus** *coll* like blazes, like mad; **in ~s Küche kommen** *coll* get into a hell of a mess; **es müßte doch mit dem ~ zugehen, wenn ...** *coll* it would be very strange if ...; **zum ~!** damn!; **wer** *etc* **zum ~ ...?** *coll* who *etc* the devil ...?; **zum ~ gehen** *coll* go west; **zum ~ jagen** *coll* send packing; **zum ~ sein** *coll* have had it; have gone west; **zum ~ mit ...!** to hell with ...! || **der ~s|kerl, –e** *coll* devil of a fellow; **der ~s|kreis, –e** vicious circle
die **Teufelei, –en** devilry; devilish trick
teuflisch diabolical, devilish
teur.. = teuer..
der **Teutone, –n** (*wk masc*) Teuton
teutonisch Teutonic
der **Text, –e** text; (advertising *etc*) copy; caption; *cin etc* script; *mus* words, (of pop song) lyrics; libretto; **aus dem ~ bringen** put off; **aus dem ~ kommen** lose the thread; **weiter im ~!** (let's) carry on!
Text– text ...; textual ...; **das ~buch, ¨er** libretto; **der ~dichter, –** librettist; **die ~kritik** textual criticism; **die ~stelle, –n** passage; **das ~system, –e** word-processor; **die ~ver|arbeitung** word processing
texten write (copy, *mus* lyrics)
der **Texter, –** copywriter; *mus* songwriter
Textil– textile ...; **t~frei** *joc* nude; **das ~geschäft, –e** clothes shop; **die ~waren** *pl* textiles
die **Textilien** [–iən] *pl* textiles

Tezett *coll*: **bis ins/zum ~** down to the last detail
TGL (= **Technische Normen, Gütevorschriften und Lieferbedingungen**) *EGer* Industrial Standard
die **TH, –(s)** = **Technische Hochschule**
Thai–: ~land Thailand; **der ~länder, –, t~ländisch** Thai
das **Theater, –** theatre; performance; *coll* fuss; **~ spielen** act; put on an act; **ins ~ gehen** go to the theatre; **zum ~ gehen** go on the stage || **der ~besucher, –** playgoer; **die ~kasse, –n** box-office; **das ~stück, –e** (stage) play
die **Theatralik** [–ɪk] theatricality
theatralisch theatrical (*also* = histrionic)
Theben Thebes
die **Theke, –n** bar; counter
das **Thema, –(m)en/–ta** subject; topic; *mus* theme
die **Thematik** [–ɪk] subject-matter
thematisch thematic (*also mus*); as regards subject-matter
die **Themse** the Thames
der **Theologe, –n** (*wk masc*) theologian
die **Theologie** theology
theologisch theological
der **Theoretiker, –** theorist
theoretisch theoretical
theoretisieren theorize
die **Theorie, –(ie)n** theory
der **Therapeut, –en** (*wk masc*) therapist
die **Therapeutik** [–ɪk] therapeutics
therapeutisch therapeutic
die **Therapie, –(ie)n** therapy
Thermal– thermal ...
die **Therme, –n** thermal spring
die **Thermik** [–ɪk] thermal
thermisch thermal
Thermo– thermo–
die **Thermodynamik** [–ɪk] thermodynamics
das **Thermometer, –** thermometer
thermonuklear thermonuclear
die **Thermopylen** *pl* Thermopylae
die **Thermos|flasche** [–ɔs–], **–n** (*trade-mark*) thermos (flask)
der **Thermostat, –e** (*or* **–en** (*wk masc*)) thermostat
die **These, –n** thesis; proposition
Thomas ['toːmas] Thomas; **ungläubiger ~** doubting Thomas
der **Thriller** ['θrɪlɐ], **–** thriller
die **Thrombose, –n** thrombosis
der **Thron, –e** throne; *joc* (child's) pot; **der ~erbe, –n** (*wk masc*) heir to the throne; **die ~folge** succession (to the throne); **der ~folger, –** successor to the throne
thronen sit in state; tower (above sth.)
Thukydides [–ɛs] Thucydides
der **Thun|fisch, –e** tuna(-fish)
Thüringen Thuringia

^der **Thüringer, –, thüringisch** Thuringian
^der **Thymian** thyme
^die **Tiara, –(r)en** tiara
^der **Tiber** Tiber
Tibet ['ti:bɛt] Tibet
^der **Tibetaner, –, tibetanisch, der Tibeter, –, tibetisch,** (*language*) **Tibetisch** Tibetan
Tibull Tibullus
^der **Tick, –s** quirk; *med* tic
ticken tick
^das **Ticket** [–ət], **–s** ticket
ticktack! tick-tock!
^die **Tide, –n** *NGer* tide
tief deep; low (*also mus*); profound; (*adv*) deep; deeply; profoundly; (bow, fly) low; **~ schlafen** be fast asleep; **bis ~ in** (*acc*) well into; far into (night); **im ~en Wald** in the depths of the forest; **im ~sten Afrika** in darkest Africa
^das **Tief, –s** *meteor* low, depression
Tief– deep ...; low ...; (**tief–**) deep (blue *etc*); deeply ...;
der ~angriff, –e low-level attack; **der ~bau** civil engineering; **t~bewegt** deeply moved; **der ~druck, –e** *meteor* low pressure; *print* gravure; **die ~ebene, –n** low-lying plain; **t~empfunden** heartfelt; **tief|ernst** deadly serious; **der ~flug, ⸚e** low-altitude flight; **der ~gang** (intellectual) depth; *naut* draught; **die ~garage, –n** underground car park, basement garage *US*; **t~gefroren** deep-frozen; **t~gehend** deep; profound; (pain) acute; **t~gekühlt** deep-frozen; **t~greifend** far-reaching; profound; **t~gründig** profound; **das ~kühl|fach, ⸚er** freezer compartment; **die ~kühl|kost** deep-frozen food; **die ~kühl|truhe, –n** deep-freeze, freezer; **der ~lader, – = der ~lade|wagen, –** low-loader; **das ~land, ⸚er** lowland(s); **t~liegend** low-lying; (eyes) deep-set; **der ~punkt, –e** low (point) (**seinen T. erreichen** reach rock-bottom); **der ~schlag, ⸚e** blow below the belt; body-blow (**für** to) ((+*dat*) **einen T. versetzen** hit below the belt); **t~schürfend** profound; **~see–** deep-sea ...; **der ~sinn** profundity; melancholy; **t~sinnig** profound; melancholy; **t~sitzend** deep-seated; **der ~stand** low (point); nadir; **t~stapeln** (*sep*) be modest; **der ~start, –s** crouch start; **t~stehend** low; inferior; **tief|traurig** extremely sad; **t~verwurzelt** deep-rooted

^die **Tiefe, –n** depth; lowness; depths; profundity; **auf ~ gehen** *naut* dive
Tiefen– depth ...; **die ~struktur, –en** *ling* deep structure; **die ~wirkung** deep action; *art* effect of depth
tiefer–: ~gehend *etc*: *comp of* **tiefgehend** *etc*
Tiefst– lowest ...
^der **Tiegel, –** *tech* crucible; *print* platen
^das **Tier, –e** animal; (= person) beast, brute; **großes/hohes ~** *coll* big shot || **der ~arzt, ⸚e** veterinary surgeon, veterinarian *US*; **der ~freund, –e** animal-lover; **der ~garten, ..gärten** zoo; **die ~handlung, –en** pet shop; **die ~heil|kunde** veterinary science; **der ~kreis** zodiac; **das ~kreis|zeichen, –** sign of the zodiac; **die ~kunde** zoology; **t~liebend** animal-loving; **die ~quälerei** cruelty to animals; **das ~reich, –e** animal kingdom; **das ~schutz|gebiet, –e** wildlife sanctuary; **der ~schutz|verein** society for the prevention of cruelty to animals; **die ~welt** animal kingdom
tierisch animal; bestial; **~er Ernst** *coll* deadly seriousness
Tiflis [–ɪs] Tbilisi
^der **Tiger, –** tiger
^die **Tigerin, –nen** tigress
tigern (*see also* **getigert**) (*sn*) *coll* traipse
^der **Tigris** [–ɪs] (*gen* –) the Tigris
tilgen wipe out; erase; pay off
^die **Tilgung, –en** *vbl noun*; *also* erasure; repayment
^das **Timbre** ['tɛ̃:brə, –bʁ], **–s** timbre
Timbuktu Timbuctoo
timen ['taɪ–] (*p/part* **getimt**) time
^das **Timing** ['taɪ–], **–s** timing
tingeln perform in small clubs, discos, *etc*; **~ durch** (*sn*) tour (country *etc*) performing in small clubs, discos, *etc*
^das **Tingeltangel, –** (*also* **der**) *dated* cheap dance-hall, honky-tonk *US*
^die **Tinktur, –en** tincture
^der **Tinnef** [–ɛf] *coll* junk, rubbish
^die **Tinte, –n** ink; **in der ~ sitzen** *coll* be in the soup || **das ~n|faß, ⸚(ss)er** inkpot; inkwell; **der ~n|fisch, –e** cuttlefish; squid; octopus; **der ~n|fleck, –e(n)** ink stain; = **der ~n|klecks, –e** (ink-)blot; **der ~n|stift, –e** indelible pencil
tintig inky
^der **Tip** [–ɪ–], **–s** tip; tip-off
Tipp–: der ~fehler, – typing error; **das ~fräulein, –** *coll* typist; **tipp|topp** *coll* tip-top (**t. in Ordnung** spick-and-span); **der ~zettel, –** pools/lottery coupon
^der **Tippel|bruder, ..brüder** *coll* gentleman of the road
tippeln (*sn*) *coll* foot it
tippen type; (*v/i*) do the pools/lottery; type; **~ an** (*acc*) tap; touch; touch on (matter); **~ auf** (*acc*) tap; *coll* tip; (**darauf**) **~, daß ...** *coll* bet (that) ...
^die **Tippse, –n** *coll* (mere) typist
tipp, tapp! pitter-patter
^die **Tirade, –n** tirade
tirilieren warble
^das **Tirol** the Tyrol

der **Tiroler, –, tirolisch** (*Aust* **tirolerisch**) Tyrolean, Tyrolese

der **Tisch, –e** table; desk; **reinen ~ machen** *coll* sort things out; **bei ~** at table; **nach/vor ~** after/before the meal; **unter den ~ fallen** *coll* go by the board; **unter den ~ fallen lassen** *coll* forget about; **unter den ~ trinken** *coll* drink under the table; **vom ~ fegen** brush aside; **vom grünen ~ aus** bureaucratically; **getrennt von ~ und Bett** separated; **zu ~ bitten** ask to come to table; **sich zu ~ setzen** sit down to a meal || **die ~dame, –n** dinner partner; **die ~decke, –n** tablecloth; **das ~gebet, –e** grace; **das ~gespräch, –e** table talk; **der ~herr, –en** (*like* **Herr**) dinner partner; **die ~lampe, –n** table-lamp; **die ~platte, –n** table-top; **die ~rede, –n** after-dinner speech; **das ~tennis** table tennis; **der ~tennis|schläger, –** table tennis bat; **das ~tuch, ¨-er** tablecloth; **der ~wein, –e** table wine

der **Tischler, –** joiner; cabinet-maker

die **Tischlerei, –en** joinery; cabinet-making; joiner's/cabinet-maker's workshop

tischlern *coll* make (piece of furniture); (*v/i*) do woodwork

das **Titan** titanium

der **Titan, –en** (*wk masc*) (intellectual *etc*) giant; *myth* Titan

der **Titel, –** title; **der ~anwärter, –** *sp* contender (for title); **das ~bild, –er** cover picture; frontispiece; **das ~blatt, ¨-er** title-page; **das ~mädchen, –** cover-girl; **die ~rolle, –n** title role; **die ~seite, –n** front page; **der ~träger, –** person with a title; *sp* title-holder; **der ~verteidiger, –** defending champion

die **Titte, –n** (*usu pl*) *vulg* tit

die **Titulatur, –en** title (= form of address)

titulieren = ~ als/mit call (s.o. sth.)

Tizian ['ti:tsĭa:n] Titian; **t~rot** titian

tja! (*reflective*, *resigned*, *etc*) hm!, well!

der **Toast** [–o:–], **–e/–s** slice of toast; toast (to s.o.); **einen ~ ausbringen auf** (*acc*) propose a toast to

toasten [–o:–] toast (bread); **~ auf** (*acc*) drink a toast to

der **Toaster** [–ɐ], **–** toaster

Tob–: die ~sucht raving madness; **t~süchtig** raving mad; **der ~suchts|anfall, ¨-e** fit of rage

Tobak [–ak] *coll*: **das ist starker ~** that's a bit much

toben rage; rave; (child) romp about, (*sn*) rampage (through sth.); **~ vor** (*dat*) go wild with

die **Tochter,** *pl* **Töchter** daughter; *Swiss* girl; maid; waitress; **die ~firma, –(m)en** subsidiary

töchterlich daughterly; filial

der **Tod, –e** death; **den ~ finden** be killed; **(ein Kind) des ~es sein** be doomed; **eines (natürlichen** *etc*) **~es sterben** die a (natural *etc*) death; **auf den ~ krank** dangerously ill; **auf den ~ nicht leiden können** *coll* be unable to abide; **zu ~e** to death; **sich zu ~e langweilen/schämen** be bored to death/utterly ashamed || **tod|ernst** deadly serious; **der ~feind, –e** mortal enemy; **t~geweiht** doomed; **tod|krank** dangerously ill; **tod|müde** dead tired; **tod|schick** *coll* dead smart; **tod|sicher** *coll* dead certain; sure-fire; (*adv*) for sure (**t~sichere Sache** dead certainty, cinch); **die ~sünde, –n** mortal sin; **tod|unglücklich** *coll* desperately unhappy

Todes– ... of death; death ...; mortal ...; fatal ...; **die ~angst** fear of death; mortal fear (**~ängste ausstehen** be scared to death); **die ~anzeige, –n** obituary notice; **der ~fall, ¨-e** death; **die ~gefahr, –en** deadly peril; **der ~kampf, ¨-e** death throes; **der ~kandidat, –en** (*wk masc*) man/woman at death's door; **t~mutig** absolutely fearless; **das ~opfer, –** fatality; victim; **der ~stoß, ¨-e** death-blow; **die ~strafe** capital punishment; **der ~tag, –e** day/anniversary of s.o.'s death; **die ~ursache, –n** cause of death; **das ~urteil, –e** death sentence; **die ~ver|achtung** defiance of death (**mit T.** *coll* without batting an eyelid); **die ~zelle, –n** condemned cell

tödlich fatal; mortal; deadly; lethal; (*adv*) (offend) mortally; (be bored) to death; **~ verunglücken** be killed in an accident

das **Töff, –s** (*also* **der**) *Swiss coll* motor-bike

tofte *NGer coll* 'great'

die **Toga, –(g)en** toga

das **Tohuwabohu** (*gen* –(s)) **–s** *coll* shambles

die **Toilette** [tŏa–], **–n** lavatory; toilet (= dressing *etc*); (lady's formal) dress; **auf die ~ gehen** go to the lavatory || **die ~n|artikel** *pl* toiletries; **das ~n|papier** lavatory paper; **der ~n|tisch, –e** dressing-table

toi, toi, toi! good luck!; touch wood!

Tokio Tokyo

die **Töle, –n** *NGer coll* cur

tolerant tolerant (**gegen** of)

die **Toleranz, –en** tolerance (*also tech*) (**gegen** of)

tolerieren tolerate

toll wild; *arch* (person, dog) mad; *coll* crazy, mad; *coll* terrific; *coll* awful; **wie ~** *coll* like mad; **es zu ~ treiben** *coll* go too far || **~dreist** bold; **das T~haus, ¨-er** madhouse; **die T~kirsche, –n** deadly nightshade; **~kühn** daredevil; **die T~wut** rabies; **~wütig** rabid

die **Tolle, –n** quiff

tollen romp about; (*sn*) romp (through streets *etc*)

der **Tolpatsch, -e** *coll* clumsy fellow
tolpatschig *coll* clumsy
der **Tölpel, -** (clumsy) fool; *ornith* gannet
tölpelhaft dull-witted (and clumsy)
Tolstoi Tolstoy
die **Tomate, -n** tomato; **das ~n|mark = das ~n|püree** tomato puree
der **Ton**[1], **-e** clay
der **Ton**[2], **⸗e** sound (*also cin, rad, TV*); tone (*also ling*); stress; tone (of voice); tone, shade; *mus* note; **ganzer ~** whole tone, **halber ~** semitone; **der gute ~** good form; **den ~ angeben** set the tone; *mus* give the note; **einen anderen ~ anschlagen** change one's tune; **keinen ~ von sich geben** not utter a sound; **dicke/große Töne reden/spucken** *coll* talk big; **hast du Töne!** did you ever!; **~ in ~** in shades of the same colour
Ton–: der ~abnehmer, - pick-up; **t~angebend** who/which set(s) the tone (**t. sein** set the tone); **der ~arm, -e** pick-up arm; **die ~art, -en** tone (adopted by speaker); *mus* key; (Dorian *etc*) mode (**eine andere T. anschlagen** change one's tune); **das ~band, ⸗er** tape (**mit** of) (**auf T.** on tape); **die ~band|aufnahme, -n** tape-recording; **das ~band|gerät, -e** tape-recorder; **die ~dichtung, -en** tone-poem; **die ~erde** aluminium oxide, aluminum oxide *US*; **der ~fall** tone of voice; intonation; **der ~film, -e** sound-film; **die ~folge, -n** sequence of notes; melody; **das ~gefäß, -e** earthenware vessel; **das ~geschirr** earthenware; **das ~geschlecht, -er** *mus* scale; **die ~höhe, -n** *ling, mus* pitch; **der ~kopf, ⸗e** sound-head; **die ~lage, -n** *mus* pitch; **die ~leiter, -n** *mus* scale; **t~los** toneless; (voice) flat; (*adv*) in a flat voice; **der ~meister, -** sound engineer; recordist; **die ~spur, -en = der ~streifen, -** sound-track; **die ~taube, -n** clay pigeon; **die ~waren** *pl* earthenware
tonal tonal
die **Tonalität** tonality
tönen tint; (*v/i*) sound; resound; *coll* boast; **~d** sonorous; (words) empty
tönern clay
die **Tonnage** [-ʒə], **-n** tonnage
die **Tonne, -n** barrel; tonne, metric ton; *naut* buoy
die **Tonsur, -en** tonsure
die **Tönung, -en** *vbl noun*; *also* tint, tone
Top– [-ɔ-] top (model *etc*); **top|fit** in top form
der **Topas** (*gen* **-es**), **-e** topaz
der **Topf, ⸗e** pot; **in einen ~ werfen** lump together || **die ~blume, -n** pot plant; **der ~gucker, -** *coll* person who looks into the cooking pots to see what meal is being prepared; nosey parker; **der ~lappen, -** oven-cloth; **die ~pflanze, -n** pot plant
der **Topfen, -** *SGer* = **Quark**
der **Töpfer, -** potter; **die ~scheibe, -n** potter's wheel; **die ~waren** *pl* pottery
die **Töpferei, -en** pottery
töpfern throw (vase *etc*); (*v/i*) do pottery
die **Topographie, -(ie)n** topography
topographisch topographic
der **Topp, -e(n)/-s** *naut* masthead; **das ~segel, -** top-sail
das **Tor, -e** gate (*also comput*); door (of garage *etc*); gateway; *sp* goal, *ski* gate; **ein ~ schießen** score a goal
der **Tor, -en** (*wk masc*) fool
Tor–: der ~bogen, -/..bögen archway; **der ~hüter, -** goalkeeper; **der ~lauf, ⸗e** slalom; **die ~linie, -n** goal-line; **t~los** goalless; **der ~mann, ⸗er** goalkeeper; **~schluß (kurz vor T.** at the eleventh hour); **die ~schluß|panik** last-minute panic; fear of being left on the shelf; **der ~schütze, -n** (*wk masc*) goal-scorer; **das ~verhältnis, -se** score; **der ~wart, -e** goalkeeper
Tores|schluß = Torschluß
der **Torf** peat; **das ~moos** sphagnum; **der ~mull** garden peat
die **Torheit, -en** folly
töricht foolish
die **Törin, -nen** foolish woman
torkeln (*also sn*; *if indicating direction*, *only sn*) stagger
der **Tornister, -** *mil* knapsack
torpedieren torpedo
der **Torpedo, -s** torpedo; **das ~boot, -e** torpedo-boat
die **Torsion, -en** torsion
der **Torso, -s/Torsi** torso
die **Torte, -n** gâteau; **der ~n|boden, ..böden** flan-case; **der ~n|heber, -** cake-slice
die **Tortur, -en** torture (= great ordeal)
tosen rage; (*sn if indicating direction*) roar, thunder; **~d** (applause) thunderous
die **Toskana** Tuscany
der **Toskaner, -, toskanisch** Tuscan
tot dead; **das T~e Meer** the Dead Sea; **~er Punkt** (*see* **Punkt**); **~es Rennen** dead heat; **der/die Tote** (*decl as adj*) dead person; **die T~en** *pl* the dead || **~arbeiten** (*sep*): **sich t.** *coll* work oneself to death; **~ärgern** (*sep*): **sich t.** *coll* be livid; **~fahren*** (*sep*) knock down and kill; **~geboren** stillborn (**ein ~geborenes Kind sein** *coll* be doomed to failure); **die T~geburt, -en** stillbirth; stillborn child; **~kriegen** *coll* (**nicht ~zukriegen** irrepressible); **~lachen** (*sep*): **sich t.** *coll* kill oneself laughing (**... ist zum T. ...** is killing); **~laufen*** (*sep*): **sich t.** *coll* peter out; **~machen** (*sep*) *coll* kill; **~sagen** (*sep*) declare dead; **~schießen*** (*sep*) shoot dead; **der T~schlag, ⸗e** manslaughter;

~schlagen* (*sep*) kill; **der T~schläger, -** cosh, blackjack *US*; **~schuften** (*sep*): **sich t.** *coll* work oneself to death; **~schweigen*** (*sep*) hush up; **~stellen** (*sep*): **sich t.** pretend to be dead; **~treten*** (*sep*) tread on and kill; trample to death

total total; (war) all-out

das **Total, -e** *Swiss* total

Total- total ...; **die ~operation, -en** *med* extirpation; hysterectomy; **der ~schaden, ..schäden** write-off

der **Totalisator, -(or)en** totalizator

totalitär totalitarian

der **Totalitarismus** totalitarianism

die **Totalität** totality

das **Totem** [-ɛm], **-s** totem; **der ~pfahl, ⸗e** totem pole

töten kill

Toten- ... of the dead; **das ~amt, ⸗er** requiem (mass); **das ~bett, -en** death-bed; **toten|blaß** deathly pale; **die ~blässe** deathly pallor; **toten|bleich** deathly pale; **die ~feier, -n** funeral rites; **die ~glocke, -n** funeral bell; **der ~gräber, -** gravedigger; **das ~hemd, -en** shroud; **der ~kopf, ⸗e** skull; death's head; skull and crossbones; *ent* death's-head moth; **der ~kult, -e** cult of the dead; **die ~maske, -n** death-mask; **die ~messe, -n** requiem mass; **der ~schein, -e** death-certificate; **die ~starre** rigor mortis; **toten|still** deathly silent; **die ~stille** deathly silence; **der ~tanz, ⸗e** dance of death; **die ~wache, -n** wake

das **Toto, -s** (*also* **der**) (state-run) football pools; **im ~ gewinnen** win the pools || **der ~schein, -e** pools coupon

die **Tötung** killing; **fahrlässige ~** *approx* = manslaughter

das **Toupet** [tu'pe:], **-s** toupee

toupieren [tu-] back-comb

die **Tour** [-u:-], **-en** tour; trip; *mech* revolution; *danc* figure; *knit* row; *coll* ploy; **wieder seine ~ haben** *coll* be in one of one's moods again; **auf ~** away on a trip; **auf die (freundliche** *etc*) **~** *coll* the (friendly *etc*) way; **auf die krumme ~** *coll* by dishonest means; **auf 'die ~ darfst du mir nicht kommen!** don't try that one on me; **auf vollen ~en laufen** run at full speed; *coll* be in full swing; **auf ~en bringen** rev up; *coll* get (s.o.) going/worked up; **auf ~en kommen** pick up speed; *coll* get into one's/its stride; get worked up; **in 'einer ~** *coll* incessantly

Touren- touring ...; **die ~zahl, -en** number of revolutions; **der ~zähler, -** rev counter

der **Tourismus** [tu-] tourism

der **Tourist** [tu-], **-en** (*wk masc*) tourist; **die ~en|klasse** tourist class

die **Touristik** [tu-, -ɪk] tourism, tourist industry

die **Tournee** [tʊr-], **-s/-(ee)n** *mus*, *theat* tour; **auf ~ (gehen)** (go) on tour

tour-retour ['tu:ɐre'tu:ɐ] *Aust* return, round-trip *US*

der **Tower** ['taʊɐ], **-** *aer* control tower

der **Trab** trot; **auf ~** *coll* on the go; **auf ~ bringen** *coll* make (s.o.) get a move on; **im ~** at a trot; **sich in ~ setzen** break into a trot || **das ~rennen, -** trotting race; trotting

der **Trabant, -en** (*wk masc*) satellite (*also* = hanger-on); **die ~en|stadt, ⸗e** satellite town

traben (*also sn*; *if indicating direction, only sn*) trot

die **Trachee** [-'xe:ə], **-n** *bot*, *zool* trachea

die **Tracht, -en** (traditional) costume; dress; (nurse's) uniform; *arch* load; **eine ~ Prügel** *coll* a thrashing

trachten: ~ nach strive after; (+*dat*) **nach dem Leben ~** be out to kill; **(danach) ~ zu ...** endeavour to ...

trächtig with young, *eg* in calf/farrow/foal; **~ von** laden with; **-trächtig** '*full of...*'

tradieren hand down

die **Tradition, -en** tradition; **... ist ~** ... is a tradition

traditionell traditional

traditions-: ~gemäß traditionally; **~reich** rich in tradition

traf (träfe) *p/t* (*subj*) *of* **treffen**

die **Trafik, -en** *Aust* tobacconist's, tobacco store *US* (also selling stamps, newspapers, *etc*)

der **Trafikant, -en** (*wk masc*) *Aust* tobacconist

der **Trafo, -s** transformer

Trag-: die ~bahre, -n stretcher; **t~fähig** able to support a load; acceptable; **die ~fläche, -n** *aer* wing; *naut* hydrofoil; **das ~flächen|boot, -e** hydrofoil; **der ~flügel, -** *aer* wing; **das ~flügel|boot, -e** hydrofoil; **der ~korb, ⸗e** pannier; **die ~kraft, ⸗e** load-bearing capacity; **die ~last, -en** load; **der ~riemen, -** strap; *mil* sling; **der ~sessel, -** sedan chair; **die ~weite** range; significance; (possible) implications; **das ~werk, -e** *aer* wing assembly

tragbar portable; wearable; tolerable; acceptable (**für** to)

die **Trage, -n** litter; **die ~tasche, -n** carrier-bag

träge sluggish; lethargic; *phys* inert

tragen (träg(s)t, *p/t* **trug** (*subj* **trüge**), *p/part* **getragen)** (*see also* **getragen**) carry; take (to a place); wear; bear (name, title); support; bear (fruit), *fin* yield (interest *etc*); bear, endure; bear (cost), take (consequences); (*v/i*) be with young; (tree) bear; (gun, voice) carry; (ice) take (s.o.'s) weight

~ an (*dat*): **schwer ~ an** have a job carrying; be weighed down by

bei sich ~ carry with one

in sich ~ contain within itself

sich ~ wear (well *etc*); dress; *comm* pay its way; **sich leicht/schwer ~** be easy/hard to carry; **sich ~ mit** entertain (idea); **sich mit der Absicht ~ zu ...** contemplate (+*ger*)

tragend (idea *etc*) fundamental, basic; (voice) that carries well; *theat* leading; *tech* load-bearing; *zool* = **trächtig**

der **Träger, –** wearer; bearer, porter, *med* stretcher-bearer; (shoulder-)strap; bearer (of name, title); representative; person/body responsible (*gen* for); vehicle (for); *med* carrier; *tech* support; *build* beam; girder || **das ~kleid, –er** pinafore dress, jumper *US*; **t~los** strapless; **die ~rakete, –n** booster (rocket)

die **Trägheit** sluggishness; lethargy; *phys* inertia

die **Tragik** [–ɪk] tragedy

der **Tragiker, –** tragedian

die **Tragikomödie** [–ĭə], **–n** tragicomedy

tragikomisch tragicomic

tragisch tragic; **~ nehmen** *coll* take to heart

die **Tragödie** [–ĭə], **–n** tragedy (*also theat*)

träg(s)t (*2nd*,) *3rd sing pres of* **tragen**

der **Trainer** ['trɛː–, 'treː–], **–** coach; trainer; *footb* manager; *Swiss* track-suit

trainieren [trɛ–, tre–] train; coach; practise; (*v/i*) train; **trainiert auf** (*acc*) trained to do

das **Training, –s** ['trɛː–, 'treː–] training; work-out; training session; practice; **der ~s|-anzug, ⸚e** track-suit; **die ~s|hose, –n** track-suit trousers; **die ~s|jacke, –n** track-suit top

Trajan Trajan

der **Trakt, –e** *archit* wing

die **Traktanden|liste, –n** *Swiss* agenda

das **Traktandum, –(d)en** *Swiss* item (on agenda)

das **Traktat, –e** (*also* **der**) treatise; tract

traktieren maltreat; torment; **~ mit** *coll* belabour with

der **Traktor, –(or)en** tractor

der **Traktorist, –en** (*wk masc*) *EGer* tractor-driver

trällern (*also v/i*) warble

das **Tram** [–a–], **–s** *Swiss*, **die Tram, –s** *SGer* tram, streetcar *US*; **die ~bahn, –en** *SGer* = **die ~way** [–vaɐ̯], **–s** *Aust* tram, streetcar *US*; tramway, streetcar line *US*

Tramp–: das ~schiff, –e *naut* tramp

der **Trampel, –** (*also* **das**) *coll* clumsy creature; **der ~pfad, –e** beaten path; **das ~tier, –e** (Bactrian) camel; *coll* clumsy creature

trampeln trample (path); stamp (from one's feet); (*v/i*) stamp one's feet; (*sn*) tramp

trampen [–ɛ–] (*sn*) hitch-hike

der **Tramper** [–ɛ–], **–** hitch-hiker

das **Trampolin** [*also* –'liːn], **–e** trampoline

der **Tran** whale-oil; **im ~** *coll* tipsy; dopey || **die ~funzel, –n** *coll* slowcoach, slowpoke *US*

die **Trance** ['trãːs(ə)], **–n** trance

Tranchier– [trãʃ–] carving ...; **das ~besteck, –e** carving-set

tranchieren [trãʃ–] carve

die **Träne, –n** tear; **~n lachen** laugh till one cries; **den ~n nahe** close to tears; **zu ~n rühren** move to tears

tränen (eye) water

Tränen–: die ~drüse, –n lachrymal gland (**auf die ~drüsen drücken** *coll* be a tear-jerker); **das ~gas** tear-gas; **t~reich** tearful

tranig (smell, taste) of whale-oil; *coll* sluggish

trank (tränke) *p/t* (*subj*) *of* **trinken**

der **Trank, ⸚e** *poet* drink; potion

die **Tränke, –n** watering-place

tränken water (animals); **~ mit** soak with; impregnate with

der **Tranquilizer** ['trɛŋkvɪlaɪ̯zɐ], **–** tranquillizer

die **Trans|aktion, –en** transaction

trans|atlantisch transatlantic

der **Transfer, –s** *fin*, *footb*, *tourism* transfer

transferieren *fin*, *footb*, *Aust admin* transfer

die **Transformation, –en** *math*, *phys*, *etc* transformation; **die ~s|grammatik** transformational grammar

der **Transformator, –(or)en** transformer

transformieren *math*, *phys*, *etc* transform

die **Transfusion, –en** transfusion

der **Transistor, –(or)en** transistor; = **das ~gerät, –e** = **das ~radio, –s** transistor (radio)

transistorisieren transistorize

der **Transit, –e** transit

transitiv transitive

transkribieren transcribe (*also mus*); transliterate

die **Transkription, –en** transcription (*also mus*); transliteration

transparent transparent

das **Transparent, –e** banner; transparency

die **Transparenz** transparency; openness (in government *etc*)

transpirieren perspire; *bot* transpire

das **Transplantat, –e** *med* transplant (=organ *etc*)

die **Transplantation, –en** *med* transplant

transplantieren *med* transplant

transponieren *mus* transpose

der **Transport, –e** transport(ation); moving (of patient *etc*); shipment; **auf dem/beim ~** in transit || **das ~band, ⸚er** conveyor belt; **t~fähig** transportable, movable; **die ~kosten** *pl* carriage; **das ~mittel, –** means of transport; **das ~unternehmen, –** haulage contractor; **das ~wesen** transport(ation) (system)

transportabel portable; transportable

der **Transporter, –** transport vehicle/aircraft/vessel; *mil* transport

transportieren transport; move (patient *etc*); *phot* wind on

transsexuell transsexual

der **Transvestit, –en** (*wk masc*) transvestite

der **Transvest(it)ismus** transvestism

transzendent transcendent(al)
die **Transzendenz** transcendence
das **Trapez, –e** trapeze; *math* trapezium
die **Trappe, –n** bustard
trappeln (hooves) clatter; (*sn*) patter; clip-clop
trapp, trapp! clip-clop!; clitter-clatter!
das **Trara** *coll* 'song and dance'
die **Trasse, –n** route (of new road *etc*)
trassieren mark out the route of
trat (träte) *p/t* (*subj*) *of* **treten**
der **Tratsch** [–aː–] *coll*, **tratschen** *coll* gossip
Trau– marriage ...; wedding ...; **der ~ring, –e** wedding-ring; **der ~schein, –e** marriage certificate; **der ~zeuge, –n** (*wk masc*) witness (at wedding ceremony)
die **Traube, –n** grape; bunch of grapes; cluster; **die ~n|lese, –n** grape-harvest; **der ~n|saft, ⸚e** grape-juice; **der ~n|zucker** glucose
trauen marry, wed (couple); (+*dat*) trust; **seinen Augen/Ohren nicht ~** be unable to believe one's eyes/ears; **sich ~ zu ...** dare to ...; **sich ~ lassen** get married
die **Trauer** sorrow, grief; mourning (**um** for); **~ tragen** wear mourning
Trauer– mourning ...; funeral ...; **die ~anzeige, –n** obituary notice; **die ~botschaft, –en** sad news; **der ~fall, ⸚e** bereavement; **die ~feier, –n** funeral service; **der ~flor, –e** mourning band; **die ~kleidung** mourning; **der ~kloß, ⸚e** *coll* wet blanket; **der ~marsch, ⸚e** funeral march; **der ~rand, ⸚er** black border; (*pl*) *coll* dirty fingernails; **die ~rede, –n** funeral oration; **das ~spiel, –e** tragedy; **t~voll** mournful; **die ~weide, –n** weeping willow; **die ~zeit** (period of) mourning; **der ~zug, ⸚e** funeral procession
trauern mourn; wear mourning; **~ über** (*acc*) mourn (over) (loss); **~ um** mourn (for); mourn (s.o.'s death)
die **Traufe, –n** eaves
träufeln pour out (in drops); (*v/i, also sn*) drip
traulich cosy
der **Traum, ⸚e** dream; **böser ~** nightmare; **aus der ~!** it's all over!; **das fällt mir nicht im ~ ein!** I wouldn't dream of it! || **das ~bild, –er** vision; **t~verloren** lost in dreams; (*adv*) dreamily
das **Trauma, –(m)en/–(m)ata** trauma
traumatisch traumatic
träumen (*also v/i*) dream; **das hätte ich mir nicht ~ lassen** I would never have thought it possible
der **Träumer, –** dreamer
die **Träumerei, –en** day-dreaming; reverie
träumerisch dreamy
traumhaft dreamlike; *coll* fabulous; **~ schön** *coll* ... dream of a ...
traurig sad; pathetic
traut cosy; *poet* beloved
Traute *coll*: **(keine) ~ haben zu ...** (not) have the guts to ...
die **Trauung, –en** marriage ceremony
die **Travestie, –(ie)n** *liter* travesty
der **Trawler** ['trɔːlɐ], – trawler
der **Treck, –s** trek; train (of refugees *etc*)
trecken (*sn*) trek
der **Trecker, –** tractor
der **Treff, –s** *coll* get-together; = **der ~punkt, –e** meeting-place; **t~sicher** accurate; unerring; to the point
treffen (triff(s)t, *p/t* **traf** (*subj* **träfe**), *p/part* **getroffen)** hit (*also* = affect), (lightning) strike, hit; meet; make (preparations, selection, *etc*), take (decision *etc*); reach (agreement); hit on; capture (sense, mood, *etc*); (remark *etc*) hurt; (news) shake; (blame) attach to; **es gut/schlecht ~** be lucky/unlucky (with weather *etc*); **auf dem Foto ist ... gut getroffen** it's a good picture of ...; **sich getroffen fühlen** take it personally; feel hurt
~ an (*dat*) touch on (tender spot)
~ auf (*acc*) (*sn*) come across; meet with, encounter; *sp* meet
sich ~ (mit) meet; **ihre Blicke trafen sich** their eyes met; **es trifft sich (gerade), daß ...** it (just) so happens that ...; **wie es sich gerade traf** as chance would have it
das **Treffen, –** meeting; *mil, sp* encounter; **ins ~ führen** put forward (as argument)
treffend apt
der **Treffer, –** hit (*also box, fenc, etc*), *footb* goal; winning ticket
trefflich *arch* excellent
Treib– *mech* driving ...; **das ~eis** drift-ice; **das ~haus, ⸚er** hothouse; **der ~haus|effekt** greenhouse effect; **das ~holz** drift-wood; **die ~jagd, –en** *hunt* battue; *pol* witch-hunt; **das ~mittel, –** (aerosol) propellant; *cul* raising agent; **der ~sand** quicksand; **der ~schlag, ⸚e** *sp* drive; **der ~stoff, –e** fuel
treiben (*p/t* **trieb,** *p/part* **getrieben)** drive; push (= urge); go in for; do; pursue (studies); be up to; *tech* chase (metal); *hort* force; *hunt* rouse (game); *bot* sprout; *cul* make (dough) rise; (*v/i*) *bot* sprout; *cul* rise; (*also sn*; *if indicating direction, only sn*) drift; **es ~** carry on (in a certain way); **es toll ~** have a wild time of it; **es/einen Spaß zu weit ~** carry things/a joke too far; **es so weit ~, daß ...** carry things to such lengths that ...; **es treibt mich (dorthin** *etc*) I feel drawn (there *etc*); **es treibt mich zu ...** I feel impelled to ...; **sich ~ lassen** drift; **+von** let oneself be carried along by
~ durch drive (nail, tunnel, *etc*) through
~ in (*acc*) drive into; **in die Höhe ~** force up (prices *etc*); (+*dat*) **die Tränen in**

die Augen/die Schamröte ins Gesicht ~ bring tears to (s.o.'s) eyes/a blush to (s.o.'s) cheeks; (+*dat*) **das Blut ins Gesicht** ~ send the blood rushing to (s.o.'s) face

mit: es ~ mit *coll* carry on with

~ **zu** drive to (despair *etc*); **zur Arbeit/Eile** ~ make (s.o.) work/hurry up

das **Treiben** *vbl noun*; *also* doings; goings-on; what (s.o.) is up to; hustle and bustle; *hunt* battue

treibend: ~e Kraft driving force

der **Treiber, –** drover; *hunt* beater

treideln tow (barge)

das **Trema, –s/–ta** diaeresis

der **Trend** [–t], **–s** trend

Trenn–: die ~schärfe *rad* selectivity; **die ~wand, ⸗e** partition

trennbar *gramm* separable

trennen (*see also* **getrennt**) separate, divide; segregate; distinguish (between), differentiate (between); *needlew* unpick (seam); *chem* separate; ~ **von** separate from; detach from; sever from

sich ~ divide; separate, split up; **sich ~ von** part with; part company with; **sich von einem Anblick nicht ~ können** be unable to take one's eyes off sth.

die **Trennung, –en** *vbl noun*; *also* separation; division; segregation; distinction (between concepts); **die ~s|entschädigung, –en** separation allowance; **der ~s|strich, –e** hyphen (**einen T. ziehen zwischen** draw a clear distinction between); **die ~s|wand, ⸗e** partition; **das ~s|zeichen, –** hyphen (at end of line)

die **Trense, –n** snaffle

trepp|auf: ~, treppab up and down the stairs

die **Treppe, –n** (flight of) stairs; steps; **die ~ hinauf/hinunter** upstairs/downstairs || **das ~n|geländer, –** banisters; **das ~n|haus, ⸗er** stairway; **der ~n|schritt, –e** *ski* sidestepping; **die ~n|stufe, –n** step; **der ~n|witz, –e** esprit de l'escalier (**T. der Weltgeschichte** irony of history)

der **Tresen, –** *NGer* counter; bar

der **Tresor, –e** safe; = **der ~raum, ⸗e** strongroom

die **Tresse, –n** braid

Tret–: das ~auto, –s pedal car; **das ~boot, –e** pedalo; **der ~eimer, –** pedal-bin; **die ~mühle, –n** treadmill; **das ~rad, ⸗er** treadwheel

treten (**tritt(st),** *p/t* **trat** (*subj* **träte**), *p/part* **getreten**) kick; operate (pedal *etc*); tread (path); kick (subordinate *etc*) around; *sp* take; *zool* tread; (*v/i sn*) tread; step; **Wasser** ~ tread water

~ **an** (*acc*) (*sn*) step over to

~ **auf** (*acc*) (*also sn*) step/tread on; (*sn*) step out onto (balcony)

~ **aus** (*sn*) step out of; come out of

~ **gegen** kick

~ **hinter** (*acc*) (*sn*) step behind; (moon) pass behind

~ **in** (*acc*) tread (seed *etc*) into; (*v/i, also sn*) step in(to); (*sn*) enter; (sap) rise in; (tears) come to (s.o.'s eyes); **sich** *dat* **... in den Fuß** ~ get (splinter *etc*) in one's foot

~ **nach** kick out at

~ **über** (*acc*) (*sn*) step over; overflow (its banks)

~ **vor** (*acc*) (*sn*) step in front of

die **Treter** *pl coll* (old) shoes

treu faithful; loyal; true; trusting; **zu ~en Händen** for safe keeping; ~ **und brav** faithfully || **der T~bruch, ⸗e** breach of faith; **treu|deutsch** typically German; (*adv*) in true German fashion; **der T~eid, –e** oath of allegiance; **~ergeben** = **~gesinnt** loyal; **T~hand–** trust (company, territory, *etc*); **der T~händer, –** trustee; **~herzig** trusting; **~los** disloyal, faithless; **die T~losigkeit** disloyalty, faithlessness

die **Treue** faithfulness; loyalty; (+*dat*) **die ~ brechen/halten** break/keep faith with; be untrue/faithful to; **auf Treu und Glauben** in good faith

treulich faithfully, loyally

der **Triangel, –** *mus* triangle

das **Tribunal, –e** tribunal

die **Tribüne, –n** platform, rostrum; *sp* stand

der **Tribut, –e** tribute; toll (**an** *acc* of); (+*dat*) **(seinen) ~ zollen** pay tribute to

der **Trichter, –** funnel; crater; **auf den (richtigen) ~ kommen** *coll* get the hang of it

der **Trick, –s** trick; ploy; (sales) gimmick; *cin* animation; **der ~film, –e** trick film; animated cartoon; **die ~kiste, –n** box of tricks; **t~reich** artful

tricksen *coll* fiddle; *sp* feint

trieb *p/t of* **treiben**

der **Trieb, –e** urge; drive; propensity; *bot* shoot; **die ~feder, –n** mainspring; driving force; **die ~kraft, ⸗e** motive power; driving force; **das ~leben** sex-life; **das ~rad, ⸗er** driving-wheel; **der ~sand** quicksand; **das ~verbrechen, –** sex crime; **der ~verbrecher, –** sex offender; **der ~wagen, –** railcar; **das ~werk, –e** engine; driving mechanism

triebhaft motivated/ruled by one's physical urges

trief–: ~äugig watery-eyed; **trief|naß** dripping wet

triefen (*p/t* **triefte**/*lit* **troff** (*subj* **triefte/tröffe**)) be dripping wet; (eye) water; (nose) run; (*sn*) drip; ~ **von/vor** (*dat*) be dripping with; ooze (with); **~d naß** dripping wet

Trient Trento

Triest Trieste

triezen *coll* plague

triff *imp sing*, **triff(s)t** (*2nd*,) *3rd sing pres of* **treffen**

triftig cogent, convincing; (excuse) valid

die **Trigonometrie** trigonometry

trigonometrisch trigonometrical

die **Trikolore, –n** tricolour

das **Trikot** [–'ko:], **–s** stockinet; leotard; *sp* jersey

der **Trikot** [–'ko:], **–s** cotton jersey

die **Trikotagen** [–ʒ–] *pl* cotton jersey garments (*esp* underwear)

der **Triller, –** trill; **die ~pfeife, –n** whistle

trillern trill

die **Trillion, –en** trillion, quintillion *US*

die **Trilogie, –(ie)n** trilogy

Trimm-dich– keep-fit ...

trimmen trim (dog); *coll* train; **~ auf** (*acc*) *coll* groom for; (**auf Pünktlichkeit** *etc*) train to be (punctual *etc*); (*with adj*) do up to look; **sich ~** do keep-fit exercises

Trink– drinking ...; **t~fest** *coll* able to hold one's liquor; **das ~geld, –er** tip; **die ~halle, –n** refreshment kiosk; pump-room (of spa); **der ~halm, –e** (drinking) straw; **der ~spruch, ⸚e** toast; **das ~wasser** drinking-water

trinkbar drinkable

trinken (*p/t* **trank** (*subj* **tränke**), *p/part* **getrunken**) drink; **~ auf** (*acc*) drink to; drink (s.o.'s health); (+*dat*) **zu ~ geben** give (s.o.) a drink

der **Trinker, –** drinker

das **Trio, –s** trio (*also mus*)

die **Triole, –n** *mus* triplet

der **Trip** [–ɪ–], **–s** trip; *coll* 'trip'

Tripoli (*Lebanon*), **Tripolis** [–ɪs] (*Libya*) Tripoli

trippeln (*sn*) trip along

der **Tripper, –** gonorrhoea

das **Triptychon** [–çɔn], **–(ch)en/–(ch)a** triptych

das **Triptyk** [–ʏk], **–s** triptyque

trist dismal, dreary

tritt *imp sing*, *3rd sing pres of* **treten**

der **Tritt, –e** step; tread; kick; (small) step-ladder; **~ fassen** find one's feet; *mil* fall into step; **im ~** *mil* in step || **das ~brett, –er** running-board; step (on train *etc*); **die ~leiter, –n** step-ladder

trittst *2nd sing pres of* **treten**

der **Triumph, –e** triumph; **~e feiern** be a great success; **im ~** in triumph || **der ~bogen, ..bögen** triumphal arch; **der ~zug, ⸚e** triumphal procession

triumphal triumphant

triumphieren exult; **~ über** (*acc*) triumph over; **~d** triumphant

trivial trivial; trite; **die T~literatur** light fiction

die **Trivialität, –en** triviality; triteness

trocken dry; arid; **sich ~ rasieren** use an electric shaver; **~ werden** dry; **auf dem ~en sitzen** *coll* be on the rocks; **im T~en sein/sitzen** be out of the rain

Trocken– dry ...; drying ...; dried ...; **der ~automat, –en** (*wk masc*) tumble-drier; **die ~beeren|auslese** (*exquisite wine made from selected grapes left to dry on the vine*); **der ~boden, ..böden** drying-loft; **das ~dock, –s** dry dock; **das ~ei, –er** dried egg; **das ~element, –e** dry cell; **die ~haube, –n** hair-drier; **der ~kurs, –e** preparatory (indoor) course (for intending skiers *etc*); **t~legen** (*sep*) drain; change (baby); **die ~milch** dried milk; **der ~rasierer, –** electric shaver; **t~reiben*** (*sep*) rub dry; **die ~schleuder, –n** spin-drier; **das ~shampoo, –s** dry shampoo; **t~stehen*** (*sep*) (cow) be dry

die **Trockenheit** dryness; aridity; drought

trocknen (*sn if v/i*) dry

die **Troddel, –n** tassel

der **Trödel** = **der ~kram** junk; **der ~laden, ..läden** junk shop

trödeln (*sn if indicating direction*) dawdle

der **Trödler, –** junk dealer; dawdler

troff (tröffe) *p/t* (*subj*) *of* **triefen**

der **Trog, ⸚e** trough; tub

trog (tröge) *p/t* (*subj*) *of* **trügen**

Troja Troy

der **Trojaner, –, trojanisch** Trojan

trollen: sich ~ *coll* push off

die **Trommel, –n** drum (*also tech, comput*); **die ~ rühren für** *coll* push || **das ~fell, –e** drum-head; *anat* ear-drum; **das ~feuer, –** barrage; **der ~revolver, –** revolver; **der ~schlag, ⸚e** drum-beat; drumming; **der ~schlegel, – = der ~stock, ⸚e** drum-stick; **der ~wirbel, –** drum-roll

trommeln drum; beat out (on drum); (*v/i*) (beat the) drum; **~ auf** (*acc*) beat out (rhythm) on; (*v/i* person, rain) drum on; **~ gegen** hammer on; (rain) drum on

der **Trommler, –** drummer

die **Trompete, –n** trumpet

trompeten (*p/part* **trompetet**) play on the trumpet; shout from the rooftops; (*v/i*) play the trumpet; (elephant) trumpet; *coll* blow one's nose loudly

Trompeten–: das ~geschmetter blare of trumpets; **der ~stoß, ⸚e** blast on the trumpet

der **Trompeter, –** trumpeter

die **Tropen** *pl* the tropics; *in compds* tropical ...; **der ~helm, –e** pith-helmet

der **Tropf, ⸚e** *coll* simpleton; (*pl* **–e**) *med* drip; **armer ~** poor devil; **am ~ hängen** be on a drip || **die ~infusion, –en** *med* intravenous drip; **tropf|naß** dripping wet; **die**

~**stein|höhle, -n** stalactitic/stalagmitic cave

tröpfchen|weise in dribs and drabs

tröpfeln pour out in drops; (*v/i sn*) drip; **es tröpfelt** it is spitting (with rain)

tropfen pour out in drops; (*v/i*) (nose) run, (tap *etc*) drip; (*sn*: water *etc*) drip; **es tropft** it is spitting (with rain)

der **Tropfen, -** drop; drip; (*pl*) *med* drops; ~ **auf den heißen Stein** *coll* drop in the ocean; **bis auf den letzten** ~ to the last drop || **t~weise** in drops, drop by drop; in dribs and drabs

die **Trophäe, -n** trophy

tropisch tropical

der **Troß, -(ss)e** hangers-on; *hist* baggage-train

die **Trosse, -n** hawser

der **Trost** [-oː-] consolation, comfort; (+*dat*) ~ **zusprechen** console; **zum** ~ by way of consolation; **nicht ganz/recht bei** ~ **sein** *coll* be off one's head || **t~bedürftig** in need of consolation; **t~los** hopeless; miserable; bleak; disconsolate; **das ~pflästerchen, -** tiny consolation; **der ~preis, -e** consolation prize; **t~reich** comforting

trösten [-øː-] console, comfort; **sich ~ mit** console oneself with; find consolation with

tröstlich [-øː-] comforting

der **Trott** slow trot (of horse); plod; routine; rut

der **Trottel, -** *coll* nitwit

trottelig *coll* dopey

trotten (*sn*) trudge, plod

der **Trotteur** [-'tøːɐ], **-s** casual (shoe)

das **Trottinett, -e** *Swiss* (child's) scooter

das **Trottoir** [-'tŏaːɐ], **-e/-s** *arch exc Aust, Swiss* pavement, sidewalk *US*

trotz (+*gen*/(*SGer*) *dat*; +*dat* – *eg* ~ **Verboten** – *when gen pl form not distinctive*) in spite of; ~ **allem** in spite of everything

der **Trotz** defiance; obstinacy; (+*dat*) ~ **bieten** defy; (+*dat*) **zum** ~ in defiance of

trotz-: ~dem 1 *adv* nevertheless; 2 *conj* (*widely regarded as incorrect*) even though; **der T~kopf, ¨-e** stubborn child/person; **~köpfig** stubborn; **die T~reaktion, -en** act of defiance

trotzen be obstinate; (+*dat*) defy; brave (elements)

trotzig obstinate, stubborn; defiant

Trotzki Trotsky

trüb-: ~selig dreary; gloomy; **der T~sinn** gloom; **~sinnig** gloomy

trüb(e) dull; dim; (liquid) cloudy; gloomy; **im trüben fischen** *coll* fish in troubled waters

der **Trubel** bustle

trüben make cloudy; dull; cloud; mar; **sich ~** go cloudy; grow dull; cloud over; (relations) become strained

die **Trübsal** affliction; grief, sorrow; ~ **blasen** *coll* mope

trudeln (*also sn*) *aer* spin

die **Trüffel, -n** (*coll* **der**, *pl* -) truffle (= prized fungus, sweetmeat)

trug (trüge) *p/t* (*subj*) *of* **tragen**

der **Trug** deception; delusion; **das ~bild, -er** delusion; illusion; **der ~schluß, ¨-(ss)e** false conclusion; fallacy

trügen (*p/t* **trog** (*subj* **tröge**), *p/part* **getrogen**) deceive; (*v/i*) be deceptive; **wenn mich nicht alles trügt** unless I'm very much mistaken

trügerisch deceptive; illusory; treacherous

die **Truhe, -n** chest

die **Trümmer** *pl* debris, rubble; ruins; wreckage; remnants; **in ~ gehen** be wrecked; **in ~n liegen** be in ruins; **in ~ schlagen** smash to pieces || **das ~grund|stück, -e** bomb site; **der ~haufen, -** pile of rubble

der **Trumpf, ¨-e** trump (card); ~ **sein** be trumps; *coll* be the in thing

trumpfen trump; (*v/i*) play a trump (card)

der **Trunk** drink; **dem ~ ergeben** addicted to drink; **im ~** while drunk || **die ~sucht** alcoholism; **t~süchtig** addicted to drink

trunken intoxicated; ~ **von/vor** (*dat*) drunk with || **der T~bold, -e** drunkard

die **Trunkenheit** drunkenness; ~ **am Steuer** drunken driving

der **Trupp, -s** squad; gang (of workers)

die **Truppe, -n** *theat* troupe; *mil* unit; (*pl*) troops; *in compds* **~n-** ... of troops; troop ...; **die ~n|schau, -en** military review; **der ~n|teil, -e** unit; **die ~n|übung, -en** field exercise; **der ~n|übungs|platz, ¨-e** military training area

der **Trust** [-a-], **-s/-e** *fin* trust

Trut-: der ~hahn, ¨-e turkey(-cock); **die ~henne, -n** turkey-hen

Tschaikowski [-'kɔf-] Tchaikovsky

der **Tscheche** [-ç-], **-n** (*wk masc*) Czech

tschechisch [-ç-], (*language*) **T~** Czech

Tschecho- [-ç-]: **der ~slowake, -n** (*wk masc*) Czechoslovakian; **die ~slowakei** Czechoslovakia; **t~slowakisch** Czechoslovak(ian)

Tschechow [-xɔf] Chekhov

der **Tschick, -(s)** *Aust coll* 'fag-end'; 'fag'

tschilpen chirrup

die **Tschinellen** *pl SGer* cymbals

tschüs! 'bye!

der **Tschusch** [-uː-], **-en** (*wk masc*) *Aust coll* wog

Tsd. = **Tausend**

die **Tsetse|fliege** ['tsɛtse-], **-n** tsetse fly

das **T-Shirt** ['tiːʃøːɐt], **-s** T-shirt

die **TU, -(s)** = **Technische Universität**

die **Tuba, -(b)en** *mus* tuba; *anat* tube

die **Tube, -n** tube; **auf die ~ drücken** *coll* step on it

der **Tuberkel, -** tubercle

tuberkulös tubercular

die **Tuberkulose** tuberculosis

das **Tuch** [–uː–], **⁼er** cloth; scarf; shawl; handkerchief; towel; (*pl* **–e**) *arch* cloth, fabric; **wie ein rotes ~ wirken auf** (*acc*) be like a red rag to a bull to || **~fühlung (T. haben mit = T. halten mit/zu** be in physical contact with; be in close contact with; **auf T. gehen** move closer together); **der ~händler, –** cloth merchant

die **Tuchent** [–ʊ–], **–en** *Aust* duvet

tüchtig able, capable; efficient; *coll* sizable; (appetite) hearty; (*adv*) (work) hard; *coll* soundly; good and proper; (eat) heartily

die **Tüchtigkeit** ability; efficiency; **körperliche ~** physical fitness

die **Tücke, –n** malice; malicious act; (*pl*) perils; **seine ~n haben** have its snags; be temperamental/treacherous

tuckern (*sn if indicating direction*) chug

tückisch malicious; treacherous

der **Tuff, –e = der ~stein** tuff

die **Tüftelei, –en** *coll* fiddly job/work

tüftelig *coll* fiddly

tüfteln *coll*: **~ an** (*dat*) fiddle about with; puzzle over

die **Tugend, –en** virtue; **der ~bold, –e** *iron* paragon of virtue; **der ~wächter, –** guardian of virtue

tugendhaft virtuous

der **Tukan, –e** toucan

der **Tüll, –e** tulle; (for curtains) net

die **Tülle, –n** spout

die **Tulpe, –n** tulip

–tum:

(*i*) (*eg* **das Römer~** Roman) way of life, civilization;

(*ii*) –ism, –ry, *eg* **das Nomaden~** nomadism, **das Luther~** Lutheranism, **das Helden~** heroism, **das Ritter~** chivalry;

(*iii*) (*office*) *eg* **das Papst~** papacy;

(*iv*) (*collective*) *eg* **das Beamten~** officialdom, civil servants

---

tumb [–p] *archaistic* naïve

Tummel–: der ~platz, ⁼e playground

tummeln: sich ~ romp about

der **Tümmler, –** bottle-nosed dolphin

der **Tumor, –(or)en** tumor

der **Tümpel, –** pond

der **Tumult, –e** commotion; tumult, uproar

tumultuarisch tumultuous

tun (*pres* **tue, tust** [–uː–], **tut, tun, tut, tun;** *subj 3rd sing* **tue;** *p/t* **tat,** *subj* **täte;** *p/part* **getan**)

1 (*a*) do; make (remark *etc*); give (shout *etc*); take (look, step, *etc*); go on (journey); *coll* (*with indication of place*) put;

etw. ~ gegen do sth. about; **Sie täten gut daran zu ...** you would do well to ...; **so etwas tut man nicht** that's not done; **... tut's auch** ... will do; **... tut es nicht** ... is not enough; **... tut es nicht mehr** *coll* ... has had it; **das tut nichts** it doesn't matter; **das tut nichts zur Sache** that makes no difference; **was tut's?** what does it matter?; **damit ist es nicht getan** that's not enough; **nach getaner Arbeit** when the day's work is done;

(*b*) (*with adv*) pretend to be; assume a ... air; *or expressed by* feign + *noun* (*eg* **erstaunt ~** feign surprise); **(so) ~, als (ob/wenn) ...** act as if ...; pretend that .../to + *infin*; **er/sie tut nur so** he's/she's only pretending; **tu (doch) nicht so!** stop pretending!;

(*c*) (+*dat*) do to; do (s.o. a favour); **(der Hund** *etc*) **tut dir nichts** (the dog *etc*) won't hurt you;

2 (*as auxiliary – following infin in emphatic initial position*) do (*eg* **übersetzen tut er gern** he does like translating); *or rendered by emphasis* (*eg* **wissen ~ wir alle nichts** none of us *knows* anything);

3 *constructions with* **zu ~: zu ~ haben** have work to do; have things to attend to; **(es) zu ~ haben mit** have dealings with; be dealing with; *coll* have (stomach *etc*) trouble; **etwas/nichts zu ~ haben mit** have something/nothing to do with; **nichts zu ~ haben wollen mit** want nothing to do with; **es zu ~ bekommen/kriegen mit** *coll* get into trouble with; **es mit der Angst zu ~ bekommen** get the wind up; **es ist mir um ... zu ~** I'm concerned about

sich ~ *coll*: **es tut sich etwas/nichts** something/nothing is happening; **sich leicht ~ mit** find easy; **sich schwer ~ mit** have difficulty with

das **Tun** activities; actions; **jmds. ~ und Treiben** s.o.'s doings

die **Tünche, –n** whitewash; veneer (= superficial appearance)

tünchen whitewash

die **Tundra, –(r)en** tundra

das **Tunell, –e** *SGer* tunnel

Tunesien [–ĭən] Tunisia

der **Tunesier** [–ĭɐ], **–, tunesisch** Tunisian

der **Tu|nicht|gut, –e** good-for-nothing

die **Tunika, –(k)en** tunic

Tunis [–ɪs] Tunis

die **Tunke, –n** sauce; gravy

tunken dip; dunk

tunlich expedient; practicable; **~st** if possible; **~st bald** as soon as possible

der **Tunnel, –, einen ~ bauen** tunnel || **der ~bau** tunnelling

tunnelieren *Aust* tunnel (hill *etc*)

die **Tunte, –n** *coll* prim female; 'pansy', 'fairy'

das **Tüpfelchen, –** small spot; dot; **das ~ auf dem**

i dot on the i; finishing touch; **bis aufs ~** to a T
tüpfeln spot
tupfen dab; **getupft** (dress) with polka dots
der **Tupfen, –** spot; dot; polka dot
der **Tupfer, –** swab
die **Tür, –en** door; (+*dat*) **~ und Tor öffnen** open the way to; **~ an ~ wohnen mit** live next door to; **mit der ~ ins Haus fallen** *coll* blurt out what one has to say; **vor die ~ setzen** *coll* throw out; **vor der ~ stehen** (Christmas *etc*) be just around the corner; **zwischen ~ und Angel** in passing || **der ~griff, –e** = **die ~klinke, –n** door-handle; **der ~öffner, –** (electric) buzzer (for opening the door); **der ~pfosten, –** doorpost; **die ~schnalle, –n** *Aust* door-handle
der **Turban, –e** turban
die **Turbine, –n** turbine; **das ~n|flugzeug, –e** turbojet
turbulent turbulent (*also phys*)
die **Turbulenz, –en** turbulence (*also phys*)
die **Türe, –n** = **Tür**
der **Turf** [–ʊ–] *horse rac* turf; racecourse
Turgenjew [–ɛf] Turgenev
–türig –door
Turin Turin
der **Türke, –n** (*wk masc*) Turk
die **Türkei** Turkey
türkis (*indecl*) turquoise
das **Türkis** (*colour*), **der Türkis, –e** *miner*, **t~farben** turquoise
türkisch, (*language*) **T~** Turkish
der **Turm, ¨–e** tower; *chess* castle, rook; *swim* diving platform; **der ~falke, –n** (*wk masc*) kestrel; **turm|hoch** towering ((+*dat*) **t. überlegen sein** be head and shoulders above); **das ~springen** high diving
das **Türmchen, –** turret
türmen pile (up); (*v/i sn*) *coll* skedaddle; **sich ~** pile up
Turn– gymnastic ...; **das ~fest, –e** gymnastic display; **das ~gerät, –e** piece of gymnastic apparatus; (*pl*) gymnastic apparatus; **die ~halle, –n** gymnasium; **das ~hemd, –en** gym shirt; **die ~hose, –n** gym shorts; **der ~saal, ..säle** *Aust* gymnasium; **der ~schuh, –e** gym shoe; **der ~ver|ein, –e** gymnastics club
turnen perform (exercise); (*v/i*) do gymnastics; *coll* romp about; (*sn*) *coll* climb (over *etc* sth.); **das Turnen** gymnastics
der **Turner, –** gymnast
turnerisch gymnastic
das **Turnier, –e** tournament; *equest* (horse) show; *danc* competition
der **Turnus, –se** rotation; *Aust* shift; **im ~** in rotation || **t~mäßig** rotatory (**t~mäßiger Wechsel** rotation; **t. auswechseln** rotate)
Turtel–: die ~taube, –n turtle-dove
turteln bill and coo
der **Tusch, –e** fanfare; **die ~zeichnung, –en** pen-and-ink drawing
die **Tusche, –n** Indian ink
tuscheln (*also v/i*) whisper
tuschen draw in Indian ink; paint in water-colours
tut! toot!; **tut, tut!** toot-toot!
die **Tute, –n** *coll* horn
die **Tüte, –n** (paper/plastic) bag; (ice-cream) cone; *coll* breathalyser, drunkometer *US*; **~n kleben** *coll* be in clink
tuten toot; **von Tuten und Blasen keine Ahnung haben** *coll* not have a clue
Tutenchamun [tutɛnˈçaːmʊn] Tutankhamen
der **TÜV** [tʏf] = **Technischer Überwachungs-Verein** (West German) vehicle inspection authority (*cf* M.O.T. in U.K.)
TV– T.V. (series *etc*)
der **Tweed** [tviːt], **–s/–e** tweed
der **Twen** [tvɛn] (*gen* –(s)), **–s** young person (*esp* man) in his/her twenties
der **Typ, –en** type; *aer*, *mot*, *etc* model; *coll* guy, character; **der ~ des ...** a typical ...
die **Type, –n** *print* character, *pl* type; *Aust aer*, *mot*, *etc* model; *coll* (odd) character
Typen *pl of* **Typ, Type, Typus; die ~scheibe, –n** daisy-wheel
der **Typhus** [ˈtyː–] typhoid
typisch typical (**für** of); **das ist (wieder einmal) ~ (Hans** *etc*)! that's (Hans *etc*) all over; **~ Mann/Frau!** just like a man/woman!
der **Typograph, –en** (*wk masc*) typographer
die **Typographie** typography
typographisch typographical
das **Typoskript, –e** typescript
der **Typus, –(p)en** type
der **Tyrann, –en** (*wk masc*) tyrant
die **Tyrannei, –en** tyranny
tyrannisch tyrannical
tyrannisieren tyrannize; bully, browbeat
Tz [teːˈtsɛt] = **Tezett**

U

[das] **U** [uː] (*gen, pl* –, *coll* [uːs]) U

u. = **und**

u. a. (= **und andere/anderes**) and others/ other things, (= **unter anderem/anderen**) among other things/others; **u. ä.** (= **und ähnliche(s)**) and the like; **u. A. w. g.** (= **um Antwort wird gebeten**) R.S.V.P.

[die] **U-Bahn, –en** (= **Untergrundbahn**) underground, subway *US*

übel bad; nasty; **nicht ~** *coll* not bad; **ich hätte nicht ~ Lust zu ...** I wouldn't mind (+*ger*); **~ dran sein** be in a bad way; **mir ist/wird ~** I feel sick; **~ aufnehmen** take badly; (+*dat*) **~ bekommen** do (s.o.) no good; (food *etc*) disagree with; **~ vermerken** take amiss

[das] **Übel, –** evil, ill; ailment; **zu allem ~** to make matters worse

übel– ill–; **~gelaunt** ill-tempered; **~nehmen*** (*sep*) take amiss; resent; (+*dat*) hold against; **~nehmerisch** touchy, easily offended; **~riechend** evil-smelling; **der Ü~stand, ⸚e** bad state of affairs; **der Ü~täter, –** wrongdoer; **~wollen*** (*sep*) (+*dat*) wish ill; **~wollend** malevolent

[die] **Übelkeit** nausea; (+*dat*) **~ erregen** make (s.o.) feel sick

üben (*see also* **geübt**) practise; exercise; (*v/i*) practise; **Geduld ~** be patient; **Kritik ~ an** (*dat*) criticize; **sich ~ in** (*dat*) practise

über 1 *prep* (+*acc*) (*a*) (*indicating motion etc*) over; across; (reach *etc*) beyond, (be) over (crisis *etc*); (tears: run) down; (cars: race) along; (hang, place) above, over; (travel) via; over (radio); through (intermediary);

(*b*) (*indicating time*) over (Christmas, the week-end, *etc*); (*following noun*) = **hindurch; die ganze Zeit ~** all the time;

(*c*) over, more than; (*age*) over (*eg* **Kinder ~ 10** children over 10); **~ alles lieben** love more than anything;

(*d*) (= '*concerning*') about; on; (amazed, laugh, *etc*) at; (news, details) of; (cheque, bill) for;

(*e*) (victory, superiority, *etc*) over; (mastery) of;

(*f*) ... after ... (*eg* **Gerüchte ~ Gerüchte** rumour after rumour);

2 *prep* (+*dat*) (*a*) (*indicating place*) over, above;

(*b*) (*indicating time, circumstances*) over (glass *etc* of ...); (*followed by vbl noun*) while (+*ger*); (*cause*) in (the excitement *etc*); as a result of;

3 *adv coll*: (+*dat*) **~ sein** be superior to (**in** *dat* in), be more than a match for; **... ist mir ~** I'm sick (and tired) of ...

~ ... (*acc*) **hin** over; across

~ ... (*acc*) **hinaus** beyond; past

~ ... (*acc*) **hinweg** over; across; for (years *etc*); in spite of (difficulties)

~ und ~ all over

von ... ~ (*acc*) **... bis zu ...** (ranging) from ... through ... to ...

über–[1] *sep* (*stressed*) *and insep* (*unstressed*) *pref – general senses*:

(*i*) ... across, ... over (*eg* **~pinseln** paint over, **~fliegen** fly across/over)

(*ii*) (*insep*) *indicates spending of time* (*eg* **~nachten** stay overnight, **~wintern** winter, hibernate);

(*iii*) over– (*eg* **~bewerten** overrate, **~heizen** overheat);

(*iv*) (*insep*) out– (*eg* **~listen** outsmart, **~spielen** *sp* outplay)

über–[2] (*prefixed to adj*) over–; super–; supra–; too ...

über|all everywhere; **~ in** (*dat*) all over; **~ wo ...** wherever ...

über|all–: **~her** (**von ü.** from all parts); **~hin** everywhere

über|altert with too many old people; outdated

[das] **Über|angebot** surplus (**an** *dat* of)

über|ängstlich over-anxious

über|anstrengen overstrain; overtax; strain; **sich ~** over-exert oneself

über|antworten (+*dat*) hand over to; **sich ~** (+*dat*) give oneself up to

über|arbeiten revise; **sich ~** overwork; **überarbeitet** overworked; revised

über|aus extremely

überbacken (*p/part* **überbacken**) bake lightly; **mit Käse überbacken** au gratin

[der] **Überbau, –e/–ten** *civ eng*, *Marxist philos* (*pl* **–e** *rare*) superstructure

überbe|anspruchen (*insep*) overtax, make too many demands on

[das] **Überbein, –e** ganglion

überbekommen* *coll* get tired of
überbelasten (*insep*) overload; overtax
überbelegt overcrowded
überbelichten (*insep*) *phot* over-expose
überbesetzt overstaffed; overcrowded
überbetonen (*insep*) over-emphasize
überbewerten [–eː–] (*insep*) overrate
überbieten* surpass; beat; outbid; **sich ~ in** (*dat*) vie with one another in
das **Überbleibsel, –** remains; relic; survival
der **Überblick, –e** overall view; survey (**über** *acc* of)
überblicken have a view of; grasp, take in
überborden (*also sn*) *Swiss* get out of hand
überbringen* (+*dat*) deliver to
der **Überbringer, –** bringer; bearer
überbrücken bridge; tide oneself over (shortage of cash); fill in (time); reconcile
überbürden overburden
überdachen roof
überdauern survive
überdecken cover over; disguise, mask; **~d** *biol* dominant; **überdeckt** *biol* recessive
überdehnen over-stretch
überdenken* think over, consider
überdies moreover; anyway
überdimensional outsize
die **Überdosis, –(s)en** overdose
überdrehen overwind; *mech* race (engine); **überdreht** *also* overexcited
der **Überdruck**[1], **–e** overprint
der **Überdruck**[2], **⸗e** *phys* excess pressure; **die ~kabine, –n** pressurized cabin
der **Überdruß** weariness (**an** *dat* of); **bis zum ~** till one is sick of it; ad nauseam
überdrüssig: (+*gen*) **~ sein/werden** be tired/tire of
überdurchschnittlich above-average
über|eck diagonally
der **Über|eifer** over-zealousness
über|eifrig over-zealous
über|eignen (+*dat*) make over to
über|eilen rush; **übereilt** precipitate, over-hasty
über|ein– *sep pref*
über|einander above/on top of/about/at one another; **~liegen*** (*sep*) lie on top of one another; **~schlagen*** (*sep*) cross (legs)
über|einkommen* (*sn*) agree
das **Über|einkommen, – = die Über|einkunft, ⸗e** agreement
über|einstimmen agree (*also gramm*); tally; match; **~ mit** agree with (**über** *acc* about); tally with; match; **darin ~, daß ...** agree that ..., be agreed that ...; **~d** concurring; matching; (*adv*) unanimously; **~d mit** in accordance with
die **Über|einstimmung, –en** agreement (*also gramm*); harmony; **in ~ mit** in agreement with; in accordance with; **in ~ bringen** harmonize
über|empfindlich over-sensitive
über|erfüllen (*insep*) *EGer* overfulfil (quota)
über|essen* (*cf next entry*): **sich** *dat* **... ~** grow sick of
über|essen* (*p/part* **übergessen**) (*cf previous entry*): **sich ~** overeat; **sich ~ an** (*dat*) eat too much ...
überfahren* (*cf next entry*) ferry across; (*v/i sn*) cross
überfahren* (*cf previous entry*) run over; go through (signal *etc*); cross; *coll* stampede (into doing sth.)
die **Überfahrt, –en** crossing
der **Überfall, ⸗e** attack, assault (**auf** *acc* on); raid (on bank), hold-up; *mil* (surprise) attack (on); **das ~kommando, –s** flying squad
überfallen* attack (*also mil*); raid, hold up; come over; overtake; *coll* descend on; **~ mit** *coll* bombard with
überfällig overdue
das **Überfalls|kommando, –s** *Aust* flying squad
überfeinert over-refined
überfliegen* fly across/over; overfly; glance through, skim
überfließen* (*sn*) overflow; **~ vor** (*dat*) overflow with; **ineinander ~** (colours) run
überflügeln outstrip
der **Überfluß** abundance (**an** *dat* of); superfluity (of); **im ~ vorhanden** in plentiful supply; **im ~ leben** live in luxury; **zu allem/zum ~** to crown it all
überflüssig superfluous; unnecessary
überfluten flood; inundate
die **Überflutung, –en** *vbl noun*; *also* inundation
überfordern ask too much of; overtax
die **Überfracht** excess freight
überfrachten: ~ mit overload with
überfragt: da bin ich ~ you've got me there
überfremdet (excessively) infiltrated by foreign influences
die **Überfremdung, –en** (excessive) infiltration by foreign influences/foreign capital/foreigners
die **Überfuhr, –en** *Aust* ferry
überführen (*cf next entry*) transport
überführen (*cf previous entry*) transport; *leg* convict (*gen* of); **~ in** (*acc*) change/*chem* convert into
die **Überführung, –en** *vbl noun*; *also* transport; *leg* conviction; *chem* conversion; (= bridge) overpass, *rail* bridge (over railway)
die **Überfülle** profusion
überfüllt overcrowded
überfüttern overfeed
die **Übergabe** handing over; *mil* surrender
der **Übergang, ⸗e** crossing (**über** *acc* of); (for pedestrians, *rail*) crossing; footbridge; transition; *rail* supplementary ticket (for transfer to 1st class)

Übergangs– transitional ...; interim ...; *cost* ... for spring/autumn wear; **die ~zeit, –en** period of transition; spring *or* autumn (**in der Ü.** in spring and autumn)

die **Übergardinen** *pl* curtains

übergeben* (+*dat*) hand over to; open to (the public, traffic); commit to (flames); *mil* surrender to; **sich ~** vomit

übergehen* (*cf next entry*) (*sn*): **~ auf** (*acc*) pass to; **~ in** (*acc*) turn into; pass into (s.o.'s possession); **~ zu** go over to; proceed to; **die Augen gingen ihm über** his eyes almost popped out of his head; *poet* his eyes filled with tears

übergehen* (*cf previous entry*) ignore; pass over

übergenug more than enough

überge|ordnet *p/part*; *also* higher, superior

übergeschnappt *p/part*; *coll* crazy

übergessen *p/part of* **überessen**

das **Übergewicht** excess weight/*aer* baggage; predominance; **~ bekommen** overbalance; **das ~ bekommen** gain the upper hand (**über** *acc* over); (**... Pfund**) **~ haben** be (... pounds) overweight

übergewichtig overweight

übergießen* (*cf next entry*) (+*dat*) pour over

übergießen* (*cf previous entry*): **~ mit** pour (water *etc*) over; **mit Fett ~** baste; **übergossen von** suffused with

überglücklich overjoyed

übergreifen* *mus* cross hands; **~ auf** (*acc*) spread to

der **Übergriff, –e** encroachment (**auf** *acc* on)

übergroß huge, tremendous

die **Übergröße, –n** outsize

überhaben* *coll* have on (cape *etc*); have left; be sick of

überhandnehmen* (*sep*) spread (alarmingly)

der **Überhang, ⸚e** projection; overhang; overhanging rock; *comm* surplus (**an** *dat* of)

überhängen (+*dat*) put around (s.o.'s) shoulders; (*v/i*: **~***, *like* **hängen** *v/i*) project; overhang; **sich** *dat* **... ~** put around one's shoulders; sling over one's shoulder

überhasten rush; **überhastet** over-hasty

überhäufen: ~ mit swamp with; heap on; lavish on

überhaupt altogether; anyway; for that matter; (first *etc*) ever; (*with interrog*, *neg*) at all; **~ nicht** not at all/in the least; **und ~** and anyway; and indeed; **wenn ... ~** if indeed ...; if ... at all

überheben*: sich ~ strain oneself (lifting sth.); be presumptuous; **sich ~ über** (*acc*) consider oneself superior to

überheblich arrogant

die **Überheblichkeit** arrogance

überheizen overheat

überhitzt overheated (*also econ*); (steam) superheated; (imagination) wild, (tempers) heated

überhöhen bank (curve); **überhöht** *also* excessive

Überhol– overtaking ...; **die ~spur, –en** outside lane

überholen (*cf next entry*) ferry across; (*v/i*) *naut* heel

überholen (*cf previous entry*) overtake, pass; overtake, leave behind (competition); *mech* overhaul; **überholt** *also* outdated

die **Überholung, –en** overhaul

überhören not hear; ignore

das **Über-Ich** (*gen* **–(s)**), **–(s)** super-ego

über|irdisch supernatural; (beauty) divine

überkandidelt *coll* slightly crazy

überkippen (*sn*) tip over; (voice) crack

überkleben stick something over

überklug too clever by half

überkochen (*sn*) boil over

überkommen[1]* come over; overcome (*esp pass*)

überkommen[2] *p/part*; traditional; handed down

überkompensieren (*insep*) over-compensate for

überkreuzen: sich ~ cross

überkriegen *coll* get sick of

überkrustet: ~ mit covered with a layer of

überladen* overload; **überladen** *also* cluttered; over-elaborate

überlagern push into the background; *geol* overlie; *rad* blot out; **sich ~** overlap

Überland– cross-country ...; overland ...

überlang exceptionally long

überlappen, sich ~ overlap

überlassen* (+*dat*) leave to; entrust to (s.o.'s) care; let (s.o.) have; **sich ~** (+*dat*) abandon oneself to; **sich** *dat* **selbst überlassen** left to oneself

überlasten overload; overtax

die **Überlastung** *vbl noun*; *also* strain (*gen* on)

der **Überlauf, ⸚e** overflow (*also comput*)

überlaufen* (*cf next entry*) (*sn*) overflow; boil over; **~ zu** go over to (enemy)

überlaufen* (*cf previous entry*) overrun; (fear *etc*) overcome (*esp pass*); **es überläuft mich kalt** a shiver runs down my spine; **überlaufen** overcrowded; overrun; inundated

der **Überläufer, –** deserter

überlaut too loud

überleben outlive; survive; **sich überlebt haben** have had its day; **das Überleben** survival; **der/die Überlebende** (*decl as adj*) survivor

die **Überlebens|chancen** *pl* chances of survival

überlebens|groß larger than life-size

überlegen (*cf next entry*) put across one's knee; (+*dat*) put (blanket *etc*) over; **sich ~**

naut heel

überlegen[1] (*cf previous entry*; *see also* **überlegt**) think over, consider; (*v/i*) think; **es sich** *dat* **anders** ~ change one's mind; **hin und her** ~ give sth. a great deal of thought; ~, **(ob** *etc*) **...** consider (whether *etc*) ...; wonder (whether *etc*) ...; **das will gut überlegt sein** that wants thinking about

überlegen[2] superior; self-possessed; (victory) convincing; (+*dat*) ~ **sein** be superior to **(an** *dat* in)

die **Überlegenheit** superiority; self-possession

überlegt *p/part*; *also* well-considered; (*adv*: act) with deliberation

die **Überlegung, –en** consideration, thought; ~**en anstellen über** (*acc*) consider; **mit** ~ with deliberation; **nach reiflicher** ~ after careful consideration

überleiten: ~ **zu** lead up to

die **Überleitung, –en** *vbl noun*; *also* transition; link

überlesen* glance through; overlook

überliefern (+*dat*) hand down to; hand over to; **überliefert** *also* traditional

die **Überlieferung, –en** *vbl noun*; *also* tradition

überlisten outsmart, outwit

überm = **über dem**

die **Übermacht** superiority, superior strength

übermächtig extremely powerful; overwhelming

übermalen paint over

übermannen overcome

das **Übermaß** excess **(an** *dat* of); **im** ~ to excess

übermäßig excessive; inordinate; *mus* augmented; (*adv*) *also* to excess; over–

der **Übermensch, –en** (*wk masc*) superman

übermenschlich superhuman

übermitteln transmit; convey (*dat* to)

übermorgen the day after tomorrow; **morgen oder** ~ tomorrow or the day after

übermüdet overtired

die **Übermüdung** overtiredness

der **Übermut** high spirits

übermütig high-spirited

übern *coll* = **über den**

übernächst [–ɛːç–] next ... but one; (week *etc*) after next

übernachten spend the night; stay **(bei** with)

übernächtig *esp Aust*, **übernächtigt** worn out (from lack of sleep)

die **Übernachtung, –en** overnight stay; night (at hotel); **die** ~**s|möglichkeit, –en** overnight accommodation

die **Übernahme** taking over, *comm* take-over; assumption; adoption

übernational supranational

übernatürlich supernatural

übernehmen* take over; adopt; assume; take on, undertake; accept (responsibility); bear (costs *etc*); *Aust coll* put one over on; **es** ~ **zu ...** undertake to ...; **sich** ~ take on too much; overdo it; overreach oneself; **übernimm dich nur nicht!** don't overdo it!

über|ordnen (*see also* **übergeordnet**) (+*dat*) place over; put before

über|organisiert over-organized

überparteilich non-party; (newspaper) independent

überpinseln paint over

der **Überpreis, –e** excessive price

die **Überproduktion** over-production

überprüfen check **(auf** *acc* for); examine; scrutinize; screen, vet

die **Überprüfung, –en** check(ing); examination; scrutiny; screening, vetting

überquellen* (*sn*) overflow **(von** with); ~ **in** (*acc*) spill over into

überqueren cross

überragen (*cf next entry*) jut out

überragen (*cf previous entry*) be taller than; tower above; **(weit)** ~ **an** (*dat*) (far) outstrip in; ~**d** outstanding

überraschen surprise; take by surprise; (storm *etc*) overtake (*esp pass*); (*v/i*) come as a surprise; ~ **bei** catch (doing sth.)

überraschend surprising; surprise; unexpected; **... kam völlig** ~ **für ...** came as a total surprise to

überrascht *p/part*; *also* surprised **(über** *acc* at); (*adv*) in surprise

die **Überraschung, –en** surprise; **zu jmds.** ~ to s.o.'s surprise

Überraschungs– surprise ...; **das** ~**moment, –e** element of surprise

die **Überreaktion, –en** overreaction

überreden persuade (to); ~ **zu** (*followed by vbl noun*) talk into (+*ger*)

die **Überredung** persuasion; **die** ~**s|kunst, ¨–e** powers of persuasion

überregional national

überreich abundant, lavish; ~ **sein an** (*dat*) abound in; ~ **beschenken** lavish presents on

überreichen (+*dat*) hand over to; present (s.o.) with; **überreicht von** presented by

überreichlich ample; ~ **Zeit** ample time

überreif overripe

die **Überreife** overripeness

überreizen overstrain; overexcite; **überreizt** *also* overwrought; **sich** ~ *cards* overbid

überrennen* bowl over; *mil* overrun

der **Überrest, –e** remnants; (*pl*) remains

überrieseln trickle over; (shiver) run down (s.o.'s) spine

der **Überroll|bügel, –** roll bar

überrollen (train *etc*) run over; (avalanche) sweep over; *mil* overrun

überrumpeln take by surprise; *mil* make a surprise attack on; **sich** ~ **lassen** be caught napping

überrunden outstrip; *sp* lap
übers = über das
übersät: ~ mit dotted with; studded with; strewn with
übersatt more than full
übersättigen satiate; *chem* supersaturate; **übersättigt von** sated with
Überschall– supersonic ...; **der ~knall, –e** sonic bang
überschatten overshadow; cast a shadow over
überschätzen overestimate; overrate
die **Überschau** overview (**über** *acc* of)
überschauen have a view of; have a grasp of
überschäumen (*sn*) froth over; **~ vor** (*dat*) bubble over with; **vor Wut ~** foam with anger; **~d** exuberant
die **Überschicht, –en** extra shift
überschlafen* sleep on (problem *etc*)
der **Überschlag, ⸚e** rough estimate; *gym* handspring
überschlagen* (*cf next entry*) cross (legs); (*v/i sn*) (waves) break; (spark) flash over; **~ in** (*acc*) (*sn*) turn into; **mit übergeschlagenen Beinen** cross-legged
überschlagen[1]***** (*cf previous entry*) skip; estimate roughly; **sich ~** tumble head over heels, (vehicle) overturn; fall over oneself (in one's eagerness); (voice) crack; (*recip*: events) come thick and fast
überschlagen[2] *p/part*; *also* lukewarm; moderately warm
überschlägig (calculation) rough
überschnappen (*see also* **übergeschnappt**) (*sn*) *coll* crack up; (voice) crack
überschneiden*: sich ~ intersect; overlap
die **Überschneidung, –en** intersection; overlap
überschreiben* head; (+*dat*/**auf** *acc*) make over to
überschreien* shout down; **sich ~** shout oneself hoarse
überschreiten* cross; exceed; go beyond
die **Überschrift, –en** title, heading; headline
die **Überschuhe** *pl* overshoes, galoshes
überschuldet heavily in debt
der **Überschuß, ⸚(ss)e** surplus (**an** *dat* of); profit; **–überschuß** *esp* surplus ...
überschüssig surplus
überschütten: ~ mit cover with; pour (water *etc*) over; heap (praise *etc*) on, shower with
der **Überschwang** exuberance
überschwappen (*sn*) slop over
überschwemmen flood; inundate (*esp pass*)
die **Überschwemmung, –en** *vbl noun*; *also* flood; inundation
überschwenglich effusive, gushing
Übersee: aus ~ from overseas; **in/nach ~** overseas
Übersee– overseas ...; **das ~telegramm, –e** cablegram
überseeisch overseas
übersehbar clear; assessable; **... ist gut ~** one gets a good view of ...
übersehen* (*cf next entry*): **sich** *dat* **... ~** grow tired of (seeing)
übersehen* (*cf previous entry*) have a view of; take in, grasp; overlook, fail to see; ignore
übersenden* (+*dat*) send to; **in der Anlage übersende ich Ihnen ...** enclosed please find ...
übersetzen (*cf next entry*) ferry across; (*v/i, also sn*) cross (to other bank/shore)
übersetzen (*cf previous entry*) translate (**aus dem Deutschen** *etc* **ins Englische** *etc* from German *etc* into English *etc*); **sich (gut** *etc*) **~ lassen** translate (well *etc*)
der **Übersetzer, –** translator
die **Übersetzung, –en** translation; *mech* gear ratio; **der ~s|fehler, –** mistranslation
die **Übersicht, –en** overall view; survey, outline (**über** *acc* of); table
übersichtlich (terrain) open; clear; clearly laid out
die **Übersichts|karte, –n** general map
übersiedeln, übersiedeln (*sn*): **~ in** (*acc*)/**nach** move to
übersinnlich supernatural
überspannen put too much strain on; (bridge) span; **~ mit** cover with; **überspannt** *also* extravagant; exaggerated; (person) eccentric
überspielen cover up (nervousness *etc*); transfer (recording); outmanoeuvre; *sp* outplay, beat
überspitzen exaggerate; carry too far
überspringen* (*cf next entry*) (*sn*) (spark) jump; **~ auf** (*acc*) switch (abruptly) to (another topic); spread to
überspringen* (*cf previous entry*) jump (over), clear; skip
übersprudeln (*sn*) bubble over (**von/vor** *dat* with); **~d** (temperament) effervescent
übersprühen spray
die **Übersprung|handlung, –en** displacement activity
überspülen wash (over)
überstaatlich supranational
überstehen* (*cf next entry*) project, jut out
überstehen* (*cf previous entry*) come through; survive; get over
übersteigen* climb over; exceed, be beyond
übersteigern force up; push too far; **übersteigert** exaggerated; excessive
übersteuern *rad* overmodulate; (*v/i*) *mot* oversteer
überstimmen outvote; vote down
überstrahlen shine on; outshine
überstrapazieren overwork (slogan *etc*)
überstreichen* paint over

überstreifen (+*dat*) slip (ring *etc*) on; **sich** *dat* **...** ~ slip on

überströmen (*cf next entry*) (*sn*) overflow

überströmen (*cf previous entry*) flood; **überströmt von** streaming with

überstülpen (+*dat*) place over; clap on (s.o.'s) head; **sich** *dat* **...** ~ clap on

die **Überstunden** *pl* overtime

überstürzen rush (into); **sich** ~ be in too much of a hurry; (*recip*) (events) follow in rapid succession; (words) come tumbling out; **überstürzt** over-hasty, precipitate

übertäuben dull

die **Überteuerung** overcharging

übertölpeln dupe

übertönen drown (sound *etc*)

der **Übertrag, ⸚e** amount carried forward; *comput* carry

übertragbar transferable; *comput* portable; *med* infectious; contagious

übertragen[1]* transfer; translate; transcribe (into longhand); *med* transmit; *comput* transmit; transfer; carry over (error); step; *rad*, *TV* broadcast; (+*dat*) assign to; ~ **auf** (*acc*) transfer to, *med* transmit to; apply (principle *etc*) to; **auf Band** ~ tape; **sich** ~ **auf** (*acc*) be communicated to; spread to; *med* be transmitted to

übertragen[2] *p/part*; *also* figurative; *Aust* worn

die **Übertragung, –en** transfer; translation; transcription; application (**auf** *acc* to); *med* transmission; *comput* transmission; transfer; *rad*, *TV* broadcast

übertrainiert [–trɛ–, –tre–] overtrained

übertreffen* surpass (**an** *dat* in), excel (in); exceed (expectations); **sich selbst** ~ excel oneself; **nicht zu** ~ unsurpassable

übertreiben* (*see also* **übertrieben**) exaggerate; overdo; **es** ~ **mit** overdo

die **Übertreibung, –en** exaggeration

übertreten* (*cf next entry*) (*also sn*) *athl* commit a foot-fault; (*sn*) overflow; ~ **in** (*acc*) (*sn*) *med etc* pass into, enter; ~ **zu** (*sn*) go over to; *relig* become a convert to

übertreten* (*cf previous entry*) infringe; **sich** *dat* **den Fuß** ~ sprain one's ankle

die **Übertretung, –en** infringement

übertrieben *p/part*; *also* exaggerated; excessive

der **Übertritt, –e** crossing (of border); shift of allegiance (to another party); *relig* conversion

übertrumpfen outdo; *cards* overtrump

übertünchen whitewash

über|übermorgen *coll* in three days' time

übervölkert overpopulated

die **Übervölkerung** overpopulation

übervoll overfull

übervorteilen swindle

überwachen supervise; monitor; keep under observation

überwachsen [–ks–]: ~ **von** overgrown with

überwältigen overpower; overcome; overwhelm; ~**d** overwhelming

überwälzen *esp Aust* = **abwälzen**

überwechseln [–ks–] (*sn*): ~ **auf** (*acc*) cross over to; switch to; transfer to; ~ **in** (*acc*) go over to; ~ **zu** switch to

überweisen* remit (*dat*/**an** *acc* to); (+*dat*/**an** *acc*) refer (proposal) to; ~ **an** (*acc*)/**zu** refer (patient) to; ~ **auf** (*acc*) transfer to (account)

die **Überweisung, –en** remittance; transfer; referral

überwerfen* (*cf next entry*) (+*dat*) throw over (s.o.'s) shoulders

überwerfen* (*cf previous entry*): **sich** ~ fall out (**mit** with)

überwiegen* outweigh; (*v/i*) predominate; prevail; ~**d** predominant; (*adv*) chiefly; **die** ~**de Mehrheit** the great majority

überwinden* overcome; get over (shock *etc*); negotiate (steep hill *etc*); **sich** ~ **zu ...** bring oneself to ...

die **Überwindung** *vbl noun*; *also* effort; strength of mind

überwintern (spend the) winter; hibernate

die **Überwinterung, –en** *vbl noun*; *also* hibernation

überwölben arch over

überwölken: sich ~ cloud over

überwuchern overgrow; **überwuchert von** overgrown with

der **Überwurf, ⸚e** wrap; *Aust* counterpane; *wrestl* sit-back

Überzahl: in der ~ in the majority

überzählig surplus; superfluous

überzeichnen overdraw; *fin* oversubscribe

überzeugen convince (**von** of); (*v/i*) be convincing; **sich** ~ satisfy oneself (**von** of); see for oneself; ~**d** convincing; ~**d wirken** carry conviction; **überzeugt** convinced (**von** of); confident (of); **von sich (selbst) überzeugt sein** be very sure of oneself

die **Überzeugung, –en** conviction; **aus** ~ from conviction || **die** ~**s|kraft, ⸚e** powers of persuasion; force (of argument)

überziehen* (*cf next entry*): (**sich** *dat* **...**) ~ put on; **jmdm. eins** ~ *coll* wallop s.o.

überziehen* (*cf previous entry*; *see also* **überzogen**) cover, (with layer) coat, *metall* plate; suffuse (face); carry too far; overrun (time); *fin* overdraw (bank account); (*v/i*) overrun the allotted time; **ein Bett (frisch)** ~ change the bed-linen; **neu** ~ re-cover; ~ **mit** cover with; coat with; subject to; **mit Guß** ~ ice (cake *etc*); **mit Krieg** ~ turn into a battlefield

sich ~ become overcast; **sich** ~ **mit** become covered with

der **Überzieher, –** overcoat
überzogen *p/part*; *also* exaggerated; excessive
überzüchtet overbred
überzuckern (sprinkle with) sugar
der **Überzug, ⸗e** (chair *etc*) cover; coat(ing); icing; *metall* plating
üblich usual; **wie ~** as usual
das **U-Boot, –e** (= **Unterseeboot**) submarine
übrig remaining, rest of; other; (*pred*) left (over); **~ haben** have left/to spare; **etwas/viel ~ haben für** have a soft spot/great liking for; **wenig/nichts ~ haben für** have little/no time for; **das ~e** the rest; **alles ~e** everything else; **ein ~es tun** do one more thing; be a further factor; **im ~en** besides; for the rest; otherwise || **~behalten*** (*sep*) have left (over); **~bleiben*** (*sep*; *sn*) be left (over) (**es bleibt mir nichts anderes ~ als zu ...** I have no choice but to ...); **~lassen*** (*sep*) leave (*dat* for) (**viel zu wünschen ü.** leave much to be desired; **nichts zu wünschen ü.** be all that could be desired)
übrigens by the way, incidentally
die **Übung, –en** practice; exercise; *univ* class; **aus der ~ (kommen)** (get) out of practice; **in ~ bleiben** keep in practice || **der ~s|platz, ⸗e** training-ground, *mil* parade ground; **das ~s|stück, –e** *mus* exercise
u. dgl. (= **und dergleichen**) and suchlike
u. d. M./ü. d. M. (= **unter/über dem Meeresspiegel**) below/above sea level
die **UdSSR** [u:de:ˀɛsˀɛsˈˀɛr] (= **Union der Sozialistischen Sowjetrepubliken**) the U.S.S.R.
das **Ufer, –** shore; bank; **ans ~** (go, wash, *etc*) ashore || **u~los** interminable; boundless (**... geht ins u~lose** there is no end to ...)
uff! phew!
die **Uffizien** [–ĭən] *pl* the Uffizi
Uffz. (= **Unteroffizier**) N.C.O.
das **UFO, Ufo** [ˈu:fo] (*gen* –(s)), **–s** U.F.O.
U-förmig U-shaped
Uganda Uganda
der **Ugander, –, ugandisch** Ugandan
ugs. (= **umgangssprachlich**) coll.
uh! ugh!; (*fright*) oh!
die **U-Haft** = **Untersuchungshaft**
die **Uhr, –en** clock; watch; meter; (*expressing time of day*) (**8** *etc*) **~** (8 *etc*) o'clock; **nach meiner ~** by my watch; **rund um die ~** round the clock; **um wieviel ~?** what time?; **wieviel ~ ist es?** what's the time? || **der ~macher, –** watchmaker; **das ~werk, –e** works (of clock, watch); **der ~zeiger, –** hand (of clock, watch); **~zeiger|sinn** (**entgegen dem U.** anti-clockwise, counterclockwise *US*; **im U.** clockwise); **die ~zeit, –en** time (of day)
der **Uhu, –s** eagle-owl
die **Ukraine** [*also* –aˈi:–] the Ukraine
der **Ukrainer** [*also* –aˈi:–], **–, ukrainisch** Ukrainian
UKW (= **Ultrakurzwelle**) V.H.F.
der **Ulan, –en** (*wk masc*) *hist* uhlan
der **Ulk, –e** lark; fun; **aus ~** for fun/a lark; **~ machen** lark about
ulken lark about
ulkig funny
die **Ulme, –n** elm; **das ~n|sterben** Dutch elm disease
die **Ultima ratio** [–ts–] last resort
ultimativ in the form of an ultimatum; **~ fordern** deliver an ultimatum demanding ...
das **Ultimatum, –s/–(t)en** ultimatum
der **Ultimo, –s** *comm* last day of the month
der **Ultra, –s** right-wing extremist; **die ~kurz|welle, –n** ultra-short wave; very high frequency; **u~marin, das ~marin** ultramarine; **der ~schall** ultrasound; **~schall–** ultrasonic ...; **die ~schall|untersuchung, –en** *med* scan (using ultrasound); **u~violett** ultraviolet
um [ʊm] **1** *prep* (+*acc*) (*a*) (*indicating place*) (a)round; about (axis); through (... degrees);
(*b*) (*indicating time*) at (... o'clock); around (Christmas, lunchtime, *etc*);
(*c*) (year *etc*) after (year *etc*); **einen Tag ~ den anderen** every other day;
(*d*) (*indicating amount*) about, roughly;
(*e*) (*indicating extent*) by (*eg* **~ 1 Meter gekürzt** shortened by 1 metre); *or not translated* (*eg* **~ eine Nuance zu laut** a shade too loud, **~ 2 Grad wärmer** 2 degrees warmer);
(*f*) (= '*in exchange for*') *esp SGer* for (... marks *etc*); *also in certain set phrases*, *eg* **~ nichts in der Welt** not for anything in the world, **~ jeden Preis** at all costs;
(*g*) (*indicating loss*) (cheat *etc*) out of; (deprive) of;
(*h*) (*other senses*) (worry *etc*) about, (haggle, quarrel) over; (ask, strike, play, *etc*) for; *Aust* (send) for, (go) to get;
2 *adv*: **... ist ~** (time *etc*) is up
~ die ... about ..., roughly ...
~ ... her around
~ ... herum around; *coll* (*of amount, time*) round about, around
so ~ round about (... o'clock)
~ so (+ *comp*) all the; **~ so besser!** so much the better!; **~ so mehr, als ...** all the more so since ...; **je ..., ~ so ...** the ..., the ...
~ ... (*gen*) **willen** for ...'s sake, for the sake of
~ zu ... (in order) to ...; only to ...; **zu ..., ~ zu ...** too ... to ...

um– *sep* (*stressed*) *and insep* (*unstressed*) *pref* – *general senses*:
(*i*) ... round (*eg* **~segeln** sail round, **sich ~drehen** turn round); (*sep*) ... on, ... round one (*eg* **~binden** put on (tie *etc*), **~nehmen** wrap round one);
(*ii*) (*sep*) ... over (*eg* **~kippen** tip over); ... down (*eg* **~blasen** blow down);
(*iii*) (*sep*) *indicates a turning over* (*eg* **~graben** dig over, **~pflügen** plough up);
(*iv*) (*sep*) *indicates a change of state or location* re–, change ... (*eg* **~gruppieren** regroup, **~steigen** change (trains *etc*), **sich ~ziehen** change (one's clothes), **ein Pferd ~satteln** change a horse's saddle)

um|adressieren re-address
um|ändern alter
die **Um|änderung, –en** alteration
um|arbeiten remodel; recast; **zu einem Drama/Drehbuch/einer TV-Serie ~** adapt for the stage/screen/for T.V.
die **Um|arbeitung, –en** *vbl noun*; *also* adaptation
um|armen embrace; hug; **sich ~** embrace; hug one another
die **Um|armung, –en** embrace; hug
der **Umbau, –ten** alterations (to building); conversion; reorganization; *theat* scene change
umbauen (*cf next entry*) make alterations to; convert (**zu** into); rebuild (apparatus); reorganize; *theat* change (scenery)
umbauen (*cf previous entry*): **~ mit** surround with (buildings *etc*); **umbauter Raum** enclosed area
umbehalten* *coll* keep on (shawl, bra, *etc*)
umbenennen* rename; **~ in** (*acc*) rename (sth. sth.)
umbesetzen appoint someone else to (post); *theat* give (role) to someone else; *sp* change (team)
umbetten transfer to another bed/grave
umbiegen* bend; (*v/i sn*) double back
umbilden reorganize; recast; *pol* reshuffle
die **Umbildung, –en** *vbl noun*; *also* reorganization; *pol* reshuffle
umbinden* (*cf next entry*) put on (tie *etc*)
umbinden* (*cf previous entry*): **~ mit** tie (string *etc*) round
umblasen* blow down
umblättern turn (page); (*v/i*) turn the page; **bitte ~** please turn over
umblicken: sich ~ look round
umbrechen* (*cf next entry*) break down; *agr* break up (soil); (*v/i sn*) break
umbrechen* (*cf previous entry*) *print* make up
umbringen* kill; **nicht umzubringen** *coll* indestructible; **sich ~** kill oneself
der **Umbruch, ⸚e** radical change; revolution (in sth.); *print* make-up; = **die ~korrektur, –en** page-proof
umbuchen [–uː–] change one's reservation for; *fin* transfer to another account
umdenken* rethink
umdeuten re-interpret
umdisponieren change one's plans
umdrängen crowd around
umdrehen turn; turn over; turn round; turn inside out; wring (neck); *coll* 'turn round' (spy); (*v/i*, *also sn*) turn back; (+*dat*) **das Wort im Munde ~** twist (s.o.'s) words; **sich ~** turn; turn round (**nach** to look at); turn over
die **Umdrehung, –en** turn; *phys* revolution, rotation; *mech* revolution
um|einander around/about/for each other
um|erziehen* re-educate
die **Um|erziehung** re-education
umfahren* (*cf next entry*) *mot* knock down
umfahren* (*cf previous entry*) go/drive/sail round; bypass
die **Umfahrung, –en** *vbl noun*; *Aust*, *Swiss* = **die ~s|straße, –n** *Aust*, *Swiss* bypass
umfallen* (*sn*) fall over/down; collapse; *coll* cave in (= yield)
der **Umfang, ⸚e** circumference; size; area; extent; range; scope; volume; **in vollem ~ überblicken** grasp the full extent of; **in (größerem** *etc*) **~** on a (larger *etc*) scale || **u~reich** (book) substantial; extensive; voluminous
umfangen* embrace
umfärben dye (sth.) another colour
umfassen clasp; embrace; comprise; contain; cover; *mil* surround, encircle; **~d** extensive; comprehensive; (confession) full
umfliegen* (*cf next entry*) (*sn*) *coll* fall over
umfliegen* (*cf previous entry*) fly around
umfließen* flow around
umflort misted with tears
umformen recast; (experience *etc*) transform; **~ in** (*acc*) *elect* convert into
der **Umformer, –** *elect* converter
die **Umfrage, –n** opinion poll
umfrieden enclose
umfüllen: ~ in (*acc*) pour/put into (another container)
umfunktionieren change the function of; **~ in** (*acc*)/**zu** turn into; convert into
der **Umgang** company (one keeps); *archit* circular gallery; **~ mit** association with; dealings with; dealing with; handling (of); how to deal with/handle; **~ haben/pflegen mit** associate with
umgänglich affable; sociable
Umgangs–: die ~formen *pl* manners; **die ~sprache** colloquial language; **u~sprachlich** colloquial; **der ~ton** tone
umgarnen ensnare

umgeben* surround; enclose; **sich ~ mit** surround oneself with

die **Umgebung** surrounding area; surroundings; environment; people around one; circle of acquaintances

die **Umgegend** surrounding area

umgehen* (*cf next entry*; *see also* **umgehend**) (*sn*) go round, circulate; **es geht dort um** the place is haunted

~ **in** (*dat*) haunt

~ **mit** associate with; be (gentle/economical *etc*) with; handle; **mit dem Gedanken ~ zu ...** be thinking of (+*ger*); **(es) verstehen, mit ... umzugehen** have a way with

umgehen* (*cf previous entry*) avoid; bypass; get round, bypass (law *etc*), avoid, dodge (difficulty *etc*)

umgehend immediate

die **Umgehung** *vbl noun*; *also* avoidance; **die ~s|straße, -n** bypass; ring road, beltway *US*

umgekehrt *p/part*; *also* reverse; opposite; (*adv*) the other way round; conversely; on the contrary; **und ~** and vice versa; **~ proportional** inversely proportional; **im ~en Verhältnis stehen zu** be in inverse proportion to

umgestalten rearrange; reorganize; recast; reshape; **~ zu** convert into

die **Umgestaltung, -en** *vbl noun*; *also* rearrangement; reorganization

umgewöhnen: sich ~ adapt

umgießen* pour into something else; *metall* recast; *coll* spill; **~ in** (*acc*) pour into

umgraben* dig over

umgrenzen bound; enclose; delimit

umgruppieren regroup

umgucken: sich ~ *coll* look around; look back; **du wirst dich noch ~!** you're in for a surprise!

umhaben* *coll* have (coat, tie, *etc*) on

umhalsen throw one's arms around (s.o.'s) neck

der **Umhang, -̈e** cape

Umhänge-: die ~tasche, -n shoulder-bag

umhängen (*cf next entry*) hang up somewhere else; rehang; (+*dat*) put round (s.o.'s) shoulders; **sich** *dat* **... ~** put round one's shoulders; sling (gun) over one's shoulder

umhängen (*cf previous entry*): **~ mit** drape with

umhauen* cut down; (*p/t only* **haute um**) *coll* knock for six; *coll* bowl over; knock out

umher: weit ~ all around

umher– *sep pref* ... around; ... about

umherblicken look about/around

umhergehen* (*sn*) walk about/around

umher|irren (*sn*) wander about/around

umherliegen* lie about/around

umherziehen* (*sn*) wander about/around; travel about/around

umhinkönnen*: ich kann nicht umhin zu ... I cannot help (+*ger*)

umhören: sich ~ ask around

umhüllen: ~ mit wrap up in

U/min (= Umdrehungen pro Minute) r.p.m.

umkämpft: heiß ~ hotly contested

die **Umkehr** turning back, (decide *etc*) to turn back; turning over a new leaf

umkehren (*see also* **umgekehrt**) turn inside out; (searcher) turn upside down; reverse; *mus* invert; (*v/i sn*) turn back; turn over a new leaf; **sich ~** be reversed

die **Umkehrung, -en** *vbl noun*; *also* reversal; *mus* inversion

umkippen knock over; upset; (*v/i sn*) tip over; overturn; *coll* pass out; *coll* cave in (= yield); *coll* (atmosphere) change suddenly

umklammern clasp; cling to; *mil* envelop; **sich ~** *wrestl* go into/be in a clinch; **umklammert halten** clutch

umklappen fold back; fold down; (*v/i sn*) *coll* pass out

Umkleide-: die ~kabine, -n changing cubicle; **der ~raum, -̈e** changing-room

umkleiden (*cf next entry*) change (s.o.'s) clothes; **sich ~** change

umkleiden (*cf previous entry*): **~ mit** cover with

umknicken bend over; fold over; (*v/i sn*) sprain one's ankle; get bent over

umkommen* (*sn*) die, be killed; *coll* (foodstuff) go bad

der **Umkreis** vicinity, neighbourhood; *math* circumcircle; **im ~ von** within a radius of

umkreisen circle round; *astron* orbit, revolve round; *space* orbit

umkrempeln turn up; turn inside out; turn upside down (in search of sth.); *coll* change (completely); shake up

umladen* transship

die **Umlage, -n** share of the costs

umlagern (*cf next entry*) transfer to another place of storage

umlagern (*cf previous entry*) (fans *etc*) besiege

das **Umland** surrounding countryside

der **Umlauf, -̈e** circulation; circular; *astron* revolution; **im ~** in circulation; **in ~ bringen** put into circulation; spread, circulate (rumour) || **die ~bahn, -en** orbit **(in eine U. bringen** put into orbit)

umlaufen* (*cf next entry*) knock over (while running); (*v/i sn*) circulate

umlaufen* (*cf previous entry*) run round; *astron* revolve round

der **Umlaut, -e** *ling* umlaut (*also* = symbol ¨), vowel mutation

umlauten *ling* umlaut, mutate (vowel)
umlegen (*cf next entry*) turn down (collar), turn up (cuffs); fold back (car seat); turn (lever); (hail *etc*) beat down; fell (tree), pull down (wall); lower (funnel, mast); relay; move (patient); change (appointment); *tel* transfer; *coll* floor; *vulg* do in; (+*dat*) put round (s.o.'s) shoulders; put (bandage) on; **~ auf** (*acc*) apportion (costs) among
umlegen (*cf previous entry*): **~ mit** garnish with
umleiten divert
die **Umleitung, -en** diversion (of); *mot* diversion, detour *US*
umlenken turn round
umlernen change one's ideas; retrain
umliegend surrounding
ummauern wall in
ummelden re-register; **jmdn./sich (polizeilich) ~** notify the authorities of s.o.'s/one's change of address
ummodeln change, alter
ummünzen: ~ in (*acc*) turn into; = **~ zu** reinterpret (*usu* wrongly) as
umnachtet: geistig ~ mentally deranged
die **Umnachtung: geistige ~** derangement
umnebeln surround with smoke; befog
umnehmen* wrap round one
um|organisieren reorganize
um|orientieren: sich ~ reorientate oneself
umpflanzen (*cf next entry*) replant; transplant
umpflanzen (*cf previous entry*): **~ mit** plant (bushes *etc*) round
umpflügen plough up
umpolen *phys* reverse the polarity of
umprogrammieren *comput* reprogram
umpusten [-u:-] *coll* blow over
umquartieren move to other accommodation/*mil* quarters; move (patient)
umrahmen (*cf next entry*) reframe
umrahmen (*cf previous entry*) frame (face *etc*)
umranden border, edge; ring (word *etc*)
umrändert: rot ~ sein (eyes) have red rings around them; **-umrändert** -rimmed
die **Umrandung, -en** border, edging
umrangieren [-ŋʒ-] *rail* shunt
umranken twine round; **von Efeu umrankt** ivy-clad
umräumen rearrange; shift
umrechnen convert (**in** *acc* into); **umgerechnet (100 Mark** *etc*) the equivalent of (100 marks *etc*)
die **Umrechnung, -en** conversion; **der ~s|kurs, -e** rate of exchange
umreisen travel (round)
umreißen* (*cf next entry*) knock down
umreißen* (*cf. previous entry*) outline; **fest/scharf umrissen** clear-cut

umrennen* knock down (while running)
umringen surround
der **Umriß, -(ss)e** outline, contour; **in Umrissen** in outline; outline of ...; **in groben Umrissen darstellen** outline || **die ~linie, -n** contour
umrühren stir
umrunden go round; *astron, space* orbit
umrüsten adapt; *mil* re-equip; **~ auf** (*acc*) convert to; *mil* re-equip with; (*v/i*) change over to
ums = um das
umsatteln change (horse's) saddle; (*v/i*) *coll* change jobs/*univ* courses; **~ auf** (*acc*) switch to
der **Umsatz, ⸚e** turnover
umsäumen (*cf next entry*) hem
umsäumen (*cf previous entry*) border; *sew* edge
umschalten switch over; *elect* switch; (*v/i*) change gear, shift *US*; **~ auf** (*acc*) switch over to; (*v/i*) (traffic lights) change to; *coll* readjust to; **~ nach** *rad, TV* go over to
Umschau: ~ halten nach look out for, be on the look-out for
umschauen: sich ~ *esp SGer* = **sich umsehen**
umschichtig in shifts
die **Umschichtung, -en** regrouping; restructuring
umschiffen (*cf next entry*) transship; transfer (passengers)
umschiffen (*cf previous entry*) (sail) round
der **Umschlag, ⸚e** envelope; (dust) jacket; turn-up, cuff *US*; sudden change (*gen* in); *comm* transfer (of goods); *med* compress; **der ~hafen, ..häfen** port of transshipment; **das ~tuch, ⸚er** shawl
umschlagen* turn (over) (page); turn up (sleeve *etc*); turn down (collar); turn back (carpet *etc*); cut down (tree); *comm* transfer (goods); (*v/i sn*) change (abruptly); (wind) veer round; (voice) crack; overturn; **jmdm./sich** *dat* **... ~** wrap round s.o.'s/one's shoulders; **~ in** (*acc*) (*sn*) turn into; **ins Gegenteil ~** change completely
umschleichen* creep round
umschließen* surround; enclose; embrace
umschlingen* embrace, clasp in one's arms; twine round
umschnallen: (sich *dat* **...) ~** buckle on
umschreiben* (*cf next entry*) rewrite; transcribe; **~ auf** (*acc*) transfer to
umschreiben* (*cf previous entry*) paraphrase; define (duties *etc*)
die **Umschrift, -en** transcription; (on coin) legend
umschulen send to another school; retrain; *pol* re-educate
umschütten pour into another container; spill
umschwärmen swarm around; surround

(admiringly)

Umschweife: keine ~ machen not beat about the bush; **ohne ~** straight out

umschwenken (*sn*) swing round; veer round; change one's tune

der **Umschwung, ⸚e** (sudden) change; swing (in opinion); *gym* circle

umsegeln sail round

umsehen*: sich ~ look round; **sich ~ in** (*dat*) look around; see (world); **sich ~ nach** look back at; look around for

umseitig overleaf

umsetzen move (pupil); transplant; repot; *comm* turn over, sell; **~ in** (*acc*) turn into; *chem*, *phys* convert into; *mus* transpose into; **in die Tat ~** put into action; **sich ~ in** (*acc*) *phys* be converted into

die **Umsicht** prudence, circumspection

umsichtig prudent, circumspect

umsiedeln resettle; **~ in** (*acc*)/**nach** (*sn*) move to

umsinken* (*sn*) sink to the ground

umso *Aust* = **um so** (*see* **um**)

umsonst in vain; free of charge; **nicht ~** not without reason; not for nothing

umsorgen look after

umspannen (*cf next entry*) change (horses); *elect* transform

umspannen (*cf previous entry*) reach round; encompass; span

der **Umspanner, –** *elect* transformer

umspielen (smile) play about; (waves) lap about; *sp* dribble round

umspringen* (*cf next entry*) (*sn*) (wind) veer round; suddenly change; *ski* jump-turn; **~ mit** treat (roughly *etc*)

umspringen* (*cf previous entry*) jump around

umspulen rewind

umspülen (waves) wash round

der **Umstand, ⸚e** circumstance; fact; (*pl*) bother, trouble; fuss; (+*dat*) **Umstände machen** put out, inconvenience; **sich** *dat* **Umstände machen** put oneself out; **wenn es dir keine Umstände macht** if it's no trouble; **viel Umstände machen mit** take a lot of trouble over; **in anderen Umständen** in the family way; **ohne Umstände** without any fuss; **unter diesen Umständen** under these circumstances; **unter allen/keinen Umständen** at all costs/on no account; **unter Umständen** possibly

umstände|halber owing to circumstances

umständlich long-winded; involved; ponderous; (*adv*) in a roundabout way

Umstands–: die ~bestimmung, –en adverbial phrase; **das ~kleid, –er** maternity dress; **die ~kleidung** maternity wear; **der ~krämer, –** *coll* fusspot; **das ~wort, ⸚er** adverb

umstehen* stand round, surround

umstehend standing around; overleaf (*also adv*); **die Umstehenden** the bystanders

Umsteige–: der ~bahnhof, ⸚e interchange station; **die ~karte, –n** transfer ticket

umsteigen* (*sn*) (passenger) change (**nach** for); **~ auf** (*acc*) switch to

der **Umsteiger, –** *coll* transfer ticket

umstellen (*cf next entry*) change round, rearrange; shift (lever), reset (clock); **~ auf** (*acc*) convert to; change (diet) to; (*also v/i*) switch to; **auf Computer/Container/elektrischen Betrieb ~** computerize/containerize/electrify; **sich ~ auf** (*acc*) switch to; adapt to

umstellen (*cf previous entry*) surround

die **Umstellung, –en** *vbl noun*; *also* changeover, conversion (**auf** *acc* to); adjustment (to)

umstimmen get (s.o.) to change his/her mind; *mus* retune

umstoßen* knock over; upset (plan); *leg* reverse; annul (will)

umstrahlen bathe in light

umstricken ensnare

umstritten controversial; disputed

umstrukturieren restructure

umstülpen turn upside down; turn inside out

der **Umsturz, ⸚e** coup (d'état), putsch

umstürzen overturn; *pol* overthrow, topple; (*v/i sn*) fall over; overturn

der **Umstürzler, –, umstürzlerisch** subversive

umtaufen rename

der **Umtausch** exchange (of goods, currency); **... ist vom ~ ausgeschlossen** ... cannot be exchanged

umtauschen exchange (**gegen** for); change (money: **in** *acc* into)

umtopfen repot

die **Umtriebe** *pl* machinations; **staatsfeindliche ~** subversive activities

der **Umtrunk** drink

umtun* *coll* (+*dat*) put on; put round (s.o.'s) shoulders; **sich** *dat* **... ~** put on; put round one's shoulders; **sich ~ nach** look around for

die **U-Musik = Unterhaltungsmusik**

umverteilen redistribute

die **Umverteilung, –en** redistribution

umwälzen roll over; revolutionize; **~d** revolutionary

die **Umwälzung, –en** radical change; (technological *etc*) revolution

umwandeln (*cf next entry*): **~ in** (*acc*) convert into (*also chem*, *phys*); *leg* commute to; **wie umgewandelt** a changed man/woman; **sich ~** be transformed

umwandeln (*cf previous entry*) walk round

die **Umwandlung, –en** change; conversion; *leg* commutation

umwechseln [–ks–]: **~ in** (*acc*) change (notes, lire, *etc*) into

der **Umweg, -e** detour; roundabout route; **einen ~ machen** make a detour; **auf ~en** by a roundabout route; indirectly; **auf dem ~ über** (*acc*) indirectly via

umwehen (*cf next entry*) blow over

umwehen (*cf previous entry*) blow round

die **Umwelt** environment; (the) world/people around one; *in compds* environmental ...; ecological ...; **u~feindlich** harmful to the environment; **u~freundlich** environment-friendly; **der ~schutz** conservation; **der ~schützer, –** conservationist; **die ~verschmutzung** pollution (of the environment)

umwenden* turn (over); (*v/i*: *p/t* **wendete um,** *p/part* **umgewendet**) *mot* turn; **sich ~** turn round (**nach** to look at)

umwerben* woo, court

umwerfen* knock over; upset (plan); *coll* bowl over; (drink) knock out; **sich** *dat* **... ~** throw round one's shoulders; **~d** staggering; devastating

umwerten [–eː–] re-evaluate

die **Umwertung, -en** re-evaluation

umwickeln: ~ mit wind (bandage *etc*) round

umwinden*: ~ mit twine round

umwittert: ~ von surrounded by; shrouded in

umwohnend neighbouring

umwölken: sich ~ cloud over

umwühlen root up; churn up; ransack (drawer *etc*)

umzäunen fence in

umziehen* (*cf next entry*) change (s.o.'s) clothes; (*v/i sn*) move (house); (firm) move; **sich ~** change (one's clothes), get changed

umziehen* (*cf previous entry*) surround; **sich ~** cloud over

umzingeln encircle, surround

der **Umzug, ⸚e** move, removal; procession

die **UN** the U.N.

---

un– [ʊn–] (*prefixed to adjectives*) un–, in– (*Note: where the stress is shown as falling on the stem, eg in* **unabwendbar,** *the word concerned may be stressed on the prefix* **un–** *instead*)

---

un|ab|änderlich irrevocable; unalterable

un|abdingbar inalienable; indispensable

un|abhängig independent (**von** of); **~ davon,** (**ob** *etc*) **...** irrespective of (whether *etc*) ...

die **Un|abhängigkeit** independence

un|abkömmlich engaged

un|ablässig incessant; unremitting

un|absehbar unforeseeable; endless; **auf ~e Zeit** for an indefinite period

un|absichtlich unintentional

un|abweisbar inescapable; imperative

un|abwendbar inevitable

un|achtsam careless; inattentive

un|ähnlich (*following dat*) unlike

un|anfechtbar incontestable

un|angebracht unsuitable; inappropriate

un|angefochten undisputed; unchallenged

un|angemeldet unannounced; unexpected

un|angemessen unsuitable; inappropriate

un|angenehm unpleasant, disagreeable

un|angetastet untouched

un|angreifbar unassailable

un|annehmbar unacceptable

die **Un|annehmlichkeiten** *pl* trouble

un|ansehnlich unsightly; plain

un|anständig indecent

die **Un|anständigkeit, -en** indecency

un|antastbar inviolable; unassailable; unimpeachable

un|appetitlich unappetizing; unsavoury

die **Un|art, -en** bad habit; naughtiness

un|artig naughty

un|artikuliert inarticulate

un|ästhetisch unsightly

un|aufdringlich unobtrusive

un|auffällig inconspicuous; unobtrusive

un|auffindbar nowhere to be found; untraceable

un|aufgefordert without being asked

un|aufhaltsam unstoppable; inexorable

un|aufhörlich incessant, constant

un|auflösbar = un|auflöslich indissoluble; insoluble (*also chem*)

un|aufmerksam inattentive

die **Un|aufmerksamkeit** inattention, inattentiveness

un|aufrichtig insincere

die **Un|aufrichtigkeit** insincerity

un|ausbleiblich inevitable

un|ausgefüllt (form *etc*) blank; unfulfilled

un|ausgeglichen unstable; unbalanced

die **Un|ausgeglichenheit** instability; imbalance

un|ausgegoren immature; half-baked

un|ausgeschlafen: ~ sein not have had enough sleep

un|ausgesetzt incessant, constant

un|ausgesprochen unspoken; implicit

un|ausgewogen unbalanced

un|auslöschlich indelible

un|ausrottbar ineradicable

un|aussprechbar unpronounceable

un|aussprechlich inexpressible; unspeakable, indescribable

un|ausstehlich intolerable, insufferable

un|ausweichlich inevitable; inescapable

unbändig unruly; unrestrained

unbarmherzig merciless

unbe|absichtigt unintentional

unbe|achtet unnoticed; unheeded; **~ bleiben** go unnoticed; be ignored; **~ lassen** disregard

unbe|antwortet unanswered
unbedacht rash; thoughtless
unbedarft inexperienced; naïve
unbedenklich harmless; (*adv*) without hesitation; ~ **sein** (state of health *etc*) give no cause for alarm
unbedeutend insignificant; minor
unbedingt absolute; unconditional (*also comput*); (*adv*) absolutely; really; at all costs; ~ **wollen** insist on (+*ger*) (*eg* **sie wollte es ~ wissen** she insisted on knowing); **nicht** ~ not necessarily; **wenn's ~ sein muß** if you insist; ~**!** most definitely!
unbe|eindruckt unimpressed
unbe|einflußt uninfluenced
unbefahrbar impassable
unbefangen impartial; natural; uninhibited
die **Unbefangenheit** impartiality; naturalness; uninhibitedness
unbefleckt unsullied; **die U~e Empfängnis** the Immaculate Conception
unbefriedigend unsatisfactory
unbefriedigt dissatisfied (**von** with); unsatisfied
unbefugt unauthorized; **der/die Unbefugte** (*decl as adj*) unauthorized person
unbegabt untalented
unbegreiflich incomprehensible; inconceivable
unbegrenzt unlimited; boundless
unbegründet groundless, unfounded
das **Unbehagen** (feeling of) uneasiness
unbehaglich uncomfortable; uneasy
unbehelligt undisturbed; unhindered; ~ **lassen** leave alone
unbeherrscht lacking self-control; unrestrained
unbehindert unhindered; (view) uninterrupted
unbeholfen clumsy, awkward
unbe|irrbar unwavering
unbe|irrt without wavering
unbekannt unknown; unfamiliar; ~**e Größe** unknown quantity; **ich bin hier** ~ I'm a stranger here; **Verfahren gegen Unbekannt** proceedings against person or persons unknown; **die Unbekannte** (*decl as adj*) unknown quantity || **unbekannter|weise** although we haven't met
unbekleidet bare; (*adv*) with nothing on
unbekümmert carefree; unconcerned
die **Unbekümmertheit** carefreeness; unconcern
unbelastet unladen; free from care; *pol* with a clean record; *fin* unencumbered
unbelebt (nature) inanimate; (street *etc*) quiet
unbeleckt *coll*: ~ **von** untouched by
unbelehrbar incorrigible
unbelesen unread
unbeliebt unpopular (**bei** with)
die **Unbeliebtheit** unpopularity
unbemannt unmanned
unbemerkbar imperceptible
unbemerkt unnoticed; unobserved; ~ **bleiben** go unnoticed
unbemittelt without means
unbenommen: es bleibt/ist mir ~ zu ... I am at liberty to ...
unbenutzt unused
unbe|obachtet unobserved
unbequem uncomfortable; awkward; disagreeable
unberechenbar unpredictable; incalculable
unberechtigt unjustified; unfounded; unauthorized
unberücksichtigt not taken into account; ~ **bleiben** not be considered; ~ **lassen** leave out of account
unberufen! touch wood!
unberührt untouched; (forest, snow) virgin; unspoiled; unaffected; unmoved; ~ **sein** (girl) be a virgin
unbeschadet (+*gen*) notwithstanding
unbeschädigt undamaged
unbeschäftigt unoccupied; unemployed
unbescheiden immodest
unbescholten irreproachable
unbeschrankt *rail* without gates
unbeschränkt absolute; unlimited
unbeschreiblich indescribable
unbeschrieben blank; ~**es Blatt** blank sheet; **ein ~es Blatt sein** *coll* be inexperienced/an unknown quantity
unbeschwert carefree; (conscience) clear
unbesehen without seeing it/them first; (buy) sight unseen
unbesetzt vacant; unoccupied
unbesiegbar invincible
unbesiegt undefeated, unbeaten
unbesonnen rash
unbesorgt unconcerned; **sei ~!** don't worry!
unbespielt (tape *etc*) blank
unbeständig changeable; fickle; inconstant; *fin* unsettled
unbestechlich incorruptible; unerring
unbestimmbar indeterminable; (age *etc*) indeterminate
unbestimmt vague; (age) indeterminate; uncertain; undecided; *gramm* indefinite; **auf ~e Zeit** indefinitely
die **Unbestimmtheit** vagueness; uncertainty
unbestraft unpunished; ~ **bleiben** go unpunished
unbestreitbar indisputable, incontrovertible
unbestritten undisputed
unbeteiligt detached; not involved (**an** *dat* in)
unbetont unstressed
unbeträchtlich insignificant; **nicht** ~ not inconsiderable
unbeugsam unyielding, unbending; (will)

indomitable
unbewacht unattended; unguarded
unbewaffnet unarmed
unbewältigt unmastered; **die ~e Vergangenheit** (*the* (*Nazi*) *past with which Germany has yet to come to terms*)
unbeweglich immovable (*also leg*), fixed; (feast) immovable; motionless; (expression) fixed; inflexible
die **Unbeweglichkeit** immovability; motionlessness; inflexibility
unbeweibt *coll* without a wife
unbewohnt uninhabited; unoccupied
unbewußt unconscious; **das Unbewußte** (*decl as adj*) the unconscious
unbezahlbar prohibitively expensive; priceless; *coll* worth its weight in gold; (person) priceless
unbezahlt unpaid
unbezähmbar uncontrollable
unbezwingbar = **unbezwinglich** invincible, (fortress) impregnable; uncontrollable
die **Unbilden** *pl* rigours; trials and tribulations
die **Unbildung** lack of education
die **Unbill** *arch* wrong (done to s.o.); rigours
unbillig unreasonable; unfair
unblutig bloodless; (*adv*) without bloodshed
unbotmäßig refractory
unbrauchbar useless, no use; unusable, unserviceable
unchristlich [-kr-] unchristian
und and; (*indicating simultaneity*) *expressed by pres/part* (*eg* **sie standen da ~ warteten** they stood there waiting, **... ~ stotterte dabei vor Verlegenheit** ... stuttering with embarrassment); (*with inversion*) even if/ though (*eg* **~ sollte ich dabei zugrunde gehen** even if it should be the ruin of me); (*where verb is repeated, with neg*) *expressed by* simply, just (*eg* **ich kann ~ kann es nicht fassen!** I simply can't grasp it!, **der Zug kam ~ kam nicht** the train just wouldn't come); (*after* **so** + *adj/adv*: *replacing infin* + **zu**) as to (*eg* **seien Sie bitte so freundlich ~ ...** would you be so kind as to ...); *coll* (*ellipt, pouring scorn on notion*) *not translated* (*eg* **ich ~ arbeiten!** me work?, **der ~ pünktlich (sein)/~ ein guter Tänzer!** him punctual/a good dancer?)
  ~? what then?; so (what)?
  na ~? so what?
  ~ (wäre es *etc*) **noch so ...** no matter how ... (it was *etc*)
  ~ ob/wie! you bet!
  ~ so weiter and so on
  ~ wenn ... even if/though ...; **~ wenn ... noch so ...** no matter how (much) ..., however (much) ...
  ~ zwar (*see* **zwar**)
der **Undank** ingratitude
undankbar ungrateful; (task *etc*) thankless
die **Undankbarkeit** ingratitude; thanklessness
undatiert undated
undefinierbar indefinable
undeklinierbar indeclinable
undemokratisch undemocratic
undenkbar inconceivable
undenklich: seit ~en Zeiten since time immemorial
das **Understatement** [andɐ'ste:tmənt] understatement
undeutlich unclear; indistinct; vague, hazy
undicht leaky; not airtight; **~e Stelle** leak
Unding: es ist ein ~ zu ... it's absurd to ...
undiszipliniert undisciplined
die **Undiszipliniertheit** lack of discipline
undramatisch undramatic
unduldsam intolerant
undurchdringlich impenetrable; inscrutable
undurchführbar unfeasible, impracticable
undurchlässig impermeable
undurchschaubar unfathomable; inscrutable
undurchsichtig opaque; non-transparent; obscure
un|eben uneven; bumpy; **nicht ~** *coll* not bad
die **Un|ebenheit, -en** unevenness; bumpy patch
un|echt false; not genuine; artificial; imitation; *math* improper
un|edel ignoble; (metal) base
un|ehelich illegitimate; **~ geboren** born out of wedlock
die **Un|ehelichkeit** illegitimacy
die **Un|ehre** dishonour; (+*dat*) **~ machen/zur ~ gereichen** disgrace
un|ehrenhaft dishonourable
un|ehr|erbietig disrespectful
un|ehrlich dishonest
die **Un|ehrlichkeit** dishonesty
un|eigennützig unselfish
un|eingeschränkt absolute; unqualified
un|eingeweiht uninitiated
un|einig divided; in disagreement; **~ sein** disagree
die **Un|einigkeit** disagreement
un|einnehmbar impregnable
un|eins in disagreement
un|empfänglich: ~ für unreceptive to
un|empfindlich insensitive (**gegen** to); (colour *etc*) practical; *med* immune (to)
die **Un|empfindlichkeit** insensitivity; *med* immunity
un|endlich infinite (*also math*); endless; no end of; (*adv*) *also* extremely; **~ klein** infinitesimal; **~ viel(e)** no end of; **bis ins ~e** ad infinitum, endlessly
die **Un|endlichkeit** infinity
un|entbehrlich indispensable
un|entgeltlich free (of charge)
un|entrinnbar inescapable; ineluctable
un|entschieden undecided; *sp* drawn; (*adv*)

sp (end) in a draw

das **Un|entschieden, –** *sp* draw

un|entschlossen undecided; indecisive, irresolute

un|entschuldigt without an excuse

un|entwegt constant; tireless, untiring

un|entwirrbar that cannot be disentangled; inextricable

un|entzifferbar undecipherable

un|erbittlich unrelenting; pitiless; inexorable

un|erfahren inexperienced

die **Un|erfahrenheit** inexperience

un|erfindlich inexplicable; **aus ~en Gründen** for some obscure reason

un|erforschlich unfathomable; (divine will) unsearchable

un|erforscht unexplored

un|erfreulich unpleasant, disagreeable

un|ergiebig unproductive; poor

un|ergründlich unfathomable; inscrutable

un|erheblich insignificant; unimportant

un|erhört outrageous; unheard-of, unprecedented; tremendous; (*adv*) outrageously; tremendously; incredibly; **~ viel** a tremendous amount

un|erklärlich inexplicable

un|erläßlich imperative

un|erlaubt not allowed; unauthorized; illegal; illicit; (*adv*) without permission

un|ermeßlich immense, vast

die **Un|ermeßlichkeit** immensity, vastness

un|ermüdlich untiring, tireless

un|erquicklich disagreeable

un|erreichbar unattainable, out of reach; inaccessible; *tel* unobtainable

un|erreicht unequalled

un|ersättlich insatiable

un|erschlossen untapped; (region) undeveloped

un|erschöpflich inexhaustible

un|erschrocken fearless, intrepid

un|erschütterlich imperturbable; unshakeable

un|erschwinglich prohibitive, beyond one's means; **~ teuer** prohibitively expensive

un|ersetzbar = **un|ersetzlich** irreplaceable; (damage, loss) irreparable

un|ersprießlich unproductive, unfruitful

un|erträglich intolerable, unbearable

un|erwähnt unmentioned

un|erwartet unexpected; (+*dat*) **~ kommen** come as a surprise to

un|erwidert unanswered; (greetings *etc*) not returned; (love) unrequited

un|erwünscht unwelcome; unwanted

un|erzogen ill-mannered

die **UNESCO** [u'nɛsko] UNESCO

unfähig incompetent; **~ zu** incapable of; **~ zu ...** unable to ...; incapable of (+*ger*)

die **Unfähigkeit** incompetence; inability

unfair [–fɛːɐ] unfair

der **Unfall, ⸚e** accident; **bei einem ~** in an accident || **die ~flucht** failure to stop after an accident; hit-and-run offence; **u~frei** accident-free; **die ~station, –en** casualty ward; **die ~stelle, –n** scene of an/the accident; **der ~wagen, –** ambulance; car damaged in an accident

unfaßbar = **unfaßlich** incomprehensible

unfehlbar infallible; (instinct) unerring; (*adv*) without fail

die **Unfehlbarkeit** infallibility

unfein unrefined, indelicate; bad form

unfertig unfinished, incomplete; immature

der **Unflat** filth

unflätig filthy, obscene

unfolgsam disobedient

unförmig shapeless; unshapely

unförmlich informal

unfrankiert unstamped

unfrei not free, *hist* in bondage; constrained; self-conscious; *post* unfranked; **~willig** compulsory; involuntary; unintentional

die **Unfreiheit** lack of freedom

unfreundlich unfriendly (**zu** to); unkind; cheerless; (weather) inclement

der **Unfrieden** strife; **~ stiften** sow discord

unfrisiert uncombed, unkempt; *coll* undoctored; not souped-up

unfruchtbar infertile; fruitless

die **Unfruchtbarkeit** infertility; fruitlessness

der **Unfug** mischief; nonsense; **grober ~** breach of the peace; **~ treiben** get up to mischief

---

–ung (*pl* **–en**) –ing, –tion, *etc* (*activity or result of an activity*), *eg* **die Atmung** breathing (**atmen** = breathe), **die Erklärung** explanation (= act of explaining, explanation given; **erklären** = explain)

---

der **Ungar** [–ŋg–], **–n** (*wk masc*) Hungarian

ungarisch [–ŋg–], (*language*) **U~** Hungarian

Ungarn [–ŋg–] Hungary

ungastlich inhospitable

unge|achtet (+*gen*; *often following noun*) notwithstanding

unge|ahnt unsuspected; undreamt-of

ungebärdig unruly

ungebeten uninvited; **~er Gast** gatecrasher

ungebeugt unbowed; *gramm* uninflected

ungebildet uneducated; uncultured

ungebräuchlich unusual, uncommon

ungebraucht unused

ungebrochen unbroken

ungebührlich improper

ungebunden free; unattached; (book) unbound, (flowers) loose; **in ~er Rede** in prose

ungedeckt (table) unlaid; uncovered (*also fin*); *chess, mil* unprotected; *sp* (player)

unmarked
die **Ungeduld** impatience
ungeduldig impatient
unge|eignet unsuitable
ungefähr approximate, rough; (*adv*) about, roughly; **so** ~ more or less; roughly; **von** ~ by chance; **nicht von** ~ ... it is no coincidence that ...
ungefährdet safe
ungefährlich harmless; safe; **nicht** ~ not without its dangers
ungefärbt undyed; (truth) unvarnished; *cul* without colouring
ungeflügelt wingless
ungefragt unasked
ungefüge cumbersome
ungehalten indignant (**über** *acc* about)
ungeheizt unheated
ungehemmt uninhibited; unrestrained; (*adv*) *also* without restraint
ungeheuer enormous; tremendous; **ins ~e steigen** skyrocket
das **Ungeheuer, –** monster
ungeheuerlich monstrous; outrageous; *occ* = **ungeheuer**
ungehindert unhindered
ungehobelt unplaned; uncouth
ungehörig improper; impertinent
die **Ungehörigkeit** impropriety; impertinence
ungehorsam disobedient
der **Ungehorsam** disobedience
der **Ungeist** evil ideology
ungeklärt not cleared up; unsolved
ungekocht uncooked; raw
ungekünstelt unaffected, natural
ungekürzt unabridged; *cin* uncut
ungeladen uninvited; unloaded; *elect* uncharged
ungelegen inconvenient; (+*dat*) ~ **kommen** be inconvenient for
die **Ungelegenheiten** *pl*, (+*dat*) ~ **bereiten/ machen** inconvenience
ungelenk awkward, ungainly
ungelenkig stiff (in the joints)
ungelernt unskilled
ungelogen! no kidding!
ungemein tremendous
ungemischt unmixed
ungemütlich uncomfortable; disagreeable; ~ **werden** *coll* turn nasty
ungenannt anonymous
ungenau inaccurate, inexact; imprecise, vague
die **Ungenauigkeit, –en** inaccuracy, inexactitude; imprecision, vagueness
ungeniert [–ʒe–] free and easy; uninhibited; (*adv*) *also* freely; **langen Sie bitte** ~ **zu!** please feel free to help yourself
die **Ungeniertheit** free and easy manner; lack of inhibition

ungenießbar not fit to eat/drink; *coll* (person) unbearable
ungenügend insufficient
ungenutzt unused; ~ **lassen** let slip (opportunity)
unge|ordnet disordered
ungepflegt untidy; neglected
ungerade uneven, odd
ungeraten ill-behaved
ungerechnet (+*gen*) not counting
ungerecht unjust
ungerechtfertigt unjustified
die **Ungerechtigkeit, –en** injustice
ungereimt unrhymed; nonsensical
die **Ungereimtheit, –en** inconsistency; absurdity
ungern reluctantly; *or conveyed by* ... is *etc* reluctant to ... (*eg* **sie kam** ~ she was reluctant to come); ... dislike(s) ... (*eg* **ich fahre (nicht) ~ Auto** I (don't) dislike driving)
ungerührt unmoved
ungesalzen unsalted
ungesättigt unsatisfied; *chem* unsaturated; **mehrfach** ~ polyunsaturated
ungeschehen: ~ **machen** undo
das **Ungeschick** clumsiness; ineptitude
die **Ungeschicklichkeit, –en** clumsy/inept act; = **Ungeschick**
ungeschickt clumsy, awkward; inept
ungeschlacht hulking great; (manner) uncouth
ungeschlechtlich asexual
ungeschliffen (diamond) uncut; unpolished
ungeschmälert undiminished
ungeschminkt without make-up; (truth) unvarnished
ungeschoren unshorn; ~ **davonkommen** get away with it; ~ **lassen** leave in peace
ungeschrieben unwritten
ungeschult untrained
ungeschwächt undiminished
ungesehen without being seen
ungesellig unsociable
ungesetzlich illegal
ungesittet unmannerly
ungestempelt unstamped; *post* unfranked
ungestört undisturbed; uninterrupted
ungestraft unpunished; (*adv*) with impunity; ~ **davonkommen** get away with it
ungestüm impetuous
das **Ungestüm** impetuosity
ungesund unhealthy
ungetan: ~ **lassen** leave undone
ungeteilt undivided; unanimous
ungetrübt unclouded; perfect
das **Ungetüm, –e** monster; monstrosity
unge|übt unpractised
ungewandt awkward
ungewiß uncertain; **im ungewissen** in the dark
die **Ungewißheit** uncertainty

ungewöhnlich unusual
ungewohnt unfamiliar; unusual; **... ist mir ~** I'm not accustomed to ...
ungewollt unintentional
ungezählt countless; uncounted
ungezähmt untamed
das **Ungeziefer** pests, vermin
ungezogen naughty
die **Ungezogenheit, -en** naughtiness, bad behaviour; (*pl*) naughtiness
ungezügelt unrestrained, unbridled
ungezwungen casual; natural, unaffected
der **Unglaube** (*like* **Glaube**) disbelief; *relig* unbelief
unglaubhaft incredible
ungläubig disbelieving, incredulous; *relig* unbelieving; **~er Thomas** doubting Thomas
unglaublich incredible
unglaub|würdig implausible
ungleich unequal; dissimilar; (socks *etc*) odd; (*adv*) *also* incomparably; **~artig** dissimilar; **~mäßig** uneven; irregular
die **Ungleichheit, -en** inequality; dissimilarity
das **Unglück, -e** accident; disaster; bad luck; misfortune; **zu allem ~** to make matters worse || **u~selig** unfortunate; disastrous
unglücklich unhappy; unfortunate; **unglücklicher|weise** unfortunately
Unglücks-: der ~fall, ⸚e accident; **der ~mensch, -en** (*wk masc*) unlucky person; **der ~rabe, -n** (*wk masc*) *coll* unlucky fellow; **der ~tag, -e** fateful day; **der ~vogel, ..vögel** *coll* = **der ~wurm, ⸚er** *coll* unlucky fellow
die **Ungnade** disfavour; **in ~ fallen** fall out of favour (**bei** with)
ungnädig ungracious; bad-tempered; **~ aufnehmen** take in bad part
ungültig invalid; void; (ballot-paper) spoilt; *sp* disallowed; **für ~ erklären** declare null and void; annul (marriage)
die **Ungültigkeit** invalidity; *leg* nullity
die **Ungunst** disfavour; inclemency (of weather); unpropitiousness; **zu jmds. ~en** to s.o.'s disadvantage
ungünstig unfavourable; adverse
ungut bad; (feeling) uneasy; **nichts für ~!** no offence!
unhaltbar intolerable; untenable; (promise) impossible to keep; *mil* indefensible; *sp* unstoppable
unhandlich unwieldy
unharmonisch inharmonious
das **Unheil** disaster; harm; **~ anrichten/stiften** do mischief || **u~bringend** unlucky; **u~voll** disastrous, calamitous
unheilbar *med* incurable; terminal
der **Unheils|prophet, -en** (*wk masc*) prophet of doom
unheimlich uncanny; eerie; *coll* tremendous; (*adv*) *coll* incredibly
unhistorisch unhistorical
unhöflich impolite, rude
die **Unhöflichkeit, -en** impoliteness, rudeness
der **Unhold, -e** fiend; monster; sex fiend
unhörbar inaudible
unhygienisch unhygienic
uni [y'ni:] (*indecl*) = **~farben** self-coloured
die **Uni** ['ʊ-], **-s** *coll* = **Universität**
die **Uniform, -en** uniform
uniformiert uniformed
das **Unikum, -s/Unika** unique thing; *coll* character, original
un|interessant uninteresting; of no interest; (offer *etc*) unattractive
un|interessiert uninterested (**an** *dat* in)
die **Union, -en** union; **die ~** (*in W. Germany*) *pol* the C.D.U. || **die ~s|parteien** *pl* the C.D.U. and C.S.U.; **die ~s|republik, -en** union republic (of the U.S.S.R.)
universal universal; *in compds* **U~-** universal ...; all-purpose ...; **das U~mittel, -** panacea
universell universal
die **Universität, -en** university; **auf die ~ gehen** go to university
das **Universum** universe
die **Unke, -n** toad; *coll* prophet of doom
unken *coll* prophesy ill
unkenntlich unrecognizable; **~ machen** disguise; obliterate
Unkenntlichkeit: bis zur ~ beyond recognition
die **Unkenntnis** ignorance; **in ~ lassen/sein** keep/be in the dark (**über** *acc* about)
der **Unken|ruf, -e** dire prophecy
unkindlich unchildlike
unklar unclear; indistinct; obscure; vague; **im ~en lassen/sein über** (*acc*) leave/be in the dark about
die **Unklarheit, -en** lack of clarity; indistinctness; obscurity; vagueness
unklug unwise
unkompliziert uncomplicated
unkontrollierbar uncontrollable
unkonzentriert lacking concentration
unkorrekt incorrect
die **Unkosten** *pl* expenses; cost(s); **sich in ~ stürzen** *coll* go to a lot of expense
das **Unkraut, ⸚er** weed; weeds; **~ jäten** weed || **der ~vernichter, -** weedkiller
unkritisch uncritical
unkultiviert uncultivated; uncultured
unkündbar permanent; not terminable; irredeemable
unkundig (+*gen*) ignorant of; **des (Englischen** *etc*) **~** unacquainted with (English *etc*); **des Lesens/Schreibens ~** unable to read/write
unlängst recently

unlauter dishonest; *comm* unfair
unleidlich (person) disagreeable
unlesbar = **unleserlich** illegible
unleugbar undeniable
unlieb: es ist mir nicht ~, daß ... I'm quite glad that ...
unliebsam disagreeable; unwelcome; (person) undesirable
unlin(i)iert unruled
unlogisch illogical
unlösbar insoluble (*also chem*); indissoluble
unlöslich *chem* insoluble
die **Unlust** reluctance; listlessness; *comm* slackness; **mit ~** with reluctance
unlustig reluctant; listless; *comm* slack
unmanierlich unmannerly
unmännlich unmanly
die **Unmasse, -n** *coll* masses
unmaß|geblich unauthoritative; **nach meiner ~en Meinung** in my humble opinion
unmäßig excessive, immoderate; inordinate; (*adv*) excessively, to excess
die **Unmenge, -n** vast amount/number
der **Unmensch, -en** (*wk masc*) brute, monster
unmenschlich inhuman; *coll* (heat *etc*) terrible
die **Unmenschlichkeit** inhumanity
unmerklich imperceptible
unmißverständlich unequivocal; (*adv*) in no uncertain terms
unmittelbar immediate; direct; **in ~er Nähe** in the immediate vicinity
unmöbliert unfurnished
unmodern old-fashioned; **~ werden** go out of fashion
unmodisch unfashionable
unmöglich [*emot* -'mø:k-] impossible; (*adv*) not possibly; **~ machen** make impossible; make (s.o.) look a fool; **sich ~ machen** make a fool of oneself; **U~es/das U~e** the impossible
die **Unmöglichkeit** impossibility; **das ist ein Ding der ~** that's quite impossible
die **Unmoral** immorality
unmoralisch immoral
unmündig under age
unmusikalisch unmusical
der **Unmut** displeasure (**über** *acc* at)
unnach|ahmlich inimitable
unnachgiebig unyielding, intransigent
unnachsichtig merciless; unrelenting
unnahbar unapproachable
unnatürlich unnatural
unnormal abnormal
unnötig unnecessary; needless; **~ zu sagen, daß ...** needless to say, ... || **unnötiger|weise** unnecessarily, needlessly
unnütz useless; (talk) idle
die **UNO** ['u:no] the U.N.
un|ordentlich untidy; disorderly
die **Un|ordnung** disorder; mess; **in ~ bringen** mess up; **in ~ geraten** get in a mess
un|orthodox unorthodox
unparteiisch impartial; **der/die Unparteiische** (*decl as adj*) impartial person; *sp* referee
die **Unparteilichkeit** impartiality
unpassend unsuitable; improper
unpassierbar impassable
unpäßlich indisposed
die **Unpäßlichkeit, -en** indisposition
unpersönlich impersonal (*also gramm*); (person) distant
unpolitisch apolitical, unpolitical
unpraktisch impractical
unproduktiv unproductive
unproportioniert ill-proportioned
unpünktlich unpunctual
unrasiert unshaven
die **Unrast** restlessness
der **Unrat** rubbish; **~ wittern** *coll* smell a rat
unrationell inefficient
unrecht wrong; **~ bekommen** prove wrong; (+*dat*) **~ geben** contradict; **~ haben** be wrong; (+*dat*) **~ tun** wrong
das **Unrecht** wrong, injustice; **im ~** in the wrong; **(sich) ins ~ setzen** put (oneself) in the wrong; **zu ~** wrongly, unjustly; **nicht zu ~** not without good reason || **u~mäßig** unlawful
unredlich dishonest
die **Unredlichkeit** dishonesty
unreell [-reɛl] *comm* dishonest
unreflektiert spontaneous
unregel|mäßig irregular (*also gramm*)
die **Unregel|mäßigkeit, -en** irregularity
unreif unripe; immature
die **Unreife** unripeness; immaturity
unrein not clean, dirty; impure; unclean (*also relig*); *mus* false; (*adv*) *mus* out of tune; **ins ~e schreiben** write out in rough
die **Unreinheit, -en** dirtiness; impurity; uncleanness
unreinlich not clean, dirty
unrentabel unprofitable
unrettbar: ~ verloren irretrievably lost
unrichtig wrong, incorrect
die **Unrichtigkeit, -en** incorrectness; mistake, error
die **Unruh, -en** balance-wheel
die **Unruhe, -n** restlessness; uneasiness; commotion; (*pl*) unrest; **~ stiften** stir up trouble; **in ~** restless; anxious || **der ~herd, -e** trouble-spot; **der ~stifter, -** troublemaker
unruhig restless; anxious; troubled; (pattern) busy; (street *etc*) noisy
unrühmlich inglorious
uns (*acc/dat of* **wir:** *see p. xxvi*) (*a*) us; (*dat*) (to/for) us; (*b*) (*refl*) ourselves, (*recip*) each other, one another; (*dat*) (to/for) ourselves, (*recip*) (to/for) each other/one

another
unsach|gemäß inexpert; improper
unsachlich not objective; biased; **~ werden** become personal
unsagbar = unsäglich unspeakable
unsanft rough; rude
unsauber dirty; untidy; impure; (transaction *etc*) shady; *sp* dirty
unschädlich harmless; **~ machen** put a stop to (thief's *etc*) activities
unscharf blurred, *phot* out of focus; imprecise
unschätzbar invaluable; priceless
unscheinbar inconspicuous
unschicklich unseemly
unschlagbar unbeatable
unschlüssig undecided; **~ sein** *also* waver
die **Unschlüssigkeit** indecision
unschön unsightly; ugly; unpleasant; unkind
die **Unschuld** innocence; virginity; **~ vom Lande** naïve country girl; **seine Hände in ~ waschen** wash one's hands of it; **in aller ~** in all innocence
unschuldig innocent; a virgin; **~ an** (*dat*) innocent of (crime); not to blame for
Unschulds–: die ~miene, –n air of innocence; **u~voll** (air) innocent
unschwer not difficult; (*adv*) without difficulty
der **Unsegen** misfortune; curse
unselb|ständig dependent, unable to stand on one's own two feet
die **Unselb|ständigkeit** dependence
unselig fateful; ill-fated
unser 1 *poss adj* (*see p. xxxiii*) our; 2 *pron* (*gen of* **wir**: *see p. xxvi*) of us; **~ aller ...** ... of all of us; **uns(e)rer/uns(e)re/uns(e)res** (*see p. xxviii*; *also* **der/die/das uns(e)re**) ours; **das Uns(e)re** what is ours; **das Uns(e)re tun** do our bit; **die Uns(e)ren** our family || **~einer** *coll* = **~eins** *coll* the likes of us; **~(er)seits** for/on our part
unser(e)s|gleichen people like us/ourselves
unseriös untrustworthy; frivolous; not to be taken seriously; *comm* dubious
unsert–: ~wegen because of us; = **(um) ~willen** for our sake
unsicher uncertain; unsafe; unstable; insecure; unsteady; **~ machen** make (s.o.) feel unsure of himself/herself; *coll* terrorize (district); be on the loose in
die **Unsicherheit, –en** uncertainty; unsafeness; instability; insecurity; unsteadiness || **der ~s|faktor, –en** element of uncertainty
unsichtbar invisible; **sich ~ machen** *joc* vanish into thin air
der **Unsinn** nonsense; **~ machen/treiben** do silly things; **~ reden** talk nonsense
unsinnig absurd; *coll* terrific
die **Unsitte, –n** bad habit
unsittlich immoral; indecent
die **Unsittlichkeit** immorality; indecency
unsolide (life, person) loose; (construction *etc*) unsound; *comm* dubious
unsozial anti-social
unsportlich unathletic; unsporting
unsr.. = unser..
unsrige: der/die/das ~ = der/die/das uns(e)re (*at* **unser**)
unstabil unstable
unstatthaft inadmissible
unsterblich immortal; (love) undying; (*adv*) *coll* utterly; madly (in love); **~ machen** immortalize
die **Unsterblichkeit** immortality
der **Unstern** unlucky star; **unter einem ~ stehen** be ill-starred
unstet restless; (life) unsettled; unsteady
die **Unstetigkeit** restlessness; unsettled nature; unsteadiness
unstillbar insatiable; unquenchable; *med* unstaunchable
die **Unstimmigkeit, –en** disagreement; discrepancy
unstreitig indisputable
die **Unsumme, –n** vast sum
unsymmetrisch asymmetrical
unsympathisch unpleasant; **... ist mir ~** I don't like ...
unsystematisch unsystematic
untad(e)lig irreproachable; unexceptionable
untalentiert untalented
die **Untat, –en** heinous crime
untätig idle; inactive; **~ herumsitzen/herumstehen** sit/stand about doing nothing
die **Untätigkeit** idleness; inactivity
untauglich unsuitable; *mil* unfit (for military service)
unteilbar indivisible
unten below; downstairs; at the bottom; down (*indicating position*, *eg* **ist er schon ~?** is he down yet?); **~ an** (*dat*) down by; at the foot of; **~ auf** (*dat*) down on (street *etc*); at the bottom of (list *etc*); **da/hier ~** down there/here; **~ in** (*dat*) down in (valley *etc*); at the bottom of (glass, league table, *etc*); **nach ~** down(wards); downstairs; **nach ~ hin/zu** towards the bottom; **von ~** from below/the bottom/downstairs; **weiter ~** further down; **... ist bei mir ~ durch** *coll* I'm through with ... || **unten|drunter** *coll* underneath; **~erwähnt** mentioned below; **~stehend** standing below; following
unter (*a*) (+*acc indicating direction*, +*dat indicating place*) under; below; among; (+ *dat* = '*less than*') under, below; (+*dat*) under (Stalin, s.o.'s leadership, *etc*);
(*b*) (+*dat*) *SGer* during;
(*c*) (+*dat*, *indicating circumstances etc*)

under (circumstances, oath, assumed name, *etc*); on (condition, pretext, *etc*); from (point of view); with (*eg* ~ **schweren Verlusten/heiseren Schreien** with heavy losses/hoarse cries); with (tears) in one's eyes; to (applause *etc*); (*followed by vbl noun*) *expressed by Eng pres/part* ...ing (*eg* ~ **Mißachtung aller ethischen Gesichtspunkte** disregarding all ethical considerations); while (+*pres/part*) (*eg* **man bringe das Wasser ~ Beigabe von etwas Essig zum Kochen** bring the water to the boil while adding a little vinegar)

~ **anderem** among other things
bis ~ (*acc*) up to; to below
~ **einem** *Aust* at the same time
~ **sich** *dat* **sein** be on their own
~ **'uns** *dat* **(gesagt)** between ourselves; ~ **'uns sein** be on our own; ~ **'uns bleiben** keep ourselves to ourselves

---

unter–[1] *sep* (*stressed*) *and insep* (*unstressed*) *pref – general senses*:
(*i*) ... under(neath) (*eg* ~**halten** hold underneath);
(*ii*) *indicates mixing* (*eg* ~**mischen** mix in);
(*iii*) under– (*eg* ~**bezahlen** underpay)

---

unter–[2] (*prefixed to adj*) under–
Unter– lower ...; under–; sub–; *for* ~**prima**, ~**sekunda**, *etc see* **Prima, Sekunda**, *etc*
unter.. (*see also* **unterst..**) lower; **das ~e Ende** the bottom (of road, table, *etc*)
die **Unter|abteilung, –en** subdivision
der **Unter|arm, –e** forearm
die **Unter|art, –en** sub-species
der **Unterbau, –ten** substructure; foundations; roadbed
unterbauen underpin (*also* theory *etc*)
unterbelichten (*insep*) *phot* under-expose; **(geistig) unterbelichtet** *coll* 'dim'
die **Unterbelichtung, –en** *phot* under-exposure
unterbesetzt understaffed
unterbewerten [–e:–] (*insep*) underrate
unterbewußt subconscious; **das U~sein** subconscious (mind) (**im U.** subconsciously)
unterbezahlen (*insep*) underpay
unterbieten* *comm* undersell, undercut; *sp* lower (record)
die **Unterbilanz, –en** *econ* adverse balance
unterbinden* (*cf next entry*) tie underneath
unterbinden* (*cf previous entry*) stop, put a stop to; *med* ligature
unterbleiben* (*sn*) not take place; stop
der **Unterboden|schutz** *mot* underseal, undercoat *US*
unterbrechen* interrupt; stop (temporarily); break (journey *etc*); *med* terminate (pregnancy); *comput* interrupt; *elect* interrupt, break; *tel* disconnect, cut off; *sp* stop (play)
der **Unterbrecher, –** *elect* interrupter; *mot* contact-breaker; *comput* circuit-breaker
die **Unterbrechung, –en** *vbl noun*; *also* interruption; break (*gen* in); *med* termination; *comput* interrupt; *elect* interruption; *tel* disconnection; *sp* stoppage; **ohne ~** without a break
unterbreiten (*cf next entry*) spread underneath
unterbreiten (*cf previous entry*) (+*dat*) put to; submit to
unterbringen* accommodate; put up; house; find room for, fit in; place (= recognize); ~ **bei** place with
die **Unterbringung** *vbl noun*; *also* accommodation
unterbrochen *p/part*; *also* (line) broken
der **Unterbruch, ¨–e** *Swiss* = **Unterbrechung**
unterbuttern *coll* throw in; walk all over
das **Unterdeck, –s** lower deck
unterderhand secretly
unterdes(sen) in the meantime
der **Unterdruck, ¨–e** *phys* vacuum; *med* low blood pressure; *in compds* vacuum ...
unterdrücken suppress; oppress
der **Unterdrücker, –** oppressor
die **Unterdrückung** suppression; oppression
unterdurchschnittlich below average
unter|einander one below the other; (connect) with one another; among ourselves/ yourselves/themselves; **sich ~** one another
unter|entwickelt underdeveloped
unter|ernährt undernourished
die **Unter|ernährung** malnutrition
unterfangen*: sich ~ zu ... dare to ...; **das Unterfangen, –** undertaking, venture
unterfassen take (s.o.'s) arm; **sich ~** link arms
der **Unterflur|motor, –en** underfloor engine
die **Unterführung, –en** underpass; subway
das **Unterfutter, –** interlining
unterfüttern interline; underpin
der **Untergang, ¨–e** sinking; setting; downfall; destruction; fall; **dem ~ geweiht** doomed
die **Untergattung, –en** subgenus
der **Untergebene** (*fem* **die ~**) (*decl as adj*) subordinate
untergehen* (*sn*) go down; set; perish; ~ **in** (*dat*) be lost in; (voice *etc*) be drowned by
unterge|ordnet *p/part*; *also* subordinate; **von ~er Bedeutung** of secondary importance
das **Untergeschoß, –(ss)e** basement
das **Untergestell, –e** chassis; *coll* 'pins'
das **Untergewicht** underweight; **~ haben** be underweight
untergliedern subdivide (**in** *acc* into)
die **Untergliederung, –en** subdivision
untergraben* (*cf next entry*) dig in

untergraben* (*cf previous entry*) undermine

der **Untergrund, ⸚e** subsoil; *art* ground; *pol etc* underground; **im ~** underground; **in den ~ gehen** go underground

Untergrund– *pol etc* underground ...; **die ~bahn, –en** underground (railway), subway *US*; **die ~bewegung, –en** underground (movement)

die **Untergruppe, –n** subgroup

unterhaken take (s.o's) arm; **sich ~** link arms

unterhalb (+*gen*) below

der **Unterhalt** maintenance; alimony; livelihood; upkeep

unterhalten* (*cf next entry*) hold underneath

unterhalten* (*cf previous entry*) support, keep; maintain (*also* relations *etc*); run; entertain; **sich ~** amuse oneself; talk (**mit** to); **~d** entertaining

Unterhalts– maintenance ...

unterhaltsam entertaining

die **Unterhaltung, –en** conversation; entertainment; upkeep, maintenance; **die ~s|kosten** *pl* maintenance costs; **die ~s|lektüre** light reading; **die ~s|musik** light music; **das ~s|programm, –e** programme featuring light entertainment

unterhandeln negotiate

der **Unterhändler, –** negotiator

die **Unterhandlung, –en** negotiation

das **Unterhaus** the House of Commons

das **Unterhemd, –en** vest, undershirt *US*

unterhöhlen undermine

das **Unterholz** undergrowth

die **Unterhose, –n** (pair of) underpants/panties

unter|irdisch underground, subterranean

Unter|italien Southern Italy

unterjochen subjugate

unterjubeln (+*dat*) *coll* palm off on

unterkellern build with a cellar

der **Unterkiefer, –** lower jaw, mandible

das **Unterkleid, –er** full-length slip

die **Unterkleidung** underclothes

unterkommen* (*sn*) find accommodation; find work (**bei** at, with)

das **Unterkommen** accommodation

der **Unterkörper** lower part of the body

unterkriechen* (*sn*) *coll* find shelter (**bei** with)

unterkriegen *coll* get the better of; **sich nicht ~ lassen** keep one's end up; **nicht unterzukriegen** irrepressible

unterkühlen *chem* supercool; **unterkühlt** *also* suffering from hypothermia; (style *etc*) unemotional

die **Unterkühlung, –en** *chem* supercooling; *med* hypothermia

die **Unterkunft, ⸚e** accommodation; *mil* quarters; billet

die **Unterlage, –n** base; underlay; something to rest on; something to lie on; (waterproof) sheet; *hort* stock; *tech* bed; (*pl*) documents, papers

Unterlaß: ohne ~ incessantly

unterlassen* refrain from (making); **es ~ zu ...** fail to ...; refrain from (+*ger*)

die **Unterlassungs|sünde, –n** sin of omission

der **Unterlauf, ⸚e** lower reaches

unterlaufen[1]* subvert; undermine; *sp* get in under (s.o.'s) guard; (*v/i sn*: error) be made, occur; **mir ist ein Fehler unterlaufen** I've made a mistake

unterlaufen[2]: mit Blut ~ bloodshot

unterlegen (*cf next entry*) put underneath; (+*dat*) attribute (meaning) to

unterlegen[1] (*cf previous entry*) (+*dat*) attribute (meaning) to; **einer Melodie einen Text ~** put words to a tune; **~ mit** back with

unterlegen[2] *p/part*; *also* inferior (**an** *dat* in); **der/die Unterlegene** (*decl as adj*) loser; underdog

die **Unterlegenheit** inferiority

der **Unterleib, –er** abdomen; lower abdomen; *in compds* **~s–** abdominal ...

das **Unterlid, –er** lower eyelid

unterliegen* (*see also* **unterlegen[2]**) (*sn exc* = 'be subject to') be defeated, lose; (+*dat*) be defeated by, lose to; succumb to; be subject to; **es unterliegt keinem Zweifel, daß ...** there is no doubt that ...

die **Unterlippe, –n** lower lip

unterm = unter dem

untermalen: mit Musik ~ provide with background music

die **Untermalung, –en** background music

untermauern underpin (*also* argument *etc*)

untermengen (*cf next entry*) mix in

untermengen (*cf previous entry*): **mit (Sand** *etc*) ~ mix (sand *etc*) with

der **Untermensch, –en** (*wk masc*) *esp Nazi* subhuman creature

Untermiete: zur ~ wohnen be a subtenant

der **Untermieter, –** subtenant

unterminieren undermine

untermischen (*cf next entry*) mix in

untermischen (*cf previous entry*): **mit (Sand** *etc*) ~ mix (sand *etc*) with

untern *coll* = **unter den**

unternehmen* undertake; do; take (steps); **alles ~, um zu ...** do all one can to ...

das **Unternehmen, –** undertaking, enterprise; venture; project; *comm* business; *mil* operation

unternehmend *pres/part*; *also* enterprising

der **Unternehmens|berater, –** management consultant

der **Unternehmer, –** entrepreneur; industrialist; employer

unternehmerisch entrepreneurial

das **Unternehmertum** employers; **freies ~** free

enterprise

die **Unternehmung, –en = Unternehmen; der ~s|geist** enterprise, initiative; **u~s|lustig** enterprising, go-ahead

der **Unter|offizier, –e** non-commissioned officer; sergeant; (air force) corporal, airman first class *US*

unter|ordnen (*see also* **untergeordnet**) (+*dat*) subordinate to; place under; **sich ~** accept a subordinate role; (+*dat*) submit to

das **Unterpfand, ⸗er** pledge

unterpflügen plough under

unterprivilegiert underprivileged

das **Unterprogramm, –e** *comput* subprogram, subroutine

die **Unterredung, –en** discussion; talks

unterrepräsentiert under-represented

der **Unterricht** lessons; teaching; instruction

unterrichten teach; inform (**über** *acc*/**von** of); **sich ~ über** (*acc*) inform oneself about; **in unterrichteten Kreisen** in well-informed circles

Unterrichts– teaching ...; educational ...; **das ~fach, ⸗er** subject; **die ~stunde, –n** lesson; **das ~wesen** educational system

der **Unterrock, ⸗e** petticoat, slip

unterrühren stir in

unters = unter das

untersagen prohibit; **jmdm. ~ zu ...** forbid s.o. to ...

der **Untersatz, ⸗e** stand; mat; *philos* minor premise; **fahrbarer ~** *coll* 'wheels'

Unterschall– subsonic ...

unterschätzen underestimate

unterscheiden* (*also v/i*) distinguish; **sich ~** differ (**von** from)

die **Unterscheidung, –en** distinction; **das ~s|-merkmal, –e** distinctive feature

der **Unterschenkel, –** shank

die **Unterschicht, –en** lower classes; *geol* substratum

unterschieben* (+*dat*) (*cf next entry*) push under; foist on

unterschieben* (+*dat*) (*cf previous entry*) attribute (falsely) to

der **Unterschied, –e** difference; distinction; **einen ~ machen** differentiate; **im ~ zu** unlike; **mit dem ~, daß ...** with the difference that ...; **ohne ~** indiscriminately; (treat) alike; (+*gen*) irrespective of; **zum ~ von** unlike

unterschiedlich different; varying; **~ sein** vary

unterschieds|los indiscriminate

unterschlagen* (*cf next entry*) cross (legs)

unterschlagen* (*cf previous entry*) embezzle; suppress

die **Unterschlagung, –en** embezzlement; suppression

der **Unterschlupf, –e** shelter; hideout

unterschlüpfen (*sn*) take shelter; go into hiding

unterschreiben* (*also v/i*) sign; **das kann ich ~!** I'll subscribe to that!

unterschreiten* fall short of

die **Unterschrift, –en** signature; caption; **u~s|reif** ready for signature

unterschwellig subliminal

das **Untersee|boot, –e, unterseeisch** submarine

die **Unterseite, –n** underside; bottom

untersetzen place underneath

der **Untersetzer, –** mat; stand

untersetzt stocky

untersinken* (*sn*) sink

unterspülen (river *etc*) undermine

unterst.. lowest; bottom

der **Unterstaats|sekretär, –e** under-secretary of state

der **Unterstand, ⸗e** shelter (from rain *etc*; *Aust also* = roof over one's head); *mil* dugout; **u~s|los** *Aust* homeless

unterstehen* (+*dat*) be under (person, s.o.'s control); come under; be subject to; **sich ~ zu ...** dare to ...; **untersteh dich!** you dare!

unterstellen (*cf next entry*) put (bicycle in shed *etc*); garage; **sich ~** take shelter

unterstellen (*cf previous entry*) assume (that ...); (+*dat*) put under; put (s.o.) in charge of, *mil* place under (s.o.'s) command; attribute (falsely) to

die **Unterstellung, –en** *vbl noun*; *also* assumption; (false) assertion, suggestion

untersteuern understeer

unterstreichen* underline; stress

die **Unterströmung, –en** undercurrent

die **Unterstufe, –n** lower school

unterstützen support; back; encourage

die **Unterstützung, –en** support; aid; benefit

untersuchen investigate; examine (*also med*) (**auf** *acc* for); test (for); *chem* analyse; **sich ärztlich ~ lassen** have a medical/check-up

die **Untersuchung, –en** investigation; inquiry; study; examination; test; *chem* analysis; *med* examination, check-up; **der ~s|ausschuß, ⸗(ss)e** committee of inquiry; **der/die ~s|gefangene** (*decl as adj*) prisoner awaiting trial; **die ~s|haft** detention pending trial (**in U.** on remand); **der ~s|richter, –** examining magistrate

Untertage– *min* underground ...

untertags *Aust*, *Swiss* during the day

untertan (*following dat*) subservient (to); **sich** *dat* **... ~ machen** subjugate; master

der **Untertan, –en** (*also wk masc*) subservient, uncritical citizen; *hist* subject; **der ~en|-geist** subservient mentality

untertänig obsequious

die **Untertasse, –n** saucer; **fliegende ~** flying saucer

untertauchen dip (**in** *dat* in); duck; (*v/i sn*) dive; disappear (**in** *dat* in); go underground

[das] **Unterteil, -e** bottom part
unterteilen subdivide (**in** *acc* into)
[die] **Unterteilung, -en** subdivision
[der] **Untertitel, -, untertiteln** subtitle (*also cin*); caption
[der] **Unterton, ⸚e** undertone
untertreiben* understate
[die] **Untertreibung, -en** understatement
untertunneln tunnel under
untervermieten (*insep*) sublet
unterversichern (*insep*) underinsure
unterwandern infiltrate
[die] **Unterwanderung** infiltration
[die] **Unterwäsche** *pl* underwear
unterwaschen* (river *etc*) undermine
Unterwasser- underwater ...
unterwegs on the/one's/its way; ~ **sein** *also* be out and about; be on the move; travel; **von** ~ (send greetings *etc*) while one is away
unterweisen* instruct (**in** *dat* in)
[die] **Unterweisung, -en** instruction
[die] **Unterwelt, unterweltlich** underworld
unterwerfen* (*see also* **unterworfen**) subjugate; (+*dat*) subject to; **sich** ~ (+*dat*) submit to
[die] **Unterwerfung, -en** subjugation; subjection; submission
unterworfen *p/part*; *also* (*following dat*) subject (to)
unterwürfig obsequious
unterzeichnen sign; **der/die Unterzeichnete** (*decl as adj*) undersigned
[der] **Unterzeichner, -** signatory
unterziehen* (*cf next entry*) put on underneath; *cul* fold in
unterziehen* (*cf previous entry*) (+*dat*) subject to; **sich** ~ (+*dat*) undergo; undertake; take (examination)
[das] **Unterzeug** *coll* underwear
[die] **Untiefe, -n** shallow; great depth
[das] **Untier, -e** monster; brute
untilgbar irredeemable; indelible
untragbar intolerable; prohibitive
untrennbar inseparable (*also gramm*)
untreu unfaithful; disloyal; (+*dat*) ~ **werden** be unfaithful to; betray (principle *etc*)
[die] **Untreue** unfaithfulness; disloyalty
untröstlich inconsolable
untrüglich unmistakable; unerring
[die] **Untugend, -en** bad habit
untypisch untypical (**für** of)
un|überbrückbar unbridgeable; irreconcilable
un|überlegt thoughtless; rash
un|übersehbar vast; incalculable; obvious
un|übersetzbar untranslatable
un|übersichtlich unclear; (bend) blind; (ground) broken; confused, muddled
un|übertrefflich unsurpassable
un|übertroffen unsurpassed
un|überwindlich insuperable; invincible
un|üblich not customary
un|umgänglich unavoidable; essential
un|umschränkt unlimited; absolute
un|umstößlich irrevocable; incontrovertible
un|umstritten undisputed
un|umwunden straight out
un|unterbrochen uninterrupted; unbroken, continuous; steady; incessant
unver|änderlich unchanging; invariable
unver|ändert unchanged
unver|antwortlich irresponsible
unver|äußerlich inalienable
unverbesserlich incorrigible
unverbindlich not binding; without obligation; non-committal; (person, manner) not very friendly
unverblümt outspoken; (truth) unvarnished; (*adv*) in plain terms; (+*dat*) ~ **die Meinung sagen** give (s.o.) it straight from the shoulder
unverbrüchlich steadfast
unverbürgt unconfirmed
unverdaulich indigestible
unverdaut undigested
unverdient undeserved; **unverdienter|maßen** undeservedly
unverdorben unspoiled
[die] **Unverdorbenheit** unspoiled state
unverdrossen indefatigable; undaunted
unverdünnt undiluted
unver|einbar incompatible
unverfälscht unadulterated; pure; genuine
unverfänglich harmless
unverfroren impudent, insolent
[die] **Unverfrorenheit** impudence, insolence
unvergänglich immortal; everlasting
unvergessen unforgotten
unvergeßlich unforgettable
unvergleichlich incomparable
unverhältnis|mäßig disproportionately; excessively
unverheiratet unmarried
unverhofft unexpected; **völlig** ~ **kommen** be quite unexpected
unverhohlen unconcealed
unverhüllt unclad; undisguised
unverkäuflich unsaleable; not for sale
unverkennbar unmistakable
unverlangt unsolicited
unverletzlich inviolable
unverletzt unhurt; (seal) unbroken
unvermeidlich unavoidable; inevitable
unvermindert undiminished
unvermischt unmixed; unadulterated
unvermittelt sudden
[das] **Unvermögen** inability
unvermögend without means; unable (to)
unvermutet unexpected

die **Unvernunft** folly, foolishness
unvernünftig foolish
unver|öffentlicht unpublished
unverrichtet: ~er Dinge = unverrichteter|dinge without achieving one's object; (come away) empty-handed
unverrückbar unshakeable, unalterable
unverschämt impudent; barefaced; *coll* outrageous
die **Unverschämtheit, –en** impudence, impertinence
unverschuldet free from debt; that is not one's own fault; (*adv*) through no fault of one's own
unversehens all of a sudden
unversehrt unhurt; undamaged, intact
unversöhnlich irreconcilable; (hatred) implacable
unversorgt unprovided-for
der **Unverstand** lack of judgement; foolishness
unverstanden misunderstood
unverständig unwise
unverständlich incomprehensible; unintelligible
das **Unverständnis** lack of understanding
unversteuert untaxed
unversucht: nichts ~ lassen try everything
unverträglich quarrelsome; incompatible (*also med*); indigestible
unverwandt (look) fixed, intent
unverwechselbar [–ks–] unmistakable
unverwertbar unusable
unverwindbar that one cannot get over
unverwischbar indelible
unverwundbar invulnerable
unverwüstlich indestructible; irrepressible; **~e Gesundheit** iron constitution
unverzagt undaunted
unverzeihlich inexcusable
unverzichtbar indispensable; that cannot be given up
unverzinslich interest-free
unverzollt duty-free
unverzüglich immediate
unvoll|endet incomplete, unfinished; **die „Unvollendete"** (Schubert's) 'Unfinished' Symphony
unvollkommen imperfect; incomplete
die **Unvollkommenheit** imperfection; incompleteness
unvollständig incomplete; *gramm* defective
unvorbereitet unprepared
unvordenklich: seit ~en Zeiten since time immemorial
unvor|eingenommen unbiased, impartial
die **Unvor|eingenommenheit** impartiality
unvorhergesehen unforeseen; unexpected
unvorsichtig careless; rash
unvorstellbar unimaginable, inconceivable
unvorteilhaft disadvantageous; (dress) unbecoming, unflattering
unwägbar incalculable; imponderable
unwahr untrue
unwahrhaftig untruthful
die **Unwahrheit, –en** untruth; untruthfulness
unwahrscheinlich unlikely, improbable; *coll* incredible
die **Unwahrscheinlichkeit** improbability
unwandelbar immutable; unswerving
unwegsam (terrain) difficult
unweiblich unfeminine
unweigerlich inevitable
unweit (+*gen*) not far from
der **Unwert** unworthiness; **Wert oder/und ~** merits and demerits
das **Unwesen** deplorable practice; **–unwesen** (*eg* **das Verbrecher~**) nefarious activities (of criminals *etc*); **sein ~ treiben** be up to mischief; go about one's shady business
unwesentlich immaterial; insignificant
das **Unwetter, –** storm
unwichtig unimportant
unwiderlegbar = unwiderleglich irrefutable
unwiderruflich irrevocable; (*adv*) *also* positively; absolutely
unwidersprochen uncontradicted; **~ bleiben** go unchallenged
unwiderstehlich irresistible
unwiederbringlich irretrievable
der **Unwille** (*like* **Wille**) indignation, displeasure (**über** *acc* at)
unwillig indignant; unwilling
unwillkommen unwelcome
unwillkürlich involuntary
unwirklich unreal
die **Unwirklichkeit** unreality
unwirksam ineffective
unwirsch surly
unwirtlich inhospitable
unwirtschaftlich uneconomic
unwissend ignorant
die **Unwissenheit** ignorance
unwissenschaftlich unscholarly; unscientific
unwissentlich unwittingly
unwohl unwell; uneasy; **mir ist ~** I don't feel well || **das U~sein** indisposition
unwürdig unworthy; degrading; (*following gen*) unworthy (of)
die **Unzahl** vast number
unzählbar countless; *gramm* uncountable; **~ viele** hosts of
unzählig countless; **~ viele** hosts of; **~e Male = unzählige|mal** countless times
unzart [–a:–] ungentle; (remark *etc*) indelicate
die **Unze, –n** ounce
Unzeit: zur ~ at an inopportune moment || **u~gemäß** outmoded; unseasonable
unzerbrechlich unbreakable
unzerreißbar untearable
unzerstörbar indestructible

unzertrennlich inseparable
unziemlich unseemly
unzivilisiert uncivilized
die **Unzucht** fornication; illicit sexual relations; **gewerbsmäßige ~** prostitution; **widernatürliche ~** unnatural sexual act
unzüchtig lewd; indecent
unzufrieden dissatisfied
die **Unzufriedenheit** dissatisfaction
unzugänglich inaccessible; unapproachable; (*following dat*) impervious (to)
unzukömmlich *Aust* insufficient; undue
die **Unzukömmlichkeiten** *pl Aust, Swiss* trouble
unzulänglich inadequate
die **Unzulänglichkeit, –en** inadequacy; (*pl*) shortcomings
unzulässig inadmissible
unzumutbar unreasonable
unzurechnungs|fähig not responsible for one's actions, *leg* of unsound mind
unzureichend insufficient
unzusammen|hängend incoherent, disjointed
unzuständig not competent
unzustellbar undeliverable; (letter) dead
unzuträglich (*following dat*) bad (for)
unzutreffend incorrect; inapplicable; **„U~es bitte streichen"** 'delete where not applicable'
unzuverlässig unreliable
die **Unzuverlässigkeit** unreliability
unzweck|mäßig inexpedient; inappropriate
die **Unzweck|mäßigkeit** inexpediency; inappropriateness
unzwei|deutig unambiguous
unzweifelhaft undoubted, indubitable
üppig luxuriant, lush; (hair) thick; sumptuous; lavish; voluptuous, (bosom) ample; (imagination) fertile; **~ leben** live in style
up to date ['ap tu 'de:t] up-to-date
der **Ur, –e** aurochs

Ur– original ...; primitive ...; primeval ...; proto–; true (Berliner *etc*); (ur–) extremely ...; thoroughly (German *etc*)

---

die **Ur|abstimmung, –en** strike ballot
der **Ur|ahn, –en** (*wk masc*), **der Ur|ahne, –n** (*wk masc*) forefather; *SGer* great-grandfather
die **Ur|ahne, –n** (female) forebear; *SGer* great-grandmother
der **Ural** (*gen* –(s)) the Urals
ur|alt ancient; age-old
das **Uran** uranium
der **Ur|anfang, ⸚e** very beginning
der **Uranus** (*gen* –) Uranus
ur|aufführen (*only infin and p/part* **uraufgeführt**), **die Ur|aufführung, –en** première
urban urbane
Urban ['ʊr–] Urban
urbar: ~ machen = urbarisieren *Swiss* cultivate
der **Urbeginn** very beginning
das **Urbild, –er** archetype
das **Urchristentum** [–kr–] early Christianity
urchristlich [–kr–] early Christian
ur|eigen(st) very own
der **Ur|einwohner, –** original inhabitant; (*Australia*) aborigine
der **Ur|enkel, –** great-grandson; **die Ur|enkelin, –nen** great-granddaughter
ur|ewig *coll*: **seit ~en Zeiten** for ages and ages
die **Urform, –en** archetype
urgemütlich really cosy
die **Urgeschichte** prehistory
die **Urgesellschaft** primitive society
das **Urgestein, –e** primary rocks
die **Urgewalt, –en** elemental force
urgieren *Aust* press for
Urgroß–: die ~eltern *pl* great-grandparents; **die ~mutter, ..mütter** great-grandmother; **der ~vater, ..väter** great-grandfather
der **Urheber, –** author, originator; author, *art* painter, *mus* composer; **das ~recht, –e** copyright
die **Urheberschaft** authorship
urig *coll* earthy
der **Urin, –e** urine
urinieren urinate
die **Urkirche** early Church
der **Urknall** big bang
urkomisch wildly funny
die **Urkraft, ⸚e** elemental force
die **Urkunde, –n** document; deed; charter; certificate
urkundlich documentary; (*adv*) in a document; **~ belegen** document
der **Urkunds|be|amte** (*decl as adj*) registrar
der **Urlaub** holiday(s), vacation *US*; *mil etc* leave; **auf/im/in ~** on holiday/vacation *US*; on leave; **auf/in ~ fahren** go on holiday/vacation *US*/leave
der **Urlauber, –** holidaymaker, vacationist *US*; *mil* soldier on leave
die **Urlaubs|zeit, –en** holiday season, vacation season *US*; (person's) holiday(s), vacation *US*
der **Urmensch, –en** (*wk masc*) primitive man
die **Urne, –n** urn; ballot-box; **zur ~ gehen** go to the polls
die **Ur|oma, –s** *coll* great-grandma
der **Ur|opa, –s** *coll* great-grandpa
urplötzlich very sudden; (*adv*) all of a sudden
der **Urquell, –e** *poet* fountainhead
die **Ursache, –n** cause (*gen*/**für** of); **keine ~!** don't mention it!; **~ und Wirkung** cause and effect; (+*dat*) **~ geben zu ...** give (s.o.) cause to ...; **(alle) ~/keine ~ haben zu ...** have (every)/no reason to ...
ursächlich causal
die **Urschrift, –en** original

urschriftlich original; (*adv*) in the original
urspr. = **ursprünglich**
der **Ursprung, ⸚e** origin; **seinen ~ haben in** (*dat*) have its origin in
ursprünglich original; initial; natural, pristine
Ursprungs– ... of origin; *comput* source ...
Urständ: fröhliche ~ feiern (old custom *etc*) make a comeback
das **Urteil** ['ʊr–], **–e** judgement; opinion; *leg* verdict; judgement; sentence; award; decree; **sich** *dat* **ein ~ bilden über** (*acc*) form an opinion about; **ein ~ fällen** pass judgement (**über** *acc* on); **zu dem ~ kommen, daß ...** come to the conclusion that ...
urteilen ['ʊr–] judge (**nach** by); **~ über** (*acc*) judge; give one's opinion on
Urteils–: die ~kraft judgement; **der ~spruch, ⸚e** verdict; sentence; **das ~vermögen** judgement
der **Urtext, –e** original (text)
das **Urtierchen, –** protozoon
der **Urtrieb, –e** basic drive
urtümlich primeval; unspoilt
der **Urtyp, –en** prototype
Uruguay [–'güaːi] Uruguay
der **Uruguayer** [–'gŭaːjɐ], **–, uruguayisch** Uruguayan
Ur|ur– great-great-
urverwandt cognate
das **Urvieh, ..viecher** *coll* real character
der **Urvogel, ..vögel** archaeopteryx
der **Urwald, ⸚er** primeval forest; jungle
die **Urwelt** primeval world
urweltlich primeval
urwüchsig [–ks–] unspoilt; (force) elemental; (humour, language, *etc*) earthy
die **Urzeit** earliest times; **seit ~en** *coll* for donkey's years
die **Urzeugung, –en** spontaneous generation
der **Urzustand, ⸚e** original state
die **USA** *pl* the U.S.A.
US-amerikanisch [uː'ʔɛs–] U.S.
die **Usance** [y'zãːs], **–n** custom; *comm* practice
usf. (= **und so fort**) etc.
die **Usurpation, –en** usurpation
der **Usurpator, –(or)en** usurper
usurpieren usurp
der **Usus** custom; **... ist ~** ... is customary
usw. (= **und so weiter**) etc.
die **Utensilien** [–ĭən] *pl* utensils, implements
der **Utilitarismus** utilitarianism
der **Utilitarist, –en** (*wk masc*), **utilitaristisch** utilitarian
die **Utopie, –(ie)n** utopia; pipe-dream
utopisch utopian
der **Utopismus** utopianism
der **Utopist, –en** (*wk masc*) utopian
u. U. = **unter Umständen**
UV = **ultraviolett**
u. v. a. (m.) (= **und viele(s) andere (mehr)**) etc. etc.
der **Ü-Wagen, –** (= **Übertragungswagen**) *rad*, *TV* O.B. van, mobile unit *US*
der **Uz** *coll* teasing
uzen *coll* tease
die **Uzerei, –en** *coll* teasing

V

das V [fao̯] (*gen, pl* –, *coll* [fao̯s]) V
V (= **Vers**) l., v., (= **Volt**) V
v. = **vom, von**
v. a. = **vor allem**
va banque [va'bã:k]: ~ **spielen** gamble everything; **das Vabanque|spiel** huge gamble
der **Vagabund, –en** (*wk masc*) vagabond
vagabundieren live as a vagabond; (*sn*) roam, rove
der **Vagant, –en** (*wk masc*) *hist* wandering scholar
vage vague
die **Vagheit** vagueness
die **Vakanz, –en** vacancy
das **Vakuum** ['va:–], **–(ku)en/–(ku)a** vacuum; **v~verpackt** vacuum-packed
der **Valentins|tag** ['va:lɛnti:ns–], **–e** St Valentine's Day
die **Valenz, –en** *chem, ling* valency
die **Valuta, –(t)en** *comm* foreign currency
der **Vampir, –e** vampire; *zool* vampire (bat)
der **Vandale, –n** (*wk masc*) Vandal
der **Vandalismus** vandalism
die **Vanille** [–ljə] vanilla
variabel variable
die **Variante, –n** variant
die **Variation, –en** variation (*also biol, math, mus*)
das **Varieté, –s** variety theatre; variety show
variieren (*also v/i*) vary (*also mus*)
der **Vasall, –en** (*wk masc*) *hist* vassal
die **Vase, –n** vase
der **Vater,** *pl* **Väter** father; **die ~figur, –en** father-figure; **das ~haus, ⸚er** parental home; **das ~land, ⸚er** native land; fatherland; **v~ländisch** patriotic; **die ~lands|liebe** patriotism; **die ~liebe** paternal love; **v~los** fatherless; **der ~mord, –e** parricide; **der ~mörder, –** parricide; *joc* stand-up collar; **das ~recht** patriarchy; **die ~stadt, ⸚e** home town; **~stelle (V. vertreten bei** be a father to); **das ~unser, –** Lord's Prayer
väterlich paternal; fatherly; one's father's; **~er|seits** on one's/the father's side
die **Vaterschaft** paternity; **die ~s|klage, –n** paternity suit
der **Vati, –s** *coll* dad(dy)
der **Vatikan** (*gen* **–s**) the Vatican; **die ~stadt** Vatican City
der **V-Ausschnitt, –e** V-neck

v. Chr. (= **vor Christus**) B.C.
VDR *EGer* = **Volksdemokratische Republik**
der **VEB, –(s)** *EGer* = **Volkseigener Betrieb**
das **VEG, –(s)** *EGer* = **Volkseigenes Gut**
der **Vegetarier** [–ĭɐ], **–, vegetarisch** vegetarian
der **Vegetarismus** vegetarianism
die **Vegetation, –en** vegetation
vegetieren vegetate; eke out a bare existence
vehement vehement
die **Vehemenz** vehemence
das **Vehikel, –** ancient vehicle; vehicle (for ideas *etc*)
das **Veilchen, –** violet; *joc* 'shiner'; **blau wie ein ~** *coll* drunk as a lord || **veilchen|blau** violet
der **Veits|tanz** St Vitus's dance
der **Vektor, –(or)en** *math, phys* vector
der **Velar, –e** velar
das **Velo, –s** *Swiss* bicycle; ~ **fahren** cycle
das **Velours** [və'lu:ɐ] (*gen* – [–s]), – [–s] suede
der **Velours** [və'lu:ɐ] (*gen* – [–s]), – [–s] velour(s)
das **Velours|leder** suede
die **Vendetta, –(tt)en** vendetta
die **Vene, –n** vein
Venedig Venice
venerisch venereal
der **Venezianer, –, venezianisch** Venetian
der **Venezolaner, –, venezolanisch** Venezuelan
Venezuela [–ŭ–] Venezuela
venös venous
das **Ventil, –e** valve; outlet, safety-valve (for emotions)
die **Ventilation** ventilation
der **Ventilator, –(or)en** (electric) fan; *mot* fan
ventilieren ventilate; examine (question)
Venus *myth*, **die ~** *astron* Venus; **der ~berg, –e** mons Veneris

---

ver– [fɛɐ–] *insep pref* (*unstressed*) – *general senses*:
(*i*) *forms verbs from nouns or adjectives* (*eg* **~barrikadieren** barricade (*see* **Barrikade**), **~einheitlichen** standardize (*see* **einheitlich**), **~stummen** go silent (*see* **stumm**));
(*ii*) mis–, ... the wrong way (*eg* **sich ~rechnen** miscalculate);
(*iii*) spend ... (*eg* **~plaudern** spend chatting, **~trinken** spend on drink);
(*iv*) ... away (*eg* **~schenken** give away, **~reisen** go away);
(*v*) (*in adjectives*) full of ..., covered in

... (*eg* ~**raucht** full of smoke (**Rauch** = smoke), ~**laust** lice-ridden (**Laus** = louse))

ver|aasen *coll* squander

ver|abfolgen (+*dat*) administer to; *joc* give (s.o. box on the ears *etc*)

ver|abreden arrange; **sich ~ mit** arrange to meet; make an appointment/a date with; **verabredet sein mit** have arranged to meet; have an appointment/a date with; **schon verabredet sein** have a prior engagement

die **Ver|abredung, –en** appointment; date (with member of opposite sex); arrangement

ver|abreichen (+*dat*) administer to; *joc* give (s.o. box on the ears *etc*)

ver|absäumen neglect (to)

ver|abscheuen detest, loathe

ver|abscheuungs|würdig detestable

ver|abschieden say goodbye to; (officially) discharge; *parl* pass (law); **sich ~** say goodbye (**von** to)

ver|absolutieren attribute absolute validity to

ver|achten despise; scorn; **nicht zu ~** *coll* not to be sneezed at || ~**s|wert** despicable, contemptible

ver|ächtlich scornful; despicable

die **Ver|achtung** disdain, contempt

ver|albern *coll* make fun of

ver|allgemeinern generalize

die **Ver|allgemeinerung, –en** generalization

ver|alten (*sn*) go out of date; become obsolete/antiquated; **veraltet** out-of-date; obsolete; antiquated

die **Veranda, –(d)en** veranda(h)

ver|änderlich changeable; *math* variable

ver|ändern change; **sich ~** change; change one's job

die **Ver|änderung, –en** change

ver|ängstigt scared

ver|ankern anchor; establish firmly; **verankert in** (*dat*) *also* enshrined in (constitution *etc*)

ver|anlagen assess (for tax purposes); (**fröhlich** *etc*/**musikalisch** *etc*/**praktisch** *etc*) **veranlagt sein** have a (cheerful *etc*) disposition/be (musically *etc*) inclined/be (practically *etc*) minded

die **Ver|anlagung, –en** disposition; predisposition (*also med*); bent; *fin* (tax) assessment

ver|anlassen give rise to; arrange for (... to be done); induce (to); get (to); **~ zu** induce to make (statement *etc*)/take (step *etc*); (*followed by vbl noun*, *eg* **zur Auswanderung/zum Nachdenken** ~) induce to (emigrate/think *etc*); **zu der Annahme ~, daß ...** lead (s.o.) to suppose that ...; **sich veranlaßt fühlen/sehen zu ...** feel compelled to ...

die **Ver|anlassung, –en** cause (for doing sth.); **auf ~** (+*gen*) at the instance of; **~ geben zu** give cause for

ver|anschaulichen illustrate

ver|anschlagen estimate (**auf** *acc* at); **zu hoch/niedrig ~** overestimate/underestimate

ver|anstalten organize; hold; *coll* make (scene)

der **Ver|anstalter, –** organizer

die **Ver|anstaltung, –en** organization (of); event; function

ver|antworten take the responsibility for; **sich ~ für/wegen** answer for; **nicht zu ~** irresponsible

ver|antwortlich responsible; **~ machen für** hold responsible for; blame for; **~ zeichnen für** be responsible for

die **Ver|antwortung** responsibility; **auf eigene ~** on one's own responsibility; **zur ~ ziehen** call to account || **v~s|bewußt** responsible; **das ~s|bewußt|sein** = **das ~s|gefühl** sense of responsibility; **v~s|los** irresponsible; **die ~s|losigkeit** irresponsibility; **v~s|voll** responsible

ver|äppeln *coll* take the mickey out of

ver|arbeiten process (*also comput*); use (in manufacture); digest; assimilate; **~ zu** turn into; **verarbeitet** (hands) worn with work; **gut/schlecht verarbeitet** well/badly-finished

die **Ver|arbeitung** processing; use; digestion; assimilation; finish; workmanship

ver|argen (+*dat*) hold against

ver|ärgern annoy; **verärgert** annoyed (**über** *acc* at)

die **Ver|ärgerung** annoyance

ver|armen (*sn*) become impoverished; **verarmt** impoverished

die **Ver|armung** impoverishment

ver|arschen *vulg* take the mickey out of

ver|arzten *joc* treat (medically); see to

ver|ästeln: sich ~ branch out; ramify; **verästelt** ramified

ver|ausgaben spend; **sich ~** spend all one's money; exhaust oneself

ver|auslagen disburse

ver|äußerlich saleable

ver|äußerlichen trivialize; (*v/i sn*) become superficial

ver|äußern dispose of (by selling)

die **Ver|äußerung, –en** disposal (by sale)

das **Verb, –en** verb

verbal verbal (*also gramm*)

verballhornen *coll* mangle (word *etc*) (in the mistaken belief that one is correcting it, or for comic effect)

der **Verband, ⸚e** association; *med* bandage; dressing; *build* bond; *mil* unit; *aer*, *naut* formation; **der ~(s)|kasten, ..kästen** first-aid box; **das ~(s)|material** dressing material

verbannen banish; exile; **der/die Verbannte** (*decl as adj*) exile

die **Verbannung, –en** *vbl noun*; *also* banishment; exile; **in der ~** in exile

verbarrikadieren barricade; **sich ~** barricade oneself in

verbauen block, obstruct; use up in building; build badly; *coll* bungle (exam *etc*); (+*dat*) spoil (s.o.'s chances); (+*dat*) **den Weg ~** bar (s.o.'s) way; **sich** *dat* **die Zukunft ~** spoil one's prospects

verbeißen* (*see also* **verbissen**): **sich** *dat* **... ~** stifle, suppress; **sich ~ in** (*acc*) sink its teeth into; devote oneself with dogged determination to; stick doggedly to

verbergen* (*see also* **verborgen**[2]) hide, conceal (*dat*/**vor** *dat* from); **sein Gesicht in den Händen ~** bury one's face in one's hands; **sich ~** hide (**vor** *dat* from)

verbessern improve; reform; correct; *sp* improve on (record); **sich ~** improve; better oneself; correct oneself; *sp* improve one's position; **zweite, verbesserte Auflage** second edition, revised

die **Verbesserung, –en** improvement; correction

verbeugen: sich ~, die Verbeugung, –en bow (**vor** *dat* to)

verbeulen dent

verbiegen* bend (out of shape); buckle; warp (s.o.'s character); **sich ~** bend; buckle; (wood) warp

verbiestert *coll* put out

verbieten* (*see also* **verboten**) forbid; prohibit; ban; **jmdm. ~ zu ...** forbid s.o. to ...; ban s.o. from (+*ger*); (s.o.'s position, pride, *etc*) not allow s.o. to ...; (+*dat*) **den Mund ~** order to be quiet; **sich (von selbst) ~** be ruled out

verbilden deform; miseducate

verbildlichen illustrate

verbilligen reduce the price of

verbimsen *coll* give (s.o.) a walloping

verbinden* connect; join; link; combine; *med* bandage; *tel* put through (**mit** to); (+*dat*) **die Augen ~** blindfold; (+*dat*) **verbunden sein** be obliged to; **verbunden sein mit** *also* involve; **falsch verbunden!** wrong number!; **mit verbundenen Augen** blindfold

sich ~ join forces; *chem* combine

verbindlich binding (**für** on); friendly

die **Verbindlichkeit, –en** binding nature; friendliness; (*pl*) civilities; *comm* obligations; liabilities

die **Verbindung, –en** connection; contact; communication; combination; association; (marriage) union; *univ* students' association; *mil* liaison; *rail etc* service; *chem* compound; combination; *tel* line; **eine ~ eingehen** *chem* combine; **in ~ mit** combined with; in conjunction with; **in ~ bringen mit** link with; **in ~/sich in ~ setzen mit** put/get in touch with; **in ~ stehen mit** be in touch with; be connected with; **in ~ treten mit** get in touch with

Verbindungs– *also* connecting ...; **der ~mann, ⸗er/..leute** contact; intermediary; **der ~offizier, –e** liaison officer; **die ~stelle, –n** junction; **das ~stück, –e** connecting piece; **die ~tür, –en** connecting door

verbissen *p/part*; *also* grim; dogged

verbitten*: sich *dat* **... ~** refuse to tolerate; **diesen Ton verbitte ich mir** I will not be spoken to like that

verbittern embitter; (*v/i sn*) become embittered; **verbittert** embittered, bitter

die **Verbitterung** bitterness, embitterment

verblassen (*sn*) fade; (star) pale; **~ neben** (*dat*) pale beside; **verblaßt** (meaning) weakened

der **Verbleib** whereabouts; remaining (within organization *etc*)

verbleiben* (*sn*) remain; **... verbleibt mir I** have ... left; **wir sind so verblieben, daß ...** we agreed that ...

verbleichen (*p/t* **verblich,** *p/part* **verblichen**) (*sn*) fade; (star) pale; *poet* pass away; **der/die Verblichene** (*decl as adj*) deceased

verbleien *tech* lead; coat with lead

verblenden blind (= rob of judgement); *build* face

die **Verblendung, –en** blindness (= lack of judgement); *build* facing

verbleuen *coll* give (s.o.) a licking

verblich(en) *p/t* (*p/part*) *of* **verbleichen**

verblöden (*sn*) become feeble-minded; *coll* turn into a zombie

verblüffen amaze, nonplus; **~d** amazing; **verblüfft** amazed, nonplussed

die **Verblüffung** amazement; **zu jmds. ~** to s.o.'s amazement

verblühen (*sn*) fade

verbluten (*sn*) bleed to death

verbocken *coll* bungle; get up to

verbohren: sich ~ in (*acc*) *coll* become obsessed with; **verbohrt** stubborn

verborgen[1] lend

verborgen[2] *p/part*; *also* hidden; (+*dat*) **nicht ~ bleiben** not escape (s.o.'s) notice; **sich ~ halten** hide; **im ~en** secretly, in secret; in obscurity; behind the scenes

die **Verborgenheit** seclusion

das **Verbot, –e** ban (*gen* on); prohibition (of)

verboten *p/part*; *also* forbidden; prohibited; banned; **~ aussehen** *coll* look a sight; **„... ~!"** '... prohibited'; 'no ...' || **verbotener|weise** although it is/was forbidden/prohibited

Verbots–: das ~schild, –er sign prohibiting

something; **v~widrig** unlawful

verbrämen trim (with fur *etc*); wrap up (in less offensive words)

der **Verbrauch** consumption (**an** *dat* of)

verbrauchen use up; consume; **verbraucht** *also* worn-out; spent; (air) stale

der **Verbraucher, –** consumer; **der ~schutz** consumer protection

die **Verbrauchs|güter** *pl* consumer goods

verbrechen* do (wrong, *eg* **was soll ich denn schon wieder verbrochen haben?** what am I supposed to have done now?); *joc* perpetrate

das **Verbrechen, –** crime

der **Verbrecher, –, verbrecherisch** criminal

das **Verbrechertum** criminality

verbreiten, sich ~ spread; **sich ~ über** (*acc*) spread across; hold forth on; **~ lassen, daß ...** let it be known that ...; **verbreitet** *also* common, widespread; widely-read

verbreitern, sich ~ widen

die **Verbreitung** *vbl noun*; *also* spread; diffusion

verbrennen* burn; cremate (body); (*v/i sn*) burn; burn down; burn to death; be scorched (by sun); **sich ~** burn oneself; **~ lassen** burn (toast *etc*); **verbrannte Erde** *mil* scorched earth

die **Verbrennung, –en** *vbl noun*; *also* cremation; combustion; *med* burn; **der ~s|motor, –en** internal combustion engine; **der ~s|ofen, ..öfen** incinerator; combustion furnace

verbriefen confirm by document (*eg* charter)

verbringen* spend (time) (**mit** *ger*, *eg* **mit Arbeit/Lesen** working/reading)

verbrüdern: sich ~ mit fraternize with

verbrühen scald; **sich ~** scald oneself

verbuchen enter (amount); notch up (success)

das **Verbum, –(b)a** verb

verbummeln *coll* idle away; mislay; forget (appointment); (*v/i sn*) go to seed

der **Verbund, –e** *econ* combine; *civ eng* bond; **im ~ mit** in conjunction with || **das ~glas** laminated glass; **das ~netz, –e** *elect* grid

verbünden: sich ~ mit form an alliance with; **der/die Verbündete** (*decl as adj*) ally

die **Verbundenheit** closeness (**mit** to); attachment (to)

verbürgen guarantee; **sich ~ für** vouch for; **verbürgt** *also* authenticated

verbürgerlichen (*sn*) become bourgeois

verbüßen serve (sentence)

verbuttern make into butter; *coll* squander

verchromen [–kr–] chromium-plate

der **Verdacht** suspicion; **–verdacht** *med* suspected case of ...; **~ schöpfen** become suspicious (**gegen** of); **auf ~** *coll* on spec; **in ~ geraten/kommen** come under suspicion; **im/in ~ haben** suspect; **im ~ ...** (*gen*) **stehen** be suspected of; **über jeden ~ erhaben** above suspicion

verdächtig suspicious; (*following gen*) suspected (of); **–verdächtig** suspected of ...; liable to ...; in the running for ...; *med* suspected of having ...; **sich ~ machen** arouse suspicion; **der/die Verdächtige** (*decl as adj*) suspect

verdächtigen suspect (*gen* of)

die **Verdächtigung, –en** suspicion

Verdachts–: der ~grund, ¨e grounds for suspicion; **das ~moment, –e** suspicious circumstance

verdammen (*see also* **verdammt**) condemn; *relig* damn; **~s|wert** damnable

die **Verdammnis** damnation

verdammt *p/part*; *coll* damned (*also adv*); **~ viel** a hell of a lot (of); **~ (noch mal)!** damn it!; **die V~en** the damned

die **Verdammung, –en** condemnation; *relig* damnation

verdampfen (*sn if v/i*) vaporize

verdanken (*Swiss in 1st sense*) express one's thanks for; (+*dat*) owe to; **es ist ...** (*dat*) **zu ~, daß ...** it's thanks to ... that ...

verdarb *p/t of* **verderben**

verdattert *coll* flabbergasted

verdauen digest (*also* mentally)

verdaulich digestible; **leicht/schwer ~** easy/hard to digest

die **Verdauung** digestion; *in compds* **~s–** digestive ...; **der ~s|kanal, ¨e** alimentary canal; **der ~s|spazier|gang, ¨e** constitutional; **die ~s|störung, –en** indigestion

das **Verdeck, –e** hood (of pram/baby carriage *US*); *mot* hood, top; *naut* upper deck

verdecken conceal; cover (up); obscure; **verdeckt** concealed; hidden

verdenken* (+*dat*) hold against

verderben (verdirb(s)t, *p/t* **verdarb** (*subj* **verdürbe**), *p/part* **verdorben)** (*see also* **verderbt, verdorben**) spoil; ruin; corrupt; (*v/i sn*) go bad; be corrupted; **sich** *dat* **den Magen ~** upset one's stomach; **es** (*Aust* **sich** *dat*) **~ mit** get on the wrong side of

das **Verderben** ruin; **ins ~ rennen** rush headlong into disaster; **ins ~ stürzen** bring ruin upon

verderblich pernicious; perishable

verderbt (*also* text) corrupt

die **Verderbtheit** corruption, depravity

verdeutlichen make clear, elucidate

verdeutschen translate into German; *coll* explain in simple language

verdichten compress; extend (network); put into artistic form; **sich ~** thicken; (rumours *etc*) increase; (feeling *etc*) grow stronger

der **Verdichter, –** compressor

die **Verdichtung** compression; extension

verdicken thicken; **sich ~** thicken; swell

verdienen (*see also* **verdient**) earn; deserve; (*v/i*) make money; **(gut** *etc*) **~** earn (a lot *etc*); ~ **an** (*dat*) make on; make out of; (*v/i*) make money out of; **sich** *dat* **das Studium** ~ finance one's own studies; **dabei ist nicht viel zu** ~ there's not much money in that; **es nicht besser** ~ deserve no better; **er hat es nicht anders verdient** he had it coming to him; **das habe ich nicht um dich verdient** I didn't deserve that from you

der **Verdiener, –** breadwinner

das **Verdienst, –e** merit; (*pl*) services (**um** to); **es ist sein** ~**, daß …** it is thanks to him that …; **jmdm./sich** *dat* **…** **als** ~ **anrechnen** give s.o./take credit for; **sich** *dat* **große** ~**e erwerben um** render great service to; **nach** ~ on merit

der **Verdienst, –e** earnings, income

Verdienst–: der ~**ausfall, ⸚e** loss of earnings; **die** ~**möglichkeit, –en** opportunity for earning money; **die** ~**spanne, –n** profit margin; **v**~**voll** deserving; meritorious

verdient *p/part*; *also* well-deserved; meritorious; **V**~ *EGer* Honoured (*eg* **V**~**er Künstler** Honoured Artist); **sich** ~ **machen um** render great services to || **verdienter|maßen** deservedly

das **Verdikt, –e** (negative) verdict (on s.o., sth.)

verdinglichen put in concrete terms; objectify; *philos* reify

verdirb *imp sing*, **verdirb(s)t** (*2nd*,) *3rd sing pres of* **verderben**

verdolmetschen translate; (+*dat*) explain to

verdonnern *coll*: ~ **zu** sentence to; fine; **verdonnert** *also* flabbergasted

verdoppeln double; redouble (efforts); **sich** ~ double

verdorben *p/part of* **verderben;** *also* bad, (gone) off; (stomach) upset; corrupt; (child) spoiled

die **Verdorbenheit** corruption, depravity

verdorren (*sn*) wither

verdösen *coll* doze away; forget (appointment *etc*); **verdöst** drowsy

verdrängen drive out; oust; replace, supplant; *psych* repress; *phys* displace

die **Verdrängung, –en** *vbl noun*; *also* replacement; *psych* repression; *phys* displacement

verdreckt filthy

verdrehen twist; roll (one's eyes); distort (s.o.'s words *etc*); (+*dat*) **den Kopf** ~ turn (s.o.'s) head; **verdreht** *coll* crazy

die **Verdrehung, –en** *vbl noun*; *also* distortion

verdreifachen, sich ~ treble

verdreschen* *coll* beat up; thrash

verdrießen (*p/t* **verdroß** (*subj* **verdrösse**), *p/part* **verdrossen**) (*see also* **verdrossen**) annoy; **sich** *dat* **keine Mühe** ~ **lassen** spare no effort

verdrießlich surly, morose; disagreeable

verdrossen *p/part of* **verdrießen;** *also* surly

verdrücken *coll* polish off; **sich** ~ slink off

der **Verdruß** (*gen* **..sses**) annoyance; **zu jmds.** ~ to s.o.'s annoyance

verduften (*sn*) lose its scent/aroma; *coll* make oneself scarce

verdummen dull (s.o.'s) mind; (*v/i sn*) stultify

verdunkeln darken; black out; obscure; **sich** ~ darken

die **Verdunk(e)lung, –en** *vbl noun*; *also* blackout

verdünnen thin; dilute; rarefy; **(mit Wasser)** ~ water down; **sich** ~ become thinner/diluted/rarefied

der **Verdünner, –** thinner

die **Verdünnung, –en** *vbl noun*; *also* dilution; rarefaction; thinner; **bis zur** ~ *coll* ad nauseam

verdunsten (*sn*) evaporate

die **Verdunstung** evaporation

verdürbe *p/t subj of* **verderben**

verdursten (*sn*) die of thirst

verdüstern, sich ~ darken

verdutzt nonplussed

ver|ebben (*sn*) subside

ver|edeln ennoble; *tech* refine; *hort* graft

ver|ehelichen: sich ~ **(mit)** wed

die **Ver|ehelichung** marriage

ver|ehren revere; worship, adore; (+*dat of pers*) present with; **verehrt** (*as form of address*) dear; honoured; **verehrte Anwesende!** ladies and gentlemen

der **Ver|ehrer, –** admirer

die **Ver|ehrung** veneration; worship, adoration

ver|eidigen swear in; **vereidigt** sworn

der **Ver|ein, –e** society; association; club; *coll* bunch; **im** ~ **mit** in conjunction with

ver|einbar compatible

ver|einbaren agree (on); arrange; **sich (nicht)** ~ **lassen mit** be (in)compatible with; **nicht zu** ~ **mit** incompatible with

die **Ver|einbarung, –en** *vbl noun*; *also* agreement; arrangement; **laut** ~ as agreed; **nach** ~ by arrangement

ver|einen unite; **in sich** ~ combine (qualities); **sich (nicht)** ~ **lassen mit** be (in)compatible with; **die Vereinten Nationen** the United Nations

ver|einfachen simplify

ver|einheitlichen standardize; unify

ver|einigen unite; combine; *comm* merge; **die Vereinigten Arabischen Emirate** the United Arab Emirates; **die Vereinigten Staaten (von Amerika)** the United States (of America)

auf sich ~ poll (votes)

in sich ~ combine (qualities)

~ **mit** reconcile with; **sich (nicht)** ~ **lassen mit** be (in)compatible with

sich ~ unite; join forces; fuse; (rivers *etc*) meet; have intercourse; **sich** ~ **mit** join forces with; be combined with; (river *etc*) join; **sich** ~ **zu** get together for the purpose of; join together to form

[die] **Ver|einigung, -en** *vbl noun*; *also* union; association; (sexual) intercourse; *comm* merger; **die ~s|freiheit** freedom of association

ver|einnahmen collect (receipts); *coll* take over, monopolize

Ver|eins- club ...; **der ~meier, -** *coll* person who is too preoccupied with club life; **die ~meierei** *coll* excessive preoccupation with club activities

ver|einsamen (*sn*) grow lonely

[die] **Ver|einsamung** isolation

ver|einzelt occasional; isolated; *meteor* scattered; (*adv*) sporadically; here and there

ver|eisen *med* freeze; (*v/i sn*) freeze over; ice over; *aer* ice up; **vereist** *also* ice-covered; icy; *aer* iced-up

ver|eiteln thwart, foil

ver|eitern (*sn*) fester

ver|ekeln (+*dat of pers*) put off

ver|elenden (*sn*) be reduced to poverty

ver|enden (*sn*) (animal) die

ver|engen narrow; **sich ~** narrow; *physiol* contract

ver|engern take in (clothes); narrow; **sich ~** narrow

ver|erben (+*dat*) leave to; *biol* transmit (gene *etc*) to; **sich ~** be hereditary; **vererbt** *also* hereditary

[die] **Ver|erbung** *vbl noun*; *biol* transmission; heredity; **die ~s|lehre** genetics

ver|ewigen immortalize; perpetuate; **sich ~** immortalize oneself

Verf. = **Verfasser**

verfahren[1]* spend (money, time) in driving/travelling; use up (petrol/gasoline *US*); (*v/i sn*) act, proceed; be (ruthless *etc*); **~ mit** deal with (in a certain manner); **sich ~** lose one's way

verfahren[2] *p/part*; *also* muddled; **~e Situation** muddle

[das] **Verfahren, -** procedure; method; *tech* process; *leg* proceedings; **die ~s|weise, -n** method; procedure

[der] **Verfall** decline; deterioration; *comm* expiry

verfallen[1]* (*sn*) fall into disrepair; deteriorate; decline; (ticket *etc*) expire; (right *etc*) lapse; (+*dat*) become addicted to; become (s.o.'s) slave; become the property of; **~ auf** (*acc*) hit on; **~ in** (*acc*) make (mistake); fall into (sleep *etc*); lapse into (dialect, silence, *etc*)

verfallen[2] *p/part*; *also* dilapidated; ruined; (features) worn

Verfalls-: die ~erscheinung, -en symptom of decline; **der ~tag, -e** expiry date

verfälschen falsify; adulterate

verfangen*: nicht ~ bei cut no ice with; **sich ~ in** (*dat*) get caught up in; **sich in Widersprüchen ~** contradict oneself

verfänglich awkward; tricky; insidious

verfärben discolour; **sich ~** change colour; (person, s.o.'s face) go red/white

verfassen write

[der] **Verfasser, -** author

[die] **Verfasserin, -nen** authoress

[die] **Verfassung, -en** *vbl noun*; *also* condition, state; frame of mind; *pol* constitution; **v~gebend** (assembly) constituent; **v~s|mäßig** constitutional; **das ~s|recht** constitutional law; **v~s|widrig** unconstitutional

verfaulen (*sn*) decay; rot; **verfault** decayed; rotten

verfechten* stand up for; champion

[der] **Verfechter, -** advocate, champion

verfehlen miss; fail to achieve; **das Thema ~** get right off the subject; **seine Wirkung ~** fail to have the desired effect; **sich ~** miss each other (= fail to meet); **verfehlt** wrong, mistaken; (life) wasted

[die] **Verfehlung, -en** *vbl noun*; *also* misdemeanour

verfeinden: sich ~ mit fall out with; **verfeindet** at daggers drawn (**mit** with)

verfeinern refine; *cul* improve; **sich ~** become more refined; **verfeinert** refined, sophisticated

[die] **Verfeinerung, -en** refinement

verfemen ostracize

verfertigen produce

verfestigen solidify; reinforce; **sich ~** solidify; be reinforced

verfetten (*sn*) grow fat; (organ) become fatty

verfeuern burn (as fuel); use up (ammunition)

verfilmen film, make a film of

[die] **Verfilmung, -en** *vbl noun*; *also* film version

verfilzen (*sn*) mat; felt; **verfilzt** matted; felted

[die] **Verfilzung** *vbl noun*; *also* (suspect) close links

verfinstern darken; *astron* eclipse; **sich ~** darken

verflachen flatten; (*v/i sn*) flatten out; (conversation *etc*) become trivial; **sich ~** flatten out

verflechten* interweave; interlink; **~ in** (*acc*) involve in; **sich ~** intertwine

[die] **Verflechtung, -en** *vbl noun*; *also* interconnection

verfliegen* (*sn exc* **sich ~**) evaporate; vanish; (time) fly by; **sich ~** lose one's/its bearings (while flying)

verfließen* (*see also* **verflossen**) (*sn*) (time) pass by; (colour) run; (contours *etc*) become blurred

verflixt *coll* darned (*also adv*); **~ (noch mal)!** drat it!; **das ~e siebte Jahr** *approx* = the seven-year itch

[die] **Verflochtenheit** interconnectedness

verflossen *p/part*; *also* last; bygone; *coll* ex- (boy-friend *etc*); **ihr Verflossener/seine Verflossene** (*decl as adj*) *coll* her/his ex
verfluchen curse; **verflucht** *coll* damned (*also adv*); **verflucht (noch mal)!** damn it!
verflüchtigen evaporate; **sich ~** evaporate; be dispelled; *joc* vanish
verflüssigen, sich ~ liquefy
die **Verflüssigung** liquefaction
Verfolg: im/in ~ (+*gen*) in pursuance of; in the course of
verfolgen pursue; follow; track (animal); badger (with request *etc*); persecute; (memory *etc*) haunt; **strafrechtlich ~** prosecute; **vom Unglück verfolgt werden** be dogged by ill fortune
der **Verfolger, –** pursuer; persecutor
die **Verfolgung, –en** *vbl noun*; *also* pursuit; persecution; **strafrechtliche ~** prosecution || **die ~s|jagd, –en** chase; **der ~s|wahn** persecution mania
verformen deform; *tech* work (steel *etc*)
verfrachten transport; *coll* bundle off
der **Verfremdungs|effekt** *theat* alienation effect
verfressen[1]* *coll* spend on food
verfressen[2] *p/part*; *coll* greedy
verfroren sensitive to cold; (hands *etc*) frozen; **~ sein** feel the cold
verfrühen: sich ~ come early; **verfrüht** premature
verfügbar available
verfügen order; decree; **~ über** (*acc*) have at one's disposal; have; be possessed of; decide what is to happen to; **frei ~ können über** (*acc*) be able to do what one likes with; **~ Sie über mich!** I am at your disposal
die **Verfügung, –en** order; decree; *leg* injunction; **einstweilige ~** temporary injunction; **zur ~ haben** have at one's disposal; (+*dat*) **zur ~ stehen** be at (s.o.'s) disposal; **zur ~ stellen** make available; (+*dat*) place at (s.o.'s) disposal; **sich zur ~ stellen** volunteer || **das ~s|recht, –e** right of disposal (**über** *acc* of)
verführen tempt; seduce; lead astray; **~ zu** tempt into (+*ger*); *joc* tempt to (glass *etc* of …)
der **Verführer, –** seducer
die **Verführerin, –nen** seductress
verführerisch seductive; tempting
die **Verführung, –en** *vbl noun*; *also* seduction; temptation; **die ~s|künste** *pl* wiles; powers of seduction
verfünffachen quintuple
verfuttern *coll* spend on food
verfüttern use as animal food; **~ an** (*acc*) feed to
die **Vergabe** allocation; awarding
vergaffen: sich ~ in (*acc*) *coll* be smitten with, fall for
vergällen denature; (+*dat*) spoil (s.o.'s pleasure *etc*)
vergaloppieren: sich ~ *coll* blunder
vergammeln *coll* idle away; (*v/i sn*) go to the dogs; go bad; **vergammelt** *coll* scruffy
vergangen *p/part*; *also* past; (year *etc*) last
die **Vergangenheit** past; *gramm* past (tense); **der ~ angehören** be a thing of the past || **die ~s|bewältigung** coming to terms with the past
vergänglich transitory
vergasen gas; *chem* gasify
der **Vergaser, –** carburettor
vergaß (vergäße) *p/t* (*subj*) *of* **vergessen**
vergeben* give away; award; allocate; throw away (chance); *cards* misdeal; (+*dat*) forgive (s.o.'s …), forgive for (+*ger*); **sich** *dat* **etwas ~** compromise one's dignity; **ein Amt ~ an** (*acc*) appoint to an office; **sich ~** *cards* misdeal; **(schon) vergeben** *also* taken; (post) filled; *coll* (person) spoken for
vergebens (*adv*) in vain
vergeblich futile; (*adv*) in vain
die **Vergebung** *vbl noun*; *also* forgiveness
vergegenwärtigen: sich *dat* **… ~** visualize
vergehen* (*see also* **vergangen**) (*sn exc* **sich ~**) pass; wear off; **~ vor** (*dat*) die of (shame *etc*); **der Appetit ist mir vergangen** I've lost my appetite; **das Lachen wird dir noch ~** you'll soon be laughing on the other side of your face; **… daß mir Hören und Sehen verging** … that it quite took my breath away
sich ~ an (*dat*) commit indecent assault on; **sich ~ gegen** violate
das **Vergehen, –** offence; passing (of time *etc*)
vergeistigen spiritualize; **vergeistigt** *also* spiritual
vergelten* repay; (+*dat of pers*) repay for; **Böses mit Gutem ~** return good for evil; **Gleiches mit Gleichem ~** give tit for tat
die **Vergeltung** retaliation; **~ üben** retaliate
Vergeltungs– retaliatory …; **die ~maß|nahme, –n** reprisal
vergesellschaften nationalize, take into public ownership
vergessen (*2nd/3rd sing pres* **vergißt**, *p/t* **vergaß** [–a:–] (*subj* **vergäße**), *p/part* **vergessen**) forget; leave behind; **~ auf** (*acc*) *SGer* forget (about); **daß ich's nicht vergesse** before I forget; **nicht zu ~ …** not forgetting …; **sich ~** forget oneself; **Vergessen suchen** try to forget
die **Vergessenheit** oblivion; **in ~ geraten** fall into oblivion
vergeßlich forgetful
vergeuden squander, waste
vergewaltigen rape; do violence to
die **Vergewaltigung, –en** *vbl noun*; *also* rape
vergewissern: sich ~ make sure (*gen* of)

vergießen* spill; shed
vergiften poison; **sich ~** poison oneself
Vergil Virgil
vergilben (*sn*) turn yellow; **vergilbt** yellowed
vergipsen fill with plaster
vergiß *imp sing of* **vergessen**
das **Vergiß|mein|nicht, -(e)** forget-me-not
vergißt *2nd/3rd sing pres of* **vergessen**
vergittern put bars/a grille over; **vergittert** barred
verglasen glaze; **verglast** (*also* eyes, look) glazed
der **Vergleich, -e** comparison; simile; *leg* settlement; **einen ~ anstellen/ziehen mit** draw a comparison with; **den ~ aushalten mit** bear comparison with, compare with; **einen ~ schließen** reach a settlement; **das ist doch gar kein ~!** there's no comparison!; **im ~ mit/zu** in comparison with
vergleichbar comparable
vergleichen* compare; **sich ~ mit** compare oneself with; *leg* settle with; **sich ~ lassen mit** compare with; **~d** comparative
Vergleichs-: die ~form, -en *gramm* comparative form; **die ~möglichkeit, -en** basis for comparison; **v~weise** comparatively; by comparison; for the sake of comparison
vergletschern (*sn*) glaciate
die **Vergletscherung, -en** glaciation
verglimmen* (*sn*) gradually cease glowing; die away; fade
verglühen (*sn*) (fire) die out; (meteor *etc*, *space*) burn up
vergnügen (*see also* **vergnügt**): **sich ~** enjoy oneself; amuse oneself
das **Vergnügen, -** pleasure; *dated* entertainment; **~ finden an** (*dat*) take pleasure in; (+*dat*) **~ machen** give (s.o.) pleasure; **viel ~!** have a good time!; *iron* I wish you joy!; **mit (dem größten) ~** with (the greatest of) pleasure; **zum ~** for the fun of it
vergnüglich enjoyable; amusing
vergnügt enjoyable; cheerful, jolly
die **Vergnügungen** *pl* entertainments; pleasures
Vergnügungs- entertainment ...; pleasure ...; **der ~park, -s** amusement park; **die ~reise, -n** pleasure-trip; **die ~stätte, -n** place of entertainment; **v~süchtig** pleasure-seeking
vergolden gild; gold-plate; (sun) turn golden; **vergoldet** *also* gilt
vergönnen (+*dat*) not begrudge; **es war ihm nicht vergönnt zu ...** it was not granted to him to ...
vergöttern idolize
vergraben* bury; **das Gesicht in den Händen ~** bury one's face in one's hands; **sich ~** bury oneself/itself; hide oneself away; **sich hinter seinen Büchern/in seine Arbeit ~** bury oneself in one's books/work
vergrämen antagonize; *hunt* scare; **vergrämt** *also* careworn
vergraulen *coll* scare away
vergreifen* (*see also* **vergriffen**): **sich ~** make a mistake; *mus* play the wrong note; **sich ~ an** (*dat*) assault; misappropriate; **sich im Ausdruck ~** use the wrong expression; **sich im Ton ~** adopt the wrong tone
vergreisen (*sn*) turn senile
vergriffen *p/part*; *also* out of print
vergröbern, sich ~ coarsen
vergrößern enlarge (*also phot*); magnify; increase; **sich ~** increase; expand
die **Vergrößerung, -en** enlargement (*also phot*); magnification; increase; **das ~s|glas, ⸗er** magnifying-glass
vergucken: sich ~ *coll* make a mistake; **sich ~ in** (*acc*) fall for
vergünstigt (price) reduced
die **Vergünstigung, -en** privilege; (price) reduction
vergüten *tech* coat (lens); *metall* quench and temper; (+*dat of pers*) pay for; reimburse for; compensate for
die **Vergütung, -en** *vbl noun*; *also* payment; reimbursement; compensation
verhaften arrest; **verhaftet** (*following dat*) rooted in; deeply attached to; **der/die Verhaftete** (*decl as adj*) person under arrest
die **Verhaftung, -en** arrest
verhageln (*sn*) be ruined by hail
verhallen (*sn*) die away
verhalten[1]* restrain; hold back; suppress; (*v/i*) stop; **sich ~** (*with adv*) behave; act; be (passive, sceptical, *etc*); keep (quiet); **A verhält sich zu B wie C zu D** A is to B as C is to D; **die Sache/es verhält sich so** this is how things stand; **mit ... verhält es sich ähnlich/anders/folgendermaßen** the situation regarding ... is similar/different/as follows; **wie verhält es sich mit ...?** what is the situation regarding ...?
verhalten[2] *p/part*; *also* restrained; suppressed; (breath) bated; (voice) low
das **Verhalten** behaviour, conduct; **die ~s|forschung** behavioural science; **v~s|gestört** disturbed; **die ~s|maßregel, -n** rule of conduct; **das ~s|muster, -** behaviour pattern; **die ~s|weise, -n** behaviour
das **Verhältnis, -se** relationship; relations; proportion; *math* ratio; *coll* (love-)affair; lady-friend; (*pl*) circumstances; conditions; **klare ~se schaffen** get things straight; **kein ~ haben zu** not relate to; **für meine ~se** by my standards; **im ~ zu** in proportion to; compared with; **in keinem ~ stehen zu** be out of all proportion to; **über seine ~se leben** live beyond one's means || **v~mäßig** relative; proportional; **die ~wahl** proportional representation;

das ~wahl|recht (system of) proportional representation; das ~wort, ⸚er preposition
verhandeln negotiate about; *leg* hear; try (case); ~ gegen *leg* try; ~ über (*acc*) negotiate about; *leg* hear; try (case)
die Verhandlung, –en negotiation; *leg* hearing; trial || die ~s|bereitschaft readiness to negotiate; der ~s|tisch negotiating table; ~s|weg (auf dem V. by negotiation)
verhangen overcast
verhängen cover (window *etc*); *sp* award; ~ über (*acc*) impose on; declare (state of emergency) in
das Verhängnis, –se disaster; (+*dat*) zum ~ werden be (s.o.'s) undoing || v~voll disastrous, fatal; fateful
verharmlosen play down
verhärmt careworn
verharren remain (in a certain position); ~ auf (*dat*)/bei stick to; ~ in (*dat*) persist in
verharschen (*sn*) (snow) crust
verhärten, sich ~ harden; sich ~ gegen harden one's heart against
verhaspeln: sich ~ *coll* (speaker) get into a muddle
verhaßt hated; hateful, odious; sich ~ machen make oneself unpopular (bei with)
verhätscheln mollycoddle
der Verhau, –e (*also* das) shack; *mil* entanglement
verhauen* (*p/t only* verhaute) *coll* give (s.o.) a walloping; make a hash of; sich ~ slip up
verheddern: sich ~ *coll* get entangled; get into a tangle
verheeren devastate; ~d devastating; *coll* ghastly
die Verheerung, –en devastation; ~en anrichten wreak havoc
verhehlen conceal (*dat* from)
verheilen (*sn*) heal up
verheimlichen keep secret (*dat* from)
verheiraten marry (off) (an *acc*/mit to); sich ~ get married (mit to); (glücklich) verheiratet (happily) married
verheißen* promise
verheißungs|voll promising
verheizen burn (as fuel); *coll* send to the slaughter
verhelfen*: (+*dat*) ~ zu help to get/find
verherrlichen glorify
die Verherrlichung glorification
verhetzen incite
verheult *coll* red with crying
verhexen bewitch; put a jinx on; es ist wie verhext *coll* it's jinxed
verhindern prevent; verhindert *coll* would-be; (dienstlich) verhindert unable to come (because of work); an (der Teilnahme *etc*) verhindert unable to (take part *etc*)
die Verhinderung prevention

verhohlen concealed; secret
verhöhnen ridicule
verhohnepipeln *coll* ridicule
verhökern *coll* 'flog'
das Verhör, –e interrogation; *leg* examination; ins ~ nehmen interrogate; *leg* examine
verhören interrogate; *leg* examine; sich ~ hear wrongly
verhornen (*sn*) become horny; verhornt horny
verhüllen veil; cover; ~d (expression) euphemistic; verhüllt *also* (threat) veiled
verhundertfachen increase a hundredfold
verhungern (*sn*) starve
verhunzen *coll* ruin; murder (language)
verhüten prevent
verhütten smelt
die Verhütung prevention; das ~s|mittel, – contraceptive
verhutzelt shrivelled; wizened
verifizieren verify
ver|innerlichen give a deeper meaning to; make (s.o.) (excessively) introspective; *psych etc* internalize
ver|irren: sich ~ get lost; go astray; (animal) stray; verirrt *also* stray
die Ver|irrung, –en *vbl noun*; *also* aberration
verjagen chase away; drive out; dispel
verjähren (*sn*) *leg* come under the statute of limitations; verjährt statute-barred
die Verjährungs|frist, –en *leg* limitation (fixed by statute of limitations)
verjazzen [–'dʒɛs–] jazz up
verjubeln *coll* 'blow'
verjüngen rejuvenate; sich ~ be rejuvenated; taper
die Verjüngung, –en rejuvenation
verjuxen *coll* 'blow'
verkalken (*sn*) calcify; *med* (artery) harden; *coll* grow senile; verkalkt *coll* gaga
verkalkulieren: sich ~ miscalculate
verkappt hidden; in disguise
verkapseln: sich ~ cut oneself off; *med* become encapsulated
verkatert *coll* suffering from a hangover, hung over
der Verkauf, ⸚e sale; sales (department); zum ~ for sale
verkaufen sell; sich ~ sell oneself; (goods) sell; zu ~ for sale
der Verkäufer, – seller; salesman; shop assistant, salesclerk *US*; *leg* vendor
die Verkäuferin, –nen shop assistant, salesclerk *US*
verkäuflich for sale; leicht/schwer ~ easy/hard to sell
Verkaufs– sales ...; selling ...; die ~bedingungen *pl* conditions of sale; der ~leiter, – sales manager; v~offen open for business; das ~personal sales force; der

~preis, -e retail price; **der ~schlager, -** big seller

der **Verkehr** traffic; trade; dealings; contact; (sexual) intercourse; *rail etc* service; **... ist kein ~ für dich** ... is not the right kind of company for you; **aus dem ~ ziehen** withdraw from circulation/service; **in brieflichem ~ stehen** correspond (**mit** with)

verkehren (*see also* **verkehrt**) twist (**ins Gegenteil** to mean the opposite), distort; (*v/i, also sn*) run; ply; operate; **~ bei** visit regularly; **~ in** (*dat*) frequent; **~ mit** associate with; have intercourse with; **brieflich ~ mit** correspond with; **sich ~ in** (*acc*) turn into

Verkehrs- traffic ...; road ...;

die ~ader, -n major thoroughfare; **die ~ampel, -n** traffic lights/light *US*; **das ~büro, -s** tourist (information) office; **das ~flugzeug, -e** commercial aircraft; **die ~insel, -n** traffic island; **der ~minister, -** minister of transport; **das ~ministerium, -(i)en** ministry of transport; **das ~mittel, -** means of transport (**öffentliche V.** public transport); **das ~opfer, -** road casualty (**die Zahl der V.** the toll on the roads); **die ~regel, -n** traffic regulation; **v~reich** (road) busy; **der ~rowdy, -s** road-hog; **das ~schild, -er** road-sign; **v~schwach** with little traffic; **v~sicher** roadworthy; safe; **die ~sicherheit** roadworthiness; road safety; **die ~sprache, -n** lingua franca; **v~stark** busy; **der ~stau, -e = die ~stauung, -en = die ~stockung, -en** traffic-jam; **die ~straße, -n** thoroughfare; **der ~sünder, -** *coll* traffic offender; **der ~teil|nehmer, -** road-user; **v~tüchtig** fit to drive; roadworthy; **der ~unfall, ¨e** road accident; **der ~verbund, -e** transport authority; **der ~ver|ein, -e** tourist (information) office; **der ~weg, -e** highway; **das ~wesen** transport system; **v~widrig** in violation of traffic regulations

verkehrt *p/part*; *also* wrong; (world) topsy-turvy; (*adv*) wrongly; (do) the wrong way; **~ (herum)** the wrong way round; inside out; upside down; **~ herum** *coll* 'queer'; **gar nicht ~** *coll* not at all bad

verkeilen wedge; *coll* thrash

verkennen* fail to appreciate, misjudge; mistake; **nicht zu ~** unmistakable; **es ist nicht zu ~, daß ...** it is undeniable that ...; **verkannt** (genius) unrecognized

verketten secure with a chain; chain together; link; **sich ~** become interlinked

die **Verkettung** *vbl noun*; *also* chain (of events)

verketzern denounce

verkitschen make kitschy; **verkitscht** kitschy

verkitten fill with putty; put putty round

verklagen sue (**wegen** for); **der/die Verklagte** (*decl as adj*) defendant

verklären transfigure; **sich ~** be transfigured; **verklärt** (face) radiant

die **Verklärung** transfiguration

verklatschen *coll* tell on; spend gossiping

verklausulieren limit by provisos; **verklausuliert** *also* involved

verkleben stick down; stick adhesive tape *etc* over; put a plaster on; use up (stamps, wallpaper, *etc*); (*v/i sn*) stick together; (hair) become matted; (eye) close (as a result of secreted pus *etc*); **verklebt** *also* sticky; matted

verkleckern *coll* spill; fritter away

verkleiden disguise; cover; panel; *build* face; **sich ~** disguise oneself; dress up

die **Verkleidung, -en** *vbl noun*; *also* disguise; covering; panelling; *build* facing

verkleinern reduce (in size); scale down; belittle; **sich ~** be reduced; *coll* move to a smaller place/smaller premises

die **Verkleinerungs|form, -en** diminutive

verklemmen: sich ~ get stuck; jam; **verklemmt** jammed; inhibited

verklingen* (*sn*) fade away; (enthusiasm *etc*) fade

verkloppen *coll* 'flog'; give (s.o.) a hiding

verknacken *coll*: **~ zu** send down for (... months *etc*); **zu ... Mark Geldstrafe ~** fine (s.o.) ... marks

verknacksen *coll*: **sich** *dat* **den Fuß ~** sprain one's ankle

verknallen: sich ~ in (*acc*) *coll* fall madly in love with

verknappen cut down on; **sich ~** grow scarce

die **Verknappung, -en** *vbl noun*; *also* scarcity (**an** *dat* of)

verkneifen*: sich *dat* **... ~** *coll* suppress; deny oneself; **es sich nicht ~ können zu ...** be unable to resist (+*ger*); **verkniffen** (face) pinched

verknöchern (*sn*) ossify

verknoten knot; tie up

verknüpfen tie together; link; combine; **verknüpft sein mit** entail; **eng verknüpft mit** closely bound up with

verknusen *esp NGer coll*: **nicht ~ können** be unable to stomach

verkochen use for cooking; (*v/i sn*) boil away; **~ zu** boil down to

verkohlen char; *tech* carbonize; *coll* 'have on', 'put on' *US*; (*v/i sn*) char

verkoken coke

verkommen[1]* (*sn*) go to the dogs; become degenerate; go to rack and ruin; run wild; (food) go bad

verkommen[2] *p/part*; *also* degenerate; dilapidated; (garden) wild

die **Verkommenheit** degeneracy; dilapidation; wild state

verkonsumieren *coll* get through (food *etc*)
verkoppeln join together; combine
verkorken cork
verkorksen *coll* make a hash of; ruin; **sich** *dat* **den Magen ~** upset one's stomach; **verkorkst** *also* 'screwed up'
verkörpern embody; *cin*, *theat* play (the part of)
die **Verkörperung, -en** embodiment; *cin*, *theat* portrayal
verköstigen feed
verkrachen: sich ~ *coll* fall out (**mit** with); **verkracht** at loggerheads; (actor, student, *etc*) failed; **verkrachte Existenz** *coll* failure
verkraften cope with; manage; take (bad news *etc*)
verkramen *coll* mislay
verkrampfen: sich ~ become cramped; become tense; **verkrampft** tense; uptight; (laugh) forced
die **Verkrampfung, -en** *vbl noun*; *also* tension
verkriechen*: sich ~ creep away; hide (away); **ich hätte mich am liebsten verkrochen** I wished the ground would open and swallow me up
verkrümeln crumble; **sich ~** *coll* slip away; disappear
verkrümmen bend; (*v/i sn*) bend; become curved
die **Verkrümmung, -en** *vbl noun*; *anat* curvature
verkrüppelt crippled; stunted
verkrustet encrusted
verkühlen: sich ~ *Aust or coll* catch cold
die **Verkühlung, -en** *Aust or coll* cold
verkümmern (*sn*) become stunted; waste away; (talent) go to waste
verkünd(ig)en announce; proclaim; promulgate (law); preach (gospel); prophesy; herald; *leg* pronounce
der **Verkünd(ig)er, -** harbinger; preacher (of gospel)
die **Verkünd(ig)ung, -en** *vbl noun*; *also* announcement; proclamation; promulgation; *leg* pronouncement; **Mariä Verkündigung** the Annunciation; Lady Day
verkupfern copper-plate
verkuppeln couple; **~ an** (*acc*) procure (girl) for; marry off (daughter) to
verkürzen shorten; reduce; cut short; *art* foreshorten; **sich** *dat* **die Zeit ~** while away the time; **sich ~** be shortened; grow shorter; be reduced; **verkürzte Arbeitszeit** shorter working hours
die **Verkürzung, -en** *vbl noun*; *also* reduction
verlachen deride
Verlade- loading …
verladen* load; *mil* entrain; embark
der **Verlag, -e** publishing house; publishers; **das Buch ist im ~ X erschienen** the book was published by X
verlagern shift (**auf** *acc* to); transfer (to); **sich ~** shift (**auf** *acc* to)
Verlags- publishing …; publisher's …; **der ~buch|händler, -** publisher; **die ~buch|handlung, -en** publishing house; **das ~programm, -e** (publisher's) list; **das ~wesen** publishing
verlangen demand; require; want; ask for; ask to see (passport *etc*); **~ nach** ask for; long for; **es verlangt mich nach** I long for; **das ist zuviel/ein bißchen viel verlangt** that's asking too much/rather a lot; **Sie werden am Telefon verlangt** you're wanted on the phone; **es wird von ihm verlangt, daß er …** he is expected to …
das **Verlangen** longing (**nach** for); desire (for); request; **auf ~** on demand; (+*gen*) at the request of; by order of
verlangend longing
verlängern extend; lengthen; (official) renew (passport *etc*); *cul* make (gravy *etc*) go further; **~ zu** *sp* pass the ball on to; **sich ~** be extended/lengthened; **~ lassen** (holder of passport *etc*) renew
die **Verlängerung, -en** extension; lengthening; renewal (of passport *etc*); *sp* extra time, overtime *US*; **die ~s|schnur, ⸚e** extension lead/cord *US*
verlangsamen slow down; **die Geschwindigkeit/das Tempo ~** slow down, reduce speed; **sich ~** slow down
verläppern *coll* fritter away; **sich ~** be frittered away
Verlaß: es ist ~/kein ~ auf (*acc*) … can/cannot be relied on
verlassen[1]* leave; desert, abandon; (courage *etc*) desert; **sich ~ auf** (*acc*) rely on; **verlaß dich drauf!** take it from me
verlassen[2] *p/part*; *also* deserted; desolate; forlorn
die **Verlassenheit** desertedness; desolation; forlornness
die **Verlassenschaft, -en** *Aust*, *Swiss* estate
verläßlich reliable
die **Verläßlichkeit** reliability
verlatschen *coll* wear out (shoes)
Verlaub: mit ~ (zu sagen) if you'll pardon my saying so
der **Verlauf** course; progress; **einen guten/schlimmen ~ nehmen** go well/badly; **im ~** (+*gen*) in the course of; **nach ~** (+*gen*) after
verlaufen* (*sn exc* **sich ~**) go (well, badly, **wie geplant** according to plan); go off (without incident *etc*); (time) pass; (boundary *etc*) run (along *etc* sth.); (colour, ink) run; **ergebnislos ~** come to nothing; **normal ~** take its normal course; **im Sand(e) ~** peter out
sich ~ lose one's way, get lost; disperse;

drain away

die **Verlaufs|form** continuous form (of verb)

verlaust lice-ridden, lousy

verlautbaren announce; ~ **lassen, daß ...** let it be known that ...

die **Verlautbarung, –en** announcement

verlauten (*also sn*): **es verlautet, daß ...** it is reported that ...; **wie aus ... verlautet** according to reports from; ~ **lassen** say (**über** *acc* about)

verleben (*see also* **verlebt**) spend (holidays *etc*)

verlebendigen bring to life

verlebt *p/part*; *also* worn-out (through loose living)

verlegen[1] transfer; shift; postpone (**auf** *acc* until); mislay; lay (cable, tiles, track, *etc*); publish; block (s.o.'s way *etc*); **die (elektrischen) Leitungen ~ in** (*dat*) wire; **die Handlung in (die Antike** *etc*)/**nach (Athen** *etc*) ~ set the action in (antiquity/Athens *etc*)

sich ~ auf (*acc*) resort to; take up (zoology *etc*)

verlegen[2] embarrassed; ~ **um** short of; **nie ~ um** never at a loss for

die **Verlegenheit, –en** embarrassment; awkward situation, predicament; **in ~ bringen** embarrass; **in ~ kommen** get embarrassed || **die ~s|pause, –n** awkward silence

der **Verleger, –** publisher

die **Verlegung, –en** *vbl noun*; *also* transfer; postponement

verleiden* (+*dat*) spoil for

der **Verleih, –e** hire service, *cin* distributors; hiring out, *cin* distribution

verleihen* lend (**an** *acc* to); hire out (to); (+*dat*) confer on; award to; give (meaning *etc*) to; lend (dignity *etc*) to; (+*dat*) **Ausdruck ~** give expression to

der **Verleiher, –** lender; hirer; *cin* distributor

verleimen glue together

verleiten tempt (to); induce (to); ~ **zu** induce to commit/make; (*followed by vbl noun, eg* **zum Kauf von ... ~**) induce to (purchase ... *etc*)

verlernen forget (one's French *etc*); (*eg* **das Lachen/Schwimmen ~**) forget how to (laugh/swim *etc*)

verlesen[1]* read out; **sich ~** make a mistake in reading

verlesen[2]* sort out

verletzbar vulnerable

verletzen injure, hurt; wound; (= distress) hurt, wound; violate; offend against; fail in (duty); **sich ~** injure oneself; **~d** hurtful, wounding

verletzlich vulnerable

die **Verletzung, –en** *vbl noun*; *also* injury (*gen* to); violation

verleugnen deny; disown; **sich ~ lassen** not be at home (to s.o.)

die **Verleugnung, –en** denial; disowning

verleumden slander; libel

der **Verleumder, –** slanderer; libeller

verleumderisch slanderous; libellous

die **Verleumdung, –en** *vbl noun*; *also* slander; libel

verlieben: sich ~ in (*acc*) fall in love with

verliebt *p/part*; *also* in love (**in** *acc* with); amorous; **die V~en** the lovers

die **Verliebtheit** being in love

verlieren (*p/t* **verlor** (*subj* **verlöre**), *p/part* **verloren**) (*see also* **verloren**) lose; shed; (*v/i*) lose; (on closer acquaintance) not be so impressive, (dress *etc*) not be the same (without a belt *etc*), (novel *etc*) lose (in translation); ~ **an** (*dat*) lose (ground, height, prestige, *etc*); lose some of one's (charm *etc*)/its (effect *etc*); **sie hat sehr verloren** she is not the good-looking woman she once was; **du hast** *etc* **hier nichts verloren** *coll* you've *etc* no business to be here; **darüber braucht man kein Wort zu ~** we needn't waste any words on that

sich ~ get lost; disappear; disperse; (scent, sound) fade away; **sich ~ in** (*acc/dat*) lose oneself in

der **Verlierer, –** loser

das **Verlies, –e** dungeon

verlisch(s)t (*2nd,*) *3rd sing pres of* **verlöschen**

verloben: sich ~ get engaged (**mit** to); **verlobt** engaged; **der/die Verlobte** (*decl as adj*) fiancé/fiancée

die **Verlobung, –en** engagement; **der ~s|ring, –e** engagement ring

verlocken entice; tempt (to); **~d** tempting

die **Verlockung, –en** enticement, temptation

verlogen untruthful; false

verlor (verlöre) *p/t* (*subj*) *of* **verlieren**

verloren *p/part of* **verlieren;** lost; *cul* (egg) poached; **der ~e Sohn** *bibl* the prodigal son; **in den Anblick von ... ~** lost in contemplation of; ~ **geben** give up for lost || **~gehen*** (*sep*; *sn*) get/be lost (**... geht mir ~** I lose ...; **an ...** (*dat*) **ist ein Lehrer** *etc* **~gegangen** ... would have made a good teacher *etc*)

verlöschen (verlisch(s)t, *p/t* **verlosch** (*subj* **verlösche**), *p/part* **verloschen)** (*sn*) go out; (memory *etc*) fade

verlosen raffle (off); draw lots for

die **Verlosung, –en** *vbl noun*; *also* raffle; draw

verlöten solder

verlottern (*sn*) *coll* go to the dogs; **verlottert** scruffy; dissolute; run-down

verludern *coll* fritter away; (*v/i sn*) go to the dogs

verlumpen *coll* fritter away; (*v/i sn*) go to the dogs

der **Verlust, -e** loss (**an** *dat* of); (*pl*) *mil* casualties; **mit** ~ (sell *etc*) at a loss || **v~bringend** loss-making; **das ~geschäft, -e** loss-maker; **die ~liste, -n** casualty list

verlustieren: sich ~ *coll* amuse oneself

verlustig: (+*gen*) ~ **gehen** lose, forfeit

vermachen (+*dat*) leave to (in will)

das **Vermächtnis, -se** legacy, bequest

vermag *1st/3rd sing pres of* **vermögen**

vermählen: sich ~ **mit** wed

die **Vermählung, -en** marriage

vermaledeit accursed

vermännlichen make/(*v/i sn*) become masculine

vermarkten market

vermasseln *coll* make a hash of, make a mess of; mess up

vermassen (*sn*) lose one's individuality

die **Vermassung** loss of individuality

vermauern wall up

vermehren increase; **sich** ~ increase; *zool* multiply, breed; *bot* propagate; **vermehrt** *also* increasingly

die **Vermehrung, -en** *vbl noun*; *also* increase (*gen* in); *bot* propagation

vermeidbar avoidable

vermeiden* avoid; **es** ~ **zu ...** avoid (+*ger*); **es läßt sich nicht** ~**, daß ...** it is inevitable that ...

vermeidlich avoidable

die **Vermeidung** avoidance

vermeinen believe, imagine

vermeintlich supposed; putative

vermelden report

vermengen mix; mix up; **sich** ~ **mit** mix with

vermenschlichen humanize; anthropomorphize

der **Vermerk, -e** note

vermerken note down; make a (mental) note of; **übel** ~ take amiss

vermessen[1]* measure; survey; **sich** ~ measure incorrectly; presume (to)

vermessen[2] *p/part*; *also* presumptuous; bold

die **Vermessung, -en** *vbl noun*; *also* measurement; survey; **der ~s|ingenieur, -e** land surveyor

vermiesen (+*dat*) *coll* spoil for

vermieten hire out; let, rent *US*; **„zu ~"** 'to let', 'for rent' *US*

der **Vermieter, -** landlord; hirer

vermindern reduce; diminish (*also mus*); **sich** ~ decrease; lessen

die **Verminderung, -en** reduction; diminution

verminen mine

vermischen mix; blend; **sich** ~ mix; mingle; blend; **vermischt** *also* miscellaneous; **„Vermischtes"** 'miscellaneous'

die **Vermischung, -en** *vbl noun*; *also* mixture

vermissen miss; be unable to find; note the absence of, (at party *etc*) not see; see that (s.o.) does not have; ~ **lassen** be lacking in; **vermißt** missing; **vermißt werden** be missing; **als vermißt melden** report missing; **der/die Vermißte** (*decl as adj*) missing person

vermitteln arrange; be agents for (flats/apartments *US*); place (with firm *etc*); convey, communicate; pass on (knowledge, values, *etc*); *tel* put through (call); (+*dat*) obtain for; arrange for; (*v/i*) mediate; **~d eingreifen** intervene

vermittels (+*gen*) by means of

der **Vermittler, -** mediator, go-between; agent

die **Vermittlung, -en** *vbl noun*; *also* communication; mediation; agency; *tel* exchange; **die ~s|gebühr, -en** commission; **die ~s|stelle, -n** agency; *tel* exchange

vermöbeln *coll* give (s.o.) a hiding

vermocht(e) *p/part* (*p/t*) *of* **vermögen**

vermodern (*sn*) moulder (away)

vermöge (+*gen*) by virtue of

vermögen* be capable of; be able (to)

das **Vermögen, -** (private) means; fortune, wealth; capital, assets; ability; **ein** ~ **kosten/wert sein** cost/be worth a fortune; **nach bestem** ~ to the best of one's ability

vermögend wealthy

Vermögens-: die ~steuer, -n wealth tax; **die ~verhältnisse** *pl* financial circumstances; **der ~verwalter, -** trustee; **die ~werte** *pl* assets

vermorschen (*sn*) rot; **vermorscht** rotten

vermummen wrap up; disguise; **sich** ~ wrap (oneself) up; disguise oneself

die **Vermummung, -en** *vbl noun*; *also* disguise

vermurksen *coll* make a botch of

vermuten assume, suppose; surmise; suspect (arson *etc*); expect to find (in a place, *eg* **nicht gerade der Ort, wo man einen de la Tour** ~ **würde** not exactly the place one would expect to find a de la Tour); think that (s.o., sth.) is (in a place, *eg* **ich habe dich in Sevilla vermutet** I thought you were in Seville); ~ **hinter** (*dat*) *also* suspect that (s.o., sth.) is behind; ~ **in** (*dat*) *also* suspect that (s.o., sth.) is; **es ist/steht zu** ~**, daß ...** it may be supposed that ...; ~ **lassen, daß ...** lead one to suppose that ...

vermutlich presumable; (*adv*) presumably; I suppose

die **Vermutung, -en** supposition; conjecture; suspicion

vernachlässigen neglect; **sich** ~ neglect one's appearance

die **Vernachlässigung** neglect

vernageln nail up; **mit Brettern** ~ board up; **vernagelt** *coll* block-headed

vernähen sew up (*also med*); use up (in sewing)

vernarben (*sn*) scar over; **vernarbt** scarred

vernarren: sich ~ in (*acc*) fall madly in love with; go overboard for; **vernarrt in** (*acc*) crazy about

die **Vernarrtheit** infatuation (**in** *acc* with)

vernaschen spend on sweets; *coll* 'make' (girl, woman)

vernebeln obscure (facts); *mil* cover with a smoke-screen

vernehmbar audible

vernehmen* hear; *leg* examine; **~, daß ...** hear that ...; **dem Vernehmen nach** from what one hears

die **Vernehmlassung, –en** *Swiss* statement

vernehmlich clear(ly audible)

die **Vernehmung, –en** *leg* examination

verneigen: sich ~ bow (**vor** *dat* to)

die **Verneigung, –en** bow

verneinen answer in the negative; reject; deny; *gramm* negate; **~d** negative (*also gramm*); **~d den Kopf schütteln** shake one's head

die **Verneinung, –en** negative answer; rejection; denial; *gramm* negation; negative; **doppelte ~** *gramm* double negative

vernichten destroy; exterminate; annihilate; **~d** *also* devastating; withering; crushing

die **Vernichtung** destruction; extermination; annihilation

vernickeln nickel-plate

verniedlichen play down

vernieten rivet

die **Vernunft** good sense; reason; **~ annehmen** see reason; (+*dat*) **~ predigen** plead with (s.o.) to be reasonable; **zur ~ bringen** bring to his/her senses; **zur ~ kommen** come to one's senses || **die ~ehe, –n** marriage of convenience; **v~widrig** irrational

vernünftig sensible; reasonable; rational; *coll* 'decent'

ver|öden *med* obliterate; (*v/i sn*) become desolate; (person) become stultified

ver|öffentlichen publish

die **Ver|öffentlichung, –en** publication

ver|ordnen *med* prescribe (*dat* for); order (to be done); (+*dat*) **Bettruhe ~** order to stay in bed

die **Ver|ordnung, –en** *vbl noun*; *also* order; *med* prescription

verpachten lease

verpacken pack; package; wrap

die **Verpackung, –en** *vbl noun*; *also* packing (material); wrapping

verpäppeln *coll* mollycoddle

verpassen miss (bus, cue, opportunity, *etc*); (+*dat*) *coll* give (s.o. injection, kick, *etc*); (+*dat*) **eine Ohrfeige ~** *coll* give (s.o.) a clout

verpatzen *coll* spoil, ruin; make a hash of, mess up

verpesten pollute

die **Verpestung** pollution

verpetzen *coll* tell on (**bei** to)

verpfänden pawn; pledge (one's word)

verpfeifen* *coll* squeal on (**bei** to)

verpflanzen transplant (*also med*)

die **Verpflanzung, –en** transplantation; *med* transplantation; transplant

verpflegen feed

die **Verpflegung** *vbl noun*; *also* food; **mit voller ~** with full board

verpflichten oblige (to); bind (by oath); engage; *sp* sign on; **~ zu** commit to; enjoin (silence *etc*) on; **Adel verpflichtet** noblesse oblige; **~d** binding; **verpflichtet** (*following dat*) under an obligation to; indebted to; committed to (ideal *etc*); **verpflichtet zu** obliged to do; **sich verpflichtet fühlen zu ...** feel obliged to ...

sich ~ commit oneself; sign on; undertake (to); **sich ~ zu** commit oneself to; (*followed by vbl noun, eg* **sich zur Zahlung von ... ~**) undertake to (pay ... *etc*)

die **Verpflichtung, –en** *vbl noun*; *also* obligation; commitment

verpfuschen *coll* make a botch of; mess up (life *etc*)

verpimpeln *coll* mollycoddle

verplanen plan how one is going to spend, budget *US*; plan wrongly; **verplant** *also* booked up

verplappern: sich ~ *coll* let the cat out of the bag

verplaudern spend chatting

verplempern *coll* fritter away

verplomben seal

verpönt frowned upon

verprassen 'blow' (**für** on)

verprellen antagonize

verproviantieren provision

verprügeln thrash

verpuffen (*sn*) go pop; (enthusiasm *etc*) evaporate; fall flat

verpulvern [–f–, –v–] *coll* squander

verpumpen *coll* lend

verpuppen: sich ~ pupate

die **Verpuppung, –en** pupation

verpusten: (sich) ~ *coll* get one's breath back

der **Verputz** plaster

verputzen plaster; *coll* polish off; **rauh ~** rough-cast

verqualmen fill with smoke; *coll* spend on smoking; smoke; **verqualmt** smoke-filled

verquellen* (*sn*) swell; warp; **verquollene Augen** swollen eyes

verquer *coll*: (+*dat*) **~ gehen** go wrong for; (+*dat*) **~ kommen** come at an awkward moment for

verquicken link

verrammeln barricade

verramschen *coll* sell off cheap

[der] **Verrat** treachery; betrayal (**an** *dat* of); *leg* treason (against); ~ **begehen an** (*dat*) betray

verraten* betray (friend, ideal, *etc*); give away, betray; reveal; **sich** ~ give oneself away; **sich** ~ **in** (*dat*) be revealed in; **verraten und verkauft** 'sunk'

[der] **Verräter,** – traitor (*gen* to); **zum** ~ **werden** turn traitor

verräterisch treacherous; telltale; *leg* treasonable

verrauchen spend on smoking; (*v/i sn*) disperse; (anger) blow over

verräuchern fill with smoke; **verräuchert** smoke-filled

verrauschen (*sn*) die away

verrechnen credit to s.o.'s account; ~ **mit** offset against; **sich** ~ miscalculate; be mistaken

Verrechnungs–: der ~**scheck, –s** non-negotiable cheque (*cf* crossed cheque); **die** ~**stelle, –n** clearing-house

verrecken (*sn*) *coll* (animal) die; *vulg* kick the bucket; die a miserable death

verregnen (*sn*) be spoiled by rain

verreiben* rub in (ointment *etc*)

verreisen (*sn*) go away (on journey); **(geschäftlich) verreist** away (on business)

verreißen* (critic) 'pan', 'slate'

verrenken dislocate; crick (neck); **sich** *dat* **den Hals** ~ **nach** crane one's neck to see; **sich** *dat* **die Zunge** ~ twist one's tongue; **sich** ~ contort oneself

[die] **Verrenkung, –en** dislocation; contortion

verrennen*: sich ~ **in** (*acc*) stick doggedly to

verrichten perform, carry out; say (prayer)

[die] **Verrichtung, –en** *vbl noun*; *also* performance; (*pl*) tasks

verriegeln bolt

verringern reduce (**auf** *acc* to); **sich** ~ lessen, decrease

[die] **Verringerung, –en** reduction

verrinnen* (*sn*) trickle away; (time *etc*) pass

[der] **Verriß, –(ss)e** 'slating'

verrohen brutalize; (*sn*) become brutalized

verrosten (*sn*) rust; **verrostet** rusty

verrotten (*sn*) rot; **verrottet** rotten

verrucht wicked, infamous

verrücken move, shift

verrückt *p/part*; *also* mad; *coll* crazy (**auf** *acc*/**nach** about); ~ **machen** *coll* drive crazy; **wie** ~ *coll* like mad; **der/die Verrückte** (*decl as adj*) madman/woman || **V~werden** *coll* (**... ist zum V.** ... is enough to drive you mad)

Verruf: in ~ **bringen/kommen** bring/fall into disrepute

verrufen disreputable

verrühren: ~ **in** (*dat*) stir into

verrußen (*sn*) become sooty

verrutschen (*sn*) slip out of place

[der] **Vers** [f–], **–e** line (of poetry); verse (of Bible, hymn); *coll* verse (= stanza); (*pl*) verse (*opp* prose); **sich** *dat* **keinen** ~ **auf ...** (*acc*) **machen können** *coll* not be able to make head or tail of; ~**e machen** write verses; **in** ~**e bringen** put into verse || **das** ~**drama, –(m)en** verse drama; **der** ~**fuß, ⸚e** (metrical) foot; **die** ~**kunst** versification; **die** ~**lehre** prosody; **das** ~**maß, –e** metre

versachlichen make objective

versacken (*sn*) *coll* sink; go to the dogs

versagen (+*dat*) deny; (*v/i*) fail; (legs *etc*) give way; **es sich** *dat* ~ **zu ...** refrain from (+*ger*); **... bleibt mir versagt** I am denied ...

[das] **Versagen** failure; **menschliches** ~ human error

[der] **Versager,** – failure, washout; (= cartridge *etc*) dud

Versailler [vɛr'saɐ̯ɐ]: **der** ~ **Vertrag** the Treaty of Versailles

versalzen (*p/part* **versalzen**) oversalt; (+*dat*) *coll* spoil for

versammeln assemble; gather together; **um sich** ~ gather around one; **sich** ~ assemble; meet

[die] **Versammlung, –en** *vbl noun*; *also* assembly; meeting; gathering

[der] **Versand** dispatch; dispatch department; *coll* mail-order firm; *in compds* dispatch ...; mail-order ...; **das** ~**haus, ⸚er** mail-order firm

versanden (*sn*) silt up; fizzle out

Versatz–: das ~**amt, ⸚er** *SGer* pawn-shop; **das** ~**stück, –e** *theat* set piece; *Aust* pledge (= pawned object)

versauen *vulg* mess up; foul up

versauern (*sn*) turn sour; (soil) sour, turn acid; *coll* (person) stagnate

versaufen* (*see also* **versoffen**) *coll* guzzle away; **seinen Verstand** ~ drink oneself silly

versäumen miss (opportunity, train, school, *etc*); lose (time); neglect; fail (to); **nichts** ~, **um zu ...** do everything to ...

[das] **Versäumnis, –se** omission; absence (from school)

verschachern *coll* sell off

verschachtelt *gramm* complex; **ineinander** ~ interlocking

verschaffen (+*dat*) obtain for; **sich** *dat* **...** ~ obtain; get; gain; **sich Gewißheit** ~ make sure of sth.; **sich Klarheit** ~ **über** (*acc*) get clear about

verschalen board

verschämt bashful

verschandeln *coll* spoil; disfigure

verschanzen *mil* entrench; **sich** ~ *mil* entrench oneself; **sich** ~ **hinter** (*dat*) entrench oneself behind (*also mil*); use as an excuse

verschärfen increase; intensify; tighten up; exacerbate (situation); **sich ~** increase; intensify; (tension) mount; (situation) become more critical; **verschärft** *also* (arrest) close; (*adv*) more closely/intensively

die **Verschärfung** *vbl noun*; *also* increase; intensification; exacerbation

verscharren bury (hurriedly)

verschätzen: sich ~ miscalculate

verschauen: sich ~ *Aust* make a mistake; **sich ~ in** (*acc*) fall for

verschaukeln *coll* con

verscheiden* (*sn*) pass away

verschenken give away

verscherbeln *coll* 'flog'

verscherzen: sich *dat* **… ~** forfeit

verscheuchen scare away; dispel, banish

verscheuern *coll* 'flog'

verschicken send off; send away; deport

verschiebbar movable; sliding

der **Verschiebe|bahnhof, ⸚e** marshalling yard, switchyard *US*

verschieben* move, shift (*also comput*), *rail* shunt; alter (perspective); postpone (**auf** *acc* until); *coll* traffic in; **sich ~** move (out of place); (perspective) alter; be postponed; *ling* shift

die **Verschiebung, –en** *vbl noun*; *also* shift (*also comput*, *ling*); postponement

verschieden different; (*pl*) *also* various; **~ (groß/lang/stark** *etc*) of different (sizes/lengths/strengths *etc*); **~ (groß/lang/stark** *etc*) **sein** vary in (size/length/strength *etc*); **das ist ~** it varies; **… ist (landschaftlich/von Geschäft zu Geschäft** *etc*) **~ …** varies from (region/shop *etc*) to (region/shop *etc*); **die ~sten …** a great variety of …; **~e** various people; **~es** various things; **„Verschiedenes"** 'miscellaneous' || **~artig** different; various (**die ~artigsten …** all manner of …); **die V~artigkeit** different nature; diversity; **verschiedener|lei** various (things); **~farbig,** *Aust* **~färbig** different-coloured

die **Verschiedenheit, –en** difference; diversity

verschiedentlich on various occasions

verschießen* fire off; use up (ammunition); *sp* miss (penalty); (*v/i sn*) fade; **sich ~ in** (*acc*) *coll* fall for; **verschossen in** (*acc*) *coll* crazy about

verschiffen ship

verschimmeln (*sn*) go mouldy

verschlafen¹* sleep through; miss by (over)-sleeping; (*v/i*) = **sich ~** oversleep

verschlafen² *p/part*; *also* sleepy

der **Verschlag, ⸚e** shed; shack; partitioned-off area

verschlagen¹* lose (place in book); (storm *etc*) drive (ship *etc*) (to place); (fate *etc*) bring (person) (to place); *sp* mishit; **mit Brettern ~** board up; **an einen Ort verschlagen werden** end up in a place; (+*dat*) **den Atem ~** take (s.o.'s) breath away; (+*dat*) **die Sprache ~** leave speechless

verschlagen² *p/part*; *also* cunning

die **Verschlagenheit** cunning

verschlammen (*sn*) be filled with mud; silt up

verschlampen *coll* mislay (through carelessness); (*v/i sn*) go to seed

verschlechtern make worse; impair; **sich ~** worsen, deteriorate; be worse off

die **Verschlechterung, –en** worsening, deterioration

verschleiern veil; conceal; blur; **sich ~** veil oneself; cloud over; (voice) become husky; **verschleiert** *also* husky

die **Verschleierung, –en** *vbl noun*; *also* concealment; cover-up

verschleifen* slur

verschleimt congested with phlegm

der **Verschleiß** wear (and tear); *Aust* retail trade; **~ an** (*dat*) consumption of

verschleißen (*p/t* **verschliß,** *p/part* **verschlissen**) wear out; *Aust* retail; (*v/i sn*) wear out; **sich ~** wear out; wear oneself out; **verschlissen** worn (out)

verschleppen carry off; abduct; protract; delay; spread (disease); **verschleppt** *also* (illness) protracted (through neglect)

verschleudern squander; sell off dirt-cheap

verschließen* (*see also* **verschlossen**) lock; lock up; lock away; cork (bottle); **die Augen ~ vor** (*dat*) close one's eyes to; **sein Herz ~ vor** (*dat*) harden one's heart against; **in sich ~** keep (thoughts *etc*) to oneself; **hinter verschlossenen Türen** behind closed doors

sich ~ (+*dat*) close one's mind to; ignore; be distant towards

verschlimmbessern *coll* make worse while attempting to improve it

verschlimmern make worse; **sich ~** get worse

verschlingen* devour; gulp down; engulf; swallow up; intertwine; **sich ~** intertwine

verschliß *p/t*, **verschlissen** *p/part of* **verschleißen**

verschlossen *p/part*; *also* (person) withdrawn

die **Verschlossenheit** reserve

verschlucken swallow; swallow up; **ich habe mich verschluckt** something has gone down the wrong way

der **Verschluß, ⸚(ss)e** lock; (airtight *etc*) seal; lid, top; stopper; fastener; clasp; catch; *phot* shutter; *med* occlusion; **unter ~** under lock and key || **der ~laut, –e** plosive

verschlüsseln encode

verschmachten (*sn*) languish; **vor Durst ~** be dying of thirst

verschmähen scorn, spurn; **verschmähte**

Liebe unrequited love
verschmelzen* fuse; blend; (*v/i sn*) fuse; merge; blend; ~ **zu** fuse (copper and zinc *etc*) to make (brass *etc*); weld into (integrated whole); (*v/i sn*) fuse/merge/blend to form
verschmerzen get over (disappointment *etc*)
verschmieren fill (hole); scribble all over; smear; smudge; **verschmiert** smeary
verschmitzt roguish, mischievous
verschmutzen soil; pollute; (*v/i sn*) get dirty; **verschmutzt** dirty; polluted
die **Verschmutzung** *vbl noun*; *also* pollution
Verschnauf–: die ~pause, –n breather
verschnaufen: (sich) ~ *coll* take a breather
verschneiden* clip; cut wrongly; blend (wine *etc*); geld, castrate (animal)
verschneit snow-covered
der **Verschnitt, –e** blend; *text* off-cuts
verschnörkeln adorn with flourishes; **verschnörkelt** ornate
verschnupfen *coll* peeve; **verschnupft sein** have a cold; *coll* be peeved
verschnüren tie up
verschollen missing; long past
verschonen spare; ~ **mit** spare (s.o. one's jokes *etc*); **verschont bleiben von** escape, be spared
verschönern beautify; improve the appearance of
verschorfen (*sn*) scab
verschränken cross (one's legs); fold (one's arms); clasp (one's hands)
verschrauben screw (into position); **miteinander** ~ screw together
verschrecken scare away (customers *etc*)
verschreiben* use up (paper *etc* in writing); *med* prescribe; (+*dat*) make over to; *med* prescribe for; **sich** ~ make a slip of the pen; (+*dat*) devote oneself to
der **Verschrieb, –e** *Swiss* spelling mistake
verschrie(e)n notorious; ~ **sein als** (+*adj*) be notoriously ...; (+*noun*) be a notorious ...
verschroben odd, eccentric
die **Verschrobenheit** eccentricity
verschrotten scrap
verschrumpeln (*sn*) shrivel up
verschüchtern intimidate
verschulden cause (accident *etc*); be responsible for; (*v/i sn*) get into debt; **sich** ~ incur debts; **verschuldet** in debt
das **Verschulden** fault; **ohne eigenes** ~ through no fault of one's own
die **Verschuldung** *vbl noun*; *also* indebtedness
verschusseln *coll* mislay; forget; **verschusselt** scatterbrained
verschütt–: ~gehen* (*sep*; *sn*) *coll* get lost
verschütten spill; fill in; (avalanche *etc*) bury
verschwägert related by marriage (**mit** to)
verschweigen* (*see also* **verschwiegen**) conceal (fact *etc*) (*dat* from); **ich habe nichts zu** ~ I've nothing to hide
verschweißen weld together
verschwenden waste (**an** *acc*/**auf** *acc*/**für** on)
der **Verschwender, –** spendthrift
verschwenderisch wasteful; extravagant; lavish
die **Verschwendung** waste; wastefulness; **die ~s|sucht** extravagance
verschwiegen *p/part*; *also* discreet; secluded
die **Verschwiegenheit** discretion; seclusion
verschwiemelt *coll* swollen
verschwimmen* (*see also* **verschwommen**) (*sn*) become blurred/hazy
verschwinden* (*sn*) disappear, vanish (**aus** from); ~ **neben** (*dat*) be eclipsed by; look tiny beside; **ich muß mal** ~ *coll* I must go to the loo/john *US*; **verschwinde!** get lost!; ~ **lassen** make (sth.) disappear; dispose of; make off with; **~d klein** minute; **~d wenig** a minute amount of; **das Verschwinden** disappearance
verschwistert: ~ sein be brother and sister/brothers/sisters; ~ **mit** married to (= combined with)
verschwitzen soak with perspiration; *coll* forget all about
verschwollen swollen
verschwommen *p/part*; *also* blurred; hazy; vague
verschwören*: sich ~ conspire (**mit** with); (+*dat*) dedicate oneself to; **der/die Verschworene** (*decl as adj*) conspirator
der **Verschwörer, –** conspirator
verschwörerisch conspiratorial
die **Verschwörung, –en** conspiracy
Verse–: der ~schmied, –e rhymester
versehen* hold (post); perform (duty); look after; ~ **mit** provide/equip/fit with; *often rendered by Eng denominative verb* (*eg* **mit einem Etikett/Stempel/Viehbestand** ~ label/stamp/stock, **mit Teppichen** ~ carpet); **versehen sein mit** be provided/equipped/fitted with; have; **gut versehen mit** well supplied/stocked with
sich ~ make a mistake; **sich** ~ **mit** provide/equip oneself with; **ehe man sich's versieht** before you know it
das **Versehen, –** oversight; mistake; **aus** ~ by mistake
versehentlich by mistake, inadvertently
der **Versehrte** (*fem* **die** ~) (*decl as adj*) disabled person
verselbständigen make independent; **sich** ~ become independent
versenden* send out; dispatch
versengen singe; scorch
versenken sink; scuttle; *tech* countersink; ~ **in** (*acc*) lower into; thrust (one's hands) into (pockets); bury (one's head) in

(book); **sich ~ in** (*acc*) become immersed in

die **Versenkung, -en** *vbl noun*; *also* immersion (in one's work *etc*); *theat* trap-door; **aus der ~ auftauchen** *coll* reappear on the scene; **in der ~ verschwinden** *coll* disappear from the scene; sink into oblivion

versessen *p/part*; ~ **auf** (*acc*) crazy about

versetzen move; transfer; transplant; stagger; pawn; sell; retort; *educ* move up, promote *US*; *mus* transpose; *coll* stand up (one's date); (+*dat*) deal (s.o. blow)

~ **in** (*acc*): *frequently signifies that s.o. or sth. is put into a certain state* (*eg* **in Bewegung ~** set in motion, **in Entzücken/Wut ~** send into raptures/a rage, **in gute Laune ~** put in a good mood, **in Angst/Erstaunen/Unruhe ~** frighten/amaze/disturb, **in den Ruhestand ~** retire, **in die Lage ~ zu ...** put in a position to ...)

~ **mit** mix with

sich in jmds. Lage ~ put oneself in s.o.'s place; **sich (an den Hof Heinrich VIII.** *etc*) ~ imagine oneself (at the court of Henry VIII *etc*)

die **Versetzung, -en** *vbl noun*; *also* transfer; *mus* transposition; **das ~s|zeichen, -** *mus* accidental

verseuchen contaminate; infect

die **Verseuchung, -en** contamination; infection

der **Versicherer, -** insurer

versichern insure (**bei** with, **gegen** against); affirm; assure; (+*dat of pers*) assure of; **sich ~** insure oneself (**bei** with, **gegen** against, **mit** for); (+*gen*) make sure of; secure; **zu hoch/niedrig ~** overinsure/underinsure; **seien Sie versichert, daß ...** rest assured that ...; **der/die Versicherte** (*decl as adj*) insured

die **Versicherung, -en** insurance; assurance; insurance company; **der ~s|beitrag, ⸚e** insurance contribution/premium; **die ~s|karte, -n (grüne V.** green card); **der ~s|nehmer, -** policyholder; **v~s|pflichtig** subject to compulsory insurance; **die ~s|police** (*Aust* **-polizze**), **-n** insurance policy; **die ~s|prämie, -n** insurance premium; **der ~s|schutz** insurance cover; **v~s|statistisch** actuarial; **die ~s|summe, -n** sum insured; **das ~s|wesen** insurance (business)

versickern (*sn*) seep away; (interest *etc*) peter out

versieben *coll* make a mess of; mislay

versiegeln seal (up)

versiegen (*sn*) dry up; **nie ~d** never-failing

versiert experienced; ~ **in** (*dat*) well versed in

versilbern silver-plate; *poet* (moon) silver; *coll* turn into cash

versimpeln oversimplify; (*v/i sn*) become simple-minded

versinken* (*sn*) sink; ~ **in** (*acc*) sink into (silence, sleep, *etc*); become immersed in; **versunken in** (*acc*) immersed in; lost in (contemplation of ...); **in Gedanken versunken** lost in thought

versinnbildlichen symbolize

die **Version, -en** version

versippt related by marriage

versitzen* (*see also* **versessen**) *coll* spend (time) sitting about; crease (by sitting on it)

versklaven enslave

die **Versklavung** enslavement

versnobt [-p-] snobbish

versoffen *p/part*; *vulg* boozy

versohlen *coll* give (s.o.) a hiding

versöhnen reconcile; propitiate (gods); **sich ~** be(come) reconciled, make it up

der **Versöhnler, -** *EGer pej* compromiser

versöhnlerisch *EGer pej* compromising

das **Versöhnlertum** *EGer pej* spirit of compromise

versöhnlich conciliatory; forgiving

die **Versöhnung, -en** reconciliation

versonnen lost in thought; (smile *etc*) dreamy

versorgen provide for; look after; ~ **mit** supply with

der **Versorger, -** supplier; breadwinner

die **Versorgung** *vbl noun*; *also* provision, supply; care

verspachteln fill (in); *coll* tuck away

verspannen *tech* brace, stay

verspäten: sich ~ be late; **verspätet** late; belated

die **Verspätung, -en** lateness; delay; ~ **haben** (train *etc*) be late; **(10 Minuten** *etc*) ~ **haben** be (10 minutes *etc*) late

verspeisen consume

verspekulieren lose through speculation; **sich ~** ruin oneself by speculation; miscalculate

versperren block; bar; *esp Aust* lock up

verspielen gamble away; throw away (chance); spend playing; **verspielt haben** have had it; **er hat bei mir verspielt** he's had it as far as I'm concerned; **verspielt** playful; **sich ~** play a wrong note

verspinnen* spin; use up in spinning; **sich ~ in** (*acc*) become wrapped up in; **versponnen** *also* airy-fairy

verspotten, die Verspottung ridicule

versprechen* promise (*also* = show signs of, *eg* **es verspricht ein netter Abend zu werden** it promises to be a nice evening); **nichts Gutes ~** be ominous; **sich** *dat* **... ~ von** expect to get out of/gain from; **sich** *dat* **viel/wenig ~ von** have high hopes/no great hopes of; **sich ~** make a slip of the tongue

das **Versprechen, –** promise
der **Versprecher, –** *coll* slip of the tongue
die **Versprechungen** *pl* promises
versprengen sprinkle; *esp mil* scatter, disperse
verspritzen splatter; spray
versprochener|maßen as promised
versprühen spray
verspüren feel; be conscious of
verstaatlichen nationalize
die **Verstaatlichung, –en** nationalization
verstädtern urbanize; (*v/i sn*) become urbanized
die **Verstädterung** urbanization
der **Verstand** intellect, mind; (common) sense; **den ~ verlieren** go out of one's mind; **da steht einem der ~ still!** that leaves me speechless!; **nicht ganz/recht bei ~** not quite all there; **mit ~ essen/trinken** savour to the full; **das geht über meinen ~** it's beyond me; **um den ~ bringen** drive out of his/her mind; **(wieder) zu ~ kommen** come to one's senses
Verstandes–: die ~kraft intellectual powers; **v~mäßig** rational; **der ~mensch, –en** (*wk masc*) rational person; **die ~schärfe** perspicacity
verständig sensible; understanding
verständigen inform (**von** of); **sich ~** make oneself understood; (*recip*) communicate; reach agreement
die **Verständigung, –en** notification; communication; agreement; **das ~s|mittel, –** means of communication
verständlich understandable; comprehensible; intelligible; **leicht/schwer ~** easy/hard to understand; (+*dat*) **~ machen** get across to; **sich ~ machen** make oneself heard/understood (*dat* by) || **verständlicher|weise** understandably
das **Verständnis** understanding (**für** of); appreciation (of: art, music, *etc*); **~ haben für** show understanding for; appreciate; **kein ~ haben für** have no understanding for; not appreciate; have no time for || **v~innig** knowing; **v~los** uncomprehending, (expression, look) blank; unappreciative; **die ~losigkeit** lack of understanding/appreciation; **v~voll** understanding; sympathetic; knowing
der **Verstands|kasten, ..kästen** *joc* brain-box
verstänkern *coll* stink out
verstärken strengthen; reinforce (*also mil*); intensify (*also phot*); boost (*also elect*); *rad* amplify; *chem* concentrate; **sich ~** increase; intensify; **verstärkt** *also* increased; (*adv*) increasingly
der **Verstärker, –** *rad* amplifier; *phot* intensifier
die **Verstärkung** *vbl noun*; *also* reinforcement (*also mil*); intensification (*also phot*); *rad* amplification; *chem* concentration; *mil* reinforcements
verstauben (*sn*) grow dusty; gather dust; **verstaubt** dusty; old-fashioned
verstauchen: sich *dat* **... ~** sprain
verstauen stow (away)
das **Versteck, –e** hiding-place; hideout; **~ spielen** play hide-and-seek || **das ~spiel, –e** hide-and-seek
verstecken, sich ~ hide (**vor** *dat* from); **sich ~ können/müssen vor** (*dat*) be no match for; **versteckt** hidden; secret; veiled; covert; **sich versteckt halten** be in hiding; **Verstecken spielen** play hide-and-seek
verstehen¹* understand; hear, understand; know (subject *etc*); **~ als** regard as; **~ unter** (*dat*) understand by; **etwas/nichts/viel ~ von** know something/nothing/a good deal about; **falsch ~** misunderstand; misconstrue; **das kann ich (aber auch) gut ~** I don't blame him/her *etc*; **es ~ zu ...** know how to ...; (+*dat*) **zu ~ geben, daß ...** give (s.o.) to understand that ...; **verstanden?** get it?; (is that) understood?
sich ~ *comm* (price) be (inclusive of *etc* ...); (*recip*) understand each other; get on (together); **sich ~ als** see oneself as; (thing) be intended as; **sich ~ auf** (*acc*) be (an) expert at; have a way with; **sich ~ mit** get on with; **das versteht sich (von selbst)** that goes without saying; **versteht sich!** of course!
verstehen²* *coll* spend standing
verstehend (look *etc*) knowing
versteifen stiffen; reinforce; **sich ~** stiffen; (attitude) harden; **sich ~ auf** (*acc*) insist on
versteigen* (*see also* **verstiegen**): **sich ~** get lost while climbing; **sich zu der Behauptung ~, daß ...** go so far as to claim that ...
der **Versteigerer, –** auctioneer
versteigern auction (off); **~ lassen** put up for auction
die **Versteigerung, –en** *vbl noun*; *also* auction
versteinern (*sn exc* **sich ~**) fossilize; petrify; **sich ~** (face, smile) freeze; **wie versteinert** petrified
die **Versteinerung, –en** *vbl noun*; *also* fossilization; petrification; fossil
verstellbar adjustable
verstellen move (from its proper place); put in the wrong place; adjust; block; disguise (handwriting, voice); **sich ~** pretend
die **Verstellung, –en** *vbl noun*; *also* adjustment; disguise; obstruction
versterben* (*see also* **verstorben**) (*only p/t and p/part*) (*sn*) pass away
versteuern pay tax on
verstiegen *p/part*; *also* eccentric; extravagant; high-flown

verstimmen put out; *mus* put out of tune; **sich** ~ get out of tune; **verstimmt put** out; (stomach) upset; *mus* out of tune

die **Verstimmung, -en** *vbl noun*; *also* disgruntlement; ill-feeling

verstockt stubborn

verstohlen surreptitious, furtive

verstopfen stop up; block, clog; *med* constipate; **verstopft** *also* congested

die **Verstopfung, -en** *vbl noun*; *also* blockage; (traffic) jam, congestion; *med* constipation

verstorben *p/part*; *also* late; **der/die Verstorbene** (*decl as adj*) the deceased

verstören (event *etc*) disturb; **verstört** *also* distraught

der **Verstoß, ⸚e** offence (**gegen** against); infringement (of)

verstoßen* turn out (of the house); repudiate; ~ **gegen** offend against; infringe

verstreben *tech* brace

verstreichen* spread; fill in; (*v/i sn*) elapse

verstreuen scatter; spill; **über das ganze Land verstreut** dotted about the country

verstricken use up in knitting; ~ **in** (*acc*) involve in; **sich** ~ **in** (*acc*) get caught up/entangled in

die **Verstrickung, -en** *vbl noun*; *also* involvement; entanglement

verströmen exude; radiate

verstümmeln mutilate; garble (text *etc*)

die **Verstümmelung, -en** *vbl noun*; *also* mutilation

verstummen (*sn*) go silent; (applause *etc*) stop

der **Versuch, -e** attempt; effort; experiment; test; *liter* essay; *rugby* try; **-versuch** *also* attempted ...; **einen** ~ **machen** make an attempt; do an experiment; **es auf einen** ~ **ankommen lassen** give it a try

versuchen try; tempt; **es** ~ **mit** give (s.o., sth.) a try; **sich** ~ **als** try one's hand as; **sich** ~ **an** (*dat*)/**in** (*dat*) try one's hand at; **sein Glück** ~ try one's luck; **versucht zu ...** tempted to ...; **versuchter Diebstahl/Mord** attempted theft/murder

der **Versucher, -** tempter

die **Versucherin, -nen** temptress

Versuchs- experimental ...; test ...; trial ...; **der ~ballon, -s** sounding-balloon; ballon d'essai (**einen V. steigen lassen** fly a kite); **das ~kaninchen, -** *coll* guinea-pig; **die ~person, -en** subject (of experiment); **die ~reihe, -n** series of experiments; **die ~strecke, -n** test track; **das ~tier, -e** laboratory animal; **v~weise** experimentally; on a trial basis; on trial

die **Versuchung, -en** temptation; **in** ~ **geraten** be tempted; **in** ~ **zu ...** tempted to ...

versumpfen (*sn*) become marshy; *coll* go to the dogs

versündigen: sich ~ **an** (*dat*) sin against

die **Versunkenheit** absorption in one's thoughts

versüßen (+*dat*) sweeten for

vertagen adjourn; defer (**auf** *acc* until); **sich** ~ adjourn

die **Vertagung, -en** adjournment; deferment

vertändeln fritter away

vertäuen *naut* moor

vertauschbar exchangeable; interchangeable

vertauschen exchange (**mit** for); interchange; mix up (hats *etc*)

die **Vertäuung, -en** *vbl noun*; *also* moorings

verteidigen defend (*also leg*, *sp*) (**gegen** against, from); **sich** ~ defend oneself; *leg* conduct one's own defence

der **Verteidiger, -** defender (*also sp*); *leg* counsel for the defence

die **Verteidigung** defence (*also leg*, *sp*); **in die** ~ **drängen** force onto the defensive; **zu jmds.** ~ in s.o.'s defence

Verteidigungs- defence ...; defensive ...; **die ~rede, -n** apologia; *leg* speech for the defence; **die ~schrift, -en** apologia; *leg* (written) defence

verteilen distribute; share out; spread; *theat* allot (parts); ~ **über** (*acc*) spread (costs *etc*) over; **sich** ~ spread out; **sich** ~ **auf** (*acc*) be divided among; disperse to; **ein Stück mit verteilten Rollen lesen** do a play-reading

der **Verteiler, -** distributor (*also mot*); distribution list; *comput* distributor; dispatcher

die **Verteilung** *vbl noun*; *also* distribution

vertelefonieren *coll* spend phoning

verteuern raise the price of; **sich** ~ become dearer

die **Verteuerung, -en** *vbl noun*; *also* price increase

verteufeln condemn; **verteufelt** *coll* tricky; devil of a ...; (*adv*) darned

vertiefen, sich ~ deepen; **sich** ~ **in** (*acc*) become engrossed in; **vertieft in** (*acc*) engrossed in; **in Gedanken vertieft** deep in thought

die **Vertiefung, -en** *vbl noun*; *also* hollow, depression; absorption, engrossment

vertiert brutish, bestial

vertikal, die Vertikale, -n vertical

vertilgen eradicate; exterminate; *joc* 'demolish'

die **Vertilgung, -en** eradication; extermination; **das ~s|mittel, -** pesticide; weed-killer

vertippen: sich ~ *coll* make a typing error

vertonen set to music; *cin* add a sound-track to

vertrackt awkward, tricky

der **Vertrag, ⸚e** contract, agreement; *pol* treaty; **unter** ~ **nehmen** sign up

vertragen* (be able to) stand/take; *Swiss* deliver (newspapers); **sich** ~ get on (together); go together; **sich ~ mit** get on with; go with; be consistent with; **sich wieder ~** make it up; **ich kann kein Eis/keinen Alkohol** *etc* **~** ice-cream/alcohol *etc* doesn't agree with me

vertraglich contractual; (*adv*) by contract; **~ gebunden** bound by contract

verträglich affable, easy to get on with; digestible; *med* well-tolerated

Vertrags– ... of a/the contract/*pol* treaty; **der ~bruch, ⸗e** breach of contract; **v~brüchig** (**v. werden** be in breach of contract); **der ~entwurf, ⸗e** draft contract/treaty; **v~gemäß** in accordance with the contract/treaty; **der ~partner, –** contracting party; **die ~strafe, –n** penalty for breach of contract; **v~widrig** contrary to the terms of the contract/treaty

vertrauen (*see also* **vertraut**) (+*dat*) trust; **~ auf** (*acc*) trust in; trust to; **auf sein Glück ~** trust to luck

das **Vertrauen** trust (**auf** *acc*/**in** *acc*/**zu** in); confidence (in); **sein ~ setzen auf** (*acc*)/**in** (*acc*) place one's trust in; **im ~ (gesagt)** in confidence; **ein Wort im ~** a word in your ear; **im ~ auf** (*acc*) trusting to; **im ~ darauf, daß ...** confident that ...; **ins ~ ziehen** take into one's confidence || **v~erweckend** inspiring confidence

Vertrauens– ... of confidence/trust; **der ~arzt, ⸗e** medical examiner (employed by health insurance company); **der ~bruch, ⸗e** breach of confidence/faith; **die ~frage** *parl* (**die V. stellen** ask for a vote of confidence); **der ~mann, ⸗er/..leute** (confidential) agent; spokesman; shop steward; **die ~person, –en** person in whom one can confide; **die ~sache, –n** confidential matter; matter of trust; **v~selig** (too) trusting; **v~voll** trusting; **das ~votum, –(t)en** vote of confidence; **v~würdig** trustworthy

vertraulich confidential; familiar

die **Vertraulichkeit, –en** confidentiality; familiarity; **mit aller ~** in strict confidence

verträumen dream away; **verträumt** *also* dreamy; (place) sleepy

vertraut *p/part*; *also* intimate; (face *etc*) familiar; **~ mit** familiar with; **(sich) ~ machen mit** familiarize (oneself) with; **der/die Vertraute** (*decl as adj*) confidant/confidante

die **Vertrautheit** intimacy; familiarity

vertreiben* chase/drive away; expel; banish (cares); *comm* sell; **sich** *dat* **die Zeit ~** while away the time

vertretbar justifiable; tenable

vertreten* represent (*also parl*); stand in for; hold (view); advocate (policy); justify; *leg* plead (s.o.'s) case; (+*dat*) **den Weg ~** bar (s.o.'s) way; **sich** *dat* **den Fuß ~** sprain one's ankle; **sich** *dat* **die Beine/Füße ~** *coll* stretch one's legs; **sich ~ lassen durch** be represented by; **vertreten sein** be represented

der **Vertreter, –** representative; deputy, *med* locum; champion (of); *comm* agent; (sales) representative

die **Vertretung, –en** *vbl noun*; *also* representation; replacement, stand-in; *comm* agency; *sp* team; **diplomatische ~** diplomatic mission; **die ~ haben/übernehmen für** stand in for; **die ~ der Firma X haben** represent Messrs X; **in ~** (+*gen*) on behalf of || **v~s|weise** as a stand-in

der **Vertrieb, –e** *comm* sale; sales department

der **Vertriebene** (*fem* **die**) (*decl as adj*) expellee

vertrimmen *coll* wallop

vertrinken* spend on drink; drink (cares) away

vertrocknen (*sn*) dry up; wither; go dry

vertrödeln *coll* dawdle away

vertrösten put off (with excuse, promise)

vertrotteln (*sn*) *coll* go gaga

vertrusten [–'tra–] *comm* form into a trust

vertun* waste (time *etc*: **mit** *ger*, *eg* **die Zeit mit Trinken und Kartenspiel ~** waste one's time drinking and playing cards); **sich ~** *coll* make a mistake

vertuschen hush up, cover up

ver|übeln (+*dat*) take amiss; **ich kann es ihm nicht ~** I can't blame him

ver|üben commit

ver|ulken *coll* make fun of

ver|unfallen (*sn*) *esp Swiss* have an accident

ver|unglimpfen denigrate

ver|unglücken (*sn*) have an accident; *joc* be a flop; **tödlich ~** be killed in an accident; **verunglückt** *joc* abortive; **der/die Verunglückte** (*decl as adj*) casualty

ver|unmöglichen *esp Swiss* prevent, make impossible

ver|unreinigen soil, dirty; pollute

die **Ver|unreinigung, –en** *vbl noun*; *also* pollution

ver|unsichern make (s.o.) feel insecure

ver|unstalten spoil the look of

ver|untreuen embezzle

die **Ver|untreuung, –en** embezzlement

ver|unzieren spoil the look of

ver|ursachen cause; give rise to

ver|urteilen condemn; *leg* sentence; **~ wegen** convict of; **~ zu** sentence to; impose (fine) on; **zum Scheitern verurteilt** doomed to failure

die **Ver|urteilung, –en** condemnation; *leg* conviction; sentencing

ver|uzen *coll* make fun of

die **Verve** verve, spirit

vervielfachen multiply

vervielfältigen duplicate; mimeograph; photocopy

die **Vervielfältigung, -en** *vbl noun*; *also* duplication; **der ~s|apparat, -e** duplicator

vervierfachen, sich ~ quadruple

vervollkommnen perfect; **sich ~** perfect oneself

die **Vervollkommnung** perfection (of)

vervollständigen complete; **sich ~** be completed

verwachsen[1]* [–ks–] (*sn*) grow together; heal (over); **~ mit** grow into (job); become closely bound up with; **~ zu** grow into (community *etc*)

verwachsen[2] [–ks–] *p/part*; *also* deformed; overgrown

verwackeln blur (by moving camera)

verwählen: sich ~ dial the wrong number

verwahren keep (in a safe place); **sich ~ gegen** protest against

verwahrlosen (*sn*) fall into disrepair; go to the dogs; run wild; **~ lassen** neglect; **verwahrlost** neglected; dilapidated; unkempt; degenerate

die **Verwahrlosung** *vbl noun*; *also* neglect; dilapidation; degeneration

die **Verwahrung** *vbl noun*; *also* custody; protest; (*+dat*) **in ~ geben** hand over to (s.o.) for safekeeping; **in ~ nehmen** take into safekeeping

verwaisen (*sn*) be orphaned; **verwaist** orphaned; (house) deserted

verwalten administer; manage; hold (office)

der **Verwalter, -** administrator; manager; trustee

die **Verwaltung, -en** administration; management; (municipal *etc*) authorities; *in compds* **~s-** *also* administrative ...

verwandeln change (completely), transform; *theat* change (scene); **~ in** (*acc*) change/convert/turn into; reduce to (pile of rubble); **(einen Elfmeter/die Vorlage** *etc*) **(zum 1:0** *etc*) **~** score (off a penalty/the pass *etc*) (to make it 1-0 *etc*); **sich ~** change (completely), be transformed; *theat* (scene) change; **sich ~ in** (*acc*) change/turn into; turn oneself into; **wie verwandelt sein** be a changed man/woman

die **Verwandlung, -en** *vbl noun*; *also* (complete) change, transformation; conversion; metamorphosis; *theat* scene change

verwandt *p/part*; *also* related (**mit** to); kindred; *ling* cognate; (*following dat*) akin to; **~e Seelen** kindred spirits; **der/die Verwandte** (*decl as adj*) relative

die **Verwandtschaft, -en** relationship; affinity; relatives, relations

verwandtschaftlich (ties *etc*) family

verwanzt bug-ridden

verwarnen warn, caution

die **Verwarnung, -en** *vbl noun*; *also* warning, caution; **gebührenpflichtige ~** fine (for minor traffic offence)

verwaschen faded (through washing); pale, watery; wishy-washy

verwässern water down; dilute

die **Verwässerung, -en** *vbl noun*; *also* dilution

verweben (*p/t* **verwebte**/(*esp in fig senses*) **verwob**, *p/part* **verwebt**/(*esp in fig senses*) **verwoben**) use in weaving; **~ in** (*acc*) weave into; **~ mit** interweave with

verwechseln [–ks–] mix up; **~ mit** mix up with; mistake for; **zum Verwechseln ähnlich** as like as two peas in a pod; (*following dat*) the spitting image of

die **Verwechslung, -en** *vbl noun*; *also* mix-up, confusion; mistake

verwegen audacious, daring; rakish

die **Verwegenheit** audacity, daring

verwehen blow away; obliterate (tracks *etc*); (*v/i sn*: words *etc*) be carried away (by wind *etc*); **„Vom Winde verweht“** 'Gone With the Wind'

verwehren (*+dat*) deny (s.o. access *etc*); bar (s.o.'s view), (*followed by vbl noun*, *eg* **jmdm. die Teilnahme an etw. ~**) bar from (taking part in sth. *etc*); **jmdm. ~ zu ...** bar s.o. from (*+ger*)

verweichlichen make soft; (*v/i sn*) grow soft

verweigern refuse to give/grant/carry out/take (oath) *etc*; (*followed by vbl noun*, *eg* **die Ausführung von ... ~**) refuse to (carry out ... *etc*); (*+dat*) refuse to give/grant; refuse (s.o. access, permission, *etc*); **die Aussage ~** refuse to make a statement/to testify; **(das Hindernis) ~** (horse) refuse

die **Verweigerung, -en** refusal

verweilen stay; linger; **~ bei** dwell on

verweint tear-stained; red with crying; **~ aussehen** look as though one has been crying

der **Verweis, -e** reprimand, rebuke; reference (**auf** *acc* to); (*+dat*) **einen ~ erteilen** reprimand, rebuke

verweisen* (*+dat of pers*) admonish for; **~ an** (*acc*) refer to (person, body) (*also leg* case to appropriate court); **~ auf** (*acc*) refer to (regulation *etc*); *sp* beat into (2nd *etc* place); (*v/i*) refer to; **auf die Plätze ~** *sp* beat; **des Landes/aus dem Lande ~** expel from the country; **vom Platz ~** *sp* send off; **von der Schule ~** expel

verwelken (*sn*) wilt; fade; **verwelkte Schönheit** faded beauty

verweltlichen secularize; (*v/i sn*) become secularized

verwendbar usable

verwenden* use; **~ auf** (*acc*) spend (time) on; put (effort, hard work) into; **gut ~** put to good use; **sich ~ für** use one's influence (**bei** with) on behalf of

die **Verwendung, -en** use; **keine ~ haben für** have no use for; **in ~ nehmen** *Aust* put into use; **in ~ sein** *Aust* be in use || **die ~s|möglichkeit, -en** (possible) use; **der ~s|zweck, -e** purpose
verwerfen* (*see also* **verworfen**) reject; condemn; *leg* dismiss (appeal); quash (verdict); (*v/i*) *vet* abort; **sich ~** warp; *geol* fault
verwerflich reprehensible
die **Verwerfung, -en** rejection; condemnation; *leg* dismissal; quashing; *geol* fault
verwertbar usable
verwerten make use of; utilize
die **Verwertung, -en** use; utilization
verwesen (*sn*) decompose
der **Verweser, -** *hist* administrator
verweslich liable to decompose
die **Verwesung** decomposition
verwetten gamble away
verwichsen [-ks-] *coll* thrash; squander
verwickeln tangle up; **~ in** (*acc*) involve in; embroil in (quarrel); **verwickelt werden in** (*acc*) get mixed up in; **sich ~** become entangled; **sich ~ in** (*acc*) become entangled in; get mixed up in; **verwickelt** *also* complex, intricate
die **Verwicklung, -en** *vbl noun*; *also* involvement; entanglement; complication
verwildern (*sn*) become overgrown; run wild; (domestic animal) become wild; **verwildert** *also* wild; overgrown; unkempt
verwinden* get over (disappointment *etc*)
verwinkelt full of nooks and crannies; twisting
verwirken forfeit
verwirklichen realize (goal *etc*); **sich ~** be realized; fulfil oneself
die **Verwirklichung** realization
verwirren tangle (up); confuse; **sich ~** become tangled (up); (mind, thoughts, *etc*) become confused; **~d** confusing; **verwirrt** tangled; confused
die **Verwirrung, -en** *vbl noun*; *also* confusion; **in ~ bringen** confuse; **in ~ geraten** become confused
verwirtschaften squander (fortune *etc*)
verwischen smudge; blur; cover up (traces); **sich ~** become blurred
verwittern (*sn*) weather; **verwittert** weather-beaten
verwitwet widowed
verwöhnen spoil; (life *etc*) be good to; **sich ~** spoil oneself; **verwöhnt** spoilt; discriminating
verwohnt (furniture *etc*) the worse for wear
verworfen *p/part*; *also* depraved
die **Verworfenheit** depravity
verworren (situation *etc*) confused
die **Verworrenheit** confusion
verwundbar vulnerable
verwunden wound; **der/die Verwundete** (*decl as adj*) casualty; **die Verwundeten** *mil* the wounded
verwunderlich surprising
verwundern (fact *etc*) surprise; **sich ~ über** (*acc*) be surprised at; **es ist nicht zu ~, daß ...** it's not surprising that ...
die **Verwunderung** surprise
die **Verwundung, -en** *vbl noun*; *also* wound
verwunschen enchanted
verwünschen curse; (in fairy-tales) enchant; **verwünscht** confounded
die **Verwünschung, -en** *vbl noun*; *also* curse; enchantment
verwursteln *coll* make a mess of
verwurzelt: ~ in (*dat*) deeply rooted in
verwüsten devastate, ravage
die **Verwüstung, -en** devastation
verzagen (*usu sn*) lose heart; **~ an** (*dat*) despair of
verzagt despondent
die **Verzagtheit** despondency
verzählen: sich ~ miscount
verzahnen interlink; *carp* dovetail; *mech* cut teeth in; **sich ~** become interlinked
verzanken: sich ~ fall out (**mit** with)
verzapfen sell on draught; *carp* mortise; *coll* concoct; **Unsinn ~** *coll* talk rot
verzärteln mollycoddle, pamper
verzaubern bewitch; enchant; **~ in** (*acc*) turn into (swan, frog, *etc*)
die **Verzauberung, -en** bewitchment; enchantment
verzehnfachen, sich ~ increase tenfold
der **Verzehr** consumption
verzehren consume; **sich ~ nach** pine for; **sich vor Gram ~** eat one's heart out; **~d** (passion *etc*) consuming
verzeichnen draw wrong, *liter* misrepresent; note; record; show (profit, loss); *comm* quote; **in einer Liste ~** list; **zu ~ haben** have notched up (success, victory); have sustained (defeat); **es sind ... Todesfälle zu ~** there have been ... fatalities
sich ~ make a mistake in drawing
das **Verzeichnis, -se** list; register; index; catalogue
verzeigen *Swiss* report (**bei** to)
verzeihen* forgive; (+*dat*) forgive (s.o.'s ...), forgive for; **~ Sie!** excuse me!; **~ Sie die Störung!** sorry to disturb you; **nicht zu ~** unforgivable
verzeihlich forgivable; pardonable
die **Verzeihung** forgiveness; **~!** sorry!; **um ~ bitten** apologize to; **ich bitte (Sie) tausendmal um ~** a thousand apologies
verzerren distort; contort; pull (muscle); **sich ~** become distorted/contorted; **verzerrt darstellen** give a distorted picture of; **-verzerrt** contorted with ...

^die^ **Verzerrung, –en** *vbl noun*; *also* distortion; contortion

verzetteln fritter away; dissipate; card-index; **sich ~** dissipate one's energies; **sich ~ in** (*dat*) get bogged down in

^der^ **Verzicht, –e** renunciation (**auf** *acc* of); sacrifice (of); **~ auf** (*acc*) *also* giving up, doing without; **~ leisten/üben = verzichten; unter ~ auf** (*acc*) renouncing; giving up || **die ~erklärung, –en** disclaimer; waiver

verzichten: ~ auf (*acc*) do/go without; dispense with; abstain from; give up; renounce; waive

verziehen* twist (one's lips *etc*) (**zu** into); pull out of shape; spoil (child); *hort* thin out; (*v/i sn*) move (house); **das Gesicht ~** pull a face; **ohne eine Miene zu ~** without turning a hair; **„verzogen"** 'gone away'

sich ~ go out of shape; (wood) warp; (s.o.'s mouth *etc*) twist (**zu** into); (clouds *etc*) disperse; (pain *etc*) pass; *coll* slip away

verzieren decorate; embellish

^die^ **Verzierung, –en** decoration; embellishment; *mus* ornament, grace-note

verzinken galvanize

verzinnen tin; tin-plate

verzinsen pay interest on; **mit ... % verzinst** yielding interest at ... %; **sich (mit ... %) ~** yield (... %) interest

verzinslich yielding interest

^die^ **Verzinsung** payment of interest; interest

verzögern delay; slow down; **sich ~** be delayed

^die^ **Verzögerung, –en** *vbl noun*; *also* delay; **die ~s|taktik** delaying tactics

verzollen pay duty on; **haben Sie etwas zu ~?** have you anything to declare?

verzottelt shaggy

verzückt ecstatic

^die^ **Verzückung, –en** ecstasy; **in ~ geraten** go into ecstasies (**wegen** over)

^der^ **Verzug** delay; **im ~** (danger) imminent; **+mit** behind with; **in ~ geraten mit** fall behind with; **ohne ~** without delay

verzwackt *coll* tricky

verzweifeln (*sn*) despair (**an** *dat* of); **verzweifelt** desperate; (glance *etc*) despairing; **... ist zum Verzweifeln!** ... is enough to make one despair!

^die^ **Verzweiflung** despair; **aus/in/vor ~** in desperation; **zur ~ bringen** drive to despair || **die ~s|tat, –en** act of desperation

verzweigen: sich ~ branch; **verzweigt** with many branches; ramified

verzwickt *coll* tricky

^die^ **Vesper** [f–], **–n** vespers; *SGer* (*also* **das,** *pl* **–**) afternoon snack

vespern [f–] *SGer* have an afternoon snack

^das^ **Vestibül, –e** vestibule

^der^ **Vesuv** (*gen* **–(s)**) Vesuvius

^der^ **Veteran, –en** (*wk masc*) veteran (*also mil*); veteran/vintage car

veterinär veterinary; **die V~medizin** veterinary medicine

^das^ **Veto, –s, sein ~ einlegen gegen** veto || **das ~recht** (power of) veto

^die^ **Vettel, –n** old hag

^der^ **Vetter, –n** cousin; **die ~n|wirtschaft** nepotism, 'jobs for the boys'

Vexier–: das ~bild, –er picture-puzzle; **der ~spiegel, –** distorting mirror

Vf. = Verfasser

^die^ **V-Form, –en** V-shape; **V-förmig** V-shaped

vgl. (**= vergleiche**) cf.

v. H. (**= vom Hundert**) per cent

^der^ **Viadukt, –e** viaduct

^die^ **Vibration, –en** vibration

vibrieren vibrate

Video– video (cassette, recording, tape, *etc*)

^das^ **Viech, –er** *coll* creature, beast

^das^ **Vieh** livestock; cattle; *coll* creature, beast; *vulg* brute, beast; **der ~bestand** livestock; **der ~händler, –** cattle-dealer; **der ~wagen, –** cattle truck, stock car *US*; **das ~zeug** *coll* animals, creatures; **die ~zucht** stock/cattle-breeding; **der ~züchter, –** stock/cattle-breeder

viehisch bestial, brutish

viel (*comp* **mehr**, *superl* **meist../am meisten**) much; a great deal (of), a lot (of); (*adv*) much, a lot; **der/die/das ~e ...,** *pl* **die ~en ...** all this/that ..., *pl* all these/those ...; **~e** *pl* many, a lot (of); many people; **~es** much, a great deal, a lot; many things; (**unheimlich** *etc*) **~** a (tremendous *etc*) amount (of); **~** (**Neues** *etc*) many (new *etc*) things; **in ~em** in many respects; **um ~es (reicher** *etc*) much (richer *etc*)

viel– much–; many–; multi–; poly–;

~deutig ambiguous; **die V~deutigkeit** ambiguity; **~diskutiert** much-discussed; **das V~eck, –e** polygon; **die V~ehe** polygamy; **~fach** multiple; multifarious; (*adv*) many times; in many ways; *coll* frequently (**~facher Millionär** multimillionare; **auf ~fache Weise** in many different ways; **auf ~fachen Wunsch** by popular request; **das V~fache** (*decl as adj*) *math* multiple; **kleinstes gemeinsames V~faches** lowest common multiple; **ein V~faches (der Menge** *etc*) many times (the amount *etc*); **um ein V~faches (schöner** *etc*) (lovelier *etc*) by far); **die V~falt** variety; diversity; **~fältig** various, diverse; multifarious; **~farbig,** *Aust* **~färbig** multicoloured; **der V~flächner, –** polyhedron; **der V~fraß, –e** glutton; **~geliebt** much-loved; **~geprüft** sorely-tried; **~gereist** much-travelled; **~gerühmt** much-vaunted;

~geschmäht much-maligned; **~gestaltig** polymorphic, polymorphous; varied; **die V~götterei** polytheism; **~köpfig** many-headed; (family, crowd, *etc*) large; **~mals** (**danke v.!** many thanks!; **ich bitte v. um Entschuldigung!** I do apologize!; **er läßt v. grüßen** he sends his kindest regards); **die V~männerei** polyandry; **~mehr** rather; **~sagend** (glance *etc*) meaningful; **~schichtig** many-layered; many-faceted, complex; **die V~schichtigkeit** complexity; **~seitig** many-sided; versatile; (interests *etc*) varied; (education) all-round (**auf ~seitigen Wunsch** by popular request; **~ anwendbar/interessiert sein** have many uses/varied interests); **die V~seitigkeit** many-sidedness; versatility; varied/all-round nature; **~silbig** polysyllabic; **~sprachig** polyglot; multilingual; **~stimmig** many-voiced; **~umstritten** highly controversial; **~umworben** much-sought-after; **~verheißend** = **~versprechend** promising; **der V~völker|staat, –en** multinational state; **die V~weiberei** polygamy; **die V~zahl** multiplicity; **~zellig** multicellular; **~zitiert** oft-quoted; **V~zweck–** multi-purpose …

vieler–: ~lei (*indecl*) all sorts of (things); **~orts** in many places

vielleicht [fi–] perhaps; by any chance; (*as emotive particle*: *intensifying*) *coll* … I *must* say! (*eg* **das ist ~ originell!** that *is* original, I *must* say!); … I can tell you!; what …!, some (= impressive), *or conveyed by inversion* (*eg* **das war ~ ein Rennen!** what a race!, that was some race!, **da hab' ich ~ gelacht!** did I laugh!); (*in question*) really (*eg* **ist das ~ dein Ernst?** are you really serious?); (*expressing command*) kindly (*eg* **~ hältst du mal den Mund!** would you kindly shut up!); **~, daß …** it could be that …

vier four; **alle ~e von sich strecken** *coll* stretch out; give up the ghost; **auf allen ~en** *coll* on all fours; **die Vier, –en** four (*also* = *fourth grade* – **'ausreichend'** – *in marking scale*) || **der V~beiner, –** *coll* four-legged friend; **~beinig** four-legged; **das V~eck, –e** quadrangle; square; **~eckig** quadrangular; square; **~fach** fourfold, quadruple; **der V~füßer, –** quadruped; **~füßig** four-legged; **das V~gespann, –e** four-in-hand; **~händig** *mus* four-handed (**v. spielen** play a duet); **der/das V~kant, –e** *tech* square; **V~mächte–** four-power …; **~mal** four times; **V~rad–** four-wheel …; **~schrötig** burly; **~seitig** four-sided; quadripartite; four-page; **der V~sitzer, –** four-seater; **der V~spänner, –** four-in-hand; **~spännig** four-horse (**v. fahren** drive a four-in-hand); **~stimmig** for four voices; **der V~takt|motor, –en** four-stroke engine; **~teilen** (*insep*) *hist* quarter; **~türig** four-door; **der V~viertel|takt** [–'fɪr–] four-four time; **der V~wald|stätter See** Lake of Lucerne

der **Vierer, –** *row* four; *in compds* … of four; **der ~bob, –s** four-man bob

der **Vierling, –e** quadruplet

viert: zu ~ (*see* **zu** 1 (*i*)); **viert..** fourth

viertel [–ɪ–]: **ein ~ …** a quarter of a …

das **Viertel** [–ɪ–], **–** quarter (*also* = district; *and used in time phrases*, *eg* **~ nach/vor acht** a quarter past/to eight)

Viertel– quarter of a …; **das ~finale, –** quarter-finals; **das ~jahr, –e** quarter (of year); **~jahres–** quarterly …; **die ~jahres|schrift, –en** quarterly; **v~jährig** three-month-old; three months'; **v~jährlich** quarterly; **die ~note, –n** crotchet, quarter note *US*; **die ~stunde, –n** quarter of an hour; **v~stündig** quarter-hour; **v~stündlich** quarter-hourly; (*adv*) every quarter of an hour, quarter-hourly; **der ~ton, ¨e** quarter-tone

vierteln [–ɪ–] quarter

viertens fourthly

vierzehn [–ɪ–] fourteen; **~ Tage** two weeks, a fortnight

vierzehnt.., das Vierzehntel, – fourteenth

vierzig [–ɪ–] forty; **die V~stunden|woche** forty-hour week

vierziger: die ~ Jahre the forties; **der Vierziger, –** man in his forties; (*pl*) forties

vierzigst.., das Vierzigstel, – fortieth

Vietnam [viɛt–] Vietnam

der **Vietnamese** [viɛt–], **–n** (*wk masc*) Vietnamese

vietnamesisch [viɛt–], (*language*) **V~** Vietnamese

der **Vikar, –e** curate

Viktoria Victoria

viktorianisch Victorian

die **Villa, –(ll)en** villa

Villen–: das ~viertel, – (fashionable) residential area; **der ~vor|ort, –e** (fashionable) residential suburb

die **Viola, –(l)en** viola

violett purple; violet

Violin– violin …; **das ~konzert, –e** violin concerto; **der ~schlüssel, –** treble clef

die **Violine, –n** violin

der **Violinist, –en** (*wk masc*) violinist

das **Violoncello** [–lɔntʃ–], **–(ll)i** violoncello

die **Viper, –n** viper

Viren *pl of* **Virus**

viril virile

virtuell potential; *comput*, *phys* virtual

virtuos masterly; virtuoso; **~ spielen** give a virtuoso performance

der **Virtuose, –n** (*wk masc*) virtuoso

die **Virtuosität** virtuosity
virulent virulent
die **Virulenz** virulence
der **Virus, -(r)en** (*also* **das**) virus
Visa *pl of* **Visum**
die **Visage** [-ʒə], **-n** *vulg* 'mug'
der **Visagist** [-ʒ-], **-en** (*wk masc*) make-up artist
vis-à-vis [viza'viː] (+*dat*, *often following the noun*) *dated* opposite
das **Visavis** [viza'viː] (*gen* – [-(s)]), – [-s] *dated* person opposite
Visen *pl of* **Visum**
das **Visier, -e** visor; (gun) sight
visieren take aim (**auf** *acc* **at**)
die **Vision, -en** vision
visionär visionary
Visit-: die ~karte, -n *Aust* visiting-card
die **Visitation, -en** search; visitation
die **Visite, -n** (doctor's) round (in hospital); **~ machen** do one's round || **die ~n\|karte, -n** visiting-card
visitieren search; inspect
visuell visual
das **Visum, -(s)a/-(s)en** visa; **der ~zwang** obligation to hold a visa
vital lively, full of vitality; vital
die **Vitalität** vitality
das **Vitamin, -e** vitamin; **v~arm** poor in vitamins; **v~haltig,** *Aust* **v~hältig** containing vitamins; **der ~mangel** vitamin deficiency; **v~reich** rich in vitamins; **der ~stoß, ⸗e** massive dose of vitamins
die **Vitrine, -n** show-case; glass cabinet
die **Vivisektion, -en** vivisection
vivisezieren vivisect
Vize- ['fiːtsə-] vice-; **der ~kanzler,** – vice-chancellor; **der ~könig, -e** viceroy
v. J. = vorigen Jahres
Vjs. = Vierteljahresschrift
das **Vlies, -e** fleece
v. M. (= **vorigen Monats**) ult.
der **V-Mann, ⸗er/V-Leute** (= **Verbindungsmann**) contact
der **Vogel,** *pl* **Vögel** bird; **~ Strauß** ostrich; **den ~ abschießen** surpass everyone; **einen ~ haben** *coll* be cuckoo; (+*dat*) **den ~ zeigen** *coll* tap one's forehead (indicating to s.o. that his/her head needs examining) || **das ~bauer,** – birdcage; **der ~beer\|baum, ⸗e** mountain ash; **das ~ei, -er** bird's egg; **die ~flug\|linie** (*direct road/rail route Hamburg–Fehmarn–Copenhagen using ferry between Puttgarden and Rødby Havn*); **v~frei** fair game; *hist* outlawed (**für v. erklären** outlaw); **das ~futter** bird food; birdseed; **das ~haus, ⸗er** aviary; **die ~kunde** ornithology; **der ~liebhaber,** – bird-fancier; **das ~nest, -er** bird's nest (**~nester ausnehmen** go bird's-nesting); **die ~perspektive = die ~schau** bird's-eye view (**aus der V. betrachten** have a bird's-eye view of; **... aus der V.** a bird's-eye view of ...); **die ~scheuche, -n** scarecrow; **das ~schutz\|gebiet, -e** bird sanctuary; **die ~-Strauß-Politik** *approx* = head-in-the-sand attitude (**V. treiben** bury one's head in the sand); **die ~warte, -n** ornithological station; **der ~zug, ⸗e** migration of birds
vögeln *vulg* 'screw'
die **Vogesen** [v-] *pl* the Vosges
der **Vogt** [foːkt], **⸗e** *hist* governor; steward
die **Vokabel, -n** word (*esp* in foreign language); (*pl*) vocabulary
das **Vokabular, -e** vocabulary
vokal *mus* vocal
der **Vokal, -e** vowel
vokalisch vocalic
der **Vokativ, -e** vocative
der **Volant** [-'lãː], **-s** *dressm* flounce; *mot* steering-wheel
die **Voliere** [-'li̯eːrə, -ɛː-], **-n** aviary
das **Volk, ⸗er** people; nation; *zool* colony; *coll* (*esp with adj*) people, folk; crowd; **alles ~** everbody; **viel ~(s)** lots of people; **unters ~ bringen** spread (rumour *etc*); spend || **v~reich** populous
Völker- ... of nations; international ...; **der ~bund** the League of Nations; **die ~kunde** ethnology; **der ~kundler,** – ethnologist; **v~kundlich** ethnological; **der ~mord** genocide; **das ~recht** international law; **v~rechtlich** in/under international law; **die ~schlacht** the Battle of the Nations; **die ~wanderung, -en** *hist* migration of peoples; *coll* mass migration/exodus
die **Völkerschaft, -en** people (= ethnic community *as opposed to* nation)
völkisch *esp Nazi* (*with racial overtones, referring to Germany*) national
Volks- ... of the people; people's ...; national ...; popular ...; public ...; ethnic ...; folk ...; (*prefixed to name of country*, *eg* **~polen** *for* **~republik Polen**) *esp EGer* People's Republic of ...

die ~abstimmung, -en plebiscite; **die (Nationale) ~armee** the People's Army (*E. German armed forces*); **der ~armist, -en** (*wk masc*) soldier in the People's Army; **die ~ausgabe, -n** popular edition; **die ~befragung, -en** referendum; **das ~begehren,** – petition for a referendum; **der ~brauch, ⸗e** popular custom; **der ~charakter, -e** national character; **die ~demokratie, -n** people's democracy; **der/die ~deutsche** (*decl as adj*) ethnic German (*person of German origin but other nationality resident outside the 1937 frontiers of Germany and Austria*); **v~eigen** *EGer* state-owned; **das ~eigentum** *EGer* national property; **das ~empfinden** popular sentiment; **der ~entscheid, –e** plebiscite; **die ~etymologie** folk etymology; **das ~fest, –e** public festival; fair; **die ~front, –en** popular front; **die ~gemeinschaft** *Nazi* the national community; **der ~gerichts|hof** the People's Court (*notorious special court in Nazi Germany set up to prosecute those offering resistance to the régime*); **der ~glaube** (*like* **Glaube**) popular belief; **die ~gruppe, –n** ethnic minority; **die ~hoch|schule, –n** adult education (classes); **die ~kammer** (East German) National Assembly; **der ~korrespondent, –en** (*wk masc*) *EGer* people's correspondent (*worker who is also a contributor to radio or the press*); **die ~kunde** folklore; **der ~kundler, –** folklorist; **v~kundlich** folkloristic; **das ~lied, –er** folk-song; **das ~märchen, –** folk-tale; **die ~menge, –n** crowd; **~mund** (**im V.** in the vernacular); **die ~musik** folk-music; **die ~polizei** (East German) People's Police; **der ~polizist, –en** (*wk masc*) member of the People's Police; **~reden** *coll* (**V. halten** speechify); **die ~republik, –en** people's republic (*eg* **V. China** People's Republic of China); **die ~schule, –n** (*hist or Aust: state school incorporating primary and secondary levels, now known in W. Germany as* Grundschule *and* Hauptschule *respectively*); **die ~seuche, –n** epidemic; **der ~stamm, ⸚e** tribe; **der ~tanz, ⸚e** folk-dance; **die ~tracht, –en** national costume; **der ~trauer|tag, –e** day of national mourning; **die ~versammlung, –en** national assembly; public meeting; **die ~vertretung, –en** parliament; **der ~wirt, –e** (political) economist; **die ~wirtschaft, –en** economics; economy (of specific country); **der ~wirtschaftler, –** (political) economist; **v~wirtschaftlich** economic; **die ~wirtschafts|lehre** economics; **das ~wohl** public weal; **die ~zählung, –en** census

das **Volkstum** national traditions

volkstümlich popular; traditional; folk

die **Volkstümlichkeit** popularity; popular nature

voll full; (cheeks) chubby; (hair) thick; (colour) rich, (sound, voice) rich, full; complete; (*eg* **~e zehn Minuten**) fully (ten minutes *etc*); *coll* 'tight'; (*adv*) fully; completely; (pay) in full; **–voll** '*full of ...*', *often* –ful (*eg* **vorwurfs~** reproachful, **hoffnungs~** hopeful, **wirkungs~** effective, **wert~** valuable); *forming nouns* (*pl* **–**) –ful (*eg* **der Mund~** mouthful, **die Hand~** handful);

~(er) ..., ~ (*+gen, when noun is preceded by adj*), **~ mit/von ...** full of ...; **in ~er Fahrt** at full speed; **in ~er Höhe** (pay) in full; **in ~em Maße** fully; **mit ~em Mund** with one's mouth full; **bei ~em Tageslicht** in broad daylight; **~er werden** fill out;

nicht für ~ nehmen not take seriously; **~ und ganz** completely, fully; **aus dem ~en leben** live in lavish style; **aus dem ~en schöpfen** draw on plentiful resources

voll– full ...; fully ...;

~auf fully (**v. genug** quite enough; **v. zu tun haben** have one's hands full); **vollaufen*** (*sep*; *sn*) fill up (**v. lassen** fill (up); **sich v. lassen** *coll* get tanked up); **~automatisch** fully automatic; **die V~beschäftigung** full employment; **V~besitz** (**im V.** (*+gen*) in full possession of); **das V~blut** thoroughbred (horse); **V~blut–** thoroughbred ...; high-powered (politician *etc*); **der V~blüter, –** thoroughbred (horse); **~blütig** thoroughbred; full-blooded; **~bringen*** (*insep*) accomplish; perform; **die V~bringung** accomplishment; performance; **~busig** full-bosomed; **der V~dampf** full steam (**mit V.** at full steam; *coll* flat out; **(mit) V. voraus!** full steam ahead!); **~enden** (*insep*) complete (**sich v.** come to an end; be completed; (love) be fulfilled; **~endet** *also* perfect; consummate; **vor ~endete Tatsachen stellen** present with a fait accompli); **die V~endung** completion; perfection (**mit V.** (*+gen*) on completion of); **~entwickelt** fully-developed; **~essen*** (*sep*): **sich v.** *coll* gorge oneself; **~fett** (cheese) full-fat; **~fressen*** (*sep*): **sich v.** *coll* stuff oneself; **~führen** (*insep*) perform; create (din *etc*); **~füllen** (*sep*) fill up; **V~gas** (**V. geben** open right up; **mit V.** at full throttle; *coll* flat out); **V~gefühl** (**im V.** (*+gen*) fully conscious of); **~gießen*** (*sep*) fill up; **~gültig** fully valid; conclusive; **der V~idiot, –en** (*wk masc*) *coll* prize idiot; **~jährig** of age (**v. werden** come of age); **die V~jährigkeit** majority; **~kasko|versichert** (**v. sein** have comprehensive insurance); **die V~kasko|versicherung** comprehensive insurance; **~klimatisiert** fully air-conditioned; **~kommen** perfect; complete (*eg* **sein Glück war v.** his happiness was complete); **(vollkommen)** (agreement *etc*) complete; **die V~kommenheit** perfection; **das V~korn|brot** wholemeal bread, whole-wheat bread *US*; **~machen** (*sep*) fill (up); make up (number) (**um das Unglück ~zumachen** to crown all); **die V~macht, –en** authority (to act on s.o.'s behalf); power of attorney; letter of attorney (**unbeschränkte V~machten** plenary powers; (*+dat*) **die V. erteilen zu ...** authorize (s.o.) to ...); **der V~matrose, –n** (*wk masc*) able seaman; **die V~milch** whole milk; **die V~milch|schokolade** milk chocolate; **der**

V~mond full moon; **~mundig** full-bodied; **die V~narkose, -n** general anaesthetic; **~packen** (*sep*) pack full; **die V~pension** full board; **~pfropfen** (*sep*) cram full; **~saufen*** (*sep*): **sich v.** *vulg* get tanked up; **~saugen** (*see* **saugen;** *sep*): **sich v.** become saturated; **~schlagen*** (*sep*) *coll* (**sich** *dat* **den Bauch v.** stuff oneself); **~schlank** with a fuller figure; **~schreiben*** (*sep*) fill (with writing); **~ständig** complete; full; **die V~ständigkeit** completeness; **~stopfen** (*sep*) cram full; **~strecken** (*insep*) *leg* carry out; execute; *footb* score from; **der V~strecker, -** executor; **die V~streckung, -en** *vbl noun*; *also* execution; **der V~streckungs|befehl, -e** writ of execution; **~tanken** (*sep*) (*also v/i*) fill up (with fuel); **~tönend** resonant; **der V~treffer, -** direct hit; smash hit; **die V~versammlung, -en** plenary session; (*of U.N.*) General Assembly; **der V~waise, -n** (*wk masc*) orphan (who has lost both parents); **~wertig** of full value; adequate; (member of society *etc*) full; **~zählig** complete; all present; (*adv*) in full strength; **~ziehen*** (*insep*) execute; carry out; consummate (marriage) (**sich v.** take place; **~ziehende Gewalt** executive); **die V~ziehung = der V~zug** execution; carrying out; consummation

das **Völle|gefühl** (unpleasant) feeling of fullness

vollends [-ɛnts] completely

voller *see* **voll**

die **Völlerei** gluttony

der **Volley|ball** ['vɔlibal] volleyball

völlig complete; total; (*adv*) completely; absolutely; quite; **das genügt ~** that's quite sufficient

der **Volontär, -e** *comm, journ* trainee

volontieren *comm, journ* undergo training

das **Volt, -** volt

die **Volte, -n** *cards* sleight of hand; *equest, fenc* volte

das **Volumen, -/Volumina** volume

voluminös voluminous

vom [-ɔ-] = **von dem**

von [-ɔ-] (+*dat*) (*a*) (*indicating direction, distance, source, etc or with reference to time*) from; (*separation, removal*) from; off;

(*b*) (*indicating cause etc*) (tired *etc*) from; (covered *etc*) with; (*with passive – indicating agent – or expressing authorship etc*) by (*eg* **~ einem Hund gebissen werden** be bitten by a dog; **das Stück ist ~ Shakespeare** the play is by S., **ein Bild ~ Tizian** a picture by Titian); (*indicating means*) (buy, pay for) out of; (live) on;

(*c*) (talk, write, *etc*) about;

(*d*) (*in var contexts*) of (*as when ~ is used in place of the genitive, eg* **der Geruch ~ Tomaten** the smell of tomatoes, **der Export ~ Kohle** the export of coal, **die Hauptstadt ~ Liechtenstein** the capital of L.; *or to indicate a quality, eg* **eine Frau ~ großer Schönheit** a woman of great beauty, **ein Edelstein ~ großem Wert** a gem of great value, *also in phrases of the type* **ein Riese ~ einem Mann** a giant of a man; *or = 'on the part of', eg* **das war nett ~ ihr** that was nice of her);

(*e*) (*partitive use*) of (*eg* **einige ~ ihnen** some of them, **kein Wort ~ dem, was du sagst** not one word of what you say); out of (*eg* **in drei ~ zehn Fällen** in three cases out of ten); some of (*eg* **er hat ~ der Milch getrunken** he's drunk some of the milk);

(*f*) *as part of s.o.'s name, functions like French* de *as the nobiliary particle* (*eg* **J.W. ~ Goethe**);

(*g*) **~ Beruf/Geburt/Natur** by profession *or* trade/birth/nature; **~ ganzem Herzen** with all one's heart

~ ... ab/an (*time*) from (... onwards); (price) from; **~ Anfang an** from the start; **~ da an** from then on; **~ heute an** from today; **~ Kindheit an** from (one's) childhood; **~ nun an** from now on

~ klein auf from childhood

~ ... aus from (position, standpoint, *etc*); **~ 'mir aus, ~ 'sich aus** (*see* **aus**)

~ ... bis ... from ... to/until ...

~ ... her from (place, time); in terms of, from the point of view of; *or expressed by adv* (*eg* **vom Instinkt her** instinctively); **~ weit her** from a long way off

~ neuem (*see* **neu**)

~ ungefähr (*see* **ungefähr**)

~ ... weg (*distance*) from

~ wegen, ~ ... wegen (*see* **wegen**)

~ ... zu ... from ... to ...

voneinander from/of *etc** one another (**see* **von**); **~gehen*** (*sep; sn*) part (company)

vonnöten necessary

vonstatten: ~ gehen take place; pass off; go (well *etc*)

der **Vopo** [f-], **-s** *EGer* = **Volkspolizist**

vor 1 *prep* (+*acc, indicating direction*) in front of; outside;

2 *prep* (+*dat*) (*a*) (*indicating place*) in front of; before; (bow, make a speech) to; ahead of; off (coast, Norway, *etc*); outside; at (door); against (background);

(*b*) (*indicating time, sequence*) before; (... minutes) to; ... ago (*eg* **~ drei Minuten** three minutes ago);

(*c*) (*indicating cause*) for (joy *etc*); with (envy, pain, *etc*);

(*d*) (respect) for; (fear) of; (warn)

against; (hide, run away, protect, *etc*) from;

3 *adv* (*in command*): **... ~!** ... step forward!

~ allem = ~ allen Dingen above all

bis ~ (*acc*) up to

~ ... (*dat*) **her** in front of

~ sich: ~ sich *dat* **haben** have in front of/ahead of one; **~ sich** *dat* **her** along (in front of one); **~ sich** *acc* **hin** (hum *etc*) to oneself

---

vor–[1] *sep pref – general senses*:

(*i*) ... forward (*eg* **sich ~neigen** bend forward);

(*ii*) ... in front (of sth.) (*eg* **~bauen** build on in front (of sth.)); *cf* **~spannen** harness;

(*iii*) *indicates protrusion* (*eg* **~stehen** stick out, protrude);

(*iv*) ... in advance, pre– (*eg* **~bestellen** order/reserve in advance, **~lochen** prepunch);

(*v*) (+*dat*) ... to ... (*eg* **jmdm. etw. ~summen** hum sth. to s.o.)

---

vor–[2] (*prefixed to adj*) pre– (*eg* **~klassisch** pre-classical); **Vor–** pre–; fore–; preliminary ...; previous ...

vor|ab to start with

Vor|abend: am ~ the evening before; (+*gen*) on the eve of

die **Vor|ahnung, –en** presentiment

die **Vor|alpen** *pl* foothills of the Alps

voran (out) in front; onwards; (*following dat*) ahead of

voran– *sep pref* ... (on) ahead, ... in front

vorangegangen *p/part*; *also* previous; preceding

vorangehen* (*see also* **vorangegangen**) (*sn*) go in front; lead the way; (work *etc*) make headway; (+*dat*) go ahead of; precede; **mit gutem Beispiel ~** set a good example; **~d** *also* preceding; **im ~den** above

vorankommen* (*sn*) make headway; get ahead

die **Vor|anmeldung, –en** appointment; advance booking; **Gespräch mit ~** *tel* personal call

der **Vor|anschlag, ⸚e** estimate

voranschreiten* (*sn*) stride ahead (*dat* of); progress

voranstellen (+*dat*) put in front of; prefix to

vorantreiben* push ahead with

die **Vor|anzeige, –n** advance notice; *cin* trailer

die **Vor|arbeit, –en** preparatory work, groundwork

vor|arbeiten (*also v/i*) work in advance; (*v/i*, +*dat*) do preparatory work for; pave the way for; **sich ~** work one's way forward; work one's way up

der **Vor|arbeiter, –** foreman

vorauf = voran, voraus

voraus ahead, in front; (*following dat*) ahead of; **seiner Zeit ~** ahead of one's time; **im voraus** in advance

voraus– *sep pref* ... on ahead (*dat* of); ... in advance; **Voraus–** advance ...

voraus|ahnen anticipate

vorausfahren* (*sn*) go/drive on ahead

vorausgehen* (*sn*) go on ahead; (+*dat*) go on ahead of; precede; **~d** preceding; **im ~den** above

vorausgesetzt *p/part*; **~, (daß) ...** provided (that) ...

voraushaben* (+*dat*) have the advantage over (s.o., sth.) of

vorausreisen (*sn*) travel ahead (*dat* of)

die **Voraussage, –n** prediction; forecast

voraussagen predict; forecast

vorausschicken send on ahead; say by way of introduction; (+*dat*) send on ahead of; preface (speech) with

voraussehen* foresee

voraussetzen (*see also* **vorausgesetzt**) assume, presuppose; take for granted

die **Voraussetzung, –en** prerequisite; requirement; assumption, premise; **unter der ~, daß ...** provided that ..., on condition that ...

die **Voraussicht** foresight; anticipation; **aller ~ nach** in all probability

voraussichtlich expected; (*adv*) probably; *or expressed by* ... is *etc* expected to ...

die **Vorauszahlung, –en** advance payment

der **Vorbau, –ten** projecting structure, *esp* porch; **einen großen ~ haben** *joc* be well-stacked

vorbauen build on (in front); (+*dat*) build onto the front of; (*v/i*) take precautions; (+*dat*) guard against

Vorbedacht: mit ~ on purpose

die **Vorbedeutung, –en** omen

die **Vorbedingung, –en** precondition

der **Vorbehalt, –e** reservation; proviso; **innerer ~** mental reservation; **ohne ~** without reservation || **v~los** unreserved; (*adv*) unreservedly, without reservation

vorbehalten*: sich *dat* **... ~** reserve (right *etc*); **es bleibt ihm vorbehalten zu ...** it is left to him to ...; **„Änderungen vorbehalten“** ‘subject to alteration’

vorbehaltlich (+*gen*) subject to

vorbei past; over, finished; **an ...** (*dat*) **~** past; **es ist ~ mit ...** ... is all over; it's all up with ...

---

vorbei– *sep pref – general senses*:

(*i*) ... past (*eg* **~fahren** drive past); *with* **an** (*dat*) = ... past (s.o., sth.); *with modal auxiliary eg* **~müssen** = get past (*eg* **ich muß vorbei** I must get past);

(*ii*) *indicates failure* (*eg* **~raten** guess

wrong, **an den Schülern ~lehren** fail to get through to one's pupils, **diese Autoren schreiben an den wahren Bedürfnissen ihres Publikums vorbei** these authors fail to satisfy the real needs of their readers); *see also* **~benehmen, ~reden**

---

vorbeibenehmen*: sich ~ *coll* misbehave
vorbeifahren* (*sn*), **~ an** (*dat*) drive past; **~ bei** *coll* drop in on
vorbeiführen: ~ an (*dat*) lead past; take past; (*v/i*) pass by; bypass
vorbeigehen* (*sn*) (time, pain, *etc*) pass; **~ an** (*dat*) pass, go past; miss (target); ignore, disregard; bypass; pass by; **an der Wirklichkeit ~** be unrealistic; **~ bei** *coll* drop in on/at; **im Vorbeigehen** on one's way past; in passing
der **Vorbeigehende** (*fem* **die ~**) (*decl as adj*) passer-by
vorbeikommen* (*sn*) come past; go past; *coll* drop in; **~ an** (*dat*) go past; get past; avoid; **~ bei** *coll* drop in on; **man kommt an der Tatsache nicht vorbei, daß ...** one can't get away from the fact that ...
vorbeikönnen*: nicht ~ an (*dat*) be unable to get past; be unable to ignore
vorbeilassen* let (s.o., sth.) pass
vorbeileben: ~ an (*dat*) ignore; **aneinander ~** lead separate lives
der **Vorbeimarsch, ⸚e** march-past
vorbeimarschieren (*sn*), **~ an** (*dat*) march past
vorbeireden: ~ an (*dat*) talk round (subject); **aneinander ~** talk at cross-purposes
vorbeischauen *coll* drop in (**bei** on)
vorbeischießen* shoot wide; (*sn*) shoot past
vorbeiziehen* (*sn*), **~ an** (*dat*) file past; march past
vorbelastet: erblich ~ sein be afflicted with a hereditary taint; **ich bin** *etc* **erblich ~** it runs in the family
die **Vorbemerkung, -en** preliminary remark; prefatory note
vorbereiten prepare (**auf** *acc* for); **sich ~** prepare (oneself) (**auf** *acc* for); be in the offing; **~d** preparatory
die **Vorbereitung, -en** preparation; *in compds* **~s-** preparatory ...
die **Vorbesprechung, -en** preliminary discussion
vorbestellen order in advance; book, reserve
die **Vorbestellung, -en** advance order; booking, reservation
vorbestraft: ~ sein have a (criminal) record; **zweimal** *etc* **~ sein** have two *etc* previous convictions
vorbeten (+*dat*) *coll* recite at great length to; (*v/i*) lead the prayer
der **Vorbeter, -** prayer-leader
vorbeugen bend (one's body *etc*) forward; (*v/i*, +*dat*) prevent; forestall; **sich ~** lean forward; **~d** preventive
die **Vorbeugung** prevention; *in compds* **~s-** preventive ...
das **Vorbild, -er** model; example; **sich** *dat* **... zum ~ nehmen** model oneself on
vorbilden train; form (at an early stage)
vorbildlich exemplary; model
die **Vorbildung** (previous) training
vorbinden* put on (apron *etc*)
der **Vorbote, -n** (*wk masc*) harbinger
vorbringen* express, state; produce, bring forward (evidence *etc*); raise (objection); offer (excuse); put forward (reason *etc*); *coll* bring forward
die **Vorbühne, -n** forestage, apron
vorchristlich [-kr-] pre-Christian
das **Vordach, ⸚er** canopy (over door); awning
vordatieren postdate
vordem in former times
vorder.. (*see also* **vorderst..**) front; **der V~e Orient** the Near East
Vorder- front ...; **~asien** the Near East; **der ~gaumen|laut, -e** palatal; **der ~grund** foreground (**im V. stehen** be in the foreground; be to the fore; (person) be in the limelight; **sich in den V. drängen/schieben/spielen** push oneself forward; **in den V. stellen** bring into prominence; **in den V. treten** come to the fore); **v~gründig** superficial; obvious; (*adv*) *also* outwardly; **~indien** the Indian subcontinent; **der ~mann, ⸚er** person in front (**auf V. bringen** *coll* lick into shape; get ship-shape); **das ~rad, ⸚er** front wheel; **der ~rad|antrieb** front-wheel drive; **die ~seite, -n** front; *numis* obverse; **der ~sitz, -e** front seat; **der ~zungen|vokal, -e** front vowel
vorderhand for the present
vorderst.. front
vordrängeln: sich ~ *coll* push to the front
vordrängen: sich ~ push to the front; push oneself forward
vordringen* (*sn*) advance; gain ground; **~ in** (*acc*) penetrate; **das Vordringen** advance
vordringlich urgent; **~ behandeln** give (sth.) priority
der **Vordruck, -e** form
vor|ehelich pre-marital
vor|eilig hasty, rash; **~e Schlüsse ziehen** jump to conclusions; **~ handeln** jump the gun; **~ urteilen** make a hasty judgement
vor|einander before/in front of/from *etc** one another (* *see* **vor**)
vor|eingenommen biased (**gegen** against)
die **Vor|eingenommenheit** bias, prejudice
die **Vor|einsendung** remittance in advance
vor|enthalten* (+*dat*) withhold from; deny; keep from
die **Vor|entscheidung, -en** preliminary decision;

sp semi-final
vor|erst for the moment
das **Vor|essen, –** *Swiss* ragout
vor|exerzieren *coll* demonstrate
vorfabrizieren prefabricate
der **Vorfahr, –en** (*wk masc*) ancestor
vorfahren* move forward; drive up; (*v/i sn*) drive up; move forward; drive on ahead; ~ **lassen** order (car); *mot* give way to, yield to *US*
die **Vorfahrt = das ~(s)|recht** right of way; **die ~(s)|straße, –n** major road
der **Vorfall, ⸚e** incident; *med* prolapse
vorfallen* (*sn*) (*esp* sth. disagreeable) occur; fall forward; *med* prolapse
das **Vorfeld** preliminary stage; run-up (*gen* to: election); *aer* apron
der **Vorfilm, –e** supporting film
vorfinden* find (in a certain place/state)
die **Vorform, –en** early form
die **Vorfreude** anticipation
vorfristig ahead of schedule
der **Vorfrühling** spell of spring-like weather
vorfühlen: ~ bei sound out
Vorführ–: die ~dame, –n mannequin; **das ~gerät, –e** projector; demonstration model; **der ~raum, ⸚e** projection room; **der ~wagen, –** demonstration model
vorführen show; present; demonstrate; *fash* model; **jmdn. dem Richter ~** bring s.o. before the judge
der **Vorführer, –** projectionist
die **Vorführung, –en** *vbl noun*; *also* presentation; demonstration
die **Vorgabe, –n** *sp* start (= advantage)
der **Vorgang, ⸚e** course of events; *tech* process; *admin* file
der **Vorgänger, –** predecessor
der **Vorgarten, ..gärten** front garden
vorgaukeln create the illusion of; (+*dat*) delude into believing in
vorgeben* (*see also* **vorgegeben**) give as an excuse; claim (falsely) (to); (+*dat*) *sp* give (s.o.) a start of
das **Vorgebirge, –** foothills; cape
vorgeblich alleged
vorgefaßt preconceived
vorgefertigt prefabricated
das **Vorgefühl** presentiment; anticipation
vorgegeben *p/part*; *also* predetermined
vorgehen* (*sn*) go on ahead; go to the front; (clock) be fast; act, take action; happen, go on; come first, take precedence; ~ **gegen** take action against; *leg* take proceedings against; **was geht in … vor?** what is going through …'s mind?; ~ **lassen** let (s.o.) go first; **das Vorgehen** action
vorgelagert offshore; (*following dat*) situated in front of; (lying) off
das **Vorgericht, –e** hors d'oeuvre
vorgerückt *p/part*; **in ~em Alter** at an advanced age; **zu ~er Stunde** at a late hour
die **Vorgeschichte** prehistory; (historical) background (*gen* to); *med* history
vorgeschichtlich prehistoric
der **Vorgeschmack** foretaste
vorgeschritten (age *etc*) advanced
der **Vorgesetzte** (*fem* **die ~**) (*decl as adj*) superior
vorgestern the day before yesterday; ~ **morgen/abend** the morning/evening before last; **von ~** (newspaper *etc*) the day before yesterday's; *coll* completely outmoded
vorgestrig the day before yesterday's
vorgreifen* (+*dat*) anticipate
der **Vorgriff, –e** anticipation (**auf** *acc* of)
vorgucken *coll* (petticoat *etc*) show
vorhaben* plan; intend; *coll* have (apron *etc*) on; **hast du morgen etwas vor?** are you doing anything tomorrow?
das **Vorhaben, –** plan; project
die **Vorhalle, –n** entrance-hall; foyer; portico; *parl* lobby
vorhalten* put in front of one's mouth; hold up; (+*dat*) hold in front of; (+*dat of pers*) reproach for/with; (*v/i*) last; (+*dat*) **als Vorbild ~** hold up as an example to; **mit vorgehaltener Pistole** at gunpoint
die **Vorhaltungen** *pl* remonstrances; (+*dat*) ~ **machen** remonstrate with (**wegen** about)
die **Vorhand** *sp*, *zool* forehand; *cards* lead
vorhanden in existence; available; present; ~ **sein** exist; be available || **das V~sein** existence; presence
der **Vorhang, ⸚e** curtain; **der Eiserne ~** the Iron Curtain
Vorhänge–: das ~schloß, ⸚(ss)er padlock
vorhängen put on (lock *etc*); hang in front
das **Vorhaus, ⸚er** *Aust* hall
die **Vorhaut, ⸚e** foreskin
vorher before(hand)
vorher– *sep pref*
vorherbestimmen predetermine; predestine
vorhergehen* (*sn*) (+*dat*) precede; **~d** preceding
vorherig previous
die **Vorherrschaft** ascendancy
vorherrschen be predominant; prevail; **~d** predominant; prevalent
die **Vorhersage, –n** forecast (*also meteor*), prediction
vorhersagen forecast (*also meteor*), predict
vorhersehen* foresee
vorheucheln feign
vorhin just now
vorhinein: im ~ in advance
der **Vorhof, ⸚e** forecourt; *anat* auricle; vestibule
die **Vorhut, –en** vanguard
vorig previous; last; *Swiss* (left) over; **die V~en** *theat* the same; **im ~en** above
das **Vorjahr, –e** previous year

vorjährig the previous year's

die **Vorkammer, –n** auricle (of heart)

der **Vorkämpfer, –** pioneer

vorkauen (+*dat*) chew for; *coll* spoonfeed to

die **Vorkehr, –en** *Swiss* = **Vorkehrung**

die **Vorkehrung, –en** precaution; **~en treffen** take precautions

die **Vorkenntnisse** *pl* previous knowledge; grounding; **gute ~ haben in** (*dat*) be well grounded in

vorknöpfen *coll*: **sich** *dat* **...** ~ take to task

vorkochen precook

vorkommen* (*sn*) occur; (+*dat*) happen to; strike (s.o.) as (odd *etc*); **sich** *dat* (**blöde/ überflüssig** *etc*) ~ feel (stupid/superfluous *etc*); **sich** *dat* **sehr klug** ~ think one is very clever; **... ist mir noch nicht vorgekommen** I've never come across ...; **mir kam es vor, als hätte ich ...** I felt as if I'd ...; I had the feeling that I'd ...; **wie kommst du mir denn vor?** who do you think you are?; **es soll nicht wieder** ~ it won't happen again

das **Vorkommen, –** occurrence; incidence; *geol* deposit

das **Vorkommnis, –se** occurrence

Vorkriegs– pre-war ...

vorladen* summon (witness *etc*)

die **Vorladung, –en** summons

die **Vorlage, –n** presentation; pattern; *liter* model; *print* original; *parl* bill; *sp* pass (setting up goal); *ski* forward lean; *chem* receiver; **die ~ verwandeln** score off the pass

das **Vorland** foreshore; foothills

vorlassen* admit; let (s.o.) go first; let (s.o., sth.) pass

der **Vorlauf, ⸚e** *sp* heat

der **Vorläufer, –** forerunner

vorläufig provisional; (*adv*) for the time being; provisionally

vorlaut cheeky

vorleben (+*dat*) set an example of (sth.) to

das **Vorleben** former life, past

Vorlege– carving ...; serving ...; **das ~schloß, ⸚(ss)er** padlock

vorlegen put in front (**vor** *acc* of); produce; present; submit; (+*dat*) present to; submit to; show to; serve with; put (question) to; *parl* lay before; *sp* feed (ball *etc*) to; **den Riegel** ~ bolt the door; **ein scharfes Tempo** ~ go at a smart pace; **sich** ~ lean forward

der **Vorleger, –** mat; rug

vorlesen* read out; (+*dat*) read (out) to

die **Vorlesung, –en** *vbl noun*; *univ* lecture; course of lectures; **das ~s|verzeichnis, –se** university calendar/catalog *US*

vorletzt last ... but one, penultimate

die **Vorliebe, –n** preference, partiality; **mit** ~ *conveyed by* ... particularly like(s) to ...

vorlieb|nehmen* (*sep*): ~ **mit** make do with

vorliegen* be available; exist (in draft form *etc*); have come in/been received; (symptom) be present; **es liegt/liegen ... vor** there is/are ... (*eg* **es liegt kein Grund zur Besorgnis vor** there is no cause for anxiety, **es muß ein Irrtum** ~ there must be some mistake); **mir liegt ... vor** I have (here) ...; **~d** in hand; **im ~den Fall** in the present case

vorlügen*: jmdm. etw. ~ lie to s.o.

vorm = **vor dem**

vormachen (+*dat*) show how to do; **jmdm./ sich** *dat* **etwas** ~ kid s.o./oneself; **mir kannst du nichts** ~ you can't fool me; **sich** *dat* **nichts** ~ have no illusions; **sich** *dat* **nichts ~ lassen** be nobody's fool

die **Vormacht** dominant power; = **die ~stellung** supremacy

vormalig former

vormals in former times

der **Vormarsch, ⸚e** *mil* advance; **im** ~ gaining ground; *mil* on the advance

der **Vormärz** (*period from 1815 to the March Revolution of 1848*)

vormerken make a note of; ~ **für** put (s.o.'s) name down for; **sich ~ lassen für** put one's name down for

vormittag: gestern/heute/morgen ~ yesterday/this/tomorrow morning

der **Vormittag, –e** morning; **am** ~ in the morning

vormittägig morning; morning's

vormittags in the morning; in the morning(s)

Vormittags– morning ...

der **Vormonat** [–at], **–e** previous month

vormontieren pre-assemble

der **Vormund, –e/⸚er** guardian

die **Vormundschaft** guardianship

vorn[1] in front; at the front; ~ **in** (*dat*) at the front of; **nach** ~ forwards; to the front; **nach ~ hinaus** at the front (of house); **von** ~ from the front; **von ~ anfangen** start from the beginning; start all over again; **von ~ bis hinten** *coll* from start to finish; from top to bottom; right, left and centre || **~an** in front; at the front; **~herein** (**von v.** from the outset); **~über–** *sep pref* ... forwards; **~weg** in front

vorn[2] *coll* = **vor den**

die **Vornahme** carrying out; making

der **Vorname, –n** (*like* **Name**) Christian name

vorne = **vorn**

vornehm distinguished; refined; (area *etc*) fashionable; (character *etc*) noble; ~ **tun** put on airs; **~st..** chief || **die V~tuerei** putting on airs

vornehmen* carry out; make (change *etc*); *coll* attend to first; (*also* + **sich** *dat*) get started on; **sich** *dat* **...** ~ plan (to do); *coll* take to task; **sich** *dat* **~ zu ...** make up one's mind to ...; **sich** *dat* **zuviel** ~ take on too much

vornehmlich in particular
vorneigen, sich ~ bend forward
der **Vor|ort, –e** suburb; *in compds* **~(s)–** suburban ...
der **Vorplatz, ¨–e** forecourt
der **Vorposten, –** outpost
vorpreschen (*sn*) race ahead
das **Vorprogramm, –e** supporting programme
vorprogrammieren pre-programme
der **Vorrang** priority; precedence; *Aust mot* right of way; **(den) ~ haben** take precedence (**vor** *dat* over); (+*dat*) **den ~ geben** give priority to
vorrangig having priority; (importance) prime; **~ behandeln** give priority to
der **Vorrat, ¨–e** stock, supply (**an** *dat* of); reserve (of); **Vorräte an ...** (*dat*) **anlegen** stockpile; **auf ~ kaufen** stock up with
vorrätig in stock; **nicht mehr ~ haben** be out of
Vorrats– store ...; **die ~kammer, –n** larder; store cupboard
der **Vorraum, ¨–e** anteroom; outer office
vorrechnen (+*dat*) calculate for, work out for; enumerate (s.o.'s failings)
das **Vorrecht, –e** privilege, prerogative
die **Vorrede, –n** preface; introductory remarks
vorreden *coll*: (+*dat*) **etwas ~** tell (s.o.) a tale
der **Vorredner, –** previous speaker; **mein ~** the previous speaker
vorrevolutionär pre-revolutionary
die **Vorrichtung, –en** device; appliance
vorrücken (*see also* **vorgerückt**) move forward; (*v/i sn*) move forward; *mil* advance (**gegen** on)
die **Vorrunde, –n** *sp* first round
vors = vor das
vorsagen (+*dat*) recite to; tell (s.o. the answer); **sich** *dat* **... ~** say to oneself
die **Vorsaison** [–zɛzɔ̃:], **–s** low season
der **Vorsänger, –** *eccles* precentor
der **Vorsatz, ¨–e** (firm) intention; **den ~ fassen zu ...** make up one's mind to ...; **der Weg zur Hölle ist mit guten Vorsätzen gepflastert** the road to hell is paved with good intentions || **das ~blatt, ¨–er** end-paper
vorsätzlich intentional; *leg* wilful; premeditated
die **Vorschau, –en** preview (**auf** *acc* of); *cin* trailer
Vorschein: zum ~ bringen produce; bring to light; **zum ~ kommen** appear; come out
vorschieben* push forward; stick out; push across; use as an excuse; use as a front; **sich ~** push forward
vorschießen* (+*dat*) advance (s.o. money); (*v/i sn*) shoot forward
der **Vorschlag, ¨–e** suggestion; proposal; *mus* appoggiatura; **–vorschlag** proposed ...; suggested ...; **auf ~** (+*gen*) at the suggestion of; **in ~ bringen** propose || **der ~hammer, ..hämmer** sledgehammer
vorschlagen* propose (**für** for); suggest
die **Vorschluß|runde, –n** semi-final
vorschneiden* carve; slice
vorschnell hasty
vorschreiben* prescribe, lay down; (+*dat*) write out for (s.o.) to copy; dictate to; **sich** *dat* **nichts ~ lassen** refuse to be dictated to
die **Vorschrift, –en** regulation, rule; instruction; **... ist ~ ...** is prescribed by the regulations; (+*dat*) **~en machen** tell (s.o.) what to do; **sich** *dat* **keine ~en machen lassen von** not take orders from; **die ~en einhalten** comply with the regulations; **die ~en übertreten/verletzen** contravene the regulations; **sich an die ~en halten** comply with the regulations; **gegen die ~en verstoßen** contravene the regulations; **laut (polizeilicher) ~** according to (police) regulations; **nach ~** according to regulations; *med* as directed; **Dienst nach ~** working to rule; **sich nach den ~en richten** comply with the regulations || **v~s|gemäß = v~s|mäßig** regulation; proper; (*adv*) according to regulations; *med* as directed; **v~s|widrig** contrary to regulations
Vorschub: (+*dat*) **~ leisten** encourage
Vorschul– pre-school (education *etc*)
die **Vorschule, –n** *approx* = nursery school
vorschulisch pre-school
der **Vorschuß, ¨–(ss)e** advance (payment); **die ~lorbeeren** *pl* praise bestowed in advance (in anticipation of 'great things')
vorschützen use as a pretext; feign; **(Müdigkeit/eine Erkältung** *etc*) **~** pretend to (be tired/have a cold *etc*)
vorschwärmen: (+*dat*) **(viel) ~ von** enthuse about
vorschweben: mir schwebt ... vor I have ... in mind
vorsehen* plan; provide for; **~ für** have in mind for; earmark for; **sich ~** take care; **sich ~ vor** (*dat*) be wary of/on one's guard against
die **Vorsehung** Providence
vorsetzen put in front; move forward; (+*dat*) put in front of; serve with; dish up (scandal *etc*)
die **Vorsicht** caution; **~ üben** exercise caution; **~!** look out!; **„~, (Glas** *etc*)**!"** '(glass *etc*) – with care'; **„~, (Hochspannung** *etc*)**!"** 'danger – (high voltage *etc*)'; **„~, bissiger Hund!"** 'beware of the dog'; **„~, Stufe!"** 'mind the step'
vorsichtig careful; cautious
Vorsichts–: v~halber as a precaution; **die ~maß|nahme, –n = die ~maß|regel, –n** precaution

das **Vorsignal, -e** *rail* distant signal
die **Vorsilbe, -n** prefix
vorsingen* (+*dat*) sing to; (*v/i*) audition
vorsintflutlich *coll* antediluvian
der **Vorsitz** chairmanship; **den ~ führen/haben** preside (**bei** over)
der **Vorsitzende** (*fem* **die ~**) (*decl as adj*) chairman (-woman); **zweiter ~r (zweite ~)** vice-chairman (-woman)
die **Vorsorge** precaution; provision (for); **~ tragen/treffen für** make provision for; **zur ~** as a precaution || **die ~untersuchung, -en** medical check-up
vorsorgen: ~ für make provision for
vorsorglich precautionary; (*adv*) as a precaution
der **Vorspann, -e** (brief) introduction; *cin, TV* opening credits
vorspannen harness (*dat* to)
die **Vorspeise, -n** hors d'oeuvre
vorspiegeln feign; make a pretence of
die **Vorspiegelung: ~ falscher Tatsachen** false pretences
das **Vorspiel, -e** prelude (to event); *mus* prelude; overture; *theat* prologue; *sp* preliminary match; *sex* foreplay
vorspielen *mus* play, *theat* act (for s.o.); (+*dat*) *coll* make a show of; (*v/i*) audition; (+*dat*) *mus* play for, *theat* act for
die **Vorsprache** [-a:-], **-n** visit, call
vorsprechen* (+*dat*) show how to pronounce; (*v/i*) *theat* audition; **~ bei** call on
vorspringen* (*sn*) leap forward; leap out; jut out; **~d** projecting; prominent
der **Vorsprung, ⸚e** projection; ledge; *esp sp* lead (**vor** *dat* over); start
das **Vorstadium, -(i)en** preliminary stage
die **Vorstadt** [-t], **⸚e** [-ɛ:t-] suburb
vorstädtisch [-ɛ:t-] suburban
der **Vorstand, ⸚e** board (of directors); executive committee; governing body; head; *Aust* stationmaster
Vorsteh-: der ~hund, -e pointer; setter
vorstehen* stick out; protrude; *hunt* point; (+*dat*) be in charge of; head; manage; **~d** protruding; above; **im ~den** above
der **Vorsteher, -** head; **die ~drüse, -n** prostate gland
vorstellbar conceivable
vorstellen put in front; move forward; put (clock) on; introduce (person) (*dat* to), present (star, new model, *etc*); represent; **sich** *dat* **... ~** imagine; visualize; have in mind; **stell dir vor!** imagine!; **etwas ~** be somebody
  sich ~ introduce oneself (*dat* to); present oneself (**bei** to); go for an interview
vorstellig: ~ werden bei make representations to
die **Vorstellung, -en** idea; introduction (to person); presentation; interview (for post); *theat etc* performance; (*pl*) representations; **das ~s|gespräch, -e** interview (for post); **die ~s|kraft = das ~s|vermögen** imagination
der **Vorstopper, -** *footb*: *approx* = central defender
der **Vorstoß, ⸚e** advance, push (*also mil*)
vorstoßen* push forward; (*v/i sn*) push forward, advance (*also mil*)
die **Vorstrafe, -n** previous conviction
vorstrecken stretch forward; stretch out; put out; (+*dat*) advance (s.o. money)
die **Vorstudie** [-ĭə], **-n** preliminary study
die **Vorstufe, -n** preliminary stage
vorstülpen protrude (lips)
vorstürmen (*sn*) charge forward
der **Vortag, -e** day before; **am ~** the day before
vortanzen (+*dat*) show how to dance; (*v/i*) dance (in front of s.o.)
vortasten: sich ~ feel one's way
vortäuschen feign; fake (accident, orgasm, *etc*); pretend (that ...)
der **Vorteil, -e** advantage (**vor** *dat* over); **die Vor- und Nachteile** the pros and cons; **einen ~ ziehen aus** benefit from; **auf seinen ~ bedacht sein** have an eye to the main chance; **gegenüber jmdm. im ~ sein** have an advantage over s.o.; **von ~** advantageous; **sich zu seinem ~ verändern** change for the better
vorteilhaft advantageous, favourable; **~ sein für** (colour *etc*) suit
der **Vortrag, ⸚e** lecture; talk; recital; recitation; performance; delivery; (pianist's *etc*) execution; *comm* carry-over
vortragen* recite; perform; convey, express; *comm* carry forward
der **Vortragende** (*fem* **die ~**) (*decl as adj*) lecturer; speaker; performer
Vortrags-: die ~reihe, -n series of lectures; **die ~weise, -n** delivery; *mus* execution
vortrẹfflich splendid
vortreten* (*sn*) step forward; stick out, (eyes) protrude
der **Vortritt** precedence; *Swiss* right of way; (+*dat*) **den ~ lassen** let (s.o.) go first
der **Vortrupp, -s** advance party
vorü̱ber = vorbei
vorü̱ber- *sep pref* = **vorbei-** (*i*)
vorü̱bergehen* (*sn*) = **vorbeigehen; ~d** temporary; passing
das **Vor|urteil, -e** prejudice (**gegen** against); **v~s|frei = v~s|los** unprejudiced; (*adv*) without prejudice; **die ~s|losigkeit** open-mindedness
die **Vorväter** *pl* forefathers
die **Vorvergangenheit** pluperfect
die **Vorverhandlung, -en** preliminary negotiations/*leg* hearing

der **Vorverkauf** advance booking; **im ~ kaufen** buy (tickets) in advance
vorverlegen bring forward, advance (date *etc*); move forward
vorvorgestern *coll* three days ago
vorvorig *coll* ... before last
vorvorletzt *coll* last ... but two
vorwagen: sich ~ venture forward
die **Vorwahl, -en** preliminary selection/*pol* election; *tel* S.T.D. code, area code *US*; dialling (of code)
Vorwähl-: die ~nummer, -n S.T.D. code, area code *US*
vorwählen preselect; *tel* dial first
der **Vorwand, ¨-e** pretext; **unter dem ~ zu ...** under the pretext of (+*ger*)
vorwärmen warm; *tech* pre-heat
vorwarnen warn (in advance)
die **Vorwarnung, -en** advance warning; *mil* early warning
vorwärts forward(s); **~!** go on!
Vorwärts- forward ...; **v~bringen*** (*sep*) help (s.o.) to get on; advance; **v~gehen*** (*sep*; *sn*) progress; **v~kommen*** (*sep*; *sn*) get on; make progress
vorweg at the outset; beforehand; **die V~nahme** anticipation; **~nehmen*** (*sep*) anticipate (**um es gleich ~zunehmen** to come straight to the point); **~schicken** (*sep*) say by way of introduction
der **Vorwegweiser, -** traffic sign (at approach to junction)
vorweisen* show, produce
vorwerfen* (+*dat*) throw (food) to; (+*dat of pers*) reproach for/with; accuse of; **sich** *dat* **nichts vorzuwerfen haben** have nothing to reproach oneself with; **sie haben einander nichts vorzuwerfen** *coll* one is as bad as the other
das **Vorwerk, -e** outwork (of castle)
vorwiegen* predominate; **~d** predominant; (*adv*) predominantly, chiefly
der **Vorwitz** cheek(iness)
vorwitzig cheeky
die **Vorwoche, -n** week before; **in der ~** the week before
das **Vorwort, -e** preface, foreword; (*pl* ¨-**er**) *Aust* preposition
der **Vorwurf, ¨-e** reproach; accusation; *arts* subject; (+*dat*) **Vorwürfe machen** reproach (**wegen** for) || **v~s|voll** reproachful
vorzählen count out
das **Vorzeichen, -** omen, sign; *comput*, *math* sign; *mus* key signature; accidental; **mit umgekehrtem ~** the other way round; **unter (demokratischen** *etc*) **~** under (democratic *etc*) conditions
vorzeichnen mark out; map out (career *etc*); (+*dat*) draw for (s.o.) to copy
vorzeigen show, produce
die **Vorzeit** prehistoric times; **in grauer ~** in the dim and distant past || **der ~mensch, -en** (*wk masc*) prehistoric man
vorzeiten in olden times
vorzeitig premature
vorzeitlich prehistoric
vorziehen* pull forward, *mil* move up; draw (curtain); prefer (*dat* to); favour; *coll* do/hold/take *etc* earlier; **es ~ zu ...** prefer to ...; choose to ...; **... ist vorzuziehen** ... is preferable
das **Vorzimmer, -** anteroom; outer office; *Aust* hall; **die ~wand, ¨-e** *Aust* hall-stand
der **Vorzug**[1], ¨-**e** relief train (ahead of main train)
der **Vorzug**[2], ¨-**e** preference; advantage; merit; privilege; *Aust educ* distinction; (+*dat*) **den ~ geben** give preference to, prefer
vorzüglich excellent; exquisite
Vorzugs- preferential ...; **die ~aktien** *pl* preference shares, preferred stock *US*; **die ~milch** special-quality milk; **der ~preis, -e** special price; **v~weise** chiefly
votieren vote
Votiv- votive (tablet *etc*)
das **Votum, -(t)en** vote
der **Voyeur** [vŏa'jøːɐ], **-e** voyeur
VR = Volksrepublik
v. T. (**= vom Tausend**) per thousand
vulgär vulgar; **das V~latein** Vulgar Latin
die **Vulgarität** vulgarity
die **Vulgata** the Vulgate
der **Vulkan, -e** volcano; **der ~ausbruch, ¨-e** volcanic eruption
vulkanisch volcanic
vulkanisieren vulcanize
v. u. Z. (**= vor unserer Zeitrechnung**) B.C.
die **VVB, -(s)** *EGer* **= Vereinigung Volkseigener Betriebe**

W

das **W** [veː] (*gen*, *pl* –, *coll* [veːs]) W

W (= **West(en), Watt**) W.

die **Waadt** [–t] = **das ~land** Vaud (*Swiss canton*)

Waag–: die ~schale, –n scale-pan (**auf die W. legen** weigh (one's words); **(schwer) in die W. fallen** carry great weight; **in die W. werfen** bring to bear)

die **Waage, –n** (pair of) scales; balance; *astron*, *astrol* Libra; **sich** *dat pl* **die ~ halten** counterbalance each other || **der ~balken, –** scale-beam; **w~recht, die ~rechte** (*decl as adj*) horizontal

wabb(e)lig *coll* wobbly; flabby

wabbeln *coll* wobble (about)

die **Wabe, –n** honeycomb

wach awake; alert; **~ küssen** wake with a kiss; **~ werden** wake up; (memory) be stirred || **die W~ablösung, –en** changing of the guard; *pol* change of government; **der W~dienst** guard-duty (**W. haben** be on guard-duty); **~habend** (officer) duty; **~halten*** (*sep*) keep alive (memory *etc*); **der W~hund, –e** watchdog; **der W~mann, ⸚er/..leute** *Aust* policeman; **die W~mannschaft, –en** guard; **der W~posten, –** sentry; **~rufen*** (*sep*) arouse; bring back (memory); **~rütteln** (*sep*) arouse (**w. aus** shake out of); **die W~stube, –n** guard-room; **der W~traum, ⸚e** daydream; **die Wạch- und Schlie̲ß|gesellschaft, –en** security firm; **das W~zimmer, –** *Aust* police-station; **W~zustand** (**im W.** while awake)

die **Wache, –n** sentry; guard; guard-duty, *naut* watch; police-station, *mil* guard-room; **auf ~** on guard; **~ halten** keep watch (**bei** over); sit up (with sick person); **~ stehen** stand guard || **der ~be|amte** (*decl as adj*) *Aust* police officer

wachen be awake; keep watch; **~ bei** sit up with; **~ über** (*acc*) watch over; keep an eye on; **darüber, ~ daß ...** make sure that ...

der **Wachọlder, –** juniper; = **der ~brannt|wein** gin; **die ~drossel, –n** fieldfare; **der ~schnaps** gin

das **Wachs** [–ks], **–e** wax; **(wie) ~ in jmds. Händen sein** be wax in s.o.'s hands || **das ~figuren|kabinett, –e** waxworks; **das ~papier** wax-paper; **das ~tuch** oilcloth; **wạchs|we̲ich** as soft as wax

wachsam vigilant, watchful

die **Wachsamkeit** vigilance, watchfulness

wachseln [–ks–] *Aust* wax (skis)

wachsen[1] [–ks–] (*2nd/3rd sing pres* **wächst,** *p/t* **wuchs** [–uː–] (*subj* **wüchse** [–yː–]), *p/part* **gewachsen**) (*see also* **gewachsen**) (*sn*) grow; **sich** *dat* **... ~ lassen** grow (beard); let (one's hair) grow; **gut gewachsen sein** have a good figure

wachsen[2] [–ks–] wax (floor, skis, *etc*)

wächsern [–ks–] wax; waxen

wächst *2nd/3rd sing pres of* **wachsen**[1]

das **Wachstum** [–ks–] growth (*also econ*); **eigenes ~** wine from our/their *etc* own vineyards || **das ~s|hormon, –e** growth hormone; **die ~s|industrie, –n** growth industry; **die ~s|rate, –n** growth rate

Wacht–: der ~meister, – police constable, patrolman *US*; *Aust*, *Swiss mil* sergeant; **der ~posten, –** sentry; **der ~turm, ⸚e** watch-tower

die **Wächte, –n** snow-cornice

die **Wachtel, –n** quail

der **Wächter, –** attendant; watchman; keeper; custodian (of public morals *etc*)

Wackel–: der ~kontakt, –e loose connection; **der ~peter, –** *coll* jelly

wack(e)lig shaky; wobbly; (tooth *etc*) loose

wackeln wobble; be loose; move (while taking picture); (position) be shaky; (*sn*) totter; **~ mit** waggle

wacker stout-hearted; *arch* worthy

die **Wade, –n** calf (of leg)

die **Waffe, –n** weapon; *mil* arm; (*pl*) *mil* arms; **die ~n strecken** surrender; **unter ~n stehen** be under arms; **zu den ~n rufen** call to arms

die **Waffel, –n** waffle; wafer; **das ~eisen, –** waffle-iron

Waffen– ... of arms; arms ...; weapons ...; **die ~gattung, –en** arm (= branch of the services); **die ~gewalt** force of arms (**mit W.** by force of arms); **die ~kammer, –n** armoury; **w~los** unarmed; **die ~ruhe** cease-fire; **der ~schein, –e** gun-licence; **der ~schmied, –e** *hist* armourer; **der ~schmuggel** gun-running; **die ~-SS** (*military branch of the SS*); **der ~still|stand** armistice; **das ~system, –e** weapon system

wag–: ~halsig daredevil

Wage–: der ~mut, w~mutig daring; **das**

~stück, –e daring feat

das Wägelchen, – little cart

wagen (*see also* gewagt) risk; hazard (remark *etc*); (es) ~ zu … dare to …; sich ~ venture (into *etc* sth.); sich ~ an (*acc*) venture on

der Wagen, –/*SGer also* Wägen car; van; wagon; cart; trolley; (typewriter) carriage; *rail* carriage, car *US*; der Große/Kleine ~ the Plough, the Great/Little Bear, the Big/Little Dipper *US* || die ~burg, –en *hist* (*U.S.A.*) corral; (*S. Africa*) laager; der ~führer, – tram-driver, motorman *US*; der ~heber, – jack; der ~park, –s fleet of vehicles; das ~rad, ⸚er cart-wheel; das ~rennen, – chariot-racing; chariot race; der ~schlag, ⸚e car/carriage door; der ~stand|anzeiger, – *rail* indicator showing order and destination of carriages/cars *US*

wägen (*p/t* wog/wägte (*subj* wöge/wägte), *p/part* gewogen/gewägt) ponder (s.o.'s words); (*p/t*, *p/part only* wog, gewogen) *Aust* weigh; erst ~, dann wagen look before you leap

der Waggon [va'gɔ̃ː], –s *rail* goods wagon, freight car *US*; wagonload, carload *US*

der Wagnerianer, – Wagnerian

das Wagnis, –se risk; bold venture

die Wahl, –en choice; *pol etc* election (in *acc* to, zum/zur as); vote; ~en ausschreiben call an election; (+*dat*) die ~ lassen leave it up to (s.o.) to choose; eine/seine ~ treffen make a/one's choice; keine andere ~ haben (, als zu …) have no alternative (but to …); es bleibt mir keine andere ~ I have no choice; … (erster *etc*) ~ *comm* grade (A *etc*) …; Waren zweiter ~ seconds; in die engere ~ kommen be short-listed; nach eigener ~ of one's own choosing; vor die ~ stellen zu … give (s.o.) the choice of (+*ger*); zur ~ gehen go to the polls; … stehen zur ~ there is a choice of …; sich zur ~ stellen stand, run *esp US* (as a candidate)

Wahl– election …; electoral …; (Berliner *etc*) by adoption;

das ~alter voting age; w~berechtigt entitled to vote; die ~beteiligung poll, turn-out; der ~bezirk, –e ward; die ~eltern *pl Aust* adoptive parents; das ~fach, ⸚er option(al subject), elective *US*; w~frei optional; *comput* random; der ~gang, ⸚e ballot; das ~geheimnis secrecy of the ballot; das ~geschenk, –e election hand-out; die ~heimat adopted country/home; die ~kabine, –n polling booth; der ~kampf, ⸚e election campaign; das ~kind, –er *Aust* adopted child; der ~kreis, –e constituency; die ~liste, –n list of candidates; (*U.S.A.*) ticket; das ~lokal, –e polling-station; die ~lokomotive, –n *coll* vote-puller; w~los indiscriminate; (*adv*) at random; indiscriminately; der ~mann, ⸚er member of an electoral college, elector *US*; die ~propaganda electioneering; das ~recht (right to) vote; electoral law (allgemeines W. universal suffrage; aktives W. right to vote; passives W. eligibility for office); der ~spruch, ⸚e election slogan; motto; der ~tag, –e polling-day; die ~urne, –n ballot-box; w~weise according to choice; der ~werber, – *Aust* candidate (in election); der ~zettel, – ballot-paper; das ~zuckerl, –n *Aust coll* election hand-out

Wähl–: die ~scheibe, –n *tel* dial

wählbar eligible for office

wählen (*see also* gewählt) choose; vote for; elect; *tel* dial; (*v/i*) choose; vote; ~ in (*acc*) elect onto; *parl* return to; ~ zu elect (s.o. president *etc*)

der Wähler, – voter, elector; *tech* selector; die ~liste, –n electoral roll

wählerisch particular, choosy

die Wählerschaft electorate

der Wahn delusion; in dem ~ leben, daß … be under the delusion that … || der ~sinn madness; w~sinnig mad; *coll* awful, dreadful; (*adv*) *coll* incredibly; madly (in love) (w. werden go mad; wie w. *coll* like mad; … ist zum ~sinnigwerden *coll* … is enough to drive you round the bend); die ~vorstellung, –en delusion; der ~witz (sheer) lunacy; w~witzig (idea *etc*) mad, lunatic

wähnen imagine (to be)

wahr true; real; ~ machen carry out; ~ werden come true; …, nicht ~? …, doesn't it/won't he/aren't you *etc*?; das ist schon gar nicht mehr ~ *coll* that was ages ago; so ~ mir Gott helfe! so help me God!; im ~sten Sinne des Wortes in the true sense of the word; das einzig W~e *coll* just the thing || ~haben (nicht w. wollen not admit (to oneself)); ~nehmbar perceptible; ~nehmen* (*sep*) perceive; detect; be(come) aware of; look after (interests); avail oneself of (opportunity); die W~nehmung *vbl noun*; *also* perception; detection; ~sagen (*sep or insep*) prophesy; (*v/i*) tell fortunes; (+*dat*) tell (s.o.'s) fortune (w. aus read (cards, tea-leaves, *etc*); (+*dat*) die Zukunft w. tell (s.o.'s) fortune; sich *dat* w. lassen have one's fortune told); die W~sagerei fortune-telling; die W~sagerin, –nen fortune-teller; ~scheinlich probable, likely; (*adv*) probably; die W~scheinlichkeit, –en probability, likelihood (aller W. nach in all probability); das W~zeichen, – symbol; emblem

wahren preserve; maintain; keep; observe; safeguard (interests *etc*); das Gesicht ~ save face; den Schein ~ keep up appearances; **gewahrt bleiben** be maintained/observed

währen last

während 1 *pres/part of* **währen;** 2 *prep* (*usu* + *gen*) during; in the course of; over (period); 3 *conj* while; whereas, while; **~dem** *coll* = **~dessen** in the meantime

wahrhaft truly

wahrhaftig truthful; (*adv*) really; truly; **~!** so it is/she can/they have *etc*!

die **Wahrheit, -en** truth; (+*dat*) **die ~ sagen** tell (s.o.) the truth; *coll* give (s.o.) a piece of one's mind; **um die ~ zu sagen** to tell the truth; **in ~** in reality || **w~s|gemäß** = **w~s|getreu** truthful

wahrlich truly

die **Währung, -en** currency; *in compds* **~s-** currency …, monetary …; **~s|fonds (der Internationale W.** the International Monetary Fund); **die ~s|schlange** (for E.C. currencies) the snake; **w~s|politisch** monetary

Waid- = **Weid-**

die **Waise, -n** orphan; *pros* rhymeless line || **das ~n|haus, ¨-er** orphanage; **das ~n|kind, -er** orphan; **~n|knabe** *coll* **(ein W. sein gegen** not be a patch on)

der **Wal, -e** whale; **der ~fang** whaling; **der ~fänger, -** whaler; **der ~fisch, -e** *coll* whale; **der ~fisch|speck** blubber

der **Wald, ¨-er** forest; wood(s); woodland; **den ~ vor lauter Bäumen nicht sehen** not see the wood for the trees || **die ~ameise, -n** red ant; **die ~erd|beere, -n** wild strawberry; **das ~horn, ¨-er** hunting horn; **der ~kauz, ¨-e** tawny owl; **der ~lauf, ¨-e** cross-country run/running; **der ~lehr|pfad, -e** nature trail; **der ~meister** woodruff; **die ~rebe, -n** clematis; **w~reich** densely-wooded; **die ~schnepfe, -n** woodcock; **das ~sterben** destruction of the forests (as a result of pollution); **Wald-und-Wiesen-** *coll* common or garden …; **die ~wiese, -n** glade

Waldes- *poet* … of the forest

waldig wooded

die **Waldung, -en** woodland

Wales [we:ls] Wales

Walhall(a) [val-] Valhalla

der **Waliser, -** Welshman; **die ~** the Welsh

die **Waliserin, -nen** Welshwoman

walisisch, (*language*) **W~** Welsh

walken full (cloth); *Aust cul* roll out (dough)

die **Walküre, -n** Valkyrie

der **Wall, ¨-e** embankment; *mil* rampart; **w~fahren** (*insep*) (*sn*) go on a pilgrimage; **der ~fahrer, -** pilgrim; **die ~fahrt, -en** pilgrimage; **der ~fahrts|ort, -e** place of pilgrimage; **der ~graben, ..gräben** moat

der **Wallach, -e** gelding

wallen bubble; (*sn*) (s.o.'s hair *etc*) flow (over shoulders *etc*); **~d** (robes *etc*) flowing

das **Wallis** [-ɪs] (*gen* -) Valais (*Swiss canton*)

der **Wallone, -n** (*wk masc*), **wallonisch** Walloon

die **Wallung, -en** *vbl noun*; *med* hot flush/flash *US*; **in ~ bringen** excite greatly; make (s.o.'s blood) boil; **in ~ geraten** be greatly agitated; fly into a passion

die **Walnuß** [-a-], **¨-(ss)e** walnut

die **Walpurgis|nacht** [val'purgɪs-] Walpurgis Night

das **Walroß** [-a-], **-(ss)e** walrus

walten prevail; (forces *etc*) be at work; **seines Amtes ~** discharge one's duties; **~ lassen** show (mercy), exercise (caution *etc*); **das Walten** workings (of God *etc*)

Walz- rolled (iron *etc*); **das ~werk, -e** rolling-mill

die **Walze, -n** roller; platen (on typewriter); cylinder; barrel (of barrel-organ); **immer die gleiche ~** *coll* always the same old stuff

walzen roll (steel, lawn, *etc*); (*v/i*: *sn if indicating direction*) *coll* waltz

wälzen roll (barrel *etc*); *coll* pore over; turn over (in one's mind); **~ auf** (*acc*) shift (blame) onto; **~ in** (*dat*) *cul* coat with; **sich ~** roll; toss and turn; writhe; wallow; **sich vor Lachen ~** *coll* roll about (with laughter); **… ist zum Wälzen** *coll* … is a scream

walzen|förmig cylindrical

der **Walzer, -, ~ tanzen** waltz

der **Wälzer, -** *coll* weighty tome

die **Wamme, -n** dewlap

das **Wams, ¨-er** *hist* doublet

wand *p/t of* **winden**[1]

die **Wand, ¨-e** wall (of room; *also anat*); partition; side (of ship *etc*); (rock) face; bank of clouds; **spanische ~** (folding) screen; **sich an die ~ drängen lassen** be pushed aside; **an die ~ drücken** drive to the wall; **an die ~ spielen** upstage; outshine; **an die ~ stellen** put before a firing-squad; **mit dem Kopf gegen die ~ rennen** bang one's head against a brick wall || **der ~behang, ¨-e** wall-hanging; **das ~gemälde, -** mural; **die ~karte, -n** wall-map; **der ~schirm, -e** (folding) screen; **der ~schrank, ¨-e** built-in cupboard; **das ~schränkchen, -** wall-cabinet; **die ~tafel, -n** blackboard; **der ~teppich, -e** tapestry; **die ~verkleidung, -en** wall-covering; panelling; **die ~zeitung, -en** wall newspaper

der **Wandale, -n** (*wk masc*) Vandal

der **Wandalismus** vandalism

wände *p/t subj of* **winden**[1]

der **Wandel** change; **~ schaffen** bring about change; **im ~ der Jahrhunderte/Zeiten** down the centuries/ages || **die ~halle, -n** foyer; *parl* lobby

wandelbar changeable

wandeln change; (*v/i sn*) stroll, promenade; **sich** ~ change; ~**des Lexikon** *joc* walking encyclopaedia

Wander– hiking ...; itinerant ...; migratory ...; touring ...; travelling ...; *med* floating ...; **der** ~**arbeiter,** – migrant worker; **die** ~**bühne, –n** *theat* touring company; **die** ~**düne, –n** shifting sand-dune; **die** ~**fahne, –n** *EGer* challenge flag (awarded to the workers' brigade achieving the best results); **der** ~**falke, –n** (*wk masc*) peregrine falcon; **das** ~**leben** roving life; **die** ~**lust** wanderlust; **der** ~**pokal, –e** challenge cup; **der** ~**preis, –e** challenge trophy; ~**stab (den W. ergreifen** take to the road); **der** ~**trieb, –e** roving spirit; *zool* migratory instinct

der **Wanderer, –** hiker

wandern (*sn*) hike; migrate; (clouds, dune, *etc*) drift; (thoughts) wander, stray, (eyes, glance) wander; ~ **durch** roam (streets *etc*); ~ **in** (*acc*) *coll* end up in; **von ... zu ...** ~ pass from ... to ...

die **Wanderschaft** travels

die **Wanderung, –en** hike; migration; **eine** ~ **machen** go on a hike

–wandig -walled

die **Wandlung, –en** change; *theol* transubstantiation

wandte *p/t of* **wenden**

die **Wange, –n** cheek; ~ **an** ~ cheek to cheek

–wangig -cheeked

Wankel–: der ~**mut** fickleness; **w**~**mütig** fickle

wanken sway; rock; waver; (throne) totter; (*sn*) stagger; **nicht** ~ **und (nicht) weichen** not budge an inch; **ins Wanken bringen** cause to sway/totter; make (s.o.) falter; shake (s.o.'s belief *etc*); **ins Wanken geraten** begin to sway/totter/falter

wann when (*in direct and indirect question*); ~ **(... auch) immer** whenever; **bis** ~ **...?** when ... by?; how long ...?; **seit** ~ **...?** since when ...?, how long ...?

die **Wanne, –n** bath(-tub); *mot* sump, oil pan *US*

der **Wanst, ¨–e** *coll* paunch

die **Wanze, –n** (bed)bug; (= concealed microphone) bug

das **Wappen, –** coat of arms; *in compds* heraldic ...; **die** ~**kunde** heraldry; **der** ~**schild, –er** escutcheon

wappnen: sich ~ **gegen** prepare for; steel oneself for; **sich mit Geduld** ~ arm oneself with patience

war *p/t of* **sein**[1]

warb *p/t of* **werben**

ward *arch p/t of* **werden**

die **Ware, –n** article; goods, merchandise; (*pl*) goods, merchandise; **–waren** ... goods, ... products, *or expressed by English collective or pl noun* (*eg* **Tabakwaren** tobacco products, **Papierwaren** stationery, **Textilwaren** textiles)

wäre *p/t subj of* **sein**[1]

Waren– ... of goods; goods ...; **das** ~**angebot** range of goods; **das** ~**haus, ¨–er** department store; **das** ~**lager, –** warehouse; stocks; **das** ~**muster, –** = **die** ~**probe, –n** sample; **die** ~**sendung, –en** consignment of goods; *post* sample sent by post; **das** ~**zeichen, –** trade-mark

warf *p/t of* **werfen**

warm (*comp, superl* ¨) warm (*also* = cordial); (food, drink) hot; **mir ist** ~ I am warm; ~**er Bruder** *coll* queer; ~ **essen** have a hot meal; ~ **machen** warm up; ~ **stellen** keep hot; ~ **werden** get warm; *coll* thaw out; **nicht** ~ **werden mit** *coll* not get close to ‖ **der W**~**blüter, –** warm-blooded animal; ~**blütig** warm-blooded; **die W**~**front, –en** warm front; ~**halten*** (*sep*) *coll* (**sich** *dat* **... w.** keep in with); ~**herzig** warm-hearted; ~**laufen*** (*sep*; *sn*) (engine) warm up (**w. lassen** warm up (engine)); **die W**~**luft** warm air; **der W**~**wasser|bereiter, –** water-heater; **die W**~**wasser|heizung, –en** hot-water central heating

Wärm–: die ~**flasche, –n** hot-water bottle

die **Wärme** warmth; heat; **mit** ~ warmly

Wärme– heat ...; thermal ...; **der** ~**austauscher, –** heat-exchanger; **der** ~**leiter, –** heat-conductor; **der** ~**regler, –** thermostat

wärmen warm; warm up (food); **sich** ~ warm oneself

wärmstens (recommend) warmly

Warn– warning ...; **das** ~**schild, –er** warning sign; **der** ~**streik, –s** token strike; **das** ~**zeichen, –** warning sign/signal

warnen warn (**vor** *dat* of, against); **(davor)** ~ **zu ...** warn not to ...; **„vor Taschendieben wird gewarnt!"** 'beware of pickpockets!'

Warschau Warsaw; **der** ~**er Pakt** the Warsaw Pact

die **Warte, –n** vantage-point; **von meiner** ~ **aus** from my standpoint

Warte– waiting ...; **die** ~**halle, –n** waiting-room; *aer* departure lounge; **das** ~**häuschen, –** (bus *etc*) shelter; **die** ~**liste, –n** waiting-list; **der** ~**saal, ..säle** *rail* waiting-room; **die** ~**zeit, –en** wait; waiting period; **das** ~**zimmer, –** waiting-room (at doctor's *etc*); **die** ~**schlange, –n** *comput* queue

warten[1] wait (**auf** *acc* for); ~ **mit** leave, put off (payment *etc*); **darauf** ~**, daß ...** wait for (s.o., sth.) to ...; ~ **lassen** let (s.o.) wait; keep (s.o.) waiting; **(lange) auf sich** ~ **lassen** take a long time; be a long time in coming; **nicht lange auf sich** ~ **lassen** not be long in coming; **(die Aufnahme**

regelmäßiger Passagierdienste *etc*) **ließ (über ein Jahrzehnt** *etc*) **auf sich ~** it was (over a decade *etc*) before (regular passenger services were started *etc*)

warten[2] *tech* service; maintain

der **Wärter, –** keeper; attendant; warder, guard *US*

–wärts –wards

die **Wartung** *tech* servicing; maintenance

warum why

die **Warze, –n** wart; **der ~n|hof, ⸚e** areola; **das ~n|schwein, –e** wart-hog

was[1] [–a–] (*gen* **wessen**) 1 *interrog pron* what; 2 *rel pron* (*referring to previous clause*) which (*eg* **man bat mich zu warten, ~ ich auch tat** I was asked to wait, which I did); 3 *adv coll* (*in exclamation*) how; *coll* why; **…, ~?** …, eh?; **alles/einiges/etwas/manches/nichts/vieles, ~ …** everything/some things/something/some things/nothing/much that …; **das Beste/einzige, ~ …** the best/only thing that …; **~ … alles …!** the things …!; **~ auch (immer)** whatever; **das, ~ …** what …, that which …; **~ denn?** what is it?; **~ für (ein) …?** what kind of …?; **~ für (ein) …!** what (a) …!; **~ ist?** what's up?, what is it?; **~ nun?** what now?; **~ aber, wenn …?** but what if …?

was[2] [–a–] *coll* = **etwas 1**; **(na/nein,) 'so ~!** well I never!

Wasch– washing …; wash …

die ~anlage, –n car-wash; *min* washery; **der ~automat, –en** (*wk masc*) automatic washing-machine; **der ~bär, –en** (*wk masc*) raccoon; **das ~becken, –** wash-basin; **das ~benzin** benzine; **das ~brett, –er** wash-board; **w~echt** (material) colour-fast; (colour) fast; real, genuine; **das ~faß, ⸚(ss)er** wash-tub; **die ~frau, –en** laundress; **die ~küche, –n** utility room; *coll* pea-souper; **der ~lappen, –** face-cloth; *coll* sissy; **die ~lauge, –n** suds; **das ~leder, –** chamois-leather; **die ~maschine, –n** washing-machine; **das ~mittel, –** detergent; **das ~pulver, –** washing-powder; **der ~raum, ⸚e** wash-room; **der ~salon, –s** laundry; launderette; **der ~samt** washable velvet; **die ~schüssel, –n** wash-basin; **die ~straße, –n** car-wash; **der ~stütz|punkt, –e** *EGer* laundering facilities (for employees or tenants); **der ~tag, –e** wash-day; **der ~tisch, –e** wash-stand; **das ~weib, –er** *coll* (old) gossip; **der ~zettel, –** blurb; **das ~zeug** toilet things

waschbar washable

die **Wäsche** washing; laundry; underwear; linen; **~ waschen** do the washing; **seine schmutzige ~ (vor anderen Leuten) waschen** wash one's dirty linen in public; **dumm aus der ~ gucken** *coll* look silly; **in die ~ geben** put in the wash; send to the laundry; **in der ~** in the wash; at the laundry || **der ~beutel, –** laundry-bag; **die ~klammer, –n** clothes-peg, clothespin *US*; **der ~korb, ⸚e** laundry-basket; **die ~leine, –n** clothes-line; **die ~schleuder, –n** spin-dryer; **der ~schrank, ⸚e** linen-cupboard, linen closet *US*; **die ~tinte, –n** marking-ink

waschen (wäsch(s)t, *p/t* **wusch** [–u:–] (*subj* **wüsche** [–y:–]), *p/part* **gewaschen)** wash; pan (gold); *coll* launder (money); **sich** *dat* **das Gesicht/die Hände** *etc* **~** wash one's face/hands *etc*; **sich ~** (have a) wash; **(Wäsche) ~** do the washing; (+*dat*) **den Kopf ~** *coll* give (s.o.) a dressing-down; **eine Hand wäscht die andere** one good turn deserves another; **…, der/die/das sich gewaschen hat** *coll* (examination) stiff; (reproach *etc*) sharp; (thrashing *etc*) sound; **Waschen und Legen** shampoo and set

die **Wäscherei, –en** laundry

die **Wäscherin, –nen** washerwoman, laundress

wäsch(s)t (*2nd*,) *3rd sing pres of* **waschen**

die **Waschung, –en** washing; *relig* ablution

das **Wasser, –** water; stretch of water; (*pl* **Wässer**) scent, cologne; **die ~** *pl* the waters; **das ist ~ auf seine Mühle** it's (all) grist to his mill; **~ lassen** pass water; **~ treten** tread water; *med* paddle in cold water (as therapy); (+*dat*) **nicht das ~ reichen** *coll* not hold a candle to; **nahe am/ans ~ gebaut haben** *coll* cry easily; **ins ~ fallen** fall into the water; *coll* fall through; **ins ~ gehen** drown oneself; **mit allen ~n gewaschen sein** *coll* know every trick in the book; **sich über ~ halten** keep one's head above water; **unter ~** under water; **zu ~ lassen** launch; **zu ~ und zu Lande** by land and water

Wasser– water …; aquatic …;

w~abstoßend water-repellent; **die ~amsel, –n** dipper; **w~arm** arid; **das ~bad, ⸚er** bain-marie; *chem* water-bath; **der ~ball, ⸚e** beach-ball; *sp* water-polo (ball); **der ~behälter, –** tank; **das ~bett, –en** water-bed; **die ~bombe, –n** depth-charge; **die ~burg, –en** castle surrounded by water; **der ~dampf** water-vapour; **w~dicht** watertight; waterproof; **der ~floh, ⸚e** water-flea; **der ~fall, ⸚e** waterfall; **die ~farbe, –n** water-colour; **w~fest** waterproof; **das ~flugzeug, –e** seaplane; **w~gekühlt** water-cooled; **das ~glas, ⸚er** tumbler; *chem* water-glass; **der ~graben, ..gräben** moat; drainage-ditch; *athl*, *equest* water-jump; **der ~hahn, ⸚e** tap, faucet *US*; **w~haltig** aqueous; **die ~jungfer, –n** dragonfly; **der ~kopf, ⸚e** hydrocephalus, water on the brain; **das ~kraft|werk, –e** hydro-electric power-station; **die ~kunst, ⸚e** fountain; **der ~lauf, ⸚e** watercourse; **die**

~leitung, -en water-pipe; die ~linse, -n duckweed; w~löslich soluble in water; der ~mann, ⸚er water-sprite; *astron*, *astrol* Aquarius; die ~melone, -n water-melon; die ~pfeife, -n hookah; die ~pflanze, -n aquatic plant; die ~polizei river police; das ~rad, ⸚er water-wheel; die ~ratte, -n water-rat; *joc* keen swimmer; die ~scheide, -n watershed; w~scheu frightened of water; der ~ski, -er water-ski; water-skiing (W. laufen water-ski); der ~speier, - gargoyle; der ~sport water sports; der ~stand, ⸚e water-level; die ~stiefel *pl* waders; der ~stoff hydrogen; wasser|stoff|blond peroxide blonde; die ~stoff|bombe, -n hydrogen bomb; der ~strahl, -en jet of water; die ~straße, -n waterway; die ~sucht dropsy; die ~uhr, -en water-meter; water-clock; der ~vogel, ..vögel waterfowl; die ~waage, -n spirit-level; der ~weg, -e waterway (auf dem W. by sea/water); der ~werfer, - water-cannon; das ~werk, -e water-works; die ~wirtschaft water supply and distribution; der ~zähler, - water-meter; das ~zeichen, - watermark

Wässerchen *coll*: **aussehen, als ob man kein ~ trüben könnte** look as if butter wouldn't melt in one's mouth

wässerig watery; (+*dat*) **den Mund ~ machen** make (s.o.'s) mouth water

wassern (*also sn*) land on water; *space* splash down

wässern water (thoroughly); *cul* soak; (*v/i* eyes, mouth) water

die **Wasserung, -en** landing on water; *space* splashdown

wäßrig = wässerig

Wat-: der ~vogel, ..vögel wader

waten (*sn*) wade

die **Water|kant** (North Sea) coast

watscheln (*sn*) waddle

das **Watt**[1], - *elect* watt

das **Watt**[2], -en mud-flat (on North Sea coast)

die **Watte** cotton wool, absorbent cotton *US*; wadding

das **Watten|meer** mud-flats (on North Sea coast)

wattieren pad

wau, wau! woof, woof!

der **Wauwau, -s** (*baby-talk*) bow-wow

das **WC, -(s)** W.C.

der **WDR = Westdeutscher Rundfunk**

Web- weaving ...; **der ~stuhl, ⸚e** loom; **die ~waren** *pl* woven goods

die **Webe, -n** *Aust* (bed) linen

weben (*p/t* **webte**/(*fig poet*) **wob** (*subj* **webte/wöbe**), *p/part* **gewebt**/(*fig poet*) **gewoben**) (*also v/i*) weave

der **Weber, -** weaver; **der ~knecht, -e** daddy-long-legs; **der ~vogel, ..vögel** weaver-bird

die **Weberei, -en** weaving; weaving-mill; woven article

der **Wechsel** [-ks-], - change; alternation, *agr etc* rotation; (monthly) allowance; *sp* change of ends; substitution; *athl* changeover; *fin* bill (of exchange)

Wechsel- *esp* alternate ...; alternating ...

das ~bad, ⸚er immersion (*esp* of extremities) alternately in hot and cold water; alternation of extremes (of treatment *etc*); **die ~beziehung, -en** interrelation, correlation (**miteinander in W. stehen** be interrelated); **die ~fälle** *pl* vicissitudes, ups and downs; **das ~geld** change; **der ~gesang** antiphony; **das ~gespräch, -e** dialogue; **die ~jahre** *pl* menopause; **der ~kurs, -e** rate of exchange; **der ~rahmen, -** clipframe; **w~seitig** reciprocal; mutual; **die ~seitigkeit** reciprocity; mutuality; **das ~spiel** interplay; **der ~strom** alternating current; **die ~stube, -n** bureau de change; **das ~tierchen, -** amoeba; **w~voll** varied; **der ~wähler, -** floating voter; **w~weise** alternately, in turn; **die ~wirkung, -en** interaction (**in W. stehen mit** interact with)

wechselhaft changeable

wechseln [-ks-] change; exchange; (+*dat*) give (s.o.) change for; (*v/i*) change; vary; alternate; **~ gegen/in** (*acc*) change into (dollars, lire, *etc*); **den Arzt/die Schule** *etc* **~** change doctors/schools *etc*; **den Besitzer ~** change hands; **Briefe ~** correspond (**mit** with); **die Farbe ~** change colour; shift one's allegiance; **die Wohnung ~** move; **~d** changing; alternating; changeable; variable; (success) varying; **~d bewölkt** cloudy with sunny periods

Weck-: das ~glas, ⸚er preserving jar; **der ~ruf, -e** reveille

wecken (*see also* **geweckt**) wake; arouse; **das Wecken** reveille

der **Wecken, -** *SGer* (oblong) roll

der **Wecker, -** alarm-clock; (+*dat*) **auf den ~ gehen** *coll* get on (s.o.'s) nerves

der **Wedel, -** feather-duster; whisk; *bot* frond

wedeln whisk; (*v/i*) *ski* wedel; **~ mit** wave; wag (its tail)

weder: ~ ... noch ... neither ... nor ...

weg [-ɛ-] away; **~ sein** be away; have gone/left; *coll* have gone off (to sleep); be out (= unconscious); **ganz ~ sein** *coll* be in raptures (**von** over); **über ...** (*acc*) **~ sein** *coll* have got over; **~ da!** out of the way!; **~ damit!** get rid of it/them!; **Hände ~!** hands off!; **in einem ~** *coll* non-stop

der **Weg, -e** path; way; route; journey; road (to success *etc*); **jmdn. ein Stück ~(es) begleiten** accompany s.o. part of the way; **seines ~es/seiner ~e gehen** go on one's way; (+*dat*) **den ~ bereiten** pave the way for; **seine eigenen ~e gehen** go one's own way; (+*dat*) **den ~ versperren** bar (s.o.'s) way

in prepositional phrases:

am ~(e) by the wayside

auf (*acc*): (+*dat*) **mit auf den ~ geben** give (s.o. sth.) to take with him/her; **sich auf den ~ machen** set out

auf (*dat*): **auf dem ~** on the way (**nach/zu** to); **auf halbem ~** halfway; **auf dem rechten/falschen ~(e) sein** be on the right/wrong track; **auf dem ~(e) der Besserung** on the road to recovery; (*denoting means*) **auf ... ~(e)** by ... means, –ly (*eg* **auf chemischem/künstlichem ~(e)** by chemical/artificial means, chemically/artificially); through ... channels (*eg* **auf diplomatischem/offiziellem ~(e)** through diplomatic/official channels); **auf gütlichem ~(e)** amicably; **auf schriftlichem ~(e)** in writing; **auf dem schnellsten ~(e)** as quickly as possible; **auf dem ~(e)** (+*gen*, *eg* **der künstlichen Besamung**) by means of (artificial insemination *etc*); **auf dem (besten) ~(e) sein zu ...** be well on the way to (+*ger*)

aus: (+*dat*) **aus dem ~(e) gehen** get out of (s.o.'s) way/out of the way of; steer clear of; fight shy of; **aus dem ~(e) räumen** remove; clear up (misunderstanding); *coll* get rid of, eliminate (person)

in: (+*dat*) **im ~(e) sein/stehen** be in (s.o.'s) way; stand in (s.o.'s) way/in the way of; (+*dat*) **Hindernisse in den ~ legen** put obstacles in (s.o.'s) way; **in die ~e leiten** arrange; set in train

über: (+*dat*) **nicht über den ~ trauen** not trust (s.o.) an inch

---

weg– [–ɛ–] *sep pref – general senses*:

(*i*) ... away, ... off (*eg* **~schleichen** sneak away/off, **~blasen** blow away); *with modal auxiliary eg* **~müssen** = go, leave (*eg* **das muß weg** that must go); (+*dat*) ... away from (*eg* **jmdm. etw. ~schnappen** snatch sth. away from s.o.);

(*ii*) ... away (*eg* **~schließen** lock away)

Weg– (*for vbl nouns with prefix* **Weg–** *see separate entries*): **der ~bereiter, –** pioneer (**der W. sein für** pave the way for); **der ~genosse, –n** (*wk masc*) companion; **der ~rand, ¨er** wayside; **w~weisend** trailblazing; **der ~weiser, –** signpost; guide; **die ~zehrung** provisions for the journey; *ecclesiastical* viaticum

wegbekommen* *coll* = **wegkriegen**

wegblasen* blow away; **wie weggeblasen sein** *coll* have vanished

wegbleiben* (*sn*) stay away (**von** from); stop coming; be omitted; *coll* (engine) fail

wegbringen* take away; see off; *coll* remove (stain *etc*)

wegdenken*: sich *dat* **... ~** imagine the place *etc* without; **... ist aus** (**unserer Welt** *etc*) **nicht wegzudenken** (our world *etc*) is inconceivable without ...

Wege–: der ~lagerer, – highwayman

wegen (*usu + gen*; *in literary style sometimes following noun*) because of; for the sake of; (dismissed, famous, *etc*) for; (ask *etc*) about; **von ~** *coll* because of; **von Amts ~** by virtue of one's office; **von Berufs ~** because of one's job; **von Rechts ~** as of right; *coll* by rights; **von ~!** are you kidding!; no way!; **von ~ ...!** ... my foot/ass *US*!

der **Wegerich, –e** plantain

weg|essen* (+*dat*) eat up all (s.o.'s) ...

der **Wegfall** [–ɛ–] dropping (of); discontinuance

wegfallen* (*sn*) be discontinued; be dropped; stop; be no longer applicable

der **Weggang** [–ɛ–] departure

weggeben* give away

weggehen* (*sn*) go, leave; go out; (letter *etc*) go off; *coll* sell; *coll* (spot) come out; (pain) go (away); **~ von** leave; **von zu Hause ~** leave home; **geh mir weg mit ...!** spare me ...!

weghaben* *coll* have got; have got (spot *etc*) out; have got the hang of; **~ wollen** want to get rid of; **einen ~** be tight; have a screw loose; **was ~** be really good (at sth.); **sein Fett ~** have got what was coming to one; **die Ruhe ~** be unflappable

weghängen put away (in wardrobe *etc*)

weghelfen*: (+*dat*) **~ über** (*acc*) *coll* help (s.o.) get over

wegholen take away; **sich** *dat* **... ~** *coll* catch (cold *etc*)

weghören not listen

wegkarren cart off

wegkommen* (*sn*) *coll* get away; (thing) get lost; **~ über** (*acc*) get over; **... ist mir weggekommen** I've lost ...; **gut/schlecht ~** come off well/badly

wegkönnen* be able to get away

wegkriegen *coll* get rid of; get out (stain *etc*); (be able to) move; get (wound *etc*), catch (cold *etc*); cotton on to; **~ von** get away from

weglassen* leave out; let (s.o.) go

weglaufen* (*sn*) run away (**vor** *dat* from); (+*dat*) (wife) run away from

weglegen put away; put aside

wegmachen *coll* get rid of; **sich ~** make off

wegmüssen* have to go/leave

die **Wegnahme** [–ɛ–] taking (away); seizure (of property)

wegnehmen* take; take away; remove; take up (space *etc*); (+*dat*) take (away) from; *games* take (s.o.'s piece)

weg|operieren remove by operation

wegpacken put away

wegputzen wipe away/off; *coll* polish off

wegradieren rub out

wegrasieren shave off

wegräumen clear away

wegreißen* (river) sweep away; (storm) rip off; (+*dat*) snatch away from; **~ von** tear away from

wegrennen* (*sn*) run away

wegschaffen get rid of; remove

wegschenken *coll* give away

wegscheren: scher dich weg! buzz off!

wegschicken send away; send off

wegschleichen* (*sn*) sneak away/off

wegschließen* lock away

wegschmeißen* *coll* chuck away

wegschnappen (+*dat*) *coll* snatch away from; pinch (s.o.'s job, girl-friend, *etc*)

wegschneiden* cut away

wegschütten pour away

wegsehen* look away

wegspülen wash away; flush away

wegstecken put away; *coll* swallow

wegsterben* (*sn*) *coll* die off; **... ist/sind ihm weggestorben** he (has) lost ...

wegtragen* carry off

wegtreten* (*sn*) *mil* fall out; **~ lassen** dismiss; **weg(ge)treten!** dismiss(ed *US*)!; **(geistig) weggetreten** *coll* dead to the world

wegtun* *coll* put away; throw away

wegwenden*, sich ~ turn away

Wegwerf– [ˈvɛk–] disposable ...; **die ~windel, –n** disposable nappy/diaper *US*

wegwerfen* throw away; **das ist weggeworfenes Geld** that's money down the drain; **sich ~ an** (*acc*) throw oneself away on; **~d** disparaging

wegwischen wipe away; wipe out; brush aside

wegwollen* want to leave/go out/get away; **~ von** want to leave

wegzählen *Aust* subtract

wegzaubern make (s.o., sth.) disappear by magic

wegziehen* pull back (curtain); (+*dat*) pull away from; (*v/i sn*) move away; (birds) leave

weh[1] melancholy; *coll* sore; **mir ist ~ ums Herz** I am sick at heart; **~ tun,** (+*dat*) **~ tun** hurt

weh[2]**: o ~!** oh dear!; **~ mir!** woe is me!; *see also* **wehe**

das **Weh** woe; grief; **mit ~ und Ach** *coll* with much moaning || **das ~geschrei** cries of woe; **w~klagen** (*insep*) lament (**über** *acc* over); **w~leidig** whining; (voice) plaintive; **die ~mut** melancholy; wistfulness; **w~mütig = w~muts|voll** melancholy; wistful; **das ~wehchen, –** *coll* (imagined) ailment

wehe: ~, wenn du ...! you'll be sorry if you ...!; **weh(e) dem, der ...!** woe betide anyone who ...!

die **Wehe, –n** drift

wehen (wind) blow (**von** off); (*v/i*) (wind) blow; (flag *etc*) flutter; (s.o.'s hair) blow about; (*sn*) waft

die **Wehen** *pl* labour pains, contractions; birth pangs (of new age *etc*); **in den ~ liegen** be in labour

das **Wehr, –e** weir

Wehr: sich zur ~ setzen defend oneself

Wehr– military ...; *archit* fortified (tower *etc*); **der ~be|auftragte** (*decl as adj*) commissioner for the armed forces; **der ~dienst** military service; **der ~dienst|verweigerer, –** conscientious objector; **w~fähig** fit for military service; **w~los** defenceless; helpless; **die ~macht** (*German armed forces, 1935–45*); **der ~mann, ⸚er** *Swiss* soldier; **die ~pflicht** conscription; **w~pflichtig** liable for military service

wehren (+*dat*) check; **sich ~** put up a fight; resist; **sich ~ gegen** resist; defend oneself against; **sich seiner Haut ~** defend oneself

das **Weib, –er** *esp pej* woman; female; *arch, bibl* wife; **ein tolles ~** *coll* quite a woman

das **Weibchen, –** little woman; *zool* female; **–weibchen** female ...

Weiber– women's ...; **der ~feind, –e** misogynist; **die ~geschichten** *pl* womanizing; **der ~held, –en** (*wk masc*) ladykiller

weibisch effeminate

weiblich feminine (*also gramm, pros*); female

die **Weiblichkeit** femininity; **die holde ~** *joc* the fair sex

Weibs–: das ~bild, –er *coll* = **die ~person, –en** *coll* female; **das ~stück, –e** *coll* 'bitch'

weich soft; **~ werden** soften; relent; **die Knie werden mir ~** I go weak at the knees || **das W~bild, –er** city/town precincts; **~gekocht** soft-boiled; **~herzig** soft-hearted; **das W~holz, ⸚er** softwood; **der W~käse** soft cheese; **~klopfen** (*sep*) *coll* = **~machen** (*sep*) *coll* soften up; **der W~macher, –** softening agent; **der W~spüler, –** fabric conditioner; **die W~teile** *pl* soft parts; **das W~tier, –e** mollusc

die **Weiche**[1]**, –n** flank

die **Weiche**[2]**, –n** *rail* points, switch *US*; **die ~n stellen** switch the points, throw the switch *US*; **+für** set the course for; set the scene for (confrontation)

weichen[1] (*p/t* **wich,** *p/part* **gewichen)** (*sn*) (pressure *etc*) ease; (mist *etc*) go; *mil* fall back; (+*dat*) give way to, yield to
  ~ **aus** (blood) drain from
  unter jmds. Füßen ~ (ground) give way beneath s.o.
  ~ **von** leave; **nicht von jmdm./jmds. Seite** ~ not leave s.o.'s side; **nicht von der Stelle** ~ refuse to budge
  zur Seite ~ step aside
weichen[2] (*also sn*) soak
die **Weichheit** softness
weichlich (man) soft; (character) weak
der **Weichling, -e** weakling
die **Weichsel** [-ks-] the Vistula
Weid- *hunt* hunting ...; **der ~mann, ⸚er** *hunt* sportsman (with gun); **w~männisch** *hunt* sportsmanlike; **~manns|heil!** good hunting!; **das ~werk** hunting
die **Weide**[1], **-n** willow
die **Weide**[2], **-n** pasture; **auf die ~ treiben** put out to pasture || **das ~land** pasture-land
weiden (cattle) graze; **seine Augen ~ an** (*dat*) feast one's eyes on; ~ **lassen** graze; **sich ~ an** (*dat*) revel in; gloat over
Weiden- willow ...; **das ~kätzchen, -** willow catkin; **der ~korb, ⸚e** wicker basket; **der ~laub|sänger, -** chiffchaff; **das ~röschen, -** willow-herb
weidlich: ~ **auslachen** have a good laugh at; ~ **ausnutzen** make full use of; ~ **ausschimpfen** give (s.o.) a good scolding; **sich ~ bemühen** make a great effort; ~ **schimpfen** grumble loudly
weigern: sich ~ refuse (to)
die **Weigerung, -en** refusal
Weih-: der ~bischof, ⸚e suffragan bishop; **w~nachten (es w~nachtet** Christmas is in the air); **das ~nachten** (*esp Aust, Swiss* **die ~nachten** *pl*) Christmas (**W.** *usu occurs without article*; *treated as sing* (*eg* **W. steht vor der Tür** Christmas is just around the corner), *as sing or pl following adj* (*eg* **nächste(s) W.** next Christmas), *as pl in* **frohe/fröhliche W.!** merry Christmas!, **grüne W.** a Christmas without snow, **weiße W.** a white Christmas; **an W.** *SGer* at Christmas; **zu W.** at Christmas, (get, give) for Christmas); **w~nachtlich** Christmas; Christmassy; **~nachts-** Christmas ...; **der ~nachts|abend, -e** Christmas Eve; **das ~nachts|fest, -e** Christmas; **das ~nachts|lied, -er** Christmas carol; **der ~nachts|mann, ⸚er** Father Christmas, Santa Claus; **der ~nachts|tag, -e (der erste W.** Christmas Day; **der zweite W.** December 26th, *usu* Boxing Day; **während der ~nachtstage** over Christmas); **der ~rauch** incense; **das ~wasser** holy water
die **Weihe**[1], **-n** solemnity; *eccles* consecration; ordination; **w~voll** solemn
die **Weihe**[2], **-n** *ornith* harrier
weihen consecrate; ordain; (+*dat*) dedicate to; **dem Tode geweiht** doomed to die; **dem Untergang geweiht** doomed
der **Weiher, -** pond
weil because
weiland *arch* formerly
Weilchen: ein ~ a little while
die **Weile** while; **eine ~** for a while; **damit hat es gute ~** there's no hurry
weilen stay; sojourn; **... weilt nicht mehr unter uns** ... is no longer with us
der **Weiler, -** hamlet
Weimarer: die ~ Republik the Weimar Republic
der **Wein, -e** wine; vines; grapes; (+*dat*) **reinen ~ einschenken** tell (s.o.) the truth, come clean; **wilder ~** Virginia creeper || **der ~bau** wine-growing; **der ~bauer, -** wine-grower; **die ~beere, -n** grape; *SGer* raisin; **der ~berg, -e** vineyard; **die ~berg|schnecke, -n** edible snail, *cul* escargot; **der ~brand, ⸚e** brandy; **der ~gärtner, -** wine-grower; **die ~gegend, -en** wine-growing region; **der ~händler, -** wine merchant; **der ~hauer, -** *Aust* wine-grower; **die ~karte, -n** wine-list; **der ~keller, -** wine-cellar; wine-tavern; **der ~krampf, ⸚e** crying fit; **die ~lese, -n** grape-harvest; **die ~probe, -n** wine-tasting; **die ~rebe, -n** (grape)vine; **wein|rot** burgundy; **die ~säure** tartaric acid; **der ~schlauch, ⸚e** wine-skin; **w~selig** merry with wine; **der ~stock, ⸚e** (grape)vine; **die ~stube, -n** wine tavern; **die ~traube, -n** grape; **der ~zwang** obligation to take wine with one's meal
weinen cry, weep; ~ **um** weep for; **sich** *dat* **die Augen aus dem Kopf** ~ cry one's eyes out; **sich in den Schlaf** ~ cry oneself to sleep; **dem Weinen nahe** close to tears; **zum Weinen bringen** make (s.o.) cry; **... ist zum Weinen!** ... is enough to make you weep!; **leise ~d** crying softly; *coll* somewhat crestfallen
weinerlich whining; weepy
weis-: ~machen (*sep*) (+*dat*) make (s.o.) believe (sth. untrue) **(das kannst du anderen w.!** tell that to the marines!; **sich** *dat* **nichts w. lassen** not be taken in); **~sagen** (*insep*) prophesy; **der W~sager, -** prophet; **die W~sagerin, -nen** prophetess; **die W~sagung, -en** prophecy
weise wise; **der Weise** (*decl as adj*) wise man; sage; **die Weise** (*decl as adj*) wise woman; **die drei W~n aus dem Morgenland** the Three Wise Men from the East
die **Weise, -n** way, manner; *mus* air; **auf (geheimnisvolle** *etc*) ~ in a (mysterious *etc*)

way; **auf diese ~** in this way; **auf verschiedene ~** in various ways; **in der ~, daß ...** in such a way that ...; **in gewisser ~** in a way; **in keiner ~** in no way; by no means; **jeder nach seiner ~** each after his own fashion

---

-weise[1] *forming adverbs*:

(*i*) (*attached to adjectives, always with level stress*) -ly (enough), *eg* **natürlicherweise** naturally (enough), **merkwürdigerweise** oddly (enough), **paradoxerweise** paradoxically, **begreiflicherweise** understandably;

(*ii*) (*attached to nouns*) -ly, by way of ..., as a ..., in ..., *etc*, *eg* **annäherungs~** approximately, **ausnahms~** by way of exception, exceptionally, **beispiels~** for example, **stellen~** in places, **straf~** as a punishment, **teil~** part(ial)ly, in part; (*referring to quantities*) ... by ..., by the ..., in ...s, *eg* **ballen~** in bales, by the bale, **blatt~** leaf by leaf, sheet by sheet, **gruppen~** in groups, **löffel~** by the spoonful, **pfund~** by the pound

-weise[2] *forming adjectives*: *certain adverbs in* **-weise** *formed from nouns* (*see* (*ii*) *in the preceding entry*) *are also used adjectivally*, *eg* **schritt~** gradual, **teil~** partial, **zwangs~** compulsory

---

der **Weisel, -** queen bee

weisen (*p/t* **wies,** *p/part* **gewiesen**) (+*dat*) show (s.o. the way *etc*); (*v/i*) point (**auf** *acc* at, **in** *acc* in: direction, into: distance, **nach** towards); **~ aus** send out of; expel from (country); **von der Schule ~** expel (from school); **(weit) von sich ~** reject (emphatically); **... ist nicht von der Hand zu ~ ...** cannot be denied; (+*dat*) **die Tür ~** show (s.o.) the door

die **Weisheit, -en** wisdom; wise saying; **mit seiner ~ am Ende sein** be at one's wits' end || **der ~s|zahn, ⸚e** wisdom tooth

weiß[1] *1st/3rd sing pres of* **wissen**

weiß[2] white; **das W~e Haus** the White House; **der W~e Tod** death in the snow; **~ werden** turn white; **der/die Weiße** (*decl as adj*) white; **das Weiße** (*decl as adj*) white (of egg); **das W~e im Auge** the whites of the eyes || **das W~bier** (*light-coloured, highly effervescent beer made with top-fermentation yeast*); **das W~blech** tinplate; **das W~brot, -e** (loaf of) white bread; **das W~buch, ⸚er** *pol* white paper; **die W~buche, -n** hornbeam; **~gelb** pale yellow; **~glühend** white-hot; **die W~glut** white heat (**bis zur W. bringen/reizen** make (s.o.) see red); **~haarig** white-haired; **der W~kohl = das W~kraut** *SGer* white cabbage; **der W~macher, -** whitener; **das W~metall, -e** white metal; **der W~russe, -n** (*wk masc*), **~russisch** White Russian; **W~rußland** White Russia; **~waschen*** (*sep*) (*only infin and p/part*) (**jmdn./sich w.** clear s.o.'s/one's name); **der W~wein, -e** white wine

die **Weiße** whiteness; **Berliner ~** (*see* **Berliner**)

weißen whiten; whitewash

weißlich whitish

weißt *2nd sing pres of* **wissen**

die **Weisung, -en** instruction

weit (*see also* **weiter**) wide; extensive; (concept *etc*) broad; (journey, way, *etc*) long; loose(-fitting); (*adv*) far; widely; wide (open); well (below, over, *etc*); **... ist (1 km** *etc*) **~ ...** is (1 km. *etc*) away; **in ~er Ferne** far in the distance; **~ entfernt** (*see* **entfernt**); **mit ... ist es nicht ~ her** *coll* ... is *etc* not up to much; **von ~ her** from far away; **~ und breit** far and wide; for miles around; **bei ~em** far (better *etc*); by far (the best *etc*); **bei ~em nicht** nowhere near; **von ~em** (hear *etc*) from a long way off; **das W~e suchen** take to one's heels;

(*with verbs*): **es ~ bringen** go far; **es ~ gebracht haben** have done very well (for oneself); **zu ~ gehen** go too far; **das geht zu ~!** that's going too far!; **haben Sie es noch ~?** have you got far to go?; **~ kommen** (*with neg or interrog*) get far; **so ~ ist es also gekommen!** so it's come to that!; **zu ~ treiben** carry too far; **wie ~ sind Sie (mit ...)?** how far have you got (with ...)?

weit-: **~ab** far away (**w. von** far from); **~aus** far (better *etc*); by far (the best *etc*); **der W~blick** far-sightedness, vision; **~blickend** far-sighted; **~gehend** extensive; wide; (*adv*) largely; to a large extent; **~gereist** widely-travelled; **~gesteckt** (programme *etc*) ambitious; **~her** (**von w.** from far away); **~hergeholt** far-fetched; **~herzig** broad-minded; **~hin** over a long distance; largely; **~läufig** extensive; spacious; lengthy; (relative) distant; **~reichend** far-reaching; **~schauend** far-sighted; **~schweifig** long-winded, rambling; **die W~sicht** far-sightedness; **~sichtig** long-sighted; far-sighted; **der W~sprung** long jump, broad jump *US*; **~spurig** broad-gauge ...; **~tragend** far-reaching; *mil* long-range; **~verbreitet** widespread; commonly-held; **~verzweigt** with many branches; highly ramified; **das W~winkel|objektiv, -e** wide-angle lens

die **Weite, -n** width; expanse; breadth (of outlook *etc*); *athl* distance (jumped, thrown); **in die ~ blicken** look into the distance

weiten widen; stretch; **sich ~** widen;

(outlook) broaden

weiter (*comp of* **weit**) further; other; another (five weeks *etc*); (*adv*) further; (... kilometres *etc*) further on; (*indicating continuing action*) *conveyed by* ... continue(s) to ... (*eg* **er versprach, ~ für sie zu sorgen** he promised to continue to look after her); furthermore; **~!** go on!; **immer ~** on and on; further and further; **immer ~!** keep at it!; **nicht ~ = ~ nicht** not particularly; **nichts ~ = ~ nichts** nothing else; that's all; **+als** nothing but; **wenn es ~ nichts ist** if that's all it is; **~ nichts?** is that all?; **niemand ~ = ~ niemand** nobody else; **~ so!** keep it up!; **und ~?** and then?; **und so ~ (und so fort)** and so on (and so forth); **Weiteres** (*decl as adj*) further details; **alles W~e** everything else; **bis auf ~es** until further notice; for the time being; **ohne ~es** (*see* **ohne**); **des ~en** furthermore

---

weiter– *sep pref – general senses*:

(*i*) ... on; ... further; continue (to) ... (*eg* **~schicken** send on, **~entwickeln** develop further, **~arbeiten** continue working, **~reisen** continue one's journey); *with modal auxiliary eg* **~müssen** = go on (*eg* **ich muß weiter** I must go on);

(*ii*) *indicates transfer or transmission to a third party* (*eg* **~geben** pass on, **~verkaufen** resell)

Weiter– further ...; continued ...

weiter|arbeiten continue working

weiterbestehen* continue to exist

weiterbilden give (s.o.) further education/training; **sich ~** continue one's education/training

weiterbringen* help on; advance

weiter|empfehlen* recommend (to others)

weiter|entwickeln develop further; **sich ~** progress

weiter|erzählen pass on (what one is told)

weiterfahren* (*sn*) drive on; continue one's journey

die **Weiterfahrt** continuation of the journey

weiterfliegen* (*sn*) fly on

der **Weiterflug** continuation of the flight

weiterführen continue; **... führt uns nicht weiter** ... doesn't lead us anywhere

die **Weitergabe** passing on; transmission

weitergeben* pass on (**an** *acc* to)

weitergehen* (*sn*) go/walk on; go further; go on, continue; **so kann es nicht ~** things/we can't go on like this; **wie geht es weiter?** what happens now?

weiterhelfen* (+*dat*) help along; be of some help to

weiterhin moreover; in the future; still; *or conveyed by* ... continue(s) to ...

weiterkommen* (*sn*) get further; get on; make headway

weiterkönnen* be able to go on; **ich kann nicht weiter** I can't go on

weiterlaufen* (*sn*) run/walk on; keep on running; go on, continue; continue to be paid

weiterleben live on

weiterleiten pass on (**an** *acc* to); forward

weiterlesen* continue reading

weitermachen carry on

weitermüssen* have to go on

weiterreichen pass on

weiterreisen (*sn*) continue one's journey; **~ nach** travel on to

weiters *Aust* in addition

weitersagen pass on; **~!** pass it on!

weitersehen: ... dann wollen wir ~ ... then we'll see

die **Weiterungen** *pl* complications; difficulties

weiterverbreiten spread

weiterver|erben pass on; **sich ~** be passed on

weiterverfolgen continue to follow; follow up

der **Weiterverkauf** resale

weiterverkaufen resell

weitervermieten sublet

weiterwissen*: nicht ~ be at a loss what to do; be stuck

weiterwollen* want to go on

weiterwurs(ch)teln *coll* muddle along

weiterzahlen continue to pay

der **Weizen** wheat; **der ~keim, –e** wheat germ; **das ~keim|öl** wheat-germ oil; **die ~kleie** bran; **das ~mehl** wheat(en) flour

welch.. (*uninflected* **welch**) 1 *interrog adj* which; what; (*in exclamations*) what (a); 2 *interrog pron* which (one); 3 *indef pron* some; any; 4 *rel pron* who; which; 5 *rel adj* which; **~ ... (auch) (immer)** whichever; whatever || **~erlei** (*indecl*) whatever

der **Welfe, –n** (*wk masc*) Guelph

welk faded; withered

welken (*sn*) wilt, fade; wither

Well–: das ~blech corrugated iron; **das ~fleisch** boiled pork; **die ~pappe** corrugated cardboard

die **Welle, –n** wave (*also phys and in hair*); craze; *rad* wavelength; *tech* shaft; **grüne ~** linked traffic lights; **(hohe) ~n schlagen** cause a (considerable) stir

wellen (*see also* **gewellt**) wave (hair); **sich ~** be/become wavy

Wellen– wave ...; **das ~bad, ⸚er** swimming-pool with artificially generated waves; **der ~bereich, –e** waveband; **der ~brecher, –** breakwater; **w~förmig** wave-like; undulatory; **der ~gang** swell; **der ~kamm, ⸚e** crest of a wave; **die ~länge, –n** wavelength; **die ~linie, –n** wavy line; **das ~reiten**

surfing; **der ~reiter, –** surfer; **der ~schlag** breaking/lapping of the waves; **der ~sittich, –e** budgerigar

wellig wavy; undulating

der **Welpe, –n** (*wk masc*) pup, whelp; cub

der **Wels, –e** catfish

welsch *Swiss* French Swiss; *arch* Latin (= relating to the Latin peoples), *esp* French *or* Italian; foreign; **die ~e Schweiz** *Swiss* French Switzerland || **das W~land** *Swiss* French Switzerland; **der W~schweizer, –** *Swiss*, **~schweizerisch** *Swiss* French Swiss

die **Welt, –en** world; **die Alte/Neue/Dritte ~** the Old/New/Third World; **die große/vornehme ~** high society; **~en trennen uns/sie** we/they are worlds apart; **alle ~** everybody; (**die größte Münze** *etc*) **der ~** (the largest coin *etc*) in the world; **auf der ~** in the world; **aus aller ~** from all over the world; **aus der ~ schaffen** eliminate; **in aller ~** the world over; (**warum** *etc*) **in aller ~ ...?** (why *etc*) on earth ...?; **in die ~ setzen** bring into the world; start (rumour); **um nichts in der ~ = nicht um alles in der ~** not for the world; **Dame/Mann von ~** woman/man of the world; **vor aller ~** in front of everyone; **zur ~ bringen/kommen** bring/come into the world

Welt– world ...; international ...;

das ~all the universe; **w~anschaulich** ideological; **die ~anschauung, –en** weltanschauung, world-view; ideology; **die ~bank** the World Bank; **w~bekannt = w~berühmt** world-famous; **w~bewegend** world-shaking; **das ~bild, –er** conception of the world; view of life; **der ~bürger, –** citizen of the world, cosmopolitan; **der ~ernährungs|rat** the Food and Agriculture Organization (of U.N.); **w~erschütternd** world-shattering; **w~fremd** unworldly; **die ~geltung** international reputation; **das ~gericht** the Last Judgement; **der ~gerichts|hof** the International Court of Justice, the World Court; **das ~geschehen** world events; **die ~geschichte** world history (**in der W. umherfahren** *coll* travel about all over the place); **w~geschichtlich** (**w~geschichtliches Ereignis** historical event of great importance; **von w~geschichtlicher Bedeutung** of great importance in world history); **die ~gesundheits|organisation** the World Health Organization; **w~gewandt** urbane; **der ~handel** world trade; **die ~hilfs|sprache, –n** international auxiliary language; **der ~kirchen|rat** the World Council of Churches; **w~klug** worldly-wise; **die ~klugheit** worldly wisdom; **der ~krieg, –e** world war; **die ~macht, ⸚e** world power; **der ~mann, ⸚er** man of the world; **w~männisch** urbane; **das ~meer, –e** ocean; **der ~meister, –** world champion; **die ~meisterschaft, –en** world championship; **der ~pokal** the World Cup; **w~offen** open-minded; **der ~post|verein** the Universal Postal Union; **der ~raum** (outer) space; **~raum–** space ...; **die ~raum|fähre, –n** space shuttle; **der ~raum|fahrer, –** astronaut; **die ~raum|fahrt, –en** space-travel; **das ~raum|labor, –e** space lab; **das ~reich, –e** empire; **die ~reise, –n** world tour; **der/die ~reisende** (*decl as adj*) globe-trotter; **der ~rekord, –e** world record; **der ~rekord|inhaber, – = der ~rekordler, –** world record holder; **der ~ruf** world-wide reputation; **der ~schmerz** weltschmerz, world-weariness; **die ~stadt, ⸚e** metropolis; **der ~untergang** end of the world; **der ~verbesserer, –** do-gooder; **w~weit** world-wide, global; **der ~wirtschafts|gipfel, –** World Economic Summit; **die ~wirtschafts|krise, –n** world economic crisis; (*1929-31*) the Depression; **das ~wunder, –** wonder of the world

der **Welten|bummler, –** globe-trotter

weltlich worldly; secular

wem (*dat of* **wer**) 1 *interrog pron* (to/for) whom; 2 *rel pron* anyone/the person to/for whom; 3 *indef pron coll* (to/for) somebody; **~ ... (auch) (immer)** whoever ... to/for || **der W~fall** dative (case)

wen (*acc of* **wer**) 1 *interrog pron* whom; 2 *rel pron* anyone/the person whom; 3 *indef pron coll* somebody; **~ ... (auch) (immer)** whoever || **der W~fall** accusative (case)

die **Wende** change; turnaround; *swim* turn; *gym* front vault; **an der/um die ~ des (19.** *etc*) **Jahrhunderts** at the turn of the (19th *etc*) century || **der ~kreis, –e** *geog* tropic; *mot* turning-circle; **der ~punkt, –e** turning-point; watershed

die **Wendel|treppe, –n** spiral staircase

wenden (*p/t* **wandte/wendete** (*rare subj* **wendete**), *p/part* **gewandt/gewendet;** *senses where only* **wendete** *and* **gewendet** *are usual are marked with an asterisk*) (*see also* **gewandt**) *turn (over); *turn (vehicle, boat, *etc*); turn (one's head); (*v/i* motorist, swimmer, *etc*) *turn; **~ an** (*acc*) spend (money, time) on; take (trouble) over; **kein Auge/keinen Blick ~ von** not take one's eyes off; **bitte ~!** please turn over

sich ~ turn (round); turn (in a certain direction, *eg* **nach Norden** to the north, northwards); (weather, s.o.'s luck) *turn; **sich ~ an** (*acc*) apply to; contact; turn to (**um** for); (book *etc*) be aimed at; **sich ~ gegen** oppose; **sich ~ von** turn from; **sich ~ zu** turn to(wards); **sich zum Gehen ~** turn to go; **sich zum Besseren** ~ take a turn for the better; **es hat sich alles zum besten gewendet** everything has turned out for the best

wendig agile; manoeuvrable

die **Wendigkeit** agility; manoeuvrability

die **Wendung, -en** turn; change; turn of events; phrase; **eine (günstige** *etc*) ~ **nehmen** take a (favourable *etc*) turn; **dieses Ereignis gab seinem Leben eine neue** ~ this event changed the direction of his life; **eine** ~ **zum Besseren** a change for the better

wenig little; not much; (*adv*) little; not much; not very; ~**(e)** *pl* few; a few; ~ **(Neues** *etc*) little that is/was (new *etc*); **ein** ~ a little; **ein klein** ~ a little bit of; **nicht** ~ not a little; ~**es** little; **um ein** ~**es** a little (older *etc*); **das** ~**e, was ...** the little that ...; **einige** ~**e** a few; **nicht** ~**e** quite a few

weniger (*comp of* **wenig;** *indecl*) less (*also math*); (*pl*) fewer; (*adv*) less; not very; **nicht** ~ **als** no less/fewer than; **nichts** ~ **als** anything but

die **Wenigkeit** small amount; trifle; **meine** ~ *joc* yours truly

wenigst.. (*superl of* **wenig**) least; (*pl*) fewest; **die** ~**en** very few (people); **das** ~**e, was ...** the least ...; **am** ~**en** least

wenigstens at least

wenn (*referring to present or future, or repeated occurrence in past*) when; (*conditional*) if; *sometimes expressed by* to + *infin* (*eg* ~ **ich ehrlich sein soll** to be honest) *or* with + *participial construction* (*eg* **ich kann mich nicht konzentrieren,** ~ **ihr beide so dasteht!** I can't concentrate with you two standing there like that!); **auch** ~ **...** even if/when ...; ~ **auch ...** even if ...; albeit ...; ~ **auch nicht ...** if not ...; ~ **... auch noch so (sehr) ...** no matter how (much) ...; ~ **... bloß/doch/nur ...!** if only ...!; ~ **... (erst) einmal** once ...; **immer/jedesmal** ~ **...** whenever ...; ~ **... nicht** if ... not; unless ...; ~ **nicht** if not; ~ **... schon** if ... (at all); even if ...; '~ **schon!** what of it?, so what?; **selbst** ~ **...** even if ...; **und** '~ **...** even if ...; **das Wenn und Aber** ifs and buts || ~**gleich** even though; albeit; ~**schon (w., dennschon** if a thing's worth doing then it's worth doing properly)

Wenzel Wenceslaus

wer (*acc* **wen,** *gen* **wessen,** *dat* **wem)** 1 *interrog pron* who; 2 *rel pron* anyone who (*often followed by the demonstrative* **der** – *which is left untranslated – in the main clause*, *eg* ~ **das behauptet, (der) lügt** anyone who says that is lying); 3 *indef pron coll* somebody; ~ **... auch (immer)** whoever; ~ **da?** *mil* who goes there?; ~ **sein** *coll* be somebody; ~ **von ...?** which (one) of ...? || **der W~fall** nominative (case)

Werbe- advertising ...; publicity ...; commercial ...; **die** ~**agentur, -en** = **das** ~**büro, -s** advertising agency; **das** ~**fern|sehen** commercial television; commercials; **der** ~**gag, -s** publicity gimmick; **der** ~**graphiker, -** commercial artist; **die** ~**kampagne, -n** advertising campaign; **das** ~**plakat, -e** poster; **der** ~**slogan, -s** advertising slogan; **der** ~**spot, -s** commercial; **der** ~**text, -e** advertising copy; **der** ~**texter, -** copywriter; ~**trommel** *coll* (**die W. rühren für** push (product *etc*)); **w**~**wirksam** effective (for advertising purposes)

werben (wirb(s)t, *p/t* **warb** (*subj* **würbe),** *p/part* **geworben) win (new customers** *etc*); recruit; ~ **für** promote; *pol* campaign for; ~ **um** court; solicit

werblich (experience *etc*) advertising

die **Werbung, -en** *vbl noun*; *also* advertising; publicity; (sales) promotion; publicity department

Werde- [-eː-]: **der** ~**gang** development; career

werden [-eː-] **(wirst, wird,** *p/t* **wurde** (*subj* **würde**), *p/part* **geworden,** (*in passive construction*) **worden)** (*sn*)

1(*a*) become; get (better, wet, *etc*), go (blind, soft, *etc*), turn (pale, Communist, Muslim, *etc*); be, come (third *etc*); live to be (90 *etc*); *sometimes rendered by* be (*eg* **das Buch wurde ein großer Erfolg** the book was a great success, **1980 wurde Pluto 50** Pluto was 50 in 1980, **er wollte Rennfahrer** ~ he wanted to be a racing-driver); *coll* be coming along; *coll* (*with interrog*) happen;

es wird schon ~ it'll be all right; **es will nicht** ~ it won't work; **wie ist (der Kuchen** *etc*) **geworden?** how did (the cake *etc*) turn out?; **(die Zeichnung** *etc*) **ist nichts geworden** (the drawing *etc*) wasn't any good; **wird's bald!** get a move on!; **es muß anders** ~ things can't go on like this;

~ **lassen (zu)** make (*eg* **der Skandal hat ihn zu einer der umstrittensten Gestalten der deutschen Politik** ~ **lassen** the scandal (has) made him one of the most controversial figures in German politics);

~ **aus** become of; come of; **aus ... wird ... ...** turn(s)/grow(s) into ..., become(s) ...; **aus ... ist etwas/nichts geworden** ... has *etc* got somewhere/not got anywhere in life; **daraus wird nichts** nothing will come of it; *coll* that's out (of the question)

~ **mit: was wird mit ...?** what is to become of ...?

~ **zu** become, turn into; turn to (dust, stone); **zum Dieb/Verräter** ~ turn thief/traitor

(*b*) (+*dat*: *impers*): **mir wird (kalt/schlecht** *etc*) I feel (cold/sick *etc*);

2 (*as auxiliary*) (*a*) (*with infin*) *forms future tense* will/shall (*eg* **er wird dich verstehen** he will understand you); *may also express a supposition* (*eg* **sie wird (wohl) krank sein** I expect she's ill);

(*b*) (*with p/part*) *forms passive* be/get + *p/part* (*eg* **angegriffen ~** be attacked, **verletzt ~** get hurt, **die Brücke wird gebaut** the bridge is being built, **er ist/war angegriffen worden** he has/had been attacked, **er muß angegriffen worden sein** he must have been attacked, (*with Ger ind obj becoming Eng subj*) **mir wurde gesagt, daß ...** I was told that ...); *also used with intransitive verbs to form impersonal passive* (*eg* **es wurde getanzt/viel gelacht** there was dancing/much laughter; (*with omission of* **es** *when clause begins with another word*) **er bestimmte, wann geschlafen wurde** he decided when they *etc* would sleep, **vor dem Schwerverbrecher wurde im Rundfunk gewarnt** a warning was given on the radio about the dangerous criminal);

(*c*) **würde** (*with infin*) would

Note: *in constructions of the type* **ich werde** *etc*/**würde** *etc* **... werden,** *the infinitive is often omitted* (*eg* **werde ich abgeholt (~)?** will I be collected?, **es wird sein größter Film (~)** it will be his greatest film, **die Brücke wird gebaut (~)** the bridge will be built, **weil er einfach mißverstanden (~) würde** because he would simply be misunderstood)

das **Werden** growth; development; **im ~** in the making

werdend nascent; (mother) expectant

werfen (wirf(s)t, *p/part* **warf** (*subj* **würfe**), *p/part* **geworfen)** throw (**nach** at); cast (shadow); form (bubbles, creases); *zool* have (young); **an die Wand ~** project onto the wall; **einen Blick ~ auf** (*acc*) (cast a) glance at; **~ mit** throw (snowballs *etc*) (**auf** *acc* at); **um sich ~ mit** bandy about; **mit Geld um sich ~** *coll* throw one's money about; **von sich ~** throw off (clothes); **zu Boden ~** throw to the ground

sich ~ (wood) warp; **sich ~ auf** (*acc*) throw oneself onto; throw oneself into (task); **sich ~ in** (*acc*) throw on (clothes); **sich ~ vor** (*acc*) throw oneself in front of; **sich jmdm. zu Füßen ~** throw oneself at s.o.'s feet; **sich zu Boden ~** throw oneself to the ground

die **Werft, -en** dockyard

das **Werk, -e** work (*also arts*); deed; works, factory; mechanism, works; **-werk** *forms certain collectives* (*eg* **das Ast~** branches, **das Laub~** foliage, **das Mauer~** masonry, **das Schuh~** footwear); **das ist dein** *etc* **~** this is your *etc* doing; **ab ~** ex works; **am ~** at work; **ans ~ gehen = sich ans ~ machen** set to work; **(behutsam** *etc*) **zu ~e gehen** proceed (cautiously *etc*)

Werk- works ...; **die ~bank, ⸚e** workbench; **w~getreu** faithful to the original; **die ~kunst|schule, -n** school of arts and crafts; **der ~meister, -** foreman; **der ~schutz** works security force; **die ~spionage** industrial espionage; **die ~statt, ⸚en** workshop; garage; studio; **der ~stoff, -e** material; **das ~stück, -e** workpiece; **der ~tag, -e** working day, workday; **w~tags** on workdays; **w~tätig** working; **der/die ~tätige** (*decl as adj*) working man/woman; **der ~unterricht** handicraft lessons; **das ~zeug, -e** tool; tools

werkeln *coll* potter about

werken work (physically); do handicrafts

Werks- works ...; **w~eigen** company-owned

der **Wermut** vermouth; *bot* wormwood; **der ~s|tropfen, -** drop of bitterness

wert [-e:-] dear; *comm* (letter) esteemed; (*following acc*) worth ...; (*following gen*) worthy of ...; **-wert** -worthy; -able; worth (+*ger*, *eg* **lebens~** worth living); **einen Versuch ~** worth a try; **nicht der Mühe/Rede ~** not worth the trouble/worth mentioning; **es ~ sein, daß man** (*eg* **einem vertraut**) deserve to be (trusted *etc*); **(es) ~ sein, (veröffentlicht** *etc*) **zu werden** be worth (+*ger*, *eg* publishing)

der **Wert** [-e:-], **-e** value; worth; *philat* denomination; (*pl*) objects of value; (moral *etc*) values; **das hat keinen ~** *coll* there's no point; **~ legen auf** (*acc*) attach importance to; **im ~(e) von** to the value of, worth

Wert- ... of value; *post* registered ...; **die ~angabe, -n** declaration of value; **w~beständig** stable (in value); **der ~gegenstand, ⸚e** article of value; (*pl*) valuables; **w~los** valueless, worthless; **die ~minderung, -en** depreciation; **die ~ordnung, -en** system of values; **das ~papier, -e** *fin* security; (*pl*) stocks and shares; **die ~sachen** *pl* valuables; **die ~schätzung** esteem; **die ~schrift, -en** *Swiss fin* security; (*pl*) stocks and shares; **die ~skala, -(l)en** scale of values; **das ~urteil, -e** value judgement; **w~voll** valuable; **das ~zeichen, -** postage-stamp; **der ~zuwachs** appreciation (in value)

werten [-e:-] assess; rate; (*v/i*) *sp* award points

-wertig *chem* -valent

die **Wertigkeit** valency

die **Wertung, -en** assessment; rating; *sp*

classification; points

der **Werwolf, ⸚e** werewolf

Wes– [–ɛ–]: **der ~fall** genitive (case)

wesen (spirit *etc*) be present

das **Wesen, –** creature; being; essence; nature; (*with adj*) manner; **–wesen** ... system, *or with this sense implied by a suffix* (*eg* **das Bank~** banking, **das Steuer~** taxation, **das Verlags~** publishing); **viel ~s machen um/von** make a lot of fuss about; **sein ~ treiben** busy oneself; (thief) be at work; (ghost) be abroad || **w~los** insubstantial

wesenhaft intrinsic

Wesens–: die ~art, –en character, nature; **w~eigen** (*following dat*) inherent in (s.o.'s) character; **w~fremd** (*following dat*) alien to (s.o.'s) nature; **w~gleich** identical in character; **der ~zug, ⸚e** characteristic

wesentlich essential; fundamental; substantial; (*adv*) fundamentally; considerably (better *etc*); **das Wesentliche** (*decl as adj*) the essential thing; the essence (of sth.); **im ~en** in essence, essentially; in the main

weshalb which is why; (*interrog*) why

der **Wesir, –e** vizier

die **Wespe, –n** wasp; **das ~n|nest, –er** wasps' nest (**in ein W. stechen** stir up a hornets' nest); **der ~n|stich, –e** wasp sting; **die ~n|taille, –n** wasp-waist

wessen (*gen of* **was**) of what, (*of* **wer**) whose

West west; *in compds* west ...; western ...; **der ~fale, –n** (*wk masc*) Westphalian; **~falen** Westphalia; **w~fälisch** Westphalian; **West|indien** the West Indies; **west|indisch** West Indian; **die ~mark, –** *coll* West German mark; **der ~wall** the Siegfried Line; **w~wärts** westwards

die **Weste, –n** waistcoat, vest *US*; **eine weiße ~ haben** *coll* have a clean slate

der **Westen** west; **der ~** *pol* the West; **der Wilde ~** the Wild West

die **Westen|tasche, –n** waistcoat pocket, vest pocket *US*; **wie seine ~ kennen** *coll* know like the back of one's hand

der **Western** ['vɛstɐn] (*gen* –(s)), **–** *cin* western

der **Westler, –** *EGer coll* West German

westlich 1 *adj* western; westerly; (*adv*) (to the) west (**von** of); 2 *prep* (+*gen*) (to the) west of

weswegen which is why; (*interrog*) why

wett: ~ sein be quits

Wett– betting ...; (*eg* **das ~schwimmen** swimming) contest;

der ~bewerb, –e competition; *sp* event (**in W. treten mit** compete with); **der ~bewerber, –** competitor; **w~bewerbs|fähig** competitive; **das ~büro, –s** betting shop; **der ~eifer** competitive spirit; **w~eifern** (*insep*) compete (**um** for); **die ~fahrt, –en** race; **der ~kampf, ⸚e** competition, contest; match; **der ~kämpfer, –** competitor; **der ~lauf, ⸚e** race (**W. mit der Zeit** race against time); **der ~läufer, –** runner; **w~machen** (*sep*) make up for; make good (loss); **das ~rennen, –** race; **das ~rüsten** arms race; **der ~streit, –e** contest

die **Wette, –n** bet; wager; **was gilt die ~?** what will you bet me?; **um die ~ fahren/laufen/reiten/schwimmen** *etc* race each other

wetten bet; **~ auf** (*acc*) bet on; **auf Platz/Sieg ~** back a horse for a place/win; **mit jmdm. um ... ~** bet s.o. (... marks *etc*); **mit jmdm. ~, daß ...** bet s.o. that ...; **(wollen wir) ~?** want to bet?

das **Wetter, –** weather; storm; **bei jedem ~** in all weathers; **alle ~!** good heavens!; **gut ~ machen bei** *coll* make up to || **der ~bericht, –e** weather report; **der ~dienst** meteorological service; **die ~fahne, –n** weather-vane; **der ~fleck, –e** *Aust* waterproof cape; **der ~frosch, ⸚e** *joc* weatherman; **w~fühlig** sensitive to changes in the weather; **die ~fühligkeit** sensitivity to changes in the weather (causing headaches *etc*); **die ~kunde** meteorology; **die ~lage, –n** weather situation; **w~leuchten** (*insep*) (**es w~leuchtet** there is sheet-lightning); **das ~leuchten** sheet-lightning; **der ~satellit, –en** (*wk masc*) weather satellite; **die ~station, –en** weather station; **der ~sturz, ⸚e** sudden drop in temperature; **die ~vorhersage, –n** weather forecast; **die ~warte, –n** weather station; **w~wendisch** fickle

wettern curse and swear; **~ gegen** inveigh against; **es wettert** there is a thunderstorm

Wetz–: der ~stein, –e whetstone

wetzen sharpen; (*v/i sn*) *coll* dash

WEZ (= Westeuropäische Zeit) G.M.T.

der **Whisky** ['vɪski], **–s** whisky

das **Whist** [vɪst] whist

wich *p/t of* **weichen**[1]

Wichs– [–ks–]: **die ~leinwand** *Aust coll* oil-cloth

die **Wichse** [–ks–], **–n** polish; **~ bekommen** *coll* get a hiding

wichsen [–ks–] (*see also* **gewichst**) polish; *coll* give (s.o.) a hiding

der **Wicht, –e** goblin; scoundrel; **armer ~** poor wretch; **kleiner ~** little one

der **Wichtel, – = das ~männchen, –** gnome

wichtig important; **(zu) ~ nehmen** take (too) seriously; **sich ~ machen/tun** put on airs || **der W~macher, –** *Aust* = **der W~tuer, –** pompous ass; **die W~tuerei** pomposity; **~tuerisch** pompous

die **Wichtigkeit** importance

die **Wicke, –n** vetch; sweet pea

der **Wickel, –** curler; reel; *med* compress; **beim ~ kriegen** *coll* grab by the scruff of the neck; give (s.o.) a telling-off || **das ~kind, –er** babe-in-arms

wickeln wind; put in curlers; bandage; wrap (**in** *acc* in); put a nappy/diaper *US* on (baby); **um den (kleinen) Finger ~** *coll* twist round one's little finger; **sich ~ um** wind itself round

der **Widder, –** ram; *astron, astrol* Aries

wider (+*acc*) against; contrary to

wider– *sep (stressed) and insep (unstressed) pref*

widerborstig recalcitrant; (hair) unruly

widerfahren* (*sn*) (+*dat*) happen to; (wrong) be done to

der **Widerhaken, –** barb

der **Widerhall, –e** echo; **~ finden** meet with a response

widerhallen echo; reverberate; **~ von** echo with

widerlegen refute

die **Widerlegung, –en** refutation

widerlich repulsive; loathsome

widernatürlich unnatural

der **Widerpart, –e** *arch* adversary; (+*dat*) **~ bieten** oppose

widerraten* (+*dat*) advise against

widerrechtlich unlawful, illegal

die **Widerrede, –n** contradiction; **ohne ~** without contradiction; **keine ~!** don't argue!

der **Widerruf, –e** cancellation, countermand; retraction; **bis auf ~** until further notice

widerrufen* cancel, countermand; revoke; retract; (*v/i*) recant

der **Widersacher, –** adversary

der **Widerschein, –e** reflection

widersetzen: sich ~ (+*dat*) resist

der **Widersinn** absurdity

widersinnig absurd

widerspenstig refractory, recalcitrant; (hair) unruly

widerspiegeln reflect; mirror; **sich ~ in** (*dat*) be reflected in

die **Widerspiegelung, –en** reflection

das **Widerspiel** interaction (of opposites)

widersprechen* (+*dat*) contradict; conflict with; run counter to; **sich** *dat* **~** contradict oneself; **sich** *dat pl*/**einander ~** conflict; **~d** conflicting, contradictory

der **Widerspruch, ⸚e** contradiction; objection; **~ in sich selbst** contradiction in terms; **~ erheben** object (**gegen** to); **im ~ zu** contrary to; **im ~ stehen zu** conflict with

widersprüchlich contradictory

Widerspruchs–: der ~geist contradictoriness; **w~los** without contradiction; **w~voll** full of contradictions

der **Widerstand, ⸚e** resistance (*also elect*) (**gegen** to); opposition (to); **den Weg des geringsten ~es gehen** follow the line of least resistance; **~ leisten** offer resistance || **die ~s|bewegung, –en** resistance movement; (the) Resistance; **w~s|fähig** resistant (**gegen** to); tough; hard-wearing; (plant) hardy; **der ~s|kämpfer, –** member of the Resistance; **die ~s|kraft** resistance; **w~s|los** without resisting; **das ~s|nest, –er** pocket of resistance

widerstehen* (+*dat*) resist; withstand; (food) be repugnant to

widerstreben (+*dat*) oppose; go against; **es widerstrebt mir zu …** I am loath to …

das **Widerstreben** reluctance; **mit ~** with reluctance

widerstrebend *pres/part*; *also* reluctant; conflicting

der **Widerstreit** conflict

widerwärtig repulsive; obnoxious

der **Widerwille** (*like* **Wille**) aversion (**gegen** to); revulsion; **mit ~n** grudgingly

widerwillig reluctant, unwilling; grudging

widmen ['vɪt–] (+*dat*) dedicate to; devote to; **sich ~** (+*dat*) attend to; devote oneself to

die **Widmung, –en** dedication

widrig adverse; **–widrig** contrary to …, *or rendered by negative prefix* (*eg* **natur~** unnatural, **sinn~** nonsensical, **sitten~** immoral) || **~en|falls** failing which

die **Widrigkeit, –en** adversity

wie 1 *adv* how; what … like (*eg* **~ ist das Wetter?** what's the weather like?); (way) in which; 2 *conj* (*a*) like; as (*expressing comparison*); as if (by a miracle *etc*); as well as; such as; (*spelling on telephone*) for (*eg* **D ~ Dora** D for David); (*followed by comp: nonstandard*) than; (*b*) (*introducing clause*) as; the way; (know, learn, teach: **~ man …**) how to (+*infin*); (*following verbs of perception*) = *pres/part* (*eg* **er sieht zu, ~ zwei Ameisen eine tote Raupe schleppen** he watches two ants dragging a dead caterpillar); such as (*eg – with the addition in German of 3rd pers pron referring back to antecedent –* **Tragetaschen aus Plastik, ~ man sie heute überall kaufen kann** plastic carrier-bags such as one can buy anywhere nowadays); (*temporal: with historic present*) as; (*with past tense*) *coll*, *reg* as; when

~? what?; **…, ~?** *coll* …, wasn't it/didn't you *etc*?; **~ bitte?** pardon?; **~ bitte!** I beg your pardon!

~ … auch however (expensive *etc*); **~ auch immer** whatever way …, however …; **~ dem auch sei** be that as it may

~ ist es mit …? what about …?; **~ wär's mit …?** how about …?

~ noch nie as never before

so ~ … the way … (*eg* **so ~ die Dinge liegen** the way things are); **so ~ ich … kenne** if I know …; **so … ~ …**

as ... as ...
und ~! I'll say!
~ wenn ... ** as though ...; **~ wäre es, wenn ...? how about ... (+*ger*)?
der **Wiedehopf, -e** hoopoe
wieder again; re- (*eg* **~ auffüllen** replenish, **~ auftauchen** resurface); back; in turn
'so ... (ist er *etc*) **auch ~ nicht** (he is *etc*) not *that*.../not as ... as all that
~ da back (again)
~ ein ... another ...; **~ einmal** once again
immer ~ again and again
schon ~ again; already; **schon ~?** what, again?; **schon ~ ...!** (yet) another ...!; not ... again!; **was ... schon ~?** what ... this time?; **was gibt's denn nun schon ~?** what is it now?, whatever's the matter now?

---

wieder- *sep pref - general senses*:
(*i*) re-, ... again (*eg* **~gewinnen** regain);
(*ii*) ... back (*eg* **~kaufen** buy back);
(*iii*) *indicates reciprocation* (*eg* **jmdn. ~lieben** return s.o.'s love)

---

wieder|anknüpfen resume (relations *etc*)
der **Wieder|anlauf, ⸚e** *comput* restart, rerun
der **Wieder|aufbau** rebuilding, reconstruction
wieder|aufbauen rebuild, reconstruct
wieder|aufbereiten recycle; *nucl tech* reprocess (nuclear waste)
die **Wieder|aufbereitungs|anlage, -n** *nucl tech* reprocessing facility
wieder|aufführen *theat* revive
wieder|aufleben (*sn*), **~ lassen** revive
das **Wieder|aufleben** revival; resurgence
die **Wieder|aufnahme** resumption; readmission; *leg* reopening; *theat* revival; **das ~verfahren, -** rehearing; retrial
wieder|aufnehmen* resume; readmit; *leg* reopen; *theat* revive
die **Wieder|aufrüstung** rearmament
wieder|ausführen re-export
der **Wiederbeginn, -e** recommencement; resumption
wiederbekommen* get back
wiederbeleben revive, resuscitate
die **Wiederbelebung, -en** revival, resuscitation
wiederbringen* bring back; return
wieder|einführen reintroduce; *comm* reimport
die **Wieder|einführung, -en** reintroduction
wieder|eingliedern reintegrate (**in** *acc* into)
die **Wieder|eingliederung, -en** reintegration
der **Wieder|eintritt, -e** re-entry (*also space*) (**in** *acc* into)
wieder|entdecken rediscover
die **Wieder|entdeckung, -en** rediscovery
wieder|erhalten* get back, recover
wieder|erkennen* recognize
wieder|erlangen regain; recover
wieder|er|öffnen reopen
wieder|erstatten refund
wiederfinden* find again; regain
die **Wiedergabe, -n** reproduction; rendering
wiedergeben* reproduce; render; convey; give an account of; (+*dat*) give back to, return to
wiedergeboren reborn
die **Wiedergeburt** rebirth
wiedergewinnen* win back; regain
wiedergrüßen return (s.o.'s) greeting
wiedergutmachen make up for; redress
die **Wiedergutmachung, -en** reparation; redress
wiederhaben* have got back; have back
wiederherstellen restore; re-establish; **(völlig) wiederhergestellt** *med* (completely) recovered
die **Wiederherstellung, -en** restoration; re-establishment; *med* recovery
wiederholen (*cf next entry*) fetch back
wiederholen (*insep*) (*cf previous entry*) repeat; revise, review *US* (vocabulary *etc*); *sp* replay; retake; *comput* rerun; **sich ~** repeat oneself; be repeated; **wiederholt** repeated
die **Wiederholung, -en** repetition; revision, review *US*; *rad, TV* repeat; action replay; *sp* replay; retaking; *comput* rerun; **die ~s|impfung, -en** booster (shot); **der ~s|kurs, -e** refresher course; *Swiss mil* annual military training; **das ~s|spiel, -e** *sp* replay; **das ~s|zeichen, -** *mus* repeat
Wiederhören: auf ~! *tel* goodbye!; *rad* goodbye for now!
die **Wieder|instand|setzung** repair
wiederkäuen ruminate; *coll* repeat over and over again; (*v/i*) chew the cud
der **Wiederkäuer, -** ruminant
die **Wiederkehr** return; recurrence; anniversary
wiederkehren (*sn*) return; recur; **~d** *also* recurrent
wiederkennen* *NGer* recognize
wiederkommen* (*sn*) come back, return
wiederkriegen *coll* get back
die **Wiederkunft** return
wiederlieben return (s.o.'s) love
Wiederschauen: auf ~! goodbye!
wiedersehen* see again; meet again; **sich ~** meet again; **das Wiedersehen, -** (subsequent) meeting; reunion; **auf Wiedersehen!** goodbye!; **auf Wiedersehen in ...!** I'll see you in ...!
der **Wiedertäufer, -** Anabaptist
wiederum again; on the other hand; in turn
wiederver|einigen reunify
die **Wiederver|einigung, -en** reunification
wiederverheiraten: sich ~ remarry
der **Wiederverkauf** resale; retail

wiederverkaufen resell; retail

wiederverwenden* re-use

die **Wiederverwendung** re-use

wiederverwerten [-e:-] re-use; recycle

die **Wiederwahl** re-election

wiederwählen re-elect

die **Wiege, –n** cradle; **das ist ihm nicht an der ~ gesungen worden** he couldn't have foreseen that; **... ist ihm in die ~ gelegt worden** he inherited (aptitude *etc*)

wiegen[1] (*p/t* **wog** (*subj* **wöge**), *p/part* **gewogen**) weigh; **schwer ~** be heavy; (argument *etc*) carry great weight; **in der Hand ~** weigh in one's hand; **sich ~** weigh oneself

wiegen[2] (*see also* **gewiegt**) rock; shake (one's head) (pensively *etc*); sway (one's hips); *cul* chop up; **in den Schlaf ~** rock to sleep; **in Sicherheit ~** lull into a false sense of security

sich ~ rock; sway; **sich ~ in** (*dat*) sway (one's hips); delude oneself with (false hopes); **sich in Sicherheit ~** lull oneself into a false sense of security

Wiegen–: der ~druck, –e incunabulum; **das ~lied, –er** lullaby

wiehern neigh; whinny; *coll* bray (with laughter)

Wien Vienna

der **Wiener, –** Viennese

Wiener (*indecl*) Viennese; **der ~ Kongreß** the Congress of Vienna; **~ Schnitzel** Wiener schnitzel; **~ Würstchen** frankfurter, wiener *US*

wienerisch Viennese

wienern *coll* polish (vigorously)

wies *p/t of* **weisen**

die **Wiese, –n** meadow; (grass) field; **auf der ~** in the meadow/field; **auf der grünen ~** in the open countryside

wiese̲hr *Aust*: **~ ... auch** however much

das **Wiesel, –** weasel

Wiesen–: die ~blume, –n wild flower; **der ~grund** *poet* low-lying meadow; **der ~pieper, –** meadow pipit

wieso̲ why; how come; **~?** how come?; how do you mean?; what makes you think that?

wieviel how much/*pl* many; **~ Uhr ist es?** what's the time? || **~mal** how many times

wievielt.. which (in a sequence); **den W~en haben wir heute?** what's the date today?; **zum ~en Mal?** how many times?

wiewe̲it to what extent

wiewo̲hl *arch* although

der **Wikinger, –, wikingisch** Viking

wild wild; savage; boisterous; (battle *etc*) fierce; unauthorized, (strike) wildcat; **~ auf** (*acc*) *coll* crazy about; **in ~er Ehe leben** live in sin; **~es Fleisch** proud flesh; **~ machen** infuriate; drive wild; **~ wachsen** grow wild; **~ werden** go wild; **das ist halb so ~** *coll* it's not as bad as all that; **wie ~** *coll* like mad; **der/die Wilde** (*decl as adj*) wild man/woman, savage

das **Wild** game; deer; *cul* game; venison

wild–: der W~bach, ⸚e torrent; **die W~bahn, –en** hunting-ground **(auf/in freier W.** in the wild); **das W~bret** game; venison; **der W~dieb, –e** poacher; **die W~ente, –n** wild duck; **der W~fang, ⸚e** boisterous child; tomboy; **das W~fleisch** game; venison; **~fremd (~fremder Mensch** complete stranger); **der W~hüter, –** gamekeeper; **die W~katze, –n** wild cat; **~lebend** living in the wild; **das W~leder, ~ledern** suede; **der W~park, –s** game park; **wịld|romạntisch** wild and romantic; **die W~sau, –en** wild sow; **der W~schaden** damage caused by game; **das W~schutz|gebiet, –e** game reserve; **das W~schwein, –e** wild boar; **~wachsend** (growing) wild; **das W~wasser, –** white water; **der W~wechsel, –** game path; **W~wẹst** (*no art*) the Wild West; **der W~wẹst|film, –e, der W~wẹst|roman, –e** western

der **Wilderer, –** poacher

wildern poach; (dog *etc*) attack game

die **Wildheit** wildness; savagery; fierceness

die **Wildnis, –se** wilderness; **in der ~** (live *etc*) in the wild

Wilhelm William; **~ der Eroberer** William the Conqueror

wilhelmi̲nisch Wilhelmine (*of the reign of Kaiser Wilhelm II, 1888–1918*)

will *1st/3rd sing pres of* **wollen**[1]

will–: ~fährig compliant; **~kọmmen** welcome (**w. heißen** welcome); **das W~kọmmen, –** welcome; **die W~kür** arbitrariness; despotism (**jmds. W. ausgeliefert** at s.o.'s mercy); **die W~kür|herrschaft** tyranny; **~kürlich** arbitrary; *physiol* voluntary

der **Wille** (*acc, dat* **–n**, *gen* **–ns**) will; **–wille** (*eg* **der Lebens~, Widerstands~**) will to (live, resist, *etc*); **guter ~** good will; **guten ~ns sein** be full of good intentions; **der Letzte ~** last will and testament; **seinen ~n durchsetzen** have one's way; (+*dat*) **seinen ~n lassen** let (s.o.) have his own way; **auf seinem ~n bestehen** insist on having one's own way; **aus freiem ~n** of one's own free will; **beim besten ~n nicht** not with the best will in the world; not for the life of me; **mit ~n** deliberately; **wenn es nach meinem ~n ginge** if I had my way; **wider ~n** in spite of oneself; (+*dat*) **zu ~n sein** comply with (s.o.'s) wishes; (sexually) yield to

willen: um ... (*gen*) **~** for the sake of

Willen–: w~los weak-willed; **die ~losigkeit** lack of willpower

willens willing (to)

Willens– ... of will; **die ~freiheit** free will; **die ~kraft** willpower; **w~schwach** weak-willed; **die ~schwäche** lack of willpower; **w~stark** strong-willed; **die ~stärke** willpower, strength of will

willentlich deliberate

willig willing; **–willig** (*eg* **arbeits~**) willing to (work *etc*), (*eg* **auswanderungs~**) wishing to (emigrate *etc*)

willst *2nd sing pres of* **wollen**

Wilna Vilnius

wimmeln: ~ von be swarming/teeming with; be riddled with; **es wimmelt von** the place is swarming/teeming with; the essay *etc* is riddled with

wimmern whimper

der **Wimpel, –** pennant

die **Wimper, –n** eyelash; *bot, zool* cilium; **ohne mit der ~ zu zucken** without batting an eyelid || **die ~n|tusche, –n** mascara; **das ~tierchen, –** ciliate

der **Wind, –e** wind; **~ bekommen von** get wind of; **viel ~ machen um** *coll* make a lot of fuss about; (+*dat*) **den ~ aus den Segeln nehmen** take the wind out of (s.o.'s) sails; **sich** *dat* **den ~ um die Nase/Ohren wehen lassen** see something of the world; **bei ~ und Wetter** in all weathers; **in den ~ reden** waste one's breath; **in den ~ schlagen** turn a deaf ear to; throw (caution) to the winds; **in alle ~e** to the four winds || **der ~beutel, –** cream-puff; *coll* happy-go-lucky person; **die ~bluse, –n** windcheater, windbreaker *US*; **das ~ei, –er** wind-egg; *coll* worthless plan; **der ~fang, ⸚e** porch; **die ~hose, –n** whirlwind; **der ~hund, –e** greyhound; *coll* fly-by-night; **die ~jacke, –n** windcheater, windbreaker *US*; **die ~mühle, –n** windmill; **die ~pocken** *pl* chicken-pox; **die ~rose, –n** compass-card; **der ~sack, ⸚e** wind-sock; **der ~schatten** lee; slipstream; **w~schief** crooked; **die ~schutz|scheibe, –n** windscreen, windshield *US*; **das ~spiel, –e** greyhound; **die ~stärke, –n** wind-force; **w~still** windless; sheltered (**es ist w.** there is no wind); **die ~stille, –n** calm; **der ~stoß, ⸚e** gust of wind; **der ~surfer, –** windsurfer; **das ~surfing** windsurfing

die **Winde, –n** *tech* winch; *bot* bindweed

die **Windel, –n** nappy, diaper *US*; **wịndel|weich** *coll* (**w. schlagen** beat to a pulp)

winden[1] (*p/t* **wand** (*subj* **wände**), *p/part* **gewunden**) (*see also* **gewunden**) wind; winch; make (garland); (+*dat*) **aus den Händen ~** wrest from (s.o.'s) hands; **sich ~** wind; wind one's way; writhe; squirm

winden[2]**: es windet** the wind is blowing

Windes|eile: mit ~ in no time

windig windy; *coll* dubious; (excuse) flimsy

die **Windung, –en** bend; coil; *anat* convolution; *tech* thread

der **Wink, –e** sign; wave; nod; hint, tip; **~ mit dem Zaunpfahl** broad hint

der **Winkel, –** corner; spot; *math* angle; *tech* square; *mil* chevron; **toter ~** blind spot; *mil* dead angle; **im rechten ~** at right angles (**zu** to) || **der ~advokat, –en** (*wk masc*) incompetent lawyer; **das ~maß, –e** *tech* square; **der ~messer, –** protractor; **der ~zug, ⸚e** subterfuge; evasion

wink(e)lig full of nooks and crannies; winding; **–wink(e)lig** -angled

winken wave; *sp* signal (offside *etc*); (*v/i*) wave; (+*dat*) wave to; signal to; hail (taxi); *or expressed – with ind obj becoming subj – by* can expect (*eg* **ihm winkt ein höherer Lebensstandard** he can expect a higher standard of living); **~ mit** wave (one's hand, handkerchief, *etc*); **zu sich ~** beckon over to one

der **Winker, –** *mot* indicator; **die ~krabbe, –n** fiddler crab

wịnke-wịnke (*baby-talk*): **~ machen** wave

winseln (animal) whimper

der **Winter, –** winter; **der ~garten, ..gärten** conservatory; **der ~schlaf** hibernation (**W. halten** hibernate); **der ~schluß|verkauf, ⸚e** winter sale; **~spiele** *pl* (**die Olympischen W.** the Winter Olympics); **der ~sport** winter sports

winterlich wintry; winter; (*adv*: dressed) for the winter

winters in winter

der **Winzer, –** wine-grower

winzig tiny

der **Wipfel, –** tree-top

die **Wippe, –n** see-saw

wippen seesaw; bob up and down; **~ mit** jiggle (foot); wag (tail)

wir (*see p. xxvi*) we

wirb *imp sing of* **werben**

der **Wirbel, –** whirl; whirlpool; crown (of head); whorl; (drum-)roll; turmoil; to-do; *phys* vortex; *anat* vertebra; *mus* peg (on instrument); **der ~knochen, –** vertebra; **w~los** invertebrate; **die ~losen** *pl* the invertebrates; **die ~säule, –n** spinal column; **der ~sturm, ⸚e** whirlwind; **das ~tier, –e** vertebrate; **der ~wind, –e** whirlwind

wirb(e)lig lively; dizzy

wirbeln whirl; (*v/i*) (drum) roll; (*sn*) whirl; swirl; **mir wirbelt der Kopf** my head is spinning

wirb(s)t (*2nd*,) *3rd sing pres of* **werben**

wird *3rd sing pres of* **werden**

wirf *imp sing*, **wirf(s)t** (*2nd*,) *3rd sing pres of* **werfen**

Wirk–: der ~stoff, –e active substance; **die ~waren** *pl* knitwear

wirken do (good); *text* knit (mechanically); weave (carpet *etc*); (*v/i*) work (as a doctor, for a cause, *etc*); have an effect; be effective, work; act (as a catalyst, deterrent, *etc*); have a ... effect (*eg* **die Nachricht wirkte elektrisierend** the news had an electrifying effect); appear, seem, give the impression of being; ~ **auf** (*acc*) make a ... impression on; have a ... effect on; (alcohol *etc*) act on; **aufeinander** ~ interact; **auf sich** ~ **lassen** take in; **Wunder** ~ perform miracles; work wonders; **das Wirken** work; activity

wirklich real; actual; (*adv*) really; ~ **und wahrhaftig** really and truly

die **Wirklichkeit** reality; **in** ~ in reality || **w~s|fremd** unrealistic; divorced from reality; **w~s|nah** realistic

wirksam effective

die **Wirkung, -en** effect; **seine** ~ **tun** have the desired effect; **ohne** ~ **bleiben** have no effect; **mit** ~ **vom ...** with effect from ... || **der ~s|bereich, -e** sphere of activity; **das ~s|feld, -er** field (of activity); **der ~s|grad, -e** *phys*, *tech* efficiency; **der ~s|kreis, -e** sphere of activity; **w~s|los** ineffective; ineffectual; **die ~s|losigkeit** ineffectiveness; **w~s|voll** effective; **die ~s|weise, -n** action (of machine *etc*)

wirr confused; chaotic; dishevelled; **der W~kopf, ⸚e** scatterbrain; **der W~warr** chaos, confusion; jumble

die **Wirren** *pl* turmoil

die **Wirrnis, -se** chaos, confusion

der **Wirsing(kohl)** savoy cabbage

wirst *2nd sing pres of* **werden**

der **Wirt, -e** landlord; *biol* host

wirten *Swiss* be a landlord

die **Wirtin, -nen** landlady; landlord's wife

wirtlich hospitable

Wirts-: das ~haus, ⸚er inn; **die ~leute** *pl* landlord and landlady; **die ~pflanze, -n** host plant; **die ~stube, -n** lounge (of inn); **das ~tier, -e** host animal

die **Wirtschaft, -en** economy; industry (and commerce); business world; housekeeping; pub, saloon *US*; *NGer* (small) farm; *coll* mess, muddle; **-wirtschaft** *may also denote a branch of industry* (*eg* **die Energie~** energy industry, **die Forst~** forestry, **die Milch~** dairy-farming); **freie** ~ private enterprise; (+*dat*) **die** ~ **führen** keep house for; **was ist denn das für eine ~!** that's a fine state of affairs!

wirtschaften keep house; manage one's affairs/money; busy oneself; **sparsam** ~ budget carefully; **zugrunde** ~ ruin

die **Wirtschafterin, -nen** housekeeper

der **Wirtschaftler, -** economist

wirtschaftlich economic; economical; thrifty

die **Wirtschaftlichkeit** profitability

Wirtschafts- economic ...; industrial ...; business ...; **die ~form, -en** economic system, (socialist *etc*) economy; **der ~führer, -** captain of industry; **das ~geld** houskeeping (money); **die ~krise, -n** economic crisis; **der ~minister, -** minister for economic affairs; **das ~ministerium, -(i)en** ministry for economic affairs; **der ~plan, ⸚e** *esp EGer* economic plan; **die ~planung** economic planning; **die ~politik** economic policy; **w~politisch** (relating to) economic policy; in terms of economic policy; **der ~prüfer, -** accountant; **der ~rat, ⸚e** economic council; **die ~spionage** industrial espionage; **das ~system, -e** economic system; **der ~teil, -e** business section; **die ~wissenschaften** *pl* economics; **der ~wissenschaftler, -** economist; **das ~wunder, -** economic miracle; **der ~zweig, -e** branch of industry

der **Wisch, -e** scrap of paper; **der ~lappen, -** = **das ~tuch, ⸚er** cloth

wischen wipe; *Swiss* sweep; **sich** *dat* **die Augen/den Mund** ~ wipe one's eyes/mouth; **Staub** ~ dust; **jmdm. eine** ~ *coll* clout s.o. one

der **Wischer, -** *mot* wiper; **das ~blatt, ⸚er** wiper blade

das **Wischiwaschi** *coll* drivel

der **Wisent, -e** (European) bison

das **Wismut** [-ɪ-] bismuth

wispern (*also v/i*) whisper

Wiß-: die ~begier(de) thirst for knowledge; **w~begierig** eager for knowledge

wissen (*pres* **weiß, weißt, weiß, wissen, wißt, wissen,** *subj* **wisse** *etc*; *p/t* **wußte,** *subj* **wüßte;** *p/part* **gewußt**)

1 know (fact *etc*, that ...); know (of); remember (*eg* **weißt du noch?** do you remember?, **ich weiß ihren Namen nicht mehr** I don't remember her name); (*with complement*) know that ... is *etc* (*eg* **jmdn. glücklich/in Gefahr** ~ know that s.o. is happy/in danger, **sich beobachtet** ~ know that one is being watched); have (*eg* **sie** ~ **gern Weiße um sich** they like to have whites around them); (*eg* **geändert)** ~ **wollen** want (changed *etc*);

weißt du schon das Neueste? have you heard the latest?; **es nicht anders/besser** ~ not know any different/better; **soviel ich weiß** as far as I know; **woher weißt du das?** how do you know that?; **nicht, daß ich wüßte** not that I know of; **man kann nie** ~ you never can tell; **weder aus noch ein** ~ be at one's wits' end; **was weiß ich!** search me!; **wer weiß wie** *coll* ever so; **... ist wieder wer weiß wo** *coll* goodness knows where ... is; ~ **Gott/der Himmel!** heaven knows!;

gewußt wie! sheer genius!;
2 ~ + **zu** + *infin* know how to; be able to; **zu schätzen** ~ appreciate
~ **um** know about
~ **von** know (nothing *etc*) about; (*v/i*) know about; **von nichts** ~ not know anything about it; **nichts** ~ **wollen von** want nothing to do with
~ **lassen** let (s.o.) know

das **Wissen** knowledge; **meines** ~**s** to my knowledge; **nach bestem** ~ **und Gewissen** to the best of one's knowledge and belief; **ohne jmds.** ~ without s.o.'s knowledge; **wider besseres** ~ against one's better judgement

wissend knowing

Wissens–: der ~**drang** = **der** ~**durst** thirst for knowledge; **das** ~**gebiet, –e** field; **das** ~**gut** (body of) knowledge; **die** ~**lücke, –n** gap in one's knowledge; **der** ~**schatz** store of knowledge; **w**~**wert** worth knowing

die **Wissenschaft, –en** science; scholarship; *arch* knowledge; **–wissenschaft** *is part of the name of numerous academic disciplines* (*eg* **die Musik**~ musicology, **die Sprach**~ linguistics)

der **Wissenschafter, –** *Aust, Swiss* = **der Wissenschaftler, –** scientist; scholar

wissenschaftlich scientific; scholarly; academic

wissentlich deliberate, intentional; (*adv*) deliberately, knowingly

wittern scent, get wind of; scent (danger *etc*)

die **Witterung** weather (conditions); *hunt* scent; **bei (guter** *etc***)** ~ if the weather is (good *etc*)

die **Witwe** [–ɪ–], **–n** widow (*gen/Aust* **nach** of); **grüne** ~ lonely suburban housewife; ~ **werden** be widowed

der **Witwer** [–ɪ–], **–** widower

der **Witz, –e** joke; wit; **das ist der ganze** ~ *coll* that's all there is to it; **einen** ~ **machen** crack a joke; **mach keine** ~**e!** don't be funny! || **das** ~**blatt, ¨er** comic magazine; **der** ~**bold, –e** joker; **die** ~**figur, –en** figure of fun; **w**~**los** *coll* pointless; **w**~**sprühend** sparkling

witzeln quip

witzig funny; witty

w. L. = **westliche Länge,** *eg* **20°** ~ longitude 20° west

Wladimir Vladimir

Wladiwostok Vladivostok

wo 1 *adv* where; (day, moment, *etc*) when; *coll* somewhere; 2 *conj* when (*indicating circumstances*); ~ **(auch) immer …** wherever …; ~ **… doch** seeing that; (= even though) when; **dort,** ~ **…** where …; **jetzt,** ~ **…** now that …; with … (*eg* **jetzt,** ~ **der Streik vorbei ist** with the strike over); ~ **möglich** if possible; ~ **nicht** if not; **überall,** ~ **…** wherever …

wo– (wor–) + *prep* (*see p. xxix and the individual entries concerned*) (*relative*) … which; (*interrogative*) what …; *eg* **worunter** under *etc** which; what … under *etc**
For the full range of possible translations of the prepositional element see the preposition concerned* (*eg* **unter) *or – where appropriate – the relevant verb or adjective entry* (*eg for* **worauf war er stolz?** what was he proud *of*? *see* **stolz** proud (**auf** *acc* of), *for* **… womit ich gerechnet hatte …** which I had expected *see* **rechnen mit** expect)

wo|anders somewhere else, elsewhere; ~**hin** (go *etc*) somewhere else

wob (wöbe) *p/t* (*subj*) *of* **weben**

wobei in the course of which; (and) in doing so; *or rendered by pres/part* (*eg* ~ **er den Lachs unter seinem Schottenrock verbarg** hiding the salmon under his kilt); with (+ *participial construction*, *eg* ~ **die meisten draußen bleiben mußten** with most of them having to stay outside, ~ **all ihre Kosten vom Staat getragen werden** with all their expenses paid by the state); (*interrog*) what … at; ~ **mir einfällt, daß …** which reminds me …

die **Woche, –n** week; **heute in einer** ~ a week today

Wochen– weekly …; **das** ~**bett** lying-in; ~**end–** week-end …; **das** ~**ende, –n** week-end (**verlängertes W.** long week-end); **die** ~**karte, –n** weekly season ticket; **w**~**lang** for weeks (on end); weeks of …; **der** ~**lohn, ¨e** weekly wage; **die** ~**schau, –en** newsreel; **die** ~**schrift, –en** weekly; **der** ~**tag, –e** weekday (including Saturday); **w**~**tags** on weekdays

wöchentlich weekly; (*adv*) weekly, every week; **–wöchentlich** every … weeks

–wöchig -week

die **Wöchnerin, –nen** woman who has recently given birth

der **Wodka** [ˈvɔt–], **–s** vodka

wodurch (*see* **wo–**) by (means of)/through/as a result of *etc* which; whereby; (*interrog*) how; what … by

wofür (*see* **wo–**) for *etc* which; (*interrog*) what … for *etc*

wog (wöge) *p/t* (*subj*) *of* **wiegen**[1]

die **Woge, –n** (large) wave; surge, wave (of enthusiasm *etc*)

wogegen (*see* **wo–**) against *etc* which; (*interrog*) what … against *etc*

wogen surge; wave; (bosom) heave; **hin und her** ~ (battle) sway to and fro

woher where … from; ~ **weißt du das?** how do you know that?

wohin where (… to); ~ **(… auch)** wherever; ~ **damit?** where shall I/we put it? || **wohingegen** whereas

wohinter (*see* **wo–**) behind *etc* which; (*interrog*) what ... behind *etc*

wohl 1 *adj* well; happy; **sich ~ fühlen** feel well/happy/at home; **mir ist nicht ~** I don't feel well; **mir ist nicht ~ bei dem Gedanken, daß ...** I'm not happy at the thought that ...; 2 *adv* (*a*) (know *etc*) well; (*b*) *unstressed particle* probably, no doubt; I suppose/expect; ... must ... (*eg* **du bist ~ verrückt!** you must be mad!, **wie oft ich das ~ schon gesagt habe!** how often I must have said that!); I take it (*eg* **du willst ~ nicht mitspielen?** I take it you don't want to play?); I wonder ... (*eg* **wie er ~ mit 60 aussieht?** I wonder what he'll look like at 60?, **ob er ~ vor Spinnen Angst hat?** I wonder if he's afraid of spiders?); *occurs with imperative force in phrase* **willst du/wollt ihr ~ ...** = will you ... (*eg* **willst du ~ damit aufhören!** will you stop that!); *with concessive force, is expressed by* it is true, ... may ... (*eg* **ich decke den Tisch ~ mit ab, aber dann ist die Sache für mich erledigt** I (do) help clear the table, it's true, but then that's it as far as I'm concerned, **~ ist er noch jung, aber doch schon recht erfahren** he may still be young, but he's already pretty experienced); (*c*) about, roughly;

es sich *dat* **~ sein lassen** enjoy oneself; **~ bekomm's!** (*see* **bekommen**); **~ aber** but (on the other hand); but it does/she is/he will/they have *etc*; **~ dem, der ...!** happy the man who ...; **~ kaum** hardly; I doubt it; **~ oder übel** whether one likes it or not, willy-nilly; **sehr ~ (, mein Herr)** *arch* very good (, sir)

das **Wohl** well-being; **das allgemeine/öffentliche ~** the common weal; **das ~ und Wehe** weal and woe; **auf Ihr ~!** your health!; **auf jmds. ~ trinken** drink s.o.'s health; **zum ~!** cheers!; **zum ~e der Menschheit** for the benefit of mankind

wohl– well–;

~ an! *arch* very well then!; **~auf** well, in good health; **~bedacht** well-considered; **das W~befinden** well-being; **das W~behagen** contentment; **~behalten** safe and sound; intact; **~bekannt** well-known; **~beleibt** stout, portly; **~betucht** *coll* well-heeled; **~durchdacht** well-thought-out; **das W~ergehen** well-being; **~erzogen** well-behaved; **die W~fahrt** welfare; **der W~fahrts|ausschuß** *Fr hist* the Committee of Public Safety; **die W~fahrts|marke, –n** charity stamp; **die W~fahrts|organisation, –en** charitable organization; **der W~fahrts|staat, –en** welfare state; **~feil** *arch* cheap; **das W~gefallen** pleasure (**sein W. haben an** (*dat*) take pleasure in; **sich in W. auflösen** *joc* fall apart; come to nothing); **~gefällig** pleasing; (look *etc*) pleased; (*adv*) with pleasure/satisfaction; **das W~gefühl** sense of well-being; **~gelitten** well-liked; **~gemeint** well-meant; **~gemerkt** mark you; **~gemut** cheerful; **~genährt** well-fed; **der W~geruch, ¨e** pleasant odour; fragrance; **der W~geschmack** pleasant taste; **~gesinnt** well-disposed (*following dat* towards); **~gestaltet** well-proportioned, shapely; **~habend** well-to-do; **die W~habenheit** affluence; **der W~klang** melodiousness; **~klingend** melodious; **der W~laut** melodiousness; **~meinend** well-meaning; **~proportioniert** well-proportioned; **~riechend** fragrant; **~schmeckend** tasty; **W~sein** (**zum W.!** your health!); **der W~stand** affluence; **die W~stands|gesellschaft** affluent society; **die W~tat, –en** good deed; blessing, boon; **der W~täter, –** benefactor; **~tätig** charitable; **die W~tätigkeit** charity; **W~tätigkeits–** charity ...; **der W~tätigkeits|ver|ein, –e** charity (= organization); **~temperiert** at the right temperature („**Das W~temperierte Klavier**" 'The Well-Tempered Clavier'); **~tuend** most agreeable; **~tun*** (*sep*) (+*dat*) do (s.o.) good; **~überlegt** well-thought-out; **~verdient** well-deserved/earned; **~weislich** very wisely; **~wollen*** (*sep*) (+*dat*) wish (s.o.) well; **das W~wollen** goodwill (**mit W.** benevolently); **~wollend** benevolent

wohlig agreeable; (sigh) contented

Wohn– living ...; residential ...;

der ~anhänger, – caravan, trailer *US*; **der ~bezirk, –e** *EGer* district (of city; = *territorial and political unit*); **der ~block, –s** block of flats, apartment building *US*; **die ~gegend, –en** residential area; **die ~gemeinschaft, –en** group sharing accommodation; **das ~haus, ¨er** dwelling-house; **das ~heim, –e** home; hostel, rooming-house *US*; *univ* hall of residence, dormitory *US*; **die ~küche, –n** kitchen-cum-living-room; **die ~kultur** (modern) style of interior decoration; **das ~mobil, –e** camper, motor caravan; **das ~objekt, –e** *Aust* residential building; **der ~ort, –e** (place of) residence; **der ~raum, ¨e** room (for living in); living-space; **das ~schlaf|zimmer, –** bed-sitting room, one-room apartment *US*; **die ~siedlung, –en** housing estate/development *US*; **der ~silo, –s** (*also* **das**) concrete block; **der ~sitz, –e** (place of) residence (**ohne festen W.** of no fixed abode); **der ~turm, ¨e** (residential) tower block; **das ~viertel, –** residential area; **der ~wagen, –** caravan, trailer *US*; **das ~zimmer, –** living-room (suite)

wohnen live (= reside); stay; dwell (in s.o.'s mind *etc*)
wohnhaft resident
wohnlich comfortable
die **Wohnung, –en** flat, apartment *US*; lodging; *in compds* **~s–** housing ...; **der ~s|bau** building of flats/apartments *US*; **der ~s|-mangel = die ~s|not** housing shortage; **der ~s|zins, –e** *Aust* rent
wölben curve; *archit* vault; **sich ~** curve; (bridge *etc*) arch
die **Wölbung, –en** curvature; curve
der **Wolf, ¨–e** wolf; *cul* mincer, meat grinder *US*; **~ im Schafspelz** wolf in sheep's clothing; **durch den ~ drehen** mince, grind *US*; *coll* put through the mill; **mit den Wölfen heulen** howl with the pack
die **Wölfin, –nen** she-wolf
wölfisch wolfish
das **Wolfram** [–ram] tungsten
Wolfs–: der ~hunger *coll* ravenous appetite; **der ~rachen, –** cleft palate; **das ~rudel, –** wolf-pack
die **Wolga** the Volga
Wolgograd Volgograd
die **Wolke, –n** cloud; (in jewel) flaw; **aus allen ~n fallen** *coll* be flabbergasted || **die ~n|bank, ¨–e** bank of clouds; **der ~n|bruch, ¨–e** cloudburst; **der ~n|himmel, –** cloudy sky; **der ~n|kratzer, –** skyscraper; **das ~n|-kuckucks|heim** cloud-cuckoo-land; **w~n|-los** cloudless; **die ~n|schicht, –en** layer of cloud; **die ~n|wand, ¨–e** bank of clouds
wolkig cloudy
Woll– woollen ...; wool ...; **die ~decke, –n** (woollen) blanket; **die ~waren** *pl* woollens
die **Wolle, –n** wool; **in die ~ bringen** *coll* get (s.o.'s) back up; **sich in die ~ kriegen** *coll* fall out; **sich in der ~ haben mit** *coll* be at loggerheads with
wollen[1] (*pres* **will, willst, will, wollen, wollt, wollen,** *subj* **wolle** *etc*; *p/t* **wollte,** *subj* **wollte;** *p/part* **gewollt,** (*after dependent infin*) **wollen)** (*see p. xlvii*; *see also* **gewollt)** want (to); (I *etc*) will; intend to; be intended to; like (*eg* **ganz wie du willst** just as you like); (*ellipt*) want to go (home, to ..., *etc*); (*+perfect infin*) claim (*eg* **er will in London geboren sein/es 1939 gesehen haben** he claims to have been born in L./to have seen it in 1939); ... will admit to (having + *p/part*) (*eg* **keiner will etwas gehört haben** nobody will admit to having heard anything, **keiner will es gewesen sein** no one will admit to having done it); **~, daß ...** want (s.o., sth.) to ...; (*expressing a necessity*) **... will ...** (*p/part*) **sein** ... has to be + *p/part* (*eg* **Geld will erst mal verdient sein, ehe man es ausgibt** money has first to be earned before it can be spent); ... needs +*ger* (*eg* **die Strafe will bedacht sein** the punishment needs thinking about);
... will und will nicht ... ... simply will not ...; **so Gott will** God willing; **man wolle bitte ...** would you kindly ...; **komme, was da wolle** come what may; **wir ~ ...!** let's ...!; **~ wir ...?** shall we ...?; **das will (Soldat** *etc*) **sein!** and he calls himself a (soldier *etc*)!;
wollte wanted (to); would; was about/going to; (*ellipt*) wanted to go (home, to ..., *etc*); (*subj, in conditional clauses*) were to (*eg* **wollte man alles glauben/wenn man alles glauben wollte, was der Pfarrer sagt** if one were to believe everything the parson says); **ich wollte, ...** I wish ...; **wollte Gott, ...** I wish to goodness ...
wollen[2] woollen
das **Wollen** volition; wish(es)
wollig woolly
die **Wollust** sensuality, voluptuousness; lust
wollüstig sensual, voluptuous; lascivious
womit (*see* **wo–**) with which; (*referring to whole clause*) by which; (*interrog*) what ... with; how
womöglich (*cf* **wo möglich** *at* **wo**) possibly
wonach (*see* **wo–**) after/by/for/according to *etc* which; (*interrog*) what ... after/by/for *etc*
die **Wonne, –n** delight; bliss; **der ~proppen, –** *joc* bundle of joy
wonnig delightful; blissful
woran (*see* **wo–**) on/by/of *etc* which; (*interrog*) what ... on/by/of *etc*; **~ liegt das?** why is it?; **(nicht) wissen, ~ man ist** (not) know where one stands (**bei** with)
worauf (*see* **wo–**) on/for/of *etc* which; whereupon; (*interrog*) what ... on/for/of *etc*
woraus (*see* **wo–**) from/out of which; (*interrog*) what ... from/out of
die **Worcester|soße** ['vʊstɐ–] Worcester sauce
worden *p/part of* **werden** 2 (*b*)
worein in(to) which; (*interrog*) what ... in(to)
worin (*see* **wo–**) in which; (*interrog*) what ... in
das **Wort, –e**/(*unconnected words*) **¨–er** word (*also comput*); saying; **... kann kein ~ (Polnisch** *etc*) ... cannot speak a word of (Polish *etc*); **das ~ ergreifen** begin to speak; take the floor; **das ~ führen** do the talking; be the spokesman/woman; **sein ~ halten** keep one's word; (*+dat*) **das ~ reden** speak in favour of; **das ~ richten an** (*acc*) address; (*+dat*) **das ~ verbieten** forbid (s.o.) to speak; **sein eigenes ~ nicht verstehen** be unable to hear oneself speak; **hast du (da noch) ~e!** did you ever!
in prepositional phrases:
(*+dat*) **aufs ~ glauben** believe (s.o.'s)

every word
beim ~ nehmen take at his/her word
~ für ~ word for word
(+*dat*) **ins ~ fallen** interrupt; **in ~e fassen** put into words; **in ~en** in words
mit 'einem ~ in a word; **mit anderen ~en** in other words
ums ~ bitten ask leave to speak
zu ~(e) kommen get a chance to speak; have one's say; **sich zu ~ melden** ask leave to speak

Wort–: die ~art, –en part of speech; **der ~bruch, ⸚e** breaking one's word; **w~brüchig (w. werden** break one's word (**an** *dat* to)); **die ~folge, –n** word-order; **der ~führer, –** spokesman; **das ~gefecht, –e** battle of words; **w~getreu** word-for-word; (translation) faithful; **w~karg** taciturn; **die ~klauberei, –en** quibbling; quibble; **der ~laut** text; wording (**eine Rede im vollen W. veröffentlichen** publish the full text of a speech); **w~los** silent; (*adv*) without a word; **die ~meldung, –en** request to speak; **w~reich** wordy, verbose; with a rich vocabulary; **der ~schatz** vocabulary; **der ~schwall** flood of words; **das ~spiel, –e** play on words, pun; **die ~stellung, –en** word-order; **die ~wahl** choice of words; **der ~wechsel, –** altercation (**einen W. haben** have words); **wort|wörtlich** word-for-word; (*adv*) word for word

Wörtchen *coll*: **ein ~ mitzureden haben** have a say; **noch ein ~ zu reden haben mit** want a word with

Wörter–: das ~buch, ⸚er dictionary; **das ~verzeichnis, –se** word-index

wörtlich literal; (speech) direct

worüber (*see* **wo–**) over/about *etc* which; (*interrog*) what … over/about *etc*

worum (*see* **wo–**) about/around/for which; (*interrog*) what … about/around/for

worunter (*see* **wo–**) under/among *etc* which; (*interrog*) what … under/among *etc*

wovon (*see* **wo–**) of/from/about *etc* which; (*interrog*) what … of/from/about *etc*

wovor (*see* **wo–**) in front of *etc* which; (*interrog*) what … in front of *etc*

wozu (*see* **wo–**) for/to which; what … to do; (*interrog*) what … for; why; what … to do; **~ denn das?** what for?

das **Wrack, –s** wreck

wrang (wränge) *p/t* (*subj*) *of* **wringen**

der **Wrasen, –** *NGer* vapour

wringen (*p/t* **wrang** (*subj* **wränge**), *p/part* **gewrungen)** wring

der **Wucher** [–uː–] usury; profiteering; *in compds* exorbitant …; usurious …

der **Wucherer** [–uː–], **–** usurer; profiteer

wucherisch usurious; exorbitant; profiteering

wuchern [–uː–] grow profusely; proliferate; profiteer; practise usury; **~d** rampant

die **Wucherung, –en** rank growth; *med* growth

wuchs (wüchse) *p/t* (*subj*) *of* **wachsen**[1]

der **Wuchs** [–uːks] growth; physique, build

–wüchsig [–yːks–] *indicates stature*, *eg* **klein~** (of) small (stature)

die **Wucht** force, impact; brunt; **eine ~ sein** *coll* be terrific; **mit aller ~** with all one's might; **mit voller ~** with full force

wuchten *coll* heave

wuchtig solid; powerful

Wühl–: die ~arbeit, –en subversive activity; **die ~maus, ⸚e** vole

wühlen burrow; (*v/i*) dig; burrow; root; rummage; stir things up; **~ in** (*dat*) dig/burrow/root in; rummage through; (hunger, pain) gnaw at; **im Schmutz ~** wallow in the mire; **sich ~ durch** burrow one's way through

der **Wühler, –** subversive; *coll* slogger

der **Wulst, ⸚e** (*also* **die**) bulge; roll (of fat)

wulstig bulging; (lips) thick

wummern *coll* boom; **~ an** (*acc*)/**gegen** thump on

wund sore; **~er Punkt** sore point; **sich** *dat* **die Füße ~ laufen** get sore feet from walking; walk one's legs off; **sich ~ reiten** get saddle-sore; **sich** *dat* **die Finger ~ schreiben** *coll* write until one's fingers ache

Wund– … of a/the wound; wound …; **der ~arzt, ⸚e** *arch* surgeon; **der ~brand** gangrene; **das ~fieber** traumatic fever; **w~liegen*** (*sep*): **sich w.** get bedsores; **das ~mal, –e** stigma (of Christ); **die ~salbe, –n** ointment; **der ~starr|krampf** tetanus, lockjaw

die **Wunde, –n** wound

wunder: sich *dat* **~ was einbilden** think no end of oneself; **glauben, ~ was getan zu haben** think one has done something marvellous; **denken, ~ wer man sei** think no end of oneself; **glauben, ~ wie gescheit zu sein** think one is ever so clever

das **Wunder, –** miracle; wonder; marvel; **sein blaues ~ erleben** get the surprise of one's life; **~ wirken** perform miracles; work wonders; **es ist ein/kein ~, daß …** it's a/no wonder that …; **was ~, wenn …** small wonder that …; **wie durch ein ~** by some miracle; **~ über ~!** wonders will never cease!

Wunder– wonder …, miracle …; magic …; miraculous …; **das ~ding, –e** marvellous thing; **wunder|hübsch** very lovely; **die ~kerze, –n** sparkler; **das ~kind, –er** infant prodigy; **das ~land** wonderland; **w~nehmen*** (*sep*) surprise; (*v/i*) be surprising; **wunder|schön** very lovely; **die ~tat, –en** miraculous deed; **w~tätig** miraculous;

miracle-working; **das ~tier, -e** *coll* amazing beast (**wie ein W. anstarren** stare at (s.o.) as if he/she were a freak); **w~voll** wonderful; **das ~werk, -e** marvel

wunderbar wonderful; miraculous

wunderlich strange, odd

wundern surprise; **es wundert mich, daß ...** I'm surprised that ...; **es sollte mich nicht ~, wenn ...** I shouldn't be surprised if ...; **sich ~** be surprised (**über** *acc* at)

der **Wunsch, ⸚e** wish; desire; request; **haben Sie sonst noch einen ~?** will there be anything else (, sir/madam)?; **auf ~** by request; **auf jmds. ~ (hin)** at s.o.'s request; **auf allgemeinen/vielfachen ~** by popular request; **nach ~** as desired; **es geht alles nach ~** everything is going smoothly || **das ~bild, -er** ideal; **das ~denken** wishful thinking; **w~gemäß** as desired/requested; **das ~kind, -er** planned child; **die ~kind|pille, -n** *EGer* contraceptive pill; **das ~konzert, -e** musical request programme; **w~los** content; (happiness) perfect (**w. glücklich** perfectly happy); **der ~traum, ⸚e** (great) dream; pipe-dream; **die ~vorstellung, -en** *approx* = wishful thinking; **der ~zettel, -** list of things one would like

die **Wünschel|rute, -n** divining-rod

wünschen wish; want; (+*dat*) wish (s.o. good morning, a pleasant journey, *etc*); wish on; **sich** *dat* **... ~** want; wish for; ask for (for one's birthday, Christmas); **was wünschst du dir zum Geburtstag/zu Weihnachten?** what would you like for your birthday/for Christmas?; **Sie ~?** what can I do for you?; what would you like?; **ich wünschte, ... I** wish ...; **es wäre (sehr) zu ~, daß ...** it is (very much) to be hoped that ...; **viel zu ~ übrig lassen** leave a great deal to be desired; **sich (weit weg** *etc*) **~** wish one were (far away *etc*) || **~s|wert** desirable

würbe *p/t subj of* **werben**

wurde (würde) *p/t* (*subj*) *of* **werden**

die **Würde, -n** dignity; rank; **unter aller ~** beneath contempt; **unter jmds. ~** beneath s.o.'s dignity || **w~los** undignified; **w~voll** dignified; (*adv*) with dignity

der **Würden|träger, -** dignitary

würdig worthy (*following gen* of); dignified; **-würdig** *esp* -able, -ible (*eg* **frag~** questionable, **verabscheuungs~** detestable)

würdigen appreciate; pay tribute to; (+*gen*) deem worthy of; **jmdn. keiner Antwort/keines Blickes/keines Grußes ~** not deign to answer/look at/greet s.o.; **zu ~ wissen** appreciate

die **Würdigung, -en** appreciation; tribute

der **Wurf, ⸚e** throw; hang (of garment *etc*); *zool* litter; **großer ~** great hit; **einen großen ~ tun** score a great success; **zum ~ ausholen** get ready to throw

Wurf- throwing ...; **das ~geschoß, -(ss)e** missile, projectile; **der ~ring, -e** quoit; **der ~speer, -e** = **der ~spieß, -e** javelin (= weapon); **die ~taube, -n** clay pigeon

würfe *p/t subj of* **werfen**

der **Würfel, -** cube (*also math*); *games* dice; **die ~ sind gefallen** the die is cast; **in ~ schneiden** dice || **der ~becher, -** shaker; **w~förmig** cube-shaped; **das ~spiel, -e** game of dice; **der ~zucker** lump sugar

würf(e)lig: ~ schneiden dice

würfeln (*see also* **gewürfelt**) throw (a six *etc*); *cul* dice; (*v/i*) play at dice; **~ um** throw dice for

der **Würge|griff, -e** stranglehold

würgen strangle, throttle; choke; (*v/i*) choke; retch; **~ an** (*dat*) have difficulty in swallowing

der **Würger, -** strangler; *ornith* shrike; *poet* death

das **Wurm, ⸚er** *coll* (little) mite

der **Wurm, ⸚er** worm; maggot; (+*dat*) **die Würmer aus der Nase ziehen** *coll* worm information out of; **da ist/sitzt der ~ drin** *coll* there's something wrong with it || **der ~fortsatz, ⸚e** (vermiform) appendix; **w~stichig** maggoty; worm-eaten

wurmen *coll* rankle with

wurmig maggoty; worm-eaten

die **Wurst, ⸚e** (German) sausage; **das ist mir ~** [-ʃt] *coll* it's all the same to me; I couldn't care less; **es geht um die ~** *coll* the moment of truth has come || **die ~waren** *pl* sausages and cold meats

das **Würstchen, -** small sausage; *coll* nobody; **armes ~** *coll* poor thing

wursteln *coll* muddle along

wurstig *coll* devil-may-care

die **Wurstigkeit** *coll* devil-may-care attitude

Würz-: der ~stoff, -e seasoning

die **Würze, -n** seasoning, spice

die **Wurzel, -n** root (*also ling, math*); **~n schlagen** take root; (person) put down roots; **mit der ~ ausrotten** eradicate || **w~los** without roots; rootless; **der ~stock, ⸚e** rhizome; **das ~zeichen, -** *math* radical sign

wurzeln: ~ in (*dat*) be rooted in; have its roots in

würzen season, spice

würzig spicy; aromatic; (air) fragrant

wusch (wüsche) *p/t* (*subj*) *of* **waschen**

Wuschel-: das ~haar *coll* curly hair; **der ~kopf, ⸚e** *coll* mop of curly hair

wuschelig *coll* tousled

wußte (wüßte) *p/t* (*subj*) *of* **wissen**

der **Wust** [-u:-] *coll* jumble

WUSt, Wust [vʊst] *Swiss* (= **Warenumsatzsteuer**) sales tax

wüst [–yː–] desolate; wild; chaotic

die **Wüste** [–yː–], **–n** desert; **in die ~ schicken** *coll* send packing

wüsten [–yː–]: **~ mit** squander; ruin (one's health)

die **Wüstenei** [–yː–], **–en** wilderness; *coll* chaos

der **Wüstling** [–yː–], **–e** libertine

die **Wut** fury, rage; fury (of elements); **–wut** ... craze, ... mania; **eine ~ im Bauch haben** *coll* be hopping mad; **~ haben auf** (*acc*) be furious with; **in ~ bringen** incense; **in ~ geraten** fly into a rage ‖ **der ~anfall, ⸚e** fit of rage; tantrum; **der ~ausbruch, ⸚e** outburst of fury; **w~entbrannt** furious; **w~schäumend** foaming with rage; **w~schnaubend** snorting with rage; **w~verzerrt** distorted with rage

wüten rage; cause havoc; **~d** furious (**auf** *acc* with, **über** *acc* at); enraged; raging; **~d machen** infuriate

der **Wüterich, –e** tartar

–wütig crazy about ...

X

das X [ɪks] (*gen*, *pl* –) X; (+*dat*) **ein X für ein U vormachen** pull the wool over (s.o.'s) eyes; **der Tag X** D-day

x (*indecl*) *coll* umpteen; **die X-Beine** *pl* knock-knees (**X-Beine haben** be knock-kneed); **~-beinig** knock-kneed; **~-beliebig** *coll* any (… you like); **~-mal** *coll* umpteen times

die **Xanthippe** [ks–], **–n** shrew, virago

xenophob [ks–] xenophobic

die **Xenophobie** [ks–] xenophobia

Xenophon ['kseːnofɔn] Xenophon

Xerxes ['ksɛrksɛs] Xerxes

x-t.. *math* nth; *coll* umpteenth; **zum ~en Male/~enmal** for the umpteenth time

das **Xylophon** [ks–], **–e** xylophone

Y

das **Y** ['ʏpsilɔn] (*gen*, *pl* –, *coll* ['ʏpsilɔns]) Y
der **Yen** [jɛn] (*gen* –(s)), –(s) yen
Ypern ['iː–, 'yː–] Ypres
das **Ypsilon** ['ʏpsilɔn] Y
der **Ysop** ['iːzɔp] hyssop
der **Yuppie** ['jʊpi], –s yuppie

Z

[das] **Z** [tsɛt] (*gen, pl* –, *coll* [tsɛts]) Z
zack: ~! zap!; ~, ~! chop-chop!
Zack *coll*: **auf ~** on the ball; **auf ~ bringen** lick into shape
[die] **Zacke, -n = der Zacken, –** point; prong; tooth (of comb); jagged peak
zackig pointed; jagged; *coll* smart; snappy
zaghaft timid
[die] **Zaghaftigkeit = die Zagheit** timidity
zäh tough; tenacious; (liquid) thick, viscous; **~flüssig** thick, viscous; slow-moving; **~lebig** tough; (prejudice *etc*) persistent
[die] **Zäheit** toughness
[die] **Zähigkeit** toughness; tenacity
[die] **Zahl, -en** number; figure; **(10** *etc*) **an der ~** (10 *etc*) in number; **in großer ~** in large numbers; **in den roten ~en stecken** be in the red
Zahl-: die ~grenze, -n fare stage; **die ~karte, -n** (giro) inpayment slip, deposit slip *US*; **der ~kellner, –** waiter whom the customer pays; **z~los** innumerable; **der ~meister, –** *mil* paymaster; *naut* purser; **z~reich** numerous, a great many; (family *etc*) large; **der ~tag, -e** pay-day; **das ~wort, ¨-er** numeral
Zähl-: das ~rohr, -e Geiger counter; **das ~werk, -e** counter
zahlbar payable
zählbar *gramm* countable
zahlen (*also v/i*) pay; **(bitte) ~!** may I have the bill/check *US*, please?
zählen count; have (... inhabitants); (*v/i*) count (= recite numbers, be of consequence); **~ auf** (*acc*) count on; **~ nach** run into (thousands *etc*); **~ zu** number among; (*v/i*) be one of; be among; **seine Tage sind gezählt** his days are numbered
Zahlen- numerical ...; **die ~angaben** *pl* figures; **das ~gedächtnis** memory for figures; **z~mäßig** numerical; **das ~material** figures; **das ~verhältnis, -se** ratio
[der] **Zähler, –** counter; meter; *math* numerator
[die] **Zahlung, -en** payment; **in ~ geben** trade in; **in ~ nehmen** take in part-exchange
[die] **Zählung, -en** count
Zahlungs-: die ~bedingungen *pl* terms (of payment); **der ~befehl, -e** order to pay; **die ~bilanz, -en** balance of payments; **die ~erleichterung, -en** easy terms; **z~fähig** able to pay; *comm* solvent; **die ~fähigkeit** ability to pay; *comm* solvency; **das ~mittel, –** means of payment **(gesetzliches Z.** legal tender); **z~unfähig** unable to pay; *comm* insolvent; **die ~unfähigkeit** inability to pay; *comm* insolvency; **der ~verkehr** payment transactions
zahm tame; docile; *coll* (criticism) mild
zähmen tame; restrain
[der] **Zahn, ¨-e** tooth; perforation (on stamp); **der ~ der Zeit** the ravages of time; **Zähne bekommen** cut one's teeth; **einen ~ draufhaben** *coll* be going like the clappers; **einen ~ zulegen** *coll* step on it; **die Zähne zeigen** bare its teeth; *coll* show one's teeth; (+*dat*) **auf den ~ fühlen** sound out; **bis an die Zähne bewaffnet** armed to the teeth
Zahn- tooth ...; dental ...; **der ~arzt, ¨-e** dentist; **z~ärztlich** dental; **der ~belag** plaque; **die ~bürste, -n** toothbrush; **der ~ersatz** dentures; **die ~fäule** caries; **das ~fleisch** gums; **die ~heil|kunde** dentistry; **z~los** toothless; **die ~lücke, -n** gap between one's teeth; **die ~medizin** dentistry; **die ~pasta, -(t)en** toothpaste; **die ~pflege** dental care; **die ~prothese, -n** dentures; **das ~rad, ¨-er** cog-wheel; **die ~rad|bahn, -en** rack railway; **der ~schmelz** (tooth) enamel; **die ~schmerzen** *pl* toothache; **die ~seide** dental floss; **der ~stein** tartar; **der ~stocher, –** toothpick; **der ~techniker, –** dental technician; **das ~weh** toothache; **die ~wurzel, -n** root (of a tooth)
Zähne-: z~fletschend baring its teeth; **das ~klappern** chattering of teeth; **z~klappernd** with teeth chattering; **z~knirschend** extremely grudgingly
zahnen teethe
zähnen tooth; perforate (stamp)
Zaire [za'i:ʁ] Zaïre
[der] **Zaïrer** [za–], **–, zaïrisch** Zaïrese
[der] **Zander, –** pike-perch
[die] **Zange, -n** pliers; pincers (*also zool*); tongs; *med* forceps; **in der ~ haben** *coll* have over a barrel; **in die ~ nehmen** *coll* put the screws on; *footb* sandwich || **die ~n|bewegung, -en** *mil* pincer movement
[der] **Zank** squabble; **der ~apfel, ..äpfel** bone of contention; **die ~sucht** quarrelsomeness; **z~süchtig** quarrelsome

zanken: sich ~ squabble (**mit** with)
der **Zänker, –** squabbler
die **Zankerei, –en** squabbling
zänkisch quarrelsome
Zapf–: der ~hahn, ⸚e tap; **die ~säule, –n** petrol pump, gasoline pump *US*
das **Zäpfchen, –** *med* suppository; *anat* uvula; **das ~-R** uvular 'r'
zapfen tap
der **Zapfen, –** bung; *Swiss* cork; *bot* cone; *carp* tenon; **der ~streich, –e** last post, taps *US*
Zappel–: der ~philipp, –e/–s *coll* fidget
zapp(e)lig *coll* fidgety; wriggly
zappeln fidget; wriggle; **~ lassen** *coll* keep on tenterhooks
zappen|duster *coll* pitch-dark; **mit … sieht es ~ aus** prospects for … are bleak
der **Zar, –en** (*wk masc*) tsar
die **Zarin, –nen** tsarina
zaristisch tsarist
zart [–aː–] tender; soft; gentle; delicate; **~besaitet** highly sensitive; **~fühlend** tactful; **das Z~gefühl** tact
zärtlich [–ɛː–] tender, loving
die **Zärtlichkeit, –en** tenderness, affection; (*pl*) caresses
der **Zaster** *coll* 'dough'
die **Zäsur, –en** break; *pros* caesura
der **Zauber, –** magic; spell; charm; **der ganze ~** *coll* the whole caboodle/business; **fauler ~** *coll* humbug
Zauber– magic …; enchanted …; **die ~kunst** magic; **der ~künstler, –** magician; **das ~kunst|stück, –e** conjuring trick; **der ~spruch, ⸚e** spell; **der ~stab, ⸚e** magic wand; **der ~trank, ⸚e** magic potion; **das ~wort, –e** magic word
die **Zauberei, –en** magic; witchcraft; conjuring trick
der **Zauberer, –** magician; sorcerer
zauberhaft enchanting
die **Zauberin, –nen** (female) magician; sorceress
zaubern conjure up; (*v/i*) perform magic; do conjuring tricks
zaudern hesitate
der **Zaum, ⸚e** bridle; **im ~ halten** keep in check; curb; **sich im ~ halten** control oneself || **das ~zeug, –e** bridle
zäumen bridle
der **Zaun, ⸚e** fence; **vom ~ brechen** start (quarrel *etc*) || **der ~gast, ⸚e** onlooker (who is not invited or has not paid an entrance-fee); **der ~könig, –e** wren; **der ~pfahl, ⸚e** fence-post (**Wink mit dem Z.** broad hint; **mit dem Z. winken** drop a broad hint)
zausen ruffle; tousle
zausig *Aust* tousled
z. B. (**= zum Beispiel**) e.g.
das **ZDF = Zweites Deutsches Fernsehen** (*second W. German TV channel*)

das **Zebra, –s** zebra; **der ~streifen, –** zebra crossing
Zech–: der ~bruder, ..brüder tippler; drinking-companion; **das ~gelage, –** drinking-bout; **der ~kumpan, –e** drinking-companion; **die ~tour, –en** pub-crawl
die **Zeche, –n** bill, check *US*; *min* (coal) mine; **die ~ prellen** leave without paying; **die ~ (be)zahlen** foot the bill
zechen carouse
die **Zecherei, –en** drinking-bout
die **Zecke, –n** tick
die **Zeder, –n, zedern** cedar
die **Zehe, –n** toe; *bot* clove; (+*dat*) **auf die ~n treten** tread on (s.o.'s) toes || **der ~n|nagel, ..nägel** toe-nail; **die ~n|spitze, –n** tip of the toe (**auf ~nspitzen** on tiptoe)
–zehig –toed
zehn ten; **die Zehn, –en** ten || **das Z~finger|system** touch system; **der Z~kampf, ⸚e** decathlon; **~mal** ten times; **Z~tausend** (**die oberen Z.** high society)
der **Zehner, –** ten; *coll* ten-pfennig piece; **die ~packung, –en** pack(et) of ten; **das ~system** decimal system
zehnt: zu ~ (*see* **zu 1** (*i*)); **zehnt..** tenth
zehntel: ein ~ … a tenth of a …
das **Zehntel, –** tenth
zehntens tenthly
zehren: ~ an (*dat*) wear out; sap; undermine (health); (worry) prey on (s.o.'s) mind; **~ von** live on
das **Zeichen, –** sign; signal; mark; symbol; punctuation mark; symptom, sign; *comm* (in correspondence) reference; *comput* character; **seines ~s** by trade; **wenn nicht alle ~ trügen** unless I'm very much mistaken; **im ~** (+*gen*) *astrol* under the sign of; **im ~ stehen von** be marked/dominated by; take place against a background of; **zum ~** (+*gen*) as a sign of
Zeichen– drawing …; **das ~brett, –er** drawing-board; **die ~erklärung, –en** key; legend; **der ~lehrer, –** art teacher; **die ~setzung** punctuation; **die ~sprache** sign language; **der ~trick|film, –e** (animated) cartoon
zeichnen draw; mark; *fin* subscribe; subscribe for (shares); (*v/i*) draw; *esp comm* sign; **schön gezeichnet sein** have attractive markings
der **Zeichner, –** draughtsman; *fin* subscriber
zeichnerisch graphic; (talent) for drawing
die **Zeichnung, –en** drawing; *zool* markings; *fin* subscription
Zeige–: der ~finger, – index-finger; **der ~stock, ⸚e** pointer
zeigen show; (*v/i*) point (**auf** *acc* at); **sich ~** appear; (fear *etc*) show; be seen; be (friendly, brave, impressed, *etc*); **dem**

werd' ich's ~! I'll show him!; **es zeigt sich, daß ...** it turns out that ...; **es wird sich ~, ob ...** it remains to be seen whether ...; **daran zeigt sich, wie ...** that shows how ...

der **Zeiger, –** hand (of clock); pointer (on instrument)

zeihen (*p/t* **zieh,** *p/part* **geziehen**) (+*gen*) *arch* accuse of

die **Zeile, –n** line; row (of houses *etc*); **zwischen den ~n lesen** read between the lines || **der ~n|abstand, ⸚e** line spacing

–zeilig -line

der **Zeisig, –e** siskin

zeit: ~ seines *etc* **Lebens** in his *etc* lifetime; all his *etc* life

die **Zeit, –en** time (*also sp*); period; age; *gramm* tense; **die gute alte ~** the good old days; **... aller ~en** ... of all time; **es ist/wird höchste ~, daß ...** it's high time ...; **lange ~** for a long time; **(ach,) du liebe ~!** dear me!; **das hat ~** it can wait; **damit hat es noch ~** there's no hurry; **sich** *dat* **~ lassen** take one's time; **es wird langsam ~, daß ...** it's about time ...; **seiner ~ voraus sein** be ahead of one's time; **das waren noch ~en!** those were the days!

in prepositional phrases:

an: es ist an der ~, daß ... it's time ...

auf ~ for a limited period; (play) for time; **Beamter auf ~** temporary civil servant; **auf unbestimmte ~** for an indefinite period

für alle ~en for ever

in dieser ~ at that time; **in der ~ von ... bis ...** between ... and ...; **in letzter ~** lately; **in nächster ~** shortly

mit der ~ in (the course of) time; **mit der ~ gehen** move with the times

seit der ~ since that time; **seit einiger ~** for some time past

über: die ganze ~ über all the time

von ~ zu ~ from time to time

vor der ~ before one's time; **vor kurzer/langer ~** a short/long time ago; **vor ~en** *arch* in times past

zu der/dieser ~ at that time; **zu der ~, als ...** (at the time) when ...; in the days when ...; **zu allen ~en** at all times; **zu jeder/keiner ~** at any/no time; **alles zu seiner ~** all in good time; **zur ~** at present; (+*gen*) at the time of; = **zu ...s ~en** in ...'s day

Zeit– ... of time; time ...;

der ~abschnitt, –e period; **das ~alter, –** age, era; **die ~arbeit** temporary work; **die ~aufnahme, –n** time-exposure; **der ~aufwand** time (spent doing sth.); **z~aufwendig** time-consuming; **die ~bombe, –n** time-bomb; **der ~druck** pressure of time; **die ~form, –en** tense; **z~gebunden** dependent on a particular time; **der ~geist** spirit of the times, zeitgeist; **z~gemäß** in keeping with the times; modern, up-to-date (**nicht mehr z.** outmoded); **der ~genosse, –n** (*wk masc*) contemporary; *coll* (odd *etc*) 'customer'; **z~genössisch** contemporary; **das ~geschehen** current affairs; **die ~geschichte** contemporary history; **der ~gewinn** saving/gaining of time; **z~gleich** contemporaneous; *sp* with the same time; (*adv*) at the same time; **die ~karte, –n** season-ticket; **das ~kino, –s** *EGer* news theatre; **z~kritisch** dealing with/relating to contemporary issues; **~lang** (**eine Z.** for a while); **z~lebens** all one's life; **z~los** timeless; ageless; **die ~lupe** slow motion; **der ~mangel** lack of time; **das ~maß, –e** tempo; **die ~messung, –en** timekeeping; **z~nah(e)** topical, of contemporary interest; **die ~nahme** timekeeping; **der ~nehmer, –** timekeeper; **die ~not** shortage of time (**in Z.** short of time); **der ~plan, ⸚e** timetable; **der ~punkt, –e** time; moment; timing; **der ~raffer** time-lapse photography (**im Z.** speeded up); **z~raubend** time-consuming; **der ~raum, ⸚e** period (of time); **die ~rechnung** (Jewish *etc*) calendar; (Christian, modern) era; **die ~schrift, –en** periodical, journal; magazine; **der ~sinn** sense of time; **die ~spanne, –n** period of time; **z~sparend** time-saving; **die ~tafel, –n** chronological table; **die ~vergeudung** waste of time; **der ~verlust, –e** loss of time; **die ~verschwendung** waste of time; **der ~vertreib, –e** pastime (**zum Z.** to pass the time); **z~weilig** temporary; **z~weise** for a time; from time to time (**z. Regen** *etc* occasional rain *etc*); **die ~wende** (= **Zeitenwende**); **der ~wert, –e** current value; **das ~wort, ⸚er** verb; **das ~zeichen, –** time-signal; **die ~zone, –n** time-zone; **der ~zünder, –** time-fuse

die **Zeiten|wende** beginning of a new/the Christian era

zeitig early; *Aust* ripe; (*adv*) early

zeitigen bring about

zeitlich temporal; chronological; (interval) of time; (*adv*) from the point of view of time, (fit in *etc*) timewise, *or conveyed by* time (*eg* **der Besuch des Museums war ~ nicht mehr möglich** there was no longer enough time to visit the museum, **das paßt uns ~ nicht** the time doesn't suit us); chronologically; *Aust coll* early; **das Z~e segnen** *now joc* depart this life; (thing) have had it

die **Zeitung, –en** newspaper; **der ~s|ausschnitt, –e** (newspaper) cutting/clipping *US*; **die ~s|ente, –n** canard; **das ~s|papier** newsprint; (for wrapping *etc*) newspaper; **der ~s|verkäufer, –** news-vendor; **das**

~s|wesen the press
zelebrieren celebrate (*also RC*)
Zell– cell ...; cellular ...; **der ~kern, –e** cell nucleus; **der ~stoff** cellulose; **die ~teilung, –en** cell division; **die ~wolle** spun rayon
die **Zelle, –n** cell (*also biol, elect, pol*); cubicle; *tel* box, booth
–zellig -cell
das **Zellophan** cellophane
das **Zelluloid** celluloid
die **Zellulose** cellulose
der **Zelot, –en** (*wk masc*) zealot
das **Zelt, –e** tent; **seine ~e abbrechen** move on || **die ~bahn, –en** canvas; **der ~pflock, ⸚e** tent-peg; **der ~platz, ⸚e** camp site; **die ~stange, –n** tent-pole
zelten camp; **das Zelten** camping
der **Zement, –e** cement (*also dent*)
zementieren cement; *pol etc* make permanent
der **Zenit** zenith
zensieren censor; *educ* mark
der **Zensor, –(or)en** censor
die **Zensur, –en** censorship; censors; *educ* mark
zensurieren *Aust* censor
der **Zentaur, –en** (*wk masc*) centaur
das **Zentigramm, –e**/(*following num*) **–** centigramme
der **Zentimeter, –** centimetre; **das ~maß, –e** tape-measure
der **Zentner, –** (metric) hundredweight (50 kg.); *Aust, Swiss* 100 kg.; **die ~last, –en** heavy burden (on s.o.'s mind); **zentner|schwer** very heavy; **z~weise** by the hundredweight
zentral (*in compds* **Z~–**) central; **die Z~heizung, –en** central heating; **das Z~komitee, –s** central committee
die **Zentrale, –n** head office; headquarters; *tel* exchange
zentralisieren centralize
der **Zentralismus** centralism
zentralistisch centralist
zentrieren centre
zentrifugal centrifugal; **die Z~kraft** centrifugal force
die **Zentrifuge, –n** centrifuge
das **Zentrum, –(r)en** centre
das **Zepter, –** sceptre

---

zer– [tsɛɐ–] *insep pref* (*unstressed*) ... to pieces; ... apart

---

zerbeißen* crunch; (insects) bite all over
zerbomben flatten by bombing
zerbrechen* smash; destroy; (*v/i sn*) smash; **~ an** (*dat*) (*sn*) be destroyed by; **sich** *dat* **den Kopf ~** rack one's brains
zerbrechlich fragile; frail
zerbröckeln (*sn if v/i*) crumble
zerdrücken squash, crush; crease, crumple; *cul* mash
die **Zeremonie, –(ie)n, die Zeremonie** [–ĭə], **–n** ceremony
zeremoniell, das Zeremoniell, –e ceremonial
zerfahren scatter-brained; (road) damaged by heavy traffic
der **Zerfall** decay; disintegration; decline, (of empire *etc*) fall, collapse; *phys* disintegration, decay
zerfallen* (*sn*) fall into ruin; disintegrate; decompose; decline, (empire *etc*) collapse; *phys* disintegrate, decay; **~ in** (*acc*) divide into, fall into; **zerfallen sein mit** have fallen out with
zerfetzen tear to pieces
zerfleddert *coll* tattered
zerfleischen tear to pieces; **sich gegenseitig ~** tear each other to pieces; **sich in Selbstvorwürfen ~** torment oneself with self-reproach
zerfließen* (*sn*) (ink *etc*) run; melt away; **in Tränen ~** dissolve into tears
zerfranst frayed
zerfressen* (moth *etc*) eat holes in; eat away; corrode; consume (= obsess; *esp pass*)
zerfurcht furrowed
zergehen* (*sn*) melt; dissolve
zergliedern dissect; analyse
zerhacken chop up
zerkauen chew
zerkleinern cut up; chop up
zerklüftet rugged
zerknallen (*sn if v/i*) burst
zerknautschen *coll* crumple
zerknirscht contrite
zerknittern crumple, crease
zerknüllen crumple up
zerkochen (*sn if v/i*) cook to a pulp
zerkratzen scratch
zerkrümeln (*sn if v/i*) crumble
zerlassen* melt (butter *etc*)
zerlegen take to pieces, dismantle; *med* dissect; *cul* carve; *gramm* parse; **~ in** (*acc*) break down into; *phys* disperse into
die **Zerlegung, –en** *vbl noun*; *also* analysis
zerlesen well-thumbed
zerlöchert full of holes
zerlumpt ragged
zermahlen (*p/part* **zermahlen**) grind
zermalmen crush
zermartern: sich *dat* **den Kopf ~** rack one's brains
zermürben wear down; **~d** wearing
die **Zermürbung** *vbl noun*; *also* attrition; **der ~s|krieg, –e** war of attrition
zerpflücken pull apart (flower *etc*); pick to pieces
zerplatzen (*sn*) burst; explode
zerquält tortured
zerquetschen crush
Zerr–: das ~bild, –er distorted picture; cari-

cature; **der ~spiegel, –** distorting mirror
zerrauft dishevelled
zerreden flog (topic) to death
zerreiben* grind; crush
Zerreiß–: die ~probe, –n crucial test
zerreißen* (*see also* **zerrissen**) tear; tear up; tear to pieces; tear apart; break (thread *etc*); shatter (silence); (*v/i sn*) tear; (rope *etc*) break; (+*dat*) **das Herz ~** be heart-rending; **ich kann mich doch nicht ~!** I can't be in two places at once!
zerren drag; **~ an** (*dat*) pull at; **sich** *dat* **einen Muskel ~** pull a muscle
zerrinnen* (*sn*) melt (away); (dreams, hopes, *etc*) vanish; (+*dat*) **unter den Fingern/Händen ~** (money) run through (s.o.'s) fingers like water
zerrissen *p/part*; *also* inwardly torn; (country) strife-torn
die **Zerrissenheit** (inner) conflict; disunity
die **Zerrung, –en** *vbl noun*; *also* pulled muscle
zerrupfen pick to pieces
zerrütten wreck; destroy; shatter (nerves); **zerrüttet** (marriage) broken; **zerrüttete Familienverhältnisse** a broken home
die **Zerrüttung** *vbl noun*; *also* destruction; breakdown (of marriage)
zersägen saw up
zerschellen (*sn*) be smashed to pieces
zerschießen* riddle with bullets
zerschlagen* smash; break up; **sich ~** come to nothing; (hope) be shattered; **zerschlagen** *coll* washed out
zerschleißen (*p/t* **zerschliß,** *p/part* **zerschlissen**) wear out
zerschmeißen* *coll* smash
zerschmelzen* (*sn*) melt
zerschmettern smash, shatter; (news *etc*) shatter
zerschneiden* cut up; cut in two; (broken glass *etc*) cut
zersetzen decompose; undermine; **sich ~** decompose; **~d** subversive
die **Zersetzung** *vbl noun*; *also* decomposition
zersiedeln spoil (countryside) by uncontrolled urban development
die **Zersied(e)lung** urban sprawl
zerspalten (*p/part also* **zerspalten**) split
zersplittern splinter; dissipate (energies); (*v/i sn*) shatter; splinter; **sich ~** dissipate one's energies
zersprengen blow up; scatter
zerspringen* (*sn*) shatter; crack; *mus* (string) break; **vor Freude ~** (heart) be bursting with joy
zerstampfen trample down; pound; *cul* mash
zerstäuben spray
der **Zerstäuber, –** spray; atomizer
zerstieben* (*sn*) scatter
zerstören destroy; ruin (health); **~d** destructive
der **Zerstörer, –** destroyer
zerstörerisch destructive
die **Zerstörung, –en** destruction; (*pl*) destruction (caused); *in compds* **~s–** destructive ...
zerstoßen* pound
zerstreiten*: sich ~ fall out (**mit** with)
zerstreuen scatter, disperse, *phys* diffuse; dispel (doubts *etc*); take (s.o.'s) mind off things; **sich ~** scatter, disperse; (doubts *etc*) be dispelled; take one's mind off things
zerstreut *p/part*; *also* absent-minded
die **Zerstreutheit** absent-mindedness
die **Zerstreuung, –en** *vbl noun*; *also* dispersal, *phys* diffusion; diversion; absent-mindedness
zerstückeln cut up; dismember; carve up (land)
zerteilen cut up; divide; part (waves, clouds)
das **Zertifikat, –e** certificate
zertrampeln trample on
zertrennen undo the seams of
zertreten* crush (underfoot); stamp out
zertrümmern smash; wreck; *phys* split (atom)
die **Zervelat|wurst, ⸚e** cervelat
zerwerfen*: sich ~ fall out (**mit** with)
zerwühlen churn up; rumple; tousle
das **Zerwürfnis, –se** quarrel
zerzausen ruffle; tousle
Zeter: ~ und Mordio schreien scream blue murder || **das ~geschrei** hullabaloo
zetern wail; scold
der **Zettel, –** slip of paper; note; **die ~kartei, –en** card-index; **der ~kasten, ..kästen** card-index box; **der ~katalog, –e** card-index
das **Zeug** *coll* stuff; things; *arch* material; **–zeug** *used esp to form collectives denoting equipment, clothing, materials, etc* (*eg* **das Schreib~** writing materials, **das Rasier~** shaving tackle, **das Schlag~** drums, **das Bade~** swimming things, **das Bett~** bedding); **altes ~** junk; **dummes ~** nonsense; **das ~ haben zu** have the makings of; **er hat nicht das ~ dazu** he hasn't got it in him; **... was das ~ hält** *coll* ... for all one is worth; (work) like hell; (+*dat*) **am ~(e) flicken** pick holes in; **sich ins ~ legen** put one's shoulder to the wheel
der **Zeuge, –n** (*wk masc*) witness; (+*gen*) **~ sein/werden** witness; **~n Jehovas** Jehovah's Witnesses
zeugen[1] father; give rise to
zeugen[2] testify; give evidence; **~ von** be evidence of, testify to
Zeugen– ... of a witness/witnesses; **die ~aussage, –n** testimony; **die ~bank = der ~stand** witness-box, witness stand *US*
das **Zeugnis, –se** evidence (= sign of sth.); testimonial; *educ* (school) report, report

card *US*; *leg* testimony; ~ **geben von** be evidence of; **ein beredtes ~ sein von** bear eloquent witness to

[das] **Zeugs** *coll* = **Zeug** (*exc arch*)

[die] **Zeugung, -en** procreation; **z~s|fähig** fertile; **z~s|unfähig** sterile

[das] **ZGB** *EGer, Swiss* = **Zivilgesetzbuch**

z. H(d). (= **zu Händen**) attn.

[die] **Zichorie** [tsɪ'ço:rĭə], **-n** chicory

[die] **Zicke, -n** she-goat; *coll* 'cow'

Zicken *coll*: ~ **machen** be difficult; fool about; **mach keine ~!** no nonsense now!

zickig *coll* silly; prudish

[der] **Zickzack, -e, im ~ fahren/laufen** zigzag

[die] **Ziege, -n** goat; *coll* 'cow'

[der] **Ziegel, -** brick; tile; **das ~dach, ⸚er** tiled roof; **ziegel|rot** brick-red; **der ~stein, -e** brick

[die] **Ziegelei, -en** brickworks

Ziegen- goat ...; goat's ...; **der ~bart, ⸚e** goatee; **der ~bock, ⸚e** he-goat; **das ~leder** kid; **der ~melker, -** nightjar; **der ~peter, -** *coll* mumps

Zieh-: der ~brunnen, - well; **die ~harmonika, -s** accordion

zieh *p/t of* **zeihen**

ziehen (*p/t* **zog** (*subj* **zöge**), *p/part* **gezogen**) pull; draw (*also* comparison, conclusion); raise (hat); pull out (choke, tooth, *etc*), *med* remove (stitches); dig (ditch); grow, cultivate; breed; *chess* move (piece); (*v/i*) (tea) stand; (chimney, pipe, *etc*) draw; *mot* pull; *chess* move; *coll* (film *etc*) go down well; (excuse *etc*) work; (*sn*) move, go; march; wander, roam; (clouds) drift; (bird of passage) migrate; move (house); **es zieht** there is a draught; **mir zieht's (im Rücken** *etc*) my (back *etc*) hurts; **es zieht mich zu** *etc* I feel drawn towards *etc*; ~ **lassen** let (tea) stand; *cul* simmer; **sich** *dat* **einen Zahn ~ lassen** have a tooth out; **„ziehen"** 'pull'

~ **an** (*dat*) pull; pull at; pull at/on (pipe *etc*); **jmdn. an den Haaren ~** pull s.o.'s hair

auf sich ~ incur (s.o.'s hatred); **die Aufmerksamkeit/die Blicke auf sich ~** attract attention

~ **aus** pull out of; draw (nourishment) from; learn (lesson) from; **Nutzen ~ aus** derive benefit from

~ **bei** *coll* go down well with; **das zieht bei mir nicht** that cuts no ice with me

ins Gespräch ~ bring into the conversation; **ins Vertrauen ~** take into one's confidence; **in den Krieg ~** go to war

~ **mit** *chess* move (piece)

nach sich ~ have (consequences)

~ **zu** (*sn*) move in with

sich ~ stretch; (fence, motif, *etc*) run; (wood) warp

[die] **Ziehung, -en** draw

[das] **Ziel, -e** goal, aim, objective; destination; *esp mil* target; *sp* finish; (+*dat*) **ein ~ setzen** limit; set (s.o.) a goal; **sich** *dat* **ein ~ setzen** set oneself a goal; **am ~ seiner Wünsche (angelangt) sein** have got what one always wanted; **übers ~ hinausschießen** overshoot the mark || **das ~band, ⸚er** *sp* tape; **z~bewußt** single-minded; **das ~fern|rohr, -e** telescopic sight; **das ~flug|gerät, -e** homing device; **die ~gerade** (*decl as adj*) home straight, homestretch *US*; **die ~kurve, -n** final bend; **die ~linie, -n** finishing-line, finish line *US*; **z~los** aimless, purposeless; **die ~losigkeit** aimlessness, purposelessness; **der ~ort, -e** destination; **die ~scheibe, -n** target; butt; **die ~setzung, -en** objectives; objective; **z~sicher** unerring; purposeful; **die ~sprache, -n** target language; **die ~stellung, -en** *EGer* objectives; objective; **z~strebig** single-minded; **die ~vorrichtung, -en** sight (on gun); **die ~vorstellung, -en** objective

zielen (*see also* **gezielt**) (take) aim; ~ **auf** (*acc*) aim at; (remark *etc*) be aimed at

ziemen: sich ~ be seemly

ziemlich quite a; fair, considerable; *arch* seemly; (*adv*) quite; reasonably (certain *etc*); quite a bit; almost, nearly; **so ~** *coll* more or less

ziepen *NGer* tweak; (*v/i*) cheep; **es ziept** it hurts; ~ **an** (*dat*) tug (s.o.'s hair)

Zier- ornamental ...; **der ~affe, -n** (*wk masc*) *coll* fop; **der ~fisch, -e** ornamental fish; **die ~leiste, -n** border; moulding; *mot* trim; **die ~pflanze, -n** ornamental plant; **der ~strauch, ⸚er** ornamental shrub

[der] **Zierat, -e** decoration

[die] **Zierde, -n** decoration; credit (*gen* to)

zieren (*see also* **geziert**) decorate; adorn; **sich ~** need pressing; (girl) act coy; **zier dich nicht so!** don't be shy!

zierlich dainty; delicate

[die] **Ziffer, -n** figure; numeral; digit (*also comput*); sub-section; **das ~blatt, ⸚er** dial (on clock *etc*)

-ziff(e)rig -figure

(-)zig [tsɪç] (*indecl*) *coll* umpteen; **zig-** (*eg* **zigmal, zigtausend**) umpteen (times, thousand, *etc*)

[die] **Zigarette, -n** cigarette; **die ~n|schachtel, -n** cigarette packet/pack *US*; **die ~n|spitze, -n** cigarette-holder; **der ~n|stummel, -** cigarette end

[der] **Zigarillo, -s** (*also* **das**) cigarillo

[die] **Zigarre, -n** cigar; *coll* dressing-down; (+*dat*) **eine ~ verpassen** *coll* give (s.o.) a dressing-down || **der ~n|abschneider, -** cigar-cutter; **die ~n|kiste, -n** cigar-box; **di**

~n|spitze, –n cigar-holder; cigar-tip

der **Zigeuner, –** gipsy

zigeunerisch gipsy-like

zigeunern *coll* lead a vagabond life; (*sn*) rove

die **Zikade, –n** cicada

die **Zimbel, –n** cymbal

das **Zimmer, –** room; **die ~antenne, –n** indoor aerial/antenna *US*; **die ~decke, –n** ceiling; **die ~flucht, –en** suite of rooms; **das ~hand|werk** carpentry; **~laut|stärke (auf Z. stellen** turn down (so that neighbours are not disturbed)); **das ~mädchen, –** chambermaid; **der ~mann, ..leute** carpenter; **der ~nachweis, –e** accommodation bureau; **die ~pflanze, –n** house plant; **das ~theater, –** small theatre

-zimm(e)rig -room(ed)

zimmern make (from wood); (*v/i*) do carpentry; **~ an** (*dat*) work on

zimperlich squeamish; prim; **nicht (gerade) ~ sein** be none too fussy (in one's choice of methods *etc*); **sei nicht so ~!** don't make such a fuss!

der **Zimt** cinnamon; *coll* junk; *coll* nonsense

das **Zink** zinc; **die ~salbe** zinc ointment

die **Zinke, –n** prong; tooth (of comb)

zinken[1] mark (cards)

zinken[2] zinc

der **Zinken, –** *coll* conk, schnozzle *US*

das **Zinn** tin; pewter; **das ~geschirr** pewter (ware); **der ~soldat, –en** (*wk masc*) tin soldier

die **Zinne, –n** pinnacle; *Swiss* flat roof (used *esp* for drying washing); (*pl*) battlements

zinnern tin; pewter

die **Zinnie** [–ĭə], **–n** zinnia

der **Zinnober** cinnabar; vermilion; *coll* junk; *coll* nonsense; fuss; **zinnober|rot, das ~rot** vermilion

der **Zins, –e** *SGer* rent; *in compds* interest ...; **der ~fuß, ⸚e** rate of interest; **z~los** interest-free; **der ~satz, ⸚e** rate of interest

die **Zinsen** *pl* interest; **auf ~** (lend) at interest

die **Zinses|zinsen** *pl* compound interest

der **Zionismus** Zionism

der **Zionist, –en** (*wk masc*), **zionistisch** Zionist

der **Zipfel, –** corner; end (of sausage); tip; **die ~mütze, –n** stocking cap

der **Zipp, –s** *Aust* = **der ~verschluß, ⸚(ss)e** *Aust* zip, zipper *US*

die **Zirbel|kiefer, –n** stone-pine

zirka approximately

der **Zirkel, –** (pair of) compasses/dividers; circle (*also* = group of people); *EGer* study-group

·ᵗkeln measure exactly

·ulation, –en circulation

·en (*also sn*) circulate

–e circumflex

·us; *coll* to-do; **in den ~ gehen** go to the circus || **das ~zelt, –e** big top

zirpen chirp

die **Zirrhose** [–'roː–], **–n** cirrhosis

Zisch–: der ~laut, –e sibilant

zischeln whisper

zischen hiss; (*v/i*) hiss; sizzle; (*sn*) *coll* whizz; **einen ~** *coll* wet one's whistle

ziselieren chase (metal)

die **Zisterne, –n** (underground) cistern

der **Zisterzienser, –** Cistercian

Zisterzienser– Cistercian ...

die **Zitadelle, –n** citadel

das **Zitat, –e** quotation

die **Zither** [–ɪ–], **–n** zither

zitieren quote; summon (**vor** *acc* before)

das **Zitronat** citron peel

die **Zitrone, –n** lemon; **zitronen|gelb** lemon yellow; **die ~n|limonade, –n** lemonade; **die ~n|säure** citric acid; **die ~n|schale, –n** lemon peel

die **Zitrus|frucht, ⸚e** citrus fruit

Zitter–: der ~aal, –e electric eel; **das ~gras, ⸚er** quaking-grass; **die ~pappel, –n** aspen; **der ~rochen, –** electric ray

zitt(e)rig shaky

zittern shake, tremble; shiver; quiver; **~ für/um** tremble for; **~ vor** (*dat*) tremble/shiver with; be terrified of; **mit Zittern und Zagen** in fear and trembling

die **Zitze, –n** teat; *vulg* tit

zivil (aviation, marriage, *etc*) civil; civilian; (price) reasonable

das **Zivil** civilian/plain clothes; *in compds* civil ...; civilian ...; **die ~bevölkerung, –en** civilian population; **die ~courage** moral courage; **der ~dienst** community service (for conscientious objectors); **die ~ehe, –n** civil marriage; **das ~gesetz|buch, ⸚er** (*E. German or Swiss civil code*); **die ~kammer, –n** division of court dealing with civil cases; **die ~luft|fahrt** civil aviation; **das ~recht, z~rechtlich** civil law; **der ~schutz** civil defence; **das ~stands|amt, ⸚er** *Swiss* registry office

die **Zivilisation, –en** (modern, technological) civilization; **die ~s|krankheit, –en** illness (*eg* heart attack, stomach ulcer) associated with life in modern industrial society

zivilisatorisch relating to/caused by/(*adv*) in terms of (modern) civilization

zivilisieren civilize; **zivilisiert** civilized

der **Zivilist, –en** (*wk masc*) civilian

das **ZK, –(s) = Zentralkomitee**

der **Zobel, –** sable (*also* = fur)

die **Zofe, –n** *hist* lady's maid

zog (zöge) *p/t* (*subj*) *of* **ziehen**

zögern hesitate; **~ mit** delay; hesitate to give (consent); **mit der Antwort ~** hesitate before replying; **~d** hesitant; **das Zögern** hesitation

der **Zögling, -e** *dated* pupil
das **Zölibat** (*also* **der**) celibacy
der **Zoll**[1], - inch; **jeder ~ ...** every inch ...
der **Zoll**[2], **⸚e** customs; customs duty; toll; **-zoll ...** duty; **~ bezahlen für** pay duty on
Zoll-: die ~abfertigung customs clearance; **das ~amt, ⸚er** customs-house; **z~amtlich** customs; (*adv*) by the customs; **der ~be|amte** (*decl as adj*) customs officer; **die ~behörde, -n** customs; **~breit (keinen Z. zurückweichen** not yield an inch); **die ~erklärung, -en** customs declaration; **z~frei** duty-free; **die ~kontrolle, -n** customs examination; **z~pflichtig** dutiable; **die ~schranke, -n** customs barrier; **der ~stock, ⸚e** folding rule; **~verschluß (unter Z.** in bond); **das ~wesen** customs
zollen: (+*dat*) **Achtung/Beifall/Dank/Lob ~** respect/applaud/thank/praise
der **Zöllner, -** *bibl* publican; *dated coll* customs officer
die **Zone, -n** zone; fare-stage; **die ~** *dated coll* East Germany; **die ~n|grenze** *dated coll* border between East and West Germany
der **Zoo, -s** zoo; **die ~handlung, -en** pet shop
der **Zoologe** [tsoo-], **-n** (*wk masc*) zoologist
die **Zoologie** [tsoo-] zoology
zoologisch [tsoo-] zoological
der **Zoom** [zu:m], **-s** *cin* zoom; = **das ~objektiv, -e** zoom lens
zoomen ['zu:-] *cin* zoom (in)
der **Zootechniker** ['tso:o-, -ç-], - *EGer* livestock specialist
der **Zopf, ⸚e** plait; pigtail; **alter ~** outdated custom/view; **in Zöpfe flechten** plait || **das ~muster, -** cable-stitch
der **Zorn** anger (**auf** *acc* at); **einen ~ haben auf** (*acc*) be furious with; **im ~** in anger; **in ~ bringen** anger; **in ~ geraten** fly into a rage || **der ~ausbruch, ⸚e** fit of anger
zornig angry (**auf** *acc* with)
die **Zote, -n** dirty joke
zotig smutty
die **Zotte, -n** tuft of hair; *anat* villus
das **Zottel|haar** shaggy hair
zott(e)lig shaggy
zotteln (*sn*) *coll* dawdle along
zottig shaggy; *anat* villose
z. T. (= **zum Teil**) partly
zu 1 *prep* (+*dat*) (*a*) (*indicating place*) at, on, to (*esp in set phrases*, *eg* **~ jmds. Füßen** at s.o.'s feet, **~ beiden Seiten der Straße** on either side of the street, **~ jmds. Rechten** to s.o.'s right); in *or* out of (door, window); (enter, leave) by;

(*b*) (*indicating destination etc*) to (place, person);

(*c*) (*indicating time, occasion*) at (a certain time, Easter, the weekend, *etc*); (*followed by date*) on; by; (give notice) for; (get) for (Christmas, one's birthday); **in der Nacht (vom 1.) ~m 2. April** on the night of April 1st; **der Winter von 1986 ~ 1987** the winter of 1986/7;

(*d*) (*indicating purpose*) for; (key) to; (*with def art*) by way of; as (*eg* **~r Belohnung** as a reward, **~m Zeichen, daß ...** as a sign that ...); *with vbl noun, often translated by* to + *infin* (*eg* **Übungen ~r Entspannung der Muskeln** exercises to relax the muscles, **etwas ~m Schreiben/Lesen** something to write with/read);

(*e*) (nice, nasty, *etc*) to; (love, friendship) for; (= '*pertaining to*') relating to; (comment, decision, essay, *etc*) on; (attitude) to;

(*f*) (*indicating change of state*) (develop *etc*) into; (merge *etc*) to form; (*followed by name of language in lower case*, *eg* **~ polnisch**) in (= '*translated into*'); *sometimes not translated* (*eg* **jmdn. ~m König ausrufen/krönen** proclaim/crown s.o. king, **~m Vorsitzenden gewählt werden** be elected chairman, **~m Verräter werden** turn traitor);

(*g*) to (s.o.'s amazement, regret, satisfaction, *etc*);

(*h*) (*indicating accompaniment*) (sing) to; (drink, wear, *etc*) with;

(*i*) (*indicating price*) at; (*ratio*) to; (*score*) **(es steht) 5 ~ 1** (*usually written* **5:1**) (the score is) 5-1; **(wir** *etc*) **sind ~ (dreien/dritt** *etc*) there are (three *etc*) of (us *etc*); **~ (dreien/dritt** *etc*) in (threes *etc*); the (three *etc*) of us/you/them ...; **~r Hälfte** half; **~ Hunderten** in (their) hundreds;

2 *with infin*, *vbl noun or pres/part* (*in the infin and pres/part of separable verbs*, *inserted between prefix and simple verb*: **-zu-**):

(*a*) **~** + *infin*: to + *infin* (*eg* **der einzige Antrag, den er an~nehmen bereit war** the only application he was prepared to accept) *or translated by gerund* (*eg* **sie liebt es, Briefe ~ schreiben** she loves writing letters, **da die Affen keinen Wert darauf legen, von uns ab~stammen** as the apes attach no importance to being descended from us);

~ +*vbl noun*: to + *infin* (*eg* **jmdn. ~r Rückkehr nach ... bewegen** persuade s.o. to return to ..., **~r Landung ansetzen** prepare to land, **sich ~r Aufgabe von ... entschließen** make up one's mind to give up ...);

(*b*) (*with passive force*) **... ist/sind** *etc* **~** +*infin*: ... is/are *etc* to be + *p/part* (*eg* **die Tür ist geschlossen ~ halten** the door is to be kept closed, **es ist ~ hoffen, daß ...** it is to be hoped that ...); ... is/are *etc* ... able *or* ... can be + *p/part* (*eg* **sie ist nicht ~**

ersetzen she's irreplaceable, **sind sie doch noch ~ restaurieren?** can they be restored after all?); (*with adj*) ... is/are *etc* ... to + *infin* (*eg* **es war leicht ~ verstehen/schön an~sehen** it was easy to understand/lovely to look at);

(*c*) (*with passive force*) ~ + *pres/part*: (that is/are *etc*) to be + *p/part* (*eg* **die noch ~ lesenden Manuskripte** the manuscripts (that are) still to be read);

3 *adv* (*a*) closed, shut; **Tür ~!** shut the door!; (*b*) (*followed by adj/adv*) too; over–; **~ ..., als daß ...** too ... (for ...) to + *infin*; (*c*) (*following dat*) towards

auf ... (*acc*) ~ up to; towards

~ ... hin towards

immer/nur ~! go on!

nach ... ~ towards

um ~ ... (in order) to ...

---

zu– [*stressed* 'tsu:–, *unstressed* tsu–]; *as sep pref – general senses*:

(*i*) *indicates act of closing, sealing* ... up, ... down, ... off, ... shut (*eg* **~mauern** wall up, **~kleben** stick down, **~drehen** turn off, **~werfen** slam shut);

(*ii*) *with* **auf** (*acc*): ... up to ... (*eg* **auf jmdn. ~marschieren** march up to s.o.); ... towards ..., ... for ... (*eg* **auf etw. ~fahren/~steuern** drive towards/steer for sth.);

(*iii*) (+*dat*) ... to(wards) ..., ... at ... (*eg* **jmdm. etw. ~werfen** throw sth. to s.o., **jmdm. ~lächeln** smile at s.o.);

(*iv*) *indicates addition* (*eg* **~zählen** add)

---

zu|aller–: ~e̱rst/~lẹtzt/~me̱ist first/last/most of all

zuballern *coll* slam

zubauen build on (site); block (view with a building/buildings)

das **Zubehör** equipment; accessories; **das ~teil, –e** accessory

zubeißen* (dog *etc*) bite; *dent* bite one's teeth together

zubekommen* *coll* get shut; (manage to) do up

zubereiten prepare (meal); make up (medicine)

die **Zubereitung, –en** preparation

zubilligen (+*dat*) grant

zubinden* tie up; (+*dat*) **die Augen ~** blindfold

zubleiben* (*sn*) *coll* stay closed

zublinzeln (+*dat*) wink at

zubringen* spend (time)

der **Zubringer, –** feeder (road); *tech* feeder; = **der ~bus, –se** shuttle; airport bus; **der ~dienst, –e** shuttle service; **die ~straße, –n** feeder (road)

zubuttern *coll* contribute

die **Zucchini** [tsu'ki:ni], – courgettes

die **Zucht, –en** discipline; breeding; growing, cultivation; culture (of bacteria, pearls, *etc*); *in compds* breeding ...; **das ~buch, ⸚er** stud-book; **das ~haus, ⸚er** *hist* convict prison; = **die ~haus|strafe** *hist* penal servitude; **der ~häusler, –** convict; **der ~hengst, –e** stud horse; **z~los** undisciplined; **die ~perle, –n** cultured pearl; **das ~tier, –e** breeding animal; **die ~wahl** selective breeding

züchten breed; grow, cultivate; culture

der **Züchter, –** breeder; grower

züchtig (girl) modest

züchtigen chastise

die **Züchtigung, –en** chastisement; **körperliche ~** corporal punishment

die **Züchtung, –en** *vbl noun*; *also* cultivation; culture; breed, *bot* variety

zuckeln (*sn*) *coll* jog along

zucken shrug (one's shoulders); (*v/i*) twitch; flinch; (lightning) flash; **~ durch** (*sn*) (pain) shoot through; **~ mit** shrug (one's shoulders); **ohne mit der Wimper zu ~** without batting an eyelid; **es zuckte mir in den Fingern zu ...** I was itching to ...

zücken draw (sword *etc*); *coll* pull out (handkerchief *etc*)

der **Zucker** sugar; *coll* diabetes; **der ~bäcker, –** *SGer* confectioner; **der ~bäcker|stil** wedding-cake architecture; **~brot (mit Z. und Peitsche** with a stick and a carrot); **die ~dose, –n** sugar-bowl; **der ~gehalt** sugar content; **der ~guß, ⸚(ss)e** icing; **der ~hut, ⸚e** sugar-loaf; **z~krank, der/die ~kranke** (*decl as adj*) diabetic; **die ~krankheit** diabetes; **das ~rohr** sugar-cane; **die ~rübe, –n** sugar-beet; **zụcker|sü̱ß** as sweet as sugar; (words) honeyed; **die ~watte** candy floss, cotton candy *US*; **die ~zange, –n** sugar-tongs

zuck(e)rig sugary

das **Zuckerl, –(n)** *SGer* sweet, candy *US*

zuckern sugar

die **Zuckung, –en** twitch

zudecken cover; cover up; **~ mit** *coll* bombard with

zude̱m in addition

zudenken* (*usu perfect*) (+*dat*) intend for

zudiktieren (+*dat*) impose on

zudrehen turn off; (+*dat*) turn (one's back) on; **sich ~** (+*dat*) turn to

zudringlich pushing; importunate

zudrücken press shut; close (eyes); **ein Auge/beide Augen ~** *coll* turn a blind eye

zu|eignen (+*dat*) dedicate to

die **Zu|eignung, –en** dedication

zu|eilen (*sn*): **~ auf** (*acc*) rush towards/up to

zu|einạnder to one another

zu|erkennen* (+*dat*) award to; confer on
zu|erst first; ... is *etc* the first to ..., first; at first
zufächeln: (+*dat*) **Luft/Kühlung** ~ fan
zufahren* (*sn*): ~ **auf** (*acc*) drive towards; **fahr zu!** get a move on!
die **Zufahrt, –en** access; drive(way); **die ~s|-straße, –n** approach road
der **Zufall, ⸚e** chance; coincidence; **durch** ~ by chance; **der ~ wollte es, daß ...** it so happened that ...
zufallen* (*sn*) close; (+*dat*) go to; fall to
zufällig chance, accidental; coincidental; *stats* random; (*adv*) by chance, accidentally, *or conveyed by* ... happen(s) to ...; (*in questions*) by any chance; ~ **stoßen auf** (*acc*) stumble across || **zufälliger|weise** = **zufällig** (*adv*)
Zufalls– chance ...; *math*, *stats*, *comput* random ...
zufassen grab at s.o./sth.; **(mit)** ~ lend a hand
zufliegen* (*sn*) (*coll in 1st sense*) slam (shut); (+*dat*) come easily to; (bird) fly into (s.o.'s) home; ~ **auf** (*acc*) fly towards; **alle Herzen flogen ihm zu** he won the hearts of everyone
zufließen* (*sn*) (+*dat*) flow towards/into; (money) go to
die **Zuflucht** refuge; **(seine)** ~ **nehmen zu** resort to || **der ~s|ort, –e** (place of) refuge
der **Zufluß, ⸚(ss)e** inflow; influx; *geog* tributary
zuflüstern (+*dat*) whisper to
zufolge (*following dat*) according to
zufrieden satisfied; content(ed); **~geben*** (*sep*): **sich z. mit** content oneself with; **~lassen*** (*sep*) leave alone; **~stellen** (*sep*) satisfy; **~stellend** satisfactory
die **Zufriedenheit** satisfaction; contentment
zufrieren* (*sn*) freeze over
zufügen (+*dat*) add to; do to; cause; inflict on; (+*dat*) **Schaden** ~ harm
die **Zufuhr, –en** supply; *meteor* influx (of air); *mil* supplies
zuführen (+*dat*) bring to; supply with; infuse (new blood) into; *tech* feed into; ~ **auf** (*acc*) lead to
die **Zuführung** *vbl noun*; *also* supply
der **Zug, ⸚e** train (**aus** from, **nach** for); (*action*) pull (*also row*), tug, *phys* traction, *swim* stroke; move (in game); puff, pull (**an** *dat*/**aus** at), (at bottle) pull, swig; breath; (*movement as group*) expedition; migration; drifting (of clouds); (*of air*) draught; (*collective*) procession; team (of horses *etc*); flock; shoal; *mil* platoon; (*objects*) bell-pull; draw-string; groove (of gun-barrel); *mus* slide (of trombone); (*of pen*) stroke; (*attribute*) feature (of face); characteristic, trait, (sadistic *etc*) streak; tendency; **ich bin am** ~ it's my move; **in einem** ~ at/in one go; **im ~e** (+*gen*) in the course of; **im besten ~e** in full swing; **in großen Zügen** in broad outline; **in vollen Zügen genießen** enjoy to the full; **in den letzten Zügen liegen** be on one's last legs; **mit dem** ~ by train; ~ **um** ~ step by step; one by one; **(nicht) zum ~e kommen** (not) get a look-in || **der ~begleiter, –** guard, conductor *US*; train schedule leaflet; **das ~begleit|personal** train crew; **die ~brücke, –n** drawbridge; **die ~feder, –n** tension spring; **die ~festigkeit** tensile strength; **der ~führer, –** (chief) guard, conductor *US*; *mil* platoon leader; **die ~kraft** tractive force; appeal; **z~kräftig** with a strong appeal; **die ~luft** draught; **die ~maschine, –n** traction-engine; **die ~nummer, –n** draw; *rail* train number; **der ~ochse, –n** (*wk masc*) draught ox; **das ~personal** train crew; **das ~pferd, –e** draught-horse; draw; **das ~tier, –e** draught-animal; **die ~verbindung, –en** train connection; **der ~verkehr** train service; **der ~vogel, ..vögel** bird of passage; **der ~zwang** tight spot **(in Z. bringen/geraten** put/be put on the spot; **unter Z. stehen** be in a tight spot)
die **Zugabe, –n** extra; *comm* free gift; *mus*, *theat*, *etc* encore
der **Zugang, ⸚e** entrance; access (**zu** to); (*pl*) new arrivals/admissions/accessions *etc*; **keinen ~ finden/haben zu** have no feeling for
zugänglich accessible; approachable; (*following dat or with* **für**) amenable (to); accessible (to)
zugeben* admit; throw in, *cul* add, *mus* give as an encore; **zugegeben, ...** admittedly ...
zugegebener|maßen admittedly
zugegen present (**bei** at)
zugehen* (*sn*) (door, suitcase, *etc*) shut, close; (+*dat*) be sent to; ~ **auf** (*acc*) go up to; be getting on for; **es geht auf ... zu** (spring *etc*) is getting closer; (+*dat*) ~ **lassen** send to; **dem Ende** ~ be drawing to a close; **spitz** ~ taper off to a point; **es geht ... zu** things are ...; **so geht es nun einmal in der Welt zu** life's like that
die **Zugeh|frau, –en** *SGer* cleaning woman
zugehören (+*dat*) belong to
zugehörig belonging to it/them; appertaining to it/them
die **Zugehörigkeit** membership (**zu** of, in *US*); affiliation; **das ~s|gefühl** sense of belonging
zugeknöpft *p/part*; *coll* tight-lipped
der **Zügel, –** rein; **die ~ fest in der Hand haben** have things firmly under control; (+*dat*) ~ **anlegen** curb || **z~los** unbridled, unrestrained
zügeln rein in; curb; **sich** ~ restrain oneself

der **Zugereiste** (*fem* **die** ~) (*decl as adj*) newcomer
zugesellen: sich ~ (+*dat*) join
zugestandener|maßen admittedly
das **Zugeständnis, –se** concession (**an** *acc* to)
zugestehen* (+*dat*) grant; **~, daß ...** admit that ...
zugetan *p/part*; *also* (*following dat*) fond of
zugießen* add (more water *etc*); fill in (with cement *etc*)
zugig draughty
zügig speedy; brisk, smart
zugipsen plaster up
zugleich at the same time
zugreifen* grab hold of sth.; help oneself; jump at the offer/opportunity; take action; put one's back into it; ~ **auf** (*acc*) *comput* access
der **Zugriff, –e** action (= intervention); *comput* access; **sich jmds. ~ entziehen** elude s.o.'s grasp
zugrunde: ~ **gehen** perish; be ruined; +**an** (*dat*) die of; be destroyed by; ~ **legen** take as a basis; (+*dat*) base on; (+*dat*) ~ **liegen** underlie; **... (***dat***) liegt ... ~** ... is/are based on ...; ~ **richten** ruin || **~liegend** underlying
Zugs– *Aust*, *Swiss* = **Zug–**
zugucken *coll* = **zusehen**
zugunsten (+*gen*) in favour of; in aid of
zugute: (+*dat*) ~ **halten** make allowance(s) for; **sich** *dat* **etwas ~ halten/tun auf** (*acc*) pride oneself on; (+*dat*) ~ **kommen** benefit; be for the benefit of; (+*dat*) ~ **kommen lassen** let (s.o.) have
zuhaben* *coll* be closed
zuhalten* keep closed; **sich** *dat* **die Augen/die Ohren/den Mund** ~ put one's hands over one's eyes/ears/mouth; **sich** *dat* **die Nase** ~ hold one's nose; ~ **auf** (*acc*) head for
der **Zuhälter, –** pimp
die **Zuhälterei** procuring
zuhanden *Aust*, *Swiss*: ~ **(von) ...** for the attention of ...
zuhängen: ~ **mit** hang (curtain *etc*) over
zuhauen* *tech* (*p/t only* **haute zu**) dress (stone); (*v/i*) hit out at s.o.
das **Zuhause** home
zuheilen (*sn*) heal up
Zuhilfe|nahme: unter ~ (+*gen*) with the aid of
zuhinterst right at the back/end
zuhöchst right at the top
zuhören listen (*dat* to)
der **Zuhörer, –** listener; **die** ~ the audience
die **Zuhörerschaft** audience
zu|innerst in one's heart of hearts; deeply
zujubeln (+*dat*) cheer
zukehren (+*dat*) turn towards; turn (one's back) on; **sich** ~ (+*dat*) turn to
zuklappen (*sn if v/i*) snap shut
zukleben stick down; ~ **mit** stick (tape *etc*) over
zuknallen (*sn if v/i*) slam (shut)
zukneifen* screw up (eyes); press (lips) together
zuknöpfen (*see also* **zugeknöpft**) button up
zukommen* (*sn*) (+*dat*) be due to (as of right); befit; (importance) attach to; ~ **auf** (*acc*) come up to; be in store for; (+*dat*) ~ **lassen** send; give; **die Dinge auf sich ~ lassen** let events take their course
zukorken cork
zukriegen *coll* get (sth.) to shut
die **Zukunft** future; *gramm* future (tense); **in** ~ in future
zukünftig future; (*adv*) in future; **mein Z~er/meine Z~e** *coll* my intended
Zukunfts– ... for/of the future; **~musik** *coll* (**das ist Z.** that's all very much in the future); **z~reich** with a promising future; **der ~roman, –e** science-fiction novel
zulächeln (+*dat*) smile at
die **Zulage, –n** bonus; allowance; rise, raise *US*
zulande: bei uns *etc* ~ in our *etc* (part of the) country
zulangen *coll* help oneself
zulänglich adequate
zulassen* allow, permit; admit of; license; leave closed; ~ **zu** admit to; allow to sit (examination); **(nicht) ~, daß ...** (not) allow (s.o., sth.) to ...
zulässig permissible; permitted
die **Zulassung, –en** *vbl noun*; *also* admission; licence
der **Zulauf** rush; **großen ~ haben** be very popular
zulaufen* (*sn*) (+*dat*) (stray) adopt; ~ **auf** (*acc*) run up to; **spitz** ~ taper to a point; **lauf zu!** hurry!; ~ **lassen** run (extra water)
zulegen add; chip in; (*v/i*) *coll* get a move on; **sich** *dat* **...** ~ *coll* get oneself, acquire; **einen Schritt** ~ quicken one's pace
zuleide: (+*dat*) **etwas ~ tun** harm
zuleiten (+*dat*) supply to; pipe into; transmit to
zuletzt last; in the end; **bis** ~ to the (very) end; **nicht** ~ not least
zuliebe (*following dat*) for ...'s sake; to please
Zuliefer–: die ~industrie, –n ancillary industry
der **Zulieferer, –** sub-contractor
zum [–ʊ–] = **zu dem**
zumachen shut, close; do up (coat *etc*); (*v/i* shop) close
zumal 1 *adv* especially; 2 *conj* = ~ **da ...** especially as
zumauern wall up
zumeist mostly
zumessen* (+*dat*) measure out (s.o.'s share);

apportion to
zumindest at least
zumutbar reasonable
zumute: mir ist/wird (traurig *etc*) ~ I feel (sad *etc*); **mir ist nicht nach (Tanzen** *etc*)/**zum Lachen** ~ I'm not in the mood for (dancing *etc*)/in a laughing mood
zumuten (+*dat*) expect of; **sich** *dat* **zuviel** ~ attempt/take on too much; **jmdm. ~ zu ...** expect s.o. to ...
die **Zumutung, -en** unreasonable demand; imposition; liberty
zunächst first; at first, to begin with; for the moment
zunageln nail down; nail up; **mit Brettern** ~ board up
zunähen sew up
die **Zunahme** increase (*gen*/**an** *dat* in)
der **Zuname, -n** (*like* **Name**) surname
Zünd- ignition ...; **das ~blättchen, -** cap; **das ~holz, ⸚er** *SGer* match; **die ~kapsel, -n** detonator; **die ~kerze, -n** spark(ing) plug; **der ~schlüssel, -** ignition key; **die ~schnur, ⸚e** fuse; **die ~spule, -n** ignition coil; **der ~stoff, -e** primary explosive; (political *etc*) dynamite
zünden ignite; detonate; fire (rocket); (*v/i*) ignite; fire; (match) light; kindle enthusiasm; **der Blitz hat gezündet** lightning has struck and set fire to sth.; **es hat bei ... gezündet** *coll* ... has *etc* cottoned on at last; **~d** rousing
der **Zunder** tinder; *metall* scale
der **Zünder, -** fuse; detonator; (*pl*) *Aust* matches
die **Zündung, -en** ignition; detonation; *mot* ignition
zunehmen* increase; put on weight; (days) lengthen; (moon) wax; **~d** increasing; (moon) crescent; = **in ~dem Maße** increasingly
zuneigen: (+*dat*) incline to; **sich** ~ (+*dat*) lean towards; **sich dem Ende** ~ be drawing to a close; (+*dat*) **zugeneigt sein** be well-disposed towards
die **Zuneigung** affection
die **Zunft, ⸚e** *hist* guild; *joc* fraternity
zünftig expert; *coll* proper
die **Zunge, -n** tongue (*also* on shoe); pointer (on scales); *mus* reed; **eine feine ~ haben** have a delicate palate; **sich** *dat* **die ~ verbrennen** burn one's tongue; say too much; **das Wort liegt/schwebt mir auf der** ~ the word is on the tip of my tongue; **mit der ~ anstoßen** lisp
züngeln dart its tongue in and out; (flame) dart
Zungen- ... of the tongue; tongue ...; **der ~brecher, -** tongue-twister; **z~fertig** voluble; **der ~kuß, ⸚(ss)e** French kiss; **das ~-R, -** rolled 'r'; **der ~schlag, ⸚e (falscher Z.** slip of the tongue); **die ~spitze, -n** tip of the tongue
Zünglein: das ~ an der Waage sein tip the scales; *pol* hold the balance of power
zunichte: ~ machen wreck, ruin; dash (hope); **~ werden** be wrecked, be ruined; be dashed
zunicken (+*dat*) nod to
zunutze: sich *dat* **... ~ machen** make use of; take advantage of
zu|oberst right at the top
zu|ordnen (+*dat*) assign to
zupacken grab hold of sth.; lend a hand; knuckle down; **~d** forceful
zupaß: (+*dat*) **~ kommen** come at the right moment
zupfen pluck (*also mus*); pull up (weeds); **~ an** (*dat*) pull at
zupfropfen cork
zupressen press shut
zuprosten [-oː-] (+*dat*) raise one's glass to
zur [-uː-, -ʊ-] = **zu der**
zuraten*: jmdm. ~ zu ... advise s.o. to ...; **auf jmds. Zuraten** on s.o.'s advice
zuraunen (+*dat*) whisper (words *etc*) to
zurechnen (+*dat*) attribute to; assign to
zurechnungs-: ~fähig of sound mind; **die Z~fähigkeit** soundness of mind (**verminderte Z.** diminished responsibility)
zurecht- *sep pref* ... into shape; ... ready
zurechtbiegen* bend into shape; straighten out, sort out
zurechtfinden*: sich ~ find one's way around; find one's bearings; **sich im Leben nicht** ~ not be able to cope with life
zurechtflicken patch up
zurechtkommen* (*sn*) arrive in time; **~ mit** get on with; cope with
zurechtlegen put out (ready); **sich** *dat* **... ~** concoct (excuse *etc*)
zurechtmachen get ready; **sich ~** get ready; make up
zurechtrücken straighten; (+*dat*) **den Kopf ~** bring to his/her senses
zurechtsetzen straighten; **sich ~** settle oneself (in a comfortable position)
zurechtstutzen trim; lick into shape
zurechtweisen*, die Zurechtweisung, -en rebuke, reprimand
zurechtzimmern knock together; *coll* concoct
zureden (+*dat*) try to persuade; (+*dat*) **gut ~** talk to nicely; **das Zureden** urging
zureichen (+*dat*) pass to
zureiten* break in (horse); **~ auf** (*acc*) (*sn*) ride towards/up to
Zürich Zurich
zurichten prepare; dress (leather *etc*); **übel ~** knock about; maul
zuriegeln bolt
zürnen (+*dat*) be angry with; rage against

zurollen (*sn if v/i*): ~ **auf** (*acc*) roll towards
die **Zurschaustellung, –en** display; parading (of)
zurück back; ~ **sein** be back; lag behind; be backward; **hinter ...** (*dat*) ~ behind; **es gibt kein Zurück (mehr)** there's no going back

---

zurück– *sep pref ...* back; *with modal auxiliary eg* **~dürfen** = go back, return (*eg* **er darf nicht** ~ he's not allowed to go back/return)

---

zurückbehalten* keep back; ~ **von** have as a result of (illness)
zurückbekommen* get back; get (... marks *etc*) change
zurückbilden: sich ~ *med* regress; atrophy
zurückbleiben* (*see also* **zurückgeblieben**) (*sn*) stay behind; be left behind, lag behind; (clock, watch) lose; (scar, feeling, *etc*) remain; ~ **hinter** (*dat*) lag behind; fall short of (expectations); **hinter der Zeit** ~ be behind the times; ~ **mit** be behind with; be left with
zurückblicken look back (**auf** *acc* at; on)
zurückbringen* bring back; take back; *coll* set back
zurückdatieren antedate; ~ **auf** (*acc*) date back to
zurückdenken*: ~ **an** (*acc*) think back to, recall; **so weit ich** ~ **kann** as far as I can recall
zurückdrängen push back; repress
zurückdrehen turn back
zurück|erhalten* get back
zurück|er|obern reconquer
zurück|erstatten refund
zurück|erwarten expect back
zurück|fahren* drive back; (*v/i sn*) go back; drive back; recoil
zurückfallen* (*sn*) fall back; fall behind (*also sp*); ~ **an** (*acc*) revert to; ~ **auf** (*acc*) recoil on; reflect on; *sp* fall back to; ~ **in** (*acc*) relapse into; **sich** ~ **lassen in** (*acc*) slump back into
zurückfinden* find one's way back; ~ **zu** find one's way back to; go back to
zurückfordern demand back
zurückführen take back; ~ **auf** (*acc*) attribute to; trace back to; reduce to (formula); **zurückzuführen auf** due to; **... ist darauf zurückzuführen, daß ...** ... is due to the fact that ...
zurückgeben* give back, return (*dat* to); retort; *sp* pass back; **ich gebe zurück ins Studio** I now hand you back to the studio
zurückgeblieben *p/part*; *also* backward, retarded
zurückgehen* (*sn*) go back, return; (tide) go down; decrease, go down; fall off; ~ **auf** (*acc*) go back to; have its origin in; ~ **lassen** send back
zurückgewinnen* win back; regain
zurückgezogen *p/part*; *also* secluded; (*adv*) in seclusion
die **Zurückgezogenheit** seclusion
zurückgreifen*: ~ **auf** (*acc*) fall back on; **weit** ~ go back a long way
zurückhalten* hold back; withhold; detain; restrain, suppress; ~ **mit** hold back; **mit seiner Meinung nicht** ~ not hesitate to speak one's mind; ~ **von** stop from making/taking *etc*
  sich ~ keep in the background; restrain oneself; exercise restraint
zurückhaltend reserved; cautious; (colour *etc*) restrained
die **Zurückhaltung** reserve, reticence
zurückholen fetch back
zurückkehren (*sn*) return
zurückkommen* (*sn*) come back, return; ~ **auf** (*acc*) come back to, return to (topic)
zurücklassen* leave; leave behind; allow back
zurücklegen put back; put by, (+*dat*/**für**) keep for; cover (distance); *Aust* resign; **sich** ~ lie back
zurücklehnen put (one's head) back; **sich** ~ lean back
zurückliegen* be (... years *etc*) ago; *sp* be (... laps *etc*) behind; **mit ... Toren** ~ be ... goals down
zurückmelden: sich ~ report back
die **Zurücknahme** taking back; withdrawal
zurücknehmen* take back; withdraw; cancel; *mil* pull back, withdraw; *sp* pull back
zurückprallen (*sn*) rebound; ~ **vor** (*dat*) shrink back from
zurückreichen pass back; (*v/i* tradition *etc*) go back (**bis in** *acc* to)
zurückreisen (*sn*) return, travel back
zurückrufen* recall; call back (*also Aust tel*); (*v/i*) *tel* call back; **sich** *dat* **... ins Gedächtnis** ~ call to mind; **ins Leben** ~ revive
zurückschalten change down, shift down *US* (**in** *acc* into)
zurückschaudern (*sn*): ~ **vor** (*dat*) shrink (back) from, recoil from
zurückscheuen (*sn*): ~ **vor** (*dat*) shy away from; **vor nichts** ~ stop at nothing
zurückschicken send back
zurückschieben* push back
zurückschlagen* hit back; turn down (bedclothes); fold back; *mil* repel; (*v/i*) hit/*mil* strike back; (*sn*) swing back
zurückschneiden* *hort* cut back
zurückschnellen (*sn*) spring back
zurückschrauben cut back (on); moderate
zurückschrecken (*also – exc where marked* * – **schrick(s)t zurück,** *p/t* **schrak** (*subj* **schräke) zurück**) (*sn*) recoil; ~ **vor** (*dat*) (*sn*) shrink back from, recoil from; *(*also*

sn) flinch from; shy away from; ***vor nichts** ~ stop at nothing

zurücksehnen: sich ~ nach long to return to

zurücksenden* send back

zurücksetzen put back, move back, *mot* back, reverse (*also v/i*); neglect; **sich ~** sit further back

zurückspringen* (*sn*) jump back; bounce back; *archit* be set back

zurückstecken put back; (*v/i*) moderate one's demands; set one's sights lower

zurückstehen* be set back; **~ hinter** (*dat*) take second place to; be behind/inferior to

zurückstellen put back; move back; defer; defer (pupil's) enrolment/*mil* (s.o.'s) military service; set aside (doubt *etc*); *Aust* return; (+*dat*/**für**) put by for

zurückstoßen* push back; (conduct *etc*) repel

zurückstufen downgrade

zurücktreiben* drive back; *mil* repulse

zurücktreten* (*sn*) step back; resign; (waters) recede; **~ hinter** (*dat*) take second place to; be insignificant compared with; **~ von** step back from; resign from; withdraw from

zurückverfolgen trace back

zurückversetzen transfer back; *educ* move down; **~ in** (*acc*) restore to; **sich zurückversetzt fühlen in** (*acc*) feel as if one has been transported back to

zurückverweisen*: ~ an (*acc*) refer back to

zurückweichen* (*sn*) draw back; recede; *mil* fall back, retreat; **~ vor** (*dat*) shrink back from; yield to

zurückweisen* turn away/back; reject

die **Zurückweisung, -en** *vbl noun*; *also* rejection

zurückwenden*, sich ~ turn back

zurückwerfen* throw back; toss (one's head) back; reflect; echo (back); set back; *mil* repulse

zurückzahlen repay, pay back; (+*dat*) repay, pay back to; *coll* pay (s.o.) back for

zurückziehen* (*see also* **zurückgezogen**) pull back (*also mil*); draw back; withdraw; **sich ~** withdraw; retire (to one's room); *mil* pull back; **sich in sich ~** withdraw into oneself; **sich ~ von** retire from; withdraw from; no longer associate with

die **Zurückziehung, -en** *vbl noun*; *also* withdrawal

zurückzucken (*sn*) flinch

der **Zuruf, -e** shout; (*pl*) cheers; **durch ~** by acclamation

zurufen* (+*dat*) shout (order *etc*) at

zurzeit *Aust*, *Swiss* at present

die **Zusage, -n** acceptance; promise

zusagen (+*vbl noun*, *eg* **seine Teilnahme ~**) promise (to take part *etc*); (+*dat*) promise; (*v/i*) accept (s.o.'s invitation); (+*dat*) appeal to, be to (s.o.'s) liking; (+*dat*) (**die Lüge** *etc*) **auf den Kopf ~** accuse outright of (lying *etc*)

zusammen together; between us; altogether, all told

---

zusammen– *sep pref – general senses*:

(*i*) ... together (*eg* **~leimen** glue together, **~bleiben** stay together);

(*ii*) ... up (*eg* **~falten** fold up);

(*iii*) *indicates collapse or destruction* (*eg* **~brechen** collapse, **~schießen** shoot to pieces);

(*iv*) *indicates diminution* (*eg* **~schrumpfen** shrivel up, **~streichen** cut);

(*v*) *indicates improvization* (*eg* **~schustern** cobble together)

---

die **Zusammen|arbeit** co-operation; collaboration

zusammen|arbeiten co-operate, work together; collaborate

zusammenballen squeeze into a ball; **sich ~** mass (together); **zusammengeballt** *also* concentrated

die **Zusammenballung, -en** *vbl noun*; *also* concentration

zusammenbauen assemble

zusammenbeißen*: die Zähne ~ clench one's teeth; grit one's teeth; **sich ~** *coll* adjust to one another (despite disagreements *etc*)

zusammenbinden* tie together

zusammenbleiben* (*sn*) stay together

zusammenbrauen (*coll in 1st sense*) concoct; **sich ~** be brewing

zusammenbrechen* (*sn*) collapse; break down; come to a standstill

zusammenbringen* bring together; get together; collect; amass (fortune); *coll* string together; **~ mit** bring into contact with

der **Zusammenbruch, ⸚e** collapse (*historically*, **der ~** *denotes Germany's collapse in 1945*); breakdown (*also med*)

zusammendrängen, sich ~ crowd together; **~ auf** (*acc*)/**in** (*acc*) compress into

zusammendrücken press together; squash

zusammenfahren* (*coll in 1st sense*) smash up; (*v/i sn*) (give a) start; collide

der **Zusammenfall, ⸚e** coincidence (of events *etc*)

zusammenfallen* (*sn*) collapse; lose flesh; coincide; *Aust coll* fall down; **in sich ~** collapse

zusammenfalten fold up; fold (one's hands)

zusammenfassen summarize; combine (**zu** in); **~ unter** (*dat*) subsume under; **~d** *also* to sum up

die **Zusammenfassung, -en** *vbl noun*; *also* combination; summary

zusammenfinden*: sich ~ get together

zusammenflicken *coll* patch up; cobble together

zusammenfließen* (*sn*) (rivers) join; (colours) merge

der **Zusammenfluß, ⸗(ss)e** confluence

zusammenfügen fit together; join together; **sich ~** fit together

zusammenführen bring together; **wieder ~** reunite

zusammengehen* (*sn*) (lines) meet; join forces

zusammengehören belong together; go together; (*explaining to salesperson etc*) **wir gehören zusammen** we're together

zusammengehörig belonging together; matching

das **Zusammengehörigkeits|gefühl** fellow feeling; feeling of solidarity

zusammengesetzt *p/part*; *gramm* compound

zusammengewürfelt: bunt ~ mixed; motley

zusammenhaben* *coll* have got together

der **Zusammenhalt** cohesion; unity, solidarity

zusammenhalten* hold together; keep together; *coll* hold onto (one's money); (*v/i*) hold together; stick together

der **Zusammenhang, ⸗e** connection; context; **aus dem ~ reißen** take out of context; **im/in ~ mit** in connection with; **in ~ bringen mit** connect with; **im/in ~ stehen mit** be connected with || **z~(s)|los** disjointed; incoherent

zusammenhängen* (*like* **hängen** *v/i*): **~ mit** be joined to; be linked/connected with; **~d** coherent

zusammenhauen* (*p/t only* **haute zusammen**) *coll* smash up; beat up; knock together

zusammenkaufen buy up

zusammenkitten cement together; patch up (marriage *etc*)

zusammenklappbar collapsible; folding

zusammenklappen fold up; click (one's heels); (*v/i sn*) *coll* flake out

zusammenkleben (*also sn if v/i*) stick together

zusammenkneifen* press together; squeeze together; screw up (one's eyes)

zusammenknüllen screw up

zusammenkommen* (*sn*) meet, get together; (money) be collected; happen at once

zusammenkrachen (*sn*) *coll* crash down; crash

zusammenkratzen scrape together

die **Zusammenkunft, ⸗e** meeting

zusammenläppern: sich ~ *coll* mount up

zusammenlaufen* (*sn*) flock together; converge; run together; curdle; **mir läuft das Wasser im Mund zusammen** my mouth waters

zusammenleben live together; **~ mit** live with; **das Zusammenleben** living together

zusammenlegen fold (up); pool; amalgamate, merge; combine; (*v/i*) club together

die **Zusammenlegung, –en** *vbl noun*; *also*. amalgamation

zusammennehmen* collect (thoughts); summon up; **sich ~** pull oneself together; **alles zusammengenommen** altogether, all in all

zusammenpassen go (well) together; be well-matched

zusammenpferchen cram together

der **Zusammenprall, –e** collision; clash

zusammenprallen (*sn*) collide; clash

zusammenpressen press together

zusammenraffen collect up hurriedly; gather up (skirts); amass; **sich ~** pull oneself together

zusammenraufen: sich ~ adjust to one another (despite disagreements *etc*)

zusammenrechnen add up; **alles zusammengerechnet** all told

zusammenreimen: sich *dat* **… ~** make sense of; **wie reimt sich das zusammen?** it just doesn't add up; **wie reimt sich das zusammen mit …?** how does that square with …?

zusammenreißen*: sich ~ *coll* pull oneself together

zusammenrollen roll up; **sich ~** curl/coil up

zusammenrotten: sich ~ band together

zusammenrücken move closer together; (*v/i sn*) move closer together, squeeze up

zusammenrufen* call together

zusammensacken (*sn*): **(in sich) ~** slump; cave in

die **Zusammenschau** survey

zusammenschießen* riddle with bullets; shoot to pieces

zusammenschlagen* smash up, wreck; beat up; click (one's heels), *mus* clash (cymbals); fold up; **die Hände über dem Kopf ~** throw up one's hands; **~ über** (*acc*) (*sn*) engulf

zusammenschließen*: sich ~ combine, join forces; amalgamate, *comm* merge

der **Zusammenschluß, ⸗(ss)e** amalgamation, *comm* merger

zusammenschmelzen* fuse (metals); (*v/i sn*) melt; dwindle

zusammenschnüren tie up; **~ zu** tie into; (+*dat*) **das Herz ~** wring (s.o.'s) heart

zusammenschrecken (*also* **schrick(s)t zusammen**, *p/t* **schrak** (*subj* **schräke**) **zusammen**) (*sn*) (give a) start

zusammenschreiben* write as one word; *coll* scribble down; *coll* make (fortune) by writing; **~ aus** put together from (various sources)

zusammenschrumpfen (*sn*) shrivel up; dwindle

zusammenschustern [–ʃuː–] *coll* cobble together

zusammenschweißen weld together

das **Zusammensein** being together; get-together

zusammensetzen (*see also* **zusammengesetzt**) put together; *mech* assemble; **sich ~** sit (down) together; get together, meet; **sich ~ aus** be made up of

die **Zusammensetzung, -en** *vbl noun*; *also* composition; *mech* assembly; *gramm* compound

zusammensinken* (*sn*): **(in sich) ~** slump; cave in

zusammensitzen* sit together

zusammensparen save up

das **Zusammenspiel** interaction, interplay; co-operation; *sp etc* teamwork

zusammenstauchen *coll* give (s.o.) a dressing-down

zusammenstecken pin together; (*v/i*) *coll* be (constantly) together; **die Köpfe ~** put our/your/their heads together

zusammenstehen* stand together; stick together

zusammenstellen put together; draw up; compile; **gut zusammengestellt sein** (colours) blend well

die **Zusammenstellung, -en** *vbl noun*; *also* compilation; list; survey

zusammenstimmen harmonize; (statements *etc*) agree

der **Zusammenstoß** [-oː-], **⸚e** collision; clash

zusammenstoßen* (*sn*) collide; (lines *etc*) meet; adjoin; **~ mit** collide with; clash with

zusammenstreichen* cut (text *etc*)

zusammenströmen (*sn*) flock together

zusammenstückeln piece together

zusammenstürzen (*sn*) collapse

zusammensuchen [-zuː-] get together

zusammentragen* collect; assemble

zusammentreffen* (*sn*) meet; coincide; **~ mit** meet; **das Zusammentreffen, -** meeting; coincidence

zusammentreiben* round up

zusammentreten* trample underfoot; (*v/i sn*) meet, assemble

zusammentrommeln *coll* round up

zusammentun* *coll* put together; **sich ~** get together (for joint action)

zusammenwachsen* [-ks-] (*sn*) grow together, *med* (bone) knit; become close friends

zusammenwirken co-operate, work together; (factors *etc*) combine

zusammenzählen count up

zusammenziehen* draw/pull together; knit (one's brows); add up; *mil* concentrate, mass; (*v/i sn*) move in together; **~ mit** (*sn*) move in with; **sich ~** contract; (storm) be brewing

die **Zusammenziehung, -en** *vbl noun*; *also* contraction; *mil* concentration

zusammenzimmern knock together

zusammenzucken (*sn*) (give a) start

der **Zusatz, ⸚e** addition; rider (to document), codicil (to will); additive; *in compds* additional ...; supplementary ...; *tech* auxiliary ...; *elect* booster ...; **der ~antrag, ⸚e** *parl* amendment; **das ~gerät, -e** attachment

zusätzlich additional; supplementary; (*adv*) in addition (**zu** to)

zuschanden: ~ machen wreck, ruin; dash (hopes); **~ werden** be ruined; (hopes) be dashed; **~ fahren** wreck (car *etc*)

zuschanzen (+*dat*) *coll* wangle for

zuschauen *esp SGer* = **zusehen**

der **Zuschauer, -** onlooker; spectator, *theat etc* member of the audience, *TV* viewer; **der ~raum, ⸚e** auditorium; **die ~tribüne, -n** stand

zuschicken (+*dat*) send to

zuschieben* push/slide shut; (+*dat*) push across to; let (s.o.) have secretly; put (blame) on

zuschießen* contribute (**zu** towards); (+*dat*) dart (glance) at; *footb* kick (ball) to; **~ auf** (*acc*) (*sn*) rush up to

der **Zuschlag, ⸚e** surcharge, *rail* supplementary fare; knocking down (to bidder); *comm* award of contract; (+*dat*) **den ~ erteilen** knock the item down to; *comm* award the contract to || **die ~karte, -n** supplementary ticket; **z~pflichtig** requiring a supplementary ticket

zuschlagen* slam (shut); nail down; (+*dat*) knock down to, *comm* award to; add to (price); *sp* hit (ball) to; (*v/i*) hit out; strike; (*sn*) slam (shut); (+*dat*) **die Tür vor der Nase ~** *coll* slam the door in (s.o.'s) face; **~ auf** (*acc*)/**zu** add to (price)

zuschließen* lock (door); lock up

zuschnallen buckle; strap up

zuschnappen snap (at s.o.); (*v/i sn*) snap shut

zuschneiden* cut to size; *tail* cut out; **zugeschnitten auf** (*acc*) geared to; tailored to

der **Zuschneider, -** cutter

zuschneien (*sn*) become snowed in/over

der **Zuschnitt, -e** cut; character; calibre

zuschnüren tie up; lace up

zuschrauben screw tight; screw on the top of

zuschreiben* (+*dat*) attribute to; blame on; transfer to; **das hast du dir selbst zuzuschreiben** you've only yourself to blame

zuschreiten* (*sn*): **~ auf** (*acc*) stride up to

die **Zuschrift, -en** letter; reply (to advertisement)

zuschulden: sich *dat* **etwas ~ kommen lassen** do wrong

der **Zuschuß, ⸚(ss)e** subsidy; contribution; allowance

zuschustern [-ʃuː-] *coll* contribute; (+*dat*) wangle for

zuschütten fill in; *coll* add (water *etc*)

zusehen* watch; look on; (+*dat*) watch; **~, wie jmd./etw. ...** watch s.o./sth. (+*ger*);

~, daß ... see to it that ...
zusehends visibly
der **Zuseher, –** *Aust* = **Zuschauer**
zusenden* (+*dat*) send to
zusetzen add (*dat* to); *coll* lose (money); (*v/i*, +*dat*) keep on at; harass; (illness) take a lot out of
zusichern (+*dat of pers*) assure of; guarantee
die **Zusicherung, –en** assurance; guarantee
der **Zuspät|kommende** (*fem* **die ~**) (*decl as adj*) latecomer
zusperren *SGer* lock up; lock
das **Zuspiel** *sp* passing
zuspielen (+*dat*) pass on (information) to; leak to; *sp* pass to
zuspitzen sharpen; **sich ~** taper to a point; (situation *etc*) become critical
zusprechen* (+*dat*) award to; grant custody of (child) to; *tel* deliver a telegram to (s.o.) by telephone; (*v/i*, +*dat*) speak to (gently *etc*); **dem Essen ~** eat heartily; **dem Alkohol ~** imbibe freely; (+*dat*) **Mut ~** encourage; (+*dat*) **Trost ~** comfort
der **Zuspruch** (words of) encouragement; **großen ~ finden** be very popular/in great demand
der **Zustand, ⸗e** state; condition; (*pl*) conditions; **Zustände bekommen** *coll* have a fit; **das sind Zustände!** what a state of affairs!; **das ist doch kein ~!** this simply won't do!
zustande: ~ bringen bring about; achieve; manage; **~ kommen** come about; be achieved || **das Z~bringen** achievement (of); **das Z~kommen** coming about; materialization
zuständig responsible; competent
die **Zuständigkeit** competence; responsibility; *leg* jurisdiction
zustatten: (+*dat*) **~ kommen** stand (s.o.) in good stead
zustecken pin together; (+*dat*) slip (s.o. money *etc*)
zustehen*: ... steht mir zu I am entitled to ...; **es steht mir nicht zu zu ...** it is not for me to ...
zusteigen* (*sn*) get on (during journey)
Zustell– *post* delivery ...
zustellen deliver (mail); block; (+*dat*) *leg* serve (writ) on
die **Zustellung, –en** delivery; *leg* service
zusteuern contribute (**zu** to); **~ auf** (*acc*) (*sn*) head for
zustimmen (+*dat*) agree with; agree to; **~d** affirmative; (*adv*) in agreement
die **Zustimmung** agreement; consent
zustopfen stop up; darn
zustoßen* push (door *etc*) shut; (*v/i*) stab at s.o./sth.; (+*dat*) (*sn*) happen to; **ihm ist ein Unglück zugestoßen** he has met with an accident

zustreben (+*dat*) strive for; (*also sn*) make for
der **Zustrom** inflow; influx; stream
zuströmen (*sn*) (+*dat*) flow towards; flock to
zustürzen (*sn*): **~ auf** (*acc*) rush up to
zustutzen trim
zutage: ~ bringen/fördern unearth; bring to light; **~ kommen/treten** come to light; become apparent; **offen ~ liegen** be plain
die **Zutat, –en** *cul* ingredient; *cost* accessory
zuteil: (+*dat*) **~ werden** fall to (s.o.'s) lot; *or conveyed – with ind obj becoming subj – by* receive, be given (*eg* **ihm wurde eine hohe Auszeichnung ~** he received a high honour); (+*dat*) **~ werden lassen** bestow on; give
zuteilen ration out; (+*dat*) allocate to; assign to
die **Zuteilung, –en** *vbl noun*; *also* allocation; assignment (to s.o., sth.); ration
zutiefst deeply
zutragen* (+*dat*) carry to; report (gossip *etc*) to; **sich ~** happen
der **Zuträger, –** telltale
zuträglich (*following dat*) beneficial (to); (+*dat*) **nicht ~ sein** not be good for; (climate *etc*) not agree with
zutrauen (+*dat*) believe (s.o.) capable of; expect (s.o.) to have; **das ist ihm zuzutrauen** I wouldn't put it past him; **das hätte ich ihm nie zugetraut** I would never have thought him capable of it
das **Zutrauen** confidence (**zu** in)
zutraulich trusting; tame
zutreffen* be correct; **~ auf** (*acc*) (description) fit; = **~ für** apply to; **~d** appropriate, apt; **„Z~des bitte unterstreichen!“** 'please underline where applicable'
zutreiben* (+*dat*) drive towards; (*v/i sn*) drift towards
zutrinken* (+*dat*) drink to
der **Zutritt** access; entry; **„kein ~!“ = „~ verboten!“** 'no admittance'
zutun* (*see also* **zugetan**) (*coll in 1st sense*) add (*dat* to); **kein Auge ~** not sleep a wink; **die Augen für immer ~** pass away
Zutun: ohne jmds. ~ without s.o. having a hand in it
zu|ungunsten (+*gen*) to the disadvantage of
zu|unterst right at the bottom
zuverlässig reliable
die **Zuverlässigkeit** reliability
die **Zuversicht** confidence; **seine ~ setzen auf** (*acc*) put one's trust in
zuversichtlich confident
zuviel too much/many; **~ des Guten = des Guten ~** too much of a good thing; **ein Zuviel an** (*dat*) too much/many
zuvor before; **~kommen*** (*sep*; *sn*) (+*dat*) beat (s.o.) to it; forestall; anticipate;

~kommend obliging; courteous; **die Z~kommenheit** obligingness; civility
zuvorderst right at the front
der **Zuwachs** [-ks] increase (**an** *dat* in); growth (of); *joc* addition to the family; **die ~rate, -n** growth rate
zuwachsen* [-ks-] (*sn*) heal up; become overgrown
zuwandern (*sn*) immigrate
die **Zuwanderung, -en** immigration
zuwarten *SGer* wait
zuwege: gut/schlecht ~ *coll* in good/poor shape; **~ bringen** manage; achieve; **~ kommen mit** (be able to) cope with
zuweilen sometimes
zuweisen* (+*dat*) assign to, allocate to
die **Zuweisung, -en** assignment, allocation
zuwenden* (+*dat*) turn towards; turn (one's back) on; devote to; let (s.o.) have; **...** (*dat*) **zugewandt** turning to; facing (street *etc*); **sich ~** (+*dat*) turn to; devote oneself to
die **Zuwendung, -en** *vbl noun*; *also* payment; donation; attention
zuwenig too little/few
zuwerfen* slam (shut); fill up; (+*dat*) throw to; cast (glance) at
zuwider (*following dat*) contrary to; **... ist mir ~** I loathe ... || **~handeln** (*sep*) (+*dat*) act contrary to; contravene; **die Z~handlung, -en** *vbl noun*; *also* contravention; **~laufen*** (*sep*; *sn*) run counter to
zuwinken (+*dat*) wave to; signal to
zuzahlen pay another ...; (*v/i*) pay extra
zuzählen add; (+*dat*) number among
zuzeiten sometimes
zuziehen* pull shut; draw (curtain); tighten; call in; (*v/i sn*) move here; **sich** *dat* **... ~** catch (illness); sustain (injury); incur (hatred *etc*); acquire (reputation)
der **Zuzug** influx (of people)
zuzüglich (+*gen*) plus
zuzwinkern (+*dat*) wink at
zwang (zwänge) *p/t* (*subj*) *of* **zwingen**
der **Zwang, ⸚e** compulsion (*also psych*); constraint; pressure; coercion; **-zwang** (*eg* **der Paß~, Wein~**) obligation to (carry a passport, order wine, *etc*); (*eg* **der Impf~, Schul~**) compulsory (vaccination, schooling, *etc*); **... ist ~** ... is compulsory; **sich** *dat* **~ antun** force oneself (to do sth.); restrain oneself; **seinen Gefühlen keinen ~ antun** make no secret of one's feelings; **tu dir keinen ~ an** *coll*, *often iron* don't stand on ceremony; don't force yourself; feel free; **unter ~** under duress || **z~los** informal; casual; irregular; **die ~losigkeit** informality
zwängen squeeze (into, through, *etc* sth.); **sich ~ durch/in** (*acc*) squeeze through/into
zwanghaft compulsive

Zwangs- compulsory ...; **(zwangs-)** compulsorily ...;
die ~arbeit hard labour; **z~ernähren** (*only infin and p/part* **z~ernährt**) force-feed; **die ~handlung, -en** compulsive act; **die ~herrschaft, -en** tyranny; **die ~jacke, -n** straitjacket; **die ~lage, -n** predicament; **z~läufig** inevitable; (*adv*) *also* necessarily; *or conveyed by* ... is *etc* bound to ...; **die ~läufigkeit** inevitability; **z~mäßig** compulsory; **das ~mittel, -** means of coercion; **die ~neurose, -n** obsessional neurosis; **die ~voll|streckung, -en** execution; **die ~vorstellung, -en** obsessive idea; **z~weise** compulsory; (*adv*) compulsorily; inevitably; **die ~wirtschaft** controlled economy
zwanzig twenty
zwanziger: die ~ Jahre the twenties
der **Zwanziger, -** twenty-year-old; *coll* twenty-mark note; (*pl*) twenties
zwanzigst.., das Zwanzigstel, - twentieth
zwar (*with concessive force*) it is true, *or left untranslated* (*eg* **das sagt sich ~ leicht, aber ...** that's easy to say, but ...), *or rendered by* ... may ..., ... do ... (*eg* **sie ist ~ alt, aber ...** she may be old, but ..., **er geht ~ nach Hause, aber ...** he does go home, but ...); **und ~** in fact; to be precise; at that; *or left untranslated* (*eg* **sie wohnt in Köln, und ~ hinter dem Dom** she lives in Cologne, behind the cathedral)
der **Zweck, -e** purpose; aim; point; **der ~ heiligt die Mittel** the end justifies the means; **seinem ~ entsprechen** serve its purpose; **das hat keinen ~** it's pointless; **zu diesem ~** for this purpose
Zweck-: der ~bau, -ten functional building; **z~dienlich** *esp admin* appropriate; (information) relevant; expedient; **z~entfremdet** used for a purpose other than that it was/they were intended for; **z~entsprechend** appropriate; **z~gebunden** for a specific purpose; **z~los** pointless, futile; **z~mäßig** appropriate; functional; expedient; **der ~optimismus** show of optimism; **der ~pessimismus** pretence of pessimism; **z~widrig** inappropriate
zwecks (+*gen*) for the purpose of; with a view to
zwei (*gen* **-er**) two; **die Zwei, -en** two (*also* = *second-highest grade* – **'gut'** – *in marking scale*) || **der Z~beiner, -** *joc* human being; **~deutig** ambiguous; suggestive; **die Z~deutigkeit, -en** ambiguity; double entendre; risqué joke; **die Z~drittel|mehrheit** two-thirds majority; **~fach** twofold; double; **~geschlechtig** bisexual; **das Z~gespann, -e** carriage and pair; *coll* twosome; **~jährlich** biennial; **das Z~kammer|system** bicameralism; **der Z~kampf, ⸚e** duel;

~**mal** twice; two tickets to/portions *etc* of; ~**malig** (done) twice; two (*eg* **nach ~maligem Versuch aufgeben** give up after two attempts); ~**motorig** twin-engined; **das Z~parteien|system** two-party system; ~**reihig** in two rows; *cost* double-breasted; ~**schneidig** double-edged (**das ist ein ~schneidiges Schwert** it cuts both ways); ~**seitig** two-sided, *cost* reversible; two-page; bilateral; (*adv*) on both sides; **der Z~sitzer, –** two-seater; **der Z~spänner, –** carriage and pair; ~**spännig** drawn by two horses; ~**sprachig** bilingual; **die Z~sprachigkeit** bilingualism; ~**spurig** *mot* two-lane; *rail* double-track; ~**stimmig** for two voices, two-part; ~**strahlig** twin-jet; **das Z~strom|land** Mesopotamia; **der Z~takt|motor, –en** two-stroke engine; ~**teilig** in two parts; *cost* two-piece; **die Z~teilung, –en** bisection; division (in two); **der Z~viertel|takt** [–'fɪr–] two-four time; ~**wertig** bivalent, divalent

zweier *see* **zwei**

der **Zweier, –** *row* pair-oars; *in compds* ... of two; **der ~bob, –s** two-man bob; **z~lei** (*indecl*) 1 *adj* two kinds of; two different; 2 *pron* two (different) things

der **Zweifel, –** doubt (**an** *dat* about); **außer ~ stehen** be beyond doubt; **in ~ ziehen** call in question; **ohne ~** without doubt; **über jeden ~ erhaben** beyond all doubt || **z~los** undoubtedly

zweifelhaft doubtful; dubious

zweifeln: ~ an (*dat*) doubt, have (one's) doubts about; **~, ob ...** doubt whether ...; **daran ist nicht zu ~** there's no doubt about it

Zweifels–: der ~fall, ⸚e doubtful case (**im Z.** in case of doubt); **z~frei** unequivocal; (*adv*) beyond all doubt; **z~ohne** undoubtedly

der **Zweig, –e** branch; twig; **auf keinen grünen ~ kommen** *coll* not get anywhere in life || **das ~geschäft, –e** branch; **die ~gesellschaft, –en** subsidiary; **die ~niederlassung, –en = die ~stelle, –n** branch

die **Zweisamkeit** togetherness

zweit: zu ~ (*see* **zu** 1 (*i*)); **zweit..** second; **ein ~er** (**Shakespeare** *etc*) another (S. *etc*); **~es Ich** alter ego; **der/die Zweite** (*decl as adj*) second person; runner-up

Zweit– second ...; **(zweit–)** second (highest *etc*); **die ~ausfertigung, –en** duplicate; **das ~auto, –s** second car; **z~best** second-best; **z~klassig** second-rate; **z~letzt** last ... but one; **z~rangig** second-rate; **die ~schrift, –en** duplicate

zweitens secondly

das **Zwerch|fell, –e** diaphragm; **z~erschütternd** side-splitting

der **Zwerg, –e** dwarf (*also astron*); midget; **weißer ~** white dwarf

Zwerg– dwarf ...; miniature ...; **der ~pudel, –** toy poodle; **die ~schule, –n** small rural school; **der ~staat, –en** miniature state; **der ~stern, –e** dwarf star; **das ~volk, ⸚er** pygmy tribe; **der ~wuchs** stunted growth

zwergenhaft dwarfish; diminutive

die **Zwetsch(g)e, –n,** *Aust* **die Zwetschke, –n** plum

Zwick–: die ~mühle, –n dilemma; catch-22 situation

der **Zwickel, –** gusset

zwicken *esp SGer* pinch; (rheumatism *etc*) give (s.o.) gyp; *Aust* punch (ticket); *Aust* peg, pin *US*

der **Zwicker, –** pince-nez

Zwie–: der ~back, –e/⸚e rusk; Melba toast; **das ~gespräch, –e** dialogue; **das ~licht** twilight; **z~lichtig** shady; **der ~spalt** conflict; rift; **z~spältig** conflicting; (man, woman) of contradictions; **~sprache** (**Z. halten mit** commune with); **die ~tracht** discord

die **Zwiebel, –n** onion; bulb; *joc* tight bun; *joc* watch

zwiebeln *coll* harass; drive hard

der **Zwilling, –e** twin; (*pl*) *astron*, *astrol* Gemini; **der ~s|bruder, ..brüder** twin brother; **die ~s|schwester, –n** twin sister

die **Zwinge, –n** clamp; ferrule

zwingen (*p/t* **zwang** (*subj* **zwänge**), *p/part* **gezwungen**) (*see also* **gezwungen**) force; *coll* manage; **~ zu** force to do (work *etc*)/take (holiday, step, *etc*); (*followed by vbl noun, eg* **zum Rücktritt ~**) force to (resign *etc*); **sich ~ zu ...** force oneself to ...; **~d** compelling

der **Zwinger, –** kennels

zwinkern blink; wink

zwirbeln twirl

der **Zwirn, –e** (strong) thread

zwirnen twist

der **Zwirns|faden, ..fäden** thread

zwischen (*+acc indicating direction*, *+dat indicating place*) between; among

Zwischen– intermediate ...; interim ...; **die ~bemerkung, –en** interjected remark; **der ~bericht, –e** interim report; **die ~bilanz, –en** stocktaking (of progress *etc*); *comm* interim balance; **das ~deck, –s** 'tween deck; *hist* steerage; **das ~ding** cross (between ...); **z~drin** *coll* in between; between whiles; **z~durch** between whiles; here and there; **der ~fall, ⸚e** incident; **die ~frage, –n** interposed question; **das ~futter** interlining; **das ~geschoß, –(ss)e** mezzanine; **der ~händler, –** middleman; **z~landen** (*usu only infin and p/part* **z~gelandet;** *sn*) *aer* stop over; **die ~landung, –en** *aer* stopover;

der ~lauf, ⸚e *sp* intermediate heat; **die ~lösung, –en** interim solution; **die ~mahlzeit, –en** snack; **z~menschlich** between people, interpersonal; **der ~raum, ⸚e** space; interval; **der ~ruf, –e** (shouted) interruption; (*pl*) heckling; **das ~spiel, –e** interlude; *mus* intermezzo; **z~staatlich** international; **das ~stadium, –(i)en** intermediate stage; **die ~station, –en** stopover (**Z. machen** stop over); **der ~stecker, –** *elect* adaptor; **der ~stock, ⸚e = das ~stock|werk, –e** mezzanine; **das ~stück, –e** *tech* adaptor; **der ~träger, –** telltale; **die ~wand, ⸚e** partition; **die ~zeit, –en** intervening period; *sp* intermediate/split time (**in der Z.** in the meantime); **z~zeitlich** in the meantime

der **Zwist, –e** strife; discord

die **Zwistigkeiten** *pl* quarrel

zwitschern twitter; **einen ~** *coll* wet one's whistle

der **Zwitter, –** hermaphrodite; cross (between ...)

zwitterhaft hermaphrodite

zwo: *used instead of* **zwei** *to avoid confusion with* **drei** (*eg by person telephoning, judge announcing points awarded*)

zwölf twelve; **der Z~fi̱nger|darm, ⸚e** duodenum; **die Z~ton|musik** twelve-tone music

zwölft: zu ~ (*see* **zu** 1 (*i*)); **zwölft..** twelfth

zwölftel: ein ~ ... a twelfth of a ...

das **Zwölftel, –** twelfth

zwölftens twelfthly

zwot.. (*see* **zwo**) = **zweit..**

das **Zya̱n** cyanogen; **das Zyan|ka̱li** potassium cyanide

das **Zyani̱d, –e** cyanide

die **Zykla̱den** *pl* the Cyclades

Zyklen *pl of* **Zyklus**

zyklisch cyclic

der **Zyklo̱n, –e** cyclone

der **Zyklo̱p, –en** (*wk masc*) Cyclops

der **Zyklus, –(l)en** cycle (*also comput*)

der **Zyli̥nder** [tsi–], – *math, mech* cylinder; = **der ~hut, ⸚e** top-hat; **der ~kopf, ⸚e** cylinder-head

–zyli̥ndrig –cylinder

zyli̥ndrisch [tsi–] cylindrical

der **Zyniker, –** cynic

zynisch cynical

der **Zyni̥smus** cynicism

Zypern Cyprus; **auf ~** in Cyprus

die **Zypre̥sse, –n** cypress

der **Zyprio̱t, –en** (*wk masc*), **zyprio̱tisch** Cypriot

die **Zyste, –n** cyst

z. Z(t). (= **zur Zeit**) at present